# THE COMPLETE
# Who's Who
# IN THE
# Bible

# THE COMPLETE

# Who's Who

# IN THE

# Bible

## Paul D. Gardner, Editor

ZondervanPublishingHouse

*Grand Rapids, Michigan*

*A Division of* HarperCollins*Publishers*

*The Complete Who's Who in the Bible*
Copyright © 1995 by Paul Gardner
Originally published in the U.K. by Marshall Pickering,
an imprint of HarperCollinsReligious,
a part of HarperCollinsPublishers.

Requests for information should be addressed to:

🏭 ZondervanPublishingHouse
*Grand Rapids, Michigan 49530*

   ISBN: 0-310-21122-0

*Printed in the United States*

# PREFACE

———— ⊙⊘ ————

Anyone approaching the Bible for the first time cannot fail to see that the Bible is not just a theoretical book about God. From the very first chapter we see this book is about God and his relationship with his creation and specially with *people*. We learn about God as we see him revealing himself to real men and women. God speaks to them, works with them, encourages them, disciplines them, loves them and judges them. It at once becomes clear that God has some sort of relationship with every single human being. The relationship may be one of love and fellowship or it may be one in which a person rebels against God, but the Creator God is always there and sovereignly sustains this world for as long as he chooses.

The challenge and excitement for me of leading this project is that it has allowed me to study these people in the light of their relationship with God. I hope that all who read this *Who's Who* will enjoy, as I have, learning more about God as we see him in relationship with people of different races, backgrounds, culture and beliefs. We see the weakest of people who trust in him and worship him being used by God in the most difficult and dangerous of situations. We see the strongest of the world's leaders who do not trust in him and worship him being torn from their thrones as God exercises his universal sovereignty. We see the most sinful of people being forgiven as they turn in faith to a loving God who cares for his people, and we see others being judged as they refuse even to listen to the warnings of judgment God gives.

As we look at people in the Bible we learn about how sin entered the world and how it has affected every part of every human being. We see this even in the so-called 'heroes' of the faith. In the biblical revelation there are no perfect leaders (until Christ himself). Abraham, Moses, David and other great leaders are seen to be God's people but are also seen to be sinners who need God's forgiveness.

As we read of the sin of men and women we can immediately recognize that these people are like us. But we also see God who forgave those who turned to him and so we see hope for ourselves if we too will trust in his salvation and forgiveness. As we look at our world and wonder at the horror of so much that is going on around us, we see that others have lived in times that were at least as bad or worse (look at the time of the Judges), and we take heart that God was sovereign then and remains the same today. We see the struggles of a faithful man like David asking 'How long O Lord?' and 'Why do the wicked prosper?' We relate to his emotions; we ask God the same questions and we learn of God as we see his answers to David and others down through history.

From the least significant, in human terms, to the greatest world leader we meet a sovereign Creator God who is concerned for *people*. As he reveals himself to people through the ages, it becomes more and more apparent that that concern of a holy and transcendent God for his people will lead to his provision for their salvation. As the focus of Scripture narrows down, it leads inexorably to God's eternal will to send his only Son Jesus to bring salvation to these people God has created and loves. The incarnation of Jesus becomes the greatest demonstration of all that God is concerned for *people*. As we study the individuals who knew Jesus and put their faith in him and who later followed him even if it took them to their death, so we find out what it is to be a recipient of God's grace and mercy and forgiveness. We see the joy in their lives even in the midst of persecution or illness or natural disaster as they know what it is to belong to God. As we see them tackling the world of their age, we are given a deeper understanding of God who loves, forgives, saves people from judgment, and leads his people forward to eternity with him.

It is my great hope that all who read this book will see the Bible as more real, relevant and useful than perhaps they had realized before. But I also hope that it will simply whet the appetite for a far deeper and life-time study of the God who created *people* and reveals himself, not in some abstract way, but in real life in the real world over which he remains totally sovereign.

PAUL D. GARDNER
*Cheshire, 1995*

# INTRODUCTION

## Purpose

The purpose of this book is to supply an exhaustive ready reference volume on the people mentioned in the biblical texts of the Old and New Testaments. Thus on each character there is at least a minimum entry which gives biblical references and a brief description of a person's role in the biblical narrative and of his or her possible relationship to other characters.

It is intended that the volume should be useful to as wide a range of people as possible. It will provide a useful reference volume for anyone, whether well read in the Scriptures, or a newcomer. Students at school, church people, teachers, ministers and Theological College or Seminary students should find value in the volume. It is also hoped that it will find a ready home on the reference shelves of public libraries and school libraries. It is deliberately written without a lot of technical detail.

It is intended that readers can gain a reasonable understanding of the biblical portrait of most mainstream characters. This discussion of the character is also designed to help people better understand that person's place within God's purposes and the history of his people. The biblical view of God himself and his relationship with his people is often most clearly seen as we study men and women of history in their contact and relationship with God. Of course, such objectives cannot be met in many cases where insufficient information appears in the text.

A few other helpful articles are included which support the book as a whole and contribute to a greater understanding of the biblical material related to the people mentioned in Scripture. Although the reader may immediately think of numerous other articles that might have been included, space has precluded more. However, those included take up some special issues that should help the reader. For example, there are articles on children in the Bible, on the unnamed character known as the Woman at the Well, on angels, theophanies and even on the biblical genealogies.

The volume is written on the understanding that biblical history is carefully selected history. The various authors of the books of the Bible, guided by God's Spirit, mention events and people because they are interested in the God of history who works among the people of his world and in the midst of his creation. Those writers are interested in many, many different aspects of that history, but are always primarily concerned to teach their own and future generations more about God and his relationship with his world and specially with his own covenant people. The purpose of this book is therefore to draw out as clearly as possible within the limitations of a one-volume work as much as possible about God and about human beings who live their lives before the omnipresent and omniscient Creator God.

## How to use this volume

In some ways this volume is completely straightforward to use. Simply look up a name and read! Wherever two or three or more different characters bear the same name they are simply listed as 1., 2., 3. etc., and it may be necessary to look through these to find, for example, the particular Zechariah required.

The purpose of the volume is to give, wherever possible, a little more than simple biographical detail of characters as mentioned above. With this in mind, in order to get the most out of this volume and to learn about *why* a person is mentioned in Scripture and what that mention may tell about God and his will and purposes, it will probably be necessary to look up other related names. Since *all* names in the Bible are listed, reference is only made to other useful names when the information contained in the entry is actually necessary in order to gain the full picture.

For example, a reader may be interested in knowing more about Reuel, Moses' father-in-law. A quick glance at the article refers the reader to Jethro. A longer article under Jethro shows how Jethro, a Midianite, was used by God not only to provide housing and a wife for Moses, but later to offer godly advice about the sharing of leadership in ruling the people of Israel as they travelled through the wilderness. Jethro's action demonstrates God's concern for his people and specially for God's own chosen leader. This might well lead on to reading the articles on Moses and on 'Covenant', both of which will add very considerably to an understanding of God's care for his people and the particular concerns of Moses, Jethro's son-in-law.

An interest in knowing more about King Saul may lead the reader to question why Samuel seemed so reluctant to see a king come to the throne in Israel. The articles on 'King', 'Kingship' and 'Samuel' will both help the reader come to understand better God's own attitude to Israel having a king and the dilemma with which Samuel was faced.

## Contributors

A list of contributors is provided on p. xii. Wherever an entry is more than about 100 words the initials of the contributor are given. Occasionally where there is more than one person of the same name, different contributors have written the respective entries. This is duly noted by initials at the end of each contribution.

## Question marks

Occasionally a contributor has put a question mark after a biblical reference. This simply indicates uncertainty as to whether the text refers to the same character being described.

## Issues arising

There are some obvious issues of interest, difficulty and debate that arise in the preparation of a volume like this. The aim of the contributors is to be comprehensive.

*Son or descendant?*   The word translated 'son' in the NIV can refer generally to a male descendant or to what we understand as 'son', i.e. a direct descendant of a particular man or woman. The word 'father' can also refer to the direct father or to an important ancestor. In this *Who's Who* the word 'son' has been used where it is at least reasonable to assume a direct 'son' is indicated. On other occasions the word 'descendant' is used. The same principle is applied to the word 'father'. No doubt in places some will disagree with the particular decision on these matters reached by the contributors to this volume. Sometimes there are genuine problems that cause disagreements among scholars. The reader is encouraged to read the article in this volume entitled 'Biblical Genealogies' (p. 87).

*People or places?*   In a number of texts there is difference of opinion as to whether a place is being mentioned or a person. In some genealogies it may even be that places are mixed with persons. People probably gave their name to a place, thus compounding the problem for us who live so long after the events being recounted (e.g. Mamre). Usually in this volume where such difference of opinion occurs between scholars, names have been treated as individuals although obviously very little indeed can be said about such people. In most cases we would not want to quarrel over the issue!

*Different names, different versions?*   All the names are taken with their NIV spellings. Those using different versions may find this difficult, as spellings differ considerably, but some basic pointers will help people find the name they are searching for. For example, the NIV uses a 'k' wherever a 'ch' would be pronounced as a hard sound. Thus names in other versions spelled with a 'ch' and not found in this volume should be looked up with a 'k' spelling (e.g. Kelal in the NIV is Chelal in other versions; Keluhi is Cheluhi and so on). Sometimes names ending in the NIV with 'a' have an 'ah' in other versions (e.g. Abida in the NIV is Abidah in some versions). Sometimes in the NIV an 's' may be used where other versions have an 'sh' or vice-versa (e.g. where the NIV has Asarelah some other versions have Asharelah; where the NIV has Ashhur some other versions have Ashur). These differences between versions can be confusing. Some arise because of a lack of clarity between Hebrew letters and others arise simply because there are attempts to help readers in English to pronounce the names. Once these basic and fairly frequent changes are recognized it should be possible to put this volume to good use with all other English versions.

## Names and naming

It is often supposed that all names used in the Bible contain special significance. However, this is not the case. The vast majority of names function very similarly to the way names are used today in most Western countries. They simply signify a particular individual. Thus the name Job says no more to us than that he was not Bildad; we do not get to know him through his name for it says nothing about his character.

In this volume, where it is possible, we have translated the meaning of names, but this is largely for interest's sake and no more. When I was given the name Paul by my parents they were not thinking of the original Latin meaning of the name and thus saying something about my character – at least I hope not, for it means 'little'!

On the other hand, my name did have significance to them and to many of their friends, for I came from a Christian family and they deliberately chose biblical names for all their children. No doubt something of this is seen in the choice of names for many people, specially in the OT. Parents would give names that would identify the children with a family that wished to be known as faithful to God, and so many names were compounded around 'el', meaning God, or abbreviations of Yahweh, which appear variously but often as 'Jah' or 'Jo' at some point in the name. For example, Elijah means 'My God is Yahweh [the LORD]' while Joshua means 'Yahweh [the LORD] saves'.

In some parts of the world it is still common practice for parents to name the first male child after his father. To the frequent amusement of Europeans, in whose countries this is no longer the tradition except in royal families, this practice is still quite common in the USA, where we think of such famous examples as George Hamilton IV! In Scripture too such practice is occasionally seen. For example, we see the debate at the birth of John the Baptist about his name. In this case the family expected the son to be called by his Father's name, Zechariah. In fact God had different ideas and the child was eventually called John (see *Luke 1:13, 57–66*). This incident raised an interesting issue as we put this volume together, for there are in fact very few cases indeed in the Bible where descendants carry the name of their father or grandfather. An analysis of those who do suggests that it was much more common among priestly families, such as Zechariah's. No doubt the hereditary functions of Levites and priests were largely responsible for this. There was probably great pride that the son would carry on the same work for the Lord as his father had, and the sense of continuity in the priestly and Levitical vocation was thus stressed through names.

However, there are a number of occasions in Scripture such as the naming of 'John' mentioned above, where clearly more is intended than the simple identification of an individual. In that instance God himself gave the name John meaning 'Yahweh [the LORD] has been gracious'. The name thus indicated the work and message that John would bring to Israel; it was a message of repentance and preparation for the coming of the Messiah. It was a message that would be wholly summed up in the statement 'Yahweh has been gracious'.

Apart from indicating a person's message or vocation other names also summarize the whole individual perhaps in terms of his or her character, personality, or lifestyle. The fact that names can have this significance is most clearly seen in relation to God himself. In Scripture we repeatedly see reference to the 'name' of God. The Bible talks of worshipping or calling on the 'name of the LORD' and of not blaspheming the 'name' (e.g. *Gen. 4:26; 21:33; Lev. 9:12; Ps. 9:10* etc.; see *God* for more detail). Here 'the name' is used to draw together all that is known of God himself.

The name Jesus, meaning 'Yahweh [the LORD] saves', was a name given to the Messiah by God himself and fully summed up all that Jesus came to do but also all he is. He came to save but he *is* the Lord himself. (See *Jesus* for more detail.)

There are many less remarkable examples of names which are seen to describe something of the character of the person or the circumstances prevailing at his or her birth. Sometimes these names are given by the direct guidance of God while at other times it seems to be under God's general sovereign work that appropriate names are given to individuals. For example, Nabal, whose name means 'fool', acts foolishly. Jacob, whose name means 'heel grasper', usurped the position of his brother: 'Esau said, "Isn't he rightly named Jacob? He has deceived me these two times: He took my birthright, and now he's taken my blessing!"' (Gen. 27:36). When Rachel died in child birth she named her child Ben-Oni, meaning 'son of my sorrow' (Gen. 35:18).

Some people were renamed by God or by others with names more appropriate to their calling or character. Two early examples are Abram becoming Abraham and Sarai becoming Sarah. Jacob ('heel grasper') was renamed by God 'Israel', which has to do with his 'striving with God' at Peniel (Gen. 32:28). Daniel and his friends were renamed in Babylon with names which clearly indicated their new position of dependency on Babylon. It is surely the fact that names could be changed to indicate a new status or calling that gives rise to the idea that one day God will call his people by 'another name' (Is. 56:5; 65:15; Rev. 3:12).

Another point worth mentioning is the power that can be expressed in the naming process. We have mentioned the Babylonians changing the names of Daniel and his friends and thereby expressing control. Pharaoh Neco did the same with King Eliakim whom he renamed as Johoiakim as a sign of his control and power (2 Kings 23:34). Men or women could show this power. For example, it was Pharaoh's daughter who gave the Hebrew child Moses his name. Adam was given by God the right to name the animals thus, no doubt, indicating a delegated authority from God (Gen. 2:19–20). Whatever may be thought of the implications for today's debates about the role of women, Adam is also allowed by God to name the first woman 'Eve' ('life'; Gen. 3:20).

Names and the naming process itself can be very significant in Scripture, but it is important to let the text give us some indication of where this is the case. Of the thousands of names given in this volume some are indeed significant in their meaning or indicate something of the power or authority being exercised in the naming process. The vast majority, however, may have meant much to the original mother and father when they chose the name, but serve only to identify an individual in the Bible, much as most names in our own age do.

# CONTRIBUTORS*

———— ⊙⁄⊙ ————

## The Editor

P. D. G.  **Gardner, Paul D.** M.Div., A.K.C., Ph.D. A Minister and Area Dean in the Church of England in Cheshire, England. Former lecturer in New Testament and Academic Registrar, Oak Hill Theological College, London, England. Dr. Gardner continues to preach and lecture internationally.

## Other Contributors

C. B.  **Blomberg, Craig** M.A., Ph.D. Professor of New Testament, Denver Seminary, Denver, Colorado, USA. Ordained in Southern Baptist Convention.

D. B.  **Bock, Darrell** Ph.D. Professor of New Testament Studies, Dallas Theological Seminary, Dallas, Texas, USA. Ordained associate pastor to Trinity Fellowship Church, Richarding, Texas.

S. C.  **Chapin, Shelley** B.A., M.A. Writer and broadcaster. General Manager of radio stations KVNE and KGLY, Tyler, Texas, USA. Ph.D. candidate.

M. J. G.  **Glodo, Michael, J.** M.Div., Th.M. Assistant Professor of Old Testament, Reformed Theological Seminary, Orlando, Florida, USA. Ph.D candidate. Ordained in the Evangelical Presbyterian Church.

W. H. H.  **Harris, W. Hall** Th.M., Ph.D., Professor of New Testament Studies, Dallas Theological Seminary, Dallas, Texas, USA.

R. H.  **Hess, Richard** M.Div., M.Th., Ph.D. Lecturer in Old Testament and Hebrew at Glasgow Bible College, Glasgow, Scotland.

S. J. K.  **Kistemaker, Simon, J.** B.D., Th.D. Professor of New Testament and Chairman of New Testament Department, Reformed Theological Seminary, Jackson, Mississippi, USA. Past president of the Evangelical Theological Society. Ordained in the Christian Reformed Church.

P. L.  **Long, Philip** M.Div., Ph.D., Professor of Old Testament, Covenant Theological Seminary, St. Louis, Misouri, USA. Ordained in the Presbyterian Church in America.

A. B. L.  **Luter, Boyd, A.** Th.M., Ph.D. Senior Associate Professor of Bible, Talbot School of Theology, La Mirada, California, USA. Ordained.

D. K. L.  **Lowery, David, K.** Th.M., Ph.D., Professor of New Testament Studies, Dallas Theological Seminary, Dallas, Texas, USA. Ordained associate pastor, Midlothian Bible Church, Texas.

*In most cases only second and subsequent degrees are listed.

A. M.  **Mawhinney, Allen** M.Div., Th.M., Ph.D. Professor of New Testament and Academic Dean at Reformed Theological Seminary, Orlando, Florida, USA. Ordained in the Presbyterian Church in America.

K. MCR.  **McReynolds, Kathy** B.A., M.A. Has specialized in writing on Christian women and women in the Bible. Ph.D. Candidate at Biola University, La Mirada, California, USA.

E. M.  **Merrill, Eugene** Ph.D., Professor of Old Testament Studies, Dallas Theological Seminary, Dallas, Texas, USA.

J. A. M.  **Motyer, J. Alec** M.A., B.D. Retired. Formerly Principal of Trinity Theological College, Bristol, England. Ordained in the Church of England and more recently minister of Christ Church, Westbourne, England.

R. M.  **Munro, Robert** B.A. Ordained in the Church of England and assistant minister in a church in Hartford, Cheshire, England.

M. P.  **Pickles, Mark** B.A. Ordained in the Church of England and a minister in a church in Winsford, Cheshire, England. D.Min. candidate, Reformed Theological Seminary, Orlando, Florida, USA.

R. P.  **Pratt, Richard** M.Div., Th.D., Professor of Old Testament at Reformed Theological Seminary, Orlando, Florida, USA. Ordained in the Presbyterian Church in America.

M. S.  **Silva, Moisés** B.D., Th.M., Ph.D. Professor of New Testament and Chairman of the Department of New Testament at Westminster Theological Seminary, Philadelphia, USA. Ordained in the Orthodox Presbyterian Church.

A. A. T.  **Trites, Allison, A.** Th.M., D.Phil. The John Payzant Distinguished Professor of Biblical Studies, Acadia Divinity College, Acadia University, Wolfville, Nova Scotia, Canada. Ordained in the Canadian Baptist Federation.

W. A. VG.  **VanGemeren, Willem** M.A., Ph.D. Professor of Old Testament and Semitic Languages, Trinity Evangelical Divinity School, Deerfield, Illinois, USA. Ordained in the Presbyterian Church in America.

S. V.  **Vibert, Simon** M.Th. Ordained in the Church of England and a minister in a church in Buxton, Derbyshire, England.

P. D. W.  **Wegner, Paul, D.** M.Div., Th.M., Ph.D. Associate Professor Bible Department (Old Testament), Moody Bible Institute, Chicago, Illinois, USA.

B. W.  **Winter, Bruce** Th.Scol., M.Th, Ph.D. Warden of Tyndale House and Director of the Institute for Early Christianity in the Graeco-Roman World, Tyndale House, Cambridge, England. Ordained in the Anglican Church in Australia.

# A

**AARON** Aaron was 'piggy in the middle' in a family of three, sandwiched between his strong-minded sister Miriam and his toweringly able younger brother Moses (*Exod. 6:20; 7:7*) – no wonder, then, that he grew up with the lovely grace of being amenable and with the reverse side of that grace: chronic weakness and indecision.

**Aaron's story** Aaron was born during Israel's Egyptian oppression but evidently before the genocidal edict of *Exod. 1:22*. He was three years old when Moses was born and when Miriam was already an unusually self-possessed little person (*Exod. 2:4–8*). From early on, therefore, he was caught between the baby who claimed such attention and who would yet catch the public eye in a big way, and a confident and decisive sister. Was he the family 'also ran'? We do not have details to inform us, but his later development (or lack of it) suggests that this was so. He grew up, married Elisheba and had four sons (*Exod. 6:23; Lev. 10:1, 6*): Nadab, Abihu, Eleazar and Ithamar. It is interesting to speculate whether the presumptuous act of Nadab and Abihu (*Levi. 10:1*) was at all provoked by what they may have thought was their father's too subservient attitude to Moses and by a desire to assert some independent thinking into the priestly family – and was Aaron's silence (*Lev. 10:3*) that of dumb sorrow, meek acquiescence or seething impotence?

Throughout the Exodus narrative Aaron is an adjunct to Moses. He was sent to provide a voice for Moses' words (*Exod. 4:14, 29; 7:1, 2; 16:9; etc.*) when he had to plead before Pharaoh for the Israelites' freedom. He was subordinate to Moses in all the plague-history (e.g. *Exod. 7:18; 8:5*), sharing with him the reproaches of the people (e.g. *Exod. 16:2*) – sharing too the refuge of prayer (*Num. 16:22; etc.*) and some privileges of Sinai (*Exod. 19:24; 24:1,9*). Only once is Aaron's name given the elder brother's priority (*Num. 3:1*) and only twice did the LORD speak to Aaron directly (*Exod. 4:27; Num. 18:1–20*). But on two occasions Aaron acted in independence of Moses and they were both unmitigated disasters. Firstly, when he was left in charge during Moses' sojourn on the Mount (*Exod. 24:14*), under pressure from the people (*Exod. 32:22*), he took the initiative in making the golden calf and promoting its worship (*Exod. 32:2, 5*). For this he attracted the LORD's anger and was saved by the intercession of his brother (*Deut. 9:20*). Secondly, he took part in an ill-advised family revolt against Moses (*Num. 12:1ff.*) on the ground that he and Miriam deserved more recognition as channels of divine revelation. Plainly (*v. 10*) in this Miriam was the prime mover – (and the description of Zipporah as 'a Cushite' indicates some 'needle' between the sisters-in-law as a not inconsiderable factor!) – and the easily swayed Aaron, as so often with fundamentally weak people, was persuaded to become indignant and to take a firm stand on the wrong point! Is it not typical that at the end Aaron again allowed himself to be swept away in another's hasty anger and forfeited his own entrance to Canaan (*Num. 20:1–13*)?

Aaron died on Mt Hor (*Num. 20:22–29*)

1

and was honoured by a month's national mourning.

**Aaron's priesthood.** Scripture as a whole deals gently with Aaron. In the Psalms he is a shepherd (*Ps. 77:20*), priest (*Ps. 99:6*), chosen (*Ps. 105:26*), holy (*Ps. 106:1*) and anointed (*Ps. 133:2*). In Hebrews, his priesthood is a foreshadowing of the perfect High Priest, the Lord Jesus (*Heb. 2:17–18; 4:14–16; 5:1–4; 7:11*). Such was the dignity and usefulness to which the LORD raised this weak, vacillating, inadequate man, amenable with all the attractiveness of that quality and with all its faults. Truly, God is not dependent on our powers but rather lifts us up by grace above our failings.

*Lev. 10:10* summarizes Old Testament priesthood as moral and educative. Taking the latter first, the priest was the repository of divine revelation (*Deut. 31:9*), and out of this revealed truth he instructed the people (*Mal. 2:4–7; cf. Num. 25:12–13*). But undoubtedly the main focus of the priestly life was dealing with the moral infirmities of the people and bringing them, through the appointed sacrifices, into an experience of acceptance before God (*Lev. 1:3, etc.*), atonement (*Lev. 1:4; etc.*) and forgiveness (*Lev. 4:31; etc.*).

The basic idea of 'atonement' is that of 'covering', not just in the sense of hiding something out of sight (Micah 7:18–19) but more in the sense that a payment 'covers' a debt, meeting and cancelling it. The mode of this 'covering price' was 'sin-bearing', the transference, by the will of God, of sin and its reward from the guilty to the innocent and the exaction upon the innocent of the (death) penalty that was due. In all the sacrifices the laying of the offerer's hand upon the beast's head was a central requirement (*Lev. 1:4; 3:2, 8, 13; 4:4, 15, 25; etc.*) and, as the book of Leviticus develops, the meaning of this rite is clarified as the designation of a substitute and the imposition upon that substitute of the offerer's own sin. In these sacrifices the ministry of the Aaronic priests was essential. This was their function and no other dared intrude upon it. It reached its climax – and its most dramatic exercise – on the annual Day of Atonement, the day when divine mercy made a clean sweep of all the sins, transgressions and iniquities of the previous year. The High Priest – dear, old fragile Aaron! – was the central officiant, first in bearing the blood that signified the death of the substitute-beast into the Holiest of all, there to sprinkle it where it was most needed, in the presence of the LORD and over the whole of the broken law of God (*Lev. 16:11–17*). But the priesthood was a teaching office and the people needed to understand publicly what the priest had done privately. Therefore the ceremony of the 'scapegoat' was ordained by God (*Lev. 16:20–22*) in which, openly before the watching people, Aaron performed the laying on of hands (*v. 21*), recited the full tale of sin (*v. 21*), and 'put' it all on the beast's head. In this way the goat was made to 'carry on itself all their sins'. This was Aaron's crowning glory, wherein he anticipated One who would be stricken for the transgression of his people and bear the sin of the many (*Isa. 53:8, 12*), One who 'through the eternal Spirit' would offer 'himself unblemished to God' and would both be and make 'one sacrifice for sins' for ever (*Heb. 9:14; 10:12*). J.A.M.

**ABADDON** (Heb., 'a place of destruction'). The word occurs in a number of places in the OT, where the NIV translates it as 'Destruction' (e.g. *Job 26:6; 28:22; Prov. 15:11* etc.) It is virtually a synonym in most of these places for 'death', where 'Death and Destruction' are to some extent personified. It is used as a name only in *Rev. 9:11*, where it is used of an angel who is the king of the Abyss, the place that is wholly evil and reserved for the wicked. The Greek equivalent is

Apollyon, which is also used only in this verse. Even in *Rev.* 9 the name is more of a personification of destruction and death than another name for Satan. Nevertheless, ultimately such 'destruction' comes, of course, from Satan (*v.* 1, *the fallen star*), who brings death and torment. The good news of *Rev.* 9, however, is that Satan cannot destroy those who belong to God through faith (*v.* 4). The sad news is that even having seen so much destruction and death around them in this world, there will be many people who refuse ever to repent (*v.* 21). P.D.G.

**ABAGTHA,** one of seven eunuchs who served King Xerxes (*Est.* 1:10). See *Vashti.*

**ABBA** (Heb., 'Father'), a name applied to God in three texts in the NT: *Mk.* 14:36; *Rom.* 8:15; *Gal.* 4:6. See God (*Father*).

**ABDA** (Heb., 'worshipper' or 'servant').
   **1.** The father of Adoniram, who was a chief official of King Solomon in charge of forced labour (1 *Kings* 4:6).
   **2.** The son of Shammua and one of the Levites who settled in Jerusalem (*Neh.* 11:17).

**ABDEEL** (Heb., 'servant of God'). The father of Shelemiah who was commanded by King Jehoiakim to arrest Baruch and Jeremiah (*Jer.* 36:26). However, they were safe because 'the LORD had hidden them'.

**ABDI** (Heb., 'servant of').
   **1.** The father of Kishi, the father of Ethan the Merarite, a priestly musician in the latter days of King David and at the founding of the Temple under King Solomon (1 *Chron.* 6:44).
   **2.** The father of Kish, another Merarite Levite who helped purify the Temple in the days of King Hezekiah (2 *Chron.* 29:12).
   **3.** A descendant of Elam, Abdi is listed

in *Ezra* 10:26 among those who had married foreign women.

**ABDIEL** (Heb., 'servant of God'), a Gadite who lived in Gilead and Bashan. He was the son of Guni and is listed in the genealogies of the time of King Jotham of Judah (1 *Chron.* 5:15).

**ABDON 1.** The son of Hillel, he served as one of the minor judges of Israel for eight years (*see Judg.* 12:13–15). He was known for his numerous sons and nephews and came from the tribe of Ephraim.
   **2.** Listed in the genealogy of Benjamin and King Saul as one of the sons of Shashak (1 *Chron.* 8:23).
   **3.** Acknowledged as the first-born son of Jeiel, son of Gibeon, in both of the genealogies of King Saul in 1 *Chron.* (8:30; 9:36).
   **4.** The son of Micah, he was one of the servants sent by King Josiah to seek the wisdom of Huldah the prophetess (2 *Chron.* 34:13–28; see *Ahikam* for detail). (Note: the account in 2 *Kings* 22:12, 14 names this servant as Acbor, son of Micaiah.) S.C.

**ABEDNEGO** (Heb. and Aram., 'servant of Nabu', a Babylonian god). This was the name given by the chief official of Nebuchadnezzar to Daniel's Jewish friend, Azariah (*Dan.* 1:6). It is found 14 times in *Dan.* 1–3.
   Abednego, like Daniel, Shadrach and Meshach, refused the royal food and ate only vegetables and drank only water (*Dan.* 1:12) while being prepared for court appearance. The LORD honoured their insistence on not eating what, as Israelites, would have been considered unclean food. As a result, their appearance proved to be healthier than others in the court. God gave Abednego and the others 'knowledge and understanding of all kinds of literature and learning' (*Dan.* 1:17). The king found no others with the

same abilities as these three men, who were rapidly raised to positions of power and influence under their leader Daniel.

Later, when Abednego would not bow to a statue of gold that Nebuchadnezzar had set up in the plain of Dura, he was thrown with Shadrach and Meshach into a furnace of fire. The three so trusted in the LORD that they informed the king, 'the God we serve is able to save us from it' (Dan. 3:17). Once in the furnace, God did intervene and Nebuchadnezzar saw the three walking in the fire unharmed. A fourth person was also present who, Nebuchadnezzar said, looked 'like a son of the gods' (Dan. 3:25). Clearly, some theophany occurred. Immediately Nebuchadnezzar had the men released, gave them back their positions of authority, and began to worship the true God who had 'sent his angel and rescued his servants' (Dan. 3:28). Nebuchadnezzar was so impressed by the saving power of the God of the Hebrews that he ordered that no one should say anything against these men.

Abednego and the others had a tremendous faith in their God who had saved them, and their faith had witnessed to pagans in the strongest possible way. This faith is alluded to in Heb. 11:34, and there becomes an example for Christians of all ages who trust in the same God as Abednego and the others. See also Azariah.                P.D.G. and A.B.L.

**ABEL,** the second son of Adam and Eve, and the brother of Cain. 'Abel' may be derived from a Heb. word meaning 'breath' or 'vanity', foreshadowing his life being cut short. Abel became a shepherd (Gen. 4:2), while Cain became an agriculturalist. At harvest time, while Cain offered God some of the fruit of the harvest, Abel made an offering of the fat firstborn of his flock, emphasizing its worth and cost. Abel's sacrifice was received by the LORD with favour, while Cain's was not. Despite a warning from

the LORD about the need to master sin, Cain plotted against his brother and murdered him. Yet the deed was not hidden from the LORD, and Abel's death resulted in judgment on Cain.

Abel was the first fatality subsequent to God's curse of mankind through Adam and Eve's rebellion; his physical death as a direct result of Cain's sin, fulfilled God's promise that eating of the fruit of the knowledge of good and evil would bring death. His physical death fulfilled the spiritual death already experienced by Adam and Eve in their exclusion from the Garden of Eden. This emphasized the rapid development of sin, as God gave up mankind to the consequences of his rebellion with a minimum of restraining grace.

The fact that Cain and Abel both made sacrifices demonstrated that despite God's curse, man retained a desire to worship God. That this should have involved sacrifice, indicated recognition that true worship of God was to be costly. The exact nature of the offering is not told, but the pattern inherited by Noah (Gen. 8:20) suggests an altar was built and the offering burnt. How God expressed his favourable reception of Abel's offering is not clear, but it was possibly by divine fire. Perhaps Abel's was burnt up and Cain's was not (cf. Lev. 9:24; Judg. 6:21; 1 Kings 18:38).

The LORD accepted Abel's offering in preference to Cain's because Abel was righteous (Matt. 23:35; Heb. 11:4; cf. Gen. 4:7) in offering the best of his flock, but his righteousness was not by the value of his works, but by faith (Heb. 11:4). Cain's rebuke from the LORD therefore focused on the attitude of his heart (Gen. 4:7). This was the first revelation that the LORD was concerned worship should be an outward expression of a devoted and obedient heart, rather than just religious behaviour.

Abel's murder as a man of faith, became a prototype of those martyred for their faith (Matt. 23:35; Luke 11:49–51). In this sense Abel's faith still speaks (*Heb.* 11:4), because his faith still awaits a final vindication. He never received the blessing of God's approval for his faith on this earth (*Heb.* 11:39). Abel's untimely death showed that the ultimate vindication of faith is a future hope, held with confidence in God. However, a contrast is made between the testimony of Abel's blood and the blood of Jesus in *Heb.* 12:24; Abel's blood provided testimony to God and brought a curse upon Cain (*Gen.* 4:10–12), Jesus' blood is superior because, though sacrificed for sinners, it brings blessing, not a curse. Jesus' sacrifice is not a martyrdom but an effectual means of salvation.          R.M.

**ABI-ALBON** (*2 Sam.* 23:31). See *Abiel.*

**ABIASAPH** (Heb., 'father has added'), a son of Korah a descendant of Levi (*Exod.* 6:24). His family was one of the Korahite clans led out of Egypt by Moses and Aaron. In *1 Chronicles* he is called Ebiasaph. His descendants were gatekeepers at the Tabernacle (*1 Chron.* 9:19).

**ABIATHAR** (Heb., 'father is excellent'), the sole survivor of Saul's massacre at Nob (see *Zadok* for more detail, also *Ahimelech*). Abiathar was the eleventh priest in line from Aaron and part of a group of priests who provided for David and his men as they fled from an angry King Saul (*1 Sam.* 21). When Abiathar escaped the slaughter, he took David news of all that had occurred. David felt responsible for the deaths of the priests and invited Abiathar to remain under his own care. Abiathar stayed with David and served as his high priest and adviser through the years. Toward the end of David's reign, Abiathar conspired to make Adonijah king – an act that almost cost him his life and did cost him the reputation of loyal service to the king (*1 Sam.* 22:6–13; 23:6–12; *2 Sam.* 15:24–36; 1 Kings 1–2).          S.C.

**ABIDA** (Heb., 'father of knowledge'), one of the sons of Midian and a descendant of Abraham through his wife Keturah (*Gen.* 25:4; 1 Chron. 1:33).

**ABIDAN,** the son of Gideoni and the leader of the people of Benjamin at the census of the Israelites in the wilderness of Sinai. His division of people numbered 32,200 (*Num.* 1:11; 2:22). As the representative of his tribe he also brought his tribe's fellowship offering when the Tabernacle was dedicated in the wilderness (*Num.* 7:60, 65).

**ABIEL** (Heb., 'God is my father').
  **1.** A descendant of Benjamin, Abiel was the grandfather of King Saul (*1 Sam.* 9:1). *1 Sam.* 14:51 indicates that Abiel was also the grandfather of Abner.
  **2.** Also called Abi-albon the Arbathite (i.e. he was probably from Arabath in Judah; *2 Sam.* 23:31), Abiel was one of King David's 30 'mighty men' (*1 Chron.* 11:32).

**ABIEZER** (Heb., 'father of help').
  **1.** Abiezer is mentioned as the leader of one of the clans of the tribe of Manasseh at the time when the tribal allotment of Canaan was made under the leadership of Joshua (*Josh.* 17:2). He was a son of Gilead (*1 Chron.* 7:18). His clan later received some significance when Gideon asked them to join him in the battle against the Midianites. The Ephraimites complained that, while the Abiezrites had been called upon to help, they had been excluded from the battle (*Judg.* 6:34; 8:2). He is probably the same as Iezer in *Num.* 26:30.
  **2.** Abiezer from Anathoth was one of David's 'Thirty' warriors from the tribe of Benjamin. As a commander in David's army he was on duty with his men in the ninth month of each year and had 24,000 men in his division (*2 Sam.* 23:27; 1 Chron. 11:28; 27:12).          P.D.G.

**ABIGAIL** (Heb., 'father rejoices').

**1.** Abigail was a beautiful and a wise woman. The writer of 2 Samuel hints that her true beauty was to be found in her love for the LORD and dedication to his service (2 Sam. 25:26). The account of Abigail's diplomatic hospitality towards David is set in contrast to the surly hostility of her husband Nabal, who foolishly returned polite greetings with insult. He failed to offer David customary accommodation and revealed that he had no knowledge of the LORD whom his wife served (see 1 Sam. 25; 2 Sam. 2:2; 3:3; 1 Chron. 3:1). Her kindness and quick thinking prevented an inevitable flaring of retributive anger. Nabal's death later in the chapter is epitaphed by David's conclusion that this was God's punishment for insulting the new leader in Israel. David then took Abigail to be his wife. Some have pointed out the literary polemic used in this story to create a moral allegory to show the superiority of Abigail over Bathsheba. However, the text itself makes no comment about this, other than to show that David was acting within social customs in taking this widow as his wife.

**2.** This Abigail is said to be the sister of David (1 Chron. 2:16; 2 Sam. 17:25). She is a different Abigail from his wife. However, there are unresolved textual difficulties in clearly identifying her.　s.v.

**ABIHAIL** (Heb., 'father of strength').

**1.** Num. 3:35 lists Abihail as a Levite and ancestor of the house of Merari. See *Merari*.

**2.** In the listing of Judah's descendants, Abihail was the wife of Abishur and the mother of Ahban and Molid (1 Chron. 2:29).

**3.** Abihail is listed as one of the men of Gad (1 Chron. 5:14). The Gadites lived in Gilead, Bashan and the pasturelands of Sharon (vv. 11–22).

**4.** Abihail was the wife of David's son, Jerimoth, and the mother of Rehoboam's wife, Mahalath (2 Chron. 11:18).

**5.** Abihail was the father of Queen Esther and the uncle of Mordecai (*Est.* 2:15; 9:29). Though we do not know how Abihail died, we do know that Mordecai took Esther and raised her as his own daughter (*Est.* 2:5–7).　s.c.

**ABIHU** (Heb., 'God is father'), brother of Nadab, Eleazar and Ithamar, was the second son of Aaron and his wife Elisheba (*Exod.* 6:32). At the time of the confirmation of God's covenant with Israel, he was among the 70 elders of Israel who 'saw the God of Israel' when they went part way up Sinai (only Moses approached the LORD; *Exod.* 24:1, 9 etc.). Time and again 'holiness' was stressed as of the essence of Israelite worship. God was 'holy' and therefore he could not be approached by the people. Thus any worship of God had to be a response to his commands and thus had to fulfil the requirements of holiness. Sadly, Abihu and his brother Nadab later were put to death for offering an 'unauthorized fire before the LORD, contrary to his command' (*Lev.* 10:1). The penalty for compromising the holiness of God was death.　p.d.g.

**ABIHUD** (Heb., 'my father of praise'), the grandson of Benjamin and the son of Bela (1 Chron. 8:3). He is listed in the genealogy leading to Saul.

**ABIJAH** (Heb., 'my father is the LORD').

**1.** Abijah was the younger son of Samuel and was appointed by his father to judge Beersheba, along with his brother, Joel (1 Sam. 8:2; 1 Chron. 6:28). Both brothers were ungodly in their justice, so the people asked Samuel for a king. Samuel was heartbroken by both the behaviour of his sons and the demand of the Israelites (1 Sam. 8:1–22).

**2.** Aaron's sons were separated into 24 divisions which took different duties in the service of the Tabernacle and Temple. Abijah, son of Aaron, was over the eighth division, the same division later served by John the Baptist's father, Zechariah (1 *Chron. 24:10; Luke 1:5*).

**3.** Rehoboam's son and successor, Abijah reigned over Judah for approximately three years. His mother was Maacah (2 *Chron. 13:2*). War was waged between Judah and Israel during his reign. Abijah's statement before the battle reminded the people of Israel that it was the house of David that God had promised he would bless. Because he and his people relied upon the LORD, Abijah beat back Jeroboam's army and succeeded in regaining power over several cities for Judah (2 *Chron. 13; 1 Kings 15:1–8*). Abijah had 14 wives, 22 sons and 16 daughters. However, war between the two kingdoms continued throughout his reign.

**4.** Jeroboam I, king of Israel, had a son named Abijah who became ill during childhood. Jeroboam sent his wife in disguise to Ahijah, the same prophet who had predicted the king's reign. Ahijah saw through the disguise and pronounced judgment on Jeroboam's house, resulting in the immediate death of the boy (1 *Kings 14:1–8*). Abijah was remembered as the only honourable member of Jeroboam's family (v. 13).

**5.** 1 *Chron. 7:6–11* gives a listing of Benjamin's three sons. Abijah was a son of Beker.

**6.** Abijah was the wife of Hezron. She bore a son named Ashur shortly after her husband died (1 *Chron 2:18–24*).

**7.** Abijah was the daughter of Zechariah and the mother of King Hezekiah of Judah (2 *Kings 18:2; 2 Chron. 29:1*).

**8.** Signifying his leadership in Israel during the rebuilding of the city wall, Abijah placed his seal upon the agreement which the Israelites, led by Nehemiah, made with God (*Neh. 9–10*). Due to the similarities between the lists given in *Neh. 10 and 12*, many scholars believe the Abijah mentioned in *Neh. 10* to be the same as the priest Abijah, mentioned in *Neh. 12:4, 17.*          S.C.

**ABIMAEL** (Heb., 'God is my father'), one of 13 sons of Joktan, a descendant of Shem (*Gen. 10:28; 1 Chron. 1:22*).

**ABIMELECH** (Heb., 'the king is my father').

**1.** This name was probably applied generally to Philistine rulers. The first ruler mentioned by this name was king of Gerar in the days of Abraham. In his nomadic wanderings, Abraham settled near Gerar (*Gen. 20*). In order to protect his wife he referred to her as his 'sister' rather than his 'wife'. Believing the deception, Abimelech took Sarah as his wife, but before he had had sexual intercourse with her, God appeared to him in a dream threatening death because he had taken Abraham's wife. Rightly, Abimelech appealed to God that he was ignorant and had been deceived. God responded: 'Yes, I know you did this with a clear conscience, and so I have kept you from sinning against me. That is why I did not let you touch her. Now return the man's wife, for he is a prophet, and he will pray for you and you will live. But if you do not return her, you may be sure that you and all yours will die' (*Gen. 20:6–7*). From that moment Abimelech himself became ill and his wife and slaves were unable to have children.

Abraham, when challenged by Abimelech about this deception, responded that he had been afraid that Sarah would be killed because there was no fear of the true God in Gerar. Abimelech gave Abraham many presents and paid a price to Sarah to cover his offence. Abraham then prayed to God and Abimelech was healed (*Gen. 20:14–18*). Later, when Abraham complained to Abimelech about a well of water that his men had seized, the two leaders made a covenant together (*Gen. 21:22–34*).

This strange episode of deception was overruled by God to establish his name and his power among the Philistines. God demonstrated that he was with Abraham and would protect his servant wherever he went (*Gen. 20:3, 6, 17–18*). Such action on God's part led to Abimelech and his commander Phicol acknowledging Abraham's God and realizing that he did answer Abraham's prayers (*Gen. 21:22, 33*). But such action on God's part also helped Abraham realize just how much God could be trusted in all situations and no doubt, therefore, provided him with a good training ground for the supreme test of his faith in *Gen. 22*, where God asked him to offer Isaac as a sacrifice.

**2.** Another Philistine Abimelech is mentioned in connection with Isaac, when he also went to Gerar. A very similar experience is then recounted of Isaac's encounter with this Abimelech and how the king took Rebekah as his wife (*Gen. 26:1, 8–9 etc.*). This story does not describe Abimelech's or Isaac's inter-action with God. However, eventually Isaac and his people had to move out of the area because they had become such a large number of people and too powerful to be living at such close quarters with the Philistines. This very similar experience to the one Abraham had had and the similar deliverance that God provided no doubt gave a very vivid picture of the lesson God then taught Isaac: 'I am the God of your father Abraham. Do not be afraid, for I am with you; I will bless you and will increase the number of your descendants for the sake of my servant Abraham' (*Gen. 26:24*).

**3.** Another Abimelech was the son of Gideon. This son was born of a concubine who came from Shechem (*Judg. 8:31*). As soon as Gideon had died, the Israelites once again turned to worship Baals and refused to show any kindness to Gideon's family and descendants (*Judg. 8:34–34*). Abimelech went back to his mother's town, Shechem, and won support for himself (*Judg. 9*). With the money they gave him he hired bandits who went and murdered all 70 sons of Gideon. Abimelech ruled the area for three years

(*Judg. 9:22*), but later 'God sent an evil spirit between Abimelech and the citizens of Shechem, who acted treacherously against Abimelech. God did this in order that the crime against Jerub-Baal's seventy sons . . . might be avenged' (*Judg. 9:23–24*). As the citizens of Shechem rebelled against him, he and his troops defeated the town in battle. Abimelech and his men then marched on the nearby town of Thebez. Just as they seemed to be about to defeat this town as well, a woman, hiding in the fortified tower in the centre of the town, dropped a millstone on Abimelech's head (*Judg. 9:53; 2 Sam. 11:21*). Ashamed that he had been defeated by a woman, he asked his armour-bearer to kill him (*Judg. 9:50–54*). The writer of the book of Judges then adds that in this way God brought justice both upon Abimelech for killing all his brothers, but also on the Shechemites for their original rebellion against the house of Gideon (*Judg. 9:56–57*). See also *Gideon, Gaal* and *Jotham.*

**4.** Another Abimelech is mentioned in the introduction to *Ps. 34*. This was probably the title of the Philistine king of Gath, Achish, to whom David ran when fleeing Saul. P.D.G.

**ABINADAB** (Heb., 'father is noble').

**1.** The second of eight sons of Jesse who were paraded in front of the prophet Samuel before eventually God indicated to Samuel that David was the one to be anointed king of Israel (*1 Sam. 16:8; 1 Chron. 2:13*). God taught both Samuel and the nation that he did not look on 'the outward appearance' when he was choosing someone for his work, rather 'the LORD looks at the heart' (*1 Sam. 16:7*). This Abinadab was one of David's older brothers later to be found among Saul's troops who were so scared of the challenge coming from the Philistine giant Goliath. It was to be David again who was God's choice to bring his

8

people victory over the giant and his Philistine masters (1 Sam. 17:3).

**2.** The day King Saul died in battle against the Philistines, Saul's second son Abinadab was also killed (1 Sam. 31:2; 1 Chron. 8:33; 9:39; 10:2).

**3.** This Abinadab came from Kiriath Jearim, where his house stood on a hill (1 Sam. 7:1). The ark of the covenant had been kept in his house after the Philistines had returned it to Israel. When King David ordered that the ark be brought up to Jerusalem, it was placed on a cart and Abinadab's sons, Uzzah and Ahio, led it (2 Sam. 6:3; 1 Chron. 13). See *Uzzah* and *Ahio* for more detail.   P.D.G.

**ABINOAM,** the father of Barak (Judg. 4:6, 12; 5:1, 12).

**ABIRAM** (Heb., 'exalted father').

**1.** A son of Eliab, a Reubenite. Together with his brother Dathan and Korah the Levite, they instigated a rebellion against Moses, leading 250 others to challenge his authority (Num. 16). This challenge to Moses and Aaron was a challenge to God's chosen leadership and therefore to the very holiness of God and his people. Their lack of faith in God and their disobedience led to their death as the ground opened and 'swallowed them, with their households' (Num. 16:23–35). Later this judgment was to serve as a reminder to the Israelites that they should love the LORD and keep his commands (Deut. 11:6; Ps. 106:17).

**2.** Abiram son of Hiel died because his father rebuilt Jericho in Ahab's time. In Josh. 6:26 Joshua placed a curse on anyone who would rebuild the city of Jericho, which he had destroyed by the power of God. 1 Kings 16:34 shows how this curse was fulfilled. This evil act of disobedience to the LORD's command was just one of the many evils of Ahab's day. The implication of the text is that a more godly king of Israel would have stopped the work proceeding.   P.D.G.

**ABISHAG,** a young and beautiful woman from Shunem who was chosen to help King David towards the end of his life (1 Kings 1:3, 15). She helped keep him warm in bed and waited on him, but had no sexual relations with him (v. 4). After David's death, Adonijah asked Bathsheba for permission to marry Abishag, thus tying her up with the intrigue that surrounded the succession to the throne. In fact Abishag had been present when David had promised Bathsheba that her son Solomon would succeed him (1 Kings 1:15–31). Solomon was furious at this request from his older brother, assuming that such a marriage would in effect give Adonijah the throne, and so Solomon had him put to death (1 Kings 2:17, 22–25).   P.D.G.

**ABISHAI** was the son of Zeruiah, one of David's sisters, and was Joab's brother (1 Sam. 26:6). He was one of David's most loyal warriors and led the second group of three among David's 'mighty men' (1 Chron. 11:20). Renowned in battle, some of his deeds are recounted in 1 Chron. 18:12; 19:11, 15.

Before David attained the throne, when he was fleeing from Saul, Abishai fought beside him. He is first mentioned in 1 Sam. 26, where David asked for a volunteer to go with him by night right into Saul's camp while they were all sleeping. Once there, Abishai recommended that he should immediately put Saul to death. David, however, would not hear of anyone laying a hand on the LORD's anointed. Only the LORD himself could strike Saul, and David was prepared to wait for that to happen. So Abishai picked up Saul's spear and water jug and took them back with David. From the top of a hill David called out to Saul and Abner, Saul's commander, and showed them how he had spared Saul's life. Later it was Abner who killed Asahel, and so Joab and Abishai, his brothers, pursued

Abner and killed him (2 Sam. 2:24; 3:30).

Later, when Absalom rebelled against David, still Abishai remained loyal. He was made the leader of one third of David's forces to repel Absalom's attack in Gilead (2 Sam. 18:2). On several occasions David had to calm Abishai down and try to persuade him that the LORD would oversee the end of his enemies (see also 2 Sam. 16:9–12). Although David appreciated Abishai's loyalty and needed him to fight off Absalom, he did plead with him to 'Be gentle with the young man Absalom' (2 Sam. 18:5). Finally, towards the end of David's life, Abishai was again instrumental in saving David, this time from a giant warrior of the Philistines (2 Sam. 21:17).

Abishai was fiercely loyal to David, but never exhibited David's commitment to the sovereignty of the LORD. He would rather do things himself than leave them in the hands of the LORD.

P.D.G.

**ABISHALOM,** see Maacah (1 Kings 15:2, 10).

**ABISHUA** (Heb., 'father of salvation').
**1.** A son of Bela and grandson of Benjamin (1 Chron. 8:4).
**2.** A son of Phinehas and the father of Bukki, Abishua is listed as a descendant of Aaron in 1 Chron. 6:4–5, 50 and is mentioned in Ezra 7:5 as an ancestor of Ezra.

**ABISHUR,** a son of Shammai, husband to Abihail (see 1 Chron. 2:28–29).

**ABITAL,** the mother of David's fifth son, Shephatiah, born in Hebron (2 Sam. 3:4).

**ABITUB** (Heb., 'my father is good'), a descendant of Benjamin and a son of Shaharaim and Hushim (his mother). He was born in Moab (1 Chron. 8:11).

**ABIUD** (Heb., 'my father is majesty'). In the genealogy of Jesus he is listed as the son of Zerubbabel and the father of Eliakim. In Matthew's Gospel the kingship of Jesus is established in a variety of ways, not least through this genealogy, which comes down through various kings and princes like Zerubbabel to Joseph and then to Jesus (Matt. 1:13).

**ABNER** was the masterful commander of Saul's army and later of the army that followed Saul's son, Ish-bosheth. He was the son of Ner who was Saul's uncle (1 Sam. 14:50). It was Abner who looked after the young David when he was preparing to go out to meet Goliath (1 Sam. 17:55, 57). Abner was highly thought of by Saul and ate at his table in the palace (1 Sam. 20:25) but soon had good reason to dislike David. When Saul was chasing David, David went into Saul's camp by night and stuck a spear into the ground near Saul's head, refusing to kill the LORD's anointed. On returning to his camp, David taunted Abner for not properly looking after his master (1 Sam. 26:5–16).

Following the defeat of Saul's household at the hands of the Philistines, David was anointed king, but Abner took Ish-bosheth over the Jordan to Mahanaim where he set him up as king (2 Sam. 2). When Abner and his men returned to Gibeon they were confronted by Joab, the commander of David's army. After a great battle, Abner fled (see Asahel). He continued to have great influence in Ish-bosheth's household (2 Sam. 3:6). When his loyalty was questioned he was very angry and defected to David's side (2 Sam. 3). Abner then persuaded the people of Israel and the Benjamites to give their allegiance to David.

When Joab returned he was suspicious of Abner's motives and perhaps jealously concerned that David would begin to look too highly on Abner (2 Sam. 3:22–25). But he was also determined to avenge the blood of his brother Asahel whom Abner had, albeit reluctantly, killed. Joab went to speak to Abner and stabbed him to death (2 Sam. 3:27). Effectively Abner's death was the final death-knell for any remaining hopes which Saul's son Ish-bosheth may have entertained of becoming king of Israel. Soon Ish-bosheth was killed (2 Sam. 4) and David became king over all Israel at Hebron (2 Sam. 5). David always respected Abner's loyalty to Saul's dynasty and his military ability. He was distressed at the way Abner was killed and blamed Joab, calling down a curse on Joab's family (2 Sam. 3; 1 Kings 2:5, 32). Later in David's reign Abner's son, Jaasiel, was appointed leader of the tribe of Benjamin (1 Chron. 27:21).

P.D.G.

# ABRAHAM (ABRAM)

## Abraham in Genesis

Abraham's history begins at Gen. 11:26 with his birth and continues until Gen. 25:19, when he is buried at Machpelah by his sons Isaac and Ishmael. This is the longest allocation of space to any of the patriarchs and reflects the importance of 'the father of all who believe' (Rom. 4:11–17).

### A slowly maturing faith

There is a distinct pattern in the way Abraham's story is told:

($A^1$) Gen. 11:27–32: The first things.
   Ancestry and birth. The Haran family. Abraham and Sarai.

($B^1$) Gen. 12:1–20:17: The conflict of faith.
   ($b^1$) Gen. 12:1–20: Venturing and compromising.
      Arrival in the Promised Land. The promise announced. The presence of Lot. The Land identified. The Land abandoned in time of hardship. The LORD can promise, but can he provide? The issue of faith and perseverance.
   ($b^2$) Gen. 13:1–18: Recommitment and compromise.
      Return to the Land. Lot. Strife. Some of the land ceded to Lot. The word of God adjusted to man's circumstances. The promise reiterated. The issue of faith and the unchangeable word of God.
   ($b^3$) Gen. 14:1–16:16: Reclamation and compromise.
      Resolute action reclaims the Land. The promise guaranteed by covenant. The compromise of Hagar. The issue of faith and patience.
   ($b^4$) Gen. 17:1–20:18: The covenant established.
      Detailed promises. The LORD's faithfulness to his covenant and Abraham's compromise based on fear. The issue of faith and trust.

($B^2$) Gen. 21:2–22:19: The maturing of faith.
   The birth of Isaac. A new title for the LORD. The offering of Isaac. The promise renewed yet again.

11

(A²) Gen. 22:20–25:10: The last things.
The Haran family. The death of Sarah. A Haran bride for Isaac. The death of Abraham.

Notice how the story is bracketed about (A¹, A²) by references to Haran and by the contrast between birth and death. It is a story of gradual transformation by divine grace whereby the people with old names, Abram and Sarai (A¹) become the people with new names, Abraham and Sarah (A²). But it was not a sudden transformation. The great decision of faith (Gen. 15:4–6) was instantaneous and irreversible, but the life of faith was a prolonged struggle (b¹–b⁴) with many faults and many lapses. Faith was effective from the start but only reached its maturity slowly. This point is as much insisted on in the New Testament as by the way the story of Abraham is told in the Old. Thus *Heb. 6:13* notes that the promise was not 'received' without patience, and *James 2:22* speaks of his faith being 'made complete'. The portrait of the father of faith, believing Abraham, speaks decisively against instantaneous sanctification.

The story of b¹–b⁴ is one of compromise. There was, first, fear in case, after all, the LORD who had called (Gen. 12:1) and promised (vv. 2–4, 7) could not also provide (note 'because', v. 10). Secondly, compromise entered through the understandable desire to find a quick, practical solution to a family problem (Gen. 13:8), and Abram was prepared to adjust the word of God (the promise of the whole Land) to pacify Lot. Next came the compromise involving Hagar, arising from impatient longing for the promise (Gen. 15:2–4) to be fulfilled (cf. Gen. 16:1). And, fourthly, Abraham compromised through thoughtless habit and fear for personal safety (Gen. 20:1, 11–13). This last was as culpable a compromise as any Abraham ever made. The LORD had not only committed himself by covenant to Abraham (Gen. 17:1–8), but had shown how liberal he was in keeping his covenant-undertakings: for he 'remembered Abraham and he brought Lot out' (Gen. 19:29), even though Lot was not directly embraced by the promise in Gen. 17:77? Yet when the crunch came Abraham could not be sure that the LORD would prove trustworthy when he was himself in a supposed danger (Gen. 20:11)!

The road to maturity of faith (Gen. 22:1–19; James 2:21–22) was always two steps forward and one back, a constant, testing demand in which the pressures of life – food (Gen. 12:10), family (Gen. 13:7), longings (Gen. 15:3; 16:1) and fears (Gen. 20:11) – all had their parts to play as those 'trials of many kinds' (James 1:2) which, if they are met with faith and perseverance, make us 'mature and complete' (James 1:3).

But this mixed story of progress and lapse has its distinct shape, and we owe it to the literary artistry of the Bible to take brief note of how b¹ and b⁴ share references to a deceit practised over Sarah (Gen. 12:1–13; 20:1). As long as Abraham walked the earth he was not immune from temptation – nor even from the recurrence of the same temptation. Yet, though he proved faithless, the LORD remained faithful, unable to deny himself (2 Tim. 2:13), and stepped into the situation in his own providential way not only to safeguard the promised seed but even to use Abram's error to enrich him materially (Gen. 12:16) and to establish him spiritually as prophet and intercessor (Gen. 20:7, 17). The middle sections (b² and b³) share the theme of the Land: pressed by the contentiousness of Lot's presence, Abram would even have forfeited his right to part of what God had promised him (Gen. 13:8–9) – as if it were within his competence to give away the Promised Land! By contrast, when the coalition of earthly kings came to establish what they saw as their right to the very same area (Gen. 14:1–11), Abram first acted with resoluteness to quash their claim (vv. 13–16) and then, with equal resoluteness, neither contested the king of Sodom when he calmly resumed possession of what he had lost nor accepted any part of the spoil. Just as the Land was not Abram's to give away, neither was it his to conquer. The promises of God cannot be bartered away (Gen. 13:8–9), nor can they be inherited other than at the LORD's time and by the perseverance of faith. Very touchingly, the story of Sarah's death (Gen. 23) and the purchase of Machpelah as a burying place bears on this same topic. It was the custom in the patriarchal family to take their dead home for burial (Gen. 50:4–5, 25), but Sarah was not taken back to Ur or Haran (Gen. 11:31–32). She was buried in Canaan. The cave with its treasured dead was a mute and potent statement: 'This land is home; this land is ours as the LORD has promised.'

### A plan for the world

Before we leave the subject of Abraham in Genesis we must notice the point at which he makes his first appearance. In contrast to Gen. 12–50. where this one man and his family occupy the whole foreground of the picture, Gen. 1–11 are universal, dealing as they do (following the Creation narrative, Gen. 1–2) with the world-wide events of the Fall (Gen. 3–5), the Flood (Gen. 6–9) and the dispersion at Babel (Gen. 10–11). In the narratives of Fall and Flood the element of divine forebearance and grace is quite explicit. The law under which humankind occupied and enjoyed the Garden included the warning that sin would bring death (Gen. 2:17), but when Adam and Eve fell into sin, the LORD God spoke to them in fact about on-going life and the ultimate defeat of the serpent (Gen. 3:15– 16). And when the Flood came, grace (Gen. 6:8) had already picked out one man and his family for salvation (Gen. 6:17). But at Babel we may well ask where the note of grace and hope is. Rather, it seems, the very fate they had dreaded (Gen. 11:4) had come upon them (v. 9) – with the additional calamity of a universal breakdown in communication – upon which Genesis, seemingly irrelevantly, embarks on yet another genealogy, and it looks as if humans are simply left to their scattered, divided lot. But a close look at the genealogy reveals some important points. First, it reaches back before the Babel incident to the new beginning in Noah, to trace the emerging story of the family of Shem. Secondly, it flies past eight generations (Shem to Nahor, Gen. 11:10–24) of whom it says nothing, until it reaches another virtually unknown man, Terah, who had a son called Abram (Gen. 11:26, 27–30) – to whom the LORD would presently say, 'all peoples on earth will be blessed through you' (Gen. 12:3) – literally, 'will bless themselves' or, more freely, 'will enter into the blessing they need'. Thus it is that the Babel story too has its note of grace and hope. Humanity has deteriorated; its plight is pitiable and irretrievable, but the LORD already had his plans laid (in Noah and Shem) before the sin at Babel with all its entail was committed. Because of this the book of Genesis, in its now almost exclusive focus on Abram/Abraham

13

and his family, has not turned its back on the world rather, this is how the world will yet be recovered from the curse (Gen. 3:14–20) and divisiveness (Gen. 11:9) of sin; this is the line in which will be born the seed of the woman who will crush the serpent's head (Gen. 22:18).

## The Abrahamic covenant

### Noah to Abraham

In the Bible God's covenant is his freely-given promise. In the case of Noah, where the word 'covenant' occurs for the first time, the promise was of salvation from the world-wide judgment of God (Gen. 6:17), and the four characteristic constituents of divine covenanting began to come together: promise (Gen. 6:17), sacrifice (Gen. 6:20), law (Gen. 9:1–8) and sign (Gen. 9:8–17). When the Lord covenants with Abram (Gen. 15 and 17) it becomes a little clearer how these elements are related to each other, though the fulness of the Covenant idea awaits Moses, the Exodus and Mt Sinai.

### Covenant reassurance

In the case of Abram, the Lord came to him at a time when he needed reassurance and hope, calling on him not to fear, pledging protection and a coming 'great reward' (Gen. 15:1). It is not clear why Abram needed such a word from God, but Gen. 15:1 offers a clue by dating it 'After this', i.e., following on the events of Gen. 14: the defeat of the kings (vv. 13–16), the restoration of the king of Sodom (vv. 17, 21) and the refusal of any share in the spoils (vv. 22–24). Reading between the lines, perhaps Abram was afraid of a counter-attack by the four kings. Did he begin to wonder if possibly his victory had, after all, been the Lord's intended way of bringing him into possession of the Land, and that he had thrown away his opportunity? Great victories are often followed by great depressions and mis-givings! But, for whatever reasons, Abram needed present and future reassurance, and the Lord gave it – only, however, to provoke a further rejoinder that life was not worth living without a son and heir (Gen. 15:2). How patient the Lord is! As if his earlier promises were not enough he returned to the task of comforting his servant with two specific promises: the promise of a son and a family (Gen. 15:4–5) and the promise of the land of Canaan for them to live in (v. 6). Since, however, Abram was still not reassured (v. 8), the Lord initiated covenant proceedings (vv. 9–18).

### Covenant sacrifice

As far as we are concerned, the sacrifice detailed in Gen. 15:9–17 is unexplained – though it is clear that Abram knew and understood what he was doing. But light is cast by Jer. 34:18, where people who wanted to undertake a solemn oath walked between the severed pieces of sacrificial animals, implying as they did so, 'If I do not keep my oath, so be it done to me.' In Abram's case, when he had arranged the sacrifice (Gen. 15:10), he was marginalized by a spiritual coma (v. 12), for he was not the oath-taker but only a spectator of what the LORD would do, as, reiterating the promise of descendants and land (vv. 13–16), he took this whole dire oath upon himself: he would bear the full brunt of the broken covenant. The vision of the LORD as 'a smoking brazier with a blazing torch' was not explained to Abram but, by hindsight, we know it to be a preview of the God of Sinai in fire and smoke (Exod. 19:18), the pillar of cloud and fire (Exod. 13:21–22), the holy God (Exod. 3:2–5) who by grace shrouds his holiness in order to come among his people. But all this is left unexplained. Gen. 15:18, however, is quite specific that the Abrahamic covenant was inaugurated by sacrifice.

## Law, promise and sign

Fifteen years after his arrival in Canaan (Gen. 12:4; 17:1) and 13 years after the Hagar-compromise (Gen. 16:16), the LORD came to Abram to complete the covenant arrangement. In Gen. 15:18 the technical word for 'inaugurating' a covenant is used; in Gen. 6:17 the verb means 'to implement, to put into action'; here in Gen. 17:2 'confirm' is, literally, 'put, place' and signifies that from now on the covenant will be the changeless mode of the relationship between the LORD and Abram. The passage amplifies the covenant action of Gen. 15 by spelling out the promise in detail (Gen. 17:4–8) and adding the remaining two components of law (Gen. 17:2) and sign (Gen. 17:9–14). Typically of the patriarchal period, the law (Gen. 17:1) is non-specific but is, even so, a searching requirement of holiness within divine fellowship. The promise, however, is detailed, covering four categories: personal (Gen. 17:4–5), domestic (v. 6), spiritual (v. 7) and territorial (v. 8), and is sealed with the covenant sign of circumcision (vv. 10–14). Since circumcision is specifically called 'the sign of the covenant' (Gen. 17:11), it must be interpreted in the same way as the identical words in Gen. 9:17 that is to say, circumcision signifies not what Abraham is pledging to God but what God is pledging to Abraham. For this reason Rom. 4:11 calls circumcision 'a seal of the righteousness that he had by faith': not a 'seal of faith', as if ratifying Abraham's response, but 'of righteousness', ratifying what God had done for Abraham and what he had promised to him. Henceforward, as Abraham still waited for the promised son to be born, he could strengthen himself in days of impatience or doubt by recalling that he bore in his very flesh the confirmation of the divine promises – just as, for Noah, the bow in the clouds dispelled any fears that a gathering storm might arouse. The sign in each case proclaimed the promises of God, just as the covenant signs of Baptism and the Lord's Supper continue to do today.

# Abraham's faith

## A single, steady aim

When we reviewed the history of Abraham in Genesis our emphasis fell on the conflict of faith and on Abraham's failures. It is time now to look at his faith itself, his sheer, persevering readiness to venture everything on the mere word of God. For that is what faith is, as we see it in Abraham – and in Scripture. It is not a leap in the dark, for that would be credulity, not faith. It is a leap into the light, for it rests on the word God has spoken; faith is conviction and action arising out of truth. By faith, says *Heb. 11:8*, 'Abraham, when called to go . . . went, even though he did not know where he was going.' Indeed (*Gen. 12:7*), it was not until he had well entered Canaan that the LORD finally said '. . . this land'. Nothing ever deflected Abraham from this course – not even his failures! For example, after his Egyptian compromise (*Gen. 12:10–20*) it was not sufficient to return to Canaan: he specifically went back to where he had started (*Gen. 13:3*), back to where he knew for certain that he had been on the road of faith. The whole cycle of his life is within three parameters: obeying the word of God, returning to the word of God, waiting for the word of God. This is what faith is and this is the life of faith.

Gen. 12 points to the great venture of faith (*vv. 1, 4*). Gen. 14 does not mention faith in connection with the war against the kings, but the context allows us to see it as the boldness of faith. Abram had sought to solve his family crisis (*Gen. 13:7*) by 'adjusting' the word of God to the situation (*Gen. 14:8–9*), but the LORD would have none of it. After the compromise had been made (*Gen. 14:14*) the LORD reaffirmed the word of promise: 'All the land . . . I will give to you . . . I am giving it to you' (*Gen. 13:15–17*), and it was specifically the area Abram would have ceded to Lot that he now recovers from the kings (*Gen. 14:8–12*). Faith can afford to be bold when it acts along the lines of God's promises. In *Gen. 18:23–33* we see the same principle in another way: the boldness of the prayer of faith when it rests on the known character of God (*v. 25*).

## The promised son

Genesis isolates two specific 'moments' in Abraham's life of faith for particular emphasis. First, the promise of the birth of a son was accepted by faith, and this faith was reckoned as righteousness (*Gen. 15:6*). This incident prompted one of Paul's many 'purple passages' – *Rom. 4:18–22*. Could anyone ever more perfectly express the sheer absurdity and wonder of the situation: a man and a woman who were, humanly speaking, 'past it', who acted not in wishful thinking but in full recognition of their own incapacity, but who none the less 'did not waver'? Both *Rom. 4:21* and *Heb. 11:11* underline the same core feature: 'fully persuaded that God had power to do what he had promised' . . . 'he considered him faithful who had made the promise'. Justifying faith deliberately faces up to human inability and equally deliberately, but with true simplicity, chooses to rely on the promise of God.

The other significant moment of faith which is singled out is *Gen. 22:1–19*, the sacrifice of Isaac. If it was outrageous that Abraham should face the deadness of his body and yet believe the promise that he would have a son, it was possibly even more outrageous that he should take this son, the sole focus of all the promises of God (*Heb. 11:17–18*), and, humanly speaking, put everything into irretrievable jeopardy. But he did. The heart of the matter is in *Gen. 22:5*: literally, 'I and the boy – we will go over there and we will worship and we will come back to you.' The speaker knew exactly that this 'worship' would involve the death and immolation of the boy, and yet he dared to say 'we . . . we . . . we . . .' The inspired commentary in *Heb. 11:19* says it all, and *James 2:22* points to this incident as 'faith made perfect', as, of course, it was. For the 'simple faith' of *Gen. 15:6*, faith as bare reliance on the word of God, must prove its reality in the challenges and responses of daily life. These testings are not haphazard but elements in a divine educative programme (*Heb. 12:1–10*) to make us 'partakers of his holiness'. Abram began with God (*Gen. 15:6*) and Abraham went the whole distance (*Gen. 22:15–18*).

### The family of believers

It is as the man of faith that Abraham is presented as our father and example in the New Testament. The key passages are *Rom. 4*, where Abraham is called the father of all those who believe (*Rom. 4:11–12, 16*) and *Gal. 3:1–14*, where believers are called his children (*Gal. 3:7*). Galatians insists that in this regard the New Testament has nothing to add to the Old: all the blessings of God in Christ Jesus, summed up and comprised fully in the gift of the Holy Spirit, are ours simply and solely on the ground of Abraham-like faith. Romans adds that this faith is the distinguishing mark of the people of God, his Israel. Physical descent from Abraham brings no more spiritual benefit for Paul in *Rom. 2:28–29; 9:7, 10–13* than for John the Baptist in *Matt. 3:9*. From the divine side, 'the Israel of God' is his new creation (*Gal. 6:15–16*) from the point of view of human experience and response, it 'comes by faith, so that it may be by grace and may be guaranteed to all Abraham's offspring; not only to those who are of the law but also to those who are of the faith of Abraham' (*Rom. 4:16*).

### The God of Abraham

*Who is the* LORD? In the stories of Abraham the divine Name, Yahweh (represented in NIV by 'LORD'), occurs 73 times, and references like *Gen. 15:8* show Abram personally using the Name. Yet is is also true, as we read in *Exod. 6:2–3*, that though the Name was known, no specific meaning was yet attached to it. In Genesis God did not reveal himself by explaining the meaning of 'Yahweh' but by using other styles and titles. *Gen. 17:1* puts the matter concisely: 'Yahweh appeared to him and said, "I am El Shaddai . . ."' El Shaddai (NIV, 'God Almighty') is the chief of four similar titles of God known to Abraham: Melchizedek came to Abraham as 'priest of God Most High' (El Elyon). Whether we translate El Olam as 'creator' (NIV) or 'possessor' (RV) 'of heaven and earth', he is the universal and supreme God, and Abram does not hesitate to identify him with his own God, Yahweh (*Gen. 14:22*). Again, when the LORD (*Gen. 16:13*) met with Hagar, she knew him as 'the God who sees me' (El Roi), a God of direct (and very gracious) knowledge of what was happening on earth. In *Gen. 21:22* Abimelech of Gerar negotiated a perpetual treaty of friendship with Abraham and, in commemoration of it, Abraham planted a tamarisk and worshipped 'the LORD, the Eternal God' (Yahweh El Olam) – possibly arriving at this title by concluding that only an eternal God could be invoked to superintend a treaty in perpetuity. (See section on Names in the article on God.)

## El Shaddai

But of these titles it is only El Shaddai that reappears in the rest of Genesis (28:3; 35:11; 43:14; 48:3; 49:25). What did it mean to the writers of this book? The meaning of 'Shaddai' as a word is much disputed and uncertain, but the contexts in which it is used suggest how it should be understood. For example, in Gen. 17:1 at least 14 years had elapsed since the original promise of a son to Abraham (Gen. 16:16). The passing years (Abraham was now almost 100 years old and Sarah'was past child-bearing, Gen. 18:11) had the effect of underlining human powerlessness. It was in this context that the LORD revealed himself as El Shaddai, and this same characteristic – the ability to transform situations of human helplessness – appears in other passages too. Thus, when Jacob sent his sons back to Egypt to face the unpredictable but all-powerful Joseph, he commended them to El Shaddai (Gen. 43:14). Doubtless in the same spirit, in Gen. 48:3, he says that it was El Shaddai who had met with him at Bethel – for what could be more hopeless than the situation of Jacob, the homeless wanderer and outcast? El Shaddai is the God who takes over human incapacity and transforms it – just as he did when he made the childless Abram into Abraham, the father of a multitude of nations. In every situation such a God can be trusted.

It was because he knew his God – El Shaddai, the God of limitless power to transform – that Abraham was the pre-eminent man of faith. J.A.M.

**ABSALOM** (Heb., 'father of peace') was the third of David's six sons. His mother was Maacah and he was born at Hebron. His passionate behaviour was shown in the murder of Amnon (see *Amnon*) when he discovered that the latter had raped Absalom's sister Tamar (2 Sam. 13). He was renowned for his beauty and long hair (2 Sam. 14:25–27).

The turmoil in David's crumbling kingship was compounded by disloyalty and murder in the kingdom, David's adultery (1 Sam. 11–12) and family violence and rape. The life of Absalom serves to illustrate the fact that the consequences of sin outlive sincere regret. Though David's sincere repentance over his adultery with Bathsheba was accepted by God, he could not escape the tumultuous consequences

in his own family. David's reluctance to intervene in punishing Amnon's rape of Absalom's sister (2 Sam. 13:22) lost him credibility in the eyes of his son. Anger and resentment smouldered in Absalom for two years until the opportunity for revenge arose and he killed Amnon (2 Sam. 13:28–29). Absalom was forced into exile for three years until the diplomatic Joab forced David into acknowledging his sin. Eventually a degree of reconciliation between son and father came about (see 2 Sam. 14).

However, the tension never went away. From this point onwards, Absalom tried hard to subvert his father's rule. The unresolved conflict between Absalom and David continued to plague David, and despite the severe threat that

Absalom now posed to David's rule, he was reluctant to perceive the severity of the danger to his authority. Absalom conspired to overthrow his father and succeeded in getting some support from disaffected followers of David (2 Sam. 15). Joab recognized David's vacillation and reluctance to bring about the death of his own son. It was Joab who eventually put Absalom to death. Absalom was found hanging in an oak tree by his hair and was finished off by Joab and his armour bearers (2 Sam. 18:1–18).

David mourned greatly for Absalom, until Joab persuaded David of the importance of seeing his son's life in the perspective of the havoc he had caused.

Absalom's three sons are not mentioned after 2 Sam. 14:27. It appears from 2 Sam. 18:18 that only his daughter survived, whom he named after his sister Tamar.                                        S.V.

**ACBOR** (Heb., 'mouse').

**1.** The father of one of the kings of Edom before the Israelites conquered the area. His son, Baal-Hanan, succeeded Shaul in the king list (Gen. 36:38–39; 1 Chron. 1:49).

**2.** In Josiah's reign the 'book of the law' was discovered in the Temple. Josiah sent Acbor, along with Hilkiah the priest and others, to consult the prophetess Huldah concerning the book. Huldah drew attention to the words of God's law that promised judgment on Israel if she turned from the LORD and worshipped other gods. This was what Israel had done and so judgment was coming (2 Kings 22:12–17).

Later, in Jeremiah's time, Acbor's son Elnathan became a court official. He was sent to Egypt to capture and bring back Uriah the prophet (Jer. 26:22; 36:12).
                                        P.D.G.

**ACHAICUS,** mentioned in 1 Cor. 16:17 along with Stephanas and Fortunatus. Possibly he was a slave from the family of a certain L. Mummius who had conquered Achaia (v. 15), but this is uncertain. Together with his two colleagues he brought information from Corinth to Paul. See Stephanas.

**ACHAN** (Heb., 'trouble-maker'). The son of Carmi, son of Zerah, Achan was a descendant of Judah and Tamar. Achan is noted for having 'troubled' Israel with serious sin. When Joshua had destroyed Jericho the LORD had placed it under a curse or 'ban'. Everything in the city had to be 'devoted' to the LORD. Often such 'devotion' of things to the LORD involved their complete destruction. Such commands of God taught the people several truths about themselves and the LORD God. As the 'holy' God he judges those who are 'unholy', refusing to recognize and worship him. God's judgment on Jericho was most severe. But also by insisting that no slaves be captured and no spoils taken, God was showing that the Israelites were to keep themselves holy unto his service. He would supply all their needs. For Achan the temptation to take spoil was too much, and he disobeyed the command of God through Joshua (Josh. 7).

The next town to conquer was Ai. It seemed easy, but the first brigade returned beaten. Joshua prayed and the LORD showed him that 'Israel' had sinned. By a process of casting lots the LORD led the leaders to Achan, who had hidden the spoil in the ground in his tent. He was taken out and stoned, and the LORD's anger turned from the Israelites. Following this Ai was taken. The valley of Achor where Achan was stoned became a symbol later for a place of evil. The prophets foresaw a day when the LORD would turn it into a place of hope and rest (Is. 65:10; Hos. 2:15).

Of interest in Josh. 7 is the way in which Israel seems to be held responsible *together* for the sin of the one person. Certainly, all Israel suffered for this sin, but in the end Achan alone could take responsibility. He stands as a reminder to future generations of the danger of disobedience (*Josh. 22:20*).                P.D.G

**ACHAR** (Heb., 'trouble-maker'). *1 Chron. 2:7*. An alternative form of Achan.

**ACHISH** (Heb., 'the king gives'). A king of Gath in the days of King David. His father was Maoch (*1 Sam. 27:2*) or, if the same person some years later is being referred to, Maacah (*1 Kings 2:39*). In this latter passage, in the days of Solomon, two of Shimei's slaves fled to Achish.

David twice took refuge with Achish in Gath whilst fleeing from Saul. The first time (*1 Sam. 21:10–15*) David feigned madness because he was scared of the Philistine King Achish. Having escaped Saul and been taken for a madman by Achish, David fled to the cave of Adullam. On the second occasion (*1 Sam. 27:1–12*) David fled to Achish with 600 men and all their families. Achish gave David the desert town of Ziklag in which to settle. True to his determination not to kill the LORD's anointed (Saul), David made out to Achish that he was sending raiding parties into Israel, when in fact he was raiding the cities of other Philistine kings. Later, when the Philistine kings went up to fight Israel, Achish wanted David to go with them, but the other Philistine kings refused to allow him to come, fearing that he might turn against them (*1 Sam. 28:1–2; 29:1–11*). David returned to Philistine territory.

While David had received help from Achish, he had never done anything to harm Israel. He was determined that the LORD would be the one who would eventually bring him to the throne of Israel, and he would not achieve this through joining forces with the LORD's enemies. This combined assault of the Philistines did eventually lead to the death of Saul and, in God's time, to David himself becoming king.                P.D.G.

**ACSAH,** a daughter of Caleb. Caleb had promised that whoever captured Kiriath Sepher could marry his daughter (*Josh. 15:16; Judg. 1:12*). Othniel took the city and so married her. Caleb had given her land in the Negev, and so later she asked her father for water springs. Duly these were given to her (*Josh. 15:19*).

**ADAH** (Heb., 'beauty').

**1.** Adah was one of two wives of Lamech. She was the mother of Jabal and Jubal who respectively were the progenitors of nomadic herdsmen and musicians (*Gen. 4:19–21*). She had to listen to Lamech's vengeful boast of murdering those who had wronged him (*Gen. 4:23–24*) – a reminder of the sin that already so thoroughly permeated the world.

**2.** One of Esau's wives taken from the women of Canaan. She was a daughter of Elon the Hittite. She gave birth to Eliphaz (*Gen. 36:4, 10* etc.). Whether Esau married two daughters from the same family when he married Basemath is not certain, but she is also called the daughter of Elon the Hittite. Esau's marriage into Canaanite families introduced pagan gods and culture right into an Israelite home. Such intermarriage would, time and again, lead Israelites to turn away from the LORD. Isaac and Rebekah found Esau's marriage a 'source of grief' probably for this very reason (*Gen. 26:35*).                P.D.G.

**ADAIAH** (Heb., 'pleasing to the LORD').

**1.** The grandfather of Josiah and the father of Jedidah (*2 Kings 22:1*).

**2.** The son of Ethan and the father of Zerah. One of Adaiah's descendants was Asaph, the associate of Heman the musician (*1 Chron. 6:41*).

**3.** The son of Shimei and a leader in the tribe of Benjamin (*1 Chron. 8:21*).

**4.** The son of Jehoram, he was one of the priests listed in *1 Chron. 9:12*.

**5.** The father of Maaseiah, who was the commander of a unit of 100 men

(2 Chron. 23:1). For more detail see Elishaphat.

**6.** A descendant of Bani, he is listed in Ezra 10:29 among those who had married foreign women.

**7.** A descendant of Binnui, he is listed in Ezra 10:39 among those who had married foreign women.

**8.** The ancestor of Maaseiah, a provincial leader who settled in Jerusalem (Neh. 11:5).

**9.** One of the priests listed in Neh. 11:12 who settled in Jerusalem. He was probably the same person as 4.          M.P.

**ADALIA,** one of ten sons of Haman killed in Susa by the Jews (Est. 9:8).

# ADAM

## Adam in the Old Testament

Some scholars suggest that this name comes from the Heb. word for 'ground', but it is not possible to be certain. This name can be used in the Bible as both the proper name of the first created person (Gen. 5:1; 1 Chron. 1:1) and, regularly, as a word meaning 'mankind' or 'man'. In certain texts in the opening chapters of Genesis there is some debate about whether the Heb. should be translated as the proper name 'Adam' or simply as 'mankind'. The first occurrence of the word is in Gen. 1:26–27. There the NIV has 'Let us make man,' in common with the views of many commentators. In Gen. 2:20 the NIV opts for 'Adam' but gives a footnote suggesting the alternative 'man'.

Adam was created by God and was the first man to inhabit the newly created earth. In the opening chapters of Genesis that creation is described. Man is clearly distinguished from the rest of the animal creation. He was made 'in the image of God' and was given dominion over the rest of creation (Gen. 1:26). He had the breath of God in him (Gen. 2:7) and was placed in the Garden of Eden (Gen. 2:8–17), where he was to obey the commands of God, notably the command not to eat of the tree of the knowledge of good and evil (Gen. 2:17). He had to work in this paradise, and God created a woman, Eve, to help him fulfil the tasks for which he was created. Adam decribed his wife as 'bone of my bones and flesh of my flesh' (Gen. 2:23). They were created without sin and lived in innocence.

The biblical description of Adam in these early chapters helps the readers understand the unique relationship between God and his human creation. Adam was not like the animals. The dominion over the rest of creation that was given to him from the beginning would continue to belong to his descendants as long as the earth would last. God talked to Adam (Gen. 1:28–30). Yet, in the midst of this close relationship, the first two chapters also serve to reinforce Adam's complete dependence on God. Adam needed God to create a woman for him. Adam needed God to give him food and sustenance (Gen. 1:29–30), and he needed God to put him in the Garden of Eden (Gen. 2:15).

Only a little is seen of Adam's own reactions to what was being done for him by God. He began to exercise his dominion over creation (Gen. 1:26) when he named all the animals (Gen. 2:19–20), but even here it is made clear that his dominion was always secondary. God brought the animals to Adam for him to name them. Adam clearly appreciated his new partner, and his words in Gen. 2:23 may well give rise to the idea that the apostle Paul used in Eph. 5:28–29 when he said, 'He who loves his wife loves himself.'

In Gen. 3 Adam's sin is described. The relationship with God that was so dependent and pure in the opening two chapters was suddenly destroyed. Eve was tempted by the 'serpent' (Satan) and ate the fruit of the tree of the knowledge of good and evil. In turn, she fed the fruit to Adam. Immediately the purity of creation was destroyed. Having been naked and without any shame at all (Gen. 2:25), their eyes were 'opened' and they were ashamed and covered themselves (Gen. 3:7). Their desire to cover themselves was an aspect of their desire to hide from God, whom they knew they had disobeyed. So, having been happy to talk to God and obey his commands, they hid from God as he walked through the Garden (Gen. 3:8). The only proper conversation recorded in the Bible between God and Adam is the one in which Adam tried to lay the blame for what had happened on his wife.

The punishment of God on Adam's sin is spelled out in graphic terms. The two areas where Adam had been so clearly set apart from the animals were both affected in this punishment. The work that Adam had been given to do for God's glory as part of his dominion over creation would now be painful at every turn (Gen. 3:17–19). From this point on Adam was to find it difficult to cultivate the land and to have dominion over the creatures of the earth. This remained his created task, but it was to be a trying and bruising effort that would continue until death, for he would return to the dust from which he had been formed (Gen. 3:19).

Adam also experienced judgment in being separated from God, both in being thrown out of the Garden of Eden (Gen. 3:23–24) and in beginning to see the physical manifestation of what was now a spiritual reality – death. Very soon Adam saw his sons begin to fight and he saw Cain kill Abel (Gen. 4:8).

Adam set the scene for humanity. It is a scene in which the true origins of mankind as unique in God's creation are clearly revealed, but it is also a scene in which the one who was given so much dominion by the Creator tried to deny his dependence on God. In that denial, in that sin, Adam set his sights on a life that would try to ignore and even deny God. In that sin man set himself up in the place of God. Through Adam sin entered the world and brought upon the whole of creation God's judgment curse.

It is important to note that even after the judgment and the exclusion from the Garden of Eden, Adam was still Adam. He did not regress into something no better than the animals. He was still made in the image of God and he still had the breath of God within him. However, he was sinful and, as the biblical narrative continues, it becomes clear that every aspect of man was permeated with that sin and that desire to deny God in thought, word and deed.

The Old Testament does not make much further reference to Adam by name. The creation is mentioned frequently and the status of mankind as created beings was recalled by many of the faithful as they worshipped God (see Ps. 8:3–5). However, Abraham received much more attention in Jewish history, because he was the father of the nation of Israel. It was not until the age of the New Testament that Adam once again figured prominently in discussions of God's dealings with mankind.

## Adam in the New Testament

In *Luke 3:38* Adam stands at the beginning of a genealogy leading to Jesus. The difference between this genealogy and Matthew's (*Matt. 1:1*), which goes back to Abraham, is notable and probably indicates Luke's concern to show Christ's relationship to the whole of mankind and not just to the Jewish people. There is another direct reference to the man Adam in *Jude 14*.

Jesus referred back to *Gen. 1:27* and *2:24* when talking about marriage and its permanency. God had created Adam and Eve to be together, and this was to be the pattern for married and family life. A similar use was made of these texts by the apostle Paul in *Eph. 5:31*. But there Paul added further meaning to that relationship between man and woman, indicating that in the marriage relationship itself there was a reflection of the relationship between Christ and his church (see 1 *Cor. 6:16–17*). The love, permanency and intimacy of this relationship with Christ were all drawn out by Paul as he compared it with marriage.

Paul further appealed to Adam's relationship with Eve to support his view of the place of women in the home and in worship. Women have different roles from men because Adam 'was formed first' and Eve was deceived first (1 *Tim. 2:13*; see 1 *Cor. 11:8–9*).

However, it was also in Paul's writings that a clear description was formulated of the theological place that Adam has in the affairs of man. In *Rom. 5* Paul presented his view of the relationship between Adam and Christ. Adam (*Rom. 5:14*), 'one man' (*v. 12*), brought sin to all mankind. In doing so he 'was a pattern of the one to come' (*v. 14*). 'Pattern' he may have been, but Paul's concern in this passage was, in fact, to demonstrate just how very different Christ is from Adam.

Paul's argument depended on his understanding that Adam was indeed *one* historical person. He brought sin into the world, sin which was daily reconfirmed in the lives of every individual (*Rom. 5:12*), 'because all sinned'. Then in *v. 15* the contrast begins with 'But the gift is not like the trespass'. Paul wanted people to hear his emphasis on two things through this passage. Repeatedly he talked of 'one man', referring both to Adam and to Christ. (The word 'one' is repeated eleven times in *vv. 15–19*.) And secondly he wanted the full significance of his 'how much more' argument to be grasped. Christian believers can learn about the grace of God in Christ by seeing 'how much more' grace overflows to people after many sins when compared with the judgment that followed only one sin (*vv. 15–17*). Adam was far surpassed by Christ. Christ obeyed God as Adam did not. Christ brought righteousness where Adam brought judgment. Christ brought eternal life (*v. 21*) where Adam brought death.

Paul showed that men and women face two options: they can be represented by Adam as their head or by Christ. They can receive God's grace of salvation through faith in Christ (*Rom. 5:2*) or they can receive judgment as sons of Adam. Adam is thus seen as the one who was disobedient and brought sin, judgment and death to all people (*v. 18*), while Christ brings salvation from that judgment, from the wrath of God.

This contrast between Adam and Christ was developed along similar lines in 1 *Cor. 15* in Paul's discussion about death and resurrection. *Verse 22*: 'For as in Adam all die, so in Christ all will be made alive.' The contrast which Paul made was between the natural person and the person who, by faith, is spiritual. Paul brought this out more vividly in *1 Cor. 15:45–47*, in which he contrasted the 'first man Adam [who] became a living being' with the 'last Adam, a life-giving spirit'. The first was the Adam of Genesis, 'of the dust of the earth', and the second was Christ, the 'man from heaven'.

The 'all' of *1 Cor. 15:22* has been discussed at length by commentators. It refers to two different groups of 'all'. All who are 'in Adam', all who are normal and natural human beings, do die because of God's judgment on Adam's sin and on their own daily sin. The second group, all who are 'in Christ', who have faith in him and are represented by him, will take on his nature – 'the likeness of the man from heaven' (*1 Cor. 15:49*), and this will bring eternal life and resurrection.

However, the move from death to life, dependent on faith in Jesus, began first with Jesus himself becoming a 'man'. Jesus was prepared to take the curse of God's judgment and die in order to be the 'firstfruits' of those who would rise from the dead. As Paul put it in *1 Cor. 15:21*, 'Since death came through a man, the resurrection of the dead comes also through a *man*.' It is in this sense that Jesus is indeed 'Adam' – the *last* Adam (*1 Cor. 15:45*) or *second* man (*v. 47*). Jesus succeeded where Adam had failed, and Jesus could only do this as a true man. The '*man* from heaven' lived and suffered and died as Adam did and all mankind does, in order to bring life to those who believe. Jesus identified in his death with Adam and with all mankind, who sit under the judgment of God because of sin. In doing so he was offering himself as a sacrifice for sin, a sacrifice that was accepted by God as he raised the second Adam from death, thus reversing in Christ the judgment curse put on Adam.

P.D.G.

**ADBEEL,** the third son of Ishmael and a tribal leader (*Gen. 25:13: 1 Chron. 1:29*).

**ADDAR,** a son of Bela (*1 Chron. 8:1–3*).

**ADDI** appears in Luke's genealogy of Jesus (*Luke 3:28*).

**ADIEL** (Heb., 'ornament of God').
**1.** A clan leader of the tribe of Simeon, mentioned in *1 Chron. 4:36*.
**2.** One of the priests who settled in Jerusalem following the Babylonian Exile (*1 Chron. 9:12*). He was the son of Jahzerah and the father of Maasai.
**3.** The father of Azmaveth, who was in charge of the royal storehouses under King David (*1 Chron. 27:25*).

**ADIN** (Heb., 'voluptuous'). *Ezra 2:15* says 454 of his descendants returned from the Babylonian Exile; the number given in *Neh. 7:20* is 655. *Ezra 8:6* mentions that one of his descendants, Ebed, and 50 other men came up from Babylon during the reign of King Artaxerxes. Adin is described as one of the leaders who affixed their seal to the agreement of the people recorded in *Neh. 10:16*.

**ADINA** (Heb., 'adorned') the son of Shiza, a Reubenite. He was a leader among his people and one of David's 'mighty men' (*1 Chron. 11:42*).

**ADLAI** (Heb., 'God's justice'), the father of Shaphat who was an official in the reign of David who was 'in charge of the herds in the valleys' (*1 Chron. 27:29*).

**ADMATHA,** a wise man and legal expert consulted by King Xerxes. For details see *Memucan* (*Est. 1:14*).

**ADNA** (Heb., 'pleasure').
**1.** A descendant of Pahath-Moab, Adna

is listed in *Ezra 10:30* among those who had married foreign women.

**2.** The head of a priestly family descended from Harim, mentioned in *Neh. 12:15*. He lived in the days of Joiakim.

**ADNAH** (Heb., 'pleasure').

**1.** This Adnah was one of those great fighting men who deserted Saul and came from the tribe of Manasseh to join David at Ziklag (*1 Chron. 12:20*). This passage makes it clear that the gradual desertion from Saul of such warriors from various tribes was led by the Spirit of God: 'Day after day men came to help David, until he had a great and mighty army' (*1 Chron. 12:22*).

**2.** Another Adnah came from the tribe of Judah and was one of the senior officers in Jehoshaphat's army (*2 Chron. 17:14*).

**ADONI-BEZEK** (Heb., 'Lord of Bezek'). Mentioned only in *Judg. 1*, he was a Canaanite king of the area of Bezek. The men of Judah and Simeon were among the first to continue the fight against the Canaanites and Perizzites after Joshua's death. They killed 10,000 in that first attack and captured Adoni-Bezek. They cut off his thumbs and big toes and then took him to Jerusalem, which they had also conquered, where he later died. The Bible shows that such a cruel judgment was to be seen as a just retribution by God on a man who had done the same to many others. He acknowledged that this action was of God and that he deserved it (*Judg. 1:4–7*).                   P.D.G.

**ADONIJAH** (Heb., 'the LORD is my Lord').

**1.** Following in the footsteps of his older brother Absalom, David's fourth son Adonijah also threatened the ailing kingdom of David (*2 Sam. 3:4; 1 Kings 1–2*). His bitterness over the assumption that Solomon, rather than he, would become David's successor led him to plot a political coup, which failed through Nathan's skilful intervention. Solomon showed tolerance of Adonijah, which ran out when he made a bid for David's former nurse Abishag, resulting in his execution at Solomon's hands (*1 Kings 2:19–25*). For more detail see *Abishag* and *Nathan*.

**2.** One of nine Levites who taught the people the Law in Judah during the reign of Jehoshaphat at the time of revived interest in the book of the Law in the third year of the king's reign (*1 Chron. 17:8*).

**3.** One of those who witnessed the sealing of the people's promise to obey the word of the LORD under the influence of Nehemiah during Ezra's reforms (*Neh. 10:16*).           S.V.

**ADONIKAM** (Heb., 'my Lord has risen'). *Ezra 2:13* records that 666 of his descendants returned from Exile, and *Ezra 8:13* says a number of his descendants returned from Babylon with Ezra during the reign of King Artaxerxes. In *Neh. 7:18* the number of his descendants who returned is given as 667.

**ADONIRAM** (Heb., 'the Lord is exalted'). Son of Abda, he was in charge of forced labour both at the end of David's reign and in Solomon's time (*2 Sam. 20:24; 1 Kings 4:6; 5:14*). His job was to force the Israelites to help with royal building works. When he worked for Solomon, he had 30,000 conscripted men under him, whom he sent in shifts of 10,000 at a time to bring cedars and pine logs back from Lebanon. Such forced labour came to be hated by the Israelites, although it is just what Samuel had warned would happen when Israel disobeyed God in wanting to have a king like the surrounding nations (*1 Sam. 8:16–19*).

When Rehoboam came to the throne and continued the policy of forced labour the northern tribes split off from Judah and Benjamin. Adoniram was sent north as an ambassador to pursue

Rehoboam's demands and was stoned to death (1 Kings 12:18, 2 Chron. 10:18).

P.D.G.

**ADONI-ZEDEK** (Heb., 'my lord is righteousness') is remembered because his call to battle led to a demonstration of God's great power and miraculous work for his people in Israel, and to the defeat of the Amorites. He was king of Jerusalem at the time when Joshua led the Israelites into Canaan. His fear of the Israelites increased when he heard that the people of Gibeon, a strong and well-fortified city, had made a peace treaty with Joshua. So he formed an alliance with five Amorite kings in order to attack Gibeon (Josh. 10:1–5). Gibeon called on Joshua for help, and he quickly marched from Gilgal to fight the Amorites. The LORD gave Israel a great victory (Josh. 10:6–15). P.D.G.

**ADRAMMELECH 1.** One of the gods worshipped by the Sepharvites (2 Kings 17:31). These people were among those transported by the Assyrian king to Samaria to replace the Israelites who had been exiled from the land (v. 24). They brought with them fearful practices that included child sacrifices made by fire.
**2.** One of the sons of the Assyrian king, Sennacherib, and brother to Sharezer. Hezekiah was threatened with the fall of Jerusalem at the hand of Sennacherib and so prayed to the LORD for deliverance. Isaiah prophesied that Sennacherib would not be able to take Jerusalem but would return home and be killed (2 Kings 19). The LORD killed many Assyrians and delivered Hezekiah and his people. In fulfilment of God's promise, Sennacherib was killed by his own sons, Adrammelech and Sharezer, while worshipping his god, Nisroch (2 Kings 19:37; Is. 37:38). P.D.G.

**ADRIEL,** the son of Barzillai, married Saul's daughter Merab. Merab (wrongly called Michal in some translations of

2 Sam. 21:8) had been promised to David (1 Sam. 18:19). Later, five of their children died as a revenge for Saul's breach of Joshua's treaty with the Gibeonites (2 Sam. 21:8). Saul had put many Gibeonites to death.

**AENEAS** is mentioned only in Acts 9:33–35. The name means 'praise'. Aeneas lived in Lydda and was bedridden for eight years with a paralysis. The apostle Peter spoke to him and Jesus Christ healed him. The miracle was instantaneous. As a result many in the town turned to the Lord Jesus.

**AGABUS** was a NT prophet who is noted for two prophecies. First he prophesied, 'through the Spirit', a famine spreading across the entire Roman world (Acts 11:28). External sources demonstrate that numerous famines did occur in many places in the Roman empire. However, the prophecy was specially influential in causing the disciples in Antioch immediately to begin a collection for the Christians living in Judea and Jerusalem (Acts 11:29–30). This collection, which eventually came from many churches, was taken to Jerusalem by Barnabas and Paul.

His second prophecy was given to Paul while he was staying in Caesarea on his way to Jerusalem (Acts 21:10). This time Agabus came to him from Judea and prophesied Paul's imprisonment should he proceed to Jerusalem. In spite of the appeals of the other Christians that he should not go, Paul insisted he had to go where the Lord took him. The prophecy did, of course, come true with Paul's arrest in Jerusalem and his later deportation to Rome for trial (Acts 21:27ff.).

P.D.G.

**AGAG** This name may have been a title of some sort.
**1.** Balaam's prophecy in Num. 24:7 refers to one such person.

26

**2.** Agag the king of Amalek who was defeated by King Saul (*1 Sam. 15:8–33*). Saul was ordered by God totally to destroy the Amalekites in battle. However, Saul and his army spared Agag and some of the best of the spoils of war. Through Samuel God pronounced judgment on Saul for his disobedience. Saul added to his sin by lying and saying that they had simply retained Agag and the spoils in order to sacrifice them to God. In a sad but profound speech that promised the end of Saul's kingdom, Samuel showed that the LORD desired obedience rather than sacrifice. Disobedience was a direct rejection of the LORD's word (*1 Sam. 15:22–26*). Samuel himself then killed Agag in an action that was shown to be God's justice on a man who himself had killed many innocent people (*1 Sam. 15:33*).                                   P.D.G.

**AGEE,** the father of Shammah in *2 Sam. 23:11*.

**AGRIPPA** Described as King Agrippa in *Acts 25:13–26:32*, this king was Herod Agrippa II, son of Agrippa I. He listened to Paul's defence during his Caesarean imprisonment. Agrippa was attentive to Paul's testimony and even dared to say to Paul, 'Do you think that in such a short time you can persuade me to be a Christian?' (*Acts 26:28*). See *Herod*.

**AGUR,** son of Jakeh, was a writer of various Proverbs intended for Ithiel and Ucal (*Prov. 30:1*). He turned his listeners away from his own wisdom and advocated that they heed the 'word of God [which] is flawless' (*Prov. 30:5*). Some have suggested that his name was another designation for Solomon, but this is unlikely.

**AHAB** (Heb., 'father's brother').
**1.** The infamy of King Ahab, son of Omri and ruler of Israel at a time overlapping with the great prophet Elijah, was that of being the worst king of Israel (see *1 Kings 16:30–33*). His crimes were not primarily political. His guilt lay in the failure to expunge the threat of Baal worship. God punished him through a drought that came upon the land – a direct judgment upon his participation in idolatrous practices. His marriage to Jezebel highlighted the consistent link made in the biblical narrative between idolatrous practice and immoral behaviour. See *Jezebel*, *Elijah* and *Naboth* for more detail.

The account of Ahab's reign is not concluded until *1 Kings 22:39–53*. His skilful foreign policies are interpreted negatively by the biblical writer because of the severe religious consequences of inter-religious worship. So bad was his behaviour perceived to be that the phrase 'house of Ahab' came to be the yardstick by which particularly bad kings could be judged (*2 Kings 21:2f.*; see also *Mic. 6:16*).

**2.** This Ahab was accused by the prophet Jeremiah of prophesying lies to the people of Israel in Babylon (*Jer. 29:21–13*). Like Hannaniah (*Jer. 28*), Ahab was probably guilty of predicting a quick end to the Exile, and like the other false prophets, guilty of 'healing the wound of my people lightly' (*Jer. 6:14; 23:11*) and committing adultery with their neighbour's wives (*Jer. 29:23*). The false prophets in Jeremiah are picked out for condemnation because they purport to offer hope, which in fact is no hope.
                                   S.V.

**AHARAH,** the third son of Benjamin (*1 Chron. 8:1*). Probably a form of the name Ahiram (*Num. 26:38*).

**AHARHEL,** the son of Harum was from the tribe of Judah (*1 Chron. 4:8*).

**AHASBAI,** as the father of Eliphelet, appears in a special list of David's 'mighty men' (*2 Sam. 23:34*).

**AHASUERUS**. See *Xerxes*.

**AHAZ** (shortened form of Jehoahaz), 'the LORD has possessed'.

**1.** King Ahaz was successor to his father Jotham, reigning for 16 years as king of Judah during the final troubled years of the Northern Kingdom (c. 742–727 BC). His own reign was characterized by trouble and earns the epitaph: 'Unlike David his father, he did not do what was right in the eyes of the LORD his God' (*2 Kings 16:2*).

He earned this reputation through his part in introducing Assyrian worship of the Astra Deities into the Jerusalem Temple (*2 Kings 16:10–16*). In *2 Chron. 28:23* we are told that he sacrificed to the gods of Damascus – which could just mean that he so syncretized with other religions that they took on their own form at home in Judah. Despite the reforms which would happen later under his son Hezekiah, Ahaz advanced the Southern Kingdom in exactly the same direction as the Northern Kingdom had gone before. Judah's downfall eventually happened in 587 BC.

The prophet Isaiah was active at this time and *Is. 7–10* provides a disturbing analysis of the effect of the reign of Ahaz. Ahaz did not begin his reign without considerable problems (already some kind of coalition had been formed between Syria and Israel against Judah). However, via the prophet Isaiah a promise was made which should have strengthened his resolve: 'If you do not stand firm in your faith, you will not stand at all' (*Is. 7:9b*). However, the reality was that, with that faith already compromised, Judah's fall became inevitable and God used Assyria as his instrument to bring about divine judgment (*Is. 10:5*). See also *Pekah*, *Rezin* and *Tiglath-Pileser* for detail.

**2.** The great-great-grandson of King Saul (see *1 Chron. 8:35f.; 9:41f.*).   S.V.

**AHAZIAH** (Heb., 'The LORD has sustained').

**1.** Ahaziah ruled from 850–849 BC in the Kingdom of Israel. Though his reign was short, the account is split between the end of *1 Kings 22* and the beginning of *2 Kings 2* to explain the relationships between Ahaziah and the prophet Elijah. He continued in the infamous religious policies of his father Ahab and mother Jezebel (*1 Kings 22:40, 49, 51*).

His two-year reign was dogged by tragedy. He attempted an alliance with Jehoshaphat, king of Judah, but Jehoshaphat would not agree (*1 Kings 22:49*); he fell through a window in Samaria and injured himself (*2 Kings 1:2*); and when he sent messengers to the god of Ekron to ask if he would recover from his injury, Elijah met them on the way and told them that the LORD had decreed that Ahaziah would die (*2 Kings 1:4*).

The mark of his reign was supreme folly rather than some unfortunate fate. He sent further messengers to challenge Elijah. They were killed by fire from heaven (*2 Kings 1:9ff.*). Eventually Elijah himself went down to Ahaziah and repeated the prophecy that he would die under the judgment of God. The passage makes it clear that the confrontation between Elijah and Ahaziah and his messengers was to be regarded as a confrontation between the one true LORD God and the so-called gods of the Philistines such as Baal-Zebub, a god in Ekron (*2 Kings 1:2–3*).

**2.** The nephew of 1. above, this Ahaziah was also known as Jehoahaz. He succeeded his father Jehoram as King of Judah, but for less than a year (around 844 BC). 'He walked in the ways of the house of Ahab and did evil in the eyes of the LORD ...' (*2 Kings 8:27*). Given the influence of his mother, Athaliah daughter of the evil King Ahab of Israel, his conduct was perhaps not surprising. He was murdered by Jehu's followers after visiting his sick uncle Joram (also called Jehoram), king of Israel. His body was brought to Jerusalem and buried in the tombs of the kings (2 Kings 9:27–29). The on-going struggle in Ahab's family, predicted by Elijah in 1 Kings 21, was finally fulfilled in the death of Jezebel, who was seen as the perpetrator of immorality and idolatry in Ahab's line (1 Kings 18; 2 Kings 9:36f.). Also see Jehoahaz.  s.v.

**AHBAN** (Heb., 'brother of the intelligent one'). In 1 Chron. 2:29 he is listed as the son of Abishur and his wife Abihail, of the tribe of Judah.

**AHER** (Heb., 'another'). In 1 Chron. 7:12 he is listed as a leader of the tribe of Benjamin. Among his descendants were the Hushites. He is perhaps the same person as Ahiram (Num. 26:38).

**AHI** (Heb., 'my brother').
   **1.** A Gadite who lived in Gilead and Bashan. He was the son of Abdiel and is listed in the genealogies of the time of Jotham king of Judah (1 Chron. 5:15).
   **2.** Mentioned as a son of Shomer, a 'brave warrior' and 'outstanding leader' in the tribe of Asher (1 Chron. 7:34).

**AHIAH** (Heb., 'the Lord is my brother') is listed as one of the leaders of the people in Neh. 10:26 who affixed his seal to the people's covenant to obey God's law.

**AHIAM,** the son of Sharar (or 'Sacar' 1 Chron. 11:35) the Hararite, was one of David's 'Thirty' warriors, a 'mighty man' in battle (2 Sam. 23:33).

**AHIAN** (Heb., 'a brother'), a leader of the tribe of Manasseh, and one of the sons of Shemida (1 Chron. 7:19).

**AHIEZER** (Heb., 'brother of help').
   **1.** Ahiezer was the son of Ammishaddai. He was the leader of the people of Dan in Moses' time and therefore represented them at the time of the census

(Num. 1:12). At the dedication of the Tabernacle, Ahiezer brought the offerings of his tribe on the tenth day of celebration. When the Israelites finally moved on from Sinai, Ahiezer was again in command of his people, and the Danites brought up the rear (Num. 10:25).
   **2.** A skilful and ambidextrous archer from the tribe of Benjamin who fought first for Saul and then transferred to David at Ziklag (1 Chron. 12:3).  p.d.g.

**AHIHUD 1.** Ahihud son of Shelomi was a leader from the tribe of Asher. The Lord told Moses to choose men from each tribe to help divide out the land of Canaan, and Ahihud represented his tribe (Num. 34:27).
   **2.** One of the sons of Gera, a Benjamite, mentioned in 1 Chron. 8:7.

**AHIJAH** (Heb., 'my brother is the Lord').
   **1.** The great grandson of Eli and the son of Ahitub, Ahijah was also a priest in Shiloh. He was approached by Saul for guidance, and was one of those in charge of the ark of the covenant when Jonathan won a famous victory over the Philistines (1 Sam. 14:3, 18).
   **2.** The son of Shisha, which, linguistically, may imply that he was a scribe. He held responsibility in Solomon's court as a secretary (1 Kings 4:3).
   **3.** A prophet from Shiloh who opposed the idolatry of Solomon and predicted the ultimate separation of the kingdom through the symbolic tearing of his robe. The twelve parts of the ripped garment symbolized the tearing of the kingdom. Ten tribes revolted against Solomon's son Rehoboam, leaving Jeroboam as king of Israel in the north (1 Kings 11:29–31). Rehoboam remained king in the south with the remaining two tribes. The theological reason for the split in the kingdom was the syncretism and ultimate apostasy of

Solomon (1 Kings 11:7–13; 12:15; 2 Chron. 9:29; 10:15).

Jeroboam sent his wife, in disguise, to Ahijah to discover whether their son would recover from his sickness. Ahijah reiterated his prophecy of doom against the house of Jeroboam, confirmed that their son would die and pronounced that God would give Israel up because 'they provoked the LORD to anger by making Asherah poles' (1 Kings 14:15). As for Jeroboam: 'Dogs will eat those belonging to Jeroboam who die in the city, and the birds of the air will feed on those who die in the country' (1 Kings 14:11). See Jeroboam for more detail.

**4.** The father of Baasha, king of Israel (1 Kings 15:27, 33; 21:22; 2 Kings 9:9).

**5.** A son of Jerahmeel in the tribe of Judah, this Ahijah is mentioned only in 1 Chron. 2:25.

**6.** The son of Ehud, a Benjamite (1 Chron. 8:7). This passage implies that Ahijah and his brother were exiled to Manahath.

**7.** This Ahijah was one of David's 'Thirty' mighty warriors and is listed as a 'Pelonite' (1 Chron. 11:36).          S.V.

**AHIKAM** (Heb., 'my brother has arisen'). In Josiah's reign the 'book of the law' was discovered in the Temple. Josiah sent Ahikam, along with Hilkiah the priest and others, to consult the prophetess Huldah concerning the book. Huldah drew attention to the words of God's law that promised judgment on Israel if she turned from the LORD and worshipped other gods. This is what Israel had done, and so judgment was coming (2 Kings 22:12–17).

Later, during Jehoiakim's reign, Jeremiah was also told by God to prophesy judgment on Judah. On hearing the prophecy, the people wanted to kill Jeremiah, but Ahikam saved him from death (Jer. 26:24). His son Gedaliah was appointed governor of Judah by Nebuchadnezzar after the fall of Jerusalem in

587 BC (Jer. 40:7). Jeremiah was then cared for by Gedaliah.

Ahikam and his son were both loyal servants of the kings of Israel, but they were also faithful to the LORD and supported his prophets in spite of their stinging proclamations of God's judgment on Judah.          P.D.G.

**AHILUD,** the father of a court recorder named Jehoshaphat who lived during the reign of King David. This Jehoshaphat was clearly one of the most trusted leaders of his time (2 Sam. 8:16; 20:24; 1 Kings 4:3, 12; 1 Chron. 18:15).

**AHIMAAZ 1.** Zadok was high priest to King David during most of his reign. Zadok's son Ahimaaz joined his father in serving the king. Ahimaaz joined Jonathan, Abiathar's son, in keeping watch for David to discover Absalom's plans. When Absalom died, Ahimaaz requested permission personally to carry the news to King David. In the end, he carried only the news of victory in battle and allowed another messenger to bear the news of Absalom's death (2 Sam. 16:15–19:8). See Zadok, Abiathar.

**2.** Ahimaaz was the father of Saul's wife, Ahinoam (1 Sam. 14:50).

**3.** Solomon appointed twelve provincial governors to supply provisions for the king and his royal household. Ahimaaz, married to Solomon's daughter Basemath, was selected as one of these governors for Naphtali (1 Kings 4:7–15).

          S.C.

**AHIMAN** (Heb., 'my brother is a gift').

**1.** One of three notorious descendants of Anak who lived in Hebron at the time of the conquest of Canaan by Joshua. Caleb led the attack against Hebron, defeating these three giants in battle. As a result he and his family inherited this part of the land of Canaan (Num. 13:22; Josh. 15:14; Judg. 1:10). It is particularly interesting to note how the LORD blessed Caleb in this conquest. It had been he and Joshua alone who had originally returned to Moses after spying out the land of Canaan and who had trusted the LORD sufficiently to believe that such giants could in fact be defeated. His faith was seen to be well placed and his rewards for that faith were considerable (Num. 13:30; 14:24).

**2.** One of the gatekeepers from the tribe of Levi who were responsible for guarding one of the gates of the Temple after the return to Jerusalem from the Babylonian exile (1 Chron. 9:17).          P.D.G.

**AHIMELECH** (Heb., 'brother of a king').

**1.** Ahimelech, son of Ahitub, was a priest of Nob and a friend to David. Ahimelech helped David and his men when they were fleeing from Saul, and Saul grew so angry that he ordered Doeg the Edomite to kill all of the priests. Doeg killed 85 priests that day and all of the men, women, children, infants and animals in Nob (1 Sam. 21–22). Only one priest escaped – Ahimelech's son, Abiathar (1 Sam. 22:20). David felt responsible for the deaths and took Abiathar in as his own priest and confidant.

**2.** In 1 Chron. 18:16 and 2 Sam. 8:17 Ahimelech is mentioned as the son of Abiathar and therefore the grandson of 1. above. While some scholars see this reference as meaning just what it says, others feel that the names were mistakenly 'switched', leaving the corrected version 'Abiathar, son of Ahimelech', in keeping with the events of 1 Sam. 21–22.

**3.** Ahimelech is referred to as 'a Hittite' in the service of David (1 Sam. 26:6–7).
                                              S.C.

**AHIMOTH,** a descendant of Elkanah, who was a descendant, through Kohath, of Levi (1 Chron. 6:25).

**AHINADAB** (Heb., 'noble brother'), the son of Iddo. He was one of Solomon's twelve district governors. Each governor had responsibility to find supplies from his region that would provide for the king for one month a year (1 Kings 4:7). Ahinadab's region was Mahanaim (1 Kings 4:14).

**AHINOAM** (Heb., 'my brother is good').

**1.** Ahinoam, daughter of Ahimaaz, was the wife of Saul (1 Sam. 14:50).

**2.** A woman from Jezreel whom David married when Saul gave Michal to another. Ahinoam was with David on his journey to Philistia where she, along with Abigail, was placed in captivity. Both women survived captivity and Ahinoam gave birth to David's first son, Amnon (1 Sam. 25:43; 27:3; 30:5; 2 Sam. 2:2; 3:2; 1 Chron. 3:1).

**AHIO** **1.** Ahio was one of the two sons of Abinadab who guided the cart on which the ark (the covenant box) was being carried when King David brought it from Baalah of Judah to Jerusalem (2 Sam. 6:3; 1 Chron. 13:7). Ahio walked in front of the cart. When the oxen pulling the cart stumbled, Ahio's brother Uzzah put out his hand to steady the cart and touched the ark, something which probably everyone had been strictly forbidden to do (2 Sam. 6:6; Num. 4:15). As a result God 'struck him down and he died' (2 Sam. 6:7). Ahio's fate is not mentioned. See Uzzah for detail.

**2.** One of the sons of Beriah and a leader from the tribe of Benjamin, Ahio lived in Aijalon (1 Chron. 8:14). He is listed in the genealogy of King Saul.

**3.** Mentioned in 1 Chron. 8:31 and 9:37, this was one of the sons of the Benjamite Jeiel and his wife Maacah. He is listed in the genealogy leading from Benjamin to Saul.          P.D.G.

**AHIRA** (Heb., 'brother of Ra'), the son of Enan. He was the leader of the people of Naphtali in Moses' time and therefore represented them at the time of the census (Num. 1:15). At the dedication of the

Tabernacle, Ahira brought the offerings of his tribe on the twelfth day of celebration (*Num. 7:78*). When the Israelites finally moved on from Sinai, Ahira was again at the head of his people (*Num. 10:27*).

**AHIRAM** (Heb., 'exalted brother'), the third of the five sons of Benjamin listed in *Num. 26:38*. He became the head of the Ahiramite clan. In *1 Chron. 8:1*, where these sons are also mentioned, his name is given as Aharah. In *1 Chron. 7:12* Aher probably refers to the same person, as probably does Ehi in *Gen. 46:21*, where further sons of Benjamin are mentioned.

**AHISAMACH** (Heb., 'my brother helps'), a Danite, was the father of Oholiab, a craftsman and designer who worked on the Tabernacle and its furniture (*Exod. 31:6* etc.).

**AHISHAHAR,** a great-grandson of Benjamin and a son of Bilhan (*1 Chron. 7:10*).

**AHISHAR,** one of Solomon's many important officials, was placed in charge of the palace (*1 Kings 4:6*). This list of officials helps emphasize the stability and grandeur of Israel under Solomon's rule.

**AHITHOPHEL** (Heb., 'brother of folly'), who came from Giloh near Hebron, lived up to his name in the part he played in Absalom's revolt against his father, King David. He also gave counsel to both David and Absalom (*2 Sam. 16:23*). However, he proved to be a traitor to David (*2 Sam. 15*). He encouraged Absalom in his attempted armed overthrow of David, and also encouraged him to sleep with his father's concubines to show his disdain for his father's rule (*2 Sam. 16:21–22*).

Though Ahithophel's actions are indicative of the general unrest with the reign of David at this time, he may have had more personal reasons for his foolish behaviour towards David. There is some evidence that Bathsheba may have been his granddaughter, and his attempts to overthrow David may have been motivated by revenge for the cruel murder of Uriah. However, he was born into an environment of great instability among David's followers, and his treachery could just as easily have been motivated by the feeling of betrayal felt by many in David's declining kingdom.

David frustrated Ahithophel's 'wise counsel' to Absalom by sending Hushai the Arkite to Jerusalem (*2 Sam. 15:34–35*). He succeeded in confusing Absalom, and ultimately undermining Ahithophel, whose anguish climaxed in his suicide by hanging (*2 Sam. 17:1, 6–7, 14–15, 21, 23; 1 Chron. 27:33f.*). Also see *Hushai.*                          S.V.

**AHITUB** (Heb., 'brother is good').

**1.** The grandson of Eli and son of Phinehas (*1 Sam. 14:3*). His own son was Ahimelech, who was one of the priests at the town of Nob who helped David when he was being chased by Saul. Saul had Ahimelech and 84 other priests and the people of Nob all put to death (*1 Sam. 22:9, 11–12, 20*).

**2.** This Ahitub, son of Amariah and a descendant of Aaron, was the father of Zadok, who was one of the chief officials in David's court (*2 Sam. 8:17; 1 Chron. 6:7–8, 52; 18:16; Ezra 7:2*). He was Zadok's grandfather according to *Neh. 9:11*. Zadok was a chief priest during the reigns of David and Solomon.

**3.** The son of Amariah, this Ahitub was also the father of a certain Zadok but in a generation of Levites later than that of 2. above (*1 Chron. 6:11–12; Neh. 11:11*).

P.D.G.

**AHLAI 1.** From the tribe of Judah, Ahlai was one of the daughters of Sheshan (*1 Chron. 2:31, 34*).

**2.** Ahlai was the father of Zabad, one of David's 'mighty men' (*1 Chron. 11:41*).

**AHOAH,** a grandson of Benjamin and a son of Bela. This genealogy is of special significance in leading from Benjamin through to Saul (1 Chron. 8:4). Ahoah is possibly the same person as Ahijah in 1 Chron. 8:7.

**AHUMAI,** one of the descendants of Judah and a son of Jahath. Ahumai and his brother Lahad formed the clans of the Zorathites (1 Chron. 4:2).

**AHUZZAM,** a leader in the tribe of Judah and a son of Ashhur (1 Chron. 4:6). His mother was Naarah.

**AHUZZATH,** the personal advisor to Abimelech, the Philistine king of Gerar. The two came to Isaac with Phicol, the commander of their forces (Gen. 26:26). Isaac expressed surprise and some fear, as he had recently been sent away from Gerar (Gen. 26:16). In fact Abimelech had come to sue for a covenant of peace between them (Gen. 26:28–31).

**AHZAI** (Heb., 'the LORD has grasped'), the grandfather of Amashai, he was an associate of Adaiah and one of the priests who settled in Jerusalem after the exile in Babylon (see Neh. 11:13). Jahzerah in 1 Chron. 9:12 is probably the same person.

**AIAH** (Heb., 'a bird of prey').
**1.** Aiah was a son of Zibeon and an Edomite descendant of Seir (Gen. 36:24; 1 Chron. 1:40).
**2.** The father of Rizpah, one of Saul's concubines (2 Sam. 3:7; 21:10).

**AKAN,** the third son of Ezer, was one of the tribal leaders in Seir, where Esau settled (Gen. 36:27; 1 Chron. 1:42).

**AKIM** In the genealogy establishing Jesus' kingly lineage, Akim is the father of Eliud and the son of Zadok (Matt. 1:14).

**AKKUB 1.** A son of Elioenai and part of the royal lineage of Judah following the Exile, therefore a descendant of David (1 Chron. 3:24).
**2.** A head of a family of Levitical gatekeepers of the Temple who lived in Jerusalem following the return from the Babylonian Exile (1 Chron. 9:17; Neh. 8:7; 11:19; 12:25). His descendants continued in the work (Ezra 2:42; Neh. 7:45), which also involved guarding the Temple storerooms at the gates. It is probably the same Akkub who is also listed among the Levites who helped instruct the people in the Law of God after Ezra had read it publicly. Their job was the task of priests and ministers down through the ages: to make clear the meaning of God's self revelation in his Word so that people could respond in faith and obedience (Neh. 8:7–8). The result of this work was that the whole people wept as they realized their disobedience and need for forgiveness. Nehemiah encouraged them with a reminder of the 'joy of the LORD' (v. 10).
**3.** This Akkub was a 'temple servant' whose descendants returned from the Exile in Babylon with Zerubbabel and Nehemiah (Ezra 2:45).           P.D.G.

**ALEMETH 1.** A grandson of Benjamin and a son of Beker (1 Chron. 7:8).
**2.** The son of Jehoaddah (1 Chron. 8:36), or Jadah (1 Chron. 9:42). He was from the tribe of Judah and was a descendant of King Saul.

**ALEXANDER** A common name given to four or five men in the NT:
**1.** The son of Simon from Cyrene (Mark 15:21). Simon was forced to carry the cross. Perhaps his son is mentioned because he was known to those who would read Mark's Gospel.
**2.** A member of the high priest's family who was present when Peter and John were questioned (Acts 4:6). See Annas.
**3.** A Jew involved in accusations against Paul in Ephesus (Acts 19:33). Perhaps he wanted to dissociate the Jews

of Ephesus from Paul's teachings, but the Greeks refused to hear him.

**4.** A man who with Hymenaeus, was 'handed over to Satan' (*1 Tim. 1:20*). He was a blasphemer who had rejected the Christian faith. Being 'handed over' in this way involved some form of discipline, perhaps excommunication. Both Alexander and Hymenaeus must have claimed to be Christians, and their expulsion from the church, if that was the discipline involved, was designed to restore them to Christian behaviour. See *Hymenaeus*: in his case (*2 Tim. 2:17–18*) it clearly did not work.

**5.** A metalworker and an enemy of the gospel (*2 Tim. 4:14*). A metalworker may have made his living making mementos and idols for the various temples. If so, Paul's teaching would have been interpreted as an attack on his trade. Perhaps he was the Alexander of either 3. or 4. above, or they may all be the same person. However, this would require that at some stage between 3. and 4. or 5. he had professed conversion to Christianity. Paul, well towards the end of his ministry (*2 Tim. 4:6–8*), recounted how alone he had been in his defence at trial. Alexander's 'strong' opposition had been specially harmful to him. But Paul knew that he could leave justice in the hands of the Lord (*2 Tim. 4:14*). P.D.G.

**ALLON** (Heb., 'oak'). Listed under the descendants of Simeon, Allon was the leader of a clan. He was the son of Jedaiah and the father of Shiphi (*1 Chron. 4:37*).

**ALMODAD** (Heb., 'God is a friend') is listed in both *Gen. 10:26* and *1 Chron. 1:20* as a descendant of Shem. His father was Joktan.

**ALPHAEUS 1.** Alphaeus, the father of the apostle Levi (Matthew), is mentioned just once (*Mark 2:14*).

**2.** Alphaeus, the father of James the apostle (*Matt. 10:3; Mark 3:18; Luke 6:15; Acts 1:13*). This James is sometimes called 'James the Less' or 'the younger' in order to distinguish him from the better known James, who was brother to John (see *James*). It is just possible that this James and Matthew were brothers.

The name Alphaeus may come from a similar Aramaic root to the name Clopas (*John 19:25*). Clopas was the husband of Mary, the mother of James. Whether Clopas and Alphaeus can thus be identified is widely disputed. Certainly, the evidence is weak at best. P.D.G.

**ALVAH** A descendant of Esau, Alvah was a clan leader of the Edomites (*Gen. 36:40; 1 Chron. 1:51*).

**ALVAN** A descendant of Esau, Alvan was the son of Shobal, a clan leader of the Edomites (*Gen. 36:23; 1 Chron. 1:40*).

**AMAL,** the son of Helem (*1 Chron. 7:35*), was a tribal leader and a descendant of Asher.

**AMALEK, THE AMALEKITES** Amalek was the son of Eliphaz by his concubine Timna and the grandson of Esau (*Gen. 36:12, 16; 1 Chron. 1:36*). He was an Edomite, and first among the people known as the Amalekites.

The Amelekites were the perpetual enemy of Israel, who spent much of their history in bitter combat with them. They originally occupied the Negeb and Sinai region, but later joined the Midianites in combat against God's people (*Exod. 17:8–13; Judg. 3:13; 6:33f.*). Part of the initial task of the people of Israel upon entering Canaan was to drive out the Amelekites (*Exod. 17:14; Num. 24:20; Deut. 25:19; Judg. 12:15*), although it seems that some of them remained (see *Judg. 3:12f.; 6:3, 33*; etc.). The memorable words of *Exod. 17:14* were later to have a rather hollow ring as time after time the people of Israel fell to the superior strength and aggressive tactics of the Amalekites. 'Write this on a scroll as something to be remembered and make sure that Joshua hears it, because I will completely erase the memory of Amalek from under heaven.'

The reason for the Israelites' defeat at the hands of the Amalekites is explained in term of Israel's disobedience (see Num. 14). It is a reminder that the promises of God are not there to instil complacency, rather their purpose is to motivate action. It is possible to disqualify oneself from the blessings of God when the strictures of the covenant relationship are flagrantly abused (Num. 14:10–12). Num. 14:16 is a solemn warning: 'The LORD was not able to bring these people into the land he promised them on oath . . .'

The beginning of Saul's downfall came when he refused to annihilate the Amalekites (1 Sam. 15), keeping the best of their cattle and sheep for sacrifice to the LORD and sparing King Agag. But it is not the believer's privilege to stand in judgment upon the Word of God, nor to assume that any worship of God will be acceptable if couched in pious rhetoric (1 Sam. 15:22f.). David proved to be more successful in driving out the Amalekites and, after 1 Sam. 30, they receive only scant attention (1 Chron. 4:42f.). When the Amalekites are mentioned again it is to highlight the victory Israel won over them (2 Sam. 8:12; 1 Chron. 18:11).

The Amalekites epitomized the danger of worldly compromise for God's people. A failure to destroy the enemies of God, however eloquently justified, displeased the LORD. However, the comfort is also there that God will build his own church, as he has promised, and the gates of hell will not prevail over it (Matt. 16:18).                          S.V.

**AMARIAH** (Heb., 'God says').

**1.** The son of Meraioth and father of Ahitub, Amariah is mentioned in the lists of the descendants of Levi in 1 Chron. 6:7, 52.

**2.** The son of Azariah and grandfather of Zadok, this Amariah was also a Levite and was an ancestor of Ezra (1 Chron. 6:11; Ezra 7:3).

**3.** A Levite and descendant of Kohath, this Amariah was the second son of Hebron and took part in the Kohathite duties in the Temple (1 Chron. 23:19; 24:23).

**4.** Another Amariah living in the days of King Jehoshaphat was chief priest. In his desire to see a restoration of worship of the true God, Yahweh (the LORD), in the nation, Jehoshaphat appointed Amariah to be the chief priest dealing with matters 'concerning the LORD' and Zebadiah to deal with 'any matters concerning the king'. In his commission to these important leaders who would steer the people and the nation back to the LORD, Jehoshaphat encouraged them that the LORD would be with them and that they should 'act with courage' (2 Chron. 19:11). He might be the same person as 2. above.

**5.** During the revival and turning to God in Hezekiah's reign, many Levites were assigned specific Temple duties. This Amariah was one of those with the task of helping Kore distribute the people's gifts around the towns of the priests 'according to their divisions' (2 Chron. 31:15).

**6.** This Amariah was among the descendants of Binnui. At the time of return from the Exile in Babylon, Shecaniah confessed to Ezra that many men and even descendants of the priests of Judah had married wives from other tribes and nations. Ezra and the people repented and made a covenant to serve the LORD (Ezra 10:2). Amariah is listed in Ezra 10:42 as one who divorced his foreign wife.

**7.** This Amariah joined in witnessing

the solemn covenant of obedience to the Law of God in Nehemiah's time in Jerusalem (*Neh. 10:3*).

**8.** The father of Zechariah and a descendant of Perez from the tribe of Judah. His descendants settled in Jerusalem on the return from the Exile in Babylon (*Neh. 11:4*).

**9.** One of the priests listed as returning from the Babylonian Exile with Zerubbabel (*Neh. 12:2*).

**10.** An ancestor of the prophet Zephaniah (*Zeph. 1:1*).                    P.D.G.

**AMASA 1.** Amasa was a nephew of David and son of Jether and Abigail, David's sister (*2 Sam. 17:25; 1 Chron. 2:17*). He served as a commander in Absalom's army in the rebellion against David. In an act of reconciliation on Absalom's death, Amasa was called into service by David but viewed as a rival by Joab (*2 Sam. 19:13*). During a critical moment in preparation for David's return to rule, Joab killed Amasa for no reason other than to regain his job as commander in chief in David's army (*20:4–13*). This act of treachery on Joab's part led David on his death-bed to charge Solomon that he should deal with Joab 'according to wisdom', not mercy (*1 Chron. 2:17; 1 Kings 2:5–6, 32–33*).

**2.** Amasa was an Ephraimite leader during the period when Pekah defeated Ahaz, king of Judah. Amasa protested the taking of Judean captives, reminding his fellow Israelites that God was also angry with Israel for their disobedience (*2 Chron. 28:1–5*).                    S.C.

**AMASAI 1.** Amasai was the father of Mahath and a Levite ancestor of Samuel (*1 Chron. 6:25, 35; 2 Chron. 29:12*).

**2.** This Amasai was one of the men who came to David at Ziklag, when he was banished from Saul's presence. Amasai became chief of David's 'Thirty' warriors (*1 Chron. 12:18*).

**3.** Another Amasai is listed as a Levite musician who blew a trumpet in *1 Chron. 15:24* when David brought the ark back to Jerusalem. He was a doorkeeper for the Tabernacle and later the Temple.

**AMASHSAI** was one of Adaiah's associates and a son of Azarel (*Neh. 11:13*). He was one of the priests who settled in Jerusalem following the return from Exile in Babylon. He is probably the same person as Maasai in *1 Chron. 9:12*.

**AMASIAH** From the tribe of Judah, Amasiah, son of Zicri, was a commander under King Jehoshaphat of Judah (*2 Chron. 17:16*). In Jehoshaphat's early years as king he was faithful to the LORD and inspired great confidence in his people. It is worthy of note that when he 'volunteered' himself to Jehoshaphat with 200,000 men, he regarded this as 'the service of the LORD'.

**AMAZIAH** (Heb., 'the LORD is mighty').

**1.** The son of Joash, and the ninth king of Judah. His 29-year reign is succinctly summarized in *2 Kings 12:21; 14:1, 3; 2 Chron. 25:1*: 'He did what was right in the eyes of the LORD, but not as his father David had done' (*2 Kings 14:3*). From a positive point of view, Amaziah executed the murderers of his father, sparing the children in keeping with the law. He attacked the Edomites, capturing the capital city Petra (see *Amos 1:11*). However, he did not entirely follow his forefather David: 'The high places, however were not removed' (*2 Kings 14:4*). This wrongful tolerance of pagan religion led to him further offending the LORD when he brought Edomite gods back to Jerusalem. This brought the condemnation of the 'man of God' in *2 Chron. 25:14ff*. 'Why,' the prophet reasoned, 'do you consult this people's gods, which could not save their own people from your hand?' Ultimately, the one who was enslaved was Amaziah, and God gave him over to Jehoash king of Israel who not only took Amaziah and his people captive but also plundered the Temple of its silver and gold articles (2 Chron. 25:20–24).

Amaziah's downfall is attributed to his foolish and presumptuous challenge of King Jehoash, who executed God's judgment in ransacking Jerusalem and taking hostages to Samaria. Eventually Amaziah's own leaders in Jerusalem conspired against him, pursued him to Lachish and killed him (2 Kings 14:19–20; 2 Chron. 25:27–28). He was buried in Jerusalem.

**2.** A musician in the house of David, a Levite descendant of Merari (1 Chron. 6:45).

**3.** A priest of Jeroboam II who opposed the prophet Amos and tried to silence him using royal authority (Amos 7:10–17).

**4.** A member of the tribe of Simeon, one of the princes who settled in Gedor (see 1 Chron. 4:34). s.v.

**AMI,** one of the 'servants of Solomon' whose descendants returned from Exile with Nehemiah (Ezra 2:57).

**AMITTAI,** the father of the prophet Jonah, who lived in the 8th century BC and came from Gath-Hepher (2 Kings 14:25; Jonah 1:1).

**AMMIEL** (Heb., 'God is my kinsman').

**1.** One of the twelve spies sent out by Moses from the Desert of Paran to spy out the land of Canaan (Num. 13:11). A representative of each tribe was chosen and Ammiel, the son of Gemalli, was from the tribe of Dan. For further detail on their mission see Shammua.

**2.** The father of Makir, who came from Lo Debar in the area of Gilead. Makir sheltered Mephibosheth, the crippled son of Saul, when David came to the throne (2 Sam. 9:4–5; 17:27).

**3.** The father of Bathsheba, who was the wife of King David (1 Chron. 3:5).

**4.** The sixth son of Obed-Edom, a descendant of Korah, this Ammiel was responsible for attending to the Tabernacle gates in David's administration (1 Chron. 26:5). P.D.G.

**AMMIHUD** **1.** The father of Elishama and son of Ladan. Elishama was the leader of the people of Ephraim at the census of the Israelites in the wilderness of Sinai (Num. 1:10; 2:18; 7:48, 53; 10:22; 1 Chron. 7:26).

**2.** The father of Shemuel and from the tribe of Simeon. Shemuel was chosen by Moses to organize the allocation of the Simeonite territory to the various clans and families following the conquest of Canaan (Num. 34:20).

**3.** This Ammihud was the father of Pedahel from the tribe of Naphtali. Pedahel was chosen by Moses to organize the allocation of his tribe's territory to the various clans and families following the conquest of Canaan (Num. 34:28).

**4.** The father of Talmai the king of Geshur, to whom Absalom fled after the revenge killing of his brother Amnon (2 Sam. 13:37).

**5.** The father of Uthai, one of those who returned to live in Jerusalem following the Exile in Babylon. He was a descendant of Judah (1 Chron. 9:4). P.D.G.

**AMMINADAB** (Heb., 'my kinsman is noble').

**1.** The father of Elisheba, who married Aaron (Exod. 6:23). He was also the father of Nahshon and an ancestor of Boaz and King David (Num. 1:7; 2:3; 7:12, 17; 10:14; Ruth 4:19–20). He is thus also named as an ancestor of Jesus Christ in the NT (Matt. 1:4; Luke 3:33).

**2.** An ancestor of Samuel and a son of Kohath the Levite (1 Chron. 6:22). He was Korah's father.

**3.** A leader of the Levites at the time of King David, this Amminadab was the son of Uzziel. He and 112 family relatives were chosen with those from other

Levitical families for the task of consecrating themselves and bringing the ark up to Jerusalem (1 Chron. 15:1–11). The ark had been left at Obed-Edom's home for three months after the LORD's judgment had fallen on Uzzah (1 Sam. 6; see Uzzah). P.D.G.

**AMMISHADDAI,** the father of the Danite, Ahiezer. Ahiezer was the leader of the Danites at Sinai (Num. 1:12; 2:25 etc.).

**AMMIZABAD** (Heb., 'the kinsman has given'), the son of Benaiah, who was one of David's 'mighty men' and the leader of the 'Thirty' warriors. Ammizabad was on duty and in charge of an army division during the third month of the year.

**AMNON** (Heb., 'faithful').
**1.** Amnon, whose mother was Ahinoam of Jezreel, was David's first son born in Hebron (2 Sam. 3:2; 1 Chron. 3:1). When he was older he fell in love with Tamar, Absalom's sister, and his own half-sister. He pretended to be ill in order to ask Tamar to serve him food in his bedroom. When she came he raped her and then threw her out. Tamar then withdrew and lived a desolate life with her brother Absalom (2 Sam. 13). Two years later Absalom took his revenge and had his men kill Amnon (v. 29).
**2.** Mentioned in 1 Chron. 4:20 as a son of Shimon of the clan of Judah. P.D.G.

**AMOK** (Heb., 'deep') was one of the priests who returned from Exile in Babylon with Zerubbabel and Jeshua (Neh. 12:7). One of his descendants, Eber, was the head of a priestly family in the days of Joiakim (Neh. 12:20).

**AMON 1.** The son of Manasseh (2 Kings 21:18–19; 2 Chron. 33:20–21) and the 15th king of Judah, Amon reigned for two years. He continued in his father's idolatrous practices – the worship of Moloch and continuance in fertility rites which were so abhorrent to the jealous

love of the LORD. Manasseh himself repented later in life out of desperation, following defeat at the hands of the Assyrians (see 2 Chron. 33). Evidently his conversion was too late to have a lasting influence on Amon, who 'did not humble himself before the LORD' as his father had done (2 Chron. 33:22–23). Amon was hated by the people, who had had enough of such tyranny, and was assassinated by palace servants at the age of 24 (2 Chron. 33:24). They then put Josiah on the throne instead.
**2.** A lesser Egyptian god worshipped by the priests of Amon, on whom Jeremiah pronounced destruction in Jer. 46:25.
**3.** The governor of Samaria who put Micaiah in prison on the word of King Ahab of Israel. The king had not liked Micaiah's prophecy of his death (1 Kings 22:26; 2 Chron. 18:25).
**4.** A captive who returned from the Babylonian Exile in the time of Nehemiah (Neh. 7:59; Ezra 2:57). He was a descendant of King Solomon's servants. S.V.

**AMOS.** The prophet Amos (Heb., '(burden-) bearer'), the only individual in the OT with this name, was a businessman-farmer from Judah who was called as a layman to deliver a message of condemnation and judgment to the Northern Kingdom, Israel. He tells nothing of his family or lineage but does provide more than the usual amount of information about his times in general and his own geographical, chronological and cultural setting in particular.

He came from Tekoa, a small village about six miles south of Bethlehem, and home also of the wise woman whom Joab procured to provide David with counsel regarding Absalom (2 Sam. 14:1–20). His occupation, he says, was that of a shepherd (Amos 1:1), but the word here (noqed) suggests something more than a mere watcher of the flocks. In the only other occurrence of the word in the OT

(2 Kings 3:4), it is used to describe Mesha, king of Moab, who clearly was not a shepherd. Most likely he was a sheep merchant or the like, and that is how Amos' occupation should be understood. This finds support in *Amos 7:14*, where he speaks of himself as a *boqer*, another rare term for 'shepherd'. Though *boqer* is without doubt related in some way to *baqar*, a common word for '(cattle) herd', *Amos 7:15* connects Amos's work to the flock, not to cattle. Thus, he was a sheepman but more than a shepherd.

The prophet also describes himself as 'a dresser of sycamore-fig trees' (*Amos 7:14*). The Heb. term here for the entire phrase is *boles*, a word which, on the basis of the Septuagint and classical Greek texts, probably refers to the nipping or slitting of fruit in order to make it edible. In any case, it seems that Amos was an expert in fig cultivation as well as a successful dealer in sheep. The importance of this is the fact that God called a busy and prosperous man away from his secular pursuits to undertake a mission among the Israelites, God's errant and sinful flock.

That Amos' ministry was of brief duration – perhaps only one assignment and for a few days – is clear from his opening statement that his commission from the LORD came in the time of King Uzziah of Judah (790–739 BC) and King Jeroboam of Israel (793–753 BC), more specifically 'two years before the earthquake' (*Amos 1:1*). This cataclysm, so massive as to have been recalled 240 years later by the prophet Zechariah (*Zech. 14:5*), is now known to have occurred at about 760 BC. Therefore, 762 BC would appear to be the precise date of Amos' ministry to the illicit shrines of King Jeroboam (*Amos 7:10–13*).

The only setting for his messages to which Amos refers is Bethel, one of two places of central worship established by Jeroboam I shortly after the division of the kingdom in 931 BC (*1 Kings 12:29–33*). This impious act of creating illegitimate shrines in competition to the only one authorized by the LORD (that at Jerusalem) resulted in a prophecy that the Bethel altar would eventually be destroyed and its priests slain (*1 Kings 13:1–3*). This took place as part of the reformation led by King Josiah 300 years later (*2 Kings 23:15–16*), and Amos himself helped pave the way by his denunciation of Bethel and its cult (*Amos 3:14; 5:5*). It was this stern message by the prophet that in fact led to his expulsion from Bethel by Jeroboam II and his priest Amaziah, on trumped-up charges that Amos was there for financial gain (so *Amos 7:12*).

Stung by this misreading of his motives, Amos replied that he was 'neither a prophet nor a prophet's son' (*Amos 7:14*) but a businessman whom Yahweh had called. By this disclaimer Amos disavows any connection with 'professional' or vocational prophetism. The 'sons of the prophets' (see *2 Kings 2:3, 5, 7*; etc.) were men in training for such a ministry. Amos wants Amaziah to understand that he is not part of such a movement, honourable as it might be, but simply a layman sent on an errand by the God who chooses and uses who he will. In addition to the profoundly important content of his messages in themselves is this lesson of Amos' own life. Those called and commissioned by God need not have formal credentials and qualifications in order to be successful in carrying out his purposes.                    E.M.

**AMOZ,** the father of the prophet Isaiah (*Is. 1:1* etc.).

**AMPLIATUS** Paul described this man as one 'whom I love in the Lord'. His name was common in Rome, where he lived, and he was greeted by Paul in *Rom. 16:8*. Paul's personal recognition and care for many individuals in different congregations is to be noted in most of his letters.

**AMRAM 1.** Amram was one of four sons of Kohath and a grandson of Levi (*Exod. 6:18; Num. 26:58–59; 1 Chron. 6:2–3, 18; 23:12–13*). He was a clan leader among the Kohathites (*Num. 3:19*). His wife Jochebed bore him three children: Aaron, Moses and Miriam (*Exod. 6:20; Num. 16:1; 1 Chron. 24:20*).

**2.** A descendant of Bani at the time of Nehemiah (*Ezra 10:34*). After Shecaniah confessed to Ezra that many men of Judah had married wives from other tribes and nations, Ezra and the people repented and made a covenant to serve the LORD (*Ezra 10:2*). Amram was one of those listed as having married a foreign wife.

P.D.G.

**AMRAPHEL,** one of four Mesopotamian kings who invaded Palestine at the time of Abraham (see also *Arioch, Kedorlaomer* and *Tidal*). The account given in *Gen. 14* is of particular interest, as it highlights both the desirability of the Jordan valley, that could attract an alliance of kings from so far afield, and the rapidly advancing influence of Abra(ha)m.

It is clear that the invading alliance was headed by Kedorlaomer (*Gen. 14:4–5*). The invaders had conquered several of the city-states of the Jordan valley and areas around the Dead Sea and had ruled the land for twelve years. In the thirteenth year the local kings of these cities rebelled and fought the invaders (see *Bera, Birsha, Shinab, Shemeber*). Once again, however, they were defeated and fled. The four kings seized a huge area of land, including the cities of Sodom and Gomorrah, from which they took all the spoil. In this conquest they carried off Abram's nephew, Lot, who was living in Sodom.

This brought Abram into the arena. When he heard what had happened, he went in pursuit of Kedorlaomer, chasing him far to the north. Finally, in a clever attack he defeated the alliance and returned with Lot and his family (*Gen. 14:14–17*).

The alliance, of which Amraphel was part, came from the same area that had been Abram's home. It is of great significance that Abram's defeat of these kings is seen in *Gen. 14* as God's victory, and indicates God's establishment of Abram in Canaan and his final and complete separation from his former life. From this point onwards, under God's sovereign plan Abram's influence in the 'promised land' continued to increase.

P.D.G.

**AMZI** (Heb., 'my strength').

**1.** A descendant of Levi and a son of Bani. A descendant of this Amzi was Ethan the Merarite, who served as a Temple musician (*1 Chron. 6:46*).

**2.** One of his descendants, Adaiah, was a priest who settled in Jerusalem after the Exile (*Neh. 11:12*).

**ANAH 1.** Anah was the father of Oholibamah, who became the wife of Esau (*Gen. 36:2, 14, 18, 20*). He was a member of the Canaanite tribe called the Hivites. Anah is also credited with finding hot springs in the desert while working for his father Zibeon (*Gen. 36:24*). See also *1 Chron. 1:40–41*, where he is the father of Dishon.

**2.** *Gen. 36:29* also refers to Anah, who was a Horite chief. Perhaps *Gen. 36:2* should read 'Horite' rather than 'Hivite', but this may be a different leader. See also *1 Chron. 1:38*, where he is son of Seir and brother of Zibeon.

**ANAIAH** (Heb., 'the LORD has answered').

**1.** He stood on the platform with Ezra when he read the book of the Law (*Neh. 8:4*).

**2.** Possibly the same as 1., he was one of the leaders who witnessed the agreement of the people to worship the LORD and obey his Law (*Neh. 10:22*).

**ANAK,** a figure known only in the distant past to the Israelites as they wandered through the Negev (*Num. 13:22, 28 etc.*).

Clearly of great stature, he became famous for his fighting strength and his base in Hebron, which had been founded by his forefather, Arba – hence the former name for Hebron was Kiriath-Arba (*Josh. 14:15*).

When the Israelites sent spies into Canaan, they reported back with great fear that they had seen the Nephilim, who were descendants of Anak, and 'we seemed like grasshoppers in our own eyes' (*Num. 13:33*). The formidable reputation of Anak's descendants became something of a byword among Israelites (e.g. *Deut. 1:28; 2:10* etc.).

Eventually Joshua did drive them out of Hebron, Debir and the hill country of Judah, so that none were left in Israelite territory. A few seem to have survived in the Philistine areas of Gaza, Gath and Ashdod. Just as the descendants of Anak were the first to cause real concern to the Israelites, so, with their destruction, Joshua finally conquered Canaan and brought peace to the land of Israel (*Josh. 11:21–23*). The confidence that Joshua and Caleb had shown in God's providence and power, after first spying out the land and seeing the Anakites (*Num. 14:6–9*), was at last vindicated. God had fulfilled his promises to Israel.     P.D.G.

**ANAMMELECH,** one of the gods worshipped by the Sepharvites (*2 Kings 17:31*). These people were among those transported by the Assyrian king to Samaria to replace the Israelites, who had been exiled from the land (*2 Kings 17:24*). They brought with them fearful practices that included child sacrifices made by fire.

**ANAN** (Heb., 'cloud'), one of the leaders who sealed the agreement of the people to worship the LORD and obey his Law (*Neh. 10:26*).

**ANANI,** a son of Elioenai and part of the royal lineage of Judah following the Exile,

therefore a descendant of David (*1 Chron. 3:24*).

**ANANIAH,** grandfather of Azariah, helped repair the wall in Jerusalem by his house (*Neh. 3:23*).

**ANANIAS** (Heb., 'the Lord has been gracious').

**1.** Ananias, husband to Sapphira, was one of the early converts in the Jerusalem church (*Acts 5*). In those days Christians 'had everything in common. Selling their possessions and goods; they gave to anyone as he had need' (*Acts 2:44–45*). Following this practice, Ananias and Sapphira decided to sell a property (*Acts 5:1*). With the full knowledge of his wife he decided to hold back some of the money for personal use. He then presented the proceeds to Peter who, under guidance from the Holy Spirit, realized what had happened and accused Ananias of lying to God. On hearing this Ananias fell down dead. When his wife later entered she continued the lie and also died. It is important to see that the issue here was not a law that they had to share everything. Indeed Peter made the point that what belonged to them was theirs (*Acts 5:4*). The problem was the deliberate and wilful attempt to lie 'to the Holy Spirit' and God's people (*Acts 5:3*). Sapphira's sin was spelled out by Peter: 'How could you *agree* to test the Spirit of the Lord?' (*Acts 5:9*).

For Christians one of the privileges of being a Christian is to be free from legalism. Peter and the early church were not creating some new binding law by which people might earn merit before God and the church, rather they were seeking to live lives that would reflect his love and grace seen in Jesus Christ. With such freedom, to work out what is right in individual lives by way of service, goes a great responsibility to be honest and open before the Lord and his people. The result of this sad episode in the early church was an increased understanding of and fear of the Lord's power and holiness. See *Sapphira*.

**2.** Another Ananias who had become a Christian at an early stage in the spread of the gospel of Christ lived in Damascus (*Acts 9:10–19*). Following the account of Saul's (Paul's) conversion and his resulting blindness at seeing the glory of the Lord on the road to Damascus, we read of Ananias receiving a vision. The Lord spoke to him and told him to go to the house where Saul was staying and lay hands on him so he would receive his sight. Ananias was fearful since Saul's reputation for violently persecuting Christians had driven fear into all the Christians in Damascus. The Lord, however, promised Saul was his 'chosen instrument to carry my name before the Gentiles and their kings and before the people of Israel' (*Acts 9:15*). The Lord also said that Paul would have to suffer for the faith in due course.

It is a testimony to the character and deep faith of Ananias that he was prepared to go to Saul's house and address him as 'brother' when a few hours earlier his very name would have made him fearful. Ananias laid hands on Saul who was then able to see again. He was immediately baptized, perhaps by Ananias, and stayed in Damascus a while with Ananias and the other Christian disciples. There can be few more dramatic instances in Scripture of the way a Christian's emotions can be changed through faith in God's word than the way fear was turned to strength and love in Ananias. Paul himself later recounted these events from his perspective and we see that Ananias was the one who first told Paul about his worldwide mission, his need for forgiveness and baptism (*Acts 22:14–16*). See *Paul*.

**3.** Another Ananias was high priest at the time of the apostle Paul's arrest in Jerusalem. He was a proud and cruel Sadducean leader. He was appointed by Herod and held power AD 47–59. In AD 52 he was sent to Rome to answer charges of cruelty. He was set free by Claudius, but this description helps us understand his personal intervention upon Paul's arrest. He ordered Paul to be slapped in the face during his trial (*Acts 23:2*) and later personally went down to Caesarea in order to pursue the charges against Paul before Felix (*Acts 24:1*).

P.D.G.

**ANATH,** father of Shamgar, one of the Judges of Israel (*Judg. 3:31; 5:6*). The name refers to a goddess of war.

**ANATHOTH** **1.** A grandson of Benjamin and a son of Beker (*1 Chron. 7:8*).

**2.** 128 of his family were recorded as having returned to Jerusalem from the Exile in Babylon. They returned with Zerubbabel and Nehemiah (*Ezra 2:23; Neh. 7:27*). In *Neh. 10:19* a leader of the people by this name may well have been the same person. Under the direction of Nehemiah, he signed the agreement of the people to obey the Law of the LORD and worship only him.

**ANDREW** The name comes from the Greek word for 'manly'. Andrew was the first apostle of the Twelve whom Jesus called, but he was quickly overshadowed by his brother Simon Peter, whom he brought to the Lord (*John 1:40–44*). From Bethsaida of Galilee, Andrew had previously been a follower of John the Baptist and had heard him point out Jesus as the Lamb of God. Like the other three disciples whom Jesus called in John 1, Andrew received his more formal commission to full-time itinerant apprenticeship with the Lord at the beginning of Jesus' Galilean ministry. Andrew, Peter, James and John were all fishermen at the time (*Matt. 4:18; Mark 1:16*). Andrew is paired with his brother in the lists of twelve disciples in *Matt. 10:2* and *Luke 6:14* (though not in *Mark 3:18* or *Acts*

1:13), suggesting that at least part of the time the two brothers ministered as a team (cf. Mark 6:7).

In Mark 13:3, the same four fishermen disciples are mentioned as those present for Jesus' 'Olivet Discourse'. In John 6:8 Andrew reported to Jesus with some concern the meagre provisions of fish and bread available to the multitude of 5,000 men. In John 12:22, he was one of the go-betweens who told Jesus about certain Greeks who were seeking an audience with the Lord. Despite claims to the contrary, there are no consistent patterns in Andrew's behaviour nor enough data in the pages of Scripture to deduce any significant theological principles about his overall personality or character. Various apocryphal acts are attributed to him, of no historical credence. Nothing else is known with any degree of historical probability about the man.     C.B.

**ANDRONICUS** With Junias (Rom. 16:7), Paul calls him a 'relative' and fellow prisoner. They were probably true blood relatives, though perhaps simply Jews like Paul. Where they were all prisoners together is not known. They were converted before Paul, and he considered them to be 'outstanding' among the apostles. This is probably the wider use of the term 'apostle' which referred to those sent out to preach the gospel.

**ANER,** one of three Amorite brothers (see also Mamre and Ashcol) who were allied with Abram when he pursued Kedorlaomer in order to rescue Lot from captivity (Gen. 14:13–16). Abram showed his gratitude to them later (Gen. 14:24). (See Amraphel for more on this incident.)

**THE ANGEL OF THE LORD.** The 'angel of the LORD' (sometimes called the 'angel of God') is mentioned over 60 times in the Bible, and is God's personal spokesman and representative to humanity. Some-

times in the OT the angel is practically identified with God, as in Jacob's encounter at Bethel, Moses at the burning bush and the deliverance from Egypt (Gen. 31:13; Exod. 3:2; Judg. 2:1). In other places the angel is differentiated from God (2 Sam. 24:16; Zech. 1:12–13). In the NT the angel is distinguished from God (as in Luke 1:19, where Gabriel is named), though Acts 8:26, 29 may refer to the activity of the Holy Spirit.

In Abraham's day the angel appeared to Hagar in the wilderness, told her to return to her mistress Sarai (Sarah) and promised that God would greatly multiply her offspring (Gen. 16:7–12). Divine instruction was also given concerning Ishmael. Later the angel intervened on Mt Moriah, forbidding the slaying of Isaac and promising to bless Abraham because of his obedience to God (Gen. 22:11–12, 15–18).

The angel of the LORD appears frequently in the Balaam story (Num. 22:22–35), and is mentioned in the song of Deborah and the call of Gideon (Judg. 5:23; 6:11–22). In the time of Judges, the angel instructed Manoah (Judg. 13:13–21). When David displeased God by taking a census, the angel brought destruction in the form of a pestilence that killed 70,000 (2 Sam. 24:10–16; 1 Chron. 21:1–14). When David prayed, the angel commanded the erection of an altar on the threshing floor of Araunah (Ornan) the Jebusite. This later became the site of the Jewish Temple (2 Sam. 24:16–25; 1 Chron. 21:15–22:1). The angel touched the despairing Elijah (1 Kings 19:7) and instructed him to challenge the king of Samaria and his messengers (2 Kings 1:3, 15). The angel annihilated Sennacherib's army, demonstrating God's power to the Assyrians (2 Kings 19:35; Is. 37:36).

In the Psalms the angel may bring either blessing or judgment. 'The angel of the LORD encamps around those who fear him [i.e. the LORD], and delivers them' (Ps. 34:7), but the enemies of God's people are subject to angelic judgment (*Ps. 35:5–6*). The angel is also prominent in Zechariah (*Zech. 1:11–12; 3:1, 5–6*).

In Luke's Gospel the angel of the Lord appeared to Zechariah announcing the births of John and Jesus (*Luke 1:11; 2:19*). An angel appeared in the nativity story (*Matt. 1:20, 24*) in dreams instructing Joseph concerning the holy family (*Matt. 2:13, 19*), and in Matthew's account of the resurrection (*Matt. 28:2–7*).

In the book of Acts the angel of the Lord is mentioned on several occasions. For example, he opened prison doors (*Acts 5:19; 12:7*), gave travel directions to Philip (*Acts 8:26*) and struck down King Herod Agrippa I as a judgment of God (*Acts 12:23*).

In summary, the angel of the Lord is active in both the OT and the NT, working to effect the divine purposes both to bless and to judge. Sometimes God communicates his will through the angel, who can guide and direct his people. At other times the angel may also be seen as the divine messenger who is responsible for carrying out God's will of judgment.

A.A.T.

## ANGELS

There are approximately 292 references to 'angels' in the Bible, 114 in the OT and 178 in the NT. This includes over 60 references to the 'angel of the LORD', but it does not include references to the two named angels in the Bible, Gabriel (*Dan. 8:16; 9:21; Luke 1:19, 26*) and Michael (*Dan. 10:13, 21; 12:1; Jude 9; Rev. 12:7*). There are also over 60 references to the cherubs or cherubim, celestial beings who are mentioned frequently in connection with God's symbolic enthronement in the Tabernacle or Temple (*Exod. 25:18–20; 37:7–9; 1 Kings 6:23–25; 8:6–7; 2 Chron. 3:7–14; Ezek. 10:1–20; Heb. 9:5*).

### Angels in the Old Testament

The OT word for angel meant simply a 'messenger'. Usually the messenger was an agent of God who carried out some aspect of the divine purpose as it related to humankind. For example, two angels came to Sodom to warn Lot and his family of the impending destruction of that city as a divine punishment for its depravity (*Gen. 19:1, 12–15*).

*Angels as guides, helpers and bringers of encouragement.* On other occasions, an angel could serve to guide a person into the fulfilment of God's will. For instance, Abraham's servant was sent to Mesopotamia to find a wife for Isaac from his own people, after Abraham had said that God would 'send his angel' before him to achieve the intended purpose (*Gen. 24:8, 40*).

Sometimes angels appeared in the OT to encourage God's people. Thus the patriarch Jacob, after he left Beersheba, had a dream at Bethel in which he saw 'a stairway resting on the earth, with its top reaching to heaven, and the angels of God were ascending and descending on it' (*Gen. 28:12*). God spoke to Jacob through this experience, and reassured him that he would be his God and watch over him, eventually bringing him back to the land of promise (*Gen. 28:13–15*).

This divine protection was seen by the psalmist as extended to all those who genuinely put their trust in the living God: 'The angel of the LORD encamps around those who fear him, and he delivers them' (*Ps. 34:7; cf. 91:11–12*).

44

One of the most interesting references to angels came when Moses addressed representatives from the king of Edom. In recounting the hardships of Egyptian bondage, Moses commented: 'but when we cried out to the LORD, he heard our cry and sent an angel and brought us out of Egypt' (Num. 20:16). Sadly, the reminder of divine help in the past was not sufficient, and passage through Edomite territory was denied (Num. 20:18–20).

**Angels as executors of divine judgment.** Sometimes angels were assigned punitive roles in the divine purpose (e.g. Gen. 19:12; 2 Sam. 24:16–17). A striking illustration of God using an angel to execute his judgment is found in 1 Chronicles: 'God sent an angel to destroy Jerusalem' (1 Chron. 21:15). Fortunately, in this case annihilation of the city was prevented: 'Then the LORD spoke to the angel, and he put his sword back into its sheath' (1 Chron. 21:27; cf. v. 15). The divine justice was tempered with the divine mercy. On the other hand, there were occasions when stubborn opposition to God was met with unmitigated divine fury, as in the plagues which fell upon Egypt: 'He unleashed against them his hot anger, his wrath, indignation and hostility – a band of destroying angels' (Ps. 78:49).

One of the most dramatic cases of divine retribution occurred in the defeat of Sennacherib in 701 BC in response to King Hezekiah of Judah's prayer: 'the LORD sent an angel, who annihilated all the fighting men and the leaders and officers in the camp of the Assyrian king' (2 Chron. 32:21f.; cf. 2 Kings 19:35; Is. 37:36; 1 Macc. 7:41). The same action which produced judgment upon the enemies of God brought deliverance to his people.

**Interpreting angels.** Angels appeared frequently in the book of Zechariah, where the interpreting angel is often mentioned (Zech. 1:9, 13–14, 18–19; 2:3; 4:1, 4–5; 5:5, 10; 6:4–5; cf. 2 Esd. 2:44–48; 5:31–55). When the angel of the LORD raised the question of how long the divine mercy would be withheld from Jerusalem, 'the LORD spoke kind and comforting words to the angel who talked' with the prophet (Zech. 1:13). The angel then communicated this God-given message to Zechariah (Zech. 1:14–17). This role of the angel in communicating the divine revelation to the prophet sheds light on the book of Revelation, where a similar role is given to the interpreting angel (Rev. 1:1–2; 22:6).

**Angels and the praise of God.** One of the most beautiful roles assigned to angels in the OT is the role of praise. The psalmist exhorted: 'Praise the LORD, you his angels, you mighty ones who do his bidding, who obey his word. Praise the LORD, all his heavenly hosts, you his servants who do his will' (Ps. 103:20–21). Similarly, Ps. 148 called for the angels to join all created things in the praise of God: 'Praise him, all his angels, praise him, all his heavenly hosts' (Ps. 148:2). When God created the earth, 'all the angels shouted for joy', singing in praise of the Creator (Job 38:7). In like manner the seraphs, the angelic beings who are only mentioned in Isaiah's temple vision, offered worship and adoration to God, praising his ineffable holiness: 'Holy, holy, holy is the LORD Almighty; the whole earth is full of his glory' (Is. 6:2–4). The very name of the angels ('seraphs' means 'the burning ones') may point to their purity as God's servants. Here great emphasis is placed on the holiness of God and the importance of praise on the part of the angels who serve him.

## Angels in the intertestamental period

Angels were particularly prominent in the intertestamental period (*2 Esd. 6:3; Tobit 6:5; Sus. 55, 59; 1 Macc. 7:41; 2 Macc. 11:6*). Some angels were named (e.g. Uriel in *2 Esd. 5:20*; Raphael in *Tobit 5:4*), and elaborate angelologies developed. Tobit, for example, could speak of 'seven holy angels who present the prayers of the saints and enter into the presence of the glory of the Holy One' (*Tobit 12:15*). The Similitudes of Enoch, which had a strong interest in angels, mentioned by name four leading angels who were given specific functions in the divine plan (*1 Enoch 40:9–10*). By contrast, the Bible's teaching on angels is restrained, and lacks the speculative element which became so dominant in the intertestamental period.

## Angels in the New Testament

In the NT, the Greek word *angelos* means a 'messenger' (e.g. John the Baptist, *Mark 1:2–4*) or an 'angel'. Angels are mentioned frequently in the Gospels, Acts, Hebrews and Revelation, and occasionally elsewhere.

***Angels and the births of John and Jesus.*** The element of praise has certainly made its presence felt in the NT. In Luke the birth of Jesus is heralded by the heavenly host 'praising God and saying, "Glory to God in the highest, and on earth peace . . ."' (*Luke 2:14*). Thus angels in the NT participate in the worship and praise of God, even as they did in OT times. The praise of God was one of their primary activities (*Rev. 5:11–12*).

Several other features of the nativity story deserve notice. First, the angel of the Lord played a prominent role in announcing the births of both John the Baptist and Jesus, appearing to Joseph (*Matt. 1:20, 24; 2:13*), Zechariah (*Luke 1:11–20*) and the shepherds (*Luke 2:9–12*). Second, the angel Gabriel made the annunciation to Zechariah and Mary (*Luke 1:19, 26*). Luke also noted Gabriel's role in the naming of Jesus (*2:21; cf. 1:26–38*).

***Angels and the temptation of Jesus.*** At the temptation, *Ps. 91:11–12* was quoted by the devil to tempt Jesus to put God's faithfulness to the test (*Matt. 4:5–7; Luke 4:9–12*). While Jesus refused to yield to this demonic suggestion, it is significant that Mark noted the ministry of angels in his account of the temptation (*Mark 1:13*). Similarly, Matthew declared at the end of his temptation account, 'Then the devil left him, and angels came and attended him' (*Matt. 4:11*). The divine promise of *Ps. 91* was fulfilled, but in God's own time and way (cf. *Luke 22:43*).

***Angels and the witness theme.*** Angels are mentioned several times in connection with Christian witness. Earthly witness for Christ was important, for it was viewed against the backdrop of eternity: 'If anyone is ashamed of me and my words, the Son of Man will be ashamed of him when he comes in his glory and in the glory of the Father and of the holy angels' (*Luke 9:26*). Christian witness had solemn significance, in view of the ultimate situation in the presence of God and the angels: 'whoever acknowledges me before men, the Son of Man will also acknowledge him before the angels of God. But he who disowns me before men will be disowned before the angels of God' (*Luke 12:8–9; cf. Matt. 10:32–33; Rev. 3:5*). In addition, Luke noted the joy that true repentance brought: 'there is rejoicing in the presence of the angels of God over one sinner who repents' (*Luke 15:10*).

***Angels and the day of the Lord.***   Matthew has highlighted the role of the angels in the final day of the Lord. In the Parable of the Weeds, for instance, the disciples are told: 'The harvest is the end of the age, and the harvesters are angels . . . The Son of Man will send out his angels, and they will weed out of his kingdom everything that causes sin and all who do evil' (*Matt. 13:39, 41*). Similarly, in the Parable of the Net the angels participate in the last judgment: 'The angels will come and separate the wicked from the righteous and throw them into the fiery furnace, where there will be weeping and gnashing of teeth' (*Matt. 13:49–50*). Similarly, in *Matt. 16:27* the angels are seen as agents of God who have a significant role to play in the judicial process: 'For the Son of Man is going to come in his Father's glory with his angels, and then will he reward each person according to what he has done.' At the end of time, God 'will send his angels with a loud trumpet call, and they will gather his elect from the four winds, from one end of the heavens to the other' (*Matt. 24:31*).

***Angels in death and resurrection scenes.***   Angels are noted in the intriguing passage on the rich man and Lazarus, where 'the beggar died and the angels carried him to Abraham's side'; by contrast, the 'rich man also died and was buried' (*Luke 16:22*). The eternal destinies of the two men were evidently quite different and in sharpest contrast with their earthly circumstances!

Angels appeared at the empty tomb following the resurrection of Jesus (*Matt. 28:2, 5; Luke 24:23; John 20:12*). Matthew noted that an 'angel of the Lord' was responsible for rolling away the stone, and described his impressive appearance and the fearful reaction of the guards (*Matt. 28:2–3*). He also recorded the angel's instructions to the women (*Matt. 28:5–7; cf. Mark 16:5–7; Luke 24:4–7*). In John's Gospel Mary Magdalene encountered 'two angels in white' and then the risen Lord himself (*John 20:11–18; cf. Acts 1:10–11* re the ascension).

***Angels in other places in the Gospels.***   Matthew drew attention to the role of guardian angels, who protect God's people (*Matt. 18:10; cf. Ps. 34:7; 91:11; Acts 12:11*). He also included the teaching of Jesus about marriage in the future state: 'At the resurrection people will neither marry nor be given in marriage; they will be like the angels in heaven' (*Matt. 22:29; cf. Luke 20:36*). Finally, there is the sombre dismissal of those on the King's left hand in the passage on 'the Sheep and the Goats': 'Depart from me, you who are cursed, into the eternal fire prepared for the devil and his angels' (*Matt. 25:41*). It is clear from this passage that some of the angels have sinned and joined the evil one's ranks, and consequently have been consigned to eternal judgment (*cf. Is. 14:12–17; Ezek. 28:12–19; 2 Pet. 2:4; Jude 6*).

In John's Gospel the evangelist recorded Jesus' striking comment to Nathaniel that he would 'see heaven open, and the angels of God ascending and descending on the Son of Man' (*John 1:51*). This passage recalls Jacob's dream at Bethel (*Gen. 28:10–17*), where angels were acting in a similar way. Here the claim is being made that Jesus, as the Son of Man, is the link between heaven and earth.

**Angels in the book of Acts.**   Luke made many references to angels in Acts. The 'angel of the Lord' opened prison doors for the apostles on several occasions (*Acts 5:19; 12:7–11*). Later an 'angel of the Lord' encouraged Paul amid a storm at sea with a message of comfort and the assurance of deliverance (*Acts 27:23–24*). On the other hand, an 'angel of the Lord' acted in judgment against an enemy of God's people, as in the OT: 'Immediately, because Herod did not give praise to God, an angel of the Lord struck him down, and he was eaten by worms and died' (*Acts 12:23*). God was guiding his people in mission and using angels, even though the rationalistic Sadducees denied their existence (*Acts 23:8*)!

**Angels in Paul's letters.**   Paul had less to say about angels than might have been expected, though he did acknowledge that the Christian struggle was with 'principalities and powers' (*Eph. 6:12; cf. 2:2; John 12:31; 14:30*). He was persuaded that neither angels, nor any other created powers, could separate true believers from the love of God in Christ (*Rom. 8:38–39*).

Paul did take note of the fallen angels, and reminded the sinful Corinthians that 'the saints' would judge these angels (*1 Cor. 6:3*). He also conceded that 'Satan himself masquerades as an angel of light' (*2 Cor. 11:14*). This situation meant that constant vigilance was necessary to resist such deceptive attacks. While angels had played a role in putting the divine law into effect (*Gal. 3:19*), they were certainly not to be worshipped (*Col. 2:18*). Indeed, Paul, in writing to the Galatians, insisted that 'even if we or an angel from heaven should preach a gospel other than the one we preached to you, let him be eternally condemned!' (*Gal. 1:8*). Still Paul could acknowledge with gratitude the initial kindness of the Galatian people, who 'welcomed me as if I were an angel of God . . .' (*Gal. 4:14*). In writing to the Thessalonians Paul solemnly declared that the opponents of the Christian message who had been persecuting believers would be punished 'when the Lord Jesus is revealed from heaven in blazing fire with his powerful angels' (*2 Thess. 1:7*). God was still in charge of his world.

Two passages in *1 Timothy* should be noted. In the first one, angels are mentioned in a lovely early Christian hymn (*1 Tim. 3:16*). In the second, a serious charge is given to the young Christian leader in the presence not only of God and Christ, but also of 'the elect angels' (who appear to be contrasted with Satan and the other fallen angels).

**Angels in the letter to the Hebrews.**   Angels are often mentioned in the epistle to the Hebrews (*Heb. 2:16; 12:22; 13:2*) but are considered inferior to Christ (*Heb. 1:5– 14*). They are carefully defined in the opening chapter as 'ministering spirits sent to serve those who will inherit salvation' (*Heb. 1:14*). Angels are introduced in a passage warning disciples to pay attention to the great salvation offered in Christ (*Heb. 2:2*). Innumerable angels were part of the heavenly Jerusalem, and this is adduced as one more incentive for the recipients not to relapse into Judaism (*Heb. 12:22–24; cf. Matt. 26:53*).

**Angels in 1 Peter, 2 Peter and Jude.**   The divine plan of salvation is so wonderful that it arouses the curiosity of the angels (*1 Pet. 1:12*). The ascension of Christ to heaven meant, among other things, that 'angels, authorities and powers' were placed in submission to him (1 Pet. 3:22). The sombre references to the doom of fallen angels in 2 Peter and Jude occur in solemn passages pointing out the errors of the false teachers and their certain destruction (2 Pet. 2:4; Jude 6). In 2 Pet. 2:11 a striking contrast is made between the good and bad angels.

**Angels in the book of Revelation.** In the book of Revelation, a letter is addressed to the 'angel' of each of the seven churches (Rev. 2:1, 8, 12, 18; 3:1, 7, 14). In each case the reference appears to be to the pastors of the churches, who were God's messengers to his people in a time of impending crisis. On the other hand, there are many references to angels as supernatural beings throughout the book (Rev. 5:2, 11; 7:1–2, 11; 8:3–8; 14:6–10; 19:17; 20:1).

Space limitations restrict us to four observations. First, angels here, as elsewhere in the Bible, are depicted as executing the judgments of God on the earth (Rev. 9:15; 16:3–12). Second, the role of the interpreting angel observed in Zechariah is found in the Apocalypse (Rev. 1:1–2; 10:7–9; 22:6). Third, a division is observed between the good angels and the fallen angels: 'there was war in heaven. Michael and his angels fought against the dragon, and the dragon and his angels fought back' (Rev. 12:7). In this war the divine side was victorious: the devil 'was hurled to the earth, and his angels with him' (Rev. 12:9). Finally, the true angels worship God and join in the praise of Christ around the divine throne (Rev. 5:11–12).

## Summary

The Bible has a considerable amount to say about angels. They are created beings and are not to be worshipped or praised. Rather, they are supernatural servants of God who participate in his purposes of judgment and salvation. They are his agents and messengers, and work on behalf of God's human servants and protect them. They participate in the worship of God and seek to advance his will on the earth. Some, however, have rebelled against God and now ally themselves with Satan. They will be judged with Satan.                                                    A.A.T.

**ANIAM,** the fourth son of Shemida, of the tribe of Manasseh (1 Chron. 7:19).

**ANNA** (Heb. 'grace') was the prophetess daughter of Phanuel, from the tribe of Asher. After only seven years of marriage, Anna became a widow and thereafter devoted herself to serving the Lord in his Temple, day and night. When Anna was 84, an event occurred which adorned her life with purpose. Luke 2:36–38 records that Anna was at the Temple during the presentation of the child Jesus: the long-awaited Messiah. Anna publicly gave thanks to God and proclaimed good news about her Redeemer. The account of Anna

and of Simeon in the same passage reveals the existence of people who were truly faithful to God's covenant and were trusting him to fulfil his promises of sending a Saviour King.                  S.C.

**ANNAS** is mentioned four times as 'high priest' (Luke 3:2; John 18:13, 24; Acts 4:6) and is always linked to Caiaphas. Josephus, the Jewish historian, mentions him as High Priest in Jerusalem from around AD 6 to AD 15 (Ants. XVIII.ii). The High Priest was the leader among the priests. His unique role in worship was to enter once a year into the Most Holy Place in the inner Temple, where he alone could offer the sacrifice on the Day of Atonement. In virtue of this office, he was also the leader of the Sanhedrin, thus wielding both religious and political power and having close contact with the Roman governor. The position had become a political appointment. Annas was a powerful leader whose influence continued after the office had passed on to others. His son-in-law Caiaphas and his grandson Matthias also became High Priests. Thus Annas and Caiaphas are mentioned together when God's Word came to John the Baptist (*Luke 3:2*). The Jews referred first to Annas when Jesus was arrested (*John 18:13, 24*), and Annas passed him on to Caiaphas. He was still involved in the Sanhedrin when Peter and John were questioned about their faith (*Acts 4:6*). P.D.G.

**ANTHOTHIJAH,** one of the Benjamites in the genealogy leading to Saul. He was a son of Shashak (*1 Chron. 8:24*).

**ANTIPAS 1.** See *Herod*.
**2.** Described as God's 'faithful witness' in *Rev. 2:13*. Speaking to the church in Pergamum in the province of Asia, the Lord commends the Christians for not renouncing their faith, even when Antipas was put to death as a martyr. This city is described as being 'where Satan lives'. It was a centre for Emperor worship. Tradition says Antipas died by being roasted in a large bowl.

**ANUB** From the tribe of Judah, he was the son of Koz (*1 Chron. 4:8*).

**APELLES** Paul sent greetings to this Roman Christian who was 'tested and approved in Christ' (*Rom. 16:10*). Perhaps this Christian had, like Paul, suffered persecution, but no further information is given. Paul's pastoral care and concern for individuals is often seen in his letters.

**APHIAH,** a descendant of Benjamin and father of Becorath. He was great-great-grandfather to King Saul (*1 Sam. 9:1*).

**APOLLOS** was a leading Christian worker in the early church. He was born and educated in the 'second Athens', i.e. Alexandria in Egypt, and may have been among the limited number of Jews who actually possessed Alexandrian citizenship. That he belonged to the upper 'social register' of that famous city is indicated by Luke's selection of terms in his brief but highly informative portrait in *Acts 18:24–28*. As 'a learned man' he was privately educated to 'university' level of the much-prized Greek education in rhetoric. This was open only to the elite because of the enormous fees. Luke says he was 'powerful' in his use of the Scriptures. 'Powerful' was a rhetorical term for logical and forceful delivery. He learnt the art of skilful debating in his secular education and put it to excellent use in 'demonstrating' (another rhetorical term) from the OT that Jesus was the promised Messiah (*Acts 18:24*). By first-century standards he is presented as a formidable Jewish Christian apologist and debater, combining his exhaustive knowledge of the OT and his secular education in the art of rhetoric. (Compare him with other preachers whose formal education is described as 'unschooled' *Acts 4:13*).

His arrival in Ephesus opened a ministry among fellow Jews. His coming clearly fortified the Christian witness in a city which was at the same time both receptive and antagonistic to Christianity. He had been taught 'the way of the Lord' (*cf. Mark 1:2* citing *Is. 40:3*), presumably by the disciples of John the Baptist, whose preaching was couched in terms of preparing the way for Jesus. John's message had spread well beyond the borders of Judea into Egypt as well as Asia Minor. Initially Apollos preached in the Ephesian synagogue where he was heard by those two great facilitators of Christian ministry and ministers in the early church, Priscilla and Aquila. In inviting him home they were probably using their residence as a 'house church' (Rom. 16:5). Even though Apollos taught about Jesus 'accurately', they filled in the gaps in his knowledge. Like any disciple of John who was not part of the apostolic band, he would presumably need to understand the theological implications of the final events in the life of Jesus including his death, resurrection and Kingdom.

Because Apollos wished to exercise his ministry across the Aegean Sea in the province of Achaea, of which Corinth was the capital, the Ephesian church encouraged him to go. They wrote a letter of commendation to the Corinthian Christians asking them to receive him. At that stage Priscilla and Aquila were the link between the two churches (Acts 18:2). Apollos strengthened the Corinthian church immeasurably, and helped in discussion with Jews who had brought a criminal case against Paul before the governor, Gallio. His judgment had placed Christians under a Jewish umbrella, and Apollos seems to have fulfilled the governor's injunction, perhaps unwittingly, by using the Scriptures to 'settle the matter' (Acts 18:15). In public debate, he both refuted the Jewish case and proved by the touchstone of Holy Scripture the Christians' claim that the Messiah was Jesus (Acts 18:28).

He remained in Corinth for some time, engaging in an effective ministry there. Those converted under his ministry subsequently saw themselves in secular terms as belonging to him when divisions arose after he left Corinth to return to Ephesus. His name was to be drawn into the unhappy problems in 1 Cor. 1–4 which were brought to a head when the Corinthians issued an invitation for him, in preference to Paul, to return to work there, even though the latter had ex-ercised an effective ministry in that city for 18 months (Acts 18:11). The use of the phrase 'now about' in relation to 'our brother, Apollos' (1 Cor. 16:12) indicates that Paul is responding to this request in their letter (1 Cor. 7:1). Given secular Corinth's love of oratory, the Apollos lobby was able to convince the church that its interests were best served by having Apollos return. In subsequent days what some thought of Paul's ministry was couched in rhetorical language which indicates that he possessed neither the charismatic presence of an Apollos, for his 'bodily presence' was weak, nor rhetorical style, for his actual presentation lacked the acceptable hallmarks of speech suited to an educated audience of sophisticated Corinthians (2 Cor. 10:10).

Paul bore no resentment towards Apollos as he wrote back to the Corinthian Christians. He refused to be drawn into their secular way of operating. In 1 Cor. 4:6 Paul condemns their pitting of the Paul lobby against the Apollos lobby as 'immature' and 'worldly'. Jealousy and quarrelling over their teachers was precisely what the secular teachers and their disciples did with their competitive spirit for the reputation of their schools and for influence in the political assembly (1 Cor. 3:1, 3; cf. 1:11). The Corinthians were concerned with who Paul and Apollos were, whereas Paul reveals their distinctive functions as planters and waterers respectively relative to the growth of the church because only God can create and make a congregation grow (1 Cor. 3:5–6). Both men were of such Christian stature that neither reacted to the Corinthians' power game, but operated for the good of the church. The text in 1 Cor. 16:12 indicates that Apollos refused the invitation to return having judged that 'it was not the will' (i.e. of God) for him to respond immediately to their request, although he might feel it right to respond at a later stage.

In *Titus 3:13* Apollos, whose education qualified him to operate as a lawyer, was in transit with Zenas 'the lawyer' (better perhaps 'legal assistant') in Crete. Paul commanded Titus to ensure that 'they have everything they need' for their journey, i.e. the necessary finance. This indicates that Apollos was still engaged in full-time Christian ministry and hence entitled to Christian support (1 *Cor.* 9:14). While Apollos could have secured great wealth by reason of his education by practising as an orator or lawyer, he chose to use his gifts and privileges for the sake of Christ's Kingdom and in doing so contributed greatly to Christian witness and apologetics.                              B.W.

**APOLLYON** See *Abaddon.*

## APOSTLES

The word 'apostle' (from the Greek apostolos, meaning 'messenger' or 'apostle') is the name given to one who is sent on a mission by another. In the NT this word was used to identify the original leaders of the movement which formed around Jesus of Nazareth. In time the word was broadened to include other Christian leaders who carried on the tasks of evangelism and mission.

### The selection of the Twelve

The original apostles were chosen directly by Jesus (*Mark 3:14–15; John 15:16*). They were appointed after a night spent in prayer for divine guidance (*Luke 6:12*). The four evangelists noted that there were twelve such leaders (*Matt. 10:1–2, 5; 11:1; 20:17; Mark 4:10; 6:7; 9:35; Luke 6:13; 8:1; 22:3; John 6:67, 70–71; 20:24*).

The names of the apostles are listed four times, in *Mark 3:16–19, Matt. 10:2–4, Luke 6:14–16* and *Acts 1:13*, where Matthias was appointed as a replacement for Judas (*Acts 1:12–26*). A study of these lists and apostolic names in John's Gospel reveals several interesting facts. First, four of the apostles were fishermen – Simon Peter, Andrew, James and John. Of this number Peter, James and John seemed to constitute an inner circle who were present with Christ on a number of memorable occasions, such as the healing of Jairus' daughter (*Mark 5:37; Luke 8:51*), the Transfiguration on the mountain (*Mark 9:2; Luke 9:28*) and the agony in the Garden of Gethsemane (*Mark 14:32*). Sometimes Andrew was included, as on the occasion when the four disciples asked Jesus a question about the time when the Temple would be destroyed (*Mark 13:3–4*). Second, two disciples, James and John, were called Boanerges, which meant 'sons of thunder', probably referring to their 'hot tempers' (*Mark 3:17*). Third, Matthew or Levi was probably well educated, a tax collector, and considered a collaborationist with the hated Roman authorities who controlled Palestine at the time. Fourth, Thomas was called Didymus, 'the twin' (*John 11:16; 20:24*). Fifth, Judas Iscariot was probably the only non-Galilean, and Simon called 'the zealot' or 'the Canaanean' was probably a political revolutionary. They were a mixed lot, and only a common loyalty to Jesus kept these men together. They knew and loved him, and wanted to be his followers, though they often failed miserably (*Matt. 8:26; 14:31; 16:8; 22:40–45; Mark 4:40; Luke 8:25; 12:28; John 20:24–28*).

## The unique association of the Twelve with Jesus

Jesus had many people who wanted to follow him (e.g. *Matt. 8:18–22; Luke 9:57–62*), and from this larger group he selected both the Seventy-two (*Luke 10:1–20*; some manuscripts read 'seventy' in *vv. 1, 17*) and the Twelve (*Luke 9:1–6*). The appointment of the Twelve had a dual purpose. They were chosen 'that they might be with him and that he might send them out to preach and to have authority . . .' to participate in the ministry of Jesus (*Mark 3:14–15*). It was a demanding, challenging task, but he promised to be with them and help them, even after he had left to go to the Father (*John 14:18*). He would send the Holy Spirit to teach them and enable them to bear witness (*John 14:26; 15:26–27*). They would then be able to reach out in mission to share the gospel with others. In John's Gospel the risen Lord reminded the disciples of their commission: 'As the Father has sent me, I am sending you' (*John 20:11*). This commission was repeatedly given (*Matt. 28:16–20; Luke 24:46–49; cf. Mark 16:15–16; Acts 1:8*).

In noting the place of intimacy and closeness to Jesus, some favourable recognition must be given to 'the beloved disciple', who was mentioned only in John's Gospel and never identified by name. Christian tradition has generally taken this to be a reference to John, the author of the Fourth Gospel, though this has been disputed. In any case, the fourth evangelist has noted that this disciple was close to Jesus, and asked the Lord at the Last Supper concerning the identity of the betrayer (*John 13:23–25*). The beloved disciple was also present at the crucifixion, where he was given the responsibility of caring for the mother of Jesus (*John 19:25–27*). Later he was present with Peter at the examination of the empty tomb and at the miraculous catch of fish on the Sea of Tiberias (*John 21:1, 7, 20*). He was apparently a well-known figure in the Johannine community, and had a particularly intimate connection with Christ.

Two others must be mentioned for their relationship with Jesus. In all of the apostolic lists Peter is always mentioned first and Judas Iscariot last. Peter was evidently the leader of the apostles, and clearly served as the spokesman for the group on a number of occasions (*Matt. 16:13–16; Mark 8:27–29; Luke 9:18–20; John 6:68–69*). At the opposite end of the scale was the tragic figure of Judas, whose betrayal of Jesus resulted in his being placed at the end of each list. He was viewed as betraying 'innocent blood', and had confessed his sin before his suicide (*Matt. 27:3–10; cf. Acts 1:16–19*).

## The dedication of the Twelve

Some of the apostles had come to Jesus from a previous association with John the Baptist (*John 1:35–42*). They had participated in a national back-to-God movement on the part of the covenant people (cf. *Mark 1:5; Matt. 3:5*). They were aware of the importance of repentance, and had taken the first steps to reaffirm their relationship with God (*Matt. 3:1–3; Luke 3:7–14*). In this way they had been prepared to receive Jesus as Israel's long-promised Deliverer.

Jesus too insisted that people repent, turning their back on the sins of the past and opening their lives to believe the good news (*Mark 1:15; cf. Matt. 3:2*). For the Twelve, the call to discipleship would involve leaving the familiar scenes of home and family and going off on an itinerant ministry with Jesus. Thus Simon and Andrew were summoned by Jesus to become fishers of men, and 'at once they left their nets and followed him' (Mark 1:16–18; Matt. 4:18–20). The call to discipleship made radical demands and involved a total commitment.

On one occasion Peter reminded Jesus of the sacrifices that he and the other disciples had made: 'We have left everything to follow you! What then will there be for us?' (Matt. 19:27; cf. Mark 10:28; Luke 18:28). It was quite natural that such a question should be asked when the cost of commitment appeared so high. On another occasion Thomas said rather stoically to the other disciples, 'Let us also go, that we may die with him' (John 11:16). Jesus himself had recognized their fellowship through difficult times, and had promised them great blessings in his Kingdom, where they would 'sit on thrones, judging the twelve tribes of Israel' (Luke 22:28–30). The joys of life in the Kingdom of God would more than compensate for all the trials and sufferings undertaken for his sake (Mark 10:29–30; cf. Matt. 19:28–29; Luke 18:29–30).

## The training of the Twelve

The Lord knew that his mission must be entrusted to the hands of those who would carry on after he had left the earth. For that reason he devoted a great deal of time and attention to the training of the disciples, and especially the Twelve. In public, he frequently taught in parables, but in private he explained everything to his disciples (Matt. 13:10–13, 36; Mark 4:10–20, 34; Luke 8:9–15). He taught them about the nature of his life and work, the necessity of his death, the certainty of his resurrection, and of his final return in power and great glory (Matt. 16:21; Mark 8:31; 9:31; 10:33–34; 14:62; Luke 9:21–22, 26; cf. John 5:25–30). They were superbly taught by Jesus, the Master Teacher, who was also their Lord (John 13:13). In fact, the title 'Teacher' was used of Jesus more often than any other title in the Gospels (e.g. Matt. 8:19; 12:38; 17:24; Mark 4:38; 12:14, 19, 32; Luke 7:40; 10:25; John 3:2; 20:16), and he certainly devoted a major part of his instruction to those who were nearest to him and to whom he entrusted the future of his work.

## The qualifications of the Twelve

There were definite qualifications for apostleship, and Peter outlined these succinctly in his speech in Acts 1:12–22. Several features must be noted in this statement.

First, to be an apostle one had to be a witness of the total public ministry of Jesus from his baptism to his ascension. Thus the importance of the eyewitness role of the apostles was stressed. Luke, in the introduction to his Gospel, had already highlighted the importance of the apostles as 'eyewitnesses' as well as 'servants of the word' (Luke 1:2). Thus the greatest possible emphasis was placed upon the historical foundations of the life and work of Jesus. His miracles, teaching, death and resurrection were not fairy-tales, but solidly attested facts which the apostles could certify as eyewitnesses. This same eyewitness claim was strongly made in the opening words of 1 John (1:1–4).

Second, the apostolic testimony underlined the importance of the cross and resurrection. It was public knowledge in first-century Jerusalem that Jesus of Nazareth had been put to death by crucifixion, and the superscription had informed others 'in Aramaic, Latin and Greek' (John 19:20). While the execution was attested by many people, the apostles fearlessly attested the fact of Jesus' resurrection, and this note is repeatedly sounded in their preaching (Acts 2:24, 32; 4:10; 5:30–32; 13:30). The apostles solemnly maintained that they were witnesses who could vouch for the aliveness of Jesus (Acts 3:15; 10:39–42; 13:31). Their witness, when taken with the testimony of the Scriptures (e.g. Acts 2:25–32; 3:17–26; 13:32–39), served to corroborate the Christian message. This was in harmony with the well-known Jewish law of evidence, which demanded that everything be established by the testimony of two or three witnesses – a principle which is repeatedly stated in the Bible (Num. 35:30; Deut. 17:6; 19:15; Matt. 18:16; 2 Cor. 13:1; 1 Tim. 5:19; Heb. 10:28). The Christian faith was presented in such a way that it honoured the principle of multiple witness.

## The authority of the apostles

The fact that the apostles were the original eyewitnesses of Jesus gave their message a unique authority. They had been chosen by God and by Christ as the authorized communicators of the Christian message (Luke 6:12–13; John 13:18; 15:16, 19; Acts 1:2; 10:41). Moreover, they were divinely appointed as 'servants of the word' (Luke 1:2), and they had been the ones to whom the risen Jesus had said: 'you will receive power when the Holy Spirit comes on you; and you will be my witnesses in Jerusalem, and in all Judea and Samaria, and to the ends of the earth' (Acts 1:8).

## The role of the apostle Paul

The most outstanding figure in carrying out the apostolic commission was the apostle Paul, whose conversion is recorded three times in Acts (9:1–19; 22:3–16; 26:9–18). In Luke's eyes this was an event of great significance in holy history for Paul, like the original Twelve, was divinely commissioned (Acts 9:15–16; 22:14–15; 26:15–18). Thus Luke broadened his use of the term 'apostle' to include Paul and Barnabas, two of the leading missionaries (Acts 14:4, 14).

Paul had strong convictions about his apostleship (1 Cor. 1:1; 15:9; 2 Cor. 1:1; Col. 1:1). On several occasions he had to insist that he was an apostle when his credentials were questioned (1 Cor. 9:1–2; Gal. 1:1; 1:15–2:10). While there were 'false apostles' in the early church (2 Cor. 11:13; Rev. 2:2), his role was by divine appointment. He had seen the risen Lord, and been called to his work by Christ himself.

Paul affirmed the role of the Twelve (1 Cor. 15:7; Gal. 1:17), but also recognized 'apostles' in the wider sense including James the Lord's brother (Gal. 1:19), Silas and Timothy (1 Thess. 2:6–7), Andronicus and Junia (Rom. 16:7) and the 'apostles of the churches' (2 Cor. 8:23).

## Summary

In summary, the apostles had a primary role in the proclamation of the gospel and the execution of the Great Commission. They were the original eyewitnesses and servants of the Word, and the church was certainly 'built upon the foundation of the apostles . . .' (*Eph. 2:20*). The apostles were joined by others like Stephen and Philip who shared in their evangelistic and missionary labours. The apostle Paul was an outstanding leader in bringing the gospel to the world of his day. Clearly the apostles had a special place in the mission of God. (For more detail see the individual entries by name.)
A.A.T.

**APPAIM** (Heb., 'faces'), a son of Nadab and father of Ishi (*1 Chron. 2:30–31*), was a leader in the tribe of Judah.

**APPHIA,** a woman greeted by the apostle Paul in *Philem. 2* and described as 'our sister'. Given that Paul greets her immediately after Philemon himself, she may have been Philemon's wife. She was clearly the hostess for the church that met at Philemon's house. She too was being asked to welcome back the slave Onesimus as a brother in Christ. Tradition says she was stoned to death under Nero's persecution of Christians.

**AQUILA** (Gk., 'eagle'), a Jewish Christian. It is not known when he converted to Christianity, but it probably happened in his native homeland of Pontus (an ancient district of Asia Minor along the Black Sea) or in Rome. In AD 49 he and his wife left Rome and came to Corinth (*Acts 18:2*). They were forced to leave their home in Rome when Emperor Claudius ordered the expulsion of all Jews from that region because of their constant rioting concerning 'Chrestus' (a possible reference to Christ).

A tentmaker by trade, Aquila began working in Corinth. The Apostle Paul met him when he came to Corinth and, being a tentmaker himself, he worked and stayed with him. When the time came for Paul to set sail for Syria, Aquila and his wife Priscilla went with him (*Acts 18:18–19*). Paul left the couple in Ephesus, where they met a Jew named Apollos. He was a learned man in the Scriptures, but knew only of the baptism of John. Aquila and Priscilla invited him into their home and 'explained to him the way of God more adequately' (*Acts 18:26*).

Paul considered Aquila and Priscilla to be loyal friends and fellow-workers in Christ. They 'risked their lives' for him and were a great help to the Gentile churches (*Rom. 16:3–4*). They also had a church meeting in their home (*1 Cor. 16:19*). The last time they are mentioned is in *2 Tim. 4:19*, where Paul exhorts Timothy to greet them.
K.MCR.

**ARA** (Heb., 'wild ass'), one of three sons of Jether, from the tribe of Asher (*1 Chron. 7:38*).

**ARAD,** a son of Beriah, appears in the genealogy leading from Benjamin to Saul (*1 Chron. 8:15–16*).

**ARAH** **1.** A son of Ulla and a descendant of Asher, he was among the 'brave warriors' from his tribe (*1 Chron. 7:39–40*).

**2.** *Ezra 2:5* records that 775 of his descendants returned from Exile with Nehemiah; *Neh. 7:10* says 652 returned.

**3.** His son Shecaniah was the father-in-law of Tobiah, Nehemiah's enemy. Many in Judah were under oath to Tobiah, and so reported all of Nehemiah's deeds to him (*Neh. 6:18–19*).

56

**ARAM 1.** Aram was the son of Shem (*Gen. 10:22–23; 1 Chron. 1:17*), listed in the table of nations. His descendants, such as Uz, Gether, Hul and Meshach were identified as the Aramean tribes who originally inhabited the north-eastern corner of the land of Canaan. Later they came to be identified with the Syrians. They lived in Mesopotamia and to the north-east of Israel.

Israel's relationship with the Arameans from the 10th century BC onwards was one of frequent conflict. Saul did battle with King Zobah (see *1 Sam. 14:47*, RSV). David married the daughter of King Talmai of Geshur who bore him the son Absalom in Hebron – a domestic relationship fraught with trouble (*2 Sam. 3:3; 1 Chron. 3:2*). David was later to fight against King Hadadezer, when 'The LORD gave David victory everywhere he went' (*2 Sam. 8:6b*). Under Solomon the skirmishes continued, with King Rezon of Eliada taking control of Damascus in the latter part of Solomon's reign. Following the division of the Kingdom the Arameans became an increasing threat, particularly during the reign of King Jehu.

The lasting significance of the Arameans was not primarily to be found in their battles with Israel, but in the influence of their language and culture. The fact that Aramaic was less cumbersome than Akkadian or Hebrew enabled the popularizing of their culture. Their proverbs and magical texts were many. The main god of the Arameans was Baal. Aramaic was the vernacular language in Israel during NT times. The NT records Jesus saying a number of things in Aramaic, such as '*Talitha qumi*' (meaning 'Little girl, arise') and '*Eloi, Eloi, Lama sabachthani*', the so-called cry of dereliction (meaning 'My God, My God, why have you forsaken me?').

**2.** Aram was the son of Kemuel. Nahor, Abraham's brother, was his grandfather (*Gen. 22:21*).

**3.** This Aram was one of Shomer's sons, listed as a member of the tribe of Asher (*1 Chron. 7:34*). S.V.

**ARAN,** a son of Dishan and brother to Uz. Dishan was the leader of the Horite clan, who lived in Edom (*Gen. 36:28; 1 Chron. 1:42*).

**ARAUNAH,** a Jebusite man from whom David bought a threshing floor. Contrary to the law (see *1 Chron. 27:23–24*), later in his reign David had ordered a census of the troops of Israel. The punishment God sent for this sin was a plague. David asked God how the plague could be stopped and was commanded by the LORD to build an altar on Araunah's threshing floor. Araunah wanted to give it to the King rather than sell it to him, and was even prepared to supply the oxen for sacrifice. However, David insisted on paying for it and on buying the sacrifices himself, as he did not want to make a sacrifice that cost him nothing (*2 Sam. 24:18–25; 1 Chron. 21*). Araunah could not have imagined, in his desire to serve David and the LORD, that one day the Temple would be built on the same site (*2 Chron. 3:1*). P.D.G.

**ARBA,** the forefather of Anak and the Anakites. He was based in Hebron, which was formerly called Kiriath-Arba in his honour. He was noted for his stature, and his descendants were thought to be giants by the Israelite spies when they looked over Canaan. Caleb was later given the city of Hebron as a reward for his trust that God would help the Israelites destroy the Anakites (*Josh. 14:15; 15:13; 21:11*).

**ARCHELAUS,** the tetrarch of Judea, Samaria and Idumea from 4 BC–AD 6. He is mentioned in the Bible only once, in *Matt. 2:22*. He was the son of Herod the Great by one of his several wives, Malthace. When Herod died in 4 BC, his kingdom was divided between three of his sons: Herod Philip II, who ruled

Trachonitis and Iturea (*Luke 3:1*); Herod Antipas, who was over Galilee and Perea (*Matt. 14:1*); and Archelaus. Because of his great cruelty as a governor, Archelaus was deposed after only ten years in AD 6. The reality of the tyranny of Archelaus is strongly implied in the biblical text. When Joseph was bringing Mary and the young child, Jesus, back to Israel from Egypt (*Matt. 2:21*), he heard that Archelaus had succeeded his father, Herod, as ruler of Judea (*v. 22*). Out of fear, he bypassed Judea and went to Galilee (*v. 22*).                                    A.B.L.

**ARCHIPPUS,** Paul's friend, worked with him in the cause of the gospel as a 'fellow soldier', implying perhaps that he had shared in some of the persecutions Paul had experienced (*Philem. 2*). He may have been related to Philemon. His association with the church at Colosse (*Col. 4:17*) has led some to suggest that perhaps he worked in nearby Laodicea, but the text does not clearly indicate this. Paul exhorted him to complete his 'work' or ministry which he had received from the Lord. This was not to suggest that he was somehow failing, but was rather an encouragement of the sort which Paul so often gave, that all Christian ministry should be regarded as service to the Lord, who both calls and prepares his people for this work (see *2 Tim. 4:5; Eph. 2:10*).
                                                       P.D.G.

**ARD    1.** One of the ten sons of Benjamin listed in *Gen. 46:21*.
**2.** The father of the Ardite clan, this Ard was a son of Bela and a grandson of Benjamin (*Num. 26:40*).

**ARDON,** the son of Caleb and his wife Azubah, in the genealogy of Judah (*1 Chron. 2:18*).

**ARELI,** a son of Gad through whom the clan of the Arelites arose (*Gen. 46:16; Num. 26:17*). He was one of those who went to Egypt with Jacob and the Israelites.

**ARETAS** is only mentioned once in the Bible in *2 Cor. 11:32* by the apostle Paul. The governor in Damascus had the city guarded in order to arrest Paul, and we are told that that governor was 'under King Aretas'.

Aretas was the name given to a number of Nabatean kings from the second century BC onwards. It is probable that Paul referred to Aretas IV, who was the father-in-law of Herod Antipas. However, Damascus was a Roman province at the time, and so various theories have been put forward to account for this reference to Aretas as 'King'. Perhaps he was recognized as a local king by the Romans because he collaborated with them. Others have suggested that the new Roman Emperor, Caligula, had given the oversight of that area to Aretas as part of a policy of devolved government in the hands of vassal kings.                     P.D.G.

**ARGOB** The text of *2 Kings 15:25*, where this name appears, is somewhat uncertain. Gilead is mentioned, so it is possible that 'Argob and Arieh' refer also to places. If they were men, then they were probably co-conspirators with Pekah against the evil King Pekahiah of Israel. Pekah killed Pekahiah and himself became king.

**ARIDAI** See *Est. 9:9*. One of ten sons of Haman killed in Susa by the Jews.

**ARIDATHA** See *Est. 9:8*. One of ten sons of Haman killed in Susa by the Jews.

**ARIEH** This name appears in *2 Kings 15:25. See Argob.*

**ARIEL** (Heb., 'lion of God'), one of the leaders summoned by Ezra to join him in the return from Babylon to Jerusalem. He was sent to Iddo to find attendants for the Temple (*Ezra 8:16*).

**ARIOCH** **1.** Arioch was the king of El-
lasar and one of four Mesopotamian kings
who invaded Palestine at the time of
Abraham (see also *Tidal, Amraphel* and
*Kedorlaomer; Gen. 14:1, 9*). The account
given in *Gen. 14* is of particular interest
as it highlights both the desirability of
the Jordan valley that could attract an
alliance of kings from so far afield,
and the rapidly advancing influence of
Abra(ha)m.

It is clear that the invading alliance was
headed by Kedorlaomer (*Gen. 14:4–5*).
The invaders had conquered several of
the city states of the Jordan valley and
areas around the Dead Sea and had ruled
the land for twelve years. In the 13th year
the local kings of these cities rebelled and
fought the invaders (see *Bera, Birsha,
Shinab, Shemeber*). Once again, however, they were defeated and fled. The
four kings seized a huge area of land
including the cities of Sodom and Gomorrah from which they took all the spoil. In
this conquest they carried off Abram's
nephew, Lot, who was living in Sodom.
This brought Abram into the arena. When
he heard what had happened, he went in
pursuit of Kedorlaomer, chasing him far
to the north. Finally in a clever attack he
defeated the alliance and returned with
Lot and his family (*Gen. 14:14–17*).

The alliance had come from the same
area that had been Abram's home. It is of
great significance that Abram's defeat of
these kings is seen in *Gen. 14* as God's
victory, and indicates God's establishment of Abram in Canaan and his final
and complete separation from his former
life. From this point onwards, under
God's sovereign plan Abram's influence
in the 'promised land' continued to increase.

**2.** Another Arioch was the commander
of the king's guard in Babylon in the days
of Daniel. He was ordered by the king to
execute all the wise men in Babylon
who had been unable to interpret Nebuchadnezzar's dream (*Dan. 2:14–15*).

Daniel had not heard that the king needed
his dream interpreting, so when Arioch
approached him he asked for time to
discover the interpretation (*v. 16*). After
prayer to God, Daniel was able to return to
the king and explain the dream and thus
was spared death. Indeed God used this
incident to bring Daniel to the forefront of
court life in Babylon (*vv. 24–25*).

P.D.G.

**ARISAI** See *Est. 9:9*. One of ten sons of
Haman killed in Susa by the Jews.

**ARISTARCHUS** (Gk., 'best ruler'), a
native of Thessalonica, was one of Paul's
most constant and faithful 'fellow-
workers' (*Philem. 24*) in his journeys. He
first comes to our attention in *Acts 19:29*
where, along with Gaius, he was seized
by the Ephesians, who were violently
antagonistic to the gospel, and taken to
the theatre. Eventually the crowd was
quietened and they were released. In *Acts
20:4* we find him accompanying Paul in
Macedonia, where again persecution was
threatened. On this journey he was probably the representative of the Thessalonian churches, carrying their offering for
the relief of the poor in Jerusalem. Later in
*Acts 27:2* he alone is mentioned as a
travelling companion with Paul. On this
occasion Paul was a prisoner being taken
to Rome. Perhaps at this time Aristarchus
was also a prisoner. In *Col. 4:10* we read
that he was Paul's 'fellow prisoner'.

His faith and commitment to Christ
were clearly very strong. In every place he
is mentioned, persecution was at hand,
and in the case of the Ephesian riot he and
Gaius seem to have been seized instead of
Paul. Men such as this, who exhibited
such Christian faith in times of persecution, have become examples for all Christians through the ages, as persecution has
abounded.

P.D.G.

**ARISTOBULUS** (Gk., 'best adviser'), a
Roman citizen, is mentioned by Paul in

Rom. 16:10, where his household is greeted. He may well have been the grandson of Herod the Great, who lived in Rome in the first century and was named Aristobulus. The fact that he personally is not greeted may suggest that only other members of his family or perhaps some of his slaves were Christians.

**ARMONI,** one of two sons of King Saul's concubine Rizpah. Together with his brother, he was handed over by King David to the Gibeonites, whom Saul had massacred. They put him to death in vengeance for what had happened (2 Sam. 21:8).

**ARNAN** is listed as one of the descendants of Zerubbabel and in the line of King David (1 Chron. 3:21).

**ARODI,** one of the sons of Gad listed in Gen. 46:16 among those who went with Jacob into Egypt. His descendants were called Arodites (Num. 26:17).

**ARPHAXAD,** one of the sons of Shem. This is the first recorded birth after the Flood. We are told that he lived a further 403 years after fathering Shelah and that he had other sons and daughters (Gen. 10:22, 24; 11:10–13). He is listed in the genealogies of Num. 1:17–24 and also as Shem's son in the genealogy leading from Christ to Adam in Luke 3:36.

**ARTAXERXES I LONGIMANUS,** the King of Persia, 464–424 BC. Rehum wrote to him advising that the Jews were rebuilding the wall and would no longer pay taxes. He responded by ordering the work to stop. However, he was later more supportive of Ezra and gave him a letter allowing all who wished to return to Jerusalem with him to do so. He ordered Ezra to take to Jerusalem all the articles of worship for the Temple, and empowered him to appoint magistrates and judges for all of Trans-Euphrates. This is recorded in Ezra 4:7–8, 11, 23; 6:14; 7:1, 7, 11–12,

21; 8:1. During his reign Nehemiah came to Artaxerxes to ask his permission to rebuild Jerusalem. He agreed and appointed Nehemiah governor of Judah during the 20th year of his reign. Nehemiah returned to the king in the 32nd year of his reign (Neh. 2:1; 5:14; 13:6).                                          M.P.

**ARTEMAS** Paul indicated that he would soon send Artemas (and Tychichus) to Titus on the island of Crete, apparently to take over the church leadership there for a time while Titus joined Paul at Nicopolis (Titus 3:12). Later tradition suggests that he became bishop of Lystra. The name is probably a contraction of a name meaning 'gift of Artemis'. No doubt he was a pagan convert. Such texts as these provide us with clear evidence of careful apostolic pastoral oversight of these early churches. Since Artemas and Tychichus had been with Paul, he had presumably trained them for just such responsibilities among the early churches.          P.D.G.

**ARTEMIS,** the Greek goddess of the forests and hills. Homer called her the 'lady of wild things', a virgin huntress. Her Roman equivalent was Diana. However, by NT times, her main centre of worship was in Ephesus, where she was largely a goddess of fertility. The huge temple in her honour in that city was one of the great wonders of the world at that time, and so drew pilgrims and tourists from around the Roman world.

Silversmiths and various craftsmen would manufacture images and shrines for sale to these people, and made a very healthy income (Acts 19:24). When the apostle Paul and his fellow missionaries such as Aristarchus and Gaius began to preach Christ, the challenge to the Ephesians was not just to their belief system but to their economic system as well. In Acts 19:27 it is interesting to note that as the silversmiths try to discredit Paul and the others, they appeal first to the loss of trade

**60**

and then to the religious issue that Artemis will be robbed 'of her divine majesty'. They succeeded in creating a riot and dragging Aristarchus and Gaius to the theatre, where they intimidated the missionaries with the cry 'Great is Artemis of the Ephesians!'

The implications of the gospel message were clearly understood by the people of the city as relating to the whole of their life and culture, a lesson often overlooked in modern Christianity.                    P.D.G.

**ARZA** lived in Tirzah at the time when Elah was King of Israel. He was in charge of the palace at Tirzah. Zimri, one of the King's officials, plotted against Elah. It was in Arza's home that Elah became drunk, and Zimri entered and killed the King (1 Kings 16:9–10).

**ASA 1.** Asa, the great-grandson of Solomon, succeeded his father Abijah to the throne of Judah and reigned in Jerusalem 911–870 BC. He did much that 'was right in the eyes of the LORD, as his father David had done' (1 Kings 15:8–11; 1 Chron. 3:10). The writer of Kings specially emphasizes his work in getting rid of the idols in the land and the shrine prostitutes. 'Although he did not remove the high places, Asa's heart was fully committed to the LORD all his life' (1 Kings 15:14).

During his reign, King Baasha of Israel waged war against Judah and effectively sealed off Judah, preventing people coming and going. Asa took the remaining treasures of the Temple and sent them to the king of Aram (Syria) to bribe him into siding with Judah against Israel. The king of Aram agreed and attacked Baasha's kingdom, destroying many towns.

The chronicler gives more detail of Asa's reign in 2 Chron. 14–15. There again, Asa's faithfulness to God is stressed. He called on the LORD to help him in battle, recognizing that he could

'rely' on God to help and that he was all powerful (2 Chron. 14:11). The LORD did help him and his people defeat Zerah the Cushite in spite of his large numbers of invading troops moving north. When the prophet Azariah met him he began by saying, 'The LORD is with you when you are with him. If you seek him, he will be found by you, but if you forsake him, he will forsake you' (2 Chron. 15:2). The prophet went on to promise rewards and blessings from God if the king would remain faithful. This message greatly encouraged Asa, who continued his work in faith, destroying further idols not only in Judah but also in the parts of Ephraim he had captured (2 Chron. 15:8).

Such was the light of God in the nation during this reign that people from the northern tribes were attracted to the south and came to Judah as they saw God blessing the nation. Asa led the whole people in an act of covenant renewal in which they promised to seek the LORD with 'all their heart and soul' (2 Chron. 15:12).

As this reign progressed, so the nation was blessed and peace was established. The evidence that the LORD honours those who place their faith and trust in him could not have been clearer. For a brief while the surrounding people had some taste of the 'light' that a faithful Judah should have been demonstrating to the nations around.

However, Asa's success eventually went to his head. The chronicler then shows us just how wrong it was that Asa entered into an agreement with the king of Aram. He should have known from the experience with the Cushites that the LORD could have protected him from Baasha without such alliances (2 Chron. 16). Eventually, even though Asa kept Baasha at bay, Hanani the seer was sent by God to say that due to his lack of faith Asa and his people would now constantly be at war. Asa himself fell ill and even in his illness did not return to the LORD (2 Chron. 16:12).

Clearly in this passage the illness he experienced and the war that came his way were designed by God to bring about repentance and a return to the faithfulness he had exhibited so well and for so long for most of his reign. However, as far as we are aware that repentance never came and the story remains a warning that commitment to the LORD should be full and complete, of heart and soul and through all situations.

In 1 Kings 16 the reigns of various kings of Israel are dated by reference to Asa's reign in Judah. When Asa eventually died of old age, his son Jehoshaphat became king (1 Kings 15:24; 22:41 etc.). He is mentioned in the genealogy of Jesus in Matthew (1:7–8).

**2.** Mentioned in 1 Chron. 9:16, this Asa was the father of Berekiah. Berekiah was one of the Levites listed among those returning to Judah from the Babylonian Exile (1 Chron. 9:16).     P.D.G.

**ASAHEL 1.** Asahel was one of three sons of Zeruiah. All were mighty warriors in King David's army and his brother, Joab, was David's chief army commander. Asahel is described as being 'as fleet-footed as a wild gazelle' and is listed among David's 'thirty mighty men' (2 Sam. 2:18; 23:34; 1 Chron. 2:16; 11:26). As a commander in David's army himself, he was on duty with his men in the fourth month of each year and had 24,000 men in his division (2 Sam. 23:27; 1 Chron. 11:28; 27:12). Later, his son Zebadiah succeeded him to this post (1 Chron. 27:7).

When David's troops, led by Joab, fought the Benjamites at Gibeon, they quickly began to win the battle. Abner, leader of the Benjamites and Ish-Bosheth's army, fled the scene, pursued by Asahel. Abner did not want to turn and fight Asahel, for he knew he would win. But in his zeal for David,

Asahel continued chasing down Abner until he turned to fight. Abner killed Asahel who was later buried in his father's tomb at Bethlehem (2 Sam. 2:18–32). Later Joab took revenge and killed Abner, much to David's disgust (2 Sam. 3:27, 30).

**2.** This Asahel, a Levite, lived in the days of King Jehoshaphat of Judah. During the early years of his reign Jehoshaphat served the LORD and sent out various teachers and Levites to teach the people of Judah the Book of the Law. Asahel was one of those teachers (2 Chron. 17:8).

**3.** Another Asahel was one of the Levites who were supervisors of tithes and offerings brought by the people. As a result of the extraordinary revival under King Hezekiah, so many offerings, gifts and tithes were brought to the Temple that special storehouses had to be prepared. This Asahel was one of a number of Levites chosen, under the leadership of Conaniah and Shimei, to organize the storage of what was given (2 Chron. 31:13).

**4.** The father of a certain Jonathan, who was one of the very few leaders in Judah who refused to join Ezra and the people in repenting for the sin of inter-marriage with foreign women (Ezra 10:15).     P.D.G.

**ASAIAH 1.** Asaiah was one of the family leaders of Simeon's tribe (1 Chron. 4:36).

**2.** A member of the tribe of Levi and a descendant of Merari, Asaiah helped David bring the ark to Jerusalem (1 Chron. 6:30; 15:6, 11).

**3.** Another Asaiah was an attendant to King Josiah. He and other trusted officials sought wisdom from Huldah the prophetess concerning Judah after the Book of the Law was found (2 Kings 22:12, 14; 2 Chron. 34:20).

**4.** This Asaiah is listed as the firstborn of the Shilonites who resettled in Jerusalem after the Exile in Babylon (1 Chron. 9:5).                                    s.c.

**ASAPH 1.** Along with Heman and Ethan, Asaph was placed in charge of the singing in the house of the LORD by King David (1 Chron. 6:31–40). He was a descendant of the Levites, a son of Berekiah and nominated as a leading singer when the ark was brought to Jerusalem and at several other occasions of national rejoicing (1 Chron. 15:17–19; 16:5, 7, 37; 2 Chron. 35:15). He joined with the other Levites in leading the praise of God when the Temple was consecrated (2 Chron. 5:12).

His musical influence extended far beyond the Temple and into the Jewish hymn book for all time. His name is to be found in the title of twelve of the Psalms, indicating that they are probably part of an ensemble composed either by him or for him (Pss. 50, and 73–83 inclusive). These Psalms featured in the singing during the revival under Hezekiah (2 Chron. 29:30). At the time of the return from Exile, Temple singers could simply be referred to as 'Asaphites' (Ezra 2:41; Neh. 7:44; 11:17 etc.).

**2.** The father of Joah, the secretary of state during the reign of King Hezekiah, King of Judah (2 Kings 18:18, 37; Is. 36:3, 22).

**3.** This Asaph was the keeper of the king's forest. He was approached by Nehemiah with royal authorization to request timbers to support the city gate and for the rebuilding of the wall of Jerusalem (Neh. 2:8).                          s.v.

**ASAREL,** of the tribe of Judah, was one of the sons of Jehallelel (1 Chron. 4:16).

**ASARELAH** was one of the sons of Asaph (1 Chron. 25:2). Immediately under Asaph's direction, and on the direct orders of King David (1 Chron. 25:1), he and others were among those who prophesied and led in the ministry of

music for worship. He is probably the one called Jesarelah in 1 Chron. 25:14.

**ASENATH** (Egypt., 'belonging to the god Neit'), the daughter of Potiphera, an Egyptian priest to the god On. She was given by Pharaoh to Joseph as his wife. Before the years of famine two sons were born to them – Manasseh and Ephraim (Gen. 41:45, 50; 46:20). She must have been a woman from a family of considerable standing in Egypt, as she was part of the tribute paid by Pharaoh to Joseph once Joseph had interpreted his dreams. Having been put in charge of the whole land of Egypt and having been renamed Zaphenath-Paneah, he was then given this woman as his wife. These events were all part of God's sovereign dealings both individually with Joseph but also, in the longer term, with his people the Israelites. Joseph's leadership in Egypt eventually meant that the Israelites were preserved through the great famine.

P.D.G.

**ASHBEL,** one of the ten sons of Benjamin listed in Gen. 46:21. He was the progenitor of the Ashbelites (Gen. 46:21; Num. 26:38; 1 Chron. 8:1).

**ASHER** Asher was born to Jacob and Zilpah in Padan-aram. He was Jacob's eighth son and his second by Zilpah. Zilpah was Leah's servant. Leah did not have her own children and so, following custom, gave her servant to Jacob. The children of this relationship would thus be seen as Leah's (Gen. 30:13, 26). It was Leah who gave him his name, Asher, meaning 'happy' or 'blessed'. At this time Jacob was still working for Leah's father Laban.

As a son of Jacob, Asher became the head of a tribe of Israel. Asher himself had at least four sons and a daughter (Gen. 46:17). In Num. 26:44 there were six clans descended from three sons, his daughter and two grandsons. Once the

Israelites left Mt Sinai, the tribe of Asher could muster 41,500 men for the army (*Num. 1:41*). At that time their leader was Pagiel. They took up the rearguard position as the Israelites moved out along with Dan and Naphtali (*Num. 10:26*).

When Joshua divided the land of Canaan between the tribes, Asher was given 22 towns and villages in an area of coastland north of Mt Carmel and across to the western shores of Lake Galilee. The precise boundaries are almost impossible to define from the evidence in the text, and the location of some sites mentioned is vigorously debated (*Josh. 17:10–11; 19:24–31, 34; Judg. 5:17*). However, the plain of Acre was entirely theirs.

It becomes clear in the book of Judges that, like other tribes, Asher did not actually take control of all the entitled land (*Judg. 1:31–32*). This meant that many lived in land that was still largely populated by Canaanites. This may have been the reason for Asher not coming to help fight Sisera, and thus receiving rebuke from Deborah (*Judg. 5:17*). However, they did come to the aid of Gideon in his fight with the Midianites (*Judg. 6:35, 7:23*). The tribe is mentioned again as being represented by 40,000 fighting men at David's coronation at Hebron (*1 Chron. 12:36*). After this the tribe seems to fade, and some of its land was actually given away by Solomon to Hiram King of Tyre in exchange for wood and other supplies used in building the palace and Temple (*1 Kings 9:11–14*).

Although very little is known of the commitment of the Asherites to the worship of the LORD after the dedication of the Tabernacle in the wilderness, in the time of Hezekiah some did respond to his call for a return to a true worship of the LORD. However, even here there is a clear indication that this tribe had moved far away from the LORD, for the majority 'scorned and ridiculed' the few who 'humbled themselves' and went to Jerusalem to worship (*2 Chron. 30:11*).

Their compromise with the religion of the people in whose land they lived was virtually total.

That a very small remnant of faithful people remained throughout the history of Israel is indicated in the NT, where we read that Anna, the prophetess who recognized the infant Jesus to be the Messiah, was of the tribe of Asher (*Luke 2:36*).                    P.D.G.

**ASHERAH** is the name of a Canaanite goddess, but it is often not distinguished from the implements used in her worship. Reference to the Asherah 'poles' indicates some large wooden objects used in the cult. These poles seem to have been set up alongside altars, and when the Israelites obeyed the command of the LORD, they were cut down and used as wood on their own sacrificial fires (e.g. *Exod. 34:13; Deut. 7:5; 16:21; Judg. 6:25*).

This goddess is known in several extra-biblical texts. In Ugaritic she was the goddess of the sea and closely linked with Baal. These two come together in the confrontation of Elijah and the prophets of Baal on Mt Carmel. In that challenge, Elijah called down fire from heaven to consume a sacrifice to the LORD. The fire came in answer to Elijah's prayers, but did not come in response to those of the prophets of Baal (*1 Kings 18:19*).

Regularly the people of Israel were drawn away from the LORD to worship with the Canaanites. Such 'adultery', as the prophets called it, was to issue in great judgment from God. The extent to which Asherah and Baal worship permeated Israelite life and worship is to be seen in many scriptures, but of particular note is *2 Kings 21:3, 7*, where we find the evil King Manasseh of Judah introducing an Asherah pole into the Temple itself. As a result of this great blasphemy the LORD promised to destroy Jerusalem and to let Judah's enemies conquer the land.

Perhaps more than any other cult, the long-term influence of the cult of Asherah came to be a symbol for Israelite assimilation of foreign culture and religion. The warnings given in Exod. 34:13 ('Break down their altars, smash their sacred stones and burn their Asherah poles in the fire; cut down the idols of their gods and wipe out their names from those places') and repeated many times in Deut. (see 7:5; 12:3 etc.) were ignored.

The heart of the problem with Asherah and Baal worship was that Israel refused to take seriously the need to be a 'holy' nation to the LORD, dedicated to his service alone. The problem of assimilation to the surrounding culture and its various religious manifestations always has been and remains a matter of the deepest concern to men and women of faith.                                    P.D.G.

**ASHHUR,** the father of Tekoa, was the descendant of Caleb and Hezron (1 Chron. 2:24; 4:5). We are told he had two wives: Helah and Naarah.

**ASHIMA,** a god made and worshipped by the people of Hamath (2 Kings 17:30). These people were one of several national groupings resettled in Samaria by the Assyrians. Each group had its own gods (vv. 24, 29).

**ASHKENAZ** was the grandson of Japheth and the son of Gomer, and was therefore a direct descendant of Noah. He had two brothers (Gen. 10:3; 1 Chron. 1:6). He may have been the progenitor of the people later identified with the Scythians. The kingdom of Ashkenaz is among those summonsed by the prophet to take vengeance on Babylon in Jer. 51:27.

**ASHPENAZ,** chief of the court officials under Nebuchadnezzar king of Babylon at the time when Jehoiakim, king of Judah, and much of the Temple treasury

were captured. He was ordered to search out intelligent Israelites for the king's service. Among those he recruited were Daniel and his friends (Dan. 1:3, 6). He was responsible for renaming them with Babylonian names. The text of Daniel (v. 9) reveals the sovereignty of God in these affairs, since God had caused Ashpenaz to choose the man whom God wanted to lead his people in Exile. Initially Daniel resisted the invitation from Ashpenaz to eat well, for he wished to keep himself holy for the LORD. However, the LORD blessed Daniel and led him to an important position in the kingdom.

**ASHURBANIPAL,** the King of Assyria from 669 BC. Early on he fought against Egypt and the Syrians. Around 640 BC he attacked Elam's capital Susa and deported men to Samaria, as mentioned in Ezra 4:10. There is uncertainty concerning the end of his reign. He probably died around 627 BC.

**ASHVATH,** the son of Japhlet of the tribe of Asher (1 Chron. 7:33).

**ASIEL,** a descendant of Simeon and an inheritor of some of the inheritance of the tribe of Judah. Asiel was the father of Seraiah and a clan leader (1 Chron. 4:35, 38–40; see Josh. 19:9).

**ASNAH** His descendants were among the Temple servants who returned from Exile with Nehemiah (Ezra 2:50).

**ASPATHA** See Est. 9:7. One of ten sons of Haman killed in Susa by the Jews.

**ASRIEL,** a descendant and inheritor of the tribe of Manasseh. He was the leader of the Asrielite clan. His mother was Manasseh's Aramean concubine (Num. 26:31; Josh. 17:2; 1 Chron. 7:14).

**ASSHUR,** one of Shem's sons (Gen. 10:22; 1 Chron. 1:17). This name was also the name for the people of Assyria and for their deity, since Asshur was considered to be the founder of that nation. Assyria's king lists say that the nation's founders were nomads who came from the south and the west. It is probably the nation that is referred to in *Num. 24:22, 24* and *Ezek. 27:23*.

**ASSIR** **1.** A descendant of Kohath and the leader of one of the Korahite clans (*Exod. 6:24; 1 Chron. 6:22*).

**2.** The son of Ebiasaph and the great-grandson of 1. (*1 Chron. 6:23, 37*). Both 1. and 2. were ancestors of Samuel.

**ASYNCRITUS,** the first named of a group of Roman Christians greeted by Paul in *Rom. 16:14*. The personal care and pastoral concern for individuals which is expressed in Paul's greetings is worthy of attention.

**ATARAH,** the second wife of Jerahmeel and the mother of Onam (*1 Chron. 2:26*).

**ATER** **1.** *Ezra 2:16* and *Neh. 7:21* record that 98 of his descendants returned from the Babylonian Exile with Nehemiah.

**2.** He was a Levite and a gatekeeper of the Temple. His descendants returned from Exile with Nehemiah (*Ezra 2:42; Neh. 7:45*).

**3.** From the tribe of Judah, he was one of the leaders who sealed the agreement of the people to worship the LORD and obey his Law in the days of Nehemiah (*Neh. 10:17*).

**ATHAIAH** (Heb., 'the LORD is helper') was one of the provincial leaders who settled in Jerusalem after the Exile in Babylon. From the tribe of Judah, he was the son of Uzziah (*Neh. 11:4*).

**ATHALIAH** (Heb., 'the LORD is great').

**1.** The daughter of Ahab, king of Israel, and granddaughter of Omri (*2 Kings 8:18; 2 Chron. 22:2*). By marrying Jehoram, king of Judah, she sealed an alliance between the split kingdoms of Israel and Judah. She was queen in Judah from about 842 BC for six years. She got rid of all the rest of the royal family (*2 Kings 11:1; 2 Chron. 22:10*). Her horrendous slaughter of family members brought to an end the brief alliance between Judah and Israel. She was eventually deposed by her dissatisfied subjects and killed in the royal palace, apparently taken completely by surprise (*2 Kings 11:16–20*). The revolt was led by Jehoiada the priest and the Temple guards. They promoted the young Joash as king. He had been saved by the quick thinking of King Jehoram's daughter and the sister of Athaliah, who hid him in the Temple of the LORD for six years (*2 Kings 2–3*). In the seventh year Joash was brought out of hiding and proclaimed king before the people. Athaliah was then taken out of the Temple and killed by the command of Jehoiada the priest, to the joy of all the people (*1 Kings 11:4–20; 2 Chron. 23*). Also see *Jehosheba* and *Jehoiada*.

**2.** One of the leading Benjamite families mentioned in the genealogy of King Saul (*1 Chron. 8:26*).

**3.** A returning exile from Babylon. His son, Jeshaiah, apparently accompanied Ezra down the river Ahava and on to Jerusalem (*Ezra 8:7*). 								S.V.

**ATHLAI,** a descendant of Bebai who in the days of Ezra, was guilty of marriage to a foreign woman (*Ezra 10:28*).

**ATTAI** **1.** Attai was the son of Sheshan's servant Jarha, to whom he had given his daughter in marriage because he had no sons. Such an arrangement allowed his servant in effect to have the rights of a son and to pass these on to his children, thus carrying on the line of Sheshan (*1 Chron. 2:35–36*). He was the father of Nathan and is named in the genealogy of Jerahmeel.

**2.** Attai was one of the famous Gadites who defected from Saul to David when he was at Ziklag. He was the sixth in the list, each of whom are described in vivid imagery as the bravest of warriors. They were commanders who proved of tremendous support to David in his battles (1 Chron. 12:11).

**3.** Mentioned in 2 Chron. 11:20, this Attai was a son of King Rehoboam and his wife Maacah, who was Absalom's daughter (2 Chron. 11:20).          P.D.G.

**AUGUSTUS** This name appears only in Luke 2:1. See Caesar.

**AZALIAH,** the father of Shaphan, King Josiah's scribe (2 Kings 22:3; 2 Chron. 34:8). Azaliah was a son of Meshullam.

**AZANIAH** (Heb., 'the LORD has heard'), the father of Jeshua, one of the Levites who sealed the agreement of the people to worship the LORD and obey his Law (Neh. 10:9).

**AZAREL** (Heb., 'God has helped').
**1.** One of the men who came to David at Ziklag when he was banished from Saul (1 Chron. 12:6).
**2.** One of the musicians chosen by lot to work in the Temple (1 Chron. 25:18).
**3.** The son of Jeroham, he was an officer of the tribe of Dan during David's reign (1 Chron. 27:22).
**4.** A descendant of Binnui who was guilty of marriage to a foreign woman (Ezra 10:41).
**5.** His son Amashai was one of the priests who settled in Jerusalem after the Exile (Neh. 11:13).
**6.** He was one of the procession who played musical instruments at the dedication of the wall of Jerusalem (Neh. 12:36).

**AZARIAH** (Heb., 'the LORD helps').
**1.** The great-grandson of Judah (through his son, Zerah) is mentioned only in the family tree in 1 Chron. 2:8.
**2.** A descendant of Judah (through his son, Perez), mentioned in the family tree in 1 Chron. 2:38–39.

**3.** A Levitical son of the priest Zadok and one of King Solomon's officials (1 Kings 4:2).
**4.** A chief official under King Solomon, referred to only in 1 Kings 4:5. He is 'the son of Nathan', possibly the prophet that confronted King David in 2 Sam. 12 or the brother of Solomon (by Bathsheba; 1 Chron. 3:5). He was in charge of Solomon's district officers (1 Kings 4:5).
**5.** The king of Judah (2 Kings 14–15; 1 Chron. 3:12). His other name is Uzziah (2 Chron. 26). See Uzziah.
**6.** A leader of the Judean remnant that stood against the prophet Jeremiah, mentioned only in Jer. 43:2. He is probably also known as Jezaniah (Jer. 42:1).
**7.** The son of Ahimaaz and the father of Johanan, he appears in the list of Levites in 1 Chron. 6:9–10.
**8.** Azariah, the grandfather of 7. above, appears in the same list (1 Chron. 6:10–11). He was a priest at the time of Solomon. He was the father of Amariah (Ezra 7:3).
**9.** This Azariah appears in the same list as 7. and 8. above. He was a Levite and the father of Seraiah (1 Chron. 6:13–14; Ezra 7:1).
**10.** A Levite and an ancestor of Samuel (1 Chron. 6:36).
**11.** One of the first Levitical priests to resettle in Jerusalem after the Babylonian captivity (1 Chron. 9:11).
**12.** The son of Oded, this Azariah prophesied during the reign of King Asa. 'The Spirit of God' came on him (2 Chron. 15:1) and he prophesied to Asa that the LORD would bless him if he followed God. Asa did this and received great blessing (2 Chron. 15).
**13.** One of the sons of King Jehoshaphat of Judah. He was brother to Jehoram, who succeeded his father to the throne (2 Chron. 21:2). Jehoram established his throne and then put to death all his brothers (v. 4).
**14.** One of the commanders who joined in a covenant with the priest Jehoiada to

**67**

put the child Joash on the throne of Judah and to overthrow the evil Queen Athaliah (2 Chron. 23:1). He was the son of Jeroham.

**15.** This Azariah was a priest in the time of King Uzziah. When Uzziah tried to fulfil the priestly duties of burning incense in the Temple, proudly believing he could do what he wanted (2 Chron. 26:16–18), Azariah reproached him. Uzziah was judged by God with a leprosy skin disease (v. 19). Azariah and the other priests quickly escorted him away from the Temple (v. 20).

**16.** An Ephraimite and the son of Jehohanan (2 Chron. 28:12). For more details see Berekiah (5).

**17.** The father of Joel, one of the Kohathites involved in cleaning the Temple during the revival under King Hezekiah (2 Chron. 29:12).

**18.** This Azariah was chief priest under King Hezekiah and was from the family of Zadok. He explained to Hezekiah why heaps of the people's tithes had been left around the Temple. Simply, there was too much for the priests to deal with, and so Hezekiah ordered store-rooms to be built (2 Chron. 31:9–13).　　　A.B.L. and P.D.G.

**AZARIAHU,** a son of King Jehoshaphat and a brother of Jehoram (2 Chron. 21:2). In some translations the name is given as Azariah, thus giving two brothers of the same name in this text.

**AZAZ,** the father of Bela and the son of Shema. He is listed as a leader of a clan and a descendant of Reuben (1 Chron. 5:8).

**AZAZIAH** (Heb., 'the LORD is strong').
**1.** This Azaziah was one of the family of Merarite Levites who were gate-keepers. Azaziah played the harp before the ark of the covenant as it was moved to Jerusalem by King David (1 Chron. 15:21).

**2.** The father of Hoshea (1 Chron. 27:20). This Hoshea was head of the tribe of Ephraim during the days of King David.

**3.** One of the Levites who were supervisors of tithes and offerings brought by the people. As a result of the extraordinary revival under King Hezekiah, so many offerings, gifts and tithes were brought to the Temple that special store-houses had to be built. Azaziah was one of a number of Levites chosen, under the leadership of Conaniah and Shimei, to organize the storage of what was given (2 Chron. 31:13).

**AZBUK** was the father of Nehemiah (not the Nehemiah who was the governor) who, following the return from Exile, was the ruler of a half-district of Beth Zur and helped to rebuild the wall of Jerusalem (Neh. 3:16).

**AZEL,** a descendant of King Saul through Jonathan and a son of Eleasah. He had six sons of his own and was a leader among the Benjamites (1 Chron. 8:37–38; 9:43–44).

**AZGAD** (Heb., 'Gad is strong').
**1.** Ezra 2:12 records that 1,222 of his descendants returned from Exile with Nehemiah; in Neh. 7:17 the figure is 2,322. One of Azgad's descendants, Johanan son of Hakkatan, returned from Exile with Ezra (Ezra 8:12).
**2.** From the tribe of Judah, he was one of the leaders who sealed the agreement of the people to worship the LORD and obey his Law (Neh. 10:15).

**AZIEL,** one of the Levites listed as a player of the lyre who played for the Israelite worship when David brought the ark of the covenant to Jerusalem (1 Chron. 15:20). He is probably the same person as Jaaziel in v. 18.

**AZIZA** (Heb., 'the strong one') was among those descendants of Zattu who were guilty of marriage to foreign women. Under Ezra's direction Aziza divorced his wife (*Ezra 10:27*).

**AZMAVETH 1.** Azmaveth, a Benjamite, was the son of Jehoaddah and was listed in Saul's genealogy (*1 Chron. 8:36*; in *9:42* his father is called Jadah).

**2.** Azmaveth the Barhumite was numbered as one of David's 'Thirty' military leaders (*2 Sam. 23:31; 1 Chron. 11:33*).

**3.** Another Azmaveth was the father of Jeziel and Palet, two of David's warriors who joined him at Ziklag (*1 Chron. 12:3*).

**4.** The son of Adiel, this Azmaveth was in charge of the royal storehouses during part of David's rule (*1 Chron. 27:25*). Possibly the same as 2. above.

**AZOR** In the genealogy establishing Jesus' kingly lineage, Azor is the father of Zadok and the son of Eliakim (*Matt. 1:13–14*).

**AZRIEL** (Heb., 'God is my help').

**1.** A head of a clan and valiant soldier in the tribe of Manasseh (*1 Chron. 5:24*). However, he and his people were 'unfaithful to the God of their fathers' and so God brought judgment on the tribe through the king of Assyria (*v. 25*).

**2.** The father of Jerimoth. During the reign of King David, Jerimoth was an official in the tribe of Naphtali (*1 Chron. 27:19*).

**3.** The father of Seraiah. Seraiah and Shelemiah were commanded by King Jehoiakim to arrest Baruch and the prophet Jeremiah (*Jer. 36:26*).

**AZRIKAM** (Heb., 'my help has arisen').

**1.** A descendant of King David, Azrikam is listed as one of three sons of Neariah in *1 Chron. 3:23*. This list provides a royal lineage for the kingdom of Judah following the Exile.

**2.** A Benjamite and the first of six sons of Azel (*1 Chron. 8:38; 9:44*). He was a descendant of Saul.

**3.** This Azrikam was the officer in charge of the palace during the reign of King Ahaz of Judah. He was killed by Zicri, a commander in the army of Israel who was fighting for Pekah son of Remaliah (*2 Chron. 28:7*).

**4.** A Merarite Levite whose grandson, Shemaiah, settled in Jerusalem following the return from the Exile in Babylon (*1 Chron. 9:14; Neh. 11:15*).

**AZUBAH 1.** The mother of King Jehoshaphat of Judah and the wife of King Asa. She was the daughter of Shilhi (*1 Kings 22:42; 2 Chron. 20:31*). Her son did much that was 'right in the eyes of the LORD', ridding Judah of male shrine-prostitutes and much of its pagan past (*1 Kings 22:43, 46*).

**2.** A wife of Caleb and the mother of Jesher, Shobab and Ardon. When she died, Caleb married Ephrath (*1 Chron. 2:18–19*).

**AZZAN,** of the tribe of Isaachar, was the father of Paltiel. Paltiel was the leader of his tribe chosen by the LORD, through Moses, to assign the land of Canaan to the various tribes and clans (*Num. 34:26*).

**AZZUR 1.** In *Neh. 10:17* Azzur was one of the leaders of the people who sealed the covenant with Nehemiah. This covenant was a recommitment by the people to serve the LORD God of Israel (see *Neh. 9*).

**2.** The father of the false prophet Hananiah, who prophesied during the reign of King Zedekiah of Judah and was challenged by Jeremiah. Azzur was a Gibeonite (*Jer. 28:1*).

**3.** Mentioned in *Ezek. 11:1* as the father of Jaazaniah, a leader of the Israelites who falsely prophesied peace for Israel and was challenged by Ezekiel.

# B

**BAAL** (Heb., 'master'). This Western-Semitic god provided a real threat to the pure worship of the people of Israel. He was most to be feared in Canaanite worship because he was the storm god who, if appeased, would provide for the crops and lands, if threatened would withhold rain.

In 1 Kings 18 Elijah, at the peak of his prophetic activity while the kingdom of Israel was in sad decline under the rule of King Ahab, confronted the Baal worship of the King and his people. The contest between the prophets of the LORD and the prophets of Baal on Carmel was the culmination of the growing tension between the prophets appointed by Jezebel and now in allegiance with Ahab and true prophets of the LORD God. Since the beginning of Solomon's reign Israel had been involved in religious syncretism with the nations around. Rather than proselytize, as they should have, they lived in an environment where fear of other gods had thwarted their trust in the words of the prophets, many of whom they had killed.

The issue for the people of Israel did not concern who was the chief god out of a range of gods. Rather, the question was 'Who is the God who alone lives?' In 1 Kings 18 the stance of the prophets was to mock the foolishness of worshipping a 'no-god' rather than to argue that such gods did not actually exist. The irony of this passage in comparing truth with falsehood, God with Baal, is seen in three areas:

(1) Perhaps most powerful is the irony relating to Baal's inability to send rain. It was presumed that Baal, the god who was in control of the forces of nature, went through a seasonal cycle of dying and rising. This death and life accounted for periods of drought or rain. Beginning with the challenge in 17:1, which assumed that the LORD could withhold rain to the detriment of the followers of Baal, and concluding with the scene where rain comes only at the LORD's instruction, the Bible demonstrates that God is clearly all powerful over nature.

(2) The second irony concerns the sacrifice itself. Ultimately the blood of the sacrifice would seem to be the blood of the slaughtered prophets of Baal (1 Kings 18:40). But, despite the prophets' frenetic activity (vv. 27–29), from Baal 'there was no response, no-one answered, no-one paid attention' (v. 29b). Their sacrifice was in vain, because the only sacrifice acceptable to God was the faithfulness of one prophet in a climate of a national failure to worship the true God.

(3) The conclusion, which the writer assumes will be self-evident for his audience, is the crowning irony that Baal is dead. This is not explicitly stated in 1 Kings 18:27–29, but the reader is left to formulate that inescapable conclusion. The vindication for the prophet is that only one God actually is alive. Only one God brings fire, the other gives no response.

The point was further underlined when, in 1 Kings 18:41–45 it was God who sent the rain – the task they assumed was the prerogative of their god. Canaanite religion would have rationalized their god's periodic silences with the mythological idea that Baal occasionally died, only to come back to life again. The inescapable silence from their god had to lead to the conclusion that he was in fact permanently dead!                          S.V.

**BAAL-BERITH** (Heb., 'god of the covenant'), a Canaanite god worshipped in Shechem (see *Baal*). Also called El-Berith. Mentioned only in *Judg.* 8–9, it is possible that this was a case of Caananite religion absorbing some Israelite religious ideas. Canaanites worshipped many Baals. It is at least possible that this one, with its reference to 'covenant', may have been created in order to help absorb the Israelites. Alternatively, Israelites, the people of the covenant, may have been more easily attracted to an already existing deity who was concerned with covenants. Certainly, they took no time, following the death of Gideon, to become involved in its worship (*Judg.* 8:33; 9:4, 46).

**BAAL-HANAN** (Heb., 'Baal is gracious').
**1.** One of the kings of Edom before the Israelites conquered the area. He succeeded Shaul as king and was the son of Acbor (*Gen.* 36:38–39; *1 Chron.* 1:49–50). Hadad followed him as king.
**2.** A Gederite who was an overseer during the reign of King David. He was in charge of the olive and fig trees in the 'western foothills', called the Shephelah (*1 Chron.* 27:28).

**BAALIS,** the king of the Ammonites during the early part of the Babylonian captivity. He instigated the murder of Gedaliah (*Jer.* 40:14). Jeremiah, having been freed by Nebuzaradan to stay in conquered Judah if he wished, went to stay with Gedaliah in Mizpah. Gedaliah had been appointed governor by the king of Babylon. Under this governor there was relative prosperity for the poor who had not been carted off to Babylon, but the Ammonites, led by Baalis, took

advantage of this situation to kill Gedaliah (*Jer.* 41).

**BAAL-ZEBUB** (Heb., 'lord of flies'). In 1 *Kings* Baal-Zebub is the name of the god of Ekron, whom King Ahaziah attempted to contact during his terminal illness.

**BAAL-ZEBUB**. See *Baal*.

**BAANA** (Heb., 'son of oppression').
**1.** Baana, the son of Ahilud, was one of King Solomon's district governors. His district covered Taanach and Megiddo and the area between Beth Shan and Abel Meholah (*1 Kings* 4:12).
**2.** Baana, the son of Hushai, was another of King Solomon's governors, in charge of Asher and Aloth (*1 Kings* 4:16).
**3.** This Baana was the father of Zadok, who worked on the rebuilding of the wall at Jerusalem after the Exile (*Neh.* 3:4).

**BAANAH** (Heb., 'son of oppression').
**1.** The son of Rimmon and the leader of a raiding band under Saul's son Ish-Bosheth. Along with Recab, he went to Ish-Bosheth's house and killed him while he was asleep. They cut off his head and took it to David, expecting his approval. David, however, ordered his men to kill them and hung their bodies by the pool in Hebron (*2 Sam.* 4:5–12). See *Recab* for more details.
**2.** A Netophathite, the father of Heled. Heled was among David's Thirty men (*2 Sam.* 23:29; *1 Chron.* 11:30). See *Heled*.
**3.** One of those who returned from Exile with Nehemiah, (*Ezra* 2:2; *Neh.* 7:7).
**4.** (Possibly the same as 3.) One of the leaders who sealed the agreement of the people to worship the Lord and obey his Law. (*Neh.* 10:27)                     M.P.

**BAARA**, wife to Shaharaim, a Benjamite who lived in Moab. He later divorced her and his first wife Hushim. Baara bore him no sons (*1 Chron.* 8:8).

**BAASEIAH,** an ancestor of Asaph, who is mentioned in the list of David's musicians who served at the Tabernacle in the days before the Temple had been built (*1 Chron. 6:40*).

**BAASHA** was King of Israel from around 909–886 BC. He took power in the northern Kingdom from King Nadab who was Jeroboam I's son. Baasha was the third king of the northern part of the divided kingdom. God had judged Nadab's reign because of his evil and idolatrous ways which simply followed the way his father had been (*1 Kings 15:25–26*).

Baasha was the son of Ahijah and from the tribe of Issachar, and killed Nadab while the latter was fighting the Philistines. He began his reign in Tirzah (*1 Kings 15:33; 16:8*) by killing everyone of the house of Jeroboam. Baasha's rule, though, was a further disaster for Israel. When he came to power Israel still held the lands on the east of the Jordan remaining from the days of King Solomon. He soon lost these and, after attacking Judah, King Asa of Judah made a treaty with the King of Syria (*1 Kings 15:16–22; 2 Chron. 16*). He soon found himself fighting on the northern and the southern front against this coalition and was forced to surrender some lands in Ephraim to Judah and other lands to Syria.

Baasha, like Nadab and Jeroboam, was idolatrous and evil and, although his son Elah briefly ruled for a couple of years, after 26 years Baasha's regime was overthrown in a *coup d'état* led by Zimri. This end was foretold by the prophet Jehu who warned him of the impending judgment of God that would result in the total destruction of his house and that dogs would eat the blood of those of his family who died in the city (*Kings 16:1–7, 12–13*).

The evil of his reign became almost as much a by-word for sin as had Jeroboam's reign before him and God used his name in future generations to remind kings of Israel of the dangers of idolatry and impending judgment (*1 Kings 21:22; 2 Kings 9:9*). Also see *Nadab*, *Jehu* and *Zimri*. P.D.G.

**BAKBAKKAR,** a Levite mentioned in *1 Chron. 9:15* as a descendant of Asaph, was one of the early returnees from the Exile in the time of Zerubbabel. He is possibly the same person as Bakbukiah (*Neh. 11:17*).

**BAKBUK** His descendants were among the Temple servants who returned from Exile with Nehemiah and Zerubbabel (*Ezra 2:51 and Neh. 7:53*).

**BAKBUKIAH 1.** A Levite among Mattaniah's associates who returned from Exile in Babylon with Nehemiah (*Neh. 11:17*).

**2.** Probably the same person as 1. With Mattaniah, he was in charge of the songs of thanksgiving in the Temple (*Neh. 12:9*).

**3.** He was one of the gate-keepers who guarded the store-rooms at the gates in the days of Joiakim (*Neh. 12:25*).

**BALAAM** stands as a warning of the danger of allowing an outsider (Balaam was from Pethor on the Euphrates) to infiltrate and perversely divert the community of God. Balaam typified the attitude of fickle Israel in the days of Moses. Moses' intervention on behalf of the people had prevented God annihilating them in judgment (*Num. 22:4–9*). Though they had witnessed privileged deliverance at his hands, the people soon became seduced by the practices of the Moabites (*see Num. 25*).

According to *Num. 22* Balaam was summoned by King Balak of Moab. God intervened in his journey by sending an angel to block his way. There is irony in the fact the donkey recognized the angel, and thus God's intervention, whilst Balaam did not. The story of Balaam is best remembered by the words of his donkey, which seemed to show greater wisdom than its master and utter wiser oracles! Eventually Balaam was allowed to continue his journey.

Balaam enjoyed privileged communication with God, who spoke via oracles to the people. However, like the people of Israel, he kindled God's wrath because of his reluctance to do 'only what I tell you' (Num. 22:20f.). Seduced by flattery (Num. 22:13) and more concerned to accommodate than to heed the oracles from his own mouth, Balaam entered Rabbinical tradition as the effective, but deceived, diplomat. Balak was not concerned to heed Balaam's words (Num. 24:10f.). According to Num. 31:8, 16 Balaam had advised the Mideonites to lure the people of Israel into sexual sinat Peor. For this reason he was killed by Moses and his men along with the Mideonite kings (Num. 31). Despite the mixture of true and false oracles and the mixed loyalties of the prophet, God continued to intervene, to lead and guide his people in victory over their enemies.

The episode with Balaam thus became yet another example of God's total sovereignty working for the good of his people.

2 Pet. 2:15, Jude 11 and Rev. 2:14 warn the NT people of God against allowing a smooth-talking pagan to capitalize on his knowledge of a form of religiosity and twist it to his own deadly end. A veneer of piety disguises the shallow convictions which can be bought for a price (Num. 22:17) and superficial repentance (v. 34) which is short-lived.

2 Pet. 2:15–16 views Balaam as a man of prophetic talent but with a desire to use the gifts of God to further his own ends. So, Peter warned of the danger of 'empty' words because they act as a cover for evil desires. The Christian must appreciate that such emptiness of heart will be exposed on judgment day (Jude 11). For the apostle John writing to the compromised church in Pergamum the worse sin is not actually that of self-deception, because that in the end will be exposed. Rather Balaam's leading of Balak into further spiritual adultery is far worse (see further on Balak). And so, the worst of judgments is saved for those who knowingly deceive others. Like Balaam their sin eventually catches up with them (see Num. 31:8; Josh. 13:22).

S.V.

**BALADAN,** the father of Merodach-baladan, the king of Babylon at the time when Hezekiah was king of Judah (2 Kings 20:12; Is. 39:1).

**BALAK,** the son of Zippor, was the king of Moab who summonsed Balaam to curse Israel. He was motivated by the fear of Israel's success over other tribes. He assumed that it was possible to buy a curse from Balaam, and so defeat the Israelites (Num. 22). Despite Balaam's foolishness, God used him repeatedly to denounce Balak and bless rather than curse Balak's enemies (Num. 23:11), much to Balak's consternation. The Bible writers view Balak as an example of extreme foolishness, and an illustration that pagans underestimate the power of Israel's God. To try and curse the people whom God has blessed will only result in bringing a curse on oneself! (So, Josh. 24:9; also, Judg. 11:25.) Future generations are called upon to remember Balak and thereby avoid the judgment of God (Mic. 6:5). Similarly, false teaching is to be shunned because of its harmful, seductive effect upon the congregation (Rev. 2:14).

S.V.

**BANI** (Heb., 'build').

**1.** An ancestor of Ethan, who served as a Temple musician during the time of King David (1 Chron. 6:46).

**2.** An ancestor of Uthai, who settled in Jerusalem after the Exile (1 Chron. 9:4).

**3.** 642 of his descendants returned from Exile with Nehemiah (Ezra 2:10).

**4.** An ancestor of Shelomith, who came to Jerusalem with Ezra during the reign of King Artaxerxes (*Ezra 8:10*).

**5. & 6.** A number of their descendants were guilty of marrying foreign women (*Ezra 10:29,34*). They obeyed Ezra and divorced them.

**7.** The father of Rehum, who led the Levites' repairs to the wall of Jerusalem (*Neh. 3:17*). See *Rehum.*

**8.** One of the Levites who instructed the people in the Law under Ezra (*Neh. 8:7*) and led them in their confession of sin (*Neh. 9:4–5*).

**9. & 10.** Two of the Levites who sealed the agreement of the people to worship the LORD and obey his Law (*Neh. 10:13–14*).

**11.** The father of Uzzi, who was the chief officer of the Levites in Jerusalem after the Exile (*Neh. 11:22*).     M.P.

**BAR-JESUS** (Heb., 'son of Jesus'), the Jewish name of a false prophet and sorcerer encountered by Paul and Silas in the town of Paphos on the island of Cyprus (*Acts 13:6*). His Greek name was Elymas (*v. 8*). This man was in the employ of the Roman proconsul, Sergius Paulus, whom Luke describes as an 'intelligent man' who 'wanted to hear the word of God' (*v. 7*). Bar-Jesus opposed the gospel and deliberately tried to turn Sergius Paulus against the faith. When the Christian faith is preached, there often seems to be a determined work against the gospel. But here Paul acted swiftly. 'Filled with the Holy Spirit', he called Elymas 'a child of the devil and an enemy of everything that is right' (*v. 10*) and pronounced God's judgment on him in the form of a temporary blindness. Such action, combined with the apostolic teaching, led to Sergius Paulus' conversion (*v. 12*).

The emphasis on the Holy Spirit and the particular judgment Paul pronounced provided a very clear differentiation between truth and falsehood, between that which was of the devil and deceitful and that which was of God.

P.D.G.

**BARABBAS** (Heb., 'son of the father'). This was the 'notorious prisoner' and murderer who was released instead of Jesus by Pilate. A crowd had been whipped up by the religious leaders to demand the death sentence for Jesus. Pilate could not find fault with Jesus, and so sought an excuse to release him by offering a choice to the crowd. Following the lead of 'the chief priests and the elders', the crowd, to the consternation of Pilate, demanded the release of Barabbas.

He was the leader of an insurrection, though what the intention of this was is not made clear in the Gospels. It is possible that he was a 'zealot' and that this was an attempt to overthrow the Roman power in Jerusalem. However, if this were the case, it would seem unlikely that he would be offered for release, even as a gesture of good will by Pilate. (*Matt. 27:16–26; Mark 15:7–15; Luke 23:18–19; John 18:40*).

Great significance is attached by all the Gospel writers to the fact that Barabbas was released while Jesus was crucified. That significance is well summarized by Peter in his sermon in *Acts 3*, where he calls Barabbas a 'murderer'. In making such a choice, and the fact that the religious leaders led the people in that choice, we find the ultimate rejection of God's Messiah, the 'Holy and Righteous One'. Jesus was not the grand messianic figure they were expecting. His path of peace and suffering was not one that would attract the crowds. However, ultimately the choice of the Jews and their leaders then was the same choice that men and women throughout the ages and of all races have continued to make, as they have rejected the gospel faith of 'Christ crucified' and have followed the 'wisdom of the world' (*1 Cor. 1:18–21*).     P.D.G.

**BARAK,** the son of Abinoam of Kadesh in Naphtali. Barak lived during the period of the Judges. This often anarchical period in the history of the Israelites was a time that saw Israel regularly dominated by the Canaanites with regard to both their religious and social life. The LORD had allowed this situation to arise as a punishment for their rejection of him on many occasions. However, the LORD remained true to his covenant promises to Abraham, Moses and his people and would not let them be utterly absorbed or destroyed by the surrounding peoples. When the domination became too great God would raise up a leader from among the people who would lead the Israelites to victory in battle. Those leaders then became Judges, often of only a small area of Israel.

Barak was noted as a commander who came forward, in response to the call of Deborah, to fight Jabin, a king of the Canaanites (*Judg. 4*). He brought with him volunteers from Zebulun and Naphtali. Initially Barak was not happy with the command from Deborah, and he doubted that they could win. He was only prepared to go to battle if Deborah went with him. She agreed, but prophesied that the glory of the battle would go to a woman. This eventually happened when Sisera, Jabin's general, was killed by the woman Jael. Eventually Jabin himself was killed. *Judg. 5* records what is often called 'The song of Deborah', but it was sung in tribute to the victory by Barak and Deborah (*v. 1*). However, that victory was clearly attributed to the LORD, who had raised up Deborah and Barak. Samuel looked back on the LORD's work through Barak and other Judges in *1 Sam. 12:11*, and in *Heb. 11:32* Barak is cited as an example of a great man of faith.   P.D.G.

**BARAKEL,** the father of Elihu and a Buzite of the family of Ram. Elihu was the last of the three who sought to argue with Job. He was younger than Job and was concerned that Job was trying to justify himself before God, implying that Job had to be guilty of something in order to receive such adversities from God (*Job 32:2, 6*).

**BARIAH,** a descendant of Shecaniah and a son of Shemaiah (*1 Chron. 3:22*). He was one of the royal line from Jehoiachin following the Exile.

**BARKOS** His descendants were among the Temple servants who returned from Exile with Nehemiah (*Ezra 2:53; Neh. 7:55*).

**BARNABAS** Barnabas is the surname given by the apostles to a Levite from Cyprus who became a leader in the early Christian church. His Jewish name was Joseph, but Luke interprets his apostolic name as 'Son of Encouragement' to suggest something of his character (*Acts 4:36*). Barnabas is mentioned 29 times in *Acts* and five times in *Paul*'s letters.

Barnabas first appears in Jerusalem, where he is cited as an outstanding example of generosity (*Acts 4:32–37*). When Saul of Tarsus was converted, it was Barnabas who introduced him to the apostles in Jerusalem (*Acts 9:27*).

Barnabas' gifts were recognized by the Jerusalem church, who sent him to investigate Christian activities in Antioch (*Acts 11:22*). He was thrilled at the spiritual developments there, and encouraged the believers to remain faithful (*Acts 11:23*). He recruited Saul (also known as Paul, *Acts 13:9*), and they worked together in Antioch and taught many people there (*Acts 11:25–26*).

In the midst of a famine during the reign of Claudius, Antioch sent aid to fellow Christians in Judea, entrusting it to Barnabas and Paul (*Acts 11:30*). These two were commissioned at Antioch and sent out on 'the first missionary journey' (*Acts 13:1–3*). Conscious of the Spirit's guidance, they preached throughout

Cyprus, and the proconsul Sergius Paulus believed the gospel (*Acts 13:7, 12*). They sailed on and landed at Perga in Pamphylia (in present-day Turkey), but John Mark left them and returned to Jerusalem (*Acts 13:13*). From this point on Paul appears to have been in charge, as Luke (the writer of Acts) refers to 'Paul and his companions' (*Acts 13:13*). The missionary duo pressed on, preaching in Antioch of Pisidia, Lystra, Iconium and Derbe amid both interest and opposition (*Acts 13:42–51; 14:1–7, 19–21*). They appointed elders to provide future leadership in each church (*Acts 14:23*). Evidently Barnabas was the more imposing figure, for in Lystra they called him 'Zeus' and Paul 'Hermes because he was the chief speaker' (*Acts 14:12*). On the return trip they retraced their steps and at Syrian Antioch reported on their mission (*Acts 14:21–28*).

Paul and Barnabas presented their case for the full admission of Gentiles (*Acts 15:1–5, 12*) to the church, and received the Jerusalem council's support (*vv. 22–29*). The council's decision was welcomed in Antioch, where Paul and Barnabas remained for some time, preaching and teaching (*vv. 30–35*).

Sadly, Barnabas and Paul had a sharp disagreement over John Mark. Paul refused to take him on his second missionary trip, while Barnabas gave him another chance, taking Mark with him back to Cyprus (*Acts 15:36–39*). At this point Barnabas disappears from the text of Acts.

There are three references to Barnabas in Galatians (*Gal. 2:1, 9, 13*), where he appears with Paul and Titus in a consultation with church leaders in Jerusalem. During this private meeting James, Cephas (Peter) and John gave the right hand of fellowship to Barnabas and Paul, agreeing that Paul and company 'should go to the Gentiles, and they to the Jews' (*Gal. 2:9*). Unfortunately, Peter gave in to pressure from the circum-

cision party, and 'even Barnabas was led astray' by 'their hypocrisy', which Paul confronted and rebuked (*Gal. 2:13–14*).

In *1 Corinthians* Paul discusses the rights of an apostle and raises a series of rhetorical questions designed to establish the principle that 'those who preach the gospel should receive their living from the gospel' (*1 Cor. 9:14*). Thus he asks pointedly: 'Don't we have the right to take a believing wife along with us, as do the other apostles and the Lord's brothers and Cephas? Or is it only I and Barnabas who must work for a living?' (*1 Cor. 9:6*).

The final reference to Barnabas is striking, because it relates to John Mark, the cousin of Barnabas, who sent greetings with Aristarchus, Paul's fellow prisoner. The rift with Paul had been healed, and Paul told the Colossians, 'if he [Mark] comes to you, welcome him' (*Col. 4:10*). Barnabas' patient ministry with Mark had been successful (*2 Tim. 4:11*).

What can be said about the character of Barnabas? He was a kind, generous, warm-hearted man who gave freely of his time and talents for the cause of Christ, both at home and in distant places. He was a man of prayer, who sought the guidance of the Holy Spirit in making decisions. He encouraged his fellow Christian workers, and was a friend who was willing to give someone a second chance. He saw potential in other people and was willing to enlist them, even if in time, like Paul, they might outstrip him. Like many another, Barnabas could be swayed by pressure, but generally 'He was a good man, full of the Holy Spirit and faith' (*Acts 11:24*).    A.A.T.

**BARSABBAS** (Heb., 'son of the sabbath'). See *Joseph Barsabbas* (*Acts 1:23*) and *Judas Barsabbas* (*Acts 15:22*).

**BARTHOLOMEW** (Aram., 'son of Tolmai') appears in each of the four NT lists of Jesus' twelve apostles (*Matt. 10:3; Mark 3:18; Luke 6:14; Acts 1:13*). In

Matthew he is paired with Philip. John describes Philip finding a friend named Nathanael, who also became a close follower of Jesus (*John 1:44–51*). It is possible, therefore, that Nathanael was this disciple's given name, and that Bartholomew was his patronymic. If this equation is correct, then we know that Jesus believed him to be 'a true Israelite, in whom there is nothing false' (*John 1:47*). A later apocryphal gospel is wrongly attributed to him. Nothing else is known with any degree of confidence about this individual.                     c.b.

**BARTIMAEUS,** the son of Timaeus, was a blind beggar. Jesus encountered him on the road leading out of Jericho on his route to Jerusalem for his final Passover. Jesus healed him (*Mark 10:46–52*). A very similar account is recorded on Jesus' *approach* to Jericho in *Luke 18:35–43*, and Matthew records the healing of *two* blind men on leaving Jericho in *Matt. 20:29–34*. The blind man's appeal that Jesus, as the 'son of David', should show mercy is significant. This was a recognition of Jesus' lineage back to King David, but, almost certainly, it was also a recognition of Jesus' messianic status. It is interesting that this ascription becomes the focus of a discussion between Jesus and the religious leaders of his day a little later in *Mark 12:35–36*. Unlike those leaders, this beggar had faith that the son of David could heal him. His faith was rewarded, and he was immediately healed.  p.d.g.

**BARUCH** (Heb., 'blessed').
**1.** The son of Zabbai, Baruch helped repair the walls of Jerusalem from the angle to the entrance of the house of Eliashib the high priest (*Neh. 3:20*).
**2.** This Baruch was one of those who sealed the agreement of the people to worship the LORD and obey his Law (*Neh. 10:6*). Possibly the same as 1. above.

**3.** His son Maaseiah, from the tribe of Judah, was one of those who settled in Jerusalem after the Exile in Babylon (*Neh. 11:5*).
**4.** The son of Neriah, this Baruch was Jeremiah's secretary (*Jer. 32:12–13, 16*). Under instruction from the LORD Jeremiah bought a field from his relative Hanamel. He signed and sealed the deed of purchase and gave it to Baruch, instructing him to place the sealed deed and unsealed copy of the deed in a clay jar so that they would last a long time. The significance of this act lay in its message of hope. It was an act of faith in the promises and faithfulness of God that the people would return again from Exile. In the midst of the exercising of his judgment came the promise of mercy and hope.

In *Jer. 36*, Jeremiah, unable to go to the Temple, dictated to Baruch all the words of the LORD he had received since the reign of Josiah. Baruch was to go and read it at the Temple with the hope that the prophecies would bring the people to repentance. Baruch did this from the room of Gemariah at the entrance of the new gate of the Temple. When Micaiah son of Gemariah heard this, the officials of the Temple ordered Baruch to bring the scroll to them. When they heard the messages they told Baruch and Jeremiah to hide and then went and reported the matter to the king. The king refused to listen to the words of the scroll and burnt it. Jeremiah took another scroll and wrote on it all the words that had been burnt and gave it to Baruch. Despite opposition the Word of God did endure these attempts to destroy it.

In *Jer. 43*, Jeremiah's enemies accused Baruch of inciting Jeremiah against them to hand them over to the Babylonians. He and Jeremiah were led away against their will by Johanan to Egypt, an act of disobedience to the LORD (*Jer. 43:3, 6*). In *Jer. 45*, Jeremiah warned Baruch not to seek great things for himself. Baruch had complained of his sorrow and pain, but the LORD wanted him to understand that within the context of the Exile and the destruction of Jerusalem, Baruch should have been thankful to escape with his life. Jeremiah warned him not to seek great things for himself (*Jer. 45:1–2*). M.P.

**BARZILLAI** (Heb., 'man of iron').

**1.** Barzillai 'the Gileadite from Rogelim' was one of those who remained faithful to King David when he was being chased by Absalom. When David came to Mahanaim, Barzillai was among those who brought bedding and other essential supplies for David and his men (*2 Sam. 17:27*). He was a 'very old man' aged 80 when he went out to accompany David back across the Jordan after Absalom's death. David wished to honour Barzillai's great faithfulness and suggested that he accompany him to Jerusalem where he would be well looked after. Barzillai refused this offer, as he wanted to die peacefully near his family home. David blessed him and passed on towards Jerusalem (*2 Sam. 19:31–39*). However, David also faithfully remembered his friends and those who had been kind to him. On his death bed, in a charge to his son Solomon, he reminded Solomon of the need to be kind to Barzillai's descendants (*1 Kings 2:7*).

**2.** Barzillai the Meholathite was the father of Adriel (*2 Sam. 21:8*). Adriel had married Saul's daughter Merab. Later, five of their children died as a revenge for Saul's breach of Joshua's treaty with the Gibeonites (*2 Sam. 21:1*). Saul had put many Gibeonites to death.

**3.** Another Barzillai lived after the return to Jerusalem from the Babylonian Exile. He had married a 'daughter' of Barzillai the Gileadite (1. above) and had taken her family name. Of course, this was centuries later and so 'female descendant' would probably be a better translation. He was a descendant of a priestly family but among those who could not trace their family ancestry and so were excluded from the priesthood as 'unclean' until the Urim and Thummim might be consulted (*Ezra 2:61–63; Neh. 7:63*). P.D.G.

**BASEMATH 1.** The daughter of Elon the Hittite (*Gen. 26:34*). Esau married her and another Hittite woman. V. *35* records that these marriages were a source of grief to Isaac and Rebekah, no doubt because such marriage was in breach of God's command that Abraham's descendants should keep themselves separate from the Canaanites. It was yet another example in Esau's life of his rejection of the LORD and his preparedness to compromise with those around him. It contrasts greatly with Jacob, who had returned to take a wife from Padam Aram rather than take a Canaanite woman (*Gen. 28:6–8*). Basemath's son, Ruel, later became a leader in Edom, and her grandsons were also chiefs (*Gen. 36:17*).

**2.** Another of Esau's wives, but a sister of Nebaioth and a daughter of Ishmael (*Gen. 36:3*). In spite of suggestions that this is the same person as 1., she should rather be identified with Mahalath (*Gen. 28:6–9*). Here again the point is made clearly that Esau should not have had a Canaanite wife.

**3.** The daughter of Solomon, who had married one of Solomon's twelve district officials – Ahimaaz, who was in Naphtali (*1 Kings 4:15*). P.D.G.

**BATHSHEBA,** a most beautiful woman who was the wife of Uriah the Hittite during the reign of King David. She was the daughter of Eliam (*2 Sam. 11:3*). She eventually became David's wife and the mother of King Solomon. In the events that surrounded David's death and the succession to the throne, she helped ensure that David's wish that Solomon should become king was fulfilled.

Bathsheba is best known, however, because of her adulterous relationship with

King David. David was walking one evening on the roof of the palace and saw at a distance this very beautiful woman bathing. After he found out who she was, he arranged for her to be brought to him, and she became pregnant. To try to get himself out of trouble, David arranged for her husband, who was out fighting in defence of the kingdom, to return home in the hope that the pregnancy could then be blamed on him. Out of loyalty to his fellow soldiers, who had not got time off, he refused to have sexual intercourse with his wife. As this plan failed, David sent Uriah back to the front with orders that he should be put where he would be killed. The adultery thus also led on into sins of deceit and eventually murder.

The prophet Nathan then came to David to pronounce God's judgment (2 Sam. 12). Bathsheba became David's wife, and by way of judgment the baby died in infancy. Once the baby had died, as part of his comforting of Bathsheba, David had intercourse with her again and this time she became pregnant with the child Solomon (v. 12).

Later Bathsheba and the prophet Nathan worked together to ensure that Adonijah would not usurp the throne (1 Kings 1:11–53).

The sin of all men, whatever their rank or status, is never concealed in Scripture. David was the greatest of the kings of Israel and God's own choice. He was the one with whom God had made a special covenant (2 Sam. 7) that would establish his throne for ever, and it was from his line that the Messiah would come, and yet he was human and sinful and deserving of God's judgment as much as the next man. The relationship with Bathsheba reflects this truth clearly, but it also shows that repentance leads to forgiveness from God, whatever the sin. Neither adultery nor murder are beyond God's forgiveness.                              P.D.G.

**BAZLUTH** His descendants were among the Temple servants who returned from Exile with Nehemiah and Zerubbabel (Ezra 2:52; Neh. 7:54).

**BEALIAH,** one of the fighting men who joined David at Ziklag while he was banished from Israel during the latter part of Saul's reign (1 Chron. 12:5). These men were Benjamites who had deserted Saul.

**BEBAI  1.** 623 (Ezra 2:11) or 628 (Neh. 7:16) of his descendants returned from Exile with Nehemiah.
**2.** His descendant Zechariah came to Jerusalem with Ezra during the reign of King Artaxerxes, bringing with him 28 men (Ezra 8:11).
**3.** Some of his descendants were guilty of marrying foreign women (Ezra 10:28).
**4.** One of the leaders who sealed the agreement of the people to worship the Lord and obey his Law (Neh. 10:15).

**BECORATH,** a Benjamite, was the father of Zeror and the great-grandfather of Kish, who was the father of King Saul (1 Sam. 9:1).

**BEDAD,** an Edomite king and the father of Hadad in the days before Israel had a king (Gen. 36:31, 35; 1 Chron. 1:46).

**BEDAN,** a descendant of Manasseh and a son of Ulam (1 Chron. 7:17).

**BEDEIAH,** a son of Bani, was among those who were guilty of marrying foreign women (Ezra 10:35).                    M.P.

**BEELIADA,** one of the many children born to King David in Jerusalem after he had taken 'more wives' (1 Chron. 14:7). This name was changed to Eliada, probably because of the associations of the Baal prefix with idolatry and Canaanite religion (2 Sam. 5:16; 1 Chron. 3:8).

**BEELZEBUB** The name came from a Heb. word meaning 'lord of the flies' and probably goes back to a Canaanite god (see 2 Kings 1:2–3, 16). In the days of the Lord Jesus the name had clearly become synonymous with Satan (Matt. 10:25; 12:24; Mark 3:22; Luke 11:15, 18–19). The extraordinary fact in the NT is that the word is only used in passages where Jesus was being accused of himself being Beelzebub or Satan or was talking of persecution.

The extent to which the religious leaders of his day were prepared to assign the works and words of Jesus to Satan himself reveals just how deeply ran their antagonism to the Messiah! They were happy to identify the Son of God with Satan himself. Jesus did of course debate this identification of himself with Satan (e.g. Luke 11:14–23), but the hatred against him was so ingrained that eventually it led to Jesus' crucifixion.          P.D.G.


**BEERA,** was of the tribe of Asher and was a son of Zophah (1 Chron. 7:37).

**BEERAH,** the leader of the Reubenites, was taken into Exile by King Tiglath-Pileser of Assyria (1 Chron. 5:6). 2 Kings 15:29–30 describes this invasion.

**BEERI 1.** A Hittite and the father of Judith, one of Esau's wives (Gen. 26:34).
**2.** The father of Hosea the prophet (Hosea 1:1).

**BEKER 1.** The second son of Benjamin (Gen. 46:21; 1 Chron. 7:6). His sons are listed in 1 Chron. 7:8
**2.** An Ephraimite and the leader of the Bekerite clan (Num. 26:35).

**BEL,** a Babylonian god who is to be identified with Marduk, as in Jer. 50:2; also see Is. 46:1; Jer. 51:44. The word is to be seen in the prefix to Daniel's Babylonian name, Belteshazzar.

**BELA 1.** A king of Edom and a son of Beor. He ruled in the city of Dinhabah at a time before Israel had a king. His son

Jobab succeeded him (Gen. 36:32–33; 1 Chron. 1:43).
**2.** Benjamin's first son, who became the leader of the Belaite clan (Gen. 46:21). Several of his sons were also clan leaders (Num. 26:38, 40; 1 Chron. 8:1–3).
**3.** The son of Azaz, a Reubenite. He lived in Aroer. In Saul's reign, his people were responsible for the defeat of the Hagrites. They took possession of land to the east of Gilead and even as far as the Euphrates, because they were so prosperous. (1 Chron. 5:8–10).

**BELIAL** In intertestamental Jewish writings the name refers to Satan and in the NT is used in that way by Paul in 2 Cor. 6:15. In that text the apostle Paul is emphatically insisting that Christians must be careful about who they mix with and the extent to which they become involved with non-Christians. He contrasts light and darkness in v. 15 but then asks 'what harmony is there between Christ and Belial'? Of course, there is no such harmony. Therefore, he argues, there can by rights be no harmony between believer and unbeliever. The appeal Paul made in drawing out this contrast was a call to holiness. It is not that Christians and unbelievers should have no contact, but involvement and harmony together would be quite inappropriate because each serves a different master – the one Christ and the other Belial.          P.D.G.

**BELSHAZZAR,** (Bab., 'Bel, protect the king') was the last king seen in Scripture of the neo-Babylonian empire. The name appears only in Dan. 5, the end of which (v. 30) records his slaying. Until relatively recently there was scepticism about the historicity of Dan. 5, since no extrabiblical evidence of a Babylonian king named Belshazzar had been found. In the surviving documents the last king of Babylon was Nabonidus, who is not mentioned in the Bible. However, currently it is widely held that Belshazzar was the son and co-regent of Nabonidus. Nabonidus apparently never relinquished sole authority of the empire to Belshazzar, though he withdrew to an outlying palace and left his son in charge of Babylon, the capital city.

Dan. 5 tells us little, if anything, positive about Belshazzar's character. As God's spokesman, Daniel confronted him about his pride and blasphemous behaviour (Dan. 5:22–23) and said to him, 'you did not honour the God who holds in his hand your life and all your ways'. There is no record of Belshazzar repenting, and his fate was sealed when Daniel translated the handwriting on the wall. The formerly glorious Babylonian empire was to be judged, and it was Belshazzar who was to preside over its demise. A.B.L.

**BELTESHAZZAR,** the 'new' name given to Daniel (Dan. 1:7). For detail see Daniel.

**BEN-ABINADAB** (Heb., 'son of Abinadab'), was married to Solomon's daughter Taphath and was the governor of Naphoth-Dor (1 Kings 4:11). See Ben-Hur.

**BEN-AMMI** (Heb., 'son of my kinsman'), the progenitor of the Ammonites. He was the son of Lot's younger daughter, and Lot was his father (Gen. 19:38). Following the destruction of Sodom, from which only Lot and his two daughters eventually escaped, the daughters were concerned that the family name should continue, and so they got their father drunk and both had sexual intercourse with him and became pregnant. It is perhaps significant that these daughters, who were reluctant to leave Sodom, continued to manifest serious sexual sin, for which, it seems, Sodom was renowned. Certainly, once away from Sodom, there was no new start for Lot. He and his daughters had been saved by God simply because of their relationship to Abraham, with whom God had made his covenant (Gen. 19:29). P.D.G

**BEN-DEKER** (Heb., 'son of Deker'), the governor in Makaz, Shaalbim and the surrounding areas (1 Kings 4:9). See Ben-Hur.

**BEN-GEBER** (Heb., 'son of Geber'), the governor in Ramoth Gilead and the surrounding areas (1 Kings 4:13). Special mention is made of 60 large cities in the district of Argob in Bashan that were under his control. See Ben-Hur.

**BEN-HADAD** (Heb., 'son of Hadad').

**1.** This Ben-Hadad was king of Damascus, a contemporary of Asa, king of Judah and of Baasha and Omri, kings of Israel, in about 890 BC (1 Kings 15:18, 20). King Asa appealed to Ben-Hadad for help in defending himself against King Baasha. The price of his appeal was high, not just financially ('Asa . . . took all the silver and gold that was left in the treasuries of the LORD's temple', 1 Kings 15:18), but also in terms of the sacrifice of political freedom. Whilst this brought temporary relief of hostilities between Israel and Judah, it meant that Syria later became a serious threat to Judah itself (see 2 Kings 12:17ff.).

**2.** Ben-Hadad II, King of Aram (Syria), besieged Samaria some time in the middle of the 9th century BC. King Ahab was reluctant to be drawn into battle (1 Kings 20:1–7). He agreed to Ben-Hadad's first demands (for the women and children and silver and gold), but drew the line at the demand that officials come and rout his royal residence (1 Kings 20:9). Ben-Hadad was furious at what he perceived to be insolent resistance and declared war (1 Kings 20:10–12). Ahab successfully repelled the onslaught and gained victory over the Syrians.

There were three key prophecies concerning Ahab and his relations with Ben Hadad, two positive, one negative. In the first, a prophet encouraged Ahab to take the initiative in battle. Ahab took 7,000 men and sprung a surprise attack on Ben-Hadad. A decisive victory was won, but Ben Hadad escaped on a horse (1 Kings 20:13–22).

The second prophecy warned Ahab to prepare for further battles with Ben Hadad (1 Kings 20:22). The King of Aram claimed that Israel's gods were gods of the hills so Ben-Hadad met the Israelites in the plain. There again the Israelites won a great battle as God demonstrated his kingly sovereignty over all the earth.

Thirdly, Ahab was denounced by the prophet of the LORD for dealing too leniently with the Syrians and building alliances with Ben-Hadad (1 Kings 20:34). Initially the two kings fought together against their mutual enemy, the Assyrians. However, Ahab was killed by the Syrians when he tried to regain Ramoth-Gilead. Ben-Hadad's death is recorded in 2 Kings 6:24; 8:7–9.

**3.** Ben-Hadad III came to power at a time of declining Syrian influence. The son of Hazael (c. 796–770 BC, see 2 Kings 13:3–4), he continued his father's oppressive policies. God allowed Israel to fall into Ben-Hadad's hands because Jehoahaz continued in the evil ways of Jeroboam I. Ben-Hadad was used as God's instrument to execute punishment upon Israel (2 Kings 13:3). He recovered the towns captured by the Moabite raiders in accordance with Elisha's prophecy.

According to Amos. 1:4 Ben-Hadad's defeat came because of God's judgment upon the nations surrounding Israel. During the reign of King Jehoash Ben-Hadad was defeated three times and lost control over the towns he had previously captured (2 Kings 13:24–25).     S.V.

**BEN-HAIL** (Heb., 'son of strength'), one of Jehoshaphat's officials who were sent, in the third year of his reign, to teach people in the towns of Judah about the LORD and his Law (2 Chron. 17:7).

**BEN-HANAN** (Heb., 'son of grace'), a son of Shimon of the clan of Judah (1 Chron. 4:20).

**BEN-HESED** (Heb., 'son of Hesed'), the governor in Arubboth, Socoh and Hepher (1 Kings 4:10). See Ben-Hur.

**BEN-HUR,** the first of a list of twelve district governors appointed by Solomon to oversee his kingdom (1 Kings 4:8). His area was Ephraim. The others are listed as Ben-Deker, Ben-Hesed, Ben-Abinadab, Baana, Ben-Geber, Ahinadab, Ahimaaz, Baana son of Hushai, Jehoshaphat, Shimei and Geber.

Following his coronation, Solomon was allowed to ask of God whatever he wanted (1 Kings 3:5–15). Rather than riches or long life, he chose wisdom and a discerning heart. God gave him this and added to it 'riches and honour'. The next few chapters show how these gifts of God were evidenced in Solomon's early years. An example of his wisdom is given in 1 Kings 3. In 1 Kings 4 emphasis is laid on the growing wealth and power of the king. It is in this context that we read of the appointment of the twelve governors, whose job it was to ensure the huge supplies needed for the royal household for one month in each year. In effect they did this by taxing their people in kind. Later in 1 Kings 4 the daily provisions required by Solomon are listed (vv. 22–23), and they were enormous. Both before and after this list of provisions the extent of Solomon's kingdom is emphasized, as it reached virtually to the boundaries promised by God to Moses. The overall impression conveyed in 1 Kings 4 is of the enormous blessings of God on this king.     P.D.G.

**BEN-ONI** (Heb., 'son of my sorrow') was

Rachel's name for her son, whom Jacob later named Benjamin (*Gen. 35:18*). In their nomadic life, Jacob was moving from Bethel towards Ephrath (Bethlehem) when it was time for Rachel's delivery. She had great difficulty with the birth and died shortly after seeing that the child was a boy and naming him in this way. See *Benjamin*.

**BEN-ZOHETH** (Heb., 'son of Zoheth'), a descendant of Ishi of the tribe of Judah (*1 Chron. 4:20*).

**BENAIAH** (Heb., 'the Lord has built').

**1.** Benaiah was the son of Jehoiada the priest and served David loyally throughout the king's reign. However, he was not one of the 'three mighty men', Josheb-Basshebeth, Eleazar, Shammah. He came from Kabzeel in Judah and was set over the Kerethites and Pelethites. David counted Benaiah as 'just as famous' and held in greater honour than any of the 'Thirty' great warriors (*2 Sam. 8:18; 20:23; 23:20–23; 1 Chron. 27:5, 34*). His loyalty meant he did not join the rebellion by Adonijah at the end of David's life and that he was used by David to proclaim Solomon king (*1 Kings 1:8; 26*). He was responsible also for the deaths of the traitors Joab, Adonijah and Shimei (*1 Kings 2:23–35, 46*).

**2.** A Pirathonite, Benaiah was one of David's 'Thirty' great warriors. Benaiah led 24,000 military men each year during the eleventh month (*2 Sam. 23:20; 1 Chron. 11:31; 27:34*).

**3.** Another Benaiah is named as one of the Levitical musicians during David's rule. He was assigned to play the lyre and accompanied the ark on its way to Jerusalem (*1 Chron. 15:18–20; 16:5*).

**4.** Benaiah is named as one of the Levitical musicians during David's rule, assigned to play the trumpet. This Benaiah also accompanied the ark on its way to Jerusalem (*1 Chron. 15:24; 16:6*).

**5.** This Benaiah, son of Jeiel, was a

descendant of Asaph, father of Zechariah (*2 Chron. 20:14*).

**6.** This Benaiah was a Levite whose job consisted in supervising contributions to the Temple during the revival of King Hezekiah's reign (*2 Chron. 31:13*).

**7.** During Hezekiah's rule, another Benaiah was a Simeonite leader whose family greatly increased in numbers (*1 Chron. 4:36, 24–43*).

**8.** This Benaiah was among the descendants of Parosh. At the time of return from the Exile in Babylon, Shecaniah confessed to Ezra that many men and even descendants of the priests of Judah had married wives from other tribes and nations. Ezra and the people repented and made a covenant to serve the LORD (*Ezra 10:2*). Benaiah is listed in *Ezra 10:25* as one who divorced his foreign wife.

**9.** Another Benaiah was among the descendants of Pahath-Moab. He also was listed as one of the family leaders guilty of intermarriage (*Ezra 10:30*).

**10.** Another Benaiah was among the descendants of Bani. He also was listed as one of the family leaders guilty of intermarriage (*Ezra 10:35*).

**11.** Another Benaiah was among the descendants of Nebo. He also was listed as one of the family leaders guilty of intermarriage (*Ezra 10:43*).

**12.** Benaiah was the father of Pelatiah, one of 25 men identified by Ezekiel as wicked and acting against God (*Ezek. 11:1, 13*). s.c.

**BENINU,** (Heb., 'our son') was one of the Levites who sealed the agreement of the people to worship the LORD and obey his Law (*Neh. 10:13*).

**BENJAMIN 1.** The twelfth Son of Jacob. His mother, Rachel, died as she gave birth, naming her child Ben-Oni, meaning 'son of sorrow' (*Gen. 35:18, 24; 1 Chron. 2:2*), which Jacob altered to Benjamin, meaning 'Son of my right hand'. Though Jacob had twelve sons, only two of them were by Rachel – Benjamin and Joseph. This and the fact that their mother died while they were so young accounts for the special affection between the two brothers.

Following the sale of Joseph into slavery in Egypt, Benjamin enjoyed the special favour of his father, who was hesitant to send his son with the other brothers in search for help in Egypt during the famine throughout Canaan (Gen. 42:4). During their second visit to Egypt, without them realizing it, it was the exalted Joseph who offered them help. Joseph went to great lengths to show kindness, particularly to his brother Benjamin, initially without revealing his identity (Gen. 45:12, 14, 22). The peculiar behaviour of Joseph to the brothers in hiding gifts in their luggage perturbed and worried them, until finally Joseph made himself known to them, and brought the whole family to Egypt. A move which proved significant for the future outworking of God's redemptive plans for the people of God (Gen. 46:3f.).

In his old age, Jacob (Israel) pronounced a blessing on all his sons, prophesying their eventual return to Canaan. To Benjamin, from whom the Benjamites (see below) are descended Jacob pronounced: 'Benjamin is a ravenous wolf; in the morning he devours the prey, in the evening he divides the plunder' (Gen. 49:27). A mixed blessing which would mark out the Benjamites as a bold, but perhaps at times callous tribe. Benjamin had ten sons (see Gen. 46:21).

The tribe of Benjamin had a reputation for bravery and skilful fighting ability. They were adept in left-handed use of their weaponry, which in the case of Ehud, resulted in the Israelites being delivered from the hand of the Moabites (see further Judg. 3:15ff.; 1 Sam. 9:1), so fulfilling Jacob's prophecy. Moses predicted that God would bless Benjamin and 'rest between his shoulders' (Deut.

33:12). The prey would be devoured and the plunder spoiled.

The tribe of Benjamin lived in the eastern strip of land below the hills of Judah – between Ephraim and Judah, and included major cities such as Jerusalem, Gibeah, and Mizpeh. However, like the history of the tribe of Benjamin, this was a mixed blessing. Gibeah became known for its homosexuality (Judg. 19:22), and battles over Jerusalem chequered their history. Under Saul's leadership the tribe of Benjamin had its greatest prominence, and the people of Benjamin for the most part remained loyal to Saul (although see 1 Chron. 12:2–7).

The tribes of Benjamin and Judah retained prominent influence among the people of Israel following the return from Babylon in 537 BC (see Ezra 1–2). According to Jer. 33:12–26 Benjamin and Judah were particularly singled out as the recipients of the 'gracious promises' of restoration and return made by the LORD.

The apostle Paul was a Benjamite and used himself as an example of the theology of 'a remnant' (see Rom. 11:1ff.). Despite the almost total rejection of Israel by God, a remnant would always remain, not because of their faithfulness but because it is chosen by grace (Rom. 11:5), and, just like the apostle himself, it owes its continuance to the gracious work of a saving God (see Phil. 3:4f.).

For us, today, the reminder is that even a great past, like that of the tribe of Benjamin, does not guarantee any future, except by the mercy of God. The apostle Paul's pedigree was invaluable to him, not least in understanding the way in which God had retained a remnant and ingrafted other branches (Gentile Christians, see Rom. 11). However, it was not his heritage that saved him, only the mercy of God in keeping his covenant promises (Gen. 12:1–3). In his defence before King Agrippa, Paul explained that God rescued him from his own people and from the Gentiles in order to be sent back to open their eyes (see *Acts 26:15ff.*). Like the tribe of Benjamin, the apostle came to appreciate that it was God's saving activity that meant God himself could retain a witness for himself in a hostile world.

**2.** The name given to Benjamin's great-grandson, son of Bilhan (*1 Chron. 7:10*).

**3.** A member of the tribe of Benjamin who repented of taking a foreign wife (*Ezra 10:32*). Ezra exhorted these men to come publicly before the whole town in remorse over their intermarriage. This may be the same Benjamin referred to in *Neh. 3:23; 12:34* who assisted with the construction of the Temple.     s.v.


**BENO,** a Levite, was the son of Jaaziah and the grandson of Merari (*1 Chron. 24:26–27*).


**BEOR 1.** The father of Bela, the first king of Edom, in the days before the Israelite monarchy (*Gen. 36:32; 1 Chron. 1:43*).

**2.** Always mentioned in connection with his son, Balaam the seer (*Num. 22:5; 24:15; Micah 6:9 etc.*).


**BERA,** one of five kings resident in the Jordan valley when Abraham was living near 'the great trees of Mamre'. He was king of Sodom (*Gen. 14:2*). Following their defeat at the hands of a coalition of Mesopotamian kings, these city kings were subjugated for 13 years until they finally rebelled. Their rebellion was put down by the four kings led by Kedorlaomer. (For more details see *Amraphel.*)

Their defeat involved the seizure of the people of Sodom, and Bera barely escaped with his life (*Gen. 14:10*). In the defeat of Sodom, Lot was captured, and this brought Abra(ha)m into the battle. He chased Kedorlaomer north and eventually defeated him in battle, bringing Lot

back with him and recovering all the spoil that had been taken from Sodom. On his return, Abraham was met by Bera in the valley of Shaveh. Bera offered to let Abram keep the recovered goods, provided the people were returned. In fact, the goods would have belonged to Abram as part of his victory, but Abram handed them back to Bera, insisting: 'I will accept nothing belonging to you . . . so that you will never be able to say, "I made Abram rich."' Abram attributed his victory to 'the Lord, God Most High' (*Gen. 14:17, 21–24*).

The author clearly intended a lesson to be learned from the contrast between Bera's behaviour with Abraham and Melchizedek's (*Gen. 14:18–20*). Melchizedek gave the glory where it was due, to 'God Most High', and praised God for giving Abram the victory. Bera had witnessed the same events, yet responded not with praise to God but with selfishness and arrogance. This arrogance was to become the hallmark of Sodom and would lead to its eventual destruction by the same God whom Bera had refused to acknowledge (*Ezek. 16:49*).     p.d.g.


**BERACAH** (Heb., 'blessing'), one of the warriors from the tribe of Benjamin who deserted Saul to join David at Ziklag (*1 Chron. 12:3*). They were ambidextrous in archery and with slings.


**BERAIAH** (Heb., 'the Lord has created') is listed as a son of Shimei in the geneaology from Benjamin to Saul (*1 Chron. 8:21*).


**BERED,** a descendant of Ephraim and a son of Shuthelah (*1 Chron. 7:20*). His son was Tahath. Bered is also called Beker in *Num. 26:35*.


**BEREKIAH** (Heb., 'Yahweh blesses').
**1.** The son of Iddo and the father of Zechariah the prophet (*Zech. 1:1*). Berekiah is mentioned only in the book of Zechariah. When Zechariah's ancestry is

cited elsewhere, he is called the son of Iddo, bypassing Berekiah completely (Ezra 6:14; Neh. 12:16). It is possible that Berekiah was the actual, immediate father of the prophet and that both were more remote descendants of Iddo or of his priestly family.

**2.** One of the five sons of Zerubbabel, this Berekiah is mentioned only in the genealogy of 1 Chron. 3:20.

**3.** A Levite whose son Asaph was appointed to an important religious service by King David (1 Chron. 6:39; cf. 15:17) and also served in the Temple (1 Chron. 15:23).

**4.** The son of Asa, this Berekiah was a Levite listed among those who returned to Judah from the Babylonian Exile (1 Chron. 9:16).

**5.** The son of Meshillemoth, this Berekiah was an Ephraimite who persuaded the Israelites of Pekah's day to allow the captives they had taken from Judah to return to their homes (2 Chron. 28:12).

**6.** The son of Meshezabel, this Berekiah was involved in the building of the walls of Jerusalem under Nehemiah's direction (Neh. 3:4, 30). His granddaughter married Jehohanan, a son of Tobiah, one of the adversaries of the rebuilding project (Neh. 6:17–18).                    E.M.

**BERI,** a son of Zophah, a chief in the tribe of Asher (1 Chron. 7:36).

**BERIAH 1.** A son of Asher. Beriah's sons were Heber and Malkiel, and he was the progenitor of the Beriite clan (Gen. 46:17; Num. 26:44–45; 1 Chron. 7:30–31).

**2.** A son of Ephraim (1 Chron. 7:23) who was called Beriah because the name sounds like the Heb. for 'misfortune', and misfortune had come to his family. Ephraim's two sons, Ezer and Elead, had gone to steal livestock from the men of Gath and had been killed by them.

**3.** A descendant of Benjamin and a son of Elpaal (1 Chron. 8:13). He was the head

of the families living in Aijalon and is credited with driving out the inhabitants of Gath. His sons are listed in v. 16.

**4.** A son of Shimei and a Levite (1 Chron. 23:10–11). He belonged to the clan of the Gershonites. Neither he nor his brother Jeush had sons, and so in the assignments for worship they were counted as one family.

**BERNICE,** the daughter of Herod Agrippa I and the sister of Herod Agrippa II. In Acts 25:13 we read that she came with her brother to Caesarea 'to pay their respects to Festus'. The apostle Paul had just been tried by Festus and had appealed to Caesar. This interesting legal case became a matter of discussion between Festus and his guests. Consequently Agrippa asked to meet Paul, who was then brought before Agrippa and Bernice and the high-ranking officials who accompanied them (Acts 25:23). In his explanation of the Christian faith to the king, Paul appealed to Agrippa to become a Christian. After the king and Bernice left, they agreed among themselves that Paul had done nothing that deserved death or imprisonment (Acts 25:30–31).

Bernice and Agrippa were Roman aristocrats but of Jewish birth. They were clearly held in high regard by both Festus and Paul. In time the close companionship of this brother and sister gave rise to gossip about an incestuous relationship. However, Bernice risked her life in an attempt to stop the massacre of the Jews by the Roman procurator Gessius Flavius in AD 66. His soldiers nearly killed her, and in the war that ensued, Josephus tells us, her palace was burned down.   P.D.G.

**BESAI** His descendants were among the Temple servants who returned from Exile with Nehemiah (Ezra 2:49; Neh. 7:52).

**BESODEIAH** (Heb., 'in the secret council of the LORD'), the father of Meshullam, who helped repair the Jeshanah gate in the wall of Jerusalem during the time of Nehemiah (*Neh. 3:6*).

**BETHUEL,** a son of Nahor and Milcah and therefore Abraham's nephew. He is of particular significance because he became the father of Laban and Rebekah, the future wife of Isaac (*Gen. 22:22–23; 24:15, 29*). In *Gen. 25:20* and *28:5* attention is drawn to the fact that Bethuel was from Padan-Aram. It was important that Abraham's children should not marry the Canaanites, and so he specifically sent back to his family in Padan-Aram for a suitable wife for Isaac. In fact Rebekah's brother Laban had a greater part in seeing his sister satisfactorily married than did Bethuel, but it was from his descendants, through Rebekah, that God fulfilled his promises to Abraham.

**BEZAI 1.** 323 of his descendants returned from Exile with Nehemiah (*Ezra 2:17*; in *Neh. 7:23* the number is 324).

**2.** One of the leaders who sealed the agreement of the people to worship the LORD and obey his law following the return from the Exile (*Neh. 10:18*).

**BEZALEL** (Heb., 'under the protection of God').

**1.** Bezalel, from the tribe of Judah, was the son of Uri and the grandson of Hur (*Exod. 31:2; 1 Chron. 2:20*). He was appointed by the LORD to work in the building of the Tabernacle. *Exod. 31:2–3* describes how the LORD himself had specially chosen him for the artistic work and designs needed for the Tent of Meeting (the Tabernacle). No doubt he had amazing natural skills in several different crafts, such as work with precious metals, woodwork and even embroidering cloth, but God specially 'filled him with the Spirit of God' so that he could do this work fully to the glory of God, and so that he would know exactly what was required of him. Such special filling with the Spirit of God was rare in OT times and was usually limited to prophets or kings. The spiritual significance and importance of his task are therefore emphasized. Part of the gift God had given him was the ability to teach others these crafts so that the work on the Tent of Meeting would be completed to God's glory (*Exod. 35:30–39:31*; see specially *36:1–2; 37:1; 38:22; 2 Chron. 1:5*). God also gave Bezalel a special helper in the person of Oholiab from the tribe of Dan.

**2.** This Bezalel was descended from Pahath-moab and had married a foreign wife in the time of Ezra (*Ezra 10:30*).

P.D.G.

**BEZER,** a descendant of Asher and a son of Zophah (*1 Chron. 7:37*).

## BIBLICAL GENEALOGIES

The Scriptures repeatedly present lists of various Jewish persons' ancestors or descendants. These genealogies serve a variety of purposes: (i) to demonstrate hereditary succession from a certain tribe to legitimate claims to an inheritance or a particular office; (ii) to disclose God's blessing or judgment on a particular family; (iii) to bridge the gap between one historical period and another; (iv) to show God's patterns of activity in human history; and (v) to distinguish true Israelites from Gentiles. It is common for names of relatively unimportant people to be left out of such lists and for genealogies to be schematically arranged. The words translated 'son' and 'father' can often mean 'descendant' and 'ancestor', respectively. Ancestry was normally traced through the males in a family tree; inclusion of women usually indicated some special purpose. The longevity of the antediluvian patriarchs perplexes many moderns but actually proves modest compared with Mesopotamian parallels; the decreasing ages over time probably indicates the increasing effects of the Fall.

The principal OT genealogical listings include the offspring of (i) Cain, and the technological developments associated with several of them (Gen. 4:17–22), (ii) Adam via Seth, tracing the patriarchal heritage through the more godly son of Adam (Gen. 5:3–22); (iii) Noah (Gen. 10, often called the Table of Nations because of the repopulation of the earth begun by Noah's three sons); (iv) Shem, up through Abraham, preparing the way for the particular family God would call to receive his covenant blessing (Gen. 11:10–32); (v) Lot, to show the origin of the Moabites and the Ammonites (Gen. 19:37–38); (vi) Nahor, Abraham's brother, as a foil to the barrenness of Abraham's wife Sarah (Gen. 22:20–24); (vii) Abraham, by a later wife Keturah, to show the origin of other Middle-Eastern peoples besides the Israelites (Gen. 25:1–4); (viii) Ishmael, Abraham's son by Hagar, for the same reason, and to illustrate how various nations originated from Abraham (Gen. 25:12–18); (ix) Jacob, by each of four women, calling particular attention to the founding of the twelve tribes of Israel, along with the offspring of each of Jacob's twelve sons (Gen. 46:8–27; cf. Num. 26:5–62); (x) a detailed listing of persons from Adam to Saul, stressing the purity of descent through post-exilic times and highlighting the grace and sovereignty of God's election (1 Chron. 1–9); (xi) various Levites, for example during the periods of David (1 Chron. 15:5–24), Hezekiah (2 Chron. 29:12–14), Josiah (2 Chron. 34:12–13), and Zerubbabel (Neh. 12:1–24), who thereby validated their right to officiate at worship.

Similar lists, which, though not strictly speaking genealogies, often include brief references to a person's ancestry, include, for example, military registers of the Israelites in the wilderness (Num. 1:5–16), David's mighty warriors (2 Sam. 23:8–39), tribal supervisers (1 Chron. 27:16–22), administrative officials (1 Chron. 27:25–31), repatriated Israelites in the days of Ezra and Nehemiah (Neh. 7:7–63), those who helped rebuild Jerusalem's wall (Neh. 3), those who had married foreign wives (Ezra 10:18–43), those who signed the covenant rededicating themselves to the God of Israel (Neh. 10:1–27) and those who resided in Jerusalem (Neh. 11:14–19).

Two significant genealogies appear in the NT, both of Jesus. Matt. 1:1–17 traces his line beginning with Abraham, in three groups of 14 generations, highlighting Jesus as son of David and restorer of the hopes which had fallen at the time of the deportation to Babylon. Four women figure significantly in the list: Tamar, Rahab, Ruth and Uriah's wife. Each was a Gentile, and each was included probably because of suspicions of bearing illegitimate children. The same suspicions surrounded Mary, the mother of Jesus, the fifth woman's name on the list. Matthew stresses that Jesus had all the proper Jewish credentials to be the Messiah and King but that he came to save the outcast as well.

Luke 3:23–37 begins with Jesus and works backwards to Adam and to God, stressing the universal outreach of the Messiah's mission. The discrepancies between the names on the two lists are usually accounted for by assuming that Matthew preserves Jesus' legal lineage and Luke, his biological one, or that

Matthew traces the ancestry through Joseph, Jesus' adoptive father, and Luke, through Mary. Both genealogies also imply Jesus' virginal conception (*Matt. 1:16; Luke 3:23*).

C.B.

**BICRI,** a Benjamite, was the father of Sheba (*2 Sam. 20*) and probably the leader of the clan known as the Berites (*v. 14*). Sheba led a rebellion against King David.

**BIDKAR,** King Jehu's chief chariot officer (*2 Kings 9:25*) when Jehu conspired against King Joram of Israel. Jehu had been anointed King of Israel by Elisha and had been told to destroy the house of Ahab and Jezebel (*vv. 6–10*). At a confrontation with Joram and King Ahaziah of Judah, Jehu shot Joram with his bow as judgment for the sin of idolatry and witchcraft that had been introduced to Israel by Jezebel. Bidkar was told to take Joram and throw his body on the field that belonged to Naboth.

**BIGTHA,** one of seven eunuchs who served King Xerxes (*Est. 1:10*). See *Vashti.*

**BIGTHANA,** one of two gate-keepers who guarded the palace doorway for King Xerxes. Along with his colleague, Teresh, he 'became angry and conspired to assassinate King Xerxes' (*Est. 2:21*). The reason for their inclusion in the book of Esther is that it was the Jew Mordecai who exposed them. Haman had arranged to have Mordecai hanged for not bowing down to him. That night the king read in the annals of the kingdom about Mordecai's exposure of the two conspirators and, in the morning, ordered Haman to honour Mordecai. This recognition of Mordecai by the king eventually led to the salvation of the Jews from the evil designs of Haman. See *Mordecai* and *Esther* for more detail.

**BIGVAI 1.** He returned from the Exile in Babylon with Nehemiah (*Ezra 2:2; Neh. 7:7*).

**2.** 2,056 of his descendants returned from the Exile with Nehemiah (*Ezra 2:14;* in *Neh. 7:19* the number is 2,067).

**3.** Some of his descendants came up to Jerusalem with Ezra during the reign of King Artaxerxes (*Ezra 8:14*).

**4.** One of the leaders who sealed the people's agreement to worship the LORD and obey his Law (*Neh. 10:16*).

**BILDAD,** 'the Shuhite' was one of Job's three 'friends' (*Job 2:11*). Initially the three friends went to Job to 'sympathise with him and comfort him'. When they saw the appalling troubles Job was facing under God's testing, they were unable to speak at all for a long time. Eventually they began to offer various forms of advice.

Bildad was the second friend to offer advice. He stressed the justice of God (*Job 8:1, 3*). In common with much teaching in Scripture, he suggested that Job should look to previous generations and learn from them. If he did that he would discover that they suffered because of their sin and the sin of their families. Therefore this must be the cause of Job's suffering and he would be quite wrong to deny guilt before the LORD (*Job 8:8–13*). The teaching that Bildad believed Job should accept was that the righteous are universally blessed while sinners suffer. Bildad believed that if Job was indeed righteous then these afflictions he was suffering would be temporary for quickly God would step in and bring justice again (*Job 8:20–22*).

In his second speech Bildad was clearly becoming fed up with Job's protestations of innocence (*Job 18:1–2*) and so he emphasized God's judgment on the wicked and warned Job of the danger of questioning God (*vv. 5–21*). In a final brief third speech Bildad spoke a hymn of praise to the creator God and compared that with the sin of mankind (*Job 25:1–6*).

The whole book of Job reveals very clearly how the often repeated religious explanations of cause and effect (sin, judgment; righteousness, blessing) are too simplistic by far when people confront the Almighty God whose sovereignty is total. In the end God did vindicate Job and ordered the friends to go to Job and have him offer sacrifices for their forgiveness: 'My servant Job will pray for you, and I will accept his prayer and not deal with you according to your folly. You have not spoken of me what is right, as my servant Job has' (*Job 42:7–9*).

P.D.G.

**BILGAH** (Heb., 'brightness').

**1.** A priest during the reign of David who was chosen by lot to be 15th in the order of ministering (*1 Chron. 24:14*).

**2.** One of the priests who returned from Exile with Zerubbabel and Jeshua in *Neh. 12:5*. In the days of Joiakim the head of this family was Shammua (*Neh. 12:18*).

**BILGAI,** (Heb., 'cheerfulness') was one of the priests who sealed the agreement of the people to worship the LORD and obey his Law (*Neh. 10:8*). He is probably the same person as Bilgah 2.

**BILHAH,** a servant girl given to Rachel by Laban on her wedding day (*Gen. 29:29*). She was also to become Jacob's concubine (*Gen. 30:3–7*) when Rachel was unable to bear children, although later God heard Rachel's prayer and gave her two sons in Canaan (Benjamin and Joseph). Bilhah gave birth to Dan and Naphtali, two of Jacob's twelve sons, who were to become leading tribes in Israel (*Gen. 35:25; 46:25; 1 Chron. 7:13*). She also had an incestuous relationship with Reuben, Jacob's eldest son by his first wife Leah (*Gen. 35:22*).

S.V.

**BILHAN** **1.** The first son of Ezer, one of

the tribal leaders in Seir, where Esau settled (*Gen. 36:27; 1 Chron. 1:42*).

**2.** The son of Jediael and therefore the grandson of Benjamin. Each of his seven sons listed in *1 Chron. 7:10* headed a family.

**BILSHAN** returned from Exile with Nehemiah (*Ezra 2:2; Neh. 7:7*).

**BIMHAL,** a son of Japhlet, of the tribe of Asher (*1 Chron. 7:33*). He was one of the brave warriors and the head of a family.

**BINEA,** a descendant of King Saul, was a Benjamite and the father of Raphah. He was the son of Moza (*1 Chron. 8:37; 9:43*).

**BINNUI** (Heb., 'to build').

**1.** The father of Noadiah, who was one of those who weighed out the silver and gold brought back from Exile with Ezra (*Ezra 8:33*).

**2.** A descendant of Pahath-Moab, this Binnui was among those who were guilty of marrying foreign women (*Ezra 10:30*).

**3.** This Binnui was the ancestor of some of those who were guilty of marrying foreign women (*Ezra 10:38*).

**4.** The son of Henadad, this Binnui was the ruler of one of the half-districts of Keilah. He helped in the repairs to the wall of Jerusalem after the Exile, working on a section from Azariah's house to the angle and corner (*Neh. 3:18, 24*). He was also one of the Levites who sealed the agreement of the people in *Neh. 10:9*.

**5.** 648 of this Binnui's descendants returned from Exile with Nehemiah (*Neh. 7:15*).

**6.** This Binnui was one of the Levites who returned from Exile with Zerubbabel (*Neh. 12:8*).

M.P.

**BIRSHA,** one of five kings resident in the Jordan valley when Abraham was living near 'the great trees of Mamre'. He was king of Gomorrah (*Gen. 14:2*). Following their defeat at the hands of a coalition of Mesopotamian kings, these city kings were subjugated for 13 years until they finally rebelled. Their rebellion was put down by the four kings led by Kedorlaomer. (For more details see *Amraphel*.) Their defeat involved the seizure of the people of Sodom, and Birsha barely escaped with his life (*Gen. 14:10*). In the defeat of Gomorrah all their goods and food were taken. Because Lot (a resident of Sodom) was captured, Abra(ha)m entered the battle. He chased Kedorlaomer north and eventually defeated him in battle, bringing Lot back with him and recovering all the spoil.

**BIRZAITH,** the son of Malkiel and a descendant of Asher (*1 Chron. 7:31*).

**BISHLAM,** along with Mithredath, Tabeel and his associates, wrote a letter to King Artaxerxes, lodging an accusation against the people of Judah (*Ezra 4:7*). See *Mithredath* for more detail.

**BITHIAH** (Heb., 'daughter of the Lord'), the daughter of Pharaoh. She married Mered of the tribe of Judah, so she appears in that genealogy (*1 Chron. 4:18*). Her name may suggest that she had converted to the Israelite religion.

**BIZTHA,** one of seven eunuchs who served King Xerxes (*Est. 1:10*). See *Vashti*.

**BLASTUS** is described as 'a trusted personal servant of the king [Herod Agrippa I]' (*Acts 12:20*). When Herod travelled to Caesarea the people of Tyre and Sidon, with whom he had been in disagreement, sought an audience with him in order to ask for peace. In his anger with them Herod had cut off their food and other essential exports. The audience with him was arranged by Blastus, who probably spoke on their behalf. Having listened to the king's speech, and in order to gain the king's favour, the visitors hailed Herod as a god. Herod was immediately struck down by an angel of the Lord and died because he 'did not give praise to God'. A clear contrast is then indicated between Herod, who died, and 'the word of God', which 'continued to increase and spread' (*Acts 12:21–24*).

**BOANERGES** This name was given to James and John, the sons of Zebedee, by Jesus when he called them to be disciples. Mark translates it as meaning 'sons of thunder' (*Mark 3:17*). It is not clear why Jesus gave them this name, but it is speculated that it is an indication of their fiery characters. See *James* and *John*.

**BOAZ 1.** (Heb., 'strength is in him'). The name is found in the book of Ruth and in the genealogies in *1 Chronicles*, *Matthew* and *Luke*. Boaz was a godly landowner in Bethlehem of Judah during the period of the Judges (*Ruth 1:1*). He married Ruth and became a forefather of King David and Jesus Christ.

*Ruth 1* concludes with Naomi and Ruth, her Moabitess daughter-in-law, arriving in Bethlehem widowed and penniless. Boaz is introduced in *Ruth 2:1* as 'a man of standing' who was related to Naomi's deceased husband. Boaz was the landowner onto whose property Ruth 'chanced' (a tongue-in-cheek Heb. way of speaking of divine providence) when she sought a field in which to glean (*Ruth 2:3*). Her location allowed Boaz to become initially her gracious benefactor and eventually opened the way for Ruth to propose a levirate marriage arrangement to Boaz (*Ruth 3–4*).

The stage is set for the movement of the narrative of Ruth by the descriptions of Boaz's family tie to Naomi and his exemplary character. Family members had various responsibilities to each other under the Mosaic Law, including financial support in some cases. The redeeming of the land and the changes in the family relationship, prepare the reader for the shift in perspective in the book's final verses. There attention moves from

Ruth and Boaz to God's wider purposes in history (Ruth 4:17–22).

The phrase translated 'a man of standing' in Ruth 2:1 is almost certainly multi-faceted in both meaning and purpose in the book of Ruth. Though it certainly reflects Boaz's prominence in Bethlehem (see also Ruth 4:1–2), it likely also speaks of his moral and spiritual excellence and perhaps even his recognized courage and honour. In Prov. 31:10 the counterpart to this phrase is used to speak of the excellence of the perfect wife. A similar term was also to refer to King David's 'mighty men', known as valiant warriors (2 Sam. 23:8–39).

In the narrative of Ruth the phrase also closely parallels the description of Ruth in 3:11 as 'a woman of noble character'. The differing translations in English obscure it, but the wording in the Heb. indicates that Boaz (Ruth 2:1) and Ruth (3:11) are a perfect match, from the moral-spiritual standpoint.

This observation is borne out by the interaction between Boaz and Ruth in chapters 2 and 3. In both scenes Ruth takes the initiative, but does so in such a way as greatly to impress Boaz with her character (Ruth 2:11–12; 3:10–11). In the twin scenes Boaz responds with graciousness and generosity well beyond the letter of the Law.

In Ruth 4:1–12 Boaz is required to demonstrate his wisdom and shrewdness in order that the opportunity to consummate the desired levirate marriage with Ruth might come about. He does so, tricking the unnamed kinsman into relinquishing his right to be the kinsman-redeemer for Naomi and Ruth (Ruth 4:3–10). The following marriage of Boaz and Ruth and the birth of their son, Obed, was cause for rejoicing throughout the village of Bethlehem (Ruth 4:11–17).

Obed's birth is also a crucial link in the qualification of David to be king of Israel and of Jesus to be Messiah. Because of his central role in that linkage, and probably also because of his exemplary character, Boaz is accorded the honoured seventh position in the royal genealogy of David in Ruth 4:18–22.

Boaz is merely mentioned in sequence in the family tree of David in 1 Chron. 2:11–12 and the messianic genealogy in Luke 3:32. The version of Christ's lineage in Matt. 1:5 includes not only the name of Ruth and the one placed in the position of Boaz's father, Salmon, but also his presumed mother, Rahab. Although the probability is that one or more generations may be missing from the family tree at this point in order to make the genealogy symmetrical (Matt. 1:17), it is possible that Boaz's mother is the former Canaanite prostitute, Rahab (Josh. 2), thus meaning that Boaz would have both a Gentile mother and a Gentile wife.

**2.** The name of the northern pillar erected in the building of Solomon's Temple by Huram (1 Kings 7:21; 2 Chron. 3:17). The southern pillar was called Jakin. Quite why these names were given is unclear, although it may have something to do with the meaning of the names themselves: Jakin = 'God will establish'; Boaz, see above.

A.B.L.

**BOHAN,** son of Reuben, is mentioned only in connection with 'the Stone of Bohan' (Josh. 15:6; 18:17). The stone was an important boundary marker between Judah and Benjamin. Bohan is not mentioned in the genealogies of Reuben.

**BOKERU,** a Benjamite and the second of six sons of Azel (1 Chron. 8:38; 9:44). He was a descendant of Saul.

**BUKKI 1.** The son of Jogli, this Bukki was the leader of the tribe of Dan and was one of those to whom the LORD instructed Moses to assign the land (Num. 34:22).

**2.** The father of Uzzi and the son of Abishua, he is recorded in the list of Levi's descendants in *1 Chron. 6:5, 51.* Ezra was one of his descendants (*Ezra 7:4*).

**BUKKIAH,** one of the sons of Asaph listed among those set apart for the ministry of prophesying and music during the reign of King David. He was a son of Heman, the king's seer (*1 Chron. 25:4, 13*).

**BUNAH** (Heb., 'intelligence'), a son of Ram and a grandson of Jerahmeel (*1 Chron. 2:25*). He was from the tribe of Judah.

**BUNNI 1.** A Levite who stood on the stairs as the book of the Law was read in *Neh. 9:4.*

**2.** One of the leaders who sealed the agreement of the people to worship the LORD and obey his Law (*Neh. 10:15*).

**3.** The ancestor of Shemaiah, who was one of the Levites who resettled in Jerusalem after the Exile (*Neh. 11:15*).

**BUZ 1.** A son of Milcah and Nahor and a nephew to Abraham. His brother Bethuel became the father of Rebekah (*Gen. 22:21*).

**2.** A man from the tribe of Gad, the father of Jahdo (*1 Chron. 5:14*).

**BUZI,** the father of Ezekiel the prophet and priest. He lived in Babylonia (*Ezek. 1:3*).

# C

**CAESAR** was the name of a dynasty of Roman leaders that began with the Julian family. The most famous Caesar was Caius Julius Caesar (102–44 BC). Octavius was his adopted heir. Caesar Augustus is mentioned in *Luke 2:1*, and Tiberius Caesar in *Luke 3:1*. It was probably Tiberius that the disciples of the Pharisees had in mind when they asked Jesus whether it was right to pay taxes to Caesar (*Matt. 22:17, 21; Mark 12:14, 17 etc.*). Jesus' answer was deliberately distorted by his opponents to the point that they accused Jesus of sedition against the Roman empire (*Luke 23:2*). The attempt by the religious leaders to suggest that Jesus was against Caesar was a determined policy to try to get the Romans to kill or at least imprison him, for to challenge Caesar was to challenge Imperial Rome (*John 19:12, 15*).

When persecuted by the Jews and tried before their courts, the apostle Paul appealed to Caesar and eventually stood trial in Rome (*Acts 25:8, 11–12, 21; 26:32*). The Caesar at the time of his trial would have been Nero, enough to drive fear into anyone. However, an angel of the Lord spoke to Paul telling him not to be afraid (*Acts 27:24*). It is worth noting in *Phil. 4:22* that, at a quite early stage in the life of the church, Paul knew of Christians who were part of 'Caesar's household'. Whether this meant slaves or people of a more senior position or even family members cannot be known. However, we do know that Paul brought the gospel right to the heart of the empire and to the Emperor himself (*2 Tim. 4:16–17*).                    P.D.G.

**CAIAPHAS** From the Jewish historian Josephus we learn that Caiaphas survived in the office of High Priest (a political appointment) for nearly eighteen years (*Ants* xviii. ii). His father-in-law Annas, who was High-Priest before him, seems to have maintained considerable influence throughout the years in which Caiaphas was High Priest. This may account for the strange reference in *Luke 3:2* to the 'high priesthood' (singular) of Annas and Caiaphas. It probably reflects the reality of the political situation, in which Annas may still have been regarded as the power behind the 'throne'.

After Jesus raised Lazarus from the dead, the Jewish authorities met to decide what to do. Seeing the possibility of their power-base being eroded among the people in favour of Jesus, they felt the Romans might clamp down on them and their religion (*John 11:48–53; 18:14*). Caiaphas argued: 'it is better for you that one man die for the people than that the whole nation perish'. Although Caiaphas said this simply for the sake of self-preservation, it was in fact precisely the course that God had in mind for his Son Jesus. Thus John later clearly identified this as a prophecy. *John 11:51–52*: 'He did not say this on his own, but as high priest that year he prophesied that Jesus would die for the Jewish nation, and not only for that nation but also for the scattered children of God, to bring them together and make them one.'

The sovereignty of God in bringing Jesus to the cross to die as the Lamb of God for the sin of the world is a strong theme in John's Gospel (*John 2:29* etc.)

and is further emphasized in this amazing episode. From that time on Caiaphas and the leaders plotted to kill Jesus. It was at Caiaphas' palace that the plot was hatched to arrest Jesus, and he presided in the Sanhedrin when Jesus was brought for trial (*Matt. 26:3, 57*).

In this trial, where witnesses could not agree, it was the High Priest who eventually asked the direct question: 'Are you the Christ, the Son of the Blessed One?' (*Mark 14:61*). Jesus responded 'I am'. At this they condemned him, and a time of torture began that led eventually to the cross.

Caiaphas' antagonism to the Christian faith and his persecution of Christians continued well after Jesus' death (*Acts 4:6, 21; 6:12–13* etc.). See *Annas*.  P.D.G.

**CAIN** was Adam and Eve's first son. His name is linked by his mother to her exclamation of thanks to the LORD 'With the help of the LORD I have brought forth a man' (*Gen. 4:1*). Cain 'worked the soil', unlike his brother Abel, who was a shepherd (*vv. 2–3*). As time went on both Cain and Abel brought 'offerings' to God. Cain brought some of the fruits of the soil and Abel brought 'fat portions from some of the firstborn of his flock' (*vv. 3–4*). 'The LORD looked with favour on Abel and his offering' but did not do so on Cain's. The text does not indicate why God distinguished in this way between the two offerings. Some have suggested that perhaps even by this early stage God had revealed to Adam and Eve that a blood sacrifice would be necessary in order to come before God, but it is rather more profitable to see what the text itself emphasizes.

*Gen. 4* examines Cain's behaviour following this rejection by God. Cain was angry and depressed (*v. 5*). God spoke to Cain challenging him about this reaction and pointing out that his offering would be acceptable if he did 'what is right'. The implication of God's comments with his mention of 'sin . . . crouching at your door . . . you must master it' (*v. 7*) is that the one who looks on the heart knew that Cain's heart was sinful. Cain's subsequent action confirms that impression. He was angry against both God and his brother. This understanding of Cain's problem is supported in *Heb. 11:4* where the writer distinguishes between Cain and Abel on the grounds of the faith that Abel showed.

Cain asked his brother to accompany him to a field, where he killed him. When God asked Cain what had happened to Abel he replied with the famous statement: 'I don't know. Am I my brother's keeper?' (*Gen. 4:9*). Cain was then condemned by God to be 'a restless wanderer on the earth' (*v. 12*). In order to protect Cain as he wandered the earth, God gave him some sort of mark so that he would not be killed, perhaps by the descendants of Abel. Cain then went to the land of Nod, that is, he 'wandered the land' east of Eden.

Cain and his wife gave birth to Enoch and became the ancestor of peoples who were nomads, those who played musical instruments, and others who worked with bronze and iron (*Gen. 4:17–22*). The contrast between this account of Cain (*Gen. 4*) and the account of Seth (*Gen. 5*) is significant. Seth was born to Adam and Eve after the death of Abel and, for them, took Abel's place (*Gen. 4:25–26*). Seth's descendants proved to be those who remained faithful to God while Cain's did not. Noah was a descendant of Seth. See *Lamech, Seth, Noah*.

Later generations are asked to remember Cain and learn from his sin and jealousy and lack of faith (*Heb. 11:4; 1 John 3:12; Jude 11*).  P.D.G.

**CAINAN 1.** The father of Shelah and the son of Arphaxad, he is listed in the genealogy that traces Jesus back to Adam in *Luke 3:36*. He is missing from the list in *Gen. 10*.

**CALCOL** **1.** As one of the sons of Mahol, he was renowned for his wisdom. Solomon's wisdom was greater by comparison, which is why we encounter Calcol in the text of *1 Kings 4:31*. In response to his request of God (*v. 29*), Solomon was given such extraordinary wisdom that it outshone even those known for wisdom in his day.

**2.** In *1 Chron. 2:6* he is listed as a son of Zerah and a descendant of Judah. He was probably the same person as 1.

**CALEB** **1.** Caleb, from the tribe of Judah, was the son of Jephunneh the Kenizzite. Moses asked him to represent his tribe in spying out the land of Canaan (*Num. 13:6*). This he did with twelve others. The land they saw was very fertile. They came back with large bunches of grapes and great reports of the land's wealth and prosperity. However, the land was found to be occupied by some fearful people, especially the descendants of the giant Anak, who lived around Hebron. Ten of the spies came back so disillusioned and so convinced they could never win in battle against these people that they turned on Moses. The Israelites, on hearing this, argued that they would have been better off back in Egypt (*Num. 13:26–29; 13:31–14:4*).

Of all the spies, only Caleb and Joshua had sufficient faith in God to know that he could enable them to take the land of Canaan. First they gave an alternative report to Moses, and then they appealed to the people. Their complete trust in the sovereign power of God is proclaimed aloud to the people in their speech: 'If the LORD is pleased with us, he will lead us into that land, a land flowing with milk and honey, and will give it to us. Only do not rebel against the LORD. And do not be afraid of the people . . . Their protection is gone, but the LORD is with us' (*Num. 14:7–9*).

As a judgment on the people for their lack of faith, that whole generation was never allowed to enter Canaan, but rather spent the time 'wandering' in the wilderness (*Num. 14:22–23; 26:65*). Only Caleb and Joshua were allowed to live long enough to enter the land, and both had a very significant part in the battles to take Canaan many years later (*Num. 14:24, 30*). It is of particular significance that Caleb, who so many years before had believed that the LORD would destroy the Anakites, was the leader of the attack on the Hebron area. He personally led the forces that defeated the giants, and as a result he was later given that area as an inheritance by Joshua (*Josh. 14:6–15; 15:13–14*). Caleb offered his daughter Acsah in marriage to the man who would conquer Kiriath-sepher (Debir) for him. Othniel, Caleb's nephew, did this and so married her (*Josh. 15:16–18*). His sons are listed in *1 Chron. 4:15*.

Caleb's 'wholehearted faith' (*Josh. 14:14; Deut 1:36* etc.) became an example for future generations. This faith issued in a practical and calm reliance upon the LORD God as the one who was all-powerful and whose will could not be thwarted. To believe this would be one thing, but to act on it in the face of such adversaries was of the essence of the true faith which Caleb demonstrated and from which all can learn.

**2.** This Caleb was the brother of Jerahmeel and the son of Hezron. He was of the tribe of Judah and married to Azubah. When she died he married Ephrath, by whom he had a son called Hur. His other sons were Mesha and Mareshah (*1 Chron. 2:9, 18–19, 42, 50*). Hur's grandson Bezalel was a craftsman who worked on the Tabernacle.    P.D.G.

**CANAAN** was the son of Ham and grandson of Noah (*Gen. 9:18, 22; 10:6*). Following some particularly sad and evil sexual sin involving a drunken Noah and his son Ham, Noah cursed Ham's son Canaan and, by contrast, blessed Shem (*Gen. 9:25–27*). As time progressed it was

Shem's line from which Abraham and eventually the Israelites came, while Canaan's descendants became the tribes that caused Israel so many problems and were frequently defeated in battle by Israel: the Hittites, Amorites, etc. (*Gen. 10:15–18*). The land that was later called 'Canaan' was occupied by tribes like the Amorites, and this may have been the derivation of the name.

**CANDACE,** the official title of the queens, or queen mothers, of Ethiopia. She is mentioned in *Acts 8:27*, when one of her treasury officials returning home after worshipping in Jerusalem, encountered Philip the Evangelist. She may have been Amaniterer, who was a ruler between about AD 25–41. Philip spoke of Christ to the Ethiopian, who was converted and baptized immediately. See *Ethiopian Eunuch.*

**CARCAS,** one of seven eunuchs who served King Xerxes (*Est. 1:10*). See *Vashti.*

**CARITES** These were mercenary troops in Jehoiada's army, although the derivation of the name is far from clear. They are to be regarded as a group, rather like the Hittites, but where they came from we cannot be sure (*2 Kings 11:4, 19*). They were probably the same as the Kerethites, who seem to have owned an area of land by the sea (*Zeph. 2:6; 1 Sam. 30:14*, see also *2 Sam. 15:18; 20:23* etc.).

**CARMI 1.** A son of Reuben who went to Egypt with Jacob (*Gen. 46:9*). He was a leader of the Carmite clan (*Exod. 6:14; Num. 26:6; 1 Chron. 5:3*).
**2.** From the tribe of Judah, he was the father of Achan. Achan disobeyed God and took spoils from the battle of Jericho for himself. God punished him with death (*Josh. 7:1, 18; 1 Chron. 2:7; 4:1*).

**CARSHENA,** a wise man and legal expert consulted by King Xerxes (*Est. 1:14*). For details see *Memucan.*

**CASTOR AND POLLUX** Known as the Dioscuri (sons of Zeus), these twin gods of mythology were patrons of sailors, and hence would regularly have figured on boats. In *Acts 28:11* we read that Paul had sailed from Malta on an Alexandrian ship that carried this figurehead.

**CENTURIONS** A centurion was a Roman military commander of a division of 100 men. Several appear in the Gospels and Acts.
**1.** *Matt. 8:5–13* and *Luke 7:1–10* both describe a centurion who requested Jesus to heal a paralysed servant. This man trusted that Christ could give orders to heal, just as he commanded his soldiers. The man's faith provoked both a miracle of healing and praise from Jesus. Matthew stresses that Gentiles with such faith will replace faithless Israelites in the kingdom (*Matt. 8:11–12*). Luke stresses that the man was worthy of Jesus' help, having loved the Jewish people and helped to build their synagogue in Capernaum (*Luke 7:4–5*).
**2.** A second centurion figures prominently in the crucifixion narrative. Standing guard by Jesus' cross and watching how he died, this man exclaimed, 'Surely he was the Son of God' (*Matt. 27:54; Mark 15:39*) or 'Surely this was a righteous man' (*Luke 23:47*). For a pagan, the title 'Son of God' would naturally refer to a righteous man deified upon his death. This same centurion also reported to Pilate that Christ had died (*John 19:44–45*).
**3.** In *Acts* several centurions figure in the accounts of Paul's imprisonments and trials. In *Acts 21:32*, they helped save Paul from the riotous crowds in Jerusalem. In *Acts 22:25–26*, they prevented him from being flogged, since he was a Roman citizen. In *Acts 23:17–23*, two

centurions helped thwart a plot to ambush Paul and kill him. Each of these actions fits Luke's interest in showing Rome as giving legal protection to Christianity in its early years. In *Acts 24:23*, a centurion kept Paul under guard in Caesarea. Throughout *Acts 27*, Julius, a centurion of the Imperial Regiment, was in charge of the prisoners, including Paul, on the ill-fated sea voyage to Rome (see *Julius*).

**4.** Perhaps the most famous and important centurion in the Bible is Cornelius. *Acts 10* tells the story of his conversion, and *Acts 11:1–18* finds Peter narrating it a second time for the Jewish Christians in Jerusalem. This event played a large role in the transformation of early Christianity from an exclusively Jewish sect to a multi-ethnic religion. Cornelius 'fears God' (*Acts 10:2*), which may imply that he kept all of the Jewish laws except circumcision. One day, God revealed to him in a vision that he was to find the apostle Peter, who had a message for him. Simultaneously, God gave Peter a vision that no foods were any longer 'unclean'. When Cornelius arrived at Peter's lodgings in Joppa, Peter 'put two and two together': clean foods make for clean people (*Acts 10:34*), since the Gentiles' eating habits were the major barrier to fellowship with Jews. Peter thus began to preach the gospel to Cornelius. In the middle of his sermon, at the very moment when Peter was preaching about repentance, Cornelius and his companions began to speak in tongues. Peter recognized this as a sign of their belief and of the arrival of the Holy Spirit, and so proceeded to baptize them in water. The Christian mission to the Gentiles had begun in earnest.                      C.B.

**CEPHAS** (Aram., 'rock'), the name given to Simon son of John by Jesus (*John 1:42*). He is usually referred to as Peter (Petros is the Gk. translation of Cephas). The apostle Paul sometimes calls him Cephas rather than Peter (e.g. *1 Cor. 1:12; 3:22; 9:5*). See *Peter*.

**CHALDEANS,** the name given to the people who lived in the area that came to be known as the kingdom of Babylon. It was originally the name of a district of Babylonia. The original tribal land referred to the marshlands which in modern days are often associated with the 'Marsh Arabs' – that area of land at the north of the Persian Gulf which now divides Iraq and Iran. Later Babylonian cuneiform texts call the inhabitants of these 'Sealands' the Kaldai. Abraham's father came from 'Ur of the Chaldeans' (*Gen. 11:28–31; 15:7* etc.). In Daniel, Ezekiel and Ezra the word becomes a synonym for Babylonians. The tradition of their great learning survives (e.g. *Dan. 1:4*, trans. 'Babylonians' in NIV; *Ezra 5:12; Ezek. 12:13; 23:23*).

**CHEMOSH,** the god worshipped by the Moabites. Human sacrifices were part of the cult (see *2 Kings 3:27*, where the king of Moab sacrificed his own son in an attempt to win a battle over the Israelites). Time and again the Israelites were warned to have nothing to do with foreign gods, and this god was seen to be one of the most vile (*2 Kings 23:13*). Curses are pronounced upon the people of Moab and their god (*Num. 21:29*), and yet still the Israelites from time to time began to worship this god.

The most dreadful example of this was to be found in Solomon's reign, which had started out so well with his faithfulness to the LORD. However, Solomon's various marriages, many of which probably took place as part of diplomatic moves to establish good relations with neighbours, led to his wives taking him away from worship of the LORD and towards their own gods. As he grew older his heart was no longer devoted to the LORD, and he even set up an altar on a hill to the east of Jerusalem for Chemosh

(1 Kings 11:7). Such sin led the LORD to bring punishment on the nation and eventually caused the kingdom to be divided (1 Kings 11:29–33).

It was not until the covenant renewal under Josiah that we are specifically told that these 'high places' of Chemosh were destroyed (2 Kings 23:13). Later, the prophet Jeremiah warned Moab of impending judgment on them and their god Chemosh (Jer. 48:7, 13, 46).

The danger of syncretism and idolatry was an ever-present problem for the Israelites as they tried to live peacefully among the nations. Throughout Scripture there are appeals to men and women who have faith in the LORD to be 'holy', separated from such idolatry. The gods may be different, but the problem remains as acute for modern Christians as it was for the Israelites.　　P.D.G.

## CHILDREN IN THE BIBLE

Children are frequently referred to in the Bible, and are an important element in the biblical picture of the godly family and the people of God as a larger unit. The perspective of the biblical writers, however, is not identical to that of contemporary Western society.

In general, in ancient Israel, as in most ancient societies, children were viewed as highly desirable. This was particularly true of male children. Most peoples saw their birth and growth as a guarantee of a work-force and protection from those outside the extended family unit. In Israel, they were regularly seen as a blessing from God (Gen. 15:2–5; Pss. 127:3–5; 128:2–3). They were the fulfilment of God's promise of covenant blessing to his people and at the same time the fulfilment of humanity's responsibility to 'Be fruitful and increase in number', to 'fill the earth and subdue it' (Gen. 1:28). Infanticide and abortion, though practised by other peoples, were not approved in the Bible.

The blessing of God is not merely seen in the birth of children, but in the maintenance of godly descendants from one generation to the next. God's blessing is not limited by the changing events of historical circumstances. His promise extends to the children's children (Pss. 103:17). The blessing of children is one way through which God's rule is extended through history. The passage of time does not vitiate the work of God to bless his people. God continues to call his people to repentance and loving service, and promises that his Spirit and his Word will not depart from the generations which are yet unborn (Is. 59:21).

From their earliest days, children were members of the cultus of ancient Israel. In a special sense the firstborn belonged to God (Num. 3:40–51), but in fact all were God's. Often children were given names which focused attention on God's care for the family or for the head of the family. Abijah (1 Sam. 8:2) means 'Yah(weh) is my Father'. Abihud (1 Chron. 8:3) means 'My father of praise'. Ahimelech means 'my brother (God) a king' (1 Sam. 21:1). (See also Gen. 29:32, 35 et al.). Male children were circumcised on the eighth day (Gen. 17:12). This was their symbolic entrance into the community of Israel, the people of God. Some children were dedicated to particular service in God's name by their parents (1 Sam. 1:11; Luke 1:76–79).

The promise of God's blessing was not a promise made in a vacuum. It came with commandments to raise children according to God's ways (Prov. 22:6). Because

God was the Creator of all things and his ways for his people touched on every area of life, there was no secular/sacred distinction in the training of children. Godly training involved all of life.

Parents were responsible for their children's education. They were to teach their children the mighty acts of God by which he had delivered them from Egypt and called them together to receive his word at Sinai (*Deut. 4:9–10*). As God continued to bless his people, the history of God's covenant faithfulness grew and the subject-matter of the education of the children took on new dimensions (*Josh. 4:21–24*; *2 Tim. 3:15*).

The training of children was not merely didactic. Parents nurtured their children by including them in the worship of God (*1 Sam. 1:4, 22–24*). From an early age they observed their parents participating in the rites of the Temple.

The nurture of children, however, went beyond teaching and modelling. Children also were to be disciplined. There was no naive optimism which saw children as innocent by nature. 'Every inclination of his heart is evil from childhood' (*Gen. 8:21*). 'Even from birth the wicked go astray; from the womb they are wayward and speak lies' (*Pss. 58:3*). Stories are told in the OT of disrespectful, selfish children (*2 Kings 2:23*). The Bible gives a very realistic picture of children. They need discipline; and parents are called on to supply that discipline. 'Folly is bound up in the heart of a child but the rod of discipline will drive it far from him' (*Prov. 22:15*). Children do not always obey the law of God. High demands are placed upon them. 'Honour your father and your mother' (*Exod. 20:12*; also *Eph. 6:1–3*; *Col. 3:20*). They do not, however, automatically fulfil those obligations. They need to be disciplined.

Children, however, do not need heavy-handed, unloving discipline. Fathers are clearly told not to 'exasperate' their children (*Eph. 6:4*) or to 'embitter' them (*Col. 3:21*). Instead, fathers are expected to give good gifts to their children (*Matt. 7:11*).

In all of this, children are seen as persons, not possessions; they are gifts from God to be nurtured and dedicated to his service. They are members of God's people. No one could make this much more clear than Jesus did in *Mark 10:14*: 'Let the little children come to me, and do not hinder them, for the kingdom of God belongs to such as these.' It is widely recognized that Jesus was using the children to make the theological point that his adult disciples must receive God's Kingdom and live with each other in gentleness and humility, rejoicing in God's grace. One must not, however, miss the point that Jesus really did receive the children. Children who rest in Jesus' arms are members (not just potential members) of the Kingdom of God. Similarly in *Matt. 21:15–16*, in the Temple after Jesus' triumphal entry, it is the children who are singled out as singing his praise, 'Hosanna to the Son of David'.

Since Jewish boys were circumcised as a sign of their membership in the covenant community, and since the children of Jewish proselytes were baptized, so also many understand children as involved in the household baptisms (signifying their membership in the new covenant community) of the early church (*Acts 16:15, 33*; *1 Cor. 1:16*).

In addition to stressing that children are members of God's Kingdom, texts such as *Mark 10:14* introduce the nuance that children are weak and dependent. They are among the groups in society which can be taken advantage of. They do not control their own destiny. This is why they are sometimes described along with their mothers as 'widows and fatherless' (*Is. 1:23; 10:2; Ps. 94:6*). Without a father to care for and protect them, they are helpless and at the mercy of others. In the patriarchal society of the ancient Mediterranean world there were no guarantees of nurture and provision for children except a father. Injustice was a daily threat for orphaned children. That is why God in grace is declared to be the 'father of the fatherless' (*Ps. 68:5*). Similarly, those whose religion is pure are described as those who visit orphans in their affliction (*James 1:27*). Not only God but also God's people care for children who have no protector or provider in their society.

The words 'child' and 'son' are also used metaphorically in the Bible. The inhabitants of Jerusalem are referred to as her 'children' (*Matt. 23:37; Gal. 4:25*). In this sense, 'children' has a meaning similar to the interchangeable expressions 'Abraham's children' (*John 8:39*), 'children of Abraham' (*Gal. 3:7*), 'Abraham's descendants' (*John 8:37; Gal. 3:16*) and 'children of Israel' (*Deut. 1:3*). Unfortunately some translators drop the reference to 'children' from such verses.

It is only a small step from this usage to the description of the covenant community as a family with God, not Abraham, as its Father. In the NT this usage is much more highly developed than in the OT. Not only is God the Father, but Jesus is the Son of God, and those who believe in him are children of God (*John 1:12*). The church is the household (or family) of God (*1 Tim. 3:15*). Other Christians are 'brothers' in Christ.

As 'children of God', God's people confess their weakness and humble dependence on the Father for all their needs, and in confidence rest in his loving provision and protection (*Matt. 6:26, 32; 7:11; 10:29, 32–33*). To be God's child commits one to doing the Father's will (*Matt. 12:48–50; 5:44–48; 7:21*) and living among God's other children, demonstrating the familial traits of humility, love and concern (*Eph. 5:1ff.*). The children mirror their Father.

The metaphor 'children' is used in a negative sense in phrases such as 'offspring of liars' (*Is. 57–4*), 'children of wrath' (*Eph. 2:3*, where it is obscured by the NIV translation, 'objects of wrath') and 'children of the devil' (*1 John 3:10*).

The words 'child', 'children' and 'son' are also used by teachers and writers to address their students and readers. The book of Proverbs makes extensive use of the figure in the phrase, 'My son' (notice the first verse of *Prov. 2–7*). In *1 John 2:1* the endearing phrase 'My dear children' is used in much the same sense. Paul (*Philem. 10*), the writer of Ecclesiastes (*Eccl. 12:12*) and Jesus (*Mark 2:5*) all use similar expressions.

A.M.

**CHLOE** (Heb., 'green grass'). Members of this woman's household brought Paul information regarding the state of the church in Corinth (*1 Cor. 1:11*). She may well have been a Christian herself and may have sent some of her slaves or household stewards to speak to Paul. Certainly, there were many wealthy women in the Roman empire who ran businesses and would have had their own workers. She reported that there were quarrels among the Corinthian Christians. They seemed to be worried about status, and therefore claimed to follow different church leaders, thus forming cliques or even divisions. Nothing is known of Chloe herself.

**CHRIST** (For the main article see *Jesus and Lord*). The name 'Christ', designating

Jesus, is used numerous times in the NT. The combined name 'Jesus Christ' occurs only five times in the Gospels but in the rest of the NT becomes a main designation used of Jesus (127 times). In places the name 'Christ' seems to have become little more than a surname for Jesus. However, to assume the name never means more than that is to miss much of the NT message about Jesus.

**Background.** The name Christ comes from an OT background. The Greek word *Christos*, derived from the Greek verb meaning 'to anoint', was used to translate the Heb. word *mashiach* which meant 'the anointed'. The word in Heb. described different people who had been anointed (usually with oil) for their tasks. In *Exod. 28:41* the priest was 'the anointed one' and the prophet Elisha was 'anointed' for his job (1 *Kings 19:16*). Other prophets are called 'the anointed ones' (1 *Chron. 16:22*). Even Cyrus, the king of Persia, could be referred to as God's 'anointed one' (*mashiach, Is. 45:1*). But it was the use of the concept of anointing for the *king* that provides the main background for 'Christ' being used in the NT.

Saul and David were 'anointed' as God's choice for king (1 *Sam 10:1; 16:13*), so that soon in many contexts reference to 'the Lord's anointed' became a synonym for the king (e.g. 1 *Sam. 16:13; 24:6, 10; 26:9, 11, 16; 26:23; 2 Chron. 6:42; Pss. 2:2; 18:50; Dan. 9:25–26*).

**Christ, son of David.** In the NT one of the most important statements about who Jesus is is that he is the expected son of David, the inheritor of David's kingdom: the Christ (Messiah). Although the OT rarely referred to the coming Davidic king as 'the Messiah', early followers of Christ quickly put two and two together as they heard Jesus speak and saw what he did. They recognized Jesus as one born in the line of David and who was indeed 'king of the Jews' (*Matt. 1:17; 2:2; 27:11, 29, 37; Mark 15:9, 12, 26* etc.). Stephen's prayer

as he faced death pulled together the OT background centred on promises to King David and applied it to Jesus directly (*Acts 4:25–27*).

But even during Jesus' lifetime this link between David and Jesus and the name Christ was well established. The heavenly choir sang of it to the angels (*Luke 2:11*). The Magi asked where the 'king' was to be found and Herod's priests were then asked where the 'Christ' was to be born (*Matt. 2:4–6*). As people saw the miracles Jesus did and heard his words, they identified him as the 'son of David' (*Matt. 12:23; 20:30; John 7:41–42*). Jesus himself prompted thoughts in this direction (*Matt. 22:42; Mark 12:35* etc.).

In Paul's writing it is almost inconceivable that he was not specifically thinking of this background on some occasions when he referred to 'Christ' or 'Christ Jesus'. For example, in *Rom. 1:1–4*, Paul called himself a 'servant of Christ Jesus' and then made a point of Jesus' descent from David (see also 2 *Tim. 2:8*).

**Jewish expectations.** The expectations of the Messiah in the days of Jesus were diverse, but Jesus' self-understanding of his messianic role did not fit any contemporary ideas. It appears that, with the rise of Jewish nationalism since the days of the Macabbees, many Jews longed for a victorious king of David's stature who would come and defeat the Roman overlords. But others probably looked for one who would be wise and demonstrate the wisdom of God's Spirit on him as Solomon had. Others dwelt upon the idea that he would introduce the 'last days'. But uniformly they would have seen him as having some kingly political role.

**Jesus, the Christ.** Jesus, on the other hand, interpreted the concept of Messiah in his own very special way. This may have been the reason why he seems to have been reluctant actually to use the name 'Christ' of himself (although he never denied the title). Jesus did not want his role and work to be confused with the contemporary views of Jewish nationalism about a warrior king Messiah. Perhaps this is why Jesus frequently used the term 'son of Man' of himself – a term that did not have such political overtones and which he could fill with the message of a Messiah who would have to suffer and die. It is interesting that immediately after Peter's confession in *Mark 8:29* in which he said to Jesus: 'You are the Christ', Jesus 'then began to teach them that the son of Man must suffer many things and be rejected by the elders, chief priests and teachers of the law, and that he must be killed and after three days rise again' (*Mark 8:31*).

No doubt it was also true that Jesus was reluctant to talk of himself as the Messiah until he had completed the work of the Messiah. People came gradually to acknowledge his messiahship as they witnessed his words and works, but above all after he had been raised from the dead.

**Christian belief.** Although the name 'Christ' gradually came to have little more significance than another name for Jesus, Christians know its original meaning is vital to a full understanding of the person of Jesus. It has always been one of the most important and fundamental tenets of the Christian faith that Jesus fulfilled God's promises in the OT. He is the long-awaited king who rules on David's throne forever, who was God's 'anointed' like David, and who would know God's Spirit and God's wisdom in his dominion and rule. As Jesus himself continued to teach about this role and live it out, and as this role was confirmed in his death, resurrection and ascension, so it became clear that his suffering was integral to his Messiahship. The one and only true Messiah suffered and died for his people so that, through faith in him as their King and Lord, they might be saved (*Is. 53; Mark 10:45; Luke 24:46; Acts 3:18; 17:3*).     P.D.G.

**CHRISTIANS** This name is actually very rare in the NT. It appears twice in *Acts* (*11:26; 26:28*) and once in *1 Peter* (*4:16*). *Acts 11:26* notes that the new community of believers in Jesus were first called Christians in Antioch. Apparently the name was a nickname given to them by outsiders to the group in that city. Herod Agrippa was aware of the name, according to *Acts 26:28*, so that it is clear that the name stuck and reached to the highest social levels as a way to refer to believers. *1 Peter* indicates that to suffer as a Christian, one should not be ashamed but should praise God that one is accounted worthy to suffer for that name (e.g. *Acts 4:24–31*). Thus it is clear that originally the name may have been a term of derision that outsiders used to taunt believers, a reflection of the world's rejection of Jesus. The church turned around this original use and made the name 'Christian' a badge of honour, since to be called by that name identified one with Jesus, the Christ.

D.B.

**CHUZA,** the manager of Herod's household. He is introduced into the narrative of *Luke* (*8:3*) because he was the husband of Joanna, one of the women who were helping to support Jesus and his twelve disciples 'out of their own means'. She may have had independent finances or her husband may have been sympathetic, but the mention of Chuza may partly be in order to emphasize that these were women from wealthy households. Certainly it is a common fiction these days that only the poor were attracted by Jesus' ministry. In some editions of the NIV this person is called Cuza.

**CLAUDIA,** one of Paul's friends who sent greetings to Timothy at the end of Paul's second letter to him (*2 Tim. 4:21*). Paul was writing from prison in Rome and mentions Pudens, Linus and 'all the brothers' as also sending these greetings.

It is just possible that Claudia was Pudens' wife. Whether she can be identified with the Claudia Quinctilla, wife of Claudius Pudens who, not far from Rome erected an inscription in memory of their infant son, is highly debatable.

**CLAUDIUS 1.** The fourth Roman emperor (AD 41–54). He succeeded Caligula, who had earlier made him a consul. Caligula had deeply offended Jews by having a statue of himself placed in the Temple at Jerusalem. However, Claudius pursued a more open and accepting policy to the religions and peoples of the empire. Herod Agrippa I was appointed ruler over a large area by Claudius in return for favours.

In the NT this emperor is mentioned twice. In *Acts 11:28* Luke established the historical fulfilment of Agabus' prophecy of a severe famine in the Roman world by reference to its having happened during the reign of Claudius. Then in *Acts 18:2* we read of Paul meeting Aquila and Priscilla in Corinth. They had recently come from Rome because 'Claudius had ordered all the Jews to leave Rome'. While he had been favourable to Jews elsewhere in the empire, it seems their great numbers in Rome had caused him problems and *c.* AD 49 they were either expelled or forbidden to gather together.

**2.** Claudius Lysias was a Roman tribune who was in charge of the garrison in Jerusalem at the time of Paul's arrest (*Acts 23:26*). He probably spoke Greek and initially seemed to know nothing of the disputes between Paul and the Jews (see *Acts 21:37–39*). However, he allowed Paul to address the crowd until the crowd, on hearing Paul's claim to a commission to preach to the Gentiles, called for his death. In the conversation that followed Claudius revealed that he had bought his Roman citizenship, while Paul's was by birth. After Paul's arrest, some Jews plotted to kill him, so Claudius stepped in and sent Paul under guard to be examined by Governor Felix at Caesarea. His letter (*Acts 23:27–30*) that accompanied Paul was fair and indicated his desire to see proper justice carried through.　　　　　　　　P.D.G.

**CLEMENT,** a Christian in the church at Philippi who is mentioned only in *Phil. 4:3*. He was one of Paul's 'fellow-workers' who, presumably, had helped in founding the Philippian church.

**CLEOPAS** Mentioned only in *Luke 24:18*, Cleopas was one of the disciples to whom Jesus spoke after his resurrection as he joined them on their walk to Emmaus. Initially they were surprised that he seemed to know nothing of the recent happenings in Jerusalem in which Jesus had been crucified. These disciples were very despondent. In *Luke 24:19–21* they reveal their limited understanding of Jesus. They had known him to be 'a prophet, powerful in word and deed before God and all the people', but they had not expected his death in this way. They had hoped that he would be the promised Redeemer of Israel. No doubt they had little more than a vague idea of what that might entail, but probably they thought in terms of freedom from Rome at least.

Then Jesus began to open up the Scriptures for them in such a way that he showed how everything that had happened in the previous few days was a necessary fulfilment of Scripture. Effectively these disciples were given one of the greatest sermons, replete with biblical theology, that anyone could have wished for! One of the most common modern misunderstandings of the Christian faith, both from without and within, is just how important the OT is in informing Christians about Jesus and his death and sacrifice on the cross. Speaking to faithful Jews, Jesus worked right through from the Law (*Genesis to Deuteronomy*) into the prophets to show that it was actually necessary for the Christ (Messiah) to suffer and die (*Luke 24:25–27*).

This picture of a Messiah who died for his people was not one that the Jews were expecting. Here Jesus was deliberately changing those expectations and showing that his Messiahship was in accordance with Scripture, even if not with the current theological understanding. The necessity of Jesus, the Messiah, to come to die for his people and thus redeem them from their sin has become a foundation-stone of classical Christianity. Later the apostle Paul talked of knowing nothing but Christ 'and him crucified' (*1 Cor. 2:2*). In the crucifixion lay redemption and the forgiveness of sin. This, no doubt, was what Cleopas learned that day.     P.D.G.

**CLOPAS,** the husband of Mary, Jesus' aunt (*John 19:25*). She was one of the women who stood at the foot of the cross.

**COL-HOZEH 1.** The father of Shallun, who repaired the Fountain Gate during the rebuilding of the walls of Jerusalem following the return from the Exile (*Neh. 3:15*).

**2.** The ancestor of Maaseiah, who was one of the descendants of Judah who resettled in Jerusalem following the Exile (*Neh. 11:5*). He was possibly the same person as 1.

**CONANIAH 1.** A Levite who supervised the Temple offerings during the time of King Hezekiah of Judah. As a result of the extraordinary revival under Hezekiah, so many offerings, gifts and tithes were brought to the Temple that special storehouses had to be prepared and a team of men were appointed to handle the goods. Conaniah was in charge of this team (*2 Chron. 31:12–13*). His brother Shimei helped him in the task.

**2.** A Levite (no doubt a descendant of 1.) who, along with his brothers Shemaiah and Nethanel and other leaders of the Levites, did a very similar job in the time of King Josiah during the great Passover celebration (*2 Chron. 35:9*). It is interesting to note how profuse and abundant were the offerings that were brought to the Temple on both these occasions of revival.

**CORNELIUS** was a centurion in the Italian Regiment of the Roman army. He was the first Gentile convert and his conversion is recorded in *Acts 10*. For detail see Centurion 4.

**COSAM** is mentioned in Luke's genealogy leading from Adam to Jesus (*Luke 3:28*). He was the son of Elmadam and the father of Addi.

## COVENANT

As we study the people of the Bible it is important to understand not just their social, geographical, and historical context, but also their spiritual and theological situation. Any discussion of these people in their theological setting must bear in mind God's dealings with his people as a covenant people. The word 'covenant' is a special designation for the relationship that God graciously established and whereby he has maintained a relationship with sinful and frail humans from generation to generation. The OT speaks of several such commitments. These come together under one umbrella in the 'new covenant' confirmed in the sacrificial death of the Lord Jesus Christ. All of God's covenants in the Bible are gracious in nature. The covenants of grace are conveniently divided into two eras: the era of the Old Covenant and the era of the New Covenant.

# The Old Covenant

The Old Covenant (OC) is the sovereign administration of promise and blessing by which the LORD God consecrated Israel as his people under the sanctions of his royal law. It is a good covenant and preparatory to the New Covenant (NC). The excellence of the NC can be better appreciated when studied in the light of the OC.

## Covenant in the Ancient Near East

The etymology of the Heb. word for covenant, b$^e$rît, is uncertain. Several proposals have been suggested, but so far none of them have received a general acceptance. The practice of covenant making is well known, however. The Hittites had a well-developed form which included some six parts: (i) preamble (introduction of the parties); (ii) historical prologue (background of the past relations); (iii) stipulations; (iv) preservation (details on where the document was to be kept and when it was to be read); (v) list of witnesses (often gods in the Ancient Near East [ANE]); and (vi) a list of blessings and curses. While the form of the covenant formula differed among the nations, it is an indisputable fact that the covenant concept is rooted in the legal practices of the ANE.

The word 'covenant' can be applied to the relationship between equals (parity covenant, for example, the covenant between Jonathan and David) and between a king/lord (suzerain) and his vassal (suzerainty covenant). The covenant relationship involved privileges and responsibilities. It ensured the parties involved of mutual commitment and protection by mutual observance of agreed upon stipulations. The formal occasion of the acceptance of the terms of the covenant was often accompanied by the ritual of slaughtering an animal. As the sacrificial animal was being dismembered, one or both parties submitted themselves to the curse of being dismembered at the infringement of the terms of the covenant.

## Covenant as metaphor

The biblical concept of covenant must be viewed against the background of the ANE. God took a common legal practice and used it to define the relationship between himself and his people. As such the covenant is a way of speaking or a metaphor of God's fellowship with humans. This metaphor is rich and variegated in the Bible as the covenant defines the relationship between the parties, delineates the terms (privileges and obligations), enforces allegiance to the LORD (blessings and curses), contextualizes the relationship with another generation (renewal ceremony), and transforms it (OC into the NC; family/national to a universal covenant).

## The covenant with Creation

The background of the OC is found in the two prior covenants: the covenant with Creation and the covenant with Abraham. At creation the LORD made a commitment with all of life, including humans. Though the covenant terminology is not formally used in Gen. 1–2, the idea is implicit. It is made explicit in the Flood narrative in which the LORD promised Noah that he would confirm the covenant, despite the destructive flood: 'But I will establish my covenant with you' (Gen. 6:18; cf. Hos. 2:18; Is. 54:9). After the Flood, the LORD confirmed it in the Noahic covenant, according to which he promised to preserve life upon the earth (Gen. 9:8–17), while making humans accountable for their preservation of life on earth (vv. 4–6).

### Abrahamic Covenant

**Promise and blessing.** The basis of the OC is the covenant with Abraham according to which God promised to be with Abraham, to increase his family, to be with his offspring, to protect them in the land of Canaan, and to make them a source of blessing to the nations (Gen. 12:2–3). The Great King promised to protect and to deliver his subjects (Gen. 15:1; 17). The promise of his being-with humans as the Immanuel ('God is with us') was not novel in the history of redemption. After all, he had promised to protect Cain (Gen. 4:15). What was new was that the LORD bound himself to a family to be the Protector of that family. The promise of his protection is further augmented by the promise of his blessing. As the promise was God's word to deliver his people, the blessing was his promise to ensure their prosperity, happiness, and security.

Both promises and blessings were incorporated in the Abrahamic covenant (Gen. 15; 17). The covenant was initially made between Abraham and the LORD in a solemn ceremony involving a ritual slaughter (Gen. 15). The LORD walked between the sacrificial animals so as to guarantee that the fulfilment of the conditions of the covenant was his. The promises and blessings were restated and elaborated in a confirmation of the covenant shortly before the birth of Isaac (Gen. 17).

**Renewal.** God's protection goes beyond the individual. The LORD confirmed the promises and covenant with Isaac and Jacob because he was true to his promise of being with the offspring of Abraham. Israel came to know him as the trans-generational God, 'the God of Abraham, Isaac, and Jacob' (Exod. 3:6). As God renewed his covenant with each new generation, so he wanted Israel to renew the covenant. The renewal was important in the history of redemption as the participants share in the historical identification with a legacy and an invitation to participate. The LORD opened up the privileges of the covenant to all physical descendants of Abraham. Yet, implicit in the covenant heritage was also the promise that all nations and kingdoms will share a place with the physical descendants of Abraham, 'As for me, this is my covenant with you: You will be the father of many nations' (Gen. 17:4). This dimension gave a clause of protection to all non-Israelites who sought to find shelter with the God of Abraham during the OC and prepared for the cosmic perspective of the NC.

**Living faith.** The Abrahamic covenant is the background for the OC in other ways as well. First, it holds up living faith as the requirement of covenant fidelity. Living faith is the essence of what God requires of man: 'walk before me and be blameless' (Gen. 17:1). As a summary of God's will it includes two dimensions. (1) It is a trust in the LORD and in his freedom to deliver when and however he chooses. Abraham had such faith: 'Abram believed the LORD, and he credited it to him as righteousness' (Gen. 15:6). The LORD had made promises to him, and, not knowing how the LORD would be true to his word, he submitted himself to his sovereignty. (2) Living faith also includes the active dimension of *allegiance* by demonstrating love for the LORD and by being obedient to his will. The LORD expected Abraham to be a man of integrity (Gen. 17:1) who would model and teach his children godliness: 'I have chosen him, so that he will direct his children and his household after him to keep the way of the LORD by doing what is right and just, so that the LORD will bring about for Abraham what he has promised him' (Gen. 18:19).

Living faith as an expression of submission and allegiance may be tested. Again and again the LORD tried Abraham's faith in the experiences of famine, childlessness, and rivalry. The most severe trial of *allegiance* took place when the LORD called him to offer his only son (Gen. 22). After his death, the LORD commended Abraham for having lived a godly life: 'Abraham obeyed me and kept my requirements, my commands, my decrees and my laws' (Gen.26:5).

**Election.**   Second, the idea of *election* is prevalent. As the suzerain chooses with whom he makes a covenant, God freely chose Abraham. His privileged position was unmerited: 'For I have chosen him' (Gen. 18:19). Moreover, Israel's position is also one of grace, as their entitlement came not by their righteousness: 'It is not because of your righteousness or your integrity that you are going in to take possesson of their land; but on account of the wickedness of these nations, the LORD your God will drive them out before you, to accomplish what he swore to your fathers, to Abraham, Isaac and Jacob' (Deut. 9:5).

**God's presence.**   Third, the central focus of the Abrahamic covenant is the promise of *God's presence*: 'I will establish my covenant as an everlasting covenant between me and you and your descendants after you for the generations to come, to be your God and the God of your descendants after you' (Gen. 17:7; cf. 26:3). This promise entails three aspects. (1) It is the basis for the *fulfilment* of the promises and of the enjoyment of his blessing. This dimension is further developed in the biblical teaching on the Kingdom of God. (2) It is the basis for *ethics* as God demands a proper demeanour in his presence (Gen. 17:1). This dimension is further developed in the legislation of the OC, but also in the teaching on the cost of discipleship, i.e. the requirements of entering the Kingdom of God. (3) It is the basis for *eschatology*. In the reality of adversities in life, the godly put their hope in the LORD's promise that he will 'tabernacle' among his people. His presence is the guarantee of his *protection* from adversities and the assurance of his blessing. This dimension is further developed in the Tabernacle/Temple in the OC, in the coming of Jesus Christ and the Holy Spirit under the NC, and in the hope of the glorious coming of our Lord. It should be apparent that the connections between OC and the NC are many. The OC is preparatory of the NC in that it prepares the reader of the NT to understand concepts such as the Kingdom of God, the cost of discipleship, and the importance of ethics in the light of the promise of Jesus' coming in glory.

### God's fidelity

The basis for the OC is God's immutable promise of his faithfulness. God's reputation is at stake in the experiences of his people. The event of the Exodus was the concrete context in which the LORD demonstrated his fidelity to the Abrahamic covenant. After many years of bondage to the Egyptians, he led his people out of Egypt under Moses amidst great signs and wonders. The Exodus was the historical moment that marked God's setting a people apart for himself. This dramatic moment was made even more significant by two subsequent events. First, the passage through the Red Sea confirmed the power of Yahweh over against the military and political powers of this world, as well as the religious structures of Egypt. He alone is God: 'Who among the gods is like you, O LORD? Who is like you – majestic in holiness, awesome in glory, working wonders?' (*Exod. 15:11*). Second, the revelation at Mt Sinai marked the constitution of Israel as the people of the LORD. This revelation is singularly important. It discloses the LORD's love for his people: 'You yourselves have seen what I did to Egypt, and how I carried you on eagles' wings and brought you to myself' (*Exod. 19:4*). As the Exodus marks his fidelity to the patriarchal promise of dealing kindly with their offspring, the Sinai revelation marks his purpose of establishing his Kingdom among his people; 'Although the whole earth is mine, you will be for me a kingdom of priests and a holy nation' (*Exod. 19:5–6*).

### The Law of God

The people received the high calling to be 'a kingdom of priests and a holy nation' (*Exod. 19:6*). However, for Israel to serve the LORD, they had to know how they could please him. To this end, the revelation at Sinai commenced a new relation with Israel. On the one hand, the relationship was *gracious* in that he covenanted himself to be the God of his people and to dwell in their midst (*Exod. 29:45–46*), the symbol of which was the Tabernacle. On the other hand, the relation was demanding in that the LORD set forth the requirements for living in his presence and warned Israel of the punishment (sanction) for disobedience.

The 'law' was the symbol of this relationship. Its requirements took on a more sinister note in the light of Israel's history of rebelliousness. During the 40 years in the wilderness, they resisted Yahweh's lordship – before, at, and after Sinai. These two dimensions – grace and sanction – created the tension which only found its resolution in the NC.

### The Covenant

The definition of the OC combines these two points of tension: The OC is the sovereign administration of promise and blessing by which the LORD God consecrated Israel as his people under the sanctions of his royal law.

**The Covenant is good.** According to this definition, the OC has four aspects. First, the covenant is a *sovereign and gracious relationship*. As in any covenant initiated by the LORD, the relationship is of the suzerainty type. God chooses, initiates, and determines with whom and how he relates. He commits himself to be a gracious LORD, promising and keeping promise. The Mosaic covenant is no different in this regard.

Second, *promises and blessings* are attached to the covenant. They are closely tied to the land of Israel's inheritance, 'flowing with milk and honey' (*Deut. 11:9*). The resources of the land are concrete expressions of God's goodness: 'I will send rain on your land in its season, both autumn and spring rains, so that you may gather in your grain, new wine and oil. I will provide grass in the fields for your cattle, and you will eat and be satisfied' (*Deut. 11:14–15; cf. 7:13; 28:3–6*). In the concrete experience of Israel's existence in the land, we find an important motif of God's concern for his people and for his creation. The existence of Israel in the land foreshadows the promise of God to make a new creation in which his people will find rest and security.

Third, the people are *consecrated to the* LORD. The whole nation was consecrated to the LORD, even though most of the people had no faith in him. He dealt with Israel as a nation, treating them favourably because of their descent from Abraham. He is holy in his being, i.e. *separate from* anything that he has created. As the Holy One of Israel, he chose Israel to be his, i.e. they were *separated unto* him. The close relationship between the LORD and his people was to be the basis for ethics: 'Be holy because I, the LORD your God, am holy' (*Lev. 19:2; cf. 1 Pet. 1:15–16*).

Fourth, *the Law* has a prominent place. Obedience to the law was an important aspect of the OC. The Decalogue (moral law) sets out God's expectations of the members of the covenant community toward him (worship and ceremony) and toward one another (*Exod. 20:2–17*). Other commandments amplify the Ten Commandments. They fall into two categories; laws specifying the worship of God in life (worship and ceremonial laws) and laws specifying neighbourly relations (civil laws). This way of looking at the commandments has given the traditional three-fold division of the Law: moral, ceremonial, and civil. Though the differentiation is quite neat, there is overlap. For example, on the Sabbath (ceremonial law) one was not to employ another Israelite (civil law). Many of the civil laws have distinct moral implications, such as the regulations on speaking truth (moral law) in a court of law (civil).

At the heart of the legal system is what is also the core of the covenantal relationship. It is a method of teaching Israel how they, like Abraham, must walk before God and be people of integrity (*Gen. 17:1*). This was well understood by the prophets. In the book of Jeremiah God said, 'I am the LORD, who exercises kindness, justice and righteousness on earth, for in these I delight' (*Jer. 9:24*). In the book of Micah God spoke similarly: 'He has showed you, O man, what is good. And what does the LORD require of you? To act justly and to love mercy and to walk humbly with your God' (*Mic. 6:8; cf. Hos. 6:6*). The law reflects the character of God. Through the detailed regulations, he taught his people what he means by love, justice, righteousness, fidelity, and compassion. If it were not for the Law, people would not have known what God requires of humans. Jesus' teaching on the love of God and of one's neighbour is an interpretation of what is already taught in the OT. So is also his emphasis on living faith as the essential requirement and on walking in the presence of God as a motivation for living.

The LORD also instructed his people that individual and corporate sin had to be dealt with. The laws of the offerings and the sacrifices (*Lev. 7*) bring out the gravity of any infraction of the commandments, but also God's holiness. The presence of God in their midst was incompatible with sin. Therefore, individuals had to confess their sins before God and sacrifice an animal, as prescribed by the Law of Moses, as an 'atonement' for their sins. To assure that any unconfessed sin in the community would not break God's fellowship with his people and incur his wrath, the high priest entered once a year on the Day of Atonement into the Holy of Holies in order to purgate the 'sacred dwelling of God'. In addition, individuals made thanksgiving offerings that were expressions of gratitude toward God's goodness as well as communal offerings at which time they celebrated as a community the privilege of belonging to the covenant.

**The Covenant is temporary.**   The OC was deficient at four points. First, the Law reveals sin and makes the sinner accountable (*Rom. 5:13*). The OT is not silent on the sins of the saints, as priests, kings, and people transgress against the LORD. The Law as a system is awesome because the infraction of a part becomes a transgression of the whole covenant relationship (*James 2:10*).

Second, obedience to the Law could not provide atonement for sin. Sin ruptured fellowship with God. The many stipulations regarding the offerings and sacrifices serve as a reminder of individual and corporate sin and of the constant deficiency of humans before God. The laws brought out human sinfulness and rebellion. The death of Jesus Christ satisfied this deficiency once and for all: 'Christ is the mediator of a new covenant, that those who are called may receive the promised eternal inheritance – now that he has died as a ransom to set them free from the sins committed under the first covenant' (*Heb. 9:15*; see *Heb. 8–9*).

Third, even when the saints under the OC underwent a spiritual transformation by the work of the Spirit in their lives, the Spirit was generally not present in the power and glory as he is now in Christians. The work of the Spirit since Christ's coming explains a radical change in that the Law is a guide that keeps one from transgression, whereas before Pentecost, the Law was a teacher, instructing God's people how to live by its many details.

Fourth, sanctions are attached to any infraction of the Law. The curse (*Deut. 28:15–68*) threatened God's people continuously, robbing them of the joy of their salvation. From this point onward Israel must live with the tension between obedience and disobedience, blessing and curse, deliverance and rejection. The Lord Jesus carried the curse of the law for us (*Gal. 3:13*), and, thereby, he has freed us from this negative aspect of the OC.

### A prophetic perspective

The prophets spoke of a new beginning as they forecast the end of the old era. The old was characterized by rebelliousness, idolatry, and human pride. Many Israelites felt themselves to be acceptable with God on account of their religious commitment to the Temple, sacrifices, and prayer (*Is. 1:11–16*). They were oblivious to what God really wanted: obedience rather than sacrifice and loyalty more than piety (*Mic. 6:6–8*). Little did the people understand that the judgment of

God was about to decimate them, disgrace the survivors, and force them to ask questions, such as 'have you abandoned us forever?' (Is. 64:12; Lam.). They had made the Holy One of Israel a fetish. So the prophets portrayed the people with a future in Exile, if they survived, and held the images of the ruins of Temple, palace, and Jerusalem before the unrepentant people. The Exile meant a rupture in the covenant relationship as Temple and Davidic kingship would no longer function. Priests could no longer serve as intermediaries. Kings could no longer protect them. Instead, the curses of the covenant would overtake them: adversity, lack of productivity, barrenness, diseases, natural disasters, famine, wars, death, and ultimately the Exile of the nation (Deut. 28:15–68; 30:1–5).

They also prophesied the restoration to the land and a new people returning from Exile. As Moses had foretold the Exile as a divine judgment (Deut. 28:64– 68), so Moses had spoken of a new beginning after the Exile. The experience of Exile was to bring them to their knees as anguish would overtake the survivors: 'Among those nations you will find no repose, no resting place for the sole of your foot. There the LORD will give you an anxious mind, eyes weary with longing, and a despairing heart. You will live in constant suspense, filled with dread both night and day, never sure of your life. In the morning you will say, "If only it were evening!" and in the evening, "If only it were morning!" – because of the terror that will fill your hearts and the sights that your eyes will see' (Deut. 28:65–67).

The basis for a proclamation of hope also lies in the OC. Moses had encouraged the people to return to the LORD in their distress: 'when you and your children return to the LORD your God and obey him with all your heart and with all your soul according to everything I command you today, then the LORD your God will restore your fortunes and have compassion on you and gather you again from all the nations where he scattered you' (Deut. 30:2–3). He delineated the steps of reconciliation: repentance (vv. 2–3), circumcision of heart (v. 6); whole-hearted obedience (vv. 8, 10), and God's delight in his people (v. 9). Two of these are expressions of human responsibility: repentance and obedience. The other two are the work of God: circumcision of the heart (requisite for repentance and obedience) and God's pleasure with his people. The covenant relationship was thus restored. This was essentially the gospel of Moses.

The gospel of Moses found an echo in the prophets. Isaiah spoke of the Exile and restoration motif as a change from wrath to compassion: 'For a brief moment I abandoned you, but with deep compassion I will bring you back' (Is. 54:7). The restoration from Exile was the beginning of a renewal of the covenant: 'Though the mountains be shaken and the hills be removed, yet my unfailing love for you will not be shaken nor my covenant of peace be removed says the LORD, who has compassion on you' (Is. 54:10).

Ezekiel represented the past and the future in terms of wicked shepherds (Ezek. 34:1–10) over against the Good Shepherd. The former had led the sheep to destruction. The Good Shepherd would make a covenant of peace, reversing the curse into a blessing (Ezek. 34:25–31). This covenant would be an everlasting covenant (Ezek. 37:26), promising security, spiritual transformation of the people (v. 28), and God's tabernacling with his people: 'I will put my sanctuary among them forever. My dwelling place will be with them; I will be their God, and they will be my people' (vv. 26–27).

Jeremiah alone used the phrase 'new covenant' (*Jer. 31:31; cf. Heb. 8:8–12*). The new covenant is first and foremost a renewal of the OC. The renewal is nevertheless a better covenant in that it provides for a change of heart, an internal motivation, a democratization, the knowledge of God, and forgiveness (*Jer. 31:33–34*). The citation of this passage in *Heb. 8:8–12* – the longest quote in the NT of an OT text – is an important commentary on *Jer. 31*. The author connects the new covenant not only with the return from Exile, but especially with the coming of Jesus Christ. God's fidelity to Israel in the era of restoration was a preparation for his gracious work of redemption in Jesus Christ.

Moses and the Prophets were united in their assessment of the OC. There had to be another covenant and another era, in which God's people would serve the LORD from the heart, know him, and advance his Kingdom.

## The New Covenant

### *Jesus' teaching on the New Covenant*

The Lord Jesus was born under the OC and fulfilled perfectly the Law of Moses. Contrary to the perspective of many, he did not abolish the Law of God or argue against it with the Pharisees. Instead, he set aside human traditions and interpreted the Law the way God had intended his people to learn the practice of love, compassion, righteousness, and justice. Matthew records Jesus' commitment to the Law in these words: 'Do not think that I have come to abolish the Law or the Prophets; I have not come to abolish them but to fulfil them. I tell you the truth, until heaven and earth disappear, not the smallest letter, not the least stroke of a pen, will by any means disappear from the Law until everything is accomplished. Anyone who breaks one of the least of these commandments and teaches others to do the same will be called least in the kingdom of heaven, but whoever practices and teaches these commands will be called great in the kingdom of heaven' (*Matt. 5:17–19*). Jesus was perfect in his obedience to the Father, and laid down his life so that he could bring humans into the presence of the Father. His life and teaching witness to both his zeal for the holiness of God and to his compassion for sinful humans.

The church is the body of believers for which Christ died. Jesus likened himself to a shepherd who was willing to give his life for the sheep (*John 10:11*). The death of Christ is the climactic demonstration of his loyalty to the Father, but also marks the transition from the Old to the New Covenant. The sacrifice of his life for the sake of his church ended the era of sacrifices, Temple, priesthood, and ceremonies. The church would remember his death as a confirmation of the new relationship which the Father established with all who believed in his Son. They share in the NC, of which Jesus spoke shortly before his death: 'This cup is the new covenant in my blood, which is poured out for you' (*Luke 22:20*).

### *The apostolic witness*

The apostles continued the witness of Christ. They preached that Jesus is the Messiah of God. He is the rightful descendant of David who is seated on David's throne, at the right hand of the Father (*Acts 2:30*). Jesus is the faithful priest who through his death, resurrection, life, ascension, and glorification has the privileged position of reconciling sinners with the Father. The church as the new community of God participate in the new covenant of grace which may be defined as 'an administration of grace and promise' in which the Father consecrates a people, whether Jews or Gentiles, to himself in union with his Son. In this he confirms their new position by the regenerating and sanctifying presence of the Spirit of God, and has sealed the saints for the day of redemption. The 'signs and seals' of the NC are baptism and the Lord's Supper. Baptism is the sign that seals the grace of God, confirming the new life in Christ. The Lord's Supper is the sign that seals the grace of God, confirming the benefits of the Lord Jesus in this life and for evermore.

## Paul

The apostle Paul taught that the NC relationship is based on and a continuation of the OC. In *Rom. 1–8*, he develops an extensive argument regarding the universality of sin, God's condemnation, and the state of humans without Christ. All humans are condemned to eternal death by their identity with Adam (*Rom. 5*). In Christ, however, the believer is a new creature, is a slave to righteousness (*Rom. 6:19*), is a child of God by adoption, and already shares in the new heritage by the Spirit (*Rom. 8*).

Nevertheless, the Law is still a gracious instrument leading to righteousness: 'I myself in my mind am a slave to God's law' (*Rom. 7:25*). Similarly, the apostle wrote, 'Let no debt remain outstanding, except the continuing debt to love one another, for he who loves his fellowman has fulfilled the law' (*Rom. 14:8; cf. vv. 9–10*). Clearly, the OC was an administration of grace, as Paul reflects on its many benefits: 'Theirs is the adoption as sons; theirs the divine glory, the covenants, the receiving of the law, the temple worship and the promises. Theirs are the patriarchs, and from them is traced the human ancestry of Christ, who is God over all, forever praised! Amen' (*Rom. 9:4–5*).

**The adoption as sons.**   The Jews are 'Israelites' (NIV, 'the people of Israel', *Rom. 9:4*), a designation by which Jews referred to each other. Paul, the Jew, hereby identified himself with his people most intimately: 'my brothers, those of my own race, the people of Israel' (*vv. 3–4*). The word Israel here signifies 'God's elect, the covenant people of the One God'. They are the heirs of the promises and of the covenants.

In what sense were they also God's children by adoption? While the OT is reticent in describing the relationship of God and his covenant people in terms of adoption, the apostle reads the privileged status of Israel in the light of the Roman legal fiction. The adoption belongs to Israel! Several arguments support this connection. First, God called Israel to be his son, his firstborn son (*Exod. 4:22; Deut. 14:1; 32:6, 18; Is. 1:2; 43:6; 45:11; 64:8; Jer. 31:9; Hos. 1:10; 11:1; Mal. 2:10*). Second, Isaiah argued for God's fidelity to the covenant from the Father-son relationship (*Is. 63:16; 64:8*). The apostle's extension of the metaphor of adoption to Israel is all the more important. Instead of breaking up the continuity between the OC and the NC by defining the experience of the OC as lacking adoption, he brings their experience within that of adoption!

**The divine glory.**   The NIV ('the divine glory') interprets the Greek text which simply reads 'the glory'. The phrase has been taken to refer to the revelations of God's glory to Israel (*Exod. 24:15–17; 40:34–35*). Yahweh revealed his glory at Sinai (*Exod. 19; 24:15–17; 40:34–35*). The Tabernacle/Temple was the focus of the revelation of God's glory (*Ezek. 10*) because it signified the presence of God with his people (*Exod. 29:42–46*). The glory that was lost was regained in Israel. The glory was lost because of sin (*Rom. 3:23*). It was God's gift to those who sought him and pleased him (*Rom. 2:7, 10*). Israel had received his blessings in a very special way because Yahweh had extended his presence to them. In his presence lay the possibility of enjoyment of life. This 'glory' was God's gift to Israel in the covenant relationship (*Ps. 8:5*). The hope given by the prophets included the promise of an era of glory. The prophet Isaiah spoke of the glory of God's people in terms of the fullness of salvation, joy, vitality, blessing, and light (*Is. 35:2; 59:19–60:3; 66:18– 19*). For Paul the hope of glory is Jesus Christ and the basis of hope lies in the resurrection of our Lord (*Rom. 5:2; 6:4*). Yet, in some sense Israel, too, shared in the hope of this glory.

**The covenants.**   The phrase 'and the covenants' ambiguously presents the advantage of Israel as a covenant people. The apostle may well have had all the OT covenants in mind, but his argument in Romans gives strength to the inference that the Jews by birth had a natural relationship to the OC, but also had received the oracles promising a new covenant era (*cf. 1 Cor. 11:25; 2 Cor. 3:6, 14; Gal. 4:24*).

**The receiving of the law.**   The Greek word *nomothesia* may be rendered actively ('the giving of the Law') or passively ('the receiving of the law', so NIV). For Paul both the gift and the reception of the Law were expressions of Israel's elect status and of her favour with the Lord. Here the word does not have the negative connotation. The Law is God's gift and is a special part of the special relationship of adoption, the covenants, and the promises. It is not to be viewed negatively, as in Paul's argument against the Galatians.

**The temple worship.**   The word *latreia* ('worship') is a technical designation for the worship of God in the Temple, including the rituals of purification and of the offerings and sacrifices. But the broader usage of a 'spiritual' worship may also be meant. In *Rom. 12:1* Paul encouraged the Christians at Rome to present a 'spiritual worship', that is, the service of God with heart and mind.

**The promises.**   The promises are at the heart of the covenant and of Israel's privileged status as God's children by adoption. Paul's understanding of the promises came through his knowledge of the Scriptures and through Christ's revelation of the NC. He rejoiced in the promises of the fathers (*Rom. 15:8*), while affirming that the promises were confirmed in Jesus Christ. The confirmation necessitated the incarnation. Jesus had to become a servant for the purpose of extending the covenant privileges and promises to the Gentiles (Rom. 15:8). The incarnation, ministry, death, resurrection, and glorification of Jesus Christ were the Father's demonstration of his fidelity to the promises (2 Cor. 1:20). As such the promise is still eschatological because it awaits the full revelation at the coming of our Lord. But, while waiting for the fulness of fulfilment, the Holy Spirit is the 'deposit, guaranteeing what is to come' (1 Cor. 1:22). In other words, the Holy Spirit is the token of the present and the eschatological enjoyment of the promises. He is God's eschatological gift.

The two dimensions greatly affect Paul's understanding of the promises. Since the promises are *historical* and *eschatological*, the fulfilment of the promises extends to all God's children (Jews and Gentiles) and to all of God's creation. This explains why Paul set Abraham up as 'the heir of the world' (Rom. 4:13) and as the father of all God's children (Rom. 4:16; Gal. 3:14; 4:23, 28). It also explains that Paul did not restrict the promises to Israel because the promises of God regarding Israel are still valid.

**The patriarchs and the human ancestry of Christ.** The 'patriarchs' include the Patriarchs and all the faithful Israelites. Paul alludes here to the privileged history of Israel. The history of redemption (patriarchs, Egypt, wilderness, conquest, kingdom, Exile, and restoration) is the story of Israel's roots. The apostle looks positively at his roots, as he concludes, 'As far as the gospel is concerned, they are enemies on your account; but as far as election is concerned, they are loved on account of the patriarchs, for God's call and gifts are irrevocable' (Rom. 11:28).

Abraham is the father of Gentiles (Rom. 4:11–12, 16–17; Gal. chs 3–4), so is Isaac (Rom. 9:10), and Jacob (Rom. 9:6). The unity of privileges of Jews and Christians lies in the coming of Jesus Christ. The Christ (Messiah) came in 'the flesh' (NIV, 'human ancestry'). But, it was only in the flesh that he could trace his ancestry back to Israel. This is a serious restriction in which Paul emphasized the distinction between Israel's natural position in the flesh and the spiritual nature of the privileges and of those who share in the privileges of Israel. The Messiah is God and man, Spirit and flesh, the Son of God and the seed of David (Rom. 1:3–4).

This means that while the privileges were given to Israel, they belong only to those who receive Jesus as the Messiah. Physical descent is important, but spiritual discernment is even more important. Jesus Christ is man and God, Israelite and the eternal one. Since this is so, the Israelite who rejects Jesus Christ, rejects God! Yet, this should not be interpreted in a way so as to suggest that the position of Israel is inferior.

In conclusion, the apostle does not separate the privileges of old and new. There is an inherent continuity between the OC and the NC. Clearly, the difference lies in the coming of Jesus Christ, by which the promises, the glory, the covenants, and the Law have a greater significance. Further, he has extended the benefits to Gentiles, as well. However, the point of Paul's argument here is in favour of continuity.

The apostle struggled with the apparent discontinuity. Gentiles have come to faith in Christ, have received the Spirit of adoption, and are grafted into the promises, covenants, and glory that belongs to the children of God. But, the Jews by

116

and large have rejected Jesus as the Messiah. How can this be? Has God abandoned his people?

Rom. 9–11 form Paul's reflections on the issue of God's fidelity, the gospel of righteousness, and the continuity of God's plan. The apostle stands in the gap between God and Israel. He holds on to the greatness and depth of God's love in Jesus Christ (Rom. 8:38–39), but wonders how to relate God's love to God's plan for Israel. Has God abandoned Israel and in this way changed his plan? If so, the gospel has changed. Paul rejects a change in the gospel. He looks at God's fidelity, which is the basis of hope for God's new covenant people (Rom. 8:31–39), as the basis of hope for the Jews.

## The book of Hebrews

The author of Hebrews compares God's ways in the past with God's way in Jesus Christ in terms of the OC versus the NC. In the OC God had spoken through Moses and the prophets (Heb. 1:1; 3:1–2), offered his people a sabbath rest which they did not enter (Heb. 4:11), forgiven his people through the shadows and symbols of the institution of the Tabernacle/Temple, priesthood, and animals (Heb. 9:1–10), and permitted Israel access to him, but amidst the threatenings of death (Heb. 12:18–21). However, in the NC the Father had revealed his glory in Jesus Christ (Heb. 1:2–4), opened up the true rest (Heb. 4:9–13), forgiven because Jesus is the High Priest by whose one-time atonement many will be justified (Heb. 4:14–5:10; 8:1–13; 9:11—10:18), and opened up more widely access to him (Heb. 12:22–24).

Clearly, the NC is far superior to the OC. How should we look at the NC, in terms of contrast or as an improvement (Heb. 8:6). The previous administration (OC) was good, but anticipated a better covenant (NC). The revelation of the 'better' does not completely invalidate what was good. Changes have definitely taken place. First, Jesus Christ is the focus, the superior revelation, the unique sacrifice, the exalted High Priest, and the mediator of the NC. Moses, the prophets, and the priests are still God's faithful servants, but take a secondary place in relation to Jesus Christ. Thus, the OT must take into account what God has revealed in the NT. A Christian approach to the OT cannot interpret it without the light from the NT. The opposite is equally true: the NT can only be interpreted in the light of the OT. How else can we appreciate the accomplishments, the ministry, and the message of Jesus Christ?

The OC is imperfect in that it is not God's final revelation, the ultimate embodiment of his love, the full unfolding of his glory, and the instrument of reconciling people to himself. Moses was God's servant and a faithful one, but he was also a messenger of a greater future (Heb. 3:1–5). As a messenger of a new era of God's administration, he looked forward to the coming of Jesus Christ (Heb. 3:5; 11:26). The institutions associated with Moses – Tabernacle/Temple, the priestly system, and the system of offerings and sacrifices – were temporary expressions of the revelation of God's love, glory, and reconciliation.

The revelation of God in Jesus Christ opened up a new administration: the administration of the NC. He is the 'radiance of God's glory' (Heb. 1:2), the Son (Heb. 3:6), and the High Priest-Mediator (Heb. 4:15; 5:5; 8:1–2; 12:24). Yet, the author of Hebrews gives no ground for being complacent with the present revelation of God in Jesus Christ. Far from it! He surveyed God's involvement in the past during the OC. While pointing people to the present ministry of Jesus Christ, he encouraged the Christians to persevere, to learn from the past, *and* to await the fulness of their salvation. This fulness lies in the future. It is eschatological. In other words, Moses encouraged generations to look for the Messiah. Now that the Messiah has come, the apostles, preachers, and teachers of God's Word encourage Christians to look ahead to the fulness, to the revelation of Jesus Christ, to the glorious future to which Jesus alone has the key. In other words, the message of Hebrews is *eschatological*. This explains why he spoke of the Day of the Lord as a shaking of creation (*Heb. 12:27*). This explains why he spoke of the 'rest to which we must make every effort to enter' (*Heb. 4:11*). This explains why he spoke of the greater salvation (*Heb. 9:28*). The author holds God's involvement in the past (Moses, prophets), the present (the mediatorship of Jesus Christ), and the future (salvation) together by interpreting the variety of God's acts in the OC and in the NC in terms of the unfolding of the *one* plan of God and of the manifold nature of his fidelity: 'Jesus Christ is the same yesterday and today and forever' (*Heb. 13:8*).

W.A.VG.

**COZBI,** a Midianite and the daughter of a tribal chief named Zur (*Num. 25:15, 18*). While Israel was staying near Shittim the Israelite men made contact with Moabite women and became involved in sexual immorality with them. Probably they indulged in fertility rites with these women, since *Num. 25:2* tells us that they were invited to make sacrifices to their gods, the 'Baal of Peor'. The LORD was angry and promised judgment unless Moses put to death all who had participated in this activity.

However, Zimri, son of Salu, the leader of a Simeonite family, compounded the evil by bringing Cozbi back into the Israelite camp with him just as Israel 'was weeping' over the judgment God was inflicting. Phinehas, a grandson of Aaron, determined to vindicate the LORD and to stem any further judgment, immediately took his spear and followed Zimri and Cozbi into their tent and killed them both (*Num. 25*).

The defence of the holiness of the Israelites and their separation from the other peoples for the services of the LORD alone was of the very essence of their calling as a nation. The preservation of such holiness was therefore vital if they were to remain faithful to their covenantal relationship with the LORD.

P.D.G.

**CRESCENS** (Lat., 'growing'), was a friend of the apostle Paul. He had been with Paul while he was in prison in Rome towards the end of his ministry. In the sad fourth and final chapter at the end of 2 *Timothy*, Paul describes how, for one reason or another, he was left completely alone to face his first trial. Some, like Demas, had left because they had been seduced away from the faith by materialism. Paul simply says that Crescens had left for Galatia (2 *Tim. 4:10*). However, Paul was still able to testify from the midst of his sadness, 'But the Lord stood at my side and gave me strength' (*v. 17*).

**CRETANS** The Cretans came from Crete, a large island lying off the coast of Greece. A very large Jewish community existed there as early as the mid-second century BC. It is for this reason that many Cretans would have been present in Jerusalem for the feast of Pentecost when the apostles received the Holy Spirit and began to preach. Acts 2:11 records that Cretans and Arabs heard the 'wonders of God' declared in their own tongues. Clearly they partook of a great miracle in which God enabled the words of the apostles to be heard and understood by everyone present on that day, no matter what their native language.

In *Titus 1:12* the apostle Paul said of them, 'Cretans are always liars, evil brutes, lazy gluttons'. He was quoting Epimenedes, a Cretan himself, who had written in this way c. 600 BC. In the context, Paul was speaking to Titus about his work among the churches on Crete and warning against false teachers. He applied this saying to them, and was not making the same universal statement about all Cretans that was intended in Epimenedes.                           P.D.G.

**CRISPUS** was a synagogue ruler in Corinth when Paul began his mission to the city (*Acts 18*). After 'reasoning' in the synagogue regularly on the Sabbath about faith in Christ, Paul was eventually ejected by angry Jews. However, many Jews obviously continued to listen along with the Gentiles, and Crispus 'and his entire household believed in the Lord' (*Acts 18:8*). Paul referred back to that early conversion in *1 Cor. 1:14*.

**CUSH 1.** One of four sons born to Ham. He had at least six sons of his own, most of whom were listed as progenitors of different tribes or peoples. Cush thus is both the person and a nation of people (e.g. *Est. 1:1*) who lived far to the south of Canaan (Ethiopia). His son Nimrod was a mighty warrior (*Gen. 10:6–9; 1 Chron. 1:8–10*).

**2.** A Benjamite whose name appears in the ascription of *Ps. 7*. His antagonism to David prompted David's reflections before the LORD in this Psalm.

**CUSHAN-RISHATHAIM,** a king in Aram in the early period of the Judges, who was used by God to bring judgment on the Israelites for their idolatry and lack of faith in the LORD (*Judg. 3:8–10*). For eight years God allowed them to languish under this oppression, and then, when they cried out to him for help, God raised up Othniel to deliver them. Othniel was Caleb's younger son. 'The Spirit of the LORD came upon him' and he went to war and defeated Cushan-Rishathaim. Othniel then became a judge in Israel, which had peace for 40 years.

On several occasions in the Bible, the oppression or conquest of the Israelites is understood as God's judgment on his people for idolatry. There is often the sense of God having given them up to what they really want. They worshipped the gods of other nations and sometimes intermarried with them, therefore God let them be ruled by other nations. As this happened, they experienced the oppression and lack of justice of pagan societies and were eventually caused to turn back to the LORD for deliverance. In this way God's judgment on his people was always constructive in its end.          P.D.G.

**CUSHI 1.** The great grandfather of Jehudi, who lived in Jeremiah's time (*Jer. 36:14*).

**2.** The father of the prophet Zephaniah and the son of Gedaliah (*Zeph. 1:1*).

**CUZA,** the manager of Herod's household. He is introduced into the narrative of *Luke* (*8:3*) because he was the husband of Joanna, one of the women who were helping to support Jesus and his twelve disciples 'out of their own means'. She may have had independent finances or her husband may have been sympathetic, but the mention of Cuza may partly be in order to emphasize that these were women from wealthy households. Certainly it is a common fiction these days that only the poor were attracted by Jesus's ministry. In some editions of the NIV this person is called Chuza.

**CYRUS,** Cyrus II, the Great, was king of Persia 559–530 BC. The Persian empire he founded, after defeating the Babylonians, continued for almost 200 years until Alexander the Great invaded in 330 BC. Cyrus was favourably regarded by many of his conquered people because he was magnanimous in his rule. This is seen specially in the biblical account in which the LORD so prompted Cyrus' heart that he was determined the Temple in Jerusalem should be rebuilt and that any former residents of Judah or Jerusalem dispersed around the empire should feel free to return to Jerusalem to help in the work (2 Chron. 36:22–23; Ezra 1:1–3). According to Ezra, this action was initiated in the heart of Cyrus by God in order to fulfil his word spoken through the prophet Jeremiah (Jer. 15:11–14). There is no doubt that under God's sovereign will the enlightened rule of Cyrus was used to bring the Israelites back to their home country after they had been in slavery for the promised 70 years.

It is not clear how Cyrus knew that he had heard the Word of Yahweh (the LORD). However, many have suggested that he may have heard the word from Daniel or someone like him: a person who held a high position in the empire and therefore had the ear of the king (see Dan. 1:21; 6:28; 10:1). Such a person would have brought to the king's attention prophecies about him in the book of Isaiah written some 150 years earlier. Those prophecies are remarkable in their content for they look forward through the Exile to deliverance from the Captivity in Babylon. The LORD even says of Cyrus: 'He is my shepherd and will accomplish all that I please' (Is. 44:28). In Is. 45:1 he calls Cyrus his 'anointed' whom God will use to rebuild the city and Temple (v. 13).

The details of how Cyrus oversaw the start of the Israelite return to Jerusalem and initiated work on the Temple is recounted in Ezra (Ezra 3:7; 4:3, 5; 5:13–17; 6:3, 14). Even more remarkable is that Cyrus encouraged the work by ordering gifts to be given to the returning people of Israel and by returning to them the Temple treasures that had been taken from Jerusalem when the city was conquered (Ezra 1:7–8).

There is little indication that Cyrus actually became a follower of Yahweh. Probably his enlightened policy of administration of such a huge empire meant that he showed respect for the religious beliefs of many different peoples. However, his rise to power at that particular moment in history was subject to God's authority and such a political policy was conceived within God's purposes for the sake of the protection and resettlement of his own people.          P.D.G.

# D

**DAGON** (Heb., 'grain') was one of the Philistine gods. Evidence of the worship of this pagan god is to be found in a number of very ancient texts. He is first mentioned in the Bible in *Judg. 16:23* after the Philistines had captured Samson. They took him into the temple of Dagon who they believed had delivered Samson into their hands. During their celebrations before this god they brought out the blinded Samson, bound with bronze shackles. In the midst of the celebrations in the temple, Samson asked to be taken to two pillars to lean on them. By this stage some of his strength had returned and he was able, with God's help, to pull the pillars down; the temple fell on him and the Philistines so that many were killed.

In *1 Sam. 5:2–12* the capture of the ark by the Philistines is recounted. It was taken to the temple of Dagon in Ashdod. The following morning the Philistines discovered the image of their God had fallen on his face before the 'ark of the LORD' (*1 Sam. 5:2–12*). The same happened the next day, and for as long as the ark remained in the hands of the Philistines the LORD brought great troubles and plagues on them.

Another temple of Dagon existed in Beth-Shan, where Saul's head was taken following his defeat in battle at the hands of the Philistines (*1 Sam. 31:9–10; 1 Chron. 10:10*). The Philistines soon experienced God's judgment as God's anointed, King David, attacked them and beat them in battle after battle.

Time and again the one true God is seen in the Bible to be completely sovereign.

There are no other gods (*Deut. 6:4; 32:17*), and so the LORD demonstrated this to the surrounding peoples both in the way they were defeated in battle and in vivid symbolic actions, such as the way the idol of Dagon fell on his face before the ark of the LORD.     P.D.G.

**DALPHON,** one of ten sons of Haman killed in Susa by the Jews (*Est. 9:7*).

**DAMARIS** This woman was one of the few people converted through Paul's preaching when he was in Athens (*Acts 17:34*). The fact that she is singled out may indicate that she was a 'prominent' Greek woman (*v. 12*).

**DAN** (Heb., 'judge' or 'judgment'), the older of two sons of Jacob by Rachel's servant girl Bilhah (*Gen. 30:5–6*). According to the birth account, Rachel celebrated the event by declaring, 'God has vindicated me' (*Heb. dananni*), and so 'she named him Dan'. The name thus rose out of a particular life situation and thereafter testified to God's favour towards the barren Rachel.

Dan the individual is not mentioned apart from this, but the tribe that bore his name receives notice frequently, and usually in a negative way. When the Danites could not occupy the land allotted to them in Canaan they travelled far to the north, slew and expelled the population of Laish, and then settled there (near modern Tell Dan) and established an idolatrous cult (*Judg. 18*). Dan, along with Bethel, was chosen later by King Jeroboam of Israel as the site of his anti-Jerusalem worship centre (1 Kings 12:29). Perhaps this is why Dan is not mentioned in the book of Revelation in the distribution of tribal lands in the end time (Rev. 7:5–8).

In his dying blessing, Jacob said that 'Dan will judge' his people but would also be like a snake (Gen. 49:16–17). Moses, in his farewell address, was not much more complimentary, referring to Dan as 'a lion's cub, springing out of Bashan' (Deut. 33:22).                                    E.M.

**DANIEL** Three persons in the OT are named Daniel (Heb., 'my judge is God'): (1) a son of King David, (2) the exile from Judah who became a high-ranking official in the governments of the neo-Babylonian and Medo-Persian empires, as well as a prophet of God, and (3) a Jewish leader who returned with Ezra from Babylon.

**1.** Daniel, son of David, is mentioned only in 1 Chron. 3:1. He was David's second son, Amnon being the first-born. His mother was Abigail and he was born during the seven and a half years that David reigned over Judah in Hebron (1 Chron. 13:4). It appears that this Daniel was also known as Kileab, since that is the name given to David's second son born in Hebron by Abigail in 2 Sam. 3:3.

**2.** Daniel, the exile and prophet, is only named with certainty in the book of Daniel (both in the Heb. and Aram. sections) in the OT, and in Matt. 24:15 in the NT. There is also a strong possibility that his name is found in Ezekiel.

Since the latter part of the 19th century there has existed considerable scepticism concerning historical aspects of the life of Daniel, notably the very existence of figures like Belshazzar and Darius the Mede. Also, a tendency to disregard the possibility of supernatural predictive prophecy has contributed greatly to a pervasive reticence about the reliability of the biblical portrait of Daniel. However, newer historical evidence and scholarly studies have reinforced the historicity of the book, and fresh consideration of the viability of scriptural prophecy before the fact is taking place in many quarters.

Sequential reconstruction of the life of Daniel from the scriptural book that bears his name is a challenging task. The book is topical instead of chronological in its wider movement at certain points; e.g. Dan. 7 is considerably earlier than Dan. 5 and 6. The most notable feature, however, is the scarcity of information concerning Daniel from around the age of perhaps 20–25 in Dan. 2 (before 600 BC, v. 1) until the dated incidents in Dan. 5–10 (ranging from about 553–536 BC).

The only recorded event in which Daniel is in view during that roughly 50-year period is his interpretation of the second vision of King Nebuchadnezzar in Dan. 4. It is not possible to date what occurred in Dan. 4 any more precisely than some time before the end of Nebuchadnezzar's reign in 562 BC. Thus, all that is known of approximately half a century of Daniel's life is the scanty information provided by Dan. 4.

The place and date of Daniel's birth and death are not explicitly stated in Scripture. However, since the book of Daniel begins by focusing on the initial invasion of Jerusalem by Nebuchadnezzar (Dan. 1:1–2) as the occasion of Daniel being taken to Babylon (Dan. 1:3–6), it is highly likely that Daniel was born and raised in Jerusalem. Further, since that invasion took place in 605 BC, and Daniel was at that point placed in the category of 'young men' to be educated (Dan. 1:4), he would probably have been 15–20 years old. That would make his date of birth around 625–620 BC during the middle of the reign of the last godly king of Judah, Josiah (640–609 BC; 2 Chron. 34–35).

The latest dated event of the book of Daniel is a revelation given to the prophet in 'the third year of Cyrus king of Persia' (Dan. 10:1) on the bank of the Tigris River (Dan. 10:4). Since the Babylonian empire fell to the Medo-Persian alliance in 539 BC., that would mean that the last event sequentially in the book of Daniel took place in 537–536 BC. However, at the end of that prophecy, a heavenly being (Dan. 12:7) told Daniel to 'go your way till the end' (i.e. your death). That directive implies that Daniel would live on for some period of time afterwards. Thus, it is virtually certain that Daniel lived well past 80 years old, and quite possibly past 90. And, since Daniel did not accompany the first wave of exiled Jews that returned to Jerusalem in 'the first year of Cyrus' (Ezra 1:1), he apparently died in Persia, having spent 70 (or more) years of his life away from his homeland.

It is not possible to determine anything more specific concerning Daniel's family background than that he was among those (Dan. 1:6) from 'the royal family and the nobility' (Dan. 1:3). If Daniel's childhood years were in the presence of the royal court in Jerusalem, his sense of the tragedy of Judah's fall and the Babylonian Exile would have been even greater. However, his early experience in such circles might also have been a great advantage in his later positions in the governments of Babylon and Persia.

When Daniel began the three-year programme of training for those who would enter King Nebuchadnezzar's service (Dan. 1:5), he (and his Jewish friends, v. 6) was given a Babylonian name, Belteshazzar (v. 7), which means something like 'Bel (a Babylonian god), protect his life'. Since the name is not merely the Babylonian form of Daniel, and it specifically incorporates the name of a Babylonian deity in place of that of the Jewish God (i.e. the 'El' suffix in Daniel), it seems that the renaming was part of a systematic, comprehensive reorientation of the students to embrace fully all aspects of the dominant Babylonian society.

The full nature of the educational process that Daniel went through after arriving in Babylon is not clear, though its rigour and broad outline can be surmised reasonably well. Daniel and his friends were trained among the best and the brightest of the empire (Dan. 1:4). By God's enablement (Dan. 1:17) they proved not only to be far superior to all the other students (v. 19), but also to 'all the magicians and enchanters' (v. 20) in the kingdom.

The subject-matter is stated in Dan. 1:4 to have been 'the language and literature of the Babylonians'. However, v. 17 expands the scope to 'all kinds of literature and learning,' including 'visions and dreams of all kinds'. The completion of the roughly three-year programme (i.e. the first and last years could be fractions of a year and still be spoken of as a year in the reckoning of time in that culture) was an oral examination by King Nebuchadnezzar in which 'wisdom and understanding' were measured and compared with 'all the magicians and enchanters' already in the king's service (Dan. 1:20). Those statements strongly imply that the programme included instruction in magic, divination and probably astrology, apparently as part of the revered literature of Babylon.

Following an angry decree by Nebuchadnezzar to execute 'all the wise men of Babylon' (Dan. 2:12), including Daniel and his friends (v. 13), because the senior counsellors could not detail and interpret one of the king's dreams (vv. 1–11), Daniel and his friends moved to the fore. After receiving a brief stay of execution from Arioch, the head of the royal guard (Dan. 2:14–16), the young Jewish men prayed concertedly overnight to God (vv. 17–23) and 'the mystery was revealed to Daniel in a vision' (v. 19). Daniel's explanation of the dream and its meaning not only saved the lives of the wise men, but it also prompted Nebuchadnezzar to praise the God of Daniel (Dan. 2:47) and to elevate Daniel and his friends to the highest governmental positions in the province of Babylon (vv. 48–49).

It is exceedingly difficult to determine when this incident fits into the life of Daniel. On the one hand, the reference to the second year of Nebuchadnezzar's reign in *Dan.* 2:1 would seem to place it within Daniel's initial three-year educational period spoken of in *v. 5*. If so, *Dan.* 2 functions as a kind of flashback demonstrating Daniel's special ability to 'understand visions and dreams' (*Dan.* 1:17). This understanding is slightly preferable, even though it results in Daniel being appointed to high office by Nebuchadnezzar (*Dan.* 2:48–49) even before completing his training. It does explain better, though, both the extravagance of the king's estimation of Daniel and his friends in *Dan.* 1:20 ('ten times better than all the magicians and enchanters') and the description of Daniel as merely 'a man among the exiles from Judah' (*Dan.* 2:25), rather than an honoured wise man already in the king's service (*Dan.* 1:19–20).

*Dan.* 3 is the only chapter in the book in which the man Daniel is not mentioned, and *Dan.* 4 begins with Nebuchadnezzar apparently at the zenith of his power (*Dan.* 4). The ensuing events imply that the chapter also records the high-point of Daniel's governmental influence. After Daniel interprets a vision that sternly warns the king of the consequences of his self-exaltation in place of the true God (*Dan.* 4:9–27), Nebuchadnezzar is only able to hold his pride in check for a year (vv. 28–32). His self-glorification immediately results in the predicted punishment: being given the mind of an animal and living like an animal for 'seven times' (*Dan.* 4:16, 23, 32–33).

The meaning of 'seven times' is not certain, and how the government of the Babylonian empire carried on while Nebuchadnezzar was mentally incapacitated is even less clear. The expression 'seven times' may merely speak figuratively of an indefinite period of time, or it may refer to a cycle of the calendar, such as a month or a year. If the common understanding that a 'time' was an annual harvest season is correct, then Nebuchadnezzar would have been unable to rule for seven years.

Since Daniel had been appointed a chief adviser to the royal court in *Dan.* 2:49 and is called 'chief of the magicians' in *Dan.* 4:9, it is quite possible that Daniel played a crucial role in maintaining the stable operations of the government while Nebuchadnezzar could not exercise his role as emperor. Even if the period was only weeks or months and though the empire was at peace, the vacuum caused by the absence of such an imposing and intelligent figure as Nebuchadnezzar would normally be quickly noted. Yet, since there is no indication of an internal power struggle or decline during the likely part of Nebuchadnezzar's tenure, it is plausible that highly respected officials, like Daniel, ran the day-to-day affairs of the Babylonian empire until the king regained his sanity and was restored to the throne (*Dan.* 4:34, 36–37).

The next recorded events in Daniel's life are during the early part of the reign of King Belshazzar, the last monarch (c. 553–539 BC) of the neo-Babylonian era. 'In the first year of Belshazzar' (*Dan.* 7:1) Daniel himself had a dream, which became his first recorded vision of the book. The next chapter describes Daniel's second vision, which occurred some two years later, 'In the third year of King Belshazzar's reign' (*Dan.* 8:1). Since both visions depict difficult future circumstances for the people of God, it is not surprising that Daniel was 'deeply troubled' by the first (*Dan.* 7:28) and sick and 'appalled' as a result of the second (*Dan.* 8:27).

During the decade between Nebuchadnezzar's death (562 BC) and the beginning of Belshazzar's rule (553 BC) Daniel apparently lost the bulk of his influence in the Babylonian government. Certainly, Daniel mentions returning to 'the king's business' (Dan. 8:27) in some sense at the conclusion of his second vision, which is to be dated about 551 BC. However, in the well-known handwriting on the wall episode in Dan. 5, which occurred at the point of the final defeat of Babylon by the Medes and Persians (Dan. 5:30–31; 6:28), in 539 BC, King Belshazzar does not seem to know Daniel personally (Dan. 5:13–16) or even to be aware of his fame as an interpreter of dreams and a wise man during Nebuchadnezzar's reign (Dan. 5:11–12).

It is amazing and indicative of God's providential protection in the transition of power that Daniel and his God again received great recognition (Dan. 5:29; 6:2). Not only was Daniel elevated against his wishes to the third highest position in the Babylonian empire, even after delivering his rebuke of the king's pride and his ominous interpretation of the handwriting to Belshazzar (Dan. 5:22–29), but, soon after the Medo-Persian victory over Babylon, he also was appointed as one of three primary administrators over the kingdom by the new ruler of the region, Darius the Mede. This was a role in which Daniel quickly distinguished himself (Dan. 6:1–3).

In order to prevent Daniel from being appointed to the chief administrative role by Darius, a conspiracy was carried out by many of the other Medo-Persian governmental officials to get rid of him by whatever means necessary (Dan. 6:4–5). Because of Daniel's unvarying ethical conduct and religious commitment, the other officials hatched a plan to persuade Darius to decree all prayer, except to the king, illegal for 30 days, punishable by death in the lions' den (Dan. 6:6–9).

Because of his unwillingness to cease praying to God, even on fear of death, Daniel was immediately arrested and thrown in the lions' den (Dan. 6:10–17). God protected Daniel throughout a night with the lions, however, and he was vindicated before Darius and restored to his position of authority (vv. 18–23, 28). The conspirators were then executed in the lions' den (v. 24), and an additional decree by Darius mandated that the people must 'reverence the God of Daniel' (v. 26).

During roughly the same period of time ('the first year of Darius', Dan. 9:1), Daniel prayed an amazing prayer of corporate repentance (Dan. 9:3–20) for the Jewish people. The timing seems to coincide closely with the proclamation by the supreme Persian ruler, Cyrus (Ezra 1:1), to allow Jews throughout the empire who chose to do so to return to Jerusalem and rebuild the Temple there (Ezra 1:2–4). As a result of Daniel's heart-rending prayer, fasting and mourning over the sins of his people (Dan. 9:3, 20), the aged prophet received the astoundingly detailed revelation of the 'seventy sevens' (Dan. 9:24) decreed by the LORD for Israel's future (Dan. 9:24–27). Though there is no consensus on the meaning and fulfilment of this prophecy, it does appear highly likely that the time period parallels the cumulative time in which the Jews failed to observe the divinely mandated law of 'sabbath rests' (2 Chron. 36:20–21) in regard to the planting of their farm land.

Some two years later (Dan. 10:1) Daniel again mourned, prayed and fasted, this time for three weeks (Dan. 20:2–3). That incident may be related to events in Jerusalem, where the rebuilding of the Temple had been stopped by fear and discouragement (Ezra 4:4, 24). The ensuing vision is the latest recorded event in the book of Daniel, and nothing else is recorded in Scripture about the closing period of the prophet's life.

Outside the book of Daniel, the name of Daniel is apparently included three times in Ezekiel (14:14, 20; 28:3). Though some have attributed the references to an ancient man of renown, which would parallel Noah and Job (14:14, 20), it is more likely a reference to the contemporary Daniel. If the occurrences in Ezekiel can be roughly dated to 592 BC (14:14, 20; see 8:1) and 586 BC (28:3; see 26:1), there is sufficient time for Daniel to have demonstrated his righteousness (14:14, 20) and wisdom in regard to mysteries (28:3). His recognition as the foremost counsellor in Babylon and his unyielding commitment to God would have been solidly in place by 600 BC (Dan. 1–2, esp. 2:1).

The only other mention of Daniel by name is in Matt. 24:15. There, in the middle of Matthew's version of the Olivet Discourse of Jesus (Matt. 24–25), reference is made to 'the abomination that causes desolation, spoken of through the prophet Daniel' (Matt. 24:15). Christ's manner of speaking here would seem to underline the historicity of the events and visions recorded in the book of Daniel.

A further tribute to Daniel's faith in the lions' den is also recorded in Heb. 11:33. His name is not mentioned, but the lack of another similar event in the OT, as well as the location of the phrase next to a reference to the furnace of fire episode (Heb. 11:34) from Dan. 3, makes the identification virtually certain.

An overall evaluation of the contributions of Daniel must include superlatives. Emerging from the trauma of the invasion of his childhood home in Judah, Daniel remarkably went on to occupy positions in the top levels of imperial authority and influence in both the Babylonian and Medo-Persian empires during a career that spanned over 60 years.

Yet, his even more profound legacy is in the realm of the spiritual. Daniel was the vehicle of divine revelation, both as interpreter and seer of visions, of some of the most far-reaching and detailed of biblical prophecies. Since that revelation spanned the period of the Babylonian Captivity of Judah (generally dated 605–539 BC), Daniel, more than any other biblical personality, proved to be a hinge figure between the pre-Captivity decline and the post-Captivity rebuilding of Jerusalem and Judah. That claim is justified, even though Daniel spent the vast bulk of his life at a great geographical distance from Judah. He was influential equally in the halls of power and by way of his extraordinary godly example.

Few people in Scripture exhibit the faith, courage, prayerfulness or wisdom which are seen consistently in the life of Daniel. Both in his day (Ezek. 14:14, 20) and in the remembrance of later biblical writers (Heb. 11:33), the lifestyle of Daniel, humble governmental counsellor-administrator and prophet of the one true God, is rightly revered and worthy of emulation.

**3.** Daniel, a Levitical leader of the Jews under Ezra and Nehemiah, is mentioned returning with Ezra from Babylon (Ezra 8:2) and in the signing of a solemn document of commitment to the LORD (Neh. 10:6). He was a descendant of Ithamar.

A.B.L.

**DARDA 1.** A man renowned for his wisdom as one of the sons of Mahol. Solomon's wisdom was greater by comparison, which is why we encounter Darda in the text of 1 Kings 4:31. In response to his request of God (v. 29), Solomon was given such extraordinary wisdom that it outshone even those known for wisdom in his day.

**2.** In 1 Chron. 2:6 he is listed as a son of Zerah and a descendant of Judah. He was probably the same as 1.

**DARIUS 1.** Darius, King of Persia. Known as Darius I or 'the Great', Darius reigned over the Persian Empire from 522 BC to 486. He appears in Ezra 4–6; Hag. 1:1, 15; 2:10; Zech. 1:1, 7; 7:1 as the ruler who gave permission to the Jews to rebuld their Temple.

**2.** Darius the Mede, a ruler over

Babylon in the days of Daniel. He should not be confused with the King Darius of *Dan. 9:1* and elsewhere (see 1.). He was actually governing under Cyrus, the founder of the Persian Empire (*Dan. 6:28*). Though some scholars identify Darius with Cyrus himself, it is more likely that he was a governor of Median descent known as Gubaru (Gk., Gobryas).

**DARKON,** 'servant of Solomon' whose descendants were among those who returned from Exile with Nehemiah (*Ezra 2:56; Neh. 7:58*).

**DATHAN,** son of Eliab. He is always mentioned with (see) *Abiram* (*Num. 16:1,12, 24–25 etc.*).

# DAVID

## General

David is the name of the greatest king of Israel and human ancestor of the Lord Jesus. His story, accomplishments, and problems receive extensive treatment in *1 Sam. 16–2 Kings 1* and in *1 Chron. 2–29*. The meaning of the name David is still uncertain. The connection between the Akkadian *dāwidûm* ('chief, commander') is attractive, but doubtful. More likely is the association with the Heb. root *dwd* ('love'), giving the meaning 'beloved'. Some have suggested that David is a throne name and that he is Elhanan ('God is gracious'), the hero who killed Goliath (*2 Sam. 21:19*). Though this solution may answer the seeming discrepancy between *1 Sam. 17* according to which David killed Goliath and *2 Sam. 21:19*, which commends Elhanan for killing Goliath, it creates another problem: why then is Elhanan named in the list of David's heroes? Another suggestion comes from *1 Chron. 20:5* which identifies Elhanan as the hero who killed the brother of Goliath, Lahmi. Since it is unclear whether the text in *2 Sam. 21:19* or in *1 Chron. 20:5* represents a textual corruption, the identification of Elhanan is uncertain.

## Background

David was the youngest of the eight sons born to Jesse, the Ephrathite from Bethlehem (*1 Sam. 17:11–12*). Jesse hailed from the tribe of Judah and was a great-grandson of Boaz and Ruth, the Moabitess (*Ruth 4:18–22; cf. 1 Chron. 2:1–15; Matt. 1:2–6; Luke 3:31–38*).

In his youth David took care of the family sheep. As a shepherd he learned to care for his animals as well as to protect them from wild animals. This experience taught him to depend on the Lord, as he affirmed to Saul. 'The LORD who delivered me from the paw of the lion and the paw of the bear will deliver me from the hand of this Philistine' (*1 Sam. 17:37*).

David was also a musician of note. When Saul suffered from depression or melancholia, his servants knew of David's reputation (*1 Sam. 16:16*). One of them said, 'I have seen a son of Jesse of Bethlehem who knows how to play the harp. He is a brave man and a warrior. He speaks well and is a fine-looking man. And the LORD is with him' (*v. 18*). This text bears out several characteristics of the youthful David: his musical skills, bravery, eloquence, appearance, but more than that, the evident presence of the LORD.

## God's election of David to be king

The young David was outstanding in both his love for God and in his physical appearance (1 Sam. 16:12). After Saul had been rejected from perpetual kingship by his acts of disobedience (1 Sam. 15:26), the LORD charged Samuel with the task of anointing a son of Jesse. Son after son passed before Samuel, but of none did the LORD say, 'This is my man.' When all seven sons had passed before Samuel, he wondered why the LORD had not shown him which son had to be anointed to become king. Samuel had been looking for a candidate who would qualify by his physical stature for kingship. After all, Samuel had told the people earlier that Saul was well qualified for kingship by his stature, 'Do you see the man the LORD has chosen? There is no-one like him among all the people' (1 Sam. 10:24).

Jesse told Samuel that his youngest son, David, was still taking care of the sheep. Upon his being brought before Samuel, the prophet knew that this lad met God's standard in that 'The LORD does not look at the things man looks at. Man looks at the outward appearance, but the LORD looks at the heart' (1 Sam. 16:7). David received two confirmations of his election: Samuel anointed him in a family ceremony and the Spirit of the LORD came on him in a powerful way. (v.13).

## David with Saul

1 Sam. 16–31 is a loose anthology of stories that as a collection have been entitled 'the history of David's rise'. The purpose of these stories is to vindicate David against accusations that he acted subversively in taking the throne from Saul's family by bearing responsibility for the deaths of Saul, Jonathan, Abner, and Ishbosheth. Clearly, God was working in all the circumstances of David's life that took him from being with the sheep to a musician in the king's palace, from fighting off wild animals to his victories over the Philistines, and from being a national hero to a political refugee.

First, David was invited to serve King Saul as a musician. Saul was suffering from melancholia because the Spirit of the LORD had departed from him (1 Sam. 16:14). At the court David pleased the king, so he was appointed to be his armour-bearer (v. 21).

Next, providence called again when the Philistines attacked Israel (1 Sam. 17). The Philistine giant, Goliath, challenged Saul and Israel several times a day for 40 days (1 Sam. 17:16). David 'happened' to be bringing supplies for his brothers and chanced to hear the giant's dare. Motivated by his zeal for the LORD, his love for the people, and by the high reward – wealth, marriage to Saul's daughter, and an exemption of the family from taxes – David volunteered to engage Goliath in battle. The LORD was with him. He triumphed over the Philistine, whom he killed with a sling and a stone (1 Sam. 17:50).

Third, David was invited to make the royal palace his home (1 Sam. 18:2). Members of Saul's family loved him. Jonathan 'became one in spirit with David, and he loved him as himself' (v. 1). He went so far as to make a 'covenant' with David (v. 3). As an expression of his deep love and respect for David, he gave him his clothes and armour (v. 4). Michal, too, loved David (v. 20).

As often happens, when too many good things are happening, fortune turned into fate. David's renown grew fast. Throughout Israel, the women praised David's name and made a positive comparison between the youth and the king: 'Saul has slain his thousands, and David his tens of thousands' (1 Sam. 18:7). This contrast aroused Saul's jealousy (v. 8). He knew that his days were numbered and that he had to protect the throne for his family. This was the beginning of acts of overt hostility against David. The narrator of Samuel wrote, 'from that time on Saul kept a jealous eye on David' (v. 9).

Saul's jealousy blinded him. He was deceitful in reversing his promise to give his older daughter Merab to David in marriage (1 Sam. 18:17). He required David to engage the Philistines in battle in the hope that he would lose his life. David, slow to accept a marriage into the royal family, was quick to please the king. In the mean time, Merab was given to another man in marriage (1 Sam. 18:19). Wily Saul challenged David to demonstrate his prowess again by killing 100 Philistines as a dowry. He was chagrined in giving Michal to David as a wife, because he knew that the LORD was with David and saw in his daughter's love for David a betrayal of her father (1 Sam. 18:28).

Fourth, through David's friendship with Saul's son, Jonathan, he was fore-warned of Saul's deep hatred for him as well as of Saul's plot to take his life. Jonathan loved David (1 Sam. 19:1) and was not apprehensive about his military feats and his growing popularity. He even spoke on behalf of David, invited him back to the palace (v. 7), but had to perceive gradually that his father was committed to having David killed. Saul made every attempt to kill David in the palace (v. 10) and even in his own house (v. 11). The two men separated under duress. Jonathan knew that David's life was at risk and also that God had a special plan for David. The two made a covenant and separated for life (1 Sam. 20:16, 42).

## Saul against David

Saul did everything to rid himself of David. Driven away from the court, David sought refuge with Achish, king of the Philistine city, Gath. Afraid that the goodwill of his host would change, he left for Adullam (1 Sam. 22:1). Here he headed a band of outlaws. He brought his family to safety in Moab, and returned to face the dangers of his exiled existence. Whoever came to the rescue of David was likely to be killed by Saul, as the priests of Nob were (1 Sam. 21–22). Wherever David went, Saul would hear about it and pursue him.

In the meantime, David's base of support was growing. Outlaws, many of whom were warriors, joined David. A priest who escaped the massacre at Nob, Abiathar, and the prophet Gath also united with David. Through his many exploits he put people into his debt. David reduced the Philistine threat as, for example, at Keilah (1 Sam. 23). He and his men also came to the defence of the people of Judah who were threatened by invaders. They lived from a share of the crops, herds, and livestock that they protected. Not all were willing to part with their wealth. Nabal, a wealthy farmer, had received such protection from David and his men, but was too greedy to reward them for their labours (1 Sam. 25). This angered David, but Abigail, the wife of Nabal, met him with gifts. Upon her husband's death, she became David's wife (1 Sam. 25:42).

Again and again David had occasion to avenge himself of Saul, but, instead, he spared his life. Life became so oppressive that he had to find refuge with Achish, king of Gath. He received the city of Ziklag for his asylum, from where he helped Saul in reducing the Philistine force (1 Sam. 27). So confident was Achish of David's loyalty that he took him with him on a major engagement at Gilboa (1 Sam. 28). Were it not for the Philistine apprehension of a potential conflict of interests, David would have fought his own people (1 Sam. 29). David returned to Ziklag and found that the city was burned, the property was looted, and the population had been taken captive by the Amalekites. While the Philistines crushed Israel in the north, David pursued the Amalekites and brought an end to their hostilities.

## David's rise to kingship

Saul and Jonathan lost their lives in the battle at Gilboa (2 Sam. 1:4). Rather than celebrating Saul's death, David mourned over the death of the king and of Jonathan (2 Sam. 1:19–27). The news of Saul's death travelled fast, but the reaction differed in the north from that in the south. The northern tribes recognized Ish-bosheth, Saul's son, as legitimate king (2 Sam. 2:8–9). The tribe of Judah was loyal to David and separated from the union by making Hebron the capital of the newly established kingdom (2 Sam. 2:3–4).

It did not take long for people to recognize the ineptitude of Ish-bosheth. His military commander, Abner, went over to David, as well as other leading citizens, and opened negotiations with him. These were cut short by Joab's revenge of his brother in the murder of Abner. The weakness of the north encouraged the assassination of Ish-bosheth and the overture toward a union under David (2 Sam. 5:1–3).

The newly unified kingdom was first centred at Hebron. Desirous of a more central location and realizing the strategic problem of the Canaanite presence, David set out to conquer Jerusalem. The city had never been conquered by the Israelites and was located at a strategic crossing between east and west and north and south. Joab, the military commander, was successful in penetrating the city and in handing it over to David.

David set out to consolidate his kingdom by making Jerusalem the administrative centre. It was a neutral city, not having any special allegiance to the northern or southern tribes (2 Sam. 5:9–10). The growth in his power did not go unnoticed. Hiram, king of Tyre, had his craftsmen build a palace for David (2 Sam. 5:11). This act cemented a relationship between Hiram and the house of David. Strange as it may seem, David's strengthened position also jeopardized the relative quiet of Judah. The Philistines did not bother Judah during the first two years of David's reign. However, with the growth of his strength, they set out to crush David's growing popularity. David resisted them successfully and thereby defined their boundary to the coastal plain (2 Sam. 5:19–25).

## Jerusalem as the centre of David's kingdom

The renewed quietness in Judah encouraged David to involve the tribes in recognizing Jerusalem as the religious centre by bringing the ark of the covenant, the central symbol of Israel's covenantal relationship, into the city (2 Sam. 6). See entry under Covenant. Having found rest in Jerusalem, David further sought to receive God's approval to provide a perpetual centre for Israel's worship by the construction of a Temple (2 Sam. 7). The LORD transposed David's offer by granting David the permanence of a 'house' (dynasty) and by permitting his son to build a permanent 'house' for the LORD. The promise of a dynasty was incorporated in a covenant of grant. The promise granted David a perpetual place within God's kingdom by bestowing upon him the privilege of being a 'son' of God. Ps. 2 celebrates the status of the son as one who enjoys a privileged position, receives authority to establish God's kingdom (see Ps. 72) by subduing the nations, when necessary by force, and brings God's blessing upon the faithful in all places on earth. These promises comprise the covenant God made with David. The Davidic covenant is a sovereign and gracious administration by which the LORD anointed David and his house to establish his kingdom and effectually to bring about a kingdom of peace, glory, and blessing. Our Lord and the apostles affirm that these promises find their focus and receive their confirmation in Jesus Christ (= 'messiah'). He is the 'anointed' one who has received authority and power (Matt. 28:20; Acts 2) from on high over all creation, including the church (Col. 1).

Encouraged with God's promise and enjoying the consolidation of Israel's position among the nations, David forged ahead. He fortified Jerusalem, developed a centralized administration of government, fought off any invading forces, and was aggressive in establishing the peace of Israel. He subjugated the Philistines, the Moabites, the Edomites, and the Ammonites (2 Sam. 12:29–31). He exacted tribute from the Arameans and nations that he decided not to subjugate (2 Sam. 8; 10). He deposited much of the tribute and booty in the Temple fund (2 Sam. 8:11–12). While severe in his justice with the nations, the king dealt compassionately with Mephibosheth, Jonathan's son. He provided him with a place and with sustenance for life (2 Sam. 9). It may be that a famine (2 Sam. 21:1) dates to this period. The famine was so severe that David asked the LORD for an explanation. It was revealed that the famine was a judgment on Saul's misguided zeal of trying to annihilate the Gibeonites (2 Sam. 21:2), who had sought and received protection in Israel (Josh. 9:15, 18–26). The death of seven of Saul's descendants, excluding Mephibosheth, satisfied the Gibeonite demand for justice. The LORD graciously removed the curse, and renewed the land with rain. David had the bones of Saul, Jonathan, and of the seven men buried in the tomb of Kish (2 Sam. 21:14).

### David's fall

From this point on, the story of David is a mixture of tragedy and divine providence. David is a tragic character. Raised up by God's grace to a position of immense power, he lusted after Bathsheba, had sexual relations with her, covered up his sin by having her husband killed in the line of duty, and married her legally, when she was pregnant (2 Sam. 11). The prophet Nathan bore prophetic witness, condemning David's lust, greed, and insidious behaviour (2 Sam. 12). David confessed his sin and was forgiven (2 Sam. 12:13; cf. Pss. 32; 51), but he suffered from the consequences of his perfidy for the rest of his life. The child born from his union with Bathsheba fell sick and died.

Consequently, David experienced instability and death in his family. Amnon raped his sister causing her disgrace (2 Sam. 13) and was murdered by Tamar's brother, Absalom. Absalom fled for his life and lived in exile for two years. David longed to see his son again and was encouraged by Joab, who outwitted the king by forcing him to follow up on the advice he had given to a woman from Tekoa. Upon Joab's urging, she had gone to the king and asked him for his protection for her son who had murdered his brother. Joab brought Absalom back, but not to the royal palace. After another period of two years, Absalom returned to the palace, enjoyed favour with the people, and thought of ways to get even with his father (2 Sam. 14).

Consequently, David experienced civil war within the country. Absalom had time to devise plans to upset the establishment. For four years he carefully prepared for the time when the people would favour him over his ageing father. Absalom had himself crowned at Hebron and with rapidity moved to Jerusalem (2 Sam. 15). David left Jerusalem with an entourage, leaving several trusted counsellors behind (Abiathar, Zadok, Hushai). Hushai gave Absalom poor advice and dispatched messengers to inform the king of Absalom's movements (2 Sam. 17). The war brought disastrous results for Absalom's forces. Absalom lost his life, hanging on a tree. The victory was clear, but David felt the loss of his son more than the joy of victory.

The king returned to Jerusalem with the support of the Judeans, who had earlier rallied behind Absalom. The northern tribes (Israelites) felt betrayed by the utter disregard of the Judeans. They had given support to the king and given the size of their territory, their voices should have counted. The Judeans claimed the king as theirs and offended the Israelites by their brazen arrogance (2 Sam. 19:40–43).

Consequently, the union of the tribes was fragile at best. The dissent rapidly grew into another civil war under the leadership of Sheba son of Bicri, a Benjaminite. He dispatched Amasa to gather Judean warriors and to put down the rebellion. When Amasa was delayed, David commissioned Abishai to pursue Sheba. (Joab, having lost favour by killing Absalom, was now under the command of Abishai.) After Amasa met up with Abishai, Joab murdered Amasa and resumed the command over the forces. He pursued Sheba as far as Abel Beth Maacah and laid siege to the city. A wise woman spared the city by offering to have the head of Sheba thrown from the wall. Joab returned as general to Jerusalem, having put down the rebellion (2 Sam. 20:23).

### The last days of David

By the end of his life, David had accomplished the goal of solidifying Israel against the Philistines to the south-west, the Edomites to the south-east, the Moabites and the Ammonites to the east, and the Arameans to the north. He had extended his kingdom to all areas of the land promised to Abraham (Gen. 15:18–19). He developed an administration by which he was able to govern his extensive kingdom. A standing army was ready to maintain stability within the kingdom.

Because of his successes, David was self-reliant and numbered the people. The LORD was displeased and brought a plague upon the kingdom. David was responsible for the innocent who died. He purchased a place and presented a sacrifice expressing sorrow for his high-mindedness. This place, the threshing flour of Araunah, was to become the location on which the Solomonic Temple was built (2 Sam. 24:1–25).

David prepared for his death by having Solomon anointed as king, after he was told that his son Adonijah had made an attempt to wrest the kingdom from Solomon (1 Kings 1:1–2:12). He forewarned Solomon of several people who could unsettle the stability of his kingdom: Joab, the commander-in-chief and Shimei, the rebel (1 Kings 2:5–6, 8–9). He charged Solomon to be faithful to the LORD, because in him was the source of strength and the perpetuity of the dynasty.

## Conclusions

David was a human, who remained faithful to the LORD throughout his life. Though he sinned against God and man grievously, he was a humble man. David's strength was in the LORD from the beginning to the end of his life. The psalms which are ascribed to him and his life bear out this truth. Such an affirmation of his trust in the LORD is also found toward the end of 2 Samuel: 'The LORD is my rock, my fortress and my deliverer; my God is my rock, in whom I take refuge, my shield and the horn of my salvation. He is my stronghold, my refuge and my saviour – from violent men you save me' (2 Sam. 22:2–3). The psalm also bears out the correlation between humility, obedience, and God's goodness. As David wrote: 'To the faithful you show yourself faithful, to the blameless you show yourself blameless, to the pure you show yourself pure, but to the crooked you show yourself shrewd. You save the humble, but your eyes are on the haughty to bring them low' (2 Sam. 22:27–28). Not only did the LORD show his strength to David and his contemporaries, he also committed himself to protect all his people through an anointed Davidic descendant. This is the essence of the Davidic covenant.

The NT writers witness to the connection between David and Jesus Christ. Jesus' genealogy goes back to David (Matt. 1:1). He is the ruler on David's throne whose kingdom extends to the ends of the world. He is the head of the church (Col. 1:18) and will bring all nations to acknowledge his sovereignty (1 Cor. 15:25; cf. Acts 2:35). He will establish God's Kingdom on earth (1 Cor. 15:27–28), and thereby fulfil the promises to all of God's people, whether they be Jews or Gentiles.

W.A.VG.

**DEACON/DEACONS** Many people attempt to tie the origin of the deacon office to Acts 6, but this cannot be substantiated. That text appears to address a special circumstance as opposed to the founding of a specific office. This means that two texts mention the office, Phil. 1:1, which merely names it, and 1 Tim. 3:8–14. Philippians does show that a formal office existed, since it is the leadership that is addressed at the start of this letter, and the leaders are distinguished from the saints. There is one other poten-tial text, Rom. 16:1, which names Phoebe as a deaconess. The problem is that the term used there is the same term both for the office and for naming any servant in a general sense (diakanos). In favour of the view that Rom. 16:1 refers to an office is the fact that Paul gives the sort of official-sounding commendation that the church is to welcome her that he gives to other official servants elsewhere (e.g. 1 Cor. 4:14–21).

1 Tim. 3 simply mentions qualifications of character that mirror those of an

elder. Deacons should be worthy of respect, sincere, not indulging in wine, nor pursuing dishonest gain, while holding to the truths of the faith. A deacon is to be the husband of one wife and an able manager of his children and his home. The key stipulation may be in 1 Tim. 3:10, which says they are to be tested and then made deacons. This shows that a process of recognition and 'leadership development' was in view. Social standing or the need to fill a vacancy were not alone good enough reasons for making someone a deacon.

What do deacons do? The texts do not tell us. It appears that those who became deacons took on ministry roles *without* the responsibilities of full shepherding or overall oversight in the church, such as the elders possessed. The deacons' ministry responsibilities were confined to very specific spheres, as opposed to responsibility for the entire community. Their management skill in the home is seen as a test of their suitability for larger ministry, so some 'administrative' skill to lead others is assumed. A deacon served as a recognized, effective contributor to the body. 1 Tim. 3:11 may suggest the presence of deaconesses as well (if it does not refer to the deacons' wives), something the church attests to until the 3rd century. The idea that deaconesses are at issue is suggested by the absence of a similar 'elder's wife' discussion when elders are mentioned. The deaconesses probably had responsibility for special ministry to widows and younger, single women.

In sum, a deacon is simply someone who has been an effective servant and is recognized by the church as functioning in this way. The office is a formal community recognition of someone as a church minister in the general sense of the term.                D.B.

**DEBIR,** the Canaanite king of Eglon. He had answered the call of Adoni-zedek, king of Jerusalem, to join a coalition of kings to fight the Gibonites, who had recently made a peace treaty with Joshua and the Israelites. When Gibeon was attacked, Joshua came to its aid and defeated the coalition, killing the kings (*Josh. 10:3–16; 12:12*).

**DEBORAH** (Heb., 'honey bee').

**1.** *Gen. 35:8* mentions a Deborah who was 'Rebekah's nurse', who 'died and was buried under the oak below Bethel'. She came from Mesopotamia with Rebekah and lived in Isaac's household until her death (*Gen. 24:59*).

**2.** Deborah, a prophetess and wife of Lappidoth, became a leader of Israel in the days of the Judges. She is the only female leader to be mentioned from those days. She acted as a judge, holding court 'under the Palm of Deborah between Ramah and Bethel in the hill country of Ephraim, and the Israelites came to her to have their disputes decided' (*Judg. 4:4–5*). She came to power during a time when the Israelites were once again ignoring the Law of God and were living under the oppressive rule of the Canaanite king, Jabin, and his general, Sisera (*Judg. 4:1–2*).

In her role as a prophet she called upon Barak from Naphtali and informed him that God wanted him to attack and defeat Sisera. Barak refused to go to war unless Deborah went with him. She consented but pointed out that the honour of victory would no longer lie with him but with a woman. Indeed, in the end the victory belonged to a woman called Jael, who killed Sisera as he was fleeing from his defeat in battle at the hands of Deborah and Barak (*Judg. 4:17–22*).

Deborah's commitment to and faith in the LORD to bring them victory and restore the honour of his name in Israel far exceeded that of Barak, whose fear of Sisera was considerable. Throughout, Deborah called on the LORD and gave the glory for victory to him. Her thanksgiving to God is recorded in what has become known as 'The Song of Deborah' (*Judg. 5*). There she emphasized the sovereignty of the LORD over the nations and their kings and gods. The final verse of praise recognizes God's justice in dealing with wickedness and his great love in dealing with those who love him: 'So may all your enemies perish, O LORD! But may they who love you be like the sun when it rises in its strength' (*Judg. 5:31*). See *Judges, Barak, Sisera, Jael*.  P.D.G.

**DEDAN 1.** Dedan was descended from Ham through Cush and Raamah, and was the brother of Sheba (*Gen. 10:7; 1 Chron. 1:9*).

**2.** The son of Jokshan and a grandson of Abraham and his concubine Keturah. He was the father of the Asshurites. (*Gen. 25:1–3; 1 Chron. 1:32*).

**DELAIAH 1.** One of the sons of Elioenai included among the list of the descendants of Jehoiachin the captive (*1 Chron. 3:24*).

**2.** A priest who was chosen by lot to be 23rd in the order of ministering during the reign of David (*1 Chron. 24:18*).

**3.** His descendants, along with those of Tobiah and Nekoda, numbered 652 and were among those who returned from Exile but could not show that their families were descended from Israel (*Ezra. 2:60*; the number in *Neh. 7:62* is 642).

**4.** The father of Shemaiah, whom Nehemiah went to visit during a time of opposition to the rebuilding of the wall (*Neh. 6:10*).

**5.** One of Jehoiakim's officials to whom Micaiah took the words of Jeremiah's scroll in *Jer. 36:12*. He urged the king not to burn the scroll, but the king would not listen (*Jer. 36:25*). See *Micaiah* for detail.  M.P.

**DELILAH** was a beautiful woman from the valley of Sarek in Philistine territory,

home of the Israelites' enemies (*Judg. 16:4*). Samson, having already shown his propensity to fickleness, fell foul of her snare and they married. Using devious seduction and persistent nagging, she enticed Samson to reveal the secret of his strength, which she then disclosed to the Philistines, who gouged out his eyes and bound him with bronze shackles. What Delilah eventually discovered was that Samson's strength depended on the length of his hair. While he was sleeping she cut his hair so he could be taken captive (*Judg. 16:6–22*). Her intrigue led to Samson's death, but not before the LORD had used Samson to bring destruction on hundreds of Philistines (*vv. 26–30*). Also see *Samson* and *Judges*.

S.V.

**DEMAS,** one of Paul's travelling companions and a friend of Luke (*Col. 4:14; Philem. 2:4*). However, much later, when Paul was a prisoner in Rome, he wrote to Timothy that Demas had deserted him. The sad comment in *2 Tim. 4:10* makes it clear that materialism was as much a draw for the early Christians as it is for many in the 20th century: 'for Demas, because he loved this world, has deserted me and has gone to Thessalonica'.

**DEMETRIUS** (Gk., 'belonging to Demeter').

**1.** A silversmith who lived in Ephesus (see also *Artemis*). He was among the many artisans and craftsmen who made a profitable business from exploiting the presence in Ephesus of one of the great wonders of the world – the temple of Artemis. Artemis of the Ephesians was worshipped not just by the Ephesians, but drew pilgrims and tourists from around the Roman world. These silversmiths would make images and shrines of the goddess (*Acts 19:24, 38*).

When the apostle Paul preached Christianity ('the Way', *Acts 19:23*) in the town and people began to turn to Christ,

Demetrius led those craftsmen who immediately recognized a threat to their livelihood. Paul was preaching that 'man-made gods are no gods at all' (v.26). They organized a virtual riot in which Paul's companions, Gaius and Silas, were seized and taken to the theatre to be harangued for a while by the crowd. The affront of the gospel to the deity of Artemis seems to have been added to the offence only as an afterthought (vv.27, 34). Eventually the city clerk quietened the crowd and pointed out that if Paul was breaking the law, then redress could be had through the courts. It is particularly interesting at this early stage of the gospel in Ephesus (Paul had been there about two years) to note how quickly its impact was felt in every area of life. Books (scrolls) on sorcery worth a fortune were publicly burned as people became Christians and, as we have seen, trade and commerce were quickly affected. Paul's preaching demanded a commitment to Christ that would always require such dramatic changes, as people faced up to serving a new Master.

**2.** A disciple noted by John for his Christian commitment (3 John 12).

P.D.G.

**DEUEL** (Heb., 'God knows'), the father of Eliasaph, a Gadite leader in the time of Moses. His son was a famous leader of the tribe at the time of the dedication of the Tabernacle (Num. 1:14; 2:14; 7:47 etc). Because the Heb. D is sometimes confused with the Heb. R, this man is called Reuel in Num. 2:14.

**DEVIL,** a name used regularly in the NT for Satan (Rev. 12:9). The term 'devil' appears most frequently in the Gospels, and especially to describe Satan when he came to tempt Jesus in the desert. It is this tempting and deceiving role of Satan that seems mostly to be described by the word 'devil' (Matt. 4:1; Luke 4:2–3; John 13:12; Acts 13:10 etc.). See Satan.

**DIBLAIM** (Heb., 'two cakes'), the father of Gomer, Hosea's unfaithful wife (Hos. 1:3).

**DIBRI,** a Danite. Her daughter Shelomith married an Egyptian (Lev. 24:11). Shelomith's son blasphemed the LORD and so was put to death outside the camp (vv. 13–15).

**DIDYMUS** (Gk., 'twin'), a name always associated in the NT with (see) Thomas (John 11:16; 20:24; 21:2).

**DIKLAH** (Heb., 'palm'), a descendant of Shem and a son of Joktan (Gen. 10:27; 1 Chron. 1:21).

**DINAH** (Heb., 'just') was the daughter of Leah and Jacob (Gen. 30:21; 46:15). Dinah left her family home to visit other women in the area. As she did this she was seen by Shechem, a Hivite, and ruler of that area. He caught her and raped her. Later he asked his father Hamor to acquire this young woman as his wife (Gen. 34:1–4). When Jacob's sons returned from the fields and heard what had happened they were very angry and planned their revenge. (vv. 7, 13). They pretended to go along with Shechem's request. Shechem offered anything he could give in order to marry Dinah (v. 11). So Jacob's sons demanded that all the males in Shechem should be circumcised. They agreed to go through with this (vv. 18, 24) and while they 'were still in pain . . . Simeon and Levi, Dinah's brothers, took their swords and attacked the unsuspecting city, killing every male' (v. 25).

The events recounted concerning Dinah, Hamor and Shechem demonstrate the lasting problems that the Israelites had with the Canaanites whom they had not destroyed on entering the land.

P.D.G.

**DIONYSIUS,** one of those converted through Paul's preaching when he was in Athens (Acts 17:34). The fact that he is singled out probably means that he was a 'prominent' Greek man (v. 12). He was a member of the Areopagus, which functioned as the High Court of Athens and met on Mars Hill, where Paul had preached. There is no evidence to confirm the tradition that he was the first bishop of Athens and martyred under Domitian. See also *Damaris*.

**DIOTREPHES** is mentioned in *3 John 9–10*, where John reprimands him for not receiving his letter and not welcoming Christian brothers. His sin was the desire for self-aggrandizement, which led him to 'gossip maliciously' about John and his representatives. He seemed to have a stranglehold on the people in the church, being an autocratic leader who would expel people who did not agree with him and were prepared to receive people like John.

John seems to make a deliberate contrast between him and Demetrius, whom he commends as 'well spoken of by everyone' (*3 John 12*). The problem for Diotrephes may well have been the question of apostolic authority. This became an issue for Paul in some places. An absent apostle was unlikely to be as influential as a local leader, but all church leaders were expected to follow apostolic teaching. For leaders like Diotrephes, who were more interested in their own status, this must have seemed very threatening and something to be resisted.    P.D.G.

**DISHAN** (Heb., 'a mountain goat'), a leader of the clan of the Horites and a son of Seir (*Gen. 36:21; 1 Chron. 1:38, 42*). The 'Dishan' of *Gen. 36:28* should read 'Dishon' (the son of Anah; see *1 Chron. 1:38–42*).

**DISHON 1.** A son of Seir and a chief of the Horites (*Gen. 36:21*).

**2.** A son of Anah and a grandson of Seir. Dishon's sister was Oholibamah (Esau's wife). His sons are also listed (*Gen.*

*36:25–26; 1 Chron. 1:41*). The 'Dishan' of *Gen. 36:28* should read 'Dishon'.

**DODAI** (Heb., 'his beloved'), an Ahohite and the father of Eleazar. Eleazar was one of David's 'three mighty men'. Dodai himself was also a commander in David's army, on duty with his men in the second month of each year (*2 Sam. 23:9; 1 Chron. 11:12; 27:4*).

**DODAVAHU** came from Mareshah and was the father of Eliezer (*2 Chron. 20:37*). Eliezer was a prophet who prophesied against King Jehoshaphat of Judah because he had made an alliance with Ahaziah of Israel.

**DODO 1.** From the tribe of Isaachar, he was the father of Puah and the grandfather of Israel's judge Tola, who lived in the hill country of Ephraim (*Judg. 10:1*).

**2.** The father of Elhanan from Bethlehem. Elhanan was one of David's 'Thirty', who were loyal warriors (*2 Sam. 23:24; 1 Chron. 11:26*).

**DOEG** (Heb., 'anxious, fearful'), the Edomite was one of Saul's shepherds. He was present with the priests at Nob when David and his men arrived seeking food (*1 Sam. 21:7*). Ahimelech the priest provided David with consecrated bread. Doeg later returned to Saul, who was chasing David and determined to put him to death. Doeg told Saul that he had seen David at Nob (*1 Sam. 22:9*). Saul summonsed the priests of Nob, led by Ahimelech, and ordered them to be killed for offering aid to David. Saul's guards refused to lift their swords against the LORD's anointed priests, and so Saul ordered Doeg the Edomite to kill them. That day Doeg killed 85 of the priests and then wiped out the town of Nob (*1 Sam. 22:18–19*). When David heard what had happened he was devastated, blaming himself for the deaths of all the priests (*vv. 20–23*). The massacre is remembered in the dedication to *Ps. 52*.

The incident is an illustration of how far Saul had moved from worship of the LORD. Now he was unable to hear the advice of the high priest and was even prepared to kill the LORD's representatives. The contrast is vivid between this evil king and the young David, biding his time until the LORD should choose to bring him to the throne.　　　P.D.G.

**DORCAS** was a woman who, having died, was prayed for by Peter and was raised from death (*Acts 9:36–39*). See also *Tabitha*.

**DRUSILLA,** a Jewish woman who was the third wife of governor Felix. She apparently was present with Felix when Paul spoke to him about faith in Christ (*Acts 24:24*). Josephus gives us some further information about this woman. She was the youngest daughter of Herod Agrippa I. Bernice was one of her sisters. She was born c. AD 38. Her marriage to Felix was her second, and with him she had a son, Agrippa, who died in the volcanic eruption at Vesuvius in AD 79. There is no indication that she ever followed the Christian faith.

**DUMAH,** a grandson of Abraham, was the seventh son of Ishmael and the progenitor of the people who lived in Dumah (*Gen. 25:14*). He was a tribal leader. Although the place has not been clearly identified, some have suggested that it lay near Hebron at a place called Deir ed-Domeh.

# E

**EBAL,** a descendant of Esau, was the son of Shobal, a clan leader of the Edomites (*Gen. 36:23; 1 Chron. 1:40*).

**EBED** (Heb., 'servant').
**1.** An Ephraimite and the father of Gaal. Gaal moved to Shechem, where he instigated a rebellion against Abimelech, the king (*Judg. 9:28–35*).
**2.** One of the family heads who returned to Jerusalem from Babylon with Ezra. He was a descendant of Adin and had 50 men with him (*Ezra 8:6*).

**EBED-MELECH,** a royal official in the court of Zedekiah. Following Jeremiah's prophecy to the officials that the Israelites should leave Jerusalem and go into exile in Babylon if they wanted to remain alive, the officials asked King Zedekiah for permission to put him in prison because he was discouraging the soldiers and making them want to give up. Ebed-Melech, a Cushite (from Ethiopia), heard that Jeremiah had been thrown into a wet dungeon to die, and so spoke up to Zedekiah on behalf of Jeremiah. Zedekiah ordered Ebed-Melech to take 30 men and go and pull Jeremiah out of the dungeon before he died. They threw a rope down and pulled him out (*Jer. 38:7–13*).

In supporting Jeremiah, Ebed-Melech was furthering the LORD's cause. It becomes clear that this man trusted God, and so Jeremiah was able to promise him that when the Babylonians eventually sacked the city he would not be killed (*Jer. 39:16–18*). The fall of Jerusalem could not be resisted. God's judgment on the city and on Judah had been promised, and it could not be thwarted by battle. Jeremiah's prophecy made it clear that it would compound Judah's disobedience and judgment if they refused to accept the exile. P.D.G.

**EBER** (Heb., 'across').
**1.** Eber, father of Peleg and Joktan was a descendant of Shem. He was thus an ancestor of Abraham and also enters the genealogy of Luke's Gospel leading from Jesus and Joseph back to Adam (*Gen. 10:21–25; 11:14–19; 1 Chron. 1:18–19, 25; Luke 3:35*).
**2.** A clan leader who was head of one of the seven Gadite clans settled in the area of Gilead and Bashan (*1 Chron. 5:13*)
**3.** *1 Chron. 8:12* lists Eber as a family of the tribe of Benjamin and a son of Elpaal.
**4.** A second person of the tribe of Benjamin was named Eber (*1 Chron. 8:22*).
**5.** *Neh. 12:20* lists Eber as a priest who served the LORD in the days of Joiakim, after the time of the Babylonian Exile. S.C.

**EBIASAPH**. See *Abiasaph*.

**EDEN** During the revival and turning to God in Hezekiah's reign, many Levites were assigned specific Temple duties. Eden son of Joah was one of those given the task of helping Kore distribute the people's gifts around the towns of the priests 'according to their divisions' (*2 Chron. 29:12; 31:15*).

**EDER** **1.** A son of Beriah and a family head who appears in the genealogy leading from Benjamin to Saul (1 Chron. 8:15).

**2.** A son of Mushi, this Eder was a Levite and the head of a family. He served in the Tabernacle worship during the reign of David once the ark of the covenant had found a permanent site in Jerusalem (1 Chron. 23:23; 24:30).

**EGLAH,** one of King David's wives. She gave birth to a son called Ithream at Hebron (2 Sam. 3:5; 1 Chron. 3:3).

**EGLON,** a king of Moab during the period of the Judges. This period of Israel's history was often virtually anarchic (see Judges). The Israelites turned to worship the gods of the Canaanites and the surrounding nations. God judged them by giving them over to be ruled by those whose gods they worshipped. From time to time they would then repent, and God would raise up a leader for them who would bring them their freedom again and become a judge in the land. After relative peace in Othniel's time, the Israelites 'Once again . . . did evil in the eyes of the LORD' and so God let Eglon invade Israel. He allied himself with the Ammonites and the Amalekites and conquered and ruled for 18 years, taking possession of Jericho and its surrounding areas (vv. 3:12–14). Eventually the oppression caused the Israelites to cry out to God, who once again raised up a leader for them, who was Ehud. He killed Eglon and became a judge in Israel (vv. 16–30). See also Ehud.

Time and again in Judges foreign oppression is seen to be the judgment of God for Israel's turning to foreign gods and becoming involved in idolatry, which was so strongly forbidden in the Law of Moses. God's judgment, though, caused his people to turn and repent, and God's amazing grace and forgiveness shines through the book of Judges as he yet again raises up a leader and judge to help them.

P.D.G.

**EHI** See Ahiram (Num. 26:38).

**EHUD** (See also Judges).

**1.** 'Ehud, a left-handed man, the son of Gera the Benjamite' (Judg. 3:15). Ehud was one of the judges of Israel. After the judge Othniel had died, the Israelites began once again to sin. As so often in the book of Judges, where these events are recorded, the Israelites' sin brought on them God's judgment, but that judgment had a restorative purpose. As foreign nations were allowed to invade and to oppress them, so the Israelites were supposed to turn back in repentance and seek the LORD. Sometimes it took them many years to turn and repent. On this occasion of their sin God allowed Eglon the king of Moab to invade. It was 18 years before the Israelites eventually called upon the LORD. The deliverer whom God then gave them was Ehud.

Ehud made a large double-edged sword which he strapped to his leg under his clothing. He then took the Israelite tribute to Eglon, arranged to be alone with him, drew his sword and killed him. He quickly escaped, rallied the Israelites and led them to a great victory. The tables were turned and Israel ruled Moab. Peace was restored and lasted for 80 years (Judg. 3:16–30). To what extent true worship of the LORD was restored in Israel is not discussed in the text. In fact, God in his grace gave peace to them while Ehud lived. Once he died, the old cycle of sin and rebellion and judgment began all over again.

**2.** One of the seven sons of Bilhan and a great-grandson of Benjamin. He was a clan leader and is listed in 1 Chron. 7:10.

P.D.G.

**EKER,** a grandson of Jerahmeel (1 Chron. 2:27).

**ELA,** a Benjamite, was the father of Shimei. Shimei was one of Solomon's twelve district governors (2 Kings 4:18).

**ELAH** **1.** Descended from Esau, this Elah was an Edomite clan leader (*Gen. 36:41; 1 Chron. 1:52*).

**2.** A son of Caleb and a grandson of Jephunneh (*1 Chron. 4:15*).

**3.** The fourth king of the northern kingdom of Israel. Elah succeeded his father Baasha to the throne. He ruled at Tirzah for two years before being killed by Zimri (*1 Kings 16:6–14*). Because of his father's sin in leading the Israelites into idolatry and away from the LORD, Jehu son of Hanani had prophesied that Baasha and his family would die. *1 Kings 16:13* tells us that Elah continued in the sins of Baasha, leading the people to 'worthless idols', and that this was the reason why Zimri was allowed by the LORD to kill the whole of Baasha's family. Idolatry within the royal family was bound to lead the Israelites themselves into sin, and so God always judged it severely. Eventually this rebellion against God would lead to judgment seen in the destruction of the northern kingdom by the Assyrians. God's relatively limited judgment at this stage in Israel's history should have been sufficient warning to future kings and to the people, especially as it was backed up time and again by prophets who explained God's actions to them.

The murder itself reveals the life-style to which Elah had become accustomed. He was killed while getting drunk in the house of Arza, the man in charge of his palace. Zimri then became king, but he too was quickly judged by God for the same sort of sin (*1 Kings 16:18–19*).

**4.** The father of Hoshea, the last king of Israel (*2 Kings 15:30; 17:1; 18:1, 9*).

**5.** One of the first settlers to return to Jerusalem after the Babylonian Exile. He was the son of Uzzi (*1 Chron. 9:8*). P.D.G.

**ELAM** **1.** *Gen. 10:22* and *1 Chron. 1:17* list Elam as a son of Shem and grandson of Noah.

**2.** *1 Chron. 8:24* includes Elam in the genealogy of Saul from the tribe of Benjamin.

**3.** Elam is listed as the fifth son of the Korahite gatekeeper, Meshelemiah, in David's division of duties for the Tabernacle (*1 Chron. 26:3*).

**4.** Elam was the head of one of the families that returned with Zerubbabel from the Babylonian Exile (*Ezra 2:7; 8:7; 10:2, 26; Neh. 7:12*).

**5.** Another Elam was also a head of one of the families that returned with Zerubbabel from the Babylonian Exile. He returned with 1,254 relatives (*Ezra 2:31; Neh. 7:34*).

**6.** When Nehemiah dedicated the new wall around Jerusalem, Elam was there as a priest of the LORD (*Neh. 12:42*).

**7.** This Elam was among the leaders of the people who signed the covenant under Nehemiah in which they promised to worship and obey only the LORD (*Neh. 10:14*). S.C.

**ELASAH** **1.** A descendant of Pashur who was among those guilty of marrying foreign women listed in *Ezra 10:22*.

**2.** He was the son of Shaphan to whom Jeremiah entrusted a letter to the surviving elders among the exiles (*Jer. 29:3*).

**EL-BERITH** (Heb., 'god of the covenant'), a Canaanite god worshipped in Shechem (see *Baal*). The god was also called Baal-Berith. Mentioned only in *Judg. 8–9*, it is possible that this was a case of Canaanite religion absorbing some Israelite religious ideas. The Canaanites worshipped many Baals. It is at least possible that this one, with its reference to 'covenant', may have been created in order to help absorb the Israelites. Alternatively, the Israelites, the people of the covenant, may have been more easily attracted to an already existing deity who was concerned with covenants. Certainly, they took no time, following the death of Gideon, to become involved in its worship (*Judg. 8:33; 9:4, 46*).

**ELDAAH,** a son of Midian and the grandson of Abraham and Keturah. The sons of Keturah all became leaders of tribes (*Gen. 25:4; 1 Chron. 1:33*).

**ELDAD,** mentioned twice with Medad, was one of the 70 elders of Israel appointed to help Moses with the work of leadership (*Num. 11:26–27*). The burden of leadership of the Israelites on Moses was clearly more than he could handle alone. Once again they were complaining about the lack of meat and the difficulties of their circumstances in the desert. They were longing for Egypt. So the LORD enabled others to share 'the burden of the people' with Moses (*Num. 11:17*). These men were leaders among their own clans and so had already demonstrated their God-given gifts of leadership. However, when the 70 met with Moses outside the Tabernacle, the Holy Spirit 'rested on them' and they prophesied.

Such spiritually gifted leaders were exactly what Israel needed, for their lust after Egypt revealed a deep spiritual problem – their inability to have faith and trust in God for everything they needed. Eldad and Medad had not joined the 70 at the Tabernacle for some reason, but 're-mained in the camp'. Nevertheless, the Spirit came on them as well and they prophesied. There are several Jewish documents which indicate something of what Eldad and Meded prophesied, but there is no indication of their words in Scripture. Joshua was not happy that they were prophesying and asked Moses to stop them, but Moses recognized the LORD's work and responded: 'Are you jealous for my sake? I wish that all the LORD's people were prophets and that the LORD would put his Spirit on them!' (*Num. 11:29*).

In a number of places in Scripture it seems that God never intended spiritual oversight to be in the hands of any one person. In *1 Corinthians* there is an emphasis on the fact that the Holy Spirit gives all Christians various special gifts, and several of these involve oversight of the church. The Pastoral Epistles indicate that a plurality of elders was the norm in most early churches. P.D.G.

**ELEAD** (Heb., 'God has testified'), a son of Ephraim. He was killed, together with his brother, when he went to raid livestock from the men of Gath (*1 Chron. 7:21*). See also *Ezer* and *Beriah*.

**ELEADAH** (Heb., 'God has adorned'), a descendant of Ephraim and a son of Tahath (*1 Chron. 7:20*).

**ELEASAH** (Heb., 'God made').
**1.** The son of Helez, this Eleasah is listed in Jerahmeel's genealogy and was from the tribe of Judah (*1 Chron. 2:39–40*).
**2.** This Eleasah was the son of Raphah and was from the tribe of Benjamin. He was the father of Azel and is listed in the genealogy of the descendants of King Saul (*1 Chron. 8:37; 9:43*).

**ELEAZAR** (Heb., 'God has helped').
**1.** One of the sons of Aaron and his wife Elisheba (*Exod. 6:23; Num. 3:2*). He became the head of a Levite clan and married one of the daughters of Putiel. His son was Phinehas (*Exod. 6:25; 1 Chron. 6:3–4, 50*). Along with his three brothers he was consecrated a priest to the LORD (*Exod. 28:1*). Eleazar figures prominently in the accounts of the wilderness wanderings of the Israelites. Unlike his brothers, Nadab and Abihu, who made an illegal offering to the LORD, and were killed (*Lev. 10:1–2; Num. 3:4*), Eleazar remained faithful to the LORD. He and his brother Ithamar were to be holy before the LORD, separated specifically for his service and for making offerings and sacrifices to God. It was to be their privilege to eat some of the meat of the sacrifices they offered for the people (*Lev. 10:12–20*).

Eleazar became chief of the Levites and had charge of the entire Tabernacle (*Num. 3:32; 4:16*). Throughout the wilderness years, Eleazar offered sacrifices for the worshipping community, interceding for the people when they sinned or rebelled. When Aaron died on Mount Hor, Moses gave Aaron's vestments, a sign of his office, to Eleazar (*Num. 20:25–29; Deut. 10:6*). He also seems to have had a role as adviser or judge in Israel for, as a priest he had access to the LORD and could consult the Urim (*Num. 27*). He was involved in the census ordered by Moses on the plains of Moab (*Num. 26*). He also took part in judging the case of Zelophehad's daughters and in appointing Joshua and giving him advice (*Num. 27: 18–23; Josh. 17:4*). He helped Joshua divide the land of Canaan between the tribes (*Num. 34:17; Josh. 14:1; 19:51*). Another of his tasks involved representing the people before the LORD when they went to battle (*Num. 31:6 f.*). Eventually he died and was buried at Gibeah in the hill country of Ephraim (*Josh. 24:33*).

Eleazar followed rigorously the laws of holiness that God demanded of his priests and of his holy nation. At a significant and most difficult time in the history of the Israelites he mediated between God and the people and the people and their God. Thus his priesthood pointed to the need for someone to stand between the holy God and mankind and the need to bring a sacrifice in order to enter God's presence. In due course, God's revelation showed that Eleazar's priesthood was but a foretaste of the high priesthood of Christ who came to mediate once and for all between mankind and God and to make the final great sacrifice that would never have to be repeated.

Later generations of Eleazar's family continued to have a prominent role in the worship of the nation. When David came to assign tasks for the Levites, one of the divisions was centred on the descendants of Eleazar (*1 Chron. 24:1–19*). Finally,

though, it is worth noting that this faithful man of God must have been proud of his son Phinehas who went down in history as one noted for his zeal for the LORD (*Num. 25*).

**2.** Another Eleazar was the son of Abinadab who was given charge to guard the ark of the covenant when it came to his father's house on a hill outside Kiriath Jearim (*1 Sam. 7:1*).

**3.** Eleazar son of Dodai the Ahohite was one of David's special 'three mighty men'. He was noted for his fighting abilities against the Philistines, especially at the battle of Pas Dammim. When some of the Israelites began to retreat, Eleazar stood his ground and fought hard until 'his hand grew tired and froze to the sword'. When the LORD gave the Israelites victory they found the Philistines around him had all been killed (*2 Sam. 23:9–10; 1 Chron. 11:12*).

**4.** One of the sons of Mahli, a descendant of Levi. He died leaving no sons but daughters who later married 'the sons of Kish', their cousins (*1 Chron. 23:21–22; 24:28*).

**5.** A Levitical priest who returned from Babylon to Jerusalem with Ezra. He helped in weighing out the Temple treasures when they arrived (*Ezra 8:33*).

**6.** This Eleazar was among the descendants of Parosh. At the time of return from the Exile in Babylon, Shecaniah confessed to Ezra that many men and even descendants of the priests of Judah had married wives from other tribes and nations. Ezra and the people repented and made a covenant to serve the LORD (*Ezra 10:2*). Eleazar is listed in *Ezra 10:25* as one who divorced his foreign wife.

**7.** A Levite who was part of the choir that sang at the dedication of the wall. The walls and city had been destroyed by the Babylonians when they took the Israelites into captivity. Under the direction of Nehemiah they were eventually rebuilt amidst great praises to God (*Neh. 12:42*).

**8.** One of the ancestors of Jesus mentioned in Matthew's genealogy (*Matt. 1:15*). He was the great-grandfather of Mary's husband Joseph.          P.D.G.

**ELHANAN** (Heb., 'God's grace').

**1.** One of David's great warriors, a Bethlehemite and the son of Jair. In one of the many battles with the Philistines Elhanan killed Lahmi, the brother of Goliath the Gittite (*1 Chron. 20:5*). There is a discrepancy between the account in *1 Chron. 20* and that in *2 Sam. 21:19*, where it appears that Elhanan killed Goliath himself rather than his brother. Some have suggested that Elhanan was simply another name for David. Others have thought that they are two different incidents and that, if Elhanan slew Goliath, there must have been two Goliaths. It is also suggested that the phrase 'brother of' has been lost from the text in *2 Samuel*. Perhaps the best supported resolution lies in an assumption of transcriptional mistakes in *2 Samuel*. The reader is advised to consult a good commentary.

In both *2 Sam. 21* and *1 Chron. 20* a number of battles are listed. The continuing problem that David had with the Philistines and others kept him and his commander Joab tied up for many years. David thus gathered round him many particularly able warriors whom God prepared so that the Israelites might eventually be victorious.

**2.** Elhanan son of Dodo was another of these great warriors and was listed among the group of David's 'mighty men' known as 'the Thirty'. He too was from Bethlehem (*2 Sam. 23:24; 1 Chron. 11:26*).
                                        P.D.G.

**ELI** (Heb., 'the Lord is uplifted') was a descendant of Aaron through Ithamar and became high priest at the worship centre in Shiloh toward the end of the period of the Judges. He combined the tasks of being high priest with the role of judge, for 'he judged Israel for eighteen years' (*1*

Sam. 4:18). It was he who was present in the temple there when Hannah came and prayed for a child (*1 Sam. 1:3–17*). Although he was initially concerned that she was drunk, when he heard the true cause of her prayers he comforted her and sent her away with a blessing (*v. 17*). It was to Eli that Hannah and her husband, Elkanah, returned after the young Samuel had been weaned. They brought an offering and then left the child to serve the LORD in the sanctuary alongside the elderly Eli (*1 Sam. 1:25; 2:11*). Each year when father and mother returned to see their son, Eli would bless the couple and pray that Hannah would have other children to make up for Samuel whom she had dedicated to the LORD's service (*1 Sam. 2:20*).

In spite of Eli's obvious trust and faith in the LORD, he had not succeeded in bringing up his family in this faith and his sons, Hophni and Phinehas, seriously abused their privileged position in Israel. It may be that it was not until Eli's old age that the seriousness of their evil ways became known. Eli knew what was going on and tried to prevent their sin (see *Hophni* and *Phinehas* for detail). Essentially, though, he was a weak man who lacked family control and his pleas to them fell on deaf ears (*1 Sam. 2:22–24*). As a result the word of the LORD came to the young Samuel who, by contrast, was growing up 'in favour with the LORD and with men' (*1 Sam. 2:26*). This prophecy reinforced an earlier word of the LORD against Eli and his family (*1 Sam. 2:27–36; 3:11–20*).

The words of condemnation on Eli were soon fulfilled. The Philistines attacked and captured the ark of the covenant. They defeated the Israelites in battle, killing Eli's two sons. When news came to Eli of the capture of the ark and the death of his sons he fell backwards off his stool and died.

Even during the later part of his life his faith was evident. When he heard Samuel's prophecy he was prepared to say, 'Let [the LORD] do what is good in his eyes' (1 Sam. 3:18). And when the messenger came from the battle, it was the capture of the ark, rather than the death of his sons, that caused him to fall backwards (1 Sam. 4:12–18).

Eli's life was in many ways tragic. He knew and loved the LORD, but his weakness of character and his tolerance of the evil around him was in direct contrast to what the LORD required of the priests leaders of his people (e.g. Lev. 22:1–3). With the removal by Solomon of Abiathar from the priesthood, the word of the LORD against the house of Eli had been fulfilled (1 Kings 2:27). From that time onwards, it was from the descendants of Eleazar that the high priesthood was taken.                                         P.D.G.

**ELIAB 1.** Eliab, son of Helon and leader of the tribe of Zebulun, was one of the men chosen to help Moses and Aaron take a census of the Israelite community in the Sinai (Num. 1:9; 2:7; 7:24–29; 10:16).

**2.** Eliab was the father of Dathan and Abiram. He was a Reubenite. Eliab's sons were leaders in Korah's rebellion against Moses and Aaron (Num. 16:1, 12; 26:8–9; Deut. 11:6). For detail see Korah.

**3.** An ancestor of Samuel, Eliab was the father of Jeroham and the son of Nahath. He was of the tribe of Levi (1 Chron. 6:27).

**4.** Eliab was the oldest son of Jesse and brother to David (1 Sam. 16:6; 17:13; 1 Chron. 2:13). Samuel was mourning Saul's disobedience when God spoke to his servant and sent Samuel to anoint the new king of Israel. Samuel followed God's directions and went to the home of Jesse. In Jesse's son Eliab he thought that he had found the LORD's anointed because Eliab was tall, handsome and the first-born. Then God spoke the words that have been repeated for centuries, 'Man looks at the outward appearance, but the LORD looks at the heart' (1 Sam. 16:7). We meet Eliab again in the story of David and Goliath. He was jealous of his younger brother; jealous of the goodness of David's heart (1 Sam. 17:28). Eliab and the others watched as David killed the Philistine in the name and honour of the LORD. Eliab's daughter, Abihail, had married David's son (2 Chron. 11:18).

**5.** Eliab was the third in command of the Gadites among David's army at Ziklag. They had deserted Saul (1 Chron. 12:9).

**6.** During David's reign, Eliab, a Levite, played the lyre when the ark was being brought to Jerusalem (1 Chron. 15:18, 20; 16:5).                                         S.C.

**ELIADA 1.** One of David's sons, Eliada was born in Jerusalem (2 Sam. 5:16; 1 Chron. 3:8; 14:7).

**2.** Eliada was the father of Rezon, who ruled in Aram as an adversary of Solomon (1 Kings 11:23).

**3.** During Jehoshaphat's reign, Eliada, a Benjamite, was a valiant soldier and the leader of 200,000 men (2 Chron. 17:17).

**ELIAHBA** (Heb., 'God hides'), one of David's 'Thirty', the 'mighty men' who went to battle for him and led the people of Israel to war. He was a Shaalbonite (2 Sam. 23:32; 1 Chron. 11:33).

**ELIAKIM** (Heb., 'God raises up').

**1.** The son of Hilkiah, this Eliakim held a prominent position in King Hezekiah's kingdom. In Is. 22:22–24 we see that, to all intents and purposes, he was prime minister. He held the 'key to the house of David'. He was delegated to speak to the commander of the Assyrian forces who were besieging Jerusalem in 701 BC (2 Kings 18:18, 26, 37; 19:2). They could reach no agreement for peace and so the Assyrians shouted out a message to Hezekiah in Hebrew (2 Kings 18:19–25). The message claimed that the LORD was on the Assyrians' side and sarcastically emphasized the weakness of the position in which Hezekiah now found himself. He had been depending upon Egypt which the Assyrians referred to as 'that splintered reed of a staff, which pierces a man's hand and wounds him if he leans on it!' (v. 21).

Eliakim was profoundly concerned that those on the walls of Jerusalem listening to this conversation would understand the Hebrew being spoken and would lose heart. Thus he asked the Assyrians to speak to them in Aramaic, the court language of those days. This simply provoked the commander to shout out still more threats in Hebrew directed at those on the wall. He specially appealed to them not to listen to Hezekiah and his promises (2 Kings 18:28–35). Eliakim and his secretary, Shebna, and the other officials returned to Hezekiah with great sorrow and fear. However, this sad turn of events did lead to Hezekiah's turning to the LORD for help and guidance, something he should have done much earlier on in the troubles. The LORD, who was always there to help his people when they called on him, answered Hezekiah's prayer for deliverance (2 Kings 19:14–19) and directly intervened by killing many of the Assyrian troops in their own camp during one night (vv. 35ff.). See also Is. 36:1–22; 37:2).

Hezekiah had learned a lesson far too few of the kings of Israel or Judah had been prepared to learn: that their only security and source of peace lay in a total dependence upon their covenant LORD.

**2.** Eliakim the son of Josiah king of Judah was made king of Judah by Pharaoh Neco on his father's death in battle against the Egyptians. His name was changed by Pharaoh as a sign of submission to the Egyptians, and he was called Jehoiakim (2 Kings 23:34; 2 Chron. 36:4). See Jehoiakim.

**3.** Another Eliakim, head of a priestly family in the time of Nehemiah, is mentioned in Neh. 12:41. He was a trumpet player during the worship at the dedication of the city walls.

**4.** In the genealogy of Jesus he is listed as the son of Abiud and father of Azor. In Matthew's Gospel the kingship of Jesus is established in a variety of ways, not least through this genealogy which comes down through various kings and princes like Zerubbabel to Joseph and then to Jesus (Matt. 1:13).

**5.** Mentioned in the genealogy leading from Jesus to Adam, as the father of Jonam and son of Melea (Luke 3:30).

P.D.G.

**ELIAM** (Heb., 'God's people'), also called Ammiel. He was the father of Bathsheba, the wife of Uriah the Hittite. David had Uriah killed after he had made Bathsheba pregnant. Later she became his wife (2 Sam. 11:3; 23:34).

**ELIASAPH 1.** He was the son of Deuel and the leader of the people of Gad at the census of the Israelites in the wilderness of Sinai. His division of people numbered 45,650 (Num. 1:14; 2:14). As the representative of his tribe, he also brought his tribe's fellowship offering when the Tabernacle was dedicated in the wilderness (Num. 7:42, 47; 10:20).

**2.** The leader of the Gershonites and the son of Lael (Num. 3:24). The Gershonites of the tribe of Levi, were responsible for the care of the tent of the Tabernacle, looking after its coverings and curtains. Each family grouping of Levites had different responsibilities, and these are spelled out in these chapters of Numbers.

**ELIASHIB** (Heb., 'God restores').

**1.** Eliashib was a priest who served in the Tabernacle during David's rule. He was responsible for the eleventh turn of service (1 Chron. 24:12).

**2.** During the time of Nehemiah, Eliashib, the high priest, directed the rebuilding of the Sheep Gate in the new city walls of Jerusalem. He was a priest who was son of Joiakim. However, it is an indication of the influence that foreigners like Tobiah had that even the high priesthood should be associated with him. Eliashib was in charge of the storerooms of the temple and had provided Tobiah with a room. When Nehemiah returned from a visit to King Artaxerxes, he had Tobiah thrown out. (*Neh. 3:1, 20–21; 12:10, 22–23; 13:4, 7, 28; Ezra 10:5–6*).

**3.** *Ezra 10:24* lists Eliashib as one of the Israelite singers who had married foreign women and lived in Judah following the return from the exile in Babylon.

**4.** Another Eliashib, descendant of Zattu, was one who had married a foreign woman (*Ezra 10:27*).

**5.** Another Eliashib, descendant of Bani, was one who had married foreign women (*Ezra 10:36*).

**6.** Eliashib, son of Elioenai, is listed in *1 Chron. 3:24* as a member of the royal line of Judah after the exile.          s.c.

**ELIATHAH** (Heb., 'God comes'), a grandson of Asaph and a son of Heman. Eliathah was one of many sons who came as a special gift of God to Heman in order that God might be glorified. He was one of those Levites who was set aside to prophesy and play music before the LORD. His father was King David's 'seer'. The duties in worship rotated between the Levitical families by lot, and Eliathah's lot was the 20th (*1 Chron. 25:4, 27*).

**ELIDAD,** the son of Kislon, was named by the LORD as one to be chosen by Moses as the leader of the tribe of Benjamin. His duty was to organize the allocation of the Benjamite territory to the various clans and families following the conquest of Canaan (*Num. 34:21*).

**ELIEHOENAI 1.** He was the son of Meshelemiah, who was one of the gatekeepers of the Tabernacle (*1 Chron. 26:3*).

**2.** A descendant of Pahath-Moab who came up from Babylon with Ezra along with 200 men during the reign of Artaxerxes in *Ezra 8:4*.

**ELIEL** (Heb., 'my God is God').

**1.** A head of a clan and valiant soldier in the tribe of Manasseh, who was unfaithful to the LORD and worshipped pagan gods (*1 Chron. 5:24–25*).

**2.** Mentioned in *1 Chron. 6:34*, he was the great-grandfather of Samuel and a descendant of Kohath. His descendants were listed among the Temple musicians.

**3.** Listed in the genealogy leading from Benjamin to Saul (*1 Chron. 8:2*). He was a son of Shimei.

**4.** Another listed in the genealogy leading from Benjamin to Saul (*1 Chron. 8:22*). He was a son of Shashak.

**5.** Eliel the Mahavite was one of David's 'Thirty' mighty men who went to battle for him and led the people of Israel to war (*1 Chron. 11:46*).

**6.** Another of David's 'mighty men' (*1 Chron. 11:47*).

**7.** Another Eliel was one of the famous Gadites who defected from Saul to David when he was at Ziklag. He was the seventh in the list each of whom are described in vivid imagery as the bravest of warriors. They were commanders who proved of tremendous support to David in his battles (*1 Chron. 12:11*). Later in the passage it seems that such men transferred loyalties not simply to be on the winning side but because the 'Spirit' had worked among them. As David's army grew it became 'like the army of God' (*v. 22*).

**8.** A descendant of Hebron and head of a Levitical family, this Eliel was appointed by David to help in bringing the ark of the LORD up to Jerusalem (*1 Chron. 15:9, 11*).

**9.** One of the Levites who were supervisors of tithes and offerings brought by the people. As a result of the extraordinary revival under King Hezekiah, so many offerings, gifts and tithes were brought to the Temple that special storehouses had to be prepared. Eliel was one of a number of Levites chosen, under the leadership of Conaniah and Shimei, to organize the storage of what was given (2 Chron. 31:13).  P.D.G.

**ELIENAI** (Heb., 'my eyes are God's), a son of Shimei, is mentioned in 1 Chron. 8:20 in the genealogy from Benjamin to Saul.

**ELIEZER** **1.** Eliezer of Damascus was Abra(ha)m's servant (Gen. 15:2). He stood to inherit Abraham's estate should Abraham have no children. Abraham was concerned that the LORD had not provided him with a child as he had promised. However, God specifically intervened to promise yet again that he would have his own child with his wife Sarah and Eliezer would not be the one to inherit (vv. 2–5). Abraham's belief in this promise 'was credited to him as righteousness' (v. 6).

**2.** A grandson of Benjamin and son of Beker (1 Chron. 7:8).

**3.** One of Moses' sons by his wife Zipporah. This Eliezer, brother to Gershom, was given his name by Moses who said: 'My father's God was my helper; he saved me from the sword of Pharaoh,' (Exod. 18:4). His own son was called Rehabiah who, in turn, had many sons (1 Chron. 23:15, 17). A descendant of Eliezer was Shelomith who, with his relatives, was in charge of King David's treasuries (1 Chron. 26:25–26).

**4.** A priest whose job it was to blow a trumpet before the ark of God when it was brought back to Jerusalem by David (1 Chron. 15:24).

**5.** During the reign of King David this Eliezer, son of Zicri, was an official in the tribe of Reuben (1 Chron. 27:16).

**6.** Eliezer son of Dodavahu of Mareshah prophesied against King Jehoshaphat of Judah because he had made an alliance with King Ahaziah of Israel. Jointly they had had ships built at Ezion Geber. These ships were later destroyed because the LORD did not approve of this alliance with an evil king (2 Chron. 20:37). It is a sad comment on Jehoshaphat that, after a

reign in which he followed the LORD faithfully (v. 32), he finally succumbed to the temptation to look for help against his enemies to those who did not trust in the same God.

**7.** One of the Jews, a leader among his people and a man of learning, who joined Ezra on their return from the Babylonian captivity to Jerusalem. He helped Ezra find suitable Levites to accompany them back to Judah (Ezra 8:16).

**8.** A descendant of Jeshua, this Eliezer was among those priests who joined Ezra and the people in repentance on their return to Jerusalem from Babylon. Many men of Judah had married wives from other tribes and nations. They made a covenant to serve the LORD (Ezra 10:2) and divorced their foreign wives (vv. 18–19).

**9.** A Levite who also divorced his foreign wife (Ezra 10:23).

**10.** Another Eliezer, from the descendants of Harim, also divorced his foreign wife (Ezra 10:31).

**11.** An ancestor of Jesus listed in the genealogy from Jesus to Adam. He was the son of Jorim and the father of Joshua (Luke 3:29).  P.D.G.

**ELIHOREPH** Listed as one of Solomon's 'chief officials', Elihoreph was one of the king's secretaries (1 Kings 4:3). He was the son of Shisha and held this job with his brother Ahijah.

**ELIHU** (Heb., 'he is my God').

**1.** This Elihu was an ancestor of Samuel (1 Sam. 1:1). Eliel in 1 Chron. 6:34 and Eliab in 1 Chron. 6:27 are thought to be the same person as Elihu.

**2.** Elihu was one of the leaders of the tribe of Manasseh who defected to David at Ziklag (1 Chron. 12:20).

**3.** This Elihu was a descendant of Obed-Edom with a reputation for strength to do God's work. He was a Korahite Levite (1 Chron. 26:7).

**4.** One of David's brothers, Elihu was an officer over the tribe of Judah (1 Chron. 27:18). Eliab in 1 Sam. 16:6; 17:13, 28; 1 Chron. 2:13; 2 Chron. 11:18 is the same man as Elihu.

**5.** Elihu, son of Barakel the Buzite, of the family of Ram, was one of Job's young friends who sought to advise him about his illness and loss. Elihu was angry with the first three friends because of their inability to refute and persuade Job. Because he was younger he had heard out the three older men first as they sought to tell Job what was wrong. He did not understand how Job could possibly continue to maintain his innocence before God, given all the tragedies he had suffered. He suggested how Job might offer repentance to God. Like the other speakers, however, he could not see what God could see or what Job knew deep within his heart, that something much more serious was going on here. As the opening chapters reveal, Job was caught up in the midst of a heavenly challenge. As Job remained faithful to the LORD throughout his ordeal, so he demonstrated in his own life the power of the LORD to keep his people, no matter what Satan threw at them (Job 32:2–37:24).   S.C. and P.D.G.

## ELIJAH, THE PROPHET

Elijah's name, meaning 'my God is Yahweh', reflects his character as a man totally dedicated to God. Because of this commitment God was able to use Elijah powerfully. His is one of the most colourful and exciting biographies in the Bible. His story is told in the middle of the accounts of the kings of Israel and Judah, between 1 Kings 17 and 2 Kings 2. These chapters recount three aspects essential to understanding Elijah's role and ministry: the miracles, the message and the man himself.

### Elijah's miracles

The miracles surrounding Elijah are the most vivid of the three aspects of his life. Whether raising the widow's son from the dead, or calling down fire from heaven, or ascending to the heavens himself, these are the dramas which everyone remembers. Behind these wonders, however, lies their consistent use by God to teach faith. The miracles represent 'signs' which call their witnesses to a decisive moment. They must decide for or against God. This is clearest on Mt Carmel (1 Kings 18:16–46). Elijah challenged the people, 'How long will you waver between two opinions? If the LORD is God, follow him; but if Baal is God, follow him' (1 Kings 18:21). At first the people said nothing. When they heard Elijah's challenge to the priests of Baal, they gave their consent (1 Kings 18:24). Elijah won them over to his side when he enlisted their aid in the construction of the altar and in soaking it with water (1 Kings 18:30–35). However, it was only when the fire fell from heaven that the people responded with the confession of faith, 'The LORD – he is God! The LORD – he is God!' (1 Kings 18:39). They then participated in the capture of the pagan priests. Thus the miraculous sign challenged the people to respond in faith. A similar miracle, in which Elijah called down fire from heaven to incinerate two companies of soldiers who came to arrest him (2 Kings 1:9–12), led to a confession of faith in Elijah as a 'man of God' and a plea for mercy from the captain of the third company which was sent (2 Kings 1:13–14).

The signs given to the widow at Zarephath (1 Kings 17:7–24) also led her to respond in faith. When she gave Elijah some of her flour and oil, she received back an unending supply to keep her alive during the drought. When Elijah restored her son to life, her accusation of Elijah (1 Kings 17:18, 'Did you come to remind me of my sin and kill my son?') turned into a confession of belief in his mission and ministry (1 Kings 17:24, 'Now I know that you are a man of God and that the word of the LORD from your mouth is the truth').

The last miracles of Elijah occurred in the company of his spiritual successor, Elisha (2 Kings 2:1–12). Elijah reversed the path which Israel took when it entered the Promised Land, from the hill country of Bethel and Ai to the region of Jericho, and finally to the Jordan River. As Israel first entered the Promised Land through a parting of the waters, so Elijah now left it. When Elisha saw how the waters separated for his master, he requested, 'Let me inherit a double portion of your spirit' (2 Kings 2:9). Across the Jordan, like Moses before him, Elijah was granted a special blessing at the moment of his departure from this life. He ascended to heaven in a whirlwind. Again, Elisha confessed the power of Israel's God: 'The chariots and horsemen of Israel!' (2 Kings 2:12). His further activities demonstrated the faith in Elijah's God which Elisha now possessed (2 Kings 2:14).

### Elijah's message

The miracles of Elijah served to call many in Israel back to faith in God. However, the message of Elijah had a different reception. While the miracles elicited responses from wayward and lukewarm Israelites of all levels in society, the message of the prophet was directed towards the kings (and queen, in the case of Jezebel) of Israel and of Judah. Elijah warned Ahaziah that his consultation with Baal-Zebub, the god of Ekron, for treatment of his foot injury was sin and would lead to his death (2 Kings 1:1–17). Ahaziah died with no notice of any repentance. The sole mention of Elijah in Chronicles occurs when Elijah sent a message to Jehoram king of Judah (2 Chron. 21:12–20). Elijah warned the king that his murderous and pagan practices, more like those of Ahab than those of his predecessors in Judah, would lead to a horrible death for himself. The notice that Ahaziah died of a painful bowel disease, unmourned by his subjects, affirmed the prophet's words and the absence of any repentance from the king.

Elijah's relationship with Ahab was the most significant illustration of the clarity of the prophet's message and the failure to repent on the part of the leadership. No king of Israel received as many warnings, and yet no king of Israel fell as deeply into sin. Elijah's ministry began with a warning to Ahab of drought (1 Kings 17:1). Yet all Ahab could do was to send out search parties to try to capture the prophet (1 Kings 18:1–14). In the end Elijah, led by God (1 Kings 18:1–2, 15–19), chose the time and place for their meeting. In his first explanation to Ahab of the reason for the drought, the prophet made clear that it was the king's own fault: 'I have not made trouble for Israel . . . But you and your father's family have. You have abandoned the LORD's commands and have followed the Baals' (1 Kings 18:18). The miracle on Mt Carmel demonstrated the superiority of Yahweh over the false deities. Although this was directed to all the people, God used Elijah to give a private demonstration of divine power for Ahab. While Ahab was in his chariot, hurrying back to Jezreel to celebrate the rain, Elijah appeared and outran the king's chariot (1 Kings 18:45–46). Even so,

Elijah's powerful demonstration of faith in withholding and granting the rains (*James 5:17–18*) did not turn Ahab away from his false worship.

This message led to no change of behaviour on the part of Ahab. Influenced by his Tyrian wife, Jezebel (*1 Kings 21:25*), Ahab continued his life of compromise with the Canaanite culture around him. He desired the vineyard of Naboth at Jezreel (*1 Kings 21*). Although this was the patrimony given by God to Naboth's family, it meant little to Ahab and nothing to Jezebel. This king should have what he wanted regardless of the covenant between God and his people. Naboth was falsely accused and put to death. Ahab seized the vineyard. To all this God had a message of doom for Elijah to take to Ahab. The king would die. His queen would also die and dogs would devour them both. This was a terrible judgment, for it meant they would not rest with their ancestors but would die unmourned and cursed by God. Of all the kings to whom Elijah delivered words of warning, only Ahab responded positively. We read that he tore his clothes, wore sackcloth, and fasted. He humbled himself before God, and God responded by delaying the coming doom to the days of his son (*1 Kings 21:27–29*). Yet the judgment was to come, just as Elijah had predicted. The king was killed and dogs licked his blood (*1 Kings 22:34–38*). Jezebel also shared the same fate (*2 Kings 9:30–37*). Finally, the whole dynasty of Ahab was wiped out by Jehu (*2 Kings 10*). Just as God had promised Ahab (*1 Kings 19:17*), it came to pass.

The messages of Elijah all came true. However, their true purpose was more than that of a pronouncement of doom. Elijah's prophetic ministry was to call the people to repentance at a time of national apostasy. His miracles provided visual aids which challenged the people, who perhaps were not as prepared to hear his arguments. However, their response contrasted throughout his ministry with the hard-hearted refusal of most of the leadership to listen to the prophet. The warnings of judgment were designed to produce repentance in the people who heard them, and in later generations, who would recall the prophet's words when they came to pass (*2 Kings 9:36; 10:10, 17*).

### Elijah the man

The subject of national apostasy introduces the third aspect of Elijah's life preserved in the biblical text: Elijah the man. There are two parts to this aspect: the loneliness of Elijah and the archetypal prophetic role which Elijah played. The first examines the unique relationship between Elijah and God and between Elijah and those who were called to hear his word. The archetypal role of the prophet begins with his successor, Elisha, and reaches into the NT.

The loneliness of the prophet encompasses every part of his life and ministry. It begins with his origins, for he came from Gilead, the land east of the Jordan (*1 Kings 17:1*). Thus in the capital and the chief cities of the northern kingdom he would have been a provincial. He was probably regarded by many as a fanatic from an uncivilized backwater of the kingdom. Yet it is from such 'backwaters' that God often chooses prophets and messengers, whether from Gilead or from Galilee. This often serves as a witness against the people who regard themselves as better than the rest, for God can find among them no one with sufficient faith to act as a messenger of the divine word.

In Elijah's case, his ministry brought him into contact with those who had no regard for his 'simple' religion of worshipping Yahweh alone. They preferred the sophisticated religion of the urban Canaanites, which integrated gods from such powerful and wealthy commercial centres as Tyre. The challenge on Mt Carmel may have been a sanctuary on the borders of Tyre and Israel. Thus it implied the introduction of a pagan deity into Israel as the chief god there. Elijah's call to confront this wickedness was an example of a called, lone minister standing against the power of hundreds of opponents supported by the state (1 *Kings* 18:19). God's effectiveness was not hindered by the uneven sides. Indeed, it all the more dramatically displayed the power of faith at work. But such an experience could only enhance the sense of loneliness which Elijah must have felt. For two years he had been in hiding with few companions other than a widow and her son (1 *Kings* 17:1–24). Even though he may have heard of prophets of Yahweh (1 *Kings* 18:13), they were in hiding and provided him with no support. Therefore it is no surprise when Elijah, fearing the reprisals of Jezebel, fled for his life to Horeb (1 *Kings* 19:1–8). His miraculous sustenance there for 40 days evokes the image of Moses in communion with God (*Exod.* 24:18), but it also confirms the picture of a lonely figure called out from the midst of a sinful people. Twice God asked Elijah his purpose in coming, and twice Elijah replied with the same words of complaint (1 *Kings* 19:10, 14; *cf. Rom.* 11:2–3), 'I have been very zealous for the LORD God Almighty. The Israelites have rejected your covenant, broken down your altars, and put your prophets to death with the sword. I am the only one left, and now they are trying to kill me too.'

The loneliness of Elijah reached a turning point in this scene. Until now he had been accustomed to express the presence of God through the use of magnificent 'special effects' miracles. God, however, now showed Elijah that the divine presence does not lie in such demonstrations of power but in the apparent weakness of the softly spoken word (1 *Kings* 19:11–13). Henceforth, Elijah's ministry would emphasize the word rather than the act. Further, his work would not be alone but would be performed alongside other faithful prophets.

This began with the appointment of Elisha, who carried forward the ministry after Elijah's death, including the anointing of Hazael and Jehu as kings of Aram and Israel (1 *Kings* 19:15–17). This concern to address the loneliness of the prophet is evident in the godly characters who populate the chapters which follow the scene at Mt Horeb (1 *Kings* 19). Unlike 1 *Kings* 17–18, where Elijah functioned alone, thereafter his activities were interspersed with other events and prophets. This began with Elisha's call (1 *Kings* 19:19–21). There were unnamed prophets at work in 1 *Kings* 20. Elijah reappears in the account of Naboth's vineyard (1 *Kings* 21:1–28), but this is followed by the prophecies of Micaiah son of Imlah (1 *Kings* 21:1–28), which confirm specifically what Elijah had already prophesied generally concerning the death of Ahab. In 2 *Kings* 1 Elijah reappears with a message for Ahaziah. There he delivered his message alone, but in 2 *Kings* 2 he was accompanied by Elisha and encountered groups of prophets at Bethel and Jericho. The ministry of Elijah exemplifies what one individual who hears and obeys the word of God can accomplish. It also exemplifies how the public faithfulness of one can be a catalyst to embolden others to make public their faith.

We have already noted the symbolism of Elijah as the successor of Moses, who meets God at Horeb and leaves this life in a special way. He also represents Joshua and the people of Israel, who cross the Jordan River on dry ground. Even more important is the role of Elijah as an archetypal prophet. Although prophets existed in Israel before Elijah, he takes on a special role. His miracles and his message are carried forward by Elisha, who requested a double portion of Elijah's spirit and who began his ministry by repeating Elijah's miracle of crossing the Jordan on dry ground (2 Kings 2:14). Elijah's message of judgment for the north was picked up by the writing prophets to the north, Hosea and Amos. A century after Elijah's work they brought the same message of judgment for the sins of the people and of the rulers. In the southern kingdom this warning was also carried forward by figures such as Isaiah. The very last of the writing prophets, Malachi, promised a return of Elijah to hold out hope for repentance before judgment (Mal. 4:5–6).

In the NT this prophecy is remembered and embodied in part with the coming of John the Baptist (Luke 1:17). Also a loner, he called the people to repentance from the Jordan River. John would refuse the identification (John 1:21, 25), but Jesus allowed that he was Elijah (Matt. 11:14; 17:10–13; Mark 9:11–13). Later some would confuse Jesus with the return of Elijah (Matt. 16:14; Mark 6:15; 8:28; Luke 9:8, 19). Jesus would never claim this identification, although he would liken his ministry to that of Elijah, as one sent to those outside Israel (Luke 4:24–26). Elijah himself would reappear in the Transfiguration. There he would appear alongside Moses as a representative of all the prophets who looked forward to the coming of the Messiah (Matt. 17:2–9; Mark 9:2–10; Luke 9:28–36). Elijah would talk with Jesus and encourage him on the lonely and self-sacrificing road to the cross (Luke 9:31). Thus it is clear how misconceived was the scorn of those at the crucifixion who suggested that he might be calling on Elijah and that Elijah could deliver him (Matt. 27:47–49; Mark 15:35–36). Christ's redemptive sacrifice was the purpose for which Elijah had ministered while on earth. It was the purpose of Elijah's symbolic return in the form of John. And it was the goal about which Elijah spoke to Jesus in the Transfiguration. (See Prophets and Prophecy)                    R.H.

**ELIJAH   1.** See Elijah, the prophet.

**2.** A son of Jeroham and a clan leader. He was a Benjamite who lived in Jerusalem (1 Chron. 8:27).

**3.** This Elijah was a descendant of Harim and one of those in the time of Ezra who had married a foreign wife rather than one from Judah (Ezra 10:21). He joined those who pledged to divorce their foreign wives after hearing the teaching of the Law from Ezra.

**4.** Another Elijah came from the descendants of Elam. He too had married a foreign wife in the time of Ezra (Ezra 10:26).

**ELIKA,** one of David's 'Thirty', the 'mighty men' who went to battle for him and led the people of Israel to war. He was a Harodite (2 Sam. 23:25, not mentioned in the list in 1 Chron. 11).

**ELIMELECH** (Heb., 'God is king') and his wife Naomi, from the tribe of Judah, had two sons, Mahlon and Kilion. They lived in Bethlehem until a famine in the area caused them to move into Moab. While in Moab Elimelech died. His sons married Moabite women but soon they themselves died, leaving Naomi a widow and without male family support. One of her daughters-in-law, Ruth, decided to return to Bethlehem with Naomi and worship the LORD as her relatives did. She later married Boaz who was a relative of Elimelech and who redeemed

Elimelech's property on behalf of Naomi and Ruth (*Ruth 1:2–3; 2:1, 3; 4:3, 9*). In the LORD's providence, Ruth became the great-grandmother of King David. See *Ruth*, *Boaz* and *Naomi* for detail.   P.D.G.

**ELIOENAI 1.** A descendant of King David, Elioenai is listed as one of three sons of Neariah in *1 Chron. 3:23–24*. This list provides a royal lineage for the kingdom of Judah following the Exile.

**2.** A clan leader of the tribe of Simeon, mentioned in *1 Chron. 4:36*.

**3.** A grandson of Benjamin and son of Beker (*1 Chron. 7:8*).

**4.** This Elioenai was a descendant of Pashhur and one of those in the time of Ezra who had married a foreign wife rather than one from Judah (*Ezra 10:22*).

**5.** This Elioenai was a descendant of Zattu and was also one of those who had married a foreign wife (*Ezra 10:17*).

**6.** Elioenai, a head of a priestly family in the time of Nehemiah, is mentioned in *Neh. 12:41*. He was a trumpet player during the worship at the dedication of the city walls.   P.D.G.

**ELIPHAL** (Heb., 'God had judged'), the son of Ur (*1 Chron. 11:35*). He may be the same person as Eliphelet in *2 Sam. 23:34*. He was one of David's 'Thirty', the 'mighty men' who went to battle for him and led the people of Israel to war.

**ELIPHAZ**   (Heb., 'God is victorious').
**1.** Eliphaz was the first-born son of Esau and his Hittite wife, Adah (*Gen. 36:4, 10–11, 15; 1 Chron. 1:35–36*).

**2.** Eliphaz was the first and oldest of Job's three friends. Initially the three friends went to Job to 'sympathise with him and comfort him'. When they saw the appalling troubles Job was facing under God's testing, they were unable to speak at all for a long time. Eventually they began to offer various forms of advice (*Job 2:11; 4:1; 15:1; 22:1; 42:7, 9*). Though the wisest, Eliphaz is presented throughout the dialogue as a dogmatic 'instructor', proclaiming a moralistic

view of salvation. First, Eliphaz exhorted Job to accept the losses as God's correction for sin (*Job 5:17*). Next, Eliphaz accused Job of undermining God (*Job 15:4*) and warned Job that he would be 'paid in full' by God for his sin. Finally, Eliphaz charged Job with numerous sins and concluded with an appeal for Job to 'submit to God' in order to be 'restored' (*Job 22*).

The whole book of Job reveals very clearly how the often-repeated religious explanations of cause and effect (sin, judgment; righteousness, blessing) are too simplistic by far when people confront the Almighty God whose sovereignty is total. In the end God did vindicate Job and ordered the friends to go to Job and have him offer sacrifices for their forgiveness: 'My servant Job will pray for you, and I will accept his prayer and not deal with you according to your folly. You have not spoken of me what is right, as my servant Job has' (*Job 42:7–9*).
   S.C. and P.D.G.

**ELIPHELEHU** After the ark of the covenant had been brought to Jerusalem, the worship of God was properly organized by King David. Eliphelehu was one of the family of Merarites who were gatekeepers, but the particular job he and his brothers were given was to be musicians and to play the harps and lyres (*1 Chron. 15:18, 21*).

**ELIPHELET 1.** A child of David born to him in Jerusalem (*2 Sam. 5:16; 1 Chron. 3:6, 8; 14:7*).

**2.** He was among David's 'Thirty' 'mighty men' (*2 Sam. 23:34*).

**3.** He was the son of Eshek, a descendant of Benjamin's recorded in the genealogy of Saul in *1 Chron. 8:39*.

**4.** A descendant of Adonikam who came up from Babylon with Ezra during the reign of King Artaxerxes (*Ezra 8:13*).

**5.** A descendant of Hashum who was among those guilty of marrying foreign women (*Ezra 10:33*).

# ELISHA

In the mid-9th century BC the Northern Kingdom of Israel was caught up in religious apostasy. The royal house, as represented by Ahab and his Sidonian wife Jezebel (1 Kings 16:29–2 Kings 10:17), was promoting the Canaanite religion of Baal and not hesitating to stamp out the truth by force. Elijah's complaint (1 Kings 19:10, 14) is an apt summary: national apostasy ('the Israelites have rejected your covenant'), religious persecution ('broken down your altars, and put your prophets to death'), and determination to destroy Yahwism ('I am the only one left, and now they are trying to kill me too').

In this situation Elijah and Elisha (Heb., 'my God saves') spearheaded 'the prophetic revolt' and whether they knew it or not, originated the great line of prophets who followed them. For this reason the ministry of the two men was marked by notable supernatural works. The Bible is very sparing in what we call 'miracles'. They are not spread evenly through Scripture: indeed, for the greater part, the Bible concentrates on the ordinary providences of God rather than on the special or spectacular happenings which proclaim his presence. But clusters of such events mark new beginnings – Moses, Samuel, Elijah-Elisha, the Lord Jesus, the apostles. By acting in unmistakable ways, the Lord thus seals and signalizes the special or unique nature of the times and their participants. This helps us to see Elisha, like Elijah, as one of the Lord's notable people.

## The mantle of Elijah

The first two Elisha stories (1 Kings 19:15–21; 2 Kings 2:1–17), his call and his emergence as the LORD's prophet after the ascension of Elijah, are linked by references to Elijah's cloak (1 Kings 19:19; 2 Kings 2:13–15).

Three names figure in the LORD's recommissioning of Elijah (1 Kings 19:15–18). Regarding the national apostasy of which Elijah had complained, the LORD's chastening agent (Deut. 28:25, 32–33) would be Hazael (2 Kings 8:10–13; 10:32; 12:17–18; 13:3–24). Vengeance on the royal house for their assault on the altars and prophets of the LORD would be the work of Jehu (2 Kings 9–10), and, far from the prophetic ministry ending with Elijah, Elisha would succeed him, along with the LORD's guarantee of a 7,000-strong remnant. Elisha thus came on the scene as a very significant person: he was the beginning of the prophetic succession whose ministry would separate and sustain the believing remnant of the people of God. The choice of Elisha was a sovereign directive of the LORD (1 Kings 19:16), but it required a personal response. This involved sacrifice, for Elisha belonged to a wealthy and loving family in which he had liberty to do what he chose (1 Kings 19:19–21), but the sense of call was strong. The distinctive cloak of the prophet (1 Kings 19:19; 2 Kings 1:8; Zech. 13:4) wrapped him round, separating him to the prophetic office, and Elisha left position and privilege to become the older man's 'attendant' (1 Kings 19:21).

By the time of 2 Kings 2, Elisha had his own assured knowledge of God and sufficient personal stature to refuse Elijah's commands (2 Kings 2:2–6) when the older man – a 'loner' to the last – wished to go to meet God alone. The story then focuses on Elisha's request (2 Kings 2:9) and its aftermath (vv. 13–15). In asking for a

**155**

'double portion' he was not wishing to be 'twice the man' Elijah was! Rather, the double portion was that of the firstborn son (*Deut. 21:17*), and Elisha's desire was that he should be recognized and equipped as Elijah's chosen successor. In a word, his prompt decision to follow Elijah (*1 Kings 19:21*) was no flash in the pan. To follow him as prophet had become his priority longing. God honoured this longing: the cloak fell from the departing prophet to the incoming prophet, and Elisha crossed back into the promised land with the spirit of Elijah recognizably resting on him (*2 Kings 2:15*). But his authority was not to be in authoritarianism, nor his leadership simply in decision-making. In their immaturity the company of the prophets wanted to search for Elijah and, though Elisha knew their request was foolish and time-wasting, he neither squashed what was, after all, the product of loving concern (*v. 17*) nor, in the outcome, did he turn it into a major issue (*v. 18*). This easy, amenable and peace-loving spirit continued to characterize Elisha.

## The sword of Elisha

The association of Elisha with Hazael and Jehu obviously placed a sword of judgment in his hand, and we do see the flash of that sword in the course of his ministry. But sometimes a sword has another use: it is with the touch of a sword that a monarch ennobles one of his/her subjects, and the sword of Elisha was similarly used – lifting up the needy and the downcast to a better and more fulfilled life.

The first pair of stories about Elisha show the contrasting uses of the sword: a curse removed (*2 Kings 2:19–22*) and (*2 Kings 2:23–25*) a curse inflicted. They record how Elisha was publicly validated as the LORD's prophet on both sides of his sword-ministry: restoring and condemning.

Jericho was the first opponent of Israel's possession of the promised land and, as such, had been placed under a curse by Joshua (*Josh. 6:26*). Is it not significant that it was in the days of Ahab that a man named Hiel felt he could ignore the curse, only to discover (*1 Kings 16:34*) that he must pay a dire price? But the curse prevailed also against those who lived in the cursed place: literally, 'the water is bad and the land bereaved' – a suspect water supply spreading deadly infection. Elisha had crossed Jordan where Joshua did and, like him, purposed a new beginning in and for Canaan. The time had come to indicate the LORD's favour by lifting the curse. The 'new bowl' (*2 Kings 2:20*) indicated that something new was afoot; 'salt' (though Scripture does not explain why) was a symbol of the LORD's eternal covenant (*Lev. 2:13; Num. 18:19; 2 Chron. 13:5*). Symbolically this act reversed the curse and brought the city and its people within the fresh blessings of the covenant, but the power was not that of ritual or magic but of the LORD's word by Elisha (*2 Kings 2:22*).

Bethel (*1 Kings 12:28–33*) was at the centre of Israel's heretical religion. For Elisha to go there at all required great resoluteness, but if he was to exercise an unfettered ministry it was essential that he should, from the start, assert dominance where it was needed. Equally, it was strategic for the priests of Bethel to strike the first blow, now that Elijah had gone and a new and untried man was at the helm. Consequently they arranged a 'reception committee' of 'youths' – not the 'little children' of AV but, to suit the context, 'young louts' (*2 Kings 2:23*) and 'youngsters' (*v. 24*). The meaning of their jeering chant, 'baldhead' is lost. What is certain is that Elisha's head would be covered and, even if he were bald, it could not have been observed. Maybe Elisha was wearing the uncut hair of a Nazirite (Num. 6:5) and the yobs were in fact mocking his consecration. In any case, the situation was one of confrontation and the future of his ministry depended on its outcome. To fight or to run would be to lose the day, but there is a great God who stands by his beleaguered servants, and to him the appeal went up and was magnificently heard. The victory was the LORD's, and 2 Kings 2:25 notes the complete freedom with which Elisha could travel the land in his ministry.

### Goodness and severity

The pattern of the remaining stories of Elisha displays the dimensions of his ministry in grace and power:

**A¹** 2 Kings 3:11–20 (Kings): Israel's king denounced (v. 13). Life-giving water. Moab's defeat predicted (v. 18). Wrath against Israel (v. 27).
   **B¹** 2 Kings 4:1–7, 8–37 (People): The poor widow (vv. 1–7) and the rich lady (vv. 8–37). The Shunammite's son restored (vv. 32–37).
      **C¹** 2 Kings 4:38–41, 42–44 (Prophets and others): Food made wholesome (vv. 38–41). Bread and to spare (vv. 42–44).
         **D** 2 Kings 5:1–27 (Naaman and Gehazi): Uncleanness removed, uncleanness inflicted (see vv. 14, 27).
      **C²** 2 Kings 6:1–7, 8–23; 6:24–7:20 (Prophets and others): Loss recovered (6:1–8). Bread and to spare (6:23; 7:18).
   **B²** 2 Kings 8:1–6, 7–14 (People and kings): The Shunammite's land restored. The land of Israel lost.
**A²** 2 Kings 9:1–13; 13:14–19, 20–21 (Kings): Israel's king destroyed. Aram's defeat predicted. The life-giving Elisha.

The bracketed people indicate the range of Elisha's concerns. He could intervene to influence the course of history, as his ministry brought him before kings. Indeed he was also even a king-maker – though in 2 Kings 9:1–10 we need to note carefully the difference between what Elisha told the young man to say (v. 1) and what he foolishly added to gratify his personal assumption that he possessed the prophetic gift (vv. 6–10)! But one of the lovely marks of Elisha's ministry was that he condescended to ordinary folk with love and power (B¹, ²), cared for his subordinates (C¹) and identified with their desires (C²). He was a balanced blend of the 'goodness and severity of God' (Rom. 11:22) on the one hand, sustaining the undeserving (2 Kings 3:17), supplying the poor (4:1–7), feeding the hungry (4:38f.), concerning himself over a lost tool (6:1f.), weeping over the suffering (8:11f.), restoring child (4:8–37) and land (8:1f.), using his God-given powers for the welfare of the LORD's people (6:8f.); on the other hand, stern in his denunciations (3:13f, cf. 2:23–25), resolute in promoting the just judgments of God (9:1–2) and the overthrow of his people's foes (13:14f.). The centrepiece of the whole presentation – as set out above, the story of Naaman and Gehazi – is a perfect summary of this great man on whom Elijah's 'double portion' so plainly came. When Naaman was brought to accept, believe and obey the work of God in all its simplicity, bending his pride to divine revelation and submitting his needs to divine supply, he went away blessed (2 *Kings* 5:1–19). However, when Gehazi, for all his privilege (2 *Kings* 5:20), contradicted the mind of God as revealed in Elisha (vv. 16, 20), corrupted the doctrine of free grace expressed by Elisha's refusal of reward, changed the truth of God into a lie (vv. 21–22), dissembled (v. 25) and saw the ministry of the grace of God as a means of gain (v. 26), he contracted the contagion of the world with which he had identified himself (v. 27). In the hands of Elisha, the sword of the Spirit, which is the word of God (*Eph.* 6:17), both ennobled and destroyed, bringing life to those who obeyed and death to the disobedient.

J.A.M.

**ELISHAH,** a son of Javan, the grandson of Japheth and the progenitor of a nation that carries the same name (*Gen.* 10:4; 1 *Chron.* 1:7). The 'coasts of Elishah' are mentioned in *Ezek.* 27:7 as the place from which purple dyes were obtained by the people of Tyre. It is possible that his people should be identified with the Greeks or the people of southern Italy.

**ELISHAMA** (Heb., 'my God hears').

**1.** The son of Ammihud and the leader of the people of Ephraim at the census of the Israelites in the wilderness of Sinai. His division of people numbered 40,500 (*Num.* 1:10; 2:18). As the representative of his tribe he also brought his tribe's fellowship offering when the Tabernacle was dedicated in the wilderness (*Num.* 7:48, 53). The enormous offering from this tribe was brought on the seventh day. He also led his tribe when the Israelites set out from the Sinai desert on their wanderings (*Num.* 10:22).

**2.** A son of King David. After David conquered Jerusalem and moved there from Hebron he took many wives and concubines. One of his many children was Elishama (2 *Sam.* 5:16; 1 *Chron.* 3:8; 14:7).

**3.** The father of Nethaniah and the grandfather of Ishmael, the assassin of Gedaliah (2 *Kings* 25:25; *Jer.* 41:1).

**4.** The son of Jekamiah and a leader from the tribe of Judah, he was a descendant of Jerahmeel (1 *Chron.* 2:41).

**5.** An Ephraimite who was an ancestor of Joshua. His father was Ammihud and his son was Nun (1 *Chron.* 7:26),

**6.** This Elishama, a priest, lived in the days of King Jehoshaphat of Judah. During the early years of his reign Jehoshaphat served the LORD and sent out various teachers and Levites to teach the people of Judah the Book of the Law. Elishama was one of those teachers (2 *Chron.* 17:8).

**7.** In the days of King Jehoiakim of Judah, another Elishama was secretary to the court. The scroll of prophecy that Baruch brought from Jeremiah to the king was kept in his room before being read to the king by Jehudi (*Jer.* 36:12, 20–21).

P.D.G.

**ELISHAPHAT** (Heb., 'God judges'), one of the commanders with whom Jehoiada the priest made a covenant. He commanded a unit of 100 men (2 *Chron.* 23:1) and helped Jehoiada crown Joash king. Jehoiada had helped hide the child king from Athaliah, the mother of Ahaziah, the recently deceased king of Judah. When seven years had passed the child was produced and crowned. Athaliah was put to death by Elishaphat and the other leaders and their men. Joash, who was clearly influenced by Jehoiada, repaired the Temple and restored the worship of the LORD. Later, when Jehoiada died, he was led astray, and sadly, he and the people returned to worshipping the Asherah.

**ELISHEBA** (Heb., 'my God is my oath'), a daughter of Amminadab and a sister of Nahshon. She married Aaron, the High Priest, and bore him Nadab, Abihu, Eleazar and Ithamar (*Exod. 6:23*). Eleazar, her son, succeeded Aaron to the position of High Priest (*Num. 20:28–29*).

**ELISHUA** (Heb., 'God is salvation'), a son of King David. After David conquered Jerusalem and moved there from Hebron, he took many wives and concubines. One of his many children was Elishua (*2 Sam. 5:15; 1 Chron. 3:6; 14:5*).

**ELIUD** (Heb., 'God my praise'), one of the ancestors of Jesus mentioned in Matthew's genealogy (*Matt. 1:14–15*). He appears four generations before Joseph. His father is listed as Akim and his son as Eleazar.

**ELIZABETH** (Heb., 'God is my oath') is mentioned only in *Luke 1*. She was a descendant of Aaron and the wife of Zechariah, the priest who was visited by the angel Gabriel (*Luke 1:5, 11*). She was also a relative of the Virgin Mary and the mother of John the Baptist.

While Zechariah was ministering in the Temple of the Lord, Gabriel appeared to him and told him that his wife, Elizabeth, would bear him a son (*Luke 1:13*). Elizabeth had no children and both she and her husband were well advanced in years. So Zechariah questioned the possibility of such an event, and his unbelief cost him his speech (*Luke 1:18*). He would not speak again until the baby was born (*Luke 1:19–20*).

God showed favour to Elizabeth in her old age and took away the shame and disgrace of being childless. It is clear that her barrenness was not a result of sin, since both she and her husband were 'upright in the sight of God' (*Luke 1:6*). But God was working out his greater purposes in her life and his plan was perfect.

Thus, when the timing was right, the Lord finally blessed her with no ordinary child. Her son was to be the forerunner to Christ, and the world would forever know him as John the Baptist. His mother, Elizabeth, would not be as well known as her famous son. However, there is no doubt that in the shadow of this godly man stood a godly mother, who raised him in the fear of the Lord. Her influence on his life should not be overlooked or underestimated.

After Elizabeth discovered she was pregnant, she remained in seclusion for five months. The text does not reveal why she did this, but she probably remained hidden in order fully to devote herself to the Lord in gratitude and thankfulness.

In Elizabeth's sixth month of pregnancy, Mary was visited by the angel Gabriel, who announced to her that she would supernaturally conceive and bring forth the Messiah, the Son of God. He told her that Elizabeth, her relative, was also pregnant (*Luke 1:36–40*). It is not known how Elizabeth was related to Mary, whether she was a cousin, an aunt or another relation.

So when Mary heard the good news about Elizabeth, she quickly left her home in Nazareth and went to the Judean hills to visit her. When the baby inside Elizabeth's womb heard Mary's voice, he leaped for joy. Elizabeth was filled with the Holy Spirit and, by supernatural means, knew that Mary was pregnant. She was also aware of the infant's identity and divine origin.

Filled with joy, Elizabeth blessed Mary and her baby with a loud voice. In her blessing, she humbly acknowledged the unborn child to be 'my Lord', showing forth her willingness to be obedient to him. Her blessing also points to Mary's incredible faith. For she had believed all that the Lord promised he would do (*Luke 1:39–45*).

Joy and gratitude are woven throughout this account of Elizabeth. She knew God was doing something new, and she rejoiced that she was a part of his plan. God entrusted the forerunner of his Son to her and she faithfully and joyfully responded to him in complete devotion.

When the time came for Elizabeth to give birth, her neighbours and relatives gathered around for the happy event. The boy was given his name at his circumcision, on the eighth day. It is not known why they waited eight days to name him, especially since he was given a name before he was conceived (Luke 1:13). They might have been following the Hellenistic custom of waiting a week before naming a newborn.

However, in accordance with Jewish custom, the child was going to be named after his father, Zechariah. But Elizabeth objected and insisted that his name was to be John. Disregarding her request (probably because she was a woman), they turned to Zechariah and asked him. He said the child was to be called John and, at that moment, Zechariah's tongue was loosed. Then, filled with the Holy Spirit, he prophesied about the destiny of his son (Luke 1:57–64, 67–79).

These events stirred the people of Judea, and they were filled with awe. They could sense that God was with this new family and they wondered what would come of it (Luke 1:65–66). The Lord was beginning to turn his people back to himself.

Elizabeth was a reverent woman who was joyously devoted to her Lord. God is glorified in her life and his presence is clearly seen in this short account. The miracle of this godly elderly woman conceiving a child reminds the reader of other famous women in Scripture with whom God intervened in a similar way – women such as Sarah (Gen. 17:15), Rachel (Gen. 30:22–24) and Hannah (1 Sam. 1). In each case God's work in their lives led to sons who became great leaders of his people. John the Baptist was the greatest (Matt. 11:11).          K.MCR.

**ELIZAPHAN** (Heb., 'my God has protected').

**1.** The son of Parnach, this man was a leader of the tribe of Zebulun. In Num. 34:25 he was appointed by Moses to divide up the part of the land of Canaan that had been allocated to Zebulun. V. 29 of that passage shows that the men appointed for this task were singled out for the work by the LORD himself.

**2.** One of the leaders among the Levites during the wilderness period. This man was the head of the Kohathite clan, which itself included a number of large family clans. He was the son of Uzziel. Num. 3:30–31 reveals that this clan was responsible for much of the work inside the Tabernacle, notably 'the care of the ark, the table, the lampstand, the altars, the articles of the sanctuary used in ministering, the curtain, and everything related to their use'. See also 1 Chron. 15:8; 2 Chron. 29:13.          P.D.G.

**ELIZUR** (Heb., 'my God is a rock'), the son of Shedeur and the leader of the people of Reuben at the census of the Israelites in the wilderness of Sinai. His division of people numbered 46,500 (Num. 1:5; 2:10). As the representative of his tribe, he also brought his tribe's fellowship offering when the Tabernacle was dedicated in the wilderness (Num. 7:30, 35). The enormous offering from this tribe was brought on the fourth day. He also led his tribe when the Israelites set out from the Sinai desert on their wanderings (Num. 10:18).

**ELKANAH** (Heb., 'God has protected').

**1.** A Levite, a descendant of Kohath and one of the sons of Korah, a clan leader (Exod. 6:24).

**2.** A grandson of Korah listed in 1 Chron. 6:23. If a generation is missed out or has become misplaced in the genealogies, then this person may be the same as 1. above.

**3.** Two others by the name of Elkanah are listed among the descendants of Kohath (1 Chron. 6:25–26, 35–36). A third (v. 27) by the same name is discussed in 4. below.

**4.** This Elkanah was the father of Samuel (*1 Chron. 6:27, 34*). He came from Ramathaim in the hill country of Ephraim and was the son of Jeroham. He was a faithful servant of the LORD who had two wives, Peninnah and Hannah. Annually he would take his family to worship and sacrifice at Shiloh where Eli was priest (*1 Sam. 1:1–4*). He loved Hannah very deeply although she could not have children. He was obviously very concerned for Hannah, who felt despised and was ridiculed by Peninnah. His love and care for Hannah is well described in *1 Sam. 1:8*, where he comforts her with the words: 'Why are you downhearted? Don't I mean more to you than ten sons?' Following Hannah's prayer to the LORD, she did get pregnant by Elkanah, and Samuel was born (*1 Sam. 1:19–20*). Elkanah was gracious enough to allow Hannah to give Samuel back to the service of the LORD at the sanctuary at Shiloh (*1 Sam. 1:23; 2:11, 20*). The faithfulness of Hannah and Elkanah was rewarded by God with five further children.

**5.** Another Elkanah, a Levite, was one of the ancestors of those who settled in Jerusalem after the return from the Exile in Babylon. He was the father of Asa (*1 Chron. 9:16*).

**6.** One of the warriors who deserted Saul to join David at Ziklag. They were ambidextrous in archery and with slings. They were from the tribe of Benjamin (*1 Chron. 12:6*).

**7.** A Levite whom David appointed to serve in the Tabernacle and then the Temple. He was a 'doorkeeper for the ark' (*1 Chron. 15:23*).

**8.** This Elkanah was second in command under King Ahaz's son, Maaseiah. He was killed by Zicri, an Ephraimite warrior (*2 Chron. 28:7*). P.D.G.

**ELMADAM,** one of Jesus' ancestors (*Luke 3:28*). He was the father of Cosam and the son of Er. He is listed in the 15th generation after David.

**ELNAAM** (Heb., 'God is delight'), the father of Jeribai and Joshaviah (*1 Chron. 11:46*). His two sons were among David's 'mighty men' and were renowned warriors.

**ELNATHAN** (Heb., 'God has given').
**1.** The father of Nehushta and grandfather of King Jehoiachin. Nehushta was Jehoiachin's mother (*2 Kings 24:8*). He may have been the same person as 2. below.

**2.** The son of Acbor, this Elnathan was a leader who was sent by King Jehoiakim to Egypt in pursuit of Uriah (*Jer. 26:21–23*). Uriah was a faithful prophet of the LORD who had warned of the impending judgment of God and destruction of Jerusalem by the Babylonians. He fled for his life, but Elnathan caught him and brought him back to Jerusalem, where the king had him killed. He was among the officials who listened to Baruch reading the prophesy from Jeremiah and advised Baruch and Jeremiah to hide. He then tried to prevent the king from burning the scroll (*Jer. 36:12, 25*).

**3.** One of the Jews, a leader among his people, who joined Ezra on their return from the Babylonian captivity to Jerusalem. He helped Ezra find suitable Levites to accompany them back to Judah (*Ezra 8:16*). P.D.G.

**ELON** (Heb., 'terebinth').
**1.** The father of Esau's wives Basemath and Adah, this Elon was a Hittite (*Gen. 26:34; 36:2*). These wives that Esau took from the tribes found in the area in which they had settled were 'a source of grief to Isaac and Rebekah' (*Gen. 26:35*). Esau should have returned, as did his brother Jacob, to find a wife in Mesopotamia (*Gen. 27:46–28:5–8*).

**2.** One of the sons of Zebulun and leader of the Elonite clan (*Gen. 46:14; Num. 26:26*).

**3.** Elon the Zebulunite, one of the Judges, led Israel for ten years following the death of Ibzan (*Judg. 12:11–12*). See *Judges*.

**ELPAAL** (Heb., 'God has acted'), a descendant of Benjamin and a tribal leader in the genealogy leading to King Saul. His mother was Hushim and his brother was Abitub (*1 Chron. 8:11–12, 18*).

**ELPELET,** one of the sons of David who was born in Jerusalem after the King had taken 'many wives' (*1 Chron. 14:5*). The context shows that taking many wives was probably what was expected in those days of a king who was 'highly exalted' (*v. 2*).

**ELUZAI** (Heb., 'God is my strength'), a skilful and ambidextrous archer from the tribe of Benjamin who fought first for Saul and then transferred to David at Ziklag (*1 Chron. 12:3*). He was one of David's 'Thirty' great warriors. Later in the passage it seems that such men transferred loyalties not simply to be on the winning side but because the 'Spirit' had worked among them.

**ELYMAS,** a sorcerer (*Acts 13:8–9*). See *Bar-Jesus* for further discussion.

**ELZABAD** **1.** Elzabad was the ninth in the list of the famous Gadites who defected from Saul to David when he was at Ziklag. These men are described in vivid imagery as the bravest of warriors. They were commanders who proved of tremendous support to David in his battles (*1 Chron. 12:12*).

**2.** A son of Shemaiah, he is listed among the gatekeepers of the Tabernacle in the time of King David (*1 Chron. 26:7*).

**ELZAPHAN** (Heb., 'protected by God'), a son of Aaron's uncle, Uzziel. He was a Levite and the leader of the Kohathites (*Exod. 6:22; Lev. 10:4*). Moses asked him and his brother Mishael to carry the bodies of their cousins, Nadab and Abihu, for burial outside the camp. Nadab and Abihu had died beside the Tabernacle after offering a sacrifice contrary to the LORD's command.

**ENAN,** a leader of the tribe of Naphtali. He is only mentioned in connection with his son Ahira, whom Moses later appointed leader of the tribe of Naphtali (*Num. 1:15; 2:29; 7:78 etc*).

**ENDOR** (the medium of). In *1 Sam. 28* an incident in Saul's life is related in which he consulted a female medium in the town of Endor concerning the future. Although Saul himself, no doubt under Samuel's direction, had expelled all mediums and spiritists from Israel (*1 Sam. 28:3*) in accordance with God's Law (*Deut. 18:10–11*), once Samuel died and Saul felt more and more threatened by David and by the Philistines, so he was prepared to break God's Law in an attempt to survive.

The Philistines had pitched camp at Shunem, and Saul brought his forces to Gibea ready for battle. But Saul 'was afraid' (*1 Sam. 28:5*). Although, at first, he consulted the LORD by means of the prophets, the Urim, and even by waiting for dreams, the LORD did not respond (*vv. 5–6*). Saul had moved so far from the LORD's way for himself and the nation that his looking to the LORD had become simply a 'last-ditch' attempt at survival. Since he was already under judgment, the LORD did not answer him, and so Saul confirmed his disobedience and lack of trust in God by going to a medium.

Much to her obvious surprise and dismay, the woman did indeed summon up Samuel, and also saw through Saul's disguise. She was scared by the appearance of Samuel and frightened that the king would put her to death (*1 Sam. 28:9–14*). It seems that in his providence God allowed Samuel to appear to Saul, since he was the only one whom Saul would believe. Samuel was allowed to return in order to pronounce the completion of the terrible judgment which he himself had earlier prophesied would fall on the house of Saul. Saul's disobedience to the LORD had led to his downfall: 'Because you did not obey the LORD . . . the LORD has done this to you today'. He then went on to say that Saul and his sons would die on the battlefield within 24 hours (1 Sam. 28:19). Saul fainted through fright and hunger, and the medium prevailed upon him to eat a fattened calf before he left for the battle.

Nowhere does the passage indicate that such use of a medium was acceptable under certain conditions. The contrary is indeed the case. This consultation was the final great act of disobedience by Saul, and it led to the pronouncing of his death. The passage also indicates that this medium was amazed when the spirit of Samuel did actually appear (1 Sam. 28:12–13). It seems that she had never experienced anything like this before. No doubt the whole sequence of events was allowed in the providence of God so that his judgment might be pronounced in a way that Saul, in his sin and disobedience, would understand.

P.D.G.

**ENOCH 1.** The first son born to Cain, after he had been banished by God to a punishment of wandering the land, was called Enoch. He was grandson to Adam and Eve. His father, Cain, was the first murderer and his descendants, such as Lamech, were renowned for their sin. Cain named the first city he built after his son (Gen. 4:17–18, 23–24).

**2.** In vivid contrast with Cain's son, Gen. 5 describes another Enoch who was a descendant of Seth. Seth had been born to Adam and Eve and had taken the place of Abel whom Cain had murdered (Gen. 4:22). Seth's descendants for the most part remained faithful to God and worshipped him. Notable among those in this godly line was Enoch who was the son of Jared and father of Methuselah (Gen. 5:18–19, 21–22; 1 Chron. 1:3). He lived for a total of 365 years and 'walked with God'. In other words, he led a righteous life of faith in service of God. Instead of his death being recorded, it is simply said of him: 'then he was no more, because God took him away' (Gen. 5:24).

Because he was part of the faithful line of descendants from Adam, he also appears as an ancestor of Jesus in Luke 3:37. The writer to the Hebrews, commenting on the faith of some of the great heroes of the past, says that Enoch 'did not experience death' because 'he was commended as one who pleased God' (Heb. 11:5). He goes on to make the point that 'pleasing God' is only possible by means of faith in him. Thus Enoch was counted 'righteous' before God by his faith; a teaching that the writer demonstrates is essential to a proper understanding of Christianity.

There is no doubt that Enoch was 'translated' or simply removed from earth into the presence of God without experiencing the suffering or pain of death. How this happened or why he particularly should have been chosen for this great privilege is not revealed in Scripture.

**3.** Another reference to Enoch is found in Jude 14. Jude quotes a prophecy from an intertestamental book attributed to the Enoch of Gen. 5. There is no indication that Jude regarded this book as 'inspired' or that he regarded the whole of it as reliable. Rather he quotes from it with approval as a book containing a concept with which he agreed: that the Lord would return with his angels to judge all who are evil. 

P.D.G.

**ENOSH,** the grandson of Adam and the son of Seth, lived 905 years (Gen. 4:26; 5:6–11; 1 Chron. 1:1). In his time, we are told, 'men began to call on the name of the LORD'. A direct contrast may be intended here between the sons of Seth and their obedience to the LORD and the family line of Cain, which had been mentioned earlier in *Gen. 4*. Enoch is also mentioned in Luke's genealogy leading from Jesus back to Adam (*Luke 3:38*).

**EPAPHRAS** was called 'my fellow prisoner for Christ Jesus', 'our dear fellow-servant' and 'a servant of Christ Jesus' by the apostle Paul, with whom he worked and with whom he was imprisoned in Rome (this was Paul's first Roman imprisonment; *Philem. 23; Col. 1:7; 4:12*). We learn from Paul in *Col. 1* that the Colossians had been converted to Christianity through Epaphras' preaching of the gospel. He was known for his commitment to Christ and his perseverance for the sake of the gospel not only at Colosse, but also at Hierapolis and Laodicea (*Col. 4:13*). He 'worked hard' for these churches, perhaps in raising material support for them from other churches, or perhaps simply in prayer and teaching. He also brought Paul information about the Colossian Christians to which Paul then referred in his letter. The Colossians were known for their 'faith and love', for their 'love in the Spirit' and for the evidence of God's grace at work among them.

In addition to his faithful preaching, Epaphras is singled out for praise because he was a man of prayer. He was known for 'wrestling' in prayer for those who, under his ministry, had found Christ. He knew how important continued growth in the faith was for these new Christians, especially with the prospect of confronting false teaching and even persecution. His prayer was that the Colossian Christians might 'stand firm in all the will of God, mature and fully assured' (*Col. 4:12*). His ministry seems to have been characterized by total commitment to Christ and the gospel in a way more often associated with the apostle Paul himself. Perhaps for this reason Paul called him a 'slave of Christ Jesus' (NIV, 'servant'), a term reserved by Paul for himself and (once) for Timothy.

**EPAPHRODITUS,** a Christian from Philippi mentioned only in *Phil. 2:25–30; 4:18*. He was sent by the Philippian church ('your messenger' *Phil. 2:25*) to bring an offering to support Paul's ministry. Epaphroditus stayed on assisting Paul, 'filling up the lack' of personal ministry from the other Philippians, who could not travel the distance to the imprisoned Paul.

It is not clear whether Epaphroditus was a leader in the Philippian church or simply a committed follower of Christ, but it is very evident that Paul held him in high esteem. Paul calls him a 'brother' (*Phil. 2:25*). He shared Paul's heritage, goals and service in the family of God. Paul calls him a 'fellow-worker' (*v. 25*), stressing that service which, Paul goes on to say, led to Epaphroditus becoming critically ill (*v. 26*). Paul calls him 'my fellow-soldier' because the service of the gospel in which they were both involved was a life-and-death struggle in which Epaphroditus was willing to 'risk' everything in the 'work of Christ' (*v. 30*).

Epaphroditus' life-threatening illness caused both Paul and the Philippians great concern, and Paul regarded his recovery as God's merciful intervention (*Phil. 2:27*). The Philippians were so concerned about his illness that Epaphroditus himself became worried. Thus, when he was well enough to travel, Paul sent him home with the highest of recommendations, assuring the Philippians that their apostle had fulfilled his commission beyond their expectations.

The name Epaphras is a contraction of Epaphroditus. Both were very common names in the 1st century. Epaphroditus is not to be confused with the Epaphras who was a native of Colosse (*Col. 4:12–13; Philem. 23*). Epaphroditus is the Greek equivalent of the Latin 'Venustus', both of these names indicating familial association with the cult of Aphrodite (Venus). In addition to being the goddess of love and beauty, Aphrodite was also the goddess of gamblers, who called out her name when casting their lots and risking their fortune. In *Phil. 2:30* Paul uses the word 'risking', which is found nowhere else in the NT. In extra-biblical Greek literature it is used to describe gambling. Possibly Paul used it here to affirm powerfully that Epaphroditus (with pagan name intact) risked his all not for Aphrodite but for the work of Christ. (The words 'to death' in *Phil. 2:30* are the same words used to describe Jesus' self-sacrifice in *Phil. 2:8*.)

Whether or not the connection of the name Epaphroditus with risk-taking gambling is correct, the connection of Epaphroditus' self-sacrifice with that of Christ is certain. The placement of this commendation of Epaphroditus (and Timothy) in *Phil. 2:19–30* is awkward at first glance. (Paul's commendations and greetings typically come at the end of his epistles.) In fact, these are well-placed illustrations of the kind of humble, self-denying sacrifice which Christ Jesus came to engender in his people. Epaphroditus is living proof that unity-producing humility is possible in the church of Philippi.                       A.M.

**EPENETUS** At the end of Paul's epistle to the Romans this man is greeted as a personal and 'dear friend' (*Rom. 16:5*). He must have had a very special place in Paul's heart, for he was the first convert 'in the province of Asia' and thus the first evidence of God's grace in the lives of the people there. The area being referred to was probably Ephesus.

**EPHAH** (Heb., 'darkness').

**1.** One of the sons of Midian and a descendant of Abraham through his wife Keturah (*Gen. 25:4; 1 Chron. 1:33*). The name is mentioned again in connection with Midian in *Is. 60:6*, where the prophet looks to a time when glory and wealth will come to Israel even from Sheba: 'Herds of camels [indicating great wealth] will cover your land, young camels of Midian and Ephah.'

**2.** One of Caleb's concubines. She bore him Haran, Moza and Gazaz (*1 Chron. 2:46*).

**3.** One of six sons of Jahdai and a leader in the tribe of Judah (*1 Chron. 2:47*).

**EPHAI,** the Netophathite, whose sons were among the army officers who rallied to support Gedaliah at Mizpah (*Jer. 40:8*). Gedaliah had been appointed by the king of Babylon as governor over Judah after most of the people had been taken into captivity (*v. 7*). For a while a number of other Israelites gathered to Gedaliah, who was given a measure of autonomy. Eventually, however, Gedaliah and all those who had supported him were assassinated by Ishmael, son of Nethaniah, in a *coup d'état*.

**EPHER    1.** One of the sons of Midian and a descendant of Abraham through his wife Keturah (*Gen. 25:4; 1 Chron. 1:33*).

**2.** Another Epher was the third son of Ezrah and was from the tribe of Judah (*1 Chron. 4:17*).

**3.** The head of a clan and a valiant soldier in the tribe of Manasseh. However, he was among those who were unfaithful to the LORD and worshipped idols (*1 Chron. 5:24*).

**EPHLAL,** the father of Obed and a son of Zabad. He was a descendant of Judah (*1 Chron. 2:37*).

**EPHRAIM** (Heb., 'fruitful'). Though he was the progenitor of one of the tribes of Israel, Ephraim was not a son of the patriarch but rather a grandson. Joseph, evidently in anticipation of the setting apart of Levi from the 'secular' tribes (*Num. 3*), thus reducing their number by one, brought his sons Manasseh and Ephraim before Jacob so that he might bless them (Gen. 48). This ultimately resulted in the division of Joseph into two lines of descendants, from Manasseh and Ephraim, and the restoration of the number of tribes to twelve (Gen. 49:22–26; cf. Deut. 33:13–17).

In the narrative of the birth of Joseph's sons (Gen. 41:50–52), the elder, Manasseh, is so named because, as Joseph said, the LORD had made him forget all his troubles. The younger son he called Ephraim because God had made him fruitful in the land of Egypt. When Joseph later presented his sons to Jacob for the blessing, he expected Manasseh to receive that of the first-born (Gen. 48:13), but, ironically and unexpectedly, Jacob crossed his arms and laid his right hand on Ephraim, thus assuring him of the rights of primogeniture (vv. 14, 19–20).

Though Ephraim was not specifically named in the blessing of Gen. 49, it is clear that he was in mind when Jacob blessed Joseph by saying, 'Joseph is a fruitful vine' (v. 22). 'Fruitful' is a play on words on the name Ephraim itself, 'the fruitful one'. In the Deuteronomy blessing the idea of fruitfulness was again paramount, though no form of the word exists except the name Ephraim (Deut. 33:17). Fulfilment of the prophetic blessing came about in both the size and might of the tribe of Ephraim and its favourable location in the central hill country of Canaan. Its leadership became apparent in the arrangement of the camp of Israel in the march from Egypt to the Promised Land. It was Ephraim that headed up the three tribes on the west side (Num. 2:18–24). Joshua was an Ephraimite (Num. 13:8), and under his command the tribe was able to receive and occupy one of the largest of the post-conquest allocations of land (Josh. 16:5–10). The Tabernacle was erected at the religious centre of Shiloh, which became the resting place of the ark during Joshua's time. This was also in Ephraim (Josh. 18:1; 22:12). Joshua himself was buried in the heart of that territory (Josh. 24:30).

Following the division of the kingdom, Jeroboam located one of his apostate shrines at Bethel (1 Kings 12:29), in Ephraim, and his capital at Shechem which, by then, lay within the administrative district of Ephraim as defined by Solomon (v. 25). Jeroboam, in fact, was an Ephraimite (1 Kings 11:26), and from his time onwards the centre of the political and religious life of the Northern Kingdom was in Ephraim. So much so was this the case, that the Northern Kingdom was commonly called Ephraim right up to the time of its fall and deportation under the Assyrians in 722 BC (cf. Is. 7:2, 5, 8–9, 17; Jer. 7:15; 31:9; Hos. 4:17; 5:3, 5).    E.M.

**EPHRATH** Her husband Caleb, the son of Hezron, was a descendant of the tribe of Judah. She bore him Hur (1 Chron. 2:19).

**EPHRON,** the son of Zohar, was a Hittite. When Sarah died at Hebron, right at the heart of what would later become the nation of Israel, Abraham sought to buy a burial place for her and his family from the Hittites. They acknowledged Abraham as 'a mighty prince among us', but still Abraham was a nomadic settler. Possession of this land for burial gave him lasting rights in the land the LORD had promised (Gen. 23). Ephron negotiated a fair price for the sale of his field, which contained a suitable burial site, the cave of Machpelah.

Later Abraham was buried there by his sons Ishmael and Isaac (Gen. 25:9). Many years later Jacob was taken back from Egypt and buried in the same cave, as an indication that he too still looked for the time when the land would belong properly to the descendants of Abraham (Gen. 49:29–30; 50:13). Jacob's body was first embalmed according to Egyptian custom before being taken back to Canaan under an escort led by Joseph.    P.D.G.

**EPICUREANS,** the adherents of a school of Greek philosophy that existed in NT times. Paul encountered members of this school in Athens in *Acts 17:18.* It was founded by Epicurus (341–270 BC). Its followers were indifferent to the gods: they believed in them, but regarded them as too far removed to worry about. Epicureanism was a close ancient equivalent to modern secular agnosticism in that it defined life very much in terms of current experience. In contrast to the Stoics, the Epicureans affirmed that human sensations, preconceptions and feelings were the standard of truth. There were two states of feeling, pleasure and pain; and two types of inquiry, one concerned with things, the other with words. The goal of life was to bring and experience happiness. Death was not to be contemplated. No planning should take the future into account, since no one knew what it would bring. The end of all action was to be free from pain and fear. In order to experience pleasure, it was sometimes necessary to experience pain too. The absence of pain was to be desired and pleasure was to be pursued. By pleasure the Epicureans did not mean prodigal or sensual pleasure, but rather that which takes away pain from the body and trouble from the soul. So the greatest good was prudence, searching out the ground of every choice and determining what to avoid. A life of true pleasure would be a life of prudence, honour and justice. This summary of the Epicurean philosophy reflects the description by Diogenes Laertius in *Lives of the Eminent Philosophers,* book 10. D.B.

**ER** (Heb., 'one who watches').

**1.** The first son of Judah by his Canaanite wife (the daughter of Shua), and the grandson of Jacob (*Gen. 38:3–7, 12; 46:12; Num. 26:19; 1 Chron. 2:3*). Er's father arranged a wife for him called Tamar. The Bible does not tell us anything about Er except that he 'was wicked in the LORD's sight; so the LORD put him to death'. More detail is given about the sin of his brother Onan, but much of the family seems to have rejected the LORD and been drawn into Canaanite culture and religion. *Gen. 38* is an unhappy chapter which records the sin of Judah and his family.

**2.** This Er was the son of Shelah and the father of Lecah and a grandson of Judah (*1 Chron. 4:21*). He was a leader of the clans of linen workers who lived at Beth Ashbea.

**3.** This Er is listed in Luke's genealogy of Jesus through Joseph to Adam (*Luke 3:28*). He was the son of Joshua and the father of Elmadam.

**ERAN,** a grandson of Ephraim and a son of Shuthelah. Eran became the leader of the Eranite clan (*Num. 26:36*).

**ERASTUS** was one of God's Christian 'civil servants' about whom Paul wrote in *Rom. 13:6.* He was the 'director of public works' in the Roman colony of Corinth (*Rom. 16:23*), the city from which Paul's letter to the Romans originated and from which he sent personal greetings to the Christians in Rome. The duties of the 'director of public works' were the upkeep and welfare of property such as streets and civic buildings, the collection of public revenue, and legal arbitration on commercial matters including presiding over financial litigation. In a wealthy city such as Corinth he would have needed large financial resources to put up the necessary financial guarantees for this honorary civic office.

To be elected he would also have needed to be a Roman citizen. As the post was one to which he would have been elected, Erastus must have been a well-known person who commanded the confidence of the leading citizens in Corinth. Election procedures demanded that the candidates make a promise which had to be fulfilled immediately by the winner.

We know that a substantial pavement measuring 19 by 19 metres was laid in large slabs of Acrocorinth limestone near the theatre. The words which clearly stood out in bronze read, 'Erastus laid this pavement at his own expense in exchange for the 'aedileship'. *Aedile* was the Latin equivalent of the Greek word *oikonomos* or 'director of public works'. Corinth was a Roman colony and in the time of Paul, it always used Latin terms for its public offices. It is known that the law made concessions to the religious scruples of the holders of these public offices. This meant that in Corinth, Jews, and therefore Christians (whom Gallio equated with Jews in his ruling in *Acts 18:12–15*), could hold office.

So here was a leading Christian citizen of Corinth who used his wealth and influence in order to undertake an honorary public office. This was in keeping with God's mandate that his people were to seek the welfare of the city (*Jer. 29:7*). Erastus would therefore have been regarded as a civic benefactor whom the rules would have praised for undertaking such 'good works'. There was a well-known convention which had a long history in the Roman world of the public recognition of such good works and Paul commends such benefactions by Christians, who had the resources to undertake that civic duty (*Rom. 13:3–4*).

As another of Paul's co-workers, Erastus was also actively engaged in Christian ministry. He, like Apollos, went to Ephesus in order to help in the vital ministry conducted there. Paul sent him into Macedonia with Timothy for the purpose of engaging in ministry (*Acts 19:22*). The last we hear of this leading Christian is that he stayed in Corinth (*2 Tim. 4:20*), where he undoubtedly continued to exercise an important role in the church. As a leading citizen his house would have been of the size that permitted all of the local Christians to gather together.

Erastus was a Christian of great wealth and also a Roman citizen. He used his resources for a public office which he himself funded. As a committed Christian, he willingly travelled by sea and land in order to participate in evangelistic endeavours and the strengthening of the churches. It is clear that in his case there was no sharp divide between seeing to the material welfare of the city, undertaken both as a ministry and as a public servant, and the spiritual ministry of the gospel and church planting. God's world is not divided, and he exercises his providential care over it both at the civic level and the spiritual.                    B.W.

**ERI** is listed as the fifth son of Gad and among those who went with Jacob to Egypt (*Gen. 46:16*). He was a grandson of Jacob and Zilpah. The passage gives some indication of the large number of those moving to Egypt with Jacob. Eri became the leader of the Erite clan (*Num. 26:16*).

**ESARHADDON** (Assyr., 'Ashur [a god] has given a brother') was king of Assyria (*681–669 BC*) and the son of Sennacherib. Sennacherib had been killed by his sons while worshipping his god Nisroch (*2 Kings 19:37; Is. 37:38*). Esarhaddon's dedication to his gods is recorded in various inscriptions, as is the fact that Manasseh, king of Judah, paid tribute to him. In the Biblical narrative he is recalled for his policy of deportation of the peoples he conquered. People who had been settled by him in Judah and the surrounding area were still there in Ezra's day (*Ezra 4:2*). They were not allowed to help in the rebuilding work of the Temple, even though they claimed to have worshipped the Israelite God since they had arrived in the country. The practice of deportation and the removal of whole peoples from one country to another often meant that those people would adopt the god of the land, thinking he would be more likely to bless them.

Part of the tribute required of vassal kings such as Manasseh was that they were required to teach obedience to Assyria and acknowledge Ashur as their god. The appalling evil and idolatry that this led to under Manasseh is vividly described in *2 Kings 21*.          P.D.G.

**ESAU** was what is nowadays called 'laid back'. He loved the free life of the open air (*Gen. 25:27*) and took nothing too seriously. His bluff and easy attitude to life was to be the cause of his tragic downfall. He was the firstborn of Isaac's and Rebekeh's twins (*Gen. 25:25*) and became his father's favourite son (*vv. 27–28*). The feud between the twins was sparked by Isaac's fancy that he was dying (*Gen. 27:1*) and that therefore the time had come to pass on the family blessing to his eldest son, but between them Rebekeh and Jacob (*vv. 5–19*) tricked the blind old man into blessing Jacob instead. Esau gave vent to a genuine outburst of grief and hatred (*Gen. 27:34, 41*), but it was not in his laid-back nature to sustain animosity. Thus, when Jacob returned, fearful, from Paddan-Aram, Esau greeted him as if nothing had happened (*Gen. 32:3–7; 33:1–4*).

Unfortunately, of course, his Edomite descendants proved more intractable, and the pebble which Esau and Jacob between them dropped into the pool of history went rippling on (e.g. *Ps. 137:7; Amos 1:11; Obad. 9–14*). But as for Esau, he took nothing seriously. When his parents grieved over his choice of wives (*Gen. 26:34*), off he went and married another wife, a daughter of Ishmael (*Gen. 28:6–9*). Life's problems were easily solved! Indeed, he was only able to create an uproar over Jacob's deceit because he did not take seriously his own earlier transaction in selling his birthright. Returning famished from hunting (*Gen. 25:29–34*), Esau found the domesticated Jacob busy in the kitchen. The aroma was too much for him and, typically, he saw it

all in exaggerated form: what use a birthright when he was dying of hunger! But that easy, frivolous decision had irreversible consequences. What Esau saw as 'taking a relaxed view' the Bible calls 'sexually immoral' and 'godless' (*Heb. 12:16*) – the attitude that lives this life as if there were no eternal life, no absolute values. For Esau, there was no place of repentance (*Heb. 12:17*).          J.A.M.

**ESH-BAAL,** one of the sons of Saul and a brother to Jonathan (*1 Chron. 8:33; 9:39*). He was also called Ish-Bosheth. After Saul's death, Abner took Ish-Bosheth and tried to make him king. The attempt at creating an alternative to David's reign was short-lived, and Ish-Bosheth was eventually murdered, much to David's dismay (*1 Sam. 2 and 4*; see more under *Ish-Bosheth*).

**ESHBAN,** a leader among the Horites. He was the son of Dishon and the grandson of Anah (*Gen. 36:26; 1 Chron. 1:41*).

**ESHCOL,** one of three Amorite brothers (see also *Mamre* and *Aner*) who were allied with Abram when he pursued Kedorlaomer in order to rescue Lot from captivity (*Gen. 14:13–16*). Abram showed his gratitude to them later (*v. 24*). See *Amraphel* for more on this incident.

**ESHEK** is mentioned in *1 Chron. 8:39* in Saul's genealogy of the tribe of Benjamin. His sons are listed as Ulam, Jeush and Eliphelet.

**ESHTEMOA  1.** His father was Ishbah and his grandparents were Mered and Pharoah's daughter, Bithiah (*1 Chron. 4:17*). He was of the tribe of Judah.

**2.** Also of the tribe of Judah, he was a Maacathite and the son of Hodiah (*1 Chron. 4:19*).

**ESHTON,** one of the leaders of the tribe of Judah. His father was Mehir, and he and his family lived in Recah (1 Chron. 4:11–12).

**ESLI** is mentioned in Luke's genealogy leading from Jesus and Joseph back to Adam (Luke 3:25). He was the father of Nahum and the son of Naggai. He appears in the tenth generation before Joseph.

**ESTHER,** also known as Hadassah, was a young Jewess from the tribe of Benjamin whose parents died and left her in the care of her cousin, Mordecai (Est. 2:5–7). Esther and Mordecai were among the Jews exiled to Susa, where they lived under the reign of King Xerxes. Esther's life changed when Vashti, the Queen, refused to display her beauty during one of Xerxes' banquets. Because of her rebellion, Vashti was banished from the king's house and the search began for a lovely young virgin who could take Vashti's place. After twelve long months of beauty treatments and training, Esther was chosen by the King as the most beautiful woman presented to him and she was made the new Queen. She did not divulge her Jewish background.

Esther flourished in her duties as did her cousin, Mordecai. But Esther's faith was tested when Mordecai approached her with a life-and-death responsibility. Mordecai had uncovered a plot by the king's top official, Haman, to annihilate all Jews, and Mordecai knew that only Esther could help to save God's people. Haman had persuaded the King to sign an order for the massacre of the Jews. Esther had a decision to make. She could risk her own life by approaching the King uninvited, or she could risk the life of all Jews by remaining silent. With Esther's words, 'If I perish, I perish' came the decision to speak out. With the prayers and fasting of all Jews in Susa, Esther sought her husband's help against Haman. Haman was hanged by the King and, although the original order could not be revoked, he gave the Jews special permission to defend themselves against the impending massacre. This they did and were saved (Est. 3–9).

God's care for his people, even though in Exile and under pagan rulers, is clearly seen as he used Esther and Mordecai to save his people. The two cousins lived out their service to Xerxes and to God with faithfulness, honour and the respect of all (see Mordecai, Vashti and Haman).

s.c.

**ETAM,** one of Judah's descendants and the father of Jezreel (1 Chron. 4:3).

**ETHAN** **1.** Known as Ethan the Ezrahite, this man was renowned for his wisdom. He is mentioned in a passage extolling the extraordinary God-given wisdom of Solomon. By comparison with Ethan and others, Solomon's wisdom was seen to be even greater (1 Kings 4:31). This Ethan is also credited with being the author of Ps. 89.

**2.** The grandson of Judah and Tamar and one of five sons of Zerah. Ethan's son was called Azariah (1 Chron. 2:6–8).

**3.** The son of Zimmah, this Ethan was a Levite who served in the ministry of the Tabernacle (1 Chron. 6:42).

**4.** Another Levite who served in the Tabernacle. He was the son of Kishi, and of the Merarite clan (1 Chron. 6:44). He is probably the same person as Ethan the son of Kushaiah, who was one of those appointed by David to sing and to play the bronze cymbals as the ark of the covenant was brought up to Jerusalem (1 Chron 15:17–19).

**ETHBAAL** (Heb., 'with Baal'), the king of the Sidonians. Sidon was an ancient Phoenician port city. Ethbaal is mentioned in connection with King Ahab of Israel, who did 'more evil in the eyes of the LORD than any of those before him' (1 Kings 16:30). Ahab's great sin was the worship of other gods. His marriage to Jezebel, Ethbaal's daughter, led directly to his worship of Baal.

**ETHIOPIAN EUNUCH** This man was in charge of the royal treasury under 'Candace, queen of the Ethiopians'. As a court official to the queen mother, it is likely that he was a castrated man (*Acts 8:27*; see *Candace*). *Acts 8:26–40* records a miraculous series of events that led to his conversion.

An angel appeared to Philip telling him to go south to the desert road. On that road he met the Ethiopian returning home in his chariot from worship in Jerusalem. Under the direction of the Holy Spirit (*Acts 8:29*) Philip went up to the chariot and discovered the Ethiopian was reading the prophecy of Isaiah. Philip asked whether the man understood what he was reading. The passage was from *Is. 53*. Philip then proceeded to expound the passage in the light of the suffering and death of Christ, explaining the 'good news about Jesus' to him (*Acts 8:35*). The eunuch came to believe in Christ, and when they passed a pool of water he asked Philip to baptize him. When this was done, the Holy Spirit 'suddenly took Philip away', and the eunuch 'went on his way rejoicing'.

As Luke recounts the very rapid spread of the gospel out from Jerusalem, Judea, Samaria and into Gentile territory (*Acts 1:8*), this event is clearly of great significance. Partly it is further evidence of the spread of the gospel, although the conversion of Cornelius is regarded as the main start of the gospel among Gentiles (*Acts 10*), but it is also clear evidence that the gospel is for all types of people, regardless of background or condition.

It is important to remember that *Deut. 23:1* and *Lev. 21:20* make it clear that as a eunuch this Ethiopian would not have been allowed into the assembly of Israel or to offer sacrifices, even though he had gone to Jerusalem to worship. Indeed, it is not clear whether he was a Gentile 'God-fearer' or of Jewish descent. Nevertheless, the prophet Isaiah had held the door open to eunuchs and foreigners who wished to follow the LORD and his covenant by promising them access to the LORD and his Temple. A prophecy in *Zeph. 3:10* also looked forward to the day when the LORD's worshippers would be gathered even from 'beyond the rivers of Cush' (the upper Nile; see also *Ps. 68:31*). This strange conversion fulfilled those OT prophecies and indicated that there were to be no second-class members of the assembly of those who believed in Christ. The 'good news' of the gospel was that the one who suffered, was 'led like a sheep to the slaughter' and gave his life, did so for any and every person who would turn to him in faith and trust.     P.D.G.

**ETHNAN,** of the tribe of Judah, was the son of Helah (*1 Chron. 4:7*).

**ETHNI,** a Levite, was the father of Adaiah and an ancestor of Asaph, one of David's leading musicians (*1 Chron. 6:41*).

**EUBULUS** (Gk., 'of good counsel'), a Christian who was with Paul during his second imprisonment in Rome and towards the end of his life. He added his greetings to the end of Paul's second letter to Timothy (*2 Tim. 4:21*). It is worth noting that he must have been one of the few Christians still with Paul at the time, for this very sad chapter details the fact that no one had stood with Paul at his first defence, except that the 'Lord stood at my side and gave me strength' (*v. 16*).

**EUNICE,** Timothy's mother and the daughter or daughter-in-law of his grandmother Lois (*2 Tim. 1:5*). She was a Jew whose husband was Greek (*Acts 16:1*). No doubt the fact that Timothy had not been circumcised (*Acts 16:3*) was due to the Greek father, but his name which means 'fearing God', was probably given to him by Eunice.

It is likely that Lois and Eunice were converted on Paul's first visit to Lystra (*Acts 14:8–20*), for Timothy appears to have known about the persecution which Paul suffered while there (2 Tim. 3:11; Acts 16:1). Although little is known of Eunice, her influence on Timothy in bringing him up to know and love the Lord of the Scriptures was considerable and was praised by Paul the apostle (2 Tim. 3:14–16). It was knowledge of the Scriptures that led to his understanding of salvation through faith in Christ, and it was this background that had prepared him so well for the ministry of an evangelist to which God called him through the apostle Paul.

It is one of the most wonderful rewards of Christian parenthood to see a child grow up in the knowledge and love of the Lord and begin to serve the Lord for himself or herself. This was the joy experienced by Eunice, who had carried through the task of teaching and training her son in the Scriptures even without a supportive husband. Such faithfulness to God and blessing from him should give much encouragement to the many men and women who find themselves in similar positions today, raising children either without a spouse at all or with a spouse who does not share a commitment to Christ and to the Scriptures.

P.D.G.

**EUODIA,** a Christian woman at Philippi who was one of Paul's 'loyal yoke-fellows' (Phil. 4:2–3). The conflict between Euodia and Syntyche was threatening the unity of the church, and Paul exhorted them to be reconciled. Theories that one or both were men, or deaconesses, or that they were symbols for Gentile and Jewish Christians, or that one of them was actually Lydia (Acts 16:14), are speculative hypotheses at best.

**EUTYCHUS** (Gk., 'Fortunate'). This young man fell asleep during a particularly long sermon in a hot, stuffy room. The apostle Paul had 'talked on and on' because he knew that he had to leave the area the following day (Acts 20:9). Eutychus must have been sitting by a window, for around midnight he 'fell to the ground from the third storey and was picked up dead'. The heat in the room was generated both by the number of people present and the number of lamps used to light such a large meeting (Acts 20: 7–8). The apostle Paul ran downstairs and lifted up the boy and, apparently by means of a miracle, the boy was found to be alive. Paul returned upstairs to break bread and then continue his teaching until dawn.

The passage gives some indication of the centrality of the preached word of God in the worship of the early church, even where they had gathered specifically to 'break bread' (Acts 20:7). This meeting was no doubt the main weekly gathering, since it was on the 'first day of the week'. Perhaps it started on the Saturday evening. The breaking of bread was an integral part of the whole gathering.

P.D.G.

## EVE

Eve, the first woman, is a central figure in the history of redemption, both in her lifetime and beyond it. Her significance can be seen in the various designations given her and the circumstances which surround them. She first is referred to as part of the corporate notion of 'man' (adam, Gen. 1:26–28; 5:2). This signified her as sharing equally in the image of God, that source of all human dignity which differentiates human persons from the rest of the animal kingdom. In this sense, her identity was directly derived from God. As 'woman' (isha, Gen. 2:22–23) Eve was the one created out of Adam and formed for the purpose of being a 'helper suitable for' (lit. 'corresponding to') him (Gen. 2:18). In this sense, her identity was derivative from Adam. The term translated 'helper', however, does not itself convey subordination. This term is used even of God elsewhere (Gen. 49:25).

This dual derivative character of Eve's identity – image of God and taken out of man – provides the basis of self-understanding for all women, since Eve was the forebear for her gender. However, her function with respect to Adam is the basis of much self-understanding for the male gender. God's intention in her creation was that she complement Adam, implying that there is an incompleteness to the first man without her. Rather than be a servant to the man, she was to share in a mutuality with him based upon their simultaneous similarity and dissimilarity. She was in the image of God and a co-recipient of the cultural mandate to fill the earth and subdue it by multiplying that image (Gen. 1:28). The absence of the woman from creation, in fact, brought forth a declaration from God of 'not good' (Gen. 2:18). When she was presented to the man, he sang forth the first hymn found in Scripture, extolling her and naming her 'woman' (isha, Gen. 2:23). The man saw in Eve an identical- yet-opposite mirror: he realized that she was a full bearer of the divine image and that he lacked what only she could provide. In this respect, Adam's identity was derived from Eve.

Eve's laudatory characterization by her husband provided the background for the temptation of the woman by the serpent. Gen. 3, read without this context in mind, could produce a distorted view of her. Satan's decision to tempt the woman appears in no way to reflect anything indemic to the feminine gender, much traditional interpretation notwithstanding. If there was any discernible rationale on the serpent's part, it was in his subversive method. There was a strongly implied hierarchy in the relationship between man and woman, and Satan may have chosen to tempt the woman in order to subvert this structure.

In succumbing to Satan's deception, the woman took upon herself the determinative role in good and evil. Human autonomy began here in the complementary realms of truth and morals. In an effort to vindicate herself, she gained Adam's participation in the rebellion. Eve's portrayal here as susceptible to temptation establishes one dimension of her character in Scripture, but this dimension must be seen in the context of her full characterization.

It is worth noting at this point that Adam may be seen as primarily at fault in the act of disobedience. Not only was he placed as a general representative head over creation, but it was his specific task to 'keep' the Garden (Gen. 2:15). The Heb. verb here can have a military sense, 'to guard', which is the case in the very next chapter (Gen. 3:24). Against the Ancient Near Eastern background of the temple soldier, Adam was to guard the holy Garden of God from the presence of evil and/or unclean intrusions. The presence of the satanic serpent in the Garden was a direct indication of Adam's failure in this regard. Understanding this properly corrects the mistaken notion that Eve was more morally weak and a temptress herself.

Eve shared fully in the shame of this rebellion, sensing with Adam the fracture of what was once their sufficient covering – the glory/spirit/image of God (Gen. 3:7). God brought to bear covenant curses upon her which were tailored to her identity and function (Gen. 3:16). But these curses are not in the full degree deserved. Certainly the woman's birth pangs would remind her and her female progeny of the rebellion of this day. They would also remind her of the danger that has come to be associated with childbirth. But in the curse we also see God's blessing, for the life-giving ability of the woman was sustained. Eve would continue to be a life-giver in spite of death being the due penalty for her and the man's rebellion.

Eve's burden from the Fall also included the distortion of her natural desire for her husband. 'Your desire will be for your husband, and he will rule over you' (Gen. 3:16b). Some commentators would find here the basis for male headship and female submission, crediting that arrangement strictly to the Fall. However, it is not the origination of desire that is in view here, for Eve certainly desired her husband before the Fall. It seems that her desire would become disproportionate or distorted. So also the same could be said for the man's ruling over her. It was not that there was not marital hierarchy before this, but that it was somehow warped.

The preservation of Eve as the source of life is not limited, however, merely to the biological realm. The curse upon the serpent included the promise that a seed of the woman would bruise the serpent's head while the seed of the serpent would bruise his heel (Gen. 3:15). This is, in fact, a reference to the two lines which would proceed from Adam and Eve – those belonging to God and to Satan. Eve, as the mother of the seed of the woman, was identified with that branch of her offspring which would seek after and follow God. She would be the spiritual as well as biological mother of a people who would belong to their Creator. Gen. 3:15 is commonly called the 'first gospel' because it anticipated the final defeat of Satan which Christ, the consummate seed of the woman, would accomplish. That Adam understood his wife's blessed hope is evidenced by his response to God's promise when he named her 'Eve, because she would become the mother of all the living' (Gen. 3:20). This appellation reflected the relationship between the name and the Heb. word *hayah*, which means 'to live'. Whether they are etymologically related is unclear, but at the very least Adam is employing a word play.

The last direct characterization of Eve occurs in her declaration at the birth of Cain, 'With the help of the LORD I have brought forth a man' (Gen. 4:1). This utterance revealed Eve's awareness of her dependence upon the LORD for the giving of life. This was Eve's own 'profession of faith' which expressed a fundamental attitude of one whose hope was in the promised seed.

Eve is not mentioned explicitly in the rest of the OT. However, as we will see further with the NT, she does serve as a paradigm character for subsequent episodes. Eve is the prototypical woman who looked for her deliverance through the birth of a son. She is the mother of travail. The child who is born of this character type is seen as the direct result of divine intervention on behalf of the mother. Seen thus, Sarah, Rebekah, Rachel, Samson's mother, Hannah and Elizabeth follow the pattern of Eve, even though she had not experienced barrenness. The one on whom the LORD has favour will share in the joy of Eve (Is. 54:1).

The NT makes two explicit references to Eve. In 2 Cor. 11:3 Paul cited the serpent's deception of Eve as a warning of what a false preacher might do to the Corinthian church. The point of analogy is the craftiness of the serpent compared with the false wisdom of someone who would preach a different gospel than the one Paul declared to them. Accompanying this analogy is an analogy of marriage to Christ and the church (2 Cor. 11:2). Verse 3, if taken as an extension of that analogy, sheds further light on the temptation in the Garden. If the temptation of the Corinthian church to a false gospel is analogous to marital infidelity, so might Eve's temptation be seen that way. This connects with a broad and frequent OT analogy which depicts idolatry as an act of marital infidelity toward God (cf.Ezek. 16; Hosea).

Eph. 5:22–23, though not explicitly mentioning Eve or Adam, cites Gen. 2:23–24. This is the primary place in Scripture where the analogy is made between Christ and the church and marriage. As the goal of Christ's work for the church is to sanctify here, so a husband's responsibility toward his wife is to set her apart as the exclusive object of his love.

The other explicit reference to Eve in the NT is found in 1 Tim. 2:13. In Paul's advice to Timothy on shepherding the church at Ephesus, particular instructions were to be given for each gender. Paul exhorted a woman to maintain a submissive posture before her husband on two bases – the order of creation and the order of deception. Adam was created first and Eve was deceived first. Some commentators assert that Paul's dictate no longer stands on one or all of the following tenets: (1) we live in an age where redemption has dealt with the Fall; (2) Paul's words were directed toward particular problems at Ephesus; (3) Paul was reflecting a common rabbinic chauvinism toward Eve; and (4) Paul was speaking out of the common cultural understandings of his day. Others point out that the creation order is the basis for Paul's understanding of role relationships, not the Fall, and that this hierarchy is to stand at least until the consummation of this world when redemption is completely applied.

The most relevant aspect of this pasage in 1 Tim. 2 for an understanding of Eve is v. 15. Paul's appeal is painted with hope that 'women will be kept safe through childbirth'. While obviously not a mechanical dictum that biological reproduction will result in spiritual salvation, it is a reflection back upon the great promise given to Eve – that she was the 'mother of all the living'.

Although Eve is not explicitly mentioned, as the mother of the serpent-destroying seed she is possibly the model in other NT contexts. Mary, the mother of Jesus, is the recipient of divine revelation that she would bear a child who would be the focal point of redemption and who would do battle against the forces of evil (Luke 1:30ff.; 2:34–35). Of note in this regard is the fact that Luke traced Jesus' genealogy back to Adam (Luke 3:38). Another possible NT allusion is the woman giving birth in Rev. 12. Here the offspring of this woman is associated with a cosmic warfare between God's forces and those of Satan.

In summary, mention of Eve in Scripture is fairly limited, but careful attention to the means of characterization reveals much about the source and nature of her identity. Beyond explicit mention, she may provide the background for understanding other biblical characters as well as some aspects of the redeeming work of Christ.

M.J.G.

**EVI,** one of the five kings of Midian whom Moses defeated in battle (Num. 31:2, 8; Josh. 13:21) as part of the LORD's vengeance on the Midianites for seducing the Israelites away from the LORD (Num. 25).

**EVIL-MERODACH** (Heb., 'man of Merodach'; Merodach = Marduk, a Babylonian god), mentioned in 2 Kings 25:27 and Jer. 52:31. A Babylonian king in the 6th century BC. In the 37th year of the Babylonian Exile and on the accession of Evil-Merodach, Jehoiachin, the captive king of Judah (2 Kings 24:15), was released from prison.

Apparently he became a friend of the Babylonian king, who fed him at his table and gave him a generous financial allowance.

In the context of the book of Jeremiah, this final chapter (*Jer. 53*) points forward to the fulfilment of Jeremiah's prophecy that the exiles should not be afraid of the king of Babylon (*Jer. 42:11–16*). Some had wished to flee to Egypt, but the LORD had promised nothing but death for them there. In Babylon, however, they would be spared and eventually restored to their homeland. The sovereignty of the LORD over the whole judgment of the Exile and the eventual restoration of the people to Judah is a dominant theme of this period. Evil-Merodach was just one of the kings used by the LORD to further his purposes for his people.     P.D.G.

**EZBAI,** the father of Naarai, one of David's 'mighty men' (*1 Chron. 11:37*).

**EZBON  1.** One of the seven sons of Gad listed in *Gen. 46:16* among those who went with Jacob into Egypt. In *Num. 26:16* he is called Ozni and is the founder of the Oznite clan.

**2.** A grandson of Benjamin and a son of Bela (*1 Chron. 7:7*).

## EZEKIEL

The name Ezekiel means 'El (God) is strong' (*Ezek. 3:14*), or 'El (God) strengthens' (*Ezek. 30:25; 34:16*) or 'May El (God) strengthen'. This prophet lived during one of the most difficult times of Judah's history – namely, the Babylonian Exile – and this may indicate the reason for his name. He was one of 10,000 captives from Jerusalem taken during Nebuchadnezzar's campaign of 597 BC (*2 Kings 24:10–17*), and most likely he prophesied in Babylon to the exiles in the settlement of Tel-abib on the river Kebar (*Ezek. 3:15*). However, Ezekiel's actual location has been hotly debated, largely due to the precision of the description of the Temple in his vision (*Ezek. 8–11*). Multiple residences for the prophet Ezekiel have been proposed in order to account for the detailed description of events in Jerusalem, as well as his Babylonian captivity. Perhaps the best alternative is to locate his ministry in Babylon, but that his oracle to the Judeans is indirect communication, similar to the other oracles to the nations, and that the accuracy of his description of events in Jerusalem is caused by the divine transportation to the scene in an ecstatic trance. According to *Ezek. 29:17*, Ezekiel prophesied until about 570 BC, which was the 27th year of Jehoiachin's exile in Babylon.

Ezekiel was a priest who possessed detailed knowledge of the Temple in Jerusalem and its cultus, though it is doubtful that he ever served in it. The mention of 30 years in *Ezek. 1:1* is more likely a reference to his age, informing the reader that he had reached manhood and could now begin his ministry. Originally his prophecies were very poorly received (*Ezek. 3:25*), but later the people's esteem for the prophet and his message appears to have grown (*Ezek. 8:1; 14:1; 20:1*).

The book appears to be held together by a series of dated oracles (i.e. *Ezek. 1:2; 3:16; 8:1; 20:1; 24:1; 26:1; 29:1, 17; 30:20; 31:1; 32:1, 17; 33:21; 40:1*) which mark the turning points in Ezekiel's ministry. These provide the necessary background for the oracles. However, the oracles to the nations (*Ezek. 25–32*) appear to be a separate unit, since they do not follow the chronological structure developed in the rest of the book. Ezekiel can be divided into three sections: (a) oracles of judgment against Judah (*Ezek. 1–24*); (b) oracles against the foreign nations (*25–32*); and

(c) aftermath (message of hope and restoration) oracles (33–48). However, the last two sections could be seen together as a message of hope for Israel, pronouncing doom on the foreign nations and the possibility of restoration for the nation of Israel. This structure appears to have been arranged in order of the sequence of historical events, announcing first judgment (in 586 BC, when Jerusalem was destroyed by the Babylonians, Ezek. 24:25–27), then hope and restoration (Ezek. 25–48). There are thematic repetitions in each of the major sections of the book, which provide cohesiveness: (1) the watchman (Ezek. 3:33); and (2) the glory of the LORD leaving the temple (8–11) and then returning (43).

The book begins with a clear description of Ezekiel's call and commission (Ezek. 1–3), including an awe-inspiring picture of God's glory and transcendence (1:4–28), as well as a severe warning to the watchman who does not warn of danger (3:16–21). These two messages motivate Ezekiel to carry out his difficult job, even when he apparently went unheeded. Modern scholars have questioned Ezekiel's sanity because of the lengths to which he went to act out his message; for example, making a model of Jerusalem under siege (Ezek. 4:1–3); lying down on his left side for 390 days and then turning over to his right for another 40 days (4:4–17); shaving off his hair and then burning one third of it, cutting one third of it with a sword and scattering one third of it to the wind (5:1–4). Even the death of his wife took on a prophetic significance (Ezek. 24:16–27). Ezekiel's ministry was crucial for the exiles of Judah because it warned them of the impending judgment. As Ezek. 2:5 says, 'And whether they listen or fail to listen – for they are a rebellious house – they will know that a prophet has been among them.' Ezekiel was relentless in condemning the nation of Israel for their infidelity to God. The nation's long history of rebellion started shortly after the Exodus (Ezek. 16; 20; 23) and continued into Ezekiel's day in such acts as profaning the sabbath (20:12, 24), worshipping at high places (6:13; 20:28) and defiling the sanctuary (23:37f.). It was Ezekiel's job to impress upon them the importance of obedience to God and the consequence of their sin. For those who believed and gave heed to his words there was 'life', but for the others certain judgment. Ezekiel's ministry indicated that even in the midst of severe judgment God was still speaking to them; even though they would be punished, they were not abandoned. While the prophet Jeremiah was proclaiming God's message in Jerusalem, an equally strong voice was proclaiming it in Babylon to the exiles so that they would be well aware of God's programme. This section ends with the announcement that Nebuchadnezzar, king of Babylon, had laid siege to Jerusalem in 588 BC, and the outcome was obvious.

Then Ezekiel turns his attention from the destruction of Jerusalem to that of her enemies (Ezek. 25–32) who rejoiced with all the scorn of your soul against the land of Israel! (25:6). Part of this judgment on the nations was a display of God's justice for their part in Jerusalem's destruction, or at least their approval of it. Another part served to vindicate Yahweh as the sovereign ruler over the nations (Ezek. 25:7, 11, 17). Both Israel and the other nations needed to realize that the judgment which fell upon Israel was because of their own wickedness, not because of God's powerlessness. The other nations would soon discover at first hand Yahweh's power when they were punished for their arrogance in attacking Israel. In Ezekiel's day victory of one nation over another nation was attributed to the superiority of the winning nation's god. Soon all nations who believed their gods to be superior would be defeated and from this vanquished position they would be able to see that it was not because of Yahweh's impotence that they were able to destroy Israel.

The last section (Ezek. 33–48) begins with two oracles emphasizing the need for individual responsibility and that each person will be judged according to their deeds. Then follows the devastating message of the prisoners from Jerusalem that the city has fallen (Ezek. 33:21). The wicked receive their punishment, whether they are the proud leaders of Jerusalem or the deluded who remain in Jerusalem believing that they are the remnant (vv. 23–29). From this point on, Ezekiel announces hope and the restoration of the nation which God will bring about. God is pictured as the life-giver who will restore his nation and assume the role of shepherd which the leaders of Israel had abused. He will purify the land, restore its boundaries and bring the people back from exile. A strong contrast is drawn in Ezek. 33–37 between the faithlessness of Israel and the destruction which it incurred versus the faithfulness of Yahweh and the restoration which he will bring about. The restoration is not based upon any duty or commitment to Israel, for they had clearly failed to keep the covenant; instead it is based entirely upon the faithfulness of Yahweh. This restoration would include a Davidic shepherd (Ezek. 34:23f.) who will lead them, a new heart for his people so that they will obey him (36:26f.), a reunited nation (37:17–22) and a new covenant of peace (37:26–28). The nation of Israel is pictured under one Davidic leader as a purified nation, who finally fulfil the hope expressed in Exod. 6:7 that Yahweh will be their God and they will be his people (Ezek. 37:27). This restoration can only occur after God has given the nation new heart, one which has been transformed so that they desire to keep his commands, and then God will re-establish a proper covenant relationship in which Yahweh will be the supreme overlord and rule from the sacred mountains of Israel. Seen in this light Ezek. 38 and 39 are pivotal, for Yahweh will destroy all of his enemies and it will be clear to all that he is the LORD (a title used over 400 times in Ezekiel). The final eight chapters are problematic for interpreters, but at the very least they indicate God's sovereignty over the land of Israel and present a clear picture of the holiness which Yahweh brings to the land. The following four interpretations for this passage have been proposed:

*The prophetic view*: these chapters contain the actual blueprint for the Temple that the exiles were to build when they returned to the land.

*The symbolic Christian view*: these chapters are already symbolically fulfilled in the Christian church, and the picture of the New Jerusalem in the book of Revelation is based largely upon Ezekiel's pattern.

*The dispensational view*: this passage, as well as all of the promises to Israel, will be literally fulfilled in the future; in a future dispensation all the OT festivals, sacrifices, priesthood and worship in the Temple will be reintroduced.

*The apocalyptic view*: this passage is interpreted against the background of other apocalyptic materials, using symbolism, numerical symmetry and futurism to present its message. It is a way of explaining the future in tangible terms based upon things already familiar to the listeners. This interpretation takes the context and type of literature into account more than the other three. According to this view, the Temple pictures the prominence of worship and Yahweh's presence in this new age.

The book of Ezekiel is part of the Heb. canon called the Major Prophets (along with Isaiah and Jeremiah). It corresponds most closely to Jeremiah in time and message. In fact, several themes appear in both books: i.e. oracles against the nations (Jer. 46–51; Ezek. 25–32); the destruction of Jerusalem (Jer. 39; 52; Ezek. 24:2; 33:21); the new covenant (Jer. 31:31–33; Ezek. 36:25–32); the Temple is not a guarantee of protection (Jer. 7; 26:2–9; Ezek. 8–11); etc. The critical importance of Ezekiel's message lies in the fact that the exiles in Babylon had not been abandoned by God, but that the punishment which they were experiencing was determined by him and was temporary. The greatest uncertainty that the exiles would have experienced was wondering if they would have any relationship with Yahweh now that they had broken the covenant. Would they forfeit their special status as God's chosen people? Yahweh takes the initiative and confirms to them that he will still maintain a relationship with them and bring about their deliverance. However, he makes it very clear that this restoration will be his doing and will not be left up to their own failed efforts.

There are several major themes in the book of Ezekiel:

**God's sovereignty**: God is the one controlling history; no matter what happens, his plans will not be thwarted. Even the disobedience of his chosen nation will not spoil his plans, which he will ultimately bring to fruition. This idea, as expressed in Ezek. 1 with the vision of God pictured as ruling over all of creation, is repeated several times throughout the book (in Ezek. 3:23 to confirm his ministry; in Ezek. 9–11 before Jerusalem's destruction; and in Ezek. 43–46 during Israel's restoration).

**Son of man**: This phrase is used for Ezekiel approximately 90 times and emphasizes the fact that he is merely a messenger of the divine sovereign of the universe who had planned all the events which were about to take place and which could not be hindered from being accomplished.

**Individual responsibility**: This is emphasized in the oracles of the watchman (Ezek. 3; 33) and the refutation of the proverb of the 'sour grapes' (Ezek. 18). It is always easy to blame someone else and the Israelites were no exception, but God was proclaiming that it was not acceptable to blame previous generations. Each generation had sinned enough to merit punishment. It was only because of God's patience that preceding generations had not been punished immediately. The Israelites' response in Ezek. 18:19 suggests one of two things: either the people wished to pass on the blame indefinitely to their children and their children's children, thereby avoiding accountability; or they were so hard-hearted that they did not care who finally received the punishment as long as it was not them. Both the 'watchman' and the 'sour grapes' messages confirmed that the watchman (or Ezekiel) and the Israelites would be held responsible for their actions. This was the way it was going to be – the sovereign LORD had declared it. (See *Prophets and Prophecy*)

P.D.W.

**EZER** **1.** A descendant of Esau, he was a son of Seir and a Horite chief (Gen. 36:21, 27, 30; 1 Chron. 1:38, 42).

**2.** A son of Ephraim, this Ezer was killed, together with his brother, when he went to raid livestock from the men of Gath (1 Chron. 7:21). See also *Elead* and *Beriah*.

**3.** Of the tribe of Judah, this Ezer was the father of Hushah and was descended from Hur (1 Chron. 4:4).

**4.** The chief of some Gadite warriors

who defected from Saul and joined David when he was at Ziklag (1 Chron. 12:9). These mighty men were described as the greatest of warriors, stronger than a hundred men and 'swift as gazelles in the mountains'.

**5.** A ruler of Mizpah and a son of Jeshua, this Ezer helped repair the walls of Jerusalem under Nehemiah's direction (Neh. 3:19; 12:42). He was a Levite, and probably the same Levite who later was part of the choir that sang at the dedication of the wall. The walls and city had been destroyed by the Babylonians when they took the Israelites into captivity.

P.D.G.

**EZRA** The name Ezra (also spelled Ezrah in 1 Chron. 4:17) derives from the Heb. word meaning 'help'. The name itself is probably a shortened form of Ezra-yah(weh), 'Yahweh helps'. Parents gave this sentence name to male children as a praise to the LORD for his help in times of trouble. Three people in the OT bear the name Ezra:

**1.** See *Ezrah.*

**2.** Soon after the Babylonian Exile had ended a priest named Ezra returned to the promised land with Zerubbabel (Neh. 12:1, 13). The same man was also called Azariah in Neh. 10:2. He was a Zadokite under the leadership of Joshua, the high priest at the time.

**3.** By far the most important character called Ezra was the priestly scribe who led major reforms within post-exilic Israel a generation or two after the time of Zerubbabel.

**Ezra's ministry.** The books of Ezra and Nehemiah tell us much about this well-known Ezra. First, he was a priest descended from Aaron, the original high priest of Israel (Ezra 7:2–7). Ezra belonged to the family of Seraiah, whom Nebuchadnezzar killed at Riblah (2 Kings 25:18–21). Seraiah's son Jehozadak was the high priest exiled to Babylon (1 Chron. 6:14–15). Although Ezra's genealogy does not mention Jehozadak (Ezra 7:2–7), he was either a member of this line or closely related to it.

Ezra held a place of leadership in Exile probably because of his priestly lineage. His precise office is unknown, but Ezra participated in government affairs at such high rank that Artaxerxes, the Persian emperor, gave him his full personal endorsement (Ezra 7:11–12).

Second, Ezra was described as a 'scribe' (NRSV; also translated as 'teacher' in NIV). Artaxerxes designated him 'the scribe' (Ezra 7:6, 11), perhaps indicating that his role was that of a learned royal adviser. Post-biblical Jewish tradition also ascribed this title to Ezra because of his expertise in matters of the Torah, the Law of Moses. In fact, these traditions suggest that Ezra had a prominent role in editing and composing major portions of the OT.

Ezra led a caravan of Babylonian exiles to the promised land by the decree of Emperor Artaxerxes (Ezra 7:1–12). He received authority from Artaxerxes to collect offerings from Jews living in Babylon for the Temple service in Jerusalem (vv. 12–28). This journey took place in 'the seventh year' of the reign of Artaxerxes (v. 8). Unfortunately, the biblical text is unclear whether this return was in the seventh year of Artaxerxes I (458 BC) or Artaxerxes II (397 BC). Whatever the case, Ezra came to Jerusalem at least one generation after Zerubbabel had strengthened the early returnees and led them to rebuild the Temple in 515 BC.

When Ezra arrived in Jerusalem he was horrified to learn that many priests, Levites and civil leaders had intermarried with pagan women (Ezra 9). These intermarriages had corrupted the moral and religious life of Israel. In his distress, Ezra humbly wept before the LORD and led the whole community in repentance (Ezra 9–10). Many men divorced their foreign wives and returned to the service of the LORD. At the Feast of Tabernacles, Ezra read from the Law of Moses (Neh. 7:73–8:12). The leaders of the people signed a ratification of the Law (Neh. 9:38–10:39), promising to renew their commitments to marital purity, Sabbath observances and Temple services.

The circumstances of Ezra's death are unknown. The biblical record stops short of his final days. The scriptural and traditional portrait of Ezra indicate that he served faithfully along with Nehemiah as a leader of God's people throughout his life.

**Ezra's message.** Ezra's message may be summarized under two rubrics: divorcing foreign wives and renewing full loyalty to the Law of Moses. His insistence on Sabbath observances, moral purity, and Temple service is not surprising. These issues were matters of concern throughout the history of Israel. Ezra's demand for mass divorce, however, may appear harsh and out of accord with the teachings of Scripture on marriage and divorce.

Nevertheless, the biblical record honours Ezra as a model leader of reform. Nowhere is his message questioned by biblical writers. Instead, the books of Ezra and Nehemiah marshal a number of defences for his actions. He had the support of the Persian Emperor, the righteous people of Jerusalem, and the LORD.

It is important to note that Ezra's requirement of divorce was not motivated by racial concerns. The examples of Zipporah (Exod 2:21–22), Rahab (Josh. 6:25) and Ruth (Ruth 1:4) make it evident that intermarriage with foreigners was not always forbidden in the OT. The issue at stake was inter-religious, not interracial marriage. The same prohibition appears in the NT as well (2 Cor. 6:14–7:1).

Why then did Ezra insist that these intermarriages be dissolved? Ezra's situation was desperate. He did not face a few intermarriages within a strong community. Pagan women had brought struggling post-exilic Israel to the brink of total apostasy. The entire restoration programme was near complete failure. In response to this critical circumstance Ezra wisely insisted that the men of Judah divorce their foreign wives.

Ezra's message of divorce did not violate the biblical principle of the sanctity of marriage. His instructions are harmonious with the wisdom of Paul who instructed NT believers to remain with unbelievers for the hope of their conversion (1 Cor. 7:17–24). Instead, Ezra addressed the extreme situation of the restored community with an extreme, but necessary solution.

In this sense, Ezra stands as a model for believers in every age. His zeal for the Kingdom of God took precedence over all other concerns.                    R.P.

**EZRAH** was from the tribe of Judah and was the father of various sons, including Mered, who married an Egyptian princess (1 Chron. 4:17–18).

**EZRI** (Heb., 'my help'), the son of Kelub, was one of King David's overseers and was in charge of those who farmed the King's land (1 Chron. 27:26).

# F

**FELIX** (Lat., 'happy'). 'Governor Felix' was the Roman Procurator of Judea between c. AD 52–58. He comes to our attention in *Acts 23:23–24:27*, for it was before Felix at Caesarea that Paul underwent his first trial for his Christian faith. Felix had been appointed by the Emperor Claudius and was later recalled to Rome by Nero.

The problem for Paul began in *Acts 21*, when he returned from Ephesus to Jerusalem. He was soon accosted by some Jews from the province of Asia (*Acts 21:27*) who accused him of stirring up antagonism to the Jewish faith. A near riot ensued in which Paul was captured by a crowd who tried to kill him (*Acts 21:31*). The Roman garrison intervened and protected Paul. *Acts 22* then recounts how Paul was allowed by the Roman commander to address the crowd and tell them of the Christian faith. The crowd listened until Paul talked of his mission to take the gospel to the Gentiles (*Acts 22:22*). This had been part of the original complaint against him, that he was prepared to bring Greeks into the Temple (*Acts 21:28*). In order to protect him, the Roman commander, Claudius Lysias, took Paul into his custody.

Paul appealed to his Roman citizenship, which protected him from a flogging and also gained further protection for him as he was taken to trial before the Sanhedrin (*Acts 23*). Following this trial, some Jews plotted to kill Paul when he next appeared before the Sanhedrin. The Roman commander thus decided to send Paul to Caesarea to be tried before Felix.

The high priest and some of the Jewish elders then brought their case against Paul before Felix, who allowed Paul to defend himself. The trial took place over a period of several days. Felix, we are told, 'was well acquainted with the Way' (*Acts 24:22*). He listened with his Jewish wife Drusilla as Paul spoke about Jesus Christ and about 'righteousness, self-control and the judgment to come' (*Acts 24:25*). Felix 'was afraid', perhaps at the thought of judgment. He further delayed the proceedings, hoping that a bribe would be forthcoming that would allow him to release Paul.

This disdain for the law seems to have been characteristic of Felix and was reported both by Josephus and Tacitus, who believed him to be a rather loathsome and cruel governor. Felix kept Paul under some sort of house arrest for two years, although it seems the conditions were fairly favourable. During this time Paul and Felix had regular conversations (*Acts 24:26–27*). Paul was still under arrest when Felix was replaced by Porcius Festus.

This time of arrest under Felix was seemingly of little benefit to anyone in Paul's continuing ministry. However, it was the first stage in the legal proceedings which would eventually lead to Paul's witnessing for Christ in Rome itself. That all this was part of God's plan is made clear through these chapters (*cf. Acts 21:11; 27:24*).                     P.D.G.

**FESTUS,** the Roman procurator of Judea who succeeded Felix c. AD 58 (*Acts 24:27*). Outside the NT he is only mentioned by Josephus, who regarded him as a noble leader who tried to restore some legal and administrative order following the poor administration under Felix. In the NT Festus comes to our attention as the governor who had to sort out the legal proceedings against the apostle Paul. These had rumbled on for over two years under Felix, who had apparently been waiting for a bribe before being prepared to pronounce Paul innocent of the Jewish charges against him.

Festus quickly took up the reigns of leadership and 'Three days after arriving in the province . . . went up from Caesarea to Jerusalem' (*Acts 25:1*). There he heard about Paul from the Jewish leaders who asked that Paul be transferred to Jerusalem for trial. Their intention was to ambush Paul on the way and kill him. Festus invited the leaders to return with him to Caesarea, where they laid charges against Paul. Paul appealed to Caesar in order to avoid being taken back up to Jerusalem and put to death (*Acts 25:2–12*). Because Paul was a Roman citizen, Festus had to honour such an appeal and held him in Caesarea until he was sent to Rome to stand trial.

A few days later Agrippa II arrived with his sister Bernice. Festus and Agrippa were clearly good friends, and together they discussed Paul's case. Paul was summonsed to speak before King Agrippa. Paul's defence was designed to proclaim the gospel to a king and his sister who had clear Jewish sympathies. When Paul reached a description of Jesus' death and his resurrection, Festus showed his Roman religious views by saying that Paul must be 'insane' (*Acts 26:24*). Paul replied by appealing to Agrippa's knowledge of recent Jewish events and his understanding of the prophets. Agrippa was clearly moved and asked Paul, 'Do you think that in such a short time you can persuade me to be a Christian?' (*Acts 26:28*). Paul replied that he was indeed praying for Agrippa and Festus and the others present that they would become Christians like him.

Agrippa wanted to see Paul freed, but the appeal to Caesar had to be carried through and so Paul, the prisoner, was put on a boat for Italy (*Acts 26:32*). God's plan that Paul should witness for him at the centre of the empire was gradually coming to fulfilment (*cf. Acts 21:11; 27:24*).                    P.D.G.

## THE 'FOOL' AND THE 'WISE'

Biblical wisdom is not primarily theoretical, but practical. It is an attribute of God which is revealed in the ordering of creation (*Prov. 8:22–31*) and its successful operation (*Job 39:26*); so wisdom and folly are practical attitudes which determine whether life is lived successfully in God's world. A growing biblical wisdom is the result of learning from the experiences of life while maintaining an obedient trust in the LORD.

### Wisdom literature

In Wisdom literature (Job, the Psalms, Proverbs and Ecclesiastes) the acquiring of wisdom is understood in a parental setting (*Prov. 1:8; 4:1; 6:20*) because gaining wisdom is understood as gaining skills for life in God's world. 'Wise' teachers fulfil a parental role to those who learn from them (e.g. *Gen. 45:8; Judg. 5:7*; note the use of 'my son' in *Prov. 1–9*); not all are willing to learn these skills, so the 'fool' and the 'wise' are frequently contrasted, and differ in their attitudes to the LORD, to learning, to speaking and to self-control.

'The fool says in his heart, "There is no God"' (Ps. 14:1; 53:1), while 'a wise man fears the LORD' (Prov. 14:16; cf. 1:7; 9:10; Job 28:28; Ps. 111:10). It is impossible to be wise, to live successfully in God's world, without acknowledging him. Thus the proverbs praising the 'wise' man, blend general insight from experience with obedience to God's revealed wisdom (e.g. Prov. 2:6) and consciousness of the LORD's scrutiny (e.g. Prov. 15:3, 11). The wisdom of the 'wise' comes from a life of faith in the LORD; in contrast the 'fool' finds wisdom not in the LORD but in himself (Prov. 18:12; 28:26). The folly of the 'fool' is his rejection of the LORD's wisdom, not mere stupidity. Such 'folly' brings moral culpability.

The contrast in attitude to learning is marked: the 'wise' learn from their teaching (Prov. 10:8; 19:20), listen to advice (Prov. 12:15), and accept rebukes thankfully (Prov. 9:8). The 'wise' are teachable. The 'fool' does what he wants (Prov. 12:15), rejects discipline (Prov. 15:15) and does not even learn from his mistakes (Prov. 26:11). Similarly, in speech, the 'wise' are characterized by restraint and the desire to build others up (Prov. 12:18; 13:14; 15:2); the 'fool' is depicted as chattering (Prov. 10:8, 10, 14) and foolish (Prov. 15:2) in what he says, in a way which leads him into trouble (Eccl. 10:12).

Another contrast comes with self-discipline: the 'wise' are slow to anger (Prov. 29:11), willing to overlook insults (Prov. 12:16), to avoid conflict (Prov. 20:3), they work hard (Prov. 10:5) and prepare for possible problems in advance (Prov. 21:20). The 'fool' lacks restraint to his temper (Prov. 12:16; 29:11), is 'hot-headed and reckless' (Prov. 14:16), being 'quick to quarrel' (Prov. 20:3), but he is also lazy and ill-prepared for life (Eccl. 4:5).

The Wisdom literature assumes wisdom grows primarily through acquiring experience in God's world, rooted in a theology of creation and common grace, which allows wisdom to be accessible to all nations. However, biblical wisdom is also rooted in a theology of redemption and revelation, so only God's people have a true insight into wisdom, through knowing the true God, the LORD.

## Jesus

Jesus' teaching makes the same contrast of the 'wise' and the 'fool', but with distinctive characteristics. For Jesus, the 'wise' not only live successfully in God's world, but live successfully in relation to him personally. In Matt. 7:24–27//Luke 6:47:49, the 'wise' man who builds the house on the rock is contrasted to the 'fool' on the basis of their practical response to Jesus' words. In Matt. 25:1–13, the 'wise' virgins are contrasted to the 'foolish' virgins on the basis of their readiness for Jesus' return (cf. Matt. 24:44), a point reinforced by the parable of the 'wise' manager (Luke 12:42ff.).

For Jesus, the 'wise' recognize God's wisdom in him in contrast to popular wisdom which does not acknowledge him, but this recognition comes by God's revelation (Matt. 11:25–26). The 'fool' neither lives for God (Luke 12:20) nor acknowledges Jesus.

## The New Testament

While defending his apostolic ministry, Paul argued as a 'fool' in 2 Cor. 11:16–12:10, which he defined as 'self-confident boasting' (2 Cor. 11:17). It was folly, because his ministry was a personal commission from the Lord Jesus, and needed no justification to the 'wise' who submitted to Jesus' revelation. However, Paul deliberately contrasted true wisdom with popular Greek wisdom in 1 Cor. 1–3, pointing out that the world's wisdom failed to bring true knowledge of God (1 Cor. 1:21), but that God's wisdom, the message of a crucified Messiah, though apparently a foolish message, was used by God to bring salvation (1 Cor. 1:23–24). This reinforces that true wisdom presumes practical experience but also revelation. Similarly in James, wisdom is both practical (James 3:13) and spiritual (James 3:17), while the 'fool' protests a faith which bears no practical fruit (James 2:20).

The NT emphasis on God's revelation as a prerequisite for true wisdom, means the 'wise' will grow through their study of Scripture (2 Tim. 3:15–16) and the grace of God (James 1:5f.), because ultimately only God is truly wise (Rom. 16:27).

R.M.

**FORTUNATUS** (Lat., 'blessed') is mentioned in 1 Cor. 16:17 along with Stephanas and Achaicus. At the end of the century Clement mentioned a man by this name in his epistle to the Corinthians, but this may not have been the same person. See *Stephanas*.

# G

**GAAL** (Heb., 'loathsome'), the son of Ebed, moved to Shechem after Gideon's son Abimelech had begun to rule there. In judgment on Abimelech for the way he had murdered Gideon's other sons, 'God sent an evil spirit between Abimelech and the citizens of Shechem, who acted treacherously against Abimelech' (*Judg. 9:23*). At a festival in one of their pagan temples, Gaal took advantage of the rebellious Shechemites and encouraged them to take up arms against Abimelech (*vv. 26–29*). The rebellion was reported to Abimelech by Zebul, the governor of the city. Abimelech attacked and Gaal and his family were driven from Shechem (*vv. 30–41*). The following day Abimelech attacked and destroyed Shechem in an action that was seen as God's judgment on the city for conniving in the murder of Gideon's sons (*vv. 23–24, 57*). For detail see *Abimelech, Zebul* and *Jotham*.  P.D.G.

**GABBAI,** a follower of Sallu who settled in Jerusalem after the Exile in Babylon (*Neh. 11:8*).

**GABRIEL** (Heb., 'man of God' or 'strength of God') is the name of a special messenger sent from God to Daniel, Zechariah and Mary (*Dan. 8:16; 9:21; Luke 1:19, 26*). Gabriel is one of two angels mentioned by name in the Bible (see also *Michael*).

In Daniel's apocalyptic vision Gabriel appeared and provided the interpretation: 'The two-horned ram that you saw represents the kings of Media and Persia. The shaggy goat is the king of Greece . . .' (*Dan. 8:20–21*). While Daniel was praying and confessing his sin, Gabriel came to him to give him 'insight and understanding' about the time between the order to rebuild Jerusalem and the coming of the 'Anointed One', the Messiah (*Dan. 9:20–27*).

In the intertestamental period, Jewish literature depicted Gabriel as one of the archangels or 'angels of the presence', who were viewed as standing before God to serve him and present 'the prayers of the saints' (*Jubilees 2:2; Tobit 12:15; 1 QH 6:13*).

In the Lucan nativity accounts Gabriel appeared in the Temple to predict the birth of John the Baptist, and later in Nazareth to foretell the birth of Jesus (*Luke 1:19, 26*). See also *Angels*.  A.A.T.

**GAD** (Heb., 'fortunate').
**1.** Gad was Jacob's seventh son and born to Leah's servant, Zilpah. He was therefore considered to be Leah's son (*Gen. 30:11; 35:26*). He was among those who went down to Egypt with his father and his many sons (*Gen. 46:16*). In Jacob's blessing he prophesied that Gad would be the subject of attack by raiders but would fight back (*Gen. 49:19*).

He became the leader of one of the twelve tribes of Israel named after him. The tribe went on to inherit land to the east of Jordan when finally the conquest of Canaan took place (*Num. 32*). At the Exodus from Egypt the fighting men in the tribe were numbered as 46,650 (*Num. 1:25*). The tribe of Gad is mentioned again in *Ezek. 48* and *Rev. 7:5* in texts that look forward to the last days and the fulfilment of the Lord's divine purposes for his kingdom.

**2.** Another Gad was a 'seer' or prophet during the reign of King David. He brought God's word to David on four special occasions. The first was when David was being chased by Saul before his enthronement. Gad encouraged David to return to Judah from his encampment in the caves of Adullam (1 Sam. 22:5).

On the second occasion, years later, when David was well established as king, Gad appeared to him to pronounce God's judgment on him for the census he had taken. Contrary to the Law, David wanted to number his troops and against the advice of Joab, his army commander, he had the men counted (2 Sam. 24:3–4). As soon as this had been done, David knew he had sinned and, with customary contrition, he asked the LORD for forgiveness (2 Sam. 24:10). Though forgiven his sin, the consequences still had to be faced. Gad brought him three choices: a famine for three years, fleeing from his enemies for three months or three days of plague in the land (2 Sam. 24:11–14). In deep sadness, David told Gad he would simply leave it in the hands of the LORD, 'for his mercy is great' (v. 14). A plague came on the land and spread towards Jerusalem, but the LORD stopped it at the threshing floor of Araunah the Jebusite (v. 16).

Gad's third appearance to David occurred on the day the plague ceased. He ordered David to build an altar to the LORD on that threshing floor, which David immediately did (2 Sam. 24: 18–19; 1 Chron. 21:3–23). The chronicler pays special attention to David's humble repentance and his immediate obedience to the word of the LORD through Gad (e.g. 1 Chron. 21:19).

Fourthly, Gad helped David divide the Levites and priests into groups and assign them different tasks in the maintenance of the worship of the nation. Hezekiah is said to have followed the assignment 'in the way prescribed by David and Gad the king's seer and Nathan the prophet' (2 Chron. 29:25). Gad apparently also wrote a book about the events of David's life (1 Chron. 29:29). P.D.G.

**GADDI,** one of the twelve spies sent out by Moses from the Desert of Paran to spy out the land of Canaan (Num. 13:11). A representative of each tribe was chosen, and Gaddi, the son of Susi, was from the tribe of Manasseh. For further detail on their mission see *Shammua.*

**GADDIEL,** one of the twelve spies sent out by Moses from the Desert of Paran to spy out the land of Canaan (Num. 13:10). A representative of each tribe was chosen, and Gaddiel, the son of Sodi, was from the tribe of Zebulun. For further detail on their mission see *Shammua.*

**GADI** (Heb., 'my fortune'), the father of Menahem. Menahem killed Shallum in Samaria and became king of Israel in his stead. He reigned for ten years (2 Kings 15:14–17).

**GAHAM** was a son of Abraham's brother Nahor by his concubine Reumah (Gen. 22:24).

**GAHAR** His descendants were among the Temple servants who returned from Exile in Babylon with Nehemiah (Ezra 2:47; Neh. 7:49).

**GAIUS 1.** Gaius from Macedonia was one of Paul's 'travelling companions'. In *Acts* 19:29, along with Aristarchus, he was seized by the Ephesians, who were violently antagonistic to the gospel, and taken to the theatre in what became an anti-Christian riot. Eventually the crowd was quietened and the two men were released. Gaius' faith and commitment to Christ were clearly very strong. In the Ephesian riot he and Aristarchus seem to have been seized instead of the apostle Paul (see also *Alexander*). Men like this, who exhibited such Christian faith in times of persecution have become examples for all Christians through the ages as persecution has abounded.

**2.** Gaius from Derbe is mentioned in *Acts 20:4* as one who went on ahead of Paul from Philippi and waited for him at Troas (*v. 5*). He was probably one of those chosen by local churches to accompany Paul to Jerusalem as he took the money he had collected to the poor of that city. (If a variant reading of the Greek text is adopted, Derbe is replaced with Doberus, a Macedonian town. This would mean that this Gaius might be identified with 1. above. Given that Aristarchus is mentioned in both places, this is possible. However, Gaius was a popular name and the reading is unreliable.)

**3.** Gaius from Corinth is mentioned in the greetings of *Rom. 16:23*. Paul stayed in his home while he was in Corinth, from where he wrote the letter to the Roman church. The fact that Paul says the 'whole church' enjoyed his hospitality suggests that one of the churches may have met in his home. He was almost certainly the same Gaius as the one Paul baptized in his early days of preaching in Corinth (*1 Cor. 1:14*). That baptism was obviously a rare occurrence, as Paul was more concerned to preach than to baptize. Paul had no desire to have anyone feel they 'belonged' to him, simply because he had baptized them. Paul's whole desire was that Christ alone should be glorified. Tradition holds that this Gaius later became bishop of Thessalonica.

**4.** In *3 John 1* this Gaius was an elder of the church to which John was writing and a dearly loved friend. John clearly held him in high regard spiritually (*vv. 2–3*). He had probably been converted under John's ministry, since he is called one of 'my children'. Gaius stands as an example for the church through the ages as one who was singled out for his 'faithfulness to the truth', for his obedience to the truth, and for his love. He was com-

mended for his hospitality to others and further encouraged in this direction by John.                                   P.D.G.

**GALAL 1.** One of the Levites who resettled in Jerusalem after the Exile in Babylon (*1 Chron. 9:15*).

**2.** His descendant Obadiah was a Levite who resettled in Jerusalem after the Exile (*1 Chron. 9:16*).

**3.** His descendant Abda was a Levite who resettled in Jerusalem after the Exile (*Neh. 11:17*).

**GALLIO,** born in Cordoba in Spain, was the son of the rhetorician Seneca, and the brother of the philosopher Seneca. He became proconsul of the province of Achaia c. AD 52 and governed in Corinth during the time of Paul's first visit to the city on his second missionary journey (*Acts 18:12–17*). He later died back in Rome, where he had been part of a plot to kill Nero.

The apostle Paul had begun his work in the city, as was his custom, by preaching in the synagogue to the Jews of the city. However, once the Jews became 'abusive' (*Acts 18:6*), Paul left the synagogue, went next door, and started preaching more specifically to the Gentiles in the house of Titius Justus, a God-fearer. Some Jews, like Crispus the synagogue ruler, had believed in Christ, but as more and more became Christians, so Jewish antagonism increased and a 'united attack' was made on Paul. The Jews brought Paul before Gallio, accusing him of preaching things 'contrary to the [Jewish] law' (*Acts 18:13*).

Gallio, however, would have nothing to do with what he regarded as an internal squabble among the Jews about matters of their own religion and law. While Roman law protected the rights of Jews to their own religion, it certainly did not allow the extension of that law onto other people. The incident throws an interesting light on how Christianity was regarded among the Gentile rulers of that day. Clearly, it was seen as a sect of Judaism, and this was why Gallio was not prepared to intervene, being happy to let the Jewish courts try to sort things out, and not even to interfere when the Jewish crowds seized their own leader, Sosthenes, and began to beat him (*Acts 18:14–17*). P.D.G.

**GAMALIEL** (Heb., 'God is my reward').

**1.** He was the son of Pedahzur and the leader of the people of Manasseh at the census of the Israelites in the wilderness of Sinai. His division of people numbered 46,500 (*Num. 1:10; 2:20*). As the representative of his tribe he also brought his tribe's fellowship offering when the Tabernacle was dedicated in the wilderness (*Num. 7:54, 59*). The enormous offering from this tribe was brought on the eighth day. He also led his tribe when the Israelites set out from the Sinai desert on their wanderings (*Num. 10:23*).

**2.** Another Gamaliel is mentioned in *Acts 5:34*. He was a highly educated and honoured teacher and Pharisee. In Rabbinic literature he is called 'Gamaliel the Elder' in distinction from Gamaliel II, who was his grandson. He was probably a grandson of Rabbi Hillel, founder of one of the main branches of the Pharisees.

When Peter and a number of the apostles were captured and brought to trial before the Sanhedrin, Gamaliel stood up, ordered the apostles to be put out of the room for a while, and then proceeded to argue on pragmatic grounds that it might be better to release them than pursue the prosecution, since the new sect would certainly die out quickly unless they were truly of God (*Acts 5:34–39*). Such a speech is entirely in line with the position that this more liberal school of Pharisees would have taken. He was successful in his appeal and when the apostles were ordered back in they were flogged and then released. The apostles went on their way rejoicing and continuing to proclaim 'the good news that Jesus is the Christ' (*Acts 5:40–42*). No amount of persecution could deflect the followers of Christ from their greatest goal: to see men and women won for Christ.

It was this same Gamaliel who had helped in the education of Saul, the Pharisee, who became Paul, the apostle. In debating the gospel of Christ with the crowds in Jerusalem after his arrest, Paul appealed to his credentials as one of those who was zealous for the Law of God having been 'thoroughly trained' by Gamaliel (*Acts 22:3*; see also *Gal. 1:14; Phil. 3:4–6*). P.D.G.

**GAMUL,** from the tribe of Levi, was the head of the 22nd division of priests appointed by King David for service at the Tabernacle (*1 Chron. 24:17*).

## THE GARDEN OF EDEN AND CREATION

What sort of people are we and what sort of world do we live in? These are the deeply important questions *Gen. 1–3* sets out to answer. Take an absurd illustration: we put anti-freeze into the car but not into the baby – even though both need protection from cold. Why? Because they are different and require different remedies. In other words they have to be 'defined' according to their individual natures. If we define a baby in mechanical terms we will kill the baby; if we define a car in human terms it will never run. So the question 'What is Man?' is by no means trivial. We need to arrive at a correct definition of ourselves if we are to discover how to live and thrive.

But the same applies to the world. We look at industrial wastelands with devastated landscape and polluted rivers; we learn of forests being felled at an

**189**

alarming rate, bringing topographical barrenness and climatic change; we hear of holes in the ozone layer – all because our forebears of the industrial revolution and their commercially covetous successors 'define' the environment as dead prey to be exploited at will. And, as we shall presently see, there is an additional dimension too (which we shall call 'moral vitality') in a full definition of our world. But the point is clear: without a true definition we cannot achieve personal fulfilment or environmental prosperity.

This is not to say that other questions about Gen. 1–3 are not important. How does Gen. 1 relate to cosmogony and to the hypothesis of evolution? The fact that Gen. 1–3 primarily exists to answer other questions does not mean that it has nothing to say about these. Here is another illustration: suppose an earthquake in AD 2020 reduced London to rubble and made the Thames run into the sea 50 miles south at Brighton instead of its short journey east. In AD 5020 an archaeologist unearths a document giving statistics of infant mortality in the former capital and providing comparative tables for 'north' and 'south of the river'. Such a document primarily answers a sociological question but it incidentally answers, correctly, the question 'Where did the Thames once run?' And it is the same with Gen. 1–3. Though questions of cosmogony and evolution, etc., are not its primary concern, it has divine revelation to offer on these matters also, and we shall take some note of these en route.

### The record of Creation

It is commonplace to treat Gen. 1:1–23 and 2:4–25 as separate accounts of God's creative work – different in literary style and contradictory in the order of events they record: Gen. 1, for example, puts the creation of Man last and Gen. 2 puts it first. This view of the two chapters arises from overlooking the linking statement in Gen. 2:4, literally. 'These are the generations of the heavens and the earth when they were created.' This formula occurs ten times in Genesis (e.g. 6:9; 11:10, 27; 25:19) and always with the same significance. The word 'generations' is a 'birth'-word, how one thing emerges from another – descendants sprang from an ancestor, a history from a certain beginning. So it is here. A 'situation' has been set out in Gen. 1:1–2:3 and we are about to be told (Gen. 2:4ff.) what 'emerged' from it, what it gave birth to. This both explains the differing literary style of the two chapters and also why, at first sight, they appear different in other ways too. Gen. 1:1–2:3 is a God-centred statement of the divine work of creation as it proceeded from his will (Gen. 1:3, 6, 9, 11, 14, 20, 24, 26), matched his intentions (vv. 7, 9, 11, 15, 24) and enshrined his values (vv. 10, 12, 21, 25, 31). By contrast, Gen. 2:4–25 is man-centred. To be sure, God is still over all and the advent of Man on the scene has not diminished his sovereignty. But now by the will of God Man has dominion, working the earth, ordering the beasts, setting up home: a world for and around Man to which (Gen. 3:8) the LORD God comes as if paying a call. Gen. 1 creates the theatre, erects the stage and gathers the cast; Gen. 2 is Act 1, Scene 1; Gen. 1 is a statement; Gen. 2 is a history; Gen. 1 tells how Man came to be; Gen. 2 begins the story of his life.

# God the Creator

*The verb 'to create'.*   Gen. 1:1 does not say how 'the heavens and the earth' came into being. It only divulges that God is prior to the universe and that it exists by his act of creation. Unlike cognate literatures which use 'to create' of man's workmanship as well as God's, the OT makes 'to create' exclusively a divine activity. The verb is used of things which because of their greatness or novelty (or both) can only be explained by an act of God. In Gen. 1:1–2:3 the beginning of all things was such an act and shows that in Heb. 'to create' includes creation ex nihilo, for the first 'move' in creation was to bring into being the physical substrate or 'matter' of the universe (Gen. 1:1). There was no pre-existing substance; it was called into being by God. The verb 'to create' next appears at that significant moment when animal, organic life first appears (Gen. 1:20–22); then it clusters in a triplet of occurrences at the crown of creation, when in Man, organic life appears 'in the image of God'. Finally it is used retrospectively in Gen. 2:3.

*Creating and making.*   The initial state of things was 'formless and empty'. That is to say (cf. Jer. 4:23–26), it gave no evidence of stabiity, life, order or any indication that these were potentially there. In this way Gen. 1 pictures the Creator as a sculptor who, taking a formless, meaningless block of stone, imparts shape, beauty, meaning and vitality to it so that what began as 'formless and empty' (Gen. 1:1) ended as illuminated (vv. 3–5), ordered and fertile (vv. 6–13), regular in movement (vv. 14–19) teeming with life (vv. 20–25), crowned with Man (vv. 26–30), 'very good' (v. 31), and complete (Gen. 2:1).

*One God only.*   The tiny detail that the plants (Gen. 1:12) were 'seed bearing plants' and that fruit has 'seed in it' is part of the testimony of Gen. 1 that everything can be traced back to the one Creator God. In Canaanite religion, Baal was the god of fertility. No tree could be fruitful – nor any animal or person – unless Baal stepped in to make them so. And indeed, throughout the ancient world there was a god for everything. The Bible's answer is very different: trees are fruitful because, in the beginning, the only God made them so. The genealogies also have this as part of their function (Gen. 5; 10 etc.,): all humankind is traced to the initial act of the Creator: not one god per tribe, bringing forth his 'children' by some quasi-sexual procedure, but one only God who created the first couple with an inherent capacity for fruitfulness (Gen. 1:26–28). Most remarkably of all, Gen. 1 records no pre-creation combat between the Creator and opposing 'spiritual forces' of chaos. This was a major theme of Babylonian cosmogony, where Marduk was not free to create until he had disposed of Tiamat, the monster of the deep. In Genesis there is no God but one, who does what he pleases and delights in what he does.

*A perfect work.*   The creative work took six days of activity and was crowned in a seventh day of satisfied rest. What period is tended by the word 'day'? It does not need to be said that if the Creator so decided all the creation could have been performed in 24-hour periods and in the order Genesis prescribes. In this sense older writers were correct when they said that the Bible waits at the end of the scientific process for research to catch up with it. Simplicity would be served by taking this view, but the biblical use of 'day' is too fluid. The word is used of the daylight hours (Deut. 9:18), the 24-hour period (Num. 20:29), an unspecified period (Ps. 20:1), and a time marked by some significant activity (Ps. 110:3, 5) – it is in this last sense that Gen. 2:4 (literally, 'in the day when the LORD made . . .') describes the whole creative process as taking a 'day'. But if the time-significance of the 'days' is open, their sequence and the delicate balance by which the Creator's work is rounded and perfect is plain – a 'roundedness' reaching also into the foundational narrative in Gen. 2:4–25.

| Gen. 1:1–2:3 The work of Creation | | | Gen. 2:4–25 Life on earth | | |
|---|---|---|---|---|---|
| (1) | (2) | (3) | | | |
| *Physical world* Light | Waters | Land Vegetation | *Situation*: Uncultivated terrain | *Provision*: Adam the cultivator | *Law*: The law of the Garden |
| *vv. 3–5* | *vv. 6–8* | *vv. 9–13* | *vv. 4–6* | *vv. 7–15* | *vv. 16–17* |
| (4) | (5) | (6) | | | |
| *Animal World* Lights | Fish | Animals Man | Man alone | Woman | The law of marriage |
| *vv. 14–19* | *vv. 20–23* | *vv. 24–31* | *v. 18* | *vv. 19–23* | *vv. 24–25* |

## Man the creature

Into this perfect, ordered creation Man came as both its crown and also as the creature *par excellence*. Humankind alone is stamped by a threefold 'created . . . created . . . created' (Gen. 1:27). The verb used uniquely of God expressed itself uniquely in Man, and the measure of this uniqueness is that 'God created man in his own image', an idea that the Genesis account nowhere defines but for which it provides ample clues. In particular it indicates that we should find the 'image of God' not in some one particular characteristic but in the entirety of human nature.

Starting with the words 'image' (e.g. 1 Sam. 6:5) and 'likeness' (e.g. 2 Kings 16:10) themselves, they refer to outward shape or appearance and point in the first instance to the bodily form in which God created Man. The Bible, of course, insists that God is Spirit and, in his essential being, invisible. Nevertheless it is equally insistent that when he so chooses he clothes himself with visibility. Moses saw 'the form of the LORD' (Num. 12:8 cf. Deut. 4:12). It was in this 'form' that the LORD created Man, the outward and visible shape appropriate to the divine nature itself.

Secondly, the image of God in Man is matrimonial. The creation of woman (Gen. 2:21–23), from Adam's point of view, was a loss of completeness. The LORD God took something from Adam in order to bring it back to him in the person of Eve. Thus in marriage the man recovers his completeness and the woman comes home to where she belongs. Gen. 5:1–2 associates this unity-in-diversity with the image of God: there is diversity, the distinct creation of male and female, but there is also oneness (literally, 'he called their name, Man') – and therein, says Genesis, lies the image of God.

Thirdly, Man and Woman together receive dominion. The imperatives in Gen. 1:28 are all plural and refer to the newly created couple. Just as, together, they are to 'be fruitful and increase' so, together, they are to 'subdue' and 'rule'. We know that ancient kings put images of themselves in all places of their dominion. But the reality exceeds the illustration, for a statue can only register a claim to sovereignty on behalf of someone else whereas the Man and Woman are the 'living image' of God, not only registering his claim but exercising rule on his behalf.

It is to the Man and Woman alone that the Creator addresses himself personally. In Gen. 1:22 he pronounces blessing over the animal creation: 'blessed . . . and said', but in v. 28 he 'blessed . . . and said to them'. They are conscious auditors of the word of God with a spiritual dimension to their nature whereby God speaks and they hear. This leads on to the fifth aspect of the image of God in Man, the moral factor. Alone in creation, humankind lives knowingly under the law of God. The diagram above makes this clear: the work of creation dealt in turn with the physical and animal realms and the early story of human life on earth and sets Man within each department in turn of what is now his environment (Gen. 2:4–17, 18–25), and in each department (the Garden and the home) God imposes his law of life. Not for Man the instinctive life of the beast; man lives in a yes/no situation, a life of conscious moral choice, the recognition or refusal of the word of God.

Finally, Genesis reveals humankind as rational, taking a thinking view of the world around. In Gen. 2:18 God notes Adam's aloneness and sets out to prepare him for the provision that is about to be made. First, therefore, Adam is allowed to exercise his powers of reasoning upon the animals as they are paraded before him; he is able to set like with like and to give names appropriate to what he sees. In this way he not only exercises lordship over the beasts; he also displays his powers of definition, categorization and description, a truly scientific task. In the course of this he also discovers his own loneliness, for 'no suitable helper' was found for Adam (Gen. 2:20). Presently, however, he awakes from sleep to greet the one who is his perfect 'match' (the central meaning of the expression 'suitable helper'), and he who is 'Ish hails her as "Ishshah"', his equal and exact female counterpart. Mind and emotion alike are caught up in the glory of the moment of recognition that he is no longer alone.

### The Garden enjoyed

The creation of Man in his own image, with all its distinctiveness, in no way compromised the sovereignty of God. The God who, in Gen. 1, 'spoke, and it came to be' (Ps. 33:6, 9) goes about his business in Gen. 2, ordering the world and the life of Man with the same unfettered freedom, making the earth, forming man, planning the Garden, directing man's work, seeing his loneliness, providing his wife, laying down his law. God remains God.

**Where?** The question of where this Garden was is reasonable but, on the evidence which Genesis provides, unanswerable. That a place is intended is clear from the topographical and geological information of Gen. 2:10–14, but in order to make use of it we need both to be able to make secure identification of the names and also to assume that the rivers, in so far as they are identifiable, are flowing in the same place as they were before the Flood. We must rather turn from profitless speculation to consider what the story affirms.

**Benevolence, abundance and obedience.**   In Gen. 1, God is sovereign in the work of creation; in Gen. 3 (notwithstanding the great rebellion) he is still sovereign but in judgment; in Gen. 2:4–25 he is sovereign in benevolence, providing a perfect environment (vv. 4–9), freedom and abundance (vv. 15–17), companionship, love and marriage (vv. 18–25) for his cherished vice-regent on earth. This is the theme of the story: a lavish abundance catering for every need of life – and all enjoyed on the sole condition of a minimal obedience. The story is a case-study of how the Bible relates love and law on the one hand and obedience and blessing on the other. First, the love of God provides the law of God. From God's point of view law is not a cramping imposition but a key opening the door to fulness of life. Secondly, from Man's point of view, the law is not a ladder by which to climb into divine favour but the way of life given to one already in the divine favour. It is not a cruel restriction of freedom and fulness but the condition whereby they are enjoyed. Later in Scripture, when sin has redrawn the map of divine-human relationships, the ground rules remain the same: the LORD gives his law (Exod. 20) not so that people may climb the ladder of meritorious behaviour into his good books but because he has already redeemed them (Exod. 6:6), brought them to himself (Exod. 19:4–6), freed them from bondage (Exod. 20:2) and desires them to enjoy life, liberty and abundance (Deut. 6:1–3).

The older translations caught the bountiful spirit of the story: 'Of every tree of the garden you may freely eat.' The banner flying over that lovely place spelled out the words 'Freedom and Abundance'. After the advent of Eve, the words 'Fulfilment and Love' were added to it. And the cost was minimal, for the whole law of God was contained in one negative and one positive precept: to shun the Tree of Knowledge of Good and Evil, and to 'cleave to your wife' (Gen. 2:16–17, 24–25). The way forward for Adam and Eve was to transform innocence into holiness by moral choice. We are not told what would have happened had they persevered in obedience, and it would be rash to do more than ask questions. As they began life in the Garden the LORD God revealed to them all they needed initially to know. If they had passed the probation imposed by the law of the Tree of Knowledge would they have faced a further revelation of the will of God with further testings? And what would have been the ultimate goal? Surely, to be like God, to be partakers of the divine nature! In so far as it is legitimate to read back God's later dealings into these earlier times, this has the ring of truth, for moral choices still lie at the heart of spiritual progress (Acts 5:32), divine revelation is still the way forward (2 Tim. 3:16–17), and the goal is 'that we may share his holiness' (Heb. 12:10). Had they matured in this way they would have viewed life from the point of view of a growing experience of the good, with evil only known by contrast and as something external to themselves. In grasping after the Tree of Knowledge, the first couple sought to possess wisdom without revelation and turned their whole nature upside-down in the process: for now they progressively know evil in personal experience and good only by contrast and as a thing external to themselves.

## The Garden forfeited

***The serpent.*** The choice itself should have prompted the scornful reply 'No contest', for it was a choice between life and death: on the one hand the free enjoyment of the Tree of Life, on the other, the death-bearing Tree of the Knowledge of Good and Evil! But what about the manner in which the temptation came? A talking snake! – not only a thing of absurdity prompting hilarity rather than credence, but, to Adam, who had just recently asserted his lordship over the beasts (Gen. 2:19–20), surely a glaringly obvious subversion of due order! It is a real token of divine care that everything pointed towards refusal. For sin was not yet resident in human nature and there was no way in which temptation could address humankind from within. It had to be a voice from outside and the Bible reveals that this is the way it happened.

The tempter approached the woman with a doubt and a denial: doubt whether the word of God could really mean what it said (Gen. 3:1) and denial that judgment would follow (v. 4). But in taking this course, the snake was walking into an open door. Adam and Eve had already tampered with the word of God – not by subtraction but by addition. The LORD said, 'you shall not eat'; they added 'neither shall you touch' and gave a human word the status of a divine command (Gen. 3:3). How totally safe they would have been if only they practised a simple obedience to a simple word and left it at that!

***Choice and consequences.*** The simple word of prohibition was the whole law of God. There were no other commands or requirements; this was all he asked. But as Eve looked at the Tree, first her emotions were roused to desire what God had forbidden ('good for food and pleasing to the eye', Gen. 3:6a); secondly, her mind contradicted the mind of God, for he had revealed that though the name of the Tree pointed to knowledge, its effect would be death. But Eve put her own logical construction on the Tree – after all, it was called the Tree of Knowledge, so what could it do but 'make wise' (Gen. 3:6b)? Thirdly, her will disobeyed: 'she took . . . and ate' (v. 6c). Thus the whole nature of Man – emotions, mind and will – broke the whole law of God.

Dire consequences followed: first, society was fragmented: the couple had lived in delightful openness with each other (Gen. 2:25) but now they discovered that the first product of sin is pathological and secretive individualism which made them hide from each other (Gen. 3:7). Secondly, a good conscience was lost and along with it the old easy fellowship with God (vv. 7–10). Indeed, things were more serious than the first couple thought, for while they would gladly remain hidden in the Garden (v. 8), God sees the danger that man might become immortal in his sin (v. 22). They can neither stay (v. 23) nor ever find their own way back (v. 24).

Thirdly, marriage was corrupted. The man who was enjoined to cleave to his wife (Gen. 2:24) promptly deserted her (Gen. 3:12) and would henceforth respond to her longings with domination (Gen. 3:16) – a sad declension from the glad, co-equal oneness of Gen. 2:23. This ruination of marriage was signalized by a change of the woman's name (Gen. 3:20). She is no longer 'Ishshah', the personal name of the co-equal partner (Gen. 2:23, see above), but Hawah, 'the mother of all the living', a functionary, a fertility machine! Fourthly, the economic basis of life was destroyed: the abundance of Eden became a hard-won subsistence (Gen. 3:17–18), with the soil hostile and reluctant to provide. This is the moral vitality of the environment: the very world around is the enemy of the sinner and man in sin can never find economic ease.

**Surprised by mercy.**   The voice of the law said 'when you eat of it you will surely die' (Gen. 2:17), but, remarkably, when the LORD comes he not only sovereignly imposes his curse but equally sovereignly talks to the death-deserving couple about continuing life (Gen. 3:15) and covers their sinful condition by providing adequate clothing (Gen. 3:21; cf. v. 7). We are (sadly) not told what the LORD said as he slew animals and clothed the sinners. Did he explain that the wages of sin is death and that this death could be executed on an innocent party instead of on the guilty? And did he go further to tell them anything in detail about the seed of the woman who would bruise the serpent's head (Gen. 3:15)? In context, this can only be what we call a messianic promise, for the terms of the story of the Fall require us to understand that the death blow will end the usurpation of the snake and bring Eden back. The seed of the woman will be the second Adam. See *Adam, Eve.*

J.A.M.

**GAREB,** an Ithrite, was one of David's 'Thirty' mighty men, who were warriors fighting at his side (2 Sam. 23:38; 1 Chron. 11:40). The Ithrites were a clan from Kiriath Jearim (1 Chron. 2:53).

**GATAM,** an Edomite leader, was the grandson of Esau and Adah (a Canaanite woman) and the son of Eliphaz (Gen. 36:11, 16; 1 Chron. 1:36).

**GAZEZ** (Heb., 'sheep-shearer'), Haran and Moza were sons of Caleb by his concubine, Ephah. Later Haran also had a son called Gazez (1 Chron. 2:46).

**GAZZAM** His descendants were among the Temple servants who returned from Exile with Nehemiah (Ezra 2:48; Neh. 7:51).

**GEBER,** the son of Uri, was one of Solomon's twelve district governors (1 Kings 4:19). Geber was in charge of the area of Gilead, 'the country of Sihon King of the Amorites and the country of Og King of Bashan'. Attention is drawn to the fact that he was the 'only governor' of this rather large district. See also *Ben-Hur.*

**GEDALIAH** (Heb., 'the LORD is great').
   **1.** One of the sons of Jeduthun listed among those set apart for the ministry of prophesying and music during the reign of King David. Jeduthun, with Asaph and Heman, was directly under the supervision of the King. This Gedaliah was the leader of the second group of Levitical musicians and choirs who ministered in the Tabernacle (1 Chron. 25:3, 9).
   **2.** Gedaliah son of Ahikam was appointed governor of Judah by Nebuchadnezzar king of Babylon following the final destruction of Jerusalem in 587 BC (2 Kings 25:22). Nebuchadnezzar had left behind only those who were poor and

would be of no real profit as slaves in Babylon (*Jer. 39:10; 40:7*). The king ordered his commander, Nebuzaradan, to look after Jeremiah when Jerusalem fell, and so Jeremiah was handed over to Gedaliah for safe-keeping (*Jer. 39:14; 40:5–6*). When the army officers who had fled into hiding heard that Gedaliah had been appointed they came to join him at his base at Mizpah, a few kilometres north-west of Jerusalem. Gedaliah proved to be a good ruler. Following the repeated assertions of Jeremiah that God would bless them if they submitted to the Babylonians, he encouraged peaceful relations with their political masters. He also began to draw together the remnants of the people of Israel, encouraging them to settle down again and begin to till the land and harvest crops (*2 Kings 25–25; Jer. 40:8–12*).

He was generous-hearted and was unable to comprehend that anyone would want to kill him. But this was the message that the army officer Johanan son of Kareah brought to him. Baalis king of the Ammonites was sending Ishmael son of Nethaniah to kill Gedaliah. Since Baalis was of royal blood (*2 Kings 25:25*) it is probable that the Ammonite king, with his expansionist desires, found a ready accomplice in one who had been passed over by the Babylonians. Johanan offered to pre-empt the attack, but Gedaliah declined the offer, and later he and many officers were killed by Ishmael when they were all having a meal together.

The result of this murder was effectively the final end to any leader or ruler from Judah staying in the land. Gedaliah's allies, afraid of Babylonian repercussions, fled to Egypt, against the advice of Jeremiah (*Jer. 40:13–41:18; 42–43*). Jeremiah went with them and nothing more is known of what then happened to them. It was not until the return from the Babylonian Exile that God once again raised up a leader from their own people to govern Judah.

**3.** A descendant of Jeshua, this Gedaliah was among those priests who joined Ezra and the people in repentance on their return to Jerusalem from Babylon. Many men of Judah had married wives from other tribes and nations. They made a covenant to serve the LORD (*Ezra 10:2*) and divorced their foreign wives (*Ezra 10:18–19*).

**4.** Gedaliah the son of Pashhur was one of the leaders in Jerusalem in the final days before its destruction at the hands of the Babylonians. He was among those who heard the prophet Jeremiah's pronouncements from God encouraging the people of Judah to accept the Babylonian invasion. He believed these pronouncements were treacherous and so wanted to see Jeremiah the prophet killed (*Jer. 38:1, 4*).

**5.** The grandfather of the prophet Zephaniah (*Zeph. 1:1*).   P.D.G.

**GEDOR  1.** Gedor, of the tribe of Benjamin, was one of the sons of Jeiel and his wife Macah (*1 Chron. 8:31; 9:37*). He is listed in the genealogy leading from Benjamin to Saul.

**2.** Gedor, of the tribe of Judah, was the son of Penuel and a descendant of Hur (*1 Chron. 4:4, 18*). However, given the listing in *v. 18* with Soco and Zanoah, this may well be a reference to a place called Gedor rather than a person.

**GEHAZI** (Heb., 'valley of vision'), Elisha's servant, is encountered in three incidents centred on *2 Kings 4–8*. The first of these concerned Elisha's visit to the town of Shunem, where he met a wealthy woman who urged him to stay and have a meal. Elisha hoped to repay her for her kindness and, using Gehazi as a go-between in the conversation, discovered that she did not have a child. Elisha promised her a child, who was then born the following year. When the child was older he died, and the distressed mother came and threw herself at Elisha's feet (*2 Kings*

4:18–37). Gehazi tried to move her away, but Elisha showed her love and compassion and sent Gehazi on to the house to lay his staff on the child. The child did not recover, and so Elisha himself went to the house, where a miracle was performed and the child revived. Apart from his excessively keen desire to protect his master, Gehazi was a willing and obedient servant.

The second incident involved the healing of Naaman, the commander of the army of the king of Aram. He was a leper (2 Kings 5). Following his strange and miraculous healing, Naaman offered Elisha a reward. Elisha refused the gift, but after Naaman had gone Gehazi ran after him, intent on getting some profit from the incident and quite unable to comprehend his master's attitude. Gehazi lied to Naaman about the need for some money to help two young prophets, and later lied to Elisha when asked where he had been. Miraculously, Elisha told Gehazi that his spirit had been there with him when Naaman had handed over the bags of silver and two sets of clothing. The judgment on Gehazi was that the leprosy from which Naaman had just been healed should be his (2 Kings 5:27).

Gehazi's character of covetousness was quickly judged because of the impact that this might have on Elisha's ministry and the name of the LORD among foreigners like Naaman. Naaman and his people would quickly have seen through the story, and Elisha would have been the one blamed for avarice, and they would have come to think that the LORD's favours were for sale.

The third mention of Gehazi by name is in 2 Kings 8:1–6. Elisha had told the Shunammite woman and her family to leave the country because of a seven-year famine coming on the land. They had gone to the land of the Philistines. When eventually they returned, the wealthy woman went to King Jehoram to have her land and house restored to her. On arrival she found that Gehazi was telling the King about the exploits of Elisha and had just reached the part of the story concerning her and the miracle of her son being healed. He was recounting the incident faithfully and was able to identify the Shunammite woman, so that she could receive back her lands and house. It seems that Gehazi had learned his lesson and continued to serve Elisha.

The sovereignty of the LORD in the events of Elisha's life and those with whom he came into contact was seen repeatedly. Gehazi must have realized this not only in the way he was discovered in his sin but also in how the woman was looked after by the LORD, even when Elisha himself was not present.     P.D.G.

**GEMALLI,** a Danite and the father of the spy Ammiel (Num. 13:12). Ammiel was one of the twelve spies sent from the Desert of Paran to spy out Canaan.

**GEMARIAH** (Heb., 'the LORD has accomplished').

**1.** The son of Shaphan the secretary, Gemariah was a leader in Judah. His room was in a prominent position 'in the upper courtyard at the entrance of the New Gate of the Temple' (Jer. 36:10). From that room Baruch decided to read to all the people the prophecy of judgment which Jeremiah had given him. In that position he could speak to all who came to the Temple. Gemariah's son, Micaiah, heard the LORD's words from the scroll and went to tell the officials of the royal palace (Jer. 36:11). Knowing that words of judgment such as these from the LORD would not be welcome to the King, the officials suggested that Jeremiah and Baruch should hide. When eventually the prophecy was read to King Jehoiakim, he reacted as predicted. During the reading he cut off what had been read column by column and burned it. Gemariah was present at this reading and urged the king not to burn the scroll but to listen to the message. Instead the king issued orders for the arrest of Baruch and Jeremiah. Gemariah was clearly one of the few officials who wanted to hear what the LORD had to say and to obey the prophet Jeremiah's recommendations (Jer. 36:19–26).

**2.** The son of Hilkiah, this Gemariah had stayed in Jerusalem with Jeremiah following the Exile of most of the people to Babylon. He acted as an emissary from King Zedekiah to Nebuchadnezzar in Babylon. When Jeremiah wrote a prophetic letter to the surviving elders and priests in Babylon, he chose Elasah and Gemariah to carry the letter to Babylon for him.                    P.D.G.

**GENTILE(S)** This concept appears frequently in the Bible. In the OT the term often translated as 'Gentile' simply means 'heathen', 'people' or 'nation(s)'. Often it is a way to refer to all non-Israelites, so it becomes a term designating 'outsiders'. In the OT, relations with Gentiles could be hostile (as with the residents of Canaan, Exod. 34:10–16; Josh. 4:24) or friendly (as with the portrait of Ruth). For Israel to be involved in Gentile religious practice was forbidden, and when it occurred it meant judgment and rebuke. The prophets parallel this portrait. Sometimes they predict severe judgment on the nations for their idolatries (Is. 17:12–14; 34:1–14), while they hold out hope that one day the nations will come and participate in the worship of God (Is. 2:1–4). They even predict future honour for Galilee of the Gentiles (Is. 9:1), a text which Matt. 4:15 cites with reference to Jesus' ministry.

In the NT, the concept also has a wide range of usage. In many cases, the term translated 'Gentiles' can also be translated as 'nations'. In general, the term refers to non-Israelites, just as it does in the OT. Sometimes it refers to a region that is not a part of Israel (Matt. 4:15). It is often used as a term of cultural or ethnic contrast. If the Gentiles do something, it is a way of saying that is what the world does (Matt. 5:47; 6:7, 32; Luke 12:30). Often when the term is used this way, it is a negative example or is an observation that such behaviour is not unusual or commendable. The term can also have the force of designating an outsider (Matt. 18:17). Sometimes it describes those who aided in the execution of Jesus or opposed him (Matt. 20:19; Luke 18:32; Acts 4:25–27). They also sometimes joined with Jews to oppose the church (Acts 14:5).

Yet, as a term of contrast, it can also be used positively to show the scope of the gospel clearly including all nations (Matt. 28:19; Acts 10:35, 45). Paul is an apostle specifically called to include Gentiles in his ministry (Acts 13:46–48; 18:6; 22:21; 26:23; 28:28; Rom. 1:5, 13; 11:13; Gal. 1:16; 1 Tim. 2:7; 4:17). Christ as Messiah is called to rule the nations and minister to them (Rom. 15:11–12). So Gentiles now have access to Christ's presence among them (Col. 1:27) and are equal heirs of God's provision of salvation (Eph. 3:6). So they are no longer outsiders but equals in Christ (Eph. 2:11–22). As such, Gentiles picture the reconciliation which Jesus brings to the creation. In this way the promise made to Abraham that he would be the father of many nations is fulfilled (Rom. 4:18). So God is both the God of the Jews and of the Gentiles (Rom. 3:29). In fact, Gentile inclusion becomes a means by which God will make Israel jealous and bring her back into blessing (Rom. 11:11–32).

One figure who pictures the Gentile relationship to God is Cornelius (Acts 10–11). This soldier is presented as the person whom God chose to reveal the fact that God was now reaching out to people of every nation and that ethnic barriers had come down through Jesus. So ground-breaking was this action that Luke constantly refers to it in Acts, as the church deals with how to incorporate Jew and Gentile into the new community which Christ had formed (*Acts 15:7–12*). By bringing salvation to the Gentiles, God brought his message to the ends of the earth (*Acts 13:47*).                    D.B.

**GENUBATH,** a son of Hadad the Edomite. David's commander Joab had destroyed all the men of Edom, but Hadad as a youth had escaped to Egypt, where he had been befriended by Pharaoh. Pharaoh's wife was Tahpenes, and her sister was given to Hadad in marriage. Genubath was a son of that marriage. He grew up among the royal household in Egypt (*1 Kings 11:19–20*).

**GERA 1.** The fourth of ten sons of Benjamin. This name became a family name within the tribe of Benjamin (*Gen. 46:21*).
**2.** This Gera was a Benjamite and the father of Ehud (*Judg. 3:15*). Ehud was one of the deliverers and judges that God raised up to defeat Eglon king of Moab during the time of the Judges.
**3.** Gera, the father of Shimei, was a Benjamite from Bahurim and was from the same clan as King Saul's family. Shimei cursed King David when he fled from Absalom, although he later repented of this action (*2 Sam. 16:5; 19:16; 1 Kings 2:8*).
**4.** A son of Bela and a grandson of Benjamin, mentioned in *1 Chron. 8:3, 5*. Probably the same Gera as listed again in *v. 7*.

**GERSHOM 1.** One of Moses' sons by his wife Zipporah. This Gershom, brother to Eliezer, was given his name by Moses who said: 'I have become an alien in a foreign land' (*Exod. 2:22; 18:3; 1 Chron. 23:15–16*). His son was called Jonathan and became a priest for the idolatrous Danites (*Judg. 18:30*). A descendant of Gershom was Shubael who, like the descendants of Gershom's brother Eliezer, had charge of King David's treasuries (*1 Chron. 23:16; 26:24*).

**2.** One of the heads of families who returned to Jerusalem with Ezra from the Exile in Babylon. He was a descendant of Phinehas (*Ezra 8:2*).

**GERSHON** (Heb., 'exiled') was one of the sons of Levi; his brothers were Kohath and Merari (*Gen. 46:11; Exod. 6:16; Num. 3:17; 1 Chron. 6:1 etc.*). He was the founder of the Gershonite clans, which included the clans of his own sons, Libni (the Libnites) and Shimei (the Shimeites, *Exod. 6:17; Num. 3:21; 26:57; 1 Chron. 6:17*). *Josh. 21:6* recounts the division of the land of Canaan by Joshua son of Nun and Eleazar the priest (*cf. 1 Chron. 6:62*). There the Gershonite descendants of Levi were given cities, as promised by Moses. They were allotted 13 towns from the tribes of Asher, Issachar, Nephtali and the half-tribe of Manasseh. As Levites, the Gershonites were given responsibilities for the Tabernacle (the Tent of Meeting). There were 2,630 men among them who helped in the task assigned to them of carrying the many different types of curtains belonging to the Tabernacle and looking after 'all the equipment used in its service' (*Num. 4:21–28*).

Joel was the leader of the Gershonite contingent of priests and Levites in King David's time; together with 130 others, he helped bring the ark of the covenant up to Jerusalem. Later, when David organized the ordering of worship at the Tabernacle, the Levites were divided into groups that corresponded in their main divisions to the Gershonites, Kohathites and Merarites (*1 Chron. 23:6*). Asaph was one of the most famous Gershonites, being in charge of the music (*1 Chron. 16:4–5*). The family continued in the service of the Temple for many years and was mentioned even as late as the days of the revival in King Hezekiah's time, when they were involved in purifying the Temple, which had fallen into a state of decay (*2 Chron. 29:12*).                                    P.D.G.

**GESHAN,** a son of Jahdai and a descendant of Judah and Caleb (*1 Chron. 2:47*).

**GESHEM** Along with Sanballat and Tobiah, he mocked Nehemiah when they heard he intended to rebuild the wall of Jerusalem after the Exile in Babylon. When the wall was rebuilt he and Sanballat sent Nehemiah a message to meet with them, but Nehemiah refused to come. He claimed that the Jews were plotting to revolt, but Nehemiah denied it (*Neh. 2:19, 6:1, 6:2, 6:6*). For more detail see *Sanballat*.

**GETHER,** one of the four sons of Aram listed in *Gen. 10:23* and *1 Chron. 1:17*. Aram was a son of Shem. The best Heb. manuscripts of *1 Chron. 1:17* do not separate the sons of Shem himself from the sons of Aram.

**GEUEL,** one of the twelve spies sent out by Moses from the Desert of Paran to spy out the land of Canaan (*Num. 13:11*). A representative of each tribe was chosen and Geuel, the son of Maki, was from the tribe of Gad. For further detail on their mission see *Shammua*.

**GIBBAR** (Heb., 'hero'). 95 of his descendants returned from Exile in Babylon with Nehemiah and Zerubbabel (*Ezra 2:20*).

**GIBEA,** a grandson of Caleb and his concubine Maacah, was of the tribe of Judah, and his father was Sheva (*1 Chron. 2:49*).

**GIDDALTI,** one of the sons of Asaph listed among those set apart for the ministry of prophesying and music during the reign of King David. He was a son of Heman, the king's seer (*1 Chron. 25:4, 29*).

**GIDDEL 1.** His descendants were among the Temple servants who returned from Exile with Nehemiah (*Ezra 2:47; Neh. 7:49*).

**2.** He was a servant of Solomon whose descendants returned from Exile with Nehemiah (*Ezra 2:56; Neh. 7:58*).

**GIDEON** (Heb., 'feller, hewer, smiter') is also called Jerubbaal (*Judg. 6:32* etc.), meaning 'let Baal contend' or 'may Baal strive', and Jerubbesheth (*2 Sam. 11:21*), in which the abhorred name Baal was replaced by the word 'shame'. He was the youngest son of Joash, from the obscure family of Abiezer in the tribe of Manasseh, and he lived at Ophrah. He later became a judge over the Israelites and delivered them from the Midianites, a marauding band from the eastern desert (*Judg. 6:1–8:35*).

The Israelites had turned away from God and were worshipping Baal, so God had given them over to the ravages of the Midianites for seven years. In desperation the Israelites called out to the LORD for help, and he raised up Gideon as their deliverer. Gideon was called while he was secretly beating out grain in a wine press, to save it from the Midianites. His first job was to tear down his father's Asherah idol and Baal altar and build an altar to the LORD in its place. This infuriated the men of the city, who determined to kill Gideon for such effrontery against Baal, but Joash's quick-wittedness saved the life of his son.

This event apparently had a significant impact on Gideon's life, as the name Jerubbaal or 'let Baal contend' indicates.

Gideon won a decisive night-time victory over the Midianites with 300 fighting men blowing trumpets and carrying torches. The Midianites became so disorientated that they began killing their own warriors and then fled in terror. This victory later took on proverbial status for divine deliverance without the aid of man (*cf. Is. 9:4*). In response to Gideon's victory the Israelites offered to let him set up a hereditary monarchy, which he refused, saying, 'I will not rule over you, nor will my son rule over you. The LORD will rule over you' (Judg. 8:23). He did, however, accept golden ear-rings as battle spoil. He made these into an ephod (its purpose is uncertain – possibly priestly functions or an image of Yahweh) and set it up in his own city. So while Gideon obeyed the letter of the Law in not becoming king, he took the plunder offered and started to act like a king (see Deut. 17:17). This ephod later became a source of idolatry for Gideon and his household (Judg. 8:27).

Gideon is portrayed as a timid and humble man whom God used mightily and, for his faith, he is recorded along with the other great heroes of faith in Heb. 11:32.                    P.D.W.

**GIDEONI,** a leader of the tribe of Benjamin and the father of Abidan (Num. 1:11; 2:22; 7:60, 65; 10:24). Abidan was the leader of the Benjamites who were chosen to help in the census of Israel under Moses during the wilderness wanderings. He remained leader of his tribe during the various important events. See Abidan.

**GILALAI** An associate of Zechariah who was part of the procession led by Nehemiah along the walls of Jerusalem when they were dedicated (Neh. 12:36).

**GILEAD** (Heb., 'a rocky mound').
**1.** A grandson of Manasseh and a son of Makir, he became the leader of the Gileadite clan (Num. 26:29–30; 27:1; 1 Chron. 2:21–23). His name was given to an area east of Jordan. The allotment of that land is recorded in Josh. 17.
**2.** The father of Jephthah, who became a judge in Israel: 'His father was Gilead; his mother was a prostitute' (Judg. 11:1). Gilead's sons by his official wife later drove Jephthah away from the family home, trying to ensure that he would not receive any inheritance from his father. The fact that Jephthah is also described as a Gileadite (living in the area called Gilead) has led some to question whether Gilead was actually the name of his father or simply a patronymic. The context suggests a genuine name.
**3.** The father of Jaroah and a son of Michael, he was a Gadite who lived in Bashan in Gilead. Again it is possible, given that this family lived in Gilead, to consider this another patronymic. However, the context of the name is in the middle of a genealogy, which makes this most unlikely (1 Chron.5:14–16).
                                    P.D.G.

**GINATH,** the father of Tibni, who briefly attempted to become king of Israel following the death of Zimri. Israel split into two factions, one supporting Tibni and the other backing Omri. Omri had the stronger side, and so he became king, while Tibni was killed (1 Kings 1:21–22.

**GINNETHON** **1.** One of the priests who sealed the agreement of the people to worship the LORD and obey his Law (Neh. 10:6).
**2.** One of the priests who returned from Exile with Zerubbabel. Meshullam was the head of this priestly family in the days of Joiakim (Neh. 12:4, 16).

**GISHPA** He and Ziha were in charge of the Temple servants who lived on the hill of Ophel after the return from Exile in Babylon (Neh. 11:21).

# GOD

## Introduction

(The reader should also consult the following entries: LORD; Jesus; Christ; Holy Spirit.) The God of the Bible reveals himself in his creation and above all through his Word in Scripture. Indeed the Bible can well be described as 'God's self-revelation to his people'. It is important to remember that the Bible shows that even what knowledge we can attain of God is limited and finite while God is infinite, pure and a living personal Spirit whom no-one has seen. Frequently the Bible uses 'anthropomorphisms' (words and ideas drawn from the experience of human activities, emotions etc.) in an attempt to help us understand God better. These can be very helpful indeed, but using descriptions and terms normally applied to human beings and applying them to an infinite and eternal God will always leave something to be desired. Having said that, 'knowing God' to the extent that we are able through his Word in Scripture, is at the very heart of biblical faith. According to the Bible, all people throughout history stand in some relationship to this God, whether it be one of rebellion and disbelief, or one of acceptance and faith in him.

Men and women are here on earth because of God's creating and sustaining power, and the Bible teaches that all will one day have to face him for judgment at the end of time. The nature of God and his attributes are therefore discussed in many ways in Scripture so that he will be better known by those whom he will hold accountable. For example, much is learned of God as he is seen acting in history for the support and defence of his people and in judgment upon those who sin, or live in rebellion against him. Much is also learned of God through the names the Bible applies to him. Much is learned as his creation is discussed and examined. Above all we learn of God as we study the biblical teaching on Jesus, who is 'Immanuel' ('God with us').

The sections below provide only pointers to some of what the Bible reveals about God. A life-time of study, faith and commitment to God through Christ will still only leave the believer longing for more, and especially for Christ's return, for he or she will acknowledge with the apostle Paul: 'Now we see but a poor reflection as in a mirror; then we shall see face to face. Now I know in part; then I shall know fully, even as I am fully known' (1 Cor. 13:12).

## The existence of the Only God

The Bible assumes the existence of God. There is no discussion of this within its pages, for this is a book in which God reveals himself. It is only the 'fool', the person who is evil and corrupt, who 'says in his heart "There is no God"' (Pss. 14:1; 53:1; see The fool and the wise). God's existence is frequently asserted in contexts which warn against idolatry. Here there is often special emphasis on the fact that God alone is God and that no other God exists. Deut. 6:4 asserts: 'Hear, O Israel: The LORD our God, the LORD is one'. Deut. 32:39 says: 'See now that I myself am he! There is no god besides me. I put to death and I bring to life, I have wounded and I will heal, and no one can deliver out of my hand.' It is for this reason that idolatry is such a serious sin (see also 1 Cor. 8:4). To become involved in idolatry is to live and believe a lie in direct rejection of the revelation of the one true God. The people of

Israel were expected to witness to the surrounding nations that one true God existed and no other god existed at all. This was specially to be seen in God's power to provide for them in war and peace, to extend their borders (against the power of other so-called gods) and in his justice and judgment on all who turned from him or rejected his ways or his people. The nations around needed to learn from Israel that their gods were false gods and that in fact they were worshipping demons (1 Cor. 10:20).

The psalmist and prophets also proclaimed that the LORD alone is God and that he pre-exists and self-exists. Ps. 90:2 says: 'Before the mountains were born or you brought forth the earth and the world, from everlasting to everlasting you are God.' In Isaiah we read: 'This is what the LORD says – Israel's King and Redeemer, the LORD Almighty: I am the first and I am the last; apart from me there is no God' (Is. 44:6); 'I am the LORD, and there is no other; apart from me there is no God. I will strengthen you, though you have not acknowledged me' (Is. 45:5; see also Is. 45:21 etc.). Jeremiah says: 'the LORD is the true God; he is the living God, the eternal King' (Jer. 10:10).

In the NT again God's eternal self-existence is assumed: 'In the beginning was the Word, and the Word was with God, and the Word was God. He was with God in the beginning. Through him all things were made; without him nothing was made that has been made. In him was life, and that life was the light of men' (John 1:1–4). Paul preached to the Athenians arguing, among other things, that 'in him [God] we live and move and have our being' (Acts 17:28). Paul appealed to the citizens at Lystra that even they ought to acknowledge the existence of the one true God for, 'he has not left himself without testimony: He has shown kindness by giving you rain from heaven and crops in their seasons; he provides you with plenty of food and fills your hearts with joy' (Acts 14:17). In Rom. 1:19–20 there is an assumption that even those who are evil and reject God can be held accountable 'since what may be known about God is plain to them, because God has made it plain to them. For since the creation of the world God's invisible qualities – his eternal power and divine nature – have been clearly seen, being understood from what has been made, so that men are without excuse.'

As in John 1 mentioned above, in the NT it is often as we learn about Jesus that we begin to understand more of God himself and his pre-existence and self-existence. Col. 1:17 describes both Jesus' pre-existence as 'the image of the invisible God' and his sustaining work in his creation (vv. 15–20). Both the Father God and Jesus are seen to be eternal in their existence: ' "I am the Alpha and the Omega," says the Lord God, "who is, and who was, and who is to come, the Almighty" ' (Rev. 1:8; also 11:15, 17; 2 Pet. 3:8). Heb. 13:8 also speaks of Jesus: 'Jesus Christ is the same yesterday and today and forever.'

## The Creator God

God's self-existence and eternal existence are also signalled in his creation which he brings about ex nihilo ('out of nothing', see Gen. 1; Rom. 4:17; Heb. 11:3). The Bible does not allow for anything existing side by side with God through all eternity. There is no teaching, for example, that matter has always existed, or alternatively that evil has always existed alongside God. God has always existed and will always exist, and he is the creator. He who exists brings other things into being. Reason may demand that if anything exists something must have the power of existence within itself. The Bible shows that that being who self-exists is God and God alone. Because he exists, life can exist, and creation can happen. In God is life and light. He alone has life in himself and dwells in light and glory from all eternity.

God's act of creation is described in many places in the Bible. Notably Gen. 1–2 describes God's word bringing all that we know into existence. These chapters clearly show that God existed before the creation and that it was through his creating word and power that the world came into existence. They also reveal that God did not simply start up some process that concluded, or has not yet concluded, with what we know in this world today. He actively intervened again and again to bring into being light, sun, moon, water, vegetation, fish, mammals, birds and humankind. In Gen. 1 this active work of God throughout the whole period of creation is to be noted in both the words 'And God said, "Let there be . . ."' and the words 'And God saw that it was good'. In Gen. 2 the work and words of 'the LORD God' are repeatedly mentioned. Ps. 33:4–9 personalizes the 'word of the LORD' as the one who created and who 'is faithful in all he does'. 'By the word of the LORD were the heavens made . . . Let all the earth fear the LORD; . . . for he spoke, and it came to be; he commanded, and it stood firm.' Jeremiah affirms, 'he [God] is the Maker of all things, including Israel, the tribe of his inheritance – the LORD Almighty is his name (Jer. 10:16; 51:19; also see Job 26:7; Pss. 102:25; 104:24; Neh. 9:6 etc.).

In the NT the writer of Hebrews reminds believers that 'by faith we understand that the universe was formed at God's command, so that what is seen was not made out of what was visible' (Heb. 11:3). Praise and worship are due to God the Father and to Jesus, the Word of God, for creation and for his continuing sustaining of his creation. Since his creation derives its life and existence from God himself, were God no longer to uphold it, it would cease to exist (Rev. 4:11; John 1:1–3; 1 Cor. 8:6; Col. 1:16–17; Heb. 1:2; 2 Pet. 3:5 etc.).

This work of creation that continues to need God's sustaining power provides evidence of God's sovereignty and power over everything. He is everywhere present sustaining and watching over his creation, bringing to bear his righteousness, justice, love and mercy, bringing into being and destroying according to his will and purposes. The doxology of Rom. 11:33–36 provides for the necessary response of the believer in the presence of the creating, sustaining, self-existing God: 'For from him and through him and to him are all things. To him be the glory forever! Amen' (v. 36).

## The personal God

The God who created the world and human beings and who sustains the world and all people reveals himself as a 'personal God'. The word 'personal' is nowhere applied to him in the Bible, and it is difficult for our minds to grasp what 'personality' in God might mean. Yet, this is how he is consistently revealed. He is a self-existent, self-conscious being. Attributes indicative of a personal being belong to him. He is shown to have a mind, to be free, to have will and purpose. To put it negatively, God is never portrayed in Scripture, as people often describe him today, as an ever-present energy or force. God shows himself to be 'personal' in the relationship between Father, Son and Spirit (see below on the Trinity), and in his desire that his people have a real relationship with the 'living God'. His 'personality', of course, is that of Spirit, and therefore not limited in the way human personality is. However, because he is personal his people are able to experience a genuine and personal relationship with him. God who is good 'loves' them and 'speaks' to them. He guides them and cares for them. Ps. 147:10–11 gives some feel of God as a personal God: 'His pleasure is not in the strength of the horse, nor his delight in the legs of a man; the LORD delights in those who fear him, who put their hope in his unfailing love' (see also Ps. 94:9–10). Eph. 1:9–11 also shows how God's will and purpose are specially disposed towards those he has 'chosen' and whom he 'loves'. He is the one who 'knows' his people (1 Cor. 8:3) and who can be called 'Father' by those who 'live for him' (v. 6). The revelation of God in Jesus shows again how he is a 'personal' God both in the relationship of Jesus and the Father (as the Son does the will of the Father and speaks his words) and as the Father shows his love to the world in giving 'his one and only Son that whoever believes in him shall not perish but have eternal life' (John 3:16; 14:15–31; 15:9–10 etc.).

### The providential God

Since God is eternal and self-existing, and the Creator of the universe, it is not surprising that one of the most frequent of biblical themes concerns the sovereign providential work of God. God is seen as king of the universe, the one who speaks and it happens, who judges and people die, who shows his love and brings about salvation. He is the LORD (see LORD) who controls his world and demands obedience. He seeks out those who will be his people. It is in his providential care for his world and his people that most often we discover in the Bible those great divine attributes of wisdom, justice and goodness. Here too we see his truth and his power. The Bible shows God to be in total control of all people, governments and indeed all things. He is called the King. He can establish earthly kingdoms and destroy them. So great is his sovereignty and providential care in ensuring that his will happens that even evil can be overturned by God and used to his good purposes.

As the biblical writers show their conviction that God governs the whole of his creation so the concepts of fate or chance are banished. By way of example, a good harvest does not happen by chance but is governed by God. It is God who promises: 'As long as the earth endures, seedtime and harvest, cold and heat, summer and winter, day and night will never cease' (Gen. 8:22). On the other hand God so rules his creation that he can withhold harvest to those who sin or rebel against him (Is. 5:10). In the days of King Ahab of Israel, God withheld rain and dew by his 'word' in judgment on the king and his people (1 Kings 17:1). The famine was very severe, but God's particular providential love for his people meant that he supplied Elijah the prophet with food in various miraculous ways (1 Kings 17–18).

The Bible is mostly concerned with God's providence as seen in his relationship with his people (see 2 Chron. 16:9). The apostle Paul speaks of it when he says 'we know that in all things God works for the good of those who love him, who have been called according to his purpose' (Rom. 8:28). Here we see that not only does

God's sovereign care always further his will and purpose but that that will is specially concerned for his people and their care and protection. The power of God is so great that 'in *all things*' God works for his own. Such an understanding of providence leads to the inevitable conclusion that even what might be initiated by the evil one or that might emanate from our own sinful desires can be overruled by God as he works without ceasing for the completion and fulfilment of his will. This faith and trust in God's providential care was not new to Paul's day. When Joseph was captured by his brothers and sold as a slave to Egypt, it was not coincidence that led him eventually to be Prime Minister of Egypt at a time when God's people needed to be preserved from a severe famine. It was all part of God's will. Later in discussing the matter with his somewhat fearful brothers, Joseph said: 'You intended to harm me, but God intended it for good to accomplish what is now being done, the saving of many lives' (Gen. 50:20). God's providential care of Job when Satan wished to attack and destroy is also evidence of God's sovereign power even over the spirit world and Satan himself (e.g. Job 1–2). God even controlled the actions of the king of Persia for the sake of his people (Is. 44:28; 45:1–7).

Nowhere is God's providential care more clearly seen than in his providing salvation for his people through the death of Jesus. The worst act ever committed by Satan and the most terrible of sins committed by human beings led to the crucifixion of Jesus the Son of God. Yet even this was the determined will of God, and he overruled this evil act to provide atonement for all who will turn to him (Acts 2:23–24). This will of God took place 'according to Scriptures'. Certainly God is often seen to act providentially and with sovereign power in accordance with his word (e.g. Rom 5:6; 1 Cor. 15:3; 2 Cor. 5:15).

God's providential work is also seen in the way he draws people to himself. The whole Trinity is involved in this work of drawing in and caring for God's people (John 17:11–12, 24; Eph. 1:3–14; Col. 1:12–14 etc.). Reflection on God's sovereignty over everything, his complete power to carry out whatever he wills, his providential care for nature, for the human race generally and specially for those whom he has redeemed, leads again to great praise in Scripture (e.g. Pss. 139:13–16; 145:1, 13–16; 1 Pet. 5:7; Ps. 103).

## The righteous God

The Bible shows God to be 'righteous'. It is part of his nature and has to do with his truth, justice and goodness. In practical terms in Scripture a recognition of God's righteousness enables people to trust that God's will is right and good and that he can be trusted for the right decision and action. He is righteous as Judge of the world and is righteous in showing mercy. More than this, his eternal will is entirely righteous, just and good. It is the joy of sinful men and women that they can turn to a righteous God and receive mercy. It is the fear of those who rebel that the righteous God will judge and condemn.

God's people ('righteous' people, those forgiven by God) frequently appeal to his righteousness. For example, the Psalmist prayed for mercy from God when the evil people around seemed to have the upper hand. He found it strange that the wicked seemed to prosper while the 'righteous' seemed to suffer. He therefore appealed to the righteousness of God for an answer to his dilemma: 'O righteous God, who searches minds and hearts, bring to an end the violence of the wicked and make the righteous secure' (Ps. 7:9, 11). 'Answer me when I call to you, O my righteous God. Give me relief from my distress; be merciful to me and hear my prayer' (Pss. 4:1; 129:4; 2 Thess. 1:6). It is out of his 'righteousness' that God expresses mercy to his people (Pss. 116:4–6; 37:39).

Sometimes, however, God's people tried to take issue with God when it appeared he was not helping them or that he was siding with other nations. God's response was that if he appeared to them to be unrighteous it was only because they had been faithless and sinful. God's actions are always righteous even if it leads to judgment on his own people. See, for example, Ezek. 18:25 (also v. 29): 'Yet you say, "The way of the LORD is not just." Hear, O house of Israel: Is my way unjust? Is it not your ways that are unjust?'

God is specially seen to be righteous in all that he does. This is reflected in his Law which is repeatedly affirmed to be 'righteous' (e.g. Ps. 119; Rom. 7:12). Deut. 32:4 summarizes the righteousness of God thus: 'He is the Rock, his works are perfect, and all his ways are just. A faithful God who does no wrong, upright and just is he.'

While God's people pray they will see his righteousness in his acts of mercy and help for them and in his judgment on their enemies, so they recognize that God's righteousness allows him to bring the judgment of discipline on them when they sin. In 2 Chron. 12 Rehoboam and the leaders of Israel were finally forced to admit that it was because of their sin and rebellion against God that Pharaoh Shishak had been allowed to attack Judah and even come as far as Jerusalem. God spared them from destruction only when they humbled themselves and acknowledged: 'The LORD is just' (v. 6). At the time of the Babylonian Exile the leaders became particularly aware of this aspect of God's righteousness. Daniel expressed it thus: 'The LORD did not hesitate to bring the disaster upon us, for the LORD our God is righteous in everything he does; yet we have not obeyed him' (Dan. 9:14; see also Ezra 9:15).

The prophets looked forward to seeing the revelation of God's righteousness in the future reign of the Messiah: ' "The days are coming," declares the LORD, "when I will raise up to David a righteous Branch, a King who will reign wisely and do what is just and right in the land" ' (Jer. 23:5; Is. 9:7; 11:4 etc.; see Luke 1:75; Acts 22:14). The apostle Paul discussed Christ's work in terms of God's revelation of his righteousness. In Christ's death God's judgment on sin is seen and God's mercy and love for his forgiven people is revealed. God has compromised neither his justice that requires death for sin, nor his covenant love for his people that promises forgiveness and mercy. God thus remains just and righteous in salvation (Rom. 1:17; 2:5–6; 3:5, 20–26 etc.).

In talking of the last days and the return of Christ when God will vindicate his name before the whole world including the wicked, it will be his righteousness that is at once noted and which will draw forth the praise of his people who are longing for that revelation (see Rev. 15:3; 16:7).

## The loving God

It is right that there should be a separate section on this most wonderful attribute of the God of the Bible, and yet traditionally and more accurately, God's love is seen to be an aspect of God's 'goodness'. Time and again in the Bible God is said to 'love' or show 'love' to his creation and specially to his people. It is part of God's nature that he is 'good' and that he is 'love'. God *does* what is good (*2 Sam. 10:12; 1 Chron. 19:13; Ps. 119:68*) but, more than that, he *is* good. In other words, goodness is so much part of him and his being that the Psalmist can say of God, 'your name is good' (*Ps. 52:9; 54:6*). (This word 'name' refers to the whole character of God himself.) Jesus says: 'No one is good – except God alone' (*Luke 18:19*). Thus if a person is to know what goodness and love are then he or she must look to God. *1 John 4:8, 16* say: 'Whoever does not love does not know God, because God is love . . . And so we know and rely on the love God has for us. God is love. Whoever lives in love lives in God, and God in him.'

God is the source of goodness. *James 1:17* says: 'Every good and perfect gift is from above, coming down from the Father of the heavenly lights, who does not change like shifting shadows.' The verse not only shows God to be the source of what is good but teaches that God is always good. There is no 'shadow' side to God, no Eastern view here that good and evil exist side by side and *together* form something called 'god'.

God's goodness, so frequently described as his 'love', is seen in this world in many ways. It is evident generally in this world, whether it be in the maintenance of life itself, of justice, order in creation, or even the providing of sun and rain, seedtime and harvest (*Ps. 33:5; Matt. 5:45; Acts 17:25*).

However, his goodness is most clearly evidenced in his faithful love to his people whom he protects, cares for and saves from judgment. This faithful love for his people is sometimes called his 'covenant love' or his 'faithful love' because God has bound himself to demonstrate this to his people forever. Repeatedly the Israelites praised the LORD for this extraordinary and unmerited eternal love that he showed them through their history (e.g. *1 Chron. 16:34; 2 Chron. 5:13; 7:3; Ezra 3:11; Ps. 118:1, 29; Jer. 33:11*). It is worth noting how the words 'good' and 'love' so often occur together when applied to God.

Those who seek God come to experience his goodness and love for they find his salvation (e.g. *Lam. 3:25*). God's people praise God most of all for his love shown in his mercy and forgiveness for their sin. It is to God's goodness that Hezekiah appealed when he asked for pardon for the people of Israel who were worshipping the LORD without having gone through all the ritual purification. 'Hezekiah prayed for them, saying, "May the LORD, who is good, pardon everyone"' (*2 Chron. 30:18; Num. 14:19*). God himself, speaking through the prophet Hosea, warns that the continued rebellion of his people will cause him 'no longer to show love to the house of Israel, that I should at all forgive them' (*Hos. 1:6*).

God's salvation of his people is his deepest and most amazing demonstration of his goodness and love to his people. Jesus was given by the Father as a sacrifice for the sins of all who believe. Perhaps the most famous verse in the Bible, *John 3:16*, expresses the heart of this love gift from God: 'For God so loved the world that he gave his one and only Son, that whoever believes in him shall not perish but have eternal life.' The gift is the more extraordinary since 'God demonstrates his own love for us in this: While we were still sinners, Christ died for us' (*Rom. 5:8; Titus 3:4; 1 John 3:16*). God's people know they did not deserve or merit this sacrifice. The unmerited nature of God's love is often summarized in the word 'grace'.

God's love is also seen by his people in the way he gives his Holy Spirit so that they can know him and respond to him in love (*Rom. 5:5*). They also experience his love in his providential care for them. This can mean that it is experienced in discipline (*Rev. 3:19*), but also in the fact that 'all things' work together for good for God's people, called according to his purpose. Nothing will be able to separate them from the love of God and of Christ (*Rom. 8:28, 35, 39*; see 'The providential God' above). As God's people reflect on God's grace on their behalf to achieve their salvation, so they praise him for the way he 'chose' them and 'predestined' them to 'be adopted as his sons through Jesus Christ, in accordance with his pleasure and will' (*Eph. 1:4–6; 1 John 3:1*). This great work of salvation was 'according to his good pleasure' (*v. 9*).

'Because of his great love for us, God, who is rich in mercy, made us alive with Christ even when we were dead in transgressions – it is by grace you have been saved' (*Eph. 2:4–5*). The problem is how any human mind can grasp this depth of love, for 'this love surpasses knowledge' (*Eph. 3:18–19*).

## The saving God

God's love is seen pre-eminently in his salvation through Jesus ('Jesus' means 'the LORD saves'; see *Jesus*). God is rightly described as a 'saving God'. The Bible teaches that all humankind is sinful and in need of redemption and that this can only be effected by the saving activity of God. The OT can refer to God as the 'Deliverer', 'Redeemer' and 'Saviour' of either the nation or of individuals. Individuals and nations need forgiveness if they are not to be judged. A lesson that had to be learned by all was that the righteous God alone was all powerful and sovereign and therefore ultimately he alone could save: 'there is no God apart from me, a righteous God and a Saviour; there is none but me' (*Is. 45:21; 43:11*). Sometimes the nation of Israel would turn to other nations for protection and salvation but inevitably this failed as God taught them that he alone was their Saviour (*Deut. 32:15–24; 1 Chron. 16:34–36; Is. 17:10*).

The promise God makes to his people is that when his people 'cry out to the LORD because of their oppressors, he will send them a saviour and defender, and he will rescue them' (*Is. 19:20; 43:3; 45:15*). The faithful men and women of the OT all knew of God's saving and delivering activity both in battle but also in forgiveness. The exodus and deliverance from Egypt became the great event in history that offered future generations a reminder and a picture of God's salvation and redemption. God redeemed his people from Egypt because he loved them: 'But it was because the LORD loved you and kept the oath he swore to your forefathers that he brought you out with a mighty hand and redeemed you from the land of slavery, from the power of Pharaoh king of Egypt' (*Deut. 7:8*).

That historical framework provided future generations with evidence that God does save and has the power to save, and became the basis on which they could appeal to God to save and deliver again in their generation (*Exod. 6:6; Deut. 9:26; Ps. 106:10*). But the deliverance of the Exodus also provided a warning of what happened to those in the wilderness who 'forgot their God': 'Whenever God slew them, they would seek him; they eagerly turned to him again. They remembered that God was their Rock, that God Most High was their Redeemer' (*Ps. 78:34–35*; see also *1 Cor. 10:1–12*). God himself would remind them of his saving work in bringing them from Egypt to the Promised Land and expect loyalty and service from his redeemed people (e.g. *Deut. 13:5; 15:15; 24:18; Hos. 13:4*).

As they needed physical redemption and salvation so they needed forgiveness for sin and in this too God proved to be the Saviour and Redeemer of his people. They praised his name for his forgiveness and knew that ultimately they could commit themselves to his righteousness and he would save (*Deut. 21:8; Pss. 31:5; 34:22, 44:26; Is. 54:5; 59:20*).

The prophets looked forward to the day when a saviour and redeemer would come to God's repentant people: ' "The Redeemer will come to Zion, to those in Jacob who repent of their sins," declares the LORD' (*Is. 59:20*). Isaiah looked forward to the day of the Messiah's coming when the people would praise him: 'I will praise you, O LORD. Although you were angry with me, your anger has turned away and you have comforted me. Surely God is my salvation; I will trust and not be afraid. The LORD, the LORD, is my strength and my song; he has become my salvation' (*Is. 12:1–3*; see *Jer. 23:6; Zech. 9:9*).

Jesus was the fulfilment of these promises. He was the saving God come to earth to save and redeem. When his birth was announced it was immediately his saving and redeeming activity that dominated the words of the angels, of Zechariah and of Mary. The prophecies concerning the saving of the people of God from their nemies with the coming of the Davidic king are rolled together with the forgiveness of the people and their salvation from God's judgment. The whole of 'salvation history', as some have called it, comes to its great climax with the coming of the one who will be called 'Jesus, for he will save his people from their sins' (*Matt. 1:21; Luke 1:46–47, 68–75; 2:11, 30–32, 38* etc.).

In Jesus the saving God is fully revealed. In him, and no-one else, is salvation (*Luke 3:6; 19:9–10; Acts 4:12; Heb. 2:10*). Indeed the word 'save' and 'salvation' comes to refer to the whole saving work of Christ from his incarnation, death and resurrection through to his glorification. His saving work is regarded as past (on the cross when believers 'were justified', *Rom. 5:1; 8:24; Eph. 2:8; 2 Tim. 1:9*), present (with the Spirit's progressive outworking in the believer's life of salvation in the process of sanctification, *1 Cor.1:18; 2 Cor. 2:15*), and future (on the judgment day believers will be saved from the righteous wrath of God and glorified, *Rom. 5:9–10*).

Meditation on who God is has always led to doxology, so *Jude 25* expresses praise to God as Saviour through Jesus: 'to the only God our Saviour be glory, majesty, power and authority, through Jesus Christ our Lord, before all ages, now and forevermore! Amen.'

## The Father God

As has been seen, God *is* good, he *is* love, so, too, he *is* 'Father'. He is the source of all things and Father in that sense. He is Father of creation, of his covenant people Israel, and of Christian believers. Above all he is Father of his one and only Son Jesus. In a day when it is often asked whether God should be called 'Father' because it might appear sexist speech, it is important to note again that God is Spirit. To describe him, therefore, as male or female is quite wrong. Indeed, we read of the Father actually being the 'God who gave you birth' (*Deut. 32:18*) – hardly a masculine action! Human fatherhood is derivative of God and not the other way round. To call God 'Father' is undoubtedly right biblically and, properly understood, no doubt has much to say in correction of the many abuses of human fatherhood as it is so often seen today.

First, God is in a general sense occasionally referred to as Father of all people or all people are regarded as his offspring (*Mal. 2:10; Acts 17:28–29; Heb. 12:9*). Secondly, and more frequently, God's fatherhood of Israel is mentioned or implied. As their Father he therefore has a right to be obeyed. *Deut. 32:5–6* gives some indication of this relationship: 'They have acted corruptly toward him [God]; to their shame they are no longer his children, but a warped and crooked generation. Is this the way you repay the LORD, O foolish and unwise people? Is he not your Father, your Creator, who made you and formed you?' It is his covenant relationship with his people that is specially in mind here. God takes (creates) Israel and makes them into his people and lovingly 'fathers' them, expecting obedience and love in response (*Mal. 1:6*). He warns that he will reject them if they reject their father (*v. 18*). Israel is thus his 'firstborn son' and, if he obeys, God protects him. For example, God demands of Pharaoh 'Let my *son* go' (*Exod. 4:22; Hos. 11:1*).

God's fatherhood of Israel means he has the right to expect a responsive loving relationship from the son. Sadly he all too often found a rebellious son. In *Is. 1:2* God says 'I reared children and brought them up, but they have rebelled against me'. However, Isaiah and Jeremiah both look forward to a time when God will be a father to a child who responds. God will thus show them his providential care and love: 'I will lead them beside streams of water on a level path where they will not stumble, because I am Israel's father, and Ephraim is my firstborn son' (*Jer. 31:9*). A humble child will admit that the father has rights: 'O LORD, you are our Father. We are the clay, you are the potter; we are all the work of your hand. Do not be angry beyond measure, O LORD; do not remember our sins forever. Oh, look upon us, we pray, for we are all your people' (*Is. 64:8–9*; also see *45:10–11; 63:16*). As covenant God and Father, when his son calls he will respond: 'He will call out to me, "You are my Father, my God, the Rock my Saviour." . . . I will maintain my love to him forever, and my covenant with him will never fail' (*Ps. 89:26–28*).

God is also Father to the king of Israel in a special way, for the king represents the people. The covenant God made with King David established that God would be 'father' to David's descendants: 'I will be his father, and he will be my son'. The Psalms pick up this theme. For example, *Ps. 2:7* says: 'I will proclaim the decree of the LORD: He said to me, "You are my Son; today I have become your Father."' (See also *Ps. 89:26–27*). Later, these passages about the Son took on messianic significance as people looked forward to the coming of the anointed Davidic King. Indeed they were later applied to Jesus (*Acts 13:33; Heb. 1:5*).

God is uniquely 'Father' to Jesus who is described as God's 'one and only Son' (see *Jesus*). Christ's sonship is attached in Luke to the virgin birth (*Luke 1:35*), but this is not the sum of his sonship. The father specifically speaks of Jesus' sonship at the baptism: 'a voice came from heaven: "You are my Son, whom I love; with you I am well pleased"' (*Mark 1:11*). But this serves to confirm publicly what was already true. Indeed the NT indicates a permanent relationship between God the Father as 'father' and God the Son as 'son'. 'Sonship' is as much part of Jesus' eternal nature as 'fatherhood' is to God the Father. This eternal relationship is indicated in *John*

1:18: 'No one has ever seen God, but God the One and Only, who is at the Father's side, has made him known'. In *John 17:5* Jesus addresses God as 'Father' and looks forward to receiving again the 'glory I had with you before the world began' (see *vv. 24–25; 1 John 4:9*).

Access to God as 'Father' can only occur through Jesus: 'No-one comes to the Father except through me,' says Jesus (*John 14:6*). But this also points the way to God's fatherhood of all Christian believers.

God as Father of all Christian believers is the final part of his fatherhood to be mentioned here. God is 'Father' of all who have faith in Christ. Part of the fulness of salvation, applied to the believer by the Holy Spirit, is that believers are 'adopted' sons (*Rom. 8:23; Eph. 1:5*) and can use the more personal name of 'Abba' ('Father') for God (*Rom. 8:14–17; Gal. 4:6*). It is important to note that in both these texts 'sonship' is also closely linked to inheritance. Just as Jesus, *the* Son, is heir to God's glory, says Paul, so adopted sons are 'co-heirs with Christ, if indeed we share in his sufferings in order that we may also share in his glory' (*Rom. 8:17*). It is possible for all who have faith in Christ to know the Father (*Gal. 3:26*), for Christ shows the Father to them (*John 14:6–9*). Jesus revealed the Father to this world: 'Don't you believe that I am in the Father, and that the Father is in me? The words I say to you are not just my own. Rather, it is the Father, living in me, who is doing his work' (*v. 10*).

Once again the only response appropriate for the Christian is one of doxology at the thought of the possibility of being God's sons: 'How great is the love the Father has lavished on us, that we should be called children of God! And that is what we are! The reason the world does not know us is that it did not know him. Dear friends, now we are children of God, and what we will be has not yet been made known. But we know that when he appears, we shall be like him, for we shall see him as he is' (*1 John 3:1–2*).

## The names of God

Whereas in modern Western cultures a person's name is really only used to distinguish one person from another, personal names in the Bible can be used to represent the whole person or indicate more about their character or role in life (see Introduction, section on 'Names'). Nowhere is this more clearly seen than in the expression 'name of the LORD' which occurs nearly 100 times in Scripture. It is a phrase that summarizes what can never be fully summarized – namely, God himself.

*The Name.* When Gen. 4:26 says, 'At that time men began to call on the name of the LORD', it was not simply that people used the name 'LORD'. The verse indicates that people started worshipping the LORD for all that he is. When the Law of *Exod. 20:7* says: 'You shall not misuse the name of the LORD your God, for the LORD will not hold anyone guiltless who misuses his name', it clearly has in mind more than the occasional blasphemous expression (though, of course, that would come under this prohibition as well). The Law is saying that the LORD himself must not be regarded or treated with disdain. He cannot be treated as the pagan idols mentioned in the previous command. He cannot be appealed to for magical power or referred to in worship that is not centred on him and him alone.

Thus reference to the 'Name' of the LORD carries with it a reference to the nature of God himself. In *Exod. 23:20* the 'Name' of God is present in the angel of the LORD sent to lead the people of Israel. It is thus right to assume that this angel was a 'theophany' in which somehow God was experienced or seen in the presence of the angel (see Theophanies).

When the Bible speaks of 'calling' on the name of the LORD it is usually in the context of an exhortation to worship the LORD fully in the whole of life, to see him for the transcendent and sovereign God he is and yet the loving faithful personal God who is present in every area of his world (e.g. *2 Kings 5:11; Ps. 17:7; Joel 2:32; Zeph. 3:9*).

To do something in the 'name of the LORD' is to do it in the place of God himself or to do it with the full weight of his presence and command. Thus the priests and Levites ministered 'in the Name of the LORD' and prophets spoke 'in the Name of the LORD', not that they claimed to be God but rather to speak and work with his full authority and power behind them. Even King David fought 'in the Name of the LORD' (*Deut. 18:17, 22; 21:5; 1 Sam. 17:45; 1 Kings 18:24* etc.). When the people wished to affirm the presence of God with the ark of the covenant they did so by calling it 'by the Name, the Name of the LORD Almighty' (*2 Sam. 6:2*). Solomon talked of building a temple 'for the Name of the LORD' (*1 Kings 8:20*). The 'Name' is thus a way of describing the fulness, transcendence and presence of God himself.

It is interesting to see that in the NT the 'Name' belongs to Jesus, thus recalling OT Scriptures which referred to all that God is. If the Name is God's and Jesus is called by the 'Name', then all that belongs to God belongs to Jesus and all that God is Jesus also is (e.g. compare *Joel 2:32* with *Acts 2:21; Rom. 10:13*). Just as God's authority and power were drawn together in his 'Name', so it is with Jesus. It is 'in the Name of Jesus' that people are urged towards repentance, baptism and forgiveness, and faith must be 'in the name of Jesus' (*Acts 2:38; 3:16; 9:21*). It is 'in the name of Jesus' that the apostles healed and the church must pray (*Acts 3:6; James 5:14*).

In addition to this all-encompassing way of seeking to refer to the fulness of God himself, several specific names are attributed to God in Scripture and help us understand more about him. Unlike the whole 'name', they emphasize aspects of God's nature and character, thus affirming and adding to what has been laid out above.

*El, Elohim.* A common and general name used of God and usually translated as 'God' is El or Elohim (the plural form). The root of the word probably means 'power'. The word was used in other cultures and religions as well to describe a great god. But in the Bible the name is applied to the one God – El Elohe Israel, 'God, the God of Israel' (*Gen. 33:20*). In the Bible he is the 'God of heaven and earth' (*Gen. 24:3*), 'the God of Abraham, Isaac and Jacob', 'the God of the Hebrews' (*Exod. 3:18*), 'God of gods', 'God of truth' (*Ps. 31:5*) and, of course, 'God of glory' (*Ps. 29:3*).

The plural form sometimes refers to other gods but is also used in Scripture of the one God though the word is in a plural form. The plural form indicates the fulness of the God himself. He is utterly distinct from created people in his being (e.g. *Num. 23:19*).

The name El also appears in forms such as 'El Shaddai' ('God Amighty', *Gen. 17:1; Exod. 6:3*. See section on 'The God of Abraham' in article on *Abraham* for more detail), 'El Elyon' ('Most High', *Deut. 32:8; Dan. 7:18, 22* etc.), 'El Bethel' ('God of Bethel', *Gen. 35:7*), and 'El Olam' ('the Eternal God', *Gen. 21:33*; also see *Ps. 90:2*).

*Yahweh (the* LORD). The name Yahweh, which is translated into English as 'the LORD', has rightly been called 'the covenant name of God'. It is by this name that the God of Abraham, Isaac and Jacob chose to reveal himself to Moses (*Exod. 6:3*). No doubt the faithful followers of the one true God had known him by this name Yahweh prior to the revelation to Moses, but with Moses there is further revelation of the covenant faithfulness of Yahweh and of his close and intimate relationship with his people. The name itself is derived from the Hebrew verb 'to be'. Moses had envisaged people asking him for the name of his God when he went back to his people. God responded to him, 'I AM WHO I AM. This is what you are to say to the Israelites: "I AM has sent me to you"' (*Exod. 3:14*, and see *v. 15*). Yahweh means something like 'He is' or perhaps 'He brings to pass'.

As the revealed name of God, the title 'Yahweh' thus drew on this statement of God's continuing existence and sustaining presence with his people. It was he who came to Moses and to the people of Israel down through the ages as a covenant God, one who would always remain faithful to his promises on behalf of his people. It was under this name that the covenant people worshipped God. In the NT, Christians began to see that the covenant Lord was Jesus Christ and so ideas and attributes from the OT that belonged to Yahweh were drawn over and applied to Jesus. For a detailed discussion of the great significance of this name see LORD, Lord.

*Adonai (Lord)*. Meaning 'Lord' or 'master', it can be applied to human beings in positions of authority. When applied to God, however, it is usually used together with the name 'Yahweh'. This does present some translation difficulties. It is not easy to read the phrase 'The Lord LORD'! Thus the NIV translates 'the sovereign LORD' (e.g. *2 Sam. 7:28; Is. 28:16; 56:8* etc.). See LORD, Lord.

*Rock*. The faithfulness and dependability and saving grace of the covenant God is occasionally described with the epithet, 'Rock' (*Deut. 32:4, 15, 18; 2 Sam. 22:3, 47; Ps. 62:7; Hab. 1:12* etc.).

*Other names*. Although sometimes being taken to be names, many other words applied to God are adjectival. They are used to describe God, to attribute praise to his name, and to distinguish him from pagan gods. *Judg. 6:24* refers to 'the LORD is Peace'. Other texts talk of God as 'the Holy One' or the 'Holy One of Israel', thus establishing a link made time and again in the OT between the holiness of God and the need for his people to be holy (e.g. *Job 6:10; Prov. 9:10; Is. 12:6*). God is also known as the 'King' (see *King*), 'the LORD Almighty', 'the LORD is my Banner', and so on.

*Jehovah*. This name rightly does not appear in the NIV or in most modern English versions of the Bible. However, mention should be made here of a name which lives on in some English-speaking circles as an important name for God. Suffice it to say here that in Hebrew the name YHWH appears and it is right either to translate this, as most do these days, with capitals (LORD) or to put in the vowels, thus reading Yahweh, which some of the contributors to this volume have done. 'Jehovah' comes from a misreading of Yahweh. The background to the problem with the name 'Jehovah' is explained in the entry under LORD, Lord.

## The Trinity

Christianity has traditionally argued that the weight of biblical evidence reveals God as three distinguishable persons. For some, such a definition of God has caused serious problems. The history of the church is scattered with sects who did not view Jesus as God or who refused to accept a trinitarian view of God or who did not view one of the persons of the Trinity as fully God, or who denied distinctions between the persons of the Trinity. Others have fallen foul of the biblical evidence by effectively entering the world of Tri-theism, a notion explicitly denied in, for example, the 'Shema' (*Deut. 6:4*). However, although the term Trinity is not used in the Bible, Christians have always believed that it alone does real justice to the biblical revelation of the 'fulness' of the Godhead. Starting with the OT, Christians point to indications that presage a more detailed NT teaching. Passages point towards a plurality within the God who is 'one God'. Great Messianic passages suggest an identification of the Messiah who is to come with God himself. He will be called the 'Mighty God', he will rule with complete sovereignty and will be 'everlasting' – a divine attribute (*Is. 9:6–7; Ps. 2* etc.). But indications are also present in the OT understanding of creation itself. Although some would deny its significance, it is interesting to note that God refers to himself with the plural 'elohim' in certain passages. In Gen. 1 it is God who creates by his word and by the Spirit (*Gen. 1:1–3*). Sometimes this plural reference seems more notable, being made explicit with the use of plural verbs and pronouns, for example, 'God said "Let us make man in our image"' (*Gen. 1:26*, also *3:22; 11:7*; also see *Is. 6:8*). There is also a personalizing of the creating 'word of the LORD' who created the heavens (*Ps. 33:6*). And something similar occurs in *Prov. 8* in which the wisdom of God is personalized as God working in the world, giving life and involved in creation itself (esp. *Prov. 8:12–21*).

Some suggest the 'Angel of the Lord' is also to be identified with God and yet is distinct from him (e.g. *Exod. 3:2–6*; see also *Angel of the Lord*). In *Is. 63:10–14* the Holy Spirit is identified as God's agent. This sort of evidence waits for its more complete interpretation in the NT. (See also *Theophanies*.)

In the NT aspects of the doctrine of the Trinity surface first as the disciples and followers of Jesus began to recognize the works and words of God in the works and words of Jesus. Indeed the problem for the religious leaders of Jesus' day was that some of the things Jesus did and said could only be done and said by God, and therefore they said he was blaspheming by claiming to be God. For example, Jesus forgave the sins of a paralytic, something the teachers believed only God could do, and was therefore blasphemous, and then proceeded to demonstrate his divine authority by raising the man to health (*Matt. 9:2–6*). John 8 proves specially enlightening in this, drawing together a number of claims by Jesus. His claims to have come from God and been sent by him (*vv. 14, 23*) and to be going to a place which the religious leaders did not know (*v. 14*), combined closely with his use of the phrase 'I am' and his claim to have existed before Abraham (*vv. 24, 28, 58* etc.), all led to a charge of blasphemy and an attempt to stone Jesus – the punishment for blasphemy (*v. 59*). Jesus accepted Peter's confession that he was the Christ (*Mark 8:29–30*) and claimed 'all'

216

authority and power before going on to make one of the clearest trinitarian statements in Scripture: 'Go . . . baptizing in the name of the Father and of the Son and of the Holy Spirit' (*Matt. 28:18*).

Elsewhere in the NT both the Holy Spirit and Jesus are shown to be divine. *John 1:1–14* speaks of Jesus as divine and pre-existent. *Rom. 9:5* is variously punctuated by some scholars but should probably read as in the NIV: 'Christ, who is God over all, be praised' (see also *Col. 2:9; Heb. 1:9–10* etc.). The Holy Spirit is also seen to be God (see, e.g., *Acts 5:3–4; John 15:26; Mark 3:29; 2 Cor. 3:17* etc.).

Of further interest are those passages in the NT where the apostolic writers are able to apply to Jesus the OT name of Yahweh (the LORD). See, for example, *Rom. 10:9–13* where confession of faith in Jesus is proved to be confession of faith in God by reference back to the OT and mention of Yahweh. A number of texts bear careful examination since they seem to draw on the OT understanding of Yahweh and apply this to Jesus or they apply statements concerning Yahweh in the OT to Jesus in the NT. For example, see *John 12:38–41* (compare with *Is. 6:10*); *Acts 2:34–36; 1 Cor. 1:30–31; 1 Cor. 12:3; Phil. 2:9–11* (compare with *Is. 45:23*) etc.

Elsewhere the triune God is at least implied in the text of the NT if not stated. The baptism of Jesus involved the Son, the Father and the Holy Spirit (*Matt. 3:13–17*). The baptism mentioned in *Matt. 28:19* is in the name of the three persons of the Godhead. Jesus refers to the Spirit as 'another Counsellor'. As the Father has sent Jesus, so the Father will give the Spirit (*John 14:15–23*). See also the work of Father, Son and Holy Spirit in the life of the believer (*Eph. 3:14–19*).

The Scriptures reveal a picture of God in three persons and this has been called 'God the Trinity'. The Father is distinct from the Son and both are distinct from the Holy Spirit and yet there is clear teaching in the OT and the NT that God is One. There are three persons but one God. Such teaching, when taken together, implies a mode of existence far removed from anything we can understand. It is for this reason that human analogies will invariably break down when talking of the Trinity.

Christians believe that it is to deny the clear evidence of Scripture about God himself if this doctrine is denied. One writer has summarized the biblical teaching in this way: 'The doctrine of the Trinity does not fully explain the mysterious character of God. Rather it sets the boundaries outside of which we must not step . . . It demands that we be faithful to the biblical revelation that in one sense God is one and in a different sense He is three' (R. C. Sproul).

## Conclusion

The God of the Bible is revealed as eternal, majestic, transcendent, and as the one who is all-powerful and all-knowing. He is also revealed as the Creator of the whole universe and of people and, in this context, he reveals himself in his Word as one who is personal, loving and sovereign, who is righteous, true and just. He is revealed as the Father, the Son and the Holy Spirit. He is revealed as the one who is with his people (Immanuel, 'God with us') and everywhere present in his creation, though in no way absorbed within his creation, as some Eastern religions teach. Though holy, separate and distinct from creation and created people, he does not leave the world to wallow in its sin with no hope of redemption, but rather reveals himself to be a God of love who saves and redeems all who turn to him. His saving grace is seen most clearly in his coming to this earth: Jesus, the Son of God, came to be the Saviour and Redeemer of mankind. His grace continues to be experienced through his Word (the Bible) and the presence of his Holy Spirit in the hearts and lives of those who have faith in him. The more the Bible is read, the clearer it becomes that all his people are obliged again and again to sing the praises of God Almighty who, though transcendent, is involved, sustains, cares and saves. 'To him who is able to keep you from falling and to present you before his glorious presence without fault and with great joy – to the only God our Saviour be glory, majesty, power and authority, through Jesus Christ our Lord, before all ages, now and forevermore! Amen.'

P.D.G.

**GOG 1.** A descendant of Joel and a son of Shemaiah of the tribe of Reuben (1 Chron. 5:4).

**2.** The chief prince of Meshech and Tubal, against whom Ezekiel prophesied (Ezek. 38–39). He ruled the land of Magog and was leader of the hordes of northerners (Ezek. 38:6) that Ezekiel foresaw attacking Israel during the messianic age (vv. 14ff.). These people would plunder and ransack every nation in their way. However, when Gog was about to attack Israel the LORD himself would intervene, said the prophet. He would cause earthquakes and would make brother fight brother and would bring total and devastating judgment on the people led by Gog: 'I will execute judgment upon him with plague and bloodshed; I will pour down torrents of rain, hailstones and burning sulphur on him and on his troops and on the many nations with him. And so I will show my greatness and my holiness, and I will make myself known in the sight of many nations. Then they will know that I am the LORD' (Ezek. 38:22–23).

Gog has been identified with Gyges of Lydia, with Gaga, a Babylonian deity, and with various other figures. Although Ezekiel probably had a particular leader in mind, the significance lies not so much in the person as the fact that the sovereign LORD would destroy all his enemies and the enemies of his people in the last days.

There would be a final desperate attempt to destroy Israel, but it would not succeed. In that final age the full power and glory of God would be seen both by Israel (who would be brought back by God from Exile) and by all the nations around. Ezekiel's message from the LORD for that age to come was this: 'I will no longer hide my face from them, for I will pour out my Spirit on the house of Israel, declares the Sovereign LORD' (Ezek. 39:29).

**3.** Following Ezekiel's prophecy, 'God and Magog' became symbolic names for all those who would try to destroy God's people in the messianic age. In Rev. 20:7–10 the ultimate defeat of Satan is described. In that defeat all those who are evil and have fought against the LORD's people will also be destroyed. Gog and Magog represent those hordes set against the reign of Christ.

P.D.G.

**GOLIATH,** a giant warrior representing the Philistines whom David killed with a stone from his sling in the latter part of King Saul's reign (1 Sam. 17). He was called a 'champion . . . from Gath'. His height is recorded as 'over nine feet tall' (about 3 metres, assuming a measure of a 'cubit' as about 45 cms.). It is likely that he was employed by the Philistines and may have been a descendant of the Rephaim or Anakim (see Anak). The text describes the weight of his armour in some detail and says his spear 'was like a weaver's rod', thus further emphasizing the giant's stature (1 Sam. 17:5–7).

The armies of the Philistines and Israelites faced each other across the Valley of Elah. Each day Goliath would walk out into the valley and shout up a challenge to the Israelites. If anyone could beat him in single combat, then the Philistines would submit to Israel. If the Israelite lost, then Goliath would expect the Israelites to submit to the Philistines. The challenge of one champion to another in this way was a method of dealing with battles that was commonly accepted in those days.

David came to the battle area as a young lad commissioned by his father to take food to his brothers, who were part of the Israelite army. He heard the challenge and asked what was going on and who was going to do anything about it. In fact Saul and his army were too frightened to take on the challenge. David was horrified that an 'uncircumcised Philistine' should be allowed to 'defy the armies of the living God' (1 Sam. 17:25–26). So he volunteered to take on the challenge himself. He went to see Saul, who thought the whole idea of young, small David taking on Goliath was absurd. David recounted events in his life where he had had to show his courage as a shepherd in his father's fields. But most impressive in David's argument with Saul was his emphasis that God would be with him, for it was the LORD God who had helped him before.

Saul eventually allowed David to go, but insisted that he dress in Saul's own armour, which turned out to be much too big. David took it off, picked up five smooth stones from a stream and went off to meet Goliath with a sling and his stones in his shepherd's pouch (1 Sam. 17:40). The Philistines were insulted that a young boy should be sent out to them, and Goliath made fearful threats against David. David's response was of great significance and pointed forward to the sort of king that he would one day become. He argued that while Goliath came with spear and javelin, he came 'in the name of the LORD Almighty, the God of the armies of Israel' (1 Sam. 17:45). It was God who would deliver Goliath into David's hands. But not only the Philistines were to learn about the LORD's power – so would the Israelites, for David continued: 'All those gathered here will know that it is not by sword or spear that the LORD saves; for the battle is the LORD's, and he will give all of you into our hands' (1 Sam. 17:47).

Goliath was killed by a stone slung with force and great accuracy by David right into the giant's forehead. David then cut off Goliath's head with his own sword. The Philistines were chased and defeated by the Israelites. Through this victory David's reputation was established, and very quickly Saul saw him as a threat (1 Sam. 18).

As this episode is recounted it becomes clear that the author is concerned for the development of three different relationships: between David and Goliath representing the Philistines; between David and Saul and his armies; and between David and the LORD God. David so trusted in the Almighty LORD that he knew he could have confidence in accepting the challenge of the 'uncircumcised' Philistines. For David, the Philistines represented a nation in rebellion against God. Anyone who stood against the LORD Almighty would be judged by the LORD, and David well anticipated the result by his faith. David also found himself at odds with the Israelites, who had not shown such faith. It seems that almost reluctantly Saul said to David: 'Go, and the LORD be with you.' Later Saul's reaction becomes evident as he regarded the killing of Goliath as evidence that the LORD was with David but not with him (1 Sam. 18:12). Indeed, it was the anger and jealousy of Saul at David's success that led to 'an evil spirit from God' coming on Saul (1 Sam. 18:10).

David's reliance on the LORD indicated his depth of faith and the relationship of trust that he had with his LORD. The LORD blessed David, and from this time forward David comes to the fore in the narrative as God's blessings on him become deeper and deeper. Goliath, the strong and big, had been defeated by the power of God in one who was young and weak. Later Goliath's sword was taken to Nob, where it was hidden by Ahimelech the priest and given back to David when he needed it for fighting (1 Sam. 21:9–10)

P.D.G.

**GOMER 1.** The first son of Japheth and grandson of Noah (Gen. 10:2–3; 1 Chron. 1:5–6). Gomer is mentioned again in Ezek. 38:6. There 'Gomer with all its troops' will join Gog in an attack on Israel but will be destroyed by Israel, on whose side the LORD will be fighting. See Gog.

**2.** Another Gomer was the wife of Hosea and daughter of Diblaim. Hosea, the prophet, lived in the 8th century BC. God called him to marry Gomer, a prostitute. Although Hosea rescued her from her trade, she quickly reverted to it and took other lovers. Finally she effectively became the slave of one of her lovers. Hosea left her but later was ordered by God to buy her back with the price that would have been paid for a slave (Hos. 1:2–3; 3:1–3). She had children who were given symbolic names: Jezreel (because God would soon punish the house of Jehu, Hos. 1:4); Lo-Ruhamah (because God would no longer show love to Israel, v. 6); Lo-Ammi (because 'you are not my people and I am not your God', v. 9).

Part of God's calling to Hosea was that he should act out in his own marriage the relationship that was so typical of God and his people Israel. God had called Israel from being no-one to be someone and to be loved by him. Yet Israel had rebelled again and again going after other gods: an action frequently referred to as adultery. God had repeatedly drawn her back to himself, even though there had been times when he had cut himself off from his people as part of their punishment.

The story of Hosea's life is profoundly sad: a wife whom he dearly loved and yet who continually turned elsewhere. It was a living prophecy of the profound 'sadness' experienced so often by God as his people were attracted elsewhere. Yet God's covenantal love for his people endures, and the love of Hosea for Gomer stands as a vivid picture that God will not let his people go unloved but will remain faithful to his promises. Eventually God did redeem them with the awesome price of his own Son who died for his people, paying the price for their sin (Is. 49:7; Luke 1:68; 24:21).

P.D.G.

**THE GOOD SAMARITAN** The parable of the Good Samaritan is unique to Luke's Gospel (10:25–37). To appreciate the characterization, it is important to realize that to a Jewish audience a Samaritan was a reprobate to the faith, a type of racial 'half-breed', since he had mixed Jewish-Gentile blood and represented a defection from Judaism (see Samaritans). The fact that such a 'half-breed' could show compassion was a surprise in the parable. So much so that when the lawyer replied to Jesus' question about whether the priest, the Levite or the Samaritan showed mercy to the man hit by the robbers, he could not even mention the Samaritan's race. The parable teaches two truths. First, one is to be a caring neighbour, as the Samaritan was. Rather than ask, 'Who is my neighbour?' Jesus says we should simply 'Be a neighbour.' Second, neighbours sometimes come from surprising places. The lawyer would never have expected a Samaritan to be an example, yet he was. Jesus was saying, do not wall people off simply because of their race. Sometimes a good neighbour has surprising roots.

D.B.

**GREEK/GREEKS** This term is primarily a racial term in the Bible, though it refers to slightly different groups depending on the context in which it appears. In the OT (NIV) the word 'Greeks' appears twice (Ezek. 27:19; Joel 3:6). There it probably refers to people from Greece with whom the Israelites traded.

Sometimes it simply describes a person of Greek origin (Mark 7:25; Acts 16:1; Timothy; Gal. 2:3, Titus). Elsewhere it appears to be describing Jews who live in a Hellenistic cultural context – that is, Jews whose culture is primarily Greek, not Semitic (Acts 6:1; 9:29, using the Greek term hellēnistēs). In other settings it refers to 'God-fearers', Greeks who had associated with Judaism (John 12:20; Acts 14:1, using the Greek term Hellēn). In the latter half of Acts, it refers to non-Jews (Acts 17:4, 12; 18:4; 19:10, 17; 20:21). Their inclusion in the faith was controversial for Jews, who sought to exclude Gentiles from equal participation, as the false charge against Paul about polluting the Temple with a Gentile's presence makes clear (Acts 21:28). But the predominant usage in the NT is in contrast to the Jews and refers to the racial scope of the gospel including those outside of Israel. Often it is noted that it is on the same terms that Jews and Greeks have need of Christ and on the same terms that they enter in and share participation in the gospel (Rom. 1:14, 16; 2:9–10; 3:9; 10:12; 1 Cor. 1:24; 10:32; 12:13; Gal. 3:28; Col. 3:11). Thus the term often signifies the scope of God's grace in including all ethnicities in his offer of the gospel.                           D.B.

**GUNI 1.** A son of Naphtali and a grandson of Jacob, Guni became leader of the Gunite clan (Gen. 46:24; Num. 26:48; 1 Chron. 7:13).

**2.** One of the Gadites who lived in Bashan. A son of Abdiel, he was a family leader (1 Chron. 5:15).

# H

**HAAHASHTARI** Mentioned in *1 Chron.* 4:6, he was one of the sons of Ashhur and Naarah of the tribe of Judah.

**HABAKKUK** (Heb., 'embraced'). Little or nothing can be known about the prophet Habakkuk explicitly, but one may infer certain things. First, he was not only a prophet but a gifted poet as well. In fact, his little book consists of a set of oracles (*Hab. 1–2*) and a prayer (*Hab. 3*) of a kind comparable to *Ps. 7* (*cf. Hab. 3:1*) and *Pss. 4* and *6* (*Hab. 3:19*). Moreover, there is some suggestion that Habakkuk was involved in Temple ministry, perhaps to the extent of being a Levite. Besides the allusions to musical instruments and music directors (*Hab. 3:19*) – both of which were central to Temple worship – he speaks of Yahweh being in the Temple (*Hab. 2:20*) and also employs the liturgical term *Selah* (*Hab. 3:3, 9, 13*).

What can be known more surely is that Habakkuk lived and ministered on the eve of Babylonia's rise to power in the Near Eastern world. Yahweh says that he is 'raising up the Babylonians' (*Hab. 1:6*), the verb form suggesting something already underway. The first unmistakable sign of this took place in 626 BC with the inauguration of Nabopolassar's kingship over Babylon. By 605 BC he and his son Nebuchadnezzar had completely eliminated Assyria from the arena of history and had set up the mighty Chaldean Empire. Habakkuk was witnessing this with his own eyes, apparently after Babylonia's might was already fully displayed (*Hab. 1:7–11*). A date between 620–612 BC would appear reasonable in light of all these circumstances.

It is the imminent coming of the Babylonians against Judah that gives rise to one of the major theological issues of the book, namely, how it is that the wicked (i.e. the Babylonians) can prosper and the righteous (i.e. Judah) can suffer if God is a God of justice (*Hab. 1:2–4*). It is the problem of theodicy, the same concern that occupies so much of the debate in the book of Job. The answer lies in the character of God who in time will, indeed, vindicate his own. Meanwhile, God informs the prophet, 'the righteous will live by his faith' (*Hab. 2:4*), a theological resolution picked up by Paul (*Rom. 1:17*; *Gal. 3:11*) as constituting the very heart and basis of salvation. What appears unfair and unjust in the here and now will find perfect redress in the time of God's ultimate reconciliation. E.M.

**HABAZZINIAH,** the grandfather of Jaazaniah, and a member of the Recabite family (*Jer. 35:3*). For more on this passage and the Recabite family see *Jaazaniah*.

**HACALIAH,** the father of Nehemiah (*Neh. 1:1; 10:1*). See *Nehemiah*.

**HACMONI,** the father of Jehiel (*1 Chron. 27:32*). Jehiel was one of King David's overseers and 'took care of the king's sons'.

**HADAD 1.** A son of Ishmael and grandson of Abraham and Hagar, he was a leader of his clan (*Gen. 25:15; 1 Chron. 1:30*).

**2.** Hadad son of Bedad became the king of Edom following the death of Husham (*Gen. 36:35–36; 1 Chron. 1:46–47*). He was renowned for his defeat of the Midianites in Moab. He lived in Avath and on his death was succeeded by Samlah. This was at a time before Israel had a king (*Gen. 36:31*).

**3.** Another Hadad, king of Edom, followed Baal-Hanan. His city was called Pau, and his wife's name was Mehetabel daughter of Matred (*Gen. 36:39; 1 Chron. 1:50–51*).

**4.** Hadad the Edomite, 'from the royal line of Edom', was raised up by the LORD to be an adversary for King Solomon (*1 Kings 11:14*). Solomon had been given great prosperity and wisdom while he relied totally upon the LORD during the early years of his reign. However, as he became more influential in the world, so came the temptation to marry into other royal families, no doubt mainly for political reasons. Each wife would have brought her own gods into Jerusalem. Thus not only did Solomon break God's Law in marrying foreign women but in doing so he broke further laws by allowing the introduction of foreign deities into his capital city (see *Josh. 23:12–13; Deut. 7:3*). Solomon's marriages with foreign women caused the LORD to be angry. Gradually these wives drew 'his heart after other gods' (*1 Kings 11:4–6*). He was in clear breach of his covenant duties given to him after he had finished building the Temple (*1 Kings 9:6–9*).

Under David the men of Edom had been wiped out, however, Hadad, still a young lad, had fled to Egypt where he had married one of Pharaoh's daughters, Tahpenes. His son, Genubath, lived in the Egyptian court. When Hadad heard that David was dead, he returned to fight Solomon and effectively wage guerrilla warfare against him. As the writer was only interested in showing how Solomon was being punished by God, we hear no more of Hadad, but it seems he probably resettled in Edom and continued to fight Solomon from time to time throughout the rest of Solomon's reign (*1 Kings 11:14–25*)          P.D.G.

**HADADEZER** son of Rehob was a king of Zobah who lived during David's time. His kingdom apparently stretched from near the river Euphrates down as far as Ammon and therefore was one of the Aramean (Syrian) kingdoms. On several occasions he fought King David. The first battle is mentioned in a long list of David's victories from the early part of his reign. Hadadezer had travelled north to restore his control in an area along the Euphrates. David attacked and nearly wiped out his army. When Syrians came to Hadadezer's aid, David attacked and defeated many of their towns as well (*2 Sam. 8:3–14; 1 Chron. 18:3–10*). The silver and gold he captured David dedicated to the LORD. When other kings heard that Hadadezer's army had been killed, they too came to pay tribute to David.

Another account of Hadadezer's exploits is given in *2 Sam. 10:15–19*. Again Hadadezer tried to make an alliance with the Syrians against David, but David defeated their combined forces to the extent that those kings who had been Hadadezer's vassals came and made their peace with David instead (also *1 Chron. 19:19*).          P.D.G.

**HADASSAH** was the Heb. name (meaning 'myrtle') of Esther (*Est. 2:7*). She was an orphan who had been brought up by her cousin Mordecai and is described as 'lovely in form and features'. See *Esther, Mordecai* and *Hegai*.

**HADLAI** was the father of Amasa, who led the tribe of Ephraim during the reign of King Pekah of Israel (*2 Chron. 28:12*). Amasa is mentioned in Scripture because he was one of those leaders who went out to meet Pekah's troops returning north from winning a battle against the Southern Kingdom of Judah. These men relayed a message from the LORD through a prophet called Oded, that the Northern Kingdom was also guilty of sin and so the men of Israel should release any captives they had taken from among their southern brethren (*vv. 9–15*).

**HADORAM 1.** A descendant of Shem and a son of Joktan (*Gen. 10:27; 1 Chron. 1:21*).

**2.** The son of Tou, king of Hamath. When King David defeated Hadadezer, Tou sent Hadoram to David 'to greet him and congratulate him on his victory'. He took with him many presents of precious metals (*1 Chron. 18:10*). In line with David's deep faith and his thankfulness to the LORD for these various victories he had won, he dedicated all the gifts he received to the LORD. This passage recounts several victories and reminds readers that David's victories were always part of the LORD's blessing (e.g. *v. 13*).

**HAGAB** His descendants were among those listed in Ezra who returned from Exile in Babylon with Nehemiah and Zerubbabel (*Ezra 2:46*).

**HAGABA** His descendants were among the Temple servants recorded in *Neh. 7:48* who returned from Exile in Babylon with Zerubbabel and Nehemiah.

**HAGABAH,** mentioned in *Ezra 2:45*, was the same person as *Hagaba* in *Neh. 7:48*.

**HAGAR** Within the legal norms of the time, the childless Sarai proposed that her husband Abram should take a secondary wife through whom Sarai might 'build a family' (*Gen. 16:1–2*). But although legally permissible this was spiritually disastrous, for it contradicted the way of obedient, patient faith in the

promises of God (*Gen. 15:3–4*). The consequences were tragic – to Hagar (*Gen. 16:6; 21:14–16*), to Abraham (*Gen. 21:11; cf. 17:18*), who loved his son, and to Sarah, who henceforth nourished a bitter, unrelentingly jealous spirit (*Gen. 16:5f.; 21:10*). But the LORD met with the broken in heart: he hears our misery (*Gen. 16:11; 21:17*), satisfies our needs (*Gen. 21:19*) and secures the future (*Gen. 21:20*). Hagar had a blessing never recorded of Sarah: a personal revelation of God in condescending grace (*Gen. 16:13*).

J.A.M.

**HAGGAI** (Heb., 'feast, festival'). Practically nothing is known of the prophet except for his chronological setting and the nature of his ministry and message, namely, to encourage the rebuilding of the Temple in Jerusalem following the Babylonian Exile. The early part of the prophecy is damning of those who have returned from Babylon for looking after themselves before starting on the Temple (*Hag. 1:4*). Haggai, who is called 'the LORD's messenger' (*v. 13*), is explicit in dating his various messages, all of which fall between the first day of the sixth month (Elul) of King Darius of Persia's second year (29 Aug. 520 BC) and the 24th day of the ninth month (Kislev) of the same year (18 Dec. 520). Thus, all of Haggai's recorded ministry in the book that bears his name took place in less than four months.

Ezra provides additional information to the effect that Haggai and Zechariah not only provided the impetus to rebuild the Temple (*Ezra 5:1*) but stayed with the project, apparently until its completion more than four years later (*Ezra 6:14–15*). Haggai makes no reference to this later phase of the work. The older ones present at the building remembered Solomon's Temple and its glory. The one they were now building would never match that one. However, Haggai's prophecy encouraged the workers to anticipate a future day more glorious than that of the completion of the present Temple. He envisioned one that would attract the riches and worship of the nations (*Hag. 2:6–9*) and, in the person of Zerubbabel, saw a messianic figure who would rule over the kingdoms as God's Servant King (*vv. 20–23*).  E.M.

**HAGGEDOLIM** He was the father of Zabdiel, the chief officer of 128 men who settled in Jerusalem after the Babylonian Exile (*Neh. 11:14*).

**HAGGI** One of the sons of Gad listed in *Gen. 46:16* among those who went with Jacob into Egypt. His descendants were called Haggites (*Num. 26:15*).

**HAGGIAH** (Heb., 'the LORD's feast'), a Levite who was a son of Shimea (*1 Chron. 6:30*). He was a descendant of the Merari family.

**HAGGITH** (Heb., 'festive'), the mother of Adonijah and one of King David's wives (*2 Sam. 3:4; 1 Kings 1:5, 11; 2:13; 1 Chron. 3:2*). Haggith's son was born to her while David's court was in Hebron and was David's fourth son born there. He later tried to usurp the throne.

**HAGRI,** the grandfather of Igal. Igal was one of David's 'Thirty' mighty warriors (*2 Sam. 23:36*, but see the footnote there for an alternative name). Hagri was father of Mibhar, also listed among David's 'mighty men' (*1 Chron. 11:38*).

**HAKKATAN** (Heb., 'little one'), the father of Johanan. Johanan was one of the heads of family who returned from Babylon to Jerusalem with the prophet Ezra (*Ezra 8:12*).

**HAKKOZ 1.** One of the priests appointed to minister in the Temple. The turn of service was decided by lots, and the seventh lot fell to Hakkoz (*1 Chron. 24:10*).

**2.** His descendants came back from Exile with Nehemiah but were unable to find their family records and so were excluded from the priesthood (*Ezra 2:61; Neh. 7:63*).

**3.** His grandson Meremoth repaired a section of the Fish Gate after the Exile (*Neh. 3:4*) and also repaired a section of the wall from the entrance of Eliashib's house to the end of it (*Neh. 3:21*). Perhaps he was the same person as 2. above.

**HAKUPHA** His descendants were among the Temple servants who came back to Jerusalem from Exile in Babylon with Nehemiah (*Ezra 2:51; Neh. 7:53*).

**HALLOHESH** (Heb., 'whisperer').
**1.** His son Shallum ruled a half district of Jerusalem in the days of Nehemiah and repaired a section of the walls of Jerusalem (*Neh. 3:12*).
**2.** He was one of the leaders of the people who joined Nehemiah in a binding agreement to worship the LORD and obey his Law (*Neh. 10:24*). Perhaps he was the same person as 1. above.

**HAM** Unlike Japheth, whose story he parallels until after the Flood, Ham, by his reaction to Noah's lapse, brought a curse on his family (*Gen. 9:20–25*). His offence was unfilial behaviour in publicizing his father's disgrace (*v. 22*). In cursing not Ham, but his son Canaan, Noah mirrored the existing situation: as he had a son who disgraced him, so let it be with Ham! And, as the scriptural history develops, so it was: Ham's descendants 'Mizrain' (Egypt) and 'Canaan' (*Gen. 10:6*) are both condemned for abhorrent sexual practices (*Lev. 18:3ff.*). In the later Canaan of the book of Joshua, the earlier Canaan, son of Ham, certainly became enslaved to the sons of Shem.  J.A.M.

**HAMAN,** son of Hammedatha, served in the highest position under King Xerxes of

Persia (*Est.* 3–7). When Mordecai, a Jew, refused to bow in homage to Haman, Haman grew angry and began to plot against Mordecai and all of the Jews. He persuaded the King to issue a decree for the complete annihilation of the Jews by arguing that they disobeyed the King's laws. Mordecai learned of the plot and sought help from his cousin, Queen Esther. Esther had never before confessed her Jewish heritage and she knew that such a confession might mean her own death. Still, Esther chose to help God's people. The Queen invited King Xerxes and Haman to a banquet which Haman supposed was for his own honour. Instead, Esther revealed Haman's plot and asked the King to spare the Jews from death. In a rage, King Xerxes got up and went into the garden, whereupon Haman threw himself down beside Esther, asking mercy. The King returned and thought Haman was molesting his wife, and immediately ordered Haman to be hanged on a gallows he had prepared for Mordecai (*Est.* 7). The King then complied with Esther's request, issuing a parallel decree that the Jews be allowed to defend themselves (*Est.* 9). The Jews survived and give thanks to this day for the LORD's victory over Haman in a feast called Purim. Haman's wife was Zaresh and his sons were later killed by the Jewish people.                          S.C.

**HAMMEDATHA** (Persian, 'given by the moon'), the father of the evil man Haman (*Est.* 3:1, 10 etc.). Haman was an 'Agagite' (*Est.* 8:5) and sought to kill all the Jews in the Persian empire of King Xerxes at the time of Queen Esther. God used Esther and her cousin Mordecai to thwart Haman's plans.

**HAMMOLEKETH,** the sister of Gilead and the daughter of Makir, who had three sons, Ishhod, Abiezer and Mahlah. She was from the tribe of Manasseh (*1 Chron.* 7:18).

**HAMMUEL** was a son of Mishma and was from the tribe of Simeon (*1 Chron.* 4:26).

**HAMOR,** the father of Shechem, who got caught up in defending his evil son (*Gen.* 34). He was a Hivite ruler of the area around Shechem (*v.* 2). He first appears in *Gen.* 33:19. Jacob bought a field for burial from Hamor's sons. This field is later mentioned in *Josh.* 24:32 when, on his death, Joseph's bones were brought back to the plot in Shechem for burial (see *Acts* 7:16).

Hamor's son raped Jacob's daughter Dinah and then asked his father to negotiate a marriage to her with Jacob's family. Jacob's sons were furious when they heard what had happened. Not only was the rape a most serious matter, but it could hardly be put right by intermarriage with Canaanites! In fact the brothers agreed to the suggestion, on the condition that all the men of Hamor's city should be circumcised. This was agreed. The circumcisions took place and three days later, 'while all of them were still in pain' (*Gen.* 34:25), Dinah's brothers, Simeon and Levi, attacked the men and killed them all. Hamor and his son Shechem died in the onslaught (*v.* 26).

The 'men of Hamor' mentioned in *Judg.* 9:28 were those who lived in Shechem, and at that time they were roundly defeated at the hands of Abimelech.

The events recounted concerning Hamor and his son and the people of Shechem demonstrate the lasting problems that the Israelites had with the Canaanites whom they had not destroyed on entering the land.                          P.D.G.

**HAMUL,** one of Judah's grandsons through his fourth son Perez (*Gen.* 46:12; *1 Chron.* 2:5). He was the head of what became the Hamulite clan (*Num.* 26:21). Hamul is listed among those who went with Jacob to Egypt.

**HAMUTAL** was the wife of King Josiah of

Judah, and became the mother of King Jehoahaz. She was the daughter of Jeremiah from Libnah (2 Kings 23:31). Jehoahaz only ruled three months in Jerusalem. She was also the mother of King Zedekiah, who ruled for eleven years (2 Kings 24:18; Jer. 52:1).

**HANAMEL** was the prophet Jeremiah's cousin and the son of Shallum. While Jerusalem was beseiged by the Babylonians, Jeremiah prophesied that Nebuchadnezzar would conquer and they would be taken into captivity. Zedekiah objected most strongly to such pessimistic talk. However, the LORD told Jeremiah that he should go and buy a field in Anathoth in Benjamin from Hanamel (Jer. 32). Jeremiah did this and paid Hanamel a suitable price for the land and entered into a formal deed (vv. 9, 12). As he then prayed over the dreadful circumstances they were facing, so the LORD spoke to him and showed him that it was his will to judge his people for their sin, but it would also be his will in the future to gather his people back to the land and there would once again be buying and selling of fields and they would live in peace. The purchase thus became a picture of Jeremiah's trust in the LORD's word and in the future mapped out by God himself (vv. 15, 37–44).          P.D.G.

**HANAN 1.** A son of Shashak, recorded in the genealogy of Saul (1 Chron. 8:23).

**2.** A son of Azel, recorded in the genealogy of Saul (1 Chron. 8:38).

**3.** A son of Maacah and one of David's mighty men (1 Chron. 11:43).

**4.** His descendants were among the Temple servants who returned to Jerusalem from Exile in Babylon with Nehemiah (Ezra 2:46; Neh. 7:49).

**5.** One of the Levites who instructed the people in the Book of the Law (Neh. 8:7).

**6.** One of the Levites who joined Nehemiah in a binding agreement to worship the LORD and obey his Law (Neh. 10:10).

**7.** One of the leaders who sealed the agreement of the people (Neh. 10:22).

**8.** Another of the leaders who sealed the agreement of the people (Neh. 10:26).

**9.** The assistant to Shelemiah, Zadok and Pedariah, whom Nehemiah put in charge of the storerooms (Neh. 13:13).

**10.** The son of Igdaliah the man of God. Hanan's sons had a side room at the Temple, where Jeremiah invited the Recabite family to drink some wine (Jer. 35:4). See Recab.          M.P.

**HANANI 1.** Father of Jehu, who spoke the Word of the LORD against Baasha (1 Kings 16:1, 7) and also spoke to Jehoshaphat and warned him of the LORD's wrath (2 Chron. 19:2). He recorded the events of Jehoshaphat's reign (2 Chron. 20:34).

**2.** Son of Heman, who performed the ministry of prophesying accompanied by harps, lyres and cymbals (1 Chron. 25:4). The 18th lot fell to him, his sons and relatives (1 Chron. 25:25).

**3.** A seer who spoke to King Asa and rebuked him for not trusting in God. In response Asa had him imprisoned (2 Chron. 16:7).

**4.** His descendants were among the descendants of priests who had married foreign women (Ezra 10:20).

**5.** Brother of Nehemiah, who came to him from Judah and gave details about those who had survived the Exile (Neh. 1:2). Nehemiah put him in charge of Jerusalem as the wall was being built (Neh. 7:2).

**6.** One of Zechariah's associates who played musical instruments during the dedication of the wall of Jerusalem (Neh. 12:36).

**HANANIAH** (Heb., 'the LORD shows grace or favour').

**1.** Hananiah, the son of Zerubbabel, the leader of the Jews after the Babylonian

Exile, is mentioned only in *1 Chron. 3:19, 21.*

**2.** Hananiah, a descendant of Benjamin is referred to only in *1 Chron. 8:24* in the genealogy of King Saul.

**3.** Hananiah, a son of Heman, is mentioned in *1 Chron. 25:4, 23.* He was involved in the ministry of prophesying with musical accompaniment during the reign of King David. See *Heman* for more detail.

**4.** Hananiah, a royal official under King Uzziah, is mentioned only in *2 Chron. 26:11.*

**5.** Hananiah, a false prophet, is referred to eight times in *Jer. 28.* He was son of Azzur from Gideon. In the presence of the prophet Jeremiah and various priests he prophesied the imminent demise of the Babylonians. Such prophecy was popular but wrong. Jeremiah showed the evil of Hananiah in causing people to believe a lie and predicted his death within a year (*Jer. 28:15–17*). Within seven months the false prophet was dead.

**6.** Hananiah, father of a Jewish official in the time of Jeremiah, is found only in *Jer. 36:12.*

**7.** Hananiah, grandfather of the captain of the guard in Jerusalem in the time of Jeremiah, is mentioned only in *Jer. 37:13.*

**8.** Hananiah, the Jewish friend of Daniel, is mentioned in *Dan. 1:6, 19* and *2:17.* Though his name is not stated, his act of faith in disobeying King Nebuchadnezzar and living through the fiery furnace (*Dan. 3*) is honoured in the NT in *Heb. 11:34.* See *Shadrach.*

**9.** Hananiah, a Jew guilty of intermarriage with foreigners at the time of Ezra, is spoken of only in *Ezra 10:28.*

**10.** This Hananiah was a perfume-maker who helped repair Jerusalem's walls in the time of Nehemiah (*Neh. 3:8*).

**11.** Possibly the same as 10. above, this Hananiah helped repair the walls above the horse gate (*Neh. 3:30*).

**12.** Mentioned in *Neh. 7:2,* this Hananiah was 'commander of the citadel' and 'a man of integrity' who 'feared God more than most men do'. Nehemiah appointed him governor of Jerusalem along with his brother, Hanani.

**13.** Hananiah, a leader of the Jews who was one of those that sealed the binding agreement in the time of Nehemiah, is referred to in *Neh. 10:23.*

**14.** Hananiah, head of a priestly family in the time of Nehemiah, is mentioned in *Neh. 12:12, 41.* He was a trumpet player during the worship at the dedication of the city walls. He may have been a descendant of 3. above.

A.B.L. and P.D.G.

## HANNAH

Israel's renowned prophet/judge Samuel, is the primary focus of the opening chapters of *1 Samuel.* But before his birth in *1 Sam. 1:20,* the reader is intimately introduced to his godly mother, Hannah. The reader is immediately drawn to her and made to witness her trials, sufferings, vow, and sacrifice.

Hannah's life, though mentioned only in the first two chapters of *1 Sam.*, speaks loudly. She stands, to this day, as a supreme example of devotion and sacrifice and she teaches us what true commitment to the LORD of the universe really means.

Hannah was the beloved wife of Elkanah, a Zuphite (a descendant of Kohath, son of Levi). They lived in Ramathaim in the territory of Ephraim (*1 Sam. 1:1*). Elkanah had another wife, Peninnah, who had born him several children. But Hannah was childless (*1 Sam. 1:2*).

Elkanah and his entire family went up yearly to Shiloh in order to worship the

LORD and to offer sacrifices. Elkanah loved Hannah deeply and gave her a double portion of the LORD's offering. But this did not console Hannah because, on these annual journeys, she was continually provoked and harassed by Peninnah (1 *Sam.* 1:1–7). The LORD had closed Hannah's womb and her rival kept inciting her, bringing her to tears.

On one of those occasions in Shiloh, after finishing her meal, Hannah went up to the Tabernacle of the LORD. In the anguish and bitterness of her soul, Hannah poured out her heart before God. Through many tears she prayed and asked the LORD for a son. She vowed to give him over to the LORD all the days of his life (1 *Sam.* 1:9–11).

This was no simple dedication. This vow meant that she was surrendering her privilege to raise him in her home. He would become a Nazirite, wholly devoted to the service of the LORD. This was an incredible promise made by Hannah. She would offer the LORD her only son, giving up her heart's desire to raise and nurture a child.

Eli, the high priest, who was sitting at the door of the Tabernacle, observed Hannah closely as she prayed and wept. Her lips were moving, but no words could be heard. He accused her of being drunk and reprimanded her concerning the immorality of such habits (1 *Sam.* 1:12–14). But she appropriately defended herself and Eli quickly turned his cursing into a blessing and bid her peace (1 *Sam.* 1:15–17).

Having received encouragement from Eli and comfort from the LORD, Hannah was no longer downcast. She, her husband, and Peninnah arose early the next morning, worshipped the LORD, and returned to Ramah. In due course, the LORD granted Hannah's request and she conceived and gave birth to Samuel (his name means 'asked of the LORD'; (1 *Sam.* 1:19–20). He was truly an answer to prayer.

Eventually, the time came for Hannah to make good her word. After weaning Samuel (ancient Heb. women breast-fed their children until they were two or three years old), she made preparations to bring him to the Tabernacle of the LORD in Shiloh. She brought with her a three-year-old bull, an ephah of flour, and a skin of wine for sacrifice. Then she presented Samuel to the high priest, Eli (1 *Sam.* 1:24–27).

The boy Samuel was to live under Eli's supervision and minister at the LORD's Tabernacle all the days of his life (1 *Sam.* 1:28). Every year his mother made him a little robe and brought it to him when she and her husband went to offer sacrifices (1 *Sam.* 2:19). The LORD was gracious to Hannah and she later bore Elkanah three sons and two daughters (1 *Sam.* 2:21).

Hannah was an extraordinary woman of integrity, faith, and commitment. She kept her vow at tremendous personal cost and has become a model for every generation.

Because it reveals the true heart and character of this noble woman, Hannah's prayer in 1 *Sam.* 2:1–11 deserves some attention. Also known as Hannah's song, this prayer contains many of the same elements found in other OT prayers/songs including combat motifs, deliverance from enemies, and the LORD's providential care for his people, Israel (e.g. *the Song of Moses, Exod.* 15:1–18; *Deut.* 32:1–43; *the Song of Deborah, Judg.* 5). There is also a strong emphasis on God's sovereignty and everlasting power.

Her hymn of victory and triumph certainly applies to the nation of Israel and is, in essence, Messianic (1 Sam. 2:10). Indeed, Mary's song in *Luke 2* seems, in part to be modelled on Hannah's song. But Hannah's song of praise and thanksgiving is probably more intimate in nature. The LORD gave *her* the victory and delivered her from Peninnah, her personal enemy.

The contrasts between the warrior and the weakling, the full and the hungry, the barren woman and the one who had many children (1 Sam. 2:4–5) bears out the fact that Hannah is rejoicing in her personal triumph.

Hannah humbly sought the LORD and waited for his deliverance. Therefore, the LORD eventually blessed her with six children. 1 Sam. 2:5a speaks of the childless woman having seven children; but, in the Scriptures, the number 'seven' is not always meant to be taken literally and can often symbolize 'completion or ideal'. Hence, Hannah was probably thinking of herself when she penned this verse.

Peninnah, on the other hand, was proud and arrogant. She who had many children will be stripped of her vitality and waste away (1 Sam. 2:5b). Ultimately, she will be destroyed along with all of the enemies of God (vv. 3, 9–10).

The prayer of Hannah is truly a sacrifice of thanksgiving to the God who rescued her from all her troubles, turned her weeping into rejoicing, and placed her in her home as a happy mother of many children. K.MCR.

**HANNIEL** (Heb., 'grace of God').

**1.** Hanniel, the son of Ephod, was a leader from the tribe of Manasseh. The LORD told Moses to choose men from each tribe to help divide out the land of Canaan and Hanniel represented his tribe (Num. 34:23).

**2.** A great warrior, and head of a family, Hanniel was a son of Ulla and from the tribe of Asher (1 Chron. 7:39).

**HANOCH 1.** One of the leaders of the Midian clan, Hanoch was one of five grandsons of Abraham and Keturah (Gen. 25:4; 1 Chron. 1:33)

**2.** The eldest son of Reuben and head of a family that became known as the Hanochite clan (Gen. 46:9; Exod. 6:14; Num. 26:5; 1 Chron. 5:3).

**HANUN 1.** Son of Nahash, he was king of the Ammonites to whom David sent a message of sympathy. Hanun had David's men seized and shaved off half their beards and cut off their garments and sent them away (2 Sam. 10:1–4). He then sent 1000 talents of silver to hire chariots to

protect himself from David and Joab. However, the LORD gave Joab the victory (vv. 13–15; 1 Chron. 19:2–6).

**2.** He repaired the Valley Gate in Jerusalem and 500 yards of the wall (Neh. 3:13), following the return from Babylon.

**3.** Son of Zalaph, he repaired a further section of wall (Neh. 3:30)

**HAPPIZZEZ** was one of the priests who were chosen to be officials in the sanctuary 'according to the last instructions of David'. Impartial selection from among the descendants of Eleazar and Ithamar was made by drawing lots. The 18th lot fell to Happizzez and that was the order in which he ministered when entering the sanctuary (1 Chron. 24:15)

**HARAN 1.** A brother of Abra(ha)m and Nahor and son of Terah, Haran became Lot's father. His daughters were Milcah and Iscah. He lived and died in Ur of the Chaldeans (Gen. 11:26–31). Nahor later married Milcah. Terah, Abram and Lot later settled in a town called Haran. Whether Terah gave the name to the town is not clear, but the town and area that became known as Haran figured prominently in later biblical narratives and survives even today as a small Arab village.

**2.** A leader in the tribe of Judah, this Haran was the son of Caleb and his concubine Ephah. He became the father of Gazez (1 Chron.2:46).

**3.** One of the sons of Shimei, a Levite from the Gershonite family, who was a head of one of the families of Ladan (1 Chron. 23:9). He is listed among those who were given specific duties by King David.

**HARBONA,** one of seven eunuchs who served King Xerxes (Est. 1:10; 7:9). See Vashti.

**HAREPH** was 'the father of Beth Gader', i.e. he was credited with founding this town. He was a son of Hur, a descendant of Caleb and a leader in the tribe of Judah (1 Chron. 2:51).

**HARHAIAH,** the father of Uzziel, a goldsmith who repaired part of the Jerusalem walls following the return from Exile in Babylon (Neh. 3:8).

**HARHAS** is mentioned in connection with the prophetess Huldah who was consulted about the message read from the Book of the Law in Josiah's reign. The Book had recently been rediscovered and the message seemed to contain warnings of imminent judgment on Judah. Harhas, the 'keeper of the wardrobe', was the father of Tikvah and grandfather of Shallum who was Huldah's husband (2 Kings 22:14). In the parallel passage in 2 Chron. 34:22 he is called Hasrah.

**HARHUR** His descendants were among the Temple servants who returned from Exile with Nehemiah (Ezra 2:51; Neh. 7:53).

**HARIM** **1.** One among the priests who

were chosen to be officials in the sanctuary 'according to the last instructions of David'. Impartial selection from among the descendants of Eleazar and Ithamar was made by drawing lots. The third lot fell to Harim and that was the order in which he ministered when entering the sanctuary (1 Chron. 24:8).

**2.** This Harim's descendants, numbering 320, were among those from a nonpriestly family returning from the captivity in Babylon. Some of them joined Nehemiah's covenant to serve the Lord (Ezra 10:2; Neh. 7:35; 10:27) and agreed to divorce their foreign wives (Ezra 2:32; 10:31).

**3.** In Neh. 7:42 and Ezra 2:39 another family who were descendants of a certain Harim is mentioned. This returning family numbered 1,017. They also divorced foreign wives and put their seal to the covenant (Ezra 10:21; Neh. 10:5).

**4.** Malkijah 'son of Harim' is mentioned in Neh. 3:11. He was one of those who repaired the walls of Jerusalem when the people of Judah returned from the Exile in Babylon. He was probably one of those mentioned in 2. or 3. above.

P.D.G.

**HARIPH** was a leader of a family who returned with his descendants to Jerusalem following the Exile in Babylon. Under the direction of Nehemiah, he signed the agreement of the people to obey the Law of the Lord and worship only him (Neh. 7:24; 10:19).

**HARNEPHER,** a son of Zophah and leader in the tribe of Asher (1 Chron. 7:36).

**HAROEH** (Heb., 'the seer'). From the tribe of Judah, Haroeh was a descendant of Shobal (1 Chron. 2:52).

**HARSHA** His descendants were among the Temple servants who returned from

Exile with Nehemiah (*Ezra 2:52; Neh. 7:54*).

**HARUM** A leader in the tribe of Judah, Harum was a son of Helah and father of Aharhel (*1 Chron. 4:8*).

**HARUMAPH** His son Jedaiah repaired part of the wall in Jerusalem opposite his house following the Exile in Babylon (*Neh. 3:10*).

**HARUZ,** the father of Meshullemeth, who was the mother of King Amon of Judah. Amon was a 'wicked king' who 'worshipped the idols his father [King Manasseh] had worshipped'. Certainly the whole family seems to have behaved wickedly before the LORD God and consequently their rebellion and sin led to their judgment and death (*2 Kings 21:19*).

**HASADIAH** (Heb., 'God is loving') is mentioned in the list in *1 Chron. 3:20* of the royal line following the Exile. Hasadiah was one of the sons of Zerubbabel.

**HASHABIAH** (Heb., 'the LORD has considered').
  **1.** His descendant, Ethan, served as a Temple musician under David. He was a Merarite Levite (*1 Chron. 6:45*).
  **2.** A descendant of Shemaiah who lived in Jerusalem following the Babylonian Exile (*1 Chron. 9:14; Neh. 11:15*).
  **3.** A son of Jeduthun who prophesied using the harp in thanking and praising God. He was the twelfth when lots were cast to minister in the Tabernacle during David's reign (*1 Chron. 25:3; 19*).
  **4.** He and his relatives, 1,700 Hebronites, were responsible for the LORD's work west of Jordan (*1 Chron. 26:30*).
  **5.** An officer of the tribe of Levi in David's time. He was Kemuel's son (*1 Chron. 27:17*).
  **6.** This Hashabiah was the leader of Levites who provided 5,000 Passover offerings and 500 cattle for Levites during

the great Passover celebrations during the revival under King Josiah (*2 Chron. 35:9*).
  **7.** One of those who returned from the Exile with Ezra, this Hashabiah was entrusted with offerings of silver and gold to take to the Temple in Jerusalem following the Exile (*Ezra 8:19, 24; Neh. 12:21*).
  **8.** Another Hashabiah carried out repairs on the Jerusalem walls and was the ruler of the half district of Keilah. He was also one of the Levites who sealed the agreement of the people with Nehemiah to obey the Law of God and worship only him (*Neh. 3:17; 10:11*).
  **9.** A descendant of Uzzi, he was chief officer of the Levites in Jerusalem on return from the Exile in Babylon (*Neh. 11:22*)
  **10.** This Hashabiah was a leader of the Levites and musicians in the Temple during the time of Joiakim (*Neh. 12:24*). Possibly the same as 8. above.          M.P.

**HASHABNAH** One of the leaders of the people who sealed Ezra's agreement of the people after the Exile. They agreed to worship only the LORD and obey his Law (*Neh. 10:25*).          M.P.

**HASHABNEIAH** **1.** The son of Hatush who worked on the repairs of the wall in Jerusalem after the Exile (*Neh. 3:10*).
  **2.** One of the Levites who addressed the people before signing the agreement of the people to worship only the LORD and obey his Law (*Neh. 9:5*).

**HASHBADDANAH** Mentioned only in *Neh. 8:4*, this man stood alongside Ezra when the Book of the Law was read to the men and women of Jerusalem and Judah following their return from the Babylonian Exile.

**HASHEM** 'The sons of Hashem' were among the great warriors listed among David's 'mighty men'. He is called a Gizonite (*1 Chron. 11:34*).

**HASHUBAH** (Heb., 'consideration') is mentioned in the list in *1 Chron. 3:20* of the royal line following the Exile. Hashubah was one of the sons of Zerubbabel.

**HASHUM 1.** 223 of his descendants were among those who returned from Exile with Nehemiah (*Ezra 2:19*). In *Neh. 7:22* the number is 328. Some of his descendants are listed among those guilty of intermarriage in *Ezra 10:33.*

**2.** He stood beside Ezra on the platform when Ezra read from the Book of the Law (*Ezra 8:4*).

**3.** One of the leaders of the people who sealed the agreement of the people after the Exile (*Neh. 10:18*).

**HASRAH** is mentioned in connection with the prophetess Huldah, who was consulted about the message read from the Book of the Law in Josiah's reign. The Book had recently been rediscovered and the message seemed to contain warnings of imminent judgment on Judah. Hasrah, the 'keeper of the wardrobe', was the father of Tokhath and grandfather of Shallum who was Huldah's husband (*2 Chron. 34:22*). In the parallel passage in *2 Kings 22:14* he is called Harhas.

**HASSENAAH** His son rebuilt the Fish Gate in Jerusalem after the Exile in Babylon (*Neh. 3:3*).

**HASSENUAH 1.** A Benjamite whose descendant Sallu resettled in Jerusalem after the Exile (*1 Chron. 9:7*).

**2.** His son Judah was in control of the second district of Jerusalem after the Exile (*Neh. 11:9*).

**HASSHUB** (Heb., 'considerate').
**1.** His son Shemaiah, a Levite, resettled in Jerusalem after the Exile (*1 Chron. 9:14; Neh. 11:15*).

**2.** The son of Pahath-Moab who repaired a section of the wall in Jerusalem and the Tower of the Ovens after the Exile (*Neh. 3:11*).

**3.** One of the leaders of the people who signed the agreement of the people after the exile to worship the LORD alone and obey his law (*Neh. 10:23*)

**4.** This Hasshub helped repair the walls of Jerusalem in front of his house in the days of Nehemiah (*Neh. 3:23*).

**HASSOPHERETH** (Heb., 'scribe'), a servant of Solomon whose descendants returned from Exile in Babylon with Nehemiah (*Ezra 2:55*). In *Neh. 7:57* he is called Sophereth.

**HASUPHA** His descendants were among the Temple servants who returned from Exile in Babylon with Nehemiah (*Ezra 2:43; Neh. 7:46*).

**HATHACH** was a eunuch in the court of King Xerxes when Esther was Queen. He acted as a go-between between Esther and her adoptive father, Mordecai (*Est. 4:5–6, 9*). When Haman the 'Agagite' (*Est. 8:5*) sought to kill all the Jews in the Persian empire of King Xerxes, God used Esther and his servant Mordecai to thwart Haman's plans. The first Esther knew of the Haman's plot to kill the Jews was when she saw Mordecai dressed in 'sackcloth' (a sign of mourning) and hanging around the king's gate. She sent Hathach to find out what was going on. When she heard the news of the imminent annihilation of the Jews she felt there was nothing she could do as she was not allowed to enter the king's presence without him first asking her. Mordecai sent back a message: 'who knows but that you have come to royal position for such a time as this?' (*Est. 8:14*). Throughout this book, which mentions little directly about God, lies this assumption that God in his sovereignty is able to overrule in all the affairs of men and women.          P.D.G.

**HATHATH,** one of the grandsons of Kenaz and a son of Othniel, of the tribe of Judah (1 Chron. 4:13).

**HATIPHA** (Heb., 'a captive'). His descendants were among the Temple servants who returned from Exile in Babylon with Nehemiah (Ezra 2:54; Neh. 7:56).

**HATITA** His descendants were among the gatekeepers of the Temple who returned from Exile in Babylon with Nehemiah (Ezra 2:42; Neh. 7:45).

**HATTIL,** a servant of Solomon whose descendants were among those who returned from Exile in Babylon with Nehemiah (Ezra 2:57; Neh. 7:59).

**HATTUSH   1.** A son of Shemaiah, and a descendant of Shecaniah, he is listed in the royal line of Jehoiachin (1 Chron. 3:22). He was one of the family heads who returned with Ezra during the reign of King Artaxerxes in Ezra 8:2.
**2.** This Hattush was the son of Hashabneiah who helped to repair the wall of Jerusalem (Neh. 3:10).
**3.** One of the priests who sealed the agreement of the people to worship only the Lord after they had returned from the Exile (Neh. 10:4).
**4.** This Hattush was one of the priests who returned from Exile with Zerubbabel and Jeshua (Neh. 12:2). Possibly the same as 3. above.

**HAVILAH   1.** The second son of Cush mentioned in Gen. 10:7; 1 Chron. 1:9. He was the grandson of Ham.
**2.** A descendant of Shem and son of Joktan (Gen. 10:29; 1 Chron. 1:23). These descendants of Shem became leaders of clans in Arabia.

**HAZAEL** was anointed to be king of Syria by Elijah at the specific command of the LORD (1 Kings 19:15). Hazael and Jehu between them were to be God's chosen instruments to bring judgment on Israel and the family of King Ahab who had been so idolatrous and evil. Hazael was an official under King Ben-Hadad of Syria. One day when Ben-Hadad was ill he sent Hazael to meet the prophet Elisha who was coming to Damascus. Hazael asked whether Ben-Hadad would live and Elisha wept as he said that Ben-Hadad would die but Hazael would live. Elisha wept for the great trouble he knew Hazael would bring on the Northern Kingdom of Israel. Hazael returned to Ben-Hadad and murdered him (2 Kings 8:8–15). He then ruled Syria from c. 843–798 BC.

Soon after Hazael took power, Joram son of Ahab and Ahaziah of Judah made an alliance and went to fight Hazael, but Joram was wounded in the battle (2 Kings 8:25–29; 2 Chron. 22:5–6). Joram was later killed by Jehu as God's justice against the idolatry of Ahab's family, and Jehu became king of Israel (2 Kings 9:14–15). As the LORD continued to bring judgment on Israel's religious infidelity and sin, he allowed Hazael to capture large swathes of Israel, overpowering the Israelites in those areas (2 Kings 10:32). As Hazael moved south he eventually overran most of Ephraim and turned to attack the kingdom of Judah and the city of Jerusalem (2 Kings 12:17–18). King Joash of Judah sent the Temple treasures as a tribute to Hazael so that Hazael withdrew from the attack.

For a number of years Hazael was allowed by the LORD to continue to oppress Israel until eventually King Jehoahaz of Israel turned back to the LORD and the LORD listened to his prayer (2 Kings 13:3–5). As they turned in prayer, so 'the LORD was gracious to them and had compassion and showed concern for them because of his covenant with Abraham, Isaac and Jacob' (2 Kings 13:23). Hazael died and Jehoash, son of Jehoahaz king of Israel, was able to fight Hazael's son, Ben-Hadad, and win back much of Israel's territory (2 Kings 13:3; 22, 24–25).

The prophet Amos also spoke against Hazael's family for all his evil in attacking Israel, promising that Ben-Hadad's fortresses would be smashed (*Amos 1:4*). Even though the LORD let Hazael win many battles because it was his will to draw Israel back to repentance and true worship, Hazael was still responsible for his own actions in attacking God's people and seeking to subdue them.          P.D.G.

**HAZAIAH** His descendant Maaseiah was one of the descendants of Judah who settled in Jerusalem after the Babylonian Exile (*Neh. 11:5*).

**HAZARMAVETH** (Heb., 'court of death') is listed in both *Gen. 10:26* and *1 Chron. 1:20* as a descendant of Shem. His father was Joktan.

**HAZIEL,** one of the sons of Shimei, was a Levite from the Gershonite family and was a head of one of the families of Ladan (*1 Chron. 23:9*). He is listed among those who were given specific duties by King David.

**HAZO,** a son of Nahor and Milcah and therefore Abraham's nephew (*Gen. 22:22*). See also *Bethuel*.

**HAZZELELPONI** Listed among the descendants of Judah, Hazzelelponi was the daughter of Etam and sister to Jezreel, Ishma and Idbash (*1 Chron. 4:3*).

**HAZZOBEBAH** was from the tribe of Judah and was the son of Koz (*1 Chron. 4:8*).

**HEBER** **1.** Heber, son of Beriah, is listed as a member of the tribe of Asher and was among those who went down with Jacob to Egypt. He founded the Heberite clan (*Gen. 46:17; Num. 26:45; 1 Chron. 7:31–32*).
**2.** Heber was the husband of Jael, the woman who killed Sisera (*Judg. 4:11, 17, 21; 5:24*). See *Jael*.

**3.** Heber, a leader in the tribe of Judah, was the son of Mered and his Judean wife. He was the father of Soco (although this may mean he founded the settlement there) (*1 Chron. 4:18*).
**4.** Heber is listed in King Saul's genealogy. He was the son of Elpaal (*1 Chron. 8:17*).          S.C.

**HEBREW(S)** **1.** In the OT, the word first appears in *Gen. 14:13*, where Abram is called 'the Hebrew'. Certainly this identification separated him from the indigenous people living in the area, but quite what the origin of the word is remains unclear. It has been suggested that the word was derived from the name Eber (great-grandson of Shem, *Gen. 10:24*). Perhaps more likely is the suggestion that the word was derived from a word meaning 'to cross over' or 'pass beyond'. This would mean that, in describing Abram and the later Israelites as 'Hebrews', there was an emphasis on the people as a pilgrim people who had come from far away.

The name Hebrew is sometimes used in an apparently derogatory way of Israelites by those from outside. For example, Potiphar's wife refers to Joseph in this way (*Gen. 39:14, 17*; see *43:32*), and the Philistines seem to refer to the Israelites in this way as well (e.g. *1 Sam. 4:6; 13:19; 14:11*). But this derogatory use is not common and usually it is a neutral word that is virtually synonymous with Israelite(s) (e.g. *Exod. 1:15–19*). The Egyptians regarded the Hebrews as a separate race who had their own God (*Exod. 3:18; 5:3* etc.). The Israelites could refer to their own race by reference to their being 'Hebrews' (e.g. *Deut. 15:12; Jer. 34:9, 14; Jonah 1:9*). Their language was also known as 'Hebrew' and was the main original language of the OT Scriptures. The language itself is mentioned a number of times in Scripture (e.g. *2 Kings 18:28; 2 Chron. 32:18; Is. 36:11–13*).          P.D.G.

**2.** In the NT, this ethnic term to refer to the Jews or a subset within the Jewish people is actually quite rare, since the NT prefers to use the term Jew/Jews to refer to this group. In *Acts 6:1*, the term refers to those Jewish members of the church whose dominant cultural influence was still Semitic in character as opposed to Hellenistic. They probably still spoke Aramaic as well. Paul used the designation frequently to describe himself as a member of Israel (*2 Cor. 11:22*). In fact Paul was an exemplary member, when he followed the Law to its full (*Phil. 3:5*).

The term is also used to refer to Aramaic as a 'Hebrew dialect', which is another way to refer to the main language in 1st-century Palestine (*Acts 21:40; 22:2; 26:14*). Other references to the language occur as well (*John 5:2; 19:13, 17, 20; Rev. 9:11; 16:16*). In this second list, the language in view is Hebrew itself.

D.B.

**HEBRON 1.** Hebron was one of four sons of Kohath and a grandson of Levi (*1 Chron. 6:2, 18; 23:12–13*). He was a clan leader among the Kohathites (*Num. 3:19*). His wife was Jochebed who bore him three children: Aaron, Moses and Miriam (*Exod. 6:20; Num. 16:1; 1 Chron. 24:20*).

**2.** The son of Mareshah and grandson of Caleb (*1 Chron. 2:42, 43*).

**HEGAI,** one of King Xerxes' eunuchs in charge of the King's harem (*Est. 2:8*). When Queen Vashti disobeyed the King, Hegai was commissioned to find a woman who would replace her as queen. He found 'beautiful young virgins' from around the empire and brought them to the citadel of Susa, where they were given beauty treatments and prepared for presentation to the king (*Est. 2:3*). Among those girls was Esther. Soon she became Hegai's favourite (*v. 9*). He gave her special food and beauty treatments so that eventually, when presented to the king, she was regarded as the most beautiful

and Xerxes took her as his queen. Hegai's advice on what she should wear and take with her into the King's presence was one of the decisive factors in her becoming queen (*v. 15*).

The writer of the book of Esther makes it clear that at this stage she did not reveal that she was a Jew to either Hegai or the King. Mordecai, her adoptive father, had warned Esther to be careful in this regard. With Mordecai's work in the background, and the LORD God's over-ruling in providing Hegai to favour her, Esther was to find herself in the right place at the right time to prevent the annihilation of the Jews. See *Esther*.

P.D.G.

**HELAH,** one of Ashhur's two wives. Her sons by Ashhur were Zereth, Zohar, Ethnan and Koz who were leaders in the tribe of Judah (*1 Chron. 4:5, 7*).

**HELDAI 1.** This Heldai is mentioned only in *Zech. 6:10* as one of the returnees from Babylon who made contributions of silver and gold to make crowns for Joshua the priest. The Syriac reads 'Heldai' for the 'Helem' of *v. 14*.

**2.** Heldai, the Netophathite, was a descendant of Othniel who commanded the twelfth division of David's army and was on duty in the twelfth month. There were 24,000 in his division (*1 Chron. 27:15*).

**HELED** was the son of Baanah the Netophathite (*2 Sam. 23:29; 1 Chron. 11:30*). He was one of David's 'Thirty' mighty men who went to battle for him and led the people of Israel to war.

**HELEK** (Heb., 'portion'), a descendant of Joseph and inheritor of the tribe of Manasseh through Gilead. He was the leader of the Helekite clan (*Num. 26:30; Josh. 17:2*).

**HELEM** (Heb., 'strength').

**1.** Probably the same as Heldai (*Zech. 6:14; cf. v. 10*), one of the contributors of precious metals used to make crowns for the post-exilic priest Joshua. The LXX suggests that 'Helem' is a descriptive of 'Heldai', viz., '(Heldai, the) strong one'.

**2.** Helem, the brother of Shomer, was a descendant of Asher and a leader of his tribe (1 Chron. 7:35).

**HELEZ 1.** Helez, the Paltite or Pelonite, was an Ephraimite and one of David's 'Thirty' warriors. As a commander in David's army he was on duty with his men in the seventh month of each year and had 24,000 men in his division (2 Sam. 23:26; 1 Chron. 11:27; 27:10).

**2.** From the Jerahmeelite clan of the tribe of Judah, his father was Azariah and his son Eleasah (1 Chron. 2:39).

**HELI** Mentioned in Luke's genealogy leading from Jesus to Adam, Heli was the father of Joseph, the husband of Mary (Luke 3:23).

**HELKAI** (Heb., 'the LORD is my portion') was the head of the priestly family Meremoth during the days of Joiakim following the Babylonian Exile (Neh. 12:15).

**HELON** (Heb., 'power'), the father of Eliab and a leader of the tribe of Zebulun at the time of Moses (Num. 1:9; 2:7; 7:24, 29; 10:16). See Eliab.

**HEMAN** (Heb., 'faithful').
**1.** From the tribe of Levi and the Kohathite clan, this Heman was a musician, son of Joel and grandson of the prophet Samuel (1 Chron. 6:33). He was an associate of Asaph, another famous leader of the musicians in the latter part of David's reign, first in the Tabernacle and then, in Solomon's time, after the building of the Temple (1 Chron. 6:32). When the ark was brought by David to the specially prepared place in Jerusalem, he ordered that the Levites appoint singers 'to sing joyful songs' (1 Chron. 15:16).

Heman was one of these who were to sound the cymbals (vv. 17–19).

He was also set aside by David 'for the ministry of prophesying' and became known as a 'seer'. He reported directly to the king himself. He was blessed with 14 sons and three daughters who were given to him as fulfilment of promises God had made him, and their job was also to 'exalt God' (1 Chron. 25:1, 4–6). When the ark was eventually brought to the new Temple in Solomon's time, Heman and his associates led the great 'songs of praise and thanks to the LORD' (2 Chron. 5:12–13). Much later, at the time of Hezekiah's revival, it is interesting to see that Heman's descendants were still among the first Levites to be involved in the purifying and reconsecrating of the Temple (2 Chron. 29:14–15). Still later, when Josiah found the Book of the Law and restarted worship in the Temple after a period of evil and idolatry, it was once again the descendants of Heman and Asaph who were to the fore in leading music in the Temple worship.

That this family should be so prominent on the occasion of the ark coming to Jerusalem, the bringing of the ark into the newly opened Temple, the rededication of the Temple at the time of Hezekiah and then again in Josiah's reign, is perhaps a good indication that they remained faithful to the LORD even through the terrible time of idolatry that Judah experienced after Solomon. It is also particularly interesting to note, in an era when joyous music once again forms a part of much worship, that Heman and his descendants were involved in loud, joyous and harmonious singing and playing of instruments before the LORD. It was a family gift and a special calling from God recognized across the generations by those around.

**2.** Mentioned in 1 Chron. 2:6, he was the son of Zerah and a grandson of Judah and Tamar.

**3.** This Heman was renowned for his wisdom and is mentioned in a passage extolling the extraordinary God-given wisdom of Solomon. By comparison with Heman and others, Solomon's wisdom was seen to be even greater (*1 Kings 4:31*). He may have been the Ezrahite in the introduction to *Ps. 88*. Some say he is the same as 2. above.

P.D.G.

**HEMDAN** A leader among the Horites, son of Dishon and grandson of Anah (*Gen. 36:26; 1 Chron. 1:41*; in the latter verse the Heb. uses the name Hamran).

**HEN** (Heb., 'grace, favour'). The son of Zephaniah, Hen is probably the same as Josiah, son of Zephaniah (*Zech. 6:14; cf. v. 10*). Perhaps *hen* is to be taken as a noun, thus, 'to the son of Zephaniah as a favour', etc. He was one of those who brought silver and gold from Babylon which was used in making a crown for the high priest.

**HENADAD** His sons and grandsons, all Levites were among those who supervised the working on the walls of Jerusalem and house of God after the Exile (*Ezra 3:9*).

His son Binnui was the ruler of a half-district of Keilah and was also one of the Levites who signed the agreement of the people (*Neh. 3:18, 24; 10:9*).

**HEPHER** **1.** A chief from the tribe of Manasseh, descended through Gilead, who became leader of the Hepherite clan. His son was Zelophehad (*Num. 26:32–33; 27:1*). In *Josh. 17:2–3* his clan received its allotment of the land of Canaan.

**2.** A leader in the tribe of Judah and son of Asshur (*1 Chron. 4:6*). His mother was Naarah.

**3.** Hepher the Mekerathite (*1 Chron. 11:36*) was one of David's great warriors, a 'mighty man' in battle.

**HEPHZIBAH** (*My delight is in her*). The mother of King Manasseh of Judah (*2 Kings 21:1*). See also *Is. 62:4*.

**HERESH,** a Levite mentioned in *1 Chron. 9:15* as a descendant of Asaph. He was one of the early returnees from the Exile in the time of Zerubbabel.

**HERMAS,** the fifth named of a group of Roman Christians greeted by Paul in his letter to the Romans (*16:14*). The personal care and pastoral concern for individuals reflected in Paul's greetings is worthy of attention. This person is not to be confused with the writer of the non-canonical work known as *The Shepherd of Hermas* which appeared in the first half of the 2nd century AD.

**HERMES** **1.** The third named of a group of Roman Christians greeted by Paul in his letter to the Romans (*16:14*). The personal care and pastoral concern for individuals reflected in Paul's greetings is worthy of attention.

**2.** A Greek god who was supposed to be the son of Zeus but also a divine messenger and god of oratory. The Romans called him Mercury. This relationship between Zeus and Hermes explains why, in *Acts 14:12*, the people of Lystra, amazed at a great miracle of healing performed by the apostle Paul and believing him to be a god, called him Hermes and Barnabas, Zeus. They regarded Paul as a messenger from the gods and so the priest of Zeus came from his temple outside the city to bring them sacrifices (*v. 13*). Appalled at such blasphemy and misunderstanding, Paul picked up on their understanding that he was a herald, and rushed into the crowd saying: 'Men, why are you doing this? We too are only men, human like you. We are bringing you good news, telling you to turn from these worthless things to the living God, who made heaven and earth and sea and everything in them' (*v. 15*). He showed how the God they preached was witnessed to by his kindness and grace in providing rains, harvests and food. While this at least stopped the sacrifices, we are not told whether he had opportunity to go on to expound Christ and to see people come to a saving faith in Christ.

The fact that Paul appealed to God's general self-revelation to all people, before giving details of the good news of Christ, is an excellent example of both his belief that general revelation could be seen by all and his method of speaking and preaching that often started with whatever he could show he had in common with his audience. 　　P.D.G.

**HERMOGENES** (Gk., 'born of Hermes') is mentioned, together with Phygelus, in Paul's second epistle to Timothy as being among 'everyone in the province of Asia' who had deserted him (2 Tim. 1:15). Clearly Paul did not mean that all the Christians of all the churches in the province of Asia, such as Ephesus, Colossae, and Laodicea, had deserted him. Probably Paul was referring to the time of his second imprisonment in Rome (v. 17), and had in mind the way the Christians had not stood by him at his trial. Those who did not stand by him would have included all those from the province of Asia living in Rome, such as Hermogenes and Phygelus, of whom he might have expected better things.

Paul drew a contrast between this sort of behaviour that was no doubt the result of fear of the Roman authorities, and the conduct of Onesiphorus, who, Paul said, 'often refreshed me and was not ashamed of my chains' (2 Tim. 1:16). Paul referred to these examples in order to encourage Timothy to 'be strong in the grace that is in Christ Jesus' (2 Tim. 2:1). In much the same way as Christians experience difficulty in standing strong and firm for Christ in many modern societies, so the problem was present in the early church where Christians could find themselves being persecuted or simply 'ashamed' if they spoke out for Christ. 　　P.D.G.

**HEROD** Four different generations of men, all with the dynastic title Herod, appear in the Gospels and Acts.

**1.** The Idumean Herod the Great was the first major client-king in Israel after its subjugation by Rome. He reigned from 37–4 BC, levying heavy taxes on the Jews, conscripting labour, and building massive public works projects. Paranoid about would-be usurpers to his throne, he had many of his family members and close associates executed. The story of Herod's disturbance at the report of the birth of the Christ-child and his subsequent 'massacre of the innocents' (Matt. 2:1–20) fits this pattern of behaviour.

**2.** *Antipas.* After Herod's death his territory was divided among his three sons, Archelaus (Matt. 2:22), Philip (Mark 6:17) and Antipas. The Herod who appears during Jesus' adult ministry, as tetrarch in Galilee (e.g. Luke 3:1; Acts 13:1; Mark 8:15), is this Antipas, who governed there from 4 BC to AD 39. Herod Antipas beheaded John the Baptist (Matt. 14:3–12; Mark 6:17–29; Luke 3:19–20) and later wondered if Jesus were John come to life again (Matt. 14:1–2; Mark 6:14–16; Luke 9:7–9). Luke shows some special interest in the Herodian family, as he is the only evangelist to embed his narrative in the events of empire history. Joanna, the wife of one of Antipas' officials, became a follower of Jesus (Luke 8:3). Christ rebuked Herod in absentia as 'that fox' (Luke 13:31–33) and appeared before him when Pilate unsuccessfully tried to avoid dealing with the Jewish leaders' request for Jesus' crucifixion (Luke 23:6–16).

**3.** *Agrippa I.* The son of another brother of Antipas named Aristobulus, and therefore grandson of Herod the Great, was the next ruler in Galilee until AD 44. This is the Herod who executed James the son of Zebedee and imprisoned Peter, in Acts

*12*, only to be subsequently struck down by an angel and eaten by worms (*vv. 19b–23*).

**4.** *Agrippa II*, son of Agrippa I, was the ruler who listened to Paul during his Caesarean imprisonment between A D 57–59 (*Acts 25:13–16:32*).          C.B.

**HERODIANS** An influential group of Jewish leaders mentioned in three places in the Gospels in connection with two different episodes of confrontation with Jesus. Mark mentions two occasions when they joined up with the Pharisees to plot against Jesus (*Mark 3:6; 12:13*). Matthew also records the second of those episodes in relation to the Pharisees and their attempt to catch Jesus out with their questions (*Matt. 22:16*).

Their name indicates that these people would have been supporters of the Herodian dynasty and therefore probably people of some standing and influence in the community. In supporting the dynasty of the Herodian family (see *Herod*) they would indirectly have upheld the Roman rule, which had allowed them a measure of autonomous home-rule. It is not possible to equate this group with the Sadducees, and yet it is likely that their beliefs would have been somewhat similar. Initially it may seem strange that a group like this should link up with the Pharisees to oppose Jesus. The Pharisees would have been against the Roman occupation but also strongly against the Herodian dynasty and any group that seemed to compromise religiously with the pagan overlords. We get some idea of the different religious views of the Pharisees and Saducees in *Acts 23:6ff. (cf. Matt. 12:18)*, and it is likely that these same differences would be seen between Pharisees and Herodians. However, both groups would have been very disturbed at Jesus' message, if indeed for different reasons. Neither would welcome a person teaching about the Kingdom of God and rallying people to his message.

One way they tried to discredit Jesus was to out-smart him with questions, revealing his poor education, the incoherence of his message and his inability to lead a popular movement. The questions asked of Jesus in Jerusalem in *Matt 22:16* and *Mark 12:13ff.* centred on the legality of paying taxes to Caesar. Jesus answered 'knowing their hypocrisy'. Both these groups would have liked to have been able to accuse Jesus of insurrection against the Romans and yet neither group would themselves have appreciated paying taxes to Rome. Try as they might to entrap Jesus, they were out-classed. In fact they were indeed up against the long-expected Messiah, the one of whom Isaiah had prophesied: 'The Spirit of the Lord will rest on him – the Spirit of wisdom and of understanding, the Spirit of counsel and power' (*Is. 11:2*).     P.D.G.

**HERODIAS** Renowned in Scriptures for her desire to see the death of John the Baptist, this woman was the wife of Herod Antipas and the daughter of Bernice and Aristobulus (*Matt. 14:3–12; Mark 6:17–29*). She had been married to Herod Philip but deserted him for his half-brother Herod Antipas following the latter's divorce from a Nabatean princess.

The conflict between John the Baptist and Herodias began when John started preaching about the need for repentance and the imminence of Christ's coming. Such gospel preaching provoked two reactions. Some responded with enthusiasm and asked John what they should do to be prepared (e.g. *Luke 3:10; 12, 14*). However, when Herod heard that John had pointed to specific sins and included his relationship with Herodias among them, Luke said he 'added' to his sins by locking John up in prison (*Luke 3:19–20*). The sins of the marriage were that Herod had married his niece and deliberately divorced in order to be able to do so. Given that Herodias was the one who continued to be so angry with John, perhaps he had also pointed to her sin in moving from one brother to the other.

One day Herodias' daughter, Salome, danced for Herod and his guests and won such approval that she was offered a huge reward of her choosing. Herodias told Salome to demand the head of John the Baptist. Somewhat reluctantly, it would appear, Herod obliged and John was beheaded (*Matt. 14:9*, although *cf. v. 5*). Judgment on Herodias eventually came when her ambitions went too far and Agrippa I was made tetrarch by the Roman emperor and Philip and Herodias were banished to Gaul.

The divisive nature of the preaching of the gospel is clearly exemplified in this incident. Luke specially demonstrates that, in the presence of the gospel mess-age and in particular when confronted with Christ, people are required to respond. The nature of the response, whether of faith and obedience or rejection and rebellion, will determine salvation or judgment.          P.D.G.

**HERODION** At the end of his letter to the Roman church, the apostle Paul demonstrated his pastoral concern for the people in a list of greeting to individuals. In *Rom. 16:11* he said: 'Greet Herodion, my relative'. It is not clear from the Greek whether Paul was actually greeting a blood relative or a fellow Jew among many Gentile Christians. The former is probably the more likely in the context, given that others in the list were Jews. The name Herodion may imply that this person was a freedman from the household of the Herods.

## KING HEZEKIAH

**King Hezekiah** reigned over Judah for 29 years (715–687 BC). His father was Ahaz and his mother was Abi. Hezekiah ruled together with his father from 729–715 BC and at the age of 25 he became the sole ruler.

### Hezekiah's reputation

Hezekiah was a godly king, as all biblical accounts bear out (*2 Kings 18–20; 2 Chron. 29–33; Is. 36–39*). According to the author of *Kings*, there was no king like him either before or after him, because Hezekiah trusted in the LORD (*2 Kings 18:5*). A testimony of Hezekiah's faithfulness is also given in *Jer. 26:18–19*. The elders of Jeremiah's time relate a prophecy upon which Hezekiah acted. Micah, a contemporary of Isaiah, had prophesied that Jerusalem would be destroyed (*Mic. 3:12*). Hezekiah's response to this message was one of humility. He sought the LORD. The calamity did not take place. A hundred years later, the elders in Jeremiah's day were familiar with the story of God's deliverance and of Hezekiah's faithfulness.

### Purification and Passover

While the record in *2 Kings* (*18:4, 16, 22*) is strangely brief, *2 Chron.* (*29:1–33:31*) supplements the account of his reform. A large portion of the Chronicler's account regarding Hezekiah concerns his purification of the worship of the LORD and the celebration of the Passover. Hezekiah began his reforms immediately upon his coronation (2 Chron. 29:3).

The reform effectively recentred the worship of the LORD in Jerusalem. As part of this programme, the young king had the Temple reopened and cleansed. Idolatry was removed from the Temple area, including the Nehushtan, the bronze serpent that Moses had erected to keep the people from being killed by snakes (Num. 21:6–9). The Nehushtan had become an object of worship. The Nehushtan-idolatry shows how easy it is to substitute true worship with false. While believing that God is pleased with worship, the worshippers may well have come under his condemnation.

Priests and Levites began to serve in accordance with biblical prescriptions. Music was restored in accordance with customs that hailed from David's time. Hezekiah even encouraged the people from the northern tribes to participate in the worship of Jerusalem. By this time they had lost their political centre. Samaria had been destroyed by the Assyrians (722 BC), and the Israelites, who were left behind, had to co-exist with other people groups whom Shalmaneser had brought in to fill the void. Hezekiah sent messengers throughout the land of Judah and Israel imploring them to worship the LORD. Some of those remaining in the Northern Kingdom scorned the messengers, but others humbled themselves and came to the Passover. The majority of those living in Judah attended (2 Chron. 30:12).

A great multitude of people gathered in Jerusalem to celebrate this festival. The Feast of Unleavened Bread, which follows the Passover feast, went on for seven days and was accompanied with 'great joy'. They had such a good time praising the LORD that they decided to extend the festival for another week! Nothing similar to this event had taken place since the days of Solomon (2 Chron. 30:26).

The people were filled with excitement concerning the LORD because of the wonderful time they had at the feast. This excitement spilled over into other areas of their lives. One of the results was the destruction of illegitimate places of worship throughout Judah and Israel. Another was the generous giving of the people in regard to the upkeep of the Temple.

The Chronicler sums up this section by noting that Hezekiah did what was good, right, and true. Hezekiah saw the need to restore the true worship of the LORD and did not waste a moment in getting started. His first day in office brought about results which were felt throughout the entire land.

### Sennacherib's campaign

Judah's political situation remained tense. Because Ahaz had made an alliance with the Assyrians, Hezekiah was considered to be their vassal. He successfully developed internal reforms without incurring the wrath of Sargon II. Sargon did skirt Judah in 714 and 710, but did not act aggressively against Judah. At Sargon's death in battle (705), Sennacherib succeeded him. This was a time for many vassals, including Hezekiah, to reassert their independence. Sennacherib was compelled to deal with the insurrections from Babylon to Egypt, and finally turned to subjugate Judah in 701.

In preparation for the coming of the Assyrian army Hezekiah rebuilt the city walls, raised up towers, and manufactured a large number of weapons and shields. He also made a tunnel connecting the Gihon Spring to the Pool to Siloam (2 Chron. 32:3–4). This tunnel was an engineering feat. Men working from opposite ends under the ground chipped away the rock until they met. The tunnel ensured Jerusalem's ability to resist the enemy for a longer duration because water was available during a siege.

The third campaign of the Assyrian king, Sennacherib, was directed against various rulers located on the western seaboard of the Mediterranean Sea. While Sennacherib was besieging Lachish, Hezekiah sent a letter to him. Hezekiah admitted that he was in the wrong and was willing to follow whatever terms Sennacherib imposed on him. He paid the demanded tribute of 300 talents of silver and 30 talents of gold, which would be approximately ten metric tons of silver and one metric ton of gold.

Hezekiah was a godly king and a good politician. On the one hand, Hezekiah had great confidence in the LORD's ability to deliver him: 'With the king of Assyria is an arm of flesh, but with us is the LORD our God to help us and to fight our battles' (2 Chron. 32:7–8). On the other hand, Hezekiah knew the cruelty of the Assyrians. As the Assyrian war machine moved closer, he pacified them by paying tribute. Possibly, he repented of his former rebellion against the Assyrians.

However, the Assyrian king did not keep his word. He sent Rabshakeh and a large army to Jerusalem demanding surrender. Rabshakeh attempted to demoralize the officials and citizens of Jerusalem, speaking to them directly. He claimed that God had told the Assyrians to destroy Judah. After all, God had not delivered the Northern Kingdom from the Assyrians. Why should the people of Jerusalem expect anything different?

Hezekiah went to the Temple to pray, spreading the letter before the LORD (2 Kings 19:14ff.). In his prayer he acknowledged that the LORD alone is God over the kingdoms of the earth. Hezekiah closed his prayer with the plea that the LORD deliver them from Sennacherib, thus demonstrating who is the true God.

The LORD sent his reply through the prophet Isaiah. The arrogance of the Assyrians was in their boast that God willed Judah's surrender and in their claim that all the gods were powerless before them. Yet 2 Kings 19:25–28 puts the Assyrian king in his place. This passage states that Sennacherib's arrogance had come up to the LORD's ears and for this reason the LORD would put his hook in Sennacherib's nose and bridle his lips. Ironically, Sennacherib had boasted that Ashkelon pulled the strap of his yoke! How shortsighted he was. He did not realize that he was serving by divine appointment. He carried his destruction far and wide, becoming arrogant and thinking he was building an empire in his own power.

Isaiah declared that Sennacherib would never take Jerusalem and that he would die a cruel death. That very night the angel of the LORD went forth and killed 185,000 Assyrians, after which Sennacherib packed up and went home (2 Kings 19:35). Scripture does not record precisely what took place, but it is interesting to read the legends connected with this retreat. In the account of Josephus, a plague is recorded as the cause of their retreat (*Ant. 10:2–5*). Herodotus records an amusing account of this event. He relates that field-mice ate the quivers, bowstrings, and leather handles of the shields, leaving the Assyrians weaponless (*Bk. 1, 141*)! A sudden rebellion in Babylon led to the withdrawal of the Assyrians. Twenty years later Sennacherib died at the hands of his assassins.

Apparently the salvation of Jerusalem resulted in a wide-scale acknowledgment of the LORD as God. Many brought gifts to the LORD at Jerusalem (*2 Chron. 32:23*). Hezekiah was also exalted after this incident. It was miraculous indeed to have the Assyrian army at your doorstep and then see them suddenly returning home. The LORD did a marvellous deed, and caused the surrounding nations to ponder this extraordinary occurrence.

### Hezekiah's illness and the Babylonian envoys

In the same year, 701 BC, Hezekiah fell mortally ill at the age of 39. Hezekiah prayed that the LORD might heal him. The LORD granted his petition and he was given 15 more years of life. After Hezekiah's recovery, he received a visit from the Babylonians. He gave them a grand tour of all his treasures. God used the envoys of Babylon as a means of testing what was in Hezekiah's heart (*2 Chron. 32:31*). Apparently Hezekiah failed, as Isaiah's words register a strong rebuke. Isaiah declared that all these treasures would be carried off to Babylon; even some of Hezekiah's sons would be taken away.

A clue to Hezekiah's failure may be found in *2 Chron. 32:25*. The Chronicler records that after Hezekiah's extension of life, he was not grateful, but his heart was proud. Because of this the LORD declared that his wrath would come upon king and people. Yet, Hezekiah and the inhabitants humbled themselves, thereby averting the wrath of the LORD in their generation (*2 Chron. 32:26*).

### Conclusion

The overall picture of Hezekiah's life is that of a man dedicated to serving the LORD with his whole heart. He was not perfect, but he was a man of contrite spirit, humbling himself before his LORD. Hezekiah knew the LORD and worshipped him accordingly. He was a faithful forerunner of the Lord Jesus. There are a number of parallels in the life of Jesus reminiscent of Hezekiah: the cleansing of the Temple, concern for those outside of Judah, his attitude toward those who were unclean, and his sickness/death/new life experience. The last mention of King Hezekiah is, appropriately, found in Matthew's genealogy of Christ (*Matt. 1:9*).          W.A.VG.

**HEZEKIAH** **1.** See *King Hezekiah*.

**2.** Mentioned in *Zeph. 1:1*, this Hezekiah was the father of Amariah and an ancestor of the prophet Zephaniah. Zephaniah prophesied in the reign of King Josiah of Judah.

**3.** This Hezekiah is mentioned in connection with Ater in *Ezra 2:16; Neh. 7:21; 10:17*. Ater's descendants, through Hezekiah, came back from the Babylonian captivity with Zerubbabel. Hezekiah himself is listed as one of the leaders of his people who returned to Judah and who signed the binding agreement with

Nehemiah to worship the LORD and obey his Law.

**HEZION** was the grandfather of King Ben-hadad of Aram (Syria) in the time of King Asa of Judah. Ben-hadad had made an alliance with Baasha king of Israel (the Northern Kingdom). This frightened Asa, as it brought together a formidable enemy on his northern borders. He took all the silver and gold in the Temple and palace treasuries and offered it as a present to Ben-hadad in exchange for an alliance. Ben-hadad then invaded Israel from the north and Asa took some towns in the southern part of the northern kingdom of Israel (1 Kings 15:18).

**HEZIR 1.** One among the priests who were chosen to be officials in the sanctuary 'according to the last instructions of David'. Impartial selection from among the descendants of Eleazar and Ithamar was made by drawing lots. The 17th lot fell to Hezir, and that was the order in which he ministered when entering the sanctuary (1 Chron. 24:15).
**2.** One of the leaders of the people who signed Ezra's covenant (Neh. 10:20).

**HEZRO** Known as 'the Carmelite', Hezro is mentioned in 2 Sam. 23:35 and 1 Chron. 11:37. He was one of David's 'Thirty' mighty men who went to battle for him and led the people of Israel to war.

**HEZRON 1.** The third son of Reuben and head of a family that became known as the Hezronite clan (Gen. 46:9; Exod. 6:14; Num. 26:6; 1 Chron. 5:3).
**2.** A grandson of Judah and son of Perez, he was a leader in the tribe of Judah and became head of his own Hezronite clan. By his wife Abijah he became father of Ashhur (Gen. 46:12; Num. 26:21; 1 Chron. 2:5, 9, 18, 21, 24–25; 4:1). One of his descendants was Boaz, who married Ruth, and thus he was a direct ancestor of King David (Ruth 4:18–19), and therefore,

of course, a direct ancestor to Jesus Christ (Matt. 1:3; Luke 3:33).

**HIDDAI** (also known as Hurai in the parallel passage in 1 Chron. 11:32) was 'from the ravines of Gaash' (2 Sam. 23:30). He was one of David's 'Thirty' mighty men who went to battle for him and led the people of Israel to war.

**HIEL,** a man from Bethel who is credited with having rebuilt Jericho in the time of King Ahab of Israel (1 Kings 16:34). His sons Abiram and Segub died because of this rebuilding. In Josh. 6:26 Joshua placed a curse on anyone who would rebuild Jericho which he had destroyed by the power of God. 1 Kings 16:34 shows how this curse was fulfilled. This evil act of disobedience to the LORD's command was just one of the many evils of Ahab's day. The implication of the text is that a more godly king of Israel would have stopped the work proceeding. The incident provides evidence of God's judgment on those who rebel against his word and perhaps still further evidence of the idolatry and paganism of Ahab's day, since it may well be that Hiel followed local customs and actually sacrificed his sons.                                  P.D.G.

**HILKIAH** (Heb., 'the LORD is my portion').
**1.** Hilkiah was the head of a Merarite family of Levites. He was an ancestor of those who were put in charge of music in the house of the LORD by King David (1 Chron. 6:45).
**2.** The second son of Hosah, this Hilkiah was also a Merarite and served in the Tabernacle under King David (1 Chron. 26:10–11).
**3.** This Hilkiah, the father of Eliakim, was a palace administrator during the reign of King Hezekiah (2 Kings 18:18, 26, 37; Is. 22:20; 36:3, 22).
**4.** Another Hilkiah was the father of Jeremiah the prophet and a priest at Anathoth (Jer. 1:1).

**5.** This Hilkiah was the father of Gemariah, a messenger of King Zedekiah to Nebuchadnezzar (*Jer. 29:3*).

**6.** Hilkiah, high priest during the reign of King Josiah, found the Book of the Law during Temple renovations and delivered it to the king. Hilkiah helped lead the reformation and revival that followed the reading of the Law. He led the delegation from King Josiah to the prophetess Huldah to 'enquire of the LORD'. He was the son of Shallum (*2 Kings 22:4–14; 1 Chron. 6:13; 2 Chron. 34:9–22; 35:8*).

**7.** A priest, this Hilkiah was among the exiles who returned to Jerusalem with Zerubbabel (*Neh. 12:7*).

**8.** *Neh. 8:4* records Hilkiah as one of those who stood beside Ezra at the public reading of the Law. He may be the same as 7. above.                               S.C.

**HILLEL,** the father of Abdon, who led Israel for eight years during the period of the Judges. Abdon was buried at Pirathon in Ephraim (*Judg. 12:13–15*).

**HIRAH** A friend of Judah, Hirah was an 'Adullamite' (*Gen. 38:1, 12*). While staying with Hira, Judah met a Canaanite woman called Shua who bore him a number of sons.

**HIRAM,** the king of Tyre at the time when King David began to build his palace in Jerusalem. His reign continued into Solomon's rule. Both David and Solomon looked to him for the supply of wood for the building of the palace and later the Temple. Hiram exported the famous cedars of Lebanon, but also exported the expert technology and craftsmen needed for carpentry and skilled stonemasonry. A treaty was made between Hiram and Solomon and large amounts of trade went both ways between the countries with Israel sending wheat and olive oil to Tyre (*2 Sam. 5:11; 1 Kings 5:1–18; 1 Chron. 14:1; 2 Chron. 2:11–12*).

Once palace and Temple were finished, Solomon gave Hiram 20 towns in the northern area of Galilee, but Hiram, who had given large amounts of cedar and gold to Solomon, was not pleased with the exchange (*1 Kings 9:11–14; 2 Chron. 8:2*). Relations seem to have survived this diplomatic disaster, however, for Hiram sent sailors to serve in Solomon's navy on the Red Sea. These ships and the ships of Hiram worked together finding treasure for Solomon wherever they could (*1 Kings 9:27; 10:22; 2 Chron. 8:18; 9:10*).
                                                    P.D.G.

**HIZKI** (Heb., 'strong'), one of the sons of Elpaal listed in the Benjamite genealogy leading to Saul (*1 Chron. 8:17*).

**HIZKIAH** (Heb., 'strength of the LORD'), a descendant of King David, listed as one of three sons of Neariah in *1 Chron. 3:23*. This list provides a royal lineage for the kingdom of Judah following the Exile.

**HOBAB** Whether Hobab was Moses' father-in-law or brother-in-law is not altogether clear in the two texts where the name appears (*Num. 10:29; Judg. 4:11*). Indeed it is possible, though unlikely, that two different men are in mind in the two texts. In the first passage he seems to have been a Midianite, while in the later passage he is seen to have been the forefather of Kenites (although *cf. Judg. 1:16*, where the unnamed father-in-law is called a Kenite). In other passages Moses' father-in-law is called Jethro.

The reason for mentioning Hobab in *Num. 10:29* is that Hobab was apparently well acquainted with the desert areas through which Moses and the Israelites would be travelling once they left Sinai. Although he was reluctant at first, Moses persuaded him to join them and the Israelites set out through the wilderness.
                                                    P.D.G.

**HOBAIAH** (Heb., 'the LORD has hidden'). His descendants were among the priests who returned from Exile in Babylon with Nehemiah (*Ezra 2:61; Neh. 7:63*). They could not establish their genealogy and so were forbidden to act as priests.

**HOD** (Heb., 'majesty') is mentioned in *1 Chron. 7:37* as a descendant of Asher and son of Zophah.

**HODAVIAH 1.** One of the sons of Elioenai in the royal line of the descendants of Jehoiachin the captive (*1 Chron. 3:24*).
**2.** This Hodaviah was the head of his family among a group of brave warriors from the tribe of Manasseh. Nevertheless these warriors were unfaithful to God (*1 Chron. 5:24*).
**3.** His grandson Sallu was among the first of the Benjamites to resettle after the Exile (*1 Chron. 9:7*).
**4.** Descendants of his line were among the Levites who returned from Exile with Nehemiah (*Ezra 2:40; Neh. 7:43*).
**5.** His descendants included Kadmiel, who helped rebuild the Temple after the Exile (*Ezra 3:9*). Possibly the same as 4. above.

**HODESH** (Heb., 'new moon'), one of the wives of the Benjamite Shaharaim after he had divorced Hushim and Baara. While he lived in Moab, Hodesh bore him seven sons each of whom became heads of families in their own right (*1 Chron. 8:9*).

**HODIAH** (Heb., 'splendour of the LORD').
**1.** One of the Levites who instructed the people in the Law when Ezra read from it, and who lead the people in prayer as they confessed their sins (*Neh. 8:7; 9:5*).
**2.** This Hodiah was one of the Levites who, following the return from Exile, signed the agreement of the people to worship only the Lord (*Neh. 10:10*).
**3.** Another of the Levites who signed the agreement of the people (*Neh. 10:13*).
**4.** Another of the leaders who signed the agreement of the people (*Neh. 10:18*).

**HOGLAH,** one of five daughters born to Zelophehad. These daughters married cousins on their father's side and were members of the tribe of Manasseh (*Num. 26:33; 27:1; 36:1–12; Josh. 17:3*). They faced a predicament over their inheritance, for normally inherited land would have been passed on through a son.

They approached Moses at the entrance to the Tabernacle about the problem, asking him to rule that they should be allowed to inherit their father's property, for it would not be right that his name should die out. Moses consulted the LORD about the situation, as a result of which a new law was promulgated allowing daughters to inherit land from their father. Later some of the leaders from the tribe of Manasseh appealed to Moses about the case, pointing out that if these women were now to marry outside the tribe the land would be lost forever to the tribe. The ruling which followed further defined the law of inheritance, insisting that the women should marry into their father's tribe or else lose the inheritance (*Num. 36*). Hence the daughters married cousins 'on their father's side', thus fulfilling the requirement of the LORD.

When finally the Israelites entered the land of Canaan and the land was divided up among the tribes, the daughters of Zelophehad were duly given their inheritance (*Josh. 17:3–4*). P.D.G.

**HOHAM,** the Amorite king of Hebron. He answered the call of Adoni-zedek, king of Jerusalem, to join a coalition of kings to fight the Gibeonites, who had recently made a peace treaty with Joshua and the Israelites. When Gibeon was attacked, Joshua came to its aid and defeated the coalition. The kings fled to a cave at Makkedah. When Joshua found them there he rolled stones in front of the cave and posted guards so they could not escape. When Joshua returned from battle he brought out the kings and put them to death (*Josh. 10:3–28; 12:10*).

# THE HOLY SPIRIT

Both the Hebrew and Greek words for the Holy Spirit underline the holiness of the Spirit. In the OT, the adjective *holy* preceding the noun *spirit* appears infrequently (*Ps. 51:11; Is. 63:10–11*). By contrast, the NT features this combination in most of its books as a frequently occurring name, especially in Acts. This does not mean that the emphasis on the Spirit is less in the OT than in the NT. The recurring appellation for the Spirit in the OT is the Spirit of God or the Spirit of the LORD; these expressions occur numerous times.

The Heb. and Gk. words for 'spirit' reveal a double meaning: spirit and wind. For instance, 'The Spirit of God was hovering over the waters' (*Gen. 1:2*), but God 'sent a wind over the earth so that the waters receded' (*Gen. 8:1*). And Jesus says to Nicodemus: 'The Spirit gives birth to spirit . . . The wind blows wherever it pleases' (*John 3:6; 8*). Another meaning of the Heb. and Gk. terms for 'spirit' is either divine or human breath (see *Job 4:9; 12:10; 2 Thess. 2:8*).

Throughout Scripture the expression 'spirit' is written either with a capital letter, referring to God's Spirit, or a lower case letter, pointing to the human spirit. Because ancient manuscripts do not feature capital letters, editors and translators are hard pressed at times to determine whether a writer has in mind the Spirit of God or that of man (see, e.g., varying translations of *Acts 19:21*).

## The Spirit in the Old Testament

### At creation

The first time the word 'Spirit' appears in Scripture is in the Genesis creation account. God's Spirit hovering over the waters is the creative power that brings order out of chaos (*Gen. 1:2*). The psalmist echoes this concept when he says: 'By the word of the LORD were the heavens made, their starry host by the breath of his mouth' (*Ps. 33:6*). By the breath of God, Adam became a living being (*Gen. 2:7*). Job affirms that God's Spirit created him and that he received life through the breath of the Almighty (*Job 27:3; 32:8; 33:4; 34:14–15*). When God removes his breath from human beings and animals, they die and return to dust (*Ps. 104:29; Eccl. 3:19–20; 12:7*). In the valley of dry bones, the breath of God entered the skeletons, and they came back to life (*Ezek. 37:1–14*).

### As a Person

The stress on monotheism by the OT writers seems to rule out the doctrine of the Trinity. These writers distinguish between God and God's Spirit, yet they do not consider the Spirit to be a mere emanation from God. Take, for example, the references in *Gen. 1:1–2*. God created heaven and earth, but the Spirit of God hovered over the waters. God says that his Spirit would not contend with man forever (*Gen. 6:3*). This does not mean that the writers saw two distinct divine beings; they understood the Spirit to be God's agent who exercised functions that the biblical writers expressed in human terms. Thus, the Spirit of God is synonymous with the breath of God. This synonymity is pronounced in a few passages: the Levites prayed, 'You gave your good Spirit to instruct [the Israelites]' (Neh. 9:20); David asked, 'Where can I go from your Spirit? Where can I flee from your presence?' (Ps. 139:7); and Isaiah wrote that God's people grieved his Holy Spirit and God became their enemy (Is. 63:10–12; see also 48:16).

### In prophesying

The manifestation of the Spirit is evident in the lives of the prophets who told the people what the LORD said. They became God's mouthpieces when the Spirit descended upon them. The prophet Isaiah declared that the Spirit of the Sovereign God was upon them (Is. 61:1), which was fully realized in Jesus (Luke 4:18). Ezekiel revealed that the Spirit lifted him up and brought him to places and people in a vision that God's Spirit gave him (Ezek. 11).

Even though some people did not bear the title prophet, they nevertheless spoke prophetic words through the Holy Spirit. King David uttered his last poetic testimony before he died and said: 'The Spirit of the LORD spoke through me; his word was on my tongue' (2 Sam. 23:2). When Joseph interpreted Pharaoh's dreams, Pharaoh exclaimed that the Spirit of God was in Joseph (Gen. 41:38–39). After Samuel anointed Saul king of Israel, the Spirit of God came mightily upon Saul and he prophesied. God transformed him into a different person, so that the Israelites asked the question, 'Is Saul also among the prophets?' (1 Sam. 10:5–13). This question was repeated when the Spirit of God descended on Saul while he relentlessly pursued David. Saul stripped off his robes and prophesied (1 Sam. 19:23–24).

In the camp of Israel, God took of the Spirit that rested on Moses and put the Spirit on 70 elders; they began to prophesy and so did Eldad and Medad. When Moses heard about it, he wished that the LORD would place his Spirit on all the people so that everyone might prophesy (Num. 11:25–29). The prophet Micah opposed the false prophets of his day. He said that he was filled with the Spirit of the LORD, with justice and might, to convict Israel of sin (Mic. 3:8).

The prototype of the Messiah is Moses, who was called a prophet and who revealed the Spirit of God. Moses predicted the coming of Christ when he told the Israelites that God would raise up a prophet like Moses from among their own people (Deut. 18:15; 18). Hence, Moses repeatedly introduced God's revelation with the words, 'The LORD said to Moses' (e.g. Num. 8:1; 5, 23). The Spirit took control of prophets and through them revealed the word of the LORD (see Ezek. 2:2; 13:3, 8, 13, 20; Mic. 3:8). The earlier prophets and, by implication, the minor prophets were inspired by the Spirit of the LORD Almighty (Zech. 7:12).

### With power

The Spirit often stirred a person and endowed him with power, as in the case of Samson (Judg. 13:25). The Spirit of the LORD enabled Gideon to rally Israel's tribes to take up arms against foreign oppressors and to rout them with 300 men (see especially Judg. 6:34). Elijah was filled with the Spirit of the LORD, who apparently transported him to various places (1 Kings 18:12; 2 Kings 2:16).

When Samuel anointed David to be king of Israel, 'the Spirit of the LORD came upon David in power'. But at the same time the Spirit left Saul; God gave Saul an evil spirit to torment him (1 Sam. 16:13–14). The Spirit blessed David with musical and poetic gifts, enabled him to be a fearless warrior, and endowed him with splendid leadership capabilities.

The gift of the Spirit was not limited to leaders and kings in Israel. For the construction of the Tabernacle, God appointed Bezalel, Oholiab, and others to carry out the work. The Spirit of God filled Bezalel 'with skill, ability and knowledge in all kinds of crafts' (Exod. 31:2–4; 35:31). In OT times, however, the Spirit did not rest on every Israelite and those who received this special gift had it only temporarily.

## Eschatology

Universal reception of the Holy Spirit was announced prophetically by Joel centuries before the outpouring of the Spirit at Pentecost (see Acts 2:17–21). God spoke through Joel and said: 'And afterward, I will pour out my Spirit on all people. Your sons and daughters will prophesy, your old men will dream dreams, your young men will see visions. Even on my servants, both men and women, I will pour out my Spirit in those days' (Joel 2:28–29). But Joel was not alone in predicting the future outpouring of the Holy Spirit on God's people. Also Isaiah conveyed the word of the LORD and drew the parallel of God pouring out streams of water on dry ground and pouring out his Spirit on Jacob's descendants (Is. 44:3). Through Ezekiel God told the Jewish exiles that the LORD would take them out of the nations and return them to their own land. Then he would put his Spirit in them and motivate them to obey his laws (Ezek. 36:24–28; 39:29). God revealed that the Messiah at his coming would be filled with the Spirit (Is. 11:2), who is also poured out on his covenant people (Is. 32:15; 59:21; Ezek. 37:14). And this Spirit would remain with God's children (Hag. 2:5).

## The intertestamental period

Concerning the Spirit, little can be learned from the literature of the intertestamental period. At most, we hear echoes from the OT era that now reinforce what is already known. Apocryphal and pseudepigraphal books, the so-called deuterocanonical literature, the Qumran documents, and the writings of Philo and Josephus present nothing new. They stress the Spirit's relation to the Messiah (1 Enoch 62:2; Ps. Sol. 17:37; 18:7), the inspiration of former prophets (Sir. 48:24), and a petition for the gift of the Spirit (2 Esdras 14:22). The writings reveal the hope for the coming of a true prophet (1 Macc. 14:41) because the prophets had ceased to appear (1 Macc. 9:27).

## The Spirit in the New Testament

References to the Spirit are numerous in the NT, especially in the writings of Luke and Paul. NT teaching on the holy Spirit fulfils the OT prophecies that predict the Spirit's coming. NT allusions to the Spirit cover the spectrum from the Spirit's overshadowing presence for Jesus' conception (*Matt. 1:18, 20; Luke 1:35*) to the Spirit's call for Jesus' return (*Rev. 22:17*). The NT stresses the Spirit's outpourings, gifts, work, inspiration, fellowship, and abiding presence.

The doctrine of the Trinity is evident in the account of Jesus' baptism: the Father reveals the Son in whom he is pleased, and the Holy Spirit descends on the Son in the form of a dove (*Matt. 3:16–17; Mark 1:10; Luke 3:22*). The trinitarian baptismal formula at the conclusion of Matthew's Gospel emphasizes this same doctrine (*Matt. 28:19*). In the epistolary literature, the apostles often taught the trinitarian tenet either at the beginning or the conclusion of their letters (see *2 Cor. 13;14; Eph. 1:2–11; 1 Pet. 1:1–3*).

### Matthew, Mark and Luke

Apart from the accounts of Jesus' birth, baptism, and temptation, allusions to the Spirit are few in the Gospels of Matthew and Mark. By comparison, Luke's Gospel is replete with passages that refer to the Spirit. Both Matthew and Luke relate Jesus' conception as the work of the Holy Spirit (*Matt. 1:18, 20; Luke 1:35*). John the Baptist told the people that while he baptized with water, Jesus would baptize them with the Holy Spirit and with fire (*Matt. 3:11; Mark 1:8; Luke 3:16*). Before Jesus began his ministry, the Spirit led him into the desert to be tempted by the devil (*Matt. 4:1; Mark 1:12; Luke 4:1*). In Matthew's Gospel, the Spirit of the Father spoke through the disciples (*Matt. 10:20*); in the two accounts of Mark and Luke, the Holy Spirit spoke through God's people (*Mark 13:11; Luke 12:12*). According to all three Synoptic evangelists, the sin against the Holy Spirit will never be forgiven either in this life or in the age to come (*Matt. 12:31–32; Mark 3:29; Luke 12:10*). When Jesus questioned the Pharisees concerning the Christ, he mentioned the Holy Spirit and asked, 'How is it then that David, speaking by the Spirit, calls him "Lord"?' (*Matt. 22:43; Mark 12:36*). That is, the Holy Spirit inspired David to compose *Ps. 110* and to refer to the Christ.

Luke's Gospel has many references to the Holy Spirit. Already in the first two chapters, the readers are told that the Spirit overshadowed Mary (*Luke 1:35*), and filled John the Baptist, Elizabeth, Zechariah and Simeon (*1:15, 17, 41, 67; 2:25–27*). After being tempted by Satan, Jesus returned to Galilee and was endowed with the power of the Holy Spirit, who rested upon him (*Luke 4:14, 18*). Luke mentions that Jesus experienced profound joy through the Holy Spirit (*Luke 10:21*) and told his disciples that the Father gives the Holy Spirit to those who ask him (*11:13*). Luke ends his account with a word of Jesus directed to the disciples; they are told to remain in Jerusalem until they are clothed with supernatural power, namely, with the Holy Spirit (*Luke 24:49*).

### Acts

A new era dawns in the NT with the outpouring of the Holy Spirit at Pentecost. The words that Jesus spoke about the Spirit dwelling in all his people were fulfilled in the apostles and are realized in all believers today. Jesus predicted that, within a few days after his ascension, the baptism of the Spirit would make the apostles witnesses for him in Jerusalem, Judea, Samaria, and to the ends of the world (*Acts 1:5, 8*). This prophecy was fulfilled on the day of Pentecost in Jerusalem for the Jewish people (*Acts 2:4, 33, 38*), later in Samaria for the Samaritans (*8:15–18*), and still later in Caesarea for the Roman centurion Cornelius and his household (*10:44–47; 11:15–16; 15:8*). The last people as a group to receive the outpouring of the Spirit were John the Baptist's followers who were living in Ephesus (*Acts 19:1–7*).

The words 'filled with' and 'full of' occur repeatedly in Acts. For instance, standing before the Sanhedrin, Peter was filled with the Holy Spirit (*Acts 4:8*). When he and John were released and went to their own people, the Spirit filled all of them (*Acts 4:31*). Likewise, the seven deacons were full of the Spirit (*Acts 6:3*), among whom was Stephen (*6:5, 10; 7:55*). Paul also was filled with the Holy Spirit (*Acts 9:17; 13:9*) and so was his companion Barnabas (*11:24*). The believers in Pisidian Antioch received the same blessing (*Acts 13:52*).

In the early church, the Holy Spirit testified through the revealed Word of God (*Acts 1:16; 4:25*). He spoke to Philip (*Acts 8:29*), Peter (*10:19; 11:12*), the leaders of the church in Antioch (*13:2*), and Paul (*21:4, 11*). Moreover, the Holy Spirit confirmed the testimony of the apostles before the Sanhedrin (*Acts 5:32*), and did not permit lying, testing, and resisting him (*5:3, 9; 7:51*). Simon the Sorcerer could not buy the Holy Spirit (*Acts 8:19*). Instead the Spirit strengthened the church (*Acts 9:31*), and approved the work of the Jerusalem Council (*15:28*). The Spirit sent forth Paul and Barnabas (*Acts 13:4*), but forbade Paul and companions to go into the province of Asia and enter Mysia (*16:6–7*). He compelled Paul to go to Jerusalem but warned him that dangers awaited him (*Acts 20:22–23*); even the prophet Agabus predicted Paul's imprisonment (*21:11*; see also *11:28*).

### Paul's epistles

Through his many letters, Paul presents a theology of the Holy Spirit that is more developed than that of other NT writers. He teaches the Spirit's relationship to God the Father and to the Lord Jesus Christ. He instructs the Christians in the work, gifts, power, and presence of the Spirit. In certain chapters of his epistles, Paul develops his Holy Spirit theology (*Rom. 8; 1 Cor. 2; 12; 2 Cor. 3; Gal. 5*). These selections, however, should be studied in the entire context of Paul's letters.

1. *The Spirit of God.* Paul mentioned the Spirit of God primarily in his epistles to the churches in Corinth and Ephesus. He noted that the Spirit of God revealed his wisdom to the believers, made them receptive to spiritual truths, and granted them the ability to be spiritually discerning (*1 Cor. 2:10–14*). He informed the recipients of his epistles that the Spirit of God lived within them because they themselves were God's temple (*Rom. 8:9, 11; 1 Cor. 3:16; 6:19*). Together they formed a dwelling in which the Spirit of God lived (*Eph. 2:22*), and as true believers they worshipped by God's Spirit (*Phil. 3:3*). It is God himself who gave his Spirit to his people (*1 Thess. 4:8*).

In another place, Paul told the Corinthians that they were a letter from Christ which did not show ink but rather the Spirit of the living God. That letter was the tablet of human hearts (*2 Cor. 3:3*). By the indwelling power of the Spirit, Paul was able to counsel the people concerning marital problems and speak with a confidence that the Spirit gave him (1 Cor. 7:40). Conversely, no person in whom God's Spirit dwells can ever curse Jesus. The believer confesses that Jesus is Lord through the Holy Spirit (1 Cor. 12:3).

2. *The Spirit and Jesus.* Paul often failed to distinguish clearly between the Spirit of the Lord God and the Spirit of the Lord Jesus Christ. The words 'Spirit of the Lord' may allude to either the Father or the Son; Paul described the Spirit as 'the Spirit of God', 'the Spirit of the Lord', 'the Spirit of Christ', 'the Spirit of Jesus', and simply 'the Spirit'. The context often gives the reader an understanding of these pertinent passages. To illustrate, in Rom. 8:9 Paul said, 'You, however, are controlled not by the sinful nature but by the Spirit, if the Spirit of God lives in you. And if anyone does not have the Spirit of Christ, he does not belong to Christ.' Paul intimated that the Spirit of God flowed through Christ to God's people and that the same Spirit emanated from both God and Christ. Both the Father and the Son cause the Holy Spirit to dwell in the hearts and lives of the believers.

Similarly, Paul wrote to the Corinthians, 'Now the Lord is the Spirit, and where the Spirit of the Lord is, there is freedom' (2 Cor. 3:17). The context of this verse features Moses putting a veil over his face to prevent the people from seeing God's glory fading from Moses's face (see Exod. 34:33–35). Paul explained that he and fellow believers reflect the Lord's glory by being transformed in the likeness of Christ (2 Cor. 3:18). Thus he conveyed the information that he was talking about Christ and that Christ works through the Spirit.

3. *The work of the Spirit.* Paul taught that the Spirit of God who raised Jesus from the dead is living in the believers and assures them that they also will be raised (Rom. 8:10–11). The Holy Spirit is at work in the hearts of believers when they terminate sinful deeds; they are led by the Spirit as children of God. The Spirit himself affirms the fact that God has adopted the believers as his children (Rom. 8:13–16).

The work of the Spirit is evident in the believers who are called the firstfruits of the forthcoming harvest (Rom. 8:23). In addition, Paul told God's people that the Spirit of God intercedes for them and helps them in their prayers. They themselves do not know how to pray properly, so 'the Spirit intercedes for the saints in accordance with God's will' (Rom. 8:26–27).

The Holy Spirit is instrumental in giving Christians the blessings of righteousness, peace and joy (Rom. 14:17; Gal. 5:5; 1 Thess. 1:6). He is their source of love, hope and power (Rom. 15:13, 16, 19). He sanctifies them through rebirth and renewal (Rom. 15:16; Titus 3:5), has fellowship with them (2 Cor. 13:13; Phil. 2:1), strengthens their faith (Eph. 3:16–17), and seals them in Christ (Eph. 1:13).

4. *Spiritual gifts.* Paul frequently enumerated and explained the gifts which the Holy Spirit imparts to the believers. In his epistle to the Romans, he specified the gifts of prophecy, service, teaching, encouraging, giving, governing, and showing mercy (Rom. 12:6–8). This list is not at all complete, because writing to the Corinthians Paul varied and expanded it. He recorded nine gifts: wisdom, knowledge, faith, healing, miraculous powers, prophecy, discerning of spirits, speaking in tongues, interpretation of tongues (1 Cor. 12:8–10). These nine gifts form three categories: 1. pedagogical: wisdom and knowledge; 2. supernatural: faith, miracles, healing; 3. communicative: prophecy, spirit discernment, tongues, interpretation of tongues. This catalogue shows variation in the last part of 1 Cor.

12. Here Paul enumerated the gifts God has appointed: apostles, prophets, teachers. After these three appointments he mentioned: miracle workers, those who have the gift of healing, helpers, administrators, tongue speakers, and interpreters (vv. 28–30). In another epistle, he also listed appointments Christ has made: apostles, prophets, evangelists, and pastors and teachers (Eph. 4:11).

Instead of enumerating the Spirit's gifts in the Galatian epistle, Paul cited nine fruits of the Spirit: love, joy, peace, patience, kindness, goodness, faithfulness, gentleness, self-control (Gal. 5:22–23). The difference between gifts and fruits is one of bestowal and result. That is, the Holy Spirit imparts a specific gift to a believer, but the working of the Spirit within the believer produces results in the form of spiritual fruits.

5. *The Spirit and Law.* Throughout some of his epistles (*Romans, 2 Corinthians* and *Galatians*), Paul spoke of the Spirit who sets the Christian free from the bondage of the Law. In context, he directed his message to Jewish converts, among others, who were influenced by Judaizers. His basic message was freedom from the law of sin and death through the working of the Holy Spirit (Rom. 8:2, 5–8; 2 Cor. 3:6, 17; Gal. 3:2–5; 5:3–5). This does not mean that by abolishing legalism Paul promoted a form of antinomianism. To the contrary, he taught that the law of the Spirit of life is freedom (Rom. 8:2), that love is the fulfilment of the law (Rom. 13:8–10; Gal. 5:14), and that a believer is led by the Spirit who lives in him (Gal. 5:18, 25).

6. *The Spirit and baptism.* In 1 Cor. 12:13 Paul stated that 'we were all baptized by one Spirit into one body – whether Jews or Greeks, slave or free – and we were all given the one Spirit to drink'. He emphasized the word *all* to indicate that people from every area, race and social status are included. He stressed the universality of Christ's body, that is, the church. In both text and context, he indicated that he was speaking figuratively about baptism and drinking the one Spirit and he gave no indication that he was thinking of the sacraments of baptism and the Lord's Supper. Here Paul did not allude to water baptism and Communion.

The flow of 1 Cor. 12:13 suggests that to be baptized signifies that a person becomes a living member of the church upon conversion. When spiritual regeneration takes place, one enters the body of Christ, that is, the church. Not the external observance of water baptism but the internal transformation by the Holy Spirit brings a believer into fellowship with Christ. Moreover, the Greek aorist verb which is translated as 'we were given to drink', indicates a single occurrence. If this verb were to relate to the Eucharist, as some suggest, it would be contrary to Paul's instruction to keep on observing the sacrament of Communion until Jesus returns (1 Cor. 11:25–26).

## John's Gospel and 1 John

1. *John's Gospel.* In many chapters of this Gospel, John referred to the Holy Spirit and recorded the words of Jesus concerning the Spirit. He alluded to the baptism of Jesus upon whom the Spirit descended as a dove. He noted that John the Baptist, who baptized with water, revealed that Jesus would baptize with the Holy Spirit (John 1:32–33). God gave the Spirit to Jesus without measure (John 3:34).

Jesus instructed Nicodemus that he had to be born again before he could be part of

God's Kingdom. He said, 'No one can enter the kingdom of God unless he is born of water and the Spirit. Flesh gives birth to flesh, but the Spirit gives birth to the Spirit' (John 3:5–6). John used the Greek word pneuma with two different meanings: wind and Spirit. The mysteriousness of the coming and going of the wind is similar to being born of the Spirit (John 3:8). The Spirit is the source of life (John 6:63), and that life may be compared with streams of living water that, spiritually speaking, flow forth from a believer (7:38–39).

Jesus' farewell address in the upper room stressed the principle of the Holy Spirit. This address teaches that the Spirit is given by the Father, remains with the believers forever, is another Counsellor, is a Person, and personifies the truth (John. 14:16–17). The Counsellor goes out from the Father, is sent by the Son, and testifies about Jesus (John 15:26). Also, the Counsellor convicts the world of sin, righteousness and judgment (John 16:7–11). The Spirit guides the believers in all truth, provides future revelation, and glorifies Jesus (John 16:13–15). And last, in anticipation of Pentecost, Jesus breathed the Holy Spirit on the disciples to help them in the task which they received from him (John 20:22).

2.   1 John.   The references to the Holy Spirit in this epistle do not differ much from those in John's Gospel. The Spirit given to believers creates in them an awareness that the Father, through the Son, lives within them (1 John 3:24; 4:13). How are Christians able to recognize the Spirit of God? They know him by acknowledging that Jesus Christ in human form has come from God; and they listen to God (1 John 4:2, 6). The Spirit of truth testifies that Jesus is the Son of God (1 John 5:6–8).

### The rest of the New Testament

1.   Hebrews.   The writer of the epistle to the Hebrews taught the doctrine of the Trinity especially with respect to God's revelation. Although David composed Ps. 95 and Jeremiah recorded a prophecy concerning the new covenant (Jer. 31:31–34), their words were those of the Holy Spirit who addressed the readers of the epistle to the Hebrews (Heb. 3:7; 10:15). At the proper time, the Spirit revealed that forgiveness of sins through the shedding of animal blood would end (Heb. 9:8, 14). In addition, the writer of this epistle pointed out those who sin against the Holy Spirit (6:4–6; 10:29). But he noted that God's people are recipients of the gifts which the Holy Spirit distributes to them (2:4).

2.   Peter's and Jude's epistles.   1 Pet. has five references to the Holy Spirit (1 Pet. 1:2, 11, 12; 3:18; 4:14). With the Father and the Son, the Spirit is the sanctifier of God's elect (1:2). The Spirit predicted the sufferings of Christ and the subsequent glory that would follow (1:11). And the Spirit guided and continues to guide those who preach the gospel of salvation (1:12).

Whereas the other parts of the NT taught that God the Father raised Jesus from the dead, Peter in his first epistle stated that Christ was made alive by the Spirit (1 Pet. 3:18; cf. Rom. 8:11). In short, the Trinity was involved in the resurrection. As the Spirit was with Christ, so the Spirit of glory rests on all the people who suffer for the sake of Christ (1 Pet. 4:14).

2 Pet. has only one reference to the Spirit (1:21). Peter wrote that the people who composed the Scriptures were carried along by the Holy Spirit. For the writing of

the OT and the NT, the Spirit used human beings with their talents and insights, their characteristics and training. In so doing, the Spirit kept them from sin and error.

Jude disclosed that ungodly people who were bent on dividing the church and who were led by physical desires lacked the indwelling power of the Holy Spirit (Jude 19). However, true believers strengthen their faith by praying constantly in the Holy Spirit (v. 20).

3. *Revelation.* The last book in the NT canon has a number of passages that speak of the Holy Spirit. On the island of Patmos, John was in the Spirit both on the Lord's Day and when he looked through an open door into heaven (Rev. 1:10; 4:2). Later he was carried by the Spirit into the desert and to a great and high mountain (17:3; 21:10). The Spirit addressed the seven churches in Asia Minor and everyone who has an ear is exhorted to listen (Rev. 2:7, 11, 17, 29; 3:6, 13, 22). The Holy Spirit added to the beatitude, 'Blessed are the dead who die in the Lord from now on', these words: 'Yes, they will rest from their labour, for their deeds will follow them' (14:13). And last, together with Jesus' church, the Holy Spirit addresses Christ and says, 'Come!' (22:17).

## Conclusion

In appearance, the Holy Spirit descended on Jesus in the bodily form of a dove (Luke 3:22), settled as tongues of fire on the people gathered at Pentecost in Jerusalem (Acts 2:3), and is the breath of God in both creation and re-creation (Ps. 33:6; John 3:8).

The Spirit was and is working in the formation and application of the Scriptures. He literally lifted up the writers of the OT and the NT and guided them in the very words as they wrote the Scriptures (2 Pet. 1:20–21). He addresses the people through the Scriptures (Acts 28:25; Heb. 3:7; 9:8; 10:15). The word of God is the sword of the Spirit (Eph. 6:17).

For the Christian, the Spirit is the Comforter who places his seal upon the believer to indicate ownership (2 Cor. 2:21). At the same time, the Christian has received the assurance that the Spirit is the first instalment of still more and greater blessings that are waiting for the believer (2 Cor. 1:22). The Spirit is like the dew that descends unseen on the earth yet exhibits visible results. God blesses his people through the Holy Spirit and grants them the trinitarian blessing of Christ's grace, God's love, and the fellowship of the Holy Spirit (2 Cor.13:14).

S.J.K.

**HOMAM** One of Esau's descendants through Seir the Horite. His father was Lotan (1 Chron. 1:39; Gen. 36:22, where the Heb. has Heman).

**HOPHNI** The brother of Phinehas, he was one of Eli's sons and a priest in Israel at Shiloh (1 Sam. 1:3). The sons of Eli became thoroughly corrupt and took advantage of their privileged position. 'They had no regard for the LORD' (1 Sam. 2:12). They would take meat people brought for sacrifice and, instead of waiting till the fat had been burned up, in accordance with the Law (Lev. 3:3–5; 7:29–34), they would insist on taking the meat away early in the sacrifice for roasting and eating by priests. They thus treated 'the LORD's offering with contempt' (1 Sam. 2:15–17). The sons were also guilty of having unlawful sexual intercourse with women who were serving at the door to the Tabernacle (v. 22). In the midst of all this squalor and evil the LORD answered the prayer of Hannah and Samuel was born.

It was clearly Eli's responsibility to discipline his sons and ensure proper order and obedience to the Law in Shiloh. However, he appears to have been a weak and indecisive man who did point out to his sons the error of their ways (1 Sam. 2:23–25), but who did not carry enough authority to put a stop to the sin. The sons merely 'did not listen' (v. 25). God twice warned Eli that judgment would come on his family. The first time this was through 'a man of God' whose name is not given (vv. 27–36). Even as God promised judgment, so he also promised that for the sake of Israel, his people, he would one day raise up a 'faithful priest' who would do what was right before God and who would 'minister before my anointed one always' (v. 35). The promise of God given in the midst of judgment reminded the Israelites that the covenant God would remain faithful to them and it indirectly looked forward to the time of Christ's coming.

The second warning came to Eli through the child Samuel (1 Sam. 3:11–18) whom God spoke to one night (vv. 1–10). It is indicative of how, sadly, the priesthood had moved far from obedience to the LORD that the passage in 1 Sam. 3 begins by saying, 'In those days the word of the LORD was rare'. The message this time was that, in spite of the earlier warning, there had been no repentance (v. 13) and so final judgment was to come on Eli's family. That judgment came (1 Sam. 4) when, in a battle against the Philistines at Aphek, the ark of the covenant was captured. Hophni and

Phinehas died (1 Sam. 4:11) and Eli, on hearing the news of the capture of the ark, fell off his seat and died (v. 18).

Throughout Scriptures, the responsibilities laid on those called to serve and lead the LORD's people are formidable. They are not only to perform their duties of sacrifice, teaching etc. exactly as commanded by the LORD but their life-style is to reflect this divine calling. Even in the NT those who lead God's people as elders are to live exemplary lives (cf. Mal. 2:7–9; 1 Tim. 3). It is therefore not surprising that James offers the advice: 'Not many of you should presume to be teachers, my brothers, because you know that we who teach will be judged more strictly' (James 3:1). However, the episode with Eli and his sons reminds leaders that they, of all people, should know that God is gracious and will forgive them if they repent of their sin.                P.D.G.

**HOPHRA** Pharaoh Hophra reigned in Egypt from 589–570 BC. He is mentioned in the Bible once in Jer. 44:30. Jeremiah had long prophesied that the people of Judah and Jerusalem should remain in their land and live under the Babylonian overlords. This was the LORD's judgment on them, but if they followed his word and stayed they would survive. However, when Ishmael killed Gedaliah, Johanan and other leaders from Judah fled to Egypt taking Jeremiah with them. God then pronounced judgment on those who had gone to Egypt and said that Egypt would not be a safe place for they too would be invaded and Hophra would be killed. Ezekiel also prophesied the downfall of this Pharaoh (Ezek. 29:1–16 etc.). Hophra was eventually killed in a revolt against him in Egypt. Nebuchadnezzar invaded Egypt in 568 BC.
                P.D.G.

**HORAM** was the king of Gezer in southern Canaan at the time of the conquest by Joshua. When Joshua besieged Lachish and defeated the city, Horam came up in support only to be defeated himself by Joshua (*Josh. 10:33*).

**HORI 1.** One of Esau's descendants through Seir the Horite and a leader of his people. His father was Lotan (*Gen. 36:22; 1 Chron. 1:39*).

**2.** From the tribe of Simeon, the father of Shaphat. Shaphat was one of the twelve spies sent by Joshua to spy out the land of Canaan (*Num. 13:5*).

**HOSAH** When the ark of the covenant was brought up to Jerusalem, King David made Hosah the 'gatekeeper' to the entrance to the tent in which the ark had been placed (*1 Chron. 16:38*). He was a Levite of the Merarite clan. Later he and his family became gatekeepers of the West Gate and the Shalleketh Gate to the Temple area (*1 Chron. 26:10–11, 16*).

**HOSEA** (Heb., 'help' or 'salvation'). The name is probably hypocoristic for *yᵉhosua* (Joshua), 'Yahweh is salvation'. Hosea, the prophet, is the only person in the OT with this particular name, though many others bear names with the *ys* ('salvation') element.

Little is known of the ancestry of the prophet, only that he was a son of Beeri (*Hos. 1:1*). He prophesied in the days of Uzziah (790–739 BC), Jotham (750–731), Ahaz (735–715) and Hezekiah (729–686), all kings of Judah, and in the reign of Jeroboam II of Israel (793–753). His public ministry thus covered a span of time from at least 755–715 BC. This makes Hosea a contemporary of Isaiah (639–680) and possibly of Amos (765–755) and Micah (735–700) as well. Like Amos, Hosea directed his message primarily to the Northern Kingdom, Israel, and thus most of his work must have been completed before 722 BC, the year of Samaria's fall to Assyria.

It is likely that Hosea was a citizen of Israel and not Judah, because of his in-

tense feelings for and knowledge of the Northern Kingdom. His message is filled with references to places and events that only one from Israel was likely to know about (*cf. Hos. 6:8*) or give such attention to (*7:1; 8:5–6; 9:15; 10:5; 12:5, 12; 14:1*). He focused almost exclusively on Israel in his direct address (*2:1–2; 4:1, 15; 5:1, 8; 6:1, 4; 9:1, 5, 7; 10:9, 12; 11:8; 12:9; 13:4, 9–13; 14:1, 8*) and showed relatively scant concern for Judah (*6:4, 11*). The reference to the four kings of Judah who were his contemporaries was only to underscore his belief in the legitimacy of the Davidic dynasty and to attest to its unbroken succession. As a true prophet, even from the Northern Kingdom, such an assessment by Hosea should not be surprising.

Almost unique to Hosea is his use of drama to drive home his prophetic message. But this drama was not mere role-playing, for it involved the prophet's married and family life and in most intimate and highly emotional terms. One of the most common metaphors to describe Yahweh's covenant relationship with Israel was that of marriage. In effect, when Yahweh chose Israel as a covenant partner, he 'married' her (*cf. Ezek. 16:6–14*) and when Israel proved to be disobedient she is said to have 'played the harlot' or to have 'committed adultery' (*Ezek. 23:3, 5, 11, 37, 45; cf. Jer. 3:9*).

The major theme of Hosea's message is Israel's covenant infidelity, unfaithfulness described as adultery (*Hos. 4:10; 9:1*). Normal human response to such blatant disloyalty by a spouse is divorce, a measure sanctioned in the Law itself for so serious a transgression (*Deut. 24:1–4; cf. Matt. 19:7–9*). Even Yahweh had threatened to do away with unfaithful Israel and to take a new people, a new bride as it were, as his 'wife' (*Exod. 32:7–14; Deut. 9:14, 25–29; Hos. 9:14–17*). His promise to the patriarchs of an everlasting covenant with them and their descendants made that impossible, however, and so the LORD graciously forgave the wicked nation and patiently restored it to himself (*Hos. 11:8–11*). What restoration failed to come to pass in history was promised for the eschatological age to come when Israel would be the redeemed and renewed people of the Lord (*Rom. 11:25–32.*).

In order for Hosea's message regarding Israel's adultery and the LORD's restorative grace to have maximum impact, he was commanded by the LORD to marry 'an adulterous wife' and to beget 'children of unfaithfulness' (*Hos. 1:2*). The moral question of God's asking the prophet to undertake such a tainted relationship leads many scholars to view the mandate (and indeed the whole account of marriage and children in *Hos. 1–3*) as an allegory or parable. There is, however, no literary of contextual clue whatsoever to support such a genre decision. An objective and straightforward reading of the story leaves no doubt that Hosea married such a wife and fathered such children.

However, the moral dilemma remains, giving rise to the likelihood that Hosea's wife Gomer revealed her infidelity only after their marriage had taken place. He writes of it then proleptically, after the event, but as though it had not yet happened. She was adulterous in the sense that that was what she would prove to be. It then follows that the 'children of unfaithfulness' are such because they were offspring of an adulteress in the making. What must be noted especially, however, are the names of the children, each of which is prophetically and theologically significant. The first of these, a son, was named Jezreel ('God plants'), so-called because God's judgment on the Jehu dynasty for the massacre at Jezreel (*2 Kings 10:1–14*) was about to fall (*Hos. 1:4–5*), something that took place with the death of King Zechariah in 753/52 BC (*2 Kings 15:8–12*). Jezreel also speaks of the abundant harvests that God would

bring in the end times (*Hos. 2:21–23*). The daughter's name was Lo-Ruhamah ('not loved'), for God would no longer love (i.e. show covenant favour) toward Israel (*Hos. 1:6*). The second son was Lo-Ammi ('not my people'), for Israel's sins had removed him from that relationship.

Having married Gomer and sired children by her, Hosea witnessed her unfaithfulness as she went away to other lovers (*Hos. 3:1*). But God then called the prophet to something more difficult: to bring her back to himself, redeemed and forgiven (*Hos. 3:1–3*). This he did and in so doing exemplified the love and grace of God that was so effective on Israel's behalf that Lo-Ruhamah ('not loved') became Ruhamah ('loved') and Lo-Ammi ('not my people') became Ammi ('my people') (*Hos. 2:1*).

The message of redeeming grace is at the heart of the remainder of the book of Hosea (*Hos. 4–14*). The NT picks up this theme as well and cites those very texts that clarify the meaning of the gospel. Peter and Paul both speak of the Gentiles as the non-people who are now a people and the ones who have found saving mercy (*1 Pet. 2:10; Rom. 9:25–26; cf. Hos. 1:6, 9; 2:1, 23*). Matthew linked the visit by the infant Jesus to Egypt with the Exodus deliverance of Israel, an act that displayed God's covenant love (*Matt. 2:15; cf. Hos. 11:1*). Finally, Paul compared the resurrection of God's saints to the renewal of OT Israel, a veritable restoration of the dead to life (*1 Cor. 15:55; cf. Hos. 13:14*). Hosea thus played his part and played it well, for in deed and in word he portrayed the life-changing message of divine grace. E.M.

**HOSHAIAH** **1.** He led one of the large choirs along the wall of Jerusalem when it was dedicated by Nehemiah. He was accompanied by half the leaders of Judah (*Neh. 12:32*).

**2.** His son Jezaniah was an army officer who with the other officers approached

Jeremiah for guidance as to whether or not they should flee the land (*Jer. 42:1*). They did not react favourably to Jeremiah's advice (*Jer. 43:2*). See *Jezaniah* for detail.

**HOSHAMA** (Heb., 'the LORD has heard') is listed among the royal line of descent following the Exile. He was a descendant of King David and a son of Jehoiachin (Jeconiah in some translations), the captive king of Judah (*1 Chron. 3:18*).

**HOSHEA** (Heb., 'May the LORD save').
**1.** Hoshea son of Nun was given the name Joshua by Moses when he was sent out to spy out the land of Canaan as a representative of the tribe of Ephraim (*Num. 13:8, 16; Deut. 32:44*). See *Joshua.*
**2.** Hoshea son of Elah assassinated Pekah son of Remaliah and became king of Israel (*2 Kings 15:30; 17:1*). Pekah had tried to fight off Assyria and consequently had lost territory to Tiglath-Pileser, king of Assyria. It was probably because of the declining power of the nation under his leadership that the rebellion took place, but it is also likely that Hoshea had some backing from the Assyrians. Hoshea then ruled in Samaria for nine years, having come to the throne in 732 BC (*2 Kings 17:1*). Almost the only area of the Northern Kingdom of Israel that had not been completely conquered by this stage was Samaria itself and part of Ephraim but, even so, Hoshea was nothing more than a vassal king to Assyria. He had to pay heavy taxes to Tiglath-Pileser's successor, Shalmaneser, who came to the Assyrian throne in 727 BC (*2 Kings 17:3*).
Hoshea tried to declare independence, stopped paying tribute, and appealed for help to Egypt. When Shalmaneser heard of this he invaded the land again and laid siege to Samaria for three years. Hoshea was captured and eventually, in 722 BC, the city fell and the Israelites were deported to Assyria (*2 Kings 17:4*).

The writer of *2 Kings* makes it clear that this final destruction of the Northern Kingdom was the final judgment of God on the nation because of its idolatry and sin (*2 Kings 17:7–23; 18:10*). Many prophets had prophesied the fall of the nation if they continued their worship of pagan gods (*2 Kings 17:13*; e.g. see *Hos. 7:11–16*), but they had not repented and God's judgment had finally fallen on the nation. They had violated his covenant (*2 Kings 17:15; 18:12*) and so the covenant curses had fallen on them just as God had promised would happen.
**3.** During the reign of King David, this Hoshea son of Azaziah was an official in the tribe of Ephraim (*1 Chron. 27:20*).
**4.** Another Hoshea was a leader of the Jews who, in the time of Nehemiah, was one of those who sealed the binding agreement to worship the LORD and obey his Law (*Neh. 10:23*).                    P.D.G.

**HOTHAM   1.** A grandson of Asher and a leader of that tribe. His father was Heber (*1 Chron. 7:32*).
**2.** The Aroerite father of Shama and Jeiel who were among David's mighty warriors and fought at his side, leading his men into battle (*1 Chron. 11:44*).

**HOTHIR** One of the sons of Asaph listed among those set apart for the ministry of prophesying and music during the reign of King David. He was a son of Heman, the king's seer (*1 Chron. 25:4, 28*).

**HUBBAH** Mentioned as a son of Shomer, a 'brave warrior' and 'outstanding leader' in the tribe of Asher (*1 Chron. 7:34*).

**HUL** One of the four Shemite sons of Aram listed in *Gen. 10:23* and *1 Chron. 1:17*. Aram was a son of Shem, a grandson of Adam. The best Heb. manuscripts of *1 Chron. 1:17* do not separate the sons of Shem himself from the sons of Aram.

**HULDAH** When King Josiah discovered the lost Book of the Law, his advisers sought help in understanding the books from Huldah, a prophetess and the wife of Shallum. Huldah lived in Jerusalem and prophesied two events: (1) the destruction of Judah due to idolatry, just as the Book of the Law had foretold, and (2) peace during King Josiah's lifetime because his 'heart was responsive' and he had repented and turned to the LORD (2 Kings 22:14–20; 2 Chron. 34:22–28).

**HUPHAM** A son of Benjamin who led the Huphamite clan (Num. 26:39), also called Huppim in Gen. 46:21.

**HUPPAH** (Heb., 'protection'). One among the priests who were chosen to be officials in the sanctuary 'according to the last instructions of David'. Impartial selection from among the descendants of Eleazar and Ithamar was made by drawing lots. The 13th lot fell to Huppah and that was the order in which he ministered when entering the sanctuary (1 Chron. 24:13).

**HUPPIM** A son of Benjamin listed among those who went with Jacob into Egypt in Gen. 46:21. In Num. 26:39 he is called Hupham after whom the Huphamite clan was named.

**HUR** **1.** Hur was one of the leaders of the Israelites during the time of Moses. He helped hold up Moses' hands in prayer when Joshua was fighting the Amalekites. The raising of Moses' hands became a vivid picture of the need for the Israelites to depend entirely upon the LORD. When the hands were lowered they started to lose the battle but victory came because of Moses' hands lifted in prayer by Aaron and Hur (Exod. 17:10, 12). Hur was from the tribe of Judah and seems to have been on a par with Aaron in terms of authority. Moses left him and Aaron jointly in charge when he went up Mount Sinai (Exod. 24:14). This Hur was probably the same as the Hur who was the son of Caleb and Ephrath and father of Uri. His son

was called Uri and his grandson Bezalel was later chosen by the LORD to make artistic designs for the Tabernacle. Bezalel was specially endowed with the Holy Spirit for this work (Exod. 31:2–3; 35:30; 38:22; 1 Chron. 2:19–20, 50; 4:1, 4; 2 Chron. 1:5).

**2.** One of the five kings of Midian whom Moses had defeated in battle as part of the LORD's vengeance on the Midianites for seducing the Israelites away from the LORD (Num. 31:2, 8; Josh. 13:21; see Num. 25). They had been allies of Sihon (see Sihon for more detail). Their land was given to the tribe of Reuben.

**3.** The father of Rephaiah. Rephaiah was one of the rulers in Jerusalem following the return from the Exile in Babylon (Neh. 3:9).        P.D.G.

**HURAI** (also known as Hiddai in the parallel passage in 2 Sam. 23:30) was 'from the ravines of Gaash' (1 Chron. 11:32). He was one of David's 'Thirty' mighty men who went to battle for him and led the people of Israel to war.

**HURAM** (Heb., 'my brother is exalted').

**1.** Huram, a grandson of Benjamin and a son of Bela, is mentioned in 1 Chron. 8:5 in a genealogy leading from Benjamin to King Saul.

**2.** 'Huram was highly skilled and experienced in all kinds of bronze work' (1 Kings 7:13–14). He lived in Tyre in the time of King Solomon when the Temple was being built. His reputation as a master-craftsman must have spread far and wide because Solomon specifically sent for him to come and work on bronze pillars and other artefacts of bronze for the Temple. The extraordinary size and brilliance of the pillars and other items he cast for the Temple gives some indication both of the scale of the Temple and its wealth and beauty. 'The weight of the bronze was not determined' (1 Kings 7:47). His importance in the work of the

Temple is further reflected in the space given to him by the writer (vv. 13–47).

Huram's mother was a widow from the tribe of Naphtali, but his father was a man from Tyre and had also been a great craftsman (v. 14). His half-Israelite descent was probably why he was allowed to work in the Temple. In the account of his work in 2 Chron. 4:11–18 he is also called Huram-Abi (v. 16), which was probably a mark of respect.     P.D.G.

**HURAM-ABI** A master-craftsman from Tyre who worked on the Temple. He was sent to Solomon by Hiram king of Tyre for this purpose after Solomon had written a letter to the king asking for help with raw materials (2 Chron. 2:13; 4:16). For more detail see Huram (2.) above.

**HURI** The father of Abihail. He was a leader in the tribe of Gad and son of Jaroah (1 Chron. 5:14).

**HUSHAH** A son of Ezer from the tribe of Judah and a descendant of Hur. However, the meaning is not all that clear, and it is possible that his name indicates a place where Ezer had settled (1 Chron. 4:4; see 2 Sam. 23:27).

**HUSHAI** **1.** A close friend and trusted ally of King David, he was called 'Hushai the Arkite', Archi being an area west of Bethel (2 Sam. 15:32; 16:16; 17:5 etc.). Hushai's loyalty to David was clearly seen during the time of Absalom's rebellion. Absalom had carefully cultivated the loyalty and respect of many Israelites by meeting them and sorting out their problems. Eventually Absalom drew troops to himself and went to Hebron, where he pronounced himself king (2 Sam. 15:9–10). David had to flee Jerusalem, but asked Hushai to stay and become an undercover agent by feigning allegiance to Absalom. Hushai could then use the sons of the priests Zadok and Abiathar to send messages about what Absalom and his advisor, Ahithophel, were planning (2 Sam. 15:3–36).

Hushai followed the plan as arranged and worked his way into favour with Absalom until he was able to offer contrary advice to Ahithophel. Absalom accepted Hushai's advice not to attack David immediately but rather to call all the Israelites together to Jerusalem (2 Sam. 17:1–14). Hushai passed on this information through the priests, thus allowing David time enough to prepare his response. David's men were able to plan a surprise attack on the Israelite forces and defeat them in battle (2 Sam. 18), and this led eventually to Absalom's death. Ahithophel committed suicide.

In these events the writer of 2 Samuel makes it very clear that Hushai was being used by the LORD to ensure that his chosen servant, King David, was restored to the throne, and to ensure the destruction of Absalom (2 Sam. 17:14). God's plans for the Davidic throne that would eventually lead to the coming of the Messiah were not to be thwarted. Hushai's faithfulness to David ensured that his name would live on as 'the king's friend' (1 Chron. 27:33).

**2.** Mentioned in 1 Kings 4:16 as the father of Baana. Baana was one of the twelve district governors of Israel under Solomon.     P.D.G.

**HUSHAM** (Heb., 'haste'), a descendant of Esau, is mentioned in the list of the kings of Edom in the time before Israel had a king. He followed Jobab in the succession and preceded Hadad son of Bedad. He came from the land of the 'Temanites' (Gen. 36:34–35; 1 Chron. 1:45–46).

**HUSHIM** **1.** One of the sons of Dan, and a clan leader, who travelled with Jacob to Egypt (Gen. 46:23). In Num. 26:42 he is named Shuham (a change in the consonant order has taken place).

262

**2.** Wife to Shaharaim, a Benjamite who lived in Moab. He later divorced her and his second wife Baara. Shaharaim is listed in the genealogy leading to King Saul (1 Chron. 8:8, 11).

**HYMENAEUS** It is likely the same person is in view in 1 Tim. 1:20 and 2 Tim. 2:17. He was a heretical teacher linked with Alexander and with Philetus (see *Alexander*). The heresy spread 'like gangrene' and was a distortion of Scripture. Particularly serious was their teaching that the resurrection had already happened (2 Tim. 2:18). Perhaps they believed the resurrection was simply a description of a spiritual experience rather than the resurrection of the *body* – a teaching that is fundamental to the Christian faith (e.g. see 1 Cor. 15:16–19). Such heresies have not been uncommon through history and Christians, wishing to follow Paul's example, have often had to confront the issues with a strong insistence on the bodily resurrection.

P.D.G.

# I

**IBHAR** (Heb., 'God chooses'). A son of King David. After David conquered Jerusalem and moved there from Hebron he took many wives and concubines. One of his many children was Ibhar (2 Sam. 5:15; 1 Chron. 3:6; 14:5).

**IBNEIAH** (Heb., 'the LORD builds'). Mentioned in 1 Chron. 9:8 as the son of Jeroham. After the captivity, Ibneiah was among the first returnees to Jerusalem from the tribe of Benjamin.

**IBNIJAH** (Heb., 'the LORD builds). Mentioned in 1 Chron. 9:8 as the father of Reuel. After the captivity, his great-grandson, Meshullam, was among the first returnees to Jerusalem from the tribe of Benjamin.

**IBRI** Found in the lists of 1 Chron. 24:27, Ibri was the son of Jaaziah, the son of Merari, a Levite.

**IBSAM** (Heb., 'fragrant'). A grandson of Issachar and son of Tola, Ibsam was a family leader and a valiant soldier (1 Chron. 7:2).

**IBZAN** became the tenth judge (see Judges) of Israel and came from and was later buried in Bethlehem (Judg. 12:8–10). It is probable that this Bethlehem was in Zebulun (see Judg. 19:15–16). He succeeded Jephthah and reigned for seven years. Little is known of him except that he had 30 sons and 30 daughters. These all married outside Ibzan's own clan and in this way, no doubt, Ibzan extended his influence through Israel.

**ICHABOD** (Heb., 'no glory') was the son of Phinehas and his wife. She died in giving birth to him while in premature labour. Phinehas and Hophni (see Hophni) were the evil sons of Eli and priests in Israel. When news came that both Hophni and Phinehas had been killed in the battle of Aphek and that the Philistines had captured the ark of the covenant, Eli fell down dead and Phinehas' wife went into labour. At such a moment of despair, she prophetically named her child 'Ichabod, saying, "The glory has departed from Israel"' (1 Sam. 4:21).

**IDBASH** Listed among the descendants of Judah and a leader of that tribe, Idbash was one of the sons of Etam (1 Chron. 4:3).

**IDDO** (Heb., 'timely').
**1.** The Iddo mentioned in Zech 1:1 is not to be confused with many others whose names are rendered Iddo in English but represent different Heb. forms such as Iddo, yIddo, ye do, or the like. Iddo of Zech 1:1, 7 is said to be the father of Berekiah or of Zechariah (Ezra 5:1; 6:14). By the spelling Iddo he is similarly identified in Neh. 12:16. The latter passage suggests that Iddo was head of a family of post-exilic priests. See Zechariah.
**2.** This Iddo was the Father of Ahinadab. Ahinadab was one of Solomon's twelve district governors (1 Kings 4:14).

**3.** Iddo, the son of Joah, was a descendant of Gershon, son of Levi, head of one of the Levitical clans (1 *Chron.* 6:21).

**4.** Iddo, the Son of Zechariah, was the officer over the half-tribe of Manasseh in Gilead under David's rule (1 *Chron.* 27:21). The Zechariah here is clearly not the prophet.

**5.** Iddo, the Seer, was a prophet in the days of Solomon and of Jeroboam I, king of Israel (2 *Chron.* 9:29). He was responsible, among other things, for keeping record of genealogies (2 *Chron.* 12:15; 13:22).

**6.** Iddo, the Temple servant, was a Jewish leader in Ezra's time from Casiphia, in Persia (*Ezra* 8:17). Considerations such as chronology rule out his identification with the Iddo of *Neh.* 12:4, ancestor of Zechariah (*Neh.* 12:16; *Ezra* 5:1; 6:14). E.M.

**IEZER** A contracted form of Abiezer. An inheritor of the tribe of Manasseh through Gilead, he was a clan leader (*Num.* 26:30).

**IGAL 1.** One of the twelve spies sent out by Moses from the Desert of Paran to spy out the land of Canaan (*Num.* 13:7). A representative of each tribe was chosen and Igal, the son of Joseph, was from the tribe of Issachar. For further detail on their mission see *Shammua.*

**2.** One of David's 'Thirty' mighty warriors who fought at his side. He was the son of Nathan from Zobah (2 *Sam.* 23:36).

**3.** Mentioned in 1 *Chron.* 3:22 as a descendant of Shecaniah and son of Shemaiah. He was one of the royal line from Jehoiachin following the Exile.

**IGDALIAH** (Heb., 'the LORD is great'). The father of Hanan. Hanan was a man of God who had rooms in the Temple area in Jerusalem (*Jer.* 35:4). The rooms were later used by Jeremiah.

**IKKESH** (Heb., 'crooked'). A man from Tekoa who was the father of Ira. Ira was one of David's 'Thirty' mighty warriors. As a commander in David's army, Ira was on duty with his men in the sixth month of each year and had 24,000 men in his division (2 *Sam.* 23:26; 1 *Chron.* 11:28; 27:9).

**ILAI,** an Ahohite, was one of David's mighty warriors (1 *Chron.* 11:29).

**IMLAH** The father of the prophet Micaiah. Micaiah prophesied during the reign of Ahab, the evil king of Israel, by whom he was hated because he never prophesied anything good. He was in fact a true prophet of the LORD who correctly prophesied Ahab's death (1 *Kings* 22:8–9; 2 *Chron.* 18:7–8).

## IMMANUEL

Immanuel is mentioned four times in Scripture (*Is.* 7:14; 8:8, 10; *Matt.* 1:23). The name means 'El (God) is with us', and indicates that the person(s) demonstrated the special presence of God with his people. Similar names appear on at least two occasions in ancient Jewish writings outside of Scripture.

Christians recognize Immanuel as the name for Jesus. *Matt.* 1:23 says that Jesus' virgin birth fulfilled the prophecy of *Is.* 7:14, 'The virgin will be with child and will give birth to a son, and will call him Immanuel.' From the early centuries of Christianity, however, Jewish interpreters have disputed this Christian claim. They have argued that Isaiah referred either to his own child or to Hezekiah, the son of Ahaz. Nevertheless, Christians have held tenaciously to the identification of Jesus as the Immanuel child of Isaiah's prophecy.

To understand the significance of this title for Jesus, we must first look at the original historical context of Isaiah's prophecy. The events of *Is. 7–8* took place during a time of crisis in the reign of Ahaz, king of Judah (732–715 BC). In 735/4 King Rezin of Syria and Pekah of Israel attacked Judah in an attempt to force Ahaz into joining their alliance against the Assyrian empire (*Is. 7:1–2*). The LORD sent Isaiah to tell Ahaz that Rezin and Pekah posed no serious threat (*Is. 7:3–9*). The LORD also offered Ahaz a sign of his care (*Is. 7:10*), but the king hypocritically refused because he preferred the protection of Assyria (*Is. 7:10–12*). In response, Isaiah announced that the LORD would give a sign of his own choosing, the Immanuel child (*Is. 7:13–14*).

It is common for Christian interpreters to treat *Is. 7:14* as a direct and exclusive reference to Jesus. In this view, Isaiah assured Ahaz of protection through the power of the Messiah to come. Thus Jesus is the fulfilment of the prophecy and the name Immanuel refers to no-one but him. This traditional approach, however, does not give adequate attention to the larger context of the prophecy.

Several factors suggest that this prophecy spoke of someone living in Isaiah's day as a type or foreshadowing of Jesus. First, Isaiah told Ahaz that his northern neighbours would stop threatening him before Immanuel 'knows enough to reject the wrong and choose the right' (*Is. 7:15–16*). Soon after the birth of the child, Judah would be given into the hands of Assyria because of Ahaz' infidelity (*Is. 7:17–25*). These descriptions orient the entire prophecy to Ahaz' time, not to Jesus' day 700 years later.

Second, *Is. 8:3* reports that Isaiah himself had a son, Maher-Shalal-Hash-Baz ('quick to the plunder, swift to the spoil'). In close parallel with his description of Immanuel (*Is. 7:15*), Isaiah announced that Syria and Israel will be plundered 'before the boy knows how to say "My father" or "My mother"' (*Is. 8:4*). These similar descriptions make it possible that Immanuel was Maher-Shalal-Hash-Baz. If so, Isaiah fathered this child (after his first wife died) with an unnamed second wife who met the requirement of the prophecy because she was a virgin at the time of the prediction.

Third, Isaiah called out to Immanuel in the two oracles that immediately followed the birth of Maher-Shalal-Hash-Baz (*Is. 8:8, 10*). This close association of the two names also suggests that they belonged to the same child.

From this viewpoint, the original Immanuel child was born in Isaiah's day as a prefiguring of Jesus. *Matt. 1:23* explains that Jesus was the ultimate expression of God's presence with his people. As the Messiah, Jesus was all that Isaiah's son represented and more.

The presence of God with his people is a central concept throughout the OT. God is said to be with his people at least 89 times in the OT. The LORD was with individuals and with the nation of Israel (e.g. *Gen. 21:20; 28:15; 31:3; 39:2–3; 46:4; Deut. 20:4; Josh. 1:5, 9, 22; 6:27; Judg. 1:19; 2:18; 1 Sam. 3:19; 10:7; 17:37; 18:14, 28; 2 Sam. 7:9; 2 Kings 18:7; 1 Chron. 22:11, 16, 18; 2 Chron. 1:1; Zech. 10:5*). In a world surrounded by enemies, faithful Israelites cherished the presence of God. He was their only secure hope for blessing and protection.

The presence of God with his people is also a vital NT concept. Jesus fulfilled *Is. 7:14* because he was the fullest demonstration of the Lord's presence with his people. In his earthly ministry, Jesus became God incarnate living among us (*John*

266

1:14). Never before had God so closely identified himself with his covenant people. After his ascension into heaven, Jesus sent the Holy Spirit to be with his people (*John 14:16; Acts 1:8; 2:1–41*). In the Holy Spirit Jesus continues to be with the church on earth, protecting and blessing (*Matt. 28:20*). Paul also explained that believers who die are with Christ (*2 Cor. 5:8*) and will return with him one day (*1 Thess. 3:13*). Finally, the great hope of the NT is that following the final judgment Christ will be with his people forever in the new heavens and new earth (*Rev. 21:3*).                                          R.P.

**IMMER** **1.** One among the priests who were chosen to be officials in the sanctuary 'according to the last instructions of David'. Impartial selection from among the descendants of Eleazar and Ithamar was made by drawing lots. The 16th lot fell to Immer and that was the order in which he ministered when entering the sanctuary (*1 Chron. 24:14*).

**2.** The father of Meshillemith, Immer is listed in *1 Chron. 9:12; Neh. 11:13; Ezra 2:37; Neh. 7:40* as a member of one of the six priestly families who returned to Jerusalem following the Babylonian Exile.

**3.** Immer is the father of the priest, Zadok, who made repairs to the wall when the Israelites returned from the Babylonian captivity (*Neh. 3:29*).

**4.** Immer is listed as the father of Pashhur in *Jer. 20*. Pashhur had Jeremiah beaten and put in stocks.        S.C.

**IMNA** A tribal leader and descendant of Asher, he was the son of Helem (*1 Chron. 7:35*).

**IMNAH** **1.** One of the sons of Asher. He was the progenitor of the Imnite clan (*Gen. 46:17; Num. 26:44; 1 Chron. 7:30*).

**2.** One of the Levites at the time of revival in the worship of the LORD under King Hezekiah. He was the father of Kore (*2 Chron. 31:14*).

**IMRAH** Mentioned in *1 Chron. 7:36* as a son of Zophah, a chief in the tribe of Asher.

**IMRI** **1.** From the tribe of Judah, his descendant Uthai was among the first to return from Exile (*1 Chron. 9:4*).

**2.** His son Zaccur helped to rebuild the walls of Jerusalem following the Babylonian Exile (*Neh. 3:2*).

**IPHDEIAH** (Heb., 'the LORD redeems'). From the tribe of Benjamin, in the genealogy leading to Saul. He was the son of Shashak (*1 Chron. 8:25*).

**IR** is mentioned in *1 Chron. 7:12* and is probably the same person as Iri in *v. 7*.

**IRA** **1.** Ira, the Jairite, is mentioned along with Zadok and Abiathar in *2 Sam. 20:26* as 'David's priest'. The Jairites were from the tribe of Manasseh (*Num. 32:41*). This might mean that some non-Levites were allowed to serve in some priestly role during David's reign.

**2.** Ira, son of Ikkesh, was one of David's 'Thirty' warriors and came from Tekoa. As a commander in David's army he was on duty with his men in the sixth month of each year and had 24,000 men in his division (*2 Sam. 23:26; 1 Chron. 11:28; 27:9*).

**3.** Another one of David's 'Thirty' warriors. This one was known as Ira the Ithrite (*2 Sam. 23:38; 1 Chron. 11:40*).

**IRAD** The son of Enoch and grandson of Cain. He is mentioned in *Gen. 4:18*, a passage which shows how the descendants of Cain spread out across the world after God's judgment on him.

**IRAM** One of the chiefs of Edom, mentioned in connection with Magdiel and a descendant of Esau (*Gen. 36:43; 1 Chron. 1:54*).

**IRI** A grandson of Benjamin and son of Bela (*1 Chron. 7:7*).

**IRIJAH** (Heb., 'the LORD sees'). The son of Shelemiah, Irijah, a captain in the army, was responsible for arresting Jeremiah at the Benjamin Gate at the time of the Babylonian invasion. He was arrested on suspicion of trying to desert to the invaders (*Jer. 37:13–14*).

**IRU** Mentioned in *1 Chron. 4:15* as the eldest of the sons of Caleb, son of Jephunneh, and a tribal leader.

**ISAAC** 'They also serve who only stand and wait.' That was Isaac. He lived a long life (*Gen. 35:28*) but he never moved from the same area (*Gen. 35:27; cf. 13:18; 24:62; 25:11*). Compared with the solemn incidents of the life of Abraham and the frenetic activity of Jacob, he did virtually nothing. Yet, along with the seemingly more impressive Abraham and Jacob, Isaac is an irreplaceable founding father of the people of God – one of the trio to whom descendants were promised (*Deut. 9:27* etc.), and the land was pledged (*Gen. 50:24; Exod. 33:1* etc.); with whom the covenant was made (*Exod. 2:24; Ps. 105:9* etc.); whose names are part of the self-identification of the God himself (*Exod. 3:6, 15–16*); who are guarantors of the security of their family (*Exod. 32:32; Deut. 29:13*) and themselves have a central place in the kingdom Jesus preached (*Matt. 8:11; Luke 13:28*); who are used by him as proofs of heaven (*Matt. 22:32*) and whose God raised Jesus from the dead (*Acts 3:13*). Importance in the sight of God is not dependant on 'doing' but on 'being'.

While the Bible sets Isaac before us, it does not explain him. But there are things about Isaac crying out to be slotted into some picture that makes sense of the man. He so needed a wife he loved to comfort him for the loss of a loved mother (*Gen. 24:67*); he was so content to be quiet (*1 Thess. 4:11*), to enjoy the delights of marriage (*Gen. 26:6*), to long for children (*Gen. 25:21*), to revel in fatherhood and the simple pleasures of the table (*Gen. 25:28*); to live without the excitement of travel and novelty (see above); and to pass on to his sons the memory of a man who knew and feared God. The LORD would speak to Jacob of being 'the God of your father Isaac' and he did so on two occasions where Jacob had every reason to be nervous, facing an unknown future (*Gen. 28:13; 46:1–3; cf. 32:9*). It was as if the greatest comfort that could come from heaven was 'Remember the God your father spoke of and worshipped'. But twice Jacob also spoke of 'the Fear of his father Isaac' (*Gen. 31:42, 53*). What a remarkable title for God! But somehow it lodged in Jacob's memory that when his father spoke of God it was both of One who could comfort those in uncertainty of the future and One so worthy of reverence that 'Fear' was, so to speak, his second name. Furthermore it is only in connection with Isaac that the Bible ever mentions Beer Lahai Roi (where the Angel met with Hagar, *Gen. 24:62; 35; cf. 16:13–14*). Is there significance in this? Unlike Abraham and Jacob, the LORD never 'appeared' to Isaac: did he long for such an experience and specially did he long for Hagar's experience of God coming to the downcast to comfort and reassure? Finally, *Heb. 11:20* makes its one comment on Isaac's faith that he 'blessed Esau and Jacob particularly regarding coming events'. What produced this subdued man with his quiet ways? What made him speak so personally and reverently of God? Why did he hope to meet Hagar's kindly Angel? Why was he particularly certain about the future?

Isaac is the only person in the whole Bible who was ever bound with ropes and laid upon a prepared altar, who ever saw a knife about to come down into his heart and who ever heard the voice of the LORD's Angel staying the sacrifice. Supremely, in the awful moment, he knew that God had cared for and preserved him and that therefore the promised future must come; with an equal intensity he knew that the God who preserved and cared was worthy of all reverence. And, having heard the Angel speak (Gen. 22:11), did he long to hear that voice again – at Beer Lahai Roi (Gen. 16:7–14)? But, also, would not such an experience – today it would be called a 'trauma' – produce a subdued temperament and a huge need for love, human and divine? All this too, was Isaac.

Isaac's story is simplicity itself. Born when his parents were humanly incapable of having a family (Gen. 17:17; 18:9–14; 21:1–7) he was pre-eminently the child of promise (Gal. 4:28) and, by a further divine directive, he was demarcated as such (Gen. 21:9–12; Rom. 9:17). At the age of 40 – significantly, as a result of his father's initiative and after his mother had died (Gen. 24:1–3ff., 67) – he married his cousin Rebekah, with, on his part at least, love at first sight. Isaac and Rebekah enjoyed a shared and personal spirituality (Gen. 25:21–23) but they erred as parents. First they divided their affections unequally between their twins (Gen. 25:28); secondly they did not bring the boys up with knowledge of the word of God which had preceded their birth. It would have been so easy afterward if only they had let the twins into the secret from their tiniest days that though Esau was technically 'firstborn' the LORD had decided otherwise. The tiny ones would have absorbed this information and it would have seeped into the fabric of their consciousness without ill-effect; it would have been the given framework of family life and sibling relationships. But the word of God was neglected and thereby hung the whole tale of woe that sundered the family, (Gen. 27:41), drove Esau to a further unequal marriage (Gen. 26:34–35; 28:6), bereaved Rebekah for ever of her beloved Jacob and imposed a 25-year exile on Jacob. Sadder still, having omitted to share God's word with their boys, Isaac and Rebekah forgot it themselves so that when Isaac set about passing on the treasured blessing, he followed logic and turned to Esau, though the word of God had chosen Jacob; and Rebekah, forgetting that God had decided what would happen, felt that she must wangle the blessing for Jacob.

Isaac's marriage began with bright hopes but by old age the couple were not communicating, not resting on God's word, nor really at one. This incident is the only minor key within the quiet music – a true second movement in God's patriarchal concerto – of Isaac's life. He lived to be 180 years old and died in the presence of his two sons who laid him to rest in that place of treasured bodies, the cave of Machpelah (Gen. 35:28).   J.A.M.

## ISAIAH

The prophet Isaiah was probably born and educated in Jerusalem. Apart from his father's name, Amoz, his genealogy is unknown. It has been surmised that he was related to King Uzziah (791–740 BC) because he had access to the court and was greatly concerned with the issue of leadership. It cannot be demonstrated that he was of royal birth, though his diction reveals a highly gifted person with an excellent educational background.

The prophet is without equal in his written expression as the book of Isaiah with its extensive diction, style, rhetorical devices, and literary imagery suggest. His style reflects a rich vocabulary and imagery with many words and expressions unique to Isaiah. The book also reveals a brilliance through its use of imagery: war (*Is. 63:1–6*), social (*3:1–17*) and rural life (*5:1–7*). He also personifies creation: the sun and the moon (*24:23*), the desert (*35:1*), the mountains and trees (*44:23; 55:12*). He employs taunts (*14:4–23*), apocalyptic imagery (*Is. 24–27*), sarcasm (*44:9–20*), personification, metaphors, wordplay, alliteration, and assonance.

Isaiah was an extremely gifted preacher who fully employed the riches of the Hebrew language. His poetic imagination and message evoke a reaction. His prophecy was not written down to be agreed with, but to generate a response. The godly responded in awe and worship, whereas the ungodly hardened themselves against the LORD.

The conservative position holds to the unity of Isaiah (*Is. 1–66*), based on similarity and repetition of themes and vocabulary throughout the book. Critics have come to recognize that the older arguments for isolating passages and dividing the book by different motifs are no longer tenable. This does not mean that they accept the unity of the book; rather they now acknowledge the similarity of motifs. The unifying message of judgment and salvation is such an overarching motif.

Isaiah was married to 'the prophetess' (*Is. 8:3*). It is unknown whether she was actually a prophetess by profession or was so called, being the wife of a prophet. From his union with 'the prophetess' came two sons, whose symbolic names set forth the message of the whole book. The first born was Shear-Jashub, whose name means '[only] a remnant will return' (see below). His second son was Maher-Shalal-hash-Baz, meaning 'speedily the booty will be taken away' (see below).

Isaiah ministered to God's people during an era of great political turmoil (740–686 BC). His ministry falls into five periods: (1) the period of social criticism (*Is. 1–5*), c. 740–734 BC; (2) the Syro-Ephraimite war (*Is. 7–9*), 734–732 BC; (3) the anti-Assyrian rebellion (*Is. 10–23*), 713–711 BC; (4) the anti-Assyrian rebellion and Jerusalem's siege (*Is. 28–32; 36–39*), 705–701 BC; (5) the last days of Hezekiah, and possibly, the beginning of Manasseh's reign (*Is. 1–66*), 701–686 BC. These periods correspond to the kings mentioned in the superscription: 'The vision concerning Judah and Jerusalem that Isaiah son of Amoz saw during the reigns of Uzziah, Jotham (750–731 BC), Ahaz (735–715) and Hezekiah (729–686), kings of Judah' (*Is. 1:1*). (See *Prophets and Prophecy*).

## Uzziah (Is. 6)

The beginning of Isaiah's ministry can be dated by the reference to Uzziah's death (*Is. 6:1*), approximately 740 BC. Under Uzziah, Judah had gained remarkable economic achievements (*2 Chron. 26:6–15*) and had made an attempt to reassert herself as a political power. The year of his death is mentioned in connection with the extraordinary vision Isaiah experienced (*Is. 6:1*), which also marked the beginning of a prophetic ministry that spanned a 40-year period. According to some, the vision did not constitute the original call, but signified a renewal of the prophetic call.

The vision of God transformed Isaiah into a servant of God with a unique message. It is a message of radical contrast. On the one hand, he presents God in his exaltation as king and in his perfections as being holy and glorious. On the other hand, he presents people as being unclean and under God's condemnation. Isaiah's message encompasses four emphases that flow from this visionary experience: (1) God alone is exalted and holy; but (2) as glorious King over all creation, he judges sinful humanity; and yet (3) he will maintain a remnant whom he has planned to consecrate to himself and with whom he will share his glory. These emphases are characteristic of the book as a whole, and receive their due in the opening chapters of the book (see below).

## Jotham: the period of social criticism (Is. 1–5)

Jotham ruled over Judah from 750–731 BC, first as co-ruler with Uzziah and then with his son, Ahaz. He had inherited Judah which was materially strong, but corrupt in her values and apostate. Isaiah spoke against power, greed, and injustice in Israel and Judah, prior to a rapid shift in the political make-up of the Ancient Near East. Assyria, under Tiglath-pileser III (745–727; 'Pul' in 2 Kings 15:19), subjugated the cities along the route from Nineveh to Damascus, including Damascus (732 BC). When Jotham died, the storm clouds were also forming on Judah's horizon, and soon she would be thrown into the midst of a stream of international developments that would reduce her to a vassal state of the Assyrian Empire. During this period the prophet was critical of the religiosity of the people (Is. 1:10–16), of the insensitivity to justice by their leaders (1:21ff.), of their pride (2:6ff.), and of their wanton way of life (Is. 3; 5).

The message of Is. 1–5 anticipates and undergirds the prophet's vision of God (Is. 6). The prophet presents God's exaltation and glory in contrast to human pride. Pride was a lifestyle of dependencies (religious, political, judicial, economic) that virtually excluded God. On the one hand, this lifestyle might be very religious, as the people of Judah were. They went to the Temple, brought their sacrifices, celebrated the holy days, and prayed (Is. 1:10–15), but did not find favour with the LORD. On the other hand, they structured their lives by a complex web of securities by which they sought to protect themselves from any possible adversity. Yet, the prophet declared that these would be brought down on the day of judgment, so that the LORD alone would be exalted: 'The eyes of the arrogant man will be humbled and the pride of men brought low; the LORD alone will be exalted in that day' (Is. 2:11).

*Holiness and hope.* The teaching on God's holiness serves to underscore God's wholly otherness from humans. He is unlike humans in his being and in his connections. He is holy, that is separate from all created existence. As sovereign over creation, he demands that anyone with whom he graciously establishes a relationship must come to him, denying any reliance on the created structures that shape human existence and the human quest for significance. The teaching on God's holiness has two implications. First, God's holiness is the ground for hope. Because God is holy, he will establish his rule by upholding justice ('fairness') and by creating order ('righteousness'). Over against the arbitrary judgments of human leaders and the anarchy of the social order, the prophet projected God's kingdom as characterized by justice and righteousness. Justice is the quality of fairness wherewith the LORD deals with his subjects. He rules so as to make right what people have made crooked, to pronounce judgments based on his will, rather than feelings or pragmatic results, and to uphold norms that enhance life rather than repress it. God's judgment brings positive results because he makes right and vindicates the righteous. The result of his rule is order, whereas the rule of man all too often creates disorder. Therefore, the prophet encouraged the needy who cried out for help with the comfort of the restoration of order in this world: 'Tell the righteous it will be well with them, for they will enjoy the fruit of their deeds' (Is. 3:10).

*Holiness and condemnation.* Second, God's holiness is the ground for condemnation: 'But the LORD Almighty will be exalted by his justice, and the holy God will show himself holy by his righteousness' (Is. 5:16). The prophet saw that the LORD alone is the true and faithful King whose sovereignty will extend to all humanity. No power on earth can match his dominion. This absolute contrast between God and man that pervades the message flowed out of the vision of God. The prophet had seen a vision of God as the Great King, in the year that Uzziah, a human king died: 'In the year that King Uzziah died, I saw the LORD' (Is. 6:1). Since his glory would extend to the whole earth (6:3), it excluded any vain glory of humans. They stood condemned in his presence (3:8) because they had not dealt fairly with their fellow-men. As such, they had not maintained order. Instead, the effects of their selfish and greedy ways had resulted in anarchy: 'And he looked for justice, but saw bloodshed; for righteousness, but heard cries of distress' (Is. 5:7). Exalted in holiness and fair in judgment, the LORD would hold all accountable for their actions: 'The LORD takes his place in court; he rises to judge the people. The LORD enters into judgment against the elders and leaders of his people' (Is. 3:13–14).

*The remnant.* Third, the LORD will reserve a remnant for himself. The remnant motif reinforces the biblical emphasis on God's fidelity. The LORD will be faithful to his covenants and to the promises he has made to the Patriarchs. This remnant will be washed and consecrated, restored to fellowship with the Holy God (Is. 4:3–4). They will see his glory (4:2; cf. 40:6) and enjoy his blessed protection (4:5–6).

The prophet projected God's glorious rule in the twin image of an elevated mountain (Is. 2:2–4) and of a glorified and holy people under his special protection (4:2–6). In the latter, he encouraged the remnant of the Jews with a future beyond the exile. In the former, Isaiah projected the inclusion of the Gentiles who would submit themselves to the Law of God and worship him. They would enjoy his protection. Isaiah's message was a preparation for the gospel of the Lord Jesus as he prophesied the full inclusion of Gentiles in the covenant and the promises of God.

### Ahaz (Jehoahaz I): the Syro-Ephraimite war (Is. 7–9)

Ahaz ruled over Judah from 735–715 BC and was very corrupt (2 Kings 16:3). The Chronicler lists the idolatrous practices instituted by Ahaz and explains that these were the cause of his international troubles (2 Chron. 28:2–4). Ahaz was an impudent man, who relied on political solutions rather than on God's promises. When he faced the alliance of King Rezin of Aram with Pekah or Israel and the expansionist drive of Assyria, he wanted to be his own man, independent of Yahweh, uninvolved with the Aramean-Israelite alliance, and autonomous from

Assyria. But he responded with great fear when Aram and Israel came against him for the purpose of dethroning him and to set up another king who would be sympathetic to their political scheming (2 Kings 16:5; Is. 7:6). In this context Isaiah challenged him not to fear their power (Is. 7:4), but instead to look for God's presence in Jerusalem as the strength of Judah (Is. 7:7; 8:10). Ahaz bypassed the prophet by asking Tiglath-pileser, the Assyrian, to help him (2 Kings 16:7). Tiglath-pileser, reacting swiftly to the threat of the Syro-Ephraimite alliance on the western front, marched through Phoenicia as far as Philistia (734 BC), destroyed Damascus (732 BC) and subjugated Israel. He also reduced Judah to a vassal state (2 Kings 15:29; 16:7–9; 2 Chron. 28:19; Is. 8:7–8).

When King Hoshea of Israel refused to pay tribute to Assyria, Shalmaneser (727–722 BC) campaigned against Samaria, brought her down, and exiled her population in 722 BC. Ahaz did not turn to the LORD, because his eyes were fixed on his own kingdom and its place in the changing political configurations under Shalmaneser V and Sargon II.

During this period, the prophet called on Ahaz to be a man of faith (Is. 7:9) and to look for the child 'Immanuel' ('God is with us') as the sign of God's protection of his people. He further prophesied of this child that he would become king (a clear rejection of Ahaz's leadership!). The child's government would bring peace and be characterized by justice and righteousness (Is. 9:6–7). Truly, his rule corresponded to God's rule in that the effect of his kingdom would bring the Kingdom of God to earth.

The message of the book is restated in the context of the historical events surrounding the future of Judah. It is also reiterated in the names of Isaiah and of his sons. That this was the prophetic intent comes out in Is. 8:19: 'Here am I, and the children the LORD has given me. We are signs and symbols in Israel from the LORD Almighty, who dwells on Mount Zion.' These names confirmed the dual aspects of salvation and judgment.

The name Isaiah ('Yahweh [the LORD] is salvation') bears out the theme of Yahweh's exaltation. The prophecy throughout sets before the reader the distinctive emphasis that the LORD alone is to be trusted. His way alone is to shape the lives of his people because the LORD demands exclusive faith in him alone as the only God and the only Saviour. For Isaiah faith is the absolute trust in the LORD as the only redeemer and the absolute loyalty in doing his will. This dual aspect comes to expression in these words: 'Bind up the testimony and seal up the law among my disciples. I will wait for the LORD, who is hiding his face from the house of Jacob. I will put my trust in him' (Is. 8:16–17).

The name of Isaiah's second son, Maher-shalal-hash-baz ('very quickly the spoils will be taken', Is. 8:1, 3), amplifies the message of God's sovereignty in judgment. When his people refused to do his will, they rejected the Holy One: 'They have forsaken the LORD; they have spurned the Holy One of Israel and turned their backs on him' (Is. 1:4). The nations, too, may make an attempt at establishing a 'new order', but in the end the LORD's will would prevail (Is. 8:10).

The name of the prophet's first son, Shear-jashub ('a remnant will return', Is. 7:3) brings out both a negative and a positive dimension. Negatively, there would be a small remnant left when God was through with his judgment (Is. 6:13). Positively, not all would be wiped out. At least, some would be left with whom the LORD would renew his commitment (*Is. 1:9; 4:2–4*). This remnant would be characterized by reliance on the LORD: 'In that day the remnant of Israel, the survivors of the house of Jacob, will no longer rely on him who struck them down but will truly rely on the LORD, the Holy One of Israel' (*Is. 10:20*).

## Hezekiah: the anti-Assyrian rebellion and Jerusalem's siege, 705–701 BC

Hezekiah (729–686 BC) was a godly king who sought counsel from the prophet Isaiah in times of national and personal tragedy. He ruled independently from 715 BC till his death in 686 BC. While leading Judah into an era of reforms (*2 Kings 18:4, 22*), climaxed in the celebration of the Passover Feast (*2 Chron. 30*), his was the difficult task of adjusting to the Assyrian presence. Hezekiah had to cope with the expansionist policy of Sargon II (722–705 BC), who was active in military campaigns, subjugating nations in the east (Elam, Babylon), west (Syria-Ephraim region), and further south as far as the Wadi-el-Arish on the south-west border of Judah (715 BC).

In the providence of God, Hezekiah was able to do just that! He set out to develop God's interests by inviting the remnant from the north to the Passover feast and by leading the nation into true reform. Sargon's reaction came in 711 BC, when he returned to subdue Philistia and to demand tribute from Hezekiah. In that year the LORD commissioned the prophet to walk barefoot and stripped of his sackcloth clothing (*Is. 20:2*). This unusual appearance of the prophet was to evoke the curiosity of the people and serve as an object lesson pointing to the certainty of Egypt's demise. As the prophet went about stripped and barefoot, so the Egyptians would be stripped in exile and serve the Assyrians. Further, the Judeans who relied on Egypt would be shown up as the true fools that they were, because Judah had relied on Egypt for political support, while resisting the Holy One of Israel. Of them he said, 'Woe to those who go down to Egypt for help, who rely on horses, who trust in the multitude of their chariots and in the great strength of their horsemen, but do not look to the Holy One of Israel, or seek help from the LORD' (*Is. 31:1*).

At Sargon's death (705 BC), his successor Sennacherib (705–681 BC) faced a coalition of Egypt, Philistia, and Judah (*2 Kings 18:7*). His forces moved through Judah (701 BC) and may have taken as many as 46 cities (some of which may have been listed in *Is. 10:28–32* and *Mic. 1:10–16*). Sennacherib recounts this victory in his Annals: 'But as for Hezekiah, the Jew, who did not bow in submission to my yoke, forty-six of his strong walled towns and innumerable smaller villages in their neighbourhood I besieged and conquered by stamping down earth-ramps and then by bringing up battering rams, by the assault of foot-soldiers, by breaches, tunnelling and sapper operations. I made to come out from them 200,150 people, young and old, male and female, innumerable horses, mules, donkeys, camels, large and small cattle, and counted them as the spoils of war.'

Finally, Sennacherib besieged Jerusalem. Hezekiah was locked in Jerusalem, surrounded by the Assryian forces. He was well prepared for the siege, but the Assyrians had the fortitude to wait for the surrender of Jerusalem (701 BC). Sennacherib described the situation in the following manner: 'He himself I shut up like a caged bird within Jerusalem, his royal city. I put watch-posts strictly around it and turned back to his disaster any who went out of its city gate'.

The LORD was true to his promise of being present to deliver and sent the angel of the LORD. Sennacherib retreated with an empty victory, whereas the people of Judah celebrated the miraculous deliverance from a cruel tyrant who had already destroyed Judah (2 Kings 19:35–36). This desperate situation may well be portrayed in Is. 1:5–9.

About the same time, Hezekiah became sick, but miraculously recovered and received another 15 years of life (2 Kings 20:1–19; 2 Chron. 32:24–26; Is. 38:1–22). During this time the LORD prospered Hezekiah and he did much to strengthen Jerusalem and Judah against a future Assyrian attack (2 Chron. 32:27–29). But these years turned out to be a mixed blessing. The king arrogantly showed his treasures and fortifications to the envoys of the Babylonian king, Merodach-baladan (Bab. Marduk-apla-iddina). God's condemnation would haunt Judah for another century: 'The time will surely come when everything in your palace, and all that your fathers have stored up until this day, will be carried off to Babylon. Nothing will be left' (Is. 39:6). These words set the background for interpreting Isaiah's oracles of deliverance from Babylon (Is. 40–48).

## The later message

The message that can be dated to the latter period of the prophet's ministry is remarkably consistent with the earlier chapters.

1. The prophet projected a different kind of leadership. Hezekiah represented this kind of a leader because he was faithful to the LORD and did much to bring the people back to their God. Yet, he, too, failed. The 'messianic' ideal is well portrayed in Is. 11. The Messiah is a descendant of David who, endowed with the Spirit of God, is a person of integrity, judges fairly, establishes order, and brings peace to the earth. His kingdom includes righteous Jews and Gentiles, but has no room for sinners: 'They will neither harm nor destroy on all my holy mountain, for the earth will be full of the knowledge of the LORD as the waters cover the sea' (Is. 11:9).

2. God's judgment rests on all the nations because the LORD is God over all Creation (Is. 13:1–27:13).

3. The LORD will open up a new era of salvation (Is. 25:1–27:13). Both themes (judgment and salvation) found a further development in Is. 28:1–35:10 and were illustrated in the life of Hezekiah (Is. 36–39). The significance of the new order of salvation received prophetic elaboration in Is. 40–55. This section begins on the note of comfort (Is. 40:1) and ends with an invitation freely to enjoy God's salvation, likened to bread and wine (Is. 55:1–3). Within these chapters the prophet elaborated the Servant-motif, including the well-known Suffering Servant (Is. 52:13–53:12). The true Servant is the one who suffers vicariously for others, while being innocent himself. The combination of this motif with that of the Messianic prophecy of Is. 11 presents us with the basis of the apostolic teaching that the Messiah of David had to suffer first and then to be seated in glory.

In the last part of the book, Isaiah charged the godly to persevere in godliness while awaiting the salvation of the LORD (Is. 56–66). The prophet carefully outlined the salvation of the LORD as he balanced God's sovereignty and human responsibility. On the one hand, he balanced God's promises with a socially responsible way of life (Is. 56:9–58:14). On the other hand, he balanced the reality of the delay with a perspective of God's power and of the glorious future prepared for the remnant (*Is. 59:1–62:12*). He affirmed the universal judgment of God (*Is. 63; 66*), while opening the door to Jews and Gentiles to participate in the new work of God: the creation of a new heaven and earth (*Is. 65:13–25*). The prophetic message anticipates the future unfolding of God's plan in the ministry of the Lord Jesus and of the message of the apostles.

W.A.VG.

**ISCAH** A daughter of Haran (Abram's brother) and sister of Milcah, Nahor's wife (*Gen. 11:29*). She appears in a genealogy of the descendants of Shem leading through Terah to Abraham.

**ISCARIOT** See *Judas Iscariot*.

**ISHBAH** The father of Eshtemoa and son of Mered, he was a grandson of Ezrah and a tribal leader in Judah (*1 Chron. 4:17*).

**ISHBAK** One of Abraham's sons by his wife Keturah (*Gen. 25:2*). He appears in a list of Abraham's descendants, bridging, in the narrative of *Gen. 24–25*, the death of Sarah and the death of Abraham (also *1 Chron. 1:32*).

**ISHBI-BENOB** A giant who fought, probably as a mercenary, for the Philistines during the reign of King David. He was a descendant of Rapha, one of the original tribes that inhabited the land of Canaan and was known for its men of great stature. Seeing David was tired at the end of a battle, Ishbi-Benob decided to go in and kill David. Abishai, one of David's most loyal and trusted henchmen killed the giant and saved David's life. The description of the size of this giant's bronze spear and sword give some indication of the threat he would have appeared to be to all Israelites (*2 Sam. 21:15–17*). He was one of the four giants from Gath (*v. 22*).

**ISH-BOSHETH** (Heb., 'man of shame'). It is very possible that his original name was Ish-baal ('man of Baal'), but because of the lewd sexual rites accompanying Baal worship later scribes were reluctant

to use the name Baal and thus substituted the word 'shame' in its place (*cf. 1 Chron. 8:33*). He was the son of King Saul and was made king by Abner, the commander of Saul's army, at Mahanaim (*2 Sam. 2:8–10*) after Saul and Jonathan's death on Mt Gilboa (*1 Sam. 31:1–6*). During the next two years the house of David greatly increased while Saul's house weakened. Its eventual demise came when Ish-Bosheth charged Abner with some indecency regarding one of Saul's former wives. Abner was furious and initiated an intrigue with David, but was murdered by Joab before its completion. Two of Ish-Bosheth's own captains murdered him (*2 Sam. 4:5–7*) and once again the nation was united, with David as their king.

P.D.W.

**ISHHOD** The son of Gilead's sister Hammoleketh. He was from the tribe of Manasseh (*1 Chron. 7:18*).

**ISHI** (Heb., 'salutary').
**1.** The father of Sheshan and son of Appaim. This Ishi is listed among the descendants of Jerahmeel and from the tribe of Judah (*1 Chron. 2:31*).
**2.** Another leader in the tribe of Judah, but this one was descended from Caleb (*1 Chron. 4:20*).
**3.** The father of four leaders of part of the tribe of Simeon who finally killed the remaining Amalekites in the time of King Hezekiah (*1 Chron. 4:42*).
**4.** A head of a clan and a valiant soldier in the tribe of Manasseh (*1 Chron. 5:24*).

**ISHIJAH** A descendant of Harim who was among those guilty of inter-marriage with foreign women (*Ezra* 10:31).

**ISHMA** One of the sons of Etam. A leader in the tribe of Judah and brother to Jezreel and Idbash. His sister was Hazzelelponi (1 *Chron.* 4:3).

**ISHMAEL** In Scripture several individuals have this name.

**1.** Ishmael was the first-born son of Isaac through Hagar, the concubine of Sarah. The biblical material concerning his life is found primarily in Gen. 16; 17:18–27; 21:9–21; 25:12–18. His name derives from the verb 'to hear, take heed' and 'El' which means 'god'. Hagar was provided this name in a visitation by the angel of the LORD (Gen. 16:11). It captured the circumstances in which Hagar found herself at the time. Abraham and Sarah had waited long for the fulfilment of God's promise that they would have an heir to effect the blessings of God's covenant (Gen. 12:1–3; 15:1–6). After the passage of much time Sarah, according to well-known customs of the time, presented her Egyptian handmaid to Abraham to conceive a child. Abraham accepted the offer and the intended result was achieved (Gen. 16:2–4).

Sarah became jealous, apparently exacerbated by some disrespect shown by Hagar, and demanded that Abraham ostracize the Egyptian servant from the clan (Gen. 16:4–5). Abraham left the matter in Sarah's hands with the result that Hagar fled from her harsh treatment (v. 6). Finding herself in the wilderness without resource, Hagar received comfort from the angel of the LORD (vv. 7–12) including the promise of a great posterity (v. 10). In this context, the name 'El has heard' communicates the total content of this divine assurance.

In this naming episode we see something of the character of Ishmael revealed even before his birth. 'He will be a wild donkey of a man, his hand will be against

everyone, and everyone's hand will be against him' (Gen. 16:12). Given this sweeping generalization and the fact that his dwelling would be 'to the east of all his brothers' (v. 12), a broader purpose for the original audience can be seen. It is not so much the characterization of one individual which is in view, but rather an ethnic etiology through which the nation of Israel would understand their relationship to and the character of the Ishmaelites, the descendants of Ishmael. The response of Hagar to this divine assurance (Gen. 16:13–14) and the circumcision of Ishmael to signify inclusion in the broader covenant community (Gen. 17:25) placed the Ishmaelites on a continuum closer to the full blessedness of the descendants of the patriarchs than the full cursedness of the idolatrous Canaanites. Ishmael's descendants would share in some benefits of an historical connection with the God of Abraham, though not full heirs to the promises.

This status is explicitly confirmed and reinforced in the divine assurances of Gen. 21:9–21. These events came after the birth of Isaac when the rivalry between Sarah and Hagar had extended to their sons. Sarah saw Ishmael 'mocking' Isaac. The verb used is the one from which Isaac's name is derived, possibly indicating through a play on words that Ishmael was mimicking Isaac, i.e. taking Isaac's place. This would reflect Sarah's concern that Ishmael would compete for Isaac's status as heir.

Whatever the nature of the offence, the result was clear. Abraham, under instructions from Sarah, sent them into the wilderness a second time (Gen. 21:14). God both endorsed Sarah's judgment in the matter (v. 12) and repeated his promised blessing upon Hagar and Ishmael (v. 13). When Hagar was devoid of provision and despairing for her and her son's lives, the angel of the LORD once again appeared with words of comfort and assurance (vv. 17–18). These words were followed by the divinely enabled discovery of a spring of water as a testimony to their veracity (v. 19). The rest of Ishmael's life is summarized in Gen. 21:20–21, indicating he enjoyed divine blessing, was skilled as an archer and dwelt in the wilderness (vv. 20–21).

The descendants of Ishmael are mentioned in a manner consistent with the characterization of their eponym – in terms of where they lived (Gen. 25:12–16) and of their nature (v. 18). At times Midianites are included among them (Judg. 8:24; cf. Gen. 37:25–28, 36; 39:1).

The life of Ishmael demonstrates several important principles. First, the ethnic etiology for the original Israelite audience may retain some usefulness for the modern audience in that we see certain limited blessings possessed by the ethical monotheism of Islam, spiritual heirs to Ishmael. However, these blessings are not the full redemptive benefits of heirs of the Abrahamic promise. Secondly, Ishmael's birth shows how human impatience may overreach the plan of God. Waiting upon God to fulfil his promises is a vital element of the life of faith. Paul's Isaac/Ishmael analogy to the respective lives according to faith and works develops this principle (Gal. 4:21ff.). Thirdly, we see the gentle kindness of God working for good in spite of human devisings.    M.J.G.

**2.** A Benjamite and the third of six sons of Azel (1 Chron. 8:38; 9:44). He was a descendant of Saul.

**3.** This Ishmael was a leader in the tribe of Judah and father of Zebadiah who lived during the reign of Jehoshaphat, king of Judah. The king appointed a number of Levites, priests and leaders to administer justice and to watch over the observance of the Law of the LORD in Judah. Zebadiah was in charge of all matters concerning the king (2 Chron. 19:11).

**4.** Ishmael son of Jehohanan was one of the commanders with whom Jehoiada the priest made a covenant. He commanded a unit of 100 men (2 Chron. 23:1). He helped Johoiada crown Joash king. Jehoiada had helped hide the child king from Athaliah the mother of Ahaziah, the recently deceased king of Judah. When seven years had passed the child was produced and crowned. Athaliah was put to death and Joash, who was clearly influenced by Jehoiada, repaired the Temple and restored the worship of the LORD. Later, when Jehoiada died, he was led astray and sadly he and the people returned to worshipping the Asherah.

**5.** This Ishmael was a descendant of Pashhur and one of those in the time of Ezra who had married a foreign wife rather than one from Judah. He later divorced her (Ezra 10:22).

**6.** Ishmael 'son of Nethaniah, the son of Elishama, who was of royal blood' was one of the army officers who joined Gedaliah at Mizpah, near Jerusalem, when Gedaliah was appointed governor of Judah once most of Judah had been taken into captivity in Babylon (2 Kings 25:23–25). Gedaliah tried to urge these officers to 'settle down' and not fear the Babylonians (v. 24). A few months later Ishmael returned with ten men and assassinated Gedaliah, others who were with him and some of the Babylonians in Mizpah (v. 25). More detail of what then happened is given in Jer. 40:8–41:18. There we read that some 80 men then came through Mizpah on their way to make an offering. Ishmael lured them into the town where he killed all but ten who managed to escape by offering bribes. Ishmael and his renegades then set off with many prisoners for the land of the Ammonites across the Jordan (Jer. 41:10). When Johanan son of Kareah heard about this, he and a number of army officers pursued Ishmael, releasing the captives and killing some of his men. Ishmael escaped. But when Johanan and the others got back to Mizpah they feared that the Babylonians would blame them for the murder of their people and so they fled to Egypt taking with them the prophet Jeremiah and others (*Jer. 41:16–43:7*). Jeremiah warned that fleeing to Egypt was against the LORD's will but they insisted on leaving.          P.D.G.

**ISHMAIAH** (Heb., 'the LORD hears').

**1.** One of the warriors who deserted Saul to join David at Ziklag. They were ambidextrous in archery and with slings. They were from the tribe of Benjamin. Ishmaiah was a 'mighty man' among David's famous and valiant 'Thirty' warriors (*1 Chron. 12:3*).

**2.** The administrator over Zebulun and a leader of his tribe during the reign of King David. His father was Obadiah (*1 Chron. 27:19*).

**ISHMERAI** (Heb., 'God preserves'). One of the sons of Elpaal and a leader from the tribe of Benjamin, Ishmerai lived in Jerusalem (*1 Chron. 8:18*).

**ISHPAH** One of the sons of Beriah and a leader from the tribe of Benjamin, Ishpah lived in Aijalon (*1 Chron. 8:16*).

**ISHPAN** *1 Chron. 8:22* lists Ishpan as a family leader in the tribe of Benjamin and a son of Shashak. His name appears in the genealogy of King Saul.

**ISHVAH** The second of four sons of Asher. As his clan is not mentioned in *Num. 26:44*, it is possible that he left no descendants (*Gen. 46:17; 1 Chron. 7:30*).

**ISHVI 1.** The third son of Asher and one of those who went down to Egypt with Jacob. He was the progenitor of the Ishvite clan (*Gen. 46:17; Num. 26:44; 1 Chron. 7:30*).

**2.** Mentioned in *1 Sam. 14:49*, this Ishvi was one of King Saul's sons and brother to Jonathan and Malki-shua.

**ISMAKIAH** (Heb., 'the LORD sustains'). One of the Levites who were supervisors of tithes and offerings brought by the

people. As a result of the extraordinary revival under King Hezekiah, so many offerings, gifts and tithes were brought to the Temple that special storehouses had to be prepared. Ismakiah was one of a number of Levites chosen, under the leadership of Conaniah and Shimei, to organize the storage of what was given (*2 Chron. 31:13*).

**ISRAEL** The name given to Jacob after he had 'struggled with God' at Peniel (*Gen. 32:28, 31*). See *Jacob*.

**ISSACHAR** (Heb., 'there is recompense' or 'hired man').

**1.** This fifth son of Jacob by Leah was born to his mother after she had ceased bearing (*Gen. 29:35*) and had ingested the fruit of a mandrake plant, thought by her to be a fertility enhancer (*Gen. 30:14–18*). Issachar appears in the blessing of Jacob as 'a scrawny donkey lying down between two saddlebags', one who 'will bend his shoulder to the burden and submit to forced labour' (*Gen. 49:14–15*). This prediction clearly relates to the second meaning of his name suggested above. Moses prophesies that Issachar, with Zebulun, will, as tribal entities, participate in maritime industry and serve as a setting for public worship (*Deut. 33:18–19*). Where and how this was subsequently carried out cannot be determined.

Otherwise, Issachar as an individual is rarely attested, his significance being limited to his founding of the tribe that bore his name. In the arrangement of the Israelite encampment in the desert, the tribe of Issachar was placed on the east with Judah and Zebulun (*Num. 2:3–9*), the two descending from Issachar's immediately elder and younger brothers respectively (*Gen. 29:35; 30:20*).

**2.** The seventh son of Obed-Edom, a descendant of Korah, this Issachar was responsible to attend to the Tabernacle gates in David's administration (*1 Chron. 26:5*).          E.M.

**ISSHIAH 1.** The grandson of Uzzi and one of five sons of Izrahiah, Isshiah was a chief in the tribe of Issachar (1 Chron. 7:3). Together with his sons and their wives and extended families they were able to provide large numbers of fighting men for Israel. During the reign of King David the descendants of Issachar were said to have been able to find 87,000 fighting men.

**2.** One of the warriors who deserted Saul to join David at Ziklag. They were ambidextrous in archery and with slings. They were from the tribe of Benjamin (1 Chron. 12:6).

**3.** A Levite and grandson of Kohath's fourth son, Uzziel (1 Chron. 23:20; 24:25). He is mentioned in a section dealing with the division of Levitical labour in the Tabernacle during the reign of King David.

**4.** Another Levite of the time of King David, who is mentioned only as a head of a family and a descendant of Rehabiah (1 Chron. 24:21).

**ITHAI** The son of 'Ribai from Gibeah in Benjamin' was one of David's 'Thirty' warriors (2 Sam. 23:29; 1 Chron. 11:31).

**ITHAMAR** (Heb., 'island of palms') was the son of Aaron and his wife Elisheba (Exod. 6:23; Num. 3:2; 26:20; 1 Chron. 6:3; 24:1–2). His two brothers offered an illegal sacrifice to the LORD and so only Ithamar and his brother Eleazar survived to serve as priests during Aaron's lifetime (Num. 3:4; Exod. 28:1). Ithamar was in charge of all the Levites during the time of Moses when the Tabernacle was being constructed (Exod. 38:21). In Leviticus, when rules for the behaviour of the Levites were being laid down, both Eleazar and Ithamar were singled out (Lev. 10:6, 12). The Gershonite service in the Tent of Meeting and the service of the Merarite clans were put under the leadership of Ithamar.

Later, when King David was arranging the service of the Tabernacle and ordering worship for the future in the Temple, Ahimelech, a descendant of Ithamar, figured prominently, and Ithamar's descendants were organized into eight groups (1 Chron. 24:3–6). His descendants were also among those who later returned from the Babylonian Exile and helped rebuild Jerusalem (Ezra 8:2).

P.D.G.

**ITHIEL 1.** His descendant Sallu was among the first of the tribe of Benjamin to return from Exile in Babylon (Neh. 11:7).

**2.** He is mentioned in Prov. 30:1 in the sayings of Agur, where a man declared the sayings to Ithiel. See Ucal for more detail.

**ITHMAH** One of David's 'Thirty' great warriors, he came from Moab (1 Chron. 11:46). Whether he was actually a Moabite (and therefore a member of a nation opposed to Israel) or someone who had intermarried and come back to support David is not clear.

**ITHRAN 1.** A leader among the Horites, son of Dishon and grandson of Anah (Gen. 36:26; 1 Chron. 1:41).

**2.** This Ithran was the son of Zophah and a leader in the tribe of Asher (1 Chron. 7:37).

**ITHREAM** The sixth of six sons born to King David while he was in Hebron. Ithream's mother was Eglah (2 Sam. 3:5; 1 Chron. 3:3).

**ITTAI,** the Gittite, led 600 men from Gath to join David when he was fleeing from Absalom. David wondered at such loyalty from a foreigner and kindly and graciously suggested he return to Absalom, but Ittai refused. David then allowed Ittai and his men and their families to lead the group of fleeing people (2 Sam. 15:19–22). Later David sent out three groups of warriors to fight Absalom's troops. The leaders of those divisions were Joab, Abishai and Ittai (*2 Sam. 18:2, 5, 12*). King David commanded them to protect Absalom if they found him.

**IZHAR** was one of four sons of Kohath and a grandson of Levi (*Exod. 6:18; 1 Chron. 6:2, 18, 38; 23:12*). He was a clan leader among the Kohathites (*Num. 3:19*). His own sons were Korah, Nepheg and Zicri (*Exod. 6:21; Num. 16:1*). Izhar's son, Korah, led a rebellion against Moses. In *1 Chron. 23:18* another son, Shelomith is mentioned as Izhar's first son.

**IZLIAH** One of the sons of Elpaal and a leader from the tribe of Benjamin, Izliah lived in Jerusalem (*1 Chron. 8:18*).

**IZRAHIAH** (Heb., 'the LORD appears'). The son of Uzzi and grandson of Tola, he had five sons. Izrahiah was a chief in the tribe of Issachar (*1 Chron. 7:3*). Together with his sons and their wives and extended families they were able to provide large numbers of fighting men for Israel. During the reign of King David the descendants of Issachar were said to have been able to find 87,000 fighting men.

**IZRI** A leader of the fourth group of Levitical musicians and choirs who ministered in the Temple (*1 Chron. 25:11*).

**IZZIAH** A descendant of Parosh, he was among those guilty of intermarriage with foreign women (*Ezra 10:25*).

# J

**JAAKOBAH** (Heb., 'protection'). A clan leader of the tribe of Simeon, mentioned in *1 Chron. 4:36*.

**JAALA** was one of Solomon's servants whose descendants returned from the Exile in Babylon in company with Zerubbabel (*Ezra 2:56; Neh. 7:58*).

**JAARE-OREGIM** The father of Elhanan, who was credited with killing 'Goliath the Gittite'. He came from Bethlehem (*2 Sam. 21:19*). For the problem of whether this was the same Goliath whom David killed, see *Elhanan*.

**JAARESHIAH** A son of Jeroham and clan leader. He was a Benjamite who lived in Jerusalem (*1 Chron. 8:27*).

**JAASIEL** (Heb., 'made by God').
**1.** Listed in *1 Chron. 11:47* as a 'Mezobaite', he was one of David's famous 'mighty men' who were valiant warriors.
**2.** The administrator over the tribal area of Benjamin and a leader of his tribe during the reign of King David. His father was Abner (*1 Chron. 27:21*). He may be the same as 1. above.

**JAASU** was among the descendants of Bani. At the time of return from the Exile in Babylon, Shecaniah confessed to Ezra that many men and even descendants of the priests of Judah had married wives from other tribes and nations. Ezra and the people repented and made a covenant to serve the LORD (*Ezra 10:2*). Jaasu is listed in *Ezra 10:37* as one who divorced his foreign wife.

**JAAZANIAH** (Heb., 'God hears').
**1.** Jaazaniah and his family were tested by the prophet Jeremiah who brought them into a room and offered them wine to drink. They refused to drink the wine because their forefather, Jonadab son of Recab, had ordered them not to drink wine and to continue to live in tents. This, he had told them, would lead to blessings for their family. Their obedience to their forefather, seen in their refusal to drink the offered wine, was used by Jeremiah as a picture of the problem of the disobedience of the people of Judah and Jerusalem at the time of the Babylonian invasion. While the Recabites provided an example of long-term obedience, the people of Judah had not listened to the prophets and had not obeyed the LORD and were therefore being judged. On the other hand, the Recabites were promised that they would 'never fail to have a man to serve' the LORD (*Jer. 35:3, 19*).
**2.** A Maacathite army officer who gathered with other officers at Mizpah on hearing about the appointment of Gedaliah by Nebuchadnezzar king of Babylon. Gedaliah became governor of Judah (*2 Kings 25:23; Jer. 40:8*) and, until he was assassinated some time later, these officers supported him.
**3.** Jaazaniah son of Shaphan was one of 70 elders of Israel seen by Ezekiel in a vision. Each of the 70 had a censer in his hand and incense was rising (*Ezek. 8:11*). Jaazaniah was probably the most important, as he alone is mentioned by name. These elders were involved in very serious idolatry in the Temple, 'each at the shrine of his own idol' (*v.12*). The

vision was given by the LORD so that the prophet would understand the depth of sin and idolatry for which Judah was to be judged (vv. 17-18). God's judgment is thus seen to be just and righteous for it is poured out on those who continue to rebel and worship other gods.

**4.** Jaazaniah son of Azzur is mentioned in Ezek. 11:1 and was an elder of the Judean people. The LORD showed the prophet Ezekiel that this leader, together with 25 others, was to be judged and condemned for leading the people astray with false prophecies and giving wicked advice to those in Jerusalem. Apart from the fearful judgment that is always promised in the Scriptures for false prophets who lead people away from the LORD's will, Jaazaniah's judgment was also deserved because the elders had 'conformed to the standards of the nations around' (v. 12).      P.D.G.

**JAAZIAH** (Heb., 'the LORD strengthens'). One of the sons of Merari, a Levite clan leader, whose descendants are listed as serving in the Tabernacle in the time of King David (1 Chron. 24:26–27).

**JAAZIEL** (Heb., 'God strengthens'). After the ark of the covenant had been brought by David to Jerusalem, the worship of God was properly organized by King David. Jaaziel was one of the family of Merarite Levites who were gatekeepers. The particular job he and his brothers were given was to be musicians and to play the harps and lyres before the ark of the covenant as it was moved to Jerusalem (1 Chron. 15:18, 20; in v. 20 he is called Aziel).

**JABAL** was the first son born to Lamech and Adah (Gen. 4:20). He was the earliest nomad mentioned in Scripture: 'the father of those who live in tents and raise livestock'.

**JABESH** (Heb., 'dry'). The father of Shallum. Towards the end of the Northern Kingdom of Israel, Shallum killed King Zechariah and took the throne by force. He, in turn, was assassinated by Menahem after only one month in power in Samaria (2 Kings 15:10, 13–14). The phrase 'Shallum son of Jabesh' could possibly indicate that Jabesh was the town from which Shallum came.

**JABEZ** The tribe of Judah was extending its life through the generations (1 Chron. 4:1–8), unconsciously making its way towards the crown of its existence (Heb. 7:14), when one man, making his only appearance in Scripture, achieved distinction because he prayed (1 Chron. 4:9–10). He discovered that ordinary, personal everyday needs can be brought to God: he 'cried out' and 'God granted his request'. Often in the Bible names must be taken seriously for, given seriously (as in this case, reflecting the circumstances of his birth) or thoughtlessly, they can become indexes of the person concerned. 'Jabez' means 'pain, sorrow' and he seems to have lived in dread that his name would be prophetic, a case of coming events casting their shadow before them. So he prayed about it and God granted his request. It was an inherited problem but prayer solved it. Jabez was also aware of material need: for some reason he needed more land and prayer solved this too: 'God granted his request'. All our needs – however this-worldly – are God's concerns. In addition, Jabez knew that he needed God to be with him and so he prayed 'Let your hand be with me' – the personal presence of God in power – and this also 'God granted'. 'We do not have because we do not ask' (James 4:2).      J.A.M.

**JABIN** (Heb., 'intelligent, discerning'). This word is possibly a royal title (similar to the Egyptian word 'Pharaoh').

**1.** A king of Hazor, the major city in northern Palestine, who led an alliance of princes against Joshua (Josh. 11:1–12).

But the LORD showed Joshua how to take the coalition by surprise, and Jabin was defeated at the waters of Merom. His city was taken and burned, and then he was slain.

**2.** Another king of Hazor (called 'king of Cannan' in *Judg. 4:2*) who 'cruelly oppressed' the Israelites for 20 years during the time of the Judges because of their idolatry (see *Judges*). Deborah and Barak defeated Sisera, Jabin's general and freed the Israelites from his tyranny (*Judg. 4:2–24*). Deborah sang praises to God for this great victory (*Judg. 5*), which is mentioned again in *Ps. 83:9*.    P.D.W.

**JACAN** A clan leader who was head of one of the seven Gadite clans settled in the area of Gilead and Bashan (*1 Chron. 5:13*).

# JACOB

## His birth (*Gen. 25:21–34; 27:1–45*)

Jacob was born in answer to prayer (*Gen. 25:21*) and on the wings of a promise (*vv. 22–23*). Did Isaac and Rebekah share the terms of this promise with the *twins* as they grew up? Did they let them know from the earliest days that according to the will of God 'the older will serve the younger'? They should have done, but the evidence suggests that they did not – for, as things turned out, the mode of Jacob's birth ('grasping', *Gen. 25:26*) and the name they gave him (Jacob, 'the heel-gripper') was for a long time the hallmark of his character – an opportunist, seizing the advantage by fair means and foul. Furthermore, Rebekah herself, faced with the possibility that Esau might achieve pre-eminence, did not resort to trust in the divine promise, but to her own form of unscrupulous opportunism (*Gen. 27:5–17*), and in this case it was 'like mother, like son'.

Esau was a bluff, easy-going activist, taking nothing very seriously and greatly given to an exaggerated demand for instant living. Jacob saw his chance. Esau returned from a day's hunting with roaring appetite and Jacob had the house filled with the aroma of a rich casserole. To Esau it was 'no contest' to hand over his rights as firstborn in return for a dinner – and one can see Jacob's quiet smile of satisfaction in a job well done (*Gen. 25:27–34*)!

The patriarchal family was the repository of the LORD's blessing for the world (see 'Abraham', *Gen. 12:2–3*) and the traumatic experience of *Gen. 22:1–18* must have impressed this blessing on Isaac. When, therefore, he sensed his approaching death (*Gen. 27:1–2*) – quite mistakenly, as is not unusual with the elderly (*Gen. 35:27–29*) – it was a matter of supreme importance to secure the transmission of the blessing. What tragedies would be avoided if only we would live in clear consciousness of the promises and the word of God! Rebekah felt it was incumbent on her to engineer the fulfilment of the promise made at the twins' birth, Isaac plainly forgot it altogether. A dreadful deceit was perpetrated, with Rebekah corrupting that positive approach which was such a charming mark of her girlhood (*Gen. 24:57*) and Jacob fearing discovery rather than the sin he was committing (*Gen. 27:12*). The consequences were enmity between the twins (*Gen. 27:41*), Rebekah's loss of her dear Jacob (*Gen. 25:28; 27–45*), never in fact to see him again on earth, and Jacob's exchange of a secure home for an unknown future (*Gen. 28:1–2, 10*).

## A deal with God (*Gen. 28:1–22*)

No sooner had Jacob begun to feel the desolation he had brought on himself than the LORD came to him with reassurances. For even though Jacob had wangled his way into the divine promise the LORD did not depart from his declared purpose. Much of the rest of the story of Jacob centres on this tension between the purpose of God to bless and the determination of Jacob to succeed by his own astuteness. The NIV margin is possibly nearer the meaning than NIV text when if offers 'There beside him' (Gen. 28:13), for the Bethel-blessing was 'I am with you . . . I will not leave you' (v. 15) and this suggests that the ladder is a picture of God descending to be with the man to whom he makes his promises (vv. 13–14). It was typical of Jacob to turn the promise into a bargain, literally putting the LORD on probation (vv. 20–22), withholding the commitment of personal faith until the LORD had proved himself as good as his word. What a God of grace, remaining silent and pursuing the fulfilment of his promises even when they have been flung back in his face! But opportunists and entrepreneurs do not make investments without a guaranteed return on their capital! Jacob was to walk a stony path until he learnt to trust.

## The story within the story (*Gen. 29–31*)

Gen. 29–31 tell how Jacob reached Haran in Paddan Aram, in the far north where Palestine and Mesopotamia meet across the Euphrates (29:1), how he met Rachel and was introduced to his mother's family (29:2–14), how he was tricked into marrying both Leah and Rachel (29:14–30), how he founded a large family (29:31–30:24), how he fared as Laban's employee (30:25–31:1) and finally how he left for home (31:2–55). It is a fascinating story – the opportunist and the wheeler-dealer, the self-reliant Jacob and the artful Laban. Laban schemed successfully to marry off the unprepossessing Leah (Gen. 29:17) – interestingly, the one who achieved the status of firstborn by trickery (25:29ff.) was tricked in turn on the ground of the status of the firstborn (29:26)! God is not mocked (*Gal. 6:7*) – but following this, for all that he did not have it easy (Gen. 31:38–41) Jacob was continuously successful. He knew how to outsmart Laban. Laban might decide which beasts would be Jacob's pay and take measures to ensure his own profits on the deal (30:34–36) but Jacob had a trick or two up his sleeve – as simple as stripping the bark off a few sticks (30:37–43) for, as he well knew, animal conception is influenced by what they are looking at!

Within the story of the peeled rods there was an inner story and Jacob began to learn and to respond to it. The LORD had promised to watch over Jacob (Gen. 28:15) and he did. No doubt Jacob was pleased with his cleverness with the rods but a vision of God put the record straight (Gen. 31:3, 10–13). It was not Jacob's superstitious eugenics but the LORD's faithful care which produced flocks to Jacob's advantage. Later Jacob said as much to Laban when the latter came blustering and fuming after him all the way to Mizpah on the borders of the promised land (Gen. 31:38–42). But, it seems, Jacob's learning of the lesson had not gone much beyond saying the right thing.

## Jacob's prayer (*Gen. 32:1–21*)

Is it an unjust criticism to say that Jacob had not yet learned to distrust self-effort and trust divine care? Two further questions point in one direction: why, when he had the company of two bands of angels (Gen. 32:1) was he afraid of Esau and 400 men (*vv.* 6–7)? And why, when he prayed such a magnificent prayer as Gen. 32:9–12, did he turn to rely rather on gifts and bribes (*vv.* 13–21)? It was a model prayer, pleasing the divine promises (*v.* 9), professing unworthiness and acknowledging blessing (*v.* 10), specific in its request (*v.* 11) and returning at the end to rest again on the promise of God (*v.* 12). There is hardly a more exemplary prayer in the Bible. Jacob should have awaited God's response, but, knowing how Esau was once bought by a good meal (Gen. 25:29ff.), he proceeded now to buy him again. Jacob was still in the state of keeping options open: a bit of prayer and a bit of bribery. But he was about to come to himself.

## Blessed in helplessness (*Gen. 32:22–31*)

If ever a scene summed up all that Jacob had ever been it was this: he sent his whole family across Jabbok but something kept him back. 'Jacob was left alone, and a man wrestled with him . . . ' (Gen. 32:24). It had really always been like that, 'Jacob alone' – wangling the birthright, sneaking the blessing, sparring with Laban, flying for home, negotiating (Gen. 31:44–55) a secure sphere of influence for himself – but, of course, no-one can negotiate to possess the promised land! The Lord will not have it. Therefore he came personally to oppose Jacob with a clearly implied choice: either you stay here alone or you go forward on my terms. Jacob was not minded to give up his independence easily and the match went on all night (Gen. 32:24). Had Jacob submitted at any point in the contest he could have walked on whole but his spirit of do-it-yourself arrogance drove him on until, with the consummate ease of almighty power, the touch of a finger tip put his hip out of joint (*v.* 25). The agony of it! The helplessness of it! The humiliation of only being able to stand upright because the strong arms of the Other held him!

But even opportunism can be sanctified! The helpless Jacob cried out 'I will not let you go unless you bless me' (*v.* 26) and the cry of the helpless for blessing made Jacob a new man with a new name (*v.* 28). He had indeed 'overcome' for that is the way of the ever-merciful God: he cannot be defeated by our strength but he is always overcome by our helplessness. And the helpless Jacob went limping on as Israel for he had 'seen the face of God' (*v.* 30).

## The man with a blessing to share (*Gen. 33:1–50:13*)

However, as the account of Jacob's life progresses, old things had not passed away and all things had not become new. The same man who 'saw God face to face' (Gen. 32:30) found Esau smiling at him and all the old smarm floated to the top: 'To see your face is like seeing the face of God' (Gen. 33:10)! The man who had (at last) been honest with God (32:26) was not yet honest with people, for promising to follow Esau to Edom (33:13–14) he did no such thing, nor indeed ever intended to do so (33:17). On the other hand, he was spiritually alive and faithfully kept the promise he had made, claiming the God of Bethel (*28:20–21*) as his God (*33:20*), anxious to keep his vow to the letter (*35:1–4*) and to bring his family within the same spiritual allegiance.

On his return to the promised land the Lord met him with reassurances and reaffirmations: affirming again his new name (*Gen. 35:9–10*) and repeating the promise of family and possession (*vv. 11–15*). Great mercy prompted this new beginning for Jacob had need of such assurance in the coming days: the death of Rachel (*Gen. 35:16–19*), the immorality and disloyalty of Reuben (*v. 21*), the death of Isaac (*vv. 27–29*), then that stretch of lost, desolate years, hardly more than a living death, when Joseph too was gone (*Gen. 37–45*). But the disciplines of God are educative and sanctifying (*Heb. 12:1–11*) and out of them Jacob emerged into a glorious Indian Summer of life wherein, every time we meet him, it is as a man with a blessing to share – blessing Pharaoh (*Gen. 47:7, 10*), blessing Joseph and his sons (*Gen. 48:15–20*) and blessing the whole family gathered at his deathbed (*Gen. 49*). And now his testimony too was without a shade of pretence: it was God who shepherded him, the angel who delivered him (*Gen 48:15*). The younger Jacob would have said 'I am about to die and I can't think what you will do without me to work and wangle for you'. But 'Israel', the man to whom God gave the new name, 'said to Joseph, "I am about to die, but God will be with you"' (*Gen. 48:21*). A man transformed, a lesson learned.                                       J.A.M.

**JADA** (Heb., 'the Lord cares'). The son of Onam from the tribe of Judah, Jada is mentioned in *1 Chron. 2:28, 32* as a grandson of Jerahmeel and Atarah.

**JADAH** A Benjamite and one of the descendants of King Saul. His father was Ahaz (*1 Chron. 9:42*). In other versions this name appears probably incorrectly as Jarah.

**JADDAI** (Heb., 'beloved'). A descendant of Nebo, Jaddai was one of those in the time of Ezra who had married a foreign wife rather than one from Judah and later divorced her (*Ezra 10:43*).

**JADDUA** **1.** One of the leaders of the people who had returned from Babylon, Jaddua signed Nehemiah's covenant of allegiance to the Lord and his Law (*Neh. 10:21*).
**2.** A descendant of Jeshua, one of the Levites who had returned from the Babylonian Exile with Zerubbabel. He was the son of a certain Jonathan. He was head of his family and a high priest in the days of Darius the Persian (*Neh. 12:11, 22*).

**JADON,** a man from Meronoth, helped repair the walls of Jerusalem under the direction of Nehemiah on their return from the Exile in Babylon (*Neh. 3:7*).

**JAEL** (Heb., 'a wild or mountain goat') [*cf. Ps. 104:18*]. The wife of Heber the Kenite who killed Sisera, Jabin's general (*Judg. 4:17–22*). The Israelites, led by Deborah and Barak, defeated Sisera and his army at 'Taanach by the waters of Megiddo', but Sisera escaped and fled for his life. He came to the place where Heber and his family dwelt, and assumed that he could accept Jael's hospitality since they had an alliance with Jabin king of Hazor. Sisera, exhausted from the battle and chase, fell asleep while hiding under a covering in Jael's tent. While he slept, Jael took a tent peg and ran it through his temple – a very brave deed, considering that the Israelites had not totally subdued the area and Jabin could be expected to retaliate. This battle appears to have been the turning point in delivering the Israelites from Canaanite oppression and Deborah immortalized Jael's brave deed in her song of victory (*Judg. 5:24–27*).                     P.D.W.

**JAHATH** (Heb., 'God will snatch up').

**1.** Son of Reaiah and father of Ahumai and Lahad, Jahath was from the Zorathite clan of the tribe of Judah. He was a great-grandson of Judah and a leader of his people (*1 Chron. 4:2*).

**2.** The grandson of Levi (*1 Chron. 6:43*). He is listed as one of the ancestors of Asaph, the Tabernacle choir leader in the latter days of King David. This name becomes a regular Levite family name.

**3.** The great-grandson of Levi (*1 Chron. 6:20*). However, probably this is the same person as 2. above, assuming that 'Libni his son' is omitted in *v. 43*.

**4.** Son of Shimei and grandson of Gershon, he is mentioned in *1 Chron. 23:10–11* in a passage describing the assignment of Temple work to the Levitical priests in the latter days of King David.

**5.** A son of Shelomoth, an Izharite from the tribe of Levi who served in the Tabernacle in King David's day (*1 Chron. 24:22*).

**6.** A Merarite Levite who was a skilful musician and oversaw the Temple repairs during the reign of King Josiah of Judah (*2 Chron. 34:12*).

**JAHAZIEL** (Heb., 'God sees').

**1.** A skilful and ambidextrous archer from the tribe of Benjamin who fought first for Saul and then transferred to David at Ziklag (*1 Chron. 12:4*). He was one of David's 'Thirty' great warriors. Later in the passage it seems that such men transferred loyalties not simply to be on the winning side but because the 'Spirit' had worked among them.

**2.** One of the priests appointed by King David to lead the worship as the ark of the covenant was moved up to Jerusalem. He

was to blow a trumpet regularly before the ark as part of the praises of the people to God (*1 Chron. 16:6*).

**3.** A Levite and descendant of Kohath, this Jahaziel was the third son of Hebron and took part in the Kohathite duties in the Temple (*1 Chron. 23:19; 24:23*).

**4.** A Levite from the clan of Asaph, he was the son of Zechariah, the son of Benaiah. He was famed for the fact that the Spirit of the LORD came upon him at a time of crisis for Judah and King Jehoshaphat (*2 Chron. 20:14*). An army of Moabites and Ammonites invaded Judah from Edom. Jehoshaphat and his people were frightened but the King turned to the LORD in prayer and called people to join him in a fast as they sought God's will. The King led the people in a great prayer of faith (*2 Chron. 20:1–12*). As the LORD had always promised, he heard the prayer of his people and answered through Jahaziel. He reminded the King and people of Judah that the battle depended on God not on them (*v. 15*). They were to take up their positions at the head of a valley and simply watch the LORD do his work. All the people praised God, led by the priests. As they went to battle they shouted and sang 'Give thanks to the LORD, for his love endures forever.' The LORD himself set traps for the enemy and they ended up fighting each other and were destroyed.

Clearly the impact of this chapter is the evidence it gives, as so often seen in the Bible, that when the King and his people sincerely looked to the LORD and put their faith in him, he did lead them to victory (*2 Chron. 20:13-28*). Other nations heard of the power of the LORD and so Jehoshaphat had security from them (*v. 30*).

**5.** Mentioned in Ezra 8:5, this Jehaziel was the father of Shecaniah and is listed among the exiles who returned with Ezra from Babylon to Jerusalem.     P.D.G.

**JAHDAI** (Heb., 'the LORD guides'). A descendant of Caleb from the tribe of Judah, listed in 1 Chron. 2:47.

**JAHDIEL** (Heb., 'God causes to rejoice'). A head of a clan and a valiant soldier in the tribe of Manasseh (1 Chron. 5:24).

**JAHDO** (Heb., 'the LORD rejoices'). The son of Buz and a clan leader in the tribe of Gad, which was settled in Bashan and Gilead (1 Chron. 5:14).

**JAHLEEL** (Heb., 'wait for the LORD). One of the sons of Zebulun and leader of the Jahleelite clan (Gen. 46:14; Num. 26:26).

**JAHMAI** (Heb., 'may the LORD protect'). A grandson of Issachar and son of Tola, Jahmai was a family leader and a valiant soldier (1 Chron. 7:2).

**JAHZEEL** (Heb., 'the LORD apportions'). The first son of Naphtali and head of the Jahzeelite clan (Num. 26:48). In 1 Chron. 7:13 he appears as Jahziel. He is listed among those who went to Egypt with Jacob (Gen. 46:24).

**JAHZEIAH** (Heb., 'the LORD sees'). The son of Tikvah, Jahzeiah was one of the very few leaders in Judah who refused to join Ezra and the people in repenting for the sin of intermarriage with foreign women (Ezra 10:15). Following the return from the Babylonian Exile, Ezra led the people in seeking to re-establish obedience to the Law of God. He urged the people to divorce these women, but Jahzeiah refused.

**JAHZERAH,** a Levite, is listed as an ancestor of Maasai who served among the priests living in Jerusalem after the return from the Babylonian Exile (1 Chron. 9:12). He was probably the same person as Ahzai in Neh. 11:13.

**JAHZIEL** Mentioned in Gen. 46:24; 1 Chron. 7:13. See Jahzeel.

**JAILER** See Philippian jailer.

**JAIR** (Heb., 'may he shine' or 'he enlightens'; cf. Ps. 104:18).

**1.** A descendant of Manasseh, who took several villages on the border of Bashan and Gilead in the conquest of the land east of the Jordan River under Moses and named them Havvoth Jair (Num. 32:41; Deut. 3:14; Josh. 13:30; 1 Kings 4:13; 1 Chron. 2:22).

**2.** One of the judges who judged Israel for 22 years and is said to have had 30 sons who ruled over 30 cities in Gilead, which were called Havvoth-jair (Judg. 10:3f.). He followed Tola as judge. Nothing more is known of him. See Judges.

**3.** The father of Mordecai (Est. 2:5).

**4.** The father of Elhanan, who killed Lahmi, the brother of Goliath (1 Chron. 20:5). In the parallel passage his name is said to be Jaare-oregim (2 Sam. 21:19), which may either mean 'weaver' or was mistakenly inserted by a copyist from the next line.                                    P.D.W.

**JAIRUS** was a synagogue ruler in the area of Lake Galilee and is presented by Mark and Luke as an example of a man of great faith (Mark 5:22–23, 35–43; Luke 8:40–42, 49–56; and Matt. 9:18–19, 23–26, where Jairus is not named). There are slight variations of detail between the accounts but the outline of the events is clear.

Jairus pleaded with Jesus to come and see his daughter who was gravely ill. Jesus set off with Jairus but their journey was interrupted by a sick woman who needed healing and by the large crowds surrounding him. Before he had reached the house, members of the household came to meet Jairus and Jesus to say that the young girl had died. Jesus responded: 'Don't be afraid; just believe' (Mark 5:36). In spite of ridicule from those around, he entered the house with Peter, James and John, took the twelve-year old girl by the hand and she was healed (vv. 40–42 etc.).

Significantly, given the opposition to Jesus of many of the religious leaders, this account reflects the fact that some were prepared to listen and to have faith in Christ. There is an emphasis in all the accounts on the manner in which the synagogue leader knelt (*Matt. 9:18*) or 'fell' (*Mark 5:22; Luke 8:41*) at the feet of the Saviour. Such faith in Christ and its results, evident for all to see, caused astonishment among the crowds. The way Jairus came to Christ, looking solely to him for help, became a clear example of how all people should respond to him.                                       P.D.G.

**JAKEH** A person who is mentioned in *Prov. 30:1* as the father of Agur. Agur was the writer of various Proverbs intended for Ithiel and Ucal.

**JAKIM** (Heb., 'God will establish').
**1.** Mentioned in *1 Chron. 8:19* in the genealogy leading from Benjamin to Saul. A son of Shimei.
**2.** One among the priests who were chosen to be officials in the sanctuary 'according to the last instructions of David'. Impartial selection from among the descendants of Eleazar and Ithamar was made by drawing lots. The eleventh lot fell to Huppah and that was the order in which he ministered when entering the sanctuary (*1 Chron. 24:12*).

**JAKIN** (Heb., 'God will establish').
**1.** The fourth son of Simeon and listed among those who went to Egypt with Jacob his grandfather. He was the leader of the Jakinite clan (*Gen. 46:10; Exod. 6:15; Num. 26:12*).

**2.** One among the priests who were chosen to be officials in the sanctuary 'according to the last instructions of David'. Impartial selection from among the descendants of Eleazar and Ithamar was made by drawing lots. The 21st lot fell to Jakin and that was the order in which he ministered when entering the sanctuary (*1 Chron. 9:10; 24:17*).
**3.** A priest, probably a descendant of 2. above, who lived in Jerusalem after the return from the Babylonian Exile and who served under Nehemiah (*Neh. 11:10*).
**4.** The name of the southern pillar erected in the building of Solomon's Temple by Huram (*1 Kings 7:21; 2 Chron. 3:17*). The northern pillar was called Boaz. Quite why these names were given is unclear, although it may have to do with the meaning of the names themselves: Jakin, see above; Boaz = 'strength'.
                                      P.D.G.

**JALAM** (Heb., 'young man'). The second son of Esau and Oholibamah, he became an Edomite chief (*Gen. 36:5, 14, 18; 1 Chron. 1:35*).

**JALON** was the fourth son of Ezrah and was from the tribe of Judah (*1 Chron. 4:17*).

**JAMBRES** Mentioned along with Jannes, he was supposedly one of the Egyptian magicians of Pharaoh's court who opposed Moses when he wished to lead the Israelites out of Egyptian slavery and captivity into God's promised land of Canaan (*2 Tim. 3:8*). For more detail see *Jannes*.

## JAMES, THE BROTHER OF JESUS

James, the brother of Jesus, became the most prominent leader in the church at Jerusalem by the time of the Jerusalem Council (*Acts 15*). He also is the traditional author of the Epistle of James. In the NT his name appears in *Matthew, Mark, Acts, 1 Corinthians, Galatians, James* and *Jude*.

The first mention of James by name in Scripture is in *Matt. 13:55*. Then the names of four other sons of Mary and Joseph, who was almost certainly dead at this point, besides Jesus are listed, along with a vague reference to 'sisters' in v. 56. Since the name of James is placed first among the brothers, it is fairly likely that James was the oldest of the brothers after Jesus. However, since the brother listed after James is Joseph (v. 55), and it was common for the eldest son to be named for the father (Luke 1:59–60), it is possible that James' name was placed first because of his prominence at the time of the writing of the Gospel. The name for Jesus, who was not the physical son of Mary's husband, Joseph, was previously commanded by God (Matt. 1:20–21).

An even earlier passage almost certainly also refers to James. In Matt. 12:46, Jesus' 'mother and brothers' are said to be waiting to speak with him. Upon hearing of their request (v. 47), the Saviour redefined his family as 'whoever does the will of my Father in heaven' (v. 49). Though he almost certainly did not understand the spiritual reality of Jesus' point at that time, a seed was probably planted in James' mind that contributed to his understanding of the nature of the church in his ministry as a church leader.

Because of the apparent lack of understanding of Jesus' role by James and his brethren in the Gospels, it is virtually certain that James' conversion to Christianity did not occur until after the resurrection of Christ. He was probably in the Upper Room along with the apostles, Mary and Jesus' other 'brothers,' also now converted (Acts 1:14). That season of prayer (v. 14) took place only a few days after the resurrected Lord appeared to James (1 Cor. 15:7). Prior to that, 'his brothers did not believe in him' (John 7:5), even though they were impressed by Jesus' miracles (v. 3).

It must have been a confusing, if not highly frustrating, thing to grow up in the home of Joseph and Mary, as the younger brother of Jesus Christ. Both parents certainly believed that Jesus was the long-anticipated Messiah, but even they did not always understand him. (Luke 2:49–50). The other children certainly would have noticed that Jesus was 'filled with wisdom, and the grace of God was upon him' (v. 40). That Jesus never sinned and that his growth was perfectly balanced (v. 52) probably engendered jealousy and resentment in the younger siblings.

Although Joseph and Mary undoubtedly had told James and their other children that Jesus had a very special role to play in God's plan, it was still probably baffling to them how Jesus could leave the family business around the age of 30 (Luke 3:23). If Joseph was dead by that time, as seems assured by his absence in the family passages in the Gospels (Matt. 12:46; John 2:1), Jesus, as oldest son, would have been the head of the household. Since Jesus was a 'carpenters's son' (Matt. 13:55) who had worked and become known as a carpenter himself (Mark 6:3), it would have been natural to assume that he would have continued at that trade. Perhaps the disappointment of James and the others is a large part of the reason why Jesus was not honoured 'in his home town and in his own house' (Matt. 13:57) during his public ministry.

There is no other record of James' response to Jesus and his ministry until after the resurrection. In what seems to have been the next-to-last appearance before his ascension to heaven, the glorified Saviour was manifested to his half-brother (1 Cor. 15:7). It is quite likely that James' conversion was a result of that meeting, much as Paul's was later (1 Cor. 15:8; Acts 9:3–19).

Since none of Joseph's and Mary's other sons believed in Jesus during his pre-crucifixion ministry (John 7:5), it is very plausible that James led some (or all) of his brothers to faith in Christ after his own conversion. Though their mother's belief was apparently not decisive, the transformation in their brother, James, may have been. The mention of 'brothers' (plural) in Acts 1:14 in the Upper Room requires the conversion of at least two of Jesus' half-brothers. Almost certainly included would be James and Jude (Matt. 13:55; Jude 1), the brothers who contributed books to the NT.

The next mention of James is in Acts 12:17, after Peter was miraculously freed from prison by an angel (vv. 3–17). Peter asked those gathered for prayer to get word of what had happened to 'James and the brothers'. 'Brothers' almost certainly means the wider church in Jerusalem, thus the mention of James' name probably reflects his recognized leadership role in the church.

Two other inclusions of James' name in Acts underline his prominence as a leader in the Jerusalem church. At the Jerusalem Council, James was the last leader to speak, adding biblical support to the testimony of Peter (Acts 15:7–11) and Barnabas and Paul (v. 12). Since James' approach was essentially accepted word-for-word by the other leaders and the gathered church (vv. 13–29), he must have commanded great respect from all.

The final mention of James in Acts is at the conclusion of Paul's third missionary journey. When Paul arrived in Jerusalem, he went to James and 'all the elders were present' (Acts 21:18). This wording again indicates that James was a leader of even higher station than the elders. Since the other apostles besides Paul were not referred to in Jerusalem in the book of Acts after the Jerusalem Council, the likelihood that James was, in effect, the ranking Christian leader in Jerusalem from that time forward until his death is fairly strong.

Most of the remaining references to James in the NT outside of Acts seem to fit into the time frame of the appearances of James in Acts. Probably the earliest of these are in Galatians, which most likely was written not long before the Jerusalem Council. In Gal. 2:9 James, Peter and John are termed 'pillars' of the church. Paul's interaction with those leaders in Jerusalem was very positive, as they recognized his mission to the Gentiles (v. 9). However, at a later point, men claiming the authority of James came to Syrian Antioch and caused great dissension in that primarily Gentile church (v. 12). Since the visitors even managed to persuade Peter and Barnabas to assume certain legalistic practices (vv. 12–13), it is likely that the assumed influence of James was part of the Judaizers' revenge.

In 1 Cor. 9, Paul noted that 'the Lord's brothers' were married (v. 5) and that their families were supported by the church financially (vv. 4–6). Surely James would be included in that phrase. The reference in 1 Cor. 15:7 to the appearance of the resurrected Christ to James is proof of that prominence.

The Epistle of James was almost certainly written by James, who grew up in the same household as Jesus, although he does not make mention of that relationship, but instead humbly calls himself 'a servant of God and of the Lord Jesus Christ' (James 1:1). The reference to the OT, Christ's Sermon on the Mount, and prayer (James 4:2–3; 5:13–16) fit well both the scriptural picture and the strong extra-biblical tradition about James. Because the congregation of believers is called both 'synagogue' (James 2:2) and ecclesía ('church', James 5:14), the epistle may be one of the earliest NT writings, dating from a time in which the church in Jerusalem was still more of a messianic synagogue within Judaism than a clearly distinct religious grouping.

The final reference to James in the NT is in the first verse of the short Epistle of Jude. Jude, like James, calls himself 'a servant of Jesus Christ', but also goes on to bolster his authority as a writer of Scripture by the further description 'a brother of James' (v. 1). By that point in the apostolic era, the only James that could be named without further description is the Lord's younger half-brother.

Tradition holds that James was killed for his faith in the early 60s AD by the Jews. He is said to have been thrown from the roof of the Temple in Jerusalem, though this is not certain. The developing church lost a great leader and godly example when James died.                                                                     A.B.L.

**JAMES** A Greek name which could be transliterated as Jacob. In the NT, four persons are named James. All four are closely related to Jesus Christ. The first, a younger son of Joseph and Mary, became an important leader in the early church, two are apostles, and the fourth the father of an apostle.

**1.** See above, *James, the brother of Jesus.*

**2.** James, the son of Zebeddee. An apostle and also the brother of John the apostle. He is found in the first three Gospels and in *Acts 1–12.*

It is likely that the home town of this James was Capernaum, on the Sea of Galilee. It is known that James and his brother, John, were partners with Simon Peter in a fishing business on the Sea of Galilee (*Luke 5:10*). It is also clear that Peter's home was in Capernaum (*Mark 1:29*).

The fishing partnership was multi-generational. Zebedee, James' father, was involved along with Peter, James and John (*Matt. 4:21*). It apparently was a somewhat prosperous business venture, since there were also 'hired men' (*Mark 1:20*).

It was from fishing that Jesus called James (as well as Peter and John) to be his disciple (*Mark 1:20*). Later, after praying all night, Christ chose James to be numbered among his twelve apostles (*Luke 6:12–14*). He is listed third in each of the passages that number the apostles (*Matt 10:2; Mark 3:17; Luke 6:14; Acts 1:13*).

In the list of the apostles in *Mark 3* a nickname that Jesus gave to James and John is explained. They were called Boanerges, which means 'Sons of Thunder', by the Saviour (*Mark 3:17*). Apparently this appellation was descriptive of the stormy personalities of the brothers when they met Jesus and during their period of training by him. Their desire to 'call down fire from heaven' to destroy a Samaritan village (*Luke 9:54*) is a good indication of how angry and impetuous James and John could be when they followed their natural bent.

Since the name of James is placed before John's in all three listings of the apostles in the Gospels, it is quite likely that James was John's older brother. It is of interest that John's name is placed before James' in the Upper Room scene in *Acts 1:13*. Since the name of Peter's brother, Andrew, is separated from Peter, being placed after James (*v. 13*), it seems that the two most prominent apostles in the early church, Peter and John, are honoured by being listed first (*v. 13*).

Perhaps it was difficult for James, as the older brother, to watch the younger

John gain more recognition as a leader than he did. However, there is no indication in the book of Acts of jealousy or rivalry on James' part during the early years of the church.

That is not to say that James (or John) had always been selfless. Along with being hotheads (*Mark 3:17*), they were apparently also highly ambitious. They may have inherited such ambition from one or both of their parents, as seen in an incident in which their mother, the wife of Zebedee, approached Jesus and asked for him to grant her sons the positions of honour in his kingdom (*Matt. 20:20–21*). Jesus informed all three that, in his kingdom the greatest of all are servants of all (*vv. 26–27*).

The request of James and John and their mother may have been based on a misunderstanding of the role of honour that Jesus had already bestowed on the sons of Zebedee and Simon Peter. The three comprised a sort of inner circle within the wider apostolic band. For example, they were the only apostles allowed to accompany Jesus when the daughter of Jairus, the synagogue ruler, was healed (*Mark 5:37–42*). They also were the apostles that Jesus took up with him on the Mount of Transfiguration (*Matt. 17:1–2*). Finally, the three accompanied Jesus when he removed himself from the other apostles to pray in the Garden of Gethsemane (*Matt. 26:36–37*).

Given the spotlighted leadership roles of Peter and John among the apostles and the followers of Jesus in the first half of the book of Acts, it is quite plausible that the trio were being trained for such roles by Jesus through their close privileged relationship with him. If so, James may have held a very responsible position in the leadership of the infant church, but one that is not focused upon in the book of Acts. Certainly his enumeration with the other apostles in the Upper Room (*Acts 1:13*) indicates that he had an important role on the Day of Pentecost (*Acts 2:14*),

in the foundational apostolic teaching (*Acts 2:42*), and the apostles' defence before the Sanhedrin (*Acts 5:29*).

The final mention of this James in the NT is in regard to his death at the hands of King Herod Agrippa (*Acts 12:1–2*). Other Christians were arrested along with James in Herod Agrippa's persecution (*v. 1*). Apparently, Agrippa intended to make James' death a warning to the church (*vv. 1–2*). But, whatever advantage Agrippa may have thought he gained by killing James was short-lived. Soon Peter was miraculously freed from prison (*vv. 3–19*), probably a great embarrassment to Agrippa. Then Agrippa himself died an excruciating death which Josephus described as being from violent stomach pains. Scripture attributes the death to Agrippa's failure to 'give praise to God' (*v. 23*), which may also include retribution for persecuting God's people, including the martyrdom of James.          A.B.L.

**3.** *James, the son of Alphaeus.* One of two of Jesus' twelve apostles named James – the other was James the son of Zebedee. He appears in each of the four NT lists of the Twelve (*Matt. 10:3*; *Mark 3:18*; *Luke 6:15*; *Acts 1:13*); in Matthew he is paired with Thaddaeus. *Mark 15:40* refers to him as James 'the less', which could refer to his size but more probably means that he is younger than the other apostle with the same name. This passage also calls his mother Mary; the parallel text in *John 19:25* can be interpreted as identifying this Mary as the sister of Mary, the mother of Jesus. If that is the correct reading, then James, son of Alphaeus, would have been one of Jesus' cousins. Nothing else is known with any certainty about the man.          C.B.

**4.** *James, the father of Judas (not Iscariot), the apostle.* Mentioned only in *Luke 6:16* and *Acts 1:13*. His son may also be known as Thaddaeus, who is listed as an apostle in *Matt. 10:3* and *Mark 3:18*. The name Thaddaeus is not found in the lists of Jesus' apostles in which 'Judas son of James' is included (*Luke 6:16; Acts 1:13*).

**JAMIN 1.** The second son of Simeon and listed among those who went to Egypt with Jacob his grandfather. He was the leader of the Jaminite clan (*Gen. 46:10; Exod. 6:15; Num. 26:12; 1 Chron. 4:24*).

**2.** Mentioned in *1 Chron. 2:27*, a son of Ram and a grandson of Jerahmeel from the tribe of Judah.

**3.** Soon after the Israelites had settled back in the towns around Jerusalem they came and asked Ezra to read to them from the Book of the Law. Jamin was one of the Levites present who later 'instructed' the people in the meaning of the Law and interpreted it for them (*Neh. 8:7*). The people heard the word and began to weep as they understood it. Jamin and the others encouraged them not to weep since this was a 'sacred day'. The people were to worship the LORD, 'for the joy of the LORD is your strength' (*v.10*). The more they understood of the Law the more they rejoiced. They celebrated the festival of the feast of Tabernacles. As a nation they then began to confess their sins (*Neh. 9*). Good instruction for the people was vital if they were to worship as the LORD wanted. Before the Exile the Levites and leaders had been severely castigated by the LORD for not doing this (e.g. *Jer. 23*). Now, after the Exile, they began to do what they should always have done, and the LORD brought them great blessing.

P.D.G.

**JAMLECH** (Heb., 'the LORD gives dominion'). Mentioned in *1 Chron. 4:34*, a leader of one of the clans of Simeon during the time of King Hezekiah.

**JANAI** (Heb., 'he answered'). A Gadite clan leader who lived in Bashan (*1 Chron. 5:12*).

**JANNAI** Mentioned in the genealogy leading from Jesus to Adam, as the father of Melki and son of Joseph (*Luke 3:24*).

**JANNES** Mentioned along with Jambres only in *2 Tim 3:8* in the biblical text. They were Egyptian magicians of Pharaoh's court who opposed Moses when he tried to lead the Israelites out of Egyptian slavery and captivity into God's promised land of Canaan.

In the account of Moses' confrontation with Pharaoh, the king asked his own magicians to do what Moses and Aaron had done. This they did. Aaron had thrown his stick to the ground and it had turned to a snake. The magicians did the same (*Exod. 7:10–12*). When Aaron's stick was used to hit the river, the river turned to blood and the fish died. But the magicians were able to imitate the same thing (*vv. 20–24*). The fact that the magicians were able to imitate what Aaron did led to the further 'hardening' of Pharaoh's heart against the LORD and his servant Moses. That theirs was a mere imitation was seen as Aaron's rod/snake swallowed those of the magicians (*v. 12*). Their imitation of Aaron and Moses' work continued in *Exod. 8*.

The fact that the apostle Paul used these names without further ellaboration indicates his own awareness of Jewish tradition but also his belief that his readers would have known what he was talking about. The names do appear in a number of non-biblical texts, but none of them are particularly early. They are not found in either Josephus or Philo. However, in the Targum of Jonathan on *Exod. 7:11*, and later in the Talmud traditions, their names do appear as the magicians of Pharaoh's court.

The significance of these magicians to the apostle Paul in *2 Tim. 3:8* is clear. Talking of the problems the Christian faith would face 'in the last days', Paul highlights the danger to true Christianity of people who would have an appearance of religion but not possess its power. Such people oppose the faith so strongly that even when they see it they are 'never able to acknowledge the truth' (*v. 7*). Paul warned that such obstinacy in the face of the truth of Christ and of lives lived to his glory would be a feature of the society in which Christians were called to witness. However, just as eventually God's great power was indeed seen as far greater than the powers of the Egyptian magicians, and just as the Egyptian magicians were made to seem foolish in the revelation of that power, so it will be with those who oppose the truth in the last days. God's power and salvation will indeed be victorious and the folly of those who opposed the faith will be seen by all (cf. 2 Tim 4:1, 8).

Towards the end of his life, Paul thus set the context for the church's mission. Christians and Christian teaching will be opposed just as Moses was opposed. The opposition will appear immensely powerful but Christians are not to be fearful for their victory is assured because it is in the hands of the same God who revealed the bankruptcy of the works and words of Jannes and Jambres.      P.D.G.

**JAPHETH** The third son of Noah (Gen. 5:32), Japheth was born into a sinful humanity under judgment (6:5–7). But as a son of the man who 'found favour' (6:8) he was embraced by the Noahic covenant and enjoyed divine salvation and became one of the fathers of humanity's second chance (7:13; 9:18–19; 10:2–4). For his sensitive reaction to his father's lapse (9:20–23) he was rewarded with divine blessing (9:27). In so far as Japheth's descendants can be identified, they lived at a distance from Israel, mainly to the far north.      J.A.M.

**JAPHIA 1.** Japhia, king of Lachish, answered the call of Adoni-Zedek, king of Jerusalem, to join a coalition of kings to fight the Gibeonites, who had recently made a peace treaty with Joshua and the Israelites. When Gibeon was attacked, Joshua came to its aid and defeated the coalition. The kings fled to a cave at

Makkedah. When Joshua found them there he rolled stones in front of the cave and posted guards so they could not escape. When Joshua returned from battle he brought out the kings and put them to death (Josh. 10:3–28; 12:10–12). The LORD continued to encourage Joshua in battle and to demonstrate that there was indeed no need for fear (Josh. 10:8; see 1:4–9).

**2.** A son of King David. After David conquered Jerusalem and moved there from Hebron he took many wives and concubines. One of his many children was Japhia (2 Sam. 5:15; 1 Chron. 3:7; 14:6).      P.D.G.

**JAPHLET** The son of Heber and a head of a clan in the tribe of Asher. He had three sons and was a 'brave warrior' and 'outstanding leader' (1 Chron. 7:32–33, 40).

**JARED** (Heb., 'descent'). The son of Mahalalel, Jared became the father of Enoch at the age of 162. He was one of those early leaders of a whole people who lived 962 years. He is also listed in Luke's genealogy leading from Jesus to Adam (Gen. 5:15–20; 1 Chron. 1:2; Luke 3:37).

**JARHA** was an Egyptian servant belonging to Sheshan. Sheshan, listed as a descendant of Jerahmeel of the tribe of Judah, only had daughters and so, in order to continue his family line, he gave his daughter in marriage to Jarha. They then had a child called Attai (1 Chron. 2:34–35).

**JARIB 1.** A son of Simeon and listed among those who went to Egypt with Jacob his grandfather (1 Chron. 4:24; the same person as Jakin, Gen. 46:10; Exod. 6:15; Num. 26:12).

**2.** One of the Jews, a leader among his people, who joined Ezra on their return from the Babylonian captivity to Jerusalem. He helped Ezra find suitable

Levites to accompany them back to Judah (*Ezra 8:16*).

**3.** A descendant of Jeshua, this Jarib was among those priests who joined Ezra and the people in repentance on their return to Jerusalem from Babylon. Many men of Judah had married wives from other tribes and nations. They made a covenant to serve the LORD and divorced their foreign wives (*Ezra 10:2, 18–19*).

P.D.G.

**JAROAH** A son of Gilead and descendant of Buz, a clan leader in the tribe of Gad that was settled in Bashan and Gilead (*1 Chron. 5:14*).

**JASHAR** Mentioned only in *Josh. 10:13* and *2 Sam. 1:18*, the 'Book of Jashar' was an ancient literary source that the writers of *Joshua* and *2 Samuel* drew upon. Who or what Jashar was is no longer known although the word means 'upright' and, therefore, it may have been a collection of poems about 'upright' men and women of the past.

**JASHEN** The 'sons of Jashen' are listed among David's 'Thirty' mighty men who went to battle for him and led the people of Israel to war (*2 Sam. 23:32*). The parallel passage in *1 Chron. 11:33* refers to the 'sons of Hashem'. Presumably Jashen was father of more than one of these warriors.

**JASHOBEAM 1.** When David became king in Israel, he rapidly moved to take Jerusalem. In all that he did we are told the 'LORD Almighty was with him' (*1 Chron. 11:9*). As David became more and more powerful, three mighty men were of particular support and Jashobeam, the Hacmonite, was one of these. He was appointed 'chief of the officers' and was renowned for having killed 300 men in one encounter (*1 Chron. 11:11*). The parallel passage in *2 Sam. 23:8* talks of Josheb-Basshebeth, a Tahkemonite, who

killed 800 men in one encounter. It is unclear whether this refers to the same person.

**2.** One of the warriors who deserted Saul to join David at Ziklag. They were ambidextrous in archery and with slings. They were from the tribe of Benjamin. He is called a Korahite (*1 Chron. 12:6*).

**3.** A descendant of Perez and son of Zabdiel (*1 Chron. 27:2*). He was a commander in David's army and on duty with his men in the first month of each year. Whether he is the same as 1. or 2. above is unclear.

P.D.G.

**JASHUB** (Heb., 'he returns').

**1.** The third son of Issachar who became founder of the Jashubite clan. He is listed among those who went down to Egypt with his grandfather Jacob (*Gen. 46:13; Num. 26:24; 1 Chron. 7:1*).

**2.** This Jashub was among the descendants of Binnui. At the time of return from the Exile in Babylon, Shecaniah confessed to Ezra that many men and even descendants of the priests of Judah had married wives from other tribes and nations. Ezra and the people repented and made a covenant to serve the LORD (*Ezra 10:2*). Jashub is listed in *Ezra 10:29* as one who divorced his foreign wife.

**JASON** (Gk., 'healing').

**1.** This Jason, who may be the same as 2. below, acted as host for Paul and Silas when they visited Thessalonica (*Acts 17:6*). As Paul preached in the synagogue some Jews 'were persuaded and joined Paul and Silas' and many God-fearing Greeks also became Christians (*v. 4*). As so often in Paul's ministry, this provoked serious antagonism from certain sections of the Jews. These people then went out to the market place and got together a 'rent-a-mob' in order to start a riot. They rushed to Jason's house to look for Paul and Silas. Not finding them there, they dragged out Jason and some of the other Christians in the house and made them face the city officials on a charge of being trouble-makers and defying the laws of Caesar by acknowledging another king called Jesus.

Jason and the other Christians were put on bail and released. Later that day Paul and Silas left the town, leaving the newly founded church in the hands of people like Jason (*Acts 17:7–9*). It is an interesting testimony to the depth of faith to be found among those newly converted Christians that, recently acquired though their faith was, they were prepared to be imprisoned and persecuted for the truth. This happened in a number of towns where Paul preached and such faith that was prepared to accept persecution has become an example to many Christians down the ages who have faced similar troubles on confessing the faith.

**2.** Either a fellow Jew or a blood relative of Paul and one of those who was with him when he wrote his letter to the Roman church (*Rom. 16:21*). He joined Paul, Timothy, Lucius and others in sending the church his greetings. It is likely that he had visited the Christians in Rome either when on business or as an itinerant Christian teacher.                    P.D.G.

**JATHNIEL** A Levite from the Korahite clan who is listed as one of the 'gate-keepers' of the sanctuary. He was appointed during the latter part of King David's reign and was the fourth son of Meshelemiah (*1 Chron. 26:2*).

**JAVAN** The fourth son of Japheth and grandson of Noah (*Gen. 10:2, 4; 1 Chron. 1:5, 7*). He was believed to be the ancestor of the 'Greeks' or of those living on Cyprus. The NIV version thus substitutes 'Greeks' or 'Greece' for 'Javanites' or 'sons of Javan' in a couple of texts. The Javanites were seen as enemies of the Israelites (e.g. see *Zech. 9:13; Joel 3:6*).

**JAZIZ** A Hagrite who was one of the overseers of all the King's property during the reign of King David. He was in charge of the King's flocks (*1 Chron. 27:31*).

**JEATHERAI** A descendant of Gershon son of Levi, head of one of the Levitical clans. His father was Zerah (*1 Chron. 6:21*).

**JEBEREKIAH** (Heb., 'the LORD bless'). The father of the Zechariah mentioned in *Is. 8:2*. This Zechariah was a colleague of the prophet Isaiah and, with Uriah the priest, became a witness to Isaiah's prophecies that Assyria would invade and conquer Syria and Samaria.

**JEBUSITES** This name refers to the inhabitants of the city of Jebus (*Judg. 19:10–11; 1 Chron. 11:4–5*), better known in the OT as Jerusalem. Inasmuch as the city was called Jerusalem (or some similar name such as Urusalim) long before the setting of the earliest biblical reference to it as Jebus, one cannot argue that its name underwent a change from Jebus to Jerusalem. On the other hand, there was clearly no shift from Jerusalem to Jebus. The best explanation for the contemporaneous use of the two city names is that the natives of the city in the time of the judges (i.e., the Jebusites) called it Jebus while others, including the Israelites, knew it as Jerusalem.

The Bible identifies the Jebusites as a Canaanite people (*Gen. 10:16; 15:21; Exod. 3:8, 17*) who lived in the hill country with the Amorites (*Num. 13:29*). In the conquest of Canaan Judah was unable to drive them out of Jerusalem, their major city (*Josh 15:63*). In fact, the narrative states that though Judah did at one point conquer and burn Jerusalem (*Judg. 1:8*), it was quickly reinhabited by Jebusites whom the Benjaminites were unable to evict up to the author's own time (*Judg. 1:21*). All through the era of the judges (cf. *Judg. 19:11*) and up to David's early monarchy (c. 1000 BC) the city remained Jebusite, independent of Israel.

When David came to the throne of united Israel he determined to make

Jerusalem his capital because of its central, strategic location. Unfortunately, the Jebusites refused to hand it over and only after a clever ruse was the acquisition of the city made possible (2 Sam. 5:6–9). It is quite apparent that David not only spared the city from destruction but he graciously allowed its inhabitants to live as well. Toward the end of his reign he purchased an area adjacent to the old city as the place for the Temple that Solomon would construct. Its owner was a Jebusite named Araunah (2 Sam. 24:16) or Ornan (1 Chron. 21:15), the uncertainty of whose name suggests his foreign (perhaps non-Semitic) lineage. This friendly transaction explains the continuing existence of Jebusites in Israel as late as post-exilic times (2 Chron. 8:7; Ezra 9:1; Neh. 9:8).                     E.M.

**JECOLIAH** A woman from Jerusalem who was the mother of King Uzziah (Azariah) of Judah (2 Kings 15:2; 2 Chron. 26:3). She was wife to King Amaziah.

**JECONIAH** Mentioned in *Matt. 1:11–12*, Jeconiah is an alternative form of the name Jehoiachin. Jehoiachin was king of Judah during the Babylonian Exile. He is listed as a descendant of Josiah in the genealogy which establishes Jesus' royal lineage.

**JEDAIAH** (Heb., 'the LORD knows'). A donor, with Heldai and Tobijah, of gold and silver with which to make crowns for the post-exilic priest Joshua (Zech. 6:10, 14).
**2.** A Simeonite, Son of Shimri, of the days of King Hezekiah who was involved in military activity against the Hamites and Meunites (1 Chron. 4:37).
**3.** One of the priests who returned to Judah from Babylon (1 Chron. 9:10; Neh. 12:7?).
**4.** The head of the second division of priests in the administration of David (1 Chron. 24:7; cf. Ezra 2:36; Neh. 7:39).

**5.** The son of Harumaph, this Jedaiah was one of the leaders in the rebuilding of Jerusalem's walls under Nehemiah (Neh. 3:10).
**6.** Jedaiah, the son of Joiarib, was a priest who settled in Jerusalem in the days of Nehemiah (Neh. 11:10; cf. 12:6).
                                          E.M.

**JEDIAEL 1.** Benjamin's third son who became a clan leader (1 Chron. 7:6). His son Bilhan and various grandsons were also clan leaders (1 Chron. 7:10–11).
**2.** The son of Shimri, this Jediael was one of David's 'Thirty' mighty warriors who fought at his side (1 Chron. 11:45). He was one of those great fighting men who deserted Saul and came from the tribe of Manasseh to join David at Ziklag. The passage in 1 Chron. 12 makes it clear that the gradual desertion from Saul of such warriors from various tribes was led by the Spirit of God. The last verse of the section (v. 22) says: 'Day after day men came to help David, until he had a great army, like the army of God.'
**3.** A Levite from the Korahite clan who is listed as one of the 'gatekeepers' of the sanctuary. He was appointed during the latter part of King David's reign and was the second son of Meshelemiah (1 Chron. 26:2).                     P.D.G.

**JEDIDAH** (Heb., 'beloved'). The mother of King Josiah of Judah. She was the daughter of Adaiah and came from Bizkath (2 Kings 22:1).

**JEDIDIAH** This was the name given to David's first surviving son by Bathsheba (2 Sam. 12:25). Their first son had died as a punishment for the murder and adultery committed by David in his desire to have Bathsheba for himself. Following that death, David 'comforted' Bathsheba, had sex with her, and she bore him his son Solomon (v. 24). 'The LORD loved him' and sent word through the prophet Nathan, that he should be called

Jedidiah which means 'loved by the LORD'. See *Solomon*.

**JEDUTHUN** (Heb., 'praise'). From the tribe of Levi and living in the villages of the Netophathites (*1 Chron. 9:16*), Jeduthun was a musician and a contemporary of Asaph (*25:1, 3, 6*). When the ark was brought by David to the specially prepared place in Jerusalem, Jeduthun was one of those who were to sound the trumpets and cymbals (*16:41–42*).

He was also set aside by David 'for the ministry of prophesying' and became known as a 'seer'. He reported directly to the King himself. He was blessed with six sons (*1 Chron. 25:1, 3, 6*). When the ark was eventually brought to the new Temple in Solomon's time, Jeduthun and his associates led the great 'songs of praise and thanks to the LORD' (*2 Chron. 5:12–13*). At the time of Hezekiah's revival, it is interesting to see that Jeduthun's descendants were still among the first Levites to be involved in the purifying and reconsecrating of the Temple (*2 Chron. 29:14–15*). Later descendants were also present at the time of revival under King Josiah of Judah (*35:15*). Others were also listed among the first Levites to return to Jerusalem from the Babylonian captivity in *Neh. 11:17*.

His sons were gatekeepers of the Tabernacle and later the Temple (*1 Chron. 16:38*). A few of David's psalms were probably written for Jeduthun and his musicians (*Pss. 39; 62; 77*). This man was head of a family of Levites who, over the years, proved their continuing faithfulness to the LORD and his service. Music was obviously a family gift which they were happy to use in the praise of God.                                    P.D.G.

**JEHALLELEL** (Heb., 'praising the LORD').
**1.** From the tribe of Judah and a descendant of Caleb, son of Jephunneh (*1 Chron. 4:16*).
**2.** A Merarite Levite whose descend-

ant, Azariah, helped organize the Temple worship during the revival under King Hezekiah of Judah (*2 Chron. 29:12*).

**JEHATH** A grandson of Gershon son of Levi and head of one of the Levitical clans. His father was Libni (*1 Chron. 6:20*).

**JEHDEIAH** **1.** A descendant of Levi, and son of Shubael, who worked in the service of the Tabernacle in the time of King David (*1 Chron. 24:20*).
**2.** A Meronothite who was one of the overseers of all the King's property during the reign of David. He was in charge of the King's donkeys (*1 Chron. 27:30*).

**JEHEZKEL** (Heb., 'the LORD strengthens'). One among the priests who were chosen to be officials in the sanctuary 'according to the last instructions of David'. Impartial selection from among the descendants of Eleazar and Ithamar was made by drawing lots. The 20th lot fell to Jehezkel and that was the order in which he ministered when entering the sanctuary (*1 Chron. 24:16*).

**JEHIAH** (Heb., 'the LORD lives'). One of the door-keepers for the ark when it was brought back to Jerusalem by David (*1 Chron. 15:24*).

**JEHIEL** (Heb., 'may God live').
**1.** After the ark of the covenant had been brought to Jerusalem, the worship of God was properly organized by King David. Jehiel was appointed one of the musicians, and was to play the lyre when the ark was brought up to Jerusalem (*1 Chron. 15:18, 20; 16:5*).
**2.** One of the Gershonite Levites, a son of Ladan, whose duties were assigned by David towards the end of his reign in anticipation of their work in the Temple. He was given charge of looking after precious stones that were brought as gifts

and put in the Temple treasury (1 Chron. 23:8; 29:8).

**3.** Mentioned in 1 Chron. 27:32, this Jehiel was a son of Hacmoni. He was placed in charge of the King David's sons.

**4.** One of the sons of King Jehoshaphat of Judah. He was brother to Jehoram who succeeded his father to the throne (2 Chron. 21:2). Jehoram established his throne and then put to death all his brothers (v. 4).

**5.** Mentioned in 2 Chron. 29:14, he was a son of Heman and worked in the Temple during the revival under King Hezekiah (see Heman for more detail). Probably he was a descendant of 2. above, as he too had charge of looking after the gifts being brought to the Temple treasury (2 Chron. 31:13).

**6.** Probably this Jehiel was a descendant of 2. and 5. above. During the revival in King Josiah's reign, Josiah provided sheep and animals for the sacrifices of the people. The Levite, Jehiel, along with two other 'administrators of God's temple' also voluntarily provided many animals for the people to sacrifice (2 Chron. 35:8).

**7.** One of those who returned to Jerusalem from Babylon with Ezra. He was the father of Obadiah (Ezra 8:9).

**8.** The father of Shecaniah and a descendant of Elam. Shecaniah confessed to Ezra that many men of Judah had married wives from other tribes and nations. Ezra and the people repented and made a covenant to serve the LORD (Ezra 10:2). He is probably the same Jehiel 'from the descendants of Elam' listed in v. 26 as one who himself had a foreign wife.

**9.** This Jehiel was a descendant of Harim and one of those in the time of Ezra who had married a foreign wife rather than one from Judah (Ezra 10:21).

P.D.G.

**JEHIELI** (Heb., 'may my God live'). A descendant of Ladan and a Levite of the Gershonite clan. This family was in charge of the Temple treasuries when King David assigned the Levitical tasks (1 Chron. 26:21–22).

**JEHIZKIAH,** son of Shallum, was an Ephraimite who persuaded the Israelites of Pekah's day to return to their homes the captives they had taken from Judah (2 Chron. 28:12).

**JEHOADDAH** The son of Ahaz and father of Alemeth (1 Chron. 8:36). He was from the tribe of Judah and a descendant of King Saul.

**JEHOADDIN** The mother of King Amaziah of Judah. She came from Jerusalem and was the wife of King Joash (2 Kings 14:2; 2 Chron. 25:1).

**JEHOAHAZ** (Heb., 'the LORD will possess').

**1.** In 2 Chron. 21:17 and one or two other places Ahaziah, sixth king of Judah, is called Jehoahaz, but this name is not used in the NIV which throughout simplifies the confusion of the text by giving the name Ahaziah for this king. See Ahaziah 2.

**2.** This Jehoahaz was the son of Jehu and became the eleventh king of the northern kingdom of Israel in his place. He reigned in Samaria for 17 years being co-regent with his elderly father for the first three years or so (814–797 BC). He inherited a desperate situation (2 Kings 10:32, 35; 13:1, 4, 7). For years Hazael, king of Syria had been oppressing Israel. This oppression had been allowed by God as a judgment on their religious infidelity to Yahweh in turning to pagan gods (2 Kings 13:3, 22). Jehoahaz himself also 'did evil in the eyes of the LORD' until he realized how serious his position was and 'Then Jehoahaz sought the LORD's favour, and the LORD listened to him' (v. 4). The LORD then provided a 'deliverer for Israel' in the form of an Assyrian attack on Syria (v. 5). However, it was not until his son Jehoash came to the throne that God began to allow Israel once more to go on the offensive and win back territory from Hazael (v. 25). When Jehoahaz died he was buried in Samaria (vv. 8–10).

**3.** Another King Jehoahaz was the son of King Josiah. He was 23 when he began to reign in Jerusalem, but he lasted a mere three months (609 BC). His mother was Hamutal from Libnah (2 Kings 23:30–31). His father, Josiah, had foolishly tried to stop Pharaoh Neco from marching north to confront the Babylonians in battle and Josiah had been killed by Neco in battle at Megiddo. His son Jehoahaz 'did evil in the eyes of the LORD' and, no doubt as a God-ordained consequence (v. 32), was captured by Neco and taken to Riblah in chains. Neco then imposed a burdensome tax on Judah and took Eliakim, another of Josiah's sons, and put him on the throne instead, renaming him Johoiakim. Jehoahaz later died in Egypt (2 Kings 23:34; 2 Chron. 36:2–4). These final years of the Southern Kingdom of Judah were as sad as the last years of Israel to the north. Repeatedly the writers of Kings and Chronicles remind us that the problem was that the kings and their people did not turn in repentance and faith to rely on the LORD God, even though the prophets had warned of what was to happen. In breach of their covenant duties to their God he no longer offered them protection from their enemies and indeed used their enemies as part of his judgment on his people (2 Chron. 36:15–23). P.D.G.

**JEHOASH** was the son of Jehoahaz (see *Jehoahaz 2.*) and became the twelfth king of the Northern Kingdom of Israel in 797 BC and ruled for 16 years from Samaria (2 Kings 13:9–10). (In some versions the name of this king is given as Joash. The Heb. does use both names for him but the NIV simplifies the matter and brings consistency into the translation. This is helpful, as the king of Israel's reign overlaps with a King 'Joash' of Judah!)

Hazael of Syria had been the overlord of Israel for many years. He had virtually captured the whole of the Northern Kingdom and, although under Jehoahaz the LORD had stopped the final destruction of the nation, it was not until Jehoash came to the throne that the LORD lifted his hand of judgment and allowed Israel to begin to win back some of their kingdom. Hazael of Syria died and his son Ben-Hadad had come to the throne. Meanwhile Syria had been attacked and almost completely conquered by Assyria, thus taking the Syrian pressure off Israel. At the same time the prophet Elisha was nearing death. Jehoash went to Elisha and pleaded with him about the nation: 'My father! My father!' he cried. 'The chariots and horsemen of Israel!' (2 Kings 13:14). Jehoash was probably more concerned at losing the man of God with his miraculous powers than with Elisha's God. Elisha asked Jehoash to shoot an arrow out of the window and told him that the arrows of Israel would defeat the Syrians. He then asked him to bang on the floor. Jehoash did this only three times, indicating some reluctance and lack of faith in Elisha, his commands and his LORD, and so Elisha said that he would defeat the Syrians only three times in battle (2 Kings 13:15–19). Jehoash subsequently did recapture many towns from the Syrians and won three major battles against them (v. 25).

Sadly, during his reign King Amaziah of Judah attacked Israel. Amaziah had started his reign desiring to serve the LORD and had been well blessed in defeating many of the enemies on his borders, but he had become arrogant, forgotten his faith, and had imported to Judah some of the gods of the peoples he had conquered. Although prophets came to advise him of the dangers of his actions, he ignored them. Furious that some disgruntled mercenary soldiers from Israel were raiding some of his border towns, he challenged Jehoash to a battle. Jehoash did not want this fight but he won easily and even went right up to Jerusalem, breaking down large parts of the city wall (2 Kings 14:1–14; 2 Chron. 25:5–24).

Jehoash ruled with some success even though he did much evil. He won many victories in battle and eventually died and was buried in Samaria. His son, Jeroboam II succeeded him (2 Kings 13:11–13; 14:16–17). His name is mentioned in Hos. 1:1 and Amos 1:1, for these two prophets prophesied during the reign of his son Jeroboam.　　P.D.G.

**JEHOHANAN** (Heb., 'the LORD is gracious').

**1.** A Levite from the Korahite clan who is listed as one of the 'gatekeepers' of the sanctuary. He was appointed during the latter part of King David's reign and was the sixth son of Meshelemiah (1 Chron. 26:3).

**2.** Another Jehohanan came from the tribe of Judah and was one of the senior officers in Jehoshaphat's army. He had control of 280,000 men (2 Chron. 17:15). He was probably the Jehohanan mentioned as father of Ishmael. Ishmael helped put Joash on the throne of Judah when Queen Athaliah was killed (2 Chron. 23:1).

**3.** The father of Azariah. Azariah was one of those from Israel who entreated Pekah and his men to send back the prisoners they had taken from Judah (2 Chron. 28:12). See Berekiah 5. for more detail.

**4.** The son of Eliashib, this Jehohanan owned a house to which Ezra retired for a time of prayer and fasting as he mourned for the unfaithfulness of the exiles who had returned from Babylon. Ezra was specially concerned for the way so many had married foreign wives (Ezra 10:6). He may have been the priest Johanan mentioned in Neh. 12:22.

**5.** This Jehohanan was among the descendants of Bebai. At the time of return from the Exile in Babylon, Shecaniah confessed to Ezra that many men and even descendants of the priests of Judah had married wives from other tribes and nations. Ezra and the people repented and made a covenant to serve the LORD (Ezra 10:2). Jehohanan is listed in Ezra 10:28 as one who had married a foreign wife.

**6.** Another Jehohanan, who had married the daughter of Meshullam son of Berekiah, was the son of Tobiah. Tobiah, an Ammonite, consistently tried to undermine Nehemiah's rebuilding plans for Jerusalem (Neh. 6:18).

**7.** One of the priests of Judah in the days of Joiakim, following the rebuilding of Jerusalem after the Babylonian Exile. He was head of Amariah's household (Neh. 12:13).

**8.** A Levite who was part of the choir that sang at the dedication of the wall. The walls and city had been destroyed by the Babylonians when they took the Israelites into captivity. Under the direction of Nehemiah they were eventually rebuilt amidst great praises to God (Neh. 12:42).　　P.D.G.

**JEHOIACHIN** (Heb., 'the LORD upholds'). Jehoiachin, otherwise known as Jeconiah (1 Chron. 3:16) or Coniah (Jer. 22:24), was a son of Jehoiakim and grandson of Josiah (2 Kings 24:6; cf. 23:34; 1 Chron. 3:15–16), both kings of Judah. Jehoiachin succeeded his wicked father to the Davidic throne in 597 BC, at the young age of 18, and reigned for only three months (2 Kings 24:8). He too was evil and for his sin and that of his people he was captured by the Babylonians and taken off to Babylon as a prisoner of war. From 597 until 560 BC he remained under at least house arrest but with the succession of Evil-Merodach to Babylonian regency he was released and, in fact, given a generous pension and even restored to some measure of authority (2 *Kings 25:27–30; cf. Jer. 52:31–34*). His fate following this is unclear, though it is likely that he died in Babylon.

What is clear is that though Jehoiachin had children (1 *Chron. 3:17*), none succeeded him as king. He was thus 'childless' in the sense that the Davidic kingship passed not through him but, apparently, through one of his brothers (*Jer. 22:24–30*). Comparison of the various biblical genealogies (1 *Chron. 3:16–19; Ezra 3:2; Matt. 1:12; Luke 3:27*) suggests that Shealtiel may have been a foster son of Jehoiachin so that the Davidic successor Zerubbabel, son of Shealtiel, was thus not a physical descendant of Jehoiachin but sprang from someone else in the royal ancestry.

Jehoiachin's rejection by the LORD could not and did not interrupt the messianic linkage between David and Jesus Christ for the line merely bypassed him while still retaining its unbrokenness. In this manner it is possible to demonstrate the theological principle that God's purposes will ultimately come to pass though the human means of achieving them may occasionally be set aside. E.M.

**JEHOIADA** (Heb., 'the LORD knows').
   **1.** The father of Benaiah. Benaiah was a ruler in King David's kingdom and a great warrior who had deserted Saul to join David. He remained loyal to David throughout his life (2 *Sam. 8:18; 20:23; 23:20, 22; 1 Kings 1:8, 26, 32 etc.*). Benaiah also fought for King Solomon (1 *Kings 2:29, 34 etc.; see also 1 Chron. 11:22, 24; 18:17*).
   **2.** Following the death of Ahithophel, the priest Jehoiada, son of Benaiah, became one of David's closest advisers (1 *Chron. 27:34*).
   **3.** The most famous Jehoiada was a priest during the reigns in Judah of Ahaziah, Queen Athaliah and Joash. He was a man who was faithful to the LORD through one of the most pagan periods in the history of the nation of Judah. King Ahaziah had been killed by Jehu as part of the fulfilment of God's judgment on the house of Ahab (1 *Kings 21:21–22*). When his mother, Queen Athaliah, heard this, she seized the throne of Judah and set about systematically killing the children of King Ahaziah. The people of Judah were very angry at her actions. In Jehoiada's seventh year as High Priest he rallied army commanders against Athaliah and showed them one of the King's sons whom he had hidden in the Temple when Athaliah was killing the royal family. They swore a covenant with Jehoiada to support the crowning of the young King Joash in place of Athaliah (2 *Kings 11:9; 2 Chron. 23*).

The child had originally been brought to Jehoiada by his wife Jehosheba who was the daughter of the former king Jehoram, and the child had been brought up under her and Jehoiada in the Temple precincts (2 *Chron. 22:11*).

When Jehoiada produced the child publicly, the commanders and people proclaimed him king to the great joy of the crowds (*vv. 11–12*). Athaliah quickly came to the Temple where she was seized, taken out of the building, and put to death (*vv. 13–19*). The result of putting Joash on the throne, under the tutelage of a wise and faithful High Priest was that Jehoiada was able to lead the people to recommit themselves to the LORD in a covenant renewal ceremony. The people went out and tore down the temple of Baal and smashed the pagan altars (2 *Chron. 22:17–18*). As Jehoiada instructed him in the ways of the LORD so Joash 'did what was right in the eyes of the LORD' (2 *Chron. 12:2*). Joash then ordered Jehoiada to repair the Temple (2 *Chron. 12:7, 9; 23–24*).

The account in 2 *Chron. 23* emphasizes the part Jehoiada played in restoring proper Levitical and priestly duties in the temple and the nation. To his great credit his life is summarized in the statement:

'As long as Jehoiada lived, burnt offerings were presented continually in the temple of the LORD' (2 Chron. 24:14). His son, Zechariah, also was faithful and the Spirit of the LORD was on him (v. 20).

P.D.G.

**JEHOIAKIM** (Heb., 'the LORD establishes'). A King of Judah. Following the untimely death of the good King Josiah in battle, his succession was undertaken by one of his four sons, Jehoahaz (2 Kings 23:30), who reigned for only three months (v. 31). Jehoahaz was quickly captured by Pharaoh Neco of Egypt, the very ruler whose armies had defeated and slain Josiah. At this time (609 BC) Egypt dominated Palestine but following the battle of Carchemish the newly powerful Babylonian regime expelled the Egyptians and began to occupy Palestine, including Judah.

Meanwhile, Jehoiakim, an elder brother of Jehoahaz, sat on David's throne (2 Kings 23:36). Originally named Eliakim, Jehoiakim received his better known name from Neco, the impetus for which can be only a matter of speculation (v. 34). For several years Jehoiakim and Judah remained relatively free of outside interference, but following the decisive defeat of Neco by Nebuchadnezzar of Babylon in 605 BC, Nebuchadnezzar incorporated Judah into his empire and made Jehoiakim a vassal ruler (2 Kings 24:1). For three years Jehoiakim submitted meekly, but for the last eight years of his reign he regularly rebelled against Babylonia, sometimes with impunity and sometimes with adverse repercussions (2 Chron. 36:5–8). Rare for his day and times, he did manage to die a 'natural' death, at least as far as the record of Kings (2 Kings 24:6) and Chronicles (2 Chron. 36:8) is concerned. Jeremiah, however, may imply a more violent end for the wicked king. Though he does not explicitly describe Jehoiakim's demise, he declares that the king 'will have the burial of a donkey – dragged away and thrown outside the gates of Jerusalem' (Jer. 22:19). Whether this hints of assassination of some other violent death or not, it surely underscores the humiliating plight of a Davidic ruler, who, because of his wickedness against the LORD, was consigned to burial outside the holy city (cf. 2 Kings 21:18, 26).

E.M.

**JEHOIARIB** One among the priests who were chosen to be officials in the sanctuary 'according to the last instructions of David'. Impartial selection from among the descendants of Eleazar and Ithamar was made by drawing lots. The first lot fell to Jehoiarib and that was the order in which he ministered when entering the sanctuary (1 Chron. 24:7). His family is mentioned among those who first returned from the Babylonian Exile and settled in Jerusalem (1 Chron. 9:10).

**JEHONADAB** Mentioned as a 'son of Recab' in 2 Kings 10:15, 23 (see Recab for detail; also Jonadab in Jer. 35, who was probably the same person as Jehonadab). Jehonadab was on the way to greet King Jehu of Israel when they met along the way. The King challenged him to see if Jehonadab was on his side against the descendants of Jezebel and Ahab and their ally, King Ahaziah of Judah. In Jehonadab Jehu found an ally in battle and one who was also zealous for the LORD God and joined Jehu in tearing down the shrines to Baal (2 Kings 10:23). In Jer. 35 Jeremiah the prophet upheld Jonadab as a fine example of a pious leader of his family of Recabites. It is likely that this man had originally gone to join Jehu as soon as he had realized that Jehu would try to destroy the pagan idols and pagan worship. He seems to have been a genuinely committed worshipper of the LORD, and one who was prepared to put his life on the line to see the country and its King return to true worship of the true God.　　　　P.D.G.

**JEHONATHAN** (Heb., 'the LORD has given').

**1.** A Levite, this Jehonathan lived in the days of King Jehoshaphat of Judah. During the early years of his reign Jehoshaphat served the LORD and sent our various teachers and Levites to teach the people of Judah the Book of the Law. Jehonathan was one of those teachers (2 Chron. 17:8).

**2.** This Jehonathan was the head of Shemaiah's family, and helped in the service of the Temple during Nehemiah's time (Neh. 12:19).

**JEHORAM** (Heb., 'the LORD is exalted').

**1.** A king of Judah and not to be confused with King Joram of Israel, to whom he was related and with whom he was contemporary. Occasionally Joram is also called Jehoram, thus exacerbating the confusion. However, in the NIV for the most part the King of Israel is called Joram (see 2. below), even where the Heb. may have Jehoram.

Jehoram succeeded his father Jehoshaphat as king of Judah in 848 BC and reigned for eight years, until 841 BC (1 Kings 22:50; 2 Kings 8:16–17; 2 Chron. 21). The verdict of the sacred historian is that he was an evil ruler, one unfit to represent the dynasty of David (2 Kings 8:18). There can be no doubt that his marriage to Athaliah, daughter of wicked Ahab and Jezebel of Israel, was a contributing factor (2 Kings 8:18, 26–27). A result of the marriage was Jehoram's kinship with Joram of Israel who, of course, became his brother-in-law. It is interesting to see, however, that the LORD remained faithful to his covenant with David (2 Sam. 7:12–14) and did not destroy the nation of Judah in spite of the evil work of the king (2 Kings 8:19; 2 Chron. 21:7).

After a series of disasters, especially the revolt of Edom from Judahite control, Jehoram died at the young age of 40, his epitaph reading, sadly enough, 'He walked in the ways of the kings of Israel' (2 Kings 8:18). His son Ahaziah continued a rule of evil (vv. 25–27). However, Jehoram's daughter Johosheba helped her husband, the priest Jehoiada, to restore to the throne a king faithful to the LORD (Joash, 2 Kings 11:12; 2 Chron. 22:11).　　　　E.M.

**2.** Jehoram son of Ahab, king of Israel. See Joram.

**3.** This Jehoram, a priest, lived in the days of King Jehoshaphat of Judah. During the early years of his reign Jehoshaphat served the LORD and sent our various teachers and Levites to teach the people of Judah the Book of the Law. Jehoram was one of those teachers (2 Chron. 17:8).

**JEHOSHAPHAT** (Heb., 'the LORD' has judged').

**1.** A king of Judah. Described as a king who 'did what was right in the eyes of the LORD' (1 Kings 22:43; 2 Chron. 20:32), Jehoshaphat succeeded his father Asa on the throne of David in 870 BC after a three-year vice-regency (1 Kings 15:24; cf. vv. 9–10). His reputation was not entirely unsullied, however, for Jehoshaphat was a contemporary of wicked King Ahab of Israel (874–853 BC) and frequently made unholy alliances with him (1 Kings 22:44). One unhappy result of this fraternity was the marriage of Ahab's daughter Athaliah to Jehoram, son of Jehoshaphat (2 Kings 8:18, 26–27), a relationship that brought severe consequences to the spiritual, social, and political life of the kingdom of Judah (2 Kings 8:27; 9:27; 10:14; 11:1–20; cf. 2 Chron. 22:2–3). It may also have been the Ahab-Jehoshaphat alliance that deterred Jehoshaphat from removing completely the vestiges of idolatry that he had inherited from his father Asa (1 Kings 22:43; cf. 15:14).

These caveats notwithstanding, the overriding image of Jehoshaphat that emerges from the sacred record, especially from 2 *Chron.* 17–20, is one of godly dedication to the covenant purposes of the LORD. 'He did not consult the Baals but sought the God of his father and followed his commands rather than the practices of Israel' (2 *Chron.* 17:4). The result was personal and national blessing in the form of wealth, honour, and power (*vv.* 5, 11–13). Concerned not only for Judah but for Israel as well, he established righteous judgment throughout the land (2 *Chron.* 19:4–7) and also instructed the priests and Levites to listen to and adjudicate matters pertaining to the LORD, that is, cases having to do with cultic life (*vv.* 8–11).

Jehoshaphat is seen at his best, perhaps, in the matter of the Israel-Judah campaign against the Arameans at Ramoth Gilead (1 *Kings* 22:1–36; 2 *Chron.* 18:1–34). Though subsequently rebuked for befriending Ahab, God's enemy (2 *Chron.* 19:2), Jehoshaphat did insist that no action be taken until they 'seek the counsel of the LORD' (2 *Chron.* 18:4). When Ahab brought forth his own hireling prophets for that purpose, Jehoshaphat rejected them and insisted that a true man of God be brought forth. This request was answered by the appearance of the courageous prophet Micaiah (2 *Chron.* 18:6, 8). Satisfied that God at last had spoken, Jehoshaphat moved forward and, despite the defeat of the coalition, was miraculously preserved by the LORD (*v.* 31). The story may suggest a weakness toward conformity, but it also reveals a bedrock inner conviction at the point of radical decision.

**2.** Son of Ahilud, he was a 'recorder' in the administration of both David (2 *Sam.* 8:16; 20:24; 1 *Chron.* 18:15) and Solomon (1 *Kings* 4:3). The office appears to have been that of a chronicler

of events of national interest.

**3.** The son of Paruah, he was an official from the provincial district of Issachar in charge of providing food supplies to the central government of Solomon for one month every year (1 *Kings* 4:17).

**4.** Jehoshaphat, son of Nimshi, was better known as the father of King Jehu of Israel (2 *Kings* 9:2, 14), though usually Jehu is called 'son of Nimshi' with Jehoshaphat's name omitted (2 *Kings* 9:20; *cf.* 1 *Kings* 19:16). E.M.

**JEHOSHEBA** The daughter of King Jehoram of Judah and wife of the priest Jehoiada (2 *Kings* 11:2; 2 *Chron.* 22:11). Her brother Ahaziah was killed by Jehu in his attempt to reform Israel and Judah and destroy pagan worship. Athaliah, who was Ahaziah's mother and a worshipper of Baal, was particularly distressed. When Jehu died she decided to have the whole royal family assassinated. However, Jehosheba took Joash, Ahaziah's young son, and hid him 'away from among the royal princes who were about to be murdered'. Athaliah herself ruled for six years, during which time the child was kept hidden from her in the Temple (2 *Kings* 11:3). Once the boy was seven years old, Jehoiada took him out under guard and Joash was proclaimed king. Immediately, Jehoiada and his troops set about tearing down the altars and idols of Baal. Having been brought up in the Temple by Jehosheba and her husband, he eventually had the Temple repaired and much good was done in his reign in restoring worship of the LORD (2 *Kings* 12). P.D.G.

**JEHOZABAD** (Heb., 'the LORD has given').

**1.** A servant of King Joash of Judah. He was one of those who took part in the murder of the King. Amaziah later executed him for his part in the plot (2 Kings 12:21; 2 Chron. 24:26; 25:3).

**2.** The second son of Obed-Edom a descendant of Korah responsible to attend to the Tabernacle gates in David's administration (1 Chron. 26:4).

**3.** Another Jehozabad came from the tribe of Benjamin and was one of the senior officers in Jehoshaphat's army. He had control of 180,000 men (2 Chron. 17:18).

**JEHOZADAK** (Heb., 'the LORD is righteous'). The father of Joshua, the post-exilic high priest (Hag. 1:1, 12, 14; 2:2, 4; Zech. 6:11) and a priest himself at the time of the Exile (1 Chron. 6:14, 15). Also a son of the high priest Seraiah.

**JEHU** (Heb., 'of the LORD').

**1.** Jehu son of Hanani was a prophet in the Northern Kingdom of Israel who prophesied against Baasha and his evil and idolatrous behaviour. The destruction of the family was prophesied, later fulfilled in the massacre of Baasha's family at the hands of Zimri (1 Kings 16:1, 7, 12). Jehu also prophesied in the days of King Jehoshaphat of Judah, condemning him for making an alliance with King Ahab of Israel (2 Chron. 19:2). Apparently he also kept annals of the kings of Israel (2 Chron. 20:34).

**2.** The father of Azariah and son of Obed, this Jehu was a leader from the tribe of Judah (1 Chron. 2:38).

**3.** Jehu son of Joshibiah was a clan leader of the tribe of Simeon (1 Chron. 4:35).

**4.** Jehu the Anathothite was one of the warriors who deserted Saul to join David at Ziklag. They were ambidextrous in archery and with slings. They were from the tribe of Benjamin (1 Chron. 12:3)

**5.** Jehu son of Nimshi was the tenth king of Israel and reigned for 28 years (842–814 BC). God had told Elijah the prophet to anoint Jehu, an army commander, to be king (1 Kings 19:16–17). Jehu's

God-appointed task was first to put to death Ahab and his family for the persecution they had inflicted on those worshipping the LORD. Elisha actually fulfilled this task of anointing by sending one of his fellow prophets to Jehu (2 Kings 9:2, 5–15). When Jehu's fellow officers heard what this prophet had done, they hurried out proclaiming Jehu king. Jehu then conspired against Joram. Joram had been injured in battle against the Syrians and was recovering in Jezreel, where Ahaziah, king of Judah, joined him. Jehu went there and met with the two kings. He killed Joram (2 Kings 9:17–26). Jehu's men chased Ahaziah and wounded him so that later he died (2 Kings 9:27–29; 2 Chron. 22:7–9).

Jehu returned to Jezreel where he ordered Jezebel to be killed. The dogs ate her blood just as Elijah had prophesied years before (2 Kings 9:34–37). On several occasions the writer of 2 Kings makes it very clear that all that Jehu was doing at this stage was fulfilling the commands of the LORD and the prophecy against the evil of the reign of King Ahab and Jezebel. No survivor was left to that dynasty (2 Kings 10:11, 17). Jehu deliberately contrasted his faithfulness to the LORD's command with the evil of Ahab's day (vv. 16–19). He called a ceremony of worship to Baal, ensured that no followers of the LORD were present, and then had them all killed (vv. 20–28). This faithfulness was rewarded by the LORD who promised Jehu descendants who would hold the throne of Israel until the fourth generation (2 Kings 10:30; 15:12).

Almost immediately, however, Jehu began to turn from the LORD (2 Kings 10:31). As a result Syria began to gain the upper hand and the size of the Northern Kingdom gradually diminished as Hazael overpowered Jehu. Jehu eventually died and was buried in Samaria (vv. 32–36). His son Jehoahaz became king in his place (2 Kings 13:1).

Sadly, Jehu's reign did not end as it had

begun. Perhaps it was power, or perhaps it was the forces of the invaders all around, that caused him to move away from his zeal for the LORD. Under Jehu, Israel had been spared full judgment for the sins of Ahab and Jezebel, but the people and their leaders had still not fully repented and given up their pagan ways, to which they kept reverting.     P.D.G.

**JEHUCAL** (Heb., 'the LORD is powerful'). The son of Shelemiah, he was sent with the priest Zephaniah to the prophet Jeremiah by King Zedekiah. Zedekiah wanted Jeremiah to pray for the people of Jerusalem who were under siege from the Babylonians (*Jer. 37:3*). This was despite the fact that Zedekiah would not listen to Jeremiah's prophecies (*v. 2*)! Jehucal was one of the king's officials listed in *Jer. 38:1* who heard Jeremiah's prophecy that those who stayed in Jerusalem would be destroyed while those who went into Exile with the Babylonians would live. The officials took this message to the king, arguing that this would lead to soldiers deserting. The king then let the officials take Jeremiah prisoner and put him in a water cistern in the courtyard of the guard. Whether Jehucal took an active part in this move against Jeremiah is not clear. Jeremiah's prophecy was, of course, the word of the LORD and did prove correct.     P.D.G.

**JEHUDI** A son of Nethaniah, Jehudi was sent to Baruch by the officials of Jerusalem to bring the scroll of Jeremiah's prophecy to them so they could read it (*Jer. 36:14*). Later King Jehoiakim asked Jehudi to bring the scroll to him as well. As Jehudi read it, the king burnt it piece by piece (*vv. 21, 23*).

**JEIEL** (Heb., 'God's treasure').
**1.** A clan chief of the tribe of Reuben. He lived in Aroer. In Saul's reign, his people were responsible for the defeat of the Hagrites and they took possession of

land to the east of Gilead and even as far as the Euphrates because they were so prosperous (*1 Chron. 5:7–10*).
**2.** One of the ancestors of Saul in the genealogy of the tribe of Benjamin. He lived in Gibeon and either had a son called Gibeon or was leader of the area called Gibeon. His wife was Maacah, and his first son was Abdon (*1 Chron. 8:29; 9:35*).
**3.** He and his brother Shama, sons of Hotham the Aroerite, belonged to David's 'Thirty' mighty men who went to battle for him and led the people of Israel to war (*1 Chron. 11:44*). The fact that Aroer is mentioned may indicate a family link with 1. above.
**4.** This Jeiel was one of the family of Merarite Levites who were gatekeepers. After the ark of the covenant had been brought to Jerusalem, the worship of God was properly organized by King David. The particular job he and his brothers were given was to be musicians and to play the harps and lyres before the ark of the covenant as it was moved to Jerusalem (*1 Chron. 15:18, 21; 16:5*).
**5.** This Jeiel was a Levite from the clan of Asaph, and an ancestor of Jahaziel (*2 Chron. 20:14*). Jahaziel was famed for the fact that the Spirit of the LORD came upon him at a time of crisis for Judah and King Jehoshaphat.
**6.** Living in the time of King Uzziah of Judah, this Jeiel was secretary to the king and kept a record of the 'well trained' fighting men. He organized them into divisions for battle (*2 Chron. 26:11*).
**7.** A Levite descended from Elizaphan who is mentioned among the list of those who helped purify the Temple during the revival under King Hezekiah (*2 Chron. 29:13*).
**8.** During the revival in King Josiah's reign, Josiah provided sheep and animals for the sacrifices of the people. One of the leaders of the Levites, Jeiel, along with other leaders of the people, also voluntarily provided many animals for the people

to sacrifice (2 Chron. 35:9). He is possibly the same person as Jehiel in v. 8.

**9.** A descendant of Nebo, this Jeiel was one of those in the time of Ezra who had married a foreign wife rather than one from Judah (Ezra 10:43).                    P.D.G.

**JEKAMEAM** The fourth son of Hebron, a Kohathite Levite (1 Chron. 23:19; 24:23).

**JEKAMIAH** (Heb., 'may the Lord establish').

**1.** Son of Shallum and a leader from the tribe of Judah, he was a descendant of Jerahmeel (1 Chron. 2:41).

**2.** Listed among the descendants of King Jehoiachin, and thus part of David's royal line, he seems to have returned after the Exile in Babylon (1 Chron. 3:18).

**JEKUTHIEL** (Heb., 'God sustains'). A descendant of Ezrah and leader in the tribe of Judah, Jekuthiel was the son of Mered and his Judean wife. He was the father of Zanoah (1 Chron. 4:18).

**JEMIMAH** At the end of Job's life, after all the tragedies and trials that he had faced, God once again blessed him. Among the children born to him at this stage were three daughters of whom the first was Jemimah (Job 42:14). Together with her two sisters she was considered very beautiful and they were each given part of Job's inheritance (v. 15).

**JEMUEL** The first son of Simeon and listed among those who went to Egypt with Jacob his grandfather (Gen. 46:10; Exod. 6:15). He is called Nemuel in Num. 26:12 and 1 Chron. 4:24 and was leader of the Nemuelite clan.

**JEPHTHAH** The son of Gilead and a prostitute mother, 'Jephthah the Gileadite was a mighty warrior'. His father had other legitimate sons who drove him away so he would not gain any of their father's inheritance (Judg. 11:1–3). Having fled to the land of Tob, he gathered round him a band of fighters and adventurers. When the Ammonites made war on Israel, the elders of Gilead went to Jephthah and asked for his help. Jephthah was reluctant to help those who had thrown him out even though they promised he could be their leader. In his discussions with the Gileadites, from the start Jephthah talked of 'the Lord' helping him defeat the Ammonites (v. 9). Before taking on the task, he went and prayed to the Lord and repeated the pledges that he and the men of Gilead had made to each other (v. 11).

Jephthah seems to have been a shrewd leader. First he tried to negotiate out of the battle. He gave a potted history of the land that was disputed by the Ammonites, but all to no avail. The more he warmed to his task, the more he seems to have begun to trust the Lord. In Judg. 11:27 he finally told the king of Ammon: 'I have not wronged you, but you are doing me wrong by waging war against me. Let the Lord, the Judge, decide the dispute this day between the Israelites and the Ammonites.' Then 'the Spirit of the Lord came upon Jephthah' and he made a vow to the Lord that if he won in battle, when he returned, the first thing that came out of his door he would sacrifice to the Lord (vv. 29–30). With the Lord's help, he won the battle (v. 32), returned home and saw first his young and only daughter coming towards him dancing (v. 34).

A vow could be a sign of surrender to God in faith. But this was not the nature of Jephthah's vow. For Jephthah this was a bargain with God. It was not a vow of self-surrender but of a willingness to undergo suffering provided the Lord gave him victory. The grief he experienced when he saw first his daughter (v. 35) is a clear indication of what was going on. Offerings were always supposed to be given to the Lord joyfully, but not so this one. Jephthah still had a pagan understanding of God, one absorbed from the society he had grown up in. Out of his gracious covenant love, Yahweh delivered the Israelites from their enemies at the hand of Jephthah, but he did not do so because of this vow. Jephthah thought he could buy God's mercy.

Whether he actually burned his daughter as a sacrifice is debated. The fact that it was her virginity that was specially mourned, that is that she would never live to see children, may indicate that she was banished from the community of the Israelites and made to live in the wilderness, or perhaps she became one of the women dedicated to the Tabernacle service of the LORD.

Following this incident, Jephthah warred against the Ephraimites, but again God gave him victory. He judged Israel for six years before dying and being buried in Gilead (*Judg. 12:1–7*). Like so many of the ancient heroes of the faith, Jephthah had a real faith and yet sinned deeply. Towards the end of his life, Samuel remembered how the LORD had used Jephthah for the sake of his people (*1 Sam. 12:11*) and in the NT the writer of Hebrews mentions Jephthah as among the great men and women of the past whose faith is to be imitated (*Heb. 11:32*).                                   P.D.G.

**JEPHUNNEH  1.** Jephunneh comes to prominence in the book of Numbers as the father of Caleb, the great warrior and man of faith (*Num. 13:6; 14:6, 30, 38; 26:65; 32:12; Deut. 1:36; Josh. 14:6* etc.). Jephunneh's grandsons are listed in *1 Chron. 4:15* and some of their land near Hebron is mentioned in *1 Chron. 6:56*. See *Caleb*.

**2.** From the tribe of Asher, he was the son of Jether and mentioned as a leader of the tribe and a great warrior (*1 Chron. 7:38, 40*).

**JERAH** (Heb., 'moon'). Listed in both *Gen. 10:26* and *1 Chron. 1:20* as a descendant of Shem, his father was Joktan.

**JERAHMEEL** (Heb., 'God will have mercy').

**1.** The first son of Hezron and great-grandson of Judah. He was an early tribal leader (*1 Chron. 2:9, 25, 27, 33, 42*). His wife was Atarah (*v. 26*). His descendants were known as Jerahmeelites and were referred to both in the genealogies of *1 Chronicles* and in the early days of David when there was mention of the 'Negev of Jerahmeel', indicating the extensive area of land that belonged to the clan (*1 Sam. 27:10*).

**2.** One of the descendants of Merari, son of Kish and a Levite clan leader. He served in the Tabernacle in the time of King David (*1 Chron. 24:29*).

**3.** An official who served under and was possibly related to King Jehoiakim (609–598 BC) during the time of the prophet Jeremiah. He was ordered to arrest Jeremiah and his scribe Baruch (*Jer. 36:26*). The king had received a scroll giving a prophecy from Jeremiah concerning the future of his kingdom and of Jerusalem. Jeremiah had promised that Babylon would conquer them and captivity would ensue. Jehoiakim rejected the prophecy as dangerous and undermining of the confidence he was trying to build among his people. When Jerahmeel and others came to arrest the prophet and his scribe we read that they could not be found, for 'the LORD had hidden them'.

The judgment coming on Judah had been foretold by God for many years. The people's continual rebellion against God had led to this. The Exile was about to happen and simply imprisoning the prophet could not have stopped the events that were about to unfold. Jeremiah was protected by God for he yet had much work to do in helping the nation understand what was happening to them.                                   P.D.G.

**JERED** A descendant of Ezrah and leader in the tribe of Judah, Jered was the

311

son of Mered and his Judean wife. He was the father of Gedor (1 Chron. 4:18).

**JEREMAI** A descendant of Hashum at the time of Nehemiah (Ezra 10:33). After Shecaniah confessed to Ezra that many men of Judah had married wives from other tribes and nations, Ezra and the people repented and made a covenant to serve the LORD (Ezra 10:2). Jeremai was one of those listed as having married a foreign wife.

## JEREMIAH THE PROPHET

### Jeremiah's Ministry

The OT tells us much about the life and ministry of Jeremiah the prophet. He was born in Anathoth (Jer. 1:1), a small village about 5 km (3.2 miles) north of Jerusalem. His father was a priest named Hilkiah (not to be confused with Hilkiah in Josiah's service, 1 Kings 22:8), and was probably a descendant of the high priest Abiathar whom Solomon banished to Anathoth (1 Kings 2:26). Jeremiah never married (Jer. 16:1–2) and dedicated his entire adult life to prophetic work. Jeremiah's ministry extended over four decades and addressed many different situations. It is helpful to divide his long ministry into four major stages.

The first stage of Jeremiah's ministry was during the reign of Josiah (639–609 BC). Jeremiah grew up about the same time as the king and entered prophetic service in the 13th year of Josiah's reign (Jer. 1:2). His work began five years before the king's reforms reached their height in 622 (2 Kings 22:3–23:23). 2 Chron. 35:25 mentions that Jeremiah lamented the king's death (2 Chron. 35:25). We may conclude, therefore, that the prophet must have supported the king's lengthy commitment to religious reform. During the reign of Josiah, Jeremiah openly condemned the injustice and idolatry of the nation and warned against false security (Jer. 1–20). He agreed with his contemporary, Huldah the prophetess (2 Kings 22:15–20), that Judah and Jerusalem would be destroyed for her sins.

Josiah's untimely death in 609 led to the second stage of Jeremiah's ministry. Jehoahaz (called Shallum in Jer. 22:11) became king, but reigned only three months. King Neco of Egypt removed Jehoahaz from the throne for refusing to pay tribute and installed Jehoiakim (609–598) as his vassal in Jerusalem (2 Kings, 23:31–35). During this time, Jeremiah predicted that Jehoahaz would not return from Egypt (Jer. 22:11–12). He condemned the sins and injustices of Jehoiakim's kingdom (Jer. 22:18–23). He also predicted that Jehoiachin, next in the Davidic line to reign, would be exiled to Babylon (Jer. 22:24–30). Because his ministry was so negative, the kings, government officials, and many of the common people opposed Jeremiah.

Jehoiakim's fourth year (605) was a particularly important time for Jeremiah. Nebuchadnezzar defeated the Egyptians at Carchemish. He then took control of Judah and removed selected nobles from Jerusalem to Babylon. Jeremiah announced that these events were the beginning of an Exile that would not end for 70 years (Jer. 25:1–14). Jeremiah produced a written record of his predictions with the help of his secretary Baruch (*Jer. 36:1–8*). The scroll so enraged Jehoiakim that he burned the scroll (*Jer. 36:9–26*), but Jeremiah courageously wrote again adding more words of condemnation against the king (*Jer. 36:27–23*).

The third stage of Jeremiah's ministry was during the reign of Zedekiah (597–586 BC), the last king of Judah. The Babylonians installed Zedekiah as their vassal after taking Jehoiachin to Babylon (*2 Kings 24:17–18*). His advisers, however, urged him to turn against Nebuchadnezzar (*Jer. 34:1–7*). The false prophets Hananiah (*Jer. 28:1–4*) and Shemaiah (*Jer. 29:24–28*) also proclaimed that the Babylonians were no threat. Jeremiah, however, insisted that Judah should submit to Babylon (*Jer. 21:1–7; 37:17–21; 38:7–28*). Zedekiah rejected Jeremiah's counsel and rebelled against Babylon in 589 BC. As a result, Nebuchadnezzar laid siege to Jerusalem. During this terrible siege, Jerusalem officials had Jeremiah arrested (*Jer. 37:11–21*); he was saved from death only by the kindness of Ebedmelech, an Ethiopian eunuch (*Jer. 38:1–13*). In 586 the Babylonians overran Jerusalem and destroyed the Temple just as Jeremiah had warned.

The fourth stage of Jeremiah's ministry took place after the destruction of Jerusalem. Jeremiah found favour among Babylonian officials and chose to remain in Judah. Nebuchadnezzar appointed Gedaliah as the governor of Judah (*Jer. 40:1–6*), but rebels in Judah soon assassinated him. Fearing reprisal, the rebels fled to Egypt, taking Jeremiah with them as hostage (*Jer. 42*). The prophet urged them to stay in Judah, but they refused and settled in Tahpanhes of Egypt. Little is known about Jeremiah's final years. The last oracle recorded in his book took place in Egypt (*Jer. 44:1–30*). It is likely that he died there, having never returned to his homeland.

### Jeremiah's message

The LORD called Jeremiah to proclaim a twofold message. 'I appoint you over nations and kingdoms to uproot and tear down, to destroy and overthrow, to build and to plant' (*Jer. 1:10*). As this commission indicates, the prophet's ministry was negative and positive. He was to announce the destruction and establishment of nations. Jeremiah spoke of the nations surrounding Israel (*Jer. 46–51*), but the chief concern of his ministry was the nation of Judah. He spoke primarily of Judah's fall and re-establishment.

Jeremiah addressed specific issues at different times, but his basic pattern remained consistent because he relied heavily on the covenant theology of Deuteronomy. Jeremiah was undoubtedly familiar with the deuteronomic laws that played such an important role in Josiah's reforms (*2 Kings 22:8*). He shaped the emphases and structure of his theology according to these laws.

The book of Deuteronomy depicted the relationship between God and his people on analogy with international covenant treaties of the Ancient Near East. The LORD was the supreme suzerain, or emperor, and Israel was his vassal, or servant nation. Divine benevolence formed the basis of this covenant relationship. God had brought Israel out of Egypt (e.g. *Deut. 4:20*), given them the Law (e.g. *Deut. 4:5–13*), and had brought them to the land of Canaan (e.g. *Deut. 4:14*). In response to these blessings, the people of Israel were to show gratitude by giving exclusive allegiance to the LORD and his Law (e.g. *Deut. 6:1–8*). This relationship was not an arrangement of salvation by good works for Israel had not earned deliverance from Egypt. Rather, obedience was to be the result of appreciation for gracious blessings already received. Nevertheless, the deuteronomic covenant offered further blessings to those who obeyed the Law, and curses for those who flagrantly disobeyed the Law (e.g. *Deut. 27–28*). Obedience furthered the covenant relationship, and disobedience reflected ingratitude and violated the convenant. These patterns of covenantal blessings and curses formed the fundamental structures of Jeremiah's various messages.

Deut. 4:25–31 conveniently summarizes the twofold framework of Jeremiah's message. First, Moses warned that covenant curses will be brought against Israel when future generations provoke the LORD to anger (*Deut. 4:25*). They will not experience peace in the land (*Deut. 4:26*), but will be driven into Exile (*Deut. 4:27–28*). In line with these perspectives, Jeremiah spent much time insisting that Israel's covenant was conditional. False prophets had popularized the idea that God's covenant with Israel ensured their safety (*Jer. 28:1–17*). Jerusalem would never be destroyed; the LORD would protect his Temple from devastation (*Jer. 7:1–29*). By contrast, Jeremiah frequently pointed out the severe sins of the people, especially their idolatry (e.g. *Jer. 16:10–13, 20; 22:9; 32:29; 44:2–3*). He announced the inevitability of Jerusalem's devastation and Exile because of their continuing violations of the covenant (e.g. *Jer. 6:1–30; 13:15–27; 25:1–14*). Jeremiah lived to see his predictions of judgment become reality when the Babylonians destroyed Jerusalem in 586.

Second, the deuteronomic covenant held out hope for the people of God even after suffering the punishment of Exile. Moses promised that God will forgive and return Israel to the land, if those driven away would seek God in repentance (*Deut. 4:29–30*). God would not forget the promises made to the fathers; he would be merciful once again (*Deut. 4:31*). For this reason, Jeremiah also proclaimed hope for Israel in the future. He assured the people that God would one day bring about a new era (*Jer. 30:1–33:26*). God would return both Judah and Israel to the land of promise (*Jer. 30:3–4*). He purchased land in his home town to demonstrate his certainty of this future (*Jer. 32:1–44*). He announced a renewal of the covenant (*Jer. 31:31–34*) and the restoration of the throne of David (*Jer. 33:15*). From Jeremiah's perspective, the eventual return was as certain as the fixed laws governing the day and night (*Jer. 33:25–26*).

Jeremiah's message of restoration was especially important for NT writers. Three times the 'new covenant' (or 'renewed covenant', as it may be translated) of *Jer. 31:31* is identified with the new covenant in Christ (*2 Cor. 3:3; Heb. 8:8–12; 10:16*). Jeremiah's words are often misunderstood as a prediction that Christ brought something entirely new or different from Israel's previous covenants with the LORD. The context of *Jer. 31:31–34*, however, points in a different direction. The new covenant will be different from the past because the covenant with Moses degenerated into a facade of external religion through disobedience (*Jer. 31:32–33*). The new covenant, however, will be a restoration to the original deuteronomic standard of devotion from the heart (e.g. *Deut. 6:4; 30:11–14*). The NT writers taught that this renewal of the covenant took place among those who followed Jesus, the mediator of the new and better covenant.

## Jeremiah's character

We know more about Jeremiah's character than most of the prophets in Scripture. Two sides of his personality stand out in the records of his book. On the one hand, many of Jeremiah's prophecies and the narratives about his life reveal the strength of his devotion to the LORD. Jeremiah's pronouncements of doom met such resistance in Judah. His preaching was never popular. Despite these difficulties, Jeremiah continued to announce boldly that Judah's sins had condemned Jerusalem to destruction and her population to Exile.

On the other hand, however, the book of Jeremiah presents a portrait of a man with deep inner struggles. Jeremiah was plagued by feelings of inadequacy, depression, doubt and despair. A number of passages (often called 'Jeremiah's Confessions') reveal severe inner conflicts. Jeremiah lamented the betrayal of his friends and family (*Jer. 11:18–12:6*). He wondered about the purpose of his ministry (*Jer. 15:10–21*). He grew impatient for the word of the LORD to be fulfilled (*Jer. 17:12–18*). He prayed for vindication from the LORD against his opponents (*Jer. 18:18–23*). In his last recorded complaint (*Jer. 20:7–18*), Jeremiah cried to the LORD, 'You deceived me' (*Jer. 20:7*), and cursed the day of his birth (*Jer. 20:14–18*).

These disclosures reveal important dimensions of Jeremiah's character. Jeremiah wrestled with the discouragement of a ministry not well received. He suffered for his message time and again, and seldom received much encouragement. In all of his trials, however, Jeremiah faced his misery with admirable honesty. He did not treat his difficulties superficially, but felt and expressed his deepest discouragements. Nevertheless, Jeremiah showed himself a man of faith by bringing his perplexing questions to God in prayer. He sought solace in the God who had called him to speak. (See *Prophets and Prophecy*)                                    R.P.

**JEREMIAH** Jeremiah was a common name in biblical times, but its meaning is not clear. Scholars have suggested: 'the LORD establishes', 'the LORD exults', 'the LORD loosens', and 'the LORD hurls'. Whatever the case, Jeremiah was a name of praise to the LORD of Israel. Nine people bear the name in the OT.

**1.** See *Jeremiah the prophet*.

**2.** A head of a clan and valiant soldier in the tribe of Manasseh (*1 Chron. 5:24*). However, he and his people were 'unfaithful to the God of their fathers' and so God brought judgment on the tribe through the king of Assyria (*v. 25*).

**3.** A skilful and ambidextrous archer from the tribe of Benjamin who fought first for Saul and then transferred to David at Ziklag (*1 Chron. 12:4*). He was one of David's 'Thirty' great warriors. Later in the passage it seems that such men transferred loyalties not simply to be on the winning side but because the 'Spirit' had worked among them (*v. 18*).

**4.** Mentioned in *1 Chron. 12:10*, this Jeremiah was the fifth of various Gadite warriors who defected from Saul and joined David when he was at Ziklag. These mighty men were described as the greatest of warriors, stronger than a hundred men and 'swift as gazelles in the mountains'. V. 22 makes it clear that the addition of people like this to David's army was seen to be the working of the hand of God. David's army increased daily until 'he had a great army, like the army of God'.

**5.** This Jeremiah was the tenth of the Gadite warriors mentioned in 3. above.

**6.** The father of Hamutal. Hamutal was

the mother of King Jehoahaz of Judah and wife to his father King Josiah. She was also mother of Zedekiah who became king later (2 *Kings* 23:31; 24:18).

**7.** Another Jeremiah is mentioned in *Jer*. 35:3. He was the father of Jaazaniah and son of Habazziniah. They were a Recabite family. See *Recab* and *Jaazaniah* 1. for more detail.

**8.** This Jeremiah was one of those who returned with Nehemiah from the Exile in Babylon and joined him in signing the binding agreement to worship the LORD and obey his Law. He is probably the man who was one of 'the leaders of Judah' and took part in the dedication of the wall of Jerusalem (*Neh*. 10:2; 12:34).

**9.** This Jeremiah was one of the leaders of the priests who returned from the Exile in Babylon with Zerubbabel and Jeshua (*Neh*. 12:1).                 P.D.G.

**JEREMOTH 1.** A grandson of Benjamin and son of Beker (1 *Chron*. 7:8).

**2.** One of the sons of Beriah and a leader from the tribe of Benjamin, this Jeremoth lived in Jerusalem and is listed in the genealogy of Saul (1 *Chron*. 8:14).

**3.** This Jeremoth was among the descendants of Binnui. At the time of return from the Exile in Babylon, Shecaniah confessed to Ezra that many men and even descendants of the priests of Judah had married wives from other tribes and nations. Ezra and the people repented and made a covenant to serve the LORD (*Ezra* 10:2). Jeremoth is listed in Ezra 10:29 as one who divorced his foreign wife.

**4.** Another Jeremoth was a descendant of Elam and also among those who divorced his foreign wife under Ezra's leadership (*Ezra* 10:26).

**5.** Another Jeremoth was a descendant of Zattu and also among those who divorced his foreign wife under Ezra's leadership (*Ezra* 10:27).

**6.** Another Jeremoth was a descendant of Bani and also among those who divorced his foreign wife under Ezra's leadership (*Ezra* 10:29).                 P.D.G.

**JERIAH** A Levite and descendant of Kohath, Jeriah was the first son of Hebron and took part in the Kohathite duties in the Tabernacle and later in the Temple (1 *Chron*. 23:19; 24:23). It was in the latter days of David's reign that search was made of the genealogical records to trace the families of priests to do this work. At that time it was found that Jeriah was the head of his clan and had 2,700 relatives who were family heads. This whole clan was given the duty of overseeing the worship of God and service of the king among the tribes of Reuben, Gad and Manasseh (1 *Chron*. 26:31–32).

**JERIBAI** He and his brother Joshaviah, sons of Elnaam, belonged to David's 'Thirty' mighty men who went to battle for him and led the people of Israel to war (1 *Chron*. 11:46).

**JERIEL** (Heb., 'God has watched'). A grandson of Issachar and son of Tola, Jeriel was a family leader and a valiant soldier (1 *Chron*. 7:2).

**JERIMOTH 1.** A grandson of Benjamin and son of Bela (1 *Chron*. 7:7).

**2.** A skilful and ambidextrous archer from the tribe of Benjamin who fought first for Saul and then transferred to David at Ziklag (1 *Chron*. 12:5). He was one of David's 'Thirty' great warriors. Later in the passage it seems that such men transferred loyalties not simply to be on the winning side but because the 'Spirit' of God had worked among them.

**3.** A son of Mushi, this Jerimoth was a Levite and head of a family. He served in the Tabernacle worship during the reign of David once the ark of the covenant had found a permanent site in Jerusalem (1 *Chron*. 23:23; 24:30).

**4.** One of the sons of Heman listed among those set apart for the ministry of prophesying and music during the reign of King David. Heman was the King's seer. Jerimoth and his relations were given the 15th turn of service in the sanctuary (1 *Chron. 25:4, 13*).

**5.** During the reign of King David, this Jerimoth, son of Azriel, was an official in the tribe of Naphtali (1 *Chron. 27:19*).

**6.** A son of King David and his wife Abihail. King Rehoboam of Judah married Jerimoth's daughter Mahalath (2 *Chron. 11:18*).

**7.** Mentioned in 2 *Chron. 31:13*, he worked in the Temple during the revival under King Hezekiah (see *Heman* for more detail). He helped administer the Temple treasuries.     P.D.G.

**JERIOTH** Of the tribe of Judah, and one of the wives of Caleb son of Hezron (1 *Chron. 2:18*). The other wife was Azubah.

**JEROBOAM** Two kings of Israel bore the name Jeroboam:

**1.** *Jeroboam I (930–909 BC)*. The records of Jeroboam I appear in 1 *Kings 11:26–14:20* and 2 *Chron. 10:1–13:20*. He was a prominent Ephraimite whom Solomon put in charge of his whole labour force. This royal appointment moved Jeroboam to the centre of a political struggle between the northern and southern tribes. Solomon's foreign wives had led him into false religions (1 *Kings 11:1–13*) and the LORD raised up many adversaries against him (*vv. 14–25*). Jeroboam was the greatest of these adversaries. The prophet Ahijah announced that the LORD would divide Solomon's kingdom and give Jeroboam ten of the twelve tribes (*vv. 26–39*). This division was delayed, however, when Solomon tried to kill Jeroboam and Jeroboam fled to Egypt (*v. 40*).

After Solomon's death, Jeroboam joined representatives of the northern tribes asking Rehoboam to lighten the harsh labour policies of his father (1 *Kings 12:1–24*). After three days of deliberation, Rehoboam refused and foolishly threatened even worse conditions for his workers. As a result, Jeroboam led a rebellion against the house of David and became king over the northern tribes.

The Scriptures never condemn Jeroboam for this rebellion. In fact, the biblical record indicates that Jeroboam was justified because of Rehoboam's threats of further hardship. The throne of Jerusalem had so violated its prerogatives that it was rendered illegitimate. On two occasions, the LORD explicitly approved of Jeroboam as king over the northern tribes. He specifically promised Jeroboam a dynasty as enduring as David's line, so long as Jeroboam remained faithful (1 *Kings 11:38*). Moreover, when Rehoboam mustered troops to attack Jeroboam, the prophet Shemaiah ordered the troops home by the word of the LORD (1 *Kings 12:24*).

Even so, trouble soon began for Jeroboam. He became concerned that his people would turn back to David's house if they continued to worship in the Temple at Jerusalem (1 *Kings 12:26–27*). For this reason, he constructed alternative worship centres twelve miles north of Jerusalem in Bethel and further north in Dan. This action was not simply against Rehoboam, but also in defiance of the LORD, who had established the Temple in Jerusalem as the place of his special presence and the only place of worship (1 *Kings 8:27-30*).

Beyond this, Jeroboam mixed the worship of the LORD with the worship of Baal. He erected golden calves in Dan and Bethel and announced in words reminiscent of Aaron (*Exod. 32:4–5*). 'These are your gods, O Israel, who brought you up out of Egypt' (1 *Kings 12:28*). Jeroboam also built worship shrines at many high places in his kingdom. He installed his own priesthood and created his own worship festivals (1 Kings 12:31–33).

Jeroboam's false worship stirred divine wrath against him. An unnamed prophet announced that a man called Josiah would one day destroy the altar at Bethel (1 Kings 13:2–3). This prediction took place in 2 Kings 23:15, when Josiah extended his religious reforms to the Northern Kingdom. Moreover, the prophet Ahijah, who had earlier offered a positive word to Jeroboam (1 Kings 11:29–39), announced that the king's actions would bring disaster to his dynasty (1 Kings 14:1–16). This prophecy took place when Baasha assassinated Jeroboam's son Nadab, and murdered the rest of Jeroboam's family (1 Kings 15:27–28).

Jeroboam's idolatry became a standard to which the writer of Kings compared all other northern kings. He often mentioned that they 'walked in all the ways of Jeroboam' (e.g. 1 Kings 16:26; 2 Kings 14:24). As David was his model of a righteous king, so Jeroboam was his model of a wicked king. This repeated remembrance of Jeroboam I indicated how seriously the LORD stood against idolatry throughout Israel's history.

**2.** *Jeroboam II (793–782 BC)*. Jeroboam II, the son of Joash, was the fourth king of Jehu's dynasty. His lengthy reign over the northern tribes received relatively little attention in 2 Kings (2 Kings 14:23–29), but it was the subject of many prophecies in the books of Amos and Hosea.

Jeroboam led Israel to unprecedented prosperity. The Assyrians had weakened Syria so that it could cause no trouble for Israel. The Assyrians themselves were preoccupied with fighting in Armenia. Consequently, Jeroboam was free to carry out an aggressive expansion of his territories. The prophet Jonah had predicted that Jeroboam would restore the boundaries of Solomon's day and the king reached that goal (2 Kings 14:25). The LORD used Jeroboam to save Israel from

years of hardship and trouble (2 Kings 14:27).

Nevertheless, the prosperity of Jeroboam's kingdom led to many evils. Amos condemned the large gap between rich and poor (Amos 2:6–7); he denounced empty religious rituals (Amos 5:21–24), and false security (Amos 6:1–8). These and other evils led Amos to predict the downfall of Israel (Amos 6:8–14). Jeroboam and the people refused to listen to Amos (Amos 7:10–17) and in 722 BC Samaria fell to the Assyrians.

The reign of Jeroboam II warns how easily prosperity leads to corruption. Although God had blessed the nation in many ways, these blessings became an occasion for disobedience and destruction.                                    R.P.

**JEROHAM 1.** The grandfather of Samuel from the tribe of Ephraim (1 Sam. 1:1). However, he is listed in the Levitical genealogy in 1 Chron. 6:27, 34. This may mean that he simply came from the area of Ephraim or that the period of the Judges had seen much intermarrying and confusion of tribal allegiances. He may have been a Levite who did not exercise any Levitical duties. His son was Elkanah.

**2.** This Jeroham was a Benjamite clan leader whose sons lived in Jerusalem. His name appears in the genealogy of Saul (1 Chron. 8:27).

**3.** The father of Ibneiah, mentioned in 1 Chron. 9:8. After the captivity, Ibneiah was among the first returnees to Jerusalem from the tribe of Benjamin.

**4.** The father of Adaiah, a priest mentioned in 1 Chron. 9:12 and Neh. 11:12. In the days of Nehemiah, following the return from Exile, Adaiah served in the Temple.

**5.** The father of Joelah and Zebadiah, this Jeroham came from Gedor and was from the tribe of Benjamin (1 Chron. 12:7). His sons were among the warriors who deserted Saul to join David at Ziklag. They were ambidextrous in archery and with slings.

**6.** The father of Azarel. Azarel was the administrator over the tribal area of Dan and a leader of his tribe during the reign of King David (*1 Chron. 27:22*).

**7.** The father of Azariah who lived in the time of Jehoiada the priest (*2 Chron. 23:1*). Azariah was one of the commanders of the army who obeyed the call of Jehoiada and helped depose the pagan Queen Athalia. They put the seven-year-old King Joash on the throne. He served the LORD and repaired the Temple (*2 Chron. 24:1–16*).    P.D.G.

**JERUB-BAAL** See *Gideon*. The name means 'Let Baal contend'. This name was given to Gideon by his father Joash and the men of the village of Ophrah (*Judg. 6:32*) when Gideon broke down the altars of Baal and contended against the idolatry of the Israelites (*Judg. 6–8*). Later, when Gideon's attack on paganism had been more widely felt in the country, and much 'shame' was attached to the name Baal, the name Jerub-Besheth, meaning 'Let shame contend', was used (*2 Sam. 11:21*; but see *1 Sam. 12:11*).

**JERUB-BESHETH** See *Gideon* and *Jerub-Baal*. 'Jerub-Baal' was the name given to Gideon when he attacked the idols of Baal. It meant 'Let Baal contend'. Later, when the Israelites attached much 'shame' to the name Baal, the name Jerub-Besheth, meaning 'Let shame contend', was used (*2 Sam. 11:21*).

**JERUSHA** (Heb., 'possession' or 'inheritance'). Jerusha was the daughter of Zadok and mother of King Jotham of Judah. She was wife to King Uzziah and her son Jotham was 25 years old when he came to the throne (*2 Kings 15:33*; *2 Chron. 27:1*). He followed his father Uzziah in doing 'what was right in the eyes of the LORD' (*2 Kings 15:34*). See *Jotham*.

**JESARELAH** A leader of the seventh group of Levitical musicians and choirs who ministered in the Temple (*1 Chron. 25:14*).

**JESHAIAH 1.** One of two sons of Hananiah, and a descendant of King David and of Zerubbabel. He was of the tribe of Judah and is mentioned only in the genealogy of *1 Chron. 3:21*.

**2.** One of the sons of Jeduthun listed among those set apart for the ministry of prophesying and music during the reign of King David. Jeduthun, with Asaph and Heman, was directly under the supervision of the King (*1 Chron. 25:3,6*). Jeshaiah was the leader of the eighth group of Levitical musicians and choirs who ministered in the Tabernacle (*1 Chron. 25:15*).

**3.** This Jeshaiah was a descendant of the Levite Eliezer, and part of a family that had charge of the Temple treasuries (*1 Chron. 26:25*). He was the father of Joram.

**4.** Jeshaiah son of Athaliah returned from the captivity in Babylon with Ezra (*Ezra 8:7*). He was a descendant of Elam.

**5.** This Levite came from the descendants of Merari. Ezra was concerned that in returning to Jerusalem from the Exile in Babylon there were no Levites travelling with them. He saw it as the 'gracious hand of God' that Jeshaiah and others came forward and offered themselves for this service. (*Ezra 8:19*). See also *Sherebiah*.

**6.** Another Jeshaiah was from the tribe of Benjamin and father of Ithiel. He is mentioned in *Neh. 11:7* and his descendants resettled in Jerusalem after the Exile.    P.D.G.

**JESHEBEAB** One among the priests who were chosen to be officials in the sanctuary 'according to the last instructions of David'. Impartial selection from among the descendants of Eleazar and Ithamar was made by drawing lots. The 14th lot fell to Jeshebeab and that was the order in which he ministered when entering the sanctuary (1 Chron. 24:13).

**JESHER** A son of Caleb and his wife Azubah, in the genealogy of Judah (1 Chron. 2:18).

**JESHISHAI** (Heb., 'a son of old age'). The grandson of Buz and a clan leader in the tribe of Gad that was settled in Bashan and Gilead (1 Chron. 5:14).

**JESHOHAIAH** A clan leader of the tribe of Simeon, mentioned in 1 Chron. 4:36.

**JESHUA** (Heb., 'the LORD saves').

**1.** Jeshua was a priest who served in the Tabernacle during David's rule. He was responsible for the ninth turn of service (1 Chron. 24:11).

**2.** During the revival and turning to God in Hezekiah's reign, many Levites were assigned specific Temple duties. This Jeshua was one of those with the task of helping Kore distribute the people's gifts around the towns of the priests 'according to their divisions' (2 Chron. 31:15).

**3.** One of the Israelite leaders who returned with Zerubbabel to Jerusalem and Judah following the Exile in Babylon (Ezra 2:2; Neh. 7:7).

**4.** A descendant of Pahath-Moab, some of his descendants returned from the Exile in Babylon with Zerubbabel and others (Ezra 2:6; Neh. 7:11).

**5.** An ancestor of a priestly family which returned from the Exile in Babylon with Zerubbabel and others (Ezra 2:36; Neh. 7:39).

**6.** This Jeshua was a Levite whose descendants also returned from the Exile (Ezra 2:40; Neh. 7:43).

**7.** Jeshua son of Jozadak was a priest who returned with Zerubbabel from the Exile in Babylon. He was among the very first who returned and built an altar to offer sacrifices (Ezra 3:2). He also helped organize the rebuilding of the Temple (Ezra 3:8–9; 5:2). His leading position in the community is seen in that he was among those who had to confront the enemies of the rebuilding project (Ezra 4:3; 12:7). Some of his family had married foreign wives and so had to divorce them (Ezra 10:18). He is called Joshua in Hag. 1:14; 2:2 etc. Neh. 12:10, 26 probably refer to this person.

**8.** This Jeshua was the father of Ezer, one of those who helped rebuild the walls of Jerusalem after the return from the Exile (Neh. 3:19).

**9.** Soon after the Israelites had settled back in the towns around Jerusalem they came and asked Ezra to read to them from the Book of the Law. Jeshua was one of the Levites present who later 'instructed' the people in the meaning of the Law and interpreted it for them (Neh. 8:7). The people heard the word and began to weep as they understood it. Jeshua and the others encouraged them not to weep since this was a 'sacred day'. The people were to worship the LORD, 'for the joy of the LORD is your strength' (v. 10). The more they understood of the Law the more they rejoiced. They celebrated the festival of the Feast of Tabernacles. As a nation they then began to confess their sins (Neh. 9:4–5). Good instruction for the people was vital if they were to worship as the LORD wanted. Before the Exile the Levites and leaders had been severely castigated by the LORD for not doing this (e.g. Jer. 23). Now, after the Exile, they began to do what they should always have done, and the LORD brought them great blessing. This Jeshua was probably the son of Azaniah who signed the agreement with Nehemiah to worship only the LORD and obey his Law (Neh. 10:9). See also Neh. 12:8, 10, 24, which probably also refer to this Jeshua.       P.D.G.

**JESHURUN** (Heb., 'the upright'). This name was a symbolic name for the people and nation of Israel. It is only used in poetic passages and in contexts in which

God confronts Israel as their covenant LORD, warning of judgment or promising blessings to his chosen people (*Deut. 32:15; 33:5, 26; Is. 44:2*).

**JESIMIEL** (Heb., 'may God establish').

A clan leader of the tribe of Simeon, mentioned in *1 Chron. 4:36*.

**JESSE** Son of Obed and grandson of Ruth and Boaz, Jesse was the father of David (*Ruth 4:17, 22*). He came from Bethlehem and the tribe of Judah as Ruth and Boaz had (*1 Sam. 16:1*). Of his sons, David was the youngest and a shepherd. When Samuel was ordered to go to Jesse's home to anoint God's choice for the next king, he assumed that Jesse's eldest and strong son would be God's choice. After working through seven sons and God saying that he had not yet reached the right one, David was brought to Samuel and anointed (*1 Sam 16:3–13*). Samuel and the people of Israel had to learn that 'man looks on the outward appearance, but the LORD looks at the heart' (*v. 7*). Jesse went on to have considerable links with King Saul as his son had to play the harp in Saul's presence (*vv. 18–20*). Saul even asked Jesse's permission to let him keep David with him so that he could play the harp to soothe him when an evil spirit came upon him (*vv. 21–23*). On another occasion Jesse sent David to take food to his brothers who were on the front line of the battle with the Philistines. It was through that trip that David eventually found himself fighting and killing the giant Goliath (*1 Sam 17*). Later when Saul was angry at David he called him simply 'the son of Jesse' (*1 Sam. 20:27, 30–31; 22* etc.; see also *1 Chron. 10:14; 12:18; 29:26* etc.).

The prophet Isaiah, looking forward to a new king sitting on King David's throne, spoke prophetically of a shoot coming 'up from the stump of Jesse' and of the 'Root of Jesse' (*Is. 11:1, 10*). This prophecy was taken up and applied to Jesus by Paul in *Rom 15:12*. Because he was the father of King David he is, of course, also mentioned in the genealogies of Christ in *Matt. 1:5* and *Luke 3:32*.          P.D.G.

# JESUS (THE LORD CHRIST)

## Jesus' name

Jesus comes from the Greek form of the name 'Joshua' which means 'Yahweh [the LORD] saves'. The name Joshua was no doubt a popular name in Jesus' day and this accounts for the occasional use of the expression 'Jesus of Nazareth' (as opposed to others by that name; see *Matt. 26:71* and 15 other times). This Jesus (of Nazareth) is the focal point of the Gospels (Matthew, Mark, Luke and John) and, in many ways, of the rest of the NT. As Christians study the NT they begin to see that Jesus is also the fulfilment of all towards which the OT has been pointing. Jesus, also called Christ or Jesus Christ, is seen to be the long-awaited Messiah, and hence is also called 'son of David'. (See *Christ* and *Lord*.)

In *Matt. 1:21* we read of the significance of the name. An angel came to Joseph to announce the birth and said 'you are to give him the name Jesus, because he will save his people from their sins'. However, it would appear that Jesus was rarely called 'Saviour', if at all, to his face. In Mary's Song at the announcement of the birth, she said: 'my spirit rejoices in God my Saviour' (*Luke 1:47*), but in these words she was probably reflecting more generally on God's work in sending Jesus to save. The angels specifically told the shepherds that 'a Saviour has been born to you; he is Christ the Lord' (*Luke 2:11*) and the Samaritans who came to believe in Jesus as the Messiah acknowledged that 'this man really is the Saviour of the world' (*John, 4:42*). Rather, it was a reflection on Jesus' life, death and resurrection, his words and his actions, that led the disciples, guided by the Holy Spirit, to be able to understand and explain how Jesus was indeed the Saviour that his God-given name had indicated. This article can only build a very partial picture of Jesus, highlighting some of the more important aspects of *who he is*, his life and mission.

## Jesus' life

There is a small amount of evidence of Jesus' life outside the Bible. The Roman historian Tacitus mentions Christians who took their name from Christ who was put to death under Pontius Pilate in the time of Tiberius (see *Luke 3:1*). Seutonius mentioned some Jewish arguments and quarrelling in Rome at the behest of a Chrestus. His reference is very likely to be to Christ and the Christians. This quarrelling, he said, accounted for the expulsion of the Jews from Rome (see *Acts 18:2*). There are a number of Rabinnic allusions from various later periods to Jesus, some of which say this man was really a magician or sorcerer. A reference in Josephus, the Jewish historian writing for the Romans, talks of Jesus who did 'marvellous deeds' and was 'the Christ'. He was killed by Pilate and appeared on the third day to those who loved him. Josephus goes on to say that still now 'the race of Christians' had not died out. Some have doubted whether this section of Josephus' writings is genuine and suggested it was added later by Christians. Whatever view is taken on this last reference and which parts may or may not be genuine, there is certainly enough outside evidence to know that Jesus lived and that the effect of his ministry was widespread and disliked by his opponents and that he was put to death by Pontius Pilate. The NT is, however, the main source of information. Here much information is given about Jesus' life, but it is set in a context of careful explanation of the events by the Gospel authors writing for those who want to know Jesus better.

### Jesus' birth and childhood

Little is said at all of Jesus' childhood. Matthew and Luke relate certain miraculous events announcing and surrounding his birth. An angel appeared to Mary and to Joseph on a number of occasions. Joseph was told to continue to stay with Mary even though she was pregnant and he was not the father. The child Jesus would be born to the Virgin Mary 'because what is conceived in her is from the Holy Spirit'. Luke links this conception under the power of the Spirit with the fact that Jesus is to be 'the Son of God' (*Matt. 1:20; Luke 1:35*). In Jesus God was doing something new for the salvation of the world. Humankind had been unable to achieve its own salvation. Sin permeated everyone and judgment awaited but for God's intervention that would bring salvation and forgiveness. Mary captured this in her words which emphasized that the coming salvation in Jesus was entirely of God and his work. Jesus' salvation was 'mercy' for sinners, not a long-deserved right for righteous people (*Luke 1:46–50*; also *1:68, 71–72; 2:29–32*).

That Jesus was also the long-awaited Messiah or 'anointed' son of David who would inherit the throne is emphasized throughout the infancy accounts, but especially in Matthew's Gospel. The Magi or 'wise men' from the East came to find 'the one who has been born king of the Jews'. That people who were not Jews came to visit and came under God's guidance through a star, showed that Jesus' salvation and kingship would spread out far beyond the bounds of the Jewish race. The fact that Herod killed all the little boys of the area in an attempt to stop the competition also shows how seriously the birth of Jesus was being taken by the authorities (*Matt. 2:1–17*; also *Luke 1:32–33; 2:11*).

The angel even indicated Jesus' divinity in saying that Jesus would be called ' "Immanuel" – which means God with us' (*Matt. 1:23*). John 1:1–4, 14 show that this Jesus was truly human and yet pre-existent and divine.

In accordance with tradition, Jesus was presented in the Temple as a child. Again it is important to see that this incident is recounted, not just as a pleasant childhood story, but because of its significance for Jesus' identification as the one who was Saviour and redeemer and because of what it said about his calling and mission. Simeon identified the child Jesus as God's 'salvation' and 'a light for revelation to the Gentiles', while the elderly Anna also saw the child and spoke of the redemption that had come to Jerusalem (*Luke 2:29–32, 36–38*). As he grew it is noted that he 'became strong; he was filled with wisdom, and the grace of God was upon him' (*v. 40*).

The only recorded event in Jesus' childhood concerns an annual visit his parents made to the Temple, and a clear indication of Jesus' self-awareness of being the 'Son of God' with a specific mission. When he was twelve Jesus travelled with his parents to the Temple, but on their return they lost him. It turned out he was listening to the religious leaders and astounding them with his wisdom and the questions he was asking. In answer to his parents' concerned questions he responded: 'Didn't you know I had to be in my Father's house?' (*Luke 2:41–51*).

### Jesus' adult life

While we can speculate that Jesus would have grown up working alongside his carpenter father (*Mark 6:3*), the Gospel writers are interested in his public ministry that began with his baptism by John the Baptist. (This is actually where Mark begins his Gospel.) In accepting baptism, Jesus identified himself with sinful men and women and committed himself publicly to faithful covenant obedience to the Father. He was anointed publicly by the Holy Spirit who 'descended on him like a dove'. This was accompanied by a public pronouncement from heaven: 'You are my Son, whom I love; with you I am well pleased' (*Luke 1:10–11*). Here a verse about the Messiah from *Ps. 2:7* is joined with part of a verse from *Is. 42:1* which is a prophecy about God's servant who will come. Thus right at the start of his ministry, Jesus' mission was highlighted by the Father, for it was to be the path of the king and yet the path of obedience and service to God that would end in dying for sin on the cross.

The Spirit led Jesus 'immediately' from the baptism to the wilderness, where he was tempted by Satan. There he was tempted in a way that resembled the temptation of Israelites in the wilderness under Moses. Where they had so often failed, Jesus, the one who had just identified with his people, came through without sin. He rejected the temptation to accept the Messiah's kingdom as defined by Satan. He rejected temptation to do things the 'easy' way. For Jesus, Messiahship meant following the Father's will and it was the word of the Father in Scripture that he used to rebut Satan (*Matt. 4:1–11* etc.). His complete submission to his Father's words and will was to be the way he chose even when it led eventually to the cross.

Jesus' ministry then began in earnest. It may have started with a brief ministry in the area of Judea, but following John the Baptist's imprisonment, Matthew, Mark and Luke say that Jesus returned to the area around Galilee in the north. Mark summed up Jesus' proclamation: 'The time has come, the kingdom of God is near. Repent and believe the good news!' (*Mark 1:15*). During this period of preaching, the Gospel writers build up a picture of Jesus' activity. It involved an almost ceaseless round of preaching, talking, healing, and casting out demons. It was also during this period that Jesus began to choose his disciples who then travelled with him throughout his ministry (e.g. see *Mark 1:16–45; Luke 5* etc.). Once the number of disciples was complete at twelve, Jesus designated them 'apostles' (*Luke 6:12–16*). In this busy schedule solitude was at a premium, but Jesus insisted on making time to be alone with his Father to pray. Often he could only do this by going out at night time to somewhere where he would not be disturbed. Even then his disciples would often catch up with him and bring him back into the work because everyone was looking for this miracle worker (*Mark 1:35–37*).

Jesus' work and teaching wherever he went provoked an almost immediate response. People were amazed and yet they did not know how to respond. His home town of Nazareth quickly rejected him when he expounded Isaiah in the local synagogue and stated that the prophecy was being fulfilled in their midst (*Luke 4:16–30*). As he travelled, the crowds wanted to see more miracles. The religious leaders became more and more concerned as the crowds began to follow Jesus in ever-increasing numbers, and as they began to see more clearly the fundamental challenge Jesus was offering to some of their most coveted traditions. For example, they were concerned that he healed on the Sabbath (e.g. *Mark 3:1–6, 20–30; Matt. 12:1–8*). The disciples and even Jesus' family showed how little they understood of all that was going on (*Mark 3:31–34; 4:10–20; 7:17–23; John 7:1–13*).

Jesus' ministry was not reserved during this time only for Jewish people. In John's Gospel we read of a very early incident, probably as Jesus moved up north to Galilee following his baptism, in which he preached to the Samaritans. After listening to Jesus, many were amazed at his teaching and responded with an understanding that was not shown among the Jews: 'we have heard for ourselves, and we know that this man really is the Saviour of the world' (*John 4:42*; see *The Woman at the Well*). Later during the Galilean ministry as pressure again built up against him from the religious leaders, Jesus moved into the area of Tyre, into Gentile territory. Specially significant during this brief trip was Jesus' encounter with a Syro-Phoenician woman who had a demon-possessed daughter. She was a Greek but begged Jesus to cast out the demon. Jesus' response indicated his mission was to the people of Israel. The woman, however, persisted, demonstrating an amazing level of faith and understanding of Jesus' mission and his power. He healed the daughter, revealing again that, though his current mission was to the people of Israel, the good news of the Kingdom of God and of salvation would indeed be for all people and not just the one race.

As his life moved on, Matthew, Mark and Luke all record the next major turning point in Jesus' ministry. In his travels Jesus came to Caesarea Philippi. By this stage the disciples had been taught much and had seen much. So Jesus asked them: ' "Who do people say I am?" They replied, "Some say John the Baptist; others say Elijah; and still others, one of the prophets." "But what about you?" he asked. "Who do you say I am?" Peter answered, "You are the Christ," ' (Mark 8:27–29). Matt. 16:17 records Jesus' reply: 'Blessed are you, Simon son of Jonah, for this was not revealed to you by man, but by my Father in heaven'. The disciples had at last understood at least something of Jesus' true position. From that time forward, the Gospel writers inform us, Jesus began to set his face for Jerusalem and teach that he would have to suffer and die. In other words, having elicited the right reply from Peter (Jesus is the Christ or Messiah), he now set about redefining that contemporary understanding of what a Messiah would be like. Peter was quite unable to accept this way forward and objected most strongly. He suffered a very severe rebuke from the Lord: 'Get behind me, Satan! You are a stumbling block to me; you do not have in mind the things of God, but the things of men' (Matt. 16:23).

The difference in Jesus' understanding of his calling to be Messiah and the public perception became more and more pronounced as Jesus moved towards Jerusalem. On entering Jerusalem he was hailed as an arriving Messiah, but it was the same crowd who called a few days later for his death. The faithful disciples deserted him to a man as the suffering and persecution reached its great climax during the last hours of his life. At his end, Jesus' mission, the whole purpose of his adult life, was to be accomplished all alone on the cross bearing the punishment of sinful men and women on himself as even his heavenly Father forsook him at the moment of dereliction.

## Jesus' teaching

Jesus' teaching covered almost every area of life. Some of it was aimed just at his disciples and some to the people as a whole. Some of his teaching arose in an environment of confrontation with the religious leaders of his day, and other teaching was given by way of interpretation of the miracles he performed. Jesus taught by word and by action. Below we briefly cover four of the more important areas of his teaching and then mention his use of parables in teaching.

### About himself

Jesus' teaching about himself is given in word and action. From the start he was aware of his mission and purpose in life and in death. He quickly demonstrated a unique relationship with God. From the incident at twelve years old where he revealed such wisdom and his need to be in 'his Father's house', through to his insistence that the words he spoke and the deeds he performed were the Father's words and works (John 14:10 etc.), all he said pointed to his unique standing as the 'Son of God'. His Father was the heavenly Father of whom he had an intimate and personal knowledge. His great prayer for his disciples and for all who would later believe in him in John 17 again shows the great depths of his relationship with his

Father and their unity of purpose and will. Jesus' standing as Son of God was also seen in the great authority he revealed. He was able to cast out demons and deal with the evil spirit world simply by speaking. Even before the crowds understood, the demons acknowledged Jesus as the Son of God with power over them (*Mark 3:11; 5:7*). He also controlled the violent storm with a command showing his authority over the whole created world (*Matt. 8:24–27*).

As Jesus revealed this unique relationship with the Father, so he began to teach his disciples more of the depths of who he is. The disciples had to learn that in Jesus they could know the Father. On one occasion Jesus turned to Philip and said: 'Don't you know me, Philip, even after I have been among you such a long time? Anyone who has seen me has seen the Father. How can you say, "Show us the Father?"' (*John 14:9*). He went on to say, 'Don't you believe that I am in the Father, and that the Father is in me? The words I say to you are not just my own. Rather, it is the Father, living in me, who is doing his work' (*v. 10*).

Jesus never flaunted the fact that he was God, but as his teaching about himself is examined and verses like those just mentioned are seen in context, so the Christian deduction that Jesus taught that he was God in his words and deeds seems inevitable (at least to those who trust in him and accept the word of the apostles and their interpretation of these events). The emphasis on being the 'Son of God', on being 'sent' by God, on his authority as the 'son of David', his acceptance of the title 'Christ' from Peter, his teaching in *John 14–17* of his intimate (and pre-existent, *John 17:5, 24*); relationship with the Father, all provide an accumulation of evidence that Jesus was teaching his divinity at least to his close crowd of disciples and friends.

However, the reaction of the Jewish leaders also indicates that they were beginning to grasp something of Jesus' extraordinary claims about himself as they accused him on several occasions of blasphemy. For example, John recounts a confrontation in *5:16*: 'Jesus said to them, "My Father is always at his work to this very day, and I, too, am working." For this reason the Jews tried all the harder to kill him; not only was he breaking the Sabbath, but he was even calling God his own Father, making himself equal with God.' Jesus' response was to push this teaching about himself still further. Calling himself 'the Son', he said he could do nothing by himself but 'only what he sees the Father doing'. He talked of the love of the Father for the Son and how the Father could raise from the dead and the Son too could give life to whom he pleased (*vv. 12–21*). Jesus was claiming for himself divine prerogatives and went on to list among these the fact that the Father had given him the right to judgment: 'that all may honour the Son just as they honour the Father'.

One of the clearest expressions of his claim to deity is found in the so-called 'I Am' statements. When Jesus claimed to exist before Abraham and said 'Before Abraham was, I am' he was making a reference to Yahweh himself ('I am who I am', *Exod. 3:14*). Again the religious leaders saw this as a blasphemous claim to be God and took up stones to throw at him.

Jesus also caused people to begin to think of him as the Messiah. From preaching about the fulfilment of Isaiah's prophecy in the synagogue through to his performing of wondrous miracles, everything was causing the normal Jewish people to think of him as a Messianic figure. However, he also taught bit by bit that the usual understanding of the Messiah as a political warrior who would defeat the

Romans and rule in Jerusalem was not part of his calling. He concentrated on revealing himself as the suffering servant of his people in his discussions with his disciples. Some have suggested that his preferred self-designation of 'Son of Man' was deliberately chosen so he could fill it with his own definition of his role as the Messiah who would suffer and die. Following Peter's confession of Jesus as the Christ, we read in Mark 8:31: 'He then began to teach them that the Son of Man must suffer many things and be rejected by the elders, chief priests and teachers of the law, and that he must be killed and after three days rise again' (see also 10:45). But Jesus' use of 'Son of Man' also carried with it a claim to great and heavenly authority that reminds us of the Son of Man who came into the presence of God in the prophecy of Daniel (Dan. 7:13). Perhaps it was that picture that Jesus had in mind when he said to the Jewish leaders at his trial: 'from now on, the Son of Man will be seated at the right hand of the mighty God' (Luke 22:69).

When Jesus showed and talked of his authority, it was always of the highest possible kind. Whether he was talking of the authority the Father had given him to judge the world (John 5:27), or the authority over demons (Mark 1:27) and creation (Luke 7:8) that he demonstrated in his miraculous work among the people, it was clearly an authority not possessed by others and it was derived from heaven alone.

The more Jesus' teaching about himself is examined, the more inevitable becomes the deduction that here was a perfect man who was also God. Belief and trust in Jesus, God and Man, and in his words and works and teaching, has become the basis for the Christian faith ever since.

### About God the Father

We have seen how Jesus taught of his close and intimate relationship with the Father, but he also taught much about the Father himself. The Father God is the creator of the world (Mark 13:19) who continues to sustain the world and care for it in his providence (Matt. 10:29). It is the Father's will that is sovereign and must be followed at all points even by Jesus himself (Matt. 26:39). It is the Father alone who knows the final Day, the day of Christ's return (Matt. 24:36). But Jesus taught of God's fatherhood of individual people not just in some general sense of being the Father of the nation of Israel. The Jewish people certainly understood the fatherhood of God in this last sense, but Jesus' insistence on the possibility of an individual relationship with the Father was newly emphasized. It is of course expressed in the first line of the Lord's Prayer: 'Our Father in heaven' (Matt. 6:9).

What Jesus taught was that it is possible to know the Father through knowledge of Jesus (John 14:6–7). When talking to Mary after the resurrection, Jesus spoke of 'my Father and your Father' (John 20:17). The direct concern for the individual believer was taught by Jesus in a number of places. The Father is so concerned for his children's needs even down to their food and drink, that Jesus encourages them they should not be concerned for tomorrow (Matt. 6:31–34).

Jesus also taught that there is a special relationship between God as 'Father' and the Kingdom of God. The Father, who prepared the Kingdom for the disciples of Jesus 'since the creation of the world' will give the Kingdom to them. The righteous are the ones who will enter it and who will inherit its blessings (Matt. 13:43; 25:34; Luke 12:31–32).

### About the Kingdom

Jesus' teaching about his Father's Kingdom, the Kingdom of God, has provoked considerable debate among scholars, but no-one doubts that it was a subject of the utmost importance in Jesus' teaching (*Matt. 4:17; Mark 1:15; Luke 4:43*). Referred to either as the 'Kingdom of heaven' (in Matthew's Gospel) or 'the Kingdom of God', Jesus taught that the Kingdom was present, 'near', and related directly to his coming: 'if I drive out demons by the Spirit of God, then the Kingdom of God has come upon you' (*Matt. 4:7; 2:28; 21:31; Mark 1:14–15; Luke 11:20; 17:20–21 etc.*). But he also taught that it was future and would be inherited by his disciples (*Matt. 25:34; Luke 11:2; 22:18*).

The 'Kingdom of God' is primarily a description of the dynamic rule of God over this world, seen especially in good news of the coming of the redeemer King, Jesus. In Jesus' life and ministry that rule was directly experienced by and revealed to those who had the eyes to see who Jesus was. Not all were able to see the truth of the Kingdom. Indeed Jesus' use of parables to teach about the Kingdom makes it clear that understanding came by revelation (*Mark 4:10–12*). Jesus the king was present among Jews and Gentiles alike and taught that he had *all* authority. He even had power over demons.

However, entrance to and possession of the Kingdom and all its blessings is limited to those who acknowledge Jesus as Lord, ask for God's forgiveness for their sin, and commit themselves wholeheartedly to serve him. Jesus made this point only too clear to the religious leaders of his day when he said to them, 'I tell you the truth, the tax collectors and the prostitutes are entering the kingdom of God ahead of you. For John came to you to show you the way of righteousness, and you did not believe him, but the tax collectors and the prostitutes did. And even after you saw this, you did not repent and believe him' (*Matt. 21:31–32*). The parable that then follows shows how the leaders were rejecting the King who had now come just as their ancestors had rejected his prophets.

The 'present' nature of the Kingdom is such that it works quietly among men and women as people are drawn to acknowledge the redeeming King. But at the same time Jesus looked forward in his teaching. One day this rule of God would be manifest to all people.

It is important to see here that Jesus never reduces the full sovereignty and authority of God over all people whether or not they acknowledge Jesus as Lord. However, being 'part of' the Kingdom, sharing in it, and enjoying the manifest blessings of being a member through faith in Christ is limited to God's people. At the start of the 'age to come', however, which will begin when Christ returns, then as the apostle Paul put it: 'at the name of Jesus every knee should bow, in heaven and on earth and under the earth' (*Phil. 2:10*). At that time as the King fully reveals himself to all people, he will be seen to be a King who is faithful to his people and who judges the unrighteous to eternal damnation. Those who have rejected the offer of the Kingdom through the coming of Jesus and have thus turned their backs on a loving God who has reached out to them, will stand under the judgment of the king.

Time and again as Jesus taught about the Kingdom he warned of the future day of judgment and of the different experiences of the righteous on that day and those who have never turned to Christ (*Matt. 13:37–43; 25:34, 41*, etc.). The OT had looked forward to the time when God would establish his rule on earth. That rule would be perfect and establish a whole new order. God would redeem his people Israel and judge all evil. Jesus taught that God was now acting as the saving and redeeming God, for the Messianic age had come upon them. He was the Messiah. Jesus invited people to accept the King and the Kingdom and did this by calling upon people to repent of their sins and to turn to God. But the final consummation of that Kingdom and the full inheritance of its blessings were reserved for Christ's return in glory (*Matt. 24:30–31*). Followers of Christ will pray 'your kingdom come' (*Matt. 6:10*) because they look forward to seeing the returning King and to the Day when he will be fully revealed to all people. They long for the full revelation of Christ's glory and inheriting his promises of eternal life, but also for full deliverance from evil and sin.

Jesus' teaching about the Kingdom of God was not just limited to certain long teaching sessions or parables where the phrase itself was used, but it was also evidenced in Jesus' works, his miracles, the way he cast out demons and, above all, in his authority to forgive sins (*Luke 7:48–8:1; 6:20, 24–26* etc.).

## About the Holy Spirit

The work of the Holy Spirit is clearly to be seen throughout Jesus' life. By the Spirit he was conceived (*Luke 1:15*), the Spirit came upon him publicly at his baptism (*Luke 3:22*); the Spirit led him into the desert where he was tempted (*Luke 4:1*) the Spirit empowered him to preach the good news (*Luke 4:18*); and the Spirit enabled him to drive out demons (*Matt. 12:28*). However, Jesus also taught much about the Holy Spirit.

Three Gospels recount an occasion when Jesus was accused of casting out demons by the power of Beelzebub (*Matt. 12:22–32; Mark 3:22–30; Luke 11:14–23*). Following this Jesus pronounced that blasphemy against the Holy Spirit was unforgivable. Jesus' specific pronouncement is directly linked to the casting out of demons. His work of establishing God's rule, so clearly seen in the power he has over demons, is shown here to involve the work of the Holy Spirit ('if I drive out demons by the Spirit of God, then the kingdom of God has come upon you', *Matt. 12:28*). Indeed, the Spirit's work is vital to the Kingdom of God. It is by the Spirit that evil spirits, and demons are conquered as the mission of Jesus proceeds.

Jesus also taught that the Holy Spirit works regeneration in the life of the believer in order that he may enter the Kingdom of God (*John 3:5*). He taught that the Spirit helps the Christian worship as he should, in truth and in spirit (*John 4:24*). The Spirit also inspires Scripture (*Mark 12:36*), and he enables Christians to speak boldly for the faith (*Matt. 10:19–20*). Jesus also taught that believers would receive the Holy Spirit personally once he had been glorified (*John 7:38–39*). There was, therefore, a distinction between the way the Spirit was present in the mission of Jesus and the proclamation of the Kingdom of God and how he would be present once Jesus had returned to glory. In *John 14–16* Jesus calls him both the 'Spirit of Truth' and the 'Counsellor'. The Spirit is 'another Counsellor' and lives for ever (e.g. *John 14:15–17*). The Spirit thus becomes the one who convicts the world day by day and yet stands alongside the Christian leading him into truth, interpreting

Scripture and being the guarantor of truth (*John 16:8–13*). Indeed Jesus teaches that it will be the Spirit's prerogative to bring glory to Jesus and make him known to future generations of people who have not seen Jesus in the flesh (*John 16:12–16*).

It is clear from Jesus' teaching that, in all his various works, the Holy Spirit is to witness to and bring glory to Jesus. He will do this through the work of regeneration, of testifying to the truth of Christ, of explaining the truth (*John 14:26*), and even of empowering Christians to witness to Christ (*15:26–27*). The Spirit will be given by Jesus (*15:26; 16:7*) and by the Father (*14:16, 26*).

### Jesus' use of parables

In about a third of Jesus' teaching in the Gospels he makes use of parables. Whether speaking to the crowds, his disciples or the religious leaders of the day this form of instruction was the norm (*Matt. 13:34*). Parables were stories taken from normal life which were then used to convey religious truth and many parables of Jesus did draw on aspects of local life in his day which would have caught the attention of his audience. For example, when Jesus told the parable of the sower, the picture would have been commonplace and, indeed, there may have been a sower sowing seed in a field nearby (*Matt. 13:3–13*). Parables were rarely allegorical. The detail of the stories was not that significant, rather they made one or two straightforward points. However, although undoubtedly part of their intention was to arrest people's interest in what was being said, Jesus' parables did not immediately help everyone to understand what he was saying.

In *Matt. 13:10–17* (also *Mark 4:10–12; Luke 8:9–10*) Jesus makes some notable comments on the intelligibility of his parables. After the parable of the sower it becomes clear the message had not been grasped even by the disciples. They asked why he spoke in parables and he replied: 'The knowledge of the secrets of the kingdom of heaven has been given to you, but not to them. This is why I speak to them in parables: Though seeing, they do not see; though hearing, they do not hear or understand. In them is fulfilled the prophecy of Isaiah: "You will be ever hearing but never understanding; you will be ever seeing but never perceiving. For this people's heart has become calloused; they hardly hear with their ears, and they have closed their eyes. Otherwise they might see with their eyes, hear with their ears, understand with their hearts and turn, and I would heal them."'

These strange comments must be seen in the light of Jesus' teaching about the Kingdom of God. Most of the parables are in fact used to teach an aspect of the nature of the Kingdom. The problem with understanding the parables lies not so much with whether the stories were good or bad illustrations but with the truth Jesus' was teaching. The secrets of the Kingdom of God now being revealed in Jesus himself, his teaching and his works, required a response and a mind open to see, believe and be committed to this 'secret' revealed. For those who would not respond then the parables simply served to obscure still further the nature of the Kingdom of God.

Thus there is an urgency in the parables that requires a response from the audience. They need to decide to grasp the Kingdom with its joy and its blessings, for it is like possessing buried treasure or like a pearl of great price which is so valuable it is worth selling everything in order to obtain it (*Matt. 13:44–45*). But, more than that, the Kingdom will soon come in its fulness at 'the end of the age'. When it does it will be like a net that trawls for fish and when they are lifted to the surface the good will be separated from the bad and a 'fiery furnace' awaits the unrighteous (*Matt. 13:47–49*). So Jesus presents a crisis situation. The rule of God manifests in Jesus and his ministry may have appeared small at the time, but it would increase dramatically as the parable of the mustard seed indicates (*Matt. 13:31–31* etc.). In parables such as these Jesus' own complete assurance of the success of his ministry is revealed even though the path to that fulfilment lay through the cross.

What was so difficult for the Jews of Jesus' day to grasp was not that the Kingdom of God would come into power. They had long believed in that and looked forward to it. Rather their problem lay with this revelation of the 'mystery' of the Kingdom: that it was God's will that the Kingdom be revealed in the coming of the Lord Jesus Christ, not in power, but to serve and give his life. The work of Christ, with such seemingly small and insignificant beginnings that seemed to end in suffering and shame on the cross, was, in fact, the essential precursor to the full revelation of the Kingdom in all its power and fulness at some later date (the day of Christ's return).

Taking hold of the Kingdom, therefore, meant grasping a very new understanding of God's purposes for this world. God's rule was not going to be thrust upon everyone but was being offered to the world in the person of Jesus. Becoming 'sons of the kingdom' (*Matt. 13:38*) involves believing God's revelation in Jesus Christ and receiving his Kingdom rule in humility and trust 'like a little child' (*Mark 10:15*; also see *Matt. 5:3–10*).

## Jesus' work

### The miracles

Jesus' miracles also revealed much about who he is and the nature of his Kingdom. Here is found the wonder worker, the man of great compassion and love, the man who came from God and did what his Father desired. But here too is revealed the authority and lordship of Jesus: his authority over sickness in healing miracles (e.g. *Matt. 8:1–4*); his authority over Gentiles (e.g. *Matt. 8:5–13*); his authority over the rest of the creation in, for example, his capacity to still the storm (*Matt. 8:23–27*); his authority over the spirit world in the way he was able with a word to cast out demons (e.g. *Matt. 8:28–34*); and, most amazing of all, his authority over life and death (e.g. *Matt. 9:18–26*).

Such authority no doubt speaks of the divinity of Jesus, but it also demonstrates again that the Kingdom of God has come. Those who watched and experienced the miracles were faced with one who was 'greater than Jonah' (*Luke 11:32*) and, as with the parables, found themselves needing to respond. Did they see the hand of God in what was being done and respond with faith? Did they see the 'glory' of Jesus? Did they realize that the miracles were 'signs' (a word especially used in John's Gospel) pointing to the King and the Kingdom? Examples of different responses are seen with virtually all miracles. After the first sign when the water was turned to wine at the wedding feast in Cana we read that the sign revealed Jesus' 'glory . . . and his disciples put their faith in him' (*John 2:12*).

Sometimes faith in Jesus was demonstrated by an individual before a miracle (e.g. Matt. 8:5–13) and sometimes after (e.g. John 2:12), while sometimes it didn't seem to be present at all (Matt. 13:53–58). Many regarded Jesus as a miracle-worker and yet would not look below the surface and learn about Jesus or trust in him. It is interesting that Jesus' own brothers clearly liked the idea that he was a miracle-worker (John 7:3–4) and yet 'even his own brothers did not believe in him' (John 7:5).

The response to miracles of trust and faith in Christ was, in fact, an acceptance of the Kingdom of God in their midst. The miracles were part and parcel of the coming of the Kingdom, and were the works of the King, the Messiah, himself. Hence the revelation of the 'glory' mentioned in John 2:11, and hence the recounting of miracles by John so that people may 'believe that Jesus is the Christ, the Son of God' (John 20:31). When Peter trusted Christ and walked towards him on the water, even with very inadequate faith, he had recognized in Christ's own walking on water that he was in the presence of 'Son of God' (Matt. 14:33).

The opposite response indicated directly the relationship between miracles and the Kingdom. As Jesus viewed cities such as Korazin and Bethsaida, in which he had performed so many miracles, he saw their lack of repentance and compared them with Sodom, warning of the horror that awaited them on the judgment day.

### Jesus' obedience to the Father

Sent by the Father (e.g. John 3:34 etc.), loved by the Father (5:20 etc.), and dependent upon the Father (14:28), the Gospels reveal that Jesus' work involved revealing the mind and will of the Father in heaven. Jesus alone perfectly knows the mind of the Father and perfectly does the will of his Father in heaven (Matt. 11:25–27; Mark 1:11; John 5:30; 10:18). The words he spoke were only the words the Father gave him and those words were directly linked to the works he did which also were given for him to do by the Father: 'Don't you believe that I am in the Father, and that the Father is in me? The words I say to you are not just my own. Rather, it is the Father, living in me, who is doing his work' (John 14:10).

The works and words Jesus did and spoke were those that fulfilled the Father's purposes (John 15:15), so much so that the words of Jesus were identified with those of the Father (John 14:24). Even when he was in the Garden of Gethsemane and shortly to be crucified, Jesus was found praying 'My Father, if it is possible, may this cup be taken from me. Yet not as I will, but as you will' (Matt. 26:39). Jesus, the eternal Son, knew his mission had been given by the Father and he knew his work was to fulfil that mission that involved him coming 'to seek and to save that which was lost' (Luke 19:10) and would lead him to the cross.

### Jesus' progress to the cross

Jesus revealed much about himself through his teaching, his miraculous works, and his obedience to the Father. However, his earthly ministry and work revealed again and again how he understood the end from the beginning. He had come to 'save his people from their sins' (Matt. 1:21). All people needed salvation or else they would face the wrath of God in judgment on sin. Jesus drew attention on many occasions to the need for forgiveness. He forgave sin with authority (*Luke 7:47–48; Matt. 16:24–25*). He warned those who did not respond to the miracles or to his teaching. But that greatest of works, the work of salvation, was to happen when he suffered and died on the cross. All that he did in some way or other helped him progress towards the cross.

Jesus regarded this mission as the fulfilment of Scripture (*Mark 9:12; Matt. 26:24; Luke 24:25–27*). Gently, and against some opposition even from his disciples, he began to teach that the one they were beginning to recognize as the Messiah would have to suffer and die (*Mark 8:29–33*). Six days after Peter's confession of Jesus as the Messiah and Jesus' reference to his suffering, the Transfiguration occurred. There Jesus was revealed in his glory talking to Elijah and Moses (*Mark 9:2–12*). Luke reports that the subject of conversation, in the presence of Peter, James and John, was Jesus' impending death in Jerusalem (*Luke 9:31*). When Jesus knew the time was right according to the Father's will, he steadfastly turned to travel to Jerusalem where he knew trouble was waiting (*Luke 9:51; 17:11*). He explained this move to his disciples in terms of the fulfilment of Scripture (*Luke 18:31–33*). When he arrived near Jerusalem again the deliberate nature of Jesus' mission was seen as he sent for a colt on which to ride into the city (*Luke 19:28–44*). *Matt. 21:5* shows this again to be a fulfilment of Scripture. The act of throwing the money changers and others out of the Temple also seems to have been an action designed to highlight the difference between the gospel of Christ and the accepted practice of the Jews of that day. Little could have provoked a reaction more clearly than this (*Matt. 21:12–17, 23–27*).

Jesus' work would only be completed when he hung on the cross, the weight of sin born on his shoulders, the penalty paid and salvation established. His words 'It is finished' were thus more than an acceptance of his death, for they were also an acknowledgement that this part of his work was completed and he had carried through to the end the Father's will (*John 19:30*).

## Jesus' death

The great work of Jesus on the cross needs to be examined if we are to know still more about who Jesus is and what he has done for those who trust in him. As the apostle Paul later said 'we preach Christ crucified' (*1 Cor. 1:23*). It is this work that stands at the heart of a Christian's commitment to and faith in Jesus, and it is on the cross that God's purposes of salvation are achieved and that we truly find Jesus to be the 'Saviour'.

### The crucifixion

The Romans put Jesus to death by crucifixion, an event which is recorded in all the Gospels (*Matt. 27:35–37* etc.). This extremely unpleasant and painful death was widely used in those days and came after Jesus had been severely beaten and tortured (*Matt. 27:28–31*). The initial proceedings against him were taken by the Jews. They were afraid of his power and authority among the people and also afraid of his teachings which had challenged their whole approach to God at nearly every point. After an initial trial before the Jewish Sanhedrin in which the main accusation requiring the death penalty was that he had blasphemed (*Matt. 26:57–68*), Jesus was taken before the Roman court under Pontius Pilate (*Matt. 27:11–31*). There the charge had changed somewhat. No doubt in order to procure a death penalty, the charge was that Jesus had claimed to be 'the King of the Jews' and was thus in rebellion against Rome. Jesus did not deny this charge (*vv. 11–14*). Eventually, under enormous pressure from the Jewish authorities and the crowds they had whipped up in their support, and apparently against Pilate's better judgment, Jesus was condemned to death.

It has already been seen that Jesus knew he was to die. The Gospels' account of the crucifixion further emphasizes both the *voluntary* nature of Jesus' death (he went to the cross of his own accord and laid down his own life for his friends, *John 10:18; 15:13*) and of the *necessity* of this death in God's plan. For example, when Peter drew a sword on one of Jesus' assailants, Jesus reminded Peter that, had he wanted, he could have called on his heavenly Father to send legions of angels to his defence, but in going to his death 'Scripture would be fulfilled' (*Matt. 26:53–54*; also see *John 19:28* etc.).

Jesus died between two criminals. During the lengthy and painful death, insults were heaped upon him by the watching crowds (*Matt. 27:41–44*), and yet Jesus still demonstrated his divine prerogative in pronouncing forgiveness for one of those criminals at his side who demonstrated repentance (*Luke 23:39–43*).

### A sacrifice for sins

Jesus' death on the cross was a sacrificial death, a fact that became evident, according to John, right at the start of Jesus' ministry when John the Baptist referred to Jesus as 'the Lamb of God, who takes away the sin of the world!' (*John 1:29*). The clearest evidence that Jesus understood his own death in this way is to be found in the account of the Last Supper. There Jesus drew on an OT background as he handed round the bread and wine: 'Jesus took bread, gave thanks and broke it, and gave it to his disciples, saying, "Take and eat; this is my body." Then he took the cup, gave thanks and offered it to them, saying, "Drink from it, all of you. This is my blood of the covenant, which is poured out for many for the forgiveness of sins"' (*Matt. 26:26–28*). In the OT sacrificial blood of animals had been shed both at the forming of covenants between God and his people and when they were renewed (*Gen. 15; Exod. 24* etc.). In Jesus' death, to which the bread and wine pointed, a new covenant relationship was established between God and his people in which the people would know inwardly the Law of God and experience God with them in a new and more personal way (*Jer. 31:31; Heb. 8*).

The relationship between his death and the removal of sins draws on an understanding of an OT sacrificial system in which different sacrifices were offered to meet different needs, the apostolic writings regard Christ's redemptive work on the cross as fulfilling the whole sacrificial system (*Rom. 6:10; Heb. 7:27; 9:12; 1 Pet. 3:18* etc.). Jesus died once and for all as a sacrifice of atonement (*Rom. 3:25*). He brought about reconciliation between the sinner and the Father (*Rom. 5:11; 2 Cor. 5:18–19*). On the cross the King Jesus, representing his people, died to bring salvation (*Gal. 2:20*). In his death, Jesus stood as redeemer in the place of sinful men and women (*Mark 10:45*). He met the legal judgment on sin for all who had faith in him. It is worth noting here that Luke talks of Jesus dying on a 'tree'. He was probably deliberately reminding the reader that Jesus was thus dying under the curse of the Law (*Acts 5:30; 10:39; 13:29*; see *Deut. 21:23*). This point is also made by Paul who taught that on the cross Jesus died as 'a curse for us' to redeem 'us from the curse of the law' (*Gal. 3:13*).

In regarding Jesus' death as a fulfilment of the whole sacrificial law of the OT, the time of his death should not be ignored. Jesus died at Passover, suggesting that he is also to be regarded as the fulfilment of the Passover sacrifice (*Luke 22:15*). This may well have been in the mind of John the Baptist in *John 1:29* mentioned above, but was certainly in Paul's mind in *1 Cor. 5:7*: 'For Christ, our Passover Lamb, has been sacrificed.'

### Victory over death and Satan

The work of Satan and his demonic forces is clearly demonstrated in the passion and crucifixion of Jesus. Jesus acknowledged this when he talked to those sent to arrest him and said 'this is your hour – when darkness reigns' (*Luke 22:53*). However, Jesus was also aware that his crucifixion would lead to the downfall of Satan. 'Now is the time for judgment on this world; now the prince of this world will be driven out' (*John 12:31*). In taking upon himself God's judgment on sin, Jesus has removed the fear of judgment and its penalty of death for all who bow to his authority. These people have now been freed from 'slavery' caused 'by their fear of death' (*Heb. 2:15*). Indeed, as truly human, Jesus shared in the experiences of all people 'so that by his death he might destroy him who holds the power of death – that is, the devil' (*v. 14*).

Death had entered the world as God's judgment on those who follow Satan. Thus death is the clearest evidence of the sinfulness of men and women and also becomes clear evidence of the power of Satan. Remove the judgment of death and the fear that goes with it and we have the clearest evidence of the defeat of Satan's power. In taking death on himself in his self-sacrifice, Jesus died instead of those who deserved it. Those who do trust in him and serve him no longer fear death and recognize that Satan's power was broken once and for all on the cross. Jesus' resurrection and ascension to glory have proved that victory. Death could not hold Jesus as the Father raised him to life and lifted him to glory. As the apostle Paul put it: 'Having disarmed the powers and authorities, he made a public spectacle of them, triumphing over them by the cross' (*Col. 2:15*). For all who believe in Jesus a transfer has occurred: 'For he has rescued us from the dominion of darkness and brought us into the kingdom of the Son he loves' (*Col. 1:13*).

### Jesus' resurrection

The Bible also teaches that Jesus was raised to life by God the Father. The Gospels tell us that the miracle of the resurrection happened 'on the third day', that is, after the crucifixion. The resurrection of Jesus occurred early on the morning of the first day of the week, what we now call Easter Day. There is no description of Jesus actually being raised from the dead. Indeed, though the stone of the tomb was rolled away by an angel of the Lord (*Matt. 28:2*), it revealed that the resurrection had already taken place. The Roman guards on duty at the tomb lest someone should have stolen the body fainted and 'became like dead men' (*v. 4*). Women who had come to the tomb in the early morning were then simply told that 'he is risen' and was going up to Galilee. However, as they were leaving to tell the disciples Jesus met them, and the women worshipped him, before going to tell the disciples what had happened (*Matt. 28:4–9*). The different Gospels recount different events surrounding that morning. Various attempts have been made to try to link them all together and explain the exact order of events. Whether or not that is possible with the limited information the authors give us is debatable. However, each of them recount the fact of the resurrection. Jesus had been buried but now he was seen alive (see also *Mark 16; Luke 24; John 20*).

The astonishing fact of the resurrection left many questions in the minds of the disciples. Jesus himself helped explain to two disciples walking on the road to Emmaus that his death had been necessary. Jesus explained that all that had happened was in fulfilment of Scripture. It seems that the disciples' eyes were deliberately held closed as they failed to recognize Jesus until he prayed with them over a meal. At that point 'he disappeared from their sight' (*Luke 24:31, 44, 46*).

Jesus' resurrected body was real enough and yet it was distinctly different from the frail body that had eventually died on the cross. The marks of the nails were there and yet the resurrected Jesus was able to move about at will, apparently coming and going without being seen to walk between places (*John 20:27*). John seems to suggest this by describing the 'locked' upper room where the fearful disciples were hiding and then simply: 'Jesus came and stood among them' (*v. 19*). Perhaps it was the same occasion that Luke described in *24:36–37*: Jesus stood among them and 'They were startled and frightened, thinking they saw a ghost'. Jesus had to show them his scars to help them realize it was he who stood before them. The extraordinary nature of this miracle is also to be seen in the doubts expressed by Thomas who refused to believe until he had himself seen the scars. When he did see Jesus and recognized him, Thomas' response indicated the enormous impact this was having on his whole way of thinking. He simply looked at Jesus and, ascribing divinity to him, said: 'My Lord and my God!' (*John 20:28*).

Yet, in spite of now living in a body that was more than it had been to the extent that he is recognized as God, Jesus was still human and still had a material body. He could be touched (*Luke 24:39; 1 John 1:1, 3*). He could be heard and he ate food (*Luke 24:41–42; John 21:12*). On several occasions Jesus is shown to emphasize that even the resurrection happened in accordance with Scripture.

### The witnesses to the resurrection

The Gospel writers are clearly most concerned to establish the historicity of the resurrection. They tell of numbers of witnesses. The witness of the women who first came to that tomb in the early morning is recounted with slight differences of detail in all four Gospels. There were witnesses to the empty tomb both among the disciples like Peter and John and among the Roman guards who were horrified and feared for their life (*Matt. 28:11–15*); witnesses who heard the angels speak, witnesses who saw Jesus walking on the road to Emmaus, witnesses in the upper room among the disciples; witnesses to a breakfast on a beach in Galilee (*John 21:10–14*), and many others. The apostle Paul recounts from a distance the importance of those eyewitnesses to this world-changing event in *1 Cor. 15:5–8*, mentioning that on one occasion Jesus appeared to over 500 people at the same time.

### The significance of the resurrection

Jesus' resurrection vindicated the whole of his mission that had led him to 'become flesh' (*John 1:14*), to live, suffer and die in obedience to his Father for the salvation of humanity. The suffering Messiah, the one who had died for sin, was revealed as the victor over death and the powers of the evil one. The resurrection also showed the Father's acceptance of Jesus' sacrifice of atonement for sin and attested to the fulfilment of so many of the OT promises (*Rom. 6:8–10; Rev. 1:18* etc.).

The bodily resurrection of Jesus became central to Christian preaching for all these reasons but also because it assured them of their own salvation and forgiveness through faith in him. 'Since we have now been justified by his blood, how much more shall we be saved from God's wrath through him! For if, when we were God's enemies, we were reconciled to him through the death of his Son, how much more, having been reconciled, shall we be saved through his life!' (*Rom. 5:9–10*). Furthermore, the resurrection became their guarantee that they too, through faith in Christ, would one day be raised bodily and receive eternal life (*Acts 4:2; 26:23; 1 Cor. 15:12–34* etc.).

### Jesus' glorification

The word 'glorification' can rightly be used to describe the whole work of salvation achieved by Jesus through the cross, resurrection, ascension and sending of the Spirit. It seems the apostle John talked of Jesus' glory in this inclusive way (e.g. *John 12:16, 23, 28; 13:31; 17:1*). But Jesus' glorification more specifically describes his ascension into heaven and his exaltation (e.g. *John 17:5; 1 Pet. 1:21*).

After a period during which Jesus lived on this earth and was witnessed by many as the risen Jesus, he returned to heaven. The ascension to heaven, which took place 'in the vicinity of Bethany', is recorded in *Luke 24:50–53* and *Acts 1:9–11*. The ascension describes Jesus' return to 'glory' (to the presence of the Father in heaven) and his exaltation by God. The fact that Jesus was caught up in a 'cloud' (*Acts 1:9*) probably also points to this 'glory', for in the OT God had revealed his 'glory' in the cloud (e.g. *Exod. 16:10; 24:16*). The ascension also partially fulfilled Jesus' own prayer of *John 17:5, 24* in which he prayed that the disciples would see his glory.

This glory was seen primarily in Jesus' exaltation to his position of supreme authority at the right hand of the Father where he was crowned King of kings (*Phil. 2:9–11; Col. 3:1; Rev. 17:14; 19:16*). From heaven Jesus rules not just the church but indeed all peoples and nations. It is also from heaven that he will one day return to judge (*Acts 1:11; Heb. 9:28; 2 Cor. 5:10; 2 Tim. 4:1; Rev. 1:5* etc.). However,

Jesus' ascension was not just about him becoming King of kings for it also enabled him to fulfil his unique role as High Priest. It meant that he, as first-fruits of the resurrection, gained access to heaven for all believers (1 Cor. 15:20) and it meant that he was able to send the Holy Spirit to be with his people (John 7:39; Acts 2:33).

## Jesus' continuing work

The Bible teaches that Jesus is alive today in heaven where he exercises full regal sovereignty as Lord of lords and Kings of kings. He oversees the nations, his people and the whole cosmos. As exalted and ascended Lord who has gone ahead of his people to heaven, he dispenses the blessings of his Kingdom which can be summed up in the word 'life' (e.g. 2 Tim. 1:1, 10). Jesus also continues to fulfil his role as High Priest. As mediator between God and man, Jesus had to enter heaven, bringing even the worst of repentant sinners into the presence of God. He entered the Holy of Holies, the presence of the Father. There at the throne of God he intercedes on our behalf; man in the presence of God, standing as humanity's representative in glory. In doing this he brings to completion the work of redemption that has begun in those who believe (Rom. 8:34; Heb. 6:19–20; 9:24). Jesus continues to plead for his people on the basis of the once-for-all sacrifice he has made for them, thus enabling them to continue to receive forgiveness.

Though enthroned in heaven as the Lord of glory, Jesus also continues to work by his Holy Spirit in the midst of his people on earth. Those who belong to him through faith are controlled by his Spirit which is indeed the sign that they are his: 'If anyone does not have the Spirit of Christ, he does not belong to Christ' (Rom. 8:9; see Holy Spirit).

## Conclusions

Above we have touched on some of the biblical teaching about Jesus. The more the biblical evidence is studied, the more it becomes clear that the authors of the NT see the whole of the OT being fulfilled in the birth, life, death, resurrection and exaltation of the Lord Jesus Christ. In Christ God has come into this world, truly human and yet without sin and still God. He is seen to be God, yet having temporarily set aside some of his divine prerogatives in order to mediate the great love and mercy of God to sinful men and women. In his life his awesome authority as Son of God was seen as he healed, drove out evil spirits, preached the Kingdom of God, and commanded even nature to obey him. His capacity to forgive sin, to see a person's heart and to know their mind, to challenge the hypocrisy and lack of understanding among the religious leaders of his day, all caused further considera-tion among the religious leaders of his day about who he really was. In the end it was all too much for them. They felt threatened and were unable to see that Jesus was the truth the way and the life and so brought about his crucifixion. But therein lay the ultimate fulfilment of God's great and eternal plan of salvation by grace. He offered the once and for all sacrifice for sin by dying on the cross and thus completed the work of salvation and redemption for all who would have faith in him. His resurrection demonstrated the acceptance of that sacrifice by God following which, his true status as Lord of lords and King of kings was revealed in his exaltation to the right hand of the Father. As the early Christians quickly realized, the only appropriate response is praise to Christ: 'In a loud voice they sang: "Worthy is the Lamb, who was slain, to receive power and wealth and wisdom and strength and honour and glory and praise!"' (Rev. 5:12).

P.D.G.

**JESUS JUSTUS** See *Justus*.

**JETHER** (Heb., 'abundance').

**1.** Jether was the eldest son of Gideon who was told by his father to draw his sword and kill Zebah and Zalmunna. These two were Midianite kings who were defeated by Gideon and the Israelites and had been taken prisoner. However, Jether was afraid because he was only a boy. Gideon himself then killed them both (*Judg. 8:20*).

**2.** This Jether was the father of Amasa, an Ishmaelite whom Absalom appointed as his army commander in the place of Joab. Jether married Abigail, King David's sister (*2 Sam. 17:25; 1 Chron. 2:17*). He was later killed by Joab against the wishes of David, who warned that the LORD would repay Joab for such unnecessary bloodshed (*1 Kings 2:5, 32*).

**3.** The son of Jada, this Jether was from the tribe of Judah and a descendant of Jerahmeel (*1 Chron. 2:32*).

**4.** This Jether was the first son of Ezrah and was from the tribe of Judah (*1 Chron. 4:17*).

**5.** Another Jether was from the tribe of Asher and was a brave warrior and 'outstanding leader'. He had three sons (*1 Chron. 7:38*). P.D.G.

**JETHETH** A descendant of Esau, Jetheth was a clan leader of the Edomites (*Gen. 36:40; 1 Chron. 1:51*).

**JETHRO** (Heb., 'excellence'). Jethro was Moses' father-in-law. He was 'a priest of Midian' and also known as Reuel (*Exod. 3:1*). He gave his daughter Zipporah to Moses to be his wife. Moses had helped

Jethro's seven daughters water their flocks and so had become a close family friend. Having fled Egypt, Moses stayed with the family and helped them as a shepherd for many years until eventually he returned to Egypt to confront Pharaoh (*Exod. 2:15–22; 4:18*).

When eventually the Israelites escaped across the Red Sea into the wilderness, Jethro took Zipporah and they visited Moses in the desert (*Exod. 18:1–27*). There Jethro was encouraged by what he learned of all that the LORD had done for the Israelites and he clearly grew in the faith of Yahweh, saying to Moses: 'Now I know that the LORD is greater than all other gods, for he did this to those who had treated Israel arrogantly' (*Exod. 18:11*).

It is of particular interest that this priest was obviously a priest to Yahweh. In a sacrifice of thanksgiving, at which Aaron was present, Jethro performed the sacrifice and Aaron and the other elders came and ate bread and had fellowship with him (*v. 12*).

During Jethro's stay in the camp of the Israelites he was worried about the amount of responsibility and work that Moses had. He was afraid Moses would be worn out. In a great display of wisdom, Jethro advocated a shared leadership in which Moses would fulfil the main task of coming before the LORD while other 'capable men', who feared God and were trustworthy, would be selected to help judge the land for the people. They would decide simple legal cases between people and only the worst cases would be brought to Moses (*vv. 17–26*).

This wise and godly man recognized

the great faithfulness of the LORD and helped God's people in learning how to govern themselves and in employing a plurality leaders.                    P.D.G.

**JETUR** A son of Ishmael and grandson of Abraham and Hagar (Gen. 25:15; 1 Chron. 1:31). The name occurs again as one of the family names of the Hagrites (descendants of Hagar and Ishmael), who were defeated by a coalition of the tribes of Reuben, Gad and Manasseh (1 Chron. 5:19).

**JEUEL 1.** Mentioned in 1 Chron. 9:6 as a leader of the Zerahites. After the captivity, Jeuel was among the first returnees to Jerusalem from the tribe of Judah.

**2.** Another Jeuel returned from the captivity in Babylon with Ezra (Ezra 8:13). He was a descendant of Adonikam and returned with 60 men.

**JEUSH** (Heb., 'may he protect').

**1.** The first son of Esau and Oholibamah. He was born in Canaan and became an Edomite chief (Gen. 36:5, 14, 18; 1 Chron. 1:35).

**2.** A great-grandson of Benjamin and son of Bilhan (1 Chron. 7:10).

**3.** The second son of Eshek and listed among the descendants of Benjamin and King Saul (1 Chron. 8:39).

**4.** Mentioned in 1 Chron. 23:10–11 as a son of Shimei and a Levite. He belonged to the clan of the Gershonites. Neither he nor his brother Beriah had sons and so in the assignments for worship they were counted as one family.

**5.** The son of Rehoboam and Mahalath (2 Chron. 11:19).

**JEUZ** Listed in the genealogy of Benjamin leading to King Saul, Jeuz was the head of a family and son of Shaharaim and his wife Hodesh. He was born in Moab (1 Chron. 8:10).

**JEW/JEWS** This ethnic term became a prominent way to refer to Israelites, the members of the Southern Kingdom of Israel, during the period of the Exile. Its first mention, comes in 2 Kings 16:6; 25:25 ('men of Judah') in association with the Babylonian Exile. It came to describe any post-exilic Israelite in contrast to the Gentiles. It appears frequently with this sense in Ezra, Esther, and Jeremiah, less so in Daniel and Zechariah. Esther, Mordecai, Shadrach, Meshach, and Abednego are prominent individuals identified explicitly as Jews in the OT (book of Esther; Dan. 3:12). The mixed cultural context of their story very much fits the usage of the term. As such it was a religious term also referring to the adherents of the Hebrew religion.

Those Jews who lived in Palestine preferred to call themselves members of Israel. For many Israelites 'the Jews' was the way outsiders referred to them. The contrast between the Jewish leaders mockingly calling Jesus 'the King of Israel' and the Romans' mocking title of 'King of the Jews' illustrates the difference in perspective (Mark 15:32; cf. vv. 2, 9, 12, 18, 26).

This sense of 'them' also arises in the NT, but in a fresh way. Now the Jews are viewed as a group who stand questioning Jesus, opposed to Jesus and his disciples, or whose practice differs from Christians with respect to things like eating of clean or unclean food or following Sabbath law (Matt. 28:15; Mark 7:3; John 2:18, 20; 5:10, 16, 18; 7:1; 9:22; 10:31; 19:38; Acts 9:23; 12:3; 14:19; 17:5; 18:12). Sometimes the term is a neutral description of those who ask Jesus for a favour or who are among those responding to Jesus (Luke 7:3; John 11:31–33, 45; 12:11; Acts 13:43; 14:1; 21:20). So the term is not used in a uniformly hostile way. In John 4:9, Jesus is identified as a Jew in contrast to the Samaritans. So are Paul and his company (Acts 16:20; 22:3, 12), as well as believers like Aquila, Apollos and Ananias (Acts 18:2, 24). So

Christians of Jewish descent are both called Jews and yet are distinguished from them. Paul is singled out as a target for Jewish opposition (*Acts 18:12; 21:27; 22:30; 23:12, 27; 24:9; 26:7; 2 Cor. 11:24*).

In the epistles, the term most frequently appears in Paul's letters, often standing in ethnic contrast to Gentiles or Greeks (*Rom. 1:16; 2:9–10; 10:12; 1 Cor. 1:24; 10:32; 12:13; Gal. 2:14–15; 3:28; Col. 3:11*; the only uses outside of Paul's epistles are in *Rev. 2:9: 3:9*). In some of these contexts, there is a hostility implied by the Jewish practice as compared with that of Christians (*Gal. 2:13–14*). In the Jew-Gentile pairing the point often reflects a desire to show the scope of salvation being offered to all races.          D.B.

**JEZANIAH** (Heb., 'the LORD hears'). One of the army officers left in Jerusalem in the last days of the Babylonian siege. He was the son of Hoshaiah. They were about to flee to Egypt to escape the death they imagined awaited them at the hands of the Babylonians. In one final act of desperation, they asked Jeremiah to appeal to the LORD for them and to seek his will on what they should do (*Jer. 42:1*). Jeremiah went away and consulted the LORD who told him to persuade the people to stay in Jerusalem where the LORD would protect them from death. However, if they were to flee to Egypt they would all die of 'sword, famine and plague' (*v. 17*).

The officers refused to accept Jeremiah's word as had the whole establishment of officers, court officials and kings down through the years. 'In disobedience to the LORD' they went down to Egypt (*Jer. 43:7*). However, the escape from the Babylonians was short-lived. In Egypt, where Jeremiah had gone with the Israelites, he was shown by God that the Babylonians would in fact invade that part of Egypt and destroy Egyptians and Israelites alike (*Jer. 44*).

God's judgment had been decreed and there was nowhere left for them to escape. Instead of accepting the judgment as God's discipline of his people and returning in repentance to the LORD, they worshipped the gods of the Egyptians (*Jer. 44:17–18*). Thus their actions confirmed the judgment and led to the inevitable consequences.

See also *Jaazaniah* (2.) who swore allegiance to Gedaliah and was probably the same person.          P.D.G.

**JEZEBEL** was the daughter of Ethbaal, king of Tyre and Sidon, and the wife of Ahab king of Israel (874–853 BC) (*1 Kings 16:31*). In biblical Heb. her name means, 'There is no nobility'. This name is probably an intentional distortion of her given name, 'Where is the Prince (Baal)' or 'The Prince (Baal) exists', which praised her god, the Phonecian Baal. The writer of Kings misconstrued her name to show his utter contempt for her actions and her religion. He characterized the queen as entirely evil.

Jezebel devoted herself to bringing the worship of Baal and his consort Asherah to Israel. She employed 450 prophets of Baal and 400 prophetesses of Asherah (*1 Kings 18:19*), and persecuted the prophets of the LORD, including Elijah (*1 Kings 19:1–9*). She also extended her religion by violating Israel's concept of limited monarchical power (*Deut. 17:14–20*). When Naboth refused to sell his God-given inheritance to Ahab (*1 Kings 21:3*), Jezebel arranged for Naboth's execution by hiring men to accuse him falsely of blasphemy (*1 Kings 21:8–16*).

Jezebel's defiance of the LORD led Elijah to prophesy that dogs would devour her body (*1 Kings 21:23*). Although she lived at least ten years after Ahab's death, she died as Elijah predicted when Jehu had her thrown from her window (2 Kings 9:32–33). Dogs devoured her in the street, leaving only her skull, feet, and the palms of her hands (2 Kings 9:34–37).

Jezebel's character and actions gain symbolic significance in the NT. Rev. 2:20 refers to a false prophetess in the church at Thyatira as 'that woman Jezebel' to indicate that the wrath of God was against her for her false teachings and immorality.                                    R.P.

**JEZER** The third son of Naphtali and head of the Jezerite clan (Num. 26:49; 1 Chron. 7:13). He is listed among those who went to Egypt with Jacob (Gen. 46:24).

**JEZIEL** A skilful and ambidextrous archer from the tribe of Benjamin who fought first for Saul and then transferred, with his brother Pelet, to David at Ziklag (1 Chron. 12:3). He was one of David's 'Thirty' great warriors and a son of Azmaveth. Later in the passage it seems that such men transferred loyalties not simply to be on the winning side but because the 'Spirit' had worked among them.

**JEZRAHIAH** A Levite who was part of the choir that sang at the dedication of the wall. The walls and city had been destroyed by the Babylonians when they took the Israelites into captivity. Under the direction of Nehemiah they were eventually rebuilt amidst great praises to God (Neh. 12:42).

**JEZREEL** (Heb., 'God sows').
**1.** The first son born to Hosea and his adulterous wife Gomer (Hos. 1:4). The name was given to the child by God. It referred to the terrible destruction by Jehu of the house of Ahab which took place in the city of Jezreel (2 Kings 10:11). The LORD said to Hosea: 'Call him Jezreel, because I will soon punish the house of Jehu for the massacre at Jezreel, and I will

put an end to the kingdom of Israel. In that day I will break Israel's bow in the Valley of Jezreel' (Hos. 1:4–5). And yet hope still lay on the horizon because the LORD would remain faithful to his promises. That hope is taken up in v. 11 where there is a play on the literal meaning of the place name 'Jezreel'. God will once more 'sow'. Out of the judgment on Israel the LORD would once again bring forth fruitfulness (Hos. 2:21–23).

As so often among the OT prophets, Hosea was called upon to pronounce judgment and yet to remind people of both the need to repent and the covenant faithfulness and love of the LORD for his people. This was lived out in an acted parable in his life. The names of his children help to illustrate the prophetic message. See also Lo-Ammi and Lo-Ruhamah.

**2.** One of the sons of Etam. A leader in the tribe of Judah and brother to Ishma and Idbash. His sister was Hazzelelponi (1 Chron. 4:3).                          P.D.G.

**JIDLAPH** (Heb., 'weeping'). A son of Nahor and Milcah and therefore Abraham's nephew (Gen. 22:22). See Bethuel.

**JOAB** (Heb., 'the LORD is his father').
**1.** Joab was the son of David's sister, Zeruiah, and was commander of his army. Along with his two brothers, Abishai and Asahel, he was a mighty warrior and for many years remained faithful to David (1 Chron. 2:16). He had become commander early in David's reign when he had decided to attack Jerusalem and take it from the Jebusites. David promised that whoever led the attack would become 'commander-in-chief' (1 Chron. 11:6; 2 Sam. 8:16).

The next time he is mentioned is when he faced up to Abner who was Ish-bosheth's commander. A descendant of Saul, Ish-bosheth claimed the throne of his father, but when Abner's fighters met with Joab's men in a prearranged contest, Joab's forces won and Abner fled (2 Sam. 2). Abner pleaded for peace and so Joab spared his life. When Abner fell out with Ish-bosheth, he went to see David at Hebron and made a treaty with him. When Joab returned to Hebron to find that David had not captured Abner but had let him go in peace, he was furious, called Abner back and stabbed him to death (2 Sam. 3). David was very upset with Joab and cursed his family (2 Sam. 3:29). David also walked in Abner's funeral procession. No doubt this action was partly political since David wanted to ensure that the northern tribes realized he had not killed their leader, but it was also part of the great difference between David and Joab which would continue to come between them in future incidents. Joab always wanted revenge and to put to death any enemies. To his despair, David was always willing to forgive and frequently deeply saddened when his enemies were killed.

Joab's skills as an army commander were notable, but such skills were also combined with worship of the LORD and a desire to seek the LORD's help in battle. 2 Sam. 10 describes a famous battle in which Joab found himself caught in a pincer movement between the Ammonites and their allies, the Syrians. Using his brother Abishai with a section of troops to go against the Ammonites, Joab chose some of his crack troops and turned to face the Syrians. Joab had faith that God would lead the Israelites to victory: 'Be strong and let us fight bravely for our people and the cities of our God. The LORD will do what is good in his sight' (2 Sam. 10:12). Joab achieved a remarkable success in the battle against seemingly impossible odds.

After Absalom had killed Amnon and fled from David, Joab sought to bring about a reconciliation between father and son. Through devious means Joab achieved at least part of his aim and Absalom was brought back to Jerusalem. However, Absalom had to stay in his own house. He summonsed Joab to him, but Joab refused to visit Absalom. Absalom then had his servants set fire to Joab's fields finally forcing Joab to come to him. Once again Joab was sent back to the king with a view to a full restoration of Absalom to favour. David took Absalom back but immediately Absalom began to conspire against David, and eventually David had to flee for his life from Jerusalem (2 Sam. 14–15). Joab went with him and fought for David against Absalom. In spite of the King's command that his son was not to be killed Joab deliberately killed him (2 Sam. 18).

Again Joab could not understand David's kindness and sadness for someone who had been a serious enemy. When David grieved for his son, Joab severely reprimanded him (2 Sam. 18:33–19:7). Perhaps because of his rudeness to David and his lack of understanding of David, when David returned to Jerusalem, he replaced Joab and made Abishai commander-in-chief.

Joab, obviously feeling humiliated and slighted by King David, sided with Adonijah and his supporters when David was old. David's clear instructions were that Solomon should inherit the throne rather than Adonijah. David had even warned Solomon about Joab and the way he had killed Abner and Amasa (1 Kings 2:5). When Adonijah's rebellion was finally put down, Benaiah followed Joab and killed him for his disloyalty to David.

Joab was a mixture of a great warrior, a good strategist and, at times, a faithful servant of God. Yet he was also intensely passionate and full of revenge and bitterness. The revenge and bitterness of Joab contrasted deeply with David's concern for his enemies, something Joab regarded as weakness in a King.

**2.** A descendant of Pahath-Moab, many of his descendants returned from the

Exile in Babylon with Zerubbabel and others (*Ezra 2:6; 8:9; Neh. 7:11*).

**3.** The son of Seraiah, this Joab was a craftsman and from the tribe of Judah (*1 Chron. 4:14*). P.D.G.

**JOAH** (Heb., 'the LORD's brother').

**1.** In the confrontation between King Hezekiah of Judah and the King of Assyria, Joah, the son of Asaph the recorder, went out with other leaders to meet the Assyrian field commander (*2 Kings 18:18, 26, 37; Is. 36:3, 11*). They listened to the commander challenge Hezekiah and try to destroy his trust in the LORD. At one point, Joah and the others asked the commander to speak in Aramaic rather than Hebrew so that the people on the walls of Jerusalem would not hear and so would not become discouraged. This simply encouraged the commander to shout out the challenge in Hebrew. The message of imminent destruction was carried to Hezekiah by Joah and the officials.

On hearing the challenge, Hezekiah turned to prayer (*2 Kings 19:14–19*) and through a prophecy from Isaiah was promised by God that Jerusalem would not fall to the Assyrian king (*vv. 20–34*). The LORD then proceeded to cause destruction in the camp of the Assyrians (*vv. 35–36*).

**2.** The third son of Obed-Edom, a descendant of Korah responsible to attend to the Tabernacle gates in David's administration (*1 Chron. 26:5*).

**3.** Joah, the father of Iddo and Eden and son of Zimmah, was a descendant of Gershon, son of Levi. He was head of one of the Levitical clans and helped in cleaning and purifying the Temple in the days of King Hezekiah (*1 Chron. 6:21; 2 Chron. 29:12*). He may have been a descendant of 2. above.

**4.** The son of Joahaz and a 'recorder' in Josiah's reign. He was sent by the king to help repair the Temple of the LORD (*2 Chron. 34:8*). P.D.G.

**JOAHAZ** (Heb., 'grasped by God'). The father of Joah who was a 'recorder' in Josiah's reign. Joah was sent by the king to help repair the Temple of the LORD (*2 Chron. 34:8*).

**JOANAN** One of the ancestors of Jesus listed in the genealogy from Jesus to Adam. He was apparently grandson of Zerubbabel though he is not mentioned in the OT (*Luke 3:27*).

**JOANNA** The wife of Chuza, the manager of Herod's household, Joanna had been healed by Jesus. She, and other women similarly healed by Jesus, helped to provide for Jesus and the twelve disciples out of their means (*Luke 8:2–3*). She must have stayed with Jesus through much of his ministry and accompanied him from Galilee to Jerusalem at the end of his work. She was no doubt one of the women present when Jesus was laid in the tomb (*Luke 23:55–56*) and who visited the tomb of Jesus following the crucifixion. There they were confronted by two men in dazzling clothes who told them that Jesus had been raised from the dead. Joanna and the others then went and told the eleven disciples about what they had seen (*Luke 24:10*). P.D.G.

**JOASH** (Heb., 'the LORD has given').

**1.** This Joash was a grandson of Benjamin and son of Beker (*1 Chron. 7:8*).

**2.** Mentioned in *1 Chron. 4:22*. A leader in the tribe of Judah. Together with others he is listed as being among the potters who lived in Moab.

**3.** Joash the Abiezrite was the father of Gideon. It was while Gideon was working at home for his father that an angel came to speak to him 'under the oak at Ophrah' (*Judg. 6:11*). There Gideon was challenged to lead Israel to victory against the Midianites. Joash had to intervene on his son's behalf when Gideon tore down an altar to Baal. Joash was obviously a man who had remained faithful to the LORD and was appalled that Israelites should want to kill his son for desiring to obey Yahweh (vv. 20–31). The faith expressed in his reply to the hostile crowd is impressive: 'Are you going to plead Baal's cause? Are you trying to save him? Whoever fights for him shall be put to death by morning! If Baal really is a god, he can defend himself when someone breaks down his altar' (v. 31). Gideon went on to become one of Israel's greatest judges.

**4.** A skilful and ambidextrous archer from the tribe of Benjamin who was the son of Shemaah. He fought first for Saul and then transferred to David at Ziklag (1 Chron. 12:3).

**5.** One of the overseers during the reign of King David. He was in charge of the supplies of olive oil (1 Chron. 27:28).

**6.** Joash was the ninth king of Judah and was seven years old when he came to the throne in c. 835 BC. His father had been King Ahaziah and his mother was Zibiah (2 Kings 11:2; 12:1). When Ahaziah died at the hands of Jehu, Athaliah, his mother, attempted a complete take-over. She set out to destroy the whole royal family, but Jehosheba, Joash's aunt, hid Joash away in the Temple precincts where her husband, Jehoiada, was the high priest. There Joash was brought up to know the Law of the LORD and was well cared for until Jehoiada felt he was old enough to be brought out and put on the throne with the help of some of the army commanders (2 Chron. 24:1–3).

'Jehoiada then made a covenant between the LORD and the king and people that they would be the LORD's people. He also made a covenant between the king and the people' (2 Kings 11:17). The people then tore down the temple of Baal. As he grew up and ruled the nation, the writer of the books of Kings comments: 'Joash did what was right in the eyes of the LORD all the years Jehoiada the priest instructed him' (2 Kings 12:2). During the time of Jehoiada's influence, Joash

ordered repairs to the Temple. He decided to levy a tax for this purpose in the way Moses had levied a tax in the wilderness (2 Chron. 24:9), but the Levites did not implement it immediately (2 Kings 12:7; 2 Chron. 24:4–6). Eventually, however, much money and treasure was given by the people and the Temple fully rebuilt and refurbished. While Jehoiada lived, sacrifices were offered regularly in the Temple to the LORD (2 Chron. 24:13–16).

During this period Joash married two wives and had various children (2 Chron. 24:3). Sadly, once this faithful priest had died, Joash was influenced by other leaders rather than the priesthood and so he turned, as his predecessors had, to pagan worship (2 Chron. 24:17–18). The LORD sent prophets to warn of the dangers of this, but he took no notice. One of those prophets was Zechariah the son of Jehoiada. The Spirit of the LORD came on him so that he spoke to the people of Judah warning them they and the king were disobeying the LORD's commands and that therefore the LORD would forsake them (2 Chron. 24:20). Instead of repenting, they stoned him to death in the courtyard of the Temple itself, an action for which Joash himself was held responsible (vv. 21–22). As the Chronicler records: 'Because Judah had forsaken the LORD, the God of their fathers, judgment was executed on Joash' (v. 24). Within the year the Syrians invaded. For a while Joash tried to buy his way out of trouble (2 Kings 12:17–18), but was eventually killed by the leaders of Judah after much plunder had been taken from Jerusalem to Damascus. The officials killed him because of his murder of Zechariah (2 Chron. 24).

Perhaps more clearly than with any other king, the influence of a faithful priesthood upon the nation and its rulers is revealed during the early years of Joash's reign. Jehoiada fulfilled all that the LORD expected of him as a high priest. He faithfully instructed the young king in the ways of the LORD and led the nation behind the scenes in faithful worship. This should have been the continuing function of the priesthood but, like the kings themselves, they were only too fallible, and once Jehoiada had died it seems that no one was able to replace him in terms of spiritual influence in the royal court. Joash himself was easily led. Perhaps he had relied too much on Jehoiada, having been placed on the throne at such an early age. Or perhaps his faith was never really a personal commitment to the LORD. Without a faithful king or priesthood the LORD's judgment on the nation was swift. Zechariah's dying words: 'May the LORD see this and call you to account' (2 Chron. 24:22) were prophetic and quickly fulfilled. After a reign lasting nearly 40 years, Joash died ignominiously in c. 796 BC.

**7.** In some versions the twelfth king of Israel is also called Joash. Since the NIV translates his name as Jehoash, see that name for detail.

**8.** Another Joash was the son of King Ahab of Israel and was in charge of the prison to which the prophet Micaiah was taken (1 Kings 22:26; 2 Chron. 18:25).

P.D.G.

## JOB

Job is the central character of the book of Job. The book recounts his experiences through the most terrible troubles and sufferings in life. Who he was or when he lived or even when the book was written has been the subject of much debate and no real consensus has emerged. Some have argued that the description of Job as wealthy in terms of his thousands of sheep, camels etc., and his large number of servants might suggest a time in history near the period in which Abraham lived. Others however, put the date much later in the time of King Solomon, during the time of the Exile, or even as late as the 4th century BC.

Job himself is described as a righteous man. He knew the LORD as his God whom he faithfully worshipped and who he knew would eventually be vindicated. He regularly sacrificed for his sins and even showed real spiritual concern for his children, making sacrifices for them in case they might have 'sinned and cursed God in their hearts' (Job 1:4–5). Such was Job's righteousness that he became the subject of discussion and challenge between the LORD and Satan. The LORD described Job as 'blameless and upright, a man who fears God and shuns evil' (v. 8). Satan argued that if all Job's blessings were withdrawn he would curse God. The LORD allowed Satan a certain freedom to put this theory to the test.

Satan brought upon Job's house one calamity after another. His sons and daughters were killed when their house fell on them, all their possessions were destroyed or taken by raiders. All that Job had known was taken from him and yet he did not curse God and so Satan attacked Job himself with sores and sickness. In spite of his wife's suggestion that he curse God and die, we read that his response remained that of one whose trust lay in God: 'In all this, Job did not sin in what he said' (Job 2:10).

In such tragedy, the majority of the book of Job then describes the way Job dealt with his life and how he interacted with three friends who sought to comfort him in various ways. (For detail of their different responses to Job's predicament see *Eliphaz, Bildad* and *Zophar*).

Two aspects of Job's reaction to his situation are seen in detail in the chapters that follow. On the one hand Job defended himself against his friends as 'innocent'. While his friends tended to make the simplistic equation that such calamity must be the judgment of God on Job, Job knew that he had not sinned in a way that deserved this. He knew he had been faithful to the LORD. On the other hand, Job also remonstrated with God about what was happening in his life. He knew that the answers coming from his friends were simplistic and inadequate and yet he could not understand what was happening. His honesty and openness before God provides a most moving example of a righteous man discussing his life and his fears and even his anger with his God.

The great dilemma for Job was the problem of theodicy. How could God be sovereignly good given the suffering among apparently innocent people and yet the prosperity of the wicked? Gradually Job learnt that it was indeed his duty to continue to serve God. He came to recognize his unworthiness in the presence of such a great God while still refusing to accept the simple equation that suffering is always a result of an individual's sin (Job 29–31). He learnt that he must accept God as he is and knew that, while he could always bare his heart to God, he could not answer God (Job 40:1–3).

In the book God speaks directly to Job (Job 38–41). First the LORD showed Job that he really did not and could not be expected to understand God's ways. God's great power and wisdom in creation are enough to expose a man's lack of understanding of God. Secondly, the LORD showed that he continued to be in ultimate control over everything, even over the most fearful creatures like the Behemoth or Leviathan that drive fear into mankind (Job 41). To this speech from God, Job responded again in faith and commitment to God's sovereignty.

Job had no idea of the challenge in heaven between God and Satan. He had no idea of God's overall purposes in what was happening in his life, that through his suffering Satan would be revealed as wrong and would be dishonoured and humiliated. Yet, by the end of the book, Job is back to where he was at the start. Having lived through the greatest horror imaginable, he came to a position of being able to express confidence in divine sovereignty, and sorrow that he had dared to question God: 'I know that you can do all things; no plan of yours can be thwarted. [You asked,] "Who is this that obscures my counsel without knowledge?" Surely I spoke of things I did not understand, things too wonderful for me to know . . . Therefore I despise myself and repent in dust and ashes' (Job 42:2–3, 6).

The book ends with God once again blessing Job, but also with God castigating Job's three friends for their wrong understanding of the workings of God. They are told to ask Job to make sacrifices on their behalf and to ask him to pray for them and we are told that 'the LORD accepted Job's prayer' (Job 42:9).

In an age where people seek simple answers of God and expect to be able to answer all the questions that concern them, specially when it comes to health and prosperity in their lives, it is good to be reminded that God is God and is sovereign; that his people can be open and honest before him in their pleading and questioning; and yet that there will often be no simple answers for mankind cannot ever know the whole mind of God. In spite of all this, a righteous person who looks to God in faith and prayer can rely on him to do what is right and to work out his purposes for the good of those who love him and are called according to his purposes (Rom. 8:28).                                               P.D.G.

**JOBAB** **1.** A descendant of Shem and son of Joktan (*Gen. 10:29; 1 Chron. 1:23*). These descendants of Shem became leaders of clans in Arabia.

**2.** The son of Zerah who lived in Bozrah, this Jobab became the king of Edom following the death of Bela (*Gen. 36:33–34; 1 Chron. 1:44–45*). This was at a time before Israel had a king (*Gen. 36:31*).

**3.** One of the kings in northern Canaan who was defeated by Joshua as he invaded the land with the Israelites (*Josh. 11:1*). He ruled in the town Madon and joined a coalition of Canaanite forces summonsed by Jabin king of Hazor to fight Joshua. The LORD promised Joshua a great victory. The victory was won in battle and all the Canaanites involved were killed (*vv. 6–15*).

**4.** This Jobab was the head of a family and son of Shaharaim and his wife Hodesh. Listed in the genealogy of Benjamin leading to King Saul, he was born in Moab (*1 Chron. 8:9–10*).

**5.** Mentioned in *1 Chron. 8:18*, this Jobab was a son of Elpaal, and a leader from the tribe of Benjamin. He lived in Jerusalem and appears in the genealogy of Benjamin leading to King Saul (*1 Chron. 8:18, 28*).          P.D.G.

**JOCHEBED** (Heb., 'the LORD is glory'). Jochebed was one of Levi's descendants who was born while the Israelites were in Egypt. She was wife to Amram and mother of Moses, Aaron and Miriam (*Exod. 6:20*). Her son Moses was born at a time when Pharaoh had decreed the murder of all male children born to the Israelites (*Exod. 2*). She hid the child for three months until the child was too large to hide in the house. Then she obtained a basket of papyrus which she coated in tar and pitch and placed it among the reeds along the bank of the Nile. She put the child in it for safekeeping from the Egyptian soldiers.

Pharaoh's daughter came down to the river to bathe, found the child and, realizing he was a Hebrew child, took pity on him (*Exod. 2:5–6*). Moses' sister had been told to watch the basket and, seeing what was happening, ran up to the princess and offered the services of a Hebrew woman to look after the child. Moses' mother was then asked to look after the child for the princess! Later when the child was older, he was taken to Pharaoh's court by the princess who 'named him Moses, saying, "I drew him out of the water"' (*Exod. 2:10*).          P.D.G.

**JODA** One of the ancestors of Jesus listed in the genealogy from Jesus to Adam. He was apparently the great-grandson of Zerubbabel, though he is not mentioned in the OT (*Luke 3:26*).

**JOED** (Heb., 'the LORD is witness'). Joed was from the tribe of Benjamin and father of Meshullam. He is mentioned in *Neh. 11:7* and was an ancestor of those who resettled in Jerusalem after the Exile.

**JOEL** (Heb., 'the LORD is God').

**1.** Apart from the identification of the prophet as 'son of Pethuel' (*Joel 1:1*) virtually nothing is known of him, not even his chronological setting. Unlike many of the other prophets, Joel does not link his ministry with the reigns of any kings and it is only on internal and very subjective evidence that one can make any judgments as to his provenance. Therefore, some scholars view Joel as one of the earliest prophets, perhaps as early as 800 BC, whereas others marshal strong evidence for the post-exilic period. Fortunately, the date has little or no bearing on the great issues the prophet addresses.

If the date is debatable, the immediate audience is not, for Joel speaks to the Southern Kingdom, Judah, as numerous references make clear (*Joel 1:14; 2:1, 15, 23, 32; 3:1–2, 6, 14–17, 19–21*). It is probable, therefore, that Joel was a native of Judah, no matter when he ministered.

Even so, his is a harsh message, one of impending wrath and judgment that he constantly describes as 'the day of the LORD' (*Joel* 1:15; 2:1, 11, 31; 3:14). That term, found also but less frequently in other prophetic books (*Is.* 13:6, 9; *Ezek.* 30:3; *Amos* 5:18, 20; *Obad.* 15; *Zeph.* 1:7, 14; *Zech.* 14:1), speaks particularly of war as Ancient Near Eastern occurrences of the same idiom attest. When the LORD comes 'in that day' he is coming as warrior and judge to put down earthly kingdoms and to establish his own reign. This suggests that the 'day of the LORD' also has a bright aspect, for the conquest of evil makes possible the triumph of righteousness. It will therefore be a day of renewal or recreation, one in which the landscape will be lush and productive (*Joel* 2:21–25), the people well fed (*v.* 26), and the Spirit of God outpoured abundantly upon all his redeemed ones (*vv.* 28–32). Ironically, the day that is characterized by war and bloodshed (*Joel* 2:3–11; 3:1–3, 12–13) will usher in the age of peace unparalleled in human history (*Joel* 3:9–11, 17–21).

Joel's 'day of the LORD' was understood by Peter to be fulfilled in part by the coming of the Holy Spirit upon the church on the day of Pentecost (*Acts* 2:17–21; *cf. Joel* 2:28–32). Otherwise the NT makes use of the more common OT meaning of wrath and judgment (*Rev.* 9:2–9; *cf. Joel* 2:2–10; *Rev.* 14:15; 18:20; 19:15; *cf. Joel* 3:13).

**2.** One of two named sons of the prophet Samuel who served as judges but corruptly and without popular support (*1 Sam.* 8:2–5; *1 Chron.* 6:28, 33; 15:17). It is sad that in this way Samuel seems at least partly to have followed Eli in not controlling his sons (see *Hophni* and *Phinehas*). Joel's disobedience and his perverting of justice were the precipitating causes of the

demands by the 'elders of Israel' that Samuel appoint them a king.

**3.** A leader of one of the clans of the tribe of Simeon who took part in military campaigns in the days of King Hezekiah (*1 Chron.* 4:35, 41).

**4.** A descendant of Reuben known otherwise only as the father of Shemaiah (*1 Chron.* 5:4) or Shema (*v.* 8).

**5.** A leader of the tribe of Gad, perhaps as late as the 9th century BC (*1 Chron.* 5:12, 17).

**6.** A Kohathite ancestor of Heman who is listed among the Temple musicians. He is otherwise identified as the father of a certain Elkanah (*1 Chron.* 6:36; *cf. v.* 33).

**7.** A descendant of Issachar through Tola and Uzzi and a family leader (*1 Chron.* 7:2–3).

**8.** One of David's so-called 'mighty men', a brother of a certain Nathan (*1 Chron.* 11:38).

**9.** A head of a Levitical clan of Gershon in the time of David who was charged with bringing the ark of the covenant into Jerusalem (*1 Chron.* 15:7, 11–12; *cf.* 23:8; 26:22); not to be confused with the Levite Joel of *1 Chron.* 6:36).

**10.** An officer in David's army in charge of the troops of half the tribe of Manasseh; otherwise described as a son of Pedaiah (*1 Chron.* 27:20).

**11.** A Kohathite Levite, son of Azariah, appointed by King Hezekiah to purify the Temple (*2 Chron.* 29:12).

**12.** A descendant of Nebo, he was one of the Jews who had married a foreign woman in post-exilic times and who was forced by Ezra to separate from her (*Ezra* 10:43).

**13.** A provincial leader under Nehemiah who was in charge of some 928 men of Benjamin after the return from Exile (*Neh.* 11:9).      E.M.

**JOELAH** One of the warriors who deserted Saul to join David at Ziklag. They were ambidextrous in archery and with slings. They were from the tribe of

Benjamin. Joelah was a 'mighty man' among David's famous and valiant 'Thirty' warriors (1 Chron. 12:7).

**JOEZER** One of the warriors who deserted Saul to join David at Ziklag. They were ambidextrous in archery and with slings. They were from the tribe of Benjamin. Joezer was a 'mighty man' among David's famous and valiant 'Thirty' warriors (1 Chron. 12:6).

**JOGLI** The father of Bukki mentioned in Num. 34:22. Bukki was the leader of the tribe of Dan who was chosen by God to help Moses assign Canaanite land given to the tribe.

**JOHA** **1.** One of the sons of Beriah and a leader from the tribe of Benjamin mentioned in the genealogy of Benjamin leading to King Saul (1 Chron. 8:16).
**2.** The son of Shimri, a Tizite, this Joha was one of David's 'Thirty' mighty warriors who fought at his side (1 Chron. 11:45). He was one of those great fighting men who deserted Saul and came from the tribe of Manasseh to join David at Ziklag. The passage in 1 Chron. 12 makes it clear that the gradual desertion from Saul of such warriors from various tribes was led by the Spirit of God. The last verse of the section (v. 22) says: 'Day after day men came to help David, until he had a great army, like the army of God.'

**JOHANAN** **1.** Johanan son of Kareah (Jer. 40:8, 13, 15–16; 2 Kings 25:23) lived at the time of Jeremiah when Gedaliah ruled Judah as a puppet governor under the Babylonians. He was among the army officers who, on hearing of Gedaliah's appointment, joined him at Mizpah. There he warned Gedaliah that Baalis, king of the Ammonites, had sent Ishmael son of Nethaniah to plan his assassination. Gedaliah refused to believe Johanan. Johanan even volunteered to go and kill Ishmael himself to prevent the assassination attempt, but still his word was not accepted (Jer. 40) and eventually Gedaliah was killed (Jer. 41).

Johanan and the army officers heard of Gedaliah's death and Ishmael's return to Ammonite country with many captives. They gave chase and caught up with the Ammonites at 'the great pool in Gibeon' (Jer. 41:12). They rescued the captives, but Ishmael and eight others escaped (v. 15). Johanan, the officers, and freed captives came to Geruth Kimham near Bethlehem on their way to Egypt to escape the Babylonians. There they asked the prophet Jeremiah what the LORD had in store for them (Jer. 42:1–6). They promised to abide by what the LORD said. However, when the LORD, through Jeremiah, told them to stay in Judah (Jer. 42:7–22), they claimed Jeremiah had lied and so they departed for Egypt taking the prophet with them (Jer. 43:2, 4–7). The epitaph for Johanan son of Kareah was simply that he 'disobeyed the LORD's command to stay in the Land of Judah' (v. 4).

**2.** This Johanan is listed among the descendants of King David. He was the eldest son of King Josiah (1 Chron. 3:15). Apparently he did not succeed his father to the throne, unless he was also called Jehoahaz (2 Kings 23:30–31).

**3.** One of seven sons of Elioenai and part of the royal lineage of Judah following the Exile, therefore a descendant of David (1 Chron. 3:24).

**4.** The son of Azariah who himself had a son called Azariah (1 Chron. 6:9–10). Johanan's son served as a priest in Solomon's Temple.

**5.** A skilful and ambidextrous archer from the tribe of Benjamin who fought first for Saul and then transferred to David at Ziklag (1 Chron. 12:4.) He was one of David's 'Thirty' great warriors. Later in the passage it seems that such men transferred loyalties not simply to be on the winning side but because the 'Spirit' had worked among them.

**6.** This Johanan was one of the famous Gadites who defected from Saul to David when he was at Ziklag. He was the eighth in the list each of whom are described in vivid imagery as the bravest of warriors. They were commanders who proved of tremendous support to David in his battles (*1 Chron. 12:12*).

**7.** Johanan son of Hakkatan was one of the heads of family who returned from Babylon to Jerusalem with the prophet Ezra. He brought with him 110 men (*Ezra 8:12*).

**8.** Johanan son of Eliashib was one of the prominent Levitical family heads in Nehemiah's time during the reign of Darius the Persian (*Neh. 12:22–23*).

P.D.G.

## JOHN, THE APOSTLE

John the son of Zebedee and brother of James was one of Jesus' twelve chosen disciples, later to be called apostles (*Matt. 10:2–4*). He was almost certainly also the one referred to in John's Gospel as 'the disciple whom Jesus loved' (*John 13:23* etc.) and often appears in the Gospels along with his brother James. These two are frequently mentioned in conjunction with Peter. They all knew each other from their fishing background (*Luke 5:10* etc.). John's father owned a boat and it was while in a boat with their father that Jesus called John and James to be disciples. The two immediately left the boat and followed Jesus (*Matt. 4:18–22*). It is probable that his mother was Salome who joined the women in taking spices to Jesus' tomb after the crucifixion (compare *Mark 16:1* and *Matt. 27:56*). Jesus called James and John 'Boanerges', which means 'Sons of Thunder' (*Mark 3:17*). Quite why he did this is not clear but it may reflect their somewhat fiery temperament, or their zealous commitment to Christ.

The deeply personal relationship between Jesus and John is seen in several passages in the Gospels. He was one of an 'inner circle' of three disciples who stayed with Jesus on a number of important occasions. However, the depth of Jesus' relationship with John was most clearly seen on the cross. There it was John whom Jesus singled out and to whom he said 'Here is your mother.' Then we read: 'From that time on, this disciple took her into his home' (*John 19:27*).

### John and Jesus

John quickly obeyed Jesus when he was called to follow as a disciple and is specially noted as one of a small group of disciples consisting of John, Peter and James who were singled out by Jesus to be present with him on a number of very significant occasions. The makings of that group was already present in *Mark 1:29* when it was James and John who went with Jesus to visit Peter's mother-in-law who was so ill. Jesus healed the woman in her house and she immediately got out of bed and started serving her guests (*Mark 1:29–31*). On another occasion Jesus was called to the house of a synagogue ruler called Jairus to heal his daughter. Before they arrived, the ruler's friends came to say that she had died. Jesus went on to the house taking only Peter, James and John. Once there he raised the girl from the dead (*Mark 5:37–43; Luke 8:51*).

The third and most important event that John witnessed with Peter and James is known as the Transfiguration. In this extraordinary event, Jesus and the three disciples went up a 'high mountain' where Jesus 'was transfigured before them'. Three Gospels record the incident (Matt. 17:1–9; Mark 9:2–13; Luke 9:28–36). It is not clear where this mountain was but it may have been Mount Hermon. Jesus had taken them up the mountain for prayer (Luke 9:28). No doubt in withdrawing this far from the nearest towns they were afforded some respite from the crowds. While praying, Jesus' face changed and his clothes became 'as bright as a flash of lightning'. Moses and Elijah then also appeared in glorious splendour, and 'spoke about Jesus' departure', which 'he was about to bring to fulfilment at Jerusalem' (vv. 29–31). All the writers emphasize the intense white light and glory of what was going on. This brief manifestation of God's glory in Jesus, and the fact that Moses and Elijah were seen talking to Jesus, led Peter to blurt out that perhaps he should build some sort of dwelling where such glory could be contained in some way. But quickly a cloud enveloped the scene. The cloud too was evidence of the presence of the glory of God himself (see Exod. 16:10; 24:16). As the cloud came down so John and the others heard the voice of God himself saying: 'This is my Son, whom I have chosen; listen to him' (v. 35).

In order to understand better what was going on in the Transfiguration it is important to see that all three Gospels have just recounted Peter's confession that Jesus was 'the Messiah [the Christ]'. This statement from Peter, who was no doubt the voice for John and the other disciples, signified a major step forward in their understanding of who Jesus is. However, Jesus immediately took the opportunity, much to Peter's dismay, to show that he would be going to suffer and eventually die. The way of this Messiah was not to be the expected way of national glory or of becoming king of Israel. The Transfiguration therefore very importantly taught John and the others that, though, it may not seem right to have a Messiah going to his death, this Messiah was to be glorified through this event. Jesus was preparing his disciples for his death and suffering, by showing them that it was only for a while that his true glory was hidden from the world. They had seen a revelation of the Christ of glory and now knew that, even though he would go to his death, he was superior in glory and authority to both the law-giver, Moses, and the great prophet, Elijah. The voice of God from heaven once again assured all those who listened, as they had been assured at Jesus' baptism, that here was indeed the true Son of God who needed to be heard and who was following a chosen path. Such a revelation of Jesus in his glory no doubt helped John in his later writing where he put such weight on Christ's 'glory' (John 1:14; 2:11; 11:40; 17; etc.).

In spite of his privileged position in the inner circle, there was much that John did not grasp of Jesus' mission. He informed Jesus on one occasion that he had stopped someone else using the name of Jesus in order to cast out demons because 'he was not one of us' (Mark 9:38). This incident is recorded immediately after the disciples had been arguing among themselves about who would be greatest in the Kingdom of God! Jesus, of course, said that this person should not have been stopped for it was being done in the name of Jesus and 'whoever is not against us is for us' (v. 39).

In a similarly impetuous move, John joined his brother, perhaps at the instigation of their mother, in asking Jesus whether when the Kingdom arrived they could have seats of honour, in other words, privileged positions (Mark 10:35). Perhaps remembering back to the Transfiguration, their request refers to Jesus' 'glory': 'Let one of us sit at your right and the other at your left in your glory'. Again Jesus had to teach that his Kingdom would not be like that. The Son of Man came to serve and such lording it over others was not of the nature of Christ's Kingdom at all. We are told that the other disciples were indignant when they heard this request being made (Mark 10:35–45).

Luke also records that as Jesus moved through a Samaritan village, on his way to Jerusalem, he was not welcomed. John and his brother asked: 'Lord, do you want us to call fire down from heaven to destroy them?' (Luke 9:54). Of course, Jesus did not want this, but perhaps these events indicate two things that had happened since the Transfiguration. On the one hand the faith of John and his brother in Jesus and his glory was greatly increased. They believed that they could call down fire as Jesus' disciples and they knew there would be a glory in which they would participate. On the other hand, along with this, there was a sinful arrogance and still a surprising inability to come to terms with the way of suffering and servanthood.

The closeness of John to Jesus is seen in other incidents as well. Mark 13:3 records John's presence in a conversation with Jesus about the signs of the end of the age. Luke 22:8 tells us that it was Peter and John who were asked to prepare the Passover feast at the end of Jesus' ministry. If we are right in assuming that John was 'the disciple whom Jesus loved' then he was the one who was reclining close to Jesus at that final meal together and asked him who the betrayer was (John 13:23–24). A little later it was Peter, James and John whom Jesus specially took aside with him in the Garden of Gethsemane and to whom he revealed the depth of his distress and trouble before the arrest and crucifixion (Mark 14:33).

### John in the book of Acts

It is interesting that in the book of Acts, it is John, rather than James, who figures prominently with Peter. He is listed after Peter when the disciples in the upper room are mentioned in Acts 1:13. Then, after the Day of Pentecost, it was Peter and John who were prominent in early apostolic miracles (Acts 3:1–5, 11). They thus specially came in for criticism from the Jewish authorities and were arrested (Acts 4). The rulers in the Sanhedrin were specially impressed with the two apostles when they realized that 'they were unschooled, ordinary men' and 'they took note that these men had been with Jesus' (Acts 4:13). This continual witness for Jesus even to the point of persecution rapidly became a feature of early apostolic ministry and John's strength of faith shines through (Acts 4:19, 21–23).

John also joined Peter in being sent from Jerusalem to see what was going on among Samaritans who were turning to Christ. He and Peter laid hands on the Samaritans so that those who had faith in Christ were seen to receive the Holy Spirit just as the converted Jews in Jerusalem had received the Spirit on the Day of Pentecost (Acts 8:14, 17, 25).

### John's writings

There has always been debate about which books of the NT the apostle John wrote. However, traditionally the Gospel and Epistles of John have been ascribed to the apostle John. There has been more debate about the book of Revelation because it is possible that it was another John who wrote it. Below it is assumed that the apostle was responsible for this writing and it is important to take note, albeit very briefly, of some of his teaching.

### The Gospel

The Gospel of John is surprisingly different from the Synoptic Gospels (Matthew, Mark, Luke). For example, it is really only from John's Gospel that we gather Jesus must have had nearly a three-year ministry. John records long disputes between the Jews of his day and Jesus in a detail not really seen in the other Gospels. John does not recount exorcisms and although in John's Gospel we see how Jesus used the miracles like parables from which he taught lessons, nevertheless there are no pithy quick parables like the Kingdom parables in *Matt. 13*. The prologue in *John 1* has no parallel in the other Gospels. However, John's Gospel does recount other incidents and offers particularly deep analysis and reflection on the teaching of Jesus. For many, the differences between John and the other Gospels, the apparently deeper reflection on who Jesus is, and some of the particular issues that John develops, have led them to believe the Gospel may have been written as late as the AD 90s. However, other scholars have suggested a much earlier date.

Although we cannot enter the debate here, there are good reasons for supposing that the apostle did write this Gospel and that it shows evidence of the hand of an eye-witness and someone who was well aware of Jewish customs and Palestinian practices and geography.

Various reasons have been suggested as to why John would have written this Gospel, but *John 20:31* does give a fairly clear indication of what the apostle had in mind: 'these [signs] are written that you may believe that Jesus is the Christ, the Son of God, and that by believing you may have life in his name'. The Gospel focuses on a number of 'signs'. These were miracles that John specially selected because of what they taught about Jesus. They are sometimes accompanied by a 'discourse' in which Jesus used the miracle as a basis for teaching. For example the healing of the man at the pool of Bethesda in *John 5* leads into Jesus' teaching that what he does is what the Father does (*vv. 17, 19–23*). This leads into teaching about the need to believe in Jesus' word and in the Father who sent him in order to receive eternal life (*vv. 24–30*).

The feeding of the 5,000 in *John 6* leads into a discourse on Jesus being 'the bread of life' (*v. 35*). This theme is developed at length showing people again how they need to come to Jesus and respond to him in faith. Those who do this will receive 'eternal life' (see below). Jesus' words, his teaching, are 'bread' and 'spirit and life' (*vv. 33, 63*). In *John 9* the healing of the blind man leads to a discussion of spiritual blindness. The Pharisees objected most strongly to the plain teaching of Jesus that they were the ones who were spiritually blind for they had refused to believe in him (*vv. 35–41*). Probably John intended the resurrection to be the great culmination of his list of 'signs'. His greatest desire was that people should have this believing faith in Jesus the Messiah and know forgiveness of their sins and eternal life. *John 20:31* might be translated as 'these [signs] are written that you may believe that Jesus is the Christ' or 'these [signs] are written that you may continue to believe that Jesus is the

Christ', either way the apostle's concern is that people know who Jesus is, believe in him and receive eternal life.

The Gospel also contrasts true faith with what might be called human wisdom. On several occasions people took Jesus at a material and literal level when he was talking at a more profound and spiritual level. By making this contrast John demonstrates the need for a change of heart, and for the work of the Spirit in regeneration, if an individual is to understand and acknowledge the truth. For example, in John 3 Jesus taught Nicodemus that he must be born again, by which Jesus meant the Holy Spirit had to work in his life. Nicodemus could not understand how a person could enter the womb again (*vv. 3–4*)! The Samaritan woman heard from Jesus that he could offer 'living water' which, if drunk, would mean a person never needed to drink again. She immediately wanted such water to save her having to make the trip to the well. Jesus was talking about water that led to 'eternal life' (*vv. 13–15*). Even when Jesus taught about the bread of life in John 6 still, like Nicodemus in John 3, the religious leaders could only think literally. They remembered the miracle of food provision that happened under Moses in the wilderness, but Jesus was talking of food in the form of his words leading to eternal life (see *Deut. 8:3*).

The Gospel also draws attention to Jesus' prayer at the end of his life in John 17 where we learn about those who will believe in later generations. Jesus' concern as he prayed was that they too might know of Christ's glory and of his relation to the Father.

This is but some of the content of this Gospel (see 'John's teaching' below) which throughout provokes serious thought about who Jesus is, about the nature of eternal life, and above all about the need for faith.


### The Epistles

There are three epistles of John. Although he never actually says who he is, in 2 and 3 John he calls himself 'the elder'. Some have therefore suggested that this John was not the apostle but one who should be called 'John the elder'. However, from the earliest days people have accepted that the author was the apostle. 1 John was probably written to a mixed audience of converted Jews and Gentiles. It may be that, if John lived in Ephesus later in his life as early Christian writers suggest, then this epistle would have been circulated to churches in that area. 1 John encouraged fellowship and joy in the church and sought to encourage the congregation to have assurance in their faith. But John also tackled the problem of certain false teachings that were beginning to have an impact. Two key themes that come through the epistle probably indicate two areas that false teachers were getting wrong. John taught about who Jesus is. He emphasized that he had *seen* Jesus and the events that gave rise to the Gospel message (1 John 1:1–4). He stressed that Jesus is the Son of God (1 John 1:3; 2:22; 5:5, 11), and reminded his readers that Jesus is pre-existent (he lived with God forever before being born on earth, 1 John 2:13–14). John also taught that Jesus will come again, that he is righteous and perfect and truly came in human flesh. Secondly John emphasized ethics, how Christians should behave given that they have such a wonderful Lord. Christians should live righteously (1 John 1:6–2:6, 15–17; 3:4–10). They should love each other as Jesus has loved them

(1 John 4:19; 2:7–11 etc.). The other two epistles of John emphasize similar themes with great emphasis on love among Christians and truth as the only adequate response to false teachers. 3 John seems to be directed at a particular ecclesiastical dispute and yet still the emphasis is there on 'the truth' (3 John 3–4, 12), and the lack of love is noted (vv. 9–10).

## The Book of Revelation

Few books of the Bible are more marvellous than the Book of Revelation and yet few have caused more debate as people have struggled to understand the imagery used in so much of the writing. This book was clearly written towards the end of the apostle's life during a period of intense persecution; some have suggested the time around Nero's persecutions of the Christians in (AD 54–68). Most feel that it is more likely to have come from the time of Domitian (AD 81–96). No matter how difficult some of the concepts and teachings in this book, there is a clear feel throughout of a pastor writing to a people suffering in various ways under persecution and the infiltration of false teaching. In spite of the difficulties John was not pessimistic about the world. For him the victory was already to be found in the Lamb (Jesus) who was slain as a sacrifice for sins and who had already defeated Satan (Rev. 5). This victory of Christ on the cross is now being worked out in this world by the church. There is even victory to be found in martyrdom since such witness to the truth of Christ (who has authority and has come) demonstrates God's victory (Rev. 12:11). Some of the style of the book has been called apocalyptic, but it is important also to see that it is written in a way that is similar to OT prophecy. There is an authority in John's teaching that is distinctly prophetic and apostolic. The book describes both the evil of Satan and his forces and the power they have in this world, but all the way through John trusted the sovereignty of God that inexorably leads on to the final great day of Christ's return when the new heavens and new earth will be established and Satan and evil will be banished for ever. At that time death and mourning, suffering and pain will be gone and God will be in the midst of the people (Rev. 21:3–4).

## John's teaching

It is only possible here to summarize some of the more important features of John's teaching. His reflection, under the Holy Spirit's guidance, on who Jesus is and on the believer's relationship to this world, to Jesus, and to the rest of the Christian church is extended and detailed.

### About Jesus

John 1 tells us much of John's thinking about Jesus. John knew Jesus as God. John 1:14 sums up much of what he wants to say: 'The Word became flesh and made his dwelling among us. We have seen his glory, the glory of the One and Only, who came from the Father, full of grace and truth'. Drawing on the OT picture of the Tabernacle tent in which God's glory was symbolically seen to dwell in the midst of his people in the form of the pillar of fire and the cloud, John says the Word (Jesus) came and 'pitched his tent' among us. Jesus became man and so it was possible to see in Jesus a glory that was uniquely God's (e.g. *Exod. 40:34; Num. 16:42; John 12:41* etc.). John teaches that Jesus brings people to worship God as he reveals the glory of the Father but that the glory of God belongs to the Son as well (*John 8:50–54; 11:4, 40–42; 14:13* etc.). Jesus did possess the Father's glory before he was born and received again his full glory when he ascended to heaven and was exalted at God's right hand (*John 17:5, 24*). John also teaches that, just as Jesus brought glory to the Father and had his own glory, so the Spirit will come and bring glory to the Son (*John 16:14*).

Jesus' pre-existence is probably more clearly taught in John's writings than anywhere else in the NT. He existed from eternity and not just since he became a man here on earth (*John 1:1, 4, 14; 3:17; 17:5, 24; 1 John 3:8; 4:9*). He was also directly involved with creation itself for 'Through him all things were made . . . in him was life' (*John 1:3–4*). Jesus 'appeared' (*1 John 1:2*) and was 'sent' by God the Father with whom he had a very special relationship (*John 8:42; 11:42; 1 John 4:14*).

His standing as 'Son of God' is also a special theme in John's Gospel in which the close relationship between the Father and the Son is especially demonstrated. Indeed the purpose of the Gospel, says John (*John 20:31*), is 'that you may believe that Jesus is the Christ, the Son of God, and that by believing you may have life in his name'. John shows that all Jesus said pointed to his unique standing as the 'Son of God'. From Jesus' insistence that the words he spoke and the deeds he performed were the Father's words and works (*John 14:10* etc.), through to his great prayer in *John 17*, we are repeatedly shown the intimacy of Christ's relationship with his Father and its importance in terms of our understanding of who Jesus is. It is John who related the occasion when Jesus turned to Philip and said: 'Don't you know me, Philip, even after I have been among you such a long time? Anyone who has seen me has seen the Father. How can you say, "Show us the Father"?' (*John 14:9*). He went on to say: 'Don't you believe that I am in the Father, and that the Father is in me? The words I say to you are not just my own. Rather, it is the Father, living in me, who is doing his work' (*v. 10*).

For John it was important that his readers come to understand that Jesus is God. The emphasis on Jesus' authority as 'Son of God', on his being 'sent' by God, on his being the Messiah (*John 1:41; 4:29; 20:31* etc.), his teaching in *John 14–17* of his intimate and pre-existent relationship with the Father, all provide an accumulation of evidence that Jesus is God. For John this teaching is summed up in his statements like that found in *John 1:14* and *20:31*. But John also especially drew attention to the number of times Jesus made relatively explicit claims to be God that immediately caused the religious leaders to accuse him of blasphemy. The most important of those statements included Jesus' use of the words 'I am' in certain contexts which identified him with Yahweh the 'I am' God (see *Exod. 3:14*). For example, in *John 8:58* we read: '"I tell you the truth," Jesus answered, "before Abraham was born, I am!"' This seems to be both a claim to pre-existence and to divinity by assuming the name of God.

John's most distinctive teaching about Jesus was that he is the 'Word' (*Logos*). Although some have debated about the background from which John drew this description of Jesus, a couple of points can be made. In *John 1* 'the Word' was with God, was God, and created everything. In *Gen.1* God spoke and the world was created. *Ps. 33:6* says: 'By the word of the LORD were the heavens made'. God's word is active in the OT. When God speaks it happens. Certainly this OT background lies behind some of what John was teaching in calling Jesus 'the Word'. Perhaps John was also thinking of a contrast between Jesus and the OT Law which was called God's 'Word'. This comparison is made in *John 1:17* at the end of the section in which Jesus, 'the Word', is introduced. John's main concern was that his readers come to know Jesus as the creating and revealing Word who came from glory in heaven and genuinely and completely became human and lived in this world. True God, the creating God, the pre-existent God, became a man who could be as hungry as anyone else, and who genuinely suffered. This Jesus, so glorious in all his truth, and perfection was seen, could be touched and his word was heard (*1 John 1:1*). Through belief in him and him alone it is possible, said John, for all to receive forgiveness and eternal life. Jesus, the sacrifice for sins brought salvation and deliverance so that none should 'perish' under God's judgment (*John 3:16–17*). What greater love is there, asked John, than this love of God who sends his only Son as an 'atoning sacrifice' for sin (*1 John 4:9–10*)?

### About sin and the world

This leads us to John's view of this world and sin. The word 'world' can refer to the geographical world or all people in the world but often it was used by John to describe the world that does not acknowledge Jesus as the Son of God and is in rebellion against him (*John 1:10; 14:17; 1 John 2:15–17; Rev. 12:9* etc.). Jesus is 'the light that shines in the darkness, but the darkness has not understood it' (*John 1:5*). Satan is described as 'the prince of this world' (*John 12:31*), and the world is full of sin which will one day be judged. False prophets are but one sign of the great extent of evil (*1 John 4:1–6*). Jesus had to come to bring salvation to a world that was standing under the judgment of God and John showed that Jesus had indeed overcome the world (*1 John 2:13; 5:4; Rev. 17:14* etc.). His victory over sin and the world and Satan was won on the cross and will finally be revealed at the second coming (*Rev. 21* etc.).

### About the Holy Spirit

John also wrote much about Jesus' teaching on the Holy Spirit. The Holy Spirit came on Jesus at his baptism by John the Baptist. John alone among the Gospel writers links that baptism to the fact that Jesus will himself baptize not with water alone but with the Holy Spirit (*John 1:31–34*; see *Luke 3:16*). Perhaps John was looking forward to Pentecost or even to the upper room experience following the resurrection when Jesus stood among his disciples and said: 'And with that he breathed on them and said, "Receive the Holy Spirit. If you forgive anyone his sins, they are forgiven; if you do not forgive them, they are not forgiven"' (*John 20:22*; see also *7:39*).

In *John 3* the writer tells of the encounter between Nicodemus and Jesus. The Spirit's work in salvation and providing eternal life is emphasized as Jesus showed Nicodemus he needed to be 'born again' and 'born of the Spirit'. The complete freedom the Spirit exercises in this work of regeneration was also highlighted (*John 3:3, 6, 8*).

The most interesting extended teaching on the Holy Spirit in John's writings occurs in *John 14–16*. There on five occasions the Spirit is called in Greek 'the Paraclete' (NIV: 'Counsellor'). This word really means 'one who comes alongside' but also has in mind the idea of a legal advocate or lawyer who argues a defendant's case. In *John 14:16–17* the 'Spirit of truth' is called 'another Counsellor'. He will come to people once the present counsellor, Jesus, has been glorified, that is, after he has ascended to heaven. His continual presence will be known by all the disciples and believers and thus Jesus himself will continue to be among his people by his Spirit. Apart from the Holy Spirit's work as God who is among his people, the Spirit also teaches about Jesus. Probably in a direct reference to the apostolic work of interpreting the life, death and resurrection of Christ to the wider world, Jesus told his disciples: 'But the Counsellor, the Holy Spirit, whom the Father will send in my name, will teach you all things and will remind you of everything I have said to you' (*John 14:26*). This was no doubt of particular importance to John who later wrote so much to so many explaining about Jesus and the way of salvation, but also because during Jesus' life-time John, as we noted above, had not grasped much of what Jesus' mission really was.

John further drew attention to Jesus' teaching that the Spirit would empower believers for witnessing (*John 15:26–27*). More than that, however, these verses point to the fact that, in all the Spirit does, he witnesses to and brings glory to Jesus. In *John 16:5–11* the work of the Spirit is further amplified. His work will bring conviction of sin to the world and warning of judgment and he will draw attention to Christ's defeat of Satan (*John 16:5–11*). Once again the Spirit's work is seen to continue the work of Christ himself. But the work will also develop what Jesus had been able to teach the disciples to this point. The Spirit will 'guide you into all truth' and will further reveal the truth about Jesus to the glory of Jesus (*John 16:12–15*).

John taught that the Spirit is intimately involved in the work of the gospel. He convicts people of their sin, works within them so they can be born again, reveals the truth about Christ to them, and remains with them until Christ returns. His work points people to Christ and brings them to him.

### About eternal life

Eternal life is an important theme in John's Gospel. While Matthew, Mark and Luke teach about the Kingdom of God (or heaven), John tends to favour the expression 'eternal life' which occurs 22 times in the Gospel and *1 John*. For John eternal life sums up all the blessings inherited by those who believe and are saved through Christ. The concept arises out of the teaching that starts in *John 1* that in Jesus is life (*John 1:4; 5:21, 26* etc.). People can remain in darkness and under judgment or they can believe in Jesus and his Father and receive eternal life. Those who believe 'have crossed from death to life' (*John 5:24; 8:12; 1 John 5:13*). When the Jews thought that they had eternal life through their obedience to Scripture, Jesus told them that the Scriptures pointed to himself in whom is life (*John 5:39–40; 1 John 5:11, 20*). Closely tied to this teaching about eternal life is the fact that Christ died as a sacrifice for others. He laid down his life in order that those who believe should have eternal life (*John 10:10–18, 28*). Eternal life is, thus, a gift from God received by those who have been born again of the Spirit (*Rev. 22:17*).

There are many present joys and blessings attached in John's teaching to eternal life. Although all the joys await their fulfilment at the return of Christ, nevertheless the present experience of eternal life is real enough. The fear of death and judgment no longer hangs over the believer for the true love of God has been experienced (*John 3:16–17, 36*). There is joy in both telling others of eternal life and in knowing Christ who is life (*John 4:36; 5:24*). There is the joy of knowing both God the Father and God the Son (*John 17:3, 6–7*) and there is the great comfort of knowing God's anointing of the Holy Spirit living in the believer's life (*1 John 2:25–27*).

Finally, it is most important to John that the goal of eternal life is the everlasting presence of believers in a new heaven and a new earth with God in the midst. The eternal life which starts now by the work of the Spirit in their hearts leads to its glorious culmination when 'they will be his people, and God himself will be with them and be their God' (*Rev. 21:3*). On that last day, though persecuted at present, Christians will receive the 'crown of life' (*Rev. 2:10*). Though so distressed in this world, they will be 'dressed in white' and their names will never be blotted out from 'the book of life' (*Rev. 3:5 etc.*).

### Conclusion

Throughout John's life and teaching it was his commitment to Jesus Christ that is most impressive. Whether it was during the life of Jesus, or soon after Pentecost during the persecutions, or later as he wrote his Gospel, Epistles and Revelation, his earnest desire was to see people come to faith in Christ and to continue to follow Christ in their faith and their life. He longed for people to know this Jesus he had known, heard and touched. It is not inappropriate that both the Gospel and Revelation end with an appeal to come to faith: This is 'written that you may believe that Jesus is the Christ, the Son of God, and that by believing you may have life in his name' (*John 20:31*). 'The Spirit and the bride say, "Come!" And let him who hears say, "Come!" Whoever is thirsty, let him come; and whoever wishes, let him take the free gift of the water of life' (*Rev. 22:17*). P.D.G.

### JOHN THE BAPTIST

According to *Luke 1*, the birth of John – which took place approximately six months before the birth of Jesus – was the result of direct divine intervention and signalled a momentous event in the history of redemption. A priest named Zechariah and his barren wife Elizabeth, who made their home in the hill-country south of Jerusalem, were well advanced in years and had led lives devoted to the commandments of God. During one of the weeks when Zechariah was ministering in Jerusalem, he received the rare privilege of offering the incense in the Temple, an act that symbolized the prayers of God's people.

While performing this duty, an angel appeared to him and announced that his prayers were going to be answered, for Elizabeth would have a child. The text does not actually say that Zechariah and Elizabeth were praying for a child, although it is reasonable to suppose that they had. Luke does make a point of reminding us, however, that the people outside the Temple were praying, and we have some evidence that one important element in ancient Jewish prayer was the hope that God would bring salvation to them.

The further words from the angel, moreover, make clear that God was about to grant both wishes. In effect, it was precisely by giving a child to Zechariah and Elizabeth that the final stages of redemption would be set in motion. When the angel explained that the child would turn the hearts of the fathers to the children and thus make ready a people for the Messiah, he indicated that through the ministry of John the last prophecy of the last of the OT prophets was about to be fulfilled (*Mal. 4*).

This truth was emphasized soon after the child was born, at the time of his circumcision. Zechariah, who had not been able to speak from the point when he received the vision (*Luke 1:20*), was suddenly released from that affliction, and, under the power of the Spirit, gave praise to God for bringing salvation to his people. The Lord had remembered his covenant to Abraham, and John would go before the Lord by giving his people 'the knowledge of salvation through the forgiveness of their sins' (*Luke 1:67–79*). *Luke 1* ends by telling us that John 'lived in the desert until he appeared publicly to Israel' (*v. 80*).

The ministry of John the Baptist is described briefly in all four Gospels. The narratives of the so-called Synoptic Gospels are very similar to each other, presenting John as a preacher of repentance who took as his motto the words from *Is. 40:3*, 'A voice of one calling in the desert, "Prepare the way for the LORD, make straight paths for him"' (see *Matt. 3:1–3; Mark 1:2–4; Luke 3:3–6*). Because that passage played an important role in the community that preserved the Dead Sea Scrolls (that is, in Qumran, which was close to the area where John ministered), some scholars have speculated that John may have been a member of this community.

Of course, it is impossible to prove or disprove this theory, although we can hardly doubt that John would have had at least some acquaintance with the group. What matters, however, is that the distinctives of his preaching were quite different from what one finds among the writings of the Qumran community. Their use of *Is. 40:3* reflected their separation from the nation of Israel, which they considered to be apostate. Indeed, they prepared the way of the Lord by rejecting the nation, withdrawing to the wilderness, and forming what they would have considered a new Israel.

In contrast – perhaps in direct opposition to the views of the Qumranites – John used *Is. 40:3* with an evangelistic aim. To be sure, John could speak harshly to those whose behaviour was reprehensible and who thought they had nothing to fear simply because they were descendants of Abraham. For the likes of such people, John's ministry – symbolized by the picture of an axe being laid at the root of the tree that is about to be cut down – was a harbinger of judgment (*Matt. 3:7–10; Luke 3:7–9*). Yet even to them he preached repentance and the promise of forgiveness and restoration.

The people's confession of sin, and thus their repentance and forgiveness, was ratified by baptism. The use of water rituals was not uncommon in Judaism (including Qumran). Cleansing from the impurities of sin was certainly one of the ideas conveyed by this ceremony. However, in view of the associations of water with Noah's Flood and the destruction of the Egyptians in the Red Sea, John's baptism was probably intended also to remind the people that sin requires divine judgment (cf. 1 Pet. 3:20–21; note also the connection between baptism and the bloody rite of circumcision in Col. 2:11–15, which points out that the judgment has been borne by Christ).

John himself understood and made clear that his preaching and baptism were meant to prepare the way for the coming of the Lord: 'I baptize you with water for repentance. But after me will come one who is more powerful than I, whose sandals I am not fit to carry. He will baptize you with the Holy Spirit and with fire' (Matt. 3:11; cf. Mark 1:7–8; Luke 3:16). Jesus, as the one called to bear the sufferings of the people, submitted himself to John's baptism, at which time a voice from heaven and the descent of the Holy Spirit made clear that Jesus was the one for whom the way was being prepared (Matt. 3:13–17; Mark 1:9–11; Luke 3:21–22).

John the Baptist's role in announcing the coming of the Messiah is emphasized especially by the Gospel of John (see esp. 1:19–34). When questioned whether he himself was the Messiah, he strongly denied it and instead pointed people to Jesus, whom he described as 'the Lamb of God, who takes away the sin of the world' (v. 29). Later in the same Gospel he is reported to have said regarding Jesus, 'He must become greater; I must become less' (John 3:30). In other words, the public appearing of the Lord, for whom he had prepared the way, marked the concluding stage of John the Baptist's ministry. This point needs to be stressed. John's period of service appears to have been very brief, and that fact helps us understand the theological significance of his ministry (as the following material further indicates).

Quite soon after Jesus was baptized, John was put in prison because he had rebuked Herod Antipas, ruler of Galilee and Perea (Matt. 4:12; Mark 1:14; Luke 3:19–20). Some time later, news of Jesus' growing ministry reached John, who proceeded to send two of his own disciples to Jesus with this question: 'Are you the one who was to come, or should we expect someone else?' (Matt. 11:2; Luke 7:18–19). Some readers have made much of John's apparent doubts about Jesus. Was he discouraged or even experiencing a spiritual crisis? The text does not tell us, but a reasonable explanation is that John may have expected the Messiah to take up the axe already laid at the root of the tree and bring judgment on the wicked. Since Jesus was doing nothing of the sort, John may have needed some reassurance or at least some clarification of the Messiah's role.

Jesus' response was in effect to point out how the Messianic works prophesied in Is. 61:1 were now being fulfilled (Matt. 11:4–6; Luke 7:21–23). What interests us here, however, is the sequel to this incident, for Jesus took the opportunity to speak about the significance of John the Baptist (Matt. 11:7–19; Luke 7:24–35). Through a series of rhetorical questions, Jesus indicated that John was not a delicate or easily intimidated man, nor was he someone interested in courting the good graces of powerful people. Quite the contrary. John was a prophet – indeed, his ministry had greater significance than that of the other prophets, for he was the Elijah promised in Mal. 3:1, the messenger who would prepare the Lord's way.

It was in this context that Jesus made the remarkable comment: 'Among those born of women there has not risen anyone greater than John the Baptist; yet he who is least in the kingdom of heaven is greater than he' (*Matt. 11:11; Luke 7:28*, 'in the kingdom of God'). Of course, Jesus was not suggesting that John the Baptist would not enter heaven. The point is rather that John, who had announced the coming of the Kingdom, did not have the opportunity to experience it because he belonged to an earlier era. On the other hand, those who receive the good news of the Messiah, and thus participate by faith in the blessings he brings, belong to a new and different age.

Matthew helps us to understand that Jesus' words have an 'eschatological' meaning (that is, they refer to the end-time fulfilment of the OT promises in the person of the Messiah) by recording another statement: 'From the days of John the Baptist until now, the kingdom of heaven has been forcefully advancing, and forceful men lay hold of it. For all the Prophets and the Law prophesied until John' (*Matt. 11:12*; Luke records the same basic saying, but in different form, in *16:16*, 'The Law and the Prophets were proclaimed until John. Since that time, the good news of the kingdom of God is being preached, and everyone is forcing his way into it').

Although this is a very difficult saying, and scholars are not agreed regarding some important details, the central idea is clear enough. John the Baptist occupies a unique position in the history of redemption. He is the last of the OT prophets, and as such he paves the way for the new era, the time of the fulfilment of the Kingdom. One should therefore not be surprised if Jesus' ministry looks quite different from that of John (see *Matt. 11:18–19*).

In another context, Jesus was asked why his disciples did not fast, even though the disciples of John (and of the Pharisees) did. Jesus' response included an interesting comparison: 'No one sews a patch of unshrunk cloth on an old garment, for the patch will pull away from the garment, making the tear worse. Neither do men pour new wine into old wineskins. If they do, the skins will burst, the wine will run out and the wineskins will be ruined. No, they pour new wine into new wineskins, and both are preserved' (*Matt. 9:16–17; Mark 2:21–22; Luke 5:36–39*). Here again Jesus was making clear that the distinctiveness of his work, compared with that of John, was its newness.

It would have been a great mistake to reject the ministry of Jesus on the grounds that it was different from that of John the Baptist. After all, John was not the true light but only a witness to it (*John 1:8*). On the other hand, we can hardly minimize the significance of his prophetic ministry. Not surprisingly, John's influence extended beyond the time of his death. (His infamous decapitation, by request of Salome, is related in *Matt. 14:3–12; Mark 6:14–29*). This influence was not confined to Palestine. According to *Acts 19:1–7*, there was in Ephesus, as late as the AD 50s, a group of people who considered themselves disciples of John the Baptist. Once they received proper instruction from Paul regarding the distinctive ministry of Christ, they were baptized in his name and received the Holy Spirit. That incident marks, in a dramatic way, the fulfilment of John's own wish, 'He must become greater; I must become less.'                    M.S.

**JOHN** **1.** See *John, the Apostle.*

**2.** See *John the Baptist.*

**3.** John the father of Simon Peter and Andrew is also called Jonah in *Matt. 16:17.* He was a Galilean fisherman. It is interesting to note that on each of the three occasions in the Gospel when Jesus called Peter by the full name, 'Simon son of John (Jonah)', it marked turning points in Peter's life. On the first occasion Andrew introduced his brother Simon to 'the Messiah', Jesus. Jesus looked at Simon and prophetically announced '"You are Simon son of John. You will be called Cephas" (which, when translated, is Peter)' (*John 1:42*). From that time onwards Simon Peter followed Christ. On the second occasion the full name was used, Peter had just responded to a question from Jesus by saying, 'You are the Christ, the Son of the living God'. The significance of this identification of Jesus as the Christ was so great that Jesus said: 'Blessed are you, Simon son of Jonah, for this was not revealed to you by man, but by my Father in heaven' (*Matt. 16:16–17*). The last occasion followed the resurrection when Jesus tested Peter's love for him and commissioned him with the words: 'Simon son of John . . . Feed my lambs' (*John 21:15–17*).

**4.** John, a relation of Annas the high priest, is mentioned only in *Acts 4:6.* This John was one of the rulers and elders before whom the apostles, Peter and John, were brought for questioning. The preaching of these apostles was beginning to disturb deeply the religious leaders and so they tried to silence Peter and John. The apostles' response was to say that they had to obey God rather than the religious leaders (*v. 19*). Eventually, feeling the weight of public opinion, the elders and rulers released the two.

P.D.G.

**JOHN MARK** See *Mark, John.*

**JOIADA** (Heb., 'the LORD knows').

**1.** Joiada son of Paseah was one of those who returned from the captivity in Babylon and helped to rebuild the walls of Jerusalem. He repaired the Jeshanah Gate (*Neh. 3:6*).

**2.** The son of Eliashib and father of Jonathan. Eliashib was one of the high priests in the days of Nehemiah. Nehemiah had to drive away from him one of Joiada's sons because he was son-in-law to Sanballat (*Neh. 12:10–11, 22; 13:28*).

**JOIAKIM,** (Heb., 'the LORD raises up') became a high priest following the rebuilding of the Temple after the Exile in Babylon. He was the father of the high priest Eliashib and son of Jeshua (*Neh. 12:10, 12, 26*).

**JOIARIB** (Heb., 'the LORD contends').

**1.** A leader among his people and a man of learning, he was one of the Jews who returned from the Babylonian captivity to Jerusalem with Ezra. He helped Ezra find suitable Levites to accompany them back to Judah (*Ezra 8:16*).

**2.** The father of Adaiah and son of Zechariah, this Joiarib was a descendant of Perez from the tribe of Judah. His descendants settled in Jerusalem on the return from the Exile in Babylon (*Neh. 11:5*).

**3.** The father of Jedaiah, this Joiarib was a priest whose son also returned to Jerusalem following the Exile (*Neh. 11:10; 12:6*).

**JOKIM** (Heb., 'the LORD exalts'). Mentioned in *1 Chron. 4:22.* A leader in the tribe of Judah and a son of Shelah. Together with others he is listed as being among the potters who lived in Moab.

**JOKSHAN** One of Abraham's sons by his wife Keturah (*Gen. 25:2–3*). He appears in a list of Abraham's descendants bridging, in the narrative of *Gen. 24–25*, the death of Sarah and the death of Abraham (also 1 Chron. 1:32). His sons were Sheba and Dedan.

**JOKTAN** The son of Eber and a descendant of Shem, Joktan was the father of 13 sons who gave their names to various clans that lived in the 'eastern hill country' (Gen. 10:25–26, 29; 1 Chron. 1:19–20, 23). These clans later became Arabian tribes.

**JONADAB** (Heb., 'the LORD is bounteous').

**1.** Jonadab son of Shimeah, was David's brother and was 'very shrewd' (2 Sam. 13:3, 5). He helped Amnon get Tamar to his bedroom where Amnon raped her. When Absalom later murdered Amnon in revenge, David imagined the worst. Jonadab was able to reassure David that Absalom had only killed Amnon and not 'all the princes' (vv. 32, 35).

**2.** Jonadab son of Recab was a Kenite and a leader of the Recabites. He is referred to in Jer. 35:6, 8, 10 etc. Also known as Jehonadab, he supported Jehu against Ahab. With great zeal for the LORD the two of them killed all the prophets of Baal (2 Kings 10:15–16, 23–28) and did much to promote true worship in Israel. For more detail about his descendants and their strict life style and concern for the law, see Recab 3. and Jehonadab. Because of the commitment of Jonadab's descendants to a godly lifestyle and the example they set for Judah, Jeremiah brought them the word of the LORD: 'Jonadab son of Recab will never fail to have a man to serve me' (Jer. 35:19).                    P.D.G.

## JONAH THE PROPHET

From Hebrew meaning 'dove', Jonah's name appears to be singularly ironic in light of the prophet's stubborn and recalcitrant spirit on the one hand and the harshness of his message to Nineveh on the other. The name may reflect the wishes of his parents for a docile, peaceful son or, perhaps, it is an epithet later applied to him in light of his calling to bear the message of the LORD far and wide.

Identified as a 'son of Amittai' (Jon. 1:1), Jonah was from the small village of Gath Hepher (2 Kings 14:25) in the tribal district of Zebulun (Josh. 19:13), some three miles north of Nazareth. It is worth noting that he was the only prophet of the OT from the Galilean region, an area known even in pre-Christian times for its large non-Hebrew population (cf. Is. 9:1). Perhaps this is one reason the LORD called him to minister to the pagan city Nineveh, for if any prophet was suited for such a task it should be one already familiar with foreign thought and customs.

Though Jonah's ministry to Nineveh is generally thought to have been unsuccessful, at least in terms of how he responded to and was shaped by it, it is important to note that he was instrumental in enlarging Israel's borders in the days of Jeroboam II (793–753 BC), a fact noted in 2 Kings 14:25. Apparently through his words of encouragement Jeroboam recovered land previously lost to the Arameans (cf. 2 Kings 10:32–33) and thereby brought back some of the glory of the days of David and Solomon (cf. 1 Kings 8:65).

Jonah's linkage with Jeroboam II provides at least a general chronological framework for his ministry. The scope narrows somewhat when the dates of Jeroboam's sole regency (782–753 BC) are considered. A year midpoint in that reign would be c. 768, a date most compatible with the situation described in the book and in documents from the Ancient Near East. More specifically, the narrative speaks of Nineveh's favourable response to Jonah's message, one that manifests itself in wholesale repentance from the king to the lowliest citizen (*Jon. 3:5–9*). Regardless of the nature of the repentance – whether genuine or only superficial – or of its lasting effects, it clearly must have followed some sense of foreboding and should be reflected to some extent in contemporary accounts.

Of all the documents of the relevant period (i.e. from 782–753 BC), the Assyrian Eponym Lists are most enlightening regarding the matter at hand. These consist of listings of all the years of the Neo-Assyrian Empire from 892–648 BC, giving the name of the official for whom the year was named and usually some significant event of that year. It is interesting to observe that Assyria was wracked with revolt and plague in every year from 763 to 758 BC. This period was during the reign of Assur-dan III (773–756), a time of such turmoil that hardly a text has survived to attest to any successes whatsoever. It is tempting, therefore, to view Jonah's ministry against this socio-political background.

The historical evidences notwithstanding, it is customary to regard the account of Jonah, if not the prophet himself, as fictional. At best, some argue, the book is an allegory or parable designed to teach some lesson or other, perhaps that the God of Israel is the God of all peoples or that Israel, like Jonah, must be swallowed up by the nations and regurgitated as a chastened, more compliant servant of the LORD. This does not appear to be the viewpoint of the book itself, however, for in addition to the lack of any genre clues to that effect, the NT makes it clear that Jesus understood the book to be historically factual. In speaking of his anticipated death and resurrection he said: 'For as Jonah was three days and three nights in the belly of a huge fish, so the Son of Man will be three days and three nights in the heart of the earth' (*Matt. 12:40*). He also referred to the repentance of Nineveh as an incentive for repentance in his own time (*v. 41*) and, just as remarkably, about Jonah himself being a sign to Nineveh (*Matt. 12:39; cf. Luke 11:30*). All of this suggests that the NT tradition at least took the Jonah story to be authentically historical.

Jonah as a 'sign' may imply more than merely the supernatural nature of his salvation from the sea and his ultimate arrival back on shore. It may also reflect ancient Assyrian legends as to the founding of the city of Nineveh by Oannes, the Greek form of Akkadian Ea. Oannes is described in ancient texts as being part fish and part man and, indeed, the cuneiform sign for the name Nineveh (Ninua or Nina in Assyrian) consists of a combination of two signs, one being *KU* ('fish') and the other being perhaps *ES* ('house' or 'place'). This would yield a meaning for 'Nineveh' as 'place of fish' or the like. Clearly Jonah's connection with a great fish would not be lost on those of Nineveh who knew the legends of their city's founding. In any event, Jesus linked Jonah as a sign to the conversion of Nineveh and then informed his critics that they would be given a sign no different from that, namely, his own death, burial, and resurrection. Sadly, he anticipated that that sign would not be effective in eliciting faith in those who were indisposed to believe (*Matt. 12:41; cf. Luke 16:31*).

Despite the apparent success of his mission Jonah failed as a man of God, at least as far as the canonical account is concerned. Having preached a message of judgment (*Jon. 3:4*), he was bitterly disappointed when the recipients of his message repented and were spared divine wrath (*Jon. 3:10–4:2*). In fact, he pleaded with God to let him die. The embarrassment of having preached a word that was overturned by God's intervention with mercy and grace was more than he could tolerate (*Jon. 4:3, 8*).

Jonah's 'failure' was God's success, however, for the conversion of a pagan city demonstrated a central theological thrust of this book and, indeed, the whole Bible, that God is a God of infinite love who desires that none should perish but should find in him forgiveness and life (*Jon. 4:11*). E.M.

**JONAH** 1. See *Jonah the prophet*.

**2.** Jonah son of Amittai, 'the prophet from Gath Hepher', is mentioned only once in Scripture in *2 Kings 14:25*. He is credited with having prophesied that under Jeroboam II the borders of Israel would once again be restored to their original extent. Gath Hepher was in the territory of Zebulun and it may be assumed the prophecy was given in the early part of the 8th century BC.

**3.** Jonah the father of Simon (*Matt. 16:17*) is also called John. Jonah was the Heb. form of the name. He was the father of Simon Peter and Andrew. See *John 3*.

**JONAM** Mentioned in the genealogy leading from Jesus to Adam as the father of a Joseph and son of Eliakim (*Luke 3:30*).

**JONATHAN** (Heb., 'the LORD has given').

**1.** The first Jonathan mentioned in the Bible is the young Levite of *Judg. 17–18* who, during those days in which 'Israel had no king, and everyone did as he saw fit' (*Judg. 17:6*), left his residence in Bethlehem apparently to search for greener pastures in which to carry on his profession (*Judg. 17:7–8*). Initially employed by an Ephraimite named Micah to serve as his personal priest in his home-made shrine (*Judg. 17:4–5, 10–13*), the young Levite soon found occasion to betray his employer by joining some migrating Danites in their theft of Micah's household idols and in their northward journey to Laish (*Judg. 18:14–20*). When the peaceful and unsuspecting city of Laish was captured and its name changed to Dan, the Danites lost no time in setting up their idols and

installing the young Levite as priest (*Judg. 18:27–31*). It is only at this point in the biblical narrative that the name of the Levite is given: 'Jonathan son of Gershom, the son of Moses' (*Judg. 18:30*).

**2.** The second Jonathan to appear in the Bible is by far the most familiar, namely, the son of King Saul and loyal friend of David. We know nothing of his childhood; he first appears, as an adult capable of commanding troops, in *1 Sam. 13*, where we read how he incited a war between Israel and the Philistines by attacking the Philistine presence in Geba (*1 Sam. 13:3*). This action triggered a general muster and a prearranged rendezvous between Saul and Samuel at Gilgal (*cf. 1 Sam. 10:7–8*). Saul's failure to wait until Samuel arrived caused a breach between prophet and king and left Israel without divine guidance for the ensuing battle (*1 Sam. 13:7–15*), a battle in which the Philistines' monopoly on iron-working gave them the technological advantage (*vv. 19–23*). In this dire position, it was again Jonathan who took the initiative and, accompanied only by his loyal armour-bearer, climbed a dangerous rock face to surprise a Philistine outpost on watch. So effective was Jonathan's daring assault that panic spread from the outpost back to the main Philistine camp (*1 Sam. 14:1–15*), and by the time Saul arrived on the scene, the Philistines were in such confusion that they were killing each other (*v. 20*).

Thus, in his earliest appearances Jonathan distinguished himself as a hero capable of great faith (*1 Sam. 14:6*) and great victories, and this initial impression in no way diminishes as his story continues and becomes intertwined with David's. At numerous points and in various ways Jonathan's qualities of faith and character cast into bold relief the lack of both in his father. While Saul, after his final rejection as king in 1 Sam. 15, virtually drove himself mad seeking to thwart the divine decree that he was to be replaced by a man of God's own choosing, 'a man after God's own heart' (1 Sam. 13:14), Jonathan, though crown-prince, freely transferred to David his claim upon the throne (1 Sam. 18:1–4). And although the text makes no explicit statement, it may have been Jonathan's submission to the divine rejection of the house of Saul that accounts for his lack of involvement in the face of the Philistine threat in 1 Sam. 17, in contrast to his bold exploits of 1 Sam. 13–14.

When forced to choose between his father and David, Jonathan consistently sided with David, whom he recognized as the Lord's chosen king (1 Sam. 23:17). He was nevertheless willing, as a loyal son, to accompany his father to Mt Gilboa for one final, disastrous battle against the Philistines. There he, along with his brothers, lost his life at the hand of the Philistines, while an injured Saul took his own life by falling on his sword (1 Sam. 31:1–6). As 2 Samuel opens, David eulogizes the heroism of both Saul and Jonathan, but reserves his final words to express grief for Jonathan, 'my brother', and to wonder at the astonishingly selfless quality of Jonathan's love and faithfulness (2 Sam. 1:26). Jonathan was later buried in his grandfather's tomb at Zela in Benjamin (2 Sam. 21:14).

**3.** A third Jonathan was the son of Abiathar, the high priest during the days of David. At the time of Absalom's revolt, David sent Zadok and Abiathar back to Jerusalem to gather information. Their respective sons, Ahimaaz and Jonathan, accompanied them to serve as couriers (2 Sam. 15:27, 35–36). Later, this same Jonathan brought news of Solomon's

coronation to Adonijah, thus ending the latter's bid for the throne (1 Kings 1:42–50).

**4.** This Jonathan was the 'son of Shimeah [or Shimea], David's brother' (2 Sam. 21:21; 1 Chron. 20:7). He fought for David against the Philistines and in one battle killed a giant, one of the descendants of Rapha. This giant had six fingers on each hand and six toes on each foot. It is possible he was the same man as 5. below.

**5.** One of David's 'Thirty' mighty warriors who fought at his side. He was the son of Shammah [Shagee in 1 Chronicles) the Hararite (2 Sam. 23:32–33; 1 Chron. 11:34).

**6.** The son of Jada and father of Peleth and Zaza, this Jonathan was from the tribe of Judah and a descendant of Jerahmeel (1 Chron. 2:32)

**7.** This Jonathan, son of Uzziah, was an overseer during the reign of King David. He was in charge of the king's 'storehouses in the outlying districts, in the towns, the villages and the watchtowers' (1 Chron. 27:25).

**8.** Another Jonathan, David's uncle, 'was a counsellor, a man of insight and a scribe'. He was probably involved in educating the king's sons. See Jehiel (1 Chron. 27:32).

**9.** A descendant of Adin and the father of Ebed. Ebed was one of the family leaders who came back from Babylon with Ezra following the Exile. Fifty family men came with him (Ezra 8:6).

**10.** The son of Asahel, this Jonathan was one of the very few leaders in Judah who refused to join Ezra and the people in repenting for the sin of intermarriage with foreign women (Ezra 10:15). Following the return from the Babylonian Exile, Ezra led the people in seeking to re-establish obedience to the Law of God. He urged the people to divorce these women, but Jonathan refused.

**11.** This Jonathan, the son of Joiada and father of Jaddua, was a Levite and descendant of Jeshua who returned with Nehemiah and Zerubbabel from the Exile in Babylon (Neh. 12:11).

**12.** The head of the priestly family of Malluch in the days of Joiakim and Nehemiah, following the return to Jerusalem from the Exile in Babylon (Neh. 12:14).

**13.** The father of Zechariah. This Zechariah was a priest who helped with the music for worship at the dedication of the walls of Jerusalem after they had been rebuilt in the days of Nehemiah (Neh. 12:35).

**14.** This Jonathan was a secretary in Jerusalem in the days of Jeremiah. It was in his house that Jeremiah was originally imprisoned when he was falsely accused of deserting to the Babylonians (Jer. 37:14–15). Jeremiah had prophesied, to the dismay of the leaders of Jerusalem that the LORD would bring judgment on the city of Jerusalem because of the people's sin (vv. 6–10). Clearly this was a particularly harsh imprisonment, as when Jeremiah was later brought before King Zedekiah, he pleaded not to be sent back to Jonathan's house or he would die there (Jer. 37:20; 38:26).

**15.** One of the sons of Kareah (Jer. 40:8), this Jonathan lived at the time of Jeremiah when Gedaliah ruled Judah as a puppet governor under the Babylonians. He was among the army officers who, on hearing of Gedaliah's appointment, joined him at Mizpah. For more detail see *Johanan*.                              P.D.G.

**JORAH** A family leader whose descendants were counted among those who, in the time of Ezra, returned with Zerubbabel and Nehemiah from the Babylonian Exile. Their number was 112 (Ezra 2:18).

**JORAI** A clan leader who was head of one of the seven Gadite clans settled in the area of Gilead and Bashan (1 Chron. 5:13).

**JORAM** (Heb., 'the LORD is exalted').

**1.** This Joram was a descendant of the Levite, Eliezer, and part of a family that had charge of the Temple treasuries (1 Chron. 26:25). He was the father of Zicri.

**2.** Son of Tou king of Hamath. When King David defeated Hadadezer, Tou sent Joram (called Hadoram in 1 Chron. 18:10) to David 'to greet him and congratulate him on his victory'. He took with him many presents of precious metals (2 Sam. 8:10). In line with David's deep faith and his thankfulness to the LORD for these various victories he had won, he dedicated all the gifts he received to the LORD.

**3.** The ninth king of Israel, this Joram was the son of Ahab and Jezebel. (In some versions his name is given as Jehoram.) He reigned in Samaria for twelve years from 852–841 BC (2 Kings 1:17; 3:1). He succeeded his brother Ahaziah to the throne (2 Kings 1:17). His father Ahab had subjugated the Moabites and forced them to pay him tribute, but when Joram came to the throne they seized the opportunity to rebel. Joram mobilized all his troops and called upon the King of Edom and King Jehoshaphat of Judah for help. The three kings marched round through the desert of Edom to attack Mesha, king of Moab. They ran out of water and appealed to Elisha to speak to the LORD for them. Elisha agreed he would speak only because Jehoshaphat was present. Joram's sin and paganism, that followed in the footsteps of his father Ahab, meant that Elisha would not speak to Joram. A great miracle took place. Elisha ordered the digging of ditches and the following day water filled the valleys. The Moabites were then defeated in battle but the allies were unable to follow up this defeat and later retreated again (2 Kings 3).

During Joram's reign the prophet Elisha continued to prophesy and to bring God's word to the king and the nation. 2 Kings 6 records some of the amazing miracles Elisha performed and how he often informed the king of Israel of the plans of the Syrians so that Joram was able to avoid defeat. It is almost extraordinary that Joram should have lived through these amazing works of God on his behalf and yet still have followed the paths of idolatry. His continued rebellion against God eventually led to his downfall. Syria invaded and besieged Samaria until mothers were killing and eating their children. Although the LORD miraculously lifted the siege, still the nation remained in idolatry (2 Kings 7).

Some years later Joram was involved in another alliance with the king of Judah who by then was Ahaziah. This time he went to war against Hazael king of Aram at Ramoth Gilead. In that battle Joram was wounded and went to Jezreel to recover (2 Kings 8:28–29; 2 Chron. 22:5–7). Ahaziah joined him there.

As part of God's judgment on Israel and on Ahaziah and Judah, Elisha anointed Jehu to be king of Israel. Jehu then led a conspiracy against Joram and went to Jezreel to see him. Ahaziah and Joram rode out in their chariots to meet Jehu. Joram asked Jehu whether he had come in peace, to which Jehu replied: 'How can there be peace as long as all the idolatry and witchcraft of your mother Jezebel abound?' (2 Kings 9:22). Jehu then shot Joram with an arrow and killed him.

This judgment by God on Joram demonstrated the severity with which God was determined to deal with witchcraft and idolatry. It also fulfilled Elijah's prophecy about the house of Ahab following the dreadful sins Ahab had committed against Naboth (1 Kings 21:19).

P.D.G.

**JORIM** Mentioned in the genealogy leading from Jesus to Adam, as the father of a Eliezer and son of Matthat (Luke 3:29).

**JORKEAM** The son of Raham, and a descendant of Caleb from the tribe of Judah (1 Chron. 2:44).

**JOSECH** Mentioned in the genealogy leading from Jesus to Adam, as the father of Semein and son of Joda (Luke 3:30).

## JOSEPH, THE SON OF JACOB

Joseph, whose name probably means 'may God add', was the eleventh son of the patriarch Jacob. His name is reflective of his role in the life of the nation of Israel, for Joseph was God's agent for preserving and prospering the nation in Egypt during a famine in Canaan. This prosperity brought them to the ripeness of nationhood 400 years later in the Exodus from Egypt.

### Joseph's birth and bondage

Joseph's birth is recounted in Gen. 30:22–24. He was born while Jacob still sojourned in Laban's household. He was the first child of Rachel, ending her barrenness. The name Rachel gave him refers in the immediate context to her desire to have another son, this wish being fulfilled in the birth of Benjamin (Gen. 35:17). But it foreshadowed the broader role Joseph would play in the prospering of the future nation.

The primary material dealing with Joseph's life is Gen. 37–50, comprising nearly one third of the book of Genesis. This history begins with the 17-year-old Joseph contributing to a bitter rivalry with his ten older brothers. He gave his father a bad report on his brothers on one occasion (Gen. 37:2). On another he recounted two dreams which predicted his brothers and father one day would bow down to him (vv. 5–10). The brothers were not only resentful of Joseph's attitude toward them, but highly jealous of the preferential treatment afforded him by their father (v. 4). When Jacob sent Joseph again to check on his brother, they doubtless remembered the first incident and conspired against him (vv. 18ff.). After determining to kill Joseph, the brothers were dissuaded by the eldest Reuben who arrived after the initial decision was made (vv. 21–22). Reuben persuaded them to throw Joseph in a pit, intending to rescue his young brother later.

The brothers stripped Joseph of the token of their father's favouritism, the multi-coloured tunic (Gen. 37:23) and, without Reuben's knowledge, sold Joseph to slave traders (vv. 25–28). In an ironic twist, the tunic that signified Jacob's favouritism of Joseph was soaked with goat blood and presented to Jacob as a sign that his beloved son had been killed by wild animals. A further irony is that the brothers themselves behaved as wild animals in initially conspiring to murder Joseph and in satisfying their appetites while Joseph languished naked and thirsty (vv. 24–25).

The narrative resumes in Gen. 39 after the story of Judah's injustice to Tamar. In this episode the Heb. words for 'hand' (yod) and 'prosper' (tsalach) form a subtle interplay to project the broader theme of Joseph's story. Potiphar purchased Joseph from the 'hand' of the slave traders (v. 1). God is 'with Joseph' (v. 2) such that Potiphar noticed how everything in Joseph's hand prospered (v. 3). As a result, Potiphar put everything he owned under Joseph's control (lit. 'hand', v. 4). Under this arrangement, Potiphar's household prospered dramatically.

After reiterating the fact that everything was in Joseph's 'hand' (Gen. 39:6), the narrative unfolds the attempted seduction of Joseph by Potiphar's wife. Joseph refused her efforts on the basis of the trust which Potiphar had vested in him (lit. 'in my hand', v. 8). Joseph saw this as a breech of trust and a sin against God (v. 9), indicating that he saw his stewardship of earthly responsibility as a religious duty. The extended attempt at seduction climaxed on a day when no one was at home besides Joseph and his master's wife, the implication being that she had sent away all of the servants in order to accomplish her goal. After Joseph stood firm by fleeing, the wife seized him by the garment. As Joseph's garment was left in her hand (v. 12), so also was his fate it seemed. She called witnesses and presented his clothing, first to the household servants and later to Potiphar when he returned home, as evidence that Joseph had attempted to seduce her. Once again an article of Joseph's clothing was used as testimony against him – in the first instance that he was dead, in the second that he was 'as good as dead'. (See *Potiphar* and *Potiphar's wife*.)

Joseph found himself in a similar or worse predicament than at the beginning of the episode. He was a prisoner once again when Potiphar had him thrown into jail (Gen. 39:20). But the repetition of the phrase 'with Joseph' (v. 21; cf. v. 2) indicated God's blessing rested upon the young man so that he found favour with this new master (v. 21; cf. v. 4). Joseph earned the jailor's trust such that everything there was placed into Joseph's hand (v. 22). The text tells us once again that the LORD prospered Joseph (v. 23; cf. vv. 2–3).

In this single episode we see vividly displayed the dominant theme of Joseph's life – that God was providentially preserving his life in spite of and through intense trial and injustice. No matter in whose 'hand' his life was held, ultimately it was the hand of God which saved and prospered Joseph. Divine providence was, therefore, behind all of the varied events leading to Joseph's ascendance to authority and influence as Pharaoh's trusted adviser.

It is worth noting at this point that many commentators find the contents of *Gen. 38* to be out of place in the midst of the Joseph story. Upon a surface reading, this account of Judah's unjust treatment of his daughter-in-law Tamar seems misplaced. However, this episode serves two important functions. First, it accounts for the origin of Judah's tribal history. Secondly, and more relevant for the discussion of Joseph, it provides for stark contrast between the two brothers. While Judah left family and homeland by choice (*Gen. 39:1*), Joseph was forcibly deported. While Judah willingly associated with a non-Israelite woman, Joseph resisted such temptation. Judah engaged in sexual immorality, victimized a powerless woman and, hence, incurred the judgment of God. Joseph resisted sexual immorality and was victimized by a woman of influence with the result that God preserved his interests in the end. Judah was accused justly by a woman while Joseph was falsely accused. In both cases a personal article, a staff and garment, respectively, was presented as a testimony against them. These extensive parallels/contrasts served to contrast the character of Judah with that of Joseph. Thus Joseph was even more dramatically presented as a man of virtue who looked to God to rule sovereignly over his fate. The placement of *Gen. 38* is critical for establishing this contrast.

## Joseph's rise to power

Joseph's rise to influence was the result of a special ability which brought him both weal and woe – the ability to interpret dreams. The initial display of this ability produced jealousy in his brothers (*Gen. 37:5ff*). When he found himself in an Egyptian prison it earned him a valuable ally who would bring about his deliverance from that prison. Pharaoh's chief cup-bearer and chief baker were in the same prison (*Gen. 40:3*). They were not mere kitchen servants of Pharaoh, but advisers in his inner circle who had somehow fallen out of the king's favour. The negative interpretation of the chief baker's dream and the positive interpretation of the chief cup-bearer's dream were fulfilled within the time specified by Joseph (*Gen. 40:21–22*).

Two years later Pharaoh had two dreams, the interpretation of which plagued him. At this point the cup-bearer remembered Joseph who was called upon to interpret Pharaoh's dream (*cf. Gen. 40:14, 23*). Just as with the men in prison, Joseph told Pharaoh that the ability to interpret came from God, not from himself (*cf. Gen. 40:8; 41:16*). Joseph correctly interpreted the dreams as portending seven years of abundance followed by seven years of famine (*Gen. 41:29ff*.). Joseph added to his interpretation the counsel of his widsom (*v. 33*), that Pharaoh should prepare for the years of famine by appointing an overseer to store up food during the years of plenty so that Egypt might endure the years of famine. Pharaoh, impressed by the wisdom of God vested in Joseph, appointed him over his entire kingdom (*v. 39ff*.). In a complete reversal of his fortune, Joseph found that the kingdom of Egypt was in his hand as evidenced by the signet ring Pharaoh placed upon it (*v. 42*). In the space of 13 years (*cf. Gen. 41:46; 37:2*) Joseph went from prison to the prime ministry and succeeded spectacularly in managing the affairs of Egypt (*Gen. 41:47–57*).

What remains of Joseph's story from this point is the reunion with his brothers (*Gen. 42–47*) and the varied blessings which Jacob placed on his twelve sons (*Gen. 48–50*). Seeking relief from the famine which has encompassed Canaan as well,

Jacob sent ten of his sons to Egypt to purchase grain (Gen. 42:1–2). Only Benjamin, the youngest and now the most beloved of his sons (thinking Joseph dead), did Jacob keep at home (v. 4). The ten naturally were required to present such a request to Joseph whom they did not recognize, not expecting to see him again combined with the passing of over 20 years (v. 8). Joseph from this point engaged in a series of subterfuges which were intended not to deceive his brothers per se, but rather to test their character (vv. 15, 19), to bring conviction upon them for their violence toward himself (v. 21) and to begin the process of their migration to Egypt (i.e. in asking that Benjamin be brought to him, v. 20). This honourable intention is revealed in his own concealed reaction to their dilemma (v. 24). Simeon was held as a prisoner to ensure that the other nine did as Joseph had commanded.

Jacob forbade the brothers to take Benjamin (Gen. 42:38), but when their grain was exhausted, Jacob relented (v. 11). In a stroke of irony the tribute gifts he instructed them to take included items for which Joseph was presumably sold to the Ishmaelite traders (cf. Gen. 37:25; 43:11). Joseph's deep love for his only maternal brother was displayed both in his request that the nine bring Benjamin to Egypt as well as his concealed reaction upon seeing him again (Gen. 43:30). Not only toward Benjamin, but toward all of the eleven, Joseph displayed kindness and hospitality during the banquet that constituted their reunion. He detected in their every action a fear of God and desire to deal honestly with him which set the stage dramatically for Joseph to reveal his identity.

Joseph, through the trials which he foisted upon them, both heightened the drama of their reunion and made it a joyous one through the deep sorrow they felt at what they had done to him years earlier. When Joseph revealed his identity he also revealed his inner character, for he comforted his brothers by explaining God's overriding purpose in their misdeeds – that Joseph had been brought to Egypt for the saving of their lives (Gen. 45:5–8). The brothers obediently brought Jacob and his entire household to Egypt where they were preserved from famine.

The brothers were not thoroughly convinced of Joseph's intentions, for when Jacob died, they felt certain that Joseph would then have his revenge against them (Gen. 50:15). But the character that was forged in the prisons of Egypt was of the most constant variety and Joseph resounded the assurance that sustained him in dark years 'as for you, you intended to harm me, but God intended it for good to accomplish what is now being done, the saving of many lives' (Gen. 50:20).

The effect of this migration of the family of Jacob was not simply that their lives would be spared from the famine. In Jacob's words of Gen. 46:3 he recognized that this was a divinely ordained sojourn directed toward the end that Israel would become a great nation in Egypt. Furthermore, they would have the divine presence which was of the essence of the Abrahamic covenant (Gen. 15:1; 28:15). In the fulfilment of his promise, God used Joseph as a primary agent.

### The tribe of Joseph

While Joseph's brothers each provided the patronym for eleven of Israel's twelve tribes, it was Joseph's two oldest sons who become the namesakes of the two 'half-tribes' of Israel – Ephraim and Manasseh. While all of Joseph's children were born in Egypt, Jacob laid special claim to the two born before he himself came to Egypt

(Gen. 48:5). The blessing of these two directly by their grandfather (Gen. 48:9ff.) gave Joseph, in effect, a double portion reserved only for the first-born son (v. 22). The significance of this is even greater when the Chronicler, from his post-exilic perspective, looked to this fact in promoting the reconstitution of the nation of Israel (1 Chron. 5:1–2).

The events of Joseph's life vividly displayed his strength. But such strength derived from confidence that divine providence, however smiling or frowning it might appear, was at the root of all the deeds of men and was purposed to bring about good for God's children. This is nowhere more beautifully said of Joseph than in the words of blessing dispensed by Jacob upon his death bed: 'Joseph is a fruitful vine, a fruitful vine near a spring; whose branches climb over a wall. With bitterness archers attacked him, then shot at him with hostility. But his bow remained steady, his strong arms stayed supple' (Gen. 49:22–24). Joseph was one of the principal figures in the history of redemption identified by Stephen in Acts 7. In Stephen's view, Joseph was one of the prime illustrations of his message in rebutting the Pharisees. In arguing against their false notion that God's blessing and presence was irrevocably staked to the Temple, Stephen articulated the 'Immanuel' principle that God had been with his people long before the Temple. In this context, he said simply of Joseph, 'Yet God was with him' (Acts 7:9). See Immanuel, Jacob etc.                                    M.G.

## JOSEPH OF NAZARETH

The husband of Mary, the mother of Jesus Christ, and thus the presumed human father of Jesus. His name is mentioned directly only in the birth narratives in Matt. 1–2 and Luke 1–2, as well as the family tree in Luke 3:23.

Little is known with certainty about Joseph's background. He was unquestionably from 'the house and line of David' (Luke 2:4), the lineage of the Messiah (2 Sam. 7:12, 16). However, it is not completely clear which of the two Gospel genealogies of Jesus Christ (Matt. 1:1–16; Luke 3:23–38) traces Joseph's family. The more likely possibility, though, is that Matthew's family tree relates to Joseph since it appears to be a stylized royal genealogy establishing Jesus' legal right to be King.

Even though Joseph was not Jesus' physical father (Matt. 1:22–25), he became the Saviour's adoptive father. In that capacity, he was Jesus' legal father, which placed Jesus in the line of descent of Joseph and his family, as well as Mary's (which is apparently traced in Luke 3:23–38).

It is held by some that this dual lineage understanding is necessary because of the curse placed on Jehoiachin, the last king of the Davidic house in Judah, at the beginning of the Babylonian Captivity (Jer. 22:30). If that curse is to be taken as meaning that, in an ongoing sense, 'none of his offspring' would ever 'sit on the throne of David or rule anymore in Judah' (v. 30), both genealogies are absolutely crucial. Matthew's family tree would still prove Jesus' legal claim to the throne of David, though, because of the curse, the actual ability to 'sit' and 'rule' (Jer. 22:30) would have to come through the alternative descent from David (through another son, Nathan; Luke 3:31) seen in Luke's family tree.

Besides his family background, the only other known aspects of Joseph's life prior to marrying Mary are his residence and trade. Though from the tribe of Judah he did not reside in Judea (Luke 2:4). Rather, he was from the town of Nazareth in Galilee (*v. 4*). In Nazareth, he worked as a carpenter (*Matt. 13:55*), a trade he apparently passed on to Jesus (*Mark 6:3*).

There is no way of knowing either Joseph's age in comparison to Mary, or the specific circumstances of their engagement. The absence of Joseph in *Matt. 13:55* and *John 2:1*, passages where he would be expected to be in view if still alive, implies that he was considerably older than Mary and already dead when Jesus began public ministry (or shortly thereafter; *Luke 3:23*). In that culture, the betrothal and marriage of Joseph and Mary was probably arranged by their parents, although the sovereignty of God guided the choices of all involved, as indicated by the family trees and the dreams of Joseph in *Matt. 1–2*.

The focus of the birth narrative in *Luke 1–2* is on Mary while the parallel section in *Matt. 1–2* provides the vast bulk of the information reflecting Joseph's character and role in the birth and earlier life of Jesus Christ. However, *Luke 2* does provide a few additional details about Joseph's actions related to Jesus' infancy, as well as the only glimpses of events during the period in which Jesus grew up in the home of Joseph and Mary.

In terms of personal character, *Matt. 1* reveals him to be both 'righteous' (*v. 19*) and compassionate. His righteousness undoubtedly had to do with obedience to the Law, but at least as much directly to the Lord (*v. 24*). His compassion is displayed in that, upon finding Mary pregnant before their marriage (*v. 18*), he decided to quietly divorce her, instead of opening her to public condemnation, as the Law allowed (*Deut. 22:23–24; 24:1*).

A remarkable sequence of dreams outlines Joseph's early role as earthly father to the Son of God. He was initially told not to divorce Mary 'because what is conceived in her is from the Holy Spirit' (*Matt. 1:20*). As was customary in that society, Joseph was directed to give the child his name: Jesus (*v. 21*). Upon waking from the dream Joseph obeyed the Lord (*vv. 24–25*).

Sometime well after the birth of the child, Joseph had a second dream that directed him to take Jesus and Mary to Egypt for protection from the design of Herod the Great to kill the infant Messiah (*Matt. 2:13*). Again, he did as the Lord commanded (*v. 14*).

Joseph's third dream sent him and his family back to Israel from Egypt after Herod's death (*vv. 19–20*). As he acted in obedience, his final dream supplied the guidance to resettle in Nazareth, not Judea (*v. 21*), which he did (*v. 23*). In each case, as the Lord directed, Joseph proceeded in full obedience.

Joseph is also seen in the presence of divinely provided insight concerning Jesus by others. At the event of Jesus' circumcision, Joseph and Mary heard the prophecies of Simeon (*Luke 2:28–32, 34–35*) and Anna (*v. 38*). They also marvelled at Jesus' own words about his role spoken in the Temple when he was twelve years old (*vv. 48–50*).

After the family returned to Nazareth from the Passover celebration (*v. 51*), there is no other express mention of Joseph in the NT. The name 'Joseph' in *Matt. 13:55* and *Mark 6:3*, used in relation to Jesus' family, refers to a younger son of Joseph and Mary, apparently named for his father.

There is no way of knowing when, along the way, Joseph might have died or what the circumstances might have been. The fact that Jesus is referred to as 'the carpenter' in *Mark 6:3* may be taken as implying that Jesus had taken over the family wood-working business after Joseph's death, until the beginning of Jesus' public ministry. On the other hand, it may mean nothing more than that Jesus had been trained by, and worked alongside, Joseph as a carpenter.

Considering that Joseph is not in any sense an extraordinary leader among God's people, he proves to be one of the most godly figures seen in Scripture. From all that is known about him, he is a man of obedience to the Lord and his written Word. He is also an exemplary husband and father. Other than his consideration of possibly divorcing Mary before God's guidance through a dream and his apparent bewilderment at Jesus' teaching in the Temple at the age of twelve, there is no hint of behaviour that is not in keeping with God's will.

Joseph truly was a 'righteous man' (*Matt. 1:19*), one who was well-chosen in the sovereignty of God to be the husband of Mary, the mother of Jesus. In that role, he apparently was a fine earthly parent for the unique God-man. Thus, there was much more about Jesus that was meaningful in the life of the Saviour than his legal right to the throne of his forefather, David (*v. 16*).                                        A.B.L.

**JOSEPH 1.** See *Joseph, the son of Jacob.*

**2.** See *Joseph of Nazareth.*

**3.** Joseph the father of Igal from the tribe Issachar. Igal was one of the twelve spies sent out by Moses from the Desert of Paran to spy out the land of Canaan (*Num. 13:7*).

**4.** Mentioned in *1 Chron. 25:2*, this Joseph was one of the sons of Asaph. Immediately under Asaph's direction, and on the direct orders of King David (*v. 1*), he and others were among those who prophesied and led in the ministry of music for worship. He was leader of the first group of Levitical musicians and choirs who ministered in the Temple (*v. 9*).

**5.** This Joseph was among the descendants of Binnui. At the time of return from the Exile in Babylon, Shecaniah confessed to Ezra that many men and even descendants of the priests of Judah had married wives from other nations. Ezra and the people repented and made a covenant to serve the LORD (*Ezra 10:2*). Joseph is listed in *Ezra 10:42* as one who divorced his foreign wife.

**6.** This Joseph was head of Shecaniah's family, a priestly family in the time of Nehemiah (*Neh. 12:14*).

**7.** An ancestor of Jesus listed in the genealogy from Jesus to Adam. He was the son of Mattathias and father of Jannai (*Luke 3:24*).

**8.** Another earlier ancestor of Jesus listed in the genealogy from Jesus to Adam. He was the son of Jonam and father of Judah (*Luke 3:30*).

**9.** Joseph, a brother of Jesus, is mentioned by name only in *Mark 6:3* and its parallel passage in *Matt. 13:55*. In that narrative, Jesus had arrived in his home town of Nazareth and began to teach in the synagogue. Both Gospels record the astonishment of the crowds at the wisdom displayed by Jesus. People were particularly astonished because they all knew his family who were present with them at the time. In a rhetorical question they asked, '"Isn't this the carpenter's son? Isn't his mother's name Mary, and aren't his brothers James, Joseph, Simon and Judas? Aren't all his sisters with us? Where then did this man get all these things?" And they took offence at him' (*Matt. 13:55–57*). Sadly, because of their lack of faith, Jesus did not do many miracles in the area and stated that a prophet was only without honour in his home town. For more detail on the brothers of the Lord see *Simon*.          P.D.G.

**10.** Joseph of Arimathea was a wealthy member of the Jewish Sanhedrin who became a disciple of Jesus, then buried the body of the crucified Christ in his own personal tomb. Each of the Gospels mentions Joseph of Arimathea only once, in the burial passages.

Joseph was from the Judean town of Arimathea (*Luke 23:51*). Besides being rich (*Matt. 27:57*), Joseph was also a powerful member of the Jewish ruling council (*Mark 15:43*). However, he also was looking for the Kingdom of God (*v. 43*) and stood against the Sanhedrin's verdict concerning Jesus (*Luke 23:51*).

This 'good and upright man' (*Luke 23:50*) overcame his fear (*John 19:38*), declared himself as a disciple of Christ by asking Pontius Pilate for Jesus' body, had the body prepared for burial generously (*vv. 39, 49*), then laid the body in a new garden tomb (*vv. 41–42*). These circumstances fulfilled the prophecy that the Messiah would be 'with the rich in his death' (*Is. 53:9*).         A.B.L.

**11.** Joseph Barsabbas (Justus). The candidate to replace Judas Iscariot who lost to Matthias (*Acts 1:23*). Also see *Justus*.

**12.** See *Barnabas*. Joseph was a Levite from Cyprus and is normally called Barnabas, a name given him by the apostles. He is only called Joseph in *Acts 4:36*.

**JOSES** Only mentioned in connection with his mother Mary who was present at the death and burial of Jesus. He was the brother of James the younger (*Matt. 27:56; Mark 15:40, 47*).

**JOSHAH** (Heb., 'gift of the LORD'). Mentioned in *1 Chron. 4:34*, a leader of one of the clans of Simeon during the time of King Hezekiah and a son of Amaziah.

**JOSHAPHAT** (Heb., 'the LORD has judged').

1. Joshaphat the Mithnite, was one of David's 'Thirty' mighty warriors who fought at his side (*1 Chron. 11:43*).

2. A priest whose job it was to blow a trumpet before the ark of God when it was brought back to Jerusalem by David (*1 Chron. 15:24*).

**JOSHAVIAH** (Heb., 'the LORD has settled'). Joshaviah the son of Elnaam was one of David's 'Thirty' mighty warriors who fought at his side (*1 Chron. 11:46*).

**JOSHBEKASHAH** One of the sons of Heman, the King's seer, listed among those set apart for the ministry of prophesying and music during the reign of King David. (*1 Chron. 25:4*). A leader of the 17th group of Levitical musicians and choirs who ministered in the Temple (*1 Chron. 25:24*).

**JOSHEB-BASSHEBETH** When David became king in Israel, he rapidly moved to take Jerusalem. As he became more and more powerful, three mighty men were of particular support and Josheb-Basshebeth, the Tahkemonite, was one of these. He was appointed 'chief of the Three' and was renowned for having killed 800 men in one encounter (*2 Sam. 23:8*). The parallel passage in *1 Chron. 11:11* talks of Jashobeam, who may have been the same person.

**JOSHIBIAH** (Heb., 'the LORD settles'). A Simeonite, son of Seraiah, and father of Jehu who, in the days of King Hezekiah, was involved in military activity against the Hamites and Meunites (*1 Chron. 4:37*).

## JOSHUA, SON OF NUN

Although Joshua, son of Nun, is the central human character of the book which bears his name, this figure was known by Moses long before he chose him as his successor. At some point Moses selected a man from the tribe of Ephraim whose name was Hoshea. He renamed him Joshua (*Num. 13:16; cf. Deut. 32:44*). Hoshea means 'Save!' The name Joshua means, 'Yahweh is salvation'. This act reflected Moses' discernment in recognizing in Joshua the figure whose military expertise would symbolize and enact the deliverance which Yahweh (the LORD God) would give to Israel as they fought their enemies in Canaan.

The first appearance of Joshua occurs in a military context. It was Israel's first battle after escaping from the Egyptians. The Amalekites threatened the people of God. Joshua was the warrior who led Israel to victory as he fought on behalf of Moses (*Exod. 17:8–13*) and he selected the army. He fought and overcame the enemy and represented all Israel as he led them to victory. Indeed, the army itself is mentioned only once (*Exod. 17:11*). As Moses' 'aide', Joshua ascended Mount Sinai with him (*Exod. 24:13*) and it was he who addressed Moses concerning the noise in the camp below (*Num. 32:17*). He was given a place at the Tent of Meeting. His concern for the welfare of Moses kept him away from the jealous strife which surrounded Moses' years in the wilderness. In *Num. 11:28* this concern went too far as Joshua protested the prophesying by Israelites who had not been selected by Moses.

Joshua was one of the twelve spies sent from Kadesh-Barnea to explore the land of Canaan (*Num. 13:16*). Ten of the spies returned with a report which insisted that the land was too difficult to conquer. Only Joshua and Caleb returned with a report in which they argued that the land could be conquered. A plague ended the lives of the ten doubters. Joshua and Caleb, alone among all that generation of Israel, were promised entrance into the land and an inheritance there (*Num. 14:6, 30, 38*). This promise, as well as the previous associations with Moses, provide the background for the remaining references to Joshua in the Pentateuch. These all emphasize the role of Joshua as successor to Moses who would lead the people into the Promised Land.

This succession was explicitly commissioned in *Num. 27:18–23*, where Moses publicly laid hands upon Joshua. Joshua's responsibilities included the act of standing before Eleazar the high priest who could discern God's will through the use of the Urim. They also included command over the people of Israel and their military forces. Joshua and Eleazar together received the instructions as to the allotment of the Transjordanian tribes (*Num. 32*). This provided an example of how Joshua would function as successor to Moses in the allotment of all the tribal lands west of the Jordan River (*Num. 34:17*). God commanded Moses 'to strengthen' Joshua (*Deut. 1:38*) and 'to encourage' him (*Deut. 3:28*). These two verbs, 'be strong and courageous', form the substance of the charge which Moses gave to Joshua, repeating it three times to add emphasis (*Deut. 31:6–7, 23*).

### Joshua's roles

With this background the roles of Joshua after Moses' death become clear. Joshua was the warrior who would lead the people to victory against their foes. He was the representative of the people before God and before the priest Eleazar. Joshua supervised the allotments of the tribal territories. Most importantly, he was the successor to Moses. No other figure in the Bible had this special role. In order to fulfil it Joshua would lead the people as Moses did and they would go through similar experiences as they had done with Moses.

## A spiritual and military leader

As spiritual and military leader of the people, God spoke directly and only to Joshua with the same words as Moses gave to him: 'Be strong and courageous' (repeated three times, Josh. 1:6–9). He led the people across the Jordan (Josh. 3–4), performed the circumcision and celebrated the Passover (Josh. 5), led in the defeat of Jericho (Josh. 6), identified and punished the sinner Achan (Josh. 7), led in the victories against Ai (Josh. 8), against the southern coalition (Josh. 10) and against the northern coalition (Josh. 11).

## The representative of the Israelites

As representative of the people before God, Joshua alone was given the divine instructions for organizing the people (Josh. 1:1–9), for crossing the Jordan River (Josh. 3:7–8; 4:1–3, 15–16), for bringing about the defeat of Jericho (Josh. 6:2–5), for identifying the culprit Achan (Josh. 7:10–15), for the conquest of Ai (Josh. 8:1–2, 18), for defeating the northern coalition (Josh. 11:6), for the distribution of the land (Josh. 13:1–7) and for designating cities of refuge (Josh. 20:1–6). The religious ceremonies of the crossing, the circumcision and the Passover have already been mentioned. In addition, Joshua led the people in the covenant dedication of Josh. 8:30–35 and in the renewal of their covenant (Josh. 24). Joshua represented the people before the priest Eleazar in at least two incidents. The first was to determine whose sin had led to defeat in the first assault on Ai (Josh. 7:14–18). Eleazar is not mentioned in the text. However, his use of the Urim was the only divinely approved method for determining the will of God. Thus it is likely that Joshua turned to Eleazar at this time. The second concerned the tribal allotments. The Transjordanian tribes had already been dealt with. Those west of the Jordan were also assigned by lot according to the direction of Joshua and of Eleazar (Josh. 14:1–2; 15:1; 16:1; 17:1; 18:1–11; 19:1, 10, 17, 24, 32, 40, 49).

## The successor to Moses

It was Joshua's role as successor to Moses which best illustrated the character of the man as a faithful servant of God. Like Moses, Joshua started from an uncertain beginning. While Moses was concerned about his ability to speak publicly, Joshua was concerned with how he could take the place which was left by such a hugely significant person as Moses, the servant of the LORD (Exod. 3–4; Josh. 1). Many of God's initial instructions to Joshua were designed to bolster him in this matter. In particular, at the point of crossing the Jordan River, God said to Joshua, 'Today I will begin to exalt you in the eyes of all Israel, so they may know that I am with you as I was with Moses' (Josh. 3:7). This was accomplished as Josh. 4:14 records. Like Moses, Joshua began his leadership with an uphill struggle for recognition. Like Moses, God intervened and established his choice.

Many of the activities which Joshua undertook could be understood as mirror images of earlier actions by Moses. Like Moses, Joshua sent out 'spies' to investigate the Promised Land (Num. 13; Josh. 2). Like Moses, Joshua led the people across an imposing body of water which miraculously opened before them (Exod.

13:17–15:21; Josh. 3–4). Like Moses, Joshua witnessed the circumcision of those males who were with him (Exod. 4:24–26; Josh. 5:2–9) and he celebrated the Passover with Israel (Exod. 12; Num. 9:1–14; Josh. 5:10–12). Like Moses, a figure approached Joshua when he was alone and instructed him to remove his shoes in reverence for the holy ground where he stood (Exod. 3:1–5; Josh. 5:13–15). Like Moses, Joshua led the people in military victories (Exod. 14–15; Num. 21; 31–32; Deut. 2:26–3:11; Josh. 6; 8; 10–12) and in identifying impurity among the people (Exod. 32; Num. 15:32–36; 16; 25; Josh. 7). Like Moses, Joshua built an altar, wrote down words of God's Law and gave it to the people as a covenant between them and God (Exod. 24:3–18; Josh. 8:30–35). Like Moses, Joshua allowed outsiders into the covenant community (Exod. 12:38; Josh. 6:22–25; 9). As Moses started, so Joshua completed apportioning the land as an inheritance to Israel (Num. 32; Deut. 3:12–20; Josh. 13–19), giving an inheritance to Caleb (Num. 14:24; Deut. 1:36; Josh. 14:6–15), confirming inheritances for the daughters of Zelophehad (Num. 27:1–11; 36:1–12; Josh. 17:3–6), assigning cities of refuge and giving the Levites their cities (Num. 35; Josh. 20–21), and confirming the continuing relationship between the tribes on both sides of the Jordan River (Num. 32; Josh. 22). Moses gave a farewell address to the people and so did Joshua (Deut. 1; Josh. 23). Moses renewed God's covenant with the people and so did Joshua (Deut. 29; Josh. 24). Although their deaths were different, mention is made of the passing of both Moses and Joshua in detail (Deut. 32:48–52; 34; Josh. 24:29–31).

## The covenant leader

Of special interest is the final address by Joshua to the people at Shechem. In Josh. 24 he reviews the covenant which God made with the people of Israel. Joshua goes on to describe the need for obedience to God and then to call witnesses to hear the people's declaration of loyalty toward God. In many ways this parallels the covenant which Moses made with the people in Deuteronomy. Both begin with a review of the history of Israel and of the way in which God alone provided for their needs and granted them success in their battles (Deut. 1–3; Josh. 24:2–13). Both of them then challenged the people to serve God alone. In Deuteronomy this occupies most of the book, (i.e. Deut. 4–30). In Josh. 24 it occupies only vv. 14–15. Blessings for obedience and curses for disobedience, which appear in Deut. 28, are found as warnings in Josh. 24:19–20. In Deut. 30:19, heaven and earth were called to witness before Israel that it had entered into covenant with God. In Josh. 24:22 the people agreed to be witnesses against themselves. In vv. 26–27 Joshua also erected a stone at Shechem which he claimed would serve as a witness against the people. The differences in the selection of witnesses reflected the different role which the people played at Shechem. In Deuteronomy there was no response of the people to the covenant. Instead, they were instructed to recite the blessings and curses of Deut. 27:12–26 on Mt Gerizim and Mt Ebal, when they entered the Promised Land. Joshua oversaw this activity (Josh. 8:30–35). The people completed the tasks which Moses commanded them to do. When they had finished they could respond to the covenant which God offered them. Thus their commitment to God in response to the covenant (Joshua 24:16–24) formed a conclusion to the covenant relationship which God had established with the generation of the conquest. Like the generation of the Exodus they were offered the covenant and accepted it (*Exod. 24*). Sadly, like that earlier generation, they soon fell into sin (*Exod. 32; Judg. 3:5–6*).

However, Joshua was no longer alive to see this unhappy ending to the covenant promises which the people had made. Apparently, the witness of Joshua and of the elders who outlived him was strong enough to restrain the evil during their own lifetimes but not in the following years (*Judg. 2:6–13*). The text indicates that this witness was one of the great acts of God. Joshua, like Moses, before him had led the people in God's redemption. Spiritually, their earlier experiences of crossing the Jordan and consecrating themselves had removed the 'reproach of Egypt' which the Israelites carried with them from the rebellions of their parents and from the sins of Baal-peor (*Num. 25; Josh. 5:9*). Politically, God had used Joshua to put the people of Israel in an ideal position for their own security and growth. A great fear of Israel's God had fallen upon all the Canaanites (*Josh. 2:9; 5:1; 9:24; 10:2*). This fear came because of the victories which Israel had won from the time they left Egypt until their defeat of Sihon and Og east of the Jordan River. The conquest had been accomplished thanks to this fear which prepared the way so that the Canaanites were unsure of themselves and of the protection of their gods. Joshua had witnessed this and had seen God's own hand participating in casting down the walls of Jericho (*Josh. 6*), and in the wondrous miracles in the sky in which the sun and moon were used by God as signs against the Canaanites (*Josh. 10:12–14*). What the Canaanites worshipped as divine became, through the prayer of Joshua, enemies toward their devotees. Even Baal, god of the storm, could not protect the Canaanites against the great hailstones which the God of Israel threw down from heaven (*Josh. 10:11*). In such ways divine miracles cooperated with the faithful actions of Joshua and of Israel to accomplish the task of defeating their enemies.

Joshua is mentioned again only in *1 Kings 16:34*, where the curse which he pronounced on whoever would rebuild Jericho, had its effect. He is not mentioned in the NT, although his faith is alluded to in the great chapter on the outstanding examples of people of faith, *Heb. 11*. In *v. 30* we read, 'By faith the walls of Jericho fell, after the people had marched around them for seven days.' Joshua was remembered as the outstanding example of a leader who was chosen by God and who exercised faith in a life lived in accordance with the divine will. As such he was able to represent the people before God and to lead them into a new land and a renewed covenant. It is not inappropriate to observe that Jesus bore the Greek equivalent of Joshua's Hebrew name. In the sense of a leader who showed his people the way of faith and brought them to God's covenant, Joshua's life was a foreshadowing of the anointed Son of God.                    R.H.

**JOSHUA** **1.** See *Joshua, son of Nun*.

**2.** Joshua, son of Jehozadak. He was the high priest in Judah following the Babylonian Exile and, with Zerubbabel, was responsible for re-establishing the Temple and worship between 538–516 BC (*Hag. 1:1, 12, 14; 2:4; Zech. 3:1, 3, 6, 8–9; 6:11*). His name is given as Jeshua in *Ezra 3:2* and *Neh. 12:1, 8*.

**3.** Joshua of Beth Shemesh. A citizen of that city in whose care the ark of the covenant was placed for a time following its capture by the Philistines in the time of Samuel (*1 Sam. 6:14, 18*).

**4.** Joshua, the mayor of Jerusalem. An official at the time of King Josiah's reformation at the end of the 7th century BC (*2 Kings 23:8*).                    E.M.

# KING JOSIAH OF JUDAH

Josiah (Heb., 'the LORD supports him') was king over Judah from c. 640–609 BC (2 Kings 22–23; 2 Chron. 34–35). His grandfather, the wicked Manasseh, had ruled for 55 years, and had persecuted the godly and repressed true religion in Judah. His father, Amon, had reigned only two years (2 Kings 21:19–26; 2 Chron. 33:21–25) and had continued in the evil practices of Manasseh, but his reign was cut short by court intrigue resulting in his assassination (2 Kings 21:24). At that difficult time, Josiah had come to the throne at the tender age of eight. His mother was Jedidah from Bozkath (2 Kings 22:1).

## Judah and Assyria

The years of Josiah's reign gave Judah some relief from Assyrian control. For a century Assyria had exerted pressure on Judah's political, religious and social life. By the end of the 7th century, the extensive Assyrian empire was threatened again by Babylon, when Assyria did not have the resilience to face Nabopolassar of Babylon (625–605 BC). The empire collapsed after the fall of Nineveh (612).

The political vacuum was filled by the resurgence of Judah under Josiah and of Egypt under Pharaoh Neco. The rivalry between these two powers propelled Josiah to stop the Egyptians at the Megiddo pass where he lost his life in 609.

## Religious reforms

Yet, the socio-political perspective cannot fully explain the religious transformations initiated by Josiah. According to Kings, Josiah was like David in that he 'did what was right in the eyes of the LORD and walked in all the ways of his father David, not turning aside to the right or to the left' (2 Kings 22:2). Chronicles further explains that 'he began to seek the God of his father David' (2 Chron. 34:3). The young king's search for the LORD was evidence of the work of God's Spirit in him. When he was 16 years old (c. 632 BC), he systematically eradicated paganism in its many syncretistic forms beginning in Jerusalem and Judah and extending his reform efforts to the northern territories.

At the age of 20 (c. 628 BC), he took away the defilement of the land by ridding it of its high places, Asherah poles, carved idols and cast images. The graves of the idolaters were desecrated, and the bones of the pagan priests were burned on the old altars (2 Chron. 34:3–7; cf. 1 Kings 13:2).

## Josiah in Kings

At the heart of the books of Kings is the Law. The author is concerned with the obedience, or lack thereof, of the king to the Law (Deuteronomy in particular). The author of Kings evaluates every king as righteous or wicked based upon his faithfulness to the laws of Deuteronomy. Josiah was a righteous king, so the author emphasizes the finding of the Book of the Law as motivating his reforms.

At the age of 26 (c. 622 BC), Josiah proceeded with his plan of purifying the land by restoring the Temple under the direction of Shaphan, Maaseiah, Joah, and

Hilkiah the high priest. They gave charge to the Levites to supervise the work and paid the workers from the Temple resources. During the cleansing of the Temple, Hilkiah the high-priest, found a book which he gave to Shaphan, the secretary. He took it to the king, when giving a report on the reconstruction, and read from it. Upon hearing the words of God's law, the king tore his robes as an overt expression of sorrow. He was pricked in his heart by the people's history of rebellion against the LORD and by the impending judgment spoken of in the Law of God.

Once the Law code was found, Josiah sought a word from the LORD through Huldah, the prophetess. She condemned Judah's idolatry and prophesied imminent Exile, while extending God's grace during Josiah's rule. This encouraged Josiah to begin the great reform. Josiah renewed the covenant, destroyed cultic centres, reinstituted the Passover in Jerusalem, and purged the land of paganism (2 Kings 23:4–20). Although the reform was a great success the true test came with the death of Josiah. After his death at the hand of Pharaoh Neco, the people returned to their pagan ways.

## Josiah in Chronicles

The emphases in Chronicles are different from those in Kings. Whereas Kings is mostly concerned with the Law and Josiah's faithfulness to it, Chronicles is interested in the messianic ideal and Josiah's relation to that king. Josiah's reform took place in three stages. In the eighth year of his reign, Josiah began to seek 'the God of his father David'. In the twelfth year, he began to purge Jerusalem and Judah of high places and false idols. Finally, in his 18th year as king, Josiah ordered that the Temple be repaired. During the repairs, the Book of the Law was found and brought to the king. After reading the book, Josiah sought for a word from the LORD. He went to the prophetess, Huldah, who informed him that God would curse Judah 'with all the curses written in the book' for the sin of idol worship, but would spare Judah during his life. After this prophetic warning, Josiah continued his reforms with even more vigour than before. He read the Law to all the people of Israel, and they renewed the covenant. He spread his idol-purging activities into parts of what was the Northern Kingdom of Israel. The people assembled in Jerusalem, together with priests and Levites. The law was publicly read and, under the godly leadership of Josiah, the people renewed themselves to be faithful to God's covenant with them. As a concrete expression of their being bound together in covenant to the LORD, the King decreed a celebration of the Passover in Jerusalem. He gave careful attention to all the details spelled out in the Law of Moses (2 Chron. 35:6, 12) as well as to the traditions that were associated with David and Solomon (v. 4). The priests and Levites officiated and, together with the attendants, were well provided for. The king and his officials contributed voluntarily 37,600 sheep and goats and 3,800 head of cattle. So great was the total number of animals slaughtered that it nearly doubled that of the Passover celebration under Hezekiah (2 Chron. 30:24). So great was the involvement of people, priests, and Levites that the Passover celebration compared favourably to the festivities of Samuel (v. 18).

## The Book of the Law

The authors of Kings and Chronicles do not further specify the nature of the Book of the Law. Did it contain the whole Pentateuch or a part of it? Was that part the whole book of Deuteronomy or only a part of it? It appears likely that the book was Deuteronomy because it specifies a central place of worship, the destruction of all high places (*Deut. 12*), curses resulting from disobedience (*Deut. 27–28*), the Passover celebration (*Deut. 16*), and the covenant renewal ceremony (*Deut. 27; 31; cf. 2 Chron. 34:30–32//2 Kings 23:2*).

The life of Josiah is carefully patterned after two other kings. First, the author of Chronicles includes similar activities and events in the lives of Hezekiah and Josiah. Both kings destroyed pagan high places in Judah and in the north (*2 Chron. 31:1–2; 34:3–7*). Both kings instituted the passover after years of negligence (*2 Chron. 30:13ff.; 35:1ff.*). Second, the stories of both Hezekiah and Josiah intimate that either of them might be a new David. David is Josiah's 'father' (*2 Chron. 34:2–3*). Like David, Josiah returned the ark to the Temple (*2 Chron. 35:3*). Moreover, Josiah returned the singers, the sons of Asaph, to the Temple as 'prescribed by David' (*2 Chron. 35:15*). The purpose for this distinct patterning is clear. Chronicles helps the reader to identify the new David with the messianic ideal. Hezekiah was presented as a new David, but he died and the realm passed on to the wicked Manasseh. Josiah is presented as a king similar to both Hezekiah and David, but despite all his efforts, he too died and his kingdom did eventually end up in captivity.

After having set Josiah so high in the expectations of the reader, Josiah cannot be the Messiah because he died as result of his political ambitions. When Pharaoh Neco came through Canaan on his way to fight with Assyria against Babylon, Josiah intercepted him at Megiddo (*2 Chron. 35:22*). Neco warned Josiah that his interference might result in judgment from God (*v. 21*). Josiah, however, refused to listen. In a scene reminiscent of King Saul, Josiah was struck by archers and later died in Jerusalem.

## Last days

It is unclear what happened between the celebration of the Passover (c. 622 BC) and Josiah's death at Megiddo (609 BC). The fall of Nineveh (612 BC) undoubtedly encouraged Josiah to occupy himself with international affairs. However, his political ambitions were also his undoing. When Pharaoh Neco passed through Judah on his way to fight the Babylonians at Carchemish, Josiah marched out to meet him in battle. It is far from clear why he did so. Most likely is the suggestion that he wanted to assure Judah's independence among the nations. Had he permitted the Egyptians to pass through, he could have been considered to be a collaborator against Babylon.

Neco was disturbed at Josiah's refusal. He sent a message with a religious overtone. He argued that God had told him to move quickly, that Josiah's hostile acts were a threat to the accomplishment of God's will, and that God would punish him for it. Like Ahab before him, Josiah was disobedient to the divine forewarning, disguised himself, engaged the enemy in battle, was hit by the arrow of an unknown archer, and died in the capital (1 Kings 22:29–40). Unlike Ahab, Josiah did not die on the battlefield. He died in Jerusalem. Great was Judah's loss. The prophet Jeremiah led the people in a lament (Jer. 35:25). Further, he rebuked Josiah's son Jehoahaz (Shallum) by comparing his ambitions to those of his father who 'did what was right and just, so all went well with him. He defended the cause of the poor and needy, and so all went well' (1 Kings 22:15–16). From this point onward, Judah drifted further away from the LORD and became more entangled in her attempt to survive the rapidly changing power-play in the Near East.                    W.A.VG.

**JOSIAH   1.** See *King Josiah of Judah*.
**2.** One of the three Jews from Babylonian Exile who contributed silver and gold to make crowns for the priest Joshua. He is identified as a son of Zephaniah in *Zech. 6:10* and is probably the same as 'Hen, son of Zephaniah' in *v. 14*.

**JOSIPHIAH** (Heb., 'may the LORD add'). One of the heads of family who returned to Jerusalem from Babylon with Ezra. He was a descendant of Bani and father of Shelomith who returned with 160 men (*Ezra 8:10*).

**JOTHAM** (Heb., 'the LORD is perfect').
**1.** Jotham was the son of King Uzziah and Jerusha. He was 25 years old when he came to the throne and reigned from 740–736 BC (*2 Kings 15:33; 2 Chron. 27:1*). He followed his father Uzziah in doing 'what was right in the eyes of the LORD' (*2 Kings 15:34*) and yet he still did not completely eradicate the pagan worship that took place at the 'high places'. No doubt he felt it would be politically difficult to attack the popular worship of the people.

As he 'walked steadfastly before the LORD' (*2 Chron. 27:6*) he became powerful and conquered the Ammonites, receiving huge taxes and tributes from them during the early years of his reign (*v. 5*). He reigned in Jerusalem for 16 years. Jotham added an 'upper gate' to the Temple and built various defences around the country (*2 Chron. 27:3–4*). Sadly, his son, Ahaz, turned right away from the LORD and followed the ways of the Northern Kingdom of Israel. Just as God had blessed Jotham for his obedience

and faithfulness, so all the good work was undone and God judged Ahaz and Judah for his sin (*2 Chron. 28;* see *Is. 7:1*).

Isaiah, Micah and Hosea all prophesied at times during Jotham's reign (*Is. 1:1; Hos. 1:1; Mic. 1:1*). He was an ancestor of Jesus and mentioned in the geneaology that demonstrates Jesus' royal lineage in *Matt. 1:9*.

**2.** A son of Jahdai and descendant of Judah and Caleb mentioned in *1 Chron. 2:47*.

**3.** The youngest son of Jerub-Baal (Gideon) and mentioned in *Judg. 9:5, 7, 21*. He was the only son of Gideon to escape the massacre of the family by the men of Shechem. As soon as Gideon had died, the Israelites once again turned to worship Baals and refused to show any kindness to Gideon's family and descendants (*Judg. 8:34–35*). Abimelech, the son of Gideon's Shechemite concubine, went to Shechem and won support for himself. With the money they gave him he hired bandits who went and murdered all 70 sons of Gideon. Jotham escaped and stood on Mount Gerazim opposite Shechem and shouted out a parable to the inhabitants. The parable was about various trees wanting to anoint a king, but the useful trees rejected the honour. Eventually the thornbush accepted. Jotham was likening Abimelech to the thornbush and clearly indicating that the men of Shechem would eventually be cursed. Abimelech ruled the area for three years (*Judg. 9:22*), but later 'God sent an evil spirit between Abimelech and the citizens of Shechem, who acted treacherously against Abimelech. God did this in order that the crime against Jerub-Baal's seventy sons . . . might be avenged' (vv. 23–24). The parable had been fulfilled.     P.D.G.

**JOZABAD  1.** Jozabad is listed as one of the warriors who joined David at Ziklag see (1 Chron. 12:4).
**2.** This Jozabad, of the tribe of Manasseh, was also listed as one of David's warriors at Ziklag (1 Chron. 12:20).
**3.** Another descendant of Manasseh, this Jozabad also served as one of David's warriors at Ziklag (1 Chron. 12:20).
**4.** Jozabad served as a supervisor in Hezekiah's Temple storeroom (2 Chron. 31:13).
**5.** A leader of the Levites, Jozabad was one of a group of men who gave generously to the priests during Josiah's reign (2 Chron. 35:7–9).
**6.** This Jozabad was one of the heads of the Levites who had charge over the outside work of the house of the LORD (Neh. 11:16). This Jozabad is probably the same as the one mentioned in Ezra 8:33.
**7.** Jozabad, a descendant of Pashhur, was one of the priests who married a foreign woman after the return from Exile (Ezra 10:22–23).     S.C.

**JOZADAK** The father of Jeshua who was a priest during the time of Zerubbabel. Jeshua took a leading role as a priest in setting up the worship for the returning exiles following the end of the Babylonian captivity. Some of his descendants had married foreign wives (Ezra 3:2, 8; 5:2; 10:18; Neh. 12:26). He may be the same person as *Jehozadak*.

**JUBAL** was the second son born to Lamech and Adah (Gen. 4:21). He was the earliest musician mentioned in Scripture: 'the father of all who play the harp and flute'.

**JUDAH  1.** Judah, born in Paddan-aram, was Jacob and Leah's fourth son (Gen. 29:35; 35:23). He thus became the founder of one of the twelve tribes of Israel. Little is known of him although, when his brothers decided to get rid of Joseph, Judah spoke up and refused to be party to murder of his own flesh and blood and recommended that they sell him as a slave to Midianite merchants (Gen. 37:26–27). On another occasion Judah went to stay with a friend called Hirah, where he met and married a Canaanite woman called Shua who bore him a number of sons (Gen. 38:1–11). One of his sons Er was wicked and killed by the LORD (v. 7). Er's wife was then given to his brother Onan who refused to bring up children with her, leaving her an unsupported widow with no children. Onan was put to death for not obeying the LORD in this matter. Instead of passing her on to his third son, Judah then sent Tamar back to her father's house and told her to live a widow's life. Some time later, when Judah's wife had died, he visited Hirah again. Tamar then deceitfully seduced her father-in-law and became pregnant by him. Judah acknowledged that he had not treated her well in her widowhood and so took her into his house and looked after her. There she bore him twins: Perez and Zerah (Gen. 38:26–30; 46:12).

The contrast between Judah's sexual sin in approaching a woman he presumed was a prostitute (Gen. 38) and the faithfulness of Joseph who refused to sleep with Potiphar's wife is marked. The whole account is woven by the writer into the midst of a description of Joseph's suffering in prison for his righteous behaviour (Gen. 37; 39– 40).

Judah next appears on the scene when the brothers travelled a second time to Egypt for food during the famine. Judah reminded his father Jacob that the prime minister would not see them again unless they brought their brother, Benjamin, with them. (They did not know that it was Joseph who wanted to see his brother.) Judah promised his father that he would stand as a surety himself for the safe return of Benjamin from Egypt.

No doubt both Jacob and Judah realized there was a possibility of losing another member of their family (Gen. 43:8). Judah seems to have become the leader of the brothers in their dealings with Joseph (Gen. 44:14–34). Joseph eventually revealed himself to them and brought them all down with their father, Jacob, to live in Egypt. Judah led them into the land of Goshen (Gen. 46:28).

When Jacob was dying, he blessed his sons, and promised that Judah would be the greatest of the tribes. He foretold that the sceptre would not depart from Judah (Gen. 49:8–10).

When the territory of Canaan was allocated in Moses' and Joshua's time, Judah was given land around Hebron and to the south of Jerusalem. The blessing of Jacob on his son Judah was to prove correct and long-lasting. Judah remained the tribe that God blessed and then, after the Assyrian invasion of Israel, the kingdom that God blessed. It was from Judah that King David

was descended and from his descendants that eventually the Saviour, Jesus, would also come. Thus it was that the sceptre was established for ever among the descendants of Judah (Luke 3:33).

**2.** Judah was one of the Levites who married a foreign woman after the return from Exile (Ezra 10:23).

**3.** This Judah, from the tribe of Benjamin, was the son of Hassenuah and was put over the second district of Jerusalem following the return from the Babylonian Exile (Neh. 11:9).

**4.** One of the Levites who helped with the singing in the Temple following the return to Jerusalem from Babylon (Neh. 12:8).

**5.** One of the leaders of Judah who led the worship on the rebuilt walls of Jerusalem in the time of Nehemiah (Neh. 12:34).

**6.** Another Judah was also involved in that procession, led by Ezra, in which the walls of Jerusalem were dedicated (Neh. 12:36).      P.D.G.

## JUDAS ISCARIOT

Judas Iscariot was one of the twelve original disciples of Jesus, but we know virtually nothing about him except that he handed Jesus over to the authorities. Even the meaning of the name 'Iscariot' is disputed. Some scholars relate it to the word sicarii, 'dagger-men', and speculate that he may have belonged to the revolutionary party of the Zealots. Others propose such meanings as 'false one', 'one who delivers', 'man from the city' (i.e. Jerusalem), etc. An early and widely accepted interpretation is 'man of Kerioth', which could refer either to a town in Moab or to a village in southern Judea, but even this proposal is far from certain.

The three Synoptic Gospels give basically the same picture of Judas. The Gospel of Mark, generally regarded as the earliest, presents the simplest decription. Judas is first mentioned in the list of apostles (Mark 3:19), where he is described as 'the one who betrayed him'. All the other references are in Mark 14, where the betrayal is recorded: Judas made an arrangement with the chief priests, who agreed to give him money (vv. 10–11); Jesus indirectly referred to him during the Last Supper (vv. 18–21); immediately after Jesus' experience in Gethsemane, Judas came with a crowd, gave him a kiss as a sign, and Jesus was taken away (vv. 43–46).

All this material is paralleled in the Gospels of Matthew and Luke, each of which however reflects a distinctive perspective, sometimes by the inclusion of other information. Matthew, for example, adds the detail that the chief priests paid Judas thirty pieces of silver (*Matt. 26:15*). (This is not a large amount, and some have speculated that it was only a down payment. Others have argued that this detail is not historical but rather the result of redactional development.) Matthew also is the only evangelist who relates Judas' remorse, leading to his suicide (*Matt. 27:3–5*). In addition, he records that the chief priests, with the pieces of silver thrown away by Judas, purchased a field for the burial of strangers, and that this event was a fulfilment of the Scriptures (*Matt. 27:6–7*, with a citation of *Zech. 11:12–13*).

Luke, for his part, is distinctive in making the initial comment that Judas conferred with the chief priests because Satan had entered into him (*Luke 22:3*). He also reports a little differently Jesus' indirect reference to Judas during the Last Supper (*Luke 22:21–23*) and abbreviates the narrative of the betrayal itself (*Luke 22:47–48*). In the book of Acts, however, Luke records some unique information. According to *Acts 1:15–20*, the apostle Peter, speaking to the believers some time after the death and resurrection of Jesus, pointed out that Judas' betrayal and death were a fulfilment of David's words (in *Ps. 69:25; 109:8*). This passage includes an account of the circumstances surrounding Judas' death that differs from the narrative in Matthew. Possible harmonizations of the two passages have been suggested, but it is difficult to reconstruct the details with certainty.

In contrast to the Synoptic Gospels, the Gospel of John makes a special point of highlighting negative characteristics of Judas at various points in the narrative. Interestingly, in the account of the betrayal itself, John does not record any interaction between Jesus and Judas (in particular, he makes no mention of the kiss). As early as *John 6*, however, in the context of a discussion about true and false discipleship, John reports these words of Jesus: 'Have I not chosen you, the Twelve? Yet one of you is a devil!' (*John 6:70*). In the next verse, John points out that this was a reference to Judas, who would later betray Jesus. Thus the author brings out explicitly a theological problem that faces every reader of the Gospels. How is it possible that Judas could be both chosen by Jesus and also his betrayer?

John's negative portrayal is also obvious in his account of the anointing of Jesus by Mary (*John 12:1–8*). Because Mary had poured very expensive perfume on Jesus' feet, Judas complained that the perfume should have been sold and the money given to the poor. John then comments, 'He did not say this because he cared about the poor but because he was a thief; as keeper of the money bag, he used to help himself to what was put into it' (*v. 6*). The Synoptic Gospels say nothing like that about Judas, and so the historicity of the account has been challenged by some scholars, but without sufficient reason (even sceptical scholars recognize that the Gospel of John may preserve historical traditions not recorded in the other Gospels).

The Synoptics' account of Jesus' prediction of the betrayal during the Last Supper is paralleled, but also expanded, in *John 13*. Early in the passage we are told, 'The evening meal was being served, and the devil had already prompted Judas Iscariot, son of Simon, to betray Jesus' (*v. 2*). In *v. 18*, John raises again the theological problem involved in the selection of Judas: 'I know those I have chosen. But this is to fulfil the scripture: "He who shares my bread has lifted up his heel against me"' (a quotation of *Ps. 41:9*). Only John goes on to say that 'Jesus was troubled in spirit and testified, "I tell you the truth, one of you is going to betray me"' (*v. 21*). Jesus identified the betrayer as the one to whom he would give a piece of bread. 'Then, dipping the piece of bread, he gave it to Judas Iscariot, son of Simon. As soon as Judas took the bread, Satan entered into him' (vv. 26–27). John also tells us that Jesus said to Judas, 'What you are about to do, do quickly', and that Judas then went out. The paragraph ends with the suggestive words, 'And it was night' (v. 30).

Finally, and most significantly, John tells us that Jesus, in the context of the so-called High Priestly prayer, spoke of Judas' betrayal: 'While I was with them, I protected them and kept them safe by that name you gave me. None has been lost except the one doomed to destruction so that Scripture would be fulfilled' (John 17:12). Here the puzzle about Judas is made even more acute because it is related to Jesus' protection of his disciples. How is it possible that someone whom Jesus chose to be one of the Twelve could be destroyed? More pointedly, the question must be asked from the opposite angle. How could Jesus have chosen someone he knew would be destroyed? The answer given in this passage sounds the depths of the divine mysteries: according to Scripture, Judas was destined to destruction.

To the modern mind, such an answer provides no solution at all. Indeed, throughout the centuries the figure of Judas has fascinated many thinkers, who have attempted to provide explanations for his behaviour. A common approach is to suggest that Judas was driven by the love of money. This explanation may appear to have some support from the comments in John 12:6, but it is interesting that the Gospel of John itself says nothing about the financial arrangements between Judas and the chief priests. Moreover, the relatively small amount of money involved can hardly account for an act of this magnitude.

Since the text provides no other information, additional attempts to explain Judas' behaviour involve considerable speculation: jealousy toward the other disciples, bitterness that his worldly hopes had fizzled, fear of political repercussions, and so on. One theory that has attracted interest suggests that Judas was seeking to force the issue. In other words, by means of the betrayal, Jesus would have been coerced into acknowledging his Messiahship and acting upon it (some might even see here a reflection of Satan's attempt to make Jesus display his powers improperly; see Matt. 4:1–11; Luke 4:1–13; cf. John 6:14–15).

One can hardly prove or disprove any of these suggestions, and it is of course possible that one or more of these factors did play a role in Judas' thinking. None of them, however, provides a sufficient basis to explain such a heinous act as the betrayal of the Son of God. That is why the Gospel of John is of special value in thinking through this issue.

John, who was probably the last of the evangelists to write his Gospel, often provides direct theological reflection on a variety of themes that the Synoptic Gospels treat only in descriptive fashion but that raise questions in the minds of attentive readers. One of these themes is the sovereignty of God in the work of salvation. The apparent tension between God's power and human agency is an undercurrent in much of the biblical narrative, and it surfaces in a number of passages. Note, for example, Jesus' claim that God has hidden his wisdom from some but revealed it to others (Matt. 11:25–27 and parallels), or his assurance that salvation is impossible for men but not for God (Matt. 19:26 and parallels).

It is generally recognized that the Gospel of John highlights the truth of human inability and therefore our dependence on God's will and power for salvation (cf. John 1:12–13; 3:3–9; 6:44). In view of this emphasis, one is not surprised to see that the Fourth Gospel pays special attention to the enigma of Judas. In effect, Judas personified in a dramatic fashion what is usually known as 'the problem of evil'. But if the Gospel does not ignore the problem, neither does it provide 'rational' solutions, that is, answers that satisfy our minds but only by minimizing one pole of the paradox or the other (either 'God does everything he wants, therefore Judas was not responsible' or 'Judas was responsible, therefore God only foreknew and did not foreordain the betrayal').

The biblical narrative leaves no doubt that Judas was a responsible human agent – what he did he did because he wanted to and not because he was coerced to do it against his will. On the other hand, *John 17:12* makes clear that psychological explanations do not get at the root of the betrayal. God's own will encompasses the whole of history, even including the greatest sin of mankind (*cf. Acts 2:23*). God is most certainly not the author of sin – herein lies the mystery of the problem of evil – but his purposes are never thwarted (*Prov. 19:21; Is. 46:10*). The figure of Judas serves as a reminder of both the awfulness of sin and God's power to effect the salvation of his people.

M.S.

**JUDAS** **1.** See *Judas Iscariot.*

**2.** Judas son of James is mentioned in *Luke 6:16* and *Acts 1:13* as one of the Twelve whom Jesus selected to be apostles. In the place where this name falls in the Lucan lists, *Matt. 10:3* and *Mark 3:18* have Thaddaeus. It may be another name for the man to keep him from being confused with Judas, the betrayer of Jesus. *John 14:22* may refer to him as well.

**3.** Another Judas was the half-brother of Jesus (*Matt. 13:55; Mark 6:3*). He was almost certainly not one of the apostles, as *John 7:5* says that the brothers of Jesus 'did not believe in him'. Later on, however, they did come to believe in Jesus as the son of God and were present in the upstairs room after the ascension where they prayed 'constantly' with the apostles and some of the women who had been with Jesus (*Acts 1:14*). In the epistle of Jude (*v. 1*), Jude calls himself the 'brother of James' and it is most likely that the Jude who penned that letter was indeed this Judas, the brother of Jesus. See *Jude.*

**4.** A certain 'Judas of Galilee' is mentioned in *Acts 5:37* by the Jewish leader, Gamaliel. He was a zealous Jewish patriot who had led a rebellion against a census ordered by Quirinius. In suggesting that the apostles, recently arrested by the Sadducees, should be released, Gamaliel argued that others had come before appearing to lead people. If such people were of God their work would survive, if not, they would end up like Judas of Galilee who 'led a band of people in revolt. He too was killed, and all his followers were scattered'.

**5.** Another Judas was a Christian man to whom Saul (Paul) had gone after his experience on the Damascus road. Ananias was then directed to visit Judas' house on Straight Street in Damascus and talk to Saul about his new-found faith and pray for him (*Acts 9:11*). See *Ananias.*

**6.** Judas Barsabbas was one of the most respected Christians present at the so-called 'Jerusalem Council' in *Acts 15*. At this council of early church leaders a number of deep theological issues were discussed which had largely arisen in the church at Antioch. The main one concerned the relationship between the new converts to Christianity from Judaism and the new converts from among Gentiles. Should the Gentiles be circumcised or made to eat specially slaughtered food etc. (*Acts 15:5, 19–20*)? When the leaders had decided on their course of action, which was to recognize Gentiles as full Christians without the need for circumcision, they sent a letter giving details of their decision to the church at Antioch. Judas and Silas, 'two men who were leaders among the brothers' (*Acts 15:22*), were assigned the task of taking the letter.

The Christians at Antioch were much encouraged by the contents of the letter and by the explanation and confirmation of what had been written given them by Judas and Silas. The two of them were both prophets and thus encouraged and strengthened the brothers (*vv. 27, 32*).

P.D.G.

**JUDE** It is generally accepted that the Jude referred to in *Jude 1* was the brother of James, the half-brother of Jesus (see *Mark 6:3*). There is little information in the letter that would indicate when Jude wrote this letter, but AD 90 would need to be the latest date. In this letter Jude encouraged the Christians to whom he was writing by stressing the grace of God and his faithfulness in keeping his children from falling (*Jude 1, 24*). He also had to call them to contend for the faith (*v. 3*). He also demonstrated to these Christians from Scripture that the problems and evil they were facing in their society were not new. Because God had consistently judged those who taught evil, so he would do so again. The great consolation for all Christians faced by attack from heretics is that God looks after his own and will indeed keep them. P.D.G.

## THE JUDGES

The period of the Judges followed the conquest of Canaan under Joshua, which had brought relative peace and stability (*Josh. 21:43–45*). However, the next generation failed to capitalize on Joshua's victories and failed to drive out the nations which remained in Canaan. The consequence of this failure was a growing compromise in the life of Israel, marked by tribal discord, religious syncretism and defeat by foreign powers. God's response to Israel's disobedience and idolatry was to judge them by bringing defeat at the hands of a succession of enemies (*Judg. 2:12–15*) – the Arameans (*3:8*), Moabites (*3:12*), Philistines (*3:31; 13:1*), Canaanites (*4:2*), Midianites (*6:1*) and Ammonites (*10:9*). The Judges were raised up by the LORD (*Judg. 2:16*) to save the nation from this foreign oppression and restore the worship of the LORD. However in each case, following the deliverances won by the Judges, the periods following their death resulted in a greater deterioration of the nation's commitment to the LORD (*Judg. 2:19*).

### Characteristics of the Judges

The title 'judge' comes from *Judg. 2:16*, 'the LORD raised up judges, who saved them . . .' But the title carries more than just a judicial connotation. During the Exodus from Egypt, judges were appointed by Moses as his delegates authorized to apply God's Word in situations of legal judgment (*Exod. 18:13–27*) and their judicial role was commanded for life in God's land (*Deut. 16:18*). However, in the times of national oppression throughout the book of Judges, their role was to be the agent of God's deliverance of Israel. In a time of apostasy, they were supernaturally enabled to deliver Israel in the name of the LORD (e.g. *Judg. 3:10*,

28; 7:15 etc.), while during peace time they seemed to fulfil a leadership role (Judg. 12:8–13).

The characters of those raised up to deliver Israel were varied. Othniel, Caleb's brother, functions as a model judge in the book. He was raised up by the LORD, endowed charismatically by the Spirit, defeated Israel's oppressor in battle and brought in a time of peace (Judg. 3:9–10). But each successive judge is marked by deliberate ambiguities of character. Ehud, being left-handed, triumphed by deception and assassination (Judg. 3:15–26). Barak was reluctant to obey the LORD without Deborah's presence (Judg. 4:8), so the honour of killing the opposing general fell to a Kenite woman, Jael (v. 21). Gideon needed repeated assurance from the LORD, to rely totally on him (Judg. 6:15, 27, 36–40; 7:10) and ultimately led Israel back into idolatry (Judg. 8:27). Jephthah's dubious background as a prostitute's son was compounded by the rashness of his vow (Judg. 11:30–31) to attempt to manipulate God. Samson repeatedly broke God's laws, touching and eating what was forbidden a Nazarite (Judg. 14:8f.; see 13:7), and in inappropriate sexual liaisons (Judg. 14:2–3; 16:1, 4f.). This pattern continued with one of the two judges mentioned in 1 Samuel; Eli, who is called a judge in 1 Sam. 4:18, yet honoured his rebellious sons more than the LORD (1 Sam. 2:29). Even Samuel, who combined the office of prophet and judge (1 Sam. 7:15–17), had wayward children (1 Sam. 8:5).

In each case, the Judges bore many of the flaws which were typical of the nation at the time. They function as types of Israel, typical Israelites who were equipped for the LORD's service by his grace alone. The assumption of the book is that it is the LORD who is the real Judge (Judg. 11:27), and the human agents of his salvation are called and equipped supernaturally, and used in his grace to relieve the suffering of his covenant people. The Judges prefigure the church: imperfect in character, yet commissioned by the LORD to bring his message to a rebellious people. Hence Heb. 11:32 names particular judges as models of faith.

In the sense that God is the one raising up the rulers of his people, the period of the Judges is seen to be a more immediate experience of God's rule than the period of the kingship which follows it (1 Sam. 8:7–8; Is. 1:26). Thus, the miraculous interventions of God during this period were associated with his Judges, whereas during the period of the kingship that followed, it was the prophets who were the focus of such signs.

### Characteristics of the people

Having been obedient to the LORD under Joshua, and enjoyed victory before all their enemies, as the LORD had promised (Josh. 21:43–45), the issue under-girding the book of Judges is the non-fulfilment of the LORD's patriarchal promise to give the whole land to Israel. Judg. 1 records the continuation of Joshua's campaign against the people of Canaan, with initial success (Judg. 1:4–20). However, total trust in the LORD, gave way to alliances with the inhabitants of the land (Judg. 1:23–26), forbidden by God (Exod. 23:32); and successive campaigns either were incomplete (Judg. 1:27–33) or failed (v. 34). The non-fulfilment of the promise was seen to hinge on the obedience of Israel to God's commands. God allowed certain

Canaanites to remain to test the depth of Israel's allegiance to him (Judg. 2:21–3:4), because of the disobedience of the generation succeeding Joshua.

Disobedience in the military campaign was coupled with Israel's persistent apostasy. Apparently, having been established in the land, the people began a syncretistic approach to religion, following local fertility gods as well as the LORD (Judg. 2:11–13). The pervasive nature of this apostasy is indicated by Gideon's father having been a priest of Baal and Asherah (Judg. 6:25); the overt idolatry recounted in Judg. 17 which involved a Levite priest; and the apparent merging of the worship of Baal and of the covenant LORD of Israel in Judg. 8:33 in the Baal-Berith (literally 'Baal of the covenant'). This apostasy provoked God's judgment against his people (Judg. 2:12–15; 3:7; 6:10), to bring them back to him.

Repeated disobedience and apostasy provide the narrative framework to the main part of the book of Judges. There is a common pattern repeated:

(1) Israel does evil (Judg. 2:11; 3:7, 12; 4:1; 6:1; 10:6; 13:1).

(2) The LORD sells them or gives them over to their enemy (Judg. 2:14; 3:8, 12; 4:2; 6:1; 10:9; 13:1).

(3) Israel cries to the LORD (Judg. 2:18; 3:9, 15; 4:3; 6:6; 10:10; but significantly not in the Samson episode).

(4) The LORD sends a deliverer (Judg. 2:16; 3:9, 15; implicit in 4:4; but significantly, a prophet is sent first in 6:8; God refused initially to save his people in 10:13; and the rescue was only 'begun' with Samson in 13:5).

(5) A summary of victory and peace (Judg. 3:10, 30; 4:23; 8:28; 11:33; but there is no statement of peace after Jephthah and no statement of victory or peace after Samson).

The changes in the narrative framework reflect the statement of Judg. 2:19, that after the oppression by an enemy and the salvation wrought by God's judges, the people returned to a worse state than they were in initially. Their disobedience and apostasy was a downward spiral, not just a repeated failure. This period therefore bears similarities to the ante-diluvian age (before Noah), when God allowed the consequences of man's sin to grow. Here God's permission of evil was checked by his acts of gracious rescue in the light of their repentance, but Judg. 6:8; 10:13 both reflect that the people of God were not genuinely repentant. This growing apostasy formed the background to the next great revelation of salvation history associated with Israel's kings and prophets.

The practical consequences of Israel's disobedience and apostasy are illustrated by the two-fold ending to the book. Judg. 17–18 tells of the accepted idolatry among the people (17), how one of Israel's tribes adopts an idolatrous priesthood (18:1–26), and how they abandon the portion of the land God had promised them, to violently seize another area for themselves (18:27–31). Judg. 19–21 tells of the moral breakdown of Israel, the Benjaminite sin was as serious as Sodom's (19). The effort to put this right led to the near annihilation of a tribe (20) and a series of mortally dubious decisions to try to put matters right again (21). Tribal disunity was a repeated problem (Judg. 5:17; 8:1ff., 12:1ff., 21), the unity of the covenant people of God, by which God brought them into the Promised Land, was threatened by their turning from the LORD. Disobedience and apostasy led to deteriorating morality and increasing violence, coupled by a self-centred rather than God-centred evaluation of right and wrong (Judg. 17:6; 21:25). Against this background, the rule of a king was anticipated (*Judg. 19:1; 21:25*) as a focus for the responsibility of Israel's covenant obedience.

## Characteristics of God

The repeated thrust of the book is the sovereign right and power of God to exercise judgment on his covenant people. God's justice is seen in his wrath at their sin (*Judg. 2:14*). Sin is seen in terms of covenant disobedience (*v. 20*). God is revealed as never tolerating compromise in allegiance to him, but continually disciplining his people to bring them to repentance.

Alongside the theme of God's judgment lies his compassion for his people under judgment. Sending the judges to rescue his people, demonstrates God's covenant love for his people. When judgment had thrown them back to dependence on him, he responded in love. However God's covenant love goes beyond their desire for salvation, in *Judg. 11:18* having threatened not to save them, 'he could bear Israel's misery no longer . . .' In *Judg. 16–18* there is no apparent crying to God at all under the Philistine rule. It appears Israel did not want to be rescued, yet God still took the initiative to send Samson as a judge.

The picture of the downward spiral of sin, reflects man's radical corruption and the urgency of wholehearted obedience to the LORD by his people. But in calling Judges who themselves were corrupt in varied ways, God demonstrated his sovereignty over sin, and how in his providence, he would work good out of evil.

Finally this period of Israelite history reveals the dependence of God's people on him as their LORD, to fulfil the promises. God's holiness permits no apostasy, yet God's covenant-love never ceases to provide a way of salvation for his people. Behind the human judges lies the one true Judge (*Judg. 11:27*), the sovereign LORD, who raises up nations to discipline his people, and yet whose power enables one man to defeat a thousand (*Judg. 15:15*). The history of the judges reveals the LORD of all history who purposes his people's defeat to bring about their repentance, but who raises up a way of salvation for those who turn to him.

The period of the Judges was a depressing spiral into sin, despite the privileged possibilities that God's rule mediated through the Judges afforded. However, the failure of this period to produce covenant obedience pointed beyond itself to a new revelation of God's saving purposes, not through the Judges, but through the responsibility of a God-appointed king. The failure of the Judges lay in the people's disregard for their divine authority, seen in their quick rejection of the LORD after the Judges' deaths; the king would be an abiding symbol of the LORD's right to rule, pointing to the only hope for salvation history: the coming of the divine-human King, Jesus Christ.

R.M.

**JUDITH** The daughter of Beeri the Hittite, she married Esau when he was 40 years old. Possibly because of her pagan background, we are told that she and Esau's other wife Basemath, also a Hittite, 'were a source of grief to Isaac and Rebekah' (*Gen. 26:34–35*). These marriages were yet another example in Esau's life of his rejection of the LORD and his preparedness to compromise with those around. There is a great contrast here with Jacob, who returned to take a wife from Padam

Aram rather than take a Canaanite woman (*Gen. 28:6–8*).

**JULIA** A Christian woman who lived in Rome and was greeted by the apostle Paul (*Rom. 16:15*). Her name is linked with Philologus, which means she may have been related to him, but we cannot be certain. Paul's personal recognition and care for many individuals in different congregations is to be noted in most of his letters.

**JULIUS** was the Roman centurion charged with escorting the apostle Paul from Caesarea to Rome where Paul was to be tried before Caesar. He belonged to the 'Imperial Regiment' and was clearly well disposed towards Paul (*Acts 27:1, 3*). On landing at Sidon, Julius allowed Paul to go off and find friends who would provide food and support for him. However, Julius did not listen to Paul when he warned him that it was too late in the year to set sail across the Mediterranean. In a fierce storm Paul assured Julius that everyone would be safe because it was God's will that he stand trial in Rome. They were shipwrecked on Malta, but all survived and eventually Paul came to Rome.

God's over-ruling is seen throughout Paul's time with Julius, who came to trust Paul. At one stage Julius actually stopped the other soldiers killing Paul and the prisoners (*Acts 27:42–43*). It was God's will that Paul should witness for Christ in Rome and before Caesar (*Acts 23:11*), and Julius was used by God to further in a small way that sovereign purpose (see *Acts 27:23–24; 28:28–30*).     P.D.G.

**JUNIAS** Greeted by Paul in *Rom. 16:7*. There has been some suggestion over the ages that Junias may have been a woman. It is a Latin name and may be a contraction of the masculine Junianus or from the feminine Junia. Andronicus and Junias are described as 'my relatives' and may have been blood relatives of the apostle or perhaps he was identifying them as Jews. They had become Christians before Paul and were 'fellow prisoners' with him. Paul said they were 'outstanding among the apostles'. This may mean that they had a high reputation among the apostles or that they were renowned as apostles, in which case the word 'apostle' here is used in the wider sense of what today might be called 'missionary' (see *1 Cor. 15:7*; also Barnabas in *Acts 14:14*). If this latter is the case, then the way they are mentioned together may mean that they were husband and wife (see, e.g., Priscilla and Acquila, *1 Cor. 16:19*).     P.D.G.

**JUSHAB-HESED** (Heb., 'let the constant [covenant] love return'). One of several sons of Zerubbabel, and a descendant of King David. He was of the tribe of Judah and is mentioned only in the genealogy of *1 Chron. 3:20*.

**JUSTUS** (Lat., 'just').

**1.** The surname of Joseph Barsabbas. This Justus was proposed along with Matthias as a replacement apostle for Judas Iscariot (*Acts 1:23*). He had been one of the Lord's disciples throughout his public ministry right from the time of John the Baptist. He had also been a witness to the resurrection and the ascension and thus potentially had the qualifications to be an apostle (*vv. 21–22*). After prayer for guidance, Matthias was eventually chosen by casting lots (*vv. 24–26*).

**2.** Titius Justus, a resident of Corinth, is mentioned in *Acts 18:7* as a 'worshipper of God' into whose house Paul moved when he was expelled from preaching in the synagogue. His home was next door to the synagogue, which must have provoked the Jews considerably. As usual, the apostle's outreach was to the Jews first and then to Gentiles when Jews would no longer listen. Titius Justus was probably a Roman citizen who had come to worship

God under the influence of Jewish teaching. His hospitality afforded Paul a relatively safe place from which to conduct his ministry.

**3.** Jesus Justus joined Paul in sending greetings to the church at Colosse (*Col.* 4:11). He was one of Paul's intimate friends during his first imprisonment in Rome. Paul draws attention to the fact that he was a converted Jew, and this provided a special comfort to him through his ordeal.                P.D.G.

# K

**KADMIEL 1.** Kadmiel was a Levite whose descendants were among those who returned from the Babylonian Exile to Jerusalem with Zerubbabel (*Ezra 2:40; 3:9; Neh. 7:43*).

**2.** Another Levite of the same period, this Kadmiel was among those who led the people in worship and singing following the reading of the Law and a lengthy period of confession. He also joined Nehemiah in sealing the agreement of the people to worship the LORD and obey his Law (*Neh. 9:4–5; 10:9; 12:8, 24*).   P.D.G.

**KALLAI** (Heb., 'swift') was a leader of the priestly family of Sallu and was among those who returned with Zerubbabel from the captivity in Babylon (*Neh. 12:20*).

**KAREAH** The father of the Johanan and Jonathan who were army commanders under Gedaliah (*Jer. 40:8*). Johanan disobeyed Jeremiah's prophecy that they should all remain in Judah rather than flee to Egypt (*2 Kings 25:23; Jer. 40:8, 13, 15* etc, also *Jer. 41–43*).

**KEDAR** (Heb., 'dark'). The second son of Ishmael and a tribal leader (*Gen. 25:13; 1 Chron. 1:29;* see *Nebaioth*). He gave his name to an Arabian tribe that is mentioned on a number of occasions in the Bible and may have been quite dark in appearance. In *Song of Sol. 1:5*, the dark beauty of the beloved is referred to in the expression 'like the tents of Kedar'. Elsewhere the place is mentioned in prophecy as being subject to judgment. Its distance to the east provides grounds for referring to it in the context of the great extent of God's rule (see *Ps. 120:5; Is. 21:16–17; 42:11; Jer. 2:10; 49:28; Ezek. 27:21*).

**KEDEMAH** A son of Ishmael and grandson of Abraham and Hagar, he was a leader of his clan (*Gen. 25:15; 1 Chron. 1:31*).

**KEDORLAOMER** was the king of Elam and one of four Mesopotamian kings who invaded Palestine at the time of Abraham (see also *Arioch, Amraphel* and *Tidal*). The account given in *Gen. 14* is of particular interest as it highlights both the desirability of the Jordan valley that could attract an alliance of kings from so far afield, and the rapidly advancing influence of Abra(ha)m.

It is clear that the invading alliance was headed by Kedorlaomer (*vv. 4–5*). The invaders had conquered several of the city states of the Jordan valley and areas around the Dead Sea and had ruled the land for twelve years. In the 13th year the local kings of these cities rebelled and fought the invaders (see *Bera, Birsha, Shinab, Shemeber*). Once again, however, they were defeated and fled. The four kings seized a huge area of land, including the cities of Sodom and Gomorrah, from which they took all the spoil. In this conquest they carried off Abram's nephew, Lot, who was living in Sodom.

This brought Abram into the arena. When he heard what had happened, he went in pursuit of Kedorlaomer, chasing him far to the north. Finally in a clever attack he defeated the alliance and returned with Lot and his family (*Gen. 14:14–17*).

The alliance had come from the same area that had been Abram's home. It is of great significance that Abram's defeat of these kings is seen in Gen. 14 as God's victory, and indicates God's establishment of Abram in Canaan and his final and complete separation from his former life. From this point onwards, under God's sovereign plan Abram's influence in the 'promised land' continued to increase.                              P.D.G.

**KELAIAH** also called Kelita, was one of the Levites who was married to a foreign woman. After the return from the Babylonian Exile and on the direction of Ezra, he agreed to divorce her (Ezra 10:23).

**KEILAH** From the tribe of Judah, Keilah was a Garmite and a son of Hodiah (1 Chron. 4:19).

**KELAL** was descended from Pahath-moab and had married a foreign wife in the time of Ezra. Under Ezra's teaching he agreed to divorce her (Ezra 10:30).

**KELITA,** also called Kelaiah, was one of the Levites who was married to a foreign woman. After the return from the Babylonian Exile and on the direction of Ezra, he agreed to divorce her. He also helped teach the people the Law of God and sealed the agreement of the people to worship the LORD and obey his Law (Ezra 10:23; Neh. 8:7; 10:10).

**KELUB 1.** The father of Mehir and brother of Shuhah, this Kelub is mentioned in 1 Chron. 4:11. He was from the tribe of Judah.

**2.** The father of Ezri. Ezri was one of King David's overseers and in charge of those who farmed the King's land (1 Chron. 27:26).

**KELUHI** was descended from Bani and had married a foreign wife in the time of Ezra. Under Ezra's teaching he agreed to divorce her (Ezra 10:35).

**KEMUEL 1.** A son of Milcah and Nahor and nephew to Abraham. His brothers included Uz and Buz. He became the father of Aram (Gen. 22:21).

**2.** Kemuel, the son of Shiphtan, was named by the LORD as one to be chosen by Moses as the leader of the tribe of Ephraim. His duty was to organize the allocation of the Ephraimite territory to the various clans and families following the conquest of Canaan (Num. 34:24).

**3.** The father of Hashabiah. Hashabiah was one of the leaders of the tribe of Levi in the time of David (1 Chron. 27:17).

**KENAANAH 1.** A great-grandson of Benjamin and son of Bilhan (1 Chron. 7:10).

**2.** The father of Zedekiah, a false prophet whose confrontation with the true prophet Micaiah is recounted in 1 Kings 22 and 2 Chron. 18.

**KENAN** The son of Enosh, Kenan became the father of Mahalalel at the age of 70. He was one of those early leaders of a whole people who lived 910 years. He is also listed in Luke's genealogy leading from Jesus to Adam (Gen. 5:9–14; 1 Chron. 1:2; Luke 3:37).

**KENANI** A Levite during the time of Nehemiah, Kenani was among those who led the people in worship and singing following the reading of the Law and a lengthy period of confession (Neh. 9:4).

**KENANIAH** was a Levite during the reign of King David. When David brought the ark of the covenant up to Jerusalem, he asked the leaders of the Levites to choose people to sing and play instruments before the ark. Kenaniah was given charge of choir singing because he had a good voice (1 Chron. 15:22; 27). Assuming it is he and his family who are mentioned again in 1 Chron. 26:29, then later he and his sons were assigned duties away from the Temple as 'officials and judges over Israel'.

**KENAZ 1.** An Edomite leader who was the grandson of Esau and Adah (a Canaanite woman) and son of Eliphaz (*Gen. 36:11, 15, 42; 1 Chron. 1:36, 53*).

**2.** The brother of Caleb and father of Othniel. Othniel attacked Kiriath Sepher at Caleb's suggestion and thereby won the hand in marriage of Caleb's daughter Acsah. Othniel later became a judge in Israel (*Josh. 15:17; Judg. 1:13; 3:9, 11; 1 Chron. 4:13.*

**3.** The son of Elah and grandson of Caleb son of Jephunneh (*1 Chron. 4:15*).

**KERAN** A leader among the Horites, son of Dishon and grandson of Anah (*Gen. 36:26; 1 Chron. 1:41*).

**KEREN-HAPPUCH** (Heb., 'horn of antimony'). At the end of Job's life, after all the tragedies and trials that he had faced, God once again blessed him. Among the children born to him at this stage were three daughters of whom the third was Keren-Happuch (*Job 42:14*). Together with her two sisters she was considered very beautiful and they were each given part of Job's inheritance (*v. 15*). The name suggests her beauty, for antimony was an expensive black colouring used in eye make-up.

**KEROS** A leader of one of the families of Temple servants. His descendants returned from the Babylonian Exile in the days of Ezra and worked on the Temple (*Ezra 2:44; Neh. 7:47*).

**KESED** A son of Nahor and Milcah and therefore Abraham's nephew (*Gen. 22:22*). See *Bethuel*.

**KETURAH** (Heb., 'incense'). Keturah was Abraham's second wife (his first was Sarah), although in *1 Chron. 1:32–33* she is called his concubine. By this time Sarah had died (*Gen. 23*), and Abraham was quite elderly. He may have remarried because of his loneliness after Isaac had married Rebekah (*Gen. 24*). She gave birth to a number of children who became leaders of tribes in their own right. In this way God's promise to Abraham, 'I will make nations of you and kings will come from you' (*Gen. 17:6*) began to be fulfilled. Perhaps the most notable nation mentioned in Scripture that came from Keturah was the tribe of Midian (*Gen. 25:1, 4; 1 Chron. 1:32–33*).

P.D.G.

**KEZIAH** At the end of Job's life, after all the tragedies and trials that he had faced, God once again blessed him. Among the children born to him at this stage were three daughters of whom the second was Keziah (*Job 42:14*). Together with her two sisters she was considered very beautiful and they were each given part of Job's inheritance (*v. 15*). The name refers to the perfume of a flower.

**KILEAB** was one of King David's sons and was born in Hebron. His mother was Abigail, Nabal's widow (*2 Sam. 3:3*). In *1 Chron. 3:1* he is also called 'Daniel'.

**KILION** and his brother Mahlon were sons of Elimelech and Naomi and lived in the days of the Judges in Israel. Because of a famine in Judah, Elimelech and his wife had left their home town of Bethlehem and gone to Moab for a while (*Ruth 1:1–2*). When Elimelech died, Naomi was looked after by her two sons. Later, the two sons also died, although the book of Ruth does not say how this happened. However, both Kilion and Mahlon had married Moabite wives who helped support Naomi (*Ruth 1:3–5*). Kilion had married Orpah. Mahlon's wife, Ruth, later returned with her mother-in-law to Bethlehem where she met and married Boaz. Boaz bought from Naomi all Kilion's property and the property of his father and brother (*Ruth 4:9–10*). P.D.G.

**KIMHAM** was the son of Barzillai. Barzillai had faithfully supported and helped King David while he had been away from Jerusalem fleeing from Absalom. Wanting to repay Barzillai for his kindness, when David was restored to the throne, he invited Barzillai to join him in Jerusalem where he would be well cared for. Barzillai, who came from Gilead, pleaded old-age as a reason for staying at home and offered his son Kimham instead. Kimham then went up to Jerusalem with the king where he was well treated (2 Sam. 19:37–38, 40).

## KING AND KINGSHIP

'God is king of all the earth; sing to him a psalm of praise' (Ps. 47:7). A fundamental truth taught in Scripture – perhaps the fundamental truth – is that God is king. He is king of all the earth, and his reign is everlasting (Pss. 9:7; 10:16). He is king by right, for he is the creator of the universe, and it rightly belongs to him (Job 41:11; Pss. 50:10–12; 96:10). He is reigning now, and though not all acknowledge his rule, one day all shall (Zech. 14:9). He rules not only over the earth, but in heaven as well (Ps. 103:19). Obedient allegiance is owed him by 'his angels . . . all his heavenly hosts . . . all his works everywhere in his dominion' (Ps. 103:20–21).

God's kingly rule is universal, but it is also particular. In the OT, God chose a particular people to be his 'treasured possession'. It was at Mt Sinai that the LORD called to Moses from the mountain and said, 'This is what you are to say to the house of Jacob and what you are to tell the people of Israel: "You yourselves have seen what I did to Egypt, and how I carried you on eagles' wings and brought you to myself. Now if you obey me fully and keep my covenant, then out of all nations you will be my treasured possession. Although the whole earth is mine, you will be for me a kingdom of priests and a holy nation." These are the words you are to speak to the Israelites' (Exod. 19:3–6; cf. Is. 43:15).

It was perhaps this consciousness of God as king – and in a special sense Israel's king – that caused Israel to hesitate for so long to install an earthly king; the concept of human kingship would, of course, have been well known to Israel from the practice of her neighbours (e.g. Judg. 3:12; 4:2; 8:5). Gideon, for example, when offered an opportunity to establish a ruling dynasty, refused with these words: 'I will not rule over you, nor will my son rule over you. The LORD will rule over you' (Judg. 8:23). Gideon's words gave eloquent testimony to the view that the LORD alone was rightful king, though his actions seemed to betray a pull in another direction; he did after all collect a kingly reward for his services (Judg. 8:24–46), sire 70 sons (v. 30) and name one of his sons Abimelech, which means 'my father is king' (v. 31).

The pull for human kingship came to full expression with the elders' demand in 1 Sam. 8. Judging Samuel to be past his prime and his sons to be ill-suited to follow him in leadership, the elders demanded 'a king to lead [lit. judge] us, such as all the other nations have' (1 Sam. 8:5). Samuel, the judge, hearing the word 'judge' in the elders' demand, apparently understood this as a personal rejection, and he was displeased (v. 6). But the LORD assured him that the problem was much deeper: 'it is not you they have rejected, but they have rejected me as their king' (v. 7). And so human kingship was introduced in Israel amidst human sinfulness.

And yet, from the beginning God had intended that Israel should one day have an earthly king (Gen. 49:10; Num. 24:7, 17–19; cf. Gen. 17:6, 16; 35:11).

Moses had anticipated the day when Israel would be settled in the land of promise and would desire a king, and had even given instructions to regulate kingship when it should come (*Deut. 17:14–20*). And so, despite the inappropriate timing and tone of the elders' demand in *1 Sam. 8*, the LORD agreed to give them a king. But first he had Samuel warn them of how they might suffer under a king 'such as all the other nations have' (*1 Sam. 8:10–18*). It was never, in fact, the LORD's intention that his people should have *such* a king. Rather, Israel's human king was to be subordinate to the Great King, God himself. He, just as much as his fellow Israelites, was to be obedient to the Word of the LORD (*Deut. 17:18–20*). To be sure, Israel's monarch was a 'sacral' king, the LORD's anointed, one whose life was sacrosanct (*1 Sam. 26:9*). But unlike the pharaohs of Egypt, he was not to be worshipped as God incarnate, and unlike the kings of Babylon, he was not to be viewed as divine by adoption. Rather, Israel's king was just as responsible to 'fear the LORD and serve and obey him and . . . not rebel against his commands' – in short, to 'follow the LORD' – as were all Israel's citizens (*1 Sam. 12:14–15*).

It was precisely in this matter of obedience to the Word of the LORD that Israel's first king, Saul son of Kish, fell short (*1 Chron. 10:13*). The first explicit rebuke of Saul by God's prophetic spokesman, Samuel, is recorded in *1 Sam. 13*. Specifically, Saul was charged with acting foolishly in failing to keep the 'command' (or 'charge') of the LORD (*v. 13*). The charge in view was an important two-part charge that was issued to Saul at the time of his anointing (*1 Sam. 10:7–8*) and was designed to test Saul's willingness to submit himself to the Great King (for discussion see *Saul, King of Israel*). The second explicit rebuke also centred on the issue of obedience (*1 Sam. 15*). Whereas the first rebuke dashed Saul's hopes of founding a dynasty (*1 Sam. 13:13–14*), the second signalled his personal rejection, in God's eyes, as king (*1 Sam. 15:26*). *1 Sam. 16* opens with the LORD confirming that Saul, in essence the people's king (*1 Sam. 8:18, 22; 12:13*), has been definitively rejected. The LORD then goes on to announce that he has selected his own king (in Heb. lit. 'for me'; *cf.* the 'man after his own heart/of his own choosing' of *1 Sam. 13:14* and the neighbour 'better than you' of *1 Sam. 15:28*). It is hard to avoid the conclusion that in Saul the people received the object of their sinful request for a king 'such as all the nations have' and in the same person also the punishment for that sin (perhaps *cf. Hos. 13:10–11*).

The king of God's choosing was David, son of Jesse (*1 Sam. 16:1–13*). Though no stranger to sin (e.g. *2 Sam. 11*), David had a heart for God (*cf. 1 Sam. 16:7*). More importantly, 'the LORD [was] with him' (*1 Sam. 16:18; 18:12, 14, 28*), and the LORD promised him a kingdom that would 'endure forever before me' (*2 Sam. 7:16*). God's promise to David of an enduring kingdom, recorded in *2 Sam. 7:4–17* (*cf. 1 Chron. 17:3–15*), has been called the theological summit of the OT. Looking backward, it took up the promises of blessing made to Abraham and his elect seed (*Gen. 12:2–3*) and brought them to rest on David (see esp. *2 Sam. 7:9–10, 12*). Looking forward, it set the stage for the messianic hope that would become a dominant thread in the fabric of Israel's faith both before and after the Exile (see below).

David's rule, like that of God himself, was characterized not only by subjugation of Israel's enemies (*2 Sam. 8:1–14*) but also by 'just and right' action (*v. 15*), as measured presumably by the 'regulations of the kingship' (*1 Sam. 10:25*) and the 'Law of Moses' (*1 Kings 2:3; cf. Neh. 9:13*; on God's 'just and right' rule, see *Pss. 89:14; 99:4*). As Jeroboam later came to be viewed as the quintessential wicked king

(*1 Kings 15:34; 16:2, 19*; etc.), so David came to stand for the ideal, loyal and faithful theocratic king (*1 Kings 11:4, 16; 14:8*; etc.). Yet neither David nor his descendants fully lived up to the ideal. And their very failures gave rise to a hope that one day a truly 'righteous Branch' would appear in the line of David, a 'King' who would 'reign wisely and do what is just and right in the land' (*Jer. 23:5; cf. 33:15*). This messianic expectation came frequently to expression in the prophetic writings (e.g. *Is. 11:1; Jer. 23:5–6; Ezek. 34:24; Hos. 3:5; Zech. 3:8; 6:12*) and was only heightened by the fall of Judah and the destruction of the Temple.

It was indeed in the person of a son of David that the OT's messianic expectations were fulfilled. Jesus, the Christ (which means the Messiah, the anointed one), was acclaimed by God the Father at both his baptism and his transfiguration with words rich in messianic resonances: 'This is my Son, whom I love; with him I am well pleased' (*Matt. 3:17* [baptism]; *17:5* [transfiguration]). 'This is my son' recalls 'You are my son' of *Ps. 2:7*, a royal messianic psalm. 'With him I am well pleased' recalls 'my chosen one in whom I delight' of *Is. 42:1*, the first of Isaiah's messianic suffering servant songs. 'Whom I love' may even recall 'whom you love' of *Gen. 22:2*, the verse in which God charged Abraham to take his only son and sacrifice him. Kingship, suffering, sacrifice – all these were implied in the simple words of God the Father to his one and only Son. Is it any wonder that Jesus was immediately 'led by the Spirit into the desert to be tempted by the devil' (*Matt. 4:1*)? Would Jesus accept a messianic role that would lead to a criminal's cross before a kingly crown?

Those who know and accept the testimony of Scripture know that the answer is *yes*. The apostle Paul eloquently summarizes the humiliation followed by exaltation that was the purpose of the first coming of Jesus, the Christ, 'who, being in very nature God, did not consider equality with God something to be grasped, but made himself nothing, taking the very nature of a servant, being made in human likeness. And being found in appearance as a man, he humbled himself and became obedient to death – even death on a cross! Therefore God exalted him to the highest place and gave him the name that is above every name, that at the name of Jesus every knee should bow, in heaven and on earth and under the earth, and every tongue confess that Jesus Christ is Lord, to the glory of God the Father' (*Phil. 2:6–11*). In the light of what Jesus' death accomplished, there was irony, but surely no inaccuracy, in the words Pilate posted at the head of Jesus' Cross: 'THIS IS JESUS, THE KING OF THE JEWS' (*Matt. 27:37; cf. John 18:37*).

Our discussion of kingship in the Bible began with the recognition that God, the Creator, is king by right. In *1 Tim. 6:15*, Paul acknowledges the Father as 'the blessed and only Ruler, the King of kings and Lord of lords.' *Rev. 19:16* completes the circle, describing the Son also as 'King of kings and Lord of lords.' Jesus, co-creator with the Father (*John 1:3; Col. 1:16*), entered his own creation to establish his Kingdom. It is a Kingdom that cannot be built by human striving nor entered by human effort. It is a Kingdom populated by 'a chosen people, a royal priesthood, a holy nation, a people belonging to God,' a people not only called 'out of darkness into his wonderful light' (*1 Pet. 2:9*), but a people purchased by the blood of the king (*Acts 20:28; Rev. 5:9; Col. 1:16–20*). It is this Kingdom to which the promises of the OT point and of which the Davidic kings were but a faint foreshadowing.

P.L.

**KISH** **1.** One of the sons of Jeiel and his wife Maacah, this Kish was one of the forefathers of Kish the father of Saul, and is mentioned in *1 Chron. 8:30.*

**2.** The father of King Saul and from the tribe of Benjamin (*1 Chron. 8:33; 9:39; 12:1; 26:28*). He was a 'man of standing' and the son of Abiel (*1 Sam. 9:1; 10:11, 21; 14:51*). Kish was buried in Zela in Benjamin (*2 Sam. 21:14*). On one occasion some of his donkeys went missing and so Kish sent his son Saul to travel the country to find them (*1 Sam. 9:3*). This quest was unsuccessful and so Saul was encouraged by his servant to consult Samuel the 'man of God'. Eventually the donkeys were found, but that contact between Saul and Samuel was the first of many as the prophet anointed Saul to be king of Israel (*1 Sam. 9:19–20; 10:1; Acts 13:21*).

**3.** A Levite from the clan of Merari who was the son of Mahli and the father of Jerahmeel (*1 Chron. 23:21–22; 24:29*).

**4.** This Kish was another Merarite Levite. He lived in the time of King Hezekiah of Judah and may have been a descendant of 3. above. He was called upon to help purify the Temple during the time of revival in Hezekiah's reign (*2 Chron. 29:12*).

**5.** A Benjamite who was the great-grandfather of Mordecai, the Jew responsible for helping Queen Esther save the Jewish people (*Est. 2:5*).       P.D.G.

**KISHI,** son of Abdi, was a Levite from the Merari clan and the father of Ethan. Ethan served in the Tabernacle (*1 Chron. 6:44*). In *1 Chron. 15:17–19* an Ethan son of Kushaiah is mentioned. It is possible that Kushaiah and Kishi are the same person.

**KISLON** was from the tribe of Benjamin and was the father of Eldad (*Num. 34:21*). Eldad was chosen by Moses to be the leader of the tribe of Benjamin.

**KOHATH** was Levi's second son and a grandson of Jacob (*Gen. 46:11; Exod. 6:16; Num. 3:17; 26:57; 1 Chron. 6:1, 16*). He became the progenitor of various Kohathite clans such as the Amramites and Hebronites, through his four sons. During the wilderness years the Kohathites were 'responsible for the care of the sanctuary' and they camped on the south side of the Tabernacle. The leaders of the Kohathites were responsible for caring for the ark, the table and many articles used in ministering in the sanctuary (*Exod. 6:18; Num. 3:27–32; 26:58; 1 Chron. 6:2, 18, 22, 38; 15:5; 23:12*). One of Kohath's descendants, Korah, took part in a rebellion against Moses (*Num. 16*).

In the days of Joshua, ten towns were given to the Kohathites together with their pasture lands (*Josh. 21:20–26*). Kohath's later descendants served the LORD in the work of the Tabernacle during the days of King David, when the various descendants of Levi were divided up into their main families for work in the Tabernacle and later in the Temple (*1 Chron. 23:6, 12–20*). They are mentioned again working in the Temple in the days of Solomon and Hezekiah (*2 Chron. 29:12; 34: 12*).       P.D.G.

**KOLAIAH** **1.** Kolaiah was from the tribe of Benjamin and was the father of Pedaiah. He is mentioned in *Neh. 11:7.*

**2.** The father of Ahab, who lived in the time of Zedekiah and the prophet Jeremiah (*Jer. 29:21*). Ahab was one of the false prophets who continually tried to promote a popular message of good news ahead for the people of Judah. He was condemned by Jeremiah.

## KORAH, THE CLAN LEADER

The most well-known Korah was the son of Izhar, the son of Levi (Exod. 6:21) who became a clan leader in his tribe (Exod. 6:24; 1 Chron. 6:22). Together with the Reubenites, Dathan and Abiram, and 250 other Israelite community leaders, he led an insurrection against Moses and Aaron (Num. 16:1–2). Their chief objection to Moses and Aaron appears to have been based on jealousy at the power the two kept to themselves, power that God had given them. They disliked the way in which only Aaron and his sons could burn incense. The Levites argued that all God's people were holy and thus the separation of Aaron and his family for the particular task of burning incense did not seem right (vv. 3, 7). But they also disliked the power that Moses himself wielded and objected to the way in which he now 'lorded it' over the people having brought them out of 'a land flowing with milk and honey' (Egypt) into the desert (vv. 12–14).

Moses was prepared to ask God to indicate who was right and so he summonsed the Levites the following morning to bring their censers and light them so the LORD could show who was holy (Num. 16:4–7, 16–18). Dathan and Abiram were in full rebellion and refused to come, but the following morning Korah and his company did appear before the Tent of Meeting where 'the glory of the LORD appeared to the entire assembly' (v. 19). The LORD told Moses and Aaron to step aside so he could destroy the assembly but, following the immediate intercession of both Moses and Aaron, the LORD stayed his judgment on the whole people and, through Moses, ordered that people stand away from the tents of Korah, Dathan and Abiram (vv. 20–24).

Moses called these families out of their tents and pointed out to the people that this test was not his idea. However, if these families lived to an old age then Moses would not have been sent by God. If something 'totally new' happened, that is, that the families and all their belongings were swallowed up by the ground, then they would know that these people were in sinful rebellion against the LORD.

The ground opened and the people were swallowed up. Fire came down from heaven and consumed the 250 men with their censers and the whole congregation of Israelites fled the scene. Later the bronze from their censers was taken and made into an overlay for the altar in the Tabernacle as a reminder that only Aaron and his sons could burn incense before the LORD (Num. 16:31–40). The very next day, though, the people continued their grumbling against Moses and Aaron, this time arguing that they were responsible for the deaths of the Israelite people. Again the 'glory of the LORD' was revealed and he sent a plague among the people as judgment for their continued rebellion. Once again it was only the interceding prayer and sacrifice of atonement offered by Aaron that saved the people, but not before some 14,700 people had died (vv. 41–50).

Korah's rebellion became infamous and stood as a warning to all future generations of Israelites of the dangers of obstructing or rebelling against the LORD's appointed leaders, although we are later told that not all of Korah's descendants were wiped out (Num. 26:10–11).

As a result of this rebellion and the concerns expressed about the duties of the Levites, the various priestly functions were more clearly spelled out. Aaron's place was established, but the other Levites were given clear areas of responsibility (*Num. 17–18*). These responsibilities for the descendants of Korah involved being 'gatekeepers' to the Tent of Meeting and later in the Temple (*1 Chron. 9:19; 26:19*). His descendants were also involved in the musical side of worship (*1 Chron. 6:37*; and the introductions to *Pss. 42; 44–49; 84–85; 87–88*).

The tragedy of Korah's rebellion indicates clearly the holiness, judgment and mercy of God. Because of God's holiness he is to be approached through sacrifice, but not just any sacrifice. It must be sacrifice and intercession carried out in the way he prescribes. When this is done people demonstrate their obedience and faith in him and experience his overwhelming mercy in the face of their sin. However, when people think they can reach God in their own way, they simply demonstrate clearly their lack of faith in God's appointed ways, and their rebellion against him and his laws and so judgment ensues. In spite of this, God's merciful hand is seen in rescuing from judgment many thousands of people who deserved death in their rebellion, because Aaron and Moses stood in their place and interceded for them and Aaron offered the sacrifice of atonement on their behalf.

Such priesthood in Scripture prefigures the work of Christ on the cross who died, though sinless, in the place of his sinful people. *I Pet. 3:18*: 'For Christ died for sins once for all, the righteous for the unrighteous, to bring you to God.'

P.D.G.

**KORAH** (Heb., 'bald').
**1.** See *Korah, the clan leader*.
**2.** The son of Esau and Oholibamah, Korah became an Edomite chief. He was born in Canaan (*Gen. 36:5, 14, 18; 1 Chron. 1:35*).
**3.** An Edomite leader who was the grandson of Esau and Adah (a Canaanite woman) and son of Eliphaz (*Gen. 36:16*).
**4.** A leader in the tribe of Judah and a son of Hebron (*1 Chron. 2:43*).

**KORE 1.** One of the descendants of Korah. The Korahites from the tribe of Levi were 'gatekeepers' for the Tabernacle and later for the Temple. Kore is described as the father of Shallum who was a priest in the time of King David (*1 Chron. 9:19*), which means that a number of generations

are omitted (*1 Chron. 26:1*).
**2.** Another 'gatekeeper' and son of Imnah, probably also a Korahite. He was in charge of receiving the freewill offerings from the LORD's people and distributing the gifts during the time of revival under King Hezekiah (*2 Chron. 31:14*). It is interesting to note how, when God's people truly return to worship, they give in great abundance to the LORD's work (see also *2 Chron. 34:9–11*). P.D.G.

**KOZ** From the tribe of Judah, Koz is listed as one of the sons of Helah and father of Anub (*1 Chron. 4:8*).

**KUSHAIAH** The father of Ethan, a Merarite Levite. He is probably the same person as Kishi (*1 Chron. 6:44; 15:17*).

# L

**LAADAH** Mentioned in 1 Chron. 4:21, Laadah was the father of Mareshah and a grandson of Judah. He was a leader of the clans of linen workers who lived at Beth Ashbea.

**LABAN** figures largely in the narratives of Isaac's and Jacob's marriages (Gen. 24:29; 29:5–29). The main interest in his inclusion is the clash of the opportunist, unscrupulous Jacob (Gen. 25:27–34; 27:19) with an even more efficient 'Mr Fixit' than himself (29:22–27; 30:31–36). Though Jacob deluded himself that he had outsmarted his father-in-law (Gen. 30:37–43), it was only to find that it was the watchful LORD who safeguarded his interests (31:6–12). Laban was fundamentally a money man (Gen. 24:30–31) and his daughter Rachel evidently learned from him to keep an eye on the main chance (31:19), for, possibly, the 'household gods' had some significance in property-inheritance. Laban's one essay in religion was a covenant safeguarding his 'sphere of interest' (Gen. 31:51–54).                    J.A.M.

**LADAN 1.** An Ephraimite who was an ancestor of Joshua. His father was Tahan and his son was Ammihud (1 Chron. 7:26).
**2.** One of the Gershonite Levites whose duties were assigned by David towards the end of his reign in anticipation of their work in the Temple. His descendants were given charge of looking after precious stones that were brought as gifts and put in the Temple treasury (1 Chron. 23:7–9; 26:21).

**LAEL** The father of Eliasaph who became the leader of the Gershonite family of Levites (Num. 3:24). The Gershonites became responsible for part of the care of the Tent of Meeting.

**LAHAD** (Heb., 'slow'). One of the descendants of Judah and son of Jahath. Together with his brother Ahumai they formed the clans of the Zorathites (1 Chron. 4:2).

**LAHMI** (Heb., 'warrior'). Lahmi was the brother of Goliath the Gittite and was himself a huge man, carrying a spear 'with a shaft like a weaver's rod' (1 Chron. 20:5). One of David's great warriors, Elhanan, killed him in a battle between the Israelites and Philistines. See *Elhanan*.

**LAISH** was the father of Paltiel and came from Gallim. Paltiel was husband to Saul's daughter Michal, even though Michal had been promised to David. Later Saul's son, Ishbosheth, gave Michal back to David, much to Paltiel's distress (1 Sam. 25:44; 2 Sam. 3:15–16).

**LAMECH** Two very different men bear the name Lamech: one (Gen. 4:18–24) offers proof of the presence and prevalence of sin; the other (Gen. 5:25–30; 1 Chron. 1:3) is a prophet of comfort and rest.
**1.** Lamech, son of Methushael. Gen. 4 develops the story of the Fall (Gen. 3) by tracing some of its consequences. Lamech is selected to show sin as destructive of God's ordering of society and as insatiable in its demands. He is the Bible's first recorded polygamist. One of the first

fruits of the Fall was a dislocation (Gen. 3:12) between the first married couple and a fundamental corruption of marriage itself (Gen. 3:16–20). Lamech's polygamy reveals an ongoing downward spiral from the divine ideal. But also, in addition to his sexual domination of woman, Lamech displays that savage spirit of arrogant self-centredness which is the cardinal characteristic of sin: for as little as a 'bruise' and a 'blow' he exacted a death-penalty and announced that sevenfold vengeance would be the law of his life. But one day the law of the sinner's venge-fulness would be dwarfed by the measure of the redeemed sinner's law of forgive-ness (Matt. 18:22).

**2.** Lamech, father of Noah. The Fall disrupted the economic basis of life (Gen. 3:17–19). No more now would they 'eat freely of every tree of the garden' but there would rather be an unending battle be-tween man and the environment in the mere attempt to stay alive. It would seem that Lamech longed for the day when the curse would be removed and, in faith that that day was about to dawn, called his son 'Noah', a name related to the verb 'to rest'. In Noah a 'new world' did indeed begin (Gen. 8:15), under divine blessing (Gen. 9:1) and covenant care (9:17) but Noah was not the 'son' a curse-laden world needed (9:20). That task was to devolve on an immeasurably greater Son!  J.A.M.

**LAPPIDOTH** (Heb., 'torches'). Lappidoth was the husband of Deborah, a proph-etess, who became one of the judges in Israel during the period of the Judges (Judg. 4:4). This is the only time he is mentioned. See Deborah.

**LAZARUS 1.** Lazarus, in Luke 16:19–31, was the name of a beggar in Jesus' parable. He was the only character named in a parable, probably because Lazarus is an abbreviation of the Heb. 'he whom God helps', the point the parable demonstrated.

In the parable Lazarus' wretchedness in poverty, disease and hunger is starkly contrasted to the rich man at whose gate he begged, who lived in wealth and luxury. After death, however, Lazarus was revealed to be a true member of the covenant people, and was received by angels to a place of honour beside Abraham in the messianic banquet of heaven. The rich man died and in the agony of God's judgment realized the consequences of his failure to repent, so appealed to his ancestor Abraham to send Lazarus to alleviate his suffering, but after death, judgment was decisive and contact impossible. The rich man then asked Lazarus to be sent to warn his surviving brothers of the eternal reality awaiting them, but their rejection of God's Word through Moses and the prophets, indi-cated that even a resurrection would not have persuaded them to repent.

The parable teaches through Lazarus, that earthly humiliation may yet promise eternal glorification to those faithful to God's Word; while those failing to practice the covenant responsibilities of mercy and love face an eternal punish-ment. The reference to resurrection is an ironic anticipation of the sceptical re-action Jesus' resurrection would pro-voke from the Pharisees to whom he addressed this parable (Luke 16:14).

**2.** Lazarus, in John 11:1–12:19, was the brother of Mary and Martha, living in Bethany. Jesus had previously been a guest at their home (Luke 10:38–42) and had a particularly deep affection for them (John 11:3, 5, 33, 35).

Lazarus fell severely ill, so Mary and Martha sent word to Jesus. Jesus, on hearing the news, prophesied the illness would not result in Lazarus' death, but rather in a revelation by God of Jesus' true glory (John 11:4). Thus despite his con-cern, Jesus, in obedience to his father's will, delayed his departure for two days. Knowing Lazarus had died, Jesus announced his intention to return to

Bethany, despite threats to his life in Judea, in order to 'wake' Lazarus from death (v. 11). His disciples characteristically misunderstood him (vv. 12–13), but Jesus anticipated that Lazarus' resurrection would lead them to a genuine faith in him (v. 15).

After a four-day journey (John 11:17), Jesus was met on the outskirts of Bethany, by Martha. Her continued trust in Jesus, despite believing Jesus' presence could have prevented Lazarus' death, elicited Jesus' self-revelation, 'I am the resurrection and the life' (v. 25). This confirmed for her his Messianic identity (v. 27). After fetching Mary, weeping in her grief, Jesus was deeply disturbed (v. 33 – implying anger, not just empathy) at this example of the effect of sin and death in the world. Going to the tomb, he commanded the removal of the stone seal. In faith, despite the stench, the stone was removed and Jesus prayed audibly so that Lazarus' miraculous resurrection would evoke faith. Calling into the tomb, with a word of command, the dead Lazarus was raised to life and came out.

Jesus' miracle evoked faith in some (John 11:45), but reports provoked a plot of the Sanhedrin to kill Jesus (v. 53) and the resurrected Lazarus (John 12:10). Lazarus' full recovery was emphasized by Jesus eating with them (John 12:2); and Lazarus attracted a crowd (v. 9) which fuelled popular Messianic speculation about Jesus (vv. 12–15, 17).

In Lazarus' resurrection, Jesus demonstrated his divine life-giving power and foreshadowed his authority over the promised general resurrection. Lazarus, however, was only resurrected to a renewed earthly life, while Jesus' resurrection formed the prototype of the resurrection awaiting Christians.          R.M.

**LEAH** Outshone by her sister (Gen. 29:17), married by trickery (29:22–26), less favoured by her husband – and knowing it (29:30, 31, 32, 33), even her death

and burial only referred to incidentally afterwards (49:31), Leah is one of the sad figures of sacred history. But the watchful Lord (Gen. 29:31) brought compensations and, though knowing the indignities of polygamy (30:14–16), she found fulfilment in motherhood and children (e.g., 30:13) and had her unique place in the divine purposes as the major foundress of the people of God (Ruth 4:11).

J.A.M.

**LEBANA** (Heb., 'white'). A leader of one of the families of Temple servants. His descendants returned from the Babylonian Exile in the days of Ezra and worked on the Temple (Neh. 7:48). In Ezra 2:45 the name is spelled Lebanah.

**LEBANAH** Found in Ezra 2:45. See Lebana.

**LECAH** Mentioned in 1 Chron. 4:21, Lecah was the son of Er and a grandson of Judah. He was a leader of the clans of linen workers who lived at Beth Ashbea.

**LEGION** This was the name normally applied to a Roman military company of troops numbering 4,000 to 5,000. In the NT it came to signify hosts of spiritual beings (e.g. Matt. 26:53). In Mark 5:9 and Luke 8:30 it appears as a proper name for a man who was demon possessed. Mark 5:9,15 explains the name by saying this man 'had been possessed by a legion of demons'. The name had come to signify the unusually large number of demons by which he was possessed.

In vivid detail Mark 5 describes the incident in which Jesus healed the man by casting out the demons. The man was behaving thoroughly wildly and lived among the tombs in the area of the Gerasenes. People had tried chaining him up but he had simply broken free with his abnormal power. By means of the demons within him, he identified Jesus as 'Son of the Most High God' and implicitly recognized Jesus' right to sit in judgment on him. Jesus cast out the demons which went into a herd of pigs. The pigs ran down the hillside into the lake where they were drowned, causing those in the area to ask Jesus to leave them. Jesus told the man to go home and tell his family how the Lord had had mercy on him.

In this incident, once again the right of the Son of God to judge and his power even over spiritual forces was manifest to those who were watching. That these demons were real is indicated by their ability to discern who Jesus was, something which people in their right mind had not yet understood. Once cured Legion then proclaimed the Lord's work among the cities of the Decapolis, 'and all the people were amazed' (*Mark 5:20*).

P.D.G.

**LEMUEL** (Heb., 'dedicated to God'). The author of *Prov. 31:1–9*. Some scholars used to equate King Lemuel with Solomon but this is rather unlikely. He is called 'King of Massa' in *v. 1* (not NIV), which would probably mean he was an Arab king. The proverbs were taught him by his mother and have to do largely with warnings about the dangers of spending time and energies on wine and women. He was also told to uphold justice and the rights of those who were destitute. It is not clear whether the rest of *Prov. 31*, describing the ideal wife, should also be attributed to him.

**LEPER** Leprosy is a skin disease that, though treatable these days, remains serious and takes a number of different forms. In biblical times no treatment was available for this illness that left the sufferer with obvious skin disfiguration. Often these obvious signs of the disease would appear first on the face. In the OT sufferers were required to be isolated. *Lev. 13* offers a detailed description of some of the symptoms of the diseases that were to be considered 'ceremonially unclean'. Depending on these symptoms, the person had to be in isolation from the community for a set period of time. Sometimes this could be for years and years. If eventually the symptoms disappeared, then they could return to normal life, but only after visiting the priest and being examined by him. His word was final in these matters.

In the NT a number of lepers came to Jesus for healing. As with other outcasts, Jesus accepted them, talked to them, and did heal them (e.g. *Matt. 8:2–3; 17:2; 26:6; Luke 7:22; Mark 14:3* etc.). The only leper mentioned by name was Simon (*Mark 14:3*), who provides us with an interesting example of how Jesus was quite able to accept those who were socially outcast in this way. In *Mark 14* Jesus is reclining at table eating in Simon's house. See *Simon the leper.*

P.D.G.

**LEVI 1.** Levi was the third son of Jacob, born to Leah. Scholars disagree on the etymology of his name, suggesting derivation from his mother's name (which means 'wild cow') or from the word for 'to pledge'. However, its significance is clear from his birth account. At Levi's birth Leah proclaimed, 'Now at last my husband will become attached to me' (*Gen. 29:34*). Forming a word-play based upon the verb 'to attach oneself', she declared his name. In the immediate context this reflected the continuing rivalry between Leah and Rachel (*cf. v. 30*). As the eponym of the Levite tribe, Levi's name might have connoted to Israel, the original audience, that the Levites played a significant role in preserving the bond (covenant) between God and the nation.

Only two other episodes in Scripture deal explicitly with Levi. The first, in *Gen. 34*, recounts how Simeon and Levi revenged the rape of their sister Dinah. After convincing them to circumcise themselves as part of the marriage arrangement, the two brothers attacked the Shechemites while they were recovering.

409

Although the act was condemned by Jacob (*Gen. 34:30*) and became the reason he withheld patriarchal favour (*Gen. 49:5*), yet it may not be completely such. This act of revenge is similar to the deadly zeal displayed by later Levites (*Exod. 32:25–29, Num. 25:6–13*). With the Shechemites a desirable result was achieved – the inhabitants of the land feared them and left them alone (*Gen. 35:5*). For the original audience, it would have inspired some proper fear of the Levites who were charged with guarding the Tabernacle and the holy things and with enforcing holiness within the nation.

The final mention of Levi, son of Jacob, is in the joint 'blessing' he received with Simeon at their father's deathbed (*Gen. 49:5–7*). Jacob's continued displeasure with their vengeful act reflected more self-interest than interest in divine justice (*cf. Gen. 35:30*). This interpretation is enhanced by the possibility that the 'ox' (singular) referred to in *Gen. 49:6* may be Jacob himself. The zeal of the brothers 'hamstrung', or put at risk, Jacob. See also *Levites*.                    M.G.

**2.** Mentioned in Luke's genealogy leading from Jesus and Joseph back to Adam (*Luke 3:24*). He was the father of Matthat, the son of Melki and probably the grandfather to Joseph.

**3.** Another Levi appears in Luke's genealogy leading from Jesus and Joseph back to Adam. He was the son of Simeon and the father of another Matthat (*Luke 3:29*).

**4.** The name given on occasion to the apostle Matthew (*Mark 2:14*). After hearing the call of Jesus to follow him, Levi left his work and did follow Jesus. Soon he held a great banquet for fellow tax-collectors to introduce them to Jesus (*Luke 5:27–29*). For more detail see *Matthew*.                    P.D.G.

## LEVITES AND PRIESTS

The Levites were the descendants of Levi, third son of Jacob, and thus made up one of the twelve tribes of the nation of Israel. Their name, like that of their eponym, connoted the notion of joining or attaching. In *Num. 18:2* Moses made a word-play upon the verb 'to join' in his instructions to the Levites. There they were attached to Aaron's service, who was himself a Levite, for the administration of the Tent of Meeting (Tabernacle) (*Num. 18:6; Exod. 38:21*). In their initial duties of preserving holiness in the camp, they were seen to be like their eponym in their avenging zeal for God (*Exod. 32:27–28*; see *Gen. 34:25–30; 49:5*).

Consistent with their priestly duties, they became a substitute for every first-born of Israel. Just as God claimed in judgment all the first-born of Egypt in the Passover plague, so he claimed all the first-born of the Israelites for his service (*Exod. 13:2*). But the means of effecting this service was that the Levites would be their substitutes (*Num. 3:12ff.*). As such, the tribe was allotted no tribal inheritance because 'the LORD was his inheritance' (*Deut. 10:9*). Instead, through the support of the tithe and the Levitical cities they were to live directly from the hand of God (*Lev. 27:32ff.; Num. 18:21, 24; 35:1–8*).

The significance of this substitutionary status is that they were acting, not strictly as a special professional clergy class, but as representatives of every common family of Israel. And although the Levites had certain tasks which were restricted to them, the lay person should have sought ways to imitate the Levite's functions in his or her own area of responsibility.

Three classes were distinguished within the Levites. The broadest identity belonged to those designated 'Levites'. Consisting in all of the members of the tribe, their general responsibilities pertained initially to the Tabernacle (Num. 3:6ff.). After the building of the Temple their duties were adapted to Temple worship (1 Chron. 23:24ff.). Within the Levitical tribe there were the descendants of Aaron denoted as 'priests' (Exod. 28:1; 30:30; 40:15). Their duties pertained to the offering of sacrifices and the service of the sanctuary itself – that is, the holy place (Lev. 1–7). This privilege was not automatically and perpetually reserved for Aaron's family, however, as seen in Ezekiel's promotion of the Zadokites to this status (Ezek. 44:15–16) due to the implied unfaithfulness of the Aaronites.

Within the priests was the individual designated 'high priest'. He was to be a descendant of Aaron's grandson Phinehas and served for life (Num. 25:10–14). The high priest wore the garments of Aaron (Exod. 28) which were themselves a pattern of the Tabernacle, signifying the priest as a holy dwelling of God. He performed the special duty of making the annual atonement offering in the holy of holies on the Day of Atonement (Lev. 16).

The Levites functioned in two directions. In some respects they were to represent the people before God, but in other respects to represent God before the people. The former posture is illustrated by the giving of offerings and the latter in enforcing the holy restrictions around the Tabernacle. Both dimensions of the Levites' work related to their primary function – to promote the holiness of the people. They were to carry out the implications of God's requirement that all the people be holy as he is holy (Lev. 11:44–45).

The work of the Levites may also be seen in terms of their similarity and dissimilarity with the people as a whole. They were dissimilar in terms of the unique places and functions reserved for them, e.g. the Tabernacle/Temple and the offering of sacrifices, respectively. They also had higher requirements of personal perfection to fulfil (Lev. 21:18–23). They were to guard the holy presence to keep out the laity (Num. 1:53; 3:10). In this last respect they functioned in the well-known Ancient Near Eastern office of the priest/soldier who guarded the god's temple/palace. In their unique roles they served to remind Israel that God was holy and separate.

But the Levites also were similar to the people in that Israel was to be a kingdom of priests and a holy nation (Exod. 19:5–6). Their functions as priests would have been a paradigm for the layperson to imitate. For example, just as the Levite put to death any unclean presence around the sanctuary, so also the people of Israel were to put to death any unclean presence in their assigned venue – the land as a whole (e.g. false prophets in Deut. 13:5 or the holy war in general). This principle of imitation is symbolized in how every person was to wear a blue thread (Num. 15:38) as a reminder of their function parallel to the high priest (Exod. 28:31).

In their broader responsibilities the Levites also performed teaching (Deut. 32:10; Mal. 2:5–7), judicial (2 Chron. 19:8, 11) and discerning (Deut. 33:8; 1 Sam. 23:6–12) functions. All these were directed toward the end that Israel be distinct and separate – holy – as the people of God, not only in their worship life, but in national conduct.

Through the NT, particularly the book of Hebrews, we see that believers in Christ come into full status as a kingdom of priests (Rev. 1:6; 5:10) through the high priesthood of Jesus Christ (*Heb. 7–8*). What the Levitical priesthood could never do (*Heb. 10:4*), even though it pointed toward Christ in its work (*Heb. 9:8–9*), Christ himself did once and for all (*Heb. 9:11–12*).                    M.G.

**LIBNI**  **1.** Libni was one of the two sons of Gershon, the other being Shimei. He was the head of the 'Libnite' clan and the grandson of Levi (*Exod. 6:17; Num. 3:18, 21;26:58; 1 Chron. 6:17, 20*).

**2.** A descendant of Merari and a Levite, this Libni was the son of Mahli (*1 Chron. 6:29*).

**LIKHI** A leader of the tribe of Manasseh, and one of the sons of Shemida (*1 Chron. 7:19*).

**LINUS** He was one of Paul's friends who sent greetings to Timothy at the end of Paul's second letter to him (*2 Tim. 4:21*). Paul was writing from prison in Rome and mentions Pudens, Claudia and 'all the brothers' as also sending these greetings. Irenaeus and Eusebius both wrote that Linus became the first bishop of Rome following the death of the apostles Peter and Paul.

**LO-AMMI** (Heb., 'not my people'). This is the name the LORD ordered Hosea the prophet to give to his second son by his wife Gomer (*Hos. 1:9*). The name was full of prophetic significance. Their first child, a son, had been called Jezreel because the LORD had said, 'Call him Jezreel, because I will soon punish the house of Jehu for the massacre at Jezreel, and I will put an end to the kingdom of Israel. In that day I will break Israel's bow in the Valley of Jezreel' (*vv. 4–5*). Their second child, a daughter, had been called Lo-Ruhamah (Heb., 'not pitied'). Through the prophet's words and family circumstances, the LORD was showing Israel that again and again she had been unfaithful to him and was thus going to be judged. Their disobedience would lead to the LORD no longer showing pity on Israel, the Northern Kingdom, and no longer forgiving them (*Hos. 1:6*). The LORD then told Hosea to name their second son Lo-Ammi, 'for you are not my people and I am not your God' (*v. 9*).

In spite of the dire warnings to Israel, Hosea also provided the people with the promise of future restoration: 'In the place where it was said to them, "You are not my people," they will be called "sons of the living God".' It was this promise that the apostle Paul picked up in *Rom. 9:25–26*. There he applied the promise of hope to his own times and the coming of the gospel of Christ to Jews and Gentiles of faith. The fulfilment of Hosea's message was thus seen in the coming of Christ as Saviour. Christ brought God's pity and forgiveness and made for himself a people who were to be called 'sons of the living God'.                    P.D.G.

**LO-RUHAMAH** (Heb., 'not pitied'). Hosea's second child, by his wife Gomer, was a daughter, and she was given this name by the LORD. See also the names of the other children: Lo-Ammi and Jezreel. The name was full of prophetic significance. The LORD said she was to be called this 'for I will no longer show love to the house of Israel, that I should at all forgive them' (*Hos. 1:6, 8*). The names of the children were to be a graphic picture of God's covenant rejection of his people in view of their continued rebellion and disobedience. He was about to withdraw his sustaining covenant love for his people. Their first child, a son, the LORD had called Jezreel 'because I will soon punish the house of Jehu for the massacre at Jezreel, and I will put an end to the kingdom of Israel. In that day I will break Israel's bow in the Valley of Jezreel' (*vv. 4–5*). The third child, a son, was named

Lo-Ammi, meaning 'not my people', 'for you are not my people and I am not your God' (v. 9).

However, in spite of the dire warnings to Israel, Hosea also provided the people with the promise of future restoration: 'I will show my love to the one I called "Not my loved one." I will say to those called "Not my people", "You are my people"; and they will say, "You are my God"' (Hos. 2:23). It was this promise that the apostle Paul picked up in Rom. 9:25–26. There he applied the promise of hope to his own times and the coming of the gospel of Christ to Jews and Gentiles of faith. The Gentiles were 'not my people' who were now to be called 'you are my people' as they turned in faith to Christ. The fulfilment of Hosea's message was thus seen in the coming of Christ as Saviour. Christ brought God's pity and forgiveness and made for himself a people who were to be called 'sons of the living God'.                                    P.D.G.

**LOIS** was Timothy's grandmother (2 Tim. 1:5). It is likely that Lois and Eunice, Timothy's mother, were converted on Paul's first visit to Lystra (Acts 14:8–20), for Timothy appears to have known about the persecution Paul suffered while there (2 Tim. 3:11; Acts 16:1). Although little is known of either Lois or Eunice, their influence on Timothy in bringing him up to know and love the Lord of the Scriptures was considerable and praised by the apostle Paul (2 Tim. 3:14–16). It was knowledge of the Scriptures that led to his understanding of salvation through faith in Christ and it was this background that had prepared him so well for the ministry of an evangelist to which God called him through the apostle Paul.

In an age when the 'extended family' has almost ceased to exist in most Western countries, it is of great importance to see how influential a believing grandmother and mother could be in the life of a child, seeing him grow up to be a Christian. Such encouragement in the faith across the generations is often seen in Scripture. The fact that almost certainly Timothy had a non-believing father should give much hope to the many men and women who find themselves in similar positions today. Grandparents who are Christians and see grandchildren growing up without Christian teaching should recognize the significant impact they can often have as they teach Scriptures to their grandchildren.
                                    P.D.G.

## LORD AND LORD

### The nouns and the Name

The OT uses two main nouns for 'God': one expresses 'God in his transcendent uniqueness' (Heb. 'El. e.g. Is. 40:18) and the other 'God in the fulness of his divine attributes' (Heb., 'Elohim). But either way, 'God is a common noun for a certain Being, just as 'man' (Heb., 'Adam, 'Ish) is a common noun. The word 'Lord' (when it is printed in our English versions with lower case 'ord') stands for the Heb. 'Adonai, meaning 'Sovereign' (e.g. Is. 6:1; cf. v. 5), describing a certain quality of the divine Being, namely that he rules and reigns as an actual 'managing director', total in his supremacy over people and events. But, by contrast, 'LORD' (four upper case letters in our English versions) is the proper noun or name, 'Yahweh'. It is as if 'God' were his surname. 'Lord' is his status in the order of things, and 'Yahweh' is his forename or personal name. As the relationship developed between the great God and his people, so he came to expect them to recognize him as Yahweh.

## 'Yahweh' and 'LORD'

Even in the OT itself we may very well be correct to sense the first hesitations about using the divine Name. Note how 'LORD' appears in *Ps. 14*, 'God' is used in *Ps. 53*! This is usually understood as a retreat from using the name 'Yahweh' as something too sacred. Between the Testaments, when Judaism arose, this process accelerated and when vowel-signs were added to the Hebrew Text (from the 5th century AD onwards) it was made impossible even by accident to pronounce the Name because the consonants *YHWH* were given the vowels appropriate to 'Adonai. In this way the synagogue reader, for example, coming to the Name would actually say the word for 'Lord' and English Bibles (*cf.* the Jerusalem Bible) have followed this practice, distinguishing Yahweh as 'LORD' from 'Adonai as 'Lord'. A further twist to this engaging absurdity is that if we actually tried to say the consonants *YHWH* with the vowels of 'Adonai, it would come out something like 'Jehovah' – a word that never actually existed!

## Compounds

Yahweh ('LORD') is widely used in combination with the nouns for God and with other words. In *Gen. 2:4–3:23* we meet 'the LORD God' 20 times. 'God' is here the (plural) 'Elohim', i.e. God in the fulness of the divine attributes. The compound thus means 'Yahweh in all his fulness as God.' *Is. 50:4–5, 7, 9* and many other references speak of 'the Sovereign LORD', i.e. 'Adonai Yahweh', Yahweh in his sovereign sway. *Ps. 50:1* has a three-part compound: 'The Mighty One, God, the LORD', El Elohim Yahweh, i.e. Yahweh in his unique transcendence and fulness of Deity. The threefold compound in *Is. 1:24*, 'The Lord, the LORD Almighty' used to appear as 'The Lord, the LORD of hosts' and the simpler expression 'LORD of hosts' abounds throughout the OT. It is very probable that 'of hosts' is meant as a noun in apposition alongside Yahweh, 'Yahweh who is hosts' and this is certainly its developed significance as it appears in the prophets: Yahweh who does not simply possess but in himself is every conceivable potentiality and power. The NIV catches this meaning well with 'Almighty' though the slightly more emphatic 'Yahweh the Omnipotent' is preferable.

## Drawing the map

Standing back from the Bible, a distinct pattern emerges regarding the divine Name.

### Basics

*Exod. 6:2–3* is a dividing line across our map. Up to this point, said God to Moses, 'I did not make myself known by my name "the LORD".' Since the book of Genesis abounds in references to 'the LORD' some have sought to solve the problem by proposing that two separate streams of tradition are represented in our Bibles: according to one stream the divine Name was known from the earliest times (*Gen. 4:26*); according to the other, the Name was not revealed until the time of Moses.

The solution, however, is simpler and is born out by a discerning reading of Genesis: in *Exod. 6:2–3* the topic is the revelation of the character of God. 'I appeared ("showed myself") to Abraham . . . as (in the character of) God Almighty (El Shaddai) but (in the character expressed) by my name Yahweh I did not make myself known . . .' This is precisely what we find in Genesis: the Name is known as a designation of God but wherever there is a revelation of the divine character there is a shift from Yahweh to El Shaddai or one of the other patriarchal titles (see below). *Gen. 17:1* is a case in point. 'The LORD appeared . . . and said, "I am God Almighty (El Shaddai)".'

Moses, then, was privileged to open up the meaning of the divine Name, Yahweh, to Israel and the foundation is laid in *Exod. 3:13–15*. Moses was a man of many excuses. He did not want to return to Egypt and he wriggled this way and that to escape it. His second excuse was ignorance. He envisaged his arrival in Egypt to be faced with the question 'What is the name of the God who has sent you?' Moses did not himself ask 'the God of the fathers' what his name was but somehow knew that the Hebrews would ask him this very thing. Was it that 'What is his name?' was an idiom meaning 'What revelation of our God do you bring?' – for 'name' in the Bible is often shorthand for the character of the person who bears it (e.g. *1 Sam. 25:25!*). Or was it that Moses knew that the Hebrews cherished a secret Name for their God which he would have to know if he was to gain a hearing? The excuse is as fascinating as it is mysterious but in any case it is a plea for information to which God replies by saying, 'I am who I am . . . say . . . "I AM has sent me . . ."' As a word 'I am' is the first person singular of the verb 'to be' and 'Yahweh' is the third person singular. Of himself he says 'I am'; we look at him and say 'he is'. Some have preferred to understand the verb here as the Heb. 'causative' form: 'I bring to pass/ He brings to pass' and, as we shall see, should this be correct it would not alter the basic understanding of the Name. In Heb. the verb 'to be', while it cannot help expressing existence (I am/I exist) more readily expresses active presence: I am/I am actively present. In itself this tells us nothing about the bearer of the Name but in Exodus it is linked first with the spoken revelation of God to Moses (*Exod. 3–4*) and then with the personal activity of God in bringing his people out of Egypt (*Exod. 5–12*). It is by this 'active presence' in the Exodus events that the LORD reveals who and what he is. For this reason, even if the wording means 'I cause to happen' the essential situation is not altered for it is still the Exodus events which are immediately 'caused to happen' and in which the revelation of God vouchsafed to Moses in plain words is confirmed in action. In a word, therefore, Yahweh is the redeemer (*Exod. 6:6–7*).

### Background: Abraham's God

Abraham would have spoken of his God as El, adding some other descriptive word to make a compound title. Thus we learn of El Elyon ('God Most High', *Gen. 14:18*), El Roi ('the God who sees me', *16:13*), El Shaddai ('God Almighty', *17:1; 28:3; 35:11; 43:14; 48:3; cf. 49:25*), El Olam ('the Eternal God', *21:33*), El Bethel ('the God of Bethel', *31:13*), and El Elohe Israel ('God, the God of Israel', *33:20*). But these are not 'gods many and lords many'. The God who revealed himself at Bethel, for example, announces himself as Yahweh, the God of the fathers (*Gen. 28:13*), is spoken of as

Yahweh (v. 16) and Elohim (vv. 17, 20) and in Gen. 48:3 is identified with El Shaddai. There are many similar cross-identifications.

Fundamentally the patriarchs received their knowledge of God by revelation. Sometimes this was a direct word from the LORD (Gen. 16:13; 17:1; 31:13); on other occasions the knowledge of God was mediated through experience: when Abram met Melchizedek he immediately recognized 'God Most High' as Yahweh (Gen. 14:22); or again, called by Abimelech of Gerar to enter a perpetual covenant, it would seem that this opened Abraham's eyes to the ever-changing nature of his God (Gen. 21:22–23, 31, 33). But Exod. 6:2 is surely right to single out El Shaddai as the pre-eminent revelation of Yahweh to the patriarchs. Unfortunately the meaning of Shaddai remains obscure. But where translation fails usage supplies all we need (see Abraham). The references given above reveal El Shaddai as the promise-maker (specially the promise of land and descendants, the central patriarchal promise), the God who steps into the human situation when human strength has disappeared (cf. Gen. 17:1, 'Abram was ninety-nine years old') and who comes with transforming intent and power (Gen. 17:5, 'no longer Abram . . . Abraham'). He is the God who is able when we are unable. It was in this way that the patriarchs knew Yahweh. The divine Name itself had not yet become the bearer of revelation to them but could there have been any more appropriate preparation for the revelation to come than this rich theology of El Shaddai?

### Aftermath

The section above entitled 'Basics' explored the Mosaic foundations no more than to say that at the Exodus, by word and deed, Yahweh was self-revealed as the Redeemer. We must now probe forward on that basis.

The title 'redeemer' (Exod. 6:6) is deeply important and destined to become a major element in Israel's knowledge of the LORD (e.g. Pss. 74:2; 106:10; 107:2; Is. 41:14; 43:14; 44:6; 47:4; 49:7, 26; 54:5, 8; 59:20; 63:16; etc.). The word is basically both relational and price-paying. The 'redeemer' (go'el) is the next-of-kin whose right it is to stand in for a helpless relative, taking every need upon himself as if it were his own and out of his own resources paying whatever price will cover the situation. The vigour and dynamic of the word is illustrated by its use of 'the avenger of blood' (Deut. 19:6, 12; etc.); its price-paying dimension is seen in Lev. 25:25; 27:13, 19, 31; Ps. 49:7–8; Is. 43:1, 3; etc.); and its tenderness is portrayed in the story of Boaz and Ruth (Ruth 2:20; 3:9, 12, 13; 4:1, 3–4, 6, 8,14). In the Exodus situation the divine Next-of-kin brought upon the enemy of his people the death which they would unjustly have inflicted (cf. Deut. 19:16–19), appointed the blood-price of their redemption (Exod. 12:3), identified himself with their need (3:7–8), led them in the way (13:21–22), fed them in the wilderness (16; 17), carried them on eagle's wings and brought them to himself (19:4): in a word, took upon himself the whole work of salvation from beginning to end and did so out of love for those to whom he allied himself as their nearest relative.

All this is summed up in the recurring description 'Yahweh who brought you out of the land of Egypt' (Exod. 20:2 etc.) and is the foundational revelation of God in the OT.

## The Exodus and the Bible

As we have seen there is a steady progression through Genesis to Exodus as the revelation of Yahweh as El Shaddai prepared for the full revelation of the divine Name through Moses. As we shall see more clearly in a moment, the climax of the Mosaic revelation was the Passover, so that, in Exodus, two major truths are bound together, the revelation of the divine Name and the provision of the Lamb of God. This, however, is precisely where the NT starts also. Each of the first three Gospels moves through its essential preliminaries to focus on the baptism of the Lord Jesus. In *Matt. 3:13–17*, when the Lord Jesus approached John in the waters of Jordan, the Baptist's first reaction was to reverse their roles: 'I need to be baptized by you, and do you come to me?' John did not at that point know that the Lord Jesus was the Messiah (*John 1:31, 33*); his words were simply an appraisal of the character of his cousin Jesus – that here was a human being who did not need a baptism of repentance. But the Lord Jesus corrected him: 'It is proper for us to do this to fulfil all righteousness' – i.e. 'Only in this way can we fulfil all the righteous will of God'. In what way? By the all-righteous One accepting a baptism of repentance, voluntarily identifying himself with sinners and being 'numbered with the transgressors' (*Isa. 53:12*).

It was at this point that heaven was (in Mark's vivid expression) 'ripped apart' (*Mark 1:10; cf. 15:38*) as if God himself could not hold back but must now, at this moment of identification with sinners in their need, not only authenticate the Lord Jesus as his only Son and endow him with the Holy Spirit, but by doing so reveal for the first time the full meaning of the divine Name, the Holy Trinity, Father, Son and Holy Spirit. It was as a consequence of seeing and hearing all this that John the Baptist hailed the Lord Jesus as 'the Lamb of God', the sin-bearer, the son of God (*John 1:29, 34–35*).

Two important truths follow from this, one as we look back and the other as we look forward. Looking back into the OT we now see that the God revealed there as Yahweh, the LORD, is not 'God the Father' but rather the Holy Trinity incognito. What was granted to Moses to declare was eternally true (*Exod. 3:15*): Yahweh is the Redeemer but it is not the whole truth: the full meaning of the Name and the full work of redemption is that of Father, Son and Holy Spirit. No amount of searching could discover in the OT that Yahweh is the Holy Trinity. To be sure, he is not a bare 'One' but a diversified unity; he is 'Yahweh of hosts' in whom we see the active Word (*Ps. 33:6*), the living Holy Spirit (*Is. 63:10, 14*), the gracious Angel (*Gen. 16:7*) and many another insight into the divine nature. Just as when Moses assembled all the bits and pieces of the Tabernacle it 'became one' (*Exod. 36:13*), a many faceted unity, a diversity of items brought into oneness, so we read (*Deut. 6:4*) 'The LORD is one': all the 'hosts' of the infinite divine nature in their oneness. The NT, however – like a projectionist bringing a picture into sharp focus – makes a final touch of adjustment to the progressive revelation of the LORD and we find that the essential diversity in unity of the one eternal God is Father, Son and Holy Spirit.

When we look forward into the NT, we find that, just as in the OT the divine nature presented itself as Yahweh, so there is a special point where the Holy Trinity is revealed and meets us: Jesus Christ is LORD. The divine Name,

Yahweh, was transferred to the Greek Translation of the OT as 'Lord' (kurios) and it is this very word that the NT uses, above all other, to designate Jesus. He is 'the Lord (kurios) Jesus – the one word the NT must avoid if it does not intend to accord to him his full stature and dignity as the eternal God. It is in this spirit that *Phil. 2:9–11* can echo *Is. 45:22–25*, bringing all Scripture into unity in the revelation of God and the Person of our Lord Jesus Christ.

## Who is the Lord?

The question which Pharaoh asked with dismissive scorn (*Exod. 5:2*) can now be repeated in reverence and with an enquiring mind. We have tried to draw a map of the way in which the Bible opens up the meaning of the divine Name. Can we now pinpoint a sharper definition?

### 'The Lord made the heavens' (Ps. 96:5)

In *Gen. 1:1–2:3* the noun, God (Elohim), is used for the Creator. Significantly it is not until the story of the beginnings of human life on earth (*Gen. 2:4ff.*; see *Creation/Garden*) that Yahweh is used, 'The Lord God', for as we have noted 'Yahweh' is a relational Name, the God who would yet reveal himself as Redeemer, Next-of-kin. But as the OT looks back it affirms that this Creator was indeed the Lord.

In the OT there is a 'Creation Quadrilateral': (a) The Lord originated all things: heaven, earth, humankind (*Is. 40:26; 45:12, 18*). *Ps. 33:6, 9* ('by the word of the Lord') means that the whole work of creation proceeded directly from him and was the expression of his will. (b) The Lord maintains all things in existence. *Is. 40:28; 42:5; Amos 4:13* all use the participle of the verb 'to create', teaching that the work of the Creator was not only a once-for-all past act but is also an ongoing operation (*cf. John 5:17*). This applies to the physical fabric of creation and its human component (*Is. 42:5*), to its invisible forces (*Amos 4:13*), and indeed to each event in history (*Isa. 41:20*): history in all its complexity of peace and trouble is constantly in his creatorial hand (*Is. 45:7*). (c) The Lord controls everything in operation. This is put very dramatically in *Is. 54:16* – weapons of destruction in their manufacture and use are in his creatorial control. It is typical of the Bible to marginalize second causes in this way: it acknowledges the work of the smith and the activity of the destroyer but directs the gaze past them to the sovereign Creator. In all events, in the face of all people, it is with him that we have to do; our place is to live by faith in him, not by the cleverness with which we can manipulate the system and pull the strings that activate secondary agents. (d) The Lord guides everything to its appointed destiny in the future creation of the new heaven and new earth with its new, cleansed people (*Is. 4:2–6; 65:17–25*).

### 'Holy, holy, holy is the Lord' (Is. 6:3).

*Ps. 145* offers one of the richest collections of divine attributes in the whole Bible and reaches its climax (*v. 21*) with 'his holy name'. This adjective is used to describe his name more than all others (e.g. 'glorious', Ps. 72:19; 'pleasant' Ps. 135:3) put together. Since 'name' is shorthand for character, this means that the LORD is the Holy One at the heart of this essential being.

As a word 'holy' denotes 'otherness'; the LORD belongs to an 'other' sphere. In a curious way Gen. 38:21 is a perfect illustration: NIV 'shrine prostitute' is literally 'holy woman'. The girl in question had separated herself to the god she served and now belonged to his sphere of reality; she was 'other'. We must, of course, overlook the fact that to Scripture the service she offered was unholy and concentrate on her position, the world to which she had come to belong, rather than on what she did. Just so the LORD belongs to his own unique sphere of reality: he is Holy. But Isaiah sets this holiness in its true biblical context: the moral holiness which excludes, exposes and condemns sinners (Is. 6:4–5).

The seraphic song: 'Holy, holy, holy' uses the Hebrew idiom of repetition to express a superlative (2 Kings 25:15, 'gold . . . silver', literally 'gold gold . . . silver silver', i.e. 'the purest gold . . . the finest silver') or that which is all-embracing (Deut. 16:20, 'justice and justice alone', literally 'righteousness, righteousness'). The threefold 'Holy' of Is. 6:3 is the only place in the OT where a quality is 'raised to the power of three' to express its 'super-superlative' nature. Nothing else so distinctively or satisfactorily describes the divine character's unique, transcendent moral holiness.

But, of course, when it is noted that in Is. 6 the LORD is revealed in such total moral purity that no sinner can stand in his presence or join in his praise, a third factor that Isaiah experienced must not be omitted: it was out from the presence of that LORD that the seraph flew to be a minister of atonement, cleansing and reconciliation (Is. 6:7). The Holy One is also the Saviour.

### 'The LORD our God made a covenant with us' (Deut. 5:2).

'Covenant' means promise and in particular refers to the thread of covenant making which began with Noah and advanced through Abraham to Moses (See Covenant).

Noah belonged to a race that was wicked (Gen. 6:5), grieving the LORD (v. 6) and deserving the judgment of death (v. 7), but (v. 8) 'Noah found grace in the eyes of the LORD'. As the article on Noah argues, the meaning of this perfectly accurate translation can be brought out by reading it backwards: 'Grace found Noah'. In undeserved favour, the LORD chose this one lost sinner for salvation, and when the merited flood came the LORD promised to 'implement his covenant' (v. 18). The covenant with Noah is thus a promise of God, arising out of grace, and pledging safety from divine judgment. When Noah emerged from the ark as the covenant man, he instinctively turned to the LORD in grateful dedication (Gen. 8:20) expressed in the sacrifice of a burnt offering to which the LORD responded with a statement of the law which he desired Noah to observe (Gen. 9:1–7).

When we come to the Abrahamic Covenant, these same three features are present: Covenant, Law and Sacrifice. In Gen. 15:1–7 Abraham received the covenant promise in its first definition: innumerable descendants and a land. At the LORD's behest he prepared the covenant sacrifice (Gen. 15:8–17) and the LORD as Covenant-maker passed between the carcasses of the beasts, taking upon himself (cf. Jer. 34:18–20) all the responsibilities and penalties of the covenant. 'On that day' says Gen. 15:18, (literally) 'the LORD inaugurated a covenant with Abram'. But the inauguration was followed by affirmation and amplification: in Gen. 17:1–2 the LORD appeared again, imposing on Abram the broad but searching law of patriarchal life (v. 1) and reaffirming the covenant: (literally, Gen. 17:2) the verb is different from Gen. 15:18, meaning literally 'I will set my covenant between me and you' – the covenant as the ongoing mode of their relationship. Following this, the promise is elaborated in terms of personal transformation (Gen. 17:3–5), domestic increase (v. 6), spiritual benefit (v. 7) and territorial possession (v. 8).

The LORD's dealings with Abraham marked a development of the covenant-idea for sacrifice is now not simply the response of the covenant man, as with Noah, but the foundation on which the covenant is inaugurated. The Mosaic Covenant brings the sequence to completion.

First, the function of sacrifice within the covenant is explained. At the end of Egypt's long probation, the LORD announced his coming in judgment (Exod. 12:12). He would pass through the land 'striking down every firstborn' but he would 'pass over' every house marked with the blood of the lamb for 'when I see the blood I will pass over you' (v. 13). Somehow that blood satisfied his demands and wrath would be replaced by peace. Furthermore, those sheltering under the blood (Exod. 12:22–23) would be safe. The events of Passover night not only make these truths of a satisfied God and a safe people clear but go to explain the power of the blood to secure these blessings. When v. 30 says that 'there was not a house without someone dead' it was, of course, referring to the houses of the Egyptians. But, in fact, in Israelite houses too there was a dead body: the slain lamb had been carried in to provide the substance of the passover feast (Exod. 12:8–11). This is the clue: each lamb had been almost mathematically chosen to represent the number and meet the needs of Israel – they were counted into the lamb individually (Exod. 12:3–4a) 'in accordance with what each . . . will eat' (Exod. 12:4b). Israel, the Lord's firstborn (Exod. 4:22–23), was safe because the lamb died in his place.

This then is the place of sacrifice in the divine Covenant: the LORD brings his covenant people into peace with himself and security from his wrath by the blood of the substitute lamb. But, secondly, the Mosaic Covenant elaborates the LORD's law and explains its function. Israel came out of Egypt as the LORD's redeemed and were led by the cloudy-fiery pillar (Exod. 13:21–22) to Sinai. There the LORD first announced himself as the Redeemer ('I am the LORD . . . who brought you out of Egypt', Exod. 20:2) and then, because they were his liberated people ('out of the land of slavery'), gave them his law (Exod. 20:3ff.). In other words, in the OT Law is consequent upon grace; it is not a ladder of merit to climb into divine favour but a pattern of responsive obedience for those who have been saved.

In a word, then, the LORD, Yahweh, is that God who, in all his sovereignty as Creator and in his holiness, pledges in solemn covenant that he will take a people for himself and does so through the blood of the Passover lamb. Because he is Creator, his covenant has a worldwide intent (Gen. 9:12) and all nations will come into blessing (Gen. 12:2–3; 22:18); because he is the Holy One, he gives his Law to those whom he saves, so that with responsive love they offer him their obedience.

J.A.M.

**LOT** As an orphan (*Gen. 11:27–28*), Lot was first taken into the family of his grandfather (*11:31*) and then (*12:5*) accompanied his uncle Abram into Canaan. By this time Lot had his own family and property (*Gen. 13:5*) and, in a land already thickly populated (*13:7*) the extended family became unwieldy and quarrelling broke out. At Abram's suggestion Lot made a decisive and fatal choice (*v. 8*). In essence it was the choice of prosperity (*v. 10*) at the risk of moral values and divine favour (*v. 13*). Thereafter Lot's story was a downward graph: 'near Sodom' (*Gen. 13:12*) . . . 'living in Sodom' (*14:12*) . . . 'sitting in the gateway of the city' (*19:1*) – from separation with the people of God (*12:4–5*) to advancement in Sodom in three easy stages. Peter tells us that he was in daily torment of conscience (*2 Pet. 2:7–8*) but because he was fundamentally living in compromise further compromise came readily (*Gen. 19:8*); he knew what it was to be right with God (*2 Pet. 2:7–8*), but even under threat of judgment he clung to Sodom (*Gen. 19:16*); he was too identified with his chosen city to bear an effective testimony there (*vv. 9, 14*); he had so long allowed faith to rust that now he could not exercise it (*vv. 18–20*); and his family were no longer supportive in the things of God (*vv. 26, 30–36*). His wife's heart was in Sodom and his daughters had only the world's model to follow (*v. 31*) – but they knew their father well enough to plot his moral shame with confidence that he had so lost his character that he would not resist.

However, Lot was not forgotten by the LORD (*Gen. 19:29; 2 Pet. 2:9*). At the time of Sodom's judgment, two angels were sent to the doomed city to rescue Lot and any who would leave with him. The moral corruption of the city was evidenced (*Gen. 19:5*) by its residents' prompt determination to subject the newcomers to homosexual assault, but equally Lot's personal deterioration was displayed by his readiness to sacrifice his daughters in the interest of his guests (*vv. 6–8*). Small wonder that his fellow citizens and his prospective sons-in-law alike (*vv. 9, 14*) saw in him no more than an interfering busybody and a sour joke! Compromise, so easily embarked upon, brought with it loss alike of character and influence. Yet, even for such a reluctant candidate for salvation, (*v. 16*), sovereign mercy prevailed and the incident stands as a shining example of grace. That God 'remembered Abraham and . . . brought Lot out' (*v. 29*) demonstrates the family principle that lies at the centre of the operation of the divine covenant.   J.A.M.

**LOTAN** was the son of Seir, the Horite, and a chief among his people living in Edom (*Gen. 36:20, 29; 1 Chron. 1:38*). His sister was called Timna and his sons: Hori and Homam (*Gen. 36:22; 1 Chron. 1:39*).

**LUCIUS    1.** Lucius of Cyrene is mentioned as one of the 'prophets and teachers' in the church at Antioch in *Acts 13:1*. Following a time of fasting and prayer, the Holy Spirit indicated to them that they should set apart Saul and Barnabas for the task to which the Lord was calling them (*vv. 1–3*). The two of them then set off for Cyprus where they continued to preach the gospel. The church at Antioch, of which Lucius was a member, is described in *Acts 11*. Lucius may have been among those Hellenistic Jewish Christians who were scattered due to persecution and, coming to Antioch, began to speak to the Greeks of the 'good news about the Lord Jesus' (*v. 20*). When Barnabas was sent by the leaders of the church in Jerusalem to Antioch to find out what was happening, he saw 'great evidence of the grace of God' there (*v. 23*).

**2.** Either a fellow Jew or a blood relative of Paul and one of those who was with him when he wrote his letter to the Roman church (*Rom. 16:21*). He joined

Paul, Timothy, and others in sending the church his greetings. It is likely that he had visited the Christians in Rome either when on business or as an itinerant Christian teacher. It is just possible that he was the same as 1. above.          P.D.G.

**LUD** One of Shem's sons and a grandson of Noah (*Gen. 10:22; 1 Chron. 1:17*). He is an ancestor of a people who continued to carry his name. It is possible that Lud may be identified with Lydia which was a nation on the west of Asia Minor. Lud is mentioned in *Is. 66:19* (NIV, Lydians) along with Javan and Tubal which may make this identification correct. However, others suggest that it refers to a North African nation. The NIV obscures the name by deciding in favour of Lydia in both *Is. 66* and *Ezek. 27:10*.

## LUKE

Luke, perhaps a pet name for Lucius, was the early Christian leader who accompanied Paul on several missionary journeys (note the 'we' passages in *Acts 16:10–17; 20:5–21:18; 27:1–28:16*). The two men were friends, and Luke's support was an encouragement to the apostle. Traditionally, Luke has been considered 'the beloved physician' (*Col. 4:14*), and some medical schools celebrate him in St Luke's Day services.

There are, however, only three specific references to Luke in the NT. In writing to Philemon, Paul clearly listed Luke along with Mark, Aristarchus and Demas as 'my fellow workers' (*Philem. 24*). According to 2 Timothy, Paul noted with appreciation Luke's presence when he commented from prison, 'Only Luke is with me' (*2 Tim. 4:11*). Since Luke is mentioned in the Colossians passage after all the Jewish Christian workers have been noted, it is usually concluded that he was a Gentile Christian (*Col. 4:10–14*).

The anti-Marcionite Prologue claimed that Luke was a native of Antioch in Syria who lived a single life and died in Boeotia (a district of ancient Greece) at the age of 84. Some have also pointed out the detailed references to Antioch in Acts (*6:5; 11:19–27; 13:1; 14:26; 15:22–35*). In any case, Luke was an earnest disciple and showed a great deal of interest in the background, formation and development of the early church.

While little is known of Luke's background, much light is shed on his interests and concerns by reading the two NT books attributed to him – the Gospel of Luke and the book of Acts. These two writings constitute about 27% of the NT. Certainly Luke's perspective on the life of Christ and Christian origins is most important if one is to understand the message of the NT. Nine features of that perspective may be noted.

### Luke the historian

It is important to pay strict attention to the Preface of Luke's Gospel (*Luke 1:1–4*). Here Luke, following the conventions of the Hellenistic historians of the time, outlined his historical method: (1) he acknowledged that others had attempted to do historical work on Christian origins before him; (2) he recognized the value of using the evidence provided by the original eyewitnesses and servants of the Word: (3) he believed that there existed a need for 'an orderly account' of Christian origins, which he could provide; (4) he claimed that he had investigated everything carefully from the beginning; (5) he named Theophilus as the intended recipient of his work (*cf. Acts 1:1*); and (6) he presented his material so that his readers (Theophilus and other interested people) might know 'the certainty' of the things they had been taught.

In other words, Luke attempted to present an historical account of Christian origins that had a high degree of credibility (note his use of the term, tekmeria, '[decisive] proofs' in *Acts 1:3*). Thus he paid careful attention to historical trustworthiness and has been hailed the historian par excellence of the NT. He made it clear that Christianity must be understood against the background of both Jewish and Roman history (e.g. *Luke 2:1; 3:1–2; Acts 10:1; 11:19; 26:26*).

## Luke the literary artist

Fortunately, Luke's concern for accuracy and sound historical method was not accomplished at the expense of good literary style. He painted vivid portraits in his Gospel of Zechariah, Mary, Elizabeth, Anna, Herod Antipas, the Roman centurion at the cross, and the wailing women of Jerusalem. Similarly in Acts there are moving accounts of Ananias and Sapphira, Stephen, Philip, the Ethiopian eunuch, Eutychus, Lydia, Barnabas, Elymas, Peter and Paul. Luke used his gift of convincing description to good advantage in both books.

This fresh manner of presentation was not confined to historical narration. It was also evident in the stories Jesus told. Many of the most familiar parables have come to us from Luke. These include 'the Rich Fool' (*Luke 12:16–21*), 'the Barren Fig Tree' (*13:6–9*), 'the Great Supper' (*14:16–24*), 'the Unjust Steward' (*16:1–9*) and 'the Unprofitable Servants' (*17:1–10*). Particularly unforgettable examples of Lucan parables are 'the Good Samaritan' and 'the Prodigal Son' (*10:25–37; 15:11–32*).

Luke was a powerful communicator, and his accounts of hair-raising escapes, midnight deliverances, heavenly interventions and remarkable prison escapades make gripping reading. He used a variety of materials such as historical records, oral tradition, parables, early Christian preaching and the memory of eyewitnesses to share his message about Christ and the emerging Christian community. He did so in such a winsome fashion that his Gospel has been called 'the most beautiful book in the world'.

## Luke's use of spiritual songs and praise

Closely related to Luke's artistry was his use of hymns. He has recorded the beginnings of early Christian hymnology. His nativity story is particularly rich, for here he has given us the 'Song of Mary' (the Magnificat, *Luke 1:46–55*), the 'Song of Zechariah' (the Benedictus, *Luke 1:68–79*), the 'Song of the Angel Host' (the Gloria in Excelsis, *Luke 2:14*) and the 'Song of Simeon' (the Nunc Dimittis, *Luke 2:28–32*).

Praising God was clearly important to Luke, and it is a prominent feature of both his Gospel and Acts (*Luke 2:13, 30; 18:43; 24:53; Acts 2:47; 3:8–9*). The 'glory to God' sung by the angels was reechoed by the disciples at the triumphal entry: they 'began joyfully to praise God in loud voices for all the miracles they had seen . . .' (*Luke 19:37–38*). Similarly in Acts, Luke noted that after the miraculous healing of the crippled beggar 'all the people were praising God for what had happened' (*Acts 4:21*). One of the most remarkable examples of praise occurred when Paul and Silas prayed and sang hymns late at night in a Philippian jail (*Acts 16:25*).

## Luke's emphasis on joy

This theme has already been suggested in the songs which mark the nativity story. The angel that heralded the birth of John the Baptist announced that he would be a 'joy and delight' to his parents and that 'many will rejoice because of his birth' (*Luke 1:14*). Similarly, the angel who announced the birth of Jesus said: 'I bring you good news of great joy that will be for all the people' (*2:10*). The coming of Jesus as Saviour and Lord was associated with joy.

This theme is sounded repeatedly throughout the Gospel and Acts (*Luke 8:13; 10:17, 21; 24:41, 52; Acts 13:52; 15:3*). It is striking how frequently Luke used the verb 'rejoice' (chairo) to describe the difference that Jesus made in the lives of his followers (e.g. *Luke 6:23; 10:20; 13:17; 15:5, 32; 19:6*). Luke believed that the Christian faith was intended to bring not only the forgiveness of sins but also a resulting joy and radiance to everyday living. The necessary condition to be met was repentance – a genuine sorrow for sin and an honest turning to God for forgiveness and cleansing (*Luke 13:3, 5; Acts 2:38; 3:19; 17:30*). Thus it was not surprising that Luke cited the words of Jesus at the conclusion of the parable of the lost sheep: 'I tell you that in the same way there will be more rejoicing in heaven over one sinner who repents than over ninety-nine righteous persons who do not need to repent' (*Luke 15:7; cf. v. 10; 10:17–20*).

In Acts too the reception of the gospel was accompanied by great joy. This was evident when Philip proclaimed Christ and met with a positive response in Samaria: 'So there was great joy in that city' (*Acts 8:8*). In like fashion the Ethiopian eunuch, following conversion and baptism, 'went on his way rejoicing' (*8:39*). Another moving example is the Philippian jailer, whose conversion brought new life: 'he was filled with joy because he had come to believe in God – he and his whole family' (*16:34*). The joy of this new life in Christ enabled believers to meet difficult experiences in a victorious manner. Thus when the apostles were roundly rebuked and ordered not to speak in the name of Jesus, they left the Jewish council 'rejoicing because they had been counted worthy of suffering disgrace for the Name' (*5:41*). A bold, joyous faith was not to be silenced by threats and intimidations.

## Luke's stress on prayer

Luke has been called 'the Evangelist of Prayer'. While all of the Gospels reveal Jesus as a man of prayer and stress the duty of prayer, Luke has highlighted the importance of prayer in the life of Jesus and the Christian church. This is clear both in his rich vocabulary for prayer (where at least nine different terms are used) and in the large number of prayer incidents recorded in both Luke and Acts.

In Luke's Gospel, Jesus prayed over every major decision and at every turning point in his life. He prayed at his baptism (*Luke 3:21*), before choosing his disciples (*6:12*), at Caesarea Philippi (*9:18*), on the Mount of Transfiguration (*9:28–29*), in Gethsemane (*22:39–46*) and on the cross (*23:34, 46*). Luke presented Christ's teaching on prayer in the 'Model Prayer' (*Luke 11:1–4; cf. Matt. 6:9–13*), and also included several prayer parables (*Luke 11:5–8; 18:1–14*). Jesus was transformed as he prayed (*9:29*), and Luke wanted to teach Christian disciples that prayer could make a great difference in their lives too. This dimension is evident in the Lucan account of Gethsemane, where Luke underscored Jesus' admonition to the disciples to pray; this was the divinely appointed way to escape falling 'into temptation' (*22:40, 46*).

Luke also pursued his interest in prayer in the book of Acts, where many elements of prayer are found including worship (*Acts 13:2*), adoration (*4:24*), rejoicing (*11:23; 13:48*), thanksgiving (*27:35; 28:15*), confession of sin (*19:18*), petition (*9:11, 13–16; 10:31; 22:10*) and intercession (*7:60; 12:5; 27:23–25; 28:8*). In fact, Acts contains about 25 specific examples of prayer. The birth of the church came in response to prayer (*Luke 24:49; Acts 1:4–5; 2:1–13*). The choice of Matthias to replace Judas was made after earnest prayer (*Acts 1:12–26*). The new believers 'devoted themselves to the apostles' teaching and to the fellowship, to the breaking of bread and to prayer' (*2:42; cf. 1:14*). Prayer was thus a vital part of the early church's life (*14:23; 20:36; 21:5*). When difficult times arose, these were met with united prayer, followed frequently by convincing demonstrations of divine power (e.g. *4:24–31; 6:1–7; 16:25–34*). Luke was emphatic in insisting on the importance of prayer in the ministry of both Jesus and the Christian community. In his view, God used the faithful prayers of his people in advancing the Kingdom of God in the world.

## Luke's interest in the Holy Spirit

The Holy Spirit features prominently in Luke's writings. In the Gospel the Spirit was active in the conception of Christ (*Luke 1:35*), throughout his ministry, and in the post-resurrection period, when he promised his disciples that they would receive the Spirit to empower their service (*Luke 24:49; Acts 1:8*). Jesus was indwelt by the Spirit (*Luke 3:22*), tested by the Spirit (*4:1*), anointed by the Spirit (*4:14, 18*), and the teacher of the disciples about the importance of the Spirit (*Luke 11:13; cf. Matt. 7:11*). Similarly, several other characters in Luke's Gospel were recipients of the Holy Spirit including John the Baptist (*Luke 1:15*), Mary (*1:35*), Elizabeth (*1:41*), Zechariah (*1:67*) and Simeon (*2:25–27*). Jesus not only rejoiced in the Holy Spirit, but also instructed his disciples about the Spirit's help in crisis situations (*Luke 10:21; 12:12*). While it was possible to be forgiven for words spoken against the Son of Man, 'anyone who blasphemes against the Holy Spirit will not be forgiven' (*Luke 12:10; cf. Matt. 12:31*).

Even more is said about the Holy Spirit in Acts, where the Spirit's power was stressed (*Acts 2:1–4; 4:31*), the Spirit's personality recognized (*5:3, 9, 32; 15:28*) and the Spirit's guidance acknowledged (*10:19; 11:12; 13:2, 4; 16:6–7*). In Acts tremendous emphasis was placed on the outward witness of the Holy Spirit. One expression of this witness was the signs and wonders performed by the apostles and their co-workers. Thus Peter and John in the power of the Spirit healed a crippled man (*Acts 3:1–10; 4:22; cf. 5:12*), and miraculous deeds were performed by Stephen (*6:8*), Philip (*8:6–7, 13*), Peter (*9:33–42*) and Paul (*19:11–12*). Another form of this Spirit-inspired witness was the boldness of the apostolic preaching. The Spirit took those who had hitherto been weak and powerless and gave them 'boldness' to speak out courageously for Jesus. This was true of Peter and John (*Acts 2:29; 4:9–10, 13*), Stephen (*6:10*), Philip (*8:30–35*), Barnabas and Paul (*13:46; 14:3*), and the apostles generally (*4:33; cf. vv. 29f.*). Beyond question, Luke stressed the importance of the Holy Spirit in both his Gospel and Acts.

## Luke's worldwide thrust

Luke had a strong conviction that the Christian message should not be confined to one people or one land. This led him to emphasize the universal nature of the gospel of Christ, which he believed was a message for all people and all lands. He expressed this conviction in both of his books.

In his Gospel, Luke was careful to include the larger imperial setting of the life of Christ (*Luke 2:1–3; 3:1–2*). He saw the divinely prepared salvation as one which God had prepared 'in the sight of all people', including the Gentiles (*Luke 2:31–32*). While several Gospel writers cited Isaiah, only Luke included the words, 'all mankind will see God's salvation' (*Luke 3:4–6; cf. Is. 40:3–5; Mark 1:2–3; Matt. 3:3*). Other indications of this wider perspective include the thankful Samaritan (*Luke 17:15–16*), the rebuke of party bigotry (*9:50*), the stress on unbounded neighbourliness (*10:33–37*), and the emphasis upon personal response rather than national privilege (*13:28–30*). Luke noted with favour the faith of the centurion when Jesus remarked: 'I tell you, I have not found such great faith even in Israel' (*Luke 7:9; Matt. 8:10*).

The same universal concern for all people is found in Acts. Jesus had envisaged a worldwide ministry (*Acts 1:8*). When the Spirit was outpoured on the day of Pentecost, converts would naturally take the Christian message back to their own countries (*cf. 2:5*). The course of events described in Acts indicates the gradual spread of the gospel into Gentile lands. The persecution which broke out against the church following the death of Stephen served to disperse believers throughout Judea and Samaria (*Acts 8:1*). Philip carried the good news to Samaria (*vv. 4–8*), and the eunuch took it to Ethiopia (*vv. 26–39*).

Saul's conversion was told three times in Acts to emphasize the importance of his role in the dissemination of the gospel: 'This man,' the Lord told the sceptical Ananias, 'is my chosen instrument to carry my name before the Gentiles and their kings and before the people of Israel' (*Acts 9:15; cf. 22:21; 26:17*). The Christian way was open to all: 'everyone who believes in him [Christ] receives forgiveness of sins through his name' (*Acts 10:43; cf. 4:12*). Thus the Gentile jailer at Philippi could be told, 'Believe in the Lord Jesus, and you will be saved – you and your household' (*Acts 16:31*). The church spread rapidly to Antioch, Cyprus, Asia Minor, Macedonia, Achaia, and Italy, reaching out from the religious capital of the Jews (Jerusalem) to the political capital of the Gentiles (Rome). The gospel was for all people, and Luke took delight in presenting it as a message for all people whatever their background, race or language.

## Luke's graciousness

Closely related to Luke's concern for 'all saints and all sorts' was his graciousness. He saw Jesus of Nazareth as deeply concerned for the underdog, the exploited and the disadvantaged. In Luke's portrait of Jesus one is given a window into Luke's own heart. Jesus was sensitive to the plight of the poor (Luke 6:20–25), lepers (5:12–14), widows (7:11–16), the sick (5:17–26; 14:1–4) and little children (18:15–17). Like his Lord, Luke exhibited a special concern for women (7:36–50; 8:1–3; 10:38–42; 13:10–17; 21:2–4). His Gospel expressed the compassion and loving-kindness of God in a most memorable form. Thus it is not surprising that he has depicted many banquet scenes, for table fellowship was the perfect expression of love and acceptance (Luke 7:36–50; 10:38–42; 11:37–54; 14:1–14; 19:1–10).

Similarly Acts showed the Christian message reaching out to Samaritans (Acts 8:25), to women (5:14; 8:3, 12; 13:50; 16:1, 13–14; 17:4, 12, 34), exploited folk (16:16–21; cf., 19:23–27), to Roman officials like the centurion Cornelius and the proconsul Sergius Paulus (Acts 10–11; 13:6–7, 12), and to immoral people in a seaport town like Corinth (18:1–11; cf. 1 Cor. 6:9–11). Luke believed there was 'a wideness in God's mercy', and that wideness was reflected in the grace and mercy of God reaching out to all who would respond to it.

## Luke's stress on Christ as Saviour and Redeemer

Finally, there is great emphasis on salvation in Luke's writings. Jesus was announced by the angel at the nativity as the promised Saviour and identified as 'Christ the Lord' (Luke 2:11). He was acknowledged by the aged prophetess Anna in the Temple as the child of promise 'to all who were looking forward to the redemption of Jerusalem' (2:38). This redemption was not restricted to the Jewish people, for it was to embrace the whole human family (3:6). The coming of Christ challenged people to repent if they were to experience forgiveness (5:32); Jesus as the Son of Man claimed to have the authority to proclaim that forgiveness (5:20–26). If men refused to repent, they were told they would perish (13:1–5). God's gracious salvation was not to be treated lightly, for those who rejected it would find themselves 'thrown out' (13:28). On the other hand, 'there is rejoicing in the presence of the angels of God over one sinner who repents' (15:10). Thus when Zacchaeus repented Jesus said to him, 'Today salvation has come to this house . . . For the Son of Man came to seek and to save what was lost' (19:9). The Christocentric message proclaimed by Luke is summed up beautifully at the end of his Gospel (24:45–46).

Acts powerfully announced this message of redemption. It is repeated again and again in the apostolic preaching in the great sermons of Acts (e.g. Acts 2–3; 7; 10; 13; 17; 22; 26). Peter, for example declared, 'Salvation is found in no one else, for there is no other name under heaven given to men by which we must be saved' (Acts 4:12; cf. 2:36). The apostles and their colleagues were busy 'telling the good news of peace through Jesus Christ, who is Lord of all' (10:36). This message was carried in ever-widening circles to the ends of the earth, and people were brought 'from darkness to light, and from the power of Satan to God' (26:18). This wonderful offer of new life was extended to the Gentiles, and many responded with faith and obedience (11:18, 21; 15:19).

Luke's two volumes touch many themes. While he was a good writer and a faithful historian, he was also a theologian, who perceived the plan and purpose of God and tried to make sense of it for his readers. He has done his work well.

A.A.T.

**LYDIA** The two references to this pious woman appear in *Acts 16:14, 40*. She is portrayed as a pious woman, a worshipper of God, who was the first to respond to Paul's offer of the gospel when he entered Macedonia. She was from Thyatira and made garments of purple dye, an occupation that suggests she clothed the wealthy. She was an example of hospitality, since she housed Paul after she was baptized by him. She hosted him later in his mission as well.

**LYSANIAS** is mentioned in *Luke 3:1* as part of the historical and political surroundings into which John the Baptist was born. He was 'tetrach of Abilene'. See also *Herod* and *Philip*.

**LYSIAS** See *Claudius Lysias*. This Roman tribune was in charge of the garrison in Jerusalem at the time of Paul's arrest (*Acts 23:26*). Later, at Paul's trial before Felix, the proceedings were adjourned until Lysias was able to attend (*Acts 24:22*).

# M

**MAACAH 1.** Maacah was a son of Abraham's brother Nahor by his concubine Reumah (*Gen. 22:24*).

**2.** This Maacah was the mother of Absalom, one of King David's sons born to him in Hebron. She was the daughter of King Talmai of Geshur (*2 Sam. 3:3; 1 Chron. 3:2*).

**3.** The father of the Philistine Achish, king of Gath (*1 Kings 2:39*).

**4.** The daughter of Abishalom, this Maacah was wife of King Rehoboam and became the mother of his successor, Abijah, king of Judah (*1 Kings 15:2*). Rehoboam loved Maacah more than any of his other wives. For this reason he appointed Abijah as the chief prince among his brothers and sent the others to other towns (*2 Chron. 11:20–23; 13:2*). Abijah quickly became an evil king who did not devote himself to 'the LORD his God' (*1 Kings 15:3*). Maacah obviously followed her son into idolatry. When Maacah's grandson, King Asa, came to the throne he returned to the LORD and, because of her idolatry, he deposed Maacah from her position as Queen Mother (*1 Kings 15:10, 13; 2 Chron. 15:16*).

**5.** A concubine belonging to Caleb the son of Hezron. She bore him four sons (*1 Chron. 2:48*).

**6.** Mentioned in *1 Chron. 7:15–16* among the descendants of Manasseh. Her husband was Makir, although she is called his sister in *v. 15*. Her son was named Peresh.

**7.** The wife of Jeiel, who lived in Gibeon, and is listed in the genealogy leading from Benjamin to Saul (*1 Chron. 8:29; 9:35*).

**8.** The father of Hanan who was one of David's 'mighty men' (*1 Chron. 11:43*)

**9.** The father of Shephatiah who was an officer over the Simeonites during King David's reign (*1 Chron. 27:16*).

P.D.G.

**MAADAI** A descendant of Bani at the time of Nehemiah (*Ezra 10:34*). After Shecaniah confessed to Ezra that many men of Judah had married wives from other tribes and nations, Ezra and the people repented and made a covenant to serve the LORD (*Ezra 10:2*). Maadai was one of those listed as having married a foreign wife.

**MAAI** was a leader of Judah and a priest who played musical instruments at the dedication of the rebuilt walls of Jerusalem (*Neh. 12:36*).

**MAASAI** One of the priests who first settled back in Jerusalem following the Babylonian Exile (*1 Chron. 9:12*). He was the son of Adiel.

**MAASEIAH** ( Heb., 'the LORD's work').

**1.** After the ark of the covenant had been brought to Jerusalem, the worship of God was properly organized by King David. Maaseiah was one of the family of Merarite Levites who were gatekeepers. The particular job he and his brothers were given was to be musicians and to play the harps and lyres before the ark of the covenant as it was moved to Jerusalem (*1 Chron. 15:18, 20*).

**2.** One of the commanders with whom Jehoiada the priest made a covenant. He commanded a unit of 100 men (*2 Chron.*

23:1). He helped Jehoiada crown Joash king. Jehoiada had helped hide the child king from Athaliah the mother of Ahaziah, the recently deceased king of Judah. When seven years had passed the child was produced and crowned. Athaliah was put to death by Maaseiah and the other leaders and their men. Joash, who was clearly influenced by Jehoiada, repaired the Temple and restored the worship of the LORD.

**3.** This Maaseiah was a royal official in the time of King Uzziah of Judah. He was responsible, under the direction of Hananiah, for planning the organization of the army (2 Chron. 26:11).

**4.** Another Maaseiah was son of King Ahaz of Judah and was killed in the war between Judah and Israel and its ally, Syria (2 Chron. 28:7).

**5.** This Maaseiah was the leader of the city of Jerusalem during the reign of King Josiah. Josiah ordered him and others to begin repairs on the Temple (2 Chron. 34:8).

**6.** Another Maaseiah was the father of the priest Zephaniah who figured prominently in the days of the prophet Jeremiah. His father was Shallum and he had a prominent room in the Temple area (Jer. 21:1; 29:25; 35:4; 37:3).

**7.** The father of Zedekiah who also lived in the days of Jeremiah and was condemned by him for prophesying lies (Jer. 29:21).

**8.** A descendant of Jeshua, this Maaseiah was among those priests who joined Ezra and the people in repentance on their return to Jerusalem from Babylon. Many men of Judah had married wives from other tribes and nations. They made a covenant to serve the LORD (Ezra 10:2) and divorced their foreign wives (v. 18).

**9.** Another Maaseiah was a descendant of Harim who also divorced a foreign wife in the days of Ezra (Ezra 10:21).

**10.** Another Maaseiah was a descendant of Pashhur who also divorced a foreign wife in the days of Ezra (Ezra 10:22).

**11.** Another Maaseiah was a descendant of Pahath-Moab who also divorced a foreign wife in the days of Ezra (Ezra 10:30).

**12.** The father of Azariah who helped repair the walls of Jerusalem in the days of Nehemiah (Neh. 3:23).

**13.** This Maaseiah was among those who stood on Ezra's right-hand side on a high wooden platform as he read the Book of the Law to the people of Israel. As the Law was read the people worshipped and praised God, confessed their sin, and recommitted themselves to the LORD's service (Neh. 8:4).

**14.** Another Maaseiah was one of the Levites who was married to a foreign woman. After the return from the Babylonian Exile and on the direction of Ezra, he agreed to divorce her. He also helped teach the people the Law of God and sealed the agreement of the people to worship the LORD and obey his Law (Neh. 8:7; 10:25).

**15.** The son of Baruch, this Maaseiah was from the tribe of Judah and one of the first to settle back in Jerusalem following the return from the Babylonian Exile (Neh. 11:5)

**16.** From the tribe of Benjamin, another Maaseiah was the father of Kolaiah and an ancestor of a family which returned from the Babylonian Exile to Jerusalem (Neh. 11:7).

**17.** This Maaseiah, a head of a priestly family in the time of Nehemiah, is mentioned in Neh. 12:41. He was a trumpet player during the worship at the dedication of the city walls.

**18.** A Levite who was part of the choir that sang at the dedication of the wall. The walls and city had been destroyed by the Babylonians when they took the Israelites into captivity. Under the direction of Nehemiah they were eventually rebuilt amidst great praises to God (Neh. 12:42).

P.D.G.

**MAATH** Mentioned in Luke's genealogy leading from Jesus and Joseph back to Adam (*Luke 3:26*). He was the father of Naggai and the son of Mattathias.

**MAAZ** Mentioned in *1 Chron. 2:27*, a son of Ram and a grandson of Jerahmeel from the tribe of Judah.

**MAAZIAH** **1.** One among the priests who were chosen to be officials in the sanctuary 'according to the last instructions of David'. Impartial selection from among the descendants of Eleazar and Ithamar was made by drawing lots. The 24th lot fell to Maaziah and that was the order in which he ministered when entering the sanctuary (*1 Chron. 24:18*).
**2.** One of the priests who sealed the agreement with Nehemiah to worship only the LORD and to obey his Law (*Neh. 10:8*).

**MACBANNAI** Mentioned in *1 Chron. 12:13*, Macbannai was the eleventh of various Gadite warriors who defected from Saul and joined David when he was at Ziklag. These mighty men were described as the greatest of warriors, stronger than a hundred men and 'swift as gazelles in the mountains'.

**MACBENAH** A grandson of Caleb and his concubine Maacah. He was of the tribe of Judah and his father was Sheva (*1 Chron. 2:49*).

**MACNADEBAI** was among the descendants of Binnui. At the time of return from the Exile in Babylon, Shecaniah confessed to Ezra that many men and even descendants of the priests of Judah had married wives from other tribes and nations. Ezra and the people repented and made a covenant to serve the LORD (*Ezra 10:2*). Macnadebai is listed in *v. 40* as one who divorced his foreign wife.

**MADAI** The third son of Japheth and grandson of Noah (*Gen. 10:2; 1 Chron.* 1:5*). Traditionally he was believed to be the progenitor of the Medes.

**MADMANNAH** A grandson of Caleb and his concubine Maacah. He was of the tribe of Judah and his father was Shaaph (*1 Chron. 2:49*).

**MAGDALENE** See *Mary*.

**MAGDIEL** One of the chiefs of Edom, mentioned in connection with Iram and a descendant of Esau (*Gen. 36:43; 1 Chron. 1:54*).

**MAGI, THE** A transliteration of the Greek word *magoi*, probably best translated as 'wise men'. They are found in the Bible only in *Matt. 2:1–12*. Since all that is said of the wise men is that they came in search of the newborn king of the Jews 'from the east' (*vv. 1–2*), it is impossible to know with certainty where they came from. They may have been from Arabia, though a stronger possibility is Persia. It is plausible that there was a link of transmitted Messianic prophecy from the time of Daniel, where it is known that there were 'wise men' in that geographic area (*Dan. 2:12–13*), as well as available biblical truth through Jews of the Babylonian Captivity.

Many such wise men were also astrologers, and the fact that they were following a star (*Matt. 2:2*) points in the direction of at least a partial astrological source, although the passing down of biblical prophecy cannot be ruled out, especially in light of Balaam's prophecy in *Num. 24:17*. Whatever the origin of their information, it was clearly limited in scope. The magi had to ask for guidance in Jerusalem (*Matt. 2:1–2*). Their inquiry almost allowed Herod the Great to determine the exact location of the infant Christ. However, the Magi were warned by the Lord in a dream not to report back to Herod (*vv. 7–8, 12*). That resulted in an angry slaughter of all the male childen under the age of two in and around Bethlehem (vv. 16–18).

When the Magi had left Herod, they had been guided by the start to the very house in Bethlehem where Joseph, Mary and the infant Jesus were living (Matt. 2:9–10). Then they worshipped and presented exquisite gifts fit for a king (v. 11). The naming of these gifts (i.e. gold, incense and myrrh) had led some to believe that there were three Magi. However, there is no firm basis for saying how many wise men there were and even less possibility that they were kings. Through their generosity, though, they were certainly the benefactors for Jesus' family's stay in Egypt, fleeing from Herod (vv. 13–15).          A.B.L.

**MAGOG 1.** The second son of Japheth and grandson of Noah (Gen. 10:2; 1 Chron. 1:5). He and his descendants became known as fierce warriors, probably thus accounting for the use of the name in 2. below.

**2.** Mentioned in Rev. 20:8 as a symbolic leader of the forces arrayed against Christ. In Ezek. 38–39 it is the land ruled by Gog. For more detail see Gog.

**MAGOR-MISSABIB** (Heb., 'terror everywhere'). The name given by the prophet Jeremiah to Pashhur son of Immer (Jer. 20:3). When Pashhur heard Jeremiah speak he felt that the people would be demoralized by words of judgment and defeat and so he had the prophet beaten and put in the stocks by the Temple area (v. 2). The following day, Pashhur, thinking Jeremiah would have learned his lesson, released him. Jeremiah then said to Pashhur: 'The LORD's name for you is not Pashhur, but Magor-Missabib'. The name meant 'terror everywhere' and was a play on the name Pashhur (v. 3–6). Specifically, Jeremiah prophesied that Pashhur's own family would go into Exile where Pashhur him-

self would die. See Pashhur 1. for more detail.

**MAGPIASH** In Neh. 10:20 Magpiash is listed as a leader of the people. Under the direction of Nehemiah, he signed the agreement of the people to obey the Law of the LORD and worship only him.

**MAHALALEL 1.** The son of Kenan, Mahalalel was one of those early leaders of a whole people and he lived 895 years. He was the father of Jared. He is also listed in Luke's genealogy leading from Jesus to Adam (Gen. 5:12–17; 1 Chron. 1:2; Luke 3:37).

**2.** An ancestor of Athaiah, a provincial leader in Jerusalem in the time of Nehemiah. He was from the tribe of Judah and a descendant of Perez (Neh. 11:4).

**MAHALATH 1.** One of Esau's wives. Esau had married Canaanite women against the express wishes of his father Isaac. When he realized that his brother Jacob had obeyed his father and gone for a wife back in Paddan-Aram, Esau decided to marry within the extended family as well in order to try to gain his father's approval. He married Mahalath who was the sister of Nebaioth and daughter of Ishmael, Abraham's son. Esau's evil in marrying Canaanites stemmed from the promise that Abraham extracted from Isaac that he would never take a Canaanite wife but return for a wife to Abraham's family. Isaac had done this and the LORD had led him to Rebekah (Gen. 24). It served as a reminder that Canaan was the 'promised land' and that Abraham and his descendants were not supposed to intermarry with those who were pagan and standing under the judgment of God.

**2.** The daughter of King David's son Jerimoth whom Rehoboam married (2 Chron. 11:18).          P.D.G.

**MAHARAI** the Netophathite was one of

David's 'Thirty' warriors. As a commander in David's army he was on duty with his men in the tenth month of each year and had 24,000 men in his division (2 Sam. 23:28; 1 Chron. 11:30; 27:13).

**MAHATH** **1.** A Kohathite from the tribe of Levi and listed in the genealogy of those priests who helped in King David's time with music. He was the father of Elkanah and son of Amasai (1 Chron. 6:35).

**2.** The son of Amasai. This Mahath was also a Kohathite Levite. He worked to help purify the Temple in the time of the revival under King Hezekiah (2 Chron. 29:12). He also worked under the supervision of Conaniah and Shimei in preparing storerooms for the people's gifts (2 Chron. 31:13).

**MAHAZIOTH** One of the sons of Heman listed among those set apart for the ministry of prophesying and music during the reign of King David. Heman was the king's seer. Mahazioth and his relations were given the 23rd turn of service in the sanctuary (1 Chron. 25:4, 30).

**MAHER-SHALAL-HASH-BAZ** (Heb., 'the spoil speeds, the prey hastens'). The symbolic name given to one of Isaiah's sons (Is. 8:1, 3). The name pointed to the imminent destruction of Pekah, king of Israel, and Rezin, king of Aram, by the king of Assyria as God brought judgment to the Northern Kingdom of Israel. The name was initially written on a large scroll and witnessed by two reliable witnesses, Uriah the priest and Zechariah. This was done even before the child was conceived. When the destruction finally came the tablet would witness to the truth of Isaiah's words and to the sin of Ahaz, king of Judah, and others in refusing to listen to the word of the LORD through Isaiah. P.D.G.

**MAHLAH** **1.** One of five daughters born to Zelophehad. Zelophehad had no sons. These daughters married cousins on their father's side and were members of the tribe of Manasseh (Num. 26:33; 27:1; 36:1–12; Josh. 17:3). They faced a predicament over their inheritance, for normally inherited land would have been passed on through a son.

They approached Moses at the entrance to the Tabernacle about the problem, asking him to rule that they should be allowed to inherit their father's property, for it would not be right that his name should die out. Moses consulted the LORD about the situation, as a result of which a new law was promulgated allowing daughters to inherit land from their father. Later some of the leaders from the tribe of Manasseh appealed to Moses about the case, pointing out that if these women were now to marry outside the tribe the land would be lost forever to the tribe. The ruling which followed further defined the law of inheritance, insisting that the women should marry into their father's tribe or else lose the inheritance (Num. 36). Hence the daughters married cousins 'on their father's side', thus fulfilling the requirement of the LORD.

When finally the Israelites entered the land of Canaan and the land was divided up among the tribes, the daughters of Zelophehad were duly given their inheritance (Josh. 17:3–4).

**2.** A son of Gilead's sister Hammoleketh. He was from the tribe of Manasseh (1 Chron. 7:18). P.D.G.

**MAHLI** **1.** One of the sons of Merari and a grandson of Levi. Mahli became a clan leader of the Mahlites (Exod. 6:19; Num. 3:20; 26:58; 1 Chron. 6:19, 29, 47; 24:26, 28). The Merarites, of which their clan was a part, were responsible in the days of Moses for carrying the frames of the Tabernacle, its pegs, bases etc. (Num. 4:29–33). Mahli's descendants were given duties at the Tabernacle in the days of King David and later at the Temple during the reign of King Solomon (*1 Chron. 23:21*).

**2.** One of the three Levite sons of Mushi and grandson of Merari (*1 Chron. 6:47; 23:23; 24:30*).

**MAHLON** and his brother Kilion were sons of Elimelech and Naomi and lived in the days of the Judges in Israel. Because of a famine in Judah, Elimelech and his wife had left their home town of Bethlehem and gone to Moab for a while (*Ruth 1:1–2*). When Elimelech died, Naomi was looked after by her two sons. Later, the two sons also died, although the book of Ruth does not say how this happened. However, both Kilion and Mahlon had married Moabite wives who helped support Naomi (*Ruth 1:3–5*). Kilion had married Orpah. Mahlon's wife, Ruth, later returned with her mother-in-law to Bethlehem where she met and married Boaz. Boaz bought from Naomi all Mahlon's property and the property of his father and brother (*Ruth 4:9–10*). P.D.G.

**MAHOL** (Heb., 'dance'). In the NIV this person appears as the father of three men, Heman, Calcol and Darda. When Solomon's wisdom was described, he was said to be wiser than all these. Some scholars have suggested that the word Mahol here has to do with describing people in the orchestra. They were apparently regarded as very wise and no doubt took part in musical contributions to worship (*1 Kings 4:31*).

**MAHSEIAH** (Heb., 'the LORD is my refuge'). The grandfather of Baruch the scribe and Seraiah, a staff officer. They helped Jeremiah during his life as a prophet at the end of the Southern Kingdom of Judah (*Jer. 32:12; 51:59*). Mahseiah's son was Neriah.

**MAKI** Father of one of the twelve spies sent out by Moses from the Desert of Paran to spy out the land of Canaan (*Num.*

*13:15*). A representative of each tribe was chosen and Maki's son Geuel was chosen from the tribe of Gad. For further detail on their mission see *Shammua.*

**MAKIR** (Heb., 'valuable').

**1.** This person is first named in *Gen. 50:23* when his children received a blessing from Joseph in his old age. Makir was a son of Manasseh and his Aramean concubine and head of the Makirite clan (*Num. 26:29; 1 Chron. 7:14*). His wife came from the clans of the Huppites and Shuppites (*1 Chron. 7:15*). His son, Gilead, also became a clan leader (*Num. 27:1; 1 Chron. 7:17*). His descendants captured the land that became known as Gilead and drove out the Amorites (*Num. 32:39*). The Makirites were 'great soldiers', and it was the Gilead clan that were later given that land officially in the distribution of Canaan by Moses and Joshua to the Israelites (*Josh. 17:1; 13:31; Judg. 5:14; Deut. 3:15; 1 Chron. 2:21–23*). Makir's descendants were involved in an interesting question of legal rights concerning the inheritance of a family where there were only daughters. The great-grandson of Makir (see *Zelophehad*) only had daughters and so Moses consulted the LORD concerning the inheritance laws (*Josh. 17:3* etc.).

**2.** This Makir, son of Ammiel, came from the area of Gilead and probably was named after the tribal leader mentioned above. He sheltered the crippled son of Saul, Mephibosheth, when David came to the throne. David enquired whether there was anyone in Saul's household to whom he could show favour and was pointed to Makir's home in Lo Debar (*2 Sam. 9:4–5*). Later Makir was also to help David himself when he was fleeing from his son Absalom. He provided bedding, bowls, pottery and food for David and his men (*2 Sam. 17:27*). He was clearly a faithful and compassionate man and was used in the plans of God that Mephibosheth should be provided for and that David and his men should survive and be restored to the throne.                                        P.D.G.

**MALACHI** (Heb., 'my messenger'). The very name of this last of the OT prophets is in dispute, many scholars suggesting it is an epithet of an unnamed prophet and others that it is indeed a personal name. It is frequently pointed out that human parents would not name a child 'my messenger', but if the name were an abbreviated form of the Heb. 'messenger of Yah [the LORD]' or the like the difficulty would disappear. The name then could originally and literally have been 'messenger of (Yah)' and only later vocalized as 'my messenger'.

The dating of the prophet and his book are likewise problematic. What seems quite clear is that many issues dealt with here such as corruption in the priesthood (*Mal. 1:6–14*), easy divorce from Jewish wives (*Mal. 2:10–16*), and intermarriage with pagans were addressed later by Ezra (*Ezra 9:1–4; 10:1–4*) and Nehemiah (*Neh. 10:28–31; 13:10–14, 23–37*) and not in reverse order. That is, it seems that Ezra and Nehemiah presuppose Malachi and not that Malachi presupposes them, for if the latter were the case one would have to write off the reforms of Ezra and Nehemiah as complete and total failures. Ezra's arrival in Jerusalem in 458 BC thus necessitates a date for Malachi somewhat earlier than that, perhaps about 470.

Malachi's concerns, as already noted, centre on religious and social improprieties which appear to have permeated the life of the post-exilic Jewish community of Jerusalem and Judah. Though the exiles had been chastened and thoroughly purged of any inclination to idolatry, their leaders and they themselves came back to the homeland largely unreformed in other respects. The Temple had been completed a half century before the likely date of Malachi's ministry and yet already its priests were corrupting its services and profiting from their sacred offices. The laity too were culpable, mistreating and taking advantage of one another. Malachi's assessment of the situation as a whole was that it constituted violation of Yahweh's covenant (*Mal. 2:8, 10*), a sin that invited the inevitable curses attached to it (*Mal. 2:2; 3:9*).

His appeal to his people is that they repent (*Mal. 3:7; 4:2, 4*), especially in light of the coming of God's messenger (*3:1*), the one who will precede and announce the coming of the LORD himself in judgment (*3:1; 4:1–6*). This messenger, the NT teaches, was John the Baptist, forerunner and proclaimer of Jesus Christ the Lord (*Matt. 11:9–14*). The book of Malachi, the last of the OT prophets, thus forms a most fitting bridge between the sterility of OT life and worship carried out *pro forma* and the NT Messiah whose coming made possible new life and new relationship to the Lord through the Spirit (*John 4:24*).

The burden of the book of Malachi was the glaring incongruity between the identity of the Jewish community as the people of God and the living out of all that this required of them. Theirs was not the problem of rebuilding the Temple and holy city, for that had long been done by Malachi's day; rather, it was the issue of holy living and holy service in the aftermath of all the external accomplishments. Malachi, though dead, yet speaks to the modern world about the need to bring performance into line with profession. His message therefore is current, especially in light of the coming of the One of whom the prophet so eloquently spoke.                                        E.M.

**MALCAM** was the head of a family and was the son of Shaharaim and his wife Hodesh. Listed in the genealogy of Benjamin leading to King Saul, he was born in Moab (*1 Chron. 8:9*).

**MALCHUS** Mentioned in *John 18:10*,

Malchus was a servant to the high priest at the time of the betrayal and arrest of Jesus. In a desperate bid to protect Jesus, Peter drew his sword and cut off Malchus' ear. Jesus immediately reprimanded Peter and, according to *Luke 22:50*, healed the servant. Jesus had not come as the Messiah in the way expected by many, the way of a King coming to conquer (see *Luke 22:52*). Rather he had come as one who would be 'led like a lamb to the slaughter' (*Is. 53:7*), one who was going to death deliberately to fulfil the will of his Father and save his people from their sin. Later another of the high priest's servants, a relative of Malchus, confronted Peter, asking him if he had not been with Jesus in the olive grove. Peter's subsequent denial was one of three that evening. P.D.G.

**MALKI-SHUA** Mentioned in *1 Sam. 14:49*, Malki-Shua was one of King Saul's sons and brother to Jonathan and Ishvi (*1 Chron. 8:33; 9:39*). He was later killed by the Philistines in a fierce battle on Mount Gilboa (*1 Sam. 31:2; 1 Chron. 10:2*).

**MALKIEL** (Heb., 'God is king'). The grandson of Asher and son of Beriah, Malkiel was a leader of the Malkielite clan and one of those who went to Egypt with Jacob (*Gen. 46:17; Num. 26:45*). He was the father of Bizraith (*1 Chron. 7:31*).

**MALKIJAH 1.** An ancestor of Asaph (*1 Chron. 6:40*).

**2.** One among the priests who were chosen to be officials in the sanctuary 'according to the last instructions of David'. Impartial selection from among the descendants of Eleazar and Ithamar was made by drawing lots. The fifth lot fell to Malkijah and that was the order in which he ministered when entering the sanctuary (*1 Chron. 24:9*).

**3.** Another Malkijah was an ancestor of a priest called Adaiah who was among the earliest of the priestly families to return and settle in Jerusalem following the Exile in Babylon (*1 Chron. 9:12*).

**4.** This Malkijah was King Zedekiah's son and owned the empty but muddy cistern into which Jeremiah was lowered by his enemies. 'Jeremiah sank down into the mud' (*Jer. 38:6*). He was put there by the royal officials because they refused to listen to his prophecy that Babylon would win the battle with Judah. They felt that this teaching was treacherous and would discourage the people of Judah, and so they wanted him killed.

**5.** Malkijah, the father of Pashhur, is mentioned in *Jer. 21:1; 38:1*. Pashhur was a servant to King Zedekiah, and was sent to Jeremiah to inquire about God's plans (*Jer. 21*). Jeremiah prophesied that the people of Judah would soon be sent into captivity and punished as their deeds deserved. In *Jer. 38:1–6* Pashhur and his friends sought to destroy Jeremiah.

**6.** Another by this name was one of the priests who sealed the agreement with Nehemiah to worship only the LORD and to obey his Law (*Neh. 10:3*).

**7.** Two descendants of Parosh are called Malkijah, although the name may be misplaced and therefore refer to only one person. They were among the Israelites who divorced their foreign wives following the Law of God and the instruction of Ezra (*Ezra 10:25*).

**8.** A descendant of Harim who also divorced his foreign wife following Ezra's instructions. He is probably the same man as helped repair a section of the wall of Jerusalem (*Ezra 10:31; Neh. 3:11*).

**9.** Malkijah son of Recab repaired the Dung Gate of the wall of Jerusalem after the return from the Babylonian Exile. He was a ruler of the district of Beth Hakkerem (*Neh. 3:14*).

**10.** Another Malkijah in the time of Nehemiah was one of the goldsmiths. He also helped repair the walls of Jerusalem 'as far as the house of the temple servants and the merchants, opposite the

Inspection Gate, and as far as the room above the corner' (Neh. 3:31).

**11.** This Malkijah was among those who stood on Ezra's right-hand side on a high wooden platform as he read the book of the Law to the people of Israel. As the Law was read the people worshipped and praised God, confessed their sin, and recommitted themselves to the LORD's service (Neh. 8:4). He may be the same as 9. or 10. above.

**12.** This Malkijah was an ancestor of Adaiah who was a head of a family of priests which worked on rebuilding the walls of Jerusalem during the time of Nehemiah (Neh. 11:12).

**13.** A Levite who was part of the choir that sang at the dedication of the wall. The walls and city had been destroyed by the Babylonians when they took the Israelites into captivity. Under the direction of Nehemiah they were eventually rebuilt amidst great praises to God (Neh. 12:42).                                    P.D.G.

**MALKIRAM** (Heb., 'my king is exalted'). Listed among the descendants of King Jehoiachin, and thus part of David's royal line who returned after the Exile in Babylon (1 Chron. 3:18).

**MALLOTHI** One of the sons of Heman the king's seer, listed among those set apart for the ministry of prophesying and music during the reign of King David (1 Chron. 25:4). A leader of the 19th group of Levitical musicians and choirs who ministered in the Temple (1 Chron. 25:26).

**MALLUCH   1.** The father of Abdi, a son of Hashabiah and an ancestor of Ethan, a Levite musician in the time of David (1 Chron. 6:44).

**2.** This Malluch was among the descendants of Bani. At the time of return from the Exile in Babylon, Shecaniah confessed to Ezra that many men and even descendants of the priests of Judah had married wives from other tribes and nations. Ezra and the people repented and made a covenant to serve the LORD (Ezra 10:2). Malluch is listed in v. 29 as one who divorced his foreign wife.

**3.** Another Malluch was among the descendants of Harim. He too is listed in Ezra 10:32 as one who divorced his foreign wife.

**4.** One of the priests who returned from the Babylonian Exile and who sealed the agreement with Nehemiah to worship only the LORD and to obey his Law (Neh. 10:4; 12:2, 14).

**5.** One of 'the leaders of the people' who also signed the agreement with Nehemiah (Neh. 10:27).          P.D.G.

**MAMRE** was a friend of Abraham who helped him when he had to fight off the Mesopotamian kings. Abraham had settled near this man who was an Amorite and lived near Hebron. Mamre's brothers, Eshcol and Aner, are also mentioned. Abraham appreciated their help in the battle and ensured that they received their reward from the booty retaken in war (Gen. 14:13, 24). Mamre seems to have given his name not only to the 'great trees of Mamre' by which Abraham set up camp, but also to the area (e.g. Gen. 13:18; 18:1; 23:17).          P.D.G.

**MANAEN** is mentioned as one of the 'prophets and teachers' in the church at Antioch in Acts 13:1. He had been brought up with Herod the Tetrarch. Following a time of fasting and prayer, the Holy Spirit indicated to these people that they should set apart Saul and Barnabas for the task to which the Lord was calling them (vv. 1–3). The two of them then set off for Cyprus where they continued to preach the gospel. The church at Antioch, of which Manaen was a member, is described in Acts 11. Manaen may have been among those Hellenistic Jewish Christians who were scattered due to persecution and, coming to Antioch, began to speak to the Greeks of the 'good news about the Lord Jesus' (*v. 20*). When Barnabas was sent by the leaders of the church in Jerusalem to Antioch to find out what was happening, he saw 'great evidence of the grace of God' there (*v. 23*).

P.D.G.

**MANAHATH** A descendant of Esau, Manahath was the son of Shobal, a clan leader of the Edomites (*Gen. 36:23; 1 Chron. 1:40*).

**MANASSEH** (Heb., 'causing to forget').

**1.** This Manasseh was a son of Joseph. Following Joseph's exaltation to high office in Egypt, he fathered two sons by Asenath, his Egyptian wife (*Gen. 41:50*). The first-born he named Manasseh, signifying his forgetting of the tragic circumstances that brought him to Egypt in the first place. He called his second son Ephraim, 'fruitful one', for God had not only delivered him from harm but had prospered him beyond measure (*Gen. 41:51–52*).

In time to come Jacob lay dying and Joseph requested him to impart the patriarchal blessings to Joseph's sons. Presenting them in the order of primogeniture, Joseph placed Jacob's right hand on Manasseh's head and his left on Ephraim's. Jacob stubbornly (and providentially) reversed his hands, however, thus bestowing the rights of the first-born on Ephraim rather than Manasseh (*Gen. 48*). This act was in line with a common biblical theme, that of God's gracious selection of those for salvation and service who would otherwise and by human traditions be bypassed (*cf. Gen. 25:23; Rom. 9:6–12*).

Ephraim went on, indeed, to father a tribe that dominated the Northern Kingdom of Israel (see *Ephraim*). But Manasseh was not by any means ignored. In fact, the tribe he sired eventually divided into two parts, one occupying a large region of the Transjordan (*Num. 32:33–42; Josh. 12:1–6*), and the other an important region to the north of Ephraim, one extending from the Mediterranean Sea to the Jordan river (*Josh. 17:1–13*). This bounty reflected the blessing spoken by Jacob to the tribes as he spoke of Ephraim and Manasseh under the rubric Joseph (*Gen. 49:22–26*). Moses likewise described the blessing of the two in terms of prosperity and power (*Deut. 33:13–17*).

**2.** Manasseh, the Father of Gershom is mentioned only in *Judg. 18:30*, and appears to be a scribal substitution for an original reading 'Moses'. The purpose for the change apparently was to deliver Moses from the onus of being grandfather of Jonathan, the first priest of the apostate cult at Dan.

**3.** Manasseh, a son of Pahath Moab, was one of the returning Jews who had married a foreign wife following the Exile (*Ezra 10:30*).

**4.** Manasseh, son of Hashum, was also one of the returning Jews who had married a foreign wife following the Exile (*Ezra 10:33*). E.M.

**5.** Manasseh, King of Judah. Manasseh ruled in Judah for fifty-five years (c. 696–642 BC). He came to the throne at twelve years old on the death of his father King Hezekiah. His mother's name was Hephzibah. The account of his reign is given in *2 Kings 21:1–18* and *2 Chron. 33:1–20*. Sadly, his reign did not start as had the reign of his father, with great revival and a turning back to the LORD. *2 Kings 21:2* begins by saying: 'He did evil in the eyes of the LORD'. This evil involved idolatry and pagan practices that had been learned from other nations. He did not simply let the country drift but took an active role in restoring pagan worship that had been destroyed during the early part of the reign of his father (*2 Chron. 33:3*). He set up pagan altars in the temple area and even sacrificed his own son in the fire (*v. 6*). He worshipped stars and was involved with sorcery, all in direct contravention of God's Law. He refused even to listen to prophets sent by the LORD. The prophets proceeded to warn that the LORD would bring a terrible devastation upon Jerusalem as a result of all this sin (vv. 10–15).

Both Scripture and Assryian inscriptions reveal that during most of his reign Manasseh was a vassal king under the overwhelming power of the Assyrians. Eventually, as judgment on Manasseh, the LORD allowed the Assyrians to invade again. They took the king prisoner, put a hook in his nose to disgrace him, put him in shackles and led him off to Babylon. At this point the chronicler records that Manasseh repented and the LORD heard his cry and brought him back to Jerusalem and to his kingdom, 'Then Manasseh knew that the LORD is God' (2 Chron. 33:10–13). On his return to Jerusalem he tore down the pagan altars and insisted the people worship only the LORD (vv. 15–17). The account in Chronicles indicates the depths of God's graciousness that he should forgive someone even as evil as Manasseh when he truly repented of his sins.

Tradition has it that Isaiah was martyred. Certainly he prophesied in Hezekiah's day, so perhaps he was killed for his stand against Manasseh's paganism in the earlier part of Manasseh's reign. Yet eventually Manasseh did turn back to the LORD and his people also turned to the LORD. How much really changed in the country and how long the king lived after his return from captivity is not at all clear. It may have only been a brief spell, for his son Amon was evil (v. 22) and when Josiah came to the throne just a few years later there seems to have been very little worship of the LORD going on in the country.                P.D.G

**MANOAH** (Heb., 'resting place'). Manoah was a Danite from the town of Zorah and, in the time of the Judges, became the father of the famous leader and judge, Samson. His wife was unable to have children but an angel of the LORD appeared to her and told her she would have a son (Judg. 13:2–3). The child was to be a Nazirite, a person consecrated to a period of service to the LORD. Usually people took a Nazirite vow of dedication for a specific period of time. However, Samson was to be a Nazirite for life on God's orders and was to be brought up fulfilling the rules and regulations applicable to Nazirites. These included not shaving or cutting hair, not drinking alcoholic drink, and following some of the laws on ceremonial purity expected of the priests (see Nazirite; also Num. 6).

The angel also told Manoah's wife that this child would begin the deliverance of the Israelites from the Philistines (Judg. 13:5). Manoah's wife told him what had happened and the passage shows Manoah's faith in God through his response. He prayed that God would again send his angel but this time to teach his wife how to bring him up correctly. When the angel appeared again Manoah was able to speak to him and in his conversation assumed the truth of what had been promised (v. 12). Manoah suggested a meal for the angel. He rejected a meal but asked that a burnt offering be offered to the LORD. Manoah appears to have thought the messenger from God was a man, perhaps a prophet, and so asked his name (v. 17). However, as the offering was being burned the angel ascended in the flame. At this, Manoah realized he was dealing with an angel and fell down to worship. In due course Samson was born and God's Spirit 'began to stir him' (vv. 24–25). Later Samson was buried in Manoah's tomb between Zorah and Eshtaol (Judg. 16:31).

This work of God occurred at a time when the Israelites had been doing 'evil in the eyes of the LORD' and had been serving their Philistine masters (Judg. 13:1). A number of different non-descript judges had tried to rule limited areas of Israel prior to this but the sin of the people and their rebellion against God was great.

It was therefore by God's intervention, by his grace alone, that they would ever recover from the consequences of their sin. This story indicates how God was not prepared to allow his people to die out or forever be subjugated by other peoples. God remained faithful to his covenant promises made to Abraham and Moses and himself caused a person to be born who would one day rescue his people. Manoah's trust probably shows that some people in Israel had remained faithful to the LORD throughout. The fact that his wife was known to be unable to have children also showed God's sovereignty in the affairs of his people. Like Abraham's wife Sarah and Elizabeth the mother of John the Baptist, this woman's infertility was used to demonstrate God's hand at work in the salvation of his people. P.D.G.

**MAOCH** Mentioned in 1 Sam. 27:2, Maoch was the father of Achish. Achish was a king of Gath in the days when David was being chased by King Saul. David took refuge with Achish for a while. The person named Maacah in 1 Kings 2:39 is probably the same person. See Achish.

**MAON** (Heb., 'dwelling'). Mentioned in 1 Chron. 2:45, Maon was the son of Shammai and 'father of Beth Zur'. This latter phrase means that either he founded the town or that his descendants lived there. In Judg. 10:12 a people known as Maonites are mentioned, but it is most unlikely that they are linked with this Maon who was a descendant of Caleb.

**MARA** This was the name that Naomi requested she be called on her return to Israel, following her experiences in Moab (Ruth 1:20). The name means 'bitter'. Naomi's life had indeed been quite horrific. She and her husband, Elimelech, had left Israel for Moab during a time of famine back at home. While in Moab Naomi's sons married Moabite women.

First, Elimelech died and then the two sons also died, leaving her a widow in a foreign land and without family to support her. She returned to Bethlehem with Ruth, one of her daughters-in-law, and asked to be called Mara, as opposed to Naomi (Heb., 'pleasant').

It is worth noting that the name was not given as a description of how she felt so much as a description of her life circumstances. In fact Naomi was not bitter in herself in spite of the bitterness of life. She trusted the LORD through all the catastrophes and her faith was eventually seen to be well placed as God did preserve her and brought her under the protection of Ruth and her new husband Boaz. P.D.G.

**MARDUK** was one of the Babylonian gods and mentioned only once in Scripture in Jer. 50:2. In that passage Jeremiah was proclaiming to the people of Judah who had seen relatives and friends taken prisoner by the Babylonians that, one day, God would destroy Babylon and her gods. At that time the people of Israel would return to Judah and worship the true God (v. 4). The passage affirms monotheism, that the covenant God of Israel had power even over the so-called gods of other nations. It also affirms his sovereign purposes for his people who would come back in repentance to their Promised Land and would return to their God (vv. 4–7).

Hammurabi's code shows that Marduk came to be regarded as the creator god and the head of the Babylonian pantheon. P.D.G.

**MARESHAH** (Heb., 'hill top').
**1.** One of Caleb's sons and nephew to Jerahmeel, this Mareshah was the father of Hebron (1 Chron. 2:42).
**2.** Mentioned in 1 Chron. 4:21, Mareshah was the son of Laadah and a grandson of Lecah, of the tribe of Judah. He was a leader of the clans of linen workers who lived at Beth Ashbea.

# MARK, JOHN

## New Testament references

The first reference to Mark in the NT appears in the account of Peter's miraculous rescue from Herod Agrippa's prison in Jerusalem (c. AD 44; *Acts 12:6–11*). After his release Peter made his way 'to the house of Mary, the mother of John whose other name was Mark' (*v. 12*). Like other Jews of this era (such as Saul, also called Paul, *Acts 13:9*), John Mark had both a Hebrew name (John, meaning 'God is gracious') and a Roman name (Mark, meaning 'large hammer'). The fact that his father is not mentioned in connection with the family's house probably means he was dead. That Peter went to this house immediately after his release suggests that it was a usual meeting place of the early church and a house of considerable prominence.

Mark is next associated with Barnabas and Saul, who brought a monetary gift from the church in Antioch for Judean Christians needing famine relief (c. AD 46; *Acts 11:29–30*). According to *Col. 4:10*, Barnabas and Mark were cousins. Without further elaboration the account in Acts reports that 'Barnabas and Saul returned from Jerusalem when they had fulfilled their mission, bringing with them John whose other name was Mark' (*Acts 12:25*).

At Antioch another mission commenced for these three men. Barnabas and Saul were sent out by the church on a missionary journey (c. AD 47) that began in Cyprus, where Barnabas had lived (*Acts 4:36*). But they did not leave Mark behind in Antioch. 'When they arrived at Salamis, they proclaimed the word of God in the synagogues of the Jews. And they had John to assist them' (*Acts 13:5*). The word ('to assist') used to describe Mark's role in the mission is used elsewhere by Luke of those who were 'ministers of the word' (*Luke 1:2*). The term is also applied to the Jewish synagogue assistant (*Luke 4:20*) whose work included the instruction of children. Though Mark may have been a general-purpose assistant to Barnabas and Saul, participation in some form of instruction was probably also an aspect of his contribution to the mission.

However, his involvement with this first missionary journey was apparently short-lived. After ministry in Cyprus the three sailed to Perga in Pamphylia (*Acts 13:13*). But there Mark decided to leave the venture. The reader of Acts is not informed of this departure until a return visit to all the churches founded on this first mission is proposed by Paul (*Acts 15:36*). Barnabas wanted to include Mark again 'but Paul did not think it wise to take him because he had deserted them in Pamphylia, and had not continued with them in the work' (*v. 38*). The dispute over this issue led to Paul parting with Barnabas and taking instead Silas as his partner on a second journey (c. AD 48; *v. 40*). Meanwhile 'Barnabas took Mark and sailed for Cyprus' (*v. 39*), the area in which Mark had previously served.

One might think that the firmness of Paul's resolve to bar Mark's participation in a second journey would spell the end of any future ministry together for them. But that proved not to be the case. Two letters written by Paul (c. AD 60–62), probably while awaiting trial in Rome after completing a third missionary journey, mention Mark in appreciative terms. In the letter to the Colossians Mark is described with other of Paul's fellow workers as one who had been 'a comfort to me' (*Col. 4:10–11*). And in the letter to Philemon he is again described (with Luke and others) as Paul's fellow worker (*Philem. 24*). Finally, in the last canonical letter of Paul to his protegé Timothy (c. A D 64) he instructs him to 'get Mark and bring him with you; because he is helpful to me in my ministry' (*2 Tim. 4:11*).

The final reference to Mark in the N T occurs in a letter of Peter. Mark was first mentioned in connection with Peter's release from prison in Jerusalem. Now Peter is in Rome (c. A D 64) and Mark is with him. The closeness of their relationship is indicated by Peter's reference to Mark as 'my son' (*1 Pet. 4:13*).

According to Papias of Heirapolis (c. A D 130; cited by Eusebius, *Ecclesiastical History* 3.39.15), Mark continued to minister with Peter in Rome, serving as his 'interpreter' and as the compiler of his teaching about 'the things said and done by the Lord'. This latter phrase is a summary description of Mark's Gospel. Papias' testimony serves to validate the usefulness and authority of Mark's account for the early church.

Mark is also credited with the establishment of churches in Alexandria (Eusebius, *EH*, 2.16.1). There he is said to have been martyred (*The Paschal Chronicle*) with his remains subsequently carried to Venice and placed under the Church of St Mark.

## Characteristics of Mark's Gospel and theology

Although each of the Gospels share a similar purpose in providing readers with an account of Jesus' teaching and ministry, the individual writing the Gospel also brought to that task particular pastoral or theological concerns and points of view. In this respect the Gospel accounts are like painted portraits that not only interpret their subject but also reveal something about the person who composed them. Read with this in mind, some of the characteristics of Mark's Gospel can be understood in light of the brief sketch of his life provided by the N T references to him (cited above).

### The disciples' failure

Although each of the Gospels in their own way relate the disciples' struggle with understanding Jesus' message and ministry, Mark's portrait of the disciples' repeated misunderstanding and failure is more sharply drawn than any other. He shows that the disciples routinely did not understand Jesus' parables (*Mark 4:13; 7:18*), his propositional statements (*10:10*), and his predictions about his impending death (*9:10, 32*). They failed to grasp the significance of his mighty deeds, like calming the sea (*4:40–41*) and walking on water (*6:49–52*), and ultimately forsook him in his hour of crisis (*14:50*).

Mark even ended his Gospel on a note of failure. The women who came to Jesus' tomb found it empty and were told to 'tell his disciples and Peter, "he is going ahead of you into Galilee"' (*Mark 16:7*). But as Mark described it, 'they said nothing to anyone, because they were afraid' (*v. 8*). This strange ending prompted later copyists to provide a conclusion more in keeping with the other Gospels (i.e. *vv. 9–20*), but Mark's abrupt closing is consistent with the bleak portrayal of Jesus' followers that characterize his presentation in this Gospel.

In part Mark's theme serves as a salutary reminder that the purposes of God are carried out by fallible people. Mark himself had turned back from the first missionary journey and left Paul and Barnabas to continue the work. Though no reason is given, Paul's unwillingness to take him on a second journey suggests that he at least regarded Mark's departure as inexcusable. Yet Paul's subsequent references to him show that a reconciliation took place later and that he not only welcomed but requested Mark's association in the work of the ministry.

## The Kingdom's advance

Mark summarized Jesus' message at the beginning of his gospel, 'The time has come . . . the kingdom of God is near. Repent and believe the good news!' (*Mark 1:15*). As do the other Gospels, Mark shows that the Kingdom has both present and future aspects corresponding to its spiritual and universal dimensions. God's salvation and sovereignty begin to be experienced by those who respond to the message of the gospel. Both the gospel and the Kingdom are compared to seed scattered over the earth (*Mark 4:14, 26*). Its beginning is hardly noticeable but its end is incomparably grand (*4:30–32*). The consummation is linked to the future coming of Jesus 'with great power and glory' (*13:26*) and the anticipation of fellowship with him in the Kingdom of God (*14:25*).

Mark was a witness to the early church's small beginnings, from its birth in Jerusalem, even meeting in his family's home, to the extension of the missionary enterprise that reached out into the extended Roman world. In later years as an associate of both Paul and Peter he could see the remarkable growth that resulted from a wide proclamation of the gospel. Yet he reminded his readers that this was God's doing. When the disciples asked Jesus, 'Who can be saved?' (*Mark 10:26*), the answer is: 'With man this is impossible, but not with God; all things are possible with God' (*v. 27*).

## Jesus' self-sacrifice and vindication

Mark leaves his readers in no doubt about the main subject of his Gospel, by stating in the first line of his writing: 'The beginning of the gospel about Jesus Christ, the Son of God' (*Mark 1:1*). But he goes on in the course of the Gospel to how understanding the meaning of those ascriptions for Jesus differed dramatically from popular expectation. Many Jews looked forward to the coming of a Messiah who would deliver God's people from their oppressors. The disciples shared this hope and struggled with Jesus' statements that the mission God had called him to must lead to death (*Mark 8:31; 9:31; 10:23*). When Peter sought to dissuade him, Jesus told him, 'You do not have in mind the things of God, but of men' (*8:33*).

The pattern of Jesus' life that Mark set before the disciples was summed up this way: 'The Son of Man did not come to be served but to serve, and to give his life as a ransom for many' (*Mark 10:45*). Jesus as the Son of God showed the vitality of that relationship by following the path of obedience that led to the cross. His submissive prayer to God was 'Not what I will but what you will' (*14:36*). Similarly disciples are called to take up their cross and follow him (*8:34*).

That this was the plan of God for Jesus is shown by the centurion's confession at the cross: 'Truly this man was the Son of God!' (*Mark 15:39*). The account of the resurrection (*16:1–8*) becomes the basis for the promise of Jesus' glorious return (*8:38; 13:26; 14:62*) and the vindication for the self-sacrificial life to which disciples are likewise called (*10:28–29*).                    D.K.L.

**MARSENA** A wise man and legal expert consulted by King Xerxes (*Est. 1:14*). For detail see *Memucan*.

**MARTHA** is mentioned in both Luke's Gospel and John's Gospel. She was a dear friend and faithful disciple of Christ and dearly beloved by him (*John 11:5*).

Martha lived with her sister and brother, Mary and Lazarus, in the little village of Bethany (*John 11:1*). Bethany was located on the eastern slope of the Mount of Olives and Jesus frequently visited them when he was in Jerusalem (*Luke 10:38*). In fact, Jesus stayed with them during his last week on earth (*Matt. 21:17*).

Martha is well known as the one who was always distracted by her daily tasks. This is why many people can identify with her. When she invited Jesus into her home, she was so taken up with the preparations that she missed the close fellowship with him that both her sister and brother enjoyed (*Luke 10:39–42; John 12:2*).

Nevertheless, Martha need not be criticized for her ambitious behaviour. For her actions do reveal her loyalty to the Lord Jesus. Her true character is displayed by her honesty and steadfast faith. When her brother was gravely ill, she and her sister sent word to Jesus to come quickly (*John 11:3*). However, Jesus did not come right away and their brother died (*vv. 6–15*).

When the Lord finally arrived, Martha was honest with him about how she felt, but also exercised extraordinary faith in identifying Jesus as God's Son and believing in his ability to do something to help her brother (*vv. 21–27*). Jesus honoured her faith and raised Lazarus from the dead, thus manifesting the glory of God (*vv. 38–44*).

Martha was a loyal disciple of Jesus Christ who believed in him and served him with ardour and zeal.           K.MCR.

## MARY, THE MOTHER OF JESUS

The Virgin Mary, the mother of Jesus, is one of the most prominent figures in the Bible. Her life was characterized by faith, humility and obedience to the will of God. Mary also holds a unique place in human history as the only woman to ever conceive a child supernaturally. This young woman is almost as well known today as the divine Child she bore. She is loved and admired by millions of people all over the world.

Mary was a descendant of King David. Many scholars contend that the genealogy in *Luke 3:23–37* is Mary's and the one in *Matt. 1:1–16* is Joseph's. It is clear, therefore, that Jesus was a descendant of David and rightful heir to his throne. When the apostle Paul speaks of Jesus being of the seed of David (*Rom. 1:3; 2 Tim. 2:8*), he is probably referring to the lineage of Mary.

Mary lived in a village called Nazareth, located on the southern plains of Lower Galilee. She was betrothed to Joseph, a faithful and God-fearing man who was also from Nazareth (*Matt. 1:18*). At that time the angel, Gabriel, appeared to Mary and announced that she was going to become pregnant and give birth to a son. This Child would be called the Son of God and he would be given the throne of his father, David (*Luke 1:26–33*).

Mary, being a virgin, questioned Gabriel as to how this would take place. She was told that the Holy Spirit would come upon her and bring about the conception supernaturally. Assuring her that nothing was impossible with God, Gabriel also revealed to her that Elizabeth, her older relative, was pregnant. Then Mary, in an astonishing display of faith, affirmed her servanthood to the Lord and humbly submitted to his will (*Luke 1:34–38*).

Immediately, Mary went to visit Elizabeth, the future mother of John the Baptist. As soon as Elizabeth heard Mary's voice, the baby inside her womb leaped for joy. Elizabeth praised the God of Israel because it was supernaturally revealed to her that Mary was carrying no ordinary child. Mary was the favoured one, chosen to bear God's one and only Son (*Luke 1:39–45*).

At that time, a song of praise and thanksgiving welled up within Mary's heart (*Luke 1:46–55*). This beautiful hymn, commonly known as 'The Magnificat' is similar in many ways to the ancient Hebrew hymns found in the OT (e.g. Hannah's prayer, *1 Sam. 2:1–10*; David's song, *2 Sam. 22:1–51*).

The praise and exaltation of God (*Luke 1:46–49*), his providential care for those who fear him (*v. 50*), and combat motifs (*vv. 51–52*) are just a few of the themes this hymn has in common with its ancient predecessors. It is also Messianic in that Mary sees in the coming of this Child God's concern for and mercy toward Israel, even as he promised to their forefather Abraham (*vv. 54–55*).

Mary stayed with Elizabeth for three months and returned home (*Luke 1:56*). When Joseph, Mary's future husband, discovered she was pregnant he planned to divorce her quietly, so as not to disgrace her (in Christ's day, the Jews considered betrothal and marriage to be synonymous). But the Lord revealed to Joseph in a dream that the Child in her womb was conceived by the Holy Spirit and exhorted him to take her as his wife. Joseph, being a righteous man, obeyed the Lord and married her (*Matt. 1:18–25*).

When Caesar Augustus ordered that a census be taken of the entire Roman world, Joseph took Mary and headed for Bethlehem in Judea. Both of them were of the lineage of David and were required to register in his hometown (*Luke 2:1–5*). While they were there, the time came for Mary to have her baby. Because there was no room for them in the inn, she delivered her firstborn Son, Jesus, in a manger (a trough for feeding animals) (*Luke 2:6–7*).

Despite his humble birth, the presence of this newborn King could not be kept a secret. Shepherds, who were visited by a heavenly host and told about the birth of Christ, came to adore him. They spread the good news of the Saviour's birth throughout the land and Mary cherished these things and meditated upon them in her heart (*Luke 2:8–20*).

On the eighth day after Jesus' birth, Mary and Joseph had him circumcised. According to Jewish Law, 33 days later they went up to the Temple of the Lord for purification and to present Jesus to the Lord (*Lev. 12:1–8*; *Num. 18:15*; *Luke 2:21–24*). While they were there, a devout and righteous man named Simeon spoke prophetically of Jesus' future as the Messiah (*Luke 2:25–32*).

Simeon also issued a special warning to Mary that she too would have her heart searched by her Son (*Luke 2:33–35*). She was simply amazed at the things which were spoken about him. For, in the beginning, even Mary did not fully understand his destiny. The prophetess, Anna, also spoke of the redemption of Israel through him (*Luke 2:36–38*).

When Joseph and Mary had fulfilled everything required of them at the Temple, they returned to Bethlehem. Magi from the East, who saw his star arise in the heavens, set out to find the baby Jesus and to worship him. The Magi went to Jerusalem first to inquire where the King of the Jews had been born (*Matt. 2:1–2*).

When King Herod heard of their arrival and inquiry, he was deeply disturbed. He sent for the Magi and instructed them to search for the Child and to notify him when they had found him. The Magi then proceeded to follow his star which finally led them to their desired destination (*Matt. 2:3–10*).

When they arrived at Joseph and Mary's home, they worshipped the baby Jesus and presented him with gifts. Having been warned in a dream of Herod's evil intent, the Magi did not return to him. Instead, they immediately departed for their own country, taking a different route (*Matt. 2:11–12*).

Joseph also had a dream alerting him of Herod's plans to kill Jesus. He took Mary and the baby and fled to Egypt where he was commanded to stay until Herod's death (*Matt. 2:13–15*). There is some debate among scholars as to when Herod actually died. But most agree that his death probably took place in 4 BC. This means that Joseph and Mary remained in Egypt for at least one year.

After Herod's death, Joseph received another dream summoning them back to Israel. When they arrived in their native land, they discovered that Archelaus, Herod's son, was reigning in Judea. Having been warned about him in yet another dream, Joseph took Mary and Jesus and returned to Nazareth in Galilee (*Matt. 2:19–23; Luke 2:39*).

Joseph and Mary went up to Jerusalem yearly to attend the Passover Feast. On one of those occasions, when they were returning home, they discovered that their twelve year old son, Jesus, was not in their company. They went back to Jerusalem and found Jesus in the Temple.

Mary anxiously questioned her son about his behaviour and he, in turn, spoke to her about his Father's House (the Temple). Mary did not understand him, but she quietly treasured the incident in her heart. This is yet another example of her steadfast faith and her humble submission and insight into God's will (*Luke 2:41–52*).

The next time we encounter Mary is during Jesus' ministry which began when he was about 30 years old (*Luke 3:23*). It is during this time that it truly becomes clear that Mary did not completely understand her son's identity or mission. As it was with Jesus' disciples, his Person and purpose was not fully revealed to her until after his resurrection.

There was a wedding at Cana in Galilee and Mary was there with Jesus. They ran out of wine and Mary spoke to her Son about it (*John 2:1–10*). She wanted to spare the family from the disgrace of running out of drink during the wedding. Mary knew Jesus could do something to save the situation, but, still, she did not fully comprehend the extent of his saving abilities.

On another occasion, when Jesus was ministering to a large crowd, Mary and his brothers went to challenge him because they thought he was going insane (*Mark*

3:20–21, 31–32). While this incident, once again, reveals their misunderstanding of his mission, it also shows their care and concern for him. For it seems that Mary and her other sons were afraid that overwork would affect his mental capacities.

Mary was also there during Jesus' suffering and crucifixion (*John 19:25*). She was standing close to the cross, painfully watching her son's anguish and torture. Jesus noticed his mother there at the cross and put her under the care of John, his beloved disciple (*John 19:26–27*). Apparently, Joseph had died and there was no one to look after her.

The last time Mary appears is after Christ's resurrection. She, her other sons, the apostles, and many disciples (approximately 120 people) were gathered together in an upper room participating in constant prayer (*Acts 1:14*). The one who bore the Christ and took care of him as his mother was now ready to serve him as her Lord and Saviour.

Through church history, other non-biblical traditions and teachings have been held and developed concerning Mary, especially in the Roman Catholic faith. Some of these include her perpetual virginity, her intercession on behalf of the saints, her immaculate conception, and her assumption.                        K.MCR.

**MARY 1.** See *Mary, the mother of Jesus.*

**2.** Mary, the mother of James and Joses. This Mary was probably a sister to Mary, mother of Jesus, and the wife of Clopas (*John 19:25*; see *Clopas*). She was an eyewitness of Christ's crucifixion (*Matt. 27:56; Mark 15:40, 47*) and was present at his tomb on the resurrection morning. With other women, she carried the news of the resurrection to the disciples (*Matt. 28:1; Mark 16:1; Luke 24:10*).

K.MCR.

**3.** Mary Magdalene was a close friend and disciple of Jesus Christ. It is not known whether 'Magdalene' was Mary's family name or if it represented the town she was from (Mary of Magdala). The latter is more likely.

Jesus cast seven demons out of her (*Mark 16:9; Luke 8:2*). During Christ's earthly ministry, Mary, along with the other women, followed him and cared for his needs (*Matt. 27:55; Mark 15:41*). She was present during his trials and sufferings (*Matt. 27:45–56*) and was near him in his death (*John 19:25*). She was also the first one to behold Jesus after his resurrection (*John 20:15–16*).

The devotion of Mary Magdalene to her Lord is evident through her unending service to him. For she cared for him even after his death. When the disciples had fled for fear of the Jews, she stayed behind to watch Joseph of Arimathea bury him. After the Sabbath's rest she planned to return to his tomb in order to anoint his body with spices and perfume (*Luke 23:56*).

On the third day after his crucifixion, Mary and the other women returned to his burial site and were surprised to find that the stone, which had been blocking the entrance to the tomb, had been rolled away (*John 20:1*). She and the others ran back to town and told the disciples (*John 20:2*).

Then Mary returned to the tomb and wept for her Lord. Two angels appeared and questioned her about her tears (*John 20:11–13*). Suddenly, in the moment of her greatest despair, Jesus appeared to her; but she did not recognize him. Thinking he was the gardener, she asked him for the body of Jesus (*John 20:14–15*). Then Jesus gently spoke her name, and she recognized him (*John 20:16*). She returned to the disciples, where she confirmed what she had seen: 'I have seen the Lord!'

Mary Magdalene was an extraordinary woman, lovingly devoted to her Lord in his life, death and resurrection.  K.MCR.

**4.** Mary mother of John Mark is only mentioned by name in *Acts 12:12*. The apostle Peter had been imprisoned by Herod but, miraculously, an angel of the Lord intervened and led him out of the prison. Peter went to the house of Mary, Mark's mother. The fact that a number of Christians had gathered there to pray for Peter and that it was the first place to which Peter went on his release suggests the house was probably quite large and may have been the venue for one of the 'churches' in Jerusalem. The sovereignty of God in overseeing and protecting Peter in this way must have been the subject of much rejoicing. This house belonged to Mary which suggests that not everyone had joined the move after the Day of Pentecost to have all things in common (*Acts 2:44–45*). On the other hand, clearly this lady from a wealthy family (her servants are mentioned in *v. 13*) had put her house at the disposal of the Christians in spite of the obvious danger to herself and her family from the authorities. (Also see *Mark, Rhoda.*)

**5.** Mary of Bethany was sister to Martha and Lazarus (*John 11:1*). These three were among Jesus' closest friends. Three events are described that involved this Mary and her home. The first is found in *Luke 10:38–42*. Mary and Martha opened their home to Jesus, and we are told that Mary 'sat at the Lord's feet listening to what he said' (*v. 39*). This caused her sister some concern for Martha was left to do all the cooking and preparations for their guests. When Martha suggested to Jesus that he tell Mary to join her in working to prepare the food Jesus responded: 'Martha, Martha, you are worried and upset about many things, but only one thing is needed. Mary has chosen what is better, and it will not be taken

away from her' (*vv. 41–42*). This strong affirmation of a woman's right to listen to the Lord speak and to be concerned with spiritual matters gives a clear indication that the Kingdom of God is for all who will listen and believe in Jesus. Luke's Gospel often mentions how people from all types of different backgrounds and minority groups needed to hear the Gospel of the Kingdom of God. Here is one of the clearest statements that Jesus intended women also to be recipients of his teaching and his rule.

The second incident is recounted in *John 11:1–47*. Lazarus, Mary's brother, became ill and so Mary and Martha went to find Jesus to tell him and ask him to help. Prophetically Jesus said to them that Lazarus' illness had come about 'for God's glory so that God's Son may be glorified through it' (*v. 4*). The sisters must have returned home, for Jesus delayed a further two days before moving off towards Bethany. On his way he told his disciples that Lazarus had died and 'for your sake I am glad I was not there, so that you may believe' (*v. 14*). The religious leaders of that area had been trying to find reason to kill Jesus and so rather sarcastically Thomas responded: 'Let us also go, that we may die with him.' Nevertheless, Jesus and his disciples went to Bethany and found Lazarus had been dead for four days. Mary went out to meet Jesus and fell weeping at his feet to worship him. She expressed what faith she had by saying that this death would not have happened had Jesus been present. Obviously Mary and the family were well loved and respected in the community for there were 'many Jews' involved in comforting the family. All were weeping and we are told 'Jesus wept' (*v. 35*).

Jesus then went to the tomb and ordered it to be opened. There was some objection on the grounds that the body would have started to decay. However, the stone was rolled from the tomb and Jesus prayed to his heavenly Father that the people standing by would believe. He then called 'Lazarus, come out!' and 'the dead man came out, his hands and feet wrapped with strips of linen, and a cloth around his face. Jesus said to them, "Take off the grave clothes and let him go."' Jesus' prayer was answerd for 'many of the Jews who had come to visit Mary, and had seen what Jesus did, put their faith in him' (vv. 43–44).

Shortly after this great miracle, John's Gospel recounts another incident involving Mary at Bethany. A dinner was being given in Jesus' honour and, once again it was Martha who was serving and Lazarus was present at the table, 'Then Mary took about a pint of pure nard, an expensive perfume; she poured it on Jesus' feet and wiped his feet with her hair. And the house was filled with the fragrance of the perfume' (John 12:1–3; see 11:2). In spite of criticism of the waste of money, Jesus quietly received this kindness and saw it as a pointer towards his imminent death on the cross when his body would be covered in perfumes and buried in a tomb. Indeed the passage ends with the Jews not only seeking Jesus' death but the death also of Lazarus through whose influence many were coming to believe in Jesus (vv. 7–11).

Mary is portrayed in Scriptures as a woman of deep personal commitment to Jesus who was obviously a very close friend. But she was also a woman of deep faith in Jesus. Although only mentioned in three incidents, she is seen to listen carefully to Jesus' teaching, and to fall at his feet in worship on two occasions. Jesus affirmed that his teaching and his work was for people such as her, people who believed and trusted in him. (Also see Martha, Lazarus.)

**6.** Another Mary, sometimes known as Mary of Rome, was greeted by Paul at the end of his letter to the church at Rome. Paul stated that 'she worked very hard for you', perhaps implying that she had

worked away from Rome in the cause of the gospel (Rom. 16:6).          P.D.G.

**MASSA** A grandson of Abraham, and sixth son of Ishmael, Massa was a tribal leader (Gen. 25:14; 1 Chron. 1:30).

**MATRED** The mother of Mehetabel the wife of King Hadad of Edom (Gen. 36:39; 1 Chron. 1:50).

**MATTAN** (Heb., 'gift'). **1.** Mattan was a priest of Baal in Israel at the time of Jehoiada the priest. Following the paganism of Queen Athaliah, Jehoiada sought to restore true worship to Judah. He trained the young King Joash in the ways of the LORD and put him on the throne. He led the people in renewing their covenant to serve the LORD. As a result of this the people went to the Temple of Baal, which they destroyed, and killed Mattan (2 Kings 11:18; 2 Chron. 23:17). Under King Joash, repairs to the Temple of the LORD began (2 Kings 12).

**2.** The father of Shephatiah, one of the leaders of Judah under King Zedekiah. Shephatiah was one of those who objected to Jeremiah's prophecies of destruction and invasion on the grounds that such talk would discourage the soldiers (Jer. 38:1).

**MATTANIAH** (Heb., 'gift of the LORD').
**1.** One of the sons of Heman listed among those set apart for the ministry of prophesying and music during the reign of King David. Heman was the king's seer. Mattaniah and his relations were given the ninth turn of service in the sanctuary (1 Chron. 25:4, 16).

**2.** A Levite descended from Asaph who is mentioned in the list of those who helped purify the Temple during the revival under King Hezekiah (2 Chron. 29:13).

**3.** This Mattaniah was the third son of King Josiah of Judah. Mattaniah was the original name of the man who was crowned king of Judah by Nebuchadnezzar king of Babylon and renamed Zedekiah (2 Kings 24:17; 1 Chron. 3:15). He was 21 when he was appointed king in the place of his nephew Jehoiachin, who was taken into captivity. See Zedekiah.

**4.** A Levite mentioned in 1 Chron. 9:15 as a descendant of Asaph and a son of Mica. He was one of the early returnees from the Exile in the time of Zerubbabel. This Mattaniah is also mentioned as an ancestor of Jahaziel upon whom the Spirit of the LORD came at a time of crisis for Judah and King Jehoshaphat (2 Chron. 20:14). He was prominent among those who helped lead music in the Temple, having been given charge of the songs of thanksgiving (Neh. 11:17, 22; 12:8). His other duties probably included looking after the Temple storerooms (Neh. 12:25).

**5.** In Ezra 10:26 this Mattaniah is listed among the descendants of Elam. Shecaniah confessed to Ezra that many men and even descendants of the priests of Judah had married wives from other tribes and nations. Ezra and the people repented and made a covenant to serve the LORD (Ezra 10:2). Mattaniah is listed in v. 26 as one who had a foreign wife.

**6.** Another Mattaniah from the descendants of Zattu had also married a foreign wife in the time of Ezra (Ezra 10:27).

**7.** Another Mattaniah descended from Pahath-Moab had also married a foreign wife in the time of Ezra (Ezra 10:30).

**8.** Another Mattaniah among the descendants of Bani had also married a foreign wife in the time of Ezra (Ezra 10:37).

**9.** The son of Micaiah and ancestor of a certain priest called Zechariah who was given the duty of blowing trumpets at the dedication of the city walls in the time of Nehemiah (Neh. 12:35).

**10.** A Levite who was the grandfather of Hanan. Hanan was considered 'trustworthy' and was placed in charge of the

stores of supplies for the Levites. He was also responsible for the distribution of these goods (Neh. 13:13).          P.D.G.

**MATTATHA** One of the ancestors of Jesus listed in the genealogy from Jesus to Adam. He was King David's grandson and the son of Nathan (Luke 3:31).

**MATTATHIAS** (Heb., 'a gift of God').
**1.** An ancestor of Jesus listed in the genealogy from Jesus to Adam. He was the son of Joseph and father of Amos and in the seventh generation before Jesus (Luke 3:25).
**2.** Another ancestor of Jesus listed in the genealogy from Jesus to Adam. He was the son of Semein and father of Maath (Luke 3:26).

**MATTATTAH** A descendant of Hashum at the time of Nehemiah (Ezra 10:33). After Shecaniah confessed to Ezra that many men of Judah had married wives from other tribes and nations, Ezra and the people repented and made a covenant to serve the LORD (Ezra 10:2). Mattattah was one of those listed as having married a foreign wife.

**MATTENAI** (Heb., 'gift').
**1.** A descendant of Hashum at the time of Nehemiah (Ezra 10:33). After Shecaniah confessed to Ezra that many men of Judah had married wives from other tribes and nations, Ezra and the people repented and made a covenant to serve the LORD (Ezra 10:2). Mattenai was one of those listed as having married a foreign wife.
**2.** Another Mattaniah, a descendant of Bani, is listed in Ezra 10:37 as one who had a foreign wife whom he later divorced.
**3.** He was the head of Joiarib's family, and helped in the service of the Temple during Nehemiah's time under the high priesthood of Joiakim (Neh. 12:19).
          P.D.G.

**MATTHAN** (Heb., 'gift'). One of the ancestors of Jesus mentioned in Matthew's genealogy (*Matt. 1:15*). The grandfather of Mary's husband Joseph, probably the same as the Matthat mentioned in *Luke 3:24*.

**MATTHAT** **1.** An ancestor of Jesus listed in the genealogy from Jesus to Adam. He was the son of Levi and father of Jorim (*Luke 3:29*).

**2.** Another ancestor of Jesus listed in the genealogy from Jesus to Adam. He was the grandfather of Mary's husband, Joseph (*Luke 3:24*).

# MATTHEW

## The apostle

Matthew was one of Jesus' twelve apostles, a converted tax-collector. *Matt. 9:9–13* describes his call and the reaction it caused. Jesus saw Matthew at his toll booth, probably on the edge of Capernaum, where he would have received levies or customs duties on commerce arriving from outside Galilee, probably often by boats travelling across the Sea of Galilee. As with several of the other of Jesus' disciples, Matthew responded at once when Jesus called him to follow him. Jesus subsequently had dinner with Matthew and several of his 'notorious' friends and peers, outcasts because of working for Rome and her client-rulers. The Jewish leaders were offended at this intimacy with the 'lawless' elements of society, but Jesus defended his action with the famous proverb, 'It is not the healthy who need a doctor but the sick' (*Matt. 9:12*). He had come not to call those who thought they were righteous but those who realized they were sinners (*v. 13*).

Mark and Luke describe essentially the same call and response, but they refer to Matthew as Levi (*Mark 2:14; Luke 5:25, 27*). It was common for Jewish people to have two or three names. 'Levi' harks back to the name of the third son of Jacob (*Gen. 29:34*), while 'Matthew' comes from the Aramaic for 'gift of God'. More probably Matthew was the name this man was more consistently known by as a Christian, i.e. during his own ministry after Jesus' death and resurrection. *Mark 2:14* adds that he was the son of a man named Alphaeus, apparently a different individual than the father of James the less (see *James the son of Alphaeus*). Matthew is listed in all of the four accounts of the twelve apostles (*Matt. 10:7; Mark 3:18; Luke 6:15; Acts 1:13*), consistently juxtaposed with either Thomas or Bartholomew.

As a toll collector, Matthew was probably relatively prosperous by the standards of his day. Whether he personally followed the practice of many in his profession of exacting more than what was legally required so as to 'skim off' additional profits for himself we cannot know. But it is reasonable to infer that many may have assumed he did so. To leave all and accompany Jesus in a life of itinerant discipleship was therefore perhaps more costly for Matthew than for some of the rest of the Twelve. Only a handful of traditions exist about his ministry and life following the resurrection. None may be authenticated with any significant degree of probability, save for his association with the composition of the Gospel which bears his name.

# The Gospel

## *Its background*

According to Papias, an early to mid-2nd century Christian writer, cited by Eusebius in the early 300s, 'Matthew composed his Gospel in the Hebrew language, and everyone translated as they were able.' No ancient Hebrew or Aramaic copy of Matthew, however, exists. The canonical Gospel shows signs of dependence on Mark and a better Greek style than Matthew's predecessor. Many modern scholars, therefore, discount Papias' testimony. It is not inconceivable, however, that Matthew composed a 'first draft' of his Gospel in a Semitic tongue, and then later he or someone else translated it and/or expanded it into the edition we now know, utilizing Mark's Gospel in the process. It is just barely possible that Matthew's first draft was something along the lines of 'Q' (the reconstructed sayings source of material common to Matthew and Luke). Others suggest that Papias' words should be rendered 'Matthew composed his Gospel in a Hebraic *style*', which would be true of certain portions of it, particularly where he is citing the words and teaching of Jesus. But the tradition of Matthew writing something in a Semitic tongue is widespread among ancient Christian writers, so much so that one or two apocryphal gospels attributed to Jewish-Christian milieux seem to be little more than revisions and corruptions of Matthew's narrative.

Modern scholarship has frequently asked whether the traditional association of the apostle Matthew with this Gospel is warranted. There is today widespread agreement that the author of this book was a Jewish-Christian with some degree of literacy in Greek, and this fits what is possible for a Jewish toll collector in cosmopolitan Galilee. But why would an apostle rely on a Gospel (Mark) which was not written by one of the Twelve? A plausible answer is that Mark himself, as early Christian tradition suggests, got much of his information from Peter. Given Peter's authority within the early church, and his participation in certain events (with James and John) in which the other nine disciples did not figure (e.g. the Transfiguration or Gethsemane), it is entirely understandable that Matthew should want to see how a narrative of Jesus' ministry derived from Peter should look and to follow him where appropriate for Matthew's own purposes.

## *The purposes of the Gospel*

Those purposes seem bound up with the predominantly Jewish-Christian community to which Matthew addressed his Gospel. Among various views, the most likely addressees for this narrative are probably a fledgling congregation which has recently broken away from the synagogue and is still in vigorous debate with it. Ancient writers often suggested that this church was located in Palestine; modern scholars tend to suggest Antioch in Syria, home to large numbers of Jews and eventually Jewish Christians. The truth is that we do not know. But the nature of the community is more significant than its location. And the hypothesis of a congregation still 'licking its wounds' from a recent rupture and still in dialogue and even polemic with 'the synagogue across the street' from which it separated best accounts for the blend of particularism and universalism in this Gospel.

### Matthew, Judaism and the world

In other words, Matthew uniquely combines an intense interest in things Jewish with an equal emphasis on Jesus' hostility to the Jewish leaders. Thus Matthew is the only Gospel to refer to Jesus' prohibition of his disciples to go outside Jewish lands during their initial ministry (*Matt. 10:5–6*) but also the only Gospel to give Jesus' famous great commission, after his resurrection, commanding the disciples to go into all the world and preach to every ethnic group (*28:16–20*). Only in Matthew has Jesus himself initially refused to heal the Syrophoenician woman's daughter because she was not Jewish (*15:24*), but only Matthew includes in the parable of the wicked tenants Jesus' words which suggest that the Kingdom would be taken from Israel and given to a multi-ethnic church (*21:43*). Only Matthew preserves Jesus' reminder of the constant need to evangelize Jews (*10:23*), yet only Matthew anticipates a judgment of all the nations of the world on the basis of their response to Jesus' messengers (*25:31–46*).

### Matthew and the Old Testament

So, too, Matthew's is the Gospel with more than twice as many OT quotations as any other and with a greater interest in Jesus' relationship to the Law, and yet when we see Jesus' relationship to the Law in this Gospel it is more one of contrast than of continuity (*cf.* classically *Matt. 5:17–48*). Matthew is consistently harsh in his polemic against the Jewish leaders; *Matt. 23* comes closer to anti-Semitism than perhaps any other extended portion of the Gospels, though it stops just short of it (*cf.* also *27:25*). Clearly Matthew wanted to convince his community (and help them convince those with whom they were in dialogue) that Jesus was the fulfilment of all of the hopes of Israel, despite her increasing rejection of him during his lifetime.

### Matthew and Jesus

Matthew's distinctive perspectives on Jesus portray him as impeccable in all his Jewish credentials – he is a true son of David and of Abraham and therefore qualified to be the Messiah (*Matt. 1:1*). But he received worship from the Gentile Magi, not the Jewish rulers (*2:1–12*), foreshadowing his greater reception among the Gentiles after his death and resurrection. His genealogy includes five women who all were, rightly or wrongly, suspected of bearing illegitimate children (*1:1–17*), hinting in advance at the Messiah's ministry to the outcast of his society, whom orthodox Jews rejected. Matthew reveals Jesus as preeminently a Teacher, particularly in long blocks of sermonic material (*Matt. 5–7; 10; 13; 18; 23–25*). Some have seen Matthew's desire here to portray Jesus as a new Moses, authoritatively interpreting but also transcending the Laws of what we call the OT. A few have even pointed to the parallels between the five major sermons and the five books of Moses, the Torah.

For Matthew, Jesus is also Son of God, at key junctures in his narrative (*Matt. 2:15; 4:3, 6; 14:33; 16:16; 26:63; 27:40, 43*), or more distinctively, 'Immanuel' – God with us (*1:23; 28:20*). He is Wisdom personified, who will give his people an easy burden and rest for their weary souls (*11:25–30*). He is Lord – master and God, worthy of worship, working miracles which only deity could effect (e.g. *8:2, 6, 25; 9:28*). He is king of the Jews (*27:1*) but not in a nationalistic or militaristic sense. And he is Son of man (see esp. *26:64*), but, despite widespread misconceptions, this term does not primarily refer to Jesus' humanity but to his exalted Messianic status as one who will one day return on the clouds of heaven (*cf. Dan. 7:13–14*).

### Matthew and the church

Additionally, Matthew is uniquely concerned with the nature of Christian community – of discipleship and the church. His is the only Gospel to use the word 'church' – three times (*Matt. 16:18; 18:17*, twice). Much of Jesus' teaching in Matthew gives his disciples instructions on how they are to relate in community after his departure. He envisages Christian wise men, prophets and scribes (*Matt. 10:40–42*) and warns against false teachers or prophets, particularly of an antinomian nature, who will later infiltrate the Christian community (*7:15–23*). He portrays the disciples in a more positive light than does Mark (*cf.*, e.g. *8:26* with *Mark 4:40*), though still they are often characterized as only 'of little faith' (e.g. *Matt. 8:26; 14:31; 16:8*). Matthew includes five unparalleled references to Peter in the middle chapters of his Gospel (*Matt. 14:28–31; 15:15–16; 16:16–23; 17:24–27; 18:21–22*). Traditionally, these passages, particularly *16:16–20*, have been taken as support for Peter's primacy, and for a growing institutionalization of Matthew's church along the lines of early, emerging Catholicism. But Matthew elsewhere offers little evidence of an institutionalized community, and the embarrassing light in which some of these passages portray Peter (most notably *16:21–23*) may suggest that Matthew was actually trying to tone down an overly exalted view of Peter current elsewhere in the Christianity of his day.

### Dating

A fair consensus of scholars today dates Matthew's Gospel to one of the decades between AD 70 and 100. By the beginning of the 2nd century, writers like Ignatius and works like the *Didache* were beginning to quote Matthew, so the Gospel must have been completed by then. Some see the break with Judaism implied by the Gospel as a sign that it must have been written after around AD 85, when Jewish relations with Christianity made it very hard for anyone who believed in Jesus to remain within the synagogues. This is the period to which many would date the *birkath ha-minim*, a curse on all heretics which entered the synagogue liturgy. On the other hand, it is increasingly questioned whether any empire-wide edict ever did ban Christians from Jewish houses of worship. And from as early as AD 40 on, Acts shows Paul regularly being expelled from the synagogues because of his 'inflammatory' teaching, so such tensions were certainly not limited to the end of the 1st century. Still others see in texts like *Matt. 22:6–7* clear reference to the destruction of Jerusalem by Roman armies in AD 70 and so date the Gospel at least after that year. But this argument works only if Jesus could not genuinely have predicted future events or if we assume that these verses actually refer to the fall of Jerusalem. Their language is in fact reminiscent of many Jewish descriptions of

God's judgment on his enemies, and does not actually correspond to the events of AD 70 (for the most part only the Temple, not the entire city, was burned), so it is hard to place much weight on an argument for the date of the Gospel from these verses alone.

The late 2nd-century writer Irenaeus attributes the composition of Matthew to the period 'while Peter and Paul were preaching the gospel and founding the church in Rome', which would suggest a date in the early 60s. If Mark is dated to the mid-60s, however, as many do, perhaps we should imagine a date just slightly thereafter. Certain references – to the Temple tax (*Matt.* 17:24–27), sacrificial offerings (5:23–24) and cultic rituals (23:16–22) might reinforce this identification, since after the destruction of the Temple in AD 70 they were no longer practised or as relevant.

## *An outline of the content*

Matthew's purposes are instructional, pastoral and apologetic. His genre is biographical according to good Jewish and Greco-Roman literary conventions of his day. Despite frequent scepticism in certain circles a good case can be made for his general historical trustworthiness. The plot of his narrative unfolds in three stages: *Matt.* 1:1–4:16 provides an introduction to Jesus' ministry. *Matt.* 4:17–16:20 describes the development of that ministry via samples of Jesus' authoritative preaching (*Matt.* 5–7) and healing (8:1–9:34), by predicting and illustrating rising opposition to his ministry (9:35–12:50), and by explaining and narrating the progressive polarization of positive and negative response to his work (13:1–16:20). The third and climactic section traces Jesus' journey, literally and figuratively, to the cross, and beyond (16:21–28:20). Here Matthew focuses first on Jesus' teachings about his coming death and its implications for discipleship and for the church (16:21–18:35). Then he sets out on his final and fateful journey to Jerusalem, predicting judgment on all who would reject him (*Matt.* 19–25). Finally, the Gospel closes with the narrative of his suffering and death. Yet the end is not tragic but triumphant as God raises him from the dead, vindicating his ministry and his claims and empowering him and his followers to evangelize the world (*Matt.* 28).

A more detailed subdivision of each of these sections might proceed as follows. In the introductory chapters, we learn of Jesus' origins (*Matt.* 1–2) by means of a heading (1:1), genealogy (1:2–17), and five fulfilment quotations of the OT (1:18–2:23). Then Matthew skips to the beginning of Jesus' adult ministry, starting with the preaching of his forerunner John the Baptist (3:1–12), moving on to Jesus' own baptism (3:13–17), continuing with his temptation (4:1–11), and culminating in his settling in Capernaum (4:12–16).

*Matt.* 4:17–25 inaugurates Jesus' great Galilean ministry. The Sermon on the Mount begins with beatitudes and related material (5:1–16), has as its thesis the greater righteousness demanded of Jesus' followers (5:17–48), illustrates this thesis under three additional headings: true versus hypocritical piety (6:1–18), wealth and worry (6:19–34) and how to treat others (7:1–12). The conclusion challenges Jesus' audience to accept rather than reject him (7:13–27). *Matt.* 8–9 illustrate Jesus' authoritative healing in three cycles of triads of miracles (8:1–17; 8:23–9:8; 9:18–

23), in between which are interspersed the resulting implications for discipleship (8:18–22; 9:9–17).

Jesus' Sermon on Mission (*Matt. 10:5–42*) is introduced with a statement on the need for workers and the listing of the twelve disciples (9:36:10:4). The sermon itself divides into two major sections: the immediate charge (10:5–16) and future prospects, which look ahead to the disciples' mission after Jesus' death (10:17–42). *Matt. 11–12* also subdivide into two parts: implicit opposition (11) and explicit opposition (12). *Matt. 13:1–52* explains the progressive polarization of response to Jesus by means of his speaking in parables. Those who have shown an openness to his message and person receive greater illumination; others are merely repulsed. *Matt. 13:53–16:20* illustrates this polarization as Jesus (like John) is misunderstood and rejected in Israel, coming into increasing conflict with the Jewish leaders (13:53–15:24), even as he is increasingly accepted by Gentiles during his one major sojourn in their territory and correctly and climactically identified as the Christ, the Son of the living God, by Peter, acting as spokesman for his closest followers (15:25–16:20).

*Matt. 16:21–17:27* initiates Matthew's third and final major section by interspersing Jesus' passion predictions among teachings which correct misunderstandings about the nature of the Messiah's mission. *Matt. 18* has often been called the Community Discourse, giving the Twelve instructions on how to live as a church, and focusing primarily on themes of humility (*vv. 1–14*) and forgiveness (*vv. 15–35*). *Matt. 19:1–22:46* might be entitled 'true discipleship versus harsher condemnation for the Jewish leaders'. This section includes further instructions for the disciples and responses to questions from the crowds as Jesus journeys to Judea (19:1–20:34), and judgment on the Temple in Jerusalem and the reigning leaders of Israel in enacted parables (21:1–22) and in controversial teachings (21:23–22:46). *Matt. 23–25* present Jesus' final block of extended discourse with his woes against the hypocrisy of various scribes and Pharisees (23) and his predictions about the coming destruction of the Temple, his own return and judgment of all nations (24–25).

The passion narrative proper rounds out Matthew's Gospel with successive foci on the Last Supper, betrayal, arrest and Jewish trial (*Matt. 26*), his hearing before the Roman governor, Pilate, and subsequent crucifixion (*Matt. 27*), and the glorious sequel to his ignominious death – his resurrection and final commissioning of his followers (*Matt. 28*).                                                                    C.B.

**MATTHIAS** This person was elected the twelfth apostle to take Judas' place in *Acts 1:23, 26*. Though many argue that Paul is really the twelfth, there is no indication of this in Acts, since the only time Paul is called an apostle it is with Barnabas (*Acts 14:4, 14*), where the term has a less technical meaning of an 'officially commissioned' person. In fact, the selection of Matthias seems to be approved by Luke, since it is surrounded by prayer and scriptural exposition in the midst of the disciples obediently waiting for the Spirit in Jerusalem just as Jesus commanded. As with many of the Twelve, we know little about him beyond his selection. Also see *Justus*.           D.B.

**MATTITHIAH** (Heb., 'gift of the LORD').
**1.** After the ark of the covenant had

456

been brought to Jerusalem, the worship of God was properly organized by King David. Mattithiah was one of the family of Merarite Levites who were gatekeepers. The particular job he and his brothers were given was to be musicians and to play the harps and lyres before the ark of the covenant as it was moved to Jerusalem. He was the son of Jeduthun, and was later the leader of the 14th group of Levitical musicians and choirs who ministered in the Temple (1 Chron. 15:18, 21; 16:5; 25:3, 24).

**2.** A Levite of the Korahite clan and first son to Shallum. His Temple duty, after the return from Exile in Babylon, was to bake bread for the Temple offering (1 Chron. 9:31).

**3.** One of those listed in Ezra as guilty of intermarriage with women from other nations (Ezra 10:43).

**4.** This Mattithiah was among those who stood on Ezra's right hand side on a high wooden platform as he read the Book of the Law to the people of Israel. As the Law was read the people worshipped and praised God, confessed their sin, and recommitted themselves to the Lord's service (Neh. 8:4).       P.D.G.

**ME-ZAHAB** (Heb., 'waters of gold'). The father of Matred. Matred was the mother of Mehetabel the wife of King Hadad of Edom (Gen. 36:39; 1 Chron. 1:50).

**MEBUNNAI** was one of David's 'Thirty' warriors and a Hushathite (2 Sam. 23:27). See also Sibbecai, who was probably the same person, the similarity of the names in Heb. leading perhaps to some scribal confusion.

**MEDAD** Mentioned in Num. 11:26–29. See Eldad.

**MEDAN** The third of Abraham's sons by his wife Keturah (Gen. 25:2). He appears in a list of Abraham's descendants bridging, in the narrative of Gen. 24–25, the death of Sarah and the death of Abraham (also 1 Chron. 1:32).

**MEDES** The Medes were an ancient people who lived in modern Azerbaijan and the north-west of Iran. In the 7th century BC they were absorbed by the expansion of the Persian empire. Reference to these peoples occurs in Scripture during the time of the Assyrian and later Babylonian invasions of Israel. In the Assyrian dispersion of Israelites, some were settled in the towns of the Medes (2 Kings 17:6; 18:11). The prophet Isaiah foresaw the day when God would use the Medes and others to bring down the Babylonian empire (Is. 13:17), and Jeremiah foretold the same (Jer. 51:11, 28). These peoples were to be used as part of God's plans to destroy the nation which had taken captive his people. The prophecies came to pass when the combined power of the Medes and Persians overtook the Babylonian empire.

Medes are thus also known to us in Scripture through the phrase 'Medes and Persians' which appears four times in Daniel (Dan. 5:28; 6:8, 12, 15). This interesting phrase reveals the influence of Median laws even in the days of the Persian empire. Such laws were apparently never to be repealed (Dan. 6:12).

There is a reference in Acts 2:9 to 'Medes' among the thousands who heard the gospel in their own language on the day of Pentecost.       P.D.G.

**MEHETABEL** (Heb., 'God does good').

**1.** Mehetabel was the wife of King Hadad of Edom and daughter of Matred (Gen. 36:39; 1 Chron. 1:50).

**2.** The grandfather of Shemaiah and father of Delaiah (Neh. 6:10). Shemaiah was a false prophet in the time of Nehemiah who was used by Sanballat in an attempt to scare Nehemiah and those working with him to rebuild the walls of Jerusalem.

**MEHIDA** A leader of one of the families of Temple servants whose descendants returned from the Babylonian Exile in the days of Ezra and worked on the Temple (*Ezra 2:52; Neh. 7:54*).

**MEHIR** was the son of Kelub and father of Eshton (*1 Chron. 4:11*). He was of the tribe of Judah.

**MEHUJAEL** (Heb., 'smitten by God'). The grandson of Enoch and great-grandson of Cain. His father was Irad. He is mentioned in *Gen. 4:18*, a passage which shows how the descendants of Cain spread out across the world after God's judgment on him.

**MEHUMAN** One of seven eunuchs who served King Xerxes (*Est. 1:10*). See *Vashti*.

**MELATIAH** (Heb., 'the LORD delivers'). One of the men from Gideon who, under the direction of Nehemiah, helped repair the walls of Jerusalem (*Neh. 3:7*).

## MELCHIZEDEK

In Hebrew this name means 'king of righteousness' or 'my king is righteous' and is transliterated in the Greek text of the NT. The word occurs in a historical section (*Gen. 14*), a poetic setting (*Ps. 110*), and in a doctrinal part of a NT epistle (*Heb. 5– 7*). The first mention of this word can be dated about two millennia before Christ, the second approximately one millennium before Jesus was born, and the third in the second half of the first century after his birth (*Gen. 14:18; Ps. 104:4; Heb. 5:6, 10; 6:20; 7:1, 10–11, 15, 17*).

### Abraham and Melchizedek (Gen. 14:17–20)

Kedorlaomer king of Elam (modern Iran) and three allied kings went to war against five kings who ruled territories near the Dead Sea. The four kings were victorious. They seized goods, food, and belongings from Sodom and Gomorrah. From among the residents of Sodom, they carried off Lot with family and possessions (*Gen. 14:1–12*). Abraham with 318 trained men went out and defeated the invading forces under cover of darkness. He rescued Lot and his family, and took possession of all the plundered goods (*vv. 13–16*). When Abraham returned from battle, he was greeted by the king of Sodom (*v. 17*). When the king offered him goods, he refused to take anything from him lest the king could say that he made Abraham rich. The patriarch swore an oath to God Most High, Creator of heaven and earth, (*vv. 22–24*) and thus distanced himself from the polytheistic worship of the kings living in the Dead Sea area. From Melchizedek, however, he received bread and wine and a blessing from God Most High, Creator of heaven and earth. This man was king of Salem (Jerusalem, see *Ps. 76:2*) and priest of God Most High, and Abraham gave him a tenth of everything (*Gen. 14:18–20*).

Melchizedek knew God either through a post-Flood tradition or because of a supernatural revelation. He realized that Abraham also served his God (*v. 22*). In turn, Abraham recognized him as God's priest who was worthy to receive a tithe (*v. 20*). Although the reference to Melchizedek in Genesis is brief, it appears in a context that portrays him as a historical figure.

A Qumran document identified Melchizedek with an angelic being who administered judgment. Describing him as an incarnate angel was already current in the first few centuries of the Christian church, in the time of Origen, Jerome, and Augustine. Others have equated Melchizedek with the post-diluvian Shem, and even the Messiah. But all these theories are speculative. The writer of the epistle to the Hebrews, however, contrasted the enduring priesthood of Melchizedek with the service of priests in the Levitical order, that was constantly interrupted by death. He depicted Melchizedek as Abraham's contemporary, both of whom are rooted in history.

### David writing about Melchizedek (Ps. 110:4)

Approximately a millennium after Abraham, David composed a psalm in which he portrayed his 'Lord' as both king and priest. In the first verse of this psalm the LORD invited David's Lord to sit at his right hand in royal splendour. And in the fourth verse the LORD swore an oath and said to David's Lord, 'You are a priest forever, in the order of Melchizedek.' The oath is irrevocable because the LORD will not change his mind. The person addressed in this psalm becomes both king and priest. Nonetheless in the Temple he could never fulfil priestly duties that were reserved only for the descendants of Levi. Yet after the model of Melchizedek, he could perform both royal and priestly duties. David spoke prophetically about a priesthood that was higher than that of Aaron and his successors.

Jesus clarified the words of *Ps. 110:1* by identifying David's Lord as the Messiah (*Matt. 22:41–46*), who functioned as king. Applying this psalm to himself, Jesus taught that the address 'my Lord' referred to someone who was superior to David. Nevertheless, he refrained from alluding to Melchizedek's priesthood mentioned in the second part of *Ps. 110*.

### Hebrews and Melchizedek (Heb. 5:6, 10; 6:20; 7:1, 10–11, 15, 17)

The writer of the Epistle to the Hebrews was the only author in the NT canon who set forth the doctrine of Christ's priesthood. Paul made one indirect reference to his priesthood (*Rom. 8:34*). He wrote that Christ is seated at God's right hand (as king) and is interceding for his people (as priest). The author of Hebrews, by contrast, devoted nearly his entire epistle to the priesthood of the Son of God. Christ purifies his people from their sins (*Heb. 1:3*). He is a merciful and faithful high priest who atones for the sins of his people (*2:17*). He is designated by God as priest in the order of Melchizedek (*5:10; 6:20*) and became a priest in this order when God swore an oath (*7:21*). Christ entered the Most Holy Place once for all in the presence of God (*9:12, 24, 26*) and sat down at God's right hand when he had offered one sacrifice for sins once for all (*10:12*).

Especially in *Heb. 7*, the writer expounded the superiority of the Melchizedekian priesthood over the Levitical priesthood. Melchizedek was king of Salem and priest of God Most High (*v. 1*), which meant that he was a king of righteousness (*zedek*) and peace (*Salem*). In addition to ruling as a king, Melchizedek was a priest without a genealogy. The words 'Without father or mother' (*v. 3*) mean that Melchizedek had no lineage with which to identify himself. References to his parentage, birth and death are lacking. Whereas the descendants of Levi had to show their pedigree to serve at and in the Tabernacle and Temple for a relatively few years of their lives, Melchizedek without lineage has a priesthood that lasts forever (v. 3). The writer of Hebrews stated that the Son of God resembles not Melchizedek but rather Melchizedek resembles God's Son, who is eternal (v. 3). Hence, this royal priest served as a type of Christ and foreshadowed righteousness and peace, which are the characteristics of the Messiah.

From the Genesis passage, the author of Hebrews showed that Melchizedek, the priest of God, was superior to Abraham, the father of believers. The patriarch gave the priest a tithe and received a spiritual blessing from him. Common sense teaches that the person who collects the tithe and blesses its giver is the greater of the two. So Melchizedek who is superior to Abraham, in a sense, even collects the tithe from Levi whom Abraham figuratively represents (Heb. 7:4–10). This means that the Melchizedekian priesthood is superior to the one of Levi. By enacting a law, God limited the priestly service to Levi's tribe and excluded all the other tribes of Israel. That law made nothing perfect and had to be annulled. However, God confirmed Melchizedek's priesthood with an oath to guarantee its unique timelessness. And because of that oath, Jesus is priest forever in the order of Melchizedek (vv. 11–22).

S.J.K.

**MELEA** One of the ancestors of Jesus listed in the genealogy from Jesus to Adam. He was the father of Eliakim and son of Menna (Luke 3:31).

**MELECH** (Heb., 'king'). One of King Saul's descendants and from the tribe of Benjamin, Melech was the second son of Micah (1 Chron. 8:35; 9:41).

**MELKI** **1.** An ancestor of Jesus listed in the genealogy from Jesus to Adam. He was the son of Addi and father of Neri (Luke 3:28).
**2.** Another ancestor of Jesus listed in the genealogy from Jesus to Adam. He was the son of Jannai and father of Levi (Luke 3:24).

**MEMUCAN** Apparently the leader of seven 'nobles of Persia' close to King Xerxes (Est. 1:14–21). Following Queen Vashti's refusal to obey the King's command to appear before him, these legal experts and wise men were consulted for advice. Memucan advised that, if women throughout the kingdom were to continue to respect their husbands, the King should issue and publish an edict

banning Vashti from his presence. This advice was accepted and, under God's providence, led to the introduction of Esther to the King's court as officials searched the kingdom for someone to replace Vashti.

P.D.G.

**MENAHEM** (Heb., 'comforting'). The son of Gadi, Menahem became king of the Northern Kingdom of Israel during the reign of Azariah, king of Judah, by assassinating Shallum (2 Kings 15:14). He reigned in Samaria for ten years (v. 17). Menahem's cruelty during this insurrection was appalling and is described in some detail (v. 16).

He was an evil king throughout his reign and never turned to the LORD, causing the whole of Israel to be led into sin as well. As prophesied, and as a judgment on Israel, the LORD allowed an invasion by the Assyrians. However, Menahem managed to stay the inevitable total conquest by paying huge taxes to Tiglath-Pileser (Pul, v. 19). Menahem gave the Assyrians 1,000 talents of silver (nearly 40 tons) and raised all this by heavily taxing his own people. When he died he was succeeded by his son Pekahiah (v. 22).

P.D.G.

**MENNA** An ancestor of Jesus listed in the genealogy from Jesus to Adam. He was the son of Mattatha and father of Melea (Luke 3:31).

**MEONOTHAI** One of the grandsons of Kenaz and a son of Othniel, of the tribe of Judah. He was father of Ophrah (1 Chron. 4:13–14).

**MEPHIBOSHETH** Both the meaning and the derivation of the name Mephibosheth are debated. The majority opinion is that the element 'bosheth' (meaning 'shame') is an intentional distortion of an original 'baal' (meaning 'Baal' or 'lord'; note that Jonathan's son, elsewhere called Mephibosheth, is named Merib-Baal in 1 Chron. 8:34; 9:40). On this reckoning, the name Mephibosheth would yield something like 'from the mouth of shame'. Other names that may exhibit the substitution of 'shame' for 'baal' include Ish-bosheth (2 Sam. 2:8; cf. Eshbaal in 1 Chron. 8:33) and Jerub-Besheth (2 Sam. 11:21 [Heb.]; cf. Jerub-Baal in Judg. 6:32). It is also worth noting that the Septuagint reads 'prophets of shame' for 'prophets of Baal' in 1 Kings 18:19, 25. A minority opinion holds that 'bosheth' originally connoted something like '(sexual) potency' and thus may have stood for Baal, the god of the Canaanite fertility cult, and may have only later come to be associated with 'shame'.

Two individuals in the Bible bear the name Mephibosheth.

**1.** The better known of the two was the son of Jonathan and grandson of King Saul. At the time of Saul's and Jonathan's deaths, Mephibosheth sustained a crippling injury to both feet when his nurse, upon hearing the bad news, attempted to flee (2 Sam. 4:4). David later showed kindness to him out of loyalty to Jonathan, taking him into his court and treating him like 'one of the king's sons' (2 Sam. 9:1–3).

At the time of Absalom's rebellion, Mephibosheth's steward, Ziba, accused him of treason towards David (2 Sam. 16:1–4).

Mephibosheth was later at least partially vindicated (2 Sam. 19:24–30), though David's compromise decision to 'divide the fields' between Mephibosheth and Ziba (2 Sam. 19:29) may suggest some uncertainty on David's part as to whom he should believe.

**2.** The other Mephibosheth, a son of Saul by his concubine Rizpah (2 Sam. 21:8), was delivered over by David to the Gibeonites, at their request, as restitution for Saul's earlier breach of covenant in attempting to annihilate the Gibeonites. A three-year famine in Israel and a word from the LORD that the cause of the famine was Saul's treachery towards the Gibeonites, prompted David's action. Mephibosheth, along with six other male descendants of Saul, was executed by the Gibeonites and exposed before the LORD at Gibeah of Saul. It was not until David had gathered the bones of these Saulides, as well as the bones of Saul and Jonathan from Jabesh Gilead, and given them a proper burial, however, that the LORD answered prayer on behalf of the land (2 Sam. 21:1–14). See also Rizpah.      P.L.

**MERAB** was the older daughter of King Saul and his wife Ahinoam (1 Sam. 14:49). At the height of David's popularity following his defeat of Goliath and victories in battles against the Philistines, Saul offered Merab to David for his wife (1 Sam. 17:25; 18:17). However, out of courtesy, David questioned whether he should be allowed to marry into the King's family (1 Sam. 18:18, 23). No doubt partly due to this but mainly due to Saul's jealousy at David's favour in the eyes of his people, Merab was given in marriage to Adriel of Meholah (v. 19).

Many years later when David was on the throne, the Gibeonites sought vengeance against the house of Saul for their people whom Saul had killed contrary to a treaty. Among those whom David handed over to the Gibeonites to put to death were five sons of Merab and her husband Adriel (2 Sam. 21:8).   P.D.G.

**MERAIAH** In the days of the high priest Joiakim, Meraiah was the head of Seraiah's family, and helped in the service of the Temple during Nehemiah's time (Neh. 12:12).

**MERAIOTH 1.** The son of Zerahiah and father of Amariah, Meraioth is mentioned in the lists of the descendants of Levi in 1 Chron. 6:6–7, 52. He was an ancestor of Ezra (Ezra 7:3).

**2.** The father of Zadok and son of Ahitub. Ahitub was an official in the Temple. Meraioth was an ancestor of Azariah who was among the priests who resettled in Jerusalem in the time of Nehemiah (1 Chron. 9:11; Neh. 11:11).

**MERARI** One of the sons of Levi who became head of the Merarite clan. His sons were Mahli and Mushi (Gen. 46:11; Exod. 6:16, 19; Num. 3:17, 20, 33, 35; 1 Chron. 6:1, 19, 29; 23:21; 24:26). The Merarite clan of Levites were appointed by Moses to 'take care of the frames of the Tabernacle, its crossbars, posts, bases, all its equipment, and everything related to their use' (Num. 3:36; 4:29–33; 10:17). The number of Merarites working in the service of the Tent of Meeting at that time was 3,200 (Num. 4:43–45). They all worked under Aaron but their own leader was Zuriel. The twelve towns that were given to the Merarite Levites came from the tribes of Reuben, Gad and Zebulun (Josh. 21:7, 34–40; 1 Chron. 6:63, 77).

Merarite duties were further outlined in the time of David (1 Chron. 6:44–46), and descendants of Merari are mentioned on a number of occasions in relation to their Tabernacle or Temple duties (1 Chron. 9:14; 15:6, 17; 26:10, 19; 2 Chron. 29:12; 34:12; Ezra 8:19).   P.D.G.

**MERED** (Heb., 'rebellion'). Mered was the second son of Ezrah and was from the tribe of Judah (1 Chron. 4:17). He married Pharaoh's daughter Bithiah and had a number of children including Miriam, Shammai and Ishbah (1 Chron. 4:17–18). He also had a Jewish wife.

**MEREMOTH 1.** The son of Uriah, this Meremoth had returned from the Exile in Babylon with Ezra. He was responsible for carrying the silver, gold and sacred articles that belonged in the Temple from Babylon to Jerusalem. He also helped repair a section of the wall of Jerusalem (Ezra 8:33; Neh. 3:4, 21).

**2.** Another Meremoth was one of the priests who sealed the agreement with Nehemiah to worship only the LORD and to obey his Law (Neh. 10:5). Possibly the same as 1. above.

**3.** This Meremoth was a descendant of Bani and lived at the time of Nehemiah (Ezra 10:36). After Shecaniah confessed to Ezra that many men of Judah had married wives from other tribes and nations, Ezra and the people repented and made a covenant to serve the LORD. Meremoth was one of those listed as having married a foreign wife.

**4.** This Meremoth was a priest listed as returning from the Babylonian Exile with Zerubbabel (Neh. 12:3).   P.D.G.

**MERES** A wise man and legal expert consulted by King Xerxes (Est. 1:14). For detail see Memucan.

**MERIB-BAAL** (Heb., 'Baal contends'). Mephibosheth, King Saul's grandson, was originally called Merib-Baal. He was the son of Jonathan and father of Micah (1 Chron. 8:34; 9:40). It is likely that 'bosheth' ('shame') in the name was substituted for 'Baal' in order not to pronounce the name of a Canaanite divinity. See Mephibosheth.

**MERODACH-BALADAN** (Heb., 'Marduk

462

has given a son'). The son of Baladan king of Babylon during the reign of King Hezekiah of Judah (c. 703 BC). Cunningly he gained entry to the Temple and palace storerooms in Jerusalem by sending a gift and letters to Hezekiah on hearing of the latter's illness (2 Kings 20:12; Is. 39:1). Isaiah firmly rebuked Hezekiah for having given these foreigners access to the LORD's treasuries and promised that one day the Babylonians would remove the treasures (Is. 39:3–7). The LORD expected his people and his kings to rely solely on him for defence and care. The fact that Hezekiah had welcomed foreigners and sought to gain their favour was thus a breach of the LORD's purposes for Israel.                              P.D.G.

**MESHA** (Heb., 'salvation').

**1.** Mesha, king of Moab is mentioned in 2 Kings 3:4. In 2 Sam. 8:2 we read that under King David, Moab had been conquered and become subject to and paid tribute to Israel. After the division of the kingdoms of Israel and Judah, Moab had tried to rebel, but under Ahab, king of Israel, Mesha had had to pay up. When Ahab's son, Joram came to the throne, Mesha thought he might be able to rebel successfully. In 2 Kings 3:4 we read of the huge tribute that Mesha was supposed to pay to Israel. It included a hundred thousand lambs and wool from as many rams. Joram appealed for help to quell the rebellion to the king of Edom and to Jehoshaphat king of Judah (v. 7).

The three kings went a roundabout route to avoid detection and to surprise Moab. However, they ran out of water. Jehoshaphat suggested they find a prophet to help them. They turned to Elisha who told them that the only reason he would help them was because King Jehoshaphat was there. (Joram was a wicked king who did not follow the LORD, v. 3.) By means of a miraculous intervention God brought them both water in the desert and a great victory

over Moab. Mesha was so disturbed he even sacrificed his own son in an attempt to gain the approval of the gods he worshipped (v. 27).

There is some external evidence of Mesha's rebellion recorded on the famous 'Moabite stone'. On that inscription some of the places Mesha captured are listed although there is no record of his defeat at the hands of Joram.

**2.** The first son of Caleb and father of Ziph (1 Chron. 2:42).

**3.** Born in the land of Moab, this Mesha was the son of Hodesh and Shaharaim and of the tribe of Benjamin (1 Chron. 8:9). He is listed in the genealogy leading to King Saul.                              P.D.G.

**MESHACH** The name means something like 'Who is what Aku [a moon god] is?' It was the name given by the chief official of Nebuchadnezzar to Daniel's Jewish friend, Mishael. The name is found 14 times in Dan. 1–3.

Meshach, like Daniel, Abednego and Shadrach, had been taken captive to Babylon. They refused the royal food and ate only vegetables and drank only water (Dan. 1:12) while being prepared for court appearance. The LORD honoured their insistence on not eating what, as Israelites, would have been considered unclean food. As a result, their appearance proved to be healthier than others in the court. God gave him and the others 'knowledge and understanding of all kinds of literature and learning' (v. 17). The king found none others with the same abilities as these three men who were rapidly raised to positions of power and influence under their leader Daniel.

Later, when Meshach would not bow to a statue of gold that Nebuchadnezzar set up in the plain of Dura, he was thrown with Abednego and Shadrach into a furnace of fire. The three so trusted in the LORD that they informed the king, 'the God we serve is able to save us from it' (Dan. 3:17). Once in the furnace, God did intervene and Nebuchadnezzar saw the three walking in the fire unharmed. A fourth person was also present who Nebuchadnezzar said looked 'like a son of the gods' (v. 25). It seems some theophany occurred. Immediately Nebuchadnezzar had the men released, gave them back their positions of authority, and began to worship the true God who had 'sent his angel and rescued his servants' (v. 28). Nebuchadnezzar was so impressed by the saving power of the God of the Hebrews that he ordered that no one should say anything against him.

Meshach and the others had a tremendous faith in their God who had saved them and their faith had witnessed to pagans in the strongest possible way. This faith is alluded to in Heb. 11:34, and there becomes an example for Christians of all ages who trust in the same God as Meshach and the others.

A.B.L. and P.D.G.

**MESHECH** (Heb., 'tall').

**1.** The sixth son of Japheth and grandson of Noah (Gen. 10:2; 1 Chron. 1:5). He was believed to be the founder of a kingdom in Asia Minor which is mentioned along with Tubal and Javan or Greece in Ezek. 27:13; 32:26. These peoples were regarded as the epitome of the forces of evil ranged against God's people in Israel (Ezek. 38:2–3; 39:1; Ps. 120:5–7).

**2.** One of the four Shemite sons of Aram listed in Gen. 10:23 and 1 Chron. 1:17. Aram was a son of Shem, a grandson of Adam. The best Heb. manuscripts of 1 Chron. 1:17 do not separate the sons of Shem himself from the sons of Aram.

**MESHELEMIAH** (Heb., 'the LORD repays'). The father of Zechariah, the gatekeeper at the Tent of Meeting in the days of King David. He was a Levite of the Korahite clan (1 Chron. 9:21; 26:1–2, 9).

**MESHEZABEL** (Heb., 'God saves').

**1.** The grandfather of Meshullam who helped repair the walls of Jerusalem following the return from Babylon (Neh. 3:4).

**2.** This Meshezabel was the father of Pethahiah who was the agent for the King of Persia following the return of the exiles to Jerusalem. He was from the tribe of Judah (Neh. 11:24).

**3.** One of 'the leaders of the people' who signed the agreement with Nehemiah to obey the LORD and follow his Law (Neh. 10:21).

**MESHILLEMITH** Mentioned in 1 Chron. 9:12. See Meshillemoth.

**MESHILLEMOTH** **1.** Meshillemoth was the father of Berekiah. Berekiah was an Ephraimite who persuaded the Israelites of Pekah's day to return to their homes the captives they had taken from Judah (2 Chron. 28:12).

**2.** An ancestor of one of the priestly families who took up residence in Jerusalem following the Babylonian Exile. He was the father of Ahzai and son of Immer (Neh. 11:13). In 1 Chron. 9:12 the man who is called Meshillemith would appear to be the same person.

**MESHOBAB** Mentioned in 1 Chron. 4:34, a leader of one of the clans of Simeon during the time of King Hezekiah. These clans found pasture for their flocks in the area of Gedor (v. 39).

**MESHULLAM** **1.** Meshullam was the grandfather of Shaphan, secretary to King Josiah (2 Kings 22:3).

**2.** Meshullam, son of Zerubbabel, is listed as a member of the royal line after the Exile (1 Chron. 3:19).

**3.** Another Meshullam was a Gadite who lived in Bashan (1 Chron. 5:13).

**4.** A son of Elpaal, this Meshullam is listed as a descendant of Saul, the Benjamite (1 Chron. 8:12–17).

**5.** This Meshullam was the father of Sallu and a Benjamite. Sallu was among the first of his tribe to resettle in Jerusalem following the Exile (1 *Chron.* 9:7; *Neh.* 11:7).

**6.** Meshullam, son of Shephatiah, was also a Benjamite who settled in Jerusalem after the Exile (1 *Chron.* 9:8).

**7.** Meshullam, son of Zadok and father of Hilkiah, is listed in 1 *Chron.* 9:11 as a member of the priestly family (also *Neh.* 11:11).

**8.** 1 *Chron.* 9:12 lists another Meshullam, son of Meshillemith, as a member of the priestly family (1 *Chron.* 9:10–13).

**9.** A Levite and skilled musician, Meshullam helped supervise the workers in Josiah's reconstruction of the Temple (2 *Chron.* 34:12–13).

**10.** This Meshullam was a leader among those who returned with Ezra to Jerusalem. He helped find Levites to serve in the Temple (*Ezra* 8:16).

**11.** Another Meshullam joined Jonathan and Jahzeiah in objecting to Ezra's view that the returned exiles should divorce their foreign wives (*Ezra* 10:15).

**12.** A descendant of Bani at the time of Nehemiah (*Ezra* 10:29). After Shecaniah confessed to Ezra that many men of Judah had married wives from other tribes and nations, Ezra and the people repented and made a covenant to serve the LORD (*Ezra* 10:2). This Meshullam was one of those listed as having married a foreign wife.

**13.** Meshullam, son of Berekiah, was an Israelite who helped repair the wall of Jerusalem following the Babylonian Exile and during Nehemiah's reforms (*Neh.* 3:4, 30).

**14.** This Meshullam was the son of Besodeiah. He helped repair the wall near the Jeshanah gate (*Neh.* 3:6).

**15.** Another Meshullam stood at Ezra's left hand during the reading of the Book of the Law of God (*Neh.* 8:4).

This Meshullam may be the same as another in this list.

**16.** This Meshullam was a priest who set his seal to the covenant made between the people and God after the return from Exile (*Neh.* 10:7).

**17.** Another Meshullam, a leader of the Israelite people, set his seal to the covenant between the people and God after the return from Exile (*Neh.* 10:20).

**18.** In the days of Joiakim, Meshullam was the head of the priestly family of Ezra (*Neh.* 12:13).

**19.** Meshullam was the head of the priestly house of Ginnethon in the time of Joiakim (*Neh.* 12:16).

**20.** Meshullam was one of the gatekeepers who guarded the storerooms in the time of Joiakim (*Neh.* 12:25).

**21.** This Meshullam participated in the celebration of the dedication of the rebuilt wall of Jerusalem (*Neh.* 12:33).

S.C.

**MESHULLEMETH** Mentioned in 2 *Kings* 21:19, Meshullemeth was the wife of King Manasseh and the mother of King Amon of Judah. She was the daughter of Haruz and came from Jotbah.

**MESSIAH** See *Christ.*

**METHUSELAH** (Heb., possibly 'man of the javelin'). The son of Enoch, Methuselah is renowned for having lived longer than anyone else listed in Scripture, some 969 years. He became the father of Lamech when he was 187 years old and hence the grandfather of Noah (*Gen.* 5:21–27; 1 *Chron.* 1:3). In *Luke* 3:37 he is mentioned in the genealogy leading from Jesus to Adam.

**METHUSHAEL** One of Cain's descendants, son of Mehujael and the father of Lamech. He is mentioned in *Gen.* 4:18, a passage which shows how the descendants of Cain spread out across the world after God's judgment on him. Some scholars believe he is the same person as Methuselah but this is unlikely given the differences in the genealogies.

**MEUNIM** A leader of one of the families of Temple servants whose descendants returned from the Babylonian Exile in the days of Ezra and worked on the Temple (*Ezra 2:50; Neh. 7:52*).

**ME-ZAHAB** (Heb., 'waters of gold'). The father of Matred. Matred was the mother of Mehetabel, the wife of King Hadad of Edom (*Gen. 36:39; 1 Chron. 1:50*).

**MIBHAR** One of David's 'Thirty' mighty warriors whose father is listed as Hagri (*1 Chron. 11:38*). In the parallel passage in *2 Sam. 23:36* his name does not appear.

**MIBSAM** **1.** Second of the sons of Ishmael who gave his name to an Arabian tribe (*Gen. 25:13; 1 Chron. 1:29*).
**2.** Mentioned in *1 Chron. 4:25*, this Mibsam was Shaul's son and father of Mishma. He was a descendant of Simeon.

**MIBZAR** A descendant of Esau, Mibzar was a clan leader of the Edomites (*Gen. 36:42; 1 Chron. 1:53*).

**MICA** **1.** *2 Sam. 9:12* mentions a young son of Mephibosheth who was called Mica. He is also called Micah in *8:34*.
**2.** Another Mica, a Levite, was the father of Mattaniah and a descendant of Asaph (*1 Chron. 9:15; Neh. 11:17, 22*).
**3.** This Mica was one of the Levites who joined Nehemiah, following the Babylonian Exile, in witnessing the solemn covenant promising to worship and obey the LORD (*Neh. 10:11*).          P.D.G.

**MICAH** **1.** Micah the prophet. His name means 'Who is like Yah(weh)?' A related name form is Michael: 'Who is like El(ohim)?'. The name is most suited to a prophet who himself asked the question, 'Who is a God like you, who pardons sin and forgives the transgression of the

remnant of his inheritance?' (*Mic. 7:18*). The incomparability of Israel's God provides the basis of Micah's thought and proclamation throughout his book.

Little information about Micah survives. Apart from the brief introduction to his book (*Mic. 1:1*) he is mentioned only in *Jer. 26:18* where certain elders, a century after Micah, quote *Mic. 3:12*, a word of judgment against Jerusalem in the days of King Hezekiah. Citing the repentance in Judah following Micah's word of woe, they plead with their own contemporaries to listen to God's word through Jeremiah as well.

Both Micah and Jeremiah describe Micah as a 'Morashtite', that is, a citizen of Moresheth, some 25 miles south-west of Jerusalem. Employing a pun on the name of his home town (*moreset*, *Mic. 1:14b*), the prophet predicts that the defeated city of Lachish will bestow a gift on Moresheth, the root meaning of which is 'possession' or 'gift' (*morasa*). Reference to Lachish and Moresheth helps to provide a chronological setting for Micah's ministry. He indicates that he received his prophetic commission during the reigns of Jotham (750–731 BC), Ahaz (735–715), and Hezekiah (729–686), kings of Judah, so his ministry spanned at a minimum the years 735–715. This, of course, makes Micah a contemporary of Isaiah (740–681?) and careful reading of their respective books makes clear their mutual awareness and dependence (*Mic. 4:1–3; cf. Is. 2:2–4, 12; 4:7; 5:6; 7:18; cf. Is. 37:32*). The anticipated conquest of Lachish and other towns of the Shephelah by the Assyrians (*Mic. 1:10–16*) requires a date prior to 701 BC when Sennacherib indeed swept down upon that region in a violent campaign of destruction and pillage (*cf. Is. 36:1*). However, Samaria was still standing at the time Micah's first oracle was delivered (*Mic. 1:1, 5–8*), so it must precede 722 BC, the date of the Assyrian capture of that city. The references to Lachish and the other sites of the Shephelah must be explained as prophetic revelation and/or simple reading of the inevitable outcome of the signs of the times.

Despite Micah's self-reference as a Morashtite, he appears to have been very much familiar with the political, cultural, and religious milieu of Jerusalem (cf. Mic. 1:9; 3:9–12; 4:9–5:1; 6:6–16). Nowhere is this more apparent than in the so-called 'rib-texts', those passages where Yahweh is said to be entering into a lawsuit with his people because of their covenant disobedience (Mic. 1:2–7; 3:1, 9; 6:1–5). Both Isaiah and Jeremiah make use of this legal form and both of them, of course, were residents of Jerusalem, the place of the central courts where suits were filed and court cases adjudicated. In fact, Micah shows such familiarity with the language and procedures involved that some scholars believe he may have been one of the circle of the elders to which reference is made in Jer. 26:17–18. While there is no objective way of proving this, Micah's unusually strong reaction to injustice in his own day might lend this hypothesis some support (cf. Mic. 2:1–2; 3:1–3, 5–12; 6:6–8, 10–12).

Micah's despair about the leadership of Israel and Judah is not without hope, however, for he anticipates a day when the long-awaited scion of David will come forth from Bethlehem, as insignificant a village as that had become in his own day (Mic. 5:2; cf. Matt. 2:6). This one would be the means of effecting peace between God and his people (Mic. 5:5). The God who now was about to bring judgment would, in the day of salvation, bring covenant renewal and fulfilment of all the ancient promises to the fathers (Mic. 7:18–20). Micah thus bridges the chasm between the understandable pessimism of his own time and the glorious future of messianic redemption and reconciliation.

**2.** Micah, an Ephraimite, was a principal figure in the story of the migration of the tribe of Dan from its original allotment to a place north of the Sea of Galilee (Judg. 17:1–18:31). Micah had embraced idolatry. He stole money from his own mother who then cursed the thief. At this he gave it back and she blessed him and consecrated the money to the LORD (Judg. 17:3) but took 200 pieces of silver and made an image out of them which she gave to Micah to keep in his house at his shrine (vv. 4–5). Micah wished to have a priest to officiate at his shrine. Having found one, a wandering Levite from Bethlehem (17:9), he no sooner had begun to employ him when the Danites hired him away with threats and bribes and took him with them to their new settlement (18:25–27). Ironically enough, Micah's priest turned out to be none other than Moses' own grandson, Jonathan (18:30).

**3.** Micah, a son of Shimei. He was a descendant of Reuben through Joel, Shemaiah, Gog and Shimei and was a clan leader (1 Chron. 5:3–5).

**4.** Micah, a son of Merib-Baal. He was a descendant of King Saul through Jonathan and Merib-Baal, otherwise known as Mephibosheth (1 Chron. 8:34–35; 9:40–41).

**5.** Micah, a member of the Kohathite clan of Levites through descent from Kohath's fourth son Uzziel (1 Chron. 23:20; 24:24–25).

**6.** This Micah was the father of Abdon. He was a citizen of Judah whose son assisted King Josiah in assessing the significance of the scroll found in the Temple (2 Chron. 34:20–22). In 2 Kings 22:12 it is probably the same person who is called Micaiah.                    E.M.

**MICAIAH** (Heb., 'who is like the LORD?').
**1.** Micaiah, son of Imlah, was a prophet who spoke God's word to the nations of Israel and Judah during the reigns of Ahab and Jehoshaphat (1 Kings 22:8–28;

2 Chron. 18:7–27). He was probably the person referred to in 2 Chron. 17:7 who was sent by King Jehoshaphat, with a number of Levites, to teach the people of Judah about the LORD. Meanwhile, in the Northern Kingdom, King Ahab of Israel 'did more to provoke the LORD, the God of Israel, to anger than did all the kings of Israel before him' (1 Kings 16:33). It is therefore not surprising that a true prophet from the LORD was largely condemning and critical of his rule. Ahab had become used to this and did not like to consult Micaiah because he only received bad news (1 Kings 22:8).

The one prophecy that is recounted demonstrates clearly the existence of true and false prophecy side by side in Israel even in Ahab's day. Ahab decided to try and regain some of his territory that had been taken by Syria. He appealed to Jehoshaphat, king of Judah, to join him in an expedition against Syria. Jehoshaphat agreed but wanted to consult the LORD first. Ahab's prophets all agreed that this was a good venture, no doubt knowing that was what Ahab wanted them to say. Jehoshaphat, however, distinguished between these prophets and true prophets and asked Ahab for a 'prophet of the LORD'. Ahab's answer reveals how far Israel had moved from the worship of the LORD. Speaking of Micaiah, he said, 'There is still one man through whom we can inquire of the LORD' (1 Kings 22:8). Micaiah was consulted. At first he told Ahab what he wanted to hear, but Ahab saw through his sarcasm and asked him to tell the truth (vv. 14–16). Micaiah then prophesied, 'I saw all Israel scattered on the hills like sheep without a shepherd, and the LORD said, "These people have no master. Let each one go home in peace"' (v. 17).

As he continued, Micaiah described a picture in which the LORD in heaven asked who would entice Ahab to go to battle. Eventually 'a spirit came forward' and said he would entice Ahab by becoming a 'lying spirit' in the mouths of Ahab's prophets.

For his efforts Micaiah was put in prison. Micaiah's parting shot was to appeal to the Law on prophets. If his word did not come true the LORD would not have spoken through him (1 Kings 22:28; see Deut. 18:22). Micaiah's word did come true and Ahab was killed at Ramoth-Gilead (1 Kings 22:34–37).

The problem of prophets who told people what they wanted to hear continued to plague both Israel and Judah and was symptomatic of how far the nations had moved from the true God. But the problem remained even in the church of the NT. The apostle Paul warned Timothy about teachers who would give the people 'what their itching ears want to hear' (2 Tim. 4:3). The danger for God's people through all ages is that they so often do not like to hear warnings and challenges from their LORD.

**2.** Another Micaiah was the father of Acbor. Acbor was one of the court officials in King Josiah's day (2 Kings 22:12).

**3.** Micaiah son of Gemariah heard Jeremiah's prophecy when Baruch read his scroll (Jer. 36:11). This prophecy warned of the impending judgment of God on Judah for all her sin (Jer. 35). Micaiah ordered that this scroll should be read to the other leaders of Judah (Jer. 36:13).

**4.** This Micaiah was the son of Zaccur and an ancestor of a certain priest called Zechariah who was given the duty of blowing trumpets at the dedication of the city walls in the time of Nehemiah (Neh. 12:35).

**5.** Another Micaiah was the head of a priestly family in the time of Nehemiah, and is mentioned in Neh. 12:41. He was a trumpet player during the worship at the dedication of the city walls.    P.D.G.

**MICHAEL** (Heb., 'who is like God?').
**1.** The father of Sethur. Sethur was

one of the spies sent out by Moses to look over the land of Canaan (*Num. 13:13*).

**2.** A clan leader who was head of one of the seven Gadite clans settled in the area of Gilead and Bashan (*1 Chron. 5:13*).

**3.** An ancestor of 2. above and a son of Jeshishai (*1 Chron. 5:14*).

**4.** Another Michael was the son of Baaseiah, a Levite and an ancestor of Asaph (*1 Chron. 6:40*).

**5.** This Michael was one of the sons of Izrahiah and was a chief in the tribe of Issachar (*1 Chron. 7:3*).

**6.** This Michael was one of the sons of Beriah and a leader from the tribe of Benjamin. Michael lived in Aijalon and is listed in the genealogy of King Saul (*1 Chron. 8:16*).

**7.** This Michael, of the tribe of Manasseh, was listed as one of David's warriors at Ziklag (*1 Chron. 12:20*).

**8.** Another Michael was the father of Omri. Omri was an official in the tribe of Issachar during the reign of King David (*1 Chron. 27:18*).

**9.** One of the sons of King Jehoshaphat of Judah. He was brother to Jehoram who succeeded his father to the throne (*2 Chron. 21:2*). Jehoram established his throne and then put to death all his brothers (*v. 4*).

**10.** The father of a certain Zebadiah who returned with Ezra and 80 of his family from Babylon to Jerusalem (*Ezra 8:8*).

**11.** Michael is also the name given to an archangel who had particular responsibility for the nation of Israel. He is 'one of the chief princes' and the 'one who protects your people' (*Dan. 10:13, 21; 12:1*). In Daniel's vision, Michael is revealed as the one who wars on behalf of God's people against the satanic forces at work in Persia and, later, in Greece. He acts for the Lord, protecting everyone whose names are 'found written in the book' and overseeing the work of the nations so that God's purposes for his people will be worked out in history (*12:1*).

He is referred to again in *Jude 9* and *Rev. 12:7* where he specifically fights and disputes with Satan. In *Jude 9* he disputed with 'the devil about the body of Moses'. Quite what this refers to is unclear but it is mentioned in a passage dealing with blasphemous people who 'slander celestial beings'. Moses was the leader of God's people, and hence no doubt the subject of singular and particular attack by Satan. In spite of his power, Michael is seen to be subordinate to the Lord who will eventually judge Satan. In *Rev. 12:7* it was Michael and his forces who fought against Satan in heaven and threw him down to earth so that he could no longer accuse God's people before the throne of God.                P.D.G.

**MICHAL** Introduced in *1 Sam. 14:49* as the younger daughter of Saul, Michal — whose name may be a shortened form of Michael (meaning 'Who is like God?') — became a wife of David in *1 Sam. 18:27*. She was not the first of Saul's daughters, however, to be offered to David. In keeping with an earlier promise to the one who should kill the Philistine giant Goliath (*1 Sam. 17:25*), Saul first offered David his older daughter, Merab, on the condition that David continue to fight against Saul's enemies. Saul hoped in fact that the Philistines would prevail over David and thus rid him of one whom he had begun to view as a dangerous rival (*1 Sam. 18:17*; perhaps the 'one better than you' of *15:28*). When David protested his unworthiness to marry a daughter of the king, Saul lost no time in giving Merab to someone else (*1 Sam. 18:18–19*). Subsequently, news of Michal's love for David provided Saul with a second opportunity to lay a snare for David (*1 Sam. 18:20–21*). This time Saul asked for an exorbitant bride-price measured in Philistine lives (*1 Sam. 17:25*), perhaps reasoning that David's hesitancy regarding Merab had freed him from his earlier promise. David's success in meeting the price twice-over, along with Michal's continued affection for David, confirmed Saul in his suspicion that 'the LORD was with David' and thus also in his fear of and animosity towards David (1 Sam. 18:29).

Like her brother Jonathan, Michal had occasion to protect David from her father's attempts on his life. In 1 Sam. 19 Michal warned David that her father had sent men to kill him and then helped him to escape by lowering him through a window. She delayed his pursuers by arranging an idol and some goats' hair in David's bed so as to make it appear that David was still in bed – ill, as she claimed. When Saul discovered her deception, Michal justified her action by claiming that David had threatened her life, should she refuse to help him. During David's extended absence, made necessary by Saul's continued aggression, Saul gave Michal to another man, Paltiel son of Laish (1 Sam. 25:44). After Saul's death, when Abner, formerly Saul's general and the only real power in the tenuous Northern Kingdom of Saul's son Ish-Bosheth, approached David with an offer to return the northern ten tribes to him, David set as the first condition of an agreement the return of his wife Michal (2 Sam. 3:13–14). Much to Paltiel's distress (2 Sam. 3:15–16), Ish-Bosheth complied with David's demand.

Whether David's demand for Michal's return was motivated more by affection or politics is uncertain, but in any case the reuniting of David and Michal brought little joy. At the time that the ark of God was brought to Jerusalem, Michal caught sight of David 'leaping and dancing before the LORD' (2 Sam. 6:16). Showing as little regard for the ark and its significance as her father had done during his reign (see 1 Chron. 13:3), she despised David in her heart and took the first opportunity to let him know how she felt. As David returned home, she greeted him with the sarcastic words, 'How the king has distinguished himself [lit., 'shown himself weighty'] today, disrobing in the sight of the slave girls . . .' David would have nothing of this criticism, insisting that 'it was before the LORD' that he had celebrated (2 Sam. 6:21). Indeed, he expressed willingness to be 'even more undignified than this' (or, more literally translated, 'I will humble myself [consider myself small and of little weight] even more than this', 2 Sam. 6:22). Unlike Eli and his sons (1 Sam. 2:29–30), and unlike Michal's own father Saul (1 Sam. 15:12, 30), David was willing to be abased that the LORD might receive the honour (weight) due him. Michal's vexation suggests that she, like her father, was out of sympathy with this spirit of kingly submission. But this is precisely what was required of Israel's kings (Deut. 17:18–20; 1 Sam. 12:13–15; 13:13). In concluding his response to Michal's rebuke, David repeated her own sarcastic words (2 Sam. 6:20), but with the sarcasm excised: 'by these slaves girls you spoke of, I will be held in honour [considered weighty]'. The notion that, though he humbled himself in his own eyes, he would be held in honour by those more discerning than Michal is in keeping with the general biblical truth that in God's economy 'the lowly will be exalted and the exalted will be brought low' (Ezek. 21:26; cf. 1 Sam. 2:7–8; Matt. 23:12; Luke 14:10–11; 18:14).

The above episode concludes with the sombre notice that 'Michal daughter of Saul had no children to the day of her death' (2 Sam. 6:23). Whether Michal's childlessness resulted from David's decision or the LORD's is a question that the text does not directly address, though the latter may be more likely; in 1 Chron. 26:4–5 the eight sons of Obed-Edom are listed as an indication of the LORD's blessing on this one who received the ark honourably.           P.L.

**MICRI** Mentioned in *1 Chron. 9:8* as the grandfather of Elah and father of Uzzi. After the captivity in Babylon, Elah was among the first returnees to Jerusalem from the tribe of Benjamin.

**MIDIAN** The fourth of Abraham's sons by his wife Keturah (*Gen. 25:2*). He appears in a list of Abraham's descendants bridging, in the narrative of *Gen. 24–25*, the death of Sarah and the death of Abraham (also *1 Chron. 1:32*). He was the father of the people who became known as the Midianites.

**MIJAMIN** (Heb., 'favoured one').

**1.** Mijamin was a priest who served in the Tabernacle during David's rule. He was responsible for the sixth turn of service (*1 Chron. 24:9*).

**2.** This Mijamin was a descendant of Parosh and one of those in the time of Ezra who had married a foreign wife rather than one from Judah (*Ezra 10:25*).

**3.** One of the priests who sealed the agreement with Nehemiah to worship only the LORD and to obey his Law (*Neh. 10:8*).

**4.** A Levite and leader of the priests who returned with Jeshua and Zerubbabel from the Babylonian Exile (*Neh. 12:5*). Possibly the same as 3. above.

          P.D.G.

**MIKLOTH 1.** Mikloth was the leader of Dodai's men in King David's army. Dodai was a commander who was on duty with his men in the second month of each year (*1 Chron. 27:4*).

**2.** One of the sons of Jeiel and his wife Maacah, this Mikloth was one of the forefathers of Kish the father of Saul (*1 Chron. 8:32; 9:37–38*). He was a Benjamite, the father of Shimeah, and lived near Jerusalem.

**MIKNEIAH** (Heb., 'the LORD possesses'). After the ark of the covenant had been brought to Jerusalem, the worship of God was properly organized by King David. Mikneiah was one of the family of Merarite Levites who were gatekeepers. The particular job he and his brothers were given was to be musicians and to play the harps and lyres before the ark of the covenant as it was moved to Jerusalem (*1 Chron. 15:18, 21*).

**MILALAI** was a leader of Judah and a priest who played musical instruments at the dedication of the rebuilt walls of Jerusalem (*Neh. 12:36*).

**MILCAH 1.** A daughter of Abraham's brother, Haran, she married Nahor (*Gen. 11:29; 22:20*). She had many sons and was grandmother to Rebekah (*Gen. 22:23; 24:15, 25, 47*).

**2.** One of five daughters born to Zelophehad. Zelophehad had no sons. These daughters married cousins on their father's side and were members of the tribe of Manasseh (*Num. 26:33; 27:1; 36:1–12; Josh. 17:3*). They faced a predicament over their inheritance, for normally inherited land would have been passed on through a son.

They approached Moses at the entrance to the Tabernacle about the problem, asking him to rule that they should be allowed to inherit their father's property, for it would not be right that his name should die out. Moses consulted the LORD about the situation, as a result of which a new law was promulgated allowing daughters to inherit land from their father. Later some of the leaders from the tribe of Manasseh appealed to Moses about the case, pointing out that if these women were now to marry outside the tribe the land would be lost forever to the tribe. The ruling which followed further defined the law of inheritance, insisting that the women should marry into their father's tribe or else lose the inheritance

(Num. 36). Hence the daughters married cousins 'on their father's side', thus fulfilling the requirement of the LORD.

When finally the Israelites entered the land of Canaan and the land was divided up among the tribes, the daughters of Zelophehad were duly given their inheritance (Josh.17:3–4).  P.D.G.

**MINIAMIN** (Heb., 'fortunate').

**1.** During the revival and turning to God in Hezekiah's reign, many Levites were assigned specific Temple duties. Miniamin was one of those with the task of helping Kore distribute the people's gifts around the towns of the priests 'according to their divisions' (2 Chron. 31:15).

**2.** Miniamin, a head of priestly family in the time of Nehemiah, is mentioned in Neh. 12:41. He was a trumpet player during the worship at the dedication of the city walls.

**MIRIAM 1.** Miriam was the sister of Moses and Aaron and daughter of Amram (Num. 26:59; 1 Chron. 6:3). She was a prophetess and eventually became a leader in Israel. Although unnamed, she is first encountered when she helped protect Moses from the massacre of infant boys by the Egyptians. She watched over the infant Moses whilst he was hidden in a papyrus basket among the reeds at the side of the Nile, and ran to get her mother, Jochebed, to nurse the child for Pharaoh's daughter (Exod. 2:4, 7).

She is first named when seen leading the women of Israel with a tambourine, dancing and singing praises to the LORD for the escape of the Israelites from Egypt (Exod. 15:20–21; see Mic. 6:4). The fact that she was called a 'prophetess' may indicate that she composed part of the song of praise found in Exod. 15. Her prophetic gifts are probably referred to again in Num. 12:1–4 where, together with her brother Aaron, she questioned Moses over his behaviour in marrying a Cushite wife. The two emphasized that the LORD had also spoken through them, again stressing her prophetic gifts. There appears to have been some jealousy over the leadership between her and Moses. However, the LORD then made it very clear that, though she and Aaron heard his voice as prophets, with Moses the LORD spoke 'face to face, clearly and not in riddles' (v. 8). God's judgment on Miriam's arrogance in speaking against Moses was that she became leprous for seven days (Num. 12:10–15; see Deut. 24:9). Miriam died at Kadesh near the Desert of Zin (Num. 20:1).

**2.** Another Miriam was the daughter of Mered from the tribe of Judah (1 Chron. 4:17).  P.D.G.

**MIRMAH** Listed in the genealogy of Benjamin leading to King Saul, Mirmah was the head of a family and son of Shaharaim and his wife Hodesh. He was born in Moab (1 Chron. 8:10).

**MISHAEL** (Heb., 'who is what God is?').

**1.** Mishael, a head of one of the clans of the tribe of Levi during the Exodus period, is mentioned in Exod. 6:22. In Lev. 10:4, he appears to be kin to Aaron and his sons (v. 1).

**2.** Mishael, the Jewish friend of Daniel, is mentioned in Dan. 1:6, 19; 2:17. Though not mentioned by name, his act of faith in disobeying King Nebuchadnezzar is honoured in the NT in Heb. 11:34. See Meshach for further detail.

**3.** Mishael, who stood with Ezra at the Water Gate, is mentioned only in Neh. 8:4.  A.B.L.

**MISHAM** One of the sons of Elpaal and a leader from the tribe of Benjamin, Misham lived in Aijalon and helped build Ono and Lod (1 Chron. 8:12).

**MISHMA 1.** A son of Ishmael and a tribal leader (Gen. 25:14; 1 Chron. 1:30).

**2.** Mishma was a descendant of Simeon and son of Mibsam (1 Chron. 4:25–26).

**MISHMANNAH** was one of the famous Gadites who defected from Saul to David when he was at Ziklag. He was the fourth in the list each of whom are described in vivid imagery as the bravest of warriors. They were commanders who proved of tremendous support to David in his battles (1 Chron. 12:11). Later in the passage it seems that such men transferred loyalties not simply to be on the winning side but because the 'Spirit' had worked among them. As David's army grew it became 'like the army of God' (v. 22).

**MISPAR** One of the Israelite leaders who returned with Zerubbabel to Jerusalem and Judah following the Exile in Babylon (Ezra 2:2).

**MISPERETH** was one of the Israelites returning to Jerusalem with Nehemiah and Zerubbabel after the captivity in Babylon (Neh. 7:7). Probably the same as Mispar (Ezra 2:2).

**MITHREDATH** (Persian, 'gift from Mithra').
**1.** A Persian name belonging to two people in the book of Ezra. The first, mentioned in Ezra 1:8, was treasurer to King Cyrus of Persia during the first year of his reign. In that year Cyrus made a proclamation allowing the displaced peoples from Judah and Benjamin to return to their home country. He also informed the people that God had commissioned him to build a Temple in Jerusalem. God prepared the hearts of the leaders of Judah and Benjamin to return to rebuild their Temple. As they got ready to depart many neighbours gave them presents, but Cyrus also called upon his treasurer to find the Temple artefacts that had originally come from Jerusalem and give them back to the leader of Judah, Sheshbazzar. This opening chapter of Ezra leaves the reader in no doubt that God's great purposes for his people were being worked out even through this pagan king. The whole episode initiating the return was a fulfilment of the prophecy of Jeremiah (Ezra 1:1, see Jer. 30–33, esp. 33:7–11; also Is. 44–45). It was God who moved the mind of Cyrus and God who prepared his people for the return and God who caused the people to want to return (Ezra 1:1–11).

**2.** Together with Tabeel and Bishlam, this Mithredath wrote a letter to King Artaxerxes lodging an accusation against the people of Judah who were involved in rebuilding the Temple following their Exile in Babylon (Ezra 4:7). These three officials were probably Persian officials in Samaria. They feared that the new Jerusalem would become a power base for the returnees that could be used to make a complete break from Persian rule. No doubt they were also interested in the money they made from the collection of taxes (v. 13). Their complaint to Artaxerxes led to a cessation on the rebuilding of the Temple until Darius came to the throne (v. 24).                    P.D.G.

**MIZRAIM** was one of four sons born to Ham. He had at least seven sons of his own, most of whom were listed as progenitors of different tribes or peoples. Mizraim is the usual Heb. term for Egypt, thus the Egyptians are regarded as descendants of Ham (Gen. 10:6, 13; 50:11; 1 Chron. 1:8, 11).

**MIZZAH** A grandson of Esau and Basemath, Mizzah was the son of Reuel and an Edomite clan chief (Gen. 36:13, 17; 1 Chron. 1:37).

**MNASON** came from Cyprus and was 'one of the early disciples' living in Jerusalem. This may mean that he had been converted on the Day of Pentecost or in those first few weeks. He may, therefore, have been one of those who provided Luke with much of his information about the early days, which Luke then wrote up in the early chapters of Acts.

When Paul and some of the disciples from Caesarea came to Jerusalem he provided hospitality for them. Paul arrived with his colleagues to give the poor Christians of Jerusalem the offering they had collected from other churches. (*Acts 21:16*). It is possible that Mnason was one of the more affluent Christians remaining in Jerusalem at the time. In the book of Acts and in much of the NT there is a great emphasis on hospitality which was regarded as a mark of Christian love and of service to the Lord.　　　　P.D.G.

**MOAB** (Heb., 'from my father'). This man became the progenitor of the Moabites. He was the son of Lot's older daughter and Lot was his father (*Gen. 19:37*). Following the destruction of Sodom, from which only Lot and his two daughters eventually escaped, the daughters were concerned that the family name should continue, and so got their father drunk and both had sexual intercourse with him and became pregnant. It is perhaps significant that these daughters who were reluctant to leave Sodom continued to manifest serious sexual sin for which, it seems, Sodom was renowned. Certainly, once away from Sodom, there was no new start for Lot. He and his daughters had been saved by God simply because of their relationship to Abraham, with whom God had made his covenant (*Gen. 19:29*).　　　　P.D.G.

**MOADIAH** (Heb., 'the LORD promises'). A Levite and leader of the priests who returned with Jeshua and Zerubbabel from the Babylonian Exile (*Neh. 12:5*).

**MOLECH** The name of a pagan deity which may originally have meant 'king', but scholars are uncertain. The deity was normally linked with the Ammonites (*1 Kings 11:5, 7*). From the warnings given the Israelites against worship of this deity, it is believed that the worship involved human sacrifices, specially children (*Lev. 18:21; 20:2–5*). Because God's Law was so decisive in its condemnation of this pagan religion, it was considered particularly serious when kings began to follow the cult. The latter years of King Solomon's reign were sadly far removed from the early years when both king and people had followed the LORD God in all his ways. Later, they turned to other gods and did not obey the Law. Because they did this, including worshipping Molech, the kingdom was divided and ten tribes, the Northern Kingdom, were separated from Solomon's inheritance (*1 Kings 11:33*).

When Josiah came to the throne in Judah, the Southern Kingdom, he turned back to the LORD and desecrated the altar to Molech in Topheth so that it could not be used any longer for child sacrifice (*2 Kings 23:10, 13*). Jeremiah referred back to this evil worship in the valley of Ben Hinnom in *Jer. 32:35* (also see *49:1–3; Is. 57:9*). The prophet Zephaniah also warned the people of the coming day of the LORD when judgment would come on those who tried to worship both the LORD and Molech (*Zeph. 1:5*). The worship of Molech became so notorious that it was even used as an example of rebellion and sin by Stephen when he preached the gospel to the crowds in Jerusalem in *Acts 7:43*.

Apart from the seriousness of worshipping a pagan deity, it is clear that such a brutal cult that involved human sacrifice was specially abhorrent both to God and to the Israelites. It is not much wonder that it remains an example of the abhorrence of pagan worship even into NT times.　　　　P.D.G.

**MOLID** A son of Abishur and his wife Abihail, Molid was a leader in the tribe of Judah (*1 Chron. 2:29*).

**MORDECAI 1.** Mordecai is listed in *Ezra 2:2* and *Neh. 7:7* as one of the

Israelites returning to Jerusalem with Nehemiah after the captivity in Babylon.

**2.** Mordecai was a Benjamite, son of Jair and cousin to Esther (see *Esther*). Mordecai lived in the citadel of Susa during the reign of King Xerxes, where he raised Esther as if she were his own daughter. In time, Esther became Queen and Mordecai distinguished himself in service to King Xerxes by exposing a plot to kill the king. Conflict arose for Mordecai when he refused to bow down to Haman, the king's highest official. Haman grew enraged and developed a plan that would destroy all Jews in Persia and leave Mordecai hanging on the gallows. With Esther's help, Haman was destroyed and Mordecai was given the highest position in the king's service. With Mordecai's first official decree, all Jews were spared.

Mordecai's faithfulness to his own race and his commitment to God's sovereignty in the affairs of his people is clearly seen in what he said to Esther when he persuaded her to go to the king to plead for the Jews: 'if you remain silent at this time, relief and deliverance for the Jews will arise from another place, but you and your father's family will perish. And who knows but that you have come to royal position for such a time as this?' (*Est.* 4:14). S.C.

## MOSES

Moses was the child of Amram (of the tribe of Levi) and Jochebed, and a brother of Aaron and Miriam. He was born during the terrible years when the Egyptians had ordered any Israelite baby boy to be killed. His parents hid him at home, and later in a basket among the bull rushes by the Nile. The discovery of the baby by the princess was providential as she saved his life. His name ('one who draws') is a reminder of his obscure beginning, as his mother said of him: 'I drew him out of the water'.

The LORD called him to be the leader by whom he would speak to Pharaoh, bring his people out of Egypt, and lead them to the Promised Land. In the process of these events, Israel underwent a transformation from being the servants of Pharaoh to being the people of God. They were bound together into a communion of people, better known as a covenant community, established by God's sovereign and gracious act. (See *Covenant*.)

The OT associates Moses with the covenant, the theocracy, and the revelation of Sinai. He was the mediator of the Sinaitic (Mosaic) covenant (*Exod. 19:3–8; 20:18–19*). This covenant was an administration of grace and promise by which the LORD consecrated a people to himself through the sanctions of divine Law. The LORD dealt with his people graciously, gave his promises to all who had faith in him, and consecrated them to order their lives by his holy Law. The covenant administration was a concrete expression of God's Kingdom. The LORD was present with his people and extended his special rule over them. The essence of the covenant is the promise, 'I will be your God and you will be my people' (*Exod. 6:7; Deut. 29:13; Ezek. 11:20*).

Moses was an exalted servant by his special relationship with the LORD (*Num. 12:6–8; Deut. 34:10–12*). When Aaron and Miriam complained against Moses' exalted position as Mediator between Yahweh and Israel, Moses did not respond to their charge (*Num. 12:3*). Instead the LORD spoke to defend his servant (*Num. 12:6–8*).

The LORD confirmed Moses' authority to be his chosen vehicle of communication: 'I reveal . . . I speak to him . . .' (v. 6; see Deut. 18:18). He set Moses apart as 'my servant' (Exod. 14:31; Deut. 34:5; Josh. 1:1–2) – a relationship of confidence and friendship between a superior and an inferior. Moses in a unique way remained God's servant, even after his death; he served as the 'head' of the covenant administration till the New Covenant in our Lord Jesus (Num. 12:7; see Heb. 3:2, 5). According to this prophetic epitaph of Moses' ministry, Moses occupied a unique place as God's friend. He had enjoyed the privilege of close communion with the LORD: 'The LORD would speak to Moses face to face, as a man speaks with a friend' (Exod. 33:9).

The characteristic difference between Moses and the prophets after him, lies in the directness in which the LORD spoke to his trusted servant. Moses as the 'fountainhead', was the first to receive, to write down, and to teach the revelation of God. This revelation extended to all facets of life, including the laws of holiness, purity, rituals, family life, work, and society. Through Moses the LORD had planned to shape Israel into 'a counter-community'. God's revelation was to make them immune to the detestable practices of the pagans, including divination and magic. The word of revelation by the power of Spirit was to transform Israel into mature children.

Moses' position and revelation foreshadow the unique position of the Lord Jesus Christ. Moses served in God's Kingdom as a faithful 'servant' (Heb. 3:2, 5), whereas our Lord is 'the Son' of God incarnate: 'Christ is faithful as a son over God's house' (Heb. 3:6). Moses, like our Lord, verified the revelation of God by signs and wonders (Deut. 34:12; see also Exod. 7:14–11:8; 14:5–15:21).

Although Moses did not as yet know of the revelation of God in Christ, he saw the 'glory' of God (Exod. 34:29–35). The apostle Paul confirmed the grace of God in the Mosaic covenant when he wrote to the church at Rome, 'Theirs is the adoption as sons; theirs the divine glory, the covenants, the receiving of the law, the temple worship and the promises. Theirs are the patriarchs, and from them is traced the human ancestry of Christ, who is God over all, forever praised! Amen' (Rom. 9:4–5).

Moses, the greatest prophet before Jesus' incarnation, spoke of the ministry of another prophet (Deut. 18:15–22). He was God's witness to Israel that a greater fulfilment lay ahead: 'Moses was faithful . . . testifying to what would be said in the future' (Heb. 3:5). The nature of that future was nothing less than the rest which comes (Heb. 4:1–13) in Jesus Christ, for whose sake Moses also suffered (Heb. 11:26).

The eschatological hope of the Mosaic revelation is nothing less than the presence of God among his people. Israel's eschatology begins in God's covenants with Abraham and with Israel. Moses – the servant of God, the intercessor, the mediator of the covenant – pointed beyond his administration to an era of rest. He spoke of the enjoyment of rest and ordained that all the members of the covenant fellowship should long for the rest-to-come in the celebration of the Sabbath ('rest'). The Sabbath is the sign of the covenant (Exod. 31:14–17), the sign of Israel's consecration to a holy mission (Exod. 31:13), and of their being blessed with all God's gifts in creation (Deut. 26:18–19; 28:3–14).

Moses painfully realized that the people could not enter into that rest, because of his own disobedience and because of Israel's rebelliousness (*Deut. 4:21–25*). Yet, he spoke of a new era opened up by God's grace, freedom, and fidelity (*Deut. 4:29–21; 30:5–10; 32:39–43*). Moses looked forward to an era of peace, tranquillity, and of the full enjoyment of God's presence, blessing, and protection in the promised land (*Deut. 12:9–10; 25:19; Exod. 33:14; Josh. 1:13*).

This hope, grounded in Yahweh's fidelity (*Deut. 4:31*), is most clearly expressed in Moses' final testimony, 'the Song of Witness' (*Deut. 32*). In it he recited Yahweh's loving acts and favour to Israel (*vv. 1–14*), warned against Israel's rebellion and their consequent suffering (*vv. 15–35*), and comforted the godly with the hope of Yahweh's vengeance upon the enemies and the deliverance of the remnant of Israel and of the nations (*vv. 36–43*). He even alluded to the greatness of Yahweh's love to Gentiles (*vv. 36–43; Rom. 15:10*)!

The eschatological significance of the Song of Moses reverberates in the prophetic messages of judgment and hope, justice and mercy, exclusion and inclusion, vengeance and deliverance. The Mosaic administration, therefore, was never intended to be an end in itself. It was a stage in the progress of fulfilment of the promises, and an important stage at that!

As fountainhead of the prophetic tradition, Moses saw more of God's glorious self-revelation than anyone else in the OT (*Exod. 33:18; 34:29–35*). He spoke by God's authority. Whoever questioned Moses challenged the LORD. Israel could find comfort, grace, and blessing, because in Moses the roles of covenant mediator and intercessor (*Exod. 32:1–34:10; Num. 14:13–25*) came together. He prayed for Israel, spoke boldly as their advocate in the presence of the LORD, and encouraged them to look beyond himself to Yahweh. (See *Prophets and Prophecy*)   W.A.VG.

**MOZA 1.** Mentioned in *1 Chron. 2:46*, this Moza was the son of Caleb and his concubine, Ephah, and from the tribe of Judah. He seems to have had two full brothers, Haran and Gazez (*1 Chron. 2:46*).

**2.** This Moza, from the tribe of Benjamin, was the son of Zimri and a descendant of King Saul. He is mentioned in Saul's genealogy and was the father of Binea (*1 Chron. 8:36–37; 9:42–43*).

**MUPPIM** Benjamin's eighth son who went to Egypt with him and became leader of a clan (*Gen. 46:21*). He is likely to be the same person as Shupham (*Num.*

*26:39*) and Shephuphan (*1 Chron. 8:5*).

**MUSHI** One of the sons of Merari and a grandson of Levi. Mushi became a clan leader of the Mushites (*Exod. 6:19; Num. 3:20; 26:58; 1 Chron. 6:19, 47; 24:26, 30*). The Merarites, of which their clan was a part, were responsible in the days of Moses for carrying the frames of the Tabernacle, its pegs, bases etc. (*Num. 4:29–33*). Mushi's descendants were given duties at the Tabernacle in the days of King David and later at the Temple during the reign of King Solomon (*1 Chron. 23:21, 23*).

# N

**NAAM** Mentioned in *1 Chron. 4:15* as the third of the sons of Caleb son of Jephunneh and a tribal leader of Judah.

**NAAMAH** (Heb., 'delightful').

**1.** The sister of Tubal-Cain and daughter of Zillah and Lamech (*Gen. 4:22*).

**2.** Naamah was an Ammonite and married to King Solomon. She was the mother of Rehoboam, who became king of Judah (*1 Kings 14:21, 31; 2 Chron. 12:13*).

**NAAMAN 1.** A 'son' of Benjamin and grandson of Jacob and Rachel. He was the founder of the Naamite clan, and went down to Egypt with Jacob (*Gen. 46:21; Num. 26:40; 1 Chron. 8:4*). In *Numbers* and *1 Chronicles* he is listed as the son of Bela, the son of Benjamin. While it is possible that there were two Naamans in two succeeding generations, the similarities in the other names suggest that the Genesis reference has missed a generation as often happens in Heb. genealogies.

**2.** A Benjamite and descendant of Ehud who was a head of a family in Geba (*1 Chron. 8:7*).

**3.** Naaman was a commander of the army of Syria (Aram) and had leprosy. *2 Kings 5* begins its account by relating that this great leader among his people had been given victory in battle by the LORD (*v. 1*). However, his leprosy would have alienated him from his people and he longed to be cured. His wife had an Israelite servant girl who had been captured in a raid by the Syrians, and the girl suggested that Naaman visit the prophet Elisha in Samaria. The king of Syria, who may have been Ben-hadad (*2 Kings 8:7*), agreed to Naaman visiting the prophet of Israel. When Naaman arrived with a letter of commendation from the king of Syria to the king of Israel (King Joram, *2 Kings 3:1?*), the Israelite king believed this was an attempt to provoke war because no one could cure leprosy (*2 Kings 5:7*). Elisha requested that Naaman be sent to him. When he arrived at Elisha's house in his chariots, Elisha simply sent a messenger out to Naaman to tell him to go and wash himself seven times in the river Jordan. Naaman was deeply offended at such cursory treatment but in due course his servants persuaded him to do what the prophet asked and so Naaman returned, dipped himself seven times in the Jordan, and was healed.

Naaman's response to his healing was deeply significant: 'Now I know that there is no God in all the world except in Israel . . . your servant will never again make burnt offerings and sacrifices to any other god but the LORD' (*vv. 15, 17*). His affirmation of the power and mercy of Yahweh (the LORD) led to him worshipping the LORD but also to asking for his forgiveness. In *v. 18* Naaman asked for forgiveness when the following day he would have to go, with his king leaning on his arm for support, into the temple of Rimmon and help the king bow down. He had realized that it was right only to worship the one true God. Elisha's response was 'Go in peace' (*v. 19*).

The fact that God healed someone who was not an Israelite and the fact that that person then acknowledged that Yahweh was the God to be worshipped even in Syria, draws attention to some basic teachings of the Bible. First, there is only one God in the world. Secondly, that God alone can save and forgive, something the Israelites themselves often forgot. Thirdly, that the LORD is free to work where he wills. And fourthly, that the LORD is merciful and will forgive anyone who turns to him, whatever their nationality or background.

The passage also gives an indication of the attitude that should be present in the one who desires to receive mercy and forgiveness. In this passage Naaman clearly changed from an arrogant commander, honoured by many in his own country and unable to consider washing himself in a rather dirty foreign river, to one who was prepared to humble himself before the LORD, and seek help and forgiveness. He returned home not just cured of his leprosy but with the peace of the LORD resting on him.

Such is the importance of this account in understanding that God offers salvation and forgiveness wherever he wills that Jesus referred to it right at the start of his public ministry in Luke 4:27. Preaching in the synagogue at Nazareth, he expounded Is. 61:1–2 in terms of his own presence among them. Knowing they would reject this message and that he would be 'a prophet without honour' among his own people, he rubbed salt into their wounds by suggesting that the Gospel would be given to others. Just as many lepers in Israel at the time of Naaman had not been healed while Naaman had, so these people would find the mercy and forgiveness of God in the gospel being offered elsewhere. Those who might have expected to receive it would be faced with a sovereign God who would show mercy where he willed. The crowd 'were furious when they heard this', and showed their rejection of Jesus and his message by seeking to kill him. God's freedom to bring mercy, love and forgiveness where he wills is

fundamental to a biblical understanding of the nature of God himself.

See also the article on Gehazi who tried to exact a payment out of Naaman when Elisha had refused Naaman's offers of a gift. Gehazi ended up suffering with the same leprosy as Naaman had had.

P.D.G.

**NAARAH** One of Ashhur's two wives. Her sons by Ashhur were Ahuzzam, Hepher, Temeni and Haahashtari, who were leaders in the tribe of Judah (1 Chron. 4:5–6).

**NAARAI** son of Ezbai belonged to David's 'Thirty' mighty men who went to battle for him and led the people of Israel to war (1 Chron. 11:37). In the parallel passage it would seem the same person is called Paarai the Arbite (2 Sam. 23:35).

**NABAL** (Heb., 'fool'). The meaning of Nabal's name (1 Sam. 25:25) was particularly suitable, given his foolish refusal to give due respect to David, king of Israel. He was a descendant of Caleb, but showed little of his forefather's discipline or wisdom (1 Sam. 25:3, 36).

The account of Nabal's folly in 1 Sam. 25 is tempered by the wisdom of Abigail who showed the courtesy and kindness due to the king's men. Nabal had no allegiance to David and knew nothing of his LORD (vv. 10–11). He refused to help feed David and his men in spite of his great wealth (v. 2). By way of contrast, Abigail evidently was a true believer and acted wisely (vv. 26–34). David prepared to march against Nabal with 400 men but he was appeased by Abigail's hospitality which should have been freely offered by Nabal in the first place. Nabal's death from heart failure when he heard of his wife's action illustrates the fact that the end of sin is death. The final folly of Nabal was to fail to realize that Abigail acted more wisely and graciously than he. She alone had asked for David's forgiveness and had recognized the presence of the LORD in all he did (*vv. 28–31*).  s.v.

**NABOTH** lived in the time of King Ahab of Israel (c. 874–852 BC). The account of his relationship with the king is found in *1 Kings 21*. Naboth, who came from Jezreel, owned a vineyard close to the palace. The king offered to buy the vineyard from Naboth or replace it with a better one elsewhere. Naboth refused on the grounds that it was part of his family's inheritance. His appeal to the LORD (*v. 3*) probably showed that he had in mind the prohibition of such sales under God's Law (*Lev. 25:23–28*). When the king's wife, Jezebel, saw the king was upset about this incident she drew up an evil scheme to obtain the land. She organized a feast day and had Naboth seated prominently at the feast. Two false witnesses were seated next to him and accused him of cursing God and the king. Naboth was then taken outside the city and stoned to death along with his sons (*1 Kings 21:13–14; 2 Kings 9:26*).

After Naboth's death Jezebel encouraged Ahab to possess the vineyard. He went to the vineyard where he was met by Elijah who had been sent there by God. Elijah prophesied to Ahab: 'This is what the LORD says: In the place where dogs licked up Naboth's blood, dogs will lick up your blood – yes, yours!' (*1 Kings 21:19*). The prophet warned of total destruction on Ahab and his house. As a result Ahab 'humbled himself' (*v. 29*) and the LORD relented and promised the disaster would be delayed. The LORD's word came true when Ahab was killed in battle at Ramoth-Gilead (*1 Kings 22:34–38*) and his body was brought back to Samaria where 'the dogs licked up his blood' (*v. 38*). Later Jehu killed Ahab's son, Joram, and had his body taken to Naboth's vineyard, thus fulfilling a further piece of the prophecy against Ahab and his family (*2 Kings 9:26*). Jehu then went to the palace and killed Jezebel

by throwing her from a palace window. When they came to bury her, dogs had already devoured her, so that they said, 'This is the word of the LORD that he spoke through his servant Elijah the Tishbite: On the plot of ground at Jezreel dogs will devour Jezebel's flesh' (*v. 36*).

The awesome nature of God's judgment against those who break his Law or who kill those who serve him is seen in several places in Scripture, but in few places is the detail of the fulfilment of the judgment as explicit as in this sad episode. The account served as a reminder for the Israelites of the LORD's judgment, his defence of the rights of the poor and humble and, above all, of the permanency and truth of his word that will always be carried through.  p. d. g.

**NACON** (Heb., 'correct'). The owner of a threshing floor past which the ark of the covenant travelled when David was bringing it from Baalah of Judah to Jerusalem. The oxen pulling the cart on which the ark was placed stumbled (*2 Sam. 6:6*). Uzzah put out his hand to steady the cart and touched the ark, something which everyone had been strictly forbidden to do. As a result God 'struck him down and he died' (*v. 7*).

**NADAB** (Heb., 'willing').
**1.** Nadab was the first son of Aaron and his wife Elisheba and brother of Abihu, Eleazar and Ithamar (*Exod. 6:23; Num. 3:2; 26:60; 1 Chron. 6:3; 24:1–2*). At the time of the confirmation of God's covenant with Israel, he was among the 70 elders of Israel who 'saw the God of Israel' when they went part way up Sinai (only Moses approached the LORD; *Exod. 24:1, 9* etc.). With Aaron and his brothers he was appointed a priest to serve the LORD and special garments were made for him (*Exod. 28:1–2*). As a priest he was to be holy and set apart to the service of the LORD.

Time and again in the organization of

the priesthood 'holiness' was stressed as of the essence of Israelite worship. God was 'holy' and therefore he could not be approached by the people. Any worship of God had to be a response to his commands and thus fulfil requirements of holiness. Sadly Nadab and his brother Abihu later were put to death for offering an 'unauthorized fire before the LORD, contrary to his command' (Lev. 10:1; Num. 26:61). The penalty for compromising the holiness of God was death. Since neither had sons, 'only Eleazar and Ithamar served as priests during the lifetime of their father Aaron' (Num. 3:4).

**2.** Nadab the son of Jeroboam I of Israel reigned in Israel for just two years (1 Kings 15:25) before being murdered by Baasha (c. 910 BC). He was the second king of the Northern Kingdom following the division of the monarchy and was as evil as his father, following in the same path of idolatry and evil (v. 26). Baasha attacked and killed Nadab while the latter was leading the Israelites in a siege of a Philistine town called Gibbethon (vv. 27–28). Although the LORD used Baasha to bring judgment on the house of Jeroboam because of that king's dreadful idolatry and sin, nevertheless Baasha did not follow the LORD but continued to do 'evil in the eyes of the LORD, walking in the ways of his father and in his sin, which he had caused Israel to commit' (v. 34).

**3.** A son of Shammai and brother to Abishur. This Nadab was from the tribe of Judah and appears in the genealogy of Jerahmeel. His sons were Seled and Appaim (1 Chron. 2:28, 30).

**4.** Mentioned in 1 Chron. 8:30 and 9:36, this was one of the sons of Jeiel, a Benjamite, and his wife Maacah. He is listed in the genealogy leading from Benjamin to Saul.                     P.D.G.

**NAGGAI** An ancestor of Jesus listed in the genealogy from Jesus to Adam. He

was the son of Maath and the father of Esli (Luke 3:25).

**NAHAM** (Heb., 'comfort'). The brother of Hodiah's wife and one of the leader's of the tribe of Judah (1 Chron. 4:19).

**NAHAMANI** (Heb., 'the LORD comforts') was one of the Israelites who returned to Jerusalem with Nehemiah and Zerubbabel after the captivity in Babylon (Neh. 7:7).

**NAHARAI** Mentioned in 2 Sam. 23:37 and 1 Chron. 11:39, Naharai was one of David's 'Thirty' mighty men who were warriors fighting at his side. He is particularly noted for being the armour-bearer for Joab, David's army commander.

**NAHASH** (Heb., 'serpent').

**1.** Nahash was an Ammonite leader whose attempt to conquer the Israelites led to them demanding a king for themselves. This had been forbidden the Israelites, for God alone was to be their king (see 1 Sam. 8:6–7; 12:12). Nahash's attack on the city of Jabesh Gilead in fact led to Saul being confirmed by the people as king of Israel (1 Sam. 11). When Nahash besieged the city, the men of Jabesh-Gilead sued for peace. Nahash was prepared to make a treaty subject to each man having his right eye gouged out. The elders of the city asked for seven days grace to consider the matter while they sent messengers round Israel seeking help. When Saul heard the news, he was just returning from his fields with his oxen. Immediately 'the Spirit of God came upon him in power, and he burned with anger' (1 Sam. 11:6). He mustered 330,000 men. They attacked the Ammonites, killing virtually all of them.

While Saul had been made king some time previously (1 Sam. 10), some had questioned his right to that position and he had clearly not established himself and so remained working at home. This victory led to a public affirmation of his kingship at Gilgal (1 Sam. 11:15). At this early stage in Saul's kingship he sought the LORD and found success in battle. He gave thanks to the LORD for his victory, saying, 'this day the LORD has rescued Israel' (v. 13). Sadly, he was later to turn far from the LORD and the Spirit left him (1 Sam. 16;14).

Later, in 2 Sam. 10:1–2 we read of Nahash's death (also 1 Chron. 19:1–2). It is clear from that text that King David had had better relations with the Ammonites than Saul had. As a result David wanted to show kindness to Nahash's son, Hanun. This kindness was rejected and war ensued which David won. On another occasion Shobi, Nahash's son, showed David kindness when he was fleeing from Absalom (2 Sam. 17:27).

**2.** The father of Abigail who had married Jether. Abigail is identified as the sister of Zeruiah the mother of Joab. Jether was the father of Amasa, Absalom's commander in chief (2 Sam. 17:25). In 1 Chron. 2:16–17 the two women are identified as sisters of David, but David's father was Jesse not Nahash. Perhaps Nahash was the first husband of David's mother and therefore that these women were step-sisters to David.    P. D. G.

**NAHATH 1.** A grandson of Esau and Basemath, Nahath was the son of Reuel and an Edomite clan chief (Gen. 36:13, 17; 1 Chron. 1:37).

**2.** A descendant of Kohath and a Levite. His father was Zophai and his son Eliab. This Nahath was an ancestor of Samuel (1 Chron. 6:26).

**3.** One of the Levites who were supervisors of tithes and offerings brought by the people. As a result of the extraordinary revival under King Hezekiah, so many offerings, gifts and tithes were brought to the Temple that special storehouses had to be prepared. Nahath was one of a number of Levites chosen, under the leadership of Conaniah and Shimei, to organize the storage of what was given (2 Chron. 31:13).

**NAHBI** One of the twelve spies sent out by Moses from the Desert of Paran to spy out the land of Canaan (Num. 13:14). A representative of each tribe was chosen and Nahbi, the son of Vophsi, was from the tribe of Naphtali. For further detail on their mission see *Shammua*.

**NAHOR 1.** Nahor was the son of Serug. At the age of 29 Nahor became the father of Terah and thus was the grandfather of Abraham (Gen. 11:22–26; 1 Chron. 1:26). No further information is given but his name does appear again in the genealogy of *Luke 3:34* which leads back from Jesus and Joseph to Adam.

**2.** Nahor, the brother of Abraham, was the grandson of the above (Gen. 11:27). Little further is known about him except that he married Milcah (v. 29) and continued to live in Mesopotamia where his sons were born (Gen. 22:20–24; 24:10). He also had a concubine called Reumah. Abraham and Nahor apparently kept in touch (22:20–24) so that presently Abraham's servant could seek a wife for Isaac in Nahor's family (Rebekah, 24:15, 24) and Jacob in turn could do the same (Rachel and Leah, 29:5). Gen. 31:53 suggests that Nahor shared with Abraham a personal faith in the true God.    J. A. M.

**NAHSHON** was the son of Amminadab and father of Salmon, an ancestor of Boaz and King David, and therefore is mentioned in the genealogies of Christ in the NT (Ruth 4:20; 1 Chron. 2:10–11; Matt. 1:4; Luke 3:32). He was the leader of the people of Judah in Moses' time and represented them at the time of the census (Num. 1:7). When instructions were given about how and where each tribe was to camp in relation to the Tabernacle (Tent of Meeting), Judah was to camp on the east with Nahshon at the head of a division of 74,600 people (Num. 2:3–4).

At the dedication of the Tabernacle, Nahshon brought the offerings of his tribe on the first day of celebration (*Num. 7:12, 17*). When the Israelites finally moved on from Sinai, Nahshon was again at the head of his people (*Num. 10:14*). His sister was Elisheba who married Aaron (*Exod. 6:23*)                    P. D. G.

**NAHUM** **1.** The name comes from the Heb. 'comfort, comforter', derived from the verb, 'to be sorry, to repent'. This man of God, unknown except through the testimony of the composition that bears his name, is described as 'an Elkoshite' (*Nah. 1:1*), that is, a native of the village of Elkosh. Unfortunately, despite several proposed identifications of the site it has been impossible so far to locate the town. It would appear to be reasonable to assume that Elkosh was somewhere in Judah since the prophet seems to have had Judah's (and Jerusalem's) well being in mind and in a way suggestive of close proximity (*Nah. 1:12–13, 15*).

Nahum shares with Jonah the fact that his oracle is addressed not directly to Israel or Judah but to Nineveh (*Nah. 1:1, 11; 2:1; 3:1*). Unlike Jonah, however, there is no evidence that Nahum travelled there to deliver his oracle of judgment. How the message arrived at Nineveh (if, indeed, it did at all) is not related. Perhaps it was intended more for local consumption in order to impress upon the prophet's hearers and readers that the LORD (Yahweh) is the Sovereign of all nations, even those that are powerful and threatening.

Though the date of Nahum's ministry is much debated, clues within the book suggest the middle and latter 7th century (c. 663–612 BC). Clearly, Nineveh still stood in Nahum's time, though its demise appears imminent (*cf. Nah. 1:15; 2:1, 3–13*). The city fell to the Babylonians by 612 BC so, if the book is to be viewed as predictive at all, Nahum spoke prior to that date. On the other hand, the prophet reflects back upon the conquest of No Amon (Thebes) by the Assyrians as an example of the fate awaiting Nineveh herself (*Nah. 3:8*). This occurred in 663 BC and appears to be an event somewhat remote from the prophet's own setting. A date of 615–612 BC seems likely.

Another difference between the message to or concerning Nineveh by Jonah and Nahum respectively is that Nineveh repented in Jonah's time (*Jon. 3:5–10;*), but there was no repentance at Nahum's preaching. Indeed, there is no hint that such a thing was even possible, for the book ends with the sombre note that Nineveh's condition was hopelessly incurable (*Nah. 3:18–19*). In both cases, however, the LORD showed his dominion over the nations of earth, either in their submission to him or destruction by him.        E. M.

**2.** Another Nahum is mentioned in the genealogy of Jesus in *Luke 3:25*. He was the son of Esli and the father of Amos.

**NAOMI** is best known as Ruth's mother-in-law (*Ruth 1*). Naomi was married to Elimelech and they had two sons, Mahlon and Kilion. During a famine in Judah, Elimelech took his family to live in Moab so that he could provide for them there. When Elimelech died, Naomi and her two sons stayed in Moab where the boys married Moabite women, Ruth and Orpah. After living in Moab for about ten years, Mahlon and Kilion also died, and Naomi was left without husband and without sons. Naomi saw no hope for herself and no happiness ahead, and so decided to return to Judah. It was Naomi's desire that both Ruth and Orpah stay in their home country of Moab, but Ruth would not hear of such a plan. Instead, Ruth clung to Naomi with the words of commitment we have heard so many times: 'Where you go, I will go and where you stay I will stay. Your people will be my people and your God my God' (*Ruth 1:16*). Naomi accepted Ruth's devotion and the two women found themselves in the field of Boaz and, later, in his family. Ruth married Boaz. Boaz 'redeemed' Naomi's rightful inheritance of land, and Ruth bore the child who became the father of Jesse, the father of David. Naomi indeed had hope, and God provided. See *Ruth 1–4*. See also *Maria, Ruth and Boaz*.

**NAPHISH** A son of Ishmael and grandson of Abraham and Hagar, he was a leader of his clan (*Gen. 25:15; 1 Chron. 1:31*). The name occurs again as one of the family names of the Hagrites (descendants of Hagar and Ishmael), who were defeated by a coalition of the tribes of Reuben, Gad and Manasseh (*1 Chron. 5:19*).

**NAPHTALI** (Heb., 'my wrestling'). This son of Jacob was the second born to Bilhah, the maidservant of Rachel. He received his name, according to the narrative (*Gen. 30:8*), because Rachel saw in the birth a sign that God had given her the advantage in her struggle with her antagonistic sister Leah. Following Naphtali's birth, Rachel was able to have two sons of her own, Joseph and Benjamin.

Naphtali never appears later as an indi-vidual except in the blessings of Jacob and Moses and there only as the patronym of the tribe that later bore his name. Jacob, somewhat opaquely, refers to Naphtali as 'a doe set free' (*Gen. 49:21*) whereas Moses, speaking of the tribe's anticipated favour and prosperity, specifies that his territorial allocation will be 'southward to the lake' (*Deut. 33:23*). The actual settlement later suggests that the lake in question was Galilee, for Naphtali lay to the north and north-west of that lake.

Isaiah, in one of his most glorious messianic prophecies, looked to a time when gloom and sorrow would be replaced by the radiant light of the good news of salvation (*Is. 9:1–7*). The land of Zebulun and Naphtali would especially benefit, and one cannot escape the significance of the life and labours of Christ in that area as a fulfilment of the prophetic hope (*cf. Matt. 4:12–16*).   E.M.

**NARCISSUS** This Roman citizen is mentioned by Paul in *Rom. 16:11*, where his household is greeted. The fact that he personally is not greeted may suggest that only other members of his family or perhaps some of his slaves were Christians.

## NATHAN, THE PROPHET

Nathan, the prophet, served the LORD during the reign of King David and survived well into the reign of King Solomon. He figured prominently on three important occasions in David's life.

In the first passage (*2 Sam. 7*; see also *1 Chron. 17*), David had just finished building his palace. He had been greatly blessed by God and decided that the ark of the covenant, which still sat in a tent, should have a permanent home. He consulted Nathan, who agreed that the LORD was with him and David should do whatever he wanted. Perhaps Nathan had got used to God blessing anything David set his mind to, but the night after this interchange the LORD spoke to him and told him that David was not to be the one to build the Temple and that the LORD had never asked for such a building (*2 Sam. 7:5–7*). The same prophecy, however, brought David the most wonderful statement of God's covenant love for him, in which the LORD promised David his name would be great (*v. 9*), his people would have peace, and his son would build a 'House for my Name'. The throne and kingdom of David and his son would then be established forever (*v. 13*). In *v. 14* the LORD said: 'I will be his father, and he shall be my son'. God went on to say that his love would remain on David's house and kingdom forever (vv. 15–16).

This message eventually became the basis for messianic expectation and has become known as the 'Davidic covenant'. Later generations looked for the coming of a Davidic king whose throne would be established forever (e.g. *Is. 9:6–7; 11:1–3; Jer. 23:5–6* etc.). Eventually, the fulfilment of this was seen in Scripture with the coming of Jesus as the Messiah and 'son of David' (*Matt. 1:1; 12:23; 22:42; Mark 12:35; Rom. 1:3; Rev. 5:5; 22:16* etc.). For David, who could not see even a little of the glory in store, the promises were still overwhelming and his prayer of praise and thanksgiving at this message brought by Nathan is recorded in *2 Sam. 7:18–29*.

Sadly, David's next recorded encounter with Nathan was not so pleasant (*2 Sam. 12*). David had recently committed adultery with Bathsheba and had arranged the death of her husband, Uriah. Nathan was sent by the LORD to David with a parable. A poor man had one ewe lamb. A rich man had great flocks of sheep. A traveller came to the rich man who prepared a meal for him. The rich man took the ewe lamb from the poor man rather than use one of his own for the meal. David heard the story and said to Nathan: 'As surely as the LORD lives, the man who did this deserves to die!' (*v. 5*). 'Then Nathan said to David, "You are the man!"' (*v. 7*). The judgment of God on David, pronounced by Nathan, was that his wives would be taken by someone else and the child of this union with Bathsheba would die. Also David's house would find themselves continually at war. David recognized the point of the parable: in spite of all he had, he had taken the wife of a man who had so little. He then repented of his sin (*2 Sam. 12:13;* see *Ps. 51*). The LORD forgave him (*2 Sam. 12:13*), but the consequences of his sin meant that subsequently the child born to him and Bathesheba died (*v. 15*). The sign of his forgiveness came later when David and Bathsheba had another son who became Solomon, the inheritor of the promises of *2 Sam. 7*. Nathan brought word from the LORD that he should be called Jedidiah (*2 Sam. 12:25*) because the LORD loved him.

The third time Nathan figured prominently in David's life was right at the end (*1 Kings 1*). God had made it clear that Solomon was to inherit the throne from his father. When another of David's sons, Adonijah, tried to usurp the throne, Nathan supported David rather than Adonijah. He informed Bathsheba of the plot (*vv. 8, 11*) and advised her on how to ensure the right succession (*vv. 12–14*). Nathan was called in by David and told to anoint Solomon king. This he did and it was proclaimed to the people (*vv. 22–45*).

The only other information we have about the prophet is that he kept records of the events of David's and Solomon's reign (*1 Chron. 29:29; 2 Chron. 9:29*) and that he must have given some instructions concerning music in the Temple worship (*2 Chron. 29:25*).

**NATHAN** (Heb., 'gift').

**1.** See *Nathan, the Prophet*.

**2.** A son of King David, born in Jerusalem. His mother was Bathsheba (*2 Sam. 5:14; 1 Chron. 3:5; 14:4*). This Nathan is mentioned again in a messianic passage in *Zech. 12:12* which looks forward to the day when David's and Nathan's descendants will, with weeping, seek the LORD's forgiveness for the way they have pierced him. Nathan is also listed as David's son in Luke's genealogy leading from Jesus and Joseph back to Adam (Luke 3:31).

**3.** This Nathan, from Zobah, was the father of Igal who was one of David's 'mighty men' (2 Sam. 23:36).

**4.** This Nathan may have been the same as 2. above. He was the brother of Joel one of David's 'Thirty' mighty men (1 Chron. 11:38).

**5.** This Nathan was father to two of Solomon's many important officials. His son Azariah was in charge of the district officers and his son Zabud was a priest and personal adviser to the king (1 Kings 4:5). This list of officials helps emphasize the stability and grandeur of Israel under Solomon's rule.

**6.** Mentioned in 1 Chron. 2:36, he was the father of Zabad and son of Attai. He was a descendant of Judah.

**7.** One of the Jews, a leader among his people, who joined Ezra on their return from the Babylonian captivity to Jerusalem. He helped Ezra find suitable Levites to accompany them back to Judah (Ezra 8:16).

**8.** This Nathan was among the descendants of Binnui. At the time of return from the Exile in Babylon, Shecaniah confessed to Ezra that many men and even descendants of the priests of Judah had married wives from other tribes and nations. Ezra and the people repented and made a covenant to serve the LORD (Ezra 10:2). Nathan is listed in Ezra 10:39 as one who divorced his foreign wife.

P.D.G.

**NATHANAEL** (Heb., 'God has given'). Nathanael is only mentioned in John's Gospel and was a disciple of Jesus from the earliest days. John 21:2 says he came from Cana in Galilee and counts him among the witnesses of the resurrection. John 1:45–49 recounts how he was brought to Jesus by Philip. Nathanael's first reaction, knowing Jesus' home town, was to question whether anything good could come from Nazareth. When Jesus saw him he said: 'Here is a true Israelite, in whom there is nothing false.' Immediately Nathanael perceived that Jesus knew him and so he asked him how this could be. Jesus answered, 'I saw you while you were still under the fig tree before Philip called you.' What follows is surprising for its lack of explanation or detail. Nathanael's response was extraordinary: 'Rabbi, you are the Son of God; you are the King of Israel.'

The brief explanation given for this demonstration of his belief in Jesus is found in John 1:50. Jesus said: 'You believe because I told you I saw you under the fig tree. You shall see greater things than that.' We have no information on Nathanael's experience under the fig tree, or why Jesus' knowledge of it should make such an impact on him. Some have suggested he was meditating on messianic Scriptures or even on the story of Jacob and the ladder with angels ascending and descending, a reference Jesus picked up in v. 51. Perhaps it was a combination of knowing that Jesus had miraculous knowledge of him as a person, together with Philip's introduction, 'We have found the one Moses wrote about in the Law, and about whom the prophets also wrote – Jesus of Nazareth, the son of Joseph.' Or perhaps there was more to the conversation than we are told. Whatever the detail and background of this explicit statement of faith from Nathanael, the Gospel writer uses it as a clear example of the sort of confession that he wants all his readers to acknowledge. Throughout his Gospel, John emphasizes the need for true belief in Jesus that involves commitment to him as the 'Son of God' (see John 20:31 for his stated reason for writing the Gospel, also 11:27). Nathanael was the first who is said to 'believe' and second only to John the Baptist (John 1:34) in calling Jesus the 'son of God', he thus became an example of the response expected from a devout Jew confronted with his Messiah king.

Attempts to identify Nathanael as one of the twelve disciples, known elsewhere by a different name, are at best simply speculative.                                    P. D. G.

**NATHAN-MELECH** (Heb., 'the king gives'). An official in the kingdom of Judah in the days of King Josiah. He had a room near the entrance to the Temple (*2 Kings 23:11*). During the revival of true worship under King Josiah, Josiah removed and burned the statues of horses and chariots which had been dedicated to the sun by previous evil kings of Judah. These had been placed near to Nathan-Melech's room.

**NAZARENE** This name appears three times in the Gospels (NIV) and is applied to Jesus (*Matt. 2:23; Mark 14:67; 16:6*). In *Acts 24:5* it is used by the lawyer Tertullus at Paul's trial before Felix as a description of a sect Paul was supposed to lead, in other words, to describe the Christians.

The origin of the word has long been debated. It probably arose quite simply because Jesus was known to come from Nazareth. The phrase 'of Nazareth' to describe Jesus occurs more frequently (in the NIV, 17 times in the Gospels and Acts). The fact that Nazareth was somewhat despised in those days (*John 1:46*) may indicate the disdain that came to be attached to the word towards the end of Jesus' ministry, for example, in its use in *Mark 16:6*. Indeed this may help explain the use of the word Nazarene in *Matt. 2:23* where Scriptures are 'fulfilled' to the effect that Jesus 'will be called a Nazarene'.

Matthew does go on to describe the way Jesus was despised by those around (*Matt. 11:16–19; 12:14, 24; 15:7–8*). The association of Nazareth, the place Jesus came from, with that which was despised probably helped Matthew see more deeply the fulfilment of all the prophecies that suggested a despised and rejected Messiah (e.g. *Is. 49:7; 53:3; Ps. 22:6–7;*

etc.). Hence the reference to fulfilment of prophecy: not necessarily that the prophets said the Messiah would come from Nazareth, so much as the fact that they did say he would be despised, as a person from Nazareth was in Matthew's day.                                    P. D. G.

**NAZIRITE** (Heb., 'consecrated'). 'Nazirite' was a term applied to a man or woman who took a particular set of special vows 'of separation to the LORD'. *Num. 6:1–21* describes these vows in some detail. Such a person had to abstain from alcohol and not eat anything that came from the grapevine. No razor was to touch his head and his hair was to grow long as a mark of his holiness and separation to the LORD. He was not to go near a dead body. Rules were also given so that, should he accidentally be contaminated, he would know what offerings needed to be made for atonement. A Nazirite had to present special offerings at the Tent of Meeting (Tabernacle). When he had finished his period of the vow, again he had to make a special offering and ceremonially shave his hair which itself became part of the offering. After that he was free to drink alcohol again.

The purpose of the vow was no doubt to offer more serious and committed service to the LORD for a period of time, perhaps as part of presenting a request to God or as part of offering thanks to God for his blessings. Either way the vow would have been linked to seeking God's blessing on the individual or community.

In the OT there are not many references to Nazirites. The only unambiguous one is to Samson who was designated by God a Nazirite from birth. It is interesting to note that the presence of God's Spirit with him was linked directly to his adherence to the rules of the vow (*Judg. 13:5, 7, 25; 16:17*). He was only captured by the Philistines when, eventually, his hair was cut off. As the hair gradually grew back and he prayed again to the LORD so his strength returned (*Judg. 16:22, 28*).

The prophet Amos looked back at the Nazirites as great people whom the LORD had raised up but whom Israel had perverted by making them drink wine. In other words, the loss of Nazirites and the perversion of their values and commitment became symptomatic of Israel's rejection of God and loss of holiness (*Amos 2:11–12*).

Although the word 'Nazirite' is not used of Samuel, it would seem that he too, like Samson, was committed by his mother to be a Nazirite for life (*1 Sam. 1:11*). Again, although not identified as a Nazirite, John the Baptist seems to have taken this vow in the way he lived and as such was specifically contrasted in his behaviour with Jesus who did come drinking wine (*Matt. 11:18–19*). The apostle Paul may have ended a Nazirite vow when he had his hair cut off at Cenchrea (*Acts 18:18*).          P.D.G.

**NEARIAH 1.** Mentioned in *1 Chron. 3:22–23* as a descendant of Shecaniah and son of Shemaiah. He was one of the royal line from Jehoiachin following the Exile. He had three sons.

**2.** A Simeonite who was the son of Ishi and lived in the time of King Hezekiah of Judah. He helped lead an invasion of the hill country of Seir (to the east of the Dead Sea), killing the remaining Amalekites. His people then settled the area (*1 Chron. 4:42–43*).

**NEBAI** was a leader of a family who returned with his descendants to Jerusalem following the Exile in Babylon. Under the direction of Nehemiah, he signed the agreement of the people to obey the Law of the LORD and worship only him (*Neh. 10:19*).

**NEBAIOTH** The first son of Ishmael and a tribal leader (*Gen. 25:13; 1 Chron. 1:29*).

One of his sisters, Mahalath, married Esau (*Gen. 28:9; also see 36:3*). In Isaiah's prophecy of the glorious future for God's people (*Is. 60:7*), the flocks and rams of Ishmael's sons Kedar and Nebaioth are to be brought into the service of the LORD as offerings, fulfilling the earlier prophecies that Ishmael's descendants would serve the descendants of Isaac.

**NEBAT** whose name appears many times in *1 Kings, 2 Kings* and *2 Chronicles*, was the father of Jeroboam I. The name always appears in the phrase 'Jeroboam son of Nebat' and was probably used in order to distinguish Jeroboam I (the first king of Israel after the kingdom divided) from Jeroboam II, who was the son of Joash and the 13th king of Israel.

**NEBO 1.** Nebo was one of the two most important gods in Babylon in the days of the prophet Isaiah and later at the time of the Babylonian invasion of Judah and the captivity. He had been a god of the Assyrians as well, and was considered to be a god of wisdom and writing. In *Is. 46:1* the prophet refers to the image of Nebo 'stooping low', using it as a picture of the eventual fall of the Babylonian empire.

**2.** The descendants of Nebo were among those who returned from the Exile in Babylon. Some of these had married foreign wives and, under Ezra's direction, decided to divorce them (*Ezra 10:43*).

**NEBO-SARSEKIM** One of Nebuchadnezzar king of Babylon's officials who entered Jerusalem when the walls were finally breached and the Babylonian forces invaded the city. With his colleagues he took up a position in the Middle Gate (*Jer. 39:3*). When King Zedekiah saw what had happend he fled, only to be captured quickly by the Babylonians. In some versions his name is simply Sarsekim. (See also *Nergal-Sharezer*).

**NEBUCHADNEZZAR** (Aram. and Heb., 'Oh Nabu [a Babylonian god], protect my son [or my boundary]'). Nebuchadnezzar was the second, and greatest, king of the Neo-Babylonian Empire. His name is found in the Bible in the books of 2 Kings, 2 Chronicles, Ezra, Jeremiah, Ezekiel, and Daniel. Nebuchadnezzar was the son of Nabopolassar (whose name is not mentioned in the Bible), the founder of the Babylonian dynasty that eclipsed the Assyrian Empire in 612 BC. He was crown prince and commander of the Babylonian army that defeated the forces of Pharaoh Neco of Egypt. In 605 BC, around the time that his army invaded Judah, initially capturing Jerusalem, Nebuchadnezzar became king upon his father's death. He may have been co-regent for a period of time before that.

As King, Nebuchadnezzar ruled until 562 BC, well over half the duration of the Babylonian dominance (612–539 BC). He was a great administrator and is credited with much of the splendour of the city of Babylon, including the Hanging Gardens, one of the wonders of the ancient world. After his death, the power of Babylon declined until its final defeat by the Medo-Persian alliance in 539 BC.

The references to Nebuchadnezzar's name in the largely parallel historical narrative in 2 Kings 24–25 and 2 Chron. 36 have to do with the various phases of his conquest and destruction of Judah (605, 597, 586 BC). The description of the final Babylonian attack speaks of the contents of the Temple being taken to Babylon before it was levelled and burned (2 Chron. 36:18–19). Virtually all Jews that did not die in the conflict were deported into Exile in Babylon (v. 20).

Twice his name appears in Jeremiah (25:9–11; 27:6) in prophecies of the Exile of Judah to Nebuchadnezzar's Babylon. The specific length of the period is mentioned: 70 years (25:9). The name also appears in Jer. 39, which tells of Nebuchadnezzar's decision to leave the prophet Jeremiah in Jerusalem (vv. 1, 5, 11). The references to Nebuchadnezzar in Ezekiel all have to do with prophecies of his victories over Tyre (Ezek. 26:7; 29:18) and Egypt (29:19, 30:10). In all these various historical and prophetic uses, it becomes clear that even a world ruler like Nebuchadnezzar is used to accomplish the sovereign purposes of the LORD God in history, especially his judgment.

The clearest biblical picture of Nebuchadnezzar's personality and response to the LORD is seen in the book of Daniel. Only Dan. 1–4 occurs during Nebuchadnezzar's lifetime, though there is reference back to the events of Dan. 4 in Dan. 5. The portrait that emerges is of a highly intelligent and sophisticated monarch (1:18–20), but equally of an angry despot (2:12, 3:13) whose ego was as vast as his power (4:30).

It is quite possible that Nebuchadnezzar became a full-fledged believer in the LORD God of Israel before the end of his life. His promotion of Daniel and his friends, Shadrach, Meshach and Abednego was in tanden with praise of God as the 'recreator of mysteries' (Dan. 2:47). After the fiery furnace episode, the King again expressed praise and decreed that no one could speak against the Jewish God (Dan. 3:29). Finally, after being reduced to an animal-like state because of his pride (Dan. 4:32), Nebuchadnezzar was restored (v. 34) and recognized and glorified the LORD as the ultimate King over heaven and earth (vv. 35–37). If this progression does not represent conversion, it at least clearly contrasts with the proud spiritual dullness of the last king of Babylon, Belshazzar (Dan. 5:18–23).

In historical sequence the latest reference to Nebuchadnezzar is in Ezra 5:12. There a letter from the Medo-Persian governor refers back to 'Nebuchadnezzar the Chaldean, King of Babylon'. The term 'Chaldean' probably refers to his family's geographical origins in southern Mesopotamia (i.e. Chaldea; see *Gen. 11:28*).                                       A.B.L.

**NEBUSHAZBAN** (Heb., Nabu [a Babylonian god] deliver me'). A 'chief officer' among the officials of Nebuchadnezzar king of Babylon. He was among those who entered Jerusalem when the walls were finally breached and the Babylonian forces invaded the city. With his colleagues he was instructed by Nebuchadnezzar to ensure that no harm came to the prophet Jeremiah. So the officials took Jeremiah and handed him to Gedaliah for safe-keeping (*Jer. 39:13*).

**NEBUZARADAN** (Heb., 'Nabu has given offspring'). The commander of the imperial guard under King Nebuchadnezzar of Babylon (*2 Kings 25:8*). He was charged with the final destruction of Jerusalem, burning down the Temple and houses and destroying the walls of the city. He then deported most of the remaining inhabitants of the area to Babylon, where he took them to the King at Riblah (*vv. 9–12, 20*). The account of the fall of Jerusalem and the role of Nebuzaradan is also given in *Jer. 39:8–13; 52:12–27*. One of his duties was to ensure the protection of the prophet Jeremiah. This he did by turning him over to the safe custody of Gedaliah, the governor of Judah appointed by the Babylonians (*Jer. 39:13–14*).

*Jer. 40* records that Nebuzaradan had found Jeremiah in chains and had had him released. The treatment accorded to Jeremiah was remarkable, perhaps largely due to the fact that he had prophesied what would happen and had warned the people not to resist the deportation to Babylon (e.g. *Jer. 38:17–28*). However, the events also reveal the sovereignty of the LORD in the way he used the Babylonians not only for judgment on his people but also to save his prophet from

death. Nebuzaradan himself seems to have recognized something of how the LORD was using him and his army in this process (*40:2–5*).

On this first occasion of Nebuzaradan's work in Jerusalem some of the poorest were left to till the fields and work the vineyards (*39:10*). Four years later he returned again and carried off to Babylon another 745 people (*52:30*).      P.D.G.

**NECO** Pharaoh Neco king of Egypt is referred to in *2 Kings 23* and its parallel in *2 Chron. 35–36*. He was the second king of the 26th dynasty.

In 609 BC the extent of Neco's influence north from Egypt was very considerable and *2 Kings 23:29* records that he set out to travel all the way to the Euphrates in order to help the king of Assyria defeat Babylon. It was on this journey that King Josiah led his troops out to meet Neco at Megiddo. The Chronicler records that Neco did not want a fight with Josiah and told Josiah that what he was doing was at God's command (*2 Chron. 35:21–22*). Josiah was killed during the battle and Jehoahaz, his son was made king. Unlike his father, who had served the LORD 'with all his heart' (*2 Kings 23:25*), Jehoahaz 'did evil in the eyes of the LORD' and, in judgment from God, he was taken prisoner and carried off to Egypt where he died (*vv. 31–35*). Neco took another of Josiah's sons, Eliakim (Jehoiakim) and made him a vassal king, exacting heavy dues from Jerusalem and Judah.

In 605 BC Nebuchadnezzar king of Babylon defeated Neco at Carchemish on the Euphrates River. This incident is referred to in *Jer. 46:2* at the start of a prophecy against Egypt in whch Jeremiah foresaw the defeat of Neco at the hands of the Babylonians. After this, Jehoiakim had to begin paying dues to Nebuchadnezzar instead of to Egypt (*2 Kings 24:1*). In his prophecy about God's judgment on the Philistines, Jeremiah also refers to Pharaoh Neco's attack on Gaza and Ashkelon (*Jer. 47:1–6*).

P.D.G.

**NEDABIAH** (Heb., 'the LORD has been generous'). Listed among the descendants of King Jehoiachin, and thus part of David's royal line. He seems to have returned after the exile in Babylon (*1 Chron. 3:18*).

**NEHEMIAH** The name Nehemiah means 'Yah(weh) [the LORD] has compassion'. In ancient Israel parents gave this name to their sons to praise the LORD for his mercy in their lives. Three characters in the O T bear this name.

**1.** The earliest reference to Nehemiah identifies a man who returned from Exile in Babylon with Sheshbazzar c. 533 BC (*Ezra 2:2; Neh. 7:7*).

**2.** This Nehemiah was a district governor of Beth-zur after the Exile (*Neh. 3:16*).

**3.** The most important Nehemiah in Scripture is the post-exilic governor of Judah, the main character in the biblical book of Nehemiah. He was the son of Hacaliah (*Neh. 1:1*) and his brother, Hanani (*Neh. 1:2; 7:2*), was made a ruler in Jerusalem.

Nehemiah himself rose to high standing during the reign of the Persian Emperor Artaxerxes I (464–424 BC). He was designated the 'cupbearer to the king' (*Neh. 1:11*). This honourable position involved tasting wine for the king to ensure it was not poisoned. Cupbearers were often eunuchs, though it is not certain that Nehemiah was a eunuch. In any case, Nehemiah enjoyed a position close enough to the king that he was able to communicate freely with him (*2:1–10*). As a result of his relationship with Artaxerxes, Nehemiah became instrumental in rebuilding and reforming Jerusalem in the post-exilic period.

**The building programme.** Nehemiah's work in Jerusalem began when his brother Hanani visited him in Susa. Nehemiah asked about the condition of the returnees and learned that the people of Jerusalem were troubled and the walls of the city were broken down. After prayer and fasting, he approached Artaxerxes and asked permission to rebuild the city. Permission was granted and Nehemiah left with royal edicts to authorize his effects (*Neh. 1:1–2:10*).

Nehemiah faced much opposition to his reconstruction. Resistance came from surrounding provinces, from within the Jewish community, and again from surrounding peoples. At first, governors from adjacent provinces troubled Nehemiah. Sanballat, governor of Samaria and Tobiah, governor of Ammon, mocked Nehemiah and his workers. They also raised the politically sensitive accusation that Nehemiah was in rebellion against Artaxerxes (*Neh. 2:10, 19–20*). Nehemiah resisted their efforts to dissuade him by praying and working all the more (*4:4–6*). After verbal attacks failed, Sanballat and Tobiah planned to use force (*4:8*). Yet, Nehemiah prayed and prepared his workers to defend themselves.

The second wave of resistance came from within the Jewish community. Many Jews complained that they were mistreated by the rich. Usury was widespread in Judah. Nehemiah halted the usury (*Neh. 5:1–13*) and showed great generosity toward the people. He won their favour and reconstruction continued (*vv. 14–19*).

Further opposition to the rebuilding project came once again from Sanballat. He, Geshem of Arabia, and other enemies tried to lure Nehemiah away from Jerusalem (*Neh. 6:2*), but Nehemiah refused. Geshem accused Nehemiah of treason (*v. 6*), but Nehemiah responded with utter denial (*v. 8*). Mention is also made of Noadiah and other prophets who also tried to intimidate Nehemiah, but he overcame their attempts (*v. 14*). As a result of his persistence, Nehemiah and the workers completed the walls of the city (v. 6:15–7:3). Jerusalem was secured against her enemies.

Nehemiah's devotion to rebuilding the walls of Jerusalem stands as a model for believers in every age. He consistently linked diligent prayer and hard work together. Fully aware of his inadequacy for the massive task before him, Nehemiah turned to God for help, time and again. Fully aware of his human responsibility, however, he also implemented a practical programme that led to the completion of the project.

**The reforms.** Nehemiah was not merely concerned with the external reconstruction of Jerusalem; he also devoted himself to the religious reform of Judah. With the assistance of the scribe Ezra, Nehemiah renewed the post-exilic community in fidelity to the Lord.

Reforms took place in several areas. Nehemiah appointed officers to govern the people. He arranged for the people to be instructed in the Law of Moses. He supervised the reading of the Law at the Feast of Tabernacles at which time the people promised to avoid foreign marriages, to keep Sabbaths and to support Temple services (Neh. 8–10).

In 433 BC Nehemiah returned to Persia for a year (Neh. 13:6). Upon his return, he discovered that Tobiah, perhaps his former Ammonite enemy, had found favour with Eliashib the high priest and was living in the Temple. Nehemiah expelled Tobiah from the province. Moreover, he learned that many of the Jews had intermarried again, setting the stage for further apostasy (vv. 23–27). In response, Nehemiah harshly rebuked the violators (vv. 4–7).

In all of these reforms Nehemiah showed himself to be much more than a shrewd politician. He recognized that external conformity to the will of God was not enough. The rebuilding of the city walls had to be matched by the reforming of lifestyle. In this way, Nehemiah reminds all believers that true devotion to the Lord reaches not only to externals, but stems from the hearts of his people.

R. P.

**NEHUM** was one of the Israelites who returned to Jerusalem with Nehemiah and Zerubbabel after the captivity in Babylon (Neh. 7:7).

**NEHUSHTA** (Heb., 'serpent'). The wife or concubine of Jehoiakim, the mother of King Jehoiachin of Judah and the daughter of Elnathan. She came from Jersualem (2 Kings 24:8). Along with her son, Jehoiachin, she surrendered to King Nebuchadnezzar when he laid siege to Jerusalem, and she was deported with Jehoiachin and his officials to Babylon (vv. 12–15).

**NEKODA 1.** A leader of one of the families of Temple servants whose descendants returned from the Babylonian Exile in the days of Ezra and worked on the Temple (Ezra 2:48; Neh. 7:50).

**2.** The descendants of this Nekoda are listed in Ezra 2:60 and Neh. 7:62 as among those who returned to Jerusalem with Nehemiah and Zerubbabel, following the Exile in Babylon, but who could not demonstrate that their families were of Israelite origin.

**NEMUEL 1.** Nemuel was the first son of Eliab listed in Num. 26:9. He was a descendant of Reuben and a brother to Dathan and Abiram, who rebelled against Moses and Aaron in Korah's rebellion.

**2.** One of Simeon's sons and founder of the Nemuelite clan (Num. 26:12; 1 Chron. 4:24). He appears to be the same as Jemuel, Simeon's first son and one who went to Egypt with Jacob his grandfather (Gen. 46:10; Exod. 6:15).

**NEPHEG** (Heb., 'sprout').
**1.** Nepheg was one of the sons of Izhar

and a grandson of Kohath. He was great-grandson of Levi (Exod. 6:21). His brother, Korah, led a rebellion against Moses.

**2.** A son of King David. After David conquered Jerusalem and moved there from Hebron he took many wives and concubines. One of his many children was Nepheg (2 Sam. 5:15; 1 Chron. 3:7; 14:6).

**NEPHILIM** These people are mentioned only in Gen. 6:4 and Num. 13:33. The origin of the word is not clear, but they were apparently a people of ancient history who were of huge stature. In Num. 13:33 when the twelve spies returned to Moses after spying out the land of Canaan, they reported that they had seen Nephilim. A parenthesis explains that the descendants of Anak came from these people. The Anakim were in turn considered to be giants. Certainly their stature scared off ten of the spies. Only Caleb and Joshua, with great faith in the LORD, believed that such people could be beaten (Num. 14:9).

**NEPHUSSIM** A leader of one of the families of Temple servants whose descendants returned from the Babylonian Exile in the days of Ezra and worked on the Temple (Ezra 2:50; Neh. 7:52).

**NER** (Heb., 'lamp'). The father of Abner, a Benjamite and a commander in King Saul's army. He was the son of Abiel and therefore brother to Saul's father, Kish (1 Sam. 14:50–51). He is mentioned in a number of places usually in connection with his son Abner (1 Sam. 26:5, 14; 2 Sam. 2:8, 12; 3:23 etc.). In 1 Chronicles he is listed in Saul's genealogy but there seems to be some confusion with the account in 1 Samuel. In 1 Chron. 8:30 and 9:36 Ner was the son of or descendant of Jeiel and lived near Jerusalem. In 8:33 and 9:39 we are told that 'Ner was the father of Kish'. Quite how this confusion might be resolved has been much discus-sed. It is possible that one or other list simply misses out a name or a generation, but efforts to harmonize do involve some speculation.                    P.D.G.

**NEREUS** A Christian who lived in Rome and was greeted, along with his sister, by the apostle Paul (Rom. 16:15). Paul's personal recognition and care for many individuals in different congregations is to be noted in most of his letters.

**NERGAL** A god made and worshipped by the people of Cuthah from the north-eastern part of Babylonia (2 Kings 17:30). These people were one of several national groupings resettled in Samaria by the Assyrians. Each group had its own gods (v. 30). This god is believed to have been a god of disease and catastrophe.

**NERGAL-SHAREZER** ('Nergal preserve the king'). A 'high official' among the officers of Nebuchadnezzar king of Baby-lon. He was among those who entered Jerusalem when the walls were finally breached and the Babylonian forces in-vaded the city (Jer. 39:3). With his col-leagues he took up a position in the Middle Gate and was instructed by Neb-uchadnezzar to ensure that no harm came to the prophet Jeremiah. So the officials took Jeremiah and handed him to Ged-aliah for safe-keeping (Jer. 39:13). The way the NIV reads it appears as if there are two officials of this name in v. 3. The Heb. is not clear on this.

**NERI** Mentioned in Luke's genealogy leading from Jesus and Joseph back to Adam (Luke 3:27). Neri was the father of Shealtiel and son of Melki.

**NERIAH** (Heb., 'the LORD is light'). Neriah was the son of Mahseiah (Jer. 32:12; 51:59). He was known for being the father of two sons, Baruch and Ser-aiah, both of whom served the prophet Jeremiah during the last years of the kingdom of Judah and during the fall of the city of Jerusalem to the Babylonians (*Jer. 32:16; 36:4, 8, 14, 32; 43:3, 6; 45:1*).

**NETHANEL** (Heb., 'gift of God').

**1.** Nethanel was the son of Zuar and leader of the people of Issachar in Moses' time and therefore represented them at the time of the census (*Num. 1:8*). When instructions were given about how and where each tribe was to camp in relation to the Tabernacle (Tent of Meeting), Issachar was to camp on the east, next to Judah, with Nethanel at the head of a division of 54,400 people (*Num. 2:5–6*). At the dedication of the Tabernacle, Nethanel brought the offerings of his tribe on the second day of celebration (*7:18, 23*). When the Israelites finally moved on from Sinai, Nethanel was again at the head of his people (*10:15*).

**2.** The fourth son of Jesse and brother to David (*1 Chron. 2:14*). When Samuel came to anoint David to be king, Jesse made all his sons in descending order of age pass before Samuel. David was seventh in line.

**3.** A priest whose job it was to blow a trumpet before the ark of God when it was brought back to Jerusalem by David (*1 Chron. 15:24*).

**4.** A Levite who was the father of Shemaiah the scribe (*1 Chron. 24:6*). Shemaiah recorded the names and duties of the priests and Levites when King David was ordering the worship at the Tent of Meeting.

**5.** The fifth of Obed-Edom's sons, a descendant of Korah responsible to attend to the Tabernacle gates in David's administration (*1 Chron. 26:4*). He is possibly to be identified with 3. above.

**6.** One of Jehoshaphat's officials who were sent, in the third year of his reign, to teach people in the towns of Judah about the LORD and his Law (*2 Chron. 17:7*).

**7.** During the revival in King Josiah's reign, Josiah provided sheep and animals for the sacrifices of the people. This Nethanel was one of the leaders of the

Levites who, along with other leaders of the people, also voluntarily provided many animals for the people to sacrifice (*2 Chron. 35:9*).

**8.** This Nethanel was a descendant of Pashhur and one of those in the time of Ezra who had married a foreign wife rather than one from Judah (*Ezra 10:22*).

**9.** This Nethanel was a leader of the priestly family of Jedaiah and among those who returned with Zerubbabel from the captivity in Babylon (*Neh. 12:21*).

**10.** Possibly the same as 8. above, this Nethanel was a leader of Judah and a priest who played musical instruments at the dedication of the rebuilt walls of Jerusalem (*Neh. 12:36*).          P. D. G.

**NETHANIAH** (Heb., 'the LORD has given').

**1.** Mentioned in *1 Chron. 25:2*, Nethaniah was one of the sons of Asaph. Immediately under Asaph's direction, and on the direct orders of King David (*v. 1*), he and others were among those who prophesied and led in the ministry of music for worship. He was leader of the fifth group of Levitical musicians and choirs who ministered in the Temple (*v. 12*).

**2.** A Levite, this Nethaniah lived in the days of King Jehoshaphat of Judah. During the early years of his reign Jehoshaphat served the LORD and sent out various teachers and Levites to teach the people of Judah the Book of the Law. Nethaniah was one of those teachers (*2 Chron. 17:8*).

**3.** The father of Jehudi one of the court officials in the days of King Jehoiakim (*Jer. 36:14*).

**4.** The father of Ishmael, an army officer and descendant of the royal family who served under Gedaliah, governor of Judah. Ishmael was later involved in the assassination of Gedaliah (*2 Kings 25:23, 25; Jer. 40:8, 14; 41:1–2, 6–18*).          P. D. G.

**NEZIAH** A leader of one of the families of Temple servants whose descendants returned from the Babylonian Exile in the days of Ezra and worked on the Temple (*Ezra 2:54; Neh. 7:56*).

**NIBHAZ** After the Assyrian invasion of the Northern Kingdom of Israel, the Israelites were dispersed to other parts of the empire. Meanwhile foreign groups were settled in Israel and Samaria, bringing with them their own gods. *2 Kings 17: 24–41* recounts this movement of peoples and the introduction of other gods to Israel. The Avvites were said to have introduced Nibhaz and Tartak. These two names would appear to represent their gods. The passage describes how those people and their descendants continued to try to worship both their own gods and the one they saw as the god of their newly adopted country, 'Yahweh' or 'the LORD' (*v. 32*). Such worship of course denied the Law of the LORD, the covenant, and the truth of monotheism, so fundamental to the faith of Israel (*vv. 34–41*).    P.D.G.

**NICANOR** ('conqueror'). Nicanor was one of seven men appointed to help the apostles who were finding the work of administration in the early Jerusalem church to be too burdensome (*Acts 6:5*). Many new people were becoming Christians. The new Christians of Greek-Jewish background were falling out with those of Hebrew-Jewish background over the distribution of food to widows. The disciples found that they were spending so much time sorting out these things (*v. 2*) that they were neglecting the ministry of the Word of God. Seven men were therefore to be appointed and to be chosen as those known to be 'full of the Spirit and wisdom'. The apostles prayed and laid their hands on these men and appointed them to the job of looking after the day-to-day affairs of the church.

This incident is an interesting indication of how early in the church's life there was a recognition of the fact that God gives different people different 'minis-tries' or gifts. But it also reflects the early recognition by the church that those called to 'the ministry of the Word of God' (*v. 2*) should not have other preoccupations. V. 7 indicates the success of this division of labour: 'the word of God spread. The number of disciples in Jerusalem increased rapidly.'    P. D. G.

**NICODEMUS** ('Conqueror of the people'). Mentioned only in John's Gospel, Nicodemus was a Pharisee and a member of the Jewish ruling council (*John 3:1*). His encounter with Jesus is recorded in detail in *John 3*. Clearly interested in what he had heard about Jesus, Nicodemus decided he should talk to him alone and came to see him under cover of dark, probably for fear of the comments from his colleagues were he to come openly. He began his conversation with great respect for Jesus whose miracles he had seen and teaching he had heard and who he was sure had come from God (*v. 2*). Jesus' response was to talk about those who wished to 'see the kingdom of God' needing to be 'born again' (or born 'from above'). Nicodemus took the language literally and could not understand how a second birth might take place. Jesus then explained the need for the work of the Holy Spirit in the life of an individual who wished to see the Kingdom of God. This would have contrasted with a Jewish belief that physical birth was of greatest importance – being a descendant of Abraham. Still Nicodemus seemed perplexed at what he was told and Jesus remarked ironically that Nicodemus, a teacher in Israel, ought to be able to understand these things. The real stumbling block for him would come not with such things that he ought to have understood ('earthly things') but with 'heavenly things'. How difficult Nicodemus would find it to believe in the heavenly Son of Man and his crucifixion and death (*John 3:13–14*).

Whether Nicodemus ever came to believe in Jesus is not clear although rather tentatively he did come to Jesus' defence later on. When some of the Pharisees were seeking to condemn Jesus, Nicodemus asked: 'Does our law condemn anyone without first hearing him to find out what he is doing?' (John 7:50–51). At Jesus' death Nicodemus joined Joseph of Arimathea in taking away the body and preparing it for burial. He provided expensive perfumes which indicates he was probably quite wealthy (19:39). This last reference gives some indication that he may quietly have come to believe in Jesus. Like Nicodemus who had come by night to Jesus (v. 39), Joseph was 'a disciple', 'but secretly because he feared the Jews' (v. 38). Perhaps the two identified with each other in their belief and their fear.

John uses this encounter with Jesus to further several themes which are of great significance to him. First there is the question of the relationship of the Jews to Jesus. They are seen not to understand what Jesus' message is really about or who he really is. Second, the image of rebirth in John 3 is but one of several instances in the Gospel where people misunderstand Jesus, taking literally what Jesus intended to be taken at a deeply spiritual level. In John 4 the Samaritan woman at first takes literally Jesus' promise to supply water that will stop all thirst. In John 6 they look for literal bread when Jesus offers bread that will stop all hunger. In each case Jesus was pointing to the essential need for a working of the Holy Spirit in the life (John. 3:5–8; 4:23–24; 6:63; 7:37–39 etc.). Third, John wishes to show that it is essential to 'believe' in Jesus and that many do not believe and so will not see the Kingdom of God or inherit eternal life. The themes of eternal life and belief are clearly highlighted in this passage (e.g. 3:12–15).

It is probably not without significance for John that Nicodemus, who came to Jesus under cover of dark, came also in darkness of understanding. The emphasis on Jesus as 'light' in the ensuing verses and the contrast with those who love darkness in explicit (3:19). But John shows how spiritual darkness may be remedied – in coming to believe in Jesus, the light who has come into the world (John 3:16–21; 1:6–9; 8:12; 9:5).  P. D. G.

**NICOLAITANS, THE** A heretical group either within or in close contact with some of the churches of Asia Minor in the latter part of the Apostolic Age. This sect is expressly named in Scripture only in Rev. 2:6, 15.

Attempts to determine the meaning of the name 'Nicolaitans' have not been fruitful and are quite speculative. There is a lingering tradition that connects the origin of the group to Nicolas, one of the seven selected to help the apostles in Acts 6:5. If the sect were to be traced to Nicolas, the likely scenario would involve his relocation because of ministry to Asia Minor, possibly with John, the writer of the book of Revelation according to Rev. 1:4. At some point Nicolas would have defected from the orthodox Christian faith, as indicated by God's hatred for the groups' deeds (Rev. 2:6).

Little is known of the exact beliefs and practices of the Nicolaitans. If their heresy (Rev. 2:15) can be connected to 'the teaching of Balaam' (v. 14) in the nearby church at Pergamum, elements of idolatry and sexual immorality would seemingly be involved. Some also hold that the sexual immorality and idolatry of 'the followers of Jezebel' in the church at Thyatira (v. 20) indicates that they were also Nicolaitans.

Whatever the specific nature of the heresy, it is despised by the Lord. Although Christ rebuked the church at Ephesus for departing from their 'first love', which likely means the Lord's two-pronged command to love him and 'your neighbour' (Matt. 22:36–39) – especially other Christians (*Gal.* 5:13–14), he commends them in regard to their perspective concerning the Nicolaitans (*Rev.* 2:6). It would seem that, in spite of that church body's serious spiritual fall and need for repentance (v. 5), their error was not nearly as grave as the viewpoint and behaviour of the Nicolaitans (v. 6).

The situation is similar with the church at Pergamum. Again, the glorified Lord's commendation is heard for the church's firm stand for him and the faith in the face of Satanically generated suffering (*Rev.* 2:13). Yet there has been significant infiltration of the congregation by Nicolaitan teaching (v. 15). Christ's demand for them to repent demonstrates how seriously he takes such compromise, even on the fringe of a local church (v. 16).

An additional fascinating element of these two clear references to the Nicolaitan heresy has to do with the apparent contrast between the heresy and the promises Christ makes to those who 'overcome'. The heresy is mentioned in close proximity to the promise (*Rev.* 2:6–7, 15, 17), but there also appears to be a purposeful play on words between 'Nicolaitan' (Greek *Nicolaitēs*) and 'overcome' (Greek *Nikaw*).

From this observation it appears that the Nicolaitan position is virtually the antithesis of orthodox Christian belief and behaviour. Certainly it is not too much to say that those who succumb to heretical teaching, or who take part in idolatrous or sexually impure practices, are anything but the 'overcomers' that Christ directs his people to be.     A.B.L.

**NICOLAS** ('conqueror of the people'). Nicolas was one of seven men appointed to help the apostles who were finding the work of administration in the early Jerusalem church to be too burdensome (*Acts* 6:5). Many new people were becoming Christians. The new Christians of Greek-Jewish background were falling out with those of Hebrew-Jewish back-

ground over the distribution of food to widows. The disciples found that they were spending so much time sorting out these things (v. 2) that they were neglecting the ministry of the Word of God. Seven men were therefore to be appointed and to be chosen as those known to be 'full of the Spirit and wisdom'. The apostles prayed and laid their hands on these men and appointed them to the job of looking after the day-to-day affairs of the church. Given the particular strife in the community it is worth noting how special attention is drawn to the fact that Nicolas was 'from Antioch, a convert to Judaism'. It seems the church deliberately tried to choose representatives of the two groups. Such men 'full of the Spirit' would be able to draw the two sides together around their service of the Lord. V. 7 indicates the success of this division of labour: 'the word of God spread. The number of disciples in Jerusalem increased rapidly.'     P.D.G.

**NIGER** A prophet and teacher in the church at Antioch (*Acts* 13:1). See *Simeon*.

**NIMROD** was the son of Cush, a descendant of Ham, and known as a 'mighty warrior' (*Gen.* 10:8–9; *1 Chron.* 1:10). His skill as a hunter spawned a proverb: 'Like Nimrod, a mighty hunter before the LORD'. *Gen.* 10:10–11 describes in some detail how his people and his rule extended through Babylonia and into Assyria. The prophet Micah equated the land of Nimrod with the land of the Assyrians and, in a messianic passage, warned the Assyrians that one day Israel would be delivered from their invasion (*Mic.* 5:6).

**NIMSHI** was the father of King Jehoshaphat and grandfather of King Jehu and is only mentioned in relation to one or the other (*1 Kings* 19:16; *2 Kings* 9:2, 14, 20; *2 Chron.* 22:7). Given the fact that Jehu is sometimes called the 'son of

Nimshi', it is probably right to assume that the phrase can simply mean 'descendant of'.

**NISROCH** The name of the god which Sennacherib king of Assyria was worshipping in Nineveh when he was killed by his sons (2 *Kings 19:37; Is. 37:38*). His death was attributed to the work of the LORD, who had promised King Hezekiah of Judah that the Assyrian king would not invade Jerusalem (2 *Kings 19:32–34*). As yet no positive identification of this god has been found from other sources.

**NOADIAH** (Heb., 'meeting with the LORD').

**1.** The son of Binnui, Noadiah was a Levite who returned from Babylon to Jerusalem with Ezra. He helped in weighing out the Temple treasures when they arrived (*Ezra 8:33*).

**2.** Noadiah was a prophetess mentioned as the leader of a number of prophets who tried to undermine the work of Nehemiah and the people of Judah in rebuilding the walls of Jerusalem. She joined Tobiah and Sanballat in trying to intimidate those who were building the walls (*Neh. 6:14*)

## NOAH, THE SON OF LAMECH

The history of Noah (*Gen. 6:5–9:28*) has a prologue (*6:5–8*), laying the groundwork; a main narrative recording the ark (*6:9–8:18*) and the covenant (*8:19–9:17*); and an epilogue (*9:18–28*) of declension and death. The prologue tells how Noah became the distinctive man; the main narrative reveals how that distinctiveness showed; and the epilogue records that he was not distinctive enough.

### Grace

Three verses of universal scope lead up to the first reference to Noah: '. . . man's wickedness . . . grieved that he had made man . . . I will wipe out man . . .' (*Gen. 6:5–7*). These verses admit no exceptions. 'Man' embraces every human being: each individually and all alike are wicked (*v. 5*), the cause of divine grief (*v. 6*) and the objects of an eradicating judgment (*v. 7*). The NT (*Matt. 24:37f., Luke 17:26f.*) makes these verses descriptive of the world to which the Lord Jesus will one day return. In that future day, as in the days of Noah, there will be no salvation but by grace. The translation of *Gen. 6:8* is exact: 'But' (i.e., contrary to what would have been expected, for all alike deserved doom) 'Noah found favour/grace'. The phrase occurs about 40 times in the OT. Sometimes it is hardly any more than a conventional politeness (1 *Sam. 20:29*) but even in such cases it implies an undeserved favour or one that could be withheld. When, however, it is used at its most distinctive (e.g. *Ruth 2:2, 10, 13*) and certainly where man and God are concerned (*Judg. 6:17*), it emphasizes an act of pure grace, undeserved and unprovoked. So it was with Noah. As a translation 'Noah found grace' is exact, but the meaning is more truly expressed by reversing the order, 'Grace found Noah'. Into the situation of total judgment, the LORD stepped with a free, unmerited outreach of grace.

### The ark

*Gen. 6:9*, 'This is the account of Noah', is more literally 'These are the generations of Noah'. The word 'generations' signifies 'what emerged from': earlier events 'giving birth' to later events. In Genesis this formula marks a new beginning. We are about to learn of the distinctive life that 'emerged/was born from' the initial work of grace (*Gen.* 6:8). It had three characteristics (*v.* 9): in character, 'righteous'; 'among the people of his time', distinctive; and in fellowship with God. But one characteristic of the life of grace is brought into particular prominence; detailed and prompt obedience to the word of God – commanded to build the ark (*Gen.* 6:14–16) 'Noah did everything just as God commanded him' (6:22; *cf.* 7:5, 9, 16). He did not enter the ark until the LORD commanded (7:1) nor (though he knew the Flood was over, 8:13–14) did he emerge until the LORD called (8:15). This is the characteristic of Noah which *Heb.* 11:7 underlines: 'warned' signifies, rather, 'having received a heavenly word' (e.g. *Matt.* 2:12, 22; *Luke* 2:26; *Acts* 10:22); and 'in holy fear' points to 'spiritual sensitivity to God's Word' (*Luke* 2:25; *Acts* 22:12; *Heb.* 5:7) – in other words, reverent acceptance of God's Word, coupled with the obedience of faith.

### The covenant

*Gen.* 6:17 says (literally) 'I will implement my covenant'. The promise looks back to 6:8. The LORD had taken an initiative of grace to Noah. In consequence, he considered himself bound by 'covenant', by an unconditional, freely-given promise so that when the just judgment fell, Noah would be wrapped in the safety of the ark. He would not be immune from judgment but the judgment was to fall upon him in such a way as actually and literally to bear him through to salvation – precisely our position in Christ, symbolized in baptism (*1 Pet.* 3:20–21). After the Flood, the LORD's covenant with Noah was elaborated in three ways which anticipate the fuller covenantal developments with Abraham and Moses and in the New Covenant. First, there was responsive consecration (*Gen.* 8:18–20). In gratitude for salvation by grace Noah committed himself unreservedly (*cf. Gen.* 22:2, 12) to God. Secondly, to the man who had been saved by grace the LORD outlined the law of 'an obedient life' (*Gen.* 9:1–7). And thirdly (*Gen.* 9:8–17) the LORD's continuing covenantal relationship with Noah was confirmed by a covenant sign. If, in the world as constituted before the Flood, there had been such a thing as a rainbow, the LORD here took the familiar and filled it with new meaning – just as later, he would do, with bread and wine. But the word translated 'rainbow' is actually 'bow' – the weapon. It is as if the LORD were saying 'See, the war is over; I have hung up my bow'. And ever after, as soon as a threat loomed, Noah saw too the 'sign' that no ultimate threat could again touch him: the LORD had promised.

### The inadequate man

In Noah, humanity had a new start, a second chance. This is why *Gen.* 9:1, 7 introduce echoes of Eden (*cf.* 1:28). But, sadly, Noah, notwithstanding grace, was still a sinner, the founder of a new humanity but, like his father Adam, only able to have sons in his own likeness (5:3). And so it would remain 'till a Greater Man restore us and regain the blissful seat' (*Is.* 11:1–9; *Rev.* 22:1–5).                J.A.M.

**NOAH** **1.** See *Noah, the Son of Lamech.*

**2. Noah, the daughter of Zelophehad.** One of five daughters born to Zelophehad, who had no sons. These daughters married cousins on their father's side and were members of the tribe of Manasseh (*Num. 26:33; 27:1; 36:1–12; Josh. 17:3*). They faced a predicament over their inheritance, for normally inherited land would have been passed on through a son.

They approached Moses at the entrance to the Tabernacle about the problem, asking him to rule that they should be allowed to inherit their father's property, for it would not be right that his name should die out. Moses consulted the LORD about the situation, as a result of which a new law was promulgated allowing daughters to inherit land from their father. Later some of the leaders from the tribe of Manasseh appealed to Moses about the case, pointing out that if these women were now to marry outside the tribe the land would be lost forever to the tribe. The ruling which followed further defined the law of inheritance, insisting that the women should marry into their father's tribe or else lose the inheritance (*Num. 36*). Hence the daughters married cousins 'on their father's side', thus fulfilling the requirement of the LORD.

When finally the Israelites entered the land of Canaan and the land was divided up among the tribes, the daughters of Zelophehad were duly given their inheritance (*Josh. 17:3–4*)     P. D. G.

**NOBAH** was from the tribe of Manasseh and was credited with capturing Kenath, which he then named Nobah after himself (*Num. 42:32*). The city is mentioned in *Judg. 8:11* and was in Gilead (the trans-jordan area to the north of the Dead Sea).

**NODAB** The name occurs as one of the family names of the Hagrites (descendants of Hagar and Ishmael), who were defeated by a coalition of the tribes of Reuben, Gad and Manasseh (*1 Chron. 5:19*).

**NOGAH** (Heb., 'brightness'). A son of King David. After David conquered Jerusalem and moved there from Hebron he took many wives and concubines. One of his many children was Nogah (*1 Chron. 3:7; 14:6*).

**NOHAH** (Heb., 'rest'). Benjamin's fourth son, who became a leader in his tribe (*1 Chron. 8:2*). His name is omitted from the list of sons in *Gen. 46:21*.

**NOT MY PEOPLE**. See *Lo-ammi* (*Hos. 1:9–10; 2:23; Rom. 9:25–26*).

**NOT PITIED** See *Lo-Ruhamah*. This is the translation (not used in the NIV) of the name Lo-Ruhamah (*Hos. 1:6, 8; 2:23*, where the translation 'Not my loved one' is used).

**NUN** (Heb., 'fish'). A member of the tribe of Ephraim and father of Joshua (also called Hoshea; *Num. 13:8, 16; 1 Chron. 7:27*). The name always appears in the phrase 'son of Nun' (e.g. *Exod. 33:11; Num. 14:6, 30; Neh. 8:17* etc.).

**NYMPHA** A person, greeted by Paul in *Col. 4:15*, in whose house a church met to worship. It is assumed in the NIV that Nympha was a woman. Though this is likely, it is by no means certain.

# O

**OBADIAH** (Heb., 'servant of the LORD').

**1.** Obadiah, the prophet. This writer of the shortest of the OT prophetic books shares with two others (Jonah and Nahum) the distinction of having addressed his message not to Israel or Judah but to (or about) foreign nations exclusively. In his case, Obadiah speaks of coming judgment on Edom, the nation east and south of the Dead Sea that traced its origins back to Esau, brother of Jacob (*Obad. 6, 8–10, 18–19, 21; cf. Gen. 36:1–8*).

The reason for Edom's threatened ruin is her 'violence against your brother Jacob' (*v. 10*), but because such violence characterized Edom's relationship with Israel and Judah almost continuously throughout the OT period it is impossible to specify the violence in question and therefore to date Obadiah's ministry. Moreover, he says nothing of his family, his residence, or his setting. Perhaps the reference to Sepharad (*v. 20*) favours a late date, especially if it is to be equated with Sardis or Saparda, a region of Media.

The major theological point to be made with reference to Obadiah and his ministry is the universal concern of the LORD for all peoples, either for salvation or for judgment, and his ultimate sovereignty over the entire family of nations (*v. 21*).

**2.** A contemporary of Elijah who was in charge of the palace of King Ahab. He was 'a devout believer in the LORD' who preserved 100 prophets of the LORD from Ahab's persecutions (*1 Kings 18:3–16*). He is not to be identified with 1. above.

**3.** One of the post-exilic members of the Davidic royal line who traced his lineage to David through Hananiah, Zerubbabel and Jehoiachin (*1 Chron. 3:21*).

**4.** This Obadiah was a son of Izrahiah and a descendant of Issachar through Tola, Uzzi and Izrahiah (*1 Chron. 7:3*).

**5.** A descendant of King Saul through his son Jonathan and grandson Merib-Baal (or Mephibosheth). He was a Benjamite and son of Azel (*1 Chron. 8:38; 9:44*).

**6.** A leader of the post-exilic Levitical community in Jerusalem who belonged to the clan of Merari. He was the son of Shemaiah (*1 Chron. 9:16*). He is probably to be identified with the Temple gatekeeper and guardian of the storerooms in the days of Nehemiah (*Neh. 12:25*).

**7.** A leading officer of the tribe of Gad who became second in command of David's troops while David still lived in Ziklag (*1 Chron. 12:9*).

**8.** A Zebulunite whose son, Ishmaiah, was leader of Zebulun under David's kingship (*1 Chron. 27:19*).

**9.** A leader in Judah whom Jehoshaphat sent out with the Levites to teach the people of Judah the Book of the Law (*2 Chron. 17:7*).

**10.** A Merarite Levite and director of the work of Temple restoration during the reforms of Josiah (*2 Chron. 34:12*). He is not to be confused with 6. above.

**11.** A family head who returned to Jerusalem from Babylon with Ezra (*Ezra 8:9*). He is perhaps the same person as the signatory to the covenant renewal under Nehemiah (*Neh. 10:5*).            E. M.

**OBAL** Listed in both *Gen. 10:28* and 1

*Chron. 1:22* as a descendant of Shem. His father was Joktan.

**OBED** (Heb., 'worshipper').

**1.** Obed was the father of Jesse and a son of Boaz and Ruth (*Ruth 4:17, 21–22; 1 Chron. 2:12*). Obed is later mentioned in the Gospel accounts (*Matt. 1:5; Luke 3:32*).

**2.** Another Obed is listed among Judah's sons (*1 Chron. 2:37–38*).

**3.** One of David's 'mighty men', Obed's name is recorded in *1 Chron. 11:26–47*.

**4.** Obed, the son of Shemaiah, was a Korahite gatekeeper in Solomon's Temple (*1 Chron. 26:7*).

**5.** *2 Chron. 23:1* lists Obed as the father of Azariah, a commander who helped Jehoiada in the battle which removed Athaliah from power. s.c.

**OBED-EDOM 1.** After Uzzah was killed for touching the ark of God, David was afraid to take the ark to Jerusalem and left it, instead, at the home of a Gittite named Obed-Edom. Obed-Edom kept the ark for three months and received blessings from the LORD, so David finally moved the sacred ark into the city (*2 Sam. 16:10–12; 1 Chron. 13:12–14; 15:23–39*).

**2.** *1 Chron. 15:24* lists another Obed-Edom as one of the Levites chosen to minister before the ark of the LORD through the blowing of trumpets.

**3.** *1 Chron. 14:4–6* lists Obed-Edom as one of the Levites chosen to minister before the ark of the LORD through petition, thanksgiving, praise and the playing of the lyre. (It is possible and, perhaps, likely that this is the same Obed-Edom as 2. above).

**4.** *1 Chron. 26:4* lists Obed-Edom as the family head of 62 men who were Korahite gatekeepers and hard workers in David's kingdom.

**5.** In *2 Chron. 25:24* we are introduced to Obed-Edom, a servant of God who took care of the gold, silver and other articles found in the Temple of God. Sadly,

because of Judah's sin, God allowed Jehoash king of Israel to invade Judah and he took all the Temple treasures from Obed-Edom back to Samaria with him. s.c.

**OBIL** (Heb., 'camel driver'). An Ishmaelite who was in charge of all the king's camels during the reign of King David (*1 Chron. 27:30*).

**OCRAN** (Heb., 'trouble'). Ocran was the father of Pagiel who was the leader of the people of Asher at the census of the Israelites in the wilderness of Sinai. Pagiel's division of people numbered 41,500 (*Num. 1:13; 2:27*). As the representative of his tribe Pagiel also brought his tribe's fellowship offering when the Tabernacle was dedicated in the wilderness (*Num. 7:72, 77*) and led his tribe when the Israelites set out from the Sinai desert on their wanderings (*Num. 10:26*).

**ODED** (Heb., 'restorer').

**1.** The father of Azariah the prophet. Azariah prophesied during the reign of King Asa. 'The Spirit of God' came on him (*2 Chron. 15:1*) and he prophesied to Asa that the LORD would bless him if he followed God (*v. 8*). Note that the Heb. of *v. 8* suggests Oded himself was the prophet. The context makes this impossible. Perhaps 'Oded the prophet' is a gloss to be deleted.

**2.** A prophet who prophesied during the reign of Ahaz king of Judah and Pekah king of Israel (*2 Chron. 28:9*). Ahaz was evil, following in the ways of 'the kings of Israel' rather than the ways of David (*v. 2*). Therefore the LORD allowed the Syrians and the Northern Kingdom of Israel to defeat Ahaz in battle (*vv. 5–6*). When the Israelites returned to Samaria with plunder and captives from Judah, Oded met them on the way. He pointed out to them that they too were guilty of great sin and they should let the people of Judah go. They listened to the message and let the captives return home (*vv. 12–15*). P.D.G.

**OG** The name of the Amorite king of Bashan who reigned at Ashtaroth (*Deut. 1:4; 4:47*). When the Israelites were making their way from the wilderness of Sinai up the King's Highway towards Canaan they asked to pass through the land of the Amorites, to the east of the Dead Sea. Permission was refused and Sihon, their king, and his people were defeated in battle (see *Sihon* for detail). The next people the Israelites encountered were led by Og, the king of Bashan, who also came out with his troops and fought the Israelites at Edrei (*Num. 21:33–35; Deut. 3:1–13; 29:7–8*). As the LORD had helped Moses and the Israelites in the fight with Sihon, so again he told them not to be afraid for he would deliver Og into their hands as well. In the battle that followed Og, his sons, and whole army were killed. Their land was eventually divided up between the tribes of Gad, Reuben and Manasseh (*Num. 32:33; Josh. 13:12, 30–31; 1 Kings 4:19*).

The account in *Deut. 3:11* says that Og was a descendant of the Rephaites which would indicate a man of great stature (or 'giant', see *Josh. 12:4*). His huge bed had become famous and no doubt had been kept as a momento!

News of the victory quickly spread and drove fear into the hearts of those in Canaan. Rahab, the prostitute of Jericho, was convinced the LORD had power even over that heavily fortified city because she and others had heard of the victory over Sihon and Og (*Josh. 2:10; also see 9:9–10*). Moses used the victory to encourage the Israelites as he left them in the charge of Joshua and about to enter Canaan (*Deut. 31:4*). The demonstration of God's faithfulness to his people in defeating Sihon and Og was recounted in the people's praises to the LORD down through the generations (e.g. *Neh. 9:22; Pss. 135:11; 136:20*). P.D.G.

**OHAD** The third son of Simeon and listed among those who went to Egypt with Jacob his grandfather (*Gen. 46:10; Exod. 6:15*).

**OHEL** (Heb., 'tent'). One of several sons of Zerubbabel, and a descendant of King David. He was of the tribe of Judah and is mentioned only in the genealogy of *1 Chron. 3:20*.

**OHOLAH** A symbolic name used by Ezekiel to describe Samaria (*Ezek. 23:4–5, 36, 44*). She was older sister to Oholibah who stood for Jerusalem. The allegory was part of Ezekiel's prophetic work designed to bring about repentance among the Israelites of his day. He also sought to explain why God had judged both Israel and Judah.

The allegory of *Ezek. 23* begins with the two sisters as 'daughters of the same mother' who quickly became prostitutes in Egypt. In vivid sexual imagery, Ezekiel describes the way they prostituted themselves to other gods even though they belonged to the LORD. Oholah 'lusted after her lovers – the Assyrians' (*v. 5*) and continued what she had begun in Egypt. Because of this idolatry the LORD handed her over in judgment to the Assyrians: a reference to the Assyrian invasion and the dispersion of the peoples of the Northern Kingdom (*vv. 9–10*).

Even though Oholibah (Jerusalem) watched all this happen and saw God's judgment on the Northern Kingdom, she continued in her own prostitution by lusting after first the Assyrians and then the Babylonians. They too turned to idolatry and made treaties with the Babylonians and eventually the Babylonians came to Jerusalem (*vv. 14–17*). This leads into Ezekiel's pronouncement of the LORD's judgment on Jerusalem as all her lovers turn against her and invade. They will be used by God to punish Oholibah. The way Oholah has gone will be the way of Oholibah as God brings his judgment on her as well (vv. 32–35, 46–49).

P.D.G.

**OHOLIAB** (Heb., 'the tent of my father'). Oholiab was from the tribe of Dan and was the son of Ahisamach (Exod. 31:6). He was appointed by the LORD to help Bezalel in artistic work and designs for the Tent of Meeting (Tabernacle). He obviously had outstanding skills in several different crafts such as work with precious metals, wood and even embroidering cloth. God had also given him the ability to teach others these crafts so that the work on the Tent of Meeting would be completed to God's glory (Exod. 35:34–36:2).

**OHOLIBAH** A symbolic name used by Ezekiel to describe Jerusalem (Ezek. 23:4, 11, 22, 36, 44). For detail of the allegory see Oholah.

**OHOLIBAMAH** (Heb., 'tent of the high place').
**1.** One of Esau's Canaanite wives and daughter of Anah and granddaughter to Zibeon the Hivite. She was mother to Jeush, Jalam and Korah who were born to her in Canaan. Each of these became leaders of Edomite tribes (Gen. 36:2, 5, 14, 18, 25).
**2.** A descendant of Esau, this Oholibamah was a clan leader of the Edomites (Gen. 36:41; 1 Chron. 1:52).

**OLYMPAS** A Christian who lived in Rome and was greeted by the apostle Paul along with Philologus, Julia, Nereus and his sister, and Olympas (Rom. 16:15). Paul's personal recognition and care for many individuals in different congregations is to be noted in most of his letters.

**OMAR** An Edomite leader who was the grandson of Esau and Adah (a Canaanite woman) and son of Eliphaz (Gen. 36:11, 15; 1 Chron. 1:36).

**OMRI 1.** Omri was the sixth king of the Northern Kingdom of Israel and reigned for twelve years from 885–873 BC. The main information about his reign comes from 1 Kings 16:15–28. Omri came to the throne at a time of instability for Israel. The capital of the nation was in Tirzah where Elah, son of Baasha, had reigned for a brief two years. He seems to have had a reputation for drunkenness (v. 9) and perhaps this led to him being deposed by Zimri, one of his officials (v. 10). Zimri became king and killed off all of Baasha's family, thus fulfilling the word of the LORD against Baasha for all his sin (vv. 12–13). Omri, the commander of Israel's army, was camping with his troops near Gibbethon, a Philistine town, no doubt preparing for attack when they heard the news that Zimri had taken control by murdering Elah. His troops preferred to back Omri to be king and so turned round and laid siege to Tirzah instead. After only seven days of rule (v. 15), Zimri committed suicide and Omri became king in Tirzah.

It seems, however, that not all the Israelites immediately rallied behind Omri and about half of them supported Tibni for king (v. 21). However, Omri's troops were the stronger, Tibni was killed, and Omri ruled the whole of the Northern Kingdom, restoring some measure of law and order and calm to the nation.

Omri bought the hill of Samaria from Shemer (for more detail see Shemer), and there built the city of Samaria, where later he was buried (vv. 24, 28). The strength of the fortified city was legendary and it took the Assyrians three years to conquer it. Little more is known about this king except that he was more evil in 'the eyes of the LORD' than all the kings who had gone before him, even than Jeroboam son of Nebat. He worshipped and encouraged the worship of idols, a point remembered in the prophecy of Micah (6:16). The idolatrous influence of this dynasty even affected the Southern Kingdom. Ahaziah, later king of Judah, was a son of Athaliah, a granddaughter of Omri. Under his mother's influence he too 'did evil in the eyes of the LORD' (2 Chron. 22:2–4; 2 Kings 8:26). Eventually Omri died and his son Ahab succeeded him to the throne (1 Kings 16:28–30). The dynasty Omri had founded lasted for almost 50 years.

**2.** A grandson of Benjamin and son of Beker (1 Chron. 7:7).

**3.** Mentioned in 1 Chron. 9:4 as the son of Ammihud and a descendant of Perez. After the captivity, this Omri was among the first returnees of Jerusalem from the tribe of Judah.

**4.** The administrator over Issachar and a leader of his tribe during the reign of King David. His father was Michael (1 Chron. 27:18).                    P. D. G.

**ON** (Heb., 'strength'). On was a son of Peleth, a Reubenite. Together with Dathan, Abiram and Korah he helped instigate a rebellion against Moses, leading 250 others to challenge Moses' authority (Num. 16). This challenge to Moses and Aaron was a challenge to God's chosen leadership and therefore to the very holiness of God and his people. Although On is not mentioned again, it may be assumed that he too was destroyed by God with Dathan and Abiram as the ground opened and 'swallowed them, with their households' (Num. 16:23–35). Later this judgment was to serve as a reminder to the Israelites that they should love the LORD and keep his commands (Deut. 11:6; Ps. 106:17).

**ONAM** (Heb., 'strong').

**1.** A descendant of Esau, Onam was a son of Shobal, and a clan leader of the Edomites (Gen. 36:23; 1 Chron. 1:40).

**2.** From the tribe of Judah, the son of Jerahmeel and his wife Atarah. His sons were Shammai and Jada (1 Chron. 2:26, 28).

**ONAN** (Heb., 'strong'). Onan was the second of Judah's sons by his Canaanite wife, Shua (Gen. 38:4; Num. 26:19; 1 Chron. 2:3). Onan's older brother Er had a wife called Tamar. When Er died because of his wickedness before God, Judah told Onan to take her on as his wife. This form of marriage, known as a levirate marriage, was intended to enable the brother's line and inheritance to continue. The woman would become pregnant by the brother and thus preserve the older brother's inheritance. Because Onan knew that if she became pregnant by him 'the offspring would not be his' (Gen. 38:8), every time he had sex with her 'he spilled his semen on the ground' (v. 9). 'What he did was wicked in the LORD's sight' and so Onan died (v. 10; Gen. 46:12).

In times past this story was used to show that masturbation was wrong in God's eyes. This, of course, was not at all the issue. In fact, Onan was practising *coitus interruptus* – in the hope that it would be an effective contraceptive. Given the particular context and purpose of a levirate marriage, this was a serious sin indeed.

**ONESIMUS** (Gk., 'profitable'). Onesimus was a slave in the household of a person called Philemon and is best known to us through the apostle Paul's letter to Philemon. Philemon was one of Paul's fellow-workers and a faithful Christian (Philem. 1, 5). In this letter it becomes evident that Onesimus had left his position of service at some stage and ended up supporting Paul during a period of imprisonment, probably in Rome (although some suggest it was during a period of imprisonment in Ephesus). There is some indication that Onesimus had run away from his master and perhaps even taken money with him. Paul told Philemon that if Onesimus had done anything wrong it should be charged to his (Paul's) account (v. 18). However, it may simply be that Onesimus had been sent by Philemon to help Paul and had stayed longer than was originally intended.

While in contact with Paul, Onesimus was converted to Christ and became a 'brother in the Lord' (v. 16). He had become specially useful to Paul and it is clear that Paul would like to have him sent back to carry on the work. Paul even made a play on the word Onesimus to suggest that he might 'profit' from Philemon sending Onesimus straight back. Paul's appeal that Onesimus should not be treated harshly but as a Christian brother is masterpiece of pastoral exhortation.

Onesimus is also mentioned in Col. 4:9 where he accompanied Tychicus on a mission to the Colossians, bringing them the latest news from Paul about his imprisonment. Here again Paul's commendation of Onesimus was expansive: 'Onesimus, our faithful and dear brother, who is one of you'. This last comment suggests he may well have come from Colosse.

The letter of Philemon has been much examined to see what can be learned of possible Christian attitudes to slavery. The letter tells us little and assumes that it was right for Onesimus to return to his master and carry on as a slave. However, the chain of events that eventually led to Christians believing that slavery was wrong was certainly set in motion by Paul's treatment of Onesimus. Paul said he was 'Father' to Onesimus. He said Onesimus was a 'brother', that he was of real benefit, and he trusted him as a helper on a mission to the Colossians. Paul sent him back to Philemon 'no longer as a slave but better than a slave'. Christianity was clearly causing a re-think of relationships between masters and slaves.

There is no hard evidence of what happened to Onesimus after this except that some 50 years later Ignatius wrote about an Onesimus who was bishop of Ephesus. It is possible that this was the young slave, now an older man in his seventies, but it it not possible to be sure.

P.D.G.

**ONESIPHORUS** (Gk. 'one who brings profit'). This Christian man had often shown kindness to the apostle Paul during his second imprisonment in Rome and had gone out of his way to find where the apostle was held captive (2 Tim. 1:16–18). He had also been a great help to Paul when he was in Ephesus. Paul pointed out how, in Rome, Onesiphorus had clearly shown his courage in being one of the few who 'was not ashamed of my chains'. Paul's personal prayer in v. 18 for this man is really one of thankfulness to God for what he has done and that his works will be recognized by the Lord on the day of judgment. The fact that he was therefore not with Paul when this letter was written and that only his 'household' was greeted in 2 Tim. 4:19 probably indicates that Onesiphorus was travelling elsewhere in the empire at the time. There is no reason to assume, as some have done, that Onesiphorus must have been dead and that therefore 2 Tim. 1:18 is an early example of a prayer for the dead. Paul's main reason for drawing attention to this loyal and helpful Christian was to provide an example for other Christians.

P.D.G.

**OPHIR** Listed in both Gen. 10:29 and 1 Chron. 1:23 as a descendant of Shem, his father was Joktan. He was believed to be the first inhabitant of Ophir, an area renowned for its gold and probably located on the south-west corner of Arabia.

**OPHRAH** (Heb., 'fawn'). The son of Meonothai and a leader of the tribe of Judah (1 Chron. 4:14).

**OREB** One of two Midianite leaders who were defeated by Gideon and the

Israelites. In an amazing display of reliance upon and obedience to God, Gideon had attacked the Midianite camp with a mere 300 men (*Judg. 7*). The Midianites had fled in the dark and Gideon called up Israelites from several different tribes to come and chase them down. Oreb was captured and killed at the rock of Oreb, probably called that to commemorate the victory (*v. 25*). Gideon was only too well aware that a victory of this magnitude was God's work (*Judg. 8:3*). Future generations looked back to the victory as an indication of what God could do on their behalf and therefore what they could ask him to do again for them (e.g. *Ps. 83:11*; *Is. 10:26*).

**OREN** was a leader in the tribe of Judah, the third son of Jerahmeel (*1 Chron. 2:25*).

**ORPAH** was a Moabite who lived in her home country with her mother-in-law Naomi, her husband Kilion, her brother-in-law Mahlon and her sister-in-law Ruth (*Ruth 1:1–3*). When both Kilion and Mahlon died, Orpah and Ruth wanted to accompany Naomi to Judah, but she urged them to remain with their own families. Orpah stayed in Moab.

**OTHNI** A son of Shemaiah and listed among the gatekeepers of the Tabernacle in the time of King David (*1 Chron. 26:7*).

**OTHNIEL** was the son of Kenaz, the younger brother of Caleb of Jephunneh (*Josh. 15:17*; *Judg. 1:13*) of the tribe of Judah. He lived at a time of transition in Israelite history, participating in the conquest of Canaan under Joshua and Caleb, yet living to see the first signs of compromise in the covenant relationship of the LORD and his people.

Othniel first distinguished himself under Caleb in leading the battle to capture Kiriath Sepher (subsequently Debi), a city on the edge of the Negev in southern Judah (*Josh. 15:15–17*; *Judg.*

*1:11–13*). As a result, he was given Caleb's daughter Acsah in marriage. His actions and marriage both emphasized Othniel's standing as a true faithful Israelite, following in the footsteps of Joshua.

Othniel outlived the generation who led the Israelites into the land of promise, and saw the beginnings of compromise, through tribal disunity, religious syncretism and the failure to complete the eradication of the Canaanites under the LORD's judgment. The LORD's response to his rebellious people, was to bring judgment. *Judg. 3:7–11* records how the king of Aram-Naharaim, Cushan-Rishathaim defeated and subjected the Israelites for eight years. Othniel led a rebellion against this foreign oppression and, endowed by God's Spirit, he defeated the enemy, delivering God's people and became a leader of Israel, the first 'judge'.

Othniel's significance is that he is presented in Judges as a model judge. His standing as a true Israelite was well established, but in the face of the oppression of God's people, he was raised up to leadership by the LORD (*Judg. 3:9*). He was empowered by the Spirit both to lead God's people and to fight God's enemies, against whom he was successful (*v. 10*). He overpowered the enemy and instituted a time of peace (*v. 11*), which was understood as the LORD's blessing on his people. This model of how a judge should be was one which each subsequent judge failed to attain in some significant way, either by weakness of character, dubious methods or disobedience.

Othniel embodied an ideal, a man appointed by the LORD, through whom the LORD mediated his rule of his people. However, the institution of the judges ultimately failed through the repeated disobedience of the LORD's people. This institution was succeeded by the abiding symbol of the LORD's right to rule, in the institution of the kings. For kings, too, Othniel was a model. He was faithful in leadership, Spirit-led, and directed by the LORD to lead and save his people. See also *Judges*.                                    R. M.

**OZEM** **1.** Ozem was a leader in the tribe of Judah, the fourth son of Jerahmeel (1 *Chron. 2:25*).

**2.** The sixth son of Jesse and a brother of King David (1 *Chron. 2:15*).

**OZNI** The founder of the Oznite clan (*Num. 26:16*). In *Gen. 46:16* he is named Ezbon and listed as the fifth son of Gad and among those who went with Jacob to Egypt. He was a grandson of Jacob and Zilpah.

# P

**PAARAI** One of David's 'Thirty' mighty warriors who fought at his side. He was known as 'the Arbite' (2 Sam. 23:35) and was possibly the same person as Naarai the son of Ezbai in the list in 1 Chron. 11:37.

**PADON** A leader of one of the families of Temple servants whose descendants returned from the Babylonian Exile in the days of Ezra and worked on the Temple (Ezra 2:44; Neh. 7:47).

**PAGIEL** was the son of Ocran. He was the leader of the people of Asher in Moses' time and therefore represented them at the time of the census (Num. 1:13). When instructions were given about how and where each tribe was to camp in relation to the Tabernacle (Tent of Meeting), Asher was to camp on the north beside the tribe of Dan with Pagiel at the head of a division of 41,500 people (Num. 2:27–28). At the dedication of the Tabernacle, Pagiel brought the offerings of his tribe on the eleventh day of celebration (7:72, 77). When the Israelites finally moved on from Sinai, Pagiel was again at the head of his people (10:26).

**PAHATH-MOAB** A family leader whose descendants were counted among those who, in the time of Ezra, returned with Zerubbabel and Nehemiah from the Babylonian Exile. Their number was 2,812 (Ezra 2:6; 8:4; Neh. 7:11). It was probably he, or a descendant of the same name, who sealed the agreement with Nehemiah to serve the LORD and obey only his Law (Neh. 10:14). Some of his descendants are mentioned as being among those who had intermarried with foreign women and another, Hasshub, was among those who helped repair the wall of Jerusalem (Ezra 10:30; Neh. 3:11).

**PALAL** (Heb., 'judge') son of Uza was one of the workers who helped rebuild the walls of Jerusalem following the return from the Exile in Babylon (Neh. 3:25).

**PALLU** The second son of Reuben and head of a family that became known as the Palluite clan. His son was Eliab (Gen. 46:9; Exod. 6:14; Num. 26:5, 8; 1 Chron. 5:3).

**PALTI** (Heb., 'the LORD delivers'). One of the twelve spies sent out by Moses from the Desert of Paran to spy out the land of Canaan (Num. 13:11). A representative of each tribe was chosen and Palti, the son of Raphu, was from the tribe of Benjamin. For further detail on their mission see Shammua.

**PALTIEL** (Heb., 'deliverance of God').
  **1.** Paltiel, the son of Azzan, was a leader from the tribe of Issachar. The LORD told Moses to choose men from each tribe to help divide out the land of Canaan, and Paltiel represented his tribe (Num. 34:26).
  **2.** The husband of Saul's daughter Michal and son of Laish from Gallim. He was from the tribe of Benjamin (1 Sam. 25:44). Saul had promised Michal to David as wife after David had paid the bride price (the death of 100 Philistines) and then, in his anger and jealousy at

David, Saul had given her to Paltiel. Later David asked Ish-Bosheth, Saul's son, to restore Michal to him and take her from Paltiel. When this was done Paltiel, who seems to have been an innocent party in Saul's intrigue, 'went with her, weeping behind her all the way to Bahurim' until finally he was sent home (2 Sam. 3:15–16).                     P.D.G.

**PARMASHTA** Mentioned in *Est. 9:8*, he was one of ten sons of Haman killed in Susa by the Jews.

**PARMENAS** was one of the seven men appointed to help the apostles who were finding the work of administration in the early Jerusalem church to be too burdensome (*Acts 6:5*). Many new people were becoming Christians. The new Christians of Greek-Jewish background were falling out with those of Hebrew-Jewish background over the distribution of food to widows. The disciples found that they were spending so much time sorting out these things (*v. 2*) that they were neglecting the ministry of the Word of God. Seven men were therefore to be appointed and to be chosen as those known to be 'full of the Spirit and wisdom'. The apostles prayed and laid their hands on these men and appointed them to the job of looking after the day-to-day affairs of the church.

This incident is an interesting indication of how early in the church's life there was a recognition of the fact that God gives different people different 'ministries' or gifts. But it also reflects the early recognition by the church that those called to 'the ministry of the Word of God' (*v. 2*) should not have other pre-occupations. V. 7 indicates the success of this division of labour: 'the word of God spread. The number of disciples in Jerusalem increased rapidly.                    P.D.G.

**PARNACH** was from the tribe of Zebulun and was the father of Elizaphan (*Num.*

34:25). Elizaphan was chosen by Moses as the leader of the tribe of Zebulun, and he helped assign the inheritance of land to the various families in his tribe.

**PAROSH** A family leader whose descendants were counted among those who, in the time of Ezra, returned with Zerubbabel and Nehemiah from the Babylonian Exile. Their number was 2,172 (*Ezra 2:3; 8:3; Neh. 7:8*). It was probably he, or a descendant of the same name, who sealed the agreement with Nehemiah to serve the LORD and obey only his Law (*Neh. 10:14*). Some of his descendants were guilty of marriage to foreign wives, and another of his descendants, Pedaiah, was among those who helped repair the wall of Jerusalem (*Ezra 10:25; Neh. 3:25*).

**PARSHANDATHA** Mentioned in *Est. 9:7*, he was one of ten sons of Haman killed in Susa by the Jews.

**PARUAH** Father of Jehoshaphat. Jehoshaphat was the district governor in Issachar at the time of Solomon and had the duty of supplying provisions to the palace for one month of each year (*1 Kings 4:17*).

**PASACH** Mentioned in *1 Chron. 7:33* as a son of Japhlet, of the tribe of Asher. He was one of the brave warriors and the head of a family.

**PASEAH** (Heb., 'supplication').
**1.** One of the leaders of the tribe of Judah. His father was Eshton and he and his family lived in Recah (*1 Chron. 4:12*).
**2.** A leader of one of the families of Temple servants whose descendants returned from the Babylonian Exile in the days of Ezra and worked on the Temple (*Ezra 2:49; Neh. 7:51*).
**3.** The father of Joiada. Joiada helped repair one of the gates of the city of Jerusalem during Nehemiah's time following the return to Judah from the Babylonian exile (*Neh. 3:6*).

**PASHHUR 1.** Pashhur son of Immer was a priest who was the 'chief officer in the temple of the LORD' at the time Jeremiah was prophesying judgment on Jerusalem (*Jer. 20:1*). When Pashhur heard Jeremiah he felt the people would be demoralized by such words and so he had the prophet beaten and put in the stocks by the Temple area (*v. 2*). The following day, Pashhur, thinking Jeremiah would have learned his lesson, released him. Jeremiah then said to Pashhur: 'The LORD's name for you is not Pashhur, but Magor-Missabib'. The name meant 'terror everywhere' (*vv. 3–6*). Specifically, Jeremiah prophesied that Pashhur's own family would go into Exile where Pashhur himself would die. With him would die all the friends to whom he had prophesied lies, namely that things would *not* go ill for Judah. Life in Judah and Jerusalem did go from bad to worse. When the Babylonians invaded and deported most of the inhabitants, no doubt Pashhur and his family and friends were also transported to Babylon.

**2.** Pashhur, son of Malkijah (different from 1. above) is mentioned in *Jer. 21:1*. He was sent by King Zedekiah to Jeremiah at a time when it seemed only a matter of days before the city of Jerusalem would be completely crushed by Nebuchadnezzar. Vainly they hoped that God would 'perform wonders for us as in times past' (*v. 2*). Jeremiah's response was that the judgment would happen and even God himself would fight against them (*vv. 5–6*). Later in *Jer. 38:1* we read again of this Pashhur wanting to silence what he saw as the defeatist attitude of Jeremiah and his prophecies. Jeremiah was arrested and thrown into a cistern from which he was later rescued. When the judgment of the LORD finally comes it is awesome and frightening. This was what Zedekiah, Pashhur and the others were about to experience. The Babylonians did take Jerusalem and this Pashhur, it seems, may have been among those who were taken away into Exile because a descendant of 'Pashhur son of Malkijah', is listed among the first of the priests to resettle in Jerusalem following the return from the Exile in Babylon. This descendant, Adaiah, was involved in helping rebuild the Temple (*Neh. 11:12; 1 Chron. 9:12*). He was a descendant of Immer and the head of a family.

**3.** An ancestor of one of the priestly families that returned with Zerubbabel to resettle in Jerusalem following the Exile in Babylon. Perhaps he was the same person as 2. above. 1,247 of Pashhur's descendants returned. Some of his descendants had been guilty of intermarriage with women of foreign nations and, under Ezra's guidance, later divorced their foreign wives (*Ezra 2:38; 10:22; Neh. 7:41*).

**4.** This Pashhur joined in witnessing the solemn covenant of obedience to the Law of God in Nehemiah's time in Jerusalem (*Neh. 10:3*).

**5.** Father of Gedaliah. Gedaliah was one of the princes in Judah who joined Pashhur son of Malkijah (2. above) in having Jeremiah arrested (*Jer. 38:1*).

P.D.G.

**PATROBAS** The fourth named of a group of Roman Christians greeted by Paul in his letter to the Romans (*16:14*). The personal care and pastoral concern for individuals reflected in Paul's greetings is worthy of attention.

# PAUL

## Introduction and background

This Jewish Pharisee is first encountered in the book of Acts under his Hebrew name Saul (*Acts 7:58; 13:9*). He was born in Tarsus in Cilicia which was in Asia Minor (modern southern Turkey). He was probably born around ten years after Christ, since he is referred to as a 'young man' at the time of Stephen's stoning (*Acts 7:58*). Paul's father was no doubt Jewish but must have bought or been given Roman citizenship, for Paul later made use of the fact that he was a Roman citizen by birth and therefore had the right to be tried in Rome by Caesar (*Acts 22:25*). In spite of his citizenship, Paul had been brought up in a devout Jewish family from the tribe of Benjamin. He had received careful instruction in the Jewish law and had joined the Pharisees. He also described himself as a 'Hebrew of the Hebrews'. He had been brought up in accordance with the Law, having been circumcised on the eighth day, and he had become zealous to follow every point of the Mosaic commands (*Phil. 3:5–6*).

So zealous was he for the Law and for his faith that he had travelled at some stage, probably in his early teenage years, to Jerusalem where he had studied under a famous teacher called Gamaliel. Paul later spoke to Jewish leaders of that time: 'Under Gamaliel I was thoroughly trained in the law of our fathers and was just as zealous for God as any of you are today' (*Acts 22:3*).

Even Jewish teachers were expected to have a trade to work at, and so it comes as no surprise that this highly educated religious leader had also been taught a craft by his father. He was a 'tent-maker' (*Acts. 18:3*), and from time to time mention is made of how he worked to support himself (*1 Cor. 4:12; 2 Thess. 3:8* etc.). There is ample evidence in these and other passages that Paul deliberately worked so as not to impose any burden on those among whom he wished to proclaim an absolutely 'free' gospel (*1 Cor. 9:16–19*). Also, given the way travelling teachers and philosophers would often expect people to support them with food and finances, he probably deliberately sought to avoid being regarded as just another roaming teacher (*1 Thess. 2:3–6*).

## Paul's life and travels

Being educated as he was and with such a universally acceptable trade, it is likely that Paul had travelled widely even before he became a Christian. He would, of course, have been fluent in Greek and Hebrew or Aramaic (possibly both). He is first noted in Acts, watching people's clothing as the crowds stoned Stephen to death for his faith, commitment to Christ, and his desire to promote the gospel. 'Saul was there giving his approval to his death' (*Acts 7:58–8:1*).

***Persecuting Christians.*** From the day of Stephen's death a great persecution broke out against the followers of Jesus. Saul's zealous activity as a Jew led him to join the persecutions. He needed no urging to this but rather volunteered his services to the Jewish leaders in Jerusalem. So violent was his persecution that we read: 'Saul began to destroy the church. Going from house to house, he dragged off men and women and put them in prison' (*Acts 8:3;* also see *1 Cor. 15:9; Phil. 3:6*). In *Acts 9:1* we read that Saul, 'breathing out murderous threats against the Lord's disciples', went to the high priest for letters he could take with him to the synagogues in Damascus in order to pursue the persecution there as well.

***Paul's conversion.***    It was while he was on his way to Damascus that *Acts 9* tells us a bright light from heaven flashed around him, throwing him to the ground and blinding him. As he lay on the ground a voice spoke to him saying, 'Saul, Saul, why do you persecute me?' Baffled, Saul asked, 'Who are you, Lord?' and the response he received must have truly amazed and frightened him: 'I am Jesus, whom you are persecuting' (*Acts 9:4–5*). Jesus then told Saul to go to Damascus and await further instructions. Saul waited in Damascus for three days without eating and drinking before being told to go to the house of a Christian called Ananias (see *Ananias*). This time without eating and drinking was probably a time of fasting and repentance for we are told that, when Ananias came to Paul, he found him praying (*v. 11*).

Ananias laid hands on Paul, his sight was restored, he received the Holy Spirit and he was baptized. Saul then spent several days with the disciples in Damascus, no doubt learning as much as he could about Jesus. However, there was not much time for that learning process as he 'at once began to preach in the synagogues that Jesus is the Son of God' (*Acts 9:20*). His extraordinary theological understanding coupled with the complete change in his perspective on Christ, enabled him to 'baffle the Jews' in Damascus 'by proving that Jesus is the Christ' (*v. 22*). Probably after some considerable period of preaching in the area around Damascus (Arabia), the Jews tried to put a stop to this and to assassinate Saul. He escaped by night and, eventually, came back to Jerusalem. There he found it difficult to meet with other disciples of Christ for, quite naturally, they were very afraid of him. Barnabas took him on and brought him to the apostles who gave him their approval. Paul preached widely and debated widely until once again his life was threatened and the disciples took him to Caesarea where he boarded a boat for Tarsus (*Acts 9:29–30; Gal. 1:18–24*). The extraordinary speed of Saul's change of heart, and the speed with which he understood Scriptures in a new light and started preaching the gospel of Christ, provides the most dramatic evidence of the work of the Holy Spirit in his life following his encounter with Christ on the Damascus road. Paul himself recounted this conversion experience on two other occasions. In the first instance in *Acts 22* it was following his arrest in Jerusalem when he asked to be allowed to speak to the crowds. The second instance is recorded in *Acts 26* when Paul was speaking in his own defence before King Agrippa.

***Called to the Gentiles.***    The speed with which Saul also found himself moving into Gentile territory is a further indication of the Spirit's driving him towards his ultimate calling, to be an apostle to the Gentiles. Paul made mentioned in his letters of this special calling of God to a ministry among the Gentiles (*Rom. 11:13; Gal. 2:8; 1 Tim. 2:7*). Although Peter was called to the Jews and Paul to the Gentiles (*Gal. 2:8*), we know that both apostles preached wherever they had opportunity. Paul, in fact usually went first to the synagogue in each town he visited. There he would preach, sometimes seeing some conversions, until he was ejected by antagonistic Jews. He would then preach to the Gentiles. (He thus lived out in practice what he taught in *Rom. 1:16; 2:9–10* etc.) One of Paul's earliest works among the Gentiles, after his acceptance by the apostles in Jerusalem (*Gal. 1*), was initiated by Barnabas who took him from Tarsus to Antioch in northern Syria. The church at Antioch was already established and Barnabas no doubt drew Paul into the work because of the teaching he could offer (*Acts 11:19–30*). The church work there had started among Jews but had soon spread to the Gentiles (Greeks) and Paul's debating ability and previous work among Gentiles no doubt stood him in good stead. While he was in Antioch, the prophet Agabus warned of an impending great famine so the church agreed to raise funds to help those in Jerusalem and Judea and to send the money with Saul and Barnabas (*v. 30*).

It is very difficult to be sure of an exact chronology in Paul's life at this time as Acts and Galatians only give partial pictures, but the Gentile ministry was firmly established and Paul's senior role in this work was seen almost immediately in the work at Antioch. He and Barnabas left Antioch under the guidance of the Holy Spirit (*Acts 13:2*). From this time onwards Paul's life may largely be seen as one of movement around the empire. Sometimes he stayed in cities for some period of time and on other occasions he stayed but a brief while, mostly he moved of his own volition but, specially later, he was often moved by others under guard on his way to prison, to trial, or to Rome.

**First missionary journey.**   Paul's travels are generally known as his 'missionary journeys' of which there were three. On the first of these journeys, probably made sometime between A D 47 and A D 48, he went to Barnabas' home country of Cyprus. Right across the island they preached. When they reached the town of Paphos, Paul was able to present the gospel to the pro-consul Sergius Paulus (see *Sergius*). Sergius believed, 'for he was amazed at the teaching about the Lord' (*Acts 13:12*). This conversion may have been the final confirmation for Paul that in his ministry he really would see serious and influential Gentiles become Christians. It is thus perhaps significant that from this time onwards Saul was called by his Latin name Paul (*Acts 13:9*). From Cyprus, Paul and Barnabas set sail for Perga in Asia Minor (modern Turkey). When they arrived there, John Mark who had been with them, left the group to return to Jerusalem. From there they travelled north to Pisidian Antioch, east to Iconium, south to Lystra and on to Derbe before retracing their steps and sailing back to Antioch from Attalia. The results of their work on this journey varied from place to place but are recorded in *Acts 13–14*. They must have been quite considerable over all, however, for their return journey involved them returning to the churches they had founded, 'strengthening the disciples and encouraging them to remain true to the faith'. They also warned that the new Christians would have 'to go through many hardships to enter the kingdom of God' (*Acts 14:22*). Paul and his friends were already experiencing this as they travelled, not just from antagonistic Gentiles but from the Jews, some of whom followed them around whipping up trouble for the missionary party. Nevertheless the churches were sufficiently well established for Paul and Barnabas to appoint elders in each church as they passed back through.

Back in Antioch some teachers arrived from Judea arguing that true salvation was dependant upon circumcision. Paul and Barnabas were incensed and debated the issue with them. The church at Antioch then decided to send these two back to Jerusalem to sort out the issues involved in a meeting with the other apostles.

***The Jerusalem Council.*** This meeting was attended by the Christian apostles and leaders in Jerusalem and has become known as the Jerusalem Council (*Acts 15:1–35*). The Council first heard reports of all the work of the gospel that was going on around Asia Minor, in Antioch and among the Gentiles generally and there was much praising God. But some believers who were converted Pharisees argued that believers among the Gentiles should be circumcised (*Acts 15:5*). Much discussion followed before Peter stood up to speak to the assembly. His statement, presumably agreed by the leadership of James and the apostles, made some interesting observations. He pointed out that he himself had first taken the gospel to the Gentiles (no doubt thinking of the episode of his vision and trip to see Cornelius, *Acts 10*). He then appealed to the fact that 'God, who knows the heart, showed that he accepted them by giving the Holy Spirit to them, just as he did to us' (*Acts 15:8*). In other words, just as the Holy Spirit's presence had been 'shown' to the apostles on the Day of Pentecost in Jerusalem through their speaking in tongues and praising God (*Acts 2:4, 47*), so the Spirit's presence among Gentiles had also been 'shown' again through speaking in tongues and praising God. On that occasion Luke records specifically that it had happened to the surprise of all the circumcised believers (*Acts 10:45–46*). For Peter that evidence had been all he had needed for proceeding to baptize these new Christians not into some second-rate form of Christian community but into the full Christian faith into which the disciples themselves had been baptized (*Acts 10:47–48*).

Since God had made 'no distinction between us and them', argued Peter (*Acts 15:9–11*), it would be quite improper to insist that converts among the Gentiles should be circumcised. Circumcision was clearly not a requirement for being a true Christian, indeed the mark of the Christian was possession of the Holy Spirit, not circumcision. Salvation was entirely through belief in the saving grace of the Lord Jesus Christ (*v. 11*). Paul and Barnabas then also joined in, pointing to the great work of grace that had been going on among the Gentiles and the miracles that had been performed among them. But it was left to James to draw the proceedings to a conclusion.

James stood up and expounded Scriptures, showing how the prophets had looked for the time when Gentiles would turn to the Lord. He agreed that they should not be forced into circumcision but, nevertheless, argued that they should demonstrate their love for the Jewish believers by abstaining from food polluted by being offered to idols, from sexual immorality, and from animals killed in particular ways (*Acts 15:13–21*). Since this compromise did not involve any matters of principle, it was agreed, and a letter was sent to the churches around Antioch carrying the decision to them. The great significance of this Council was the way it established once and for all the legitimate full membership among the true people of God of believing Gentiles. Paul's stand for the universal significance of the gospel message had been vindicated.

***Second and third missionary journeys.*** The second missionary journey lasted from around AD 49 to AD 52 (*Acts 15:36–18:22*). This journey was very significant for it spread the gospel much more widely taking it from Asia Minor into south-eastern Europe as well. This work began rather sadly with a difference of opinion between Paul and Barnabas. The latter wanted to take Mark with them on the trip. Perhaps Mark had originally returned to Jerusalem because of his doubts about the Gentile mission, we cannot be sure. However, Paul was adamant that John Mark should not come and so Barnabas and Mark left for Cyprus to continue the work there, and Paul took Silas north with him to Antioch in Syria, on to Tarsus and back through the recently founded churches in Derbe, Lystra, and Iconium.

While in Lystra, Paul was introduced to a young man who became one of his closest and most reliable friends, Timothy. Timothy had a Jewish mother and a Greek father and had become a disciple of Christ. The leaders of the church at Lystra urged Paul to take Timothy with him and they 'spoke well of him' (*Acts 16:1–2*). Living in a Greek family had meant that Timothy was not a circumcised Jew. Because his mother was a Jew (*v. 1*) Paul felt it would enhance Timothy's ministry among the Jewish communities if he were circumcised, so Timothy was circumcised at Paul's direction. There was no conflict here in Paul's thinking with the antagonism he showed to the circumcision party in his letter to the Galatians. It was one thing for a Jew to be circumcised in order better to reach his own people with the gospel, but altogether another to enforce circumcision on Gentiles based on some false understanding that they needed to be 'Jews' in order to be proper Christians!

The next part of their journey was into new territory. They made a rigorous overland trip to Troas, being very carefully guided by 'the Spirit of Jesus' not to work in some areas (*Acts 16:7*). While preaching in Troas, one night Paul had a vision of a man calling him to come and minister in Macedonia. Concluding this was God instructing them on the next stage of their journey, they crossed by boat into the Greek province of Macedonia where they preached in Neapolis, Philippi, Thessalonica and Berea. From there they set sail south and preached in Athens and Corinth (where he stayed for 18 months), before crossing back to Ephesus in Asia Minor and on to Caesarea, Jerusalem and back to Antioch.

The work of the gospel continued to expand rapidly during this trip. The churches founded during the first journey were settling down well and more and more were added to their number (*Acts 16–19*). There were many encouragements and some very hard times of persecution. Among the encouragements Paul saw the successful founding of many more churches. He also saw results of the gospel message in the lives of some men and women who no doubt became special friends to the missionary team. In Philippi they encountered a businesswoman called Lydia who was converted and put the team up in her house. They also saw the amazing conversion of their jailer when they were imprisoned in Philippi (see *Philippian jailer*). In Thessalonica they saw converts like Jason being imprisoned for the gospel's sake. Yet how they must have enjoyed the reception given them by the 'noble' Bereans who accepted 'the message with great eagerness and examined the Scripture [Old Testament] every day to see if what Paul said was true' (*Acts 17:11*). Here Paul and the team saw how the gospel was beginning to touch the hearts and lives of people from different social classes as a 'number of prominent Greek women and many Greek men' were converted (*v. 12*).

In Athens, Paul had seen at least a few conversions while debating with some of the greatest philosophers of the age. Back in Corinth, Paul struck up a close friendship with a Jewish couple who were also tentmakers and became great workers for Christ, Priscilla and Aquila (*Acts 18:1–3*). These two then accompanied him on his trip from Corinth over to Ephesus and, while there, were responsible for helping Apollos understand more of the truth of the gospel. Apollos was then sent back to Greece and continued the gospel ministry in Corinth. Paul meanwhile stopped just briefly in Ephesus before returning to Caesarea and Jerusalem where he greeted the church and then returned once more going to Antioch.

In each town where he preached Paul was now encountering very severe resistance to the gospel. In Philippi Paul and Silas were imprisoned because of the antagonism of the crowds and only released after the miraculous intervention of God himself which led to the jailer's conversion. In Thessalonica others were imprisoned because Paul could not be found. In Corinth, though quite quickly released, Paul was attacked by the Jews and taken before a court under Gallio (see *Gallio*).

Paul spent some time in Antioch before embarking on his third missionary journey which took place somewhere in the period between AD 53 and AD 57 (*Acts 18:23–21:16*). On this trip Paul once again travelled north and west overland revisiting the churches in Galatia and Phrygia (Derbe, Lystra, Iconium, and Antioch of Pisidia). When at last Paul arrived in Ephesus we read that he encountered 'some disciples'. They had only received the baptism of John the Baptist and when Paul filled them in on the news about Christ and receiving the Holy Spirit, they were immediately baptized 'into the name of the Lord Jesus' and the Spirit came upon them (*Acts 19:1–7*). This interesting aside gives an indication that the work of the Baptist had reached a far wider area than the Gospels' account would suggest.

Once again having begun to preach in the synagogue, Paul was ejected and preached widely to the Gentiles in the city for two years (*v. 10*). Clearly many miracles accompanied Paul's proclamation of the gospel and brief mention of these is made in *v. 11*. Numbers of people were converted during this time in Ephesus, a time which also witnessed many magicians and people who followed sorcery being converted and bringing all their books to be burned publicly. *V. 20* summarizes this period of ministry: 'In this way the word of the Lord spread widely and grew in power.'

It was during this period that a great riot occurred in Ephesus. Ephesus was famous for its temple to Artemis (see *Artemis, Alexander*). Acts does not give a full account of the persecution Paul experienced while in the city but it was probably considerable (see *1 Cor. 15:32; Rom. 16:3–4; 2 Cor. 1:8–11*). Paul then sent Timothy and Erastus on ahead to Macedonia. He expressed his intention to leave for Jerusalem via Macedonia and Achaia and (*Acts 19:21*) informed the people that at some stage he would have to go to Rome.

It was during this journey that Paul became specially concerned to raise money for the support of the very poor believers in the church in Jerusalem. Paul instructed churches to join him in contributing to this collection, seeing it as a sign of the unity of the church world-wide and especially the unity between converted Jews and converted Gentiles (e.g. *Rom. 15:25–32*).

Paul sailed over to Macedonia retracing his earlier ministry through Philippi,

Thessalonica and Berea, and encouraging the believers. A short stay in Greece, perhaps in Athens, led to further persecution and so he returned to Macedonia before setting sail again from Troas. In Troas, Paul continued to preach. In an early example of worship on the first day of the week (Sunday) we read that Paul preached after they had broken bread together (taken communion). He preached on till late at night as he was leaving the next day. In the heat of the crowded room and due to the lateness of the day, a young man called Eutychus fell asleep and fell from a window in which he was sitting to the ground three storeys below. Paul raised him to life again and continued preaching (*Acts 20:7–12*).

The following morning Paul set sail stopping at various ports on the way south, including Miletus where he met with the elders of the Ephesian church. There he taught the elders yet more of the dangers of false teaching and the need to keep watch over themselves and their faith and over their flock. He committed them to God and talked of being 'compelled by the Spirit' to go to Jerusalem. The sadness of their parting is vividly described as they all knelt in a prayer meeting together, realizing they would not see their beloved apostle again (*vv. 36–38*). The rest of this journey is described briefly by Luke in *Acts 21:1–17*. The only significant port of call was at Tyre. There the prophet Agabus warned Paul not to go to Jerusalem because his life would be in danger. It is perhaps significant that Paul's earlier statement of being compelled to go to Jerusalem by the Spirit took precedence over this warning by Agabus. It would seem that, although the prophecy itself was accurate, the interpretation was wrong. Agabus clearly expected that Paul would not go to Jerusalem, but that is where he went and that led to his arrest and imprisonment. In going this way, Paul made it clear he was prepared to die for Christ, if that was what he was called to do (*v. 13*).

This third journey had again seen many more people converted and much antagonism and persecution, but it must also have been an encouraging time. Paul was able to see many younger people beginning to come into the ministry of the gospel. Among those mentioned during this trip were people like 'Sopater son of Pyrrhus from Berea, Aristarchus and Secundus from Thessalonica, Gaius from Derbe, Timothy also, and Tychicus and Trophimus from the province of Asia' (*Acts 20:4*). Even though Paul would not return to many of these places, he now knew the work would continue in the hands of a younger generation of faithful missionaries and pastors.

***On trial and in prison.*** Once Paul arrived back in Jerusalem the prophecy of Agabus was soon fulfilled. Jews stirred up antagonism and Paul was arrested for his own protection amidst a massive demonstration against him that would have led to his death (*Acts 21:27–36*). Paul asked the Roman commander for permission to speak to the crowd and used the opportunity once again to preach the gospel of Jesus, telling them of his own conversion and calling to the Gentiles. It was at the mention of the Gentiles that once again the anger of the crowd took over and Paul was taken to the barracks. There he appealed to his Roman citizenship to avoid being flogged. The following day the commander called together the Sanhedrin and Paul defended himself before his accusers (*Acts 23*). Paul successfully managed to divide his accusers into different sides by saying that he was on trial because he believed in the resurrection. The Pharisees, who also believed in the resurrection, then started arguing with Sadducees who did not. Again, for Paul's protection in the dispute, he was taken back to barracks. That night the Lord himself stood by Paul and encouraged him, also telling him that he would yet have to go to Rome to testify to the gospel (*Acts 23:11*).

A plot to kill Paul was then discovered and the commander, Claudius Lysias, decided to transfer Paul to Caesarea where his case could be looked into by Governor Felix. *Acts 24* describes the trial before Felix. Felix appears to have been interested in what he heard from Paul concerning 'the Way', but out of deference to the Jews he continued to hold Paul in prison for around two years. When Festus arrived in the province the Jews asked him to deal with Paul. Festus suggested he should hand Paul over to the Jews, but Paul, knowing he would not get a proper trial in Jerusalem and no doubt conscious of the Lord's call that he should testify in Rome, appealed to Caesar. This effectively took him out of the Jewish legal system altogether. Shortly after this Agrippa also visited Caesarea and Festus talked to him about Paul. Paul again related his conversion and talked of the gospel of Christ. While Festus thought Paul must be mad, Agrippa seems to have been quite moved by what Paul had to say, even suggesting that he had been tempted also to become a Christian as he listened (*Acts 26:28*). Agrippa's conclusion was that Paul could have been released had he not appealed to Caesar (*v. 32*).

Paul was then transported to Rome as a prisoner under the command of a centurion called Julius. (For more detail on these times see *Agrippa, Festus, Felix* and *Julius*). After a shipwreck on Malta which again Paul used as an opportunity for the gospel, they finally arrived in Rome where Paul was placed under house arrest but allowed Christian visitors (*Acts 28*). During two years under this house arrest (probably around AD 61 to AD 63), Paul 'Boldly and without hindrance preached the kingdom of God and taught about the Lord Jesus Christ' (*Acts 28:31*).

***Paul's death.*** There are few indications of what happened after this period of house arrest in Rome. Clearly Paul used the opportunity very effectively for the gospel, but Luke finishes his book of Acts at that point having established the legal right for the gospel to be preached in Rome. There is much debate among scholars about what then occurred. Given that the pastoral epistles (see below) seem to refer to events in Paul's life not recorded in Acts and assuming that Paul wrote those epistles, many have conjectured that Paul was eventually declared innocent by the courts and released. Certainly Paul seems to anticipate release in *Phil. 1:19, 25* and *2:24*. Perhaps it was after this release that Paul achieved his ambition of travelling to Spain (see *Rom. 15:24, 28*). This period would also have seen the composition of the letters to Timothy and Titus. Once Christianity was outlawed, Paul was rearrested and taken back for a second imprisonment in Rome from where he wrote *2 Timothy*. His period of freedom would probably have lasted from around AD 63 to AD 66. *2 Tim. 4* is then a sad account of what certainly seems to be Paul's final trial before his death (*v. 18*). Even in that most sad chapter, however, it is clear that Paul continued to take advantage of every opportunity for the gospel (*2 Tim. 4:17–18*). Tradition has it that Paul died in Rome a martyr at the hands of Nero around AD 67.

## Paul's writings

Paul's legacy to the world is enormous. Apart from the fact that he introduced the wider world to the truth of the gospel of Jesus Christ, he also wrote a number of very significant epistles that have come down to us as Scripture in the NT. These letters are full of exposition about Jesus, about sin and salvation, leading a Christian life, the future, and about the nature of the church. The epistles cannot be examined in detail here and the very brief summaries below could never do justice to the depths of teaching each letter contains, but will perhaps whet the reader's appetite to examine them more closely. In many ways these epistles have provided a framework for the church of Christ across the centuries. Although some scholars these days debate about whether or not Paul was directly responsible for all those epistles attributed to him, there are 13 that are attributed to him in the NT. For convenience here they are divided into three groups.

***The early and major epistles.*** These epistles include *Galatians*, 1 and 2 *Thessalonians*, 1 and 2 *Corinthians*, and *Romans*. Galatians is the only epistle in which Paul had almost nothing positive to say to the believers to whom he was writing. This was because of his great burden that many were pursuing 'another gospel'. He was afraid for their very salvation and for the purity of the doctrine of salvation by grace alone through faith. It would appear that those arguing that a Christian must first become a Jew in order to be saved had had some success in expounding their views. They advocated circumcision, and keeping the Mosaic Law and Sabbaths. This was directly contrary to Paul's teaching that Gentiles could become Christians and be 'justified' (declared not guilty before God) through faith in Christ and still be Gentiles (*Gal. 3:8, 11, 24; 5:4*). To the Galatians Paul said: 'If anybody is preaching to you a gospel other than what you accepted, let him be eternally condemned!' (*Gal. 1:9*). Paul insisted that they were all sons of God 'through faith in Christ Jesus . . . There is neither Jew nor Greek, slave nor free, male nor female, for you are all one in Christ Jesus. If you belong to Christ, then you are Abraham's seed, and heirs according to the promise' (*Gal. 3:26–29*). Christ brings a freedom from the letter of the Law and its punishment because, said Paul, 'I have been crucified with Christ and I no longer live, but Christ lives in me. The life I live in the body, I live by faith in the Son of God, who loved me and gave himself for me' (*Gal. 2:20*). This life in Christ is a changed life of a new nature now led by the Spirit of Christ and heading for the goal of eternal life (*Gal. 5:16, 22, 25; 6:8*). Paul insisted that these truths are for all who believe in Christ, whatever their nationality, sex or social class. Christianity could never be just a sect of Judaism. The fact that the decisions of the Jerusalem Council did not form part of Paul's appeal and teaching suggests to some that it was probably written just before that Council met (perhaps AD 49). Others put the letter somewhat later.

The epistles of 1 and 2 *Thessalonians* are best known for their teaching on the second coming of Jesus. In fact, in 1 *Thessalonians* Paul spends considerable time encouraging these Christians in their faith and Christian life and witness (1 *Thess.* 4). He thanks God for them and specially for the way they accepted the preaching at the beginning 'not as the word of men, but as it actually is, the word of God which is at work in you who believe' (1 *Thess. 2:13*). Paul urged their continuation in the faith specially in the light of the coming of Christ which should provide them with great hope and joy. They should encourage each other (1 Thess. 4:18) with the knowledge that Christ would return and certainly not grieve for those who have died, as if they were like the rest of the world with no hope (1 Thess. 4:13). The second epistle was probably written during Paul's stay at Corinth. Again Paul was thankful to God for their perseverance and faith and the great love the believers demonstrated for each other (2 Thess. 1:3–12). However, part of the letter is also written to correct certain misunderstandings about the return of Christ. A fanaticism had developed that seems to have led to some even giving up work in order to wait for the imminent return of the Lord (2 Thess. 2). Paul had to insist that normal Christian life should continue to be lived even though this would be a life of persecution and difficulties. The fact that God had chosen them and saved them through the work of the Spirit should help them stand firm in the faith (2 Thess. 2:13–15).

The Corinthian epistles were probably written during Paul's extended stay in Ephesus. The first epistle to the Corinthians tackles a number of very practical problems being faced by the church. Paul expressed concern at the way they seemed to be dividing into groups (1 Cor. 1:12). He reminded them they shouldn't need to go to the secular courts in trying to sort out their differences (1 Cor. 6). He taught them about leading a pure life morally and reminded them that their bodies were 'God's temple and that the Holy Spirit lives in you' (1 Cor. 3:16; 5:1–13). He dealt with the practical issue of whether they should eat meat that had previously been offered as a sacrifice to pagan gods and also examined the way spiritual gifts should be used in the church. Those gifts needed to be used to build each other up so that true Christian love would be shown in the community (1 Cor. 12–14). The bodily resurrection of Christ is also defended at length in 1 Cor. 15.

By the time of 2 Corinthians the divisions in the church seem to have become even more pronounced. But Paul is specially concerned to discuss his own relationship with the church. It is clear that some Christians in Corinth have put him down, perhaps arguing that he was not as spiritual as some of their own leaders whom Paul refers to as 'super-apostles' (2 Cor. 11:5).

Paul demonstrated in this letter what the life of the true Christian was to be like. Taking his own life by way of example, he showed that for the sake of Christ, he had had to suffer untold persecution and difficulties (2 Cor. 10–12). He may not have been the most eloquent of speakers but nevertheless he was called to gospel ministry and God had honoured that work. Many was the time he had felt frail and almost defeated but always it had been faith in Christ and a desire to fulfil his calling that had kept him going (see esp. 2 Cor. 4–5; 7). He reminded them of the glory of the gospel (2 Cor. 3) and encouraged them to generosity in their giving for the Jerusalem appeal (2 Cor. 8).

Romans was probably written in the mid A D 50s. It is an epistle written by Paul to a church he had not at that time visited. It is full of praise for their faith and commitment to Christ. Its main theme stresses that justification is by faith in Christ for Jew and Gentile alike. There is some discussion as to why Paul wrote this letter. Some say Paul was aware of a debate between converted Jews and converted Gentiles in the church and their need for some pastoral help. Others suggest the letter formed a theological basis for his missionary strategy to take the gospel to the

Gentiles and that Paul hoped for support from the Roman Christians for his intended trip to Spain. Other views have also been proposed. The letter itself stresses that all people, Jew and Gentile, have sinned (Rom. 1:18; 3:10–11 etc.). However, salvation has come to all, 'without distinction', who have faith in Jesus. Though all have sinned, for those who believe all 'are justified freely by his grace through the redemption that came by Christ Jesus' (Rom. 3:23). The reason for this possibility of salvation for all is to be seen in the sacrificial nature of Christ's death (Rom. 3:24–26; see Jesus). Jew and Gentile alike inherit God's rich covenant blessings because God is faithful to his promises. God's righteousness is seen in his acquitting of those saved by faith but also in the way he has fulfilled his promises made to Abraham, the great example of one who was justified by faith (Rom. 4). In this epistle, Paul also talked of Christian life lived under the Spirit's guidance, or the privilege of adoption as God's sons and the eternal security that that brings (Rom. 8). He also discussed how the nation of Israel fitted into God's great plan of salvation (Rom. 9–11) and then provided instructions about how these Christians should live for Christ, as 'living sacrifices, holy and pleasing to God' (Rom. 12:1–2).

**The prison epistles.**   These epistles were written from prison. There has been some discussion as to whether they all came from a Roman imprisonment or perhaps from the time of his Caesarean imprisonment. If they all come from the Roman imprisonment then they may be dated to a period around AD 62 to AD 63. They include Ephesians, Philippians, Colossians and Philemon. (For more on Philemon see *Philemon* and *Onesimus*.)

The epistle to the Ephesians opens with one of the most glorious passages of Scripture describing the great blessings Christians experience from being 'in Christ'. These blessings have been planned by God from before creation. They include forgiveness of sins, predestination to adoption as sons of God, the joy of bringing glory to God and possession of the Holy Spirit as the guarantee of redemption and the full inheritance of eternal life (Eph. 1). The epistle meditates on these blessings and on God's wonderful love for his people that led to his greatest demonstration of grace in the salvation of those who have faith in Jesus (Eph. 2). The church is the body of Christ, united in calling and purpose (Eph. 2:11–22). The people of God should therefore live as children of light, in step with the Holy Spirit, imitating God and witnessing to him in the midst of the darkness of the world around (Eph. 4:1–5:21). Paul went on to expound how certain specific relationships would reflect this love of Christ for his people (Eph. 5:21–6:10). He then urged that these Christians stand firm in the faith putting on the whole armour of God, led by the Spirit and obedient to the Word of God (Eph. 6:1–18).

Philippians is a 'thank you' letter. Paul wrote to thank the Philippians for their most recent financial gift for his support (especially Phil. 1 and 4:10–20). The Christians at Philippi seem to have been faithful supporters of Paul's ministry and his thankfulness to God for them shines through the epistle. Personal comments in the letter about Epaphroditus and his illness reflect Paul's personal relationship with these Christians. Paul had to warn the Ephesians about Judaizers (Phil. 3:1–11) and encouraged them to stand firm and continue to live lives that were 'worthy of Christ' whatever they might have to live through (Phil. 1:27–30; 2:12–18; 3:12–4:1). The most notable passage theologically is to be found in Phil. 2:1–11. The passage speaks of Christ's humility, not a characteristic to which anyone in the ancient world or indeed in the modern world particularly aspired! This humility of Christ, who followed his calling even to the cross, provides the basis and example for Paul's appeal that the Philippians continue in humility together and without grumbling as they work out their own calling from God. That calling is summarized by Paul in *Phil. 2:14–17*. They are to 'shine like stars in the universe' as they 'hold out the word of life'.

The Colossian Christians were probably mostly Gentiles, the first of whom had been converted under the ministry of Epaphras (*Col. 1:7; 2:13*). From what Paul says, scholars have inferred that Paul was concerned in writing this letter with some particularly serious false teaching that had entered the church. Perhaps this heretical teaching had diminished the place of Christ and emphasized human wisdom. It had perhaps even begun to insist on some Jewish practices such as circumcision and Sabbath observance. The worship of angels may have played a part in their thinking and there was probably an emphasis on the mystical and secretive. In response to this Paul spoke of the pre-eminence of Christ in all things. He alone is the head of the church. He is the Creator, he is pre-existent, he is the first to rise from the dead (*Col. 1:15–23*). It was in Christ that these people had died to sin and been raised by God to life. It was 'in him' that they had been forgiven. 'In Christ' Sabbath laws and eating and drinking laws had been rendered redundant for they were but 'shadows' waiting for the time of Christ (*Col. 2:16–19*). The way forward for these Christians was not to turn away from Christ in looking for their spiritual experiences, whether to angels, legal regulations etc., but rather as Paul put it, 'Set your minds on things above, not on earthly things. For you died, and your life is now hidden with Christ in God' (*Col. 3:2–3*). They should live as God's chosen and holy children, letting 'the Word of Christ dwell' in them (*Col. 3:15–17*).

**The pastoral epistles.** The epistles under this heading are 1 and 2 *Timothy* and *Titus*. Traditionally they have been called 'pastoral' because they include instruction to the young pastors, Timothy and Titus, on the oversight of the early church. Paul called these pastors to be on their guard against false teaching that will enter the church only too quickly (*1 Tim. 1:3–20; 2 Tim. 3; Titus 1:10–16* etc.). He exhorted them to public prayer and he gave instructions about the type of people suitable to be elders and deacons in the churches (*1 Tim. 3:1–13; Titus 1:6–9*). Paul was also concerned that they knew what to teach and how to handle different groups of people. The teaching was to follow the Scriptures and could not be compromised simply because people would not always like what they heard (*2 Tim. 3:14–4:5; Titus 2* etc.). The teaching also needed to warn against quarrelling and godlessness that would be symptomatic of the 'last days' (*1 Tim. 4:1–16; 6:3–10; 2 Tim. 2:14–3:9* etc.).

## Paul's teaching

Only some of Paul's teaching can be touched upon here. What drove Paul as he taught was his own experience on the Damascus road. As he reflected upon what had happened there he had concluded that the glory he saw and that had blinded him had to do with the glory of God. Jesus had that glory, therefore Jesus must be

God, a point he makes in a number of ways, not least by applying to Jesus statements and ideas that were attributed to Yahweh in the OT. Paul had recognized that, though a Jew, he needed salvation and forgiveness for his sin and that that could only be found in the sacrifice of Christ who died in his place on the cross. This great message was for all people without regard to race or background.

**All have sinned.** This assessment of man's plight underlies the tremendous conviction that Paul had that all people needed to hear the gospel. In *Rom.* 1–3 Paul demonstrates that Gentiles (pagans) are to be held guilty for their rejection of God on the grounds of his revelation in creation. Paul puts it like this: 'since the creation of the world God's invisible qualities – his eternal power and divine nature – have been clearly seen, being understood from what has been made, so that men are without excuse' (*Rom.* 1:19–20). Sin has led to more sin for, as people have turned from God in rebellion and sin, so God has given them up to the very sin they wanted. Their end is clearly stated: 'because of your stubbornness and your unrepentant heart, you are storing up wrath against yourself for the day of God's wrath, when his righteous judgment will be revealed' (*Rom.* 2:5). It was one thing, however, for Paul to talk of such deep sin amongst the Gentiles but Paul went on to argue that the Jews were in the same situation as well for 'God does not show favouritism' (*Rom.* 2:11). The Mosaic Law cannot save either, and so Paul argues that a true Jew is one who is one inwardly. He continues: 'a man is a Jew if he is one inwardly; and circumcision is circumcision of the heart, by the Spirit, not by the written code' (*v.* 29). The advantage a Jew has lies in the fact that he has the Word of God, the Law and the OT Scriptures (*Rom.* 3:2), and yet that same Law points to God's righteousness and judgment on sin. The Law reveals just how sinful men and women are (*Rom.* 3:20). Paul's conclusions, based on what he has taught in these opening chapters, are summed up in quotations from a number of texts from the very Law that Jews thought they could rely on: 'There is no one righteous, not even one; there is no one who understands, no one who seeks God. All have turned away, they have together become worthless; there is no one who does good, not even one' (*Rom.* 3:10–12; see *Pss.* 14:1–3; 53:1–3). The result of this universal sin is therefore clear for no one will escape the wrath (righteous judgment) of God. The problem faced by all mankind is therefore fearful. Jew or Gentile, God will not distinguish between sinners.

**Christ crucified.** For Paul there was only one answer to this and he had found it in the person of Christ himself. Wherever he went Paul preached Christ. Christ was the answer to the plight of all people, not just Jews but Gentiles as well. All people standing under the judgment of God need salvation, redemption and forgiveness. However, God could not ignore his righteousness. He could not express love at the expense of his justice (see *God, Jesus*). God *is* love but God *is* just as well. Paul had learned that in Christ God's perfect righteousness, his justice, was revealed but also in Christ God's great goodness, his love, mercy and grace, were also revealed.

In *Rom.* 3:21–26 Paul expounded that this righteousness of God 'comes through faith in Jesus Christ to all who believe' (*v.* 22). Precisely because God shows no favouritism, 'for all have sinned', so men and women of whatever race can be 'justified freely by his grace through the redemption that came by Christ Jesus'

(v. 24). Jesus had been presented by God as a sacrifice. Faith in Jesus meant understanding that his life had been given as an atonement for sins and that in this way God remained just – the penalty for sin was paid on the cross. Elsewhere Paul referred to this sacrifice in different ways. For example, he saw the sacrifice as God making 'him who had no sin [Jesus]to be sin for us, so that in him we might become the righteousness of God' (2 Cor. 5:21). He also saw Jesus in this way: 'Christ, our Passover Lamb, has been sacrificed' (1 Cor. 5:7).

Paul's argument for Jews and Gentiles finding salvation in the same way is further based upon the fact that 'there is only one God' for Jew and Gentile. Therefore, since he is just and shows no favouritism, salvation will be by faith in Christ for all who have that faith (Rom. 3:29–30).

For Paul the coming of Christ fulfilled God's way of salvation: 'when the time had fully come, God sent his Son, born of a woman, born under law, to redeem those under law, that we might receive the full rights of sons' (Gal. 4:4–5). Under the Law, Christ had taken the punishment on himself redeeming people from 'the curse of the law by becoming a curse for us' (Gal. 3:13). It was Christ's sacrifice on the cross, the redemption he bought with his own blood, that became the focal point of Paul's preaching. This was the Good News: Jesus had come to bring forgiveness and had paid the penalty for sin. Paul could thus summarize his preaching by saying, 'we preach Christ crucified' (1 Cor. 1:23). His message was 'the message of the cross' (1 Cor. 1:18).

**_Justification by grace through faith._**  Access to this saving work of Christ on the cross was, for Paul, entirely by God's grace. Had redemption come by obedience to the Law it would have been possible for a person to boast that they had achieved their own salvation, but Paul was adamant that this is God's work for his people and it demonstrates God's grace (his undeserved love and mercy) for his people (Eph. 2:9). Time and again Paul insists that all individuals will have to stand before the judgment seat of God and their only hope for a 'not guilty' verdict (being justified), when faced with his righteous judgment lies in his grace. Redemption thus comes by grace and is appropriated by the individual through faith. Faith involves a commitment to God's righteousness and his right ways in Christ. Faith looks to God alone for salvation, thus admitting helplessness before God, admitting sin and the need for forgiveness, and looking to God to supply.

This justification is won at the cost of Christ's death and the payment of the penalty is confirmed by God in the resurrection (Rom. 4:25; 5:16, 18 etc.). No other cost is involved. Sinners are justified 'freely by grace'; 'For it is by grace you have been saved, through faith – and this not from yourselves, it is the gift of God' (Rom. 3:24; Eph. 2:5, 8 etc.). Because obedience to the Law cannot gain salvation, once again Paul shows that Gentiles can therefore be included. They too can have faith: 'The Scripture foresaw that God would justify the Gentiles by faith, and announced the gospel in advance to Abraham: "All nations will be blessed through you"' (Gal. 3:8). Paul does not only teach about justification by faith in Christ at the point of becoming a Christian. God has saved believers by grace for a purpose: He 'has saved us and called us to a holy life – not because of anything we have done but because of his own purpose and grace' (2 Tim. 1:9). And this justification by grace means that believers have access to all the blessings God has promised to his people summed up in the words 'eternal life': 'so that, having been justified by his grace, we might become heirs having the hope of eternal life' (*Titus 3:7*).

**Life through the Spirit.**   The work of the Holy Spirit permeates every area of the Christian's life and the church's life in Paul's writings. The Holy Spirit is first involved in the actual proclamation of the gospel of Christ crucified. Paul's preaching led to people's conversion because: 'My message and my preaching were not with wise and persuasive words, but with a demonstration of the Spirit's power' (*1 Cor. 2:4*). This work of the Spirit, says Paul, was so that faith should rest entirely on God's power (*v. 5*) for 'faith comes from hearing the message, and the message is heard through the word of Christ' (*Rom. 10:17; 1 Thess. 1:5*). But the Spirit is also active in the one who hears the message for 'The man without the Spirit does not accept the things that come from the Spirit of God, for they are foolishness to him, and he cannot understand them, because they are spiritually discerned' (*1 Cor. 2:14*). Thus the Spirit is actively present in the preaching of the gospel and in the person who hears and turns to Christ.

Those who then come to faith and are redeemed and justified know that they no longer stand condemned by God. 'There is now no condemnation for those who are in Christ Jesus' (*Rom. 8:1*). But the evidence they have of God's work in their lives lies, says Paul, in their possession of God's Holy Spirit. Life in the Spirit thus brings the believer many great blessings and many challenges. Anyone who belongs to Christ has the Spirit of Christ, and this means that they are controlled by the Spirit (*Rom. 8:9*). It is the Spirit who guarantees the fact that a person belongs to God. Indeed this is God's 'seal of ownership' that he has 'put his Spirit in our hearts as a deposit guaranteeing what is to come' says Paul (*2 Cor. 1:22*). This aspect of the Spirit's 'guaranteeing' work is mentioned on a number of occasions, specially when Paul thinks about the future, about facing death, or about the inheritance a Christian will one day receive from the Lord (*2 Cor. 5:4–5; Eph. 1:14* etc.).

The Holy Spirit helps people to pray, bringing frail and fallible believers' requests before the Father (*Rom. 8:26–27*). Since life as a Christian is to be lived in the community, the Spirit also helps in the corporate life of the church. Each person, says Paul, has been given some 'gift of the Spirit' with which to help other believers in their Christian life. These gifts will be useful for building up others in the faith in a variety of ways. Paul gives no exhaustive lift of such gifts but mentions gifts as diverse as hospitality and speaking in tongues, teaching and giving liberally, prophecy and administration (*1 Cor. 12:4–11; Rom. 12:6–8*). Closely allied to this work that enables all believers to play a full part in the life of the church is the work of ensuring Christian unity. Paul often highlights this work of the Spirit. Unity among believers is not an optional extra but of the essence of Christian faith as unity is of the essence of the Godhead: 'For we were all baptized by one Spirit into one body – whether Jews or Greeks, slave or free – and we were all given the one Spirit to drink' (*1 Cor. 12:13*). It is thus the Christian's duty to 'make every effort to keep the unity of the Spirit through the bond of peace' because 'There is one body and one Spirit – just as you were called to one hope when you were called – one Lord, one faith, one baptism; one God and Father of all, who is over all and through all and in all' (*Eph. 4:3–6*).

A major aspect of the work of the Spirit in the life of the believer is to produce awareness of sin and the need for forgiveness and to help a person live a life of holiness and righteousness to God's glory. This process of Spirit led growth is called 'sanctification'. It refers to God's Spirit setting the believer apart from the life of sin and working to produce a life ever more like the life of Christ. In 2 Thess. 2:13 Paul says: 'But we ought always to thank God for you, brothers loved by the Lord, because from the beginning God chose you to be saved through the sanctifying work of the Spirit and through belief in the truth' (also see 1 Cor. 6:11). It is this work of the Spirit that believers ignore at their peril. Paul insists that they should 'live by the Spirit' and in this way they will be protected from the evil around and from sin: 'So I say, live by the Spirit, and you will not gratify the desires of the sinful nature. For the sinful nature desires what is contrary to the Spirit, and the Spirit what is contrary to the sinful nature. They are in conflict with each other, so that you do not do what you want' (Gal. 5:16–17; Rom. 8:13–15).

As we read Paul, however, we would be hard pressed to find any work of the Spirit that excites him more than the work that confirms for the believer the fact of adoption as 'sons of God'. This clearly has to do with being full inheritors of all God's blessings but also it has to do with a new and very personal relationship with the Father: 'Because you are sons, God sent the Spirit of his Son into our hearts, the Spirit who calls out, "Abba, Father"' (see Abba). This new relationship is wonderfully liberating, 'For you did not receive a spirit that makes you a slave again to fear, but you received the Spirit of sonship. And by him we cry, "Abba, Father"' (Rom. 8:15).

According to Paul, then, the Spirit is essential to a Christian's very existence. He initiates faith, confirms faith, develops faith, establishes unity, lives in the believer, enables sanctification, guarantees the future, enables community life and fulfils many other tasks besides these. His goal is to carry out the whole will of God in the life of the individual believer and in the life of God's church.

**Life after death.** Paul was fully committed to his belief in life after death. He assumed that one day everyone would have to face the returning and judging Lord (Rom. 2:5; 14:10; Phil. 2:10). On that day there would be a division of people depending, not on their good works or lack of works, but upon whether, through faith, they had seen the saving work of God's grace in their lives (Rom. 5:1; 8:1). Because he believed that Christ had taken sin upon himself on the cross and paid the penalty, one of the great joys Paul had as a Christian was that he no longer feared death (Rom. 8:15–17). Indeed he was utterly confident of the future. Whether he died or went on living he would be with the Lord and could continue to glorify the Lord (2 Cor. 5:6–9). Of all people, Paul was conscious of the frailty of human life. On many occasions he had been near to death and had often felt bruised and battered (2 Cor. 11:23–29). He talked of 'groaning' and being 'burdened' in this body and yet he carried on in the sure knowledge that one day 'what is mortal' would be 'swallowed up by life' (2 Cor. 5:4). Again Paul turned to the Holy Spirit within him for confirmation and a guarantee of his future (v. 5).

Though Paul made it clear he would have rather been with the Lord than suffering persecution for the faith, he was never preoccupied with the afterlife. Rather his absolute confidence that one day, like Christ, he would be raised from the dead and inherit eternal life gave him purpose for this life. God had called him to proclaim this good news, that Christ had died in the place of all who would believe in him, and that he had been raised from the dead, the 'first fruits' of those who have died. The return of Christ and the resurrection of the dead will lead to a radical change in the body (1 Cor. 15:20, 35–44). This led Paul to say: 'we eagerly await a Saviour from there, the Lord Jesus Christ, who, by the power that enables him to bring everything under his control, will transform our lowly bodies so that they will be like his glorious body' (Phil. 3:20–21).

There has been much discussion about what Paul imagined would happen between the time of death and the time of the general resurrection at the return of Christ. Did Paul believe in some form of 'soul sleep', that people enter a period of unconsciousness while awaiting Christ's return, or did he believe that the human spirit went immediately into the presence of the Lord? There is not space here to examine Paul's teaching in any detail, but there are passages that make it clear that Paul believed that, for the Christian, human life was followed immediately by presence with the Lord. In talking again of his desire to serve the Lord here and yet to be with him for eternity, Paul said: 'I am torn between the two: I desire to depart and be with Christ, which is better by far' (Phil. 1:23; also see 2 Cor. 5:3).

However it was all to happen, for Paul death meant 'eternal glory', it meant being 'with the Lord', it meant 'life', it meant 'a building from God, an eternal house in heaven' (2 Cor. 4:17; 5:1, 4, 8). Is it any wonder, therefore, that he could say: 'So we fix our eyes not on what is seen, but on what is unseen. For what is seen is temporary, but what is unseen is eternal' (2 Cor. 4:18).

## Conclusions

Paul was surely the greatest teacher of the Christian faith after the Lord Jesus himself. Called and led by the Spirit to take the gospel to the Gentiles, this great theologian expounded the depths of the Christian faith in a way that has proved foundational for the church of Christ through the years. His total commitment to the gospel of Christ crucified stands as an example to all believers through the centuries. His desire to maintain truth against all heresy or anything that would diminish the truth of salvation by grace alone shines through all his writings. His deep passion for the application of the gospel truth in the life of the believer led to pages of writing on how to lead the Christian life in the midst of a pagan world. All this could only be achieved by God's Spirit who lived within the believer working out the purposes of the Father himself. His deep love for his Christian brothers and sisters, his pain at their hurt, and his sadness at their sin, is seen not only as he wrote to them often with great tenderness and encouragement, but also in his repeated reference to his prayers for them.

However, it was his deep belief that all have sinned and all stand under God's judgment and his concern that men and women around the world find the salvation they so desperately need, that caused Paul to respond to God's call to preach the gospel to the Gentiles. For Paul, Christ was the only answer. He was the focus and power of Paul's life, and above all the one who had died so Paul could be forgiven and find justification and eternal life on the last day.       P. D. G.

**PAULUS, SERGIUS** Sergius Paulus was the Roman proconsul in Paphos on the island of Cyprus in the years AD 47–48. Luke describes him as 'an intelligent man'. He asked Barnabas and Saul (Paul) to come and see him 'because he wanted to hear the word of God' (*Acts 13:7*). When he listened to the word they preached he obviously showed some signs of being interested in conversion. A sorcerer called Elymas, probably seeing part of his livelihood slipping from his grasp, tried to turn the proconsul against Paul. Paul, 'filled with the Holy Spirit' (*v. 9*), looked at Elymas in the eye and called him a 'child of the devil' and an enemy of all that is right. Paul pronounced judgment in the name of the Lord upon him and immediately he became blind. On seeing this, the proconsul 'believed, for he was amazed at the teaching about the Lord' (*v. 12*). The emphasis in this passage on hearing the word of God and on 'the teaching about the Lord' may indicate that this was a genuine conversion, and not like the initial response of Simon, which was a response more to the miracles than the word of God (*Acts 8:18*).                         P. D. G.

**PEDAHEL** (Heb., 'God delivers'), son of Ammihud, was a leader from the tribe of Naphtali. The LORD told Moses to choose men from each tribe to help divide out the land of Canaan, and Pedahel represented his tribe (*Num. 34:28*).

**PEDAHZUR** was the father of Gamaliel, who was the leader of the people of Manesseh at the census of the Israelites in the wilderness of Sinai. Gamaliel's division of people numbered 32,200 (*Num. 1:10; 2:20*). As the representative of his tribe Gamaliel also brought his tribe's fellowship offering when the Tabernacle was dedicated in the wilderness (*Num. 7:54, 59*) and led his tribe when the Israelites set out from the Sinai desert on their wanderings (*Num. 10:23*).

**PEDAIAH** (Heb., 'the LORD has redeemed').

**1.** Pedaiah was the father of Zebidah, the mother of King Jehoiakim of Judah (*2 Kings 23.36*).

**2.** Another Pedaiah was the father of Joel. This Joel was the leader of the tribe of Manasseh during the time of King David (*1 Chron. 27:20*).

**3.** This Pedaiah is listed among the descendants of King Jehoiachin and is thus part of David's royal line. He seems to have returned after the Exile in Babylon. He was the father of Zerubbabel (*1 Chron. 3:18–19*).

**4.** Pedaiah son of Parosh was among those who helped rebuild the walls of Jerusalem following the return from Babylon (*Neh. 3:25*).

**5.** This Pedaiah was among those who stood on Ezra's right-hand side on a high wooden platform as he read the Book of the Law to the people of Israel. As the Law was read the people worshipped and praised God, confessed their sin, and recommitted themselves to the LORD's service (*Neh. 8:4*).

**6.** Pedaiah, the son of Kolaiah and the father of Joed, was from the tribe of Benjamin and was an ancestor of some of those who resettled in Jerusalem after returning from Babylon (*Neh. 11:7*).

**7.** A Levite named Pedaiah who lived in Nehemiah's day was considered particularly trustworthy and so was put in charge of the storerooms of the Temple to look after the people's gifts (*Neh. 13:13*).
                                        P.D.G.

**PEKAH** (Heb., 'he has opened'). Pekah son of Remaliah was king of the Northern Kingdom of Israel from c. 740–732 BC. He came to the throne by assassinating his predecessor, Pekahiah (*2 Kings 15:25*). He was a chief officer in the army and gathered together 50 'men of Gilead' for the *coup-d'état*. It is likely that his co-conspirators were senior army officers as well and were probably among the 'wealthy men' (*v. 20*) who had no desire to pay the very heavy taxes in tribute to Tiglath-Pileser, king of Assyria, that King Menahem and more latterly King Pekahiah seemed prepared to pay (*v. 20*).

It would appear that Pekah had spent some time securing a base for his takeover. Probably he had been *de facto* leader in Gilead for some time and had apparently formed some sort of alliance with Rezin, king of Syria (Aram). This is the most likely solution to the rather vexed question of the duration of Pekah's reign. *2 Kings 15:27* says that he reigned 20 years and that he began to reign in the 52nd year of Azariah king of Judah. Comparative chronologies with the dates for the fall of Samaria and the dates of the kings of Judah would indicate fairly clearly the dates mentioned above, thus limiting his actual reign as king to some eight to ten years at most. However, if the author of Kings was aware that Pekah had been *de facto* king in large parts of Israel for some while, particularly in Transjordan areas of Gilead, before he captured Samaria then the reference to 20 years is probably correct and a description of the period during which he had considerable power and oversight in the country.

In *v. 29* there is a clear indication of the power of Tiglath-Pileser III. During Pekah's reign he captured large parts of northern and eastern Israel, including Pekah's own base of Gilead and the fortified city of Hazor in the north, which protected the junction of two important trade routes. He also transported many of the Israelites from those areas to Babylon.

Pekah's response was to ally himself with Rezin of Assyria and to build a power-base in Palestine. The two kings attacked King Ahaz of Judah because he failed to join them in their plans (*2 Chron. 28:5–21*). The Israelites did inflict a severe defeat on the northern part of Judah and carried off many prisoners. 'In one day Pekah son of Remaliah killed a hundred and twenty thousand soldiers in Judah' (*v. 6*). And they actually got as far as laying siege to Jerusalem (*2 Kings 16:5*). Ahaz appealed to Assyria for help (*v. 7; 2 Chron. 28:16*). When the king of Assyria did come he simply caused Ahaz still more trouble, but he did capture Damascus and thus relieved the siege on Jerusalem (*Is. 7; 9:8–21*). Eventually Pekah was assassinated by Hoshea, who was pro-Assyrian (*2 Kings 16:30*).

In the account of Pekah's reign the book of Kings continues to document the decline of Israel and impending inevitable judgment of God. As a succession of kings came and went with several of them being assassinated, the general degeneration of a nation that refused to return to their God and LORD is described. Even when, for a moment, Pekah seemed to be winning in battle against Judah, it was only for a short time while the LORD used him in judgment on Ahaz in the Southern Kingdom who, rather ironically, was acting like 'the kings of Israel' doing 'evil in the eyes of the LORD' (*2 Kings 16:2–3*). While in Judah there were times when the kings repented and the LORD stayed his hand of judgment, for example under Hezekiah and Josiah, such repentance did not happen in Israel. In terms of God's work, therefore, judgment had to come. Under the leadership of the King of Assyria that judgment began in earnest during Pekah's reign. It was concluded under his successor, Hoshea, the last king of Israel (*2 Kings 17:7–23*).

For more detail on some parts of these events see *Ahaz*, *Oded* and *Rezin*.

P.D.G.

**PEKAHIAH** (Heb., 'the LORD has opened'). The son of King Menahem of Israel. Pekahiah reigned in Samaria for just two years (c. 741–740 BC). Like his forebears he did 'evil in the eyes of the LORD' (*2 Kings 15:22–26*). He probably continued to pay tribute to Assyria as his father had done (*vv. 19–20*). This may have led to the rebellion that eventually resulted in his assassination by Pekah son of Remaliah. Pekah seems then to have made an alliance with Syria (e.g. *v. 37; 2 Kings 16*).

**PELAIAH** ('Heb., 'the LORD is marvellous').

**1.** Pelaiah, son of Elioenai, is listed in *1 Chron. 3:24* as a member of the royal line of Judah after the Exile.

**2.** Soon after the Israelites had settled back in the towns around Jerusalem they came and asked Ezra to read to them from the Book of the Law. This Pelaiah was one of the Levites present who later 'instructed' the people in the meaning of the Law and interpreted it for them (*Neh. 8:7*). The people heard the Word and began to weep as they understood it. Pelaiah and the others encouraged them not to weep since this was a 'sacred day'. The people were to worship the LORD, 'for the joy of the LORD is your strength' (*v. 10*). The more they understood of the Law the more they rejoiced. They celebrated the festival of the Feast of Tabernacles. As a nation they then began to confess their sins (*Neh. 9:4–5*). Good instruction for the people was vital if they were to worship as the LORD wanted. Before the Exile the Levites and leaders had been severely castigated by the LORD for not doing this (e.g. *Jer. 23*). Now, after the Exile, they began to do what they should always have done and the LORD brought them great blessing.

Pelaiah also signed the agreement with Nehemiah and the people in which they promised to obey the Law and worship only the LORD (*Neh. 10:10*). P.D.G.

**PELALIAH** was the grandfather of the priest Adaiah. Adaiah was one of those who helped rebuild the Temple in the days of Nehemiah (*Neh. 11:12*).

**PELATIAH** (Heb., 'the LORD delivers').

**1.** A Simeonite and son of Ishi who lived in the time of King Hezekiah of Judah. He helped lead an invasion of the hill country of Seir (to the east of the Dead Sea), killing the remaining Amalekites. His people then settled in the area (*1 Chron. 4:42–43*).

**2.** One of two sons of Hananiah, and a descendant of King David and of Zerubbabel. He was of the tribe of Judah and is mentioned only in the genealogy of *1 Chron. 3:21*.

**3.** Mentioned only in *Neh. 10:22*, Pelatiah was one of the leaders of the Jews who returned from the Exile in Babylon and joined Nehemiah in binding himself to an agreement to obey the Law of God.

**4.** Pelatiah son of Benaiah is mentioned in *Ezek. 11:1* and was an elder of the Judean people. The LORD showed the prophet Ezekiel that this leader, together with 25 others, was to be judged and condemned for leading the people astray with false prophecies and giving wicked advice to those in Jerusalem. Apart from the fearful judgment that is always promised in Scriptures for false prophets who lead people away from the LORD's will, Pelatiah's judgment was also deserved because the elders had 'conformed to the standards of the nations around' (*v. 12*). Even as he spoke, Pelatiah fell down dead, leading Ezekiel to ask of the LORD whether he was going to destroy even the remnant of Judah (*v. 13*). P.D.G.

**PELEG** (Heb., 'division'). The son of Eber and a descendant of Shem, Peleg was the brother of Joktan and father to Reu. He was thus an ancestor of Abraham and also enters the genealogy of Luke's Gospel leading from Jesus and Joseph back to Adam (*Gen. 10:25; 11:16–19; 1 Chron. 1:19, 25; 3:35*). The text says he was called Peleg 'because in his time the earth was divided'. Quite what this meant is not clear. Perhaps the most plausible explanation is that it refers to the time of the Tower of Babel when peoples were divided into language groupings (*Gen. 11*).

**PELET** **1.** A son of Jahdai and a descendant of Judah and Caleb mentioned in 1 Chron. 2:47.

**2.** A skilful and ambidextrous archer from the tribe of Benjamin who fought first for Saul and then transferred, with his brother Jeziel, to David at Ziklag (1 Chron. 12:3). Later in the passage it seems that such men transferred loyalties not simply to be on the winning side but because the 'Spirit' had worked among them.

**PELETH** **1.** The father of On, a Reubenite. On joined Dathan, Abiram and Korah in a rebellion against Moses (Num. 16:1).

**2.** A son of Jonathan and brother to Zaza, this Peleth was from the tribe of Judah and a Jerahmeelite (1 Chron. 2:33).

**PENINNAH** One of the two wives of Elkanah from the tribe of Ephraim. Peninnah had several children but Elkanah's other wife, Hannah, was unable to have children (1 Sam. 1:1–6). Year by year the family went to Shiloh to sacrifice to the LORD Almighty. Elkanah would give portions of the meat to Peninnah and the children but reserved a double portion for Hannah 'because he loved her and the LORD had closed her womb' (v. 5). Peninnah was jealous and ridiculed Hannah for not having children, making her life a misery (v. 6). Eventually Hannah did have children, the most famous of whom was Samuel. See *Hannah* and *Samuel*.

**PENUEL** (Heb., 'face of God').

**1.** Of the tribe of Judah, Penuel was the father of Gedor and was descended from Hur (1 Chron. 4:4).

**2.** This Penuel was from the tribe of Benjamin, and is mentioned in the genealogy leading to Saul. He was the son of Shashak (1 Chron. 8:25).

**PERESH** was a descendant of Manasseh and a leader in that tribe. He was a son of Makir and his wife Maacah (1 Chron. 7:16).

**PEREZ** (Heb., 'a bursting forth'). Perez was a twin brother to Zerah and a son of Judah. He was the founder of the Perezite clan (Gen. 38–29; Num. 26:20; 1 Chron. 9:4). Both his own sons, Hezron and Hamul, also became clan leaders in their own right (Gen. 46:12; Num. 26:21; 1 Chron. 2:4–5; 4:1). Perez and Zerah were born as a result of an incestuous relationship between their father Judah and his daughter-in-law Tamar. His unusual name was given because of the nature of his birth. When he was about to be born one of the sons' hands appeared and so a scarlet thread was put round the wrist to identify the 'first born'. The hand was withdrawn and Perez 'burst forth' ahead of his brother who had the scarlet thread round his wrist.

Perez became the most prominent member of the house of Judah. The firstborn son of Judah, Er, had died because of his wickedness (Gen. 38:7). The second son, Onan, had also died under God's judgment (v. 10). The third son, Shelah, became the leader of his own Shelanite clan, but seems not to have been regarded as the rightful heir to Judah, perhaps because his mother was a Canaanite (v. 2).

Perez is mentioned again in the account of Ruth and Boaz. There the elders of Bethlehem wished Boaz well with his new wife and said: 'may your family be like that of Perez, whom Tamar bore to Judah' (Ruth 4:12). This was probably an expression in common use at the time and reflected the fact that it was through Perez that the tribe of Judah had continued. In the genealogy at the end of Ruth that summarizes the message of the book Perez is at the head of the family line leading through Boaz to David (Ruth 4:18). Perez therefore appears again in both the genealogies of Christ in the NT (Matt. 1:3; 3:33). Some of the descendants of Judah listed as returning with Ezra and Nehemiah after the Exile in Babylon also traced their ancestry back to Perez, so that his descendants who initially returned numbered 468 men (*Neh. 11:4, 6*). See also *1 Chron. 27:3.*                    P. D. G.

**PERIDA** was one of Solomon's servants whose descendants returned from the Exile in Babylon in company with Zerubbabel (*Neh. 7:57*). He is called Peruda in *Ezra 2.55*.

**PERSIS** A woman who 'worked very

hard in the Lord' and was one of the Roman Christians greeted by Paul in his letter to the Romans as his 'dear friend' (*16:12*). The personal care and pastoral concern for individuals reflected in Paul's greetings is worthy of attention.

**PERUDA** was one of Solomon's servants whose descendants returned from the Exile in Babylon in company with Zerubbabel (*Ezra 2:55*). He is called Perida in *Neh. 7:57*.

# PETER

## Peter's background

Originally named Simon, he was the son of John (*John 1:42*), and the brother of Andrew (*Matt. 4:18; John 6:8*). He was married and his wife was a believer who accompanied him on his travels (*Matt. 8:14; 1 Cor. 9:5*). He originally worked in his father's fishing business (*Mark 1:16–20*).

He was not trained as a Rabbi and had a Galilean accent (*Matt. 26:33*). He was, therefore, regarded disparagingly as 'ignorant and unlearned' by those in Jerusalem (*Acts 4:13*).

## Peter's call and discipleship

He headed the list of disciples not because he was the first called by Jesus, but as the discussion in the following sections indicates, he was the leader of the disciples. In *Matt. 10:2* we read, 'first, Simon (who is called Peter)' (also *Mark 3:16; Luke 6:14*). He was one of the inner ring which included James and John (*Mark 5:37, 9:2, 13:3; Luke 8:51*).

Peter was a willing disciple who sought to exercise faith, although he proved to be somewhat mercurial as the incident of walking on the water shows (*Matt. 14:28*). He admitted his ignorance and his own sinfulness (*Matt. 15:15; Luke 5:8; 12:41*) and asked questions when he was curious (*John 13:24*). In spite of having had a divine revelation concerning the identity of Jesus, he rejected any notion of the death of Jesus, a statement which Jesus attributed to Satan. Peter's motivation was exposed as 'earthly', i.e. his concept of the Messiah was that of an earthly ruler in which he may have perceived himself playing a major part in the reign of Jesus (*Matt. 16:23; Mark 8:33*). He was present with James and John at the transfiguration (*Mark 9:7; Luke 9:28*) and heard the voice of God endorsing the Sonship of Jesus (an incident to which he bore witness in *2 Pet. 1:18*) and requiring obedience by the disciples to the teaching of Jesus (*Matt. 17:1–6*). Peter learnt of the importance of Jesus' disciples paying tribute to earthly kings not because they had to, but because failure to do so would create a stumbling block to the promotion of the gospel (*Matt.*

17:27). He struggled over the issue of forgiveness and was warned about what happened to the unforgiving disciple and the torture he would experience (*Matt. 18:21–35*). He was quick to remind Jesus that the disciples had abandoned everything to follow him, but was promised that the twelve would sit on thrones judging Israel (*Matt. 19:27–30; Mark 10:28; Luke 18:28*). Initially he refused to allow Jesus to wash his feet and then asked for the washing of his hands and his head also as a symbol of cleansing (*John 13:6–10*).

Peter is remembered for his contradiction of Jesus when he spoke of the disciples' denial of him. His retort was that he, like the other disciples, would face death rather than deny Jesus (*Matt. 26:33–35; Mark 14:29; Luke 22:34; John 13:36–38*). He failed to watch and pray with Jesus even though he was warned that the spirit was willing but the flesh weak (*Matt. 26:37–44; Mark 14:33–41*). In a rash moment he cut off the ear of Malchus, the High Priest's servant (*John 18:10*). In the courtyard of the house of Caiaphas, the High Priest, Peter's resolve collapsed, not in front of a court, but with a question asked by a young servant girl. The enormity of his denial following the fulfilment of Jesus' prophecy that it would happen before the following dawn caused Peter to weep bitterly (*Matt. 26:58, 69–75; Mark 14:54; 66–72; Luke 22:54–62; John 18:15–18, 25–27*). At the empty tomb the women were told to tell 'the disciples and Peter' that they would see Jesus in Galilee (*Mark 14:27*). It was Peter who subsequently ran to the empty tomb and was uncertain as to its significance (*Luke 24:12; John 20:2–10*). It was when he was with some of the disciples in Galilee that Jesus appeared to them and showed himself to be alive. Peter, who was fishing at the time, plunged into the sea to swim ashore when John recognized that it was the Lord. It was Jesus's direction from the shore as to where they should cast their nets that resulted in a full catch. After breakfast Jesus questioned the degree of Peter's love for him. On the affirmation of his loyalty he was commanded to act as a shepherd and nourish spiritually the lambs and sheep. At the same time Peter was told of the manner of his own death – crucifixion by which God would be glorified (*John 21:1–23*). This is traditionally said to have occurred in Rome.

## Peter's apostleship

Following Jesus's inquiry as to how others perceived him and what his disciples thought of him, Peter was the first to confess that Jesus was the Messiah promised in the OT. Furthermore he acknowledged he was the Son of the living God and he recognized that Jesus had the words of eternal life (*Matt. 16:16; John 6:68*). This truth was not arrived at by deduction or through any human agency, but as a result of revelation from God the Father. According to Jesus, Peter's understanding would be a great blessing to him not only because it is the truth of the gospel to understand who Jesus really is, but also because it was this message that he was commissioned to proclaim (*Matt. 16:17–19*). In a play on words, Jesus told Simon that his name was to be changed to 'Peter' to describe this role as an apostle. Jesus said that it was 'before this rock' that he would build his church. ('On this rock' is a mistranslation of the phrase. In the Greek construction this verb followed by a particular participle and its case is used of building something *in front of* and not *upon* something.) It was 'before this rock' (*petra*), Jesus would build his church (assembly). Israel had gathered in a solemn assembly before Mount Sinai to hear the Word of God, i.e. 'the Book of the covenant' spoken by Moses. They endorsed it and were formally constituted the people of God following their salvation from Egypt (*Exod. 24:1–11*). So too the Word of God, i.e. the gospel in the mouth of Peter, would be the means by which those Jews who embraced the salvation which Jesus offered would be constituted the people of God in the New Covenant. In the Old Covenant, death excluded the people of God from that assembly. However Jesus told Peter that 'the gates of Hades', i.e. death, could not exclude those who were the members of Christ's church, such is the nature of Jesus' gift of eternal life. Peter was *the* apostle to the Jews both in Palestine, possibly in Corinth (*1 Cor. 1:12*) and, according to tradition, in Rome.

We actually see this promise of Jesus realized in the book of Acts, for it was Peter who proclaimed the gospel on the day of Pentecost when some 3,000 Jerusalem and Diaspora Jews were saved. His speech showed his grasp of the OT Scriptures when he cited *Joel 2:28–32* as the explanation of the phenomenon of Jews from different parts of the Roman empire hearing 'the mighty works of God', i.e. the gospel, being proclaimed in their own language. In that speech Peter again quoted *Ps. 16:8–11* to show that death could never be victorious over Jesus and that the pouring out of God's Spirit was proof that Jesus was now exalted as Lord as *Ps. 110:1* said he would be (*Acts 2:1–42*).

Again Peter was the preacher who explained to the crowd that the miracle of the healing of the lame man at the gate Beautiful was not performed by his power, but by that of the God of Abraham, Isaac and Jacob. It was this God who had glorifed his servant Jesus and whose sufferings were prophesied in all the prophets. Peter proclaimed that Jesus was *the* prophet of whom Moses spoke in *Deut. 18:15–19* and that those who refused to accept him would suffer destruction. Again Peter declared that the blessing of all the families of the earth as predicted in the Abrahamic promise of *Gen. 12:3* was now realized in the death and resurrection of Jesus. The Jews were being given the first opportunity to receive this blessing by repenting of their sins. In the face of the subsequent inquiry of the religious leaders it was Peter who declared that the miracle was performed in the name of Jesus, the risen Messiah, and that Jesus was the rejected stone of *Ps. 118:22* but in whom alone was salvation to be found. The attempt of the authorities to muzzle Peter and John failed when they declared that they could not be silent, for their role as apostles compelled them to bear witness to what they had seen and heard (*Acts 3:1–4:22*).

The god-fearer, Cornelius, who was the first Gentile to hear the gospel did so through the preaching of Peter. That gospel was declared to be one of peace through Jesus the Messiah who was now Lord of all following his resurrection. Jesus had charged his disciples to bear witness to the fact that he was the one God ordained to be the judge of the living and the dead. Jesus had secured remission of sins for all who believed in him just as all the prophets had testified would happen (*Acts 10:34–44*).

It was also Peter who declared to the leaders of the church in Judea that God had granted repentance to the Gentiles also through the preaching of the salvation offered by Jesus. His natural reluctance as a Jew to take the gospel to them was overcome by the divine vision and the miraculous circumstances by which the messengers of Cornelius were led to the house where Peter was staying

(*Acts 10:1–23; 11:1–18*). He counselled the gathering in Jerusalem as it discussed the contentious matter of circumcision and obedience to the Jewish Law for Gentile Christians. They should not tempt God by burdening Gentile converts with the yoke of the Law that Jews themselves could not keep. He declared that they were saved through the grace of God just as Jewish Christians were (*Acts 15:7–11*).

It was Peter who instituted the election procedures for Matthias (*Acts 1:15–26*). The book of Acts also shows that Peter took the initiative and spoke out against the deception of Ananias and Sapphira (*Acts 5:1–4*). He was also miraculously delivered from imprisonment and certain death in *Acts 12:1–20*, and in Joppa a miracle was performed through him on Dorcas who was raised from the dead (*Acts 10:36–43*).

## Peter's writings

According to Papias, a 2nd-century Christian writer, Mark's Gospel reflects Peter's teaching which Mark, acting as a scribe, carefully wrote down. There are certainly striking parallels between the Gospel and the outline of the life and ministry of Jesus in the sermon Peter preached to Cornelius. In Mark also, the gospel of Jesus begins in Galilee after the preaching of John the Baptist and following Jesus' anointing by the Holy Spirit. The ministry of Jesus is described to Cornelius in terms of doing good, healing those oppressed by the devil, the crucifixion and resurrection (*Acts 10:36–43*). Certainly Peter's sermon which is only in outline in Acts, parallels the events of Mark's Gospel in a striking manner.

1 *Peter* carries the inscription of 'Peter, an apostle of Jesus Christ' who has witnessed the sufferings of Jesus (*1 Pet. 1:1; 5:1*) and is addressed to Christians scattered in what is now the northern part of Turkey. It was written out by Silvanus (*1 Pet. 5:12*) (for his role see *Silas (Silvanus)*).

One of the features of this letter is the use of the O T. Peter not only cited specific passages, but chose identical situations in the O T to those the people of God were now facing to support his discussion. We find him doing the same thing in his speeches in Acts. In fact, he begins his letter by declaring that they are the 'dispersed' (N I V: 'scattered') people of God, not dispersed in Babylon as the Jews had been while waiting to return to Jerusalem, but dispersed in the provinces of the Roman empire until they received their eternal inheritance in heaven.

In a strong Trinitarian introduction, Peter described the work of the Father, Son and Holy Spirit who have secured their salvation (*1 Pet. 1:2*). He then systematically explained the way in which each Person of the Godhead had contributed to this (*1 Pet. 1:3–12*). This foundation of their faith enabled them to wait with confidence for their inheritance of heaven.

In the face of suspicion and antagonism he told the exiled people of God how they should live. As in *Jer. 29:7* which speaks to a similar situation, they were not to be self-indulgent but to seek the welfare of the cities in which they were living. If they did this then they would present a credible life-style of good works which would authenticate the gospel when it was preached to others (*1 Pet. 2:11–12*). With this overarching theme he systematically examined various spheres of life and in each exhorted Christians to continue to do good – namely in civic life, in the household situation, in marriage and generally in society (*1 Pet. 2:13–3:12*).

Great emphasis was placed on the work of Christ as the example for loving and living the Christian life (1 Pet. 1:18ff.). He dwelt on Christ's suffering in order to demonstrate that it was not by turning one's back on the present suffering but by pressing on doing good that the Christian life would be lived (1 Pet. 3:14–4:2). It was the will of God that, by doing good, they could silence unfounded allegations against themselves and also commit their soul to God as the faithful Creator (1 Pet. 2:15; 4:19).

In a command reminiscent of Jesus' commission to Peter to 'feed My sheep' (John 20:15–17), he likewise called upon the Christian leaders to exercise their ministry not unwillingly or for money or by using their role as a means of lording it over others, but to lead by example and thus be rewarded by the chief Shepherd (1 Pet. 5:1–4). Younger members, indeed all of the congregation were exhorted to humility under the mighty hand of God, and given the promise that anxiety and suffering could be faced. God would use such adversity to develop greater stability in their Christian lives (1 Pet. 5:5–11).

1 Peter is said to be about 'the true grace of God' (cf. Acts 15:11) in which Christians were exhorted to stand firm (1 Pet. 5:12) in spite of the present difficulties and discrimination. They were not to live self-indulgent lives because these activities would ultimately be scrutinized by an impartial Father (1 Pet. 1:17; 2:11; 4:3–4).

2 Peter was written to fellow Christians who were described as having obtained a faith identical to that of the apostles by means of 'the righteousness of our God and Saviour, Jesus Christ' (2 Pet. 1:1). The recipients were the same as in 1 Peter, as he referred to 'my second letter to you' (2 Pet. 3:1). Its stress was on growth in the Christian life and the importance of the recording of Peter's witness to the events of Christ's life in order to refute false understanding. The statement made about his death suggests that his earthly life was almost finished (2 Pet. 1:14–15; cf. John 21:19–20).

The trustworthiness of God's 'very great and precious promises' would be the Christian's confidence for salvation (2 Pet. 1:2–4). He stated that Christian development was not automatic and demanded faith in God's promises. Virtue, knowledge, self-control, penitence, endurance, godliness and love were all to abound within the essential context of faith so that the knowledge of Jesus Christ as Lord would not be unproductive. The abundance of such attributes guaranteed the Christian's rich entrance into heaven (2 Pet. 1:4–11).

The stress on the remembrance of the apostolic witness to the transfiguration and God's witness to his Son was meant to refute cleverly invented fables, as indeed was Peter's use of the OT Scriptures. Clearly, there are false teachers among the Christian community whose lifestyle and exploitation of Christians were described in full with the aid of apposite incidents drawn from the OT (2 Pet. 2). The false teachers were disturbing Christians with taunts about the delay of the return of Christ, standard teaching on its certainty and the need for watchfulness (2 Pet. 3:1–13; cf. Mark 13).

There is an important reference to Paul's teaching as 'scripture', which Peter indicated was misused as were 'other scriptures', (2 Pet. 3:14–16). In spite of the problem in Antioch with Peter withdrawing from Gentile company while eating because of the arrival of fellow Jews, he bore no grudge against Paul's justified rebuke of his conduct. Indeed he referred to Paul as 'our beloved brother' who spoke according to the divine wisdom given to him (2 Pet. 3:15; cf. Gal. 2:11–14; cf. Acts 10:9–16; 11:1–8).

As an apostle charged to *feed my sheep* Peter remained faithful to that task and concluded his last letter with the exhortation to grow in grace and the knowledge of our Lord and Saviour, Jesus Christ (2 Pet. 3:18).

Peter was appointed by Jesus as the leading apostle to the Jews, a role he discharged in establishing Christ's eternal church by the preaching of the gospel and by faithfully nurturing it until the end of his life.                                    B. W.

**PETHAHIAH** (Heb., 'opened by the LORD').

**1.** One among the priests who were chosen to be officials in the sanctuary 'according to the last instructions of David'. Impartial selection from among the descendants of Eleazar and Ithamar was made by drawing lots. The 19th lot fell to Pethahiah and that was the order in which he ministered when entering the sanctuary (1 Chron. 24:16)

**2.** Another Pethahiah was one of the Levites who was married to a foreign woman. After the return from the Babylonian Exile and on the direction of Ezra, he agreed to divorce her. He also helped teach the people the Law of God and sealed the ageement of the people to worship the LORD and obey his Law (Ezra 10:23; Neh. 9:5).

**3.** Pethahiah son of Meshezabel was from the tribe of Judah and was the king's agent in all affairs dealing with the people in post-exilic Jerusalem (Neh. 11:24).

                                    P.D.G.

**PETHUEL** The father of the prophet Joel (Joel. 1:1).

**PEULLETHAI** The eighth son of Obed-Edom, a descendant of Korah, Peullethai was responsible to attend to the Tabernacle gates in David's administration (1 Chron. 26:5).

**PHANUEL** (Heb., 'face of God'). The father of Anna, a prophetess from the tribe of Asher (Luke 2:36). Anna was an elderly widow who was faithful to the Lord and was allowed to see the child Jesus in the Temple.

**PHARAOH** This is the usual title in the Bible for the kings of Egypt, meaning 'Great House'. There is substantial evidence from Egyptian sources that the word Pharaoh could be used simply as a title standing on its own, as it is often found in the Bible. Various Pharaohs are mentioned in the Bible and are only rarely identified (e.g. Neco is identified in 2 Kings 23:29, 33 etc. as the one who killed King Josiah). The earliest mentioned is the one encountered by Abraham who was afraid for Sarah's safety when he went to Egypt (Gen. 12:15, 17 etc.). Another prominent Pharaoh was the one encountered by Moses who had made life so unbearable for the Hebrew people. It is not always possible to be sure of identifying a particular Pharaoh with the king lists of Egypt mainly because not enough detail is given in Scripture, or because the events recorded in Scripture are too insignificant to be recorded in the annals of Egypt.                                    P. D. G.

**PHARAOH'S DAUGHTER. 1.** The woman best known in the Bible as 'Pharaoh's daughter' is mentioned in the account of the birth and childhood of Moses (Exod. 2:1–10). At a time when Pharaoh had ordered all the male children born to Hebrew women to be put to death, one woman hid her child by putting him in a papyrus basket and letting it float among the reeds at the side of the river Nile. The baby's sister, Miriam, looked after the child. Pharaoh's daughter came down to the river to bathe, heard the child cry, realized the baby must be a Hebrew child and retrieved him from the basket. Miriam, who was watching, went forward and offered to find a nurse for the child. This offer was accepted and so Miriam found the child's own mother to nurse him. Later when the child grew older he was taken by Pharaoh's daughter and officially became her son. 'She named him Moses, saying, "I drew him out of the water"' (v. 10).

The work of the LORD in these events is clearly seen in retrospect as he chose Moses to become leader of his people and to deal directly as the voice of God with Pharaoh. Because of his upbringing he would have known the court formalities and had an access to Pharaoh probably denied to most Hebrew slaves. See also *Acts 7:21* and *Heb. 11:24*.

**2.** King Solomon married a certain 'Pharaoh's daughter' for whom he built a special palace, since she could not live in David's palace 'because the places the ark of the LORD has entered are holy' (*1 Kings 7:8; 9;24; 11:1; 2 Chron. 8:11*). Solomon's marriages with this woman and other foreign women were eventually to lead to his downfall. Such intermarriage with other peoples had been forbidden by the Law of God and the wives gradually drew 'his heart after other gods' (*1 Kings 11:4–6*).

**3.** See *Bithiah*, Pharaoh's daughter who became Mered's wife (*1 Chron. 4:18*).

P.D.G.

## PHARISEES

One of three Jewish sects described by the 1st-century Jewish historian Josephus (along with the Sadducees and Essenes). Probably no more than 5–10% of all Jews belonged to this group, which was a cross between a political party and a religious faction. The name probably means 'separatists', and it was applied to a movement which grew out of the Maccabean era composed of religious leaders and students of the Law who tried to create a 'fence around the Torah' – an elaborate system of oral legislation and interpretation to enable the faithful Jew to obey and apply God's commandments in every area of life. Originally pious reformers, they were generally well-respected by the ordinary, less zealous Jews, even if the Pharisees at times criticized them for not being sufficiently scrupulous in heeding God's Law. Unlike the Sadducees, they continued to view Rome as an illegitimate, oppressive government which blocked Israel from receiving her divinely ordained blessings of freedom and peace in the land. They were by no means uniformly hypocritical, as Christians have often wrongly assumed. Still, later Talmudic tradition does describe seven classes of Pharisees, according to the motivation for their behaviour, and only one of the seven is said to act out of love.

In Mark, some Pharisees asked why Jesus ate with tax-collectors and sinners (*Mark 2:16*). They fasted when Jesus' disciples did not (*2:18*), charged Jesus with breaking the Sabbath (*2:24*), began to plot to kill him (*3:6*), questioned why he did not follow their traditions of ritual cleanliness (*7:1, 3, 5*), and demanded a miraculous sign to authenticate his ministry (*8:11*). Their teaching was compared to an evil, insidious force (*8:15*), and they tried to trap Jesus in asking his views on divorce (*10:2*) and on taxes (*12:13*).

Matthew repeats all these references but heightens the animosity by adding several others, in keeping with his consistently harsh polemic against the Jewish leaders. Pharisees were present to scrutinize John's ministry of baptizing (*Matt. 3:7*). Jesus declared that his disciples' righteousness must exceed that of the Pharisees (*5:20*). They charged him with casting out demons by the prince of demons (*9:34; 12:24*) and recognized themselves as the wicked tenants in Jesus' parable (*21:45*). One, a lawyer, asked Jesus about the greatest commandment (*22:34–35*). Jesus charged them with all kinds of hypocrisy in his longest sustained invective anywhere in the Gospels (*Matt. 23*), and they requested Pilate to give them a guard for Jesus' tomb (*27:52*).

Luke differs from Matthew and Mark in a number of places. Some of his references to the Pharisees remain negative. They complained about Jesus' claim to be able to forgive sins (*Luke 5:21*), rejected God's counsel (*7:30*), murmured about Christ's association with the unrepentant (*15:2*), rejected Jesus' teaching on stewardship because they 'loved money' (*16:14*) and called on Christ to rebuke his followers when they acclaimed him as the coming king (*19:39*). Jesus' parable of the Pharisee and tax collector stunned his audience because the popular Jewish leader turned out to be the one who was not justified rather than the notorious employee of imperialist Rome (*18:10–14*). On the other hand, Luke is the one Gospel writer to include a number of texts which portray the Pharisees in a more positive light, often in the context of table fellowship with Christ. Simon invited Jesus to his house for dinner, but it was Jesus who used the occasion to criticize the Pharisee's hospitality (*7:36–50*). *11:37–53* and *14:1–24* describe two similar feasts which Pharisees arranged on Jesus' behalf, but which degenerated into criticism of some aspect of their behaviour. In *13:31*, they warned Jesus against Herod's wrath, and seemed genuinely concerned for his well-being. And in *17:20–21*, they asked about the coming Kingdom of God, leading Jesus to declare that it was in their very midst, by means of his own person and ministry.

John is more like Matthew in portraying the Pharisees as mostly hostile to Jesus. They sent a Temple guard on an aborted mission to arrest him (*John 7:32–46*). They challenged Jesus' testimony as invalid, since he spoke on his own behalf (*8:13*). They investigated his healing of a blind man, rejecting that man's assessment of Jesus and revealing their own spiritual blindness in the process (*9:13–41*). They formed a council in which they decided to arrest Jesus and attempted to have him put to death, albeit secretly (*11:45–57*), they lamented how the 'whole world' had gone after Jesus, following his Triumphal Entry (*12:19*), and they appeared as part of the detachment of Jews who went to Gethsemane to arrest him (*18:3*). Fear of the Pharisees kept some Jews who believed in Christ from confessing him publicly (*12:42*). On the other hand, at least one prominent Pharisee appeared in a somewhat more positive light – Nicodemus (*3:1*), who, despite not initially understanding Jesus' claim that one must be born again (*vv. 3–4*), later came to Christ's defence (*7:50–51*) and assisted Joseph of Arimathea in Jesus' burial (*19:39*). More neutral texts involving Pharisees included their query regarding John the Baptist's identity (*1:24*) and the report that they heard that Jesus was baptizing more people than was John (*4:1*).

As in Luke, Acts mixes positive and negative references. A leading member of the Jewish high court, Gamaliel, came to the apostles' defence. Some Pharisees became Christians but wrongly believed that Gentile believers must continue to obey all of the Law (*Acts 15:5*). At his hearing before the Sanhedrin, Paul divided the court by siding with the Pharisees over against the Sadducees when he claimed that he was on trial for his belief in the resurrection. Again in *26:5*, while defending himself before Agrippa, he referred to his own upbringing as a Pharisee. *Phil. 3:5* reflects this identical testimony, but in both contexts Paul also made clear that as a Christian many of his fundamental commitments had changed.      C.B.

**PHICOL** was commander of Abimelech's forces in the days of Abraham. He accompanied Abimelech, a Philistine leader, in making a treaty with Abraham at Beersheba (*Gen. 21:22,32*). Later, when Abraham was dead and there was a famine in the land, Isaac went to Abimelech in Gerar for help and food. He stayed there a while and became powerful and a threat to the Philistines and so he was asked to move away from them. After various disputes over wells, Isaac returned to Beersheba. Once there, Abimelech and Phicol once again came to the area seeking a treaty, this time with Isaac (*Gen. 26:26*). Whether the same Philistine leaders dealt with Abraham and many years later with Isaac is not certain. It is possible that Phicol and Abimelech were both Philistine titles for their leaders, and thus two different men could have been involved.      P.D.G.

**PHILEMON** was one of Paul's fellow-workers, a 'dear friend' and a faithful Christian. He had probably been converted under Paul's ministry (*Philem. 1, 5, 19*). A house church met at his home and some of the members of that group or of his household are also greeted at the start of the epistle Paul wrote to him. Philemon's love for 'the saints' (other Christian brothers and sisters) was well known. He had refreshed the hearts of the saints (*vv. 5, 7*). One of Paul's prayers for him was that he might be active in sharing the gospel of Christ with others. This might indicate a certain timidity on his part in actually speaking out for Christ among his pagan business contacts (*v. 6*).

From a careful comparison with Paul's letter to the Colossians it can reasonably be affirmed that Philemon's household was part of the church at Colosse. In Colossians Onesimus, the subject of Paul's letter to Philemon, was said to be 'one of you' (*Col. 4:6*). Onesimus was a slave who belonged to Philemon but had either run away, possibly taking money with him, or had been loaned to the apostle Paul. Whatever the situation (see *Onesimus*), it can be assumed a slave-owner with a big enough house to contain the members of a house church was a wealthy man of some standing in the community.

Paul's epistle to this man is the shortest we have from his pen. It is a personal note requesting that Philemon take back his former slave as a 'brother' (*v. 16*). Again and again the apostle emphasized the value of Onesimus to him personally. He had become like a son to Paul while he was in chains for the gospel. Paul's letter began with a comment on how Philemon had 'refreshed the hearts of the saints' and he drew it to a conclusion asking Philemon to 'refresh my heart in Christ' (*vv. 7, 20*) by taking Onesimus back. Paul had begun with reference to Philemon's care for the saints and ended with a request that a guest room be prepared for him too (*vv. 5, 22*).

Whether Paul was in prison when he wrote this letter has been much disputed. Some have suggested he wrote it from prison in Caesarea (see *Acts 25*), others have postulated a captivity in Ephesus from which he might have written the epistle, but still the most likely situation was Paul's Roman imprisonment. A slave like Onesimus might well have tried to escape and get lost among the crowds of a large city like Rome. Perhaps while there he had been introduced to Paul from whom he had heard the gospel or had perhaps been captured and shared a cell with Paul for a while. At best such reconstructions, though, can only be possibilities.

The letter of Philemon has been much examined to see what can be learned of possible Christian attitudes to slavery. The letter tells us little and assumes that it was right for Philemon to take Onesimus back as a slave. However, the chain of events that eventually led to Christians believing that slavery was wrong was certainly set in motion by Paul's treatment of Onesimus. Paul said he was 'Father' to Onesimus. He called Onesimus a 'brother' and said he was of real 'benefit', and he trusted him as a helper on a mission to the Colossians. Paul sent him back to Philemon 'no longer as a slave but better than a slave'. Christianity was clearly causing a re-think of relationships between masters and slaves. How Philemon reacted to this challenge to his way of thinking is, sadly, not recorded.

P. D. G.

**PHILETUS** (Gk., 'beloved') was a heretical teacher linked with Hymenaeus and therefore probably with Alexander (2 Tim. 2:17; 1 Tim. 1:20). The heresy spread 'like gangrene' and was a distortion of Scripture. Particularly serious was their teaching that the resurrection had already happened (2 Tim. 2:18). Perhaps they believed the resurrection was simply a description of a spiritual experience rather than the resurrection of the body – a teaching that is fundamental to the Christian faith (e.g. see 1 Cor. 15:16–19). Such heresies have not been uncommon through history and Christians, wishing to follow Paul's example, have often had to confront the

issues with a strong insistence on the bodily resurrection.

P. D. G.

**PHILIP** In the NT four different persons are called Philip. It is important to distinguish between Philip, one of the original twelve disciples, and Philip, sometimes known as 'the evangelist', who was a minister or deacon chosen by the apostles to serve the early church (Acts 6:5).

**1. Philip the apostle** is mentioned in the Gospels and Acts. In Matt. 10:3, Mark 3:18 and Luke 6:14 he appears in the list of the twelve disciples, later called apostles. Little is known of his background except what may be determined from John's Gospel. He was from the same town as Andrew and Peter – Bethsaida in Galilee (John 1:44). This was a fishing town situated slightly east and north of where the Jordan river flows into the Sea of Galilee. There is some discussion about its precise location. Philip the tetrarch, some 30 or so years earlier, had re-established this town and had called it 'Julias' in honour of the emperor's daughter. The fact that Philip the tetrarch had such associations with the town may well explain the apostle's name. His parents may have called him Philip after this ruler.

From John's Gospel it appears that Philip was the fourth apostle to be chosen by Jesus (John 1:43). In the lists of the Synoptic Gospels he always appears fifth, probably because John and his brother James were always mentioned together. It is in John's Gospel that Philip receives some further attention. It is clear in his response to Jesus' command 'Follow me' that he quickly believed in Jesus as one who fulfilled what Moses wrote about in the OT Law. Philip's enthusiasm was immediately evident in his introduction of Nathaniel to Jesus (1:46).

Three points are worthy of note here. First, Philip is a good example, along with Andrew and Peter, of those people who did quickly and enthusiastically 'receive' Jesus, at a time when most of 'his own did not receive him' (*John 1:11*). Secondly, although there are indications that Philip was somewhat timid or lacking in faith (see below), he immediately 'witnessed' to Jesus in promptly telling Nathaniel. This theme of bearing witness to Jesus, a command laid on all Christians, is developed at length in John's Gospel (see esp. *5:31–46*). Already John the Baptist had witnessed to Jesus (*1:7f.*), as had Andrew to his brother Peter (*1:41*). Later in the Gospel the OT witness to Jesus is mentioned (*5:39*), as is the Samaritan witness to Jesus (*4:39–42*), the Holy Spirit's witness to Jesus (*15:26*) and, of course, the apostolic witness (*15:27*). Thirdly, the content of that witness becomes evident as Philip witnessed not just to an amazing man but to Jesus who was written about in the law of Moses. Perhaps Philip was thinking of Jesus as 'the prophet' (*Deut. 18:19*, a verse alluded to in *John 1:21*). Philip believed Scriptures were being fulfilled, a point that John was determined to establish throughout his Gospel.

In *John 6* Philip is mentioned again. Jesus turned to Philip to test him by asking where bread could be bought to feed 5,000 people (*6:5–6*). Whether Jesus particularly wanted to test Philip's faith rather than anyone else's, or whether Philip was the logical one to turn to because he knew this area of 'the far shore of Galilee' (*6:1*, perhaps near Bethsaida) cannot be known. But Jesus seized the opportunity, even though he had his own plans to perform a miracle. Philip neither had the faith nor the understanding to imagine any sort of feeding other than that which would cost a fortune for so many people. This lack of understanding on Philip's part was also to be seen in the other disciples on many occasions, but it was evident again in Philip in *14:8*, where he wanted Jesus to show him 'the Father'. This, he said, 'will be enough'.

Jesus' response sounds profoundly sad. Philip and the others had been with Jesus for a long time. They had seen him in action and had heard his teaching. Still they had not realized that in seeing Jesus they were seeing the Father himself. Rhetorically, Jesus asked how Philip could ask this question after so long in Jesus' presence? The answer was that Philip and the other disciples had not yet had their spiritual eyes opened properly to understand these things. It would fall to the later work of the Holy Spirit fully to open their understanding (*14:25–26*). In reporting incidents like this to his readers, John opened up the depth of Jesus' teaching and highlighted its importance. The unity of the Father and Son was firmly established in Jesus' response to Philip's question.

In *John 12:21–22* some Greeks approached Philip requesting an interview with Jesus. Perhaps they approached Philip because he had a Greek name. The Greeks are surely significant at this juncture in John's Gospel for they indicate that there were non-Jews who were interested in Jesus, and they point forward to the time when other sheep would be added to Jesus' flock, sheep that were not Jews (*10:15–16*). Before that could happen Jesus would have to die. It is therefore appropriate that in *12:23* Jesus' response was to point forward to his death and resurrection. It is not clear whether Philip managed to arrange a meeting with Jesus for these Greeks. The last time Philip is mentioned is in *Acts 1:13* where he is listed with the disciples gathered in the Upper Room.

**2. Philip the evangelist**, sometimes also called a deacon, is mentioned first in *Acts 6:5*. The apostles were finding the work of administration in the early Jerusalem church to be so burdensome that they needed help. Many new people were becoming Christians. The new Christians of Greek-Jewish background were falling out with those of Hebrew-Jewish background over the distribution of food to widows. The disciples found that they were spending so much time sorting out these things (Acts 6:2) that they were neglecting the ministry of the Word of God. Seven helpers were therefore to be appointed and were to be chosen as men known to be 'full of the Spirit and wisdom'. One of those chosen was Philip. The apostles prayed and laid their hands on these men and appointed them to the job of looking after the day-to-day affairs of the church.

This incident is an interesting indication of how early in the church's life there was a recognition of the fact that God gives different people different ministries of gifts. But it also reflects the early recognition by the church that those called to 'the ministry of the Word of God' (6:2) should not have other preoccupations. V. 7 indicates the result of this division of labour: the Word of God spread and the number of disciples increased rapidly.

When the early persecution broke out in the Jerusalem area (around the time that Stephen was martyred), Philip went to Samaria where he quickly became a prominent evangelist and missionary. At the end of the book of Acts, Paul and Luke visited Philip who was, by then, known as 'the evangelist' (Acts 21:8) and lived in Caesarea.

Acts 8 gives an idea of the sort of work in which Philip was involved in Samaria. He proclaimed the gospel, performed miracles and generally conducted a ministry more reminiscent of the apostles than of an apostolic helper or administrator. Philip's work in Samaria is of particular importance to the message of the book of Acts. In Acts, Luke shows the way in which, under the guidance of the Holy Spirit, the great commission was fulfilled. Acts 1:8 gives Jesus' commission to the disciples to be witnesses in Jerusalem, Judea and Samaria and to the whole world. With Philip this witness reached Samaria. Many people were converted through Philip's ministry and were baptized (8:12). Later an apostolic delegation of Peter and John arrived in Samaria and confirmed that the gospel had been received by those outside Jerusalem.

While in Samaria, Philip encountered problems with a magician known as Simon. When Simon saw Philip's miracles and heard him preach he believed and was baptized. Whether true conversion took place is not altogether clear as Simon was later castigated roundly by Peter (8:20–24).

Philip was also responsible for preaching to an Ethiopian Eunuch. It was probably through this man's conversion that the gospel first spread all the way to Ethiopia for the Eunuch was an important government official and on his way home (8:27–28). The fact that Philip was indeed a 'man full of the Holy Spirit' is seen in the way that the Spirit led him to speak to this man seated in his chariot. Philip expounded the OT Scriptures to him in the light of the coming of Christ, and the Ethiopian believed and was baptized. Clearly the reference to Philip as 'the evangelist' in 21:8 indicates that later in his life he was still widely known for his missionary zeal.

**3. Philip, son of Herod the Great.** In Mark 6:17 (see Matt. 14:3; Luke 3:19) the death of John the Baptist is recalled when people suggested that perhaps Jesus was John the Baptist come alive again. In recalling this incident Mark referred to Herod's marriage to Herodias who, he said, had been Herod's brother Philip's wife. The references to this ruler, whose wife Herodias had subsequently been taken by Herod, are significant in providing historical background to the challenge that John the Baptist made to Herod. John challenged Herod about this illegal marriage and was put to death as a result (Matt. 14:3–12).

It is sometimes assumed that this Philip can only be Philip Herod the tetrarch (see

544

below), the son of Herod the Great and Cleopatra. However, Josephus identified Herodias' first husband as Herod, the son of Herod the Great and Mariamne. Herod, was of course, the family name. But Josephus failed to give any second name to this son. It is certainly possible that Herodias' first husband was Herod Philip, thus accounting for Mark's designation of him as 'Philip'. It is true that this would mean that two sons of Herod the Great were called Philip, but such is not impossible given that two different mothers were involved.

**4. Philip, tetrarch of Iturea and Trachonitis.** This ruler, known as Philip Herod, was the son of Herod the Great and Cleopatra of Jerusalem. *Luke 3:1* describes his rule as having been over Iturea and Trachonitis. It is impossible now to accurately define the borders of this territory, but Josephus states that it included Auranitis, Gaulanitis and Batanaea. The area covered would therefore have stretched from a little west of the northern part of the Jordan to include a substantial area east of the Jordan but north of the Decapolis region. Lake Huleh and the city known as Caesarea Philippi would have been included within this territory. Philip ruled this area from 4 BC until his death in AD 33. During this time he was responsible for the re-establishing of Caesarea Philippi (formerly known as Peneion) and the fishing town of Bethsaida on the northern edge of the Sea of Galilee. He was regarded by the population as the best and most just of the Herodian rulers. P.D.G.

**PHILIPPIAN JAILER** One of the most extraordinary conversions recounted in the book of Acts occurred in the life of a man who was once a jailer charged with keeping Paul and Silas (*Acts 16:16–40*). Paul and Silas had been arrested on their first visit to Philippi. After being 'severely flogged' they were put into prison in the care of a jailer who was charged 'to guard them carefully' (*v. 23*). During the night Paul and Silas were heard by the other prisoners to be praying and singing hymns to God, when suddenly a violent earthquake caused the chains of all the prisoners to fall off and all the prison doors to open. The jailer awoke and, knowing he would be held accountable for the escape of the prisoners, was about to commit suicide when Paul shouted out: 'Don't harm yourself! We are all here!' (*v. 28*).

The jailer rushed in and, seeing that the prisoners were indeed there, asked Paul and Silas what he needed to do to be saved. They responded: 'Believe in the Lord Jesus, and you will be saved – you and your household' (*v. 31*). The two missionaries then preached to the jailer and other members of his household. The jailer tended the wounds of Paul and Silas from their beatings and then in the middle of the night he and his family were baptized. 'He was filled with joy because he had come to believe in God – he and his whole family' (*v. 34*).

Both the simplicity and the sheer joy of becoming a Christian are stressed in this passage. It stands as a statement down through the ages of the power of the gospel of Christ to transform people entirely when they place their faith in him. P.D.G.

**THE PHILISTINES** This name comes from the Heb. *Philistia* and *Philistine*. The Gk. *Palaistinei* gave rise to the modern name Palestine for what roughly is coterminous with the territory of OT Israel and Judah. In Akkadian texts the area is referred to as Palastu, Pilistu, or Pilista. The Philistines are mentioned prominently in New Kingdom Egyptian documents (c. 1200–1100 BC) as an element of the nefarious 'Sea Peoples' who tried unsuccessfully to invade Egypt from the Mediterranean and Libya during the reigns of Rameses III and his immediate successors. These texts call the Philistines,

Peleset, a name close to the Heb. rendering.

The term 'Sea Peoples' is aptly descriptive of the Philistines and their allies, for both the OT and extra-biblical documents place their origin in the islands and coastlands near Greece and Crete. *Gen. 10:14* links the Philistines and Caphtorim, and nearly all scholars identify Caphtor as Crete. The same identification is made in ancient Akkadian texts that describe persons from Crete as *kaptaru*. Deuteronomy suggests that Caphtorim had arrived on the Mediterranean coast at and around Gaza and had supplanted the indigenous Avvim population (*Deut. 2:23*). That, of course, is the very area consistently associated in the OT with the Philistine city-states. The linkage is complete with Jeremiah's observation that the Philistines were 'the remnant from the coasts of Caphtor' (*Jer. 47:4*). Amos adds the information that the LORD had brought the Philistines to Canaan from Caphtor just as surely as he had brought Israel there from Egypt (*Amos 9:7*).

The majority of historians date the arrival of the Philistines at the eastern Mediterranean at no earlier than 1200 BC, a conclusion that raises considerable difficulty in light of OT references to them in much earlier times. The most notable instance is the contact that both Abraham and Isaac had with Philistines as early as 2000 BC (*Gen. 21:32, 34; 26:1, 8*). They appear again in the account of the Exodus where God led Israel away from the coastal route to Canaan because that was 'the road through the Philistine country' (*Exod. 13:17*). If one accepts the traditional date for the Exodus (c. 1440 BC), the Philistines in this narrative precede the Sea Peoples' occupation of Canaan by more than two centuries.

There can be no doubt that the Philistines arrived in Canaan in great numbers at 1200 BC or later. The OT itself is reflective of this for it is only in the days of Samuel and Samson (c. 1120 BC) that they are sufficiently numerous to pose serious problems for Israel (*1 Sam. 4–6; Judg. 10:7–8; 13–16*). This does not preclude the possibility of earlier Philistines, however, exactly in line with the Genesis and Exodus passages and with the notation in Deuteronomy of the replacement of Avvim by Caphtorim, an event Moses views as in his distant past (*Deut. 2:23*). The abundant references to Caphtorim (or Kaptara or the like) in texts as early as 2000 BC is sufficient to allow the possibility of their existing in coastal Canaan in pre-Mosaic times.

Whatever their ultimate origin and chronological setting, by the 12th century the Philistines were firmly entrenched on the lower Mediterranean coast of Canaan and concentrated in five cities: Gaza, Ashkelon, Ashdod, Gath and Ekron. It is customary to refer to their political structure as a pentapolis ('five cities'), each governed not by a king but by an official described in Heb. as *seren*, perhaps to be translated as 'lord' (*Josh. 13:3; Judg. 3:3; 16:5, 8, 18, 23, 27*; etc.). Its translation in the LXX as 'tyrant' supports the Aegean origin of the Philistines. The pentapolis appears to have been a coalition of equals who could exercise some autonomy (as in Achish's dealings with David, *1 Sam. 27:5–7*) but who, in the face of national emergency, worked in concert and were subject to majority decision (again, as in the dismissal of David from battle with Saul, *1 Sam. 29*).

Recent archaeological excavation has revealed that the Philistines introduced and enjoyed a rather high level of culture and technology. Relief drawings from Medinet Habu in Egypt depict their dress and armament and artefacts from tombs, and other sites in Canaan include impressive samples of pottery, daggers, stamp seals, and sophisticated architectural features. A major Philistine achievement was the use of iron, an innovation well in advance of its use in Israel. As late as the time of Saul (1050–1010 BC), if an Israelite wanted to sharpen or repair an iron implement, he had to take it to the Philistines, who had a corner on the requisite skills (1 Sam. 13:19–21).

The OT does not emphasize the cultural achievements of the Philistines, however, but instead focuses on their negative impact on Israel. Fiercely warlike, they proved to be implacable foes of Israel to the end of OT times, overrunning Israel's territory time and again until Samuel (1 Sam. 7:12–14) and then David (2 Sam. 5:22–25) put an end to their maraudings. Even more deleterious, perhaps, was their religious practice, one centred on a half-fish, half human deity named Dagon (1 Sam. 5:1–5). The Semitic name of this god (cf. the Mari and Canaanite Dagan) and the existence of other Philistines deities such as Baal-Zebub (2 Kings 1:2) and Ashtoreth/Ashtaroth (1 Sam. 31:8–13), both Semitic, show clearly that the Philistines had assimilated their own native and original cult to that of the Canaanites.

Theologically, the Philistines typify the kind of baleful influences that Israel was to resist as the chosen people of the LORD (Yahweh). The frequent reference to them as the 'uncircumcised (Philistines)' (Judg. 15:18; 1 Sam. 14:6; 17:26; 31:4; 2 Sam. 1:20) makes it clear that they were not of the covenant people and therefore were to be strictly avoided as a contaminating evil.          E. M.

**PHILOLOGUS** (Gk., 'lover of learning'). A Christian who lived in Rome and was greeted by the apostle Paul along with Julia, Nereus and his sister, and Olympas (Rom. 16:15). It is possible that as he heads this list he was the leader of a house church, and it may be that Julia was his wife. Paul's personal recognition and care for many individuals in different congregations is to be noted in most of his letters.

**PHINEHAS 1.** Phinehas the priest was the son of Eleazar son of Aaron and one of the greatest of all Israelites. His mother was 'one of the daughters of Putiel' (Exod. 6:25). His own son was called Abishua (1 Chron. 6:4, 50). In the days of the return from the Exile in Babylon, Ezra himself and others traced their ancestry back to Phinehas (Ezra 7:5; 8:2). 1 Chron. 9:20 indicates that one of his main jobs was to be a 'gatekeeper' of the Tabernacle.

His fame centred on his 'zeal' to defend the LORD God in the face of idolatry. Num. 25 records how, while Israel was camped at Shittim 'the men began to indulge in sexual immorality with Moabite women who invited them to the sacrifices to their gods' – the Baal of Peor (vv. 1–3). The LORD's anger at such behaviour led to swift judgment. All the leaders who had been involved in this immorality and idolatry were put to death, but even while this was happening a Simeonite, Zimri son of Salu, brought a Midianite woman, Cozbi, back to his home with all his family with the intention of having sex with her. Phinehas followed them into their tent and thrust his spear through the Israelite and into the woman's body with one thrust, clearly indicating that he had caught them in the act of adultery and immorality (vv. 7–8). God's plague of judgment on the Israelites was stopped by this swift action, but not before 24,000 Israelites had died.

Of Phinehas the LORD said: 'He was as zealous as I am for my honour among them, so that in my zeal I did not put an end to them. Therefore tell him I am making my covenant of peace with him. He and his descendants will have a covenant of a lasting priesthood, because he was zealous for the honour of his God and made atonement for the Israelites' (vv. 11–13). With the exception of a short period under Eli, Phinehas' descendants continued his work of priesthood and through most of that time also provided the high priests. Phinehas himself later served before the ark of the covenant at Bethel where, once again, his zeal for the LORD was seen as he carried the word of the LORD to the people concerning the avenging of the sin of the Benjamites (Judg. 20:28).

Phinehas next appears in the account of Num. 31:6 where he went with Israelite soldiers to fight the Midianites to avenge the incident at Baal Peor. He took with him some of the articles from the sanctuary and trumpets for signalling.

In Josh. 22 Phinehas led a delegation to the tribes of Reuben, Gad and Manasseh who had built an altar near the Jordan river. Worship was only allowed at the Tabernacle and so when the rest of the Israelites heard what had happened they feared lest yet again the LORD's judgment should come on them. Phinehas and representatives from each of the ten tribes (vv. 13–14) went to speak to the tribal leaders before the whole of Israel went to war against them. The three tribes argued that their altar was to stand as a witness to the fact that they would only worship at the Tabernacle, and that it would never be used for burnt-offerings or sacrifices (v. 26). It was to serve as a reminder to all the Israelites that the tribes, largely settled on the eastern side of the Jordan, were still part of Israel and worshipped the same LORD. Phinehas and the others returned to the other Israelites praising God (vv. 30–34).

Such concern for the LORD and his Law became a model for how all Israelites and specially their leaders were to be. His zeal for the LORD is commemorated in Ps. 106:30 and in the books of Maccabees his zeal was to be emulated (e.g. 1 Macc. 2:26, 54).

**2.** Brother of Hophni, he was one of Eli's sons and a priest in Israel at Shiloh (1 Sam. 1:3; 14:3). The sons of Eli became thoroughly corrupt and took advantage of their privileged position. 'They had no regard for the LORD' (2:12). Eventually he died under God's judgment. For more detail see Hophni.

**3.** The father of Eleazar who was one of the priests who returned from the Babylonian Exile with Ezra. Eleazar helped weigh and account for all the silver and gold that they had brought back with them for the Temple (Ezra 8:33). P. D. G.

**PHLEGON** (Gk., 'burning'). The second named of a group of Roman Christians greeted by Paul in his letter to the Romans (16:14). The personal care and pastoral concern for individuals reflected in Paul's greetings is worthy of attention.

**PHOEBE** A well-known Christian woman with a ministry in Cenchraea, a port city some seven miles east of Corinth. Paul describes her both as a 'sister' and a 'minister', using the same term from which we get the term 'deaconess'. It is unclear whether this refers to a fixed office (Phil. 1:1; 1 Tim. 3:8, 12) or is a broader term to describe someone who engaged effectively in ministry (Eph. 3:7; Col. 1:7). Either way it is clear that Paul had a high regard for her work for the Lord. We do know that an order of deaconesses existed in the 2nd century, but the only possible NT reference to such a position is 1 Tim. 3:11. Paul urges that she be helped in whatever way is possible. Clearly she had a specific role to perform and the church was to give her all the help she required. D. B.

**PHYGELUS** (Gk., 'fugitive'). Mentioned, together with Hermogenes, in Paul's first epistle to Timothy as being among 'everyone in the province of Asia' who had deserted him (2 Tim. 1:15). Clearly Paul did not mean that all the Christians of all the churches in the province of Asia, such as Ephesus, Colosse, and Laodicea, had deserted him. Probably Paul was referring to the time of his second imprisonment in Rome (v. 17), and had in mind the way the Christians had not stood by him at his trial. Those who did not stand by him would have included all those from the province of Asia living in Rome, such as Hermogenes and Phygelus, of whom he might have expected better things.

Paul drew a contrast between this sort of behaviour that was no doubt frightened of the Roman authorities, and the conduct of Onesiphorus who Paul said: 'often refreshed me and was not ashamed of my chains' (v. 16). Paul referred to these examples in order to encourage Timothy to 'be strong in the grace that is in Christ Jesus' (2:1). In much the same way as Christians experience difficulty in standing strong and firm for Christ in many modern societies, so the problem was present in the early church where Christians could find themselves being persecuted or simply 'ashamed' if they spoke out for Christ.                    P. D. G.

**PILATE** Pontius Pilate was the relatively ruthless Roman governor (procurator or prefect) who ruled in Judea from AD 26–36, including the period of Christ's ministry (Luke 3:1). Luke 13:1 describes him as having slaughtered some Galileans and mingling their blood with that of the Jewish sacrifices. He figures most prominently, however, in each of the four Gospels' accounts of Jesus' crucifixion.

Mark 15 recounts how the Sanhedrin brought Jesus to Pilate for his execution. Pilate asked Jesus if he was the 'King of the Jews' as charged; Jesus replied with a qualified affirmative (v. 2). Concerning further accusations he remained silent. Following a custom of releasing one prisoner every Passover, Pilate tried to free Jesus, but the Jewish leaders clamoured instead for an insurrectionist, Barabbas. Pilate asked them what they wanted done with Jesus, and they requested his crucifixion. Despite believing that Jesus had committed no crime, Pilate consented, had Jesus scourged and delivered him over to death (v. 15). Later he agreed to let Joseph of Arimathea take the corpse off the cross and give it a proper burial (vv. 42–45). For Mark, Pilate seems not so much cruel as weak.

Matt. 27 includes the identical outline of events but adds that Pilate's wife had dreamt about Jesus and advised her husband to have nothing to do with 'that innocent man' (v. 19). Pilate subsequently washed his hands 'of this man's blood' (v. 24). Both of these additions fit Matthew's concern to place primary blame for Jesus' death on the Jewish leaders. In vv. 62–66, the Pharisees requested and received from Pilate a guard for the tomb.

Luke 23 even more clearly stresses Pilate's belief in Christ's innocence (e.g. vv. 4, 13–16, 22). Pilate tried to pawn his problem off on Herod Antipas, but to no avail, save that the two rulers became friends (vv. 6–12). Luke's mild whitewashing of Pilate fits his desire to present Christianity in a positive light to Roman rulers of his day.

John 18–19 contains the most elaborate account of Pilate's trial of Jesus. Repeatedly, Pilate moved back and forth between Jesus and the Jewish leaders in attempting to free him. 18:33–38 contain additional dialogue between Pilate and Christ. Jesus revealed that he is a king, but not of this world, sent to bear witness to the truth. But Pilate had no comprehension of truth. 19:10 illustrates a key theme for John – Jesus' sovereignty, even in his death. John also clarifies Pilate's primary motive in giving in to the Jewish authorities – fear of being called unloyal to Caesar (vv. 12, 15). Vv. 19–23 describe the title Pilate had affixed above the cross, which he refused to alter – 'Jesus of Nazareth, King of the Jews'.

Acts refers back to Pilate's treachery in crucifying Christ (3:13; 4:27; 13:28), but as part of God's sovereign will which fulfils the Scriptures. 1 Tim. 6:13 labels Jesus' admission of his kingship before Pilate as 'the good confession', exhorting believers to imitate their Lord in bold witness.                    C. B.

**PILDASH** A son of Nahor and Milcah and therefore Abraham's nephew (*Gen. 22:22*). See also *Bethuel*.

**PILHA** Mentioned only in *Neh. 10:24*, Pilha was one of the leaders of the Jews who returned from the Exile in Babylon and joined Nehemiah in binding himself to an agreement to obey the Law of God.

**PILTAI** (Heb., 'the LORD delivers') was the head of Moadiah's family, and helped in the service of the Temple during Nehemiah's time (*Neh. 12:17*).

**PINON** Descended from Esau, Pinon was a clan leader of the Edomites (*Gen. 36:41; 1 Chron. 1:52*).

**PIRAM** (Heb., 'wild ass'). Piram king of Jarmuth answered the call of Adoni-Zedek, king of Jerusalem, to join a coalition of kings to fight the Gibeonites, who had recently made a peace treaty with Joshua and the Israelites. When Gibeon was attacked, Joshua came to its aid and defeated the coalition. The kings fled to a cave at Makkedah. When Joshua found them there he rolled stones in front of the cave and posted guards so they could not escape. When Joshua returned from battle he brought out the kings and put them to death (*Josh. 10:3–28; 12:10*). The LORD continued to encourage Joshua in battle and to demonstrate that there was indeed no need for fear (*10:8; see 1:4–9*).

**PISPAH** From the tribe of Asher, he was the son of Jether and mentioned as a leader of the tribe and a great warrior (*1 Chron. 7:38, 40*).

**PITHON** One of King Saul's descendants and from the tribe of Benjamin, Pithon was the first son of Micah (*1 Chron. 8:35; 9:41*).

**POKERETH-HAZZEBAIM** (Heb., 'hunter of gazelles') was one of Solomon's servants whose descendants returned from the Exile in Babylon in company with Zerubbabel (*Ezra 2:57; Neh. 7:59*).

**POLLUX (see CASTOR)** Roman gods in a figurehead on a boat (*Acts 28:11*).

**PONTIUS** See *Pilate* for detail. Pontius may mean 'bridge'. Pontius Pilate was the Roman procurator of Judea at the time of Christ's crucifixion. The name Pontius occurs only with the second name Pilate and only in the following verses: *Luke 3:1; Acts 4:27; 1 Tim. 6:13*. The name Pilate, of course, appears many more times.

**PORATHA** Mentioned in *Est. 9:8* as one of ten sons of Haman killed in Susa by the Jews.

**PORCIUS FESTUS** (*Acts 24:27*) was the Roman procurator of Judea who succeeded Felix. He is more often simply called Festus. See *Festus* for detail.

**POTIPHAR** The name probably means 'Whom Ra [the sun god] has given'. Potiphar was an official in Pharaoh's court in Egypt. He was called 'the captain of the guard' and was responsible for buying Joseph when he was sold into slavery in Egypt by the Midianites (*Gen. 37:36*).

In Potiphar's household Joseph, with God's guidance, quickly rose to a position of great trust. Everything Joseph did prospered because the LORD was with him. Eventually even Potiphar's house experienced the blessing of the LORD because Joseph had been placed in charge (*Gen. 39:2–5*). Potiphar's trust in Joseph was shown to be well-placed when he refused the advances of the official's wife. Joseph was handsome and she wanted to seduce him. He refused her and refused to sin against God (*v. 9*). For days she kept trying to persuade him to go to bed with her, but when he continued to refuse her she grasped his cloak. He fled leaving the cloak in her hand. She then called the servants and pretended that Joseph had wanted to sleep with her and she had screamed, whereupon he had run off (vv. 14–15). When Potiphar heard this story from his wife he had Joseph thrown into prison. However, God's plans were still being worked out through all this. *Gen. 39:21* says 'the LORD was with him; he showed him kindness and granted him favour in the eyes of the prison warden'.

Gen. 50:20, perhaps more than any other verse, summarizes what was happening in Joseph's life as he was sold by his brothers into slavery, became the slave of Potiphar, was imprisoned and then went on to become prime minister of Egypt. It contains the words spoken by Joseph to his brothers after they had all settled in Egypt: 'You intended to harm me, but God intended it for good to accomplish what is now being done, the saving of many lives.' Also see *Joseph*.

P. D. G.

**POTIPHAR'S WIFE** For detail see *Potiphar*. This unnamed woman tried to seduce Joseph who had risen to a place of trust in Potiphar's household. Joseph refused to sleep with her and refused to sin against God and so she falsely accused him of wanting to have sex with her. Her husband, Potiphar, on hearing his wife's version of events put Joseph in prison (*Gen. 39:6–20*).

**POTIPHERA** A priest of On. On, later named Heliopolis by the Greeks, was the Egyptian city of the cult of the sun god, Re. Potiphera probably held a very high position in the society of Joseph's day as his daughter was given to Joseph to be his wife at a time when Joseph was, in effect, the prime minister of Egypt. The woman's name was Asenath (*Gen. 41:45, 50; 46:20*).

**PRIESTS** See *Levites*.

**PRISCILLA** was also known as 'Prisca', which was her formal name. The apostle Paul refers to her as Prisca in his writings. She was married to a Jewish Christian named Aquila. He was a tent-maker and a native of Pontus.

Priscilla and her husband, who are always mentioned together, are introduced in the book of Acts. They are also mentioned by Paul in *Romans, 1 Corinthians* and *2 Timothy*. They are the only husband and wife team recognized in Acts and the Epistles.

Of the six times that Priscilla and Aquila are mentioned, Priscilla is listed first in four of them. This had led many scholars to believe that she was from a higher social class than her husband. It is generally held that Aquila was a Jewish slave who became a freedman in Rome and that Priscilla was linked to a Roman family named 'Prisca'.

It is interesting to note that in *1 Cor. 16:19*, where Paul is talking about the church that meets in their home, Priscilla is mentioned second to her husband. Some suggest that this coincides with Paul's teaching on the order of the husband/wife relationship in the home (*Eph. 5:22–33*). (The other time she is mentioned second is at the couple's introduction in *Acts 18:2*.)

Because of the Edict of Claudius, Priscilla left Rome with her husband and came to Corinth in AD 49. She became acquainted with the apostle Paul who worked with Aquila as a tent-maker and who also lived in their home (*Acts 18:3*).

The couple accompanied Paul to Syria and then settled down in Ephesus (*Acts 18:18–19*) where they met a Jew named Apollos. He was preaching about Jesus in a synagogue and, while he possessed a thorough knowledge of the Scriptures, he knew only of the baptism of John. Priscilla and Aquila invited him into their home and taught him the rest of the gospel (*Acts 18:26*).

The above account of their encounter with Apollos reveals that Priscilla was in no way inferior to her husband in knowledge or service. She was an intelligent woman who was a vital part of the church's ministry in the 1st century. She was faithful, supportive to her husband, hospitable and honourable.

Priscilla and Aquila were dear friends of the apostle Paul throughout his ministry (*Rom. 16:3–4*). The last time they are mentioned is at the end of Paul's life when, in his final letter to Timothy, he instructs Timothy to greet them (*2 Tim. 4:19*). Also see *Aquila*.          K.MCR

**PROCORUS** was one of seven men appointed to help the apostles who were finding the work of administration in the early Jerusalem church to be too burdensome (*Acts 6:5*). Many new people were becoming Christians. The new Christians of Greek-Jewish background were falling out with those of Hebrew-Jewish background over the distribution of food to widows. The disciples found that they were spending so much time sorting out these things (*v. 2*) that they were neglecting the ministry of the Word of God. Seven men were therefore to be appointed and to be chosen as those known to be 'full of the Spirit and wisdom'. The apostles prayed and laid their hands on these men and appointed them to the job of looking after the day-to-day affairs of the church.

This incident is an interesting indication of how early in the church's life there was a recognition of the fact that God gives different people different 'ministries' or gifts. But it also reflects the early recognition by the church that those called to 'the ministry of the Word of God' (*v. 2*) should not have other preoccupations. *V. 7* indicates the success of this division of labour: 'the word of God spread. The number of disciples in Jerusalem increased rapidly.'          P.D.G.

## PROPHETS AND PROPHECY

The prophets were God's messengers in the OT. As spokes-persons for Yahweh (the LORD), they addressed human concerns from God's perspective. They had a double perspective in their preaching. On the one hand, they presented a clear portrayal of human ambition, defiance of God, and depravity. In this context, the prophets announced repentance and spoke of the imminence of God's judgment. On the other hand, they envisioned a transformed humanity and a new world order (the Kingdom of God). To this end, they spoke encouragingly to the godly, comforting them with the promise of restoration, and prompting them to persevere in their pursuit of godliness.

The prophets, as heralds of the Kingdom, form one continuous stream from Moses to John the Baptist. The course of the 'stream' through the history of redemption is altered at crucial junctures, or 'rapids.'

### Moses

Moses, the beginning of the stream, is 'the fountainhead' of the prophetic movement. He was the mediator of the Sinaitic (Mosaic) covenant (*Exod. 9:3–8; 20:18–19*) and God's chosen vehicle of communication: 'I reveal . . . I speak to him . . .' (*Num. 12:6–8;* see *Deut. 18:18*). He set Moses apart as a 'servant' (*Exod. 14:31; Deut. 34:5; Josh. 1:1–2*) – a relationship of confidence and friendship between a superior and an inferior. He enjoyed the privilege of close communion with the LORD: 'The LORD would speak to Moses face to face, as a man speaks with a friend' (Exod. 33:9). He was the faithful servant of the administration that lasted till the coming of the Son of God (Heb. 3:1–5). As fountainhead of the prophetic tradition, Moses saw more of God's glorious self-revelation than anyone else in the OT (Exod. 33:18; 34:29–35). Whoever questioned Moses challenged the LORD. Israel could find comfort, grace and blessing, because in Moses the roles of covenant mediator and intercessor (Exod. 32:1–34:10; Num. 14:13–25) came together. He prayed for Israel, spoke boldly as their advocate in the presence of the LORD, and encouraged them to look beyond himself to Yahweh.

The characteristic difference between Moses and the prophets after him, lies in the directness with which the LORD spoke to his trusted servant. Moses as the fountainhead was the first to receive, to write down, and to teach the revelation of God. This revelation extended to all facets of life, including the laws of holiness, purity, rituals, family life, work, and society. Although Moses did not as yet know of the revelation of God in Christ, he saw the 'glory' of God (Exod. 34:29–35). Moses, the greatest prophet before Jesus' incarnation spoke of the ministry of another prophet (Deut. 18:15–22). He was God's witness to Israel that a greater fulfilment lay ahead: 'Moses was faithful . . . testifying to what would be said in the future' (Heb. 3:5). The nature of that future was nothing less than the rest which comes (Heb. 4:1–13) in Jesus Christ, for whose sake Moses also suffered (Heb. 11:26). The eschatological hope of the Mosaic revelation is nothing less than the presence of God among his people.

Moses painfully realized that the people could not enter into that rest, because of his own disobedience and because of Israel's rebelliousness (Deut. 4:21–25). Yet, he spoke of a new era opened up by God's grace, freedom, and fidelity (Deut. 4:29–31; 30:5–10; 32:39–43). Moses looked forward to an era of peace, tranquillity, and of the full enjoyment of God's presence, blessing, and protection in the promised land (Deut. 12:9–10; 25:9; Exod. 33:14; Josh. 1:13). This hope, grounded in Yahweh's fidelity (Deut. 4:31), was most clearly expressed in Moses' final testimony, 'the Song of Witness' (Deut. 32). In it he recited Yahweh's loving acts and favour to Israel (vv. 1–14), warned against Israel's rebellion and their consequent suffering (vv. 15–35), and comforted the godly with the hope of Yahweh's vengeance upon the enemies and the deliverance of the remnant of Israel and of the nations (vv. 36–43). He even alluded to the greatness of Yahweh's love to Gentiles (vv. 36–43; Rom. 15:10)!

The eschatological significance of the Song of Moses reverberates in the prophetic messages of judgment and hope, justice and mercy, exclusion and inclusion, vengeance and deliverance. The Mosaic administration, therefore, was never intended to be an end in itself. It was a stage in the progress of fulfilment of the promises, and an important stage at that! The apostle Paul confirmed the grace of God in the Mosaic covenant (Rom. 9:4–5). See also Moses and Covenant.

## Prophets like Moses

The possibility of additional revelation opens the Mosaic 'canon' to further revelation from God. Moses was not the end of divine revelation, but the beginning of the prophetic movement. He gave specific instructions on the office, role, and message of the prophets. The prophets comprised a class of theocratic officers, by whom the LORD would guide the covenant community in addition to the priests (and Levites), kings (*Deut. 17:14–20*), tribal and local leadership (elders, leaders, and princes).

The prophets, like the priests and kings, were called and chosen by the LORD to serve as guardians of his Kingdom. The prophets, unlike the priestly caste and the royal dynasty, could not claim hereditary rights. Each one of them received a distinct call. As officers in God's Kingdom, they were called to shepherd God's people. The prophets in Israel conformed to seven criteria laid down in the Mosaic revelation:

**1.** The prophet as an Israelite shared fully in the heritage of covenant, the divine revelation, and the promises, and therefore, the new revelation had to be continuous with the Mosaic revelation (*Deut. 13:1–5*). This was true of all prophets, including our Lord (*Matt. 5:17–19*).

**2.** The prophet received a distinct call from the LORD. Like Moses he knew without a doubt that he had been sent with a message by the great King.

**3.** The Holy Spirit empowered the servant of God to withstand the pressures of his contemporaries, to speak the Word of God, and to discharge his office faithfully. The power of the Spirit, that had characterized the ministry of Moses (*Num. 11:17*), was also present with the prophets. Some underwent a visible change, as the Spirit 'lifted' them 'up' (*Ezek. 3:12, 14; 8:3; 11:1, 24; 43:5*), or 'came upon' them (*1 Sam. 19:20; 2 Chron. 20:14; Ezek. 11:4*). They all experienced an overpowering presence. The overwhelming sense of the Spirit's presence left them with no doubt that God had spoken and explains the prophetic sense of an inner compulsion, as in the case of Amos: 'The Sovereign LORD does nothing without revealing his plan to his servants the prophets . . . The Sovereign LORD has spoken – who can but prophesy?' (*Amos. 3:7, 8b*).

**4.** The prophet declared God's word as his spokes-person. He did not serve himself, but his LORD (*Deut. 18:18–19; Exod. 4:10–16; 7:1*).

**5.** The authority of the prophet did not lie in his personal credentials, but in the privilege of speaking in the name of the LORD (*Deut. 18:19–20, 22*).

**6.** The prophet was like Moses in that he was a good shepherd for God's people, loved them, and interceded on their behalf.

**7.** A true prophet might give a sign verifying that the LORD had sent him (*Exod. 3:12; 4:8; Deut. 13:2*). The 'sign' also witnessed to the authenticity of his message. Though the signs were diverse – a miracle (*1 Kings 13:5; 2 Kings 20:9*); a designation of a specified time (*1 Sam. 12:16–19; Is. 7:14–25*); a special event (*1 Sam. 10:3–7; see vv. 9–11; 1 Kings 13:3–5; 2 Kings 19:29*); the prophet himself (*Is. 8:18; 20:3; Ezek. 24:24*); or an object lesson (*Ezek. 4:3*) – they signified that the prophet's mission was in the service of the LORD and that the prophet was God's mouthpiece. Whether the prophet gave a sign or not, the veracity of his message was vindicated by fulfilment (*1 Kings 13:26; 16:12; 2 Kings 24:2; Jer. 28:15–17; Ezek. 33:33*).

God's people were responsible for 'testing' the new revelation by the standard ('canon') of the older revelation and by verifying the 'signs' of the prophet (*Deut. 13:1–5; 18:20–22*). The veracity of the prophetic word could also be verified by later generations, as Ezekiel writes: 'When all this comes true – and it surely will – then they will know that a prophet has been among them' (*Ezek. 33:33*).

## Samuel: the prophetic role model

Samuel bridged the space between the epoch of Moses/Joshua and that of David/ Solomon. After the death of Moses, Israel received continual reassurance that the LORD was with them through the revelation that came to Joshua (*Josh. 3:7; 4:14; 6:27*). Shortly before his death Joshua challenged the leaders of Israel to remain faithful to the LORD (*Josh. 23:1–11*), because Joshua could not bring Israel into a state of 'rest' on account of his old age (*Josh. 13:1*). In spite of the repeated warnings by Moses (Deuteronomy), Joshua (*Josh. 23–24*), and by God's servants (*Judg. 2:1– 5; 6:7–10*), Israel rebelled against the LORD and often experienced divine abandonment. The LORD had tested the loyalty of his people (*Judg. 2:22–3:1*), but Israel had failed him as individuals, as tribes, and as a nation. Since the rest, that they had begun to enjoy under Joshua (*Josh. 22:4*), had been conditioned on covenantal fidelity (*Josh. 22:5*), Yahweh suspended the fulfilment of this promise of rest (*Judg. 2:3, 21; Ps. 95:11*). Israel had come to a very low point in redemptive history.

Samuel has the distinction of being the first of the prophets (*Acts 3:24*). The LORD called him to be his prophet (*1 Sam. 3:1–14*) and as a prophet he embodied the spirit of Moses (*Jer. 15:1*). He was recognized as God's 'servant', by whom the LORD spoke to his people individually (*1 Sam. 9:6*) and nationally (*1 Sam. 7:2–4; 8:1–22*). Samuel's prophetic ministry was so unique that all the tribes heard about God's prophet: 'And all Israel from Dan to Beersheba recognized that Samuel was attested as a prophet of the LORD' (*1 Sam. 3:20*). Samuel became the role model for the prophets as the guardian of the theocracy. He showed a pastoral concern for all twelve tribes (*1 Sam. 4:1*), brought revival to Israel (*1 Sam. 7:6; 12:18–19*), led Israel in worship, and guided the tribes with his counsel. He also led Israel into a period of international stability and national peace and prosperity.

In his position as God's spokesman to the people and to the theocratic king, Samuel defined the role of the prophets as guardians of the theocracy. Samuel, like Moses and Joshua, exhorted Israel to remain faithful to Yahweh in his farewell speech, lest God's curses should overtake them (*1 Sam. 12:1–25*). The psalmist placed him next to Moses and Aaron as God's priest: 'Moses and Aaron were among his priests, Samuel was among those who called on his name; they called on the LORD and he answered them' (*Ps. 99:6*).


## Elijah: the covenant prosecutor

Elijah the Tishbite also lived during another period of crisis. Ahab had married Jezebel, a Phoenician princess, who had introduced Baal worship and pagan culture into Israel. Ahab followed the political ambitions of his father, Omri, who had begun making Israel into a political-military power of international renown. The administration of Ahab had opened Israel to a grand future of economic prosperity and military might, as Israel had become a 'power' among the nations. The people had rejected the covenant and the way of revelation and had become enamoured with a new way of life.

Elijah occupies a distinct place in the history of redemption. Though he left no prophetic book, Elijah is one of the greatest OT prophets and has a special place next to Moses. He shaped the course of the 'classical' prophets. The stories surrounding Elijah incorporated in *1 Kings 17–21* and *2 Kings 1:1–2:11* present us with one of the greatest prophets of the OT.

Alone and exhausted, persecuted after the Mt Carmel experience (*1 Kings 18*), Elijah stood on Mount Horeb (*19:7*) where Moses had received the revelation and had seen the glory of the LORD. Elijah's return to Mt Sinai marked the end of one era, characterized by divine patience, and the beginning of another, characterized by purification! Israel had shown herself to be a nation hardened in unbelief. The situation had changed dramatically from the days when Moses repeatedly interceded on her behalf. Unlike Moses, who interceded on behalf of Israel (*Exod. 31–34*), Elijah accused God's people of infidelity. He brought three charges and a personal lament against Israel: (i) '(they) have rejected your covenant, (ii) broken down your altars, and (iii) put your prophets to death with the sword. (iv) I am the only one left, and now they are trying to kill me too' (*1 Kings 19:10, 14*). Yahweh came to Elijah in a voice like 'a gentle whisper' (*1 Kings 19:12*), to which the prophet responded with awe, sensing the presence of Yahweh.

Elijah was the beginning of a long line of prophets who charged God's people with breaking the covenant and who pronounced God's judgment on them. Though Elijah mainly directed his message to the king, his ministry extended beyond Ahab to all of Israel. He was God's first covenant prosecutor, for he charged Israel with its failures to conform to the covenantal expectations (*1 Kings 18:21*). The issue was no longer between prophet and king, but between prophet and people, as it was in the days of Moses and Samuel. The prophet no longer warned and threatened; he proclaimed judgment and the reality of the covenantal curses.

As 'covenant prosecutors', the prophets stood between the LORD and the people. They listened in on the divine council, while observing God's movement in history. The prophet of God was both a man 'in his time' and 'out of his time'. As a man 'in his time' the prophetic message must be understood within its historic, geographic, and cultural contexts. As a man 'out of his time' he spoke of events that pertain to the establishment of God's Kingdom, the judgment of the wicked, and the vindication of the godly remnant.

Elijah was one of the greatest individuals in redemptive history. The Holy Spirit empowered him and gave him a concern for the spiritual condition of his people. Elijah longed for a people whose heart would be loyal to the LORD, as he discerned the necessity of judgment and purification (see *Mal. 4:5–6*). His ministry was continuous with Moses and with all the prophets who served after him as 'covenant prosecutors', including the literary or classical prophets. The Spirit of Elijah was with Amos, Hosea, Isaiah, Jeremiah, Ezekiel, and with all the other prophets before, during, and after the Exile. He was with John the Baptist (*Mal. 4:5; Matt. 11:14; 17:10–13*), the apostles, and is still present with all who proclaim God's Word faithfully.

### Interpretation of the prophets

The interpreter of the prophets must be sensitive to the historical context, language, metaphors, and literary imagery. The prophet was a real human being who shared his life with his contemporaries in a cultural context. He had received a vision of

God, but spoke of it in a language that people could understand. The prophets paint multifaceted pictures representing the acts of God from their days until the full inauguration of the Kingdom of God.

The prophetic word has a bearing on the historical context of the prophet, but its relevance goes far beyond the questions of what the prophet said and how it was fulfilled. The prophetic oracles are God's word to each new generation in its own historical context. Each generation can find its identity in the history and progression of fulfilment, while living in the hope of the great future God has prepared for his people. Each generation must get involved in the interpretation and application of the prophetic word, so that it, too, may contribute to the progress of redemption.

Interpretation of the prophets requires both an understanding of the social world of Israel and a sensitivity to God's accommodation to present his truth in human language and images. Isaiah, for example, announced the grandeur of salvation in the imagery of victory: light, brightness, and joy (Is. 51:4; 58:8,10; 59:9; 60:1,3, 19–20). He set this metaphor within the historically conditioned language of a victorious people, who receive recognition by the nations (Is. 11:11–16; 14:2; 49:22–26; 60:4). The nations will provide the redeemed with precious objects (Is. 60:4–16), will bring tribute to Jerusalem (Is. 23:17–18; 60:13–16; 66:20), and will serve them (Is. 61:4–6).

The prophets employed distinct forms of prophetic speech and rhetorical devices. They lived in a cultural milieu in which oral and literary forms were the accepted ways of communication. They spoke the message of God in ways that their contemporaries recognized as 'prophetic'; they were 'poets with a "message"'. They creatively put to use Israel's cultural and revelatory heritage as they were steeped in all the traditions of Israel: theophanic, war, legal, wisdom, and cultic.

Classical prophecy was first and foremost an oral expression, the written forms being secondary, but the process from oral to written form is far from clear. Certain speeches may have been written soon after the original pronouncement. Others may have circulated, possibly among a group of disciples. In cases where there was a significant time lapse, the prophet could summarize his oracles, paraphrase them, and polish his work into a literary masterpiece. With the fall of Samaria and Jerusalem, some prophetic books may have been edited in less than favourable conditions. For example, the prophecy of Jeremiah results from several stages of collection and editing, resulting in an 'anthology of anthologies', completed during the Exile.

The prophets proclaimed a message of tranformation in a historical context to people who were complacent with their abilities and achievements. They spoke of God's imminent judgment on all humanity – including Israel and Judah, because mankind has rebelled against the LORD, the King of glory. They announced the coming Kingdom of the LORD, the judgment, and transformation of creation.

The prophetic vision of God's glorious Kingdom shattered the reality of human kingdoms and structures, but also shaped the vision of a remnant that lives in harmony with God. They saw a radical antithesis between God and man, between the Creator and the creature, between the Kingdom of God and the kingdom of humans, and between revelation and religion. The distinction between revelation and religion is fundamental in understanding the nature of the prophetic role and in interpreting the prophetic message.

Interpretation of the prophets involves eschatology. The prophets announce the closure of one era and the opening of a new era. The new era in the progress of redemption has elements of continuity with the past era, as the new acts of grace flow out of the promises of God. Yet, the new era has elements of discontinuity as God confirms an even grander fulfilment of his promises. The prophets point beyond their time to an eternity of time, when God will fulfil the promises and covenants. He will be with his people and will rule over them together with his Messiah from age to age. The eschatological prophetic message is theocentric with its focus on the coming of the great King, the inauguration of the Davidic (Messianic) era, the outpouring of the Holy Spirit, the renewal of the covenant, the renewal of the people of God, the ingathering of both Jews and Gentiles, the glory and joy associated with the presence of the LORD, the joy of God's people, the restoration of the land of Canaan, Jerusalem, and the earth, and the removal of evil, curse, death, and any other forms of divine judgment.

The NT confirms the prophetic hope by its witness that in Jesus Christ the promises of God are true. Consequently, Jesus is 'the focus' of hope, in whom the reality and fulfilment of all divine promises are guaranteed. The salvation, of which the prophets have spoken (1 Pet. 1:10–12), is found in none other than Jesus Christ. However, only the Father knows the nature, manner, and time of the fulness of salvation (Acts 1:7). Since fulfilment is in Jesus Christ (2 Cor. 1:20), the complete fulfilment of the promises is the object of hope by both the OT and the NT saints. Both OT and NT witness to the 'salvation' to come and to the exclusive claims of Jesus that he is the way by which the Father will fully inaugurate all the promises and covenants, including the rule of David.

In the coming of Jesus, the inauguration of the Kingdom showed more clearly its eschatological dimension. The Gospels present the preaching and ministry of Jesus from the perspective of the risen Christ, who will come to fulfil the Law of Moses and the prophetic word. They integrate this with Jesus' teaching on the future – the judgment, the elect, the resurrection, the growth and joy of the Kingdom with the prophetic hope. The past, present, and future come together in Jesus Christ. Our Lord explained his mission using these OT writings. To his disciples he said, 'Everything must be fulfilled that is written about me in the Law of Moses, the Prophets and the Psalms' (Luke 24:46). From this we learn that everything in the OT has its proper focus in Jesus Christ. A Christian reading the OT cannot but pay careful attention to the relationship between the OT and our Lord. Each division of the OT relates to our Lord, including the prophetic writings. These Scriptures are God's Word to his people, and the authority of that Word has not been diminished since the coming of Jesus Christ. The very basis for apostolic preaching was the OT. In Jesus the future is full of hope, because he is now seated at the right hand of the Father. The witness of the OT and NT finds its focus in Jesus through whom the Father will complete his plan of redemption (2 Cor. 1:20). He is the One of whom the prophets have spoken (Rom. 1:2; 16:26) and he is the Alpha and Omega (Rev. 22:12–14).

## Summary

The prophetic ministry is a direct continuation of the revelation of God through Moses, the fountainhead of OT revelation. Moses desired for God's people to form a 'counter-culture', a new community transformed by divine revelation and by the Spirit. The prophetic message was consistent with the Mosaic revelation, for it applied more explicitly the blessings and the curses of which Moses had spoken, and supplemented the existing canonical writings with a new word from God.

All prophetic utterances were to be tested by God's revelation to Moses. The prophets applied and further developed the essential elements of the Mosaic revelation: the judgments and blessings, the call for covenantal loyalty, and the hope in the grand future prepared for the people of God. The prophets, like Moses, called for a commitment to Yahweh that must lead to 'conflict with civilization'.

A major development took place with Samuel. Samuel was the role model of the OT prophetic movement. He declared the Word of God to all Israel and anointed their first two kings. As a guardian of the theocracy, he led Israel into revival and peace. Samuel is the role model of the prophets, as he sought to guard the theocracy, established by God's covenant at Mt Sinai. Samuel, the guardian of the covenant, spoke God's Word to king and people alike. His ministry consisted of intercession for the people, application of the curses and blessings of the Mosaic covenant, and a godly life. And yet, Samuel, too, was an eschatological prophet, as he longed for a greater spiritual sensitivity, discernment, and a rest that would outlast him.

The prophets after Samuel spoke God's Word with little apparent result. Israel and Judah readily adopted the mantic and magical practices of the pagans. They adapted to the worship of many gods, and adulterated the revelation of Yahweh. Finally, Elijah arose and brought a covenantal suit from the LORD at Mt Sinai. From this point onward, the prophets increasingly turned away from the kings to the people, with the express purpose of calling forth a remnant.

The prophetic message of the classical prophets includes a statement of God's legal suit against his people, an announcement of judgment, a call for repentance, and a proclamation of the good news of God's deliverance. They affirmed that Yahweh is faithful in his commitment to renew the covenants, to usher in his Kingdom, and to fulfil his promises. The prophets were God's appointed covenant prosecutors, but in this function they did not cease praying that God's people might turn to the LORD, undergo a transformation by the Spirit, and enjoy the blessings of the Kingdom. See also *Covenant*.                                   W.A.VG.

**PUAH 1.** The second son of Issachar who became founder of the Puite clan. He is listed among those who went down to Egypt with his grandfather Jacob (*Gen. 46:13; Num. 26:23; 1 Chron. 7:1*).

**2.** This Puah was one of the Heb. midwives who were ordered by the king of Egypt to kill any male son they delivered to the Heb. people (*Exod. 1:15*).

However, Puah and her colleague Shiphrah feared God and refused to carry out these orders. When they were summonsed by the king to explain how it was that Heb. male children were still being born and surviving, they concocted a story saying that, unlike Egyptian mothers, Heb. mothers were very strong and gave birth before the midwives could arrive (v. 19)! God blessed the activities of these midwives so that even more male children were born and because of their faith God gave the two midwives their own children (vv. 20–21). In Exodus this order to kill the Heb. male children was eventually carried out by the Egyptians themselves. One of the few to escape the killings was Moses who became leader of his people and helped them escape the clutches of Pharaoh and the Egyptians.

The faithfulness of God's people in time of persecution is seen regularly to be rewarded in Scripture and became an example for the people of God in future generations. God's power in overcoming all that the Egyptians could throw at his people was recalled in later generations in Psalms of praise and prayer (e.g. Ps. 105:24–27).

**3.** This Puah was the son of Dodo and father of Tola and from the tribe of Issachar (Judg. 10:1). Tola became one of Israel's leaders during the time of the Judges.                                    P.D.G.

**PUBLIUS** (Lat., 'popular'). Publius was the 'chief official' appointed by the Romans on the island of Malta when the apostle Paul was shipwrecked there on his voyage to Rome. The official welcomed Paul and his colleagues to his own home and entertained them hospitably for three days (Acts 28:7). Publius' father was ill with a high fever, so Paul went into his room and prayed for him and he was cured (v. 8). When news of this miracle began to circulate, ill people came to Paul from all over the island for healing. After three months, when it was time for them to set sail again for Italy, the islanders furnished them with all the supplies they needed (vv. 9–10). Although tradition says that this official later became the first bishop of Malta who was later martyred, this has not been confirmed.

**PUDENS** He was one of Paul's friends who sent greetings to Timothy at the end of Paul's second letter to him (2 Tim. 4:21). Paul was writing from prison in Rome and mentions Linus, Claudia and 'all the brothers' as also sending these greetings. Different traditions surround who Pudens was and what part he played in early Christianity, but they cannot be confirmed.

**PUL** Another name for Tiglath-pileser III, the King of Assyria (2 Kings 15:19; 1 Chron. 5:26). It may have simply been this king's original name.

**PURAH** was the servant of Gideon who, at the LORD's suggestion, accompanied him by night to the camp of the Midianite army (Judg. 7:10–11). There the two of them overheard a man recounting a dream to a friend in which he saw a loaf of bread tumbling into their camp and striking a tent with such force that the tent collapsed. The friend interpreted the dream as an omen indicating that God had given them into Gideon's hands (vv. 13–15). Gideon returned and got his 300 men together, informing them that the LORD had already given the Midianites into their hands.

**PUT** was one of four sons born to Ham. He had at least six sons of his own most of whom were listed as progenitors of different tribes or peoples. Put thus is both the person and a nation of people (Gen. 10:6–9; 1 Chron. 1:8). The land of Put may have been modern Libya, but it is not possible to be certain.

**PUTIEL** The father of the woman whom Eleazar son of Aaron married. The woman's name is not given. She was the mother of Phinehas (Exod. 6:25).

**PYRRHUS** (Gk., 'fiery red'). Pyrrhus the father of Sopater was from Berea, a town in Macedonia. Sopater joined the apostle Paul on his travels from Greece through Macedonia and on to Jerusalem (Acts 20:4).

# Q

**QUARTUS** was one of those who joined Paul in sending greetings at the end of Paul's letter to the church in Rome. The apostle called him 'our brother' (*Rom. 16:23*).

**QUEEN OF SHEBA** David was succeeded by his son, Solomon, who was known for his wisdom, his riches and his relationship with the LORD. Another great ruler at that time was known as the Queen of Sheba. Sheba was probably in modern day Yemen in the south-west of Arabia. When the Queen heard about Solomon, she decided to visit him with the purpose of testing this Israelite king. The Queen of Sheba arrived in Jerusalem in all her splendour, but she could not confound Solomon. Scripture records that the Queen was literally 'overwhelmed' by Solomon's answers, by the orderly manner of his kingdom and by his faith. The Queen's response? She praised Solomon openly and, even more significantly, began to give the praise to Solomon's God, the one LORD. The two great rulers exchanged gifts, respect and a mutual admiration for God (*1 Kings 10:1–13*). s.c.

**QUIRINIUS** Born around 50 BC, Quirinius is mentioned in the Bible only in the Gospel of Luke as 'the governor of Syria' (*Luke 2:2*). A census took place during his rule at the command of Caesar Augustus in which everyone had to return to their home town to register. Under the guidance of God, this led to Joseph and Mary returning to Bethlehem, where Jesus was born, thus fulfilling the prophecy that the Messiah would come from David's town of Bethlehem (*Luke 2:4; Mic. 5:2; Matt. 2:6; John 7:42*).

Tacitus wrote that Publius Sulpicius Quirinius was a brave soldier whom Augustus rewarded with a consulship. He then had various imperial administrative duties. Tacitus then went on to say that in his last years he had not endeared himself to many because of his meanness. He governed Crete as proconsul for a while and then worked to bring peace in Pisidia and Cilicia in Asia Minor between about 12 BC and 3 BC, when he was made proconsul in Asia. It was not until AD 6 that he became governor of Syria and Cilicia, a post he held for about three years.

For Luke, however, the mention of Quirinius served no further function than to identify the time-frame within which Jesus was born and, for the modern historian, this has caused considerable problems. In *Acts 5:37* Gamaliel refers to a registration that must have been about AD 6. Some Roman registrations seem to have happened on a 14-year cycle which would put the previous one back in 7 or 8 BC when it would appear Quirinius was well employed elsewhere. Some scholars have insisted that Luke simply got it wrong. However, Luke's normal historical accuracy means that his information cannot easily be dismissed. Various solutions have been offered to the potential conflict of dates. One that seems plausible is that Quirinius exercised some type of authority in Syria prior to his appointment in AD 6. The list of governors in Syria seems to have some gaps one of which, say between 11–8 BC, may have been filled by Quirinius. Perhaps more likely is the suggestion that he held some extraordinary office based in Syria while conducting campaigns in Pisidia and Cilicia. Certainly Syria would have been a sensible base for such manoeuvres. Some have suggested that he might have ordered the census in about 8 BC that may have taken a year or so to complete. Jesus could then have been born c. 6–5 BC and would have been nearly two years old when Herod ordered the massacre of the infants (*Matt. 2:13–18*). (Herod died in Jericho in the spring of 4 BC). Much has been written by many scholars on this issue, but a reconstruction of this sort does justice to the evidence in Matthew relating to Herod and to Luke's usual historical accuracy. Some external evidence has been adduced to support this sort of theory, but it is sure that the last word on the subject has not yet been written!                                    P. D. G.

# R

**RAAMAH** was the fourth son of Cush and a grandson of Ham. He and his sons, Sheba and Dedan, are listed in *Gen. 10:7* and *1 Chron. 1:9*. *Ezek. 27:22* refers to merchants from Sheba and Raamah who traded spices, precious stones and gold. The location of Raamah is not known with any degree of certainty, although it is suggested that it was to be found on the western side of the Arabian peninsula, possibly in modern Yemen.

**RAAMIAH** One of the Israelite leaders who returned with Zerubbabel to Jerusalem and Judah following the Exile in Babylon (*Neh. 7:7*). He is probably the same person as Reelaiah in *Ezra 2:2*.

**RABBI** (Heb., 'my LORD', 'my master' etc.; *rab-* meant 'great'). In Scripture the word is used only in the NT, although in the OT the word *rab* occasionally occurs as a mark of respect for someone in an official position. The term gradually came to refer only to Jewish religious leaders and teachers.

Jesus gave strict instructions to his disciples that they were not to be addressed as 'Rabbi', implying that it was a title that caused pride but also arguing that the disciples had 'only one Master and you are all brothers' (*Matt. 23:7–8*). This was one of the most important lessons Jesus had to teach his disciples on several occasions about the constituency of the Kingdom of God. Status in the Kingdom was not something to be sought after by its members.

Jesus was addressed as 'Rabbi' on several occasions as a mark of respect (e.g.

*Mark 9:5; 10:51; 1:49; 3:2* etc.), although on other occasions there may have been a sense of irony about its use, for example, on the lips of Judas (*Matt. 26:25, 49*). When two disciples of John the Baptist addressed Jesus as 'Rabbi' John interpreted the term for his audience as 'teacher' (*John 1:38*). In *John 3:26* John the Baptist was also addressed respectfully in this way. Luke, who fails to use the term at all, substituted the word 'master' or 'lord'.                                    P.D.G.

**RACHEL** (Heb., 'ewe'). While Leah found fulfilment within an unpromising situation, Rachel was the pretty daughter who was a bit 'spoiled' and who could be petulant. Her sister's promptness to conceive (*Gen. 29:31–30:1*) was a real provocation and betrayed her into anger with God. Jacob's rebuke is a model of husbandly care and theological correctness (*Gen. 30:2*) but like Sarai before her (*Gen. 16*) Rachel adopted the legal expedient of a secondary wife through whom to secure a child and, as in the case of Abram, Jacob (also wrongly?) acquiesced. As a result of this – and of Leah's quite impermissible *quid pro quo* (*Gen. 30:9*) – Jacob's family increased but relationships between the sisters deteriorated. It is sadly revelatory of Rachel that she saw even motherhood in confrontational terms (*vv. 6–7*). She was all too certain about her 'rights' before God (*v. 6*) and sickeningly insensitive in her assumption of power over her husband (*v. 15*). Yet grace gave her a prominent place in the divine purposes. She produced the toweringly impressive Joseph (*v. 24*). She and Jacob are one of the great love matches of the Bible (*Gen. 29:9f., 16–18, 20, 30*). Is any sorrow so genuine as Jacob's grief at her death (*Gen. 48:7*) or any of the Bible's many re-namings as moving as when the son of Rachel's sorrow became the son of Jacob's right hand (*Gen. 35:16–20*)? Under a sometimes hard exterior beat a tender heart and fittingly it was Rachel whom Jeremiah heard weeping for her exiled children (*Jer. 31:15*) and whose tears reached their full intensity over the world's savage counterattack against the divine plan of salvation (*Matt. 2:17–18*).

J.A.M.

**RADDAI** The fifth son of Jesse and brother to David (*1 Chron. 2:14*). When Samuel came to anoint David to be king, Jesse made all his sons in descending order of age pass before Samuel. David was seventh in line.

**RAHAB 1.** Rahab's story is recorded in *Josh. 2.* Joshua was the leader of the Israelites when he sent two men from Shittim into Canaan to assess the strength of the cities there, especially the strength of Jericho. The men entered the house of a prostitute named Rahab and soon learned that she was a believer in God and afraid of what would happen to her loved ones when God's people arrived to inhabit the land. When the king of Jericho heard about the spies, he sent a message to Rahab that he wanted her to bring the men to him. She protected the two Israelites by hiding them on her roof and telling the king they had already left her home. In return for her kindness, Rahab asked for protection for her family and was prom-ised this gift of grace by the two spies. Rahab and her family were spared (*Josh. 6:22–25*) when the Israelites took control of Jericho. This commitment of Rahab to the incoming Israelites and their LORD was a commitment of faith which is acknowledged in the NT (*James 2:25; Heb. 11:31*).

**2.** Scholars are divided on the identity of the Rahab mentioned in *Matt. 1:5.* Some believe this Rahab to be the same as 1. above, while some believe her to be the wife of Salmon and the mother of Boaz.

S.C.

**RAHAM** (Heb., 'love'). A leader in the tribe of Judah and a son of Shema and grandson of Hebron. He was the father of Jorkeam (*1 Chron. 2:44*).

**RAKEM** was the son of Sheresh, a descen-dant of Manasseh and a leader in that tribe. He was a grandson of Makir and his wife Maacah (*1 Chron. 7:16*).

**RAM** ('Heb., 'exalted').
**1.** This Ram was the brother of Jerahmeel and the son of Hezron. He was of the tribe of Judah and was the father of Amminadab. He is listed in the genealogy of Perez, Boaz and David at the end of the book of Ruth and thus is one of the ancestors of Jesus Christ listed in the genealogies of both Matthew and Luke (*Ruth 4:19; 1 Chron. 2:9–10; Matt. 1:3–4; Luke 3:33*).
**2.** This second Ram to be mentioned in Scriptures was Jerahmeel's firstborn son and Hezron's grandson. He too was from the tribe of Judah and was the nephew of 1. above. His sons were Maaz, Jamin and Eker (*1 Chron. 2:25, 27*).
**3.** The name of the family to which Elihu belongs. Elihu was one of Job's friends who sought to 'comfort' him (*Job 32:2*).

**RAMIAH** (Heb., 'the LORD is high'). A descendant of Parosh. Shecaniah con-fessed to Ezra that many men of Judah had married wives from other tribes and nations. Ezra and the people repented and made a covenant to serve the LORD (*Ezra 10:2*). Ramiah was one of those who then divorced his foreign wife (*Ezra 10:25*).

**RAPHA 1.** The ancestor of the giants of the Philistines who were encountered when the Israelites went to war against them. His name normally occurs in the expression 'the descendants of Rapha' (2 Sam. 21:16, 18, 20, 22; 1 Chron. 20:6, 8). In Heb. the article is used with the name Rapha, hence 'the Rapha', implying that the name may indicate a race of people. The relationship between the giants of the wars against the Philistines in David's time and the descendants of the Rephaites (of which Og of Bashan was supposedly one of the last) is unclear. Certainly mention of Rapha or 'the giant' indicated the enormous size of some of the enemy who frightened the Israelites. The names of some of those who managed to kill such 'descendants of Rapha' were recorded for posterity in some of the verses listed above.

**2.** Benjamin's fifth son, who became a leader in his tribe (1 Chron. 8:2). His name is omitted from the list of sons in Gen. 46:21.              P.D.G.

**RAPHAH** A descendant of King Saul, a Benjamite and father of Eleasah. He was the son of Binea (1 Chron. 8:37). In 1 Chron. 9:43 he is called Rephaiah.

**RAPHU** (Heb., 'healed'). The father of Palti and from the tribe Benjamin. Palti was one of the twelve spies sent out by Moses from the Desert of Paran to spy out the land of Canaan (Num. 13:9).

**REAIAH 1.** Reaiah was the son of Shobal, one of the famous descendants of Judah. His son was named Jahath (1 Chron. 4:2).

**2.** A descendant of Joel and son of Micah of the tribe of Reuben. His son was named Baal. He lived a little before the Assyrian invasion under Tiglath-Pileser III (1 Chron. 5:4).

**3.** A leader of one of the families of Temple servants whose descendants returned from the Babylonian Exile in the days of Ezra and worked on the Temple (Ezra 2:47; Neh. 7:50).

**REBA** (Heb., 'fourth'). One of the five kings of Midian whom Moses had defeated in battle as part of the LORD's vengeance on the Midianites for seducing the Israelites away from the LORD (Num. 31:2, 8; Josh. 13:21; see Num. 25). They had been allies of Sihon (see Sihon for more detail). Their land was given to the tribe of Reuben.

**REBEKAH** Her strongmindedness showed itself in her prompt decision to leave home to marry Isaac (Gen. 24:57) and in the assured personal spirituality of Gen. 25:22. This personal self-confidence made her the perfect wife for the more retiring Isaac and they enjoyed a true marriage of the heart (Gen. 24:67; 26:7–8). But Rebekah's weakness was the other side of her strength: decisiveness put to a corrupt use (27:5–16), spirituality buried under impatience to hasten the LORD's promises (25:23), wifely dignity degenerating into dominance. And what a price she paid! – a 'curse' indeed (27:13), never to see her beloved Jacob again! Fittingly this believable and attractive woman rests with Isaac in Machpelah (49:31).       J.A.M.

**RECAB 1.** A son of Rimmon the Beerothite from the tribe of Benjamin who, together with his brother Baanah, was a leader among Saul's men. After Saul's death his son, Ish-Bosheth was made king by Abner in the Northern Kingdom of Israel, although Judah followed King David (2 Sam. 2:8–10). Later, when Abner was killed, Recab and Baanah no doubt thought they could endear themselves to David if they killed Ish-Bosheth. This they did and brought his head to David. David was extremely angry. He had not wanted to conquer Saul's family in this way but had always been prepared to wait for the LORD's timing. He killed Baanah and Recab for their treachery to their king (2 Sam. 4:2, 5–6, 9) and had Ish-Bosheth's head buried in the tomb along with Abner (*v. 12*).

**2.** The father of Malkijah who probably returned from the Exile in Babylon and lived with his son in Jerusalem in the days of Nehemiah. His son became ruler of the district Beth Hakkerem (*Neh. 3:14*).

**3.** A certain Recab also appears as the 'father of Jehonadab' (*2 Kings 10:15, 23*). Jehonadab supported Jehu against Ahab. With great zeal for the LORD the two of them killed all the prophets of Baal (*vv. 16, 23–28*) and did much to promote true worship in Israel. In the days of Jeremiah a group of people were in existence known as the 'Recabite family' (NIV). These people traced their ancestry back to Jonadab (Jehonadab) who, they said, gave them strict commands of obedience to the LORD and strict commands about life-style which included not drinking wine or building houses. Rather they were to live in tents as nomads. They came to Jerusalem only for protection from the Babylonians (*Jer. 35:3–11*). Jeremiah then used the Recabites as an example for the people of Judah of a group who had remained faithful to their forefathers, something the people of Judah had failed to do (*vv. 12–17*). It is worth noting that Jeremiah did not commend the particular commands that the Recabites followed but rather their general faithfulness to their laws and to the LORD. Because of this faithfulness the LORD promised the Recabites through Jeremiah that 'Jonadab son of Recab will never fail to have a man to serve me' (*v. 19*).

In *1 Chron. 2:55* there is a reference to Kenites who came from Hammath, 'the father of the house of Recab'. Hammath may have been Recab's father but it may also have been a place where the Kenites lived. Recab may itself have simply referred to a group or association of people whose ancestors were the Kenites.

P. D. G.

**REELAIAH** One of the Israelite leaders who returned with Zerubbabel to Jerusalem and Judah following the Exile in Babylon (*Ezra 2:2*). He is probably the same person as Raamiah in *Neh. 7:7*.

**REGEM** A son of Jahdai and a descendant of Judah and Caleb mentioned in *1 Chron. 2:47*.

**REGEM-MELECH** (Heb., 'friend[?] of the king'). With Sharezer he was part of a delegation that travelled to the Temple at Jerusalem to interrogate the priests in the early post-exilic period (*Zech. 7:2*).

**REHABIAH** (Heb., 'the LORD has broadened'). A descendant of Moses through Eliezer whose sons were 'very numerous'. One of his descendants, Isshiah was a family head at the time of King David, and others were in charge of the Tabernacle treasuries (*1 Chron. 23:17; 24:21; 26:25*).

**REHOBOAM** (Heb., 'the people expand'). The main account of the life and work of King Rehoboam, the first king of Judah in the divided kingdom, is to be found in *1 Kings 11:43–12:24; 14:21–31; 2 Chron. 10–12; 1 Chron. 3:10*. His father was King Solomon. His mother was Naamah, an Ammonite (*1 Kings 14:21, 31* etc.).

As son and successor to King Solomon, Rehoboam could have expected to rule over the whole of Israel as his father had done. However, his father's reign had not been without its problems and by the time of his death the situation in the country was far from stable. As Solomon's power and wealth had increased, he turned away from wholeheartedly following the LORD (*1 Kings 11:4*). A major contributory factor in his religious demise was his marriage, contrary to the Law of God, to a number of foreign wives. No doubt these wives, such as Pharaoh's daughter, would largely have been taken for political and diplomatic reasons to ensure stability and peace with the nations on his borders. Instead Solomon should have relied on the LORD to protect his borders. The judgment of the LORD quickly came as he raised up enemies on the borders of Israel who continually attacked and caused him problems (*vv. 14, 23* etc.), and the LORD promised that the kingdom would be divided after he died.

Meanwhile Solomon's rule needed much physical sustaining which involved the people in many duties and very heavy taxes to fund the lavish court expenditure (see *1 Kings 4; 9:15–24*). During his lifetime one of his senior officers (see *Jeroboam I*) rebelled against him unsuccessfully and fled to Egypt. Thus when Solomon died and Rehoboam took his place there was already a pretender to the throne in the wings.

On his accession Rehoboam went to Shechem where the leaders of Israel asked him whether he would continue the policy of placing heavy and burdensome labour and taxes on the people. Rehoboam's elders encouraged him to be lenient and to rule with the will of the people, but he took advice from younger men and responded, 'My father laid on you a heavy yoke; I will make it even heavier. My father scourged you with whips; I will scourge you with scorpions' (*1 Kings 12:11*). Immediately Jeroboam, who had returned from Egypt, rebelled and Rehoboam had to flee back to Jerusalem. 'This turn of events was from the LORD, to fulfil the word the LORD had spoken' (*v. 15*).

Rehoboam then ruled the southern part of the divided kingdom that became known as the kingdom of Judah, although it also included the tribe of Benjamin, and he fortified the towns of Judah (*1 Kings 12:21; 2 Chron. 11:5–12*). Rehoboam's man in charge of forced labour, Adoniram, was stoned to death in the north and, when the king tried to make war against the north, the LORD refused

the battle by sending the prophet Shemaiah to tell the people that the division was of the LORD and they should not fight each other (*1 Kings 12:22–24*).

Rehoboam reigned for 17 years from about 931–913 BC but he did not follow the LORD as David had done. He introduced idolatry to the land or was too weak to prevent it. Shrines to foreign gods and Canaanite gods were built and practices forbidden by the Law were allowed (*1 Kings 14:21–24*). As a result King Shishak of Egypt invaded and attacked Jerusalem. He took away Temple treasures (*2 Chron. 12:1–6*). The kingdom was further reduced in size. However, the people repented and so they were not destroyed by Egypt but became its vassals (*vv. 6–8*).

In summarizing the reign of Rehoboam the Chronicler emphasizes how Rehoboam repented and that 'there was some good in Judah' (*v. 12*). Worship of the LORD did continue in the Temple in Jerusalem and, as Jeroboam in the Northern Kingdom progressively turned further from the LORD, so Levites and priests even from the north came to Jerusalem (*2 Chron. 11:13–14*).

His reign seems to have been largely a time of weakness. Having tried to be strong at first and yet losing the Northern Kingdom, he seems to have allowed much to take place around him without intervening. Yet true worship did carry on in the midst of idolatry and 'he acted wisely' in the appointments he made around his kingdom (*2 Chron. 11:23*). His salvation from disaster because of his repentance should have been an example for the kings who followed.

Rehoboam had a number of wives and concubines, but the wife he loved most was Maacah daughter of Absalom, and it was her son, Abijah whom he appointed to be his successor. P.D.G.

**REHUM** (Heb., 'merciful').

**1.** One of the Israelite leaders who

returned with Zerubbabel to Jerusalem and Judah following the Exile in Babylon (*Ezra 2:2*).

**2.** Rehum was one of the Persian commanding officers during the reign of King Artaxerxes in Persia (*Ezra 4:8–9*). He and various Persian judges and officials who had charge for the Persian empire of areas around Canaan and Samaria objected to the Jews rebuilding the walls of the city of Jerusalem. They feared that the Jews would settle back within a well-fortified city and refuse to pay taxes to the empire. They wrote a letter detailing their concerns to King Artaxerxes (*vv. 12–16*). The king replied to Rehum and Shimshai his secretary (*v. 17*) that he had been through the archives and discovered that the Israelites had indeed been a most powerful people in the past and that it would be dangerous to let them continue with rebuilding the city. Rehum and Shimshai were ordered to stop the work, which they immediately did (*v. 23*).

The book of Ezra goes on to show how God overruled this decree from Artaxerxes on behalf of his people. Under the guidance of the prophets Haggai and Zechariah, in the second year of King Darius, the work started again and was eventually completed to God's great praise and glory.

**3.** This Rehum was a Levite and a son of Bani. Under Nehemiah's direction he helped in rebuilding the walls of Jerusalem after the return from Exile (*Neh. 3:17*). He may well be the same Rehum as later signed the covenant of commitment to the LORD and the Law of God (*Neh. 10:25*).

**4.** Another of the priests listed as returning from the Babylonian Exile with Zerubbabel (*Neh. 12:3*). P.D.G.

**REI** (Heb., 'friendly'). One of those men who, with Zadok the priest, Nathan the prophet, and others remained loyal to King David's wishes to put his son Solomon on the throne (*1 Kings 1:8*). Another of David's sons, Adonijah, tried to usurp the throne but, following the careful help received from Nathan and Zadok, Solomon's right of succession was ensured. For more detail see *Nathan*.

**REKEM** (Heb., 'friendship').
**1.** One of the five kings of Midian whom Moses had defeated in battle as part of the LORD's vengeance on the Midianites for seducing the Israelites away from the LORD (*Num. 31:2,8; Josh. 13:21; see Num. 25*). They had been allies of Sihon (see *Sihon* for more detail). Their land was given to the tribe of Reuben.
**2.** A leader in the tribe of Judah and a son of Hebron. He was the father of Shammai (*1 Chron. 2:43–44*).

**REMALIAH** The father of Pekah, and only mentioned in the Bible in the phrase 'Pekah son of Remaliah'. Pekah became king of Israel by assassinating Pakahiah (*2 Kings 15–16; 2 Chron. 28:6; Is. 7:1,4; 8:6* etc.). For detail see *Pekah*.

**REPHAEL** (Heb., 'healed by God'). A son of Shemaiah and listed among the gatekeepers of the Tabernacle in the time of King David (*1 Chron. 26:7*).

**REPHAH** (Heb., 'riches'). Rephah, a member of an Ephraimite family and a son of Beriah is mentioned in *1 Chron. 7:25*.

**REPHAIAH** (Heb., 'the LORD heals').
**1.** A Simeonite and son of Ishi who lived in the time of King Hezekiah of Judah. He helped lead an invasion of the hill country of Seir (to the east of the Dead Sea), killing the remaining Amalekites. His people then settled the area (*1 Chron. 4:42–43*).
**2.** A descendant of King David and of Zerubbabel. He was of the tribe of Judah and is mentioned in the genealogy of *1 Chron. 3:21*.

**3.** A grandson of Issachar and son of Tola, Rephaiah was a family leader and a valiant soldier (1 Chron. 7:2).

**4.** This Rephaiah, from the tribe of Benjamin, was the son of Binea and a descendant of King Saul. He is mentioned in Saul's genealogy and was the father of Eleasah (1 Chron. 9:43).

**5.** The son of Hur, this Rephaiah was ruler of a 'half-district of Jerusalem' and was one of the leaders in the rebuilding of Jerusalem's walls under Nehemiah (Neh. 3:9).                                  P.D.G.

**REPHAN** The name of a Babylonian deity linked to the planet Saturn. In Stephen's speech in Acts 7:43, which refers to Rephan, he quotes the Septuagint version of Amos 5:26. The Heb. passage refers to star gods or 'star of your God' (NIV). The reference to Rephan occurs in a passage where Stephen showed how the Jewish forbears had rebelled against God and needed forgiveness, just as the generation he was addressing had sinned. Such preaching led eventually to Stephen's death as the first recorded Christian martyr.

**RESHEPH** (Heb., 'flame' or 'fire') was a member of an Ephraimite family and was a son of Rephah. He and his son Telah are mentioned in 1 Chron. 7:25.

**REU** (Heb., 'friend'). The son of Peleg and a descendant of Shem, Reu was father to Serug. He was thus an ancestor of Abraham and also enters the genealogy of Luke's Gospel leading from Jesus and Joseph back to Adam (Gen. 11:18–21; 1 Chron. 1:25; Luke 3:35).

**REUBEN** was the oldest of the twelve sons of Jacob, born of Leah. His name quite possibly derives from two Heb. words which would in effect mean 'See, a son'. However, the word-play in Gen. 29:32 juxtaposes his name with the phrase translated 'the LORD has looked upon my affliction'. Leah saw the end of her barrenness as a result of God's graciousness. Of his youth we know only the incident in Gen. 30:1ff. where he found mandrakes which he brought to Leah. However, he was a minor character in the account of the continued rivalry between his mother and Rachel.

Although briefly recounted, Reuben's constitution was revealed in his tryst with Bilhah, Rachel's handmaid and a concubine of his father (Gen. 35:22). On account of this, Jacob did not grant Reuben the double portion of the first-born (Gen. 49:3–4). This incident is later referred to as the reason why the Reubenites did not receive the first-born allotment expected in the restoration from Exile (1 Chron. 5:1; 2:1).

Reuben played a primary role in the ten oldest brothers' treatment of Joseph. Though most likely sharing in their jealousy, it was he who persuaded the others not to murder Joseph (Gen. 37:21). In fact, it was Reuben's plan to rescue Joseph altogether (v. 22). Whether Reuben's authority over them was weak or their resolve was too strong we cannot tell, but the ten only partly followed his instructions, selling Joseph into slavery. Reuben was genuinely upset when he learned of this (v. 29), although more out of concern for facing their father than for Joseph's well-being. After all, he had left Joseph languishing in a waterless pit. Reuben seemed most worried about the consequences of returning home without Jacob's favourite son (v. 30).

This concern for consequences rather than misdeeds was reflected later in Egypt. He saw the predicament foisted upon them by Pharaoh's representative, not realizing that it was Joseph, as God's retribution on them (Gen. 42:22). It should be granted, however, that Reuben was the best of the ten. For though his actions were not commendable, he possessed a greater conscience than the others. Perhaps as the oldest he had learned the most from his own father's futile attempts to circumvent providence. He seemed filled with a new resolve to do right which was reflected in the pledge of his own sons to Jacob should they not bring Benjamin back from Egypt (*Gen. 42:37*).

When the tribal lands were eventually distributed in Canaan, Reuben's tribe was given land on the east of the Jordan (see Og and *Sihon*). For Moses' blessing on Reuben see *Deut. 33:6*. M.J.G.

**REUEL** (Heb., 'friend of God').
**1.** The first son of Esau and Basemath. He was born in Canaan and became an Edomite chief (*Gen. 36:4, 10; 1 Chron. 1:35*). His sons, Nahath, Zerah, Shammah and Mizzah, became chiefs of Edom in their own right (*Gen. 36:13, 17; 1 Chron. 1:37*).
**2.** This Reuel, also known as Jethro, was the Midianite priest who became Moses' father-in-law when he gave his daughter Zipporah to Moses to be his wife (*Exod. 2:18, 21; Num. 10:29*). See *Jethro*.
**3.** Mentioned in *1 Chron. 9:8* as the father of Shephatiah and son of Ibnijah. After the captivity, his grandson, Meshullam, was among the first returnees to Jerusalem from the tribe of Benjamin.
**4.** In some versions (but not NIV) Reuel is the name of the father of Eliasaph, the leader of the people of Gad in *Num. 2:14*. The NIV is correct to change this to Deuel, in line with *Num. 1:14; 7:42, 47; 10:20* etc. See *Deuel*.

**REUMAH** was the concubine of Abraham's brother Nahor. She bore Nahor four sons who were ancestors to Aramean tribes (*Gen. 22:24*).

**REZIN** (Aram., 'chief') became king of Aram (Syria) around 740 BC during the last years of the Northern Kingdom of Israel under King Pekah. The two kings allied themselves together, hoping that they might be able to fend off the Assyrians. When Ahaz in Judah refused to join them, the two attacked Judah with some success, taking many prisoners and even, for a while, besieging Jerusalem (*2 Kings 16:5–6*). This aggression against the Southern Kingdom is recorded in *2 Kings 15:37* as an act of the LORD in bringing judgment against Judah for becoming idolatrous and turning from the LORD. However, the LORD prevented Rezin and Pekah from taking Jerusalem. Ahaz appealed to Tiglath-Pileser III, and the Assyrians invaded Syria, attacking and conquering Damascus, deporting its inhabitants and killing Rezin (*2 Kings 16:6–9*) in accordance with Isaiah's prophecy (*Is. 7:1–8; 8:3–4, 6*; also see *Amos 1:3–5*).
**2.** A leader of one of the families of Temple servants whose descendants returned from the Babylonian Exile in the days of Ezra and worked on the Temple (*Ezra 2:48; Neh. 7:50*). P.D.G.

**REZON** Following Solomon's marriages to women from foreign nations, contrary to the Law of God, the writer of 1 Kings says they 'turned his heart after other gods, and his heart was not fully devoted to the LORD his God, as the heart of David his father had been' (*1 Kings 11:4*). As a result of his sin the LORD raised up adversaries to Solomon (*vv. 14, 23*). One of these was Rezon son of Eliada. He was from Aram (Syria) and had fled from Hadadezer king of Zobah. He had formed a band of men around him and they had taken control of Damascus. The account in *1 Kings 11:23–25* simply says that he added to the trouble caused by Hadad and continued to be Israel's adversary as long as Solomon lived.

This incident is but one that charts the sad decline of Solomon, who had started his reign with so many blessings from the LORD because of his faithfulness. As his power grew, so, it seems, he relied less on the LORD and more on himself. His marriages with foreign women such as

Pharaoh's daughter would largely have been for political and diplomatic reasons to ensure stability and peace with the nations on his borders. Instead he should have relied on the LORD to protect his borders. The judgment of the LORD that caused those on his borders to attack him was thus particularly meaningful and appropriate to the sin.                P.D.G.

**RHESA** One of the ancestors of Jesus listed in the genealogy from Jesus to Adam. He was apparently one of Zerubbabel's sons, though he is not mentioned in the OT (*Luke 3:27*).

**RHODA** is only mentioned in *Acts 12:13*. She was a servant girl in the house of Mary, mother of John Mark. When the apostle Peter was miraculously released from prison, he went straight to Mary's house (*Acts 12:1–12*). He knocked at the door and when Rhoda recognized his voice, she immediately ran back to tell the others who were earnestly praying for him. But, in her joy, she failed to open the door and let him in. The account draws attention to the importance of prayer in a small gathering of the persecuted early church.                K.MCR.

**RIBAI**, a Benjamite who came from Gibeah, was the father of Ithai. Ithai was one of David's 'Thirty' warriors, a 'mighty man' in battle (*2 Sam. 23:29; 1 Chron. 11:31*).

**RIMMON   1.** (Heb., 'pomegranate'.) The father of Baanah and Recab, who came from Beeroth and was from the tribe of Benjamin. His sons later killed Mephibosheth, Saul's son, much to the anger of King David (*2 Sam. 4:2, 4, 9*). See *Recab*.

**2.** (From an Akkadian source, 'thunderer'.) The god in whose temple the king of Syria, Ben-Hadad, worshipped daily. The god is known to us from various sources and may have either originated in Aram or in Mesopotamia. The context in which this god is mentioned in *2 Kings* is particularly interesting (*2 Kings 5:18*). The commander of Ben-Hadad's forces was cured by Elisha of leprosy and swore he would only worship Yahweh (the LORD) in future. Knowing he would be obliged to enter the temple of Rimmon with his king, he asked for forgiveness in advance. For detail see *Naaman*.   P.D.G.

**RINNAH** (Heb., 'song'). Mentioned in *1 Chron. 4:20* as a son of Shimon of the clan of Judah.

**RIPHATH** was the grandson of Japheth and the son of Gomer, and therefore a direct descendant of Noah. He had two brothers (*Gen. 10:3; 1 Chron. 1:6*).

**RIZIA** A great warrior, an 'outstanding leader' and the head of a family, Rizia was a son of Ulla and was from the tribe of Asher (*1 Chron. 7:39–40*).

**RIZPAH** (Heb., 'a hot stone or coal'). One of King Saul's concubines and a daughter of Aiah. When the king died, his son, Ish-Bosheth, became king of parts of Israel, since Judah followed David. During Ish-Bosheth's brief rule Abner had begun to wield more and more power, and so the king accused him of sleeping with his father's concubine, Rizpah (*2 Sam. 3:7*). Whether this accusation was fair or simply a ruse by which Ish-Bosheth believed he might rid himself of Abner is unclear. The idea of sleeping with a former king's wife or concubine would indicate a clear challenge to the throne. Abner claimed he had always been loyal to the house of Saul and was so furious that he transferred his allegiance to King David.

It is not until much later that Rizpah's name appears again (*2 Sam. 21:8, 10–11*). A three-year famine led David to ask the LORD for the cause. He was told that the famine had come because of Saul's attempt to wipe out all the Gibeonites, contrary to a treaty that Joshua had made with them (*Josh. 9*). When David asked the Gibeonites how he could make amends they asked to be given seven of Saul's descendants to put to death. Rizpah's two sons by Saul, Armoni and Mephibosheth, were among the seven male descendants of King Saul whom David handed over to them. Their bodies were left exposed in Gibeah. Rizpah took up a position on a rock near the bodies and did not let the birds or animals touch them 'from the beginning of the harvest until the rain poured down' (*2 Sam. 21:10*). David, impressed with Rizpah's devotion, then ordered that the bodies of these sons together with the bodies of Saul and Jonathan be buried together in the tomb of Saul's father Kish at Zela in Benjamin (*vv. 11–14*). P.D.G.

**ROHGAH** Mentioned as a son of Shomer, a 'brave warrior' and 'outstanding leader' in the tribe of Asher (*1 Chron. 7:34, 40*).

**ROMAMTI-EZER** One of the sons of Heman the king's seer, listed among those set apart for the ministry of prophesying and music during the reign of King David (*1 Chron. 25:4*). A leader of the 24th group of Levitical musicians and choirs who ministered in the Temple (*1 Chron. 25:31*).

**ROSH** (Heb., 'head'). Seventh of the ten sons of Benjamin and a grandson of Jacob and Rachel. He is listed as among those who went down to Egypt with his grand-father (*Gen. 46:21*).

**RUFUS** (Lat., 'red').
**1.** Rufus, son of Simon from Cyrene and brother of Alexander (*Mark 15:21*). His father was forced to carry Jesus' cross. Perhaps Rufus was mentioned because he was known to those who would read the Gospel.
**2.** Rufus (*Rom. 16:13*) is one among many greeted by Paul at the end of this epistle. His mother had apparently looked after Paul on occasion and he is singled out as 'chosen in the Lord'. It is rather unlikely that he is the same Rufus mentioned in *Mark 15*.

## RUTH

'Ruth' is a Moabite name which may mean something like 'friendship'. In the OT the name is found only in the book of Ruth, and in the NT it occurs only in the genealogy of Jesus Christ in *Matt. 1:5*. In both cases it refers to a Moabite woman who married a Jew living in Moab, was widowed, then returned with her mother-in-law, Naomi, to Bethlehem of Judah, later marrying Boaz and having a child. The genealogy at the conclusion of Ruth portrays him as King David's grandfather.

It is remarkable that Ruth plays such a positive and important role in the biblical record. After all, Israel and Moab were hardly on the best of terms. As a result of the obstacles which Moab presented to Israel in her movement from the Wilderness of Sinai to the Promised Land (*Num. 22:25*), the LORD decreed that 'no Moabite or any of his descendants may enter the assembly of the LORD, even down to the tenth generation' (*Deut. 23:3*).

Nor were the differences merely historical. The events of the book of Ruth took place 'in the days when the judges ruled' (*Ruth 1:1*). Relatively early in that difficult period the Moabites, under King Eglon, had invaded and controlled a sizeable portion of Israel for 18 years (*Judg. 3:12–14*) before Ehud, the left-handed judge, delivered them (*vv. 15–29*). Afterward, Moab was subservient to Israel for 80 years (*v. 30*).

While it is virtually impossible to place the book of Ruth within the narrative of the book of Judges because of likely gaps in the genealogy in Ruth 4:18–22, it is likely that memories of the ancient and more recent hostilities had not completely died away, especially considering the ongoing prohibition of Deut. 23:3. In that light, the inclusion of Ruth the Moabitess on the pages of Scripture can hardly be due to any other reason than God's providence, evidencing his grace and ability to work in and through the lives of anyone, no matter what his or her background may be.

The fact that the beautiful narrative has traditionally had the name of Ruth as its title is equally surprising. Esther and Ruth are the only two biblical books named after women, and Ruth is the sole book bearing the name of a Gentile woman in all of Scripture. If nothing else, that perspective increases the significance of Ruth in God's biblical revelation and purposes.

The initial mention of Ruth is in relation to her marriage to one of the sons of Elimelech and Naomi (Ruth 1:4). It is only in 4:10 that it is revealed that her husband was Mahlon (vv. 2, 5). Given the cultural background, it is fairly likely that the marriage was arranged by Elimelech before his death (1:3).

It was a tragic reversal that Mahlon and his brother Chilion, died suddenly and unexpectedly a few years after the death of Elimelech (Ruth 1:3, 5). From all appearances, Ruth, her mother-in-law Naomi, and her sister-in-law Orpah, were left penniless (vv. 5–6). It proved necessary to travel back to Judah in search of food to survive physically (vv. 6–7).

Only slightly less problematic was the childlessness of Ruth's marriage and widowhood (Ruth 1:5, 4:10). The inability to bear children was considered virtually a divine curse in many of the ancient cultures. Further, the family name could not go on without children, and childlessness greatly reduced the possibility of remarriage.

Given the lack of options, Naomi urged Ruth and Orpah to go back to their parents' homes in Moab and attempt to remarry (Ruth 1:8–9). They initially resisted, but after Naomi verbally portrayed their desperate plight (vv. 10–13), Orpah proceeded to leave (v. 14). Ruth, however, not only pledged herself to Naomi until death, but also to the God of Israel (vv. 16–17). That commitment apparently reflected Ruth's status as a believer in the LORD God and as a proselyte of sorts within the covenant people.

As early as the day after Ruth's and Naomi's bittersweet arrival in Bethlehem (Ruth 1:19–22), Ruth went out to glean in the grainfields in order to get food (Ruth 2:2–3). It is possible that such gleaning was common in the Moabite culture, but it was clearly mandated in the Law of Moses. The poor, widows and resident aliens in the midst of Israel could meet their basic physical needs with some dignity through gleaning (Lev. 23:22; Deut. 24:19).

Ruth, however, requested more than just the opportunity to glean in the field to which God led her (the Heb. idiom in Ruth 2:3 looks past the appearance of chance to divine providence). She courageously sought the privilege of following immediately behind the field hands and gathering from what they had already harvested (Ruth 2:7). The landowner, Boaz, who was aware of who Ruth was and her current circumstances (vv. 11–12), granted the unusual request (vv. 8–9) and went well beyond it in providing protection and provision (vv. 9, 14–18).

At this point, Boaz had emerged only as a temporary benefactor for Ruth and Naomi, until the end of the harvest. However, Naomi saw in Boaz's actions the strong possibility that he might be willing to enter a levirate marriage relationship with Ruth (Ruth 2:20; 3:1–5). Though scripturally limited to brothers-in-law (Deut. 25:5–7), apparently as time went on, the family responsibility to the deceased brother and his widow was applied also to other close kinsmen in the Jewish culture. Accordingly, Naomi devised a plan to discreetly, but decisively, approach Boaz on this matter.

At the end of the harvest season (Ruth 2:23), under the cover of darkness, Ruth went to the location beside the threshing floor outside Bethlehem, where Boaz was sleeping to guard the grain from his fields (3:2–6). She then lay down at Boaz's feet and waited for him to awaken, at which point she appealed to his role as a kinsman-redeemer as a basis for marriage (vv. 8–9). After their interaction, Ruth remained at Boaz's feet until rising and leaving at early dawn (vv. 13–14).

Some scholars have interpreted Ruth's actions, particularly uncovering Boaz's feet when she lay down (Ruth 3:7), then staying through the rest of the night (vv. 13–14), as subtle indications that Ruth had made a sexual advance to which Boaz was receptive. Such an idea, is, however, completely against the grain of what is seen of Ruth's and Boaz's characters throughout the book. Specifically, in the middle of Ruth's and Boaz's late-night conversation, Boaz expresses admiration for Ruth's restraint (v. 10) and 'noble character' (v. 11). Also, the nuances in the scene that have been taken by some as sexual in nature are equally capable of being understood otherwise. There is no credible evidence of sexual misconduct.

Boaz's response brought to light an additional factor in the movement of the narrative. Though Boaz was quite willing to undertake a levirate marriage with Ruth, he noted the presence of a closer kinsman-redeemer in Bethlehem (v. 12). The relinquishing of that man's right and responsibility was necessary for Boaz to proceed with his agreement with Ruth (v. 13).

Before the assembled elders of Bethlehem (Ruth 4:2), Boaz shrewdly won agreement from the unnamed kinsman for Boaz to assume the role of primary kinsman-redeemer (vv. 1–8). According to the Mosaic Law, Ruth had the right to publicly humiliate the other kinsman (Deut. 25:7–10). However, because her desire was to marry Boaz, Ruth did not come forward at all. Instead, she trusted Boaz to act in her best interest (Ruth 3:18).

As the legal transaction was completed, well-wishers in the crowd, compared Boaz's new wife, Ruth, to women with formative roles in Israel's history: Rachel and Leah (Ruth 4:11) and Tamar, a Gentile mother who had children through a levirate relationship of sorts with Judah (Ruth 4:12; Gen. 28). Perhaps the temporary childlessness and later fertility of Rachel and Tamar was another intended point of comparison.

At the time of their marriage it is not possible specifically to answer whether Boaz was already married or what the age comparison was between Boaz and Ruth. Since Boaz repeatedly refers to Ruth by the words, 'My daughter' (Ruth, 2:8; 3:10–11), as does her mother-in-law, Naomi (2:2, 22; 3:1, 16, 18), he was probably much closer to Naomi's age than Ruth's. After nearly ten years of marriage and widowhood (1:4–5), Ruth may have been in her later 20s when she married Boaz, and he may have been around 50 or even somewhat older.

At that age and in that society, it is quite likely that Boaz had been married. If so, either his wife and children are simply not mentioned or he also was widowed and perhaps childless. Certainly no concerns about confusion over Boaz's estate are mentioned, as the other kinsman does in Ruth 4:6.

Soon after their marriage, Ruth was enabled to conceive by the LORD (v. 13). The child, Obed, became a great joy to Naomi, his grandmother, as well as a forefather of King David (vv. 14–17). It is intriguing to notice that Obed was proclaimed to be Naomi's kinsman-redeemer in her old age (vv. 14–15) at the same time that the wording in vv. 16–17 indicates that Naomi not only was Obed's nurse (v. 16), but also effectively adopted him (v. 17). If that understanding is correct, Obed legally replaced one of Naomi's deceased sons (Ruth 1:5; 4:10). Perhaps the reference to Ruth as being 'better to you than seven sons' (4:15) is intended to mean that Ruth more than replaced the other son through her devotion (4:15; 1:16–17).

Because this was a patriarchal society and the ideal family size was often considered to be seven, the biblical number for completeness, the statement that Ruth was better than seven sons is extravagant praise indeed. Perhaps much as Ruth and Boaz were compared earlier in the book in regard to their excellent character (Ruth 2:1; 3:11), at the conclusion of the book they are honoured similarly. The gathered crowd had already requested that Boaz 'be famous in Bethlehem' (4:11). But, that is not all. Boaz is found in the spotlighted seventh position in the royal genealogy of David (4:21). Thus, both Ruth and Boaz are seen to be exemplary biblical figures, perfectly matched spiritually.

The lone additional scriptural reference to Ruth is particularly interesting because of the clear relationship it has to the purpose of the book in which it is found. The mention of Ruth in the family tree of Jesus Christ in Matt. 1:5 is alongside that of the only three other women: Tamar (v. 3), Rahab (v. 5) and 'Uriah's wife' (v. 6). All four women appear to be Gentiles from the OT contexts in which they are found. Thus, the first Gospel, which concludes with Christ's command to 'make disciples of all nations' (Matt. 28:19) begins with the realization that Gentiles like Ruth had contributed greatly to the bloodline of Jesus, the Messiah.     A.B.L.

# S

**SABEANS** Perhaps the name of this people is derived from Seba who was the first son of Cush and grandson of Ham (*Gen. 10:7; 1 Chron. 1:9*). It describes a tribe from the south of Arabia, perhaps from the area around modern Yemen, who had a reputation for being tall and fearsome. The description of tribes from Sheba may also refer to these people. They were obviously a trading people, living in an area that was relatively stable compared with the nations to the north and en route for Africa and the east, especially India. They were also involved at some time in trading slaves (*Job. 1:15; Ps. 72:15; Is. 45:14; 60:6; Ezek. 23:42; 27:22; Joel 3:8*). There is a problem in distinguishing between those people descended from Seba and those from Sheba, the latter being a descendant of Shem (*Gen. 10:28; also see Ps. 72:10*). It may well have been the Sabean queen (the queen of Sheba) who went to visit Solomon at the height of his power and influence in the region (*1 Kings 10:1–13*).

P. D. G.

**SABTA** An alternative spelling for Sabtah found in *1 Chron. 1:9*. This person was the third son of Cush.

**SABTAH** The third son of Cush mentioned in *Gen. 10:7*, spelled as Sabta in *1 Chron. 1:9*. He was the grandson of Ham. It is possible that the Cushites settled along the Red Sea either on the Arabian or Egyptian side.

**SABTECA** The fifth son of Cush mentioned in *Gen. 10:7* and *1 Chron. 1:9*. He was the grandson of Ham.

**SACAR 1.** Mentioned in *1 Chron. 11:35*, Sacar, the Hararite, was the father of one of David's 'mighty men', Ahiam.

**2.** The fourth son of Obed-Edom, a descendant of Korah responsible to attend to the Tabernacle gates in David's administration (*1 Chron. 26:4*).

**SADDUCEES** One of three Jewish sects described by the 1st-century Jewish historian Josephus (along with the Pharisees and Essenes). Only a tiny fraction of the Jewish leaders, particularly among the priests and aristocrats, belonged to this group, which was something of a cross between a political party and a religious faction. The name may derive from King David's priest, Zadok. In a sense the Sadducees were politically liberal and religiously conservative. They had made their peace with the occupying Roman government (unlike the Pharisees) but believed only in the written Scriptures (what Christians came to call the OT). Whereas the Pharisees gave credence to a large body of oral traditions that grew up around the written Law of Moses, the Sadducees would not believe any doctrine that could not be derived from the first five books of their Bible. Hence, their disbelief in the resurrection and in angels (*Acts 23:8*).

In Mark and Luke, the Sadducees appear only once, when they tried to ridicule the doctrine of the resurrection by asking Jesus who a woman who had been married seven times would have for a husband in the life to come (*Mark 12:18; Luke 20:7*). Matthew recounts this story, too (*Matt. 22:23–33*), but adds several unparalleled references to Sadducees. They came to where John was baptizing (*Matt. 3:7*) and later tested Jesus by asking for a sign from heaven to authenticate his ministry (*Matt. 16:1*). Jesus warned his disciples against their 'leaven' – i.e. the pervasive, evil influence of their teaching (*Matt. 16:11–12*). In each of these cases they were paired with the Pharisees. Some have questioned whether these arch-rivals would have come together as Matthew depicts them doing, but antagonists often unite against a common enemy (in this case Jesus). Matthew is clearly interested in portraying them in a negative light, however, in keeping with his generally hostile perspective toward the Jewish leaders who ultimately crucified Christ.

In Acts, Sadducees, along with other priests and the captain of the Temple guard arrested Peter and John (*Acts 4:1*) and soon afterwards all of the apostles (*Acts 5:17*), even though their imprisonment was short-lived. When Paul was on trial before the Jewish high court, he tried to divide the 'jury' by claiming to be on trial for the Pharisaic hope of the resurrection, as over against Sadducean beliefs (*Acts 23:6–7*). There is some evidence for a Sadducean persecution of Christians in Jerusalem and Rome in the decade prior to the destruction of the Temple by the Romans (AD 70); if Matthew and/or Luke were writing during this period, some of this antagonism may explain their uniformly negative portrait in these documents.    C.B.

**SAKIA** Listed in the genealogy of Benjamin leading to King Saul, Sakia was the head of a family and the son of Shaharaim and his wife Hodesh. He was born in Moab (*1 Chron. 8:10*)

**SALLAI** is known as a descendant of Benjamin who settled in Jerusalem after the Exile (*Neh. 11:8*).

**SALLU 1.** Mentioned in *1 Chron. 9:7* as the son of Meshullam. After the captivity, Sallu was among the first returnees to Jerusalem from the tribe of Benjamin (*Neh. 11:7*).

**2.** This Sallu was a leader among the priests who returned with Zerubbabel from the captivity in Babylon (*Neh. 12:7, 20*).

**SALMA**, 'the father of Bethlehem', was credited with founding this town. He was the third son of Hur, a descendant of Caleb and a leader in the tribe of Judah (*1 Chron. 2:51, 54*).

**SALMON** was the son of Nahshon and father of Boaz. He was an ancestor of Boaz and King David and therefore is mentioned in the genealogies of Christ in the New Testament (*Ruth 4:20; 1 Chron. 2:11; Matt. 1:4–5; Luke 3:32*).

**SALOME** (Heb., 'peace').

**1.** Mark alone identifies this woman by name. She was one of those women who watched the crucifixion at a distance (*Mark 15:40*) and who, after the burial, were then involved in anointing Jesus' body with spices (*Mark 16:1*). These women, who included Mary Magdalene and Mary the mother of James, had followed Jesus through Galilee and 'cared for his needs' (*Mark 15:41*). This means that Salome may have been a woman of independent means or from a fairly wealthy family. It is quite possible, given a comparison between *Mark 15:40–41* and *Matt. 27:55–56*, that Salome was the mother of the 'sons of Zebedee', James and John. If this were the case then it was she who was rebuked by Jesus for requesting that her sons be given some prominence in his Kingdom (*Matt. 20:20–21*).

**2.** The name given by Josephus to the daughter of Herodias. She danced for Herod Antipas and was promised a great reward. She took advice from her mother who demanded the death of John the

Baptist (*Mark 6:21–28*). Although distressed at this demand, Herod gave in to her wishes and John was beheaded. See *Herodias* for the detail of the incident.

P. D. G.

**SALU** The father of Zimri, Salu was leader of one of the Simeonite families (*Num. 25:14*). Zimri was put to death in Moses' time by Phinehas the priest because he married a Moabite woman. Such liaisons with foreign pagan tribes had been specifically forbidden by the LORD.

**SAMARITAN, SAMARITANS** Usually this term refers to a person who belonged to an Israelite sect located in the territory of Samaria between Judea and Galilee. The group had a sanctuary on Mt Gerazim (see *John 4:20–21*) during the intertestamental period. Their origins are generally understood to be associated with the account of the Assyrian conquest of Palestine in *2 Kings 17:24–41* which recounts how the Assyrians colonized the conquered area by settling it with people from Mesopotamia, who intermarried with Israelites that the Assyrians had left in the region. Josephus labelled the Samaritans as Jewish apostates and records how the priest Manasseh was expelled from Jerusalem and a sanctuary was built for him just after the beginning of the Hellenistic period by his father-in-law Sanballat on Mt Gerazim.

There is now a scholarly consensus that almost all of the preceding assertions cannot be maintained. While there is considerable disagreement on how and when the Samaritan sect did come into existence, the situation reflected in the NT references to Samaritans apparently developed far more recently than previously thought. The account in *2 Kings 17* probably does not refer to the Samaritans as described in the NT. The word in *17:29* translated 'Samaritans' refers merely to the inhabitants of the city or region of Samaria. There is no evidence linking the later Samaritans with Samaria; the earliest references locate them at Shechem (as would be expected from their theology, *cf. Sirach 50:26; 2 Macc. 5:22–23; 6:2*). One of Josephus' sources actually refers to them as 'Shechemites'. It is not known for certain who resettled Shechem (and possibly Mt Gerazim itself) at the start of the Hellenistic period, but it is reasonable to think that this was done by a group who were descended from the original Israelite population in the north not exiled by the Assyrians. This is consistent with Samaritan theology, which shows no pagan influences as might be expected if the Samaritans were descended from people who had intermarried with Assyrian colonists.

The Samaritans were rejected by the Jews in the intertestamental period. *Sirach 50:25–26* speaks of them as 'no nation' and 'the foolish people that dwell in Shechem', and *Testament of Levi 7:2* calls them 'City of the Senseless' (i.e. fools). This designation clarifies *John 8:48* where the Jewish leadership called Jesus a Samaritan. The Samaritans accepted as authoritative only the Pentateuch. Nevertheless they shared much in common with Jews theologically: belief in monotheism, in Moses as prophet, and in the Law of Moses. They differed in regarding Mt Gerazim as the place appointed by God for sacrifice (*cf. John 4:20*).

In the Synoptic Gospels there are references to Samaritans in *Matt. 10:5; Luke 9:52; 10:33; 17:16*. These can all be understood in light of the background mentioned above as long as one remembers that the description of the Samaritans is from a Jewish viewpoint. Thus in *Matt. 10:5* the Samaritans are regarded as a third category, distinct from Israelites and Gentiles. *Luke 9:52* portrays typical animosity between Samaritans and Jews, but it is interesting to note that Jesus himself did not subscribe to the general Jewish proced-ures of avoiding Samaritan territory when travelling from Galilee to Jerusalem (see also *John 4:4*). The parable of the Good Samaritan (*Luke 10:25–37*) is significant because it portrays a Samaritan in a posi-tive role (especially in contrast to Jewish religious figures) and achieves its 'shock value' from the reversal of popular expec-tations. Something similar occurs in *Luke 17:16* where it is the Samaritan alone who returned to thank Jesus for his cleansing from leprosy.

By far the most extensive NT treatment of Samaritans occurs in *John 4:4–42* (the only other reference in the Fourth Gospel is in *8:48*, mentioned above). The sur-prise expressed by the woman that Jesus would request a drink from her (*John 4:9*) and the evangelist's note that Jews and Samaritans had no dealings (lit., 'do not use vessels in common') are both typical of Jewish-Samaritan relations of the period. So is the woman's question about the right place to worship (*John 4:20*), which forms the basis for the re-ligious identity of the Samaritans (see *Woman at the well*). The Samaritans are portrayed positively in their response to Jesus (*John 4:42*) and for the evangelist this underscores the non-exclusive scope of Jesus' mission. In both Luke and John it is surprising how positively the Samaritans are portrayed given the nega-tive evaluation by 1st-century Judaism. They illustrate that Jesus and his message were not bound by cultural, religious, or ethnic stereotypes. w.h.h.

**SAMLAH** is mentioned in the list of the kings of Edom in the time before Israel had a king. He followed Hadad in the succession and preceded Shaul from Rehoboth. He came from Masrekah (*Gen. 36:36–37; 1 Chron. 147–48*).

**SAMSON** receives much attention in the book of Judges, perhaps because he exem-plifies the theme of the book: 'In those days Israel had no king; everyone did as he saw fit' (*Judg. 21:25*). He is best remembered for his noble exploits tainted by lack of self-control. His anger at being rejected in marriage, his riddles, his ven-geance upon his enemies by tying flaming torches to the tails of foxes and, of course, his ill-fated marriage to Delilah, still have the power to fascinate.

For the writer of Judges, there were other more prominent themes to be re-membered. Samson did indeed begin to subdue the oppressive Philistine hold upon the Israelites which would continue for much of Israel's future history. However, his success was sporadic and short-lived. Like many charismatic figures, he was in danger of fickleness much of the time, which was, perhaps, his besetting sin (e.g. *Judg. 16:20*). Never-theless, the epitaph in *Judg. 16:30* is a fitting tribute to his dying resolve: 'he killed many more when he died than while he lived'. Even in his way of death, God would be the final rescuer of Israel, despite the failing exploits of its great heroes.

The introduction of the extreme op-pression by the Philistines and the significance of Samson's Nazirite dedica-tion (see *Num. 6*) to the LORD are the main concerns of the book of Judges. The writer paints Samson as a less successful type of Samuel who was to follow him later.

The Philistines were mortal enemies of the Israelites, but were used by God to test their dedication to Him (*Judg. 3:1–3*). By the time of Samson the Philistines had gained further control of Israel, and God used Samson to bring about further conflict (*Judg. 14:4*). However, Samson only enjoyed partial success and was soon enticed into immorality and en-snared by attractive women.

Samson was a man with a fiery temper. He broke up with his wife (fiancée), Timnah, during his time of betrothal (*Judg. 14:20*). Her father's attempt to offer Samson the younger daughter instead only further angered him (15:2) and Samson vowed to get even by tying the tails of 300 foxes in pairs to flaming torches. His own people became exasperated with Samson's vengeance, and his retort, 'I merely did to them what they did to me' (15:11) was not a very mature response!

Samson appeared to be unstoppable, ruling over Israel for 20 years before he fell for the beautiful Delilah (Judg. 15:20). Delilah was a prostitute from the town of Gaza who used her seductive wiles eventually to find the way to disarm Samson. The secret of his strength was found, not in being tied up with leather thongs, new ropes or by binding his hair. Rather when his hair was cut (long hair which identified him as a Nazirite), then his strength left him, and thus Samson was defeated (15:6–20).

In accordance with the angel's promise to his parents, Samson was to be a Nazirite 'set apart to God from birth'. The requirements of Num. 6 prohibited the drinking of wine and intoxicating drinks; the cutting of the hair and going near a dead body. It may be mere conjecture that Samson drank wine at his wedding feast (Judg. 14:10), but certainly the other two prohibitions were systematically broken (see 14:8; 16:19). Num. 6 also makes provision for those who break their vows, and it may be that Samson had those in mind with his penitential prayer in 16:28. The writer had already hinted that as Samson's hair grew again, so his strength would be restored (16:22).

Samson, like the people of Israel over whom he judged, tried God's patience greatly. So easily were they seduced. However, God's graciousness was evident, not least in that he temporarily broke the cycle of defeat at the hands of the Philistines.                            S.V.

# SAMUEL

Samuel was a son of Elkanah and Hannah. Elkanah was a descendant of Levi, though not of the lineage of Aaron, the priestly line (1 Chron. 6:33–34). Hannah was barren. She prayed to the LORD and received the promise through Eli, the priest, that she would have a child. Upon this news, she returned home, vowing to dedicate this child to the LORD. She named him Samuel ('the name of God'), signifying her hope that Samuel would carry the name of God. The popular rendering, 'asked of God', as found in 1 Sam. 1:20, 'I asked the LORD for him', may be amplified by the addition of the meaning of Samuel's name: 'I asked the LORD [a name of God] for him.' Truly, Samuel placed the name of God before his people as he reminded them during national and personal crises of God's goodness and of their evil ways.

Samuel bridges the epochs of Moses/Joshua and that of David/Solomon. After the death of Moses the word of the LORD came to Joshua by whom Israel received reassurance that the LORD was still with them (Josh. 3:7; 4:14; 6:27). Shortly before his death Joshua challenged the leaders of Israel to remain faithful to the LORD (Josh. 23:1–11), because Joshua could not bring Israel into a state of 'rest' on account of his old age (Josh. 13:1).

In the period following his death, Israel rebelled against the LORD and often experienced divine abandonment. Moses (Deuteronomy), Joshua (Josh. 23–24), and God's servants (Judg. 2:1–5; 6:7–10) had challenged Israel to stay close to the LORD, but they did whatever they pleased. The LORD tested the loyalty of his people (Judg. 2:22–3:1), but they failed him as individuals, as tribes, and as a nation. The period of the Judges was an era of Israel's failings and of God's response to the cry of his people. Israel had come to a very low point in redemptive history. (See Judges.)

The LORD raised up Samuel in this period of crisis in Israel's history. He served Israel as judge, priest, and prophet. As the last of the judges (Acts 13:20), and the first of the prophets (Acts 3:24), he was a transition figure between the era of the Judges and the Kings. Samuel was God's chosen instrument whose spiritual descent links him with Joshua, Moses, and Abraham.

### Samuel the priest

At an early age, Samuel began his service at the Tabernacle in Shiloh. Surrounded by Eli's sons, whose lewd behaviour was well known (1 Sam. 2:12–17, 22–25), Samuel remained steadfast in his love for the LORD. One night he received a special revelation that concerned the end of Eli's dynasty (1 Sam. 3:11–14). This oracle was the beginning of his prophetic ministry. Samuel was set apart as a prophet in Israel as everyone began to recognize him as a man of God (1 Sam. 3:19–21).

The prophecy of God's judgment on Eli's family came true during a campaign against the Philistines. Eli's sons, Hophni and Phinehas, brought the ark of the covenant to the battle scene (1 Sam. 4). They were killed and the ark was taken by the Philistines. Upon hearing of their death and of the capture of the ark, Eli died. Both events, Eli's death and the shame of the ark's reduction to a captured fetish, brought about the end of Shiloh as the religious centre in Israel. The desolation of Shiloh shocked the nation, and the reverberation was felt well into the 6th century when Jeremiah said, 'Go now to the place in Shiloh where I first made a dwelling for my Name, and see what I did to it because of the wickedness of my people Israel' (Jer. 7:12).

Though not of Aaronic descent, Samuel served as a priest after the end of Eli's dynasty. This aspect of his life is overshadowed by his leadership as a prophet and judge in Israel. These several aspects of his ministry come together in the story of the Mizpah assembly. Samuel called the people together at Mizpah, called them to repent, prayed for them, and made an offering on their behalf (1 Sam. 7) upon which the LORD helped them in fighting off the attack of the Philistines. The victory was celebrated with the setting up of a stone by Mizpah (1 Sam. 7:12). This stone was called 'Ebenezer' ('stone of help').

Samuel, like Moses, prayed for Israel (1 Sam. 7:9; cf. 12:17, 19, 23). At the end of his public ministry, he reviewed Israel's past, exhorted the people to learn from their history, and threatened them with hail and thunder (1 Sam. 12). Upon hearing his prophetic charge and seeing the devastation caused by the storm, the people asked him again to pray for them. He did so, but not without warning them of God's impending judgment, 'But be sure to fear the LORD and serve him faithfully with all your heart; consider what great things he has done for you. Yet if you persist in doing evil, both you and your king will be swept away' (vv. 24–25).

## Samuel the seer/prophet

Samuel has the distinction of being the first of the prophets (*Acts 3:24*). The LORD called him to be his prophet (*1 Sam. 3:1–14*) and as a prophet he embodied the spirit of Moses (*Jer. 15:1*). He was recognized as God's servant', by whom the LORD spoke to his people individually (*1 Sam. 9:6*) and nationally (*1 Sam. 7:2–4; 8:1–22*). Samuel's prophetic ministry was so unique that all the tribes heard about God's prophet: 'And all Israel from Dan to Beersheba recognized that Samuel was attested as a prophet of the LORD' (*1 Sam. 3:20*). See *Prophets and Prophecy*.

## Samuel the judge

Samuel was a faithful judge, who lived up to the theocratic ideal, shaped Israel's political life, unified the tribes, and victoriously fought the Philistines (*1 Sam. 7:13b–17*). The office of judge was both political and military. As a political leader the judge preserved the unity of the tribes and dealt with judicial matters that were beyond the ken of the local leaders. As a military leader, he 'delivered' Israel from the attacks of their enemies. The LORD granted a temporary rest to Israel during Samuel's ministry.

The centre of his leadership was his birthplace, Ramah (*1 Sam. 7:17*), from where he would travel on a circuit from town to town. Little is known of his home-life, except that his two sons (Joel and Abijah) were scoundrels (*1 Sam. 8:1–3*). Their failure occasioned the leaders to decide on a new course in Israel's life. Instead of relying on a charismatic figure, such as a judge, they determined that Israel was ripe for the leadership of a royal dynasty (*1 Sam. 8*). Their request met with opposition from Samuel, but received approval from the LORD.

The prophet submitted to God's will, knowing full well how treacherous the new course would be for Israel. Providence brought Saul into Samuel's life. Saul had come to enquire of Samuel as to the whereabouts of his father's donkey. Assured by God, the prophet secretly anointed Saul as king over Israel (*1 Sam. 9*). Providence also brought Saul into the mainstream of Israel after he was chosen at a public meeting at Mizpah, where lots had been cast to determine the king (*1 Sam. 10*). Providence sealed the matter when Saul demonstrated his prowess in battle, being successful against the Philistines. However, Saul's personal ambitions were at odds with Samuel's selfless service, and, in the end, they ran completely counter to God's will. The LORD wanted obedience from his king, whereas Saul sought to placate God with offerings. On one such occasion, Saul defied Samuel's instructions to execrate all Amalekite life by keeping their animals as well as the Amalekite king alive. This incident led to a rift between the two parties, and resulted in Samuel's rejection of Saul as king: 'Does the LORD delight in burnt offerings and sacrifices as much as in obeying the voice of the LORD? To obey is better than sacrifice, and to heed is better than the fat of rams. For rebellion is like the sin of divination, and arrogance like the evil of idolatry. Because you have rejected the word of the LORD, he has rejected you as king' (*1 Sam. 15:22–23*).

The removal of Saul's family from permanent, dynastic leadership in Israel, opened up the possibility of another king. David was the man of God's choice.

He had a heart for God and was quite unlike Saul, who with his tall, masculine appearance made an impressive king. The choice of David, the shepherd-musician, was God's affirmation to Samuel. Samuel, who had wondered about the propriety of kingship in Israel and had forewarned Israel of a king's autocratic governance, was vindicated during his life. But, he was also encouraged by God's choice of a godly man.

Samuel withdrew into the background, while Saul contended with David to dominate as the main character. Saul was jealous of the young David, whose heroic acts were on the lips of the people. He made every effort to kill God's anointed servant, hoping to leave the throne to Jonathan, his son. Samuel was not privileged to live long enough to see David come to the throne. He died and was buried amidst national mourning.

We meet Samuel again the day before Saul's death. The king, being afraid of the battle against the Philistines, sought a word from Samuel through a spiritist at Endor. Samuel appeared to Saul and told him of his impending death. The next day Saul died in battle even as Samuel had said.

Samuel was a faithful servant of the LORD. His name is mentioned in the NT among the heroes of faith (*Heb. 11:32*). See also *Covenant*.　　　　W. A. VG.

**SANBALLAT** was governor of Samaria, under the Persian empire, when the Israelites returned to Jerusalem from Exile. He was also Nehemiah's main opponent during the rebuilding of the wall (*Neh. 4*). Sanballat and Tobiah the Ammonite wanted to display their power, so they taunted the people and openly predicted destruction and defeat. Nehemiah did not move from his goal or his position, and he encouraged the people by reminding them of the great and awesome God they served (*Neh. 4:14*). Nehemiah openly refuted Sanballat and continued to lead the Israelites in rebuilding both their city and their national identity. When Sanballat saw that his tactics were ineffective, he started a rumour that Nehemiah wanted to be king (*Neh. 6*). Again, Nehemiah stopped Sanballat's lies and the wall was rebuilt in honour of God's faithfulness to his people.　　S.C.

**SANHEDRIN (THE)** The Sanhedrin was the highest council and legal authority for Jews in the period up to the fall of Jerusalem. The word *Sanhedrin* is a Hebrew and Aramaic term that was a transliteration from the Greek *sunedrion*, meaning 'sitting in council'. Although the highest legal authority for Jews, under the Roman occupation its powers were limited. Information concerning the Sanhedrin largely comes from Josephus and the NT, although some information may be taken from the Mishnah. Although the Jewish teachers believed the council was a genuine continuation from the 70 rulers who were chosen to help Moses rule Israel, it had probably existed for less than 200 years in the form found in the days of the apostles.

Its members consisted of the chief priests and chief Pharisees. In the NT the phrase 'The chief priests and the whole Sanhedrin' indicates the prominent role the priests took (*Matt. 5:22, 29; Mark 14:55*). But other 'elders' and 'teachers of the law' also took part (*Mark 15:1; John 11:47; Acts 4:5*), and *Acts 5:21* refers to 'the full assembly of the elders of Israel'. It was presided over by the high priest and had up to 70 members.

The Sanhedrin had general delegated powers from the Romans over civil law and serious judicial matters that lower courts did not handle. In *Acts* 4 Peter and John were taken before the Sanhedrin and tried for their proclamation of the gospel of Jesus and his resurrection. On that occasion all the rulers felt able to do was to threaten the apostles and release them. However, in *Acts* 5:17–24 the Sanhedrin, who had their own police force, were able to imprison the apostles, at least until the Lord sent his angel to release them (*v. 19*).

As the influence of the apostles and the gospel grew wider the Sanhedrin was again called upon to judge a follower of Christ. It was this body that ruled, on the evidence of false witnesses, that Stephen should be stoned to death for blasphemy (*Acts* 6:12, 15). The Sanhedrin was the legal body to which the Romans looked for information when they were finding out about the official charges being brought against the apostle Paul (*Acts* 22:30; 23:1, 20, 28; 24:20). Given that both Pharisees and Sadducees were members of the council, it is not surprising that serious theological difference would have arisen between them from time to time. The apostle Paul was able to use this to his advantage on at least one occasion (*Acts* 23:6).

The biblical information on this council obviously shows the members set against early Christians, but much of its work would have concerned normal civil law and, if Gamaliel's comments in *Acts* 5:34–40 are examined, it was often led by wise elder statesmen.     P. D. G.

**SAPHA** Mentioned only in *2 Sam.* 21:18, Saph, a descendant of Rapha, was killed by Sibbecai in an Israelite battle against the Philistines at Gob. It is likely that Sibbecai's killing of Sippai, mentioned in *1 Chron.* 20:4, who was also a Rephaite, is a reference to the same incident. The incident was of special importance for the Israelites because the victory over the giant temporarily led to the subjugation of the Philistines by Israel.

**SAPPHIRA** (Gk., 'beautiful') was the wife of Ananias and is mentioned only in *Acts* 5:1. With her 'full knowledge' her husband kept back part of the money he had earned from the sale of some of his property. In giving his money to the apostles, he pretended that he had given them all the proceeds. For their hypocrisy and lying to the Holy Spirit (*v. 3*) they both died suddenly, creating great fear of God's judgment in the early church. The text makes it clear that it was not the fact of keeping their own property or money that was the problem but rather the lying and deception. For more detail see *Ananias*.

**SARAH/SARAI** (Heb., 'princess'). The NT sees Sarah as an example of the Lord's triumph over human deadness (*Rom.* 4:19; *Heb.* 11:11) and of wifely respect for her husband (*1 Pet.* 3:6). This latter quality she had in considerable measure: acquiescing in Abram's disruption of home and life to follow God's call into the unknown (*Gen.* 12:1–5), in his absurd weakness in the face of supposed danger (*Gen.* 12:10–13; 20:2) and making no recorded protest over his decision to sacrifice her only son (*Gen.* 22). *Gen.* 16:5 finds her hitting out in every direction but is it not the understandable trauma of facing the bitter reality of a shared husband? And is not her action in *Gen.* 21:9–10, spiteful and mean-spirited though it was, the other side of (at last) finding her own fulfilment and worth? Her laughter in *Gen.* 18:12 betrayed a doubting spirit but she laughed with open delight (*Gen.* 21:6) when the LORD proved that nothing is too hard for him (*cf. Gen.* 18:14). No wonder Abraham wept for this human, lovable woman (*Gen.* 23:2). Sarah's experience provides a case-study of the spiritual dimensions of childlessness and fertility which

remains as the Word of God even in our medically sophisticated age (*Gen. 16:2; cf. 30:2; 18:10–14; 21:1–2; cf. 25:21; 29:31; 30:17, 22*).
J. A. M.

**SARAPH** Mentioned in *1 Chron. 4:22*. A leader in the tribe of Judah. Together with others he is listed as being among the potters who lived in Moab.

**SARGON** (Assyr., 'the lawful king'). Mentioned in the Bible only in *Is. 20:1*, Sargon was king of Assyria around 722–705 BC. He was the son of Tiglath-Pileser III and succeeded his brother Shalmaneser to the throne. His exploits are well known from extra-biblical material and provide some of the background to Isaiah's prophecy of the destruction of the Northern Kingdom of Israel. Although it was Shalmaneser V who had besieged Samaria for three years, the area finally fell in 721 BC once Sargon had come to the throne. Assyrian records indicate that 27,290 Israelites were deported from Samaria and resettled in parts of Mesopotamia.

Some of this history is recounted in *2 Kings 17* where it is recorded that Hoshea, king of the Northern Kingdom of Israel, rebelled against Assyria, refused to pay tribute and sought help from King So of Egypt (*vv. 1–6*). Hoshea was imprisoned and, after the long siege, Samaria was captured (*v. 6*). In the biblical account it is clear that Sargon was used by the LORD to bring judgment on the Israelites for their sin. Particularly serious was their sin of idolatry. Nearly every hill in Samaria had sacred stones and Asherah poles for the worship of other gods. Although, through prophets like Isaiah, Israel had been warned of judgment, they had continued to sin and thus were eventually held accountable by God (*vv. 7–23*).
P.D.G.

# SATAN

## The name

***Meaning.*** The name 'Satan' is derived from a Heb. word meaning 'act as an adversary'. The verb can mean 'to accuse'. The noun is transliterated in Greek as 'Satanas', and appears in English 35 times in the NT. The word is sometimes used simply to describe a normal adversary. For example, in the Heb. of *1 Sam. 29:4* the Philistine commanders objected to the fact that David was in their midst and urged that he be sent back to his people: 'He must not go with us into battle, or he will turn against us during the fighting', i.e. 'become an adversary [Satan] to us'. Sometimes the word is used with the article and in these cases indicates 'the Satan' who is the personal adversary of God and his people. In the NT the word in effect becomes the title of this fallen but powerful angelic being. He is specifically called an 'adversary' in *1 Pet. 5:8* ('the enemy' in NIV).

***Other descriptive names.*** Frequently other names or descriptions are applied to the being known as Satan. He was of course the 'serpent' of *Gen. 3:1*. In *Rev. 12:9* and *20:2* he is again called 'that ancient serpent', but also the 'dragon' and 'the devil or Satan'. The term 'devil' (from a root word also meaning 'accuse') is used regularly in the NT (some 36 times), but other names and terms help build a picture of this evil personal being. In *Rev. 9:11* he is 'Abaddon' or, in Greek, *Apollyon*. This 'destroyer' is 'the angel of the Abyss', a 'star that had fallen from the sky' (*v. 1*). Descriptive terms such as Apollyon or 'the angel of the Abyss' are in one sense more of a personification of destruction and death than another name for Satan. Nevertheless ultimately such 'destruction' comes, of course, from Satan (*v. 1*, the fallen star) and therefore phrases, terms and names such as this all contribute to our understanding of this being. Further notable descriptions that refer to Satan include: 'the god of this age' (*2 Cor. 4:4*); 'the prince of demons' (*Matt. 12:24*); the 'ruler of the kingdom of the air' (*Eph. 2:2*); 'the ruler of darkness' (*Eph. 6:12*); the 'tempter' (*Matt. 4:3*) and 'the evil one' (*Matt. 13:19*). In *2 Cor. 6:15* he is called Belial and in *Matt. 12:24*, Beelzebub, and in *John 8:44* Jesus called him a 'murderer from the beginning', a 'liar and the father of lies'.

## The biblical description

***His person.*** The Bible describes Satan as an angelic being who rebelled against his Creator God. Surprisingly little information is given about his position in heaven and no explanation is given for his evil disposition and desire. A passage in *Ezek. 28:11–19* does provide some background, though the name Satan is not used here. This passage is directly related to a prophecy against the King of Tyre and so some would argue that it has nothing to do with Satan. However, it seems likely that the references to his being a 'cherub' and present in 'Eden, the garden of God' mean that either the author was applying truths about Satan to the King of Tyre or describing Satan who is represented in this instance by the King of Tyre. In either case it is possible directly or indirectly to learn something of Satan himself.

He was once 'the model of perfection' (*Ezek. 28:12*) and 'blameless', but always a 'created being' (*v. 15*). He lived 'on the holy mount of God' and was 'anointed as a guardian cherub' by God himself (*v. 14*). But eventually 'wickedness was found in' him (*v. 15*) and he became 'filled with violence' and 'sinned'. This led to God expelling him 'from the mount of God'. He was thrown down to earth and 'reduced to ashes on the ground in the sight of all who were watching' (*vv. 16–18*). Further descriptions of other fallen angels cast out of heaven can be found in *Jude 6; 2 Pet. 2:4*. (See also *Is. 14:12–17*, where the king of Babylon is described in very similar terms to those attached to the king of Tyre by Ezekiel.)

***His purposes.*** Satan's purpose is to gain control for himself through thwarting the will of God and destroying the people of God. He is devious and deceitful. He thinks and argues and he formulates strategies aimed at the destruction of God's people. He is seen continually to war against God but always in the context of being a created and subordinate being for whom God has a chosen destiny that Satan cannot avoid. Although there is not a hint of dualism in the Bible between good and evil or of some equality between the evil of Satan and the goodness of Jesus, nevertheless part of Satan's subtlety is to mimic the truth. He seeks to persuade those he would lead astray that he has equal authority with Jesus and equal power. Unlike Jesus, the conquering Lion of Judah, Satan prowls like a lion, 'seeking whom he may devour' (*1 Pet. 5:8*). Unlike Jesus, who is the 'light of the world', Satan appears as one who 'masquerades as angel of light' as he seeks to deceive God's people (*2 Cor. 11:14*).

In Scripture there are several incidents where his attempts to work out his purposes are vividly portrayed. In the book of Job, Satan's purpose as Job's adversary was to bring Job into disrepute before God (*Job 1–2*). God, however, knew Job's heart, his righteousness, and trust and allowed Satan a certain power over Job for a while in order to test and tempt him. All the worst that Satan could throw at Job failed to make Job deny God. Another incident in which Satan sought to lead astray one of God's people is recounted in *1 Chron.* 21:1. There Satan tempted King David into disobeying the Law of God and caused him to sin in taking a census of God's people. Unlike Job, who remained righteous, here David succumbed to the temptation and was promptly judged by God for his sin. However, even in judgment there was forgiveness, and David was again restored to a right relationship with God in spite of Satan's efforts to the contrary.

Satan's accusing role is also portrayed in *Zech.* 3. There, in the presence of God, Satan accused the high priest Joshua of sin in an attempt to disqualify him from the LORD's service (*v.* 1). As one of God's people Joshua's sins were forgiven (*v.* 4). God himself saw to it that Satan's attack came to nothing, and God was responsible for Joshua being dressed in pure and clean garments, symbolic of his right standing before God.

In the NT the focus of Satan's attack is on Jesus himself, and then on his people, the church. It started when Jesus was tempted by Satan. In an episode not entirely dissimilar to the temptation of God's people in the wilderness following their Exodus from Egypt, Jesus was led by the Spirit of God into the desert. There Jesus was put to the test by Satan. Satan's main aim was to draw Jesus away from his objective of going to the cross to bring salvation. Unlike the Israelites, however, the true and perfect Son of God would not sin and, throughout, followed the will of his heavenly Father in faithful obedience. The temptations are listed in *Matt.* 4:1–12 and in the parallels in *Mark* 1 and *Luke* 4. Jesus' obedience was specifically to the Word of God, and so he cited Scripture against Satan.

Satan's distortion of the meaning and application of Scripture in the temptations is part and parcel of his continuing work. This work of Satan is highlighted by Jesus in the parable of the sower (*Mark* 4:15). People hear God's Word, yet Satan takes it from them. Being well aware that 'faith comes from hearing the message, and the message is heard through the word of Christ' (*Rom.* 10:17), Satan therefore works his utmost to prevent people hearing the message or understanding it (*2 Cor.* 4:4).

Satan also works to deceive people into thinking that he is sovereign in this world and, to the extent that many, many people believe him and follow him and reject the Lord God, he does hold some sway within this world. His target therefore in the NT specially related to drawing people away from Christ and bringing them back under his own control or preventing people from acknowledging the truth that Christ is Lord and King of all. This is what Jesus meant when he described Satan as the 'prince of this world' (*John* 12:31; 16:11). In one sense the extraordinary power of Satan as prince or ruler of this world is most clearly seen as Jesus is taken to the cross. Jesus briefly acknowledged this power in *John* 14:30 and yet ultimately to see the cross in this way was in fact to see the cross with eyes blinded by Satan. It was at the moment of Satan's apparently greatest triumph, as Christ died on the cross, that God's extraordinary sovereign power and total control and total faithfulness to his people (the object of Satan's attack) was in fact to be seen.

***His power.*** Unlike first appearances, the cross was not the place of a great demonstration of Satan's power so much as the place where the limitation of Satan's power was most clearly to be seen. Throughout Scripture his power has always been shown to exist under the permissive will of God. In the incident with Job, Satan was limited specifically by God in what he could do. The same is clearly true in the incident with the high priest Joshua. But that limitation of Satan's power was first indicated in God's judgment on Satan following the sin of Adam and Eve in the Garden of Eden. There Satan was restricted to a desperate existence in which he would again and again fail in his attack on God's people. God's curse on Satan warned him that while he would 'strike the heel' of the offspring of the woman, that offspring would 'crush the head' of the serpent (*Gen.* 3:15). While no doubt this was the general experience of God's people through the ages, it was particularly true of Jesus himself. As Satan struck at the moment of the cross so right at that point the curse of God was fulfilled, sin was dealt with and paid for, God's people were redeemed and God overcame death with the resurrection of Jesus, the first fruits of those who have fallen asleep (*1 Cor.* 15:20). A decisive blow was inflicted on Satan.

Neither Satan nor all his demonic forces will be able to 'separate us [God's people] from the love of Christ' (*Rom.* 8:35). Throughout, God and his Christ have ultimate and complete power. Satan is not omniscient (all-knowing), nor omnipotent (all-powerful), nor even omnipresent (everywhere present). Indeed, he even admitted his own limitations in his discussions with God about Job, whom Satan acknowledged God had protected (*Job* 1:10).

However, even Satan's limited power is exceedingly dangerous for the church. Satan himself is credited with leading Ananias and Sapphira in the early church into sin that led to their death (*Acts* 5:3). Satan was able, temporarily at least, to hinder the work of the apostle Paul (*1 Thess.* 2:18), and Paul warned Timothy of those in the churches who had already turned to follow Satan's ways (*1 Tim.* 5:15).

### The Christian's defence

On many occasions the NT warns believers that they should defend themselves against Satan. The fact that during the temptation in the desert Jesus answered Satan three times with the words, 'It is written . . .' (*Matt.* 4:4, 7, 10) shows the way forward for Christians. Christ used Scripture (the Word of God) as the ultimate defence against Satan. Christians are to listen to the Word of God in Scripture both in command and in promise. They should live by faith in the sovereign God whose Word is powerful to save. They should live in obedience to that Word and so be hedged round with God's protection. The Word of God is not only a defensive weapon against Satan but is also an offensive weapon: it is 'the sword of the Spirit' (*Eph.* 6:17). Faith in God and his Word becomes a shield with which 'all the flaming arrows of the evil one' can be extinguished (*v.* 16).

Christians have already seen evidence of God's power over Satan as their own minds have been set free from Satan's tyranny so they can understand and believe the truth (Acts 26:17–18). They are also aware that the victory over Satan, won by Christ on the cross, will be finally demonstrated to the world at the return of Christ when the final crushing of Satan's head will be witnessed by all (Rom. 16:20; Rev. 20:10). But using God's Word in this way as a practical defence against the tempter and the accuser requires faithful and daily obedience. Submission to God is the other side of the coin that says 'resist the devil' (James 4:7). The practical steps of obedience to God's Word in keeping busy and looking after others, of not letting the sun go down on anger etc., all help prevent the devil from taking a 'foothold' in the Christian's life (Eph. 4:27–28). Temptation from Satan should be avoided at all costs, and again the Bible offers no mystical route to such avoidance, but rather simple practical advice, such as not unnecessarily abstaining from having sex with one's marriage partner so 'Satan will not tempt you because of your lack of self-control' (1 Cor. 7:5). Of course, such a practical defence against Satan is only possible because of the presence of the Holy Spirit: 'the one who is in you is greater than the one who is in the world' (1 John 4:4).

Ultimately, however, the Christian's defence is wonderfully glorious, for it is centred in the atoning work of Christ on the cross. Through faith in Christ the believer knows that, even if Satan briefly causes him to sin, because of Christ's death the punishment has been taken and justification is a reality. The verdict of 'not guilty' has been pronounced by God in advance ('we have been justified', Rom. 5:1). Christ's continuing intercessory work on the believer's behalf upholds and supports him and mediates the forgiveness of the Father.

### Satan's demise

The Bible not only shows the limitations of Satan's power but also reveals his end. The Lord God has promised a full and final judgment on Satan and all his followers. His end was intimated in Gen. 3:15 and Ezek. 28:19 but becomes explicit in the NT with the coming of Christ and his death and conquest of death in the resurrection to eternal life (e.g. Matt. 25:41; Luke 10:18). The book of Revelation, addressed to a persecuted church suffering under the torments of Satan and his people, pays special attention to the ultimate defeat of Satan and his casting 'into the lake of fire'. Some believe a final great flurry of activity from Satan is indicated before Christ's return, but whatever the precise way these final events in history reveal themselves, this book makes it absolutely clear that Satan's influence, power and control will be entirely defeated so that in the new heavens and the new earth he will not be known at all. Even death itself, which Satan has used to create fear and rebellion in the world, will be gone. The glory of that final banishing of Satan is difficult to comprehend. Believers have prayed for it for so long (e.g. 1 Cor. 16:22; Rev. 6:10), but it will be a day that brings the greatest of glory to God the Saviour and brings great peace and joy to all believers, for 'God will wipe every tear from their eyes. There will be no more death or mourning or crying or pain, for the old order of things has passed away' (Rev. 21:4; see also Rev. 20:7–14; 2 Thess. 2:3–12; Rev. 12:9–12 etc.). P.D.G.

**SAUL 1.** Saul, son of Kish and the first king of Israel, is one of the more enigmatic figures in the Bible. His story, recounted in 1 Sam. 9–31, has caused some interpreters to raise questions about the justice and benevolence of God, and of his prophetic spokesman Samuel. Additionally, many scholars have expressed doubts about the literary and logical coherence of the narratives depicting his career. This in turn has led to a general despair of discovering the historical truth about Saul – if the narratives do not constitute a good story, then they can hardly be expected to yield good history. Recent studies, however, are helping to resolve some of these theological, literary and historical issues, as we shall see below.

Saul, whose name sounds like '(one) asked for', is first introduced in 1 Sam. 9:1–2, though some commentators claim to detect his veiled presence even earlier. Since the Heb. verb meaning 'to ask for' occurs repeatedly in the story of Samuel's birth in 1 Sam. 1, some have supposed that the birth narrative of Samuel is actually a reworking of an original birth narrative of Saul. A more likely hypothesis, however, is that the biblical writer may have capitalized on the 'ask for' root in the Samuel birth narrative in order simply to foreshadow the significant role that Saul would later play in the book and perhaps to anticipate the fact that Samuel, the one 'asked for' by righteous Hannah (1 Sam. 2:20, 27–28), would be directly involved in the rise and fall of Saul, the one 'asked for' by the elders of sinful Israel (1 Sam. 8:4–9; 10:17–19).

In any case, Saul's explicit introduction comes in 1 Sam. 9:1–2, where he is described as a prime specimen of manhood, 'choice and good'. Although it is often assumed that Saul was but a 'diffident youth' at this time in his life, his description as being 'a head taller than any of the others' makes this unlikely. It is also worth observing that, despite its rather positive ring, this first description of Saul focuses exclusively on external qualities, in contrast, for example, to the introduction of David (1 Sam. 16:18), which adds to his fine external qualities the notices that he was 'brave' and, most significantly, that 'the LORD [was] with him.'

In keeping with the unsettling omissions in his introduction, it soon becomes apparent that Saul, though a superb physical specimen, was lacking in spiritual qualities necessary to be a successful king in Israel. A primary indicator of Saul's unsuitability was his repeated failure to obey the word of the LORD as issued by Samuel. It is often observed that the prophetic office came into its own with the inception of kingship in Israel. That is, as distinct from the situation in the book of Judges, where a Gideon, for example, would both receive the divine instructions and also carry them out (Judg. 6–8), the rise of kingship saw a division of responsibilities whereby God's instructions were often mediated through a prophet to the king, who then, in obedience to the prophet, was to carry them out. Under such an arrangement, it was of course of utmost importance that the king obey the prophet, if God's rule (i.e. the theocracy) was to be maintained. But this, as the Bible tells us, Saul failed to do.

While the better-known instances of Saul's disobedience are found in 1 Sam. 13 and 15, the first may come already in 1 Sam. 10. On the occasion of Saul's anointing by Samuel, three signs were given to serve as confirmation. According to the text, when the third and last was fulfilled, Saul was to 'do what [his] hand [found] to do' (according to Samuel's charge in 1 Sam. 10:7), after which (according to Samuel's further directive of 1 Sam. 10:8) he was to head for Gilgal to await additional instructions regarding the Philistine battle that his first action would surely provoke. Had Saul adhered to this scheme, he would have demonstrated his willingness to submit himself to a 'theocratic authority structure' and thus would have confirmed his suitability to be king. He would also have moved a step closer to the throne, following a three-part pattern of designation (by anointing), demonstration (by a deed of valour, i.e. 'what [his] hand [found] to do', 1 Sam. 10:7), and finally confirmation by the people and the prophet. Unfortunately, Saul apparently shrank back from the charge of 1 Sam. 10:7 and thus forestalled the accession process. While Saul's victory over the Ammonites in 1 Sam. 11 was sufficient to satisfy the people and to bring about the 'renewal' of Saul's kingdom (1 Sam. 11:14), it is apparent from the tone of Samuel's speech in 1 Sam. 12 that in his mind, at least, Saul's kingship had still to pass a test.

In 1 Sam. 13 Jonathan, not Saul, did what Saul's hand should have done earlier, thus throwing down the gauntlet to the Philistines. Apparently recognizing that the charge of 1 Sam. 10:7 was now fulfilled, albeit by Jonathan, Saul immediately went down to Gilgal in accordance with 1 Sam. 10:8 to await Samuel's arrival. When Samuel was slow in coming, Saul proceeded to offer pre-battle sacrifices in Samuel's absence, judging that the military situation precluded further delay. No sooner had Saul begun than Samuel arrived and, after hearing Saul's excuses, announced that Saul had acted foolishly and that his kingdom would not endure. Commentators sometimes seek to justify, or at least trivialize, Saul's actions and to criticize Samuel's reaction as overly harsh. But in the light of the significance of the charge issued in 1 Sam. 10:7–8 as a test of Saul's suitability, such interpretations fail. On the occasion of Saul's first rejection, as also on the occasion of his second (1 Sam. 15), Saul's specific deeds of disobedience were but symptomatic of his fundamental inability to accommodate himself to the necessary requirements of theocratic kingship. In short, they were symptomatic of his lack of true faith in God (cf. 1 Chron. 10:13).

After his definitive rejection in 1 Sam. 15, Saul was no longer rightful king in God's eyes (though he remained on the throne for some years), and God turned his attention to another, to David. 1 Sam. 16–31 trace Saul's emotional and psychological disintegration, a disintegration worsened by his fear of David (1 Sam. 18:29), whom he sensed to be God's choice to replace him as king (1 Sam. 18:8; 20:31). After failing in many attempts to take David's life, Saul eventually took his own (1 Sam. 31:4). David, all the while, was providentially, if circuitously, guided towards the throne.

While it is not possible in a dictionary article to go into detail, it may be observed that the Saul narratives, if interpreted along the lines suggested above, make good sense both literarily and theologically, and this in turn opens the door to a positive appraisal of their historical worth.

**2.** For Saul in the NT see *Paul*.      P.L.

**SAVIOUR** See *Jesus*.

**SCEVA** Mentioned only in *Acts* 19:14, Sceva, a Jewish 'high priest', was the father of seven sons who were travelling around Ephesus trying to cast out demons in the name of Jesus. Sceva may have been a member of a high-priestly family, but there is no actual record of him ever having been the 'high-priest' himself. On the occasion recounted in *Acts* 19, the sons attempted to cast out a demon who turned on them saying: 'Jesus I know, and I know about Paul, but who are you?' (*v.* 15). At that the man who was possessed by this demon jumped on the sons of Sceva, overpowered them and beat them until they were nearly dead. The result of this episode was that people throughout

Ephesus became very fearful and 'the name of the Lord Jesus was held in high honour' (v. 17). Many who were converted then proceeded to bring their scrolls on magic arts to be burned as a public testimony to their commitment to the Lord.

This one incident helps demonstrate a truth that is taught throughout Scripture that God is completely sovereign and that even demons operate only while permitted to do so by the Lord. The power of the Lord Jesus far exceeds any alternative power (e.g. see Rom. 8:38–39).    P.D.G.

**SEBA** The first son of Cush and a descendant of Ham (Gen. 10:7; 1 Chron. 1:9), he was probably the progenitor of the tribe known as the Sabeans. The area known as Seba and mentioned in Ps. 72:10 and Is. 43:3 probably belonged to his descendants and may have been in southern Arabia. See Sabeans.

**SECUNDUS** (Lat., 'second'). Along with Sopater, Secundus was a Christian from the Thessalonian church who joined Paul on his final journey through Greece and back eventually to Jerusalem. He may have been one of his church's representatives carrying that church's offering for the relief of the poor in Jerusalem (Acts 20:4).

**SEGUB 1.** Segub and his brother, Abiram, were sons of Hiel, the man who rebuilt Jericho during Ahab's reign (1 Kings 16:34). The writer of Kings says that Hiel laid the foundations and hung the gates at the cost of the life of his sons. This fulfilled Joshua's promise that anyone trying to rebuild Jericho would die together with his son (Josh. 6:26).

**2.** Segub, Hezron's son, was a great-grandson of Judah and a leader in his tribe (1 Chron. 2:21–22).

**SELED** A son of Nadab, who was a leader in the tribe of Judah. He had no children of his own (1 Chron. 2:30).

**SEMAKIAH** (Heb., 'the LORD sustains'). A relative of Shemaiah and among the descendants of Korah, Semakiah is listed among the gatekeepers of the Tabernacle in the time of King David (1 Chron. 26:7).

**SEMEIN** Mentioned in Luke's genealogy leading from Jesus and Joseph back to Adam (Luke 3:26). He was the father of Mattathias and the son of Josech.

**SENNACHERIB** reigned over Assyria and Babylonia from 705–681 BC, and he enjoyed much strength and success as a leader. He invaded Judah in 701 BC. When King Hezekiah refused to pay taxes, Sennacherib threatened to attack Jerusalem. Hezekiah sent three leaders to talk with Sennacherib, but Sennacherib was proud and would not listen. The same three leaders went to inquire wisdom from Isaiah, and the prophet encouraged Hezekiah not to surrender but to trust God. The Israelites waited, and God's word was fulfilled. The Egyptian army threatened Sennacherib from the south and death came to the Assyrian army through an angel sent by God. Sennacherib returned to his own country of Nineveh and there met his death at the hands of his own sons (see 2 Kings 18–19; 2 Chron. 32; Is. 36–37).    S.C.

**SEORIM** One among the priests who were chosen to be officials in the sanctuary 'according to the last instructions of David'. Impartial selection from among the descendants of Eleazar and Ithamar was made by drawing lots. The fourth lot fell to Seorim and that was the order in which he ministered when entering the sanctuary (1 Chron. 24:8).

**SERAH** (Heb., 'abundance'). A daughter of Asher who, together with her brothers, is listed among those who went down to Egypt with her grandfather Jacob (Gen. 46:17; Num. 26:46; 1 Chron. 7:30).

**SERAIAH** (Heb., 'the LORD has persisted').

**1.** When David's kingdom was at its greatest power, Seraiah served as secretary to the king (*2 Sam. 8:17*). (Most scholars agree that Sheva of *2 Sam. 20:25*, Shavsha of *1 Chron. 18:16* and Shisha of *1 Kings 4:3* are the same individual.)

**2.** *1 Chron. 4:14* names Seraiah as the father of Joab and a leader in the tribe of Judah.

**3.** *1 Chron. 4:35* names Seraiah as the father of Joshibiah and a leader in the tribe of Simeon.

**4.** Seraiah, son of Azariah and father of Jehozadak (*1 Chron. 6:14*), was the chief priest in Jerusalem in 587 BC when the Babylonians captured the city (*2 Kings 25; Jer. 52:24, 27*). Seraiah, along with other chief officials, was taken to King Nebuchadnezzar at Riblah and executed.

**5.** Seraiah, son of Tanhumeth, was the captain of a group of Israelites who escaped during the battle with Babylon but later surrendered under the promise of fair treatment from Gedaliah. The people were treated fairly until Gedaliah was assassinated. Those who were not killed along with Gedaliah then fled to Egypt (*2 Kings 25:23; Jer. 40:8*).

**6.** *Jer. 51:59–64* introduces Seraiah, son of Neriah, as a servant to Zedekiah in the fourth year of the king's reign. Seraiah received instructions from Jeremiah the prophet to read a scroll aloud when he arrived in Babylon. The scroll contained a prophecy against the great city, and Seraiah was to read the words, then tie a stone around the scroll and throw it in the Euphrates river. The sinking of the scroll was to provide a vivid picture of what would happen to the Babylonian empire.

**7.** *Ezra 2:2* records Seraiah as one of the remnant who returned from Exile with Zerubbabel (also *Neh. 12:1, 12*) .

**8.** In *Neh. 10:2* Seraiah is listed as one of the Israelite leaders who followed Nehemiah's lead and placed his seal upon the agreement between the people and their God.

**9.** Seraiah is named as one of the chief priests who served Israel during the return from Exile (*Neh. 11:11*).

**10.** This Seraiah, son of Azriel, served Jehoiakim during the days of Jeremiah. Seraiah was ordered to arrest Jeremiah and Baruch after Jeremiah delivered a prophecy which was displeasing to the king, but the LORD had hidden his servants (*Jer. 36:26*).                S.C.

**SERED** One of the sons of Zebulun and the leader of the Seredite clan (*Gen. 46:14; Num. 26:26*). He was the grandson of Jacob and Leah and was born in Paddan Aram.

**SERGIUS** A Roman proconsul who lived in Paphos on the island of Cyprus. He asked Barnabas and Saul (Paul) to come and see him 'because he wanted to hear the word of God' (*Acts 13:7*). For more detail see *Paulus, Sergius*.

**SERUG** was a descendant of Shem. He was the father of Nahor and the son of Reu, thus becoming the great-grandfather of Abraham (*Gen. 11:20–23*). He is also mentioned in Luke's genealogy leading from Jesus and Joseph back to Adam (*Luke 3:35*).

**SETH** was the third son born to Adam and Eve, when Adam was 130 years old. He was born after Cain had killed Abel. *Gen. 4:25* says that his name was given him by Eve because 'God has granted me another child in place of Abel, since Cain killed him.' The Heb. name may come from the verb meaning 'granted' or 'appointed'. Given Cain's sin and Abel's death, it was through Seth that the official line from Adam and Eve was carried. Seth was in Adam's 'own likeness, in his own image' and lived 912 years (*Gen. 5:3–8*).

Seth had a son named Enosh (*Gen. 4:26; 1 Chron. 1:1*) and it was at this time that 'men began to call on the name of the LORD'. This is probably mentioned in order to emphasize that it was through Seth that the godly line continued. Eventually that line became the Messianic line descending through Noah to Abraham, David and on down to Jesus (*Luke 3:38*).

P.D.G.

**SETHUR** One of the twelve spies sent out by Moses from the Desert of Paran to spy out the land of Canaan (*Num. 13:11*). A representative of each tribe was chosen and Sethur, the son of Michael, was from the tribe of Asher. For further detail on their mission see *Shammua*.

**SHAAPH 1.** The sixth son of Jahdai and a descendant of Judah and Caleb, mentioned in *1 Chron. 2:47*.

**2.** A son of Caleb the brother of Jerahmeel and the concubine Maacah, he was the 'father' of Madmannah. This may mean he was the founder of a town by that name (*1 Chron. 2:49*).

**SHAASHGAZ** was a eunuch who was in charge of the king's concubines during the reign of King Xerxes I of Persia. He therefore had charge of Esther, who later became queen instead of Vashti (*Est. 2:14*).

**SHABBETHAI** This man was a Levite who returned from the Exile in Babylon with Ezra and helped those returning deal with the sin of having married foreign wives contrary to God's Law. He was one of the 'heads' among the Levites and shared responsibility in teaching the people the Law, and also had charge of the outside work on the repair of the Temple (*Ezra 10:15; Neh. 8:7; 11:16*)

**SHADRACH** (Bab., 'command of Aku [a moon god]'). It was the name given by the chief official of Nebuchadnezzar to Daniel's Jewish friend, Hananiah. The name is found 14 times in *Dan. 1–3*.

Shadrach, like Daniel, Abednego and Meshach, had been taken captive to Babylon. They refused the royal food and ate only vegetables and drank only water (*Dan. 1:12*) while being prepared for court appearance. The LORD honoured their insistence on not eating what, as Israelites, would have been considered unclean food. As a result, their appearance proved to be healthier than others in the court. God gave him and the others 'knowledge and understanding of all kinds of literature and learning' (*v. 17*). The king found no others with the same abilities as these three men, who were rapidly raised to positions of power and influence under their leader Daniel.

Later, when Shadrach would not bow to a statue of gold that Nebuchadnezzar set up in the plain of Dura (*Dan. 3:12–13*), he was thrown with Abednego and Meshach into a furnace of fire. The three so trusted in the LORD that they informed the king 'the God we serve is able to save us from it' (*v. 17*). Once in the furnace, God did intervene and Nebuchadnezzar saw the three walking in the fire unharmed. A fourth person was also present who Nebuchadnezzar said looked 'like a son of the gods' (*v. 25*). It seems some theophany occurred. Immediately Nebuchadnezzar had the men released, gave them back their positions of authority, and began to worship the true God who had 'sent his angel and rescued his servants' (*v. 28*). Nebuchadnezzar was so impressed by the saving power of the God of the Hebrews that he ordered that no one should say anything against him.

Shadrach and the others had a tremendous faith in their God who had saved them and their faith had witnessed to pagans in the strongest possible way. This faith is alluded to in *Heb. 11:34*, and there becomes an example for Christians of all ages who trust in the same God as Shadrach and the others. See *Theophany*.

P.D.G.

**SHAGEE** was the father of one of David's 'Thirty' mighty men, Jonathan. He was a Hararite and is mentioned only in *1 Chron. 11:34*.

594

**SHAHARAIM** Mentioned in the genealogy of King Saul and the tribe of Benjamin, Shaharaim had sons by two wives whom he later divorced. He lived in Moab with his third wife, Hodesh (*1 Chron. 8:8–11*).

**SHALLUM** 1. Shallum, son of Sismai, was a descendant of the tribe of Judah and the family of Jerahmeel (*1 Chron. 2:40–41*).
  **2.** Another Shallum, son of Shaul, was a descendant of Simeon (*1 Chron. 4:25*).
  **3.** *1 Chron. 6:12–13* and *Ezra 7:2* list this Shallum as a high priest who was the son of Zadok and the father of Hilkiah.
  **4.** Though the NIV text records the name of Naphtali's fourth son as 'Shillem', most Heb. manuscripts record this name as 'Shallum' (*1 Chron. 7:13*).
  **5.** Another Shallum, an Ephraimite, was the father of Jehizkiah, who was one of the Israelites leaders of Pekah's day who opposed bringing Judean captives into Israel. Jehizkiah and the others reminded the Israelites that they, too, had sinned against God (*2 Chron. 28:12*).
  **6.** *1 Kings 22:14* and *2 Chron. 34:22* name Shallum as the husband of the prophetess Huldah. His father was Harhas.
  **7.** Shallum, son of Jabesh, ruled over the Northern Kingdom of Israel after murdering King Zechariah. He ruled for one month. At that time he was killed by his successor, Menaham (*2 Kings 15:8–16*). The general degeneration of political life in Israel is well signified at this time in history by the short reigns of the kings and various assassinations.
  **8.** Shallum was the fourth son and successor to King Josiah. The LORD was not pleased with his rule and delivered a prophecy concerning this king (*1 Chron. 3:15; Jer. 22:11–17*). This Shallum is usually called Jehoahaz (see *2 Kings 23:30–35; 2 Chron. 36:1–4*). See *Jehoahaz*.

  **9.** *Jer. 32* records a prophecy of Jeremiah concerning the future of Judah. God used Jeremiah's uncle, Shallum, to initiate this prophecy. He sent word to Jeremiah, that the prophet could now redeem a field that rightfully belonged in his family. Jeremiah bought the field even though he knew the land would be overrun by the Babylonians, thereby indicating that he knew the people of Judah would one day return to their land (*Jer. 32:6*).
  **10.** During Jeremiah's prophetic years, Shallum was a doorkeeper in the house of the LORD (*Jer. 35:4*).
  **11.** *1 Chron. 9:17* names Shallum as a gatekeeper and one of the first to return to Judah from Babylonian captivity. This Shallum was also head of a family of gatekeepers in the years when Jerusalem was being re-established (*Ezra 2:42; Neh. 7:45*). Possibly this is the same Shallum, also a gatekeeper, mentioned in *Ezra 10:24*, who had taken a foreign wife and later divorced her.
  **12.** Under Nehemiah's leadership, Shallum, son of Hallohesh, and his daughters helped to rebuild the wall of Jerusalem. Shallum also governed one of the half-districts of the city (*Neh. 3:12*).
  **13.** Another Shallum is listed as one of the Israelites who took foreign women as their wives while in Exile and later divorced them under Ezra's direction (*Ezra 10:42*).    S.C.

**SHALLUN** He is mentioned as one of those who helped to rebuild the walls of Jerusalem following the return of the Jews from Exile and during the time of Nehemiah. His father was Col-Hozeh and he was the ruler of the district of Mizpah. He was responsible for the 'Fountain Gate', its roof, doors and bolts. He also repaired the wall by the Pool of Siloam (*Neh. 3:15*).

**SHALMAI** A leader of one of the families of Temple servants. His descendants returned from the Babylonian Exile in the days of Ezra and worked on the Temple (*Ezra 2:46; Neh. 7:48*).

**SHALMAN** In *Hos. 10:14* Shalman is named as the king who devastated Beth Arbel in battle and destroyed even the women and children of the town. Exactly who he was is not clear, but he may have been an Assyrian king, Shalamaneser V. See *Shalmaneser*.

**SHALMANESER** (Assyr., 'Sulman [a god] is leader') was the Assyrian king whom God used to teach the Northern Kingdom about their disobedience to his ways. In approximately 730 BC Hoshea became the king of Israel and he did evil in the eyes of God. At first, Hoshea enjoyed a good relationship with Assyria through the paying of required taxes, but Shalmaneser V discovered that Hoshea had stopped paying taxes and was ruling deceitfully in Samaria. Shalmaneser took Hoshea captive and then invaded the land, marching against Samaria and beseiging it for three years. In Hoshea's ninth and final year of rule, Shalmaneser and his army captured Samaria and sent the Israelites into exile to Assyria. God made it clear to the Israelites that they were exiled for their sin, but still the Israelites refused to obey God and chose, instead, to practice their own forms of idolatry (*2 Kings 17*). See *Hoshea*.    S.C.

**SHAMA** (Heb., 'he has heard'). He and his brother Jeiel, sons of Hotham the Aroerite, belonged to David's 'Thirty' mighty men who went to battle for him and led the people of Israel to war (*1 Chron. 11:44*).

**SHAMGAR** was one of several 'judges' and deliverers mentioned in the book of Judges at a time in Israel's history when considerable anarchy reigned and regular attacks were made on the land by the surrounding peoples. Shamgar, the son of

Anath, followed Ehud who had brought a considerable time of peace to the land (*Judg. 3:31*). He was famed for killing 600 Philistines with an ox-goad. It was not until later that the main Philistine incursions seem to have taken place, so there is every possibility that this was one of the earliest encounters between the Philistines and Israelites. The anarchy of the period is mentioned in the Song of Deborah where it is said: 'In the days of Shamgar son of Anath, in the days of Jael, the roads were abandoned; travellers took to winding paths' (*Judg. 5:6*).    P.D.G.

**SHAMHUTH** the Izrahite, was one of David's army commanders. As a leader in David's army he was on duty with his men in the fifth month of each year and had 24,000 men in his division (*1 Chron. 27:8*). He might be the same as the person called Shammah in *2 Sam. 23:25* and Shammoth in the list of the 'Thirty' mighty men in *1 Chron. 11:27*.

**SHAMIR** (Heb., 'thorn'). A Levite, the son of Micah and the grandson of Kohath's fourth son, Uzziel (*1 Chron. 24:24*). He is mentioned in a section dealing with the division of Levitical labour in the Tabernacle during the reign of King David.

**SHAMMA** was one of the sons of Zophah and a leader in the tribe of Asher, renowned as an outstanding leader and a brave warrior (*1 Chron. 7:37*).

**SHAMMAH 1.** Esau's son was Reuel, father of Shammah. Shammah became an Edomite chief (*Gen. 36:13–17; 1 Chron. 1:37*).

**2.** Shammah was the third son of Jesse of Bethlehem and the father of Jonadab and Jonathan. Shammah was in Saul's army and he attended the meal when Samuel anointed David as king (*2 Sam. 13:3, 32; 21:21; 1 Chron. 20:7; 1 Sam. 16:9; 17:13*). Alternative spellings for this man's name include Shimeah (2 Sam. 13:3, 32; 21:21) and Shimea (1 Chron. 20:7).

**3.** Shammah was the third member of David's famous 'Three'. He is best known for his defeat of an entire Philistine raiding party. Shammah's son, Jonathan, was a member of David's 'Thirty' (2 Sam. 23:11–12; 1 Chron. 11:12–14).

**4.** David's 'Thirty' mighty men included Shammah. He commanded 24,000 men in the fifth month during his service for the king (2 Sam. 23:25; 1 Chron. 27:8). He might be the same as 3. above.

s.c.

**SHAMMAI 1.** Shammai, son of Onam and father of Nadab and Abishur, was a descendant of Jerahmeel (1 Chron. 2:28, 32).

**2.** Another Shammai is listed as one of Caleb's descendants (1 Chron. 2:44–45).

**3.** This Shammai was one of the children born to Mered, son of Ezrah, and his Egyptian wife (1 Chron. 4:17–18).   s.c.

**SHAMMOTH** the Harorite was one of David's 'Thirty' warriors (1 Chron. 11:27). See also Shamhuth, who may be the same person.

**SHAMMUA** (Heb., 'heard').

**1.** One of the twelve spies sent out by Moses from the Desert of Paran to spy out the land of Canaan (Num. 13:11; wrongly spelt Shammau in some editions of the NIV). A representative of each tribe was chosen and Shammua, the son of Zaccur, was from the tribe of Reuben (Num. 13:4). Their mission was to find out everything they could about the land: its inhabitants, their number, the extent of the fortifications, and the fertility of the soil (vv. 17–20). The twelve carried out their commission, bringing back enormous bunches of grapes and extolling the virtues of the land (v. 27). However, their report about the inhabitants was fearful.

The people were powerful and some of them were even giants, and the cities were well fortified (vv. 28–29). When Caleb (supported by Joshua) suggested that the land could certainly be taken, the other ten were horrified and the people rejected the idea and turned against Moses and the LORD (Num. 14:2–3). The LORD judged the people for their lack of trust and their rebellion by promising that only Caleb and Joshua of that whole generation would live to enter the land of Canaan, and thus began the 40 years of desert wanderings for the Israelites until all those like Shammua had died (vv. 20–38).

**2.** A son of King David. After David conquered Jerusalem and moved there from Hebron he took many wives and concubines. One of his children was Shammua (2 Sam. 5:14; 1 Chron. 3:5; 14:4). Shammua's mother was Bathsheba, daughter of Ammiel.

**3.** Shammua was a Levite and the father of Abda and son of Galal. Abda helped Nehemiah at the time of rebuilding the Temple in Jerusalem following return from the Babylonian Exile (Neh. 11:17).

**4.** This Shammua may have been the same as 3. above. He was the head of Bilgah's family, and helped in the service of the Temple during Nehemiah's time (Neh. 12:18).   p.d.g.

**SHAMSHERAI** A son of Jeroham and a clan leader. He was a Benjamite who lived in Jerusalem and is listed in the genealogy of King Saul (1 Chron. 8:26).

**SHAPHAM** was a Gadite who lived with his tribe in Bashan (1 Chron. 5:12).

**SHAPHAN** (Heb., 'rabbit').

**1.** Shaphan was the secretary during King Josiah's reign (2 Kings 22:3–13). When the Book of the Law was found, it was Shaphan who carried the book to the king.

**2.** When Ezekiel looked into the Temple, he saw 70 elders doing detestable things there. Jaazaniah, son of Shaphan, was one of the 70 (*Ezek. 8:7–13*).

**SHAPHAT** (Heb., 'judged').

**1.** One of the twelve spies sent out by Moses from the Desert of Paran to spy out the land of Canaan (*Num. 13:5*). A representative of each tribe was chosen and Shaphat, the son of Hori, was from the tribe of Simeon. For further detail on their mission see *Shammua*.

**2.** The father of the great prophet Elisha who came from Abel Meholah. Elijah was ordered to anoint Elisha son of Shaphat as his successor. Elisha then left his father and mother and followed Elijah (*1 Kings 19:16, 19; 2 Kings 3:11; 6:31*).

**3.** Mentioned in *1 Chron. 3:22* as a descendant of Shecaniah and son of Shemaiah. He was one of the royal line from Jehoiachin following the Exile.

**4.** A Gadite clan leader who lived in Bashan (*1 Chron. 5:12*).

**5.** Son of Adlai, this Shaphat was an overseer during the reign of King David. He was in charge 'of the herds in the valleys' (*1 Chron. 27:29*).

**SHARAI** was among the descendants of Binnui. At the time of return from the Exile in Babylon, Shecaniah confessed to Ezra that many men and even descendants of the priests of Judah had married wives from other tribes and nations. Ezra and the people repented and made a covenant to serve the LORD (*Ezra 10:2*). Sharai is listed in *Ezra 10:40* as one who divorced his foreign wife.

**SHARAR** Known as 'the Hararite', he was the father of Ahiam, one of David's 'Thirty' warriors, a 'mighty man' in battle (*2 Sam. 23:33*). His name is spelled Sacar in *1 Chron. 11:35*.

**SHAREZER** (Assyr., 'protect the king').

**1.** This Sharezer was a son of Sennacherib and a prince of Assyria who, with his brother Adrammelech, assassinated his father in 681 BC. He then escaped to the land of Ararat (*2 Kings 19:37; Is. 37:38*).

**2.** Because of certain grammatical features this name is thought by some to be Beth-el-Sharezer. This Sharezer was a contemporary of Zechariah who formed part of a delegation to the priests at Jerusalem from the people of Bethel. They were asking whether they really needed to fast in the fifth month of each year as they had done while in Babylon. The fast was originally designed to remember the destruction of Jerusalem (*Zech. 7:2–3*). The LORD's response through the prophet was that the fast had never really been kept for the sake of the LORD, and that what he really desired of his people was justice and mercy (*vv. 9–10*). E.M.

**SHASHAI** was among the descendants of Binnui. At the time of return from the Exile in Babylon, Shecaniah confessed to Ezra that many men and even descendants of the priests of Judah had married wives from other tribes and nations. Ezra and the people repented and made a covenant to serve the LORD (*Ezra 10:2*). Shashai is listed in *Ezra 10:40* as one who divorced his foreign wife.

**SHASHAK** One of the sons of Beriah and a leader from the tribe of Benjamin, Shashak lived in Aijalon and had eleven sons. He is listed in the Benjamite genealogy leading to King Saul (*1 Chron. 8:14, 25*).

**SHAUL** (Heb., 'asked').

**1.** One of the kings of Edom before the Israelites conquered the area. He succeeded Samlah and came from 'Rehoboth on the river'. Baal-Hanan son of Acbor followed him as king (*Gen. 36:37–38; 1 Chron. 1:48–49*).

**2.** The sixth son of Simeon and listed among those who went to Egypt with Jacob his grandfather. He was the leader of the Shaulite clan (*Gen. 46:10; Exod. 6:15; Num. 26:13; 1 Chron. 4:24*).

**3.** A descendant of Kohath and a Levite, this Shaul was the son of Uzziah (*1 Chron. 6:24*).

**SHAVSHA** was a secretary in the court of King David and one of his senior officials (*1 Chron. 18:16*). His name is probably mis-spelled as Seraiah in *2 Sam. 8:17*, as Sheva in *2 Sam. 20:25* and as Shisha in *1 Kings 4:3*. It is possible that Shavsha was not an Israelite, but he seems to have served David well, since his sons were later given the same appointment under Solomon. The list of court officials in *1 Chron. 18:16* gives an indication of the increasing amount of administration as the monarchy stabilized and had more contact with other countries.

**SHEAL** was among the descendants of Binnui. At the time of return from the Exile in Babylon, Shecaniah confessed to Ezra that many men and even descendants of the priests of Judah had married wives from other tribes and nations. Ezra and the people repented and made a covenant to serve the LORD (*Ezra 10:2*). Sheal is listed in *Ezra 10:29* as one who divorced his foreign wife.

**SHEALTIEL** (Heb., 'shield of God') was the father of Zerubbabel who led the people back from the captivity in Babylon to Jerusalem. He was the eldest son of Jehoiachin (Jeconiah) king of Judah (*1 Chron. 3:17; Ezra 3:2, 8; 5:2; Neh. 12:1; Hag. 1:1, 12, 14; 2:2, 23*). Zerubbabel became the governor of Judah following the return from Exile. In *1 Chron. 3:19* it is stated that Pedaiah, Shealtiel's brother was the father of Zerubbabel. It is possible that a levirate marriage gave rise to this difference between the accounts. He is mentioned in both of the NT genealogies that establish the lineage of the Messiah (*Matt. 1:12; Luke 3:27*).

**SHEAR-JASHUB** (Heb., 'a remnant will return'). This was the symbolic name given to one of Isaiah's sons (*Is. 7:3*). The LORD told Isaiah to take his son with him to meet Ahaz, king of Judah, and give him a message. The message challenged Ahaz to have faith in God while being threatened by a coalition of armies of Israel and Syria to the north. However, the LORD reminded Ahaz that if he trusted in him he would be saved. This coalition would be defeated by Assyria. The name of the child is therefore full of hope in the midst of a depressing series of prophecies. Even though judgment would be inevitable, yet the LORD would ensure that a remnant returned from the foreign lands to which they were transported.

This early mention of a 'remnant' became an important theological theme in the book of Isaiah. It began in *Is. 1:9* where there was talk of at least 'some survivors' being left, but the judgment on God's people was inevitable for their sin' and idolatrous lifestyle (*Is. 2:6–8*). It was to be extensive (*Is. 6:11–13*) and yet still, where the people had faith in the LORD he would save (*Is. 10:20–23; 11:11–16*). Faith was the key element in defining the remnant as becomes clear in the incident with Shear-Jashub. There Isaiah's message was: 'If you do not stand firm in your faith, you will not stand at all' (*Is. 7:9*; see *8:17*). If they had faith, God would, after all, remain faithful to his people and save the remnant.

Looking forward in the time of Hezekiah to judgment on the Southern Kingdom, Isaiah still always spoke with an element of hope for the future in terms of a remnant surviving (*Is. 37:4, 31–32*). Still later, looking forward to the Babylonian conquest, Isaiah preached to 'all you who remain of the house of Israel'. The fact that some remained after such serious judgment was an indication that God had sustained them and rescued them (Is. 46:3–4). Isaiah, however, also broadened the number who were left to include some non-Israelites (Is. 45:20) and at the end of his prophecy looked forward to the great eschatological hope in which other nations would be drawn in to God's people (Is. 66:19–21). It is this concept that the apostle Paul later built upon in Rom. 9–11). Isaiah's days were over but much of his prophecy had been fulfilled. Many Israelites had not shown faith but some had faith in Christ. These, together with those of faith from many other nations, had thus revealed the truth of the 'remnant' prophecy.                              P. D. G.

**SHEARIAH** A Benjamite and the fourth of six sons of Azel (1 Chron. 8:38; 9:44). He was a descendant of King Saul.

**SHEBA 1.** Sheba is listed as one of the descendants of Ham (Gen. 10:7; 1 Chron. 1:9).

**2.** Sheba, the son of Joktan, was also the name given to one of Shem's descendants (Gen. 10:28; 1 Chron. 1:22).

**3.** This Sheba is listed as a grandson of Abraham and Keturah (Gen. 25:1–4; 1 Chron. 1:32).

**4.** Sheba was a Gadite descendant, as recorded in 1 Chron. 5:13.

**5.** Sheba, a Benjamite of the hill country, rebelled against David and literally lost his head when Joab besieged the city in which he took refuge. The men decapitated Sheba and handed him over to David's commander-in-chief (2 Sam. 20:1–26).

**6.** Also see Queen of Sheba.       S.C.

**SHEBANIAH 1.** Shebaniah was chosen as one of the priests who would blow his trumpet before the ark of the LORD during David's reign (1 Chron. 15:24).

**2.** Neh. 9:4–5 names Shebaniah as one of the Levites who led the people in worship after Ezra's reading of the Law. It is likely that this is the same Shebaniah that signed the covenant agreement between the people and the LORD that they would obey only his Law and worship only him (Neh. 10:10).

**3.** Neh. 10:4 records a third Shebaniah who sealed this agreement.

**4.** Neh. 10:12 records another Shebaniah who sealed this agreement.       S.C.

**SHEBER** A son of Caleb the brother of Jarahmeel and his concubine Maacah. He was from the tribe of Judah (1 Chron. 2:48).

**SHEBNA** was secretary to King Hezekiah when Sennacharib threatened those living in Judah with captivity or death. Shebna was one of the three sent first to communicate with Sennacharib and then with Isaiah. Isaiah assured the messengers that Sennacharib would not defeat Hezekiah's army. In fact, Sennacharib would flee and be killed in his own country (2 Kings 18–19). Sennacharib's death occurred just as God prophesied through Isaiah.

Isaiah prophesied against this Shebna for cutting out a grave for himself from rock and thus making himself out to be a very important leader of Judah. Such arrogance would be judged by God and indeed he was never buried in the grave but died in Exile. The LORD put Eliakim in his place (Is. 22:15–24).       S.C.

**SHECANIAH** (Heb., 'the LORD dwells').

**1.** Shecaniah is listed as one of the descendants of Zerubbabel and in the line of King David (1 Chron. 3:21–22).

**2.** 2 Chron. 31:14–15 records Shecaniah as one of the priests during Hezekiah's reign who assisted Kore the Levite in the distribution of freewill offerings.

**3.** Ezra 8:3 lists Shecaniah as one of the

family heads who came up from Babylon with Ezra during the reign of King Artaxerxes.

**4.** *Ezra 8:5* lists another Shecaniah, son of Jahaziel, as one of the family heads who came up from Babylon with Ezra during the reign of King Artaxerxes.

**5.** *Neh. 12:3* names another Shecaniah as a priest who returned with Zerubbabel from Babylonian Exile.

**6.** This Shecaniah was a priest who served in the Tabernacle during David's rule. He was responsible for the tenth turn of service (*1 Chron. 24:11*).

**7.** While Ezra was praying and confessing the sins of the people, Shecaniah, son of Jehiel, confessed his own sin and that of other Israelite leaders – they had married foreign women during the Exile (*Ezra 10:1–4*).

**8.** *Neh. 3:29* records that Shecaniah's son, Shemaiah, helped to repair the wall of Jerusalem following the return from Babylon.

**9.** This Shecaniah was Tobiah the Ammonite's father-in-law (*Neh. 6:18*).

S. C.

**SHECHEM** (Heb., 'shoulder').

**1.** Shechem was a son of Hamor, a Hivite. Jacob had purchased a plot of land outside the city of Shechem from Hamor's sons where he had set up an altar to the 'God of Israel' (*Gen. 33:19–20; Josh. 24:32; Judg. 9:28*). Later Shechem caught sight of Dinah, daughter of Jacob and Leah, and fell in love with her. He took her away and raped her (*Gen. 34:2*). Later he asked his father Hamor to acquire this young woman as his wife (*v. 4*). When Jacob's sons returned from the fields and heard what had happened they were very angry and planned their revenge (*vv. 7, 13*). They pretended to go along with Shechem's request. Shechem offered anything he could give in order to marry Dinah (*v. 11*). So Jacob's sons demanded that all the males in Shechem should be circumcised. They agreed to go through

with this (*vv. 18, 24*) and while they 'were still in pain . . . Simeon and Levi, Dinah's brothers, took their swords and attacked the unsuspecting city, killing every male' (*v. 25*).

When the elderly Jacob came to bless his sons, he recalled this incident of extreme violence, anger and revenge. He cursed their anger and promised that they would be scattered and dispersed in Israel (*Gen. 49:7*). Revenge, in Scripture, always belongs to the LORD and whatever the circumstances it should not have been carried out in this way. The events recounted concerning Hamor and Shechem and their extended family point forward to the lasting problems that the Israelites had with the Canaanites.

**2.** A descendant of Joseph through Manasseh and founder of the Shechemite clan (*Num. 26:31; Josh. 17:2*). Possibly the same as 3. below.

**3.** A leader of the tribe of Manasseh, and one of the sons of Shemida (*1 Chron. 7:19*). P.D.G.

**SHEDEUR** (Heb., 'the Almighty is fire') was the father of Elizur, who was the leader of the people of Reuben at the census of the Israelites in the wilderness of Sinai. Elizur's division of people numbered 46,500 (*Num. 1:5; 2:10*). As the representative of his tribe Elizur also brought his tribe's fellowship offering when the Tabernacle was dedicated in the wilderness (*Num. 7:30, 35*) and led his tribe when the Israelites set out from the Sinai desert on their wanderings (*Num. 10:18*).

**SHEERAH** The daughter of Ephraim. She built Lower and Upper Beth Horon and Uzzen Sheerah (*1 Chron. 7:24*).

**SHEHARIAH** A son of Jeroham and a clan leader. He was a Benjamite who lived in Jerusalem and is listed in the genealogy of King Saul (*1 Chron. 8:26*).

**SHELAH** **1.** His father was Arphaxad and he was a grandson of Shem (*Gen. 10:24; 1 Chron. 1:18, 24*). At the age of 30 he became the father of Eber (*Gen. 11:12–15; 1 Chron. 2:3; 4:21*). Shelah is also listed in Luke's genealogy leading from Jesus to Adam (*Luke 3:35*).

**2.** Born at Kezib, this Shelah was a son of Judah and Shua, a Canaanite woman. After Judah's son Er had died as a judgment from God on his sin, Judah promised Tamar, Er's widow, that she could marry Shelah when he grew up. Judah failed to fulfil his promise (*Gen. 38:5, 11, 14, 26*). For more detail see *Tamar.* Later Shelah was listed with Jacob, his grandfather, and other members of the family who went down to Egypt (*Gen. 46:12*). He became the father of the Shelanite clan (*Num. 26:20; Neh. 11:5*). P.D.G.

**SHELEMIAH** (Heb., 'the LORD has restored').

**1.** A gatekeeper, Shelemiah was given responsibility for the East Gate during King David's reign (*1 Chron. 26:14*). This is the same man as 'Meshelemiah' listed in *v. 1.*

**2.** Shelemiah was the son of Cushi and ancestor of Jehudi, the young man who read Jeremiah's scroll to King Jehoiakim (*Jer. 36:14*).

**3.** The son of Abdeel, Shelemiah was one of three men sent to arrest Baruch and Jeremiah after the reading of Jeremiah's scroll to King Jehoiakim (*Jer. 36:26ff.*).

**4.** This Shelemiah was the son of Hananiah and the father of Irijah (*Jer. 37:13*).

**5.** Shelemiah was the father of Jehucal. Jehucal was one of the leaders of Judah who, heaving heard Jeremiah's prophecy of doom, believed he ought to be killed (*Jer. 38:1*).

**6.** Shelemiah, a descendant of Binnui, is listed as one who took a foreign wife after the Exile and then divorced her under Ezra's direction (*Ezra 10:39*).

**7.** This Shelemiah is also listed in *Ezra 10:41* as another descendant of Binnui who had a foreign wife.

**8.** Shelemiah was the father of Hananiah. Hananiah helped in rebuilding the walls of Jerusalem following the Exile in Babylon (*Neh. 3:30*).

**9.** Shelemiah was a priest appointed by Nehemiah to be in charge of the distribution of offerings among the Levites (*Neh. 13:13*). S.C.

**SHELEPH** Listed in both *Gen. 10:26* and *1 Chron. 1:20* as a descendant of Shem, his father was Joktan. His name gave rise to an Arabian tribe that possibly settled in what is today the Yemen.

**SHELESH** A tribal leader and a descendant of Asher, he was the son of Helem (*1 Chron. 7:35*).

**SHELOMI** (Heb., 'peace') was the father of Ahihud. Ahihud was chosen to be the leader of the tribe of Asher, and it was his duty to allocate the Asherite territory in Canaan to the various clans (*Num. 34:27*).

**SHELOMITH** (Heb., 'peace').

**1.** *Lev. 24:11* names Shelomith as the mother of a man who blasphemed the name of the LORD and was stoned by the entire Israelite assembly. She was from the tribe of Dan and was the daughter of Dibri.

**2.** Shelomith and his relatives were given responsibility for the care of all the treasures of David's kingdom (*1 Chron. 26:20–28*).

**3.** In *2 Chron. 11:20* another Shelomith is named as a child of Rehoboam and Maacah.

**4.** Another Shelomith was Zerubbabel's daughter (*1 Chron. 3:19*).

**5.** This Shelomith is listed as the first son of Izhar in *1 Chron. 23:18* (this is probably the same man who is called Shelomoth in *1 Chron. 24:22*).

**6.** Shelomith is listed as son of Josiphiah and a descendant of Bani. He was the leader of a family that returned with Ezra from Babylon (*Ezra 8:10*). S.C.

**SHELOMOTH** (Heb., 'peace').

**1.** *1 Chron. 23:9* lists Shelomoth, son of Shimei, as a Levite belonging to the family of Gershon. He served in the Tabernacle during the reign of King David and was the head of a 'family of Ladan'.

**2.** Shelomoth is named as a Levite from the Izharite family. He had a son called Jahath (*1 Chron. 23:22*).

**SHELUMIEL** (Heb., 'God is peace'). The son of Zurishaddai and the leader of the people of Simeon at the census of the Israelites in the wilderness of Sinai. Shelumiel's division of people numbered 59,300 (*Num. 1:6; 2:12*). As the representative of his tribe he also brought his tribe's fellowship offering when the Tabernacle was dedicated in the wilderness (*Num. 7:36, 41*). The enormous offering from this tribe was brought on the fifth day. He also led his tribe when the Israelites set out from the Sinai desert on their wanderings (*Num. 10:19*).

**SHEM** was the first son of Noah (*Gen. 5:32; 6:10; 1 Chron. 4:1, 17*). He and his wife joined Noah on the ark during the great Flood (*7:13; 9:18*). The main incident in Shem's life recorded in Scripture is found in *Gen. 9:18–26*. In spite of the destruction of evil people in the Flood and the apparently good beginnings of a new life for Noah, the heart of man remained evil. Noah was found drunk and naked in his tent. Ham, another of Noah's sons, appears to have exploited the situation, though the text does not make it clear exactly what his sin was. When he went and told Shem and Japheth, his brothers, they came into the tent, walked in backwards and laid a garment over their father 'so that they would not see their father's nakedness' (*Gen. 9:23*).

This action led to a great blessing on Shem from his elderly father Noah, while Ham was cursed. Shem, who lived around 600 years, became the ancestor of the semites and those who spoke Semitic languages (*Gen. 10:22–31*) while Ham was the ancestor of the Canaanites. Shem also became an ancestor of God's special people and heads the genealogy that introduces Terah, the father of Abraham, in *Gen. 11:10–32*. In *Luke 3:36* he is mentioned in the genealogy of Jesus.

P. D. G.

**SHEMA** (Heb., 'he has heard').

**1.** A leader in the tribe of Judah and a son of Hebron. He was the father of Raham (*1 Chron. 2:43–44*).

**2.** The father of Azaz, a Reubenite. His family settled in Aroer. In Saul's reign, his descendants were responsible for the defeat of the Hagrites. They took possession of land to the east of Gilead because they were so prosperous, and even as far as the Euphrates (*1 Chron. 5:8–10*).

**3.** Mentioned in *1 Chron. 8:13* as a descendant of Benjamin and a son of Elpaal, he was the head of families living in Aijalon and is credited with driving out the inhabitants of Gath.

**4.** This Shema was among those who stood on Ezra's right-hand side on a high wooden platform as he read the Book of the Law to the people of Israel. As the Law was read the people worshipped and praised God, confessed their sin, and recommitted themselves to the LORD's service (*Neh. 8:4*).

**SHEMAAH** was a Gibeathite and the father of Ahiezer and Joash. These two sons were leaders among the warriors who deserted Saul to join David at Ziklag. They were ambidextrous in archery and with slings and from the tribe of Benjamin (*1 Chron. 12:3*).

**SHEMAIAH** (Heb., 'the LORD hears').

**1.** Shemaiah is listed as a valiant leader of his clan and a descendant of Simeon (*1 Chron. 4:37*).

**2.** A descendant of Joel, Shemaiah is listed as one of the members of Reuben's tribe (*1 Chron. 5:4*).

**3.** This Shemaiah was head of one of the Levite families chosen by David to bring the ark to Jerusalem (*1 Chron. 15:8, 11*).

**4.** Shemaiah, the oldest son of Obed-Edom, was a Levite and the father of strong and hard-working sons (*1 Chron. 26:4–7*).

**5.** Another Shemaiah was a prophet during the reign of Rehoboam (*1 Kings 12:22; 2 Chron. 11:2*). He warned King Rehoboam not to attack Jeroboam who was beginning to rule the ten northern tribes. Through him the LORD reminded Rehoboam and the people of Judah that this division of the kingdom was the LORD's own doing (*1 Kings 12:24*). They obeyed the word of the LORD and there was no war between the divided kingdoms. In *2 Chron. 12:5* it is further recorded that Shemaiah came to Rehoboam to inform him that, since he had abandoned the LORD, the LORD would now abandon him and his people to Pharaoh Shishak. At this the leaders repented. The LORD responded by not judging Jerusalem, although the nation did become a vassal to Egypt and the treasures of the Temple were taken to Egypt by the Pharaoh (*vv. 9–11*). V. 15 says that the prophet was also involved in writing up records of the king's reign.

**6.** *2 Chron. 17:8* lists this man as one of nine Levites sent by Jehoshaphat to teach the Law in the towns of Judah.

**7.** A Levite in the family of Juduthun, Shemaiah was one of 14 Levites who played a role in purifying the Temple during the revival in King Hezekiah's reign in Judah (*2 Chron. 29:14*).

**8.** Another Shemaiah was a member of a commission of Levites and priests who distributed tithes and offerings to the families of the priests during King Hezekiah's reign (*2 Chron. 31:14–18*).

**9.** Shemaiah was one of six sons of Shecaniah in a list of the descendants of King David who lived after the Babylonian Exile (*1 Chron. 3:21–22*).

**10.** This Shemaiah is listed as the father of Uriah, the prophet (*Jer. 26:20*). Uriah spoke against Jerusalem in the days of King Jehoiakim.

**11.** A leader in Babylon, Shemaiah the Nehelamite was a false prophet who prophesied in the captivity in Babylon. He spoke against Jeremiah who had prophesied that the stay in Babylon would be lengthy. Jeremiah's response was to prophesy that Shemaiah and his family would die in captivity, never having returned to Judah (*Jer. 29:24–27*).

**12.** Shemaiah's son, Delaiah, was an official during Jehoiakim's reign and heard the reading by Baruch of Jeremiah's prophecy. He later witnessed the burning of the scroll that contained the prophecy (*Jer. 36:12*).

**13.** Shemaiah, son of Hasshub, is listed as a Levite resident of Jerusalem after the Exile (*1 Chron. 9:14; Neh. 11:15*).

**14.** This Shemaiah, son of Galal, is also listed as a Levite who returned to Jerusalem after the Exile (*1 Chron. 9:16; Shammua in Neh. 11:17*). He was the father of Obadiah.

**15.** One of the leaders of the Levites, Shemaiah helped provide 5,000 offerings and 500 head of cattle for the celebration of Passover during Josiah's reign (*2 Chron. 35:9*).

**16.** Shemaiah is listed as one who returned from the Exile with Ezra (*Ezra 8:13*). He was a descendant of Adonikam.

**17.** Shemaiah, a descendant of Harim, is listed as one of the priests who took a foreign wife after the return from Exile. Under Ezra's direction he decided to divorce her (*Ezra 10:21*).

**18.** This Shemaiah is also listed as one

who took a foreign wife after the return from Exile (*Ezra 10:31*).

**19.** Shemaiah, son of Shecaniah, is listed as one who helped repair the wall of Jerusalem after the return from Exile (*Neh. 3:29*).

**20.** Shemaiah, son of Delaiah, was hired by Sanballat and Tobiah to fill Nehemiah with fear in the hope of intimidating him into ceasing to rebuild the wall of Jerusalem (*Neh. 6:10*).

**21.** Shemaiah was a member of a family of priests. He signed the recommitment agreement offered to the LORD by those who returned from Exile (*Neh. 10:8; 12:6, 18*).

**22.** Shemaiah was a Levite who joined in the musical celebration during the dedication of the Jerusalem wall (*Neh. 12:34*). Possibly the same as 21. above.

**23.** This Shemaiah was the grandfather of Zechariah who is listed as one who joined in the musical celebration during the dedication of the Jerusalem wall in Nehemiah's time (*Neh. 12:35*).

**24.** Shemaiah is listed as a musician during the celebration at the completion of the rebuilding work on the walls of Jerusalem. Ezra led the procession (*Neh. 12:36*).

**25.** Shemaiah is listed as a Levite musician who took his place with Nehemiah in the Temple during the dedication of the Jerusalem wall (*Neh. 12:42*). This Shemaiah could be any of 22., 23. or 24. above.   s.c.

**SHEMARIAH** (Heb., 'the LORD has preserved').

**1.** Shemariah is named as a Benjamite warrior who joined David at Ziklag (*1 Chron. 12:5*).

**2.** This Shemariah was one of three sons born to Rehoboam and Mahalath (*2 Chron. 11:18–19*).

**3.** Another Shemariah, son of Harim, is listed as one of the Israelites who had a foreign wife after the Exile in Babylon.

Under Ezra's direction he later divorced her (*Ezra 10:32*).

**4.** Shemariah, son of Binnui, is also listed as one of the Israelites who had married a foreign wife (*Ezra 10:41*).   s.c.

**SHEMEBER** One of five kings resident in the Jordan valley when Abraham was living near 'the great trees of Mamre'. He was king of Zeboiim (*Gen. 14:2*). Following their defeat at the hands of a coalition of Mesopotamian kings, these city kings were subjugated for 13 years until they finally rebelled (*v. 8*). Their rebellion was put down by the four kings led by Kedorlaomer. For more details see *Amraphel*.

Their defeat involved the seizure of the people of Sodom and Gomorrah (*v. 11*). In the defeat of Gomorrah all their goods and food were taken. Because Lot (a resident of Sodom) was captured, Abra(ha)m entered the battle. He chased Kedorlaomer north and eventually defeated him in battle, bringing Lot back with him and recovering all the spoil.

P.D.G.

**SHEMED** One of the sons of Elpaal and a leader from the tribe of Benjamin, Shemed lived in Aijalon and helped build Ono and Lod (*1 Chron. 8:12*).

**SHEMER** (Heb., 'watch').

**1.** Shemer, son of Mahli, was a Levite from the Merari clan and the father of Bani. His descendant, Ethan, served as a Temple musician in the days of King David (*1 Chron. 6:46*).

**2.** The owner of the hill on which King Omri founded the city of Samaria. Omri bought the hill from Shemer for two talents of silver and called the town after Shemer. The Heb. word for the city means 'belonging to Shemer' (*1 Kings 16:24*).

**SHEMIDA** A chief from the tribe of Manasseh, descended through Gilead, who became leader of the Shemidaite clan (*Num. 26:32*). In *Josh. 17:2–3* his clan received its allotment of the land of Canaan. His sons are listed in *1 Chron. 7:19*.

**SHEMIRAMOTH 1.** After the ark of the covenant had been brought to Jerusalem, the worship of God was properly organized by King David. Shemiramoth was appointed one of the musicians, and was to play the harp and lyre before the ark. He was among a group of Levites who were the gatekeepers at the Tabernacle (*1 Chron. 15:18, 20; 16:5*).

**2.** Another Levite, this Shemiramoth lived in the days of King Jehoshaphat of Judah. During the early years of his reign Jehoshaphat served the LORD and sent out various teachers and Levites to teach the people of Judah the Book of the Law. Shemiramoth was one of those teachers (*2 Chron. 17:8*).

**SHEMUEL** (Heb., 'heard by God'). Shemuel son of Ammihud was named by the LORD as one to be chosen by Moses as the leader of the tribe of Simeon. His duty was to organize the allocation of the Simeonite territory to the various clans and families following the conquest of Canaan (*Num. 34:20*).

**SHENAZZAR** ('Sin [the moon god] protects') is listed among the descendants of King Jehoiachin and is thus part of David's royal line. He seems to have returned after the Exile in Babylon (*1 Chron. 3:18*) and is probably to be identified with Sheshbazzar (*Ezra 1:8; 5:14*).

**SHEPHATIAH** (Heb., 'the LORD has judged').
**1.** Shephatiah was the fifth son born to David at Hebron by his wife Abital (*2 Sam. 3:4; 1 Chron. 3:3*).
**2.** Shephatiah, a Haruphite, was one of the mighty warriors of Benjamin who joined David at Ziklag (*1 Chron. 12:5*).

**3.** This Shephatiah, son of Maacah, was an officer over the tribe of Simeon during David's reign (*1 Chron. 27:16*).
**4.** Another Shephatiah was brother to King Jehoram and son of King Jehoshaphat. He was later killed by Jehoram (*2 Chron. 21:2*).
**5.** In *Jer. 38:1–5*, we meet a Shephatiah who was one of the king's advisers and recommended putting Jeremiah to death. He was responsible for putting Jeremiah into the cistern where he was kept prisoner for a while.
**6.** Shephatiah, descendant of Parosh, is listed as the head of one of the exiled families who returned to Jerusalem with Nehemiah (*Ezra 2:4; 8:8; Neh. 7:9*).
**7.** This Shephatiah, who was descended from one of Solomon's servants, is listed as a member of one of the families who returned to Jerusalem with Nehemiah (*Ezra 2:57; Neh. 7:59*).
**8.** This Shephatiah was the father of Meshullam, who was among the first of the Benjamites who resettled in Jerusalem after the Exile in Babylon (*1 Chron. 9:8*).
**9.** In *Neh. 11:3–4* Shephatiah, a descendant of Judah, is listed as one who settled in Jerusalem after the Exile.  s.c.

**SHEPHO** A descendant of Esau, Shepho was the son of Shobal, a clan leader of the Edomites (*Gen. 36:23; 1 Chron. 1:40*).

**SHEPHUPHAN** (Heb., 'serpent'). A son of Bela, son of Benjamin, listed in the genealogy of King Saul (*1 Chron. 8:5*). This individual's name may appear in other lists in a different form. For example, a listing of Bela's sons in *Num. 26:39* gives the name Shupham from whom is derived the Shuphamite clan. A reference to the Shuppites in *1 Chron. 7:12* may have in mind the same clan.

**SHEREBIAH** (Heb., 'the LORD sent burning heat'). This Levite from the descendants of Mahli was considered a 'capable man' by Ezra (*Ezra 8:18*). Ezra was concerned that in returning to Jerusalem from the Exile in Babylon there were no Levites travelling with them. He saw it as the 'gracious hand of God' that Sherebiah and his 18 sons should come forward with various others and offer themselves for this service. Ezra committed to Sherebiah and others the responsibility for carrying back to Jerusalem the offerings of the people in Exile for the Temple (*v. 24*). They also took offerings of great value in silver and gold from the king. All was delivered safely to Jerusalem where the people then offered sacrifices to the LORD (*vv. 33–36*).

Later, it is probably the same Sherebiah who is mentioned as one of the Levites who 'instructed the people in the Law' in Jerusalem, who encouraged the people to worship and confess their sins, and who joined in witnessing the solemn covenant of obedience to the Law of God (*Neh. 8:7; 9:4–5; 10:12; 12:8, 24*).     P.D.G.

**SHERESH** was a descendant of Manasseh and a leader in that tribe. He was a son of Makir and his wife Maacah (*1 Chron. 7:16*).

**SHESHAI** One of three notorious descendants of Anak who lived in Hebron at the time of the conquest of Canaan by Joshua. Caleb led the attack against Hebron, defeating these three giants in battle. As a result he and his family inherited this part of the land of Canaan (*Num. 13:22; Josh. 15:14; Judg. 1:10*). It is particularly interesting to note how the LORD blessed Caleb in this conquest. It had been he and Joshua alone who had originally returned to Moses after spying out the land of Canaan and who had trusted the LORD sufficiently to believe that such giants could in fact be defeated. His faith was seen to be well-placed and his rewards for that faith were considerable (*Num. 13:30; 14:24*).     P.D.G.

**SHESHAN** was from the tribe of Judah and a descendant of Jerahmeel. He was the father of Ahlai and son of Ishi and a leader in his tribe. Sheshan had only daughters and no sons to his name. He gave his daughter in marriage to his Egyptian servant Jarha (*1 Chron. 2:34–35*). She then had a son called Attai (perhaps the same as Ahlai in *v. 31*), thus giving her father a son to carry on his name. The inclusion of this part of the lineage helps establish the tribal credentials of Elishama (*v. 41*).

**SHESHBAZZAR** is called 'the prince of Judah' in *Ezra 1:8* and is credited with leading the first group of returnees from Exile back to Jerusalem. King Cyrus of Persia gave him custody of the articles and vessels that had originally come from the Temple at Jerusalem so that he could take them back with him. The inventory of these valuable items for which he was responsible is given in *Ezra 1:9–11*. Sheshbazzar then helped lay the 'foundations of the house of God in Jerusalem' (*Ezra 5:14–16*).

There has been some considerable debate as to whether Sheshbazzar can be identified with Zerubbabel who was called 'governor of Judah' (*Hag. 1:1*) and who was also involved in laying the foundations of the temple (*Ezra 3:2, 10*). However, it seems more likely that Sheshbazzar is to be identified with Shenazzar who was one of King Jehoiachin's sons and therefore an uncle to Zerubbabel (*1 Chron. 3:18*). It is quite possible, since his name seems to disappear early on in the narrative, that Sheshbazzar died after a short while in Jerusalem and Zerubbabel took over the work.

This return to Jerusalem from Babylon had been prophesied by Isaiah and the work of Cyrus in this regard had been mentioned (*Is. 45:1–13*). The fulfilment of prophecy and the faithfulness of the covenant LORD to his people was clearly seen in their return to Jerusalem. Thus, when the first foundation stones of the Temple had been laid, the people sang a song to the LORD: 'He is good; his love to Israel endures for ever' (Ezra 3:11).

P. D. G.

**SHETHAR** A wise man and legal expert consulted by King Xerxes (Est. 1:14). For detail see Memucan.

**SHETHAR-BOZENAI** was an associate of Tattenai governor of Transeuphrates at the time of King Darius of Persia. The return of the Jews to Jerusalem from their captivity in Babylon came under the oversight of these Persian officials (Ezra 5:3). When they saw what was happening in Jerusalem, they questioned the returnees, whose response is recorded in Ezra 5:11–17. The two officials then wrote to King Darius asking whether Zerubbabel and his people genuinely had permission to rebuild the Temple. Darius found the original decree signed by Cyrus and ordered that the officials not interfere with 'the work on this temple of God' (Ezra 6:6–7). Indeed he did much more than this, for Darius ordered Tattenai and Shethar-bozenai to pay for the work out of the royal treasury. They were even to pay for animals for the sacrifices (vv. 8–12). The two officials and their associates then set about helping the Jews with the building work and carried out Darius' orders 'with dilegence' (v. 13).

As the work continued, the book of Ezra notes how the LORD helped at each stage of the work and how thanks continued to be given by the people for the way his providence was seen even in events that were under the authority of the rulers back in Persia.

P. D. G.

**SHEVA 1.** A son of Caleb the brother of Jerahmeel and his concubine Maacah, he was the 'father' of Macbenah and Gibea.

This may mean he was the founder of towns by those names (1 Chron. 2:49)

**2.** Sheva was a secretary in the court of David and one of David's senior officials (2 Sam. 20:25). His name is probably mis-spelled as Seraiah in 2 Sam. 8:17, and as Shisha in 1 Kings 4:3. See Shavsha for more detail, as that is likely to be the original name (1 Chron. 18:16).

**SHILHI** was the father of Azubah, the mother of King Jehoshaphat of Judah (1 Kings 22:42; 2 Chron. 20:31).

**SHILLEM** The fourth son of Naphtali and the head of the Shillemite clan (Num. 26:49; 1 Chron. 7:13). He is listed among those who went to Egypt with Jacob (Gen. 46:24).

**SHILSHAH** was one of the sons of Zophah and a leader in the tribe of Asher (1 Chron. 7:37).

**SHIMEA** (Heb., 'he has heard').

**1.** The third son of Jesse and a brother to King David. Shimea's son, Jonathan, was later credited with killing a giant descended from Rapha (1 Chron. 20:7). For more detail see another spelling of his name: Shimeah.

**2.** A Levite from the Merarite clan whose father was Uzzah and whose son was Haggiah (1 Chron. 6:30).

**3.** A Levite from the Gershonite clan and the grandfather of Asaph. Asaph was one of the leading musicians during the reign of King David (1 Chron. 6:39).

**SHIMEAH** (Heb., 'he has heard').

**1.** The third son of Jesse and a brother of King David (also called Shimea: 1 Chron. 20:7 where his son Jonathan was credited with slaying a giant, also 2 Sam. 21:21. Also called Shammah in 1 Sam. 17:13 where he served King Saul in the army). Shimeah's son, Jonadab, was a friend of Amnon who had fallen in love with Absalom's sister, Tamar. Jonadab encouraged Amnon in his rape of and incest with Tamar (2 Sam. 13:3, 32).

**2.** Son of Mikloth, this Shimeah is listed in the Benjamite genealogy of King Saul (1 Chron. 8:32.) In 1 Chron. 9:38 he is called Shimeam. He lived near Jerusalem.

**SHIMEAM** See Shimeah. He was a Benjamite who is listed in the genealogy of King Saul (1 Chron. 9:38).

**SHIMEATH** The Ammonite mother of Jozabad (2 Kings 12:21) or Zabad (2 Chron. 24:26). Jozabad was one of those who murdered King Joash of Judah. The murder was regarded as judgment from God on Joash who had ordered the righteous priest, Zechariah, killed and who had led the nation away from the LORD and into idolatry (2 Chron. 24:18–24). The fact that Jozabad's mother was identified as an Ammonite, and the second conspirator was identified as having a Moabite mother, reminds the reader of Chronicles how far the nation had moved from obedience to the Law of God, where such intermarriage was forbidden.

**SHIMEI 1.** Shimei was a head of the Israelite family of Gershon (Exod. 6:17; Num. 3:18, 21; 1 Chron. 6:17; 23:7, 10; Zech. 12:13). He was also an ancestor of Asaph who was David's leader of music in the Tabernacle.

**2.** Identified as a relative of Saul, Shimei, son of Gera, walked alongside David's army with anger and accusations as the army approached Bahurim. Shimei pelted David and all his officials with stones as he blamed David for Saul's death. When David was restored to the throne following Absalom's rebellion, Shimei and his men from Benjamin met David as he crossed the Jordan. They repented for their rudeness and offered their full cooperation and service to King David

(1 Sam. 28–29; 2 Sam. 16:5–13; 19:16–23).

**3.** Shimei (Shimeah) is identified in 2 Sam. 21:21 as a brother of David. He was the father of Jonathan, who killed a Philistine giant.

**4.** Shimei was counted as one who did not join Adonijah's rebellion (1 Kings 1:8).

**5.** 1 Chron. 3:19 lists Shimei as brother of Zerubbabel and son of Pedaiah.

**6.** A descendant of Simeon, Shimei is listed as the son of Zaccur and the father of 16 sons and six daughters (1 Chron. 4:26–27).

**7.** A member of the family of Reuben, this Shimei was a descendant of Joel (1 Chron. 5:4).

**8.** Another Shimei, son of Libni, was a Levite of the family of Merari (1 Chron. 6:29).

**9.** This Shimei, son of Jahath and grandson of Gershon, was a Levite and an ancestor of Asaph (1 Chron. 6:42).

**10.** This Shimei (also spelled 'Shema') was a descendant of Benjamin and listed in the genealogy of King Saul (1 Chron. 8:13, 21).

**11.** Another Shimei was a member of the family of Levitical singers after the Exile (1 Chron. 25:3, 17).

**12.** Shimei, a Ramathite, was in charge of King David's vineyards (1 Chron. 27:27).

**13.** During the period of purification and revival under Hezekiah, Shimei's descendants were among those who ministered in the Temple (2 Chron. 29:14).

**14.** Under Hezekiah's leadership, Conaniah and Shimei were two Levite brothers who were given responsibility over contributions, tithes and dedicated gifts (2 Chron. 31:12–13).

**15.** Shimei was one of the Levites guilty of intermarriage with foreign women after the return from Exile. Under Ezra's direction, they agreed to divorce these wives (Ezra 10:23).

**16.** A descendant of Hashum, another Shimei was guilty of this intermarriage after the return from the Babylonian Exile (*Ezra 10:33*).

**17.** Shimei, son of Binnui was also guilty of intermarriage after the return from Exile (*Ezra 10:38*).

**18.** This Shimei is listed as an ancestor of Mordecai, the Benjamite cousin of Esther (*Est. 2:5*).                                    S.C.

**SHIMEON** One of the descendants of Harim who is listed among those who had married non-Jewish wives while in Exile in Babylon. Along with many others, and in observance of the Law of God under Ezra's direction, he divorced his wife (*Ezra 10:31*).

**SHIMON** A descendant of Caleb, Shimon was a leader of the tribe of Judah and had four sons (*1 Chron. 4:20*).

**SHIMRATH** (Heb., 'a watcher'). In the genealogy from Benjamin to Saul he is listed as a son of Shimei (*1 Chron. 8:21*).

**SHIMRI** (Heb., 'watchful').
**1.** Mentioned in *1 Chron. 11:45*, this Shimri was the father of one of David's 'mighty men', Jediael.

**2.** A Merarite Levite who was the son of Hosah. He is listed among the gatekeepers chosen by King David who also had duties ministering in the Tabernacle worship (*1 Chron. 26:10*).

**3.** A Simeonite, Shimri was the son of Shemaiah and in the days of King Hezekiah was involved in military activity against the Hamites and Meunites. He was father of Jedaiah and lived near Gedor (*1 Chron. 4:37*).

**4.** A descendant of Elizaphan, this Shimri was a Levite who helped prepare and purify the Temple during the days of revival under King Hezekiah (*2 Chron. 29:13*).

**SHIMRITH** (Heb., 'watchful'). The Moabite mother of Jehozabad (*2 Chron.

24:26*), also called Shomer (*2 Kings 12:21*). Jehozabad was the second named of those who murdered King Joash of Judah. The murder was regarded as judgment from God on Joash who had ordered the righteous priest, Zechariah, killed and who had led the nation away from the Lord and into idolatry (*2 Chron. 24:18–24*). The fact that Jehozabad's mother was identified as a Moabite, and the first conspirator was identified as having an Ammonite mother, reminds the reader of Chronicles how far the nation had moved from obedience to the Law of God where such intermarriage was forbidden.                                    P.D.G.

**SHIMRON** The fourth son of Issachar who became founder of the Shimronite clan. He is listed among those who went down to Egypt with his grandfather Jacob (*Gen. 46:13; Num. 26:24; 1 Chron. 7:1*).

**SHIMSHAI** was secretary to Rehum, one of the Persian commanding officers during the reign of King Artaxerxes in Persia (*Ezra 4:8–9*). Rehum and various Persian judges and officials who had charge for the Persian empire of areas around Canaan and Samaria objected to the Jews rebuilding the walls of the city of Jerusalem. They feared that the Jews would settle back within a well-fortified city and refuse to pay taxes to the empire. They wrote a letter detailing their concerns to King Artaxerxes (*Ezra 4:12–16*). The king replied to Rehum and Shimshai (*v. 17*) that he had been through the archives and discovered that the Israelites had indeed been a most powerful people in the past and that it would be dangerous to let them continue with rebuilding the city. Rehum and Shimshai were ordered to stop the work, which they immediately did (*v. 23*).

The book of Ezra goes on to show how God overruled this decree from Artaxerxes on behalf of his people. Under the guidance of the prophets Haggai and

Zechariah, in the second year of King Darius, the work started again and was eventually completed to God's great praise and glory. P.D.G.

**SHINAB** One of five kings resident in the Jordan valley when Abraham was living near 'the great trees of Mamre'. He was king of Admah (*Gen. 14:2*). Following their defeat at the hands of a coalition of Mesopotamian kings, these city kings were subjugated for 13 years until they finally rebelled (*v. 8*). Their rebellion was put down by the four kings led by Kedorlaomer. For more details see *Amraphel.*

Their defeat involved the seizure of the people of Sodom and Gomorrah (*v. 11*). In the defeat of Gomorrah all their goods and food were taken. Because Lot (a resident of Sodom) was captured, Abra(ha)m entered the battle. He chased Kedorlaomer north and eventually defeated him in battle, bringing Lot back with him and recovering all the spoil. P.D.G.

**SHIPHI** A Simeonite leader and a son of Allon. His son was called Ziza. In the days of King Hezekiah, his family was involved in military activity against the Hamites and Meunites (*1 Chron. 4:37*).

**SHIPHRAH** (Heb., 'beautiful') was one of the Hebrew midwives who were ordered by the king of Egypt to kill any male son they delivered for the Hebrew people (*Exod. 1:15*). However, Shiphrah and her colleague Puah feared God and refused to carry out these orders. When they were summonsed by the king to explain how it was that Hebrew male children were still being born and surviving, they concocted a story saying that, unlike Egyptian mothers, Hebrew mothers were very strong and gave birth before the midwives could arrive (*v. 19*)! God blessed the activities of these midwives so that even more male children were born, and because of their faith God gave the two

midwives their own children (*vv. 20–21*). In Exodus this order to kill the Hebrew male children was eventually carried out by the Egyptians themselves. One of the few to escape the killings was Moses who became leader of his people and helped them escape the clutches of Pharaoh and the Egyptians.

The faithfulness of God's people in time of persecution is seen regularly to be rewarded in Scripture and became an example for the people of God in future generations. God's power in overcoming all that the Egyptians could throw at his people was recalled in later generations in Psalms of praise and prayer (e.g. *Ps. 105:24–27*). P.D.G.

**SHIPHTAN** (Heb., 'he has judged') was from the tribe of Ephraim and was the father of Kemuel (*Num. 34:24*). Kemuel was chosen by Moses as the leader of the tribe of Ephraim and helped assign the inheritance of land to the various families in his tribe.

**SHISHA** had been a secretary in the court of King David and one of his senior officials, but here in *1 Kings 4:3* it is his sons who are mentioned as secretaries during King Solomon's reign. Shisha's name is probably mis-spelled both here and as Seraiah in *2 Sam. 8:17*. The list of court officials in *1 Chron. 18:16*, where he is probably correctly called Shavsha, gives an indication of the increasing amount of administration as the monarchy stabilized and had more contact with other countries.

**SHISHAK** was King of Egypt in the days of King Solomon and the division of the kingdom between Jeroboam and Rehoboam (around 950–925 BC). In the latter part of his reign, King Solomon disobeyed God's Law and married many wives from other nations, who began to turn his heart from the LORD to worship other gods (*1 Kings 11:1–6*). The judgment of the LORD was that the kingdom would be torn away from his family and divided (vv. 9–13). The LORD raised up various adversaries against Solomon who included Jeroboam, son of Nebat, who was an Ephraimite and one of Solomon's officials. Ahijah the prophet told Jeroboam that if he obeyed the LORD the ten tribes of the Northern Kingdom would be his and he would have an enduring kingdom (vv. 29–39). When Solomon realized what was happening, he tried to kill Jeroboam, who then fled to the court of Shishak in Egypt, where he stayed until Solomon's death (v. 40).

On Solomon's death, Rehoboam tried to rule the whole kingdom but Jeroboam returned from Shishak's protection and led the northern tribes in rebellion. Rehoboam became king of the southern tribes of Benjamin and Judah and Jeroboam of the northern tribes. In the fifth year of Rehoboam's reign, because of Judah's unfaithfulness, God allowed Shishak to invade Judah and he attacked Jerusalem (1 Kings 14:25; 2 Chron. 12:2). The message of judgment was delivered by the prophet Shemaiah: 'This is what the LORD says, "You have abandoned me; therefore, I now abandon you to Shishak"' (2 Chron. 12:5). This led to their repentance (v. 7) and the LORD's judgment was stayed, so that Jerusalem was not itself captured, although the people became vassals to Egypt. Many of the Temple and palace treasures were taken back to Egypt (v. 9).

Shishak's invasion of Judah is described in some detail in 2 Chron. 12:1–4 and consisted of a large number of troops. It occurred towards the end of his own reign and some of the towns that he defeated in Judah are listed on a stele found at Karnak. He is to be identified with Sheshonq I, who founded the 22nd dynasty.                                      P.D.G.

**SHITRAI** A Sharonite who was an overseer during the reign of King David. He was in charge of the herds grazing in Sharon. The list in 1 Chronicles gives some indication of the extent to which the LORD had blessed King David personally (1 Chron. 27:28).

**SHIZA** was a Reubenite and the father of Adina, who was one of David's 'Thirty' mighty men (1 Chron. 11:42).

**SHOBAB 1.** A son of Caleb and his wife Azubah, in the genealogy of Judah (1 Chron. 2:18).
**2.** A son of King David. After David conquered Jerusalem and moved there from Hebron he took many wives and concubines. Shobab was one of his many children, and his mother was Bathsheba (2 Sam. 5:14; 1 Chron. 3:5; 14:4).

**SHOBACH** was a commander in the Syrian army under Hadadezer. In battle the Syrians had fought as mercenaries on the side of the Ammonites against King David. Joab and his brother Abishai had led David's troops to a great victory and the Syrians (Arameans) had been routed (2 Sam. 10:1–14). However, Hadadezer then brought many more of his troops together, they regrouped under the command of Shobach at Helam, across the Jordan (v. 16). David heard of this and led his troops across the Jordan to join battle. In the ensuing battle, which David won easily, Shobach was killed (v. 18). The result was that those kings who had been vassals to Hadadezer now independently sought peace with King David (v. 19).

The context in which this account occurs indicates the continued prosperity of King David under God's guidance and blessing. Both Joab and Abishai stressed the importance that the fight in which they were engaged was a fight 'for the cities of God'. They encouraged the people that 'The LORD will do what is right' (v. 12). While they continued to rely on the LORD in this way they were blessed by him and saw victories in battle. However, complacency was soon to set in as King David became too self-confident. In *2 Sam. 11*, when David should have been leading his people to battle, he stayed at home and committed adultery with Bathsheba and connived in the death of Uriah.                    P.D.G.

**SHOBAI** was a Levite and the head of one of the families who were Temple gate-keepers. His descendants were among those who returned to Jerusalem from the Babylonian Exile in the company of Zerubbabel (*Ezra 2:42; Neh. 7:45*)

**SHOBAL** **1.** Shobal was the son of Seir the Horite, and a chief among his people living in Edom (*Gen. 36:20,29; 1 Chron. 1:38*). His sons are listed in *Gen. 36:23* and *1 Chron. 1:40*.
**2.** This Shobal, son of Hur, was the founder or 'father' of Kiriath Jearim and was a descendant of Caleb (*1 Chron. 2:50*). His own descendants are listed in vv. 52–53. In *1 Chron. 4:1–2* he is named among the important descendants in the tribe of Judah and his son Reaiah is mentioned.

**SHOBEK** Mentioned only in *Neh. 10:24*, Shobek was one of the leaders of the Jews who returned from the Exile in Babylon and joined Nehemiah in binding himself to an agreement to obey the Law of God.

**SHOBI** the son of Nahash, an Ammonite, lived in Mahanaim and, together with Makir and Barzillai, hid David from Absalom. These men then provided David and his men with bedding, food and cooking utensils (*2 Sam. 17:27*).

**SHOHAM** (Heb., 'a precious stone'). Mentioned in the lists of *1 Chron. 24:27*, Shoham was the son of Jaaziah, the son of Merari, a Levite.

**SHOMER** (Heb., 'watcher').

**1.** The mother of Jehozabad (*2 Kings 12:21*), also called Shimrith (*2 Chron. 24:26*). Jehozabad was the second named of those who murdered King Joash of Judah. The murder was regarded as judgment from God on Joash who had ordered the righteous priest, Zechariah, killed and who had led the nation away from the LORD and into idolatry (*2 Chron. 24:18–24*). See *Shimrith* for more detail.
**2.** The son of Heber and the head of a clan in the tribe of Asher. He had four sons and was a 'brave warrior' and 'out-standing leader' (*1 Chron. 7:32, 34, 40*).

**SHOPHACH** The commander of the Syrian forces under Hadadezer which fled before King David. During the battle Shophach was killed (*1 Chron. 19:16, 18*). For more detail see *Shobach*, the name used for the same person in *2 Sam. 10:16, 18*.

**SHUA** **1.** Shua was the daughter of a Canaanite whom Judah encountered when staying with a man named Hirah (*Gen. 38:1–2*). Judah married her and had various children with her. Her death is recorded in *v. 12*. Er died because he 'was wicked in the LORD's sight' (*v. 7*) as did Shua's second son Onan (*v. 10; 1 Chron. 2:3*). Whether Shua's own death was linked to the death of her sons or to the general wickedness of the family is not clear. However, intermarrying with Canaanites had been prohibited by God and it is likely that this is why such sadness came upon Judah and his family.
**2.** This daughter of Heber was sister to Japhlet, Shomer and Hotham, all of whom were heads of Asherite clans. The brothers were called 'brave warriors' and 'outstanding leaders' (*1 Chron. 7:32, 40*).
                    P. D. G.

**SHUAH** One of Abraham's sons by his wife Keturah (*Gen. 25:2*). He appears in a list of Abraham's descendants in between the death of Sarah and the death of Abraham (also 1 Chron. 1:32).

**SHUAL** (Heb., 'fox'). Mentioned in 1 Chron. 7:36 as a son of Zophah, a chief in the tribe of Asher. He was among the 'brave warriors and outstanding leaders' of the tribe (v. 40).

**SHUBAEL** **1.** A Levite and a descendant of Moses, Shubael was the first son of Gershom and took part in duties in the Tabernacle and later in the Temple (1 Chron. 23:16; 24:20). He and his descendants were the officers in charge of the Temple treasuries in the days of King David (26:24).
**2.** One of the sons of Heman listed among those set apart for the ministry of prophesying and music during the reign of King David. Heman was the king's seer. Shubael and his relations were given the 13th turn of service in the sanctuary (1 Chron. 25:4, 20).

**SHUHAH** The brother of Kelub, Shuhah is listed in the genealogy of the tribe of Judah (1 Chron. 4:11).

**SHUHAM** The son of Dan who was the founder of the Shuhamite clans (Num. 26:42–43). In the census conducted under Moses, the clan numbers were 64,400. Dan's son is named as Hushim in Gen. 46:23.

**SHULAMMITE** This is the name by which the woman in the Song of Songs is known to her friends (S.of S. 6:13). The name is only used twice and in one verse. The woman's beauty is described in great detail by her lover, in a poem which demonstrates the beauty and mutuality of human love between husband and wife. The developing intimacy of this love is revealed and the onlookers, the 'friends', long to gaze on her beauty as the husband does (v. 13).

The origin of the name is not clear. It is perhaps most likely to refer to the woman's origins – 'a woman from Shunem'. The occasional interchange between 'n' and 'l' in Heb. is well documented. Two other women in Scripture were known as 'Shunammite' (from Shunem; see Shunammite). One of these was Abishag, a very beautiful girl who was brought to warm David in his old age but with whom King David never had sexual intercourse (1 Kings 1:3–4). Given that Solomon became furious when Adonijah requested her hand in marriage and saw this as a direct challenge to his throne, it is probable that he inherited Abishag. It has been suggested, therefore, that she was the beloved of the poem and hence the 'Shulammite'. However, such suggestions must remain conjectural.

Others have suggested the name is derived from a feminine form of the Heb. word for Solomon, thus being something of a title for Solomon's wife, but again we are in the realm of conjecture.     P.D.G.

**SHUNAMMITE** This is a word used to describe a person from the town of Shunem in the tribal territory of Issachar a little to the north of the valley of Jezreel. In Scripture 'the Shunammite' is used of two women. One of these was Abishag, a very beautiful girl who was brought in to warm David in his old age but with whom King David never had sexual intercourse (1 Kings 1:3–4,15). After David had died, Adonijah wanted to become king and saw the inheritance of his father's wives and concubines as one of the standard ways of establishing his credentials. He therefore asked for the hand of Abishag, the Shunammite, in marriage (1 Kings 2:17,21). For this threat to his position as king, Solomon had Adonijah killed (vv. 19–25).

The second woman to be called 'the Shunammite' was a wealthy woman from Shunem with whom Elisha and his servant Gehazi stayed. Because she was hospitable to Elisha he offered to help her. Gehazi discovered for his master that what she most desired was a child. In due course a child was born. One day the child became ill and died. 'The Shunammite' went in search of the prophet, who came to her house and raised the boy from the dead (2 Kings 4:12, 25, 36).

Use of the description 'the Shulammite' may well be a corruption of Shunammite (Song of Songs 6:13).          P.D.G.

**SHUNI** One of the sons of Gad listed in Gen. 46:6 among those who went with Jacob into Egypt. His descendants were called Shunites (Num. 26:15).

**SHUPHAM** A descendant of Benjamin mentioned in Num. 26:39 and the founder of the Shuphamite clan. A reference to the Shuppites in 1 Chron. 7:12 may mean the same clan. Also see Shephupham.

**SHUPPIM** When the ark of the covenant was brought up to Jerusalem in the time of King David, he appointed the Levites to many different positions of service. Shuppim was a gatekeeper of the West Gate of the Tabernacle area and the Shalleketh Gate. Given his close association with Hosah, he was probably a Levite of the Merarite clan (1 Chron. 26:16).

**SHUTHELAH 1.** A descendant of Ephraim and the leader of the Shuthelahite clan (Num. 26:35). His descendants included Eran, founder of the Eranite clan (v. 36). His son is listed as Bered (1 Chron. 7:20).
**2.** A descendant of 1. above (1 Chron. 7:21). While some scholars have suggested that this occurrence of the name is repeated from the previous verse, there is no necessary reason why a name should not be repeated in a family line within a couple of generations.

**SIA** A leader of one of the families of Temple servants. His descendants returned from the Babylonian Exile in the days of Ezra and worked on the Temple (Neh. 7:47). In Ezra 2:44 he is called Siaha.

**SIAHA** A leader of one of the families of Temple servants whose descendants returned from the Babylonian Exile in the days of Ezra and worked on the Temple (Ezra 2:44). In Neh. 7:47 he is called Sia.

**SIBECCAI** (Heb., 'weaver') the Hushathite was one of David's 'Thirty' warriors. As a commander in David's army he was on duty with his men in the eighth month of each year and had 24,000 men in his division (1 Chron. 11:29; 27:11). He was particularly famed for having killed Saph, one of the giants who was a descendant of Rapha and who fought for the Philistines (2 Sam. 21:18). It is likely that his killing of Sippai, mentioned in 1 Chron. 20:4, who was also a Rephaite, is a reference to the same incident. That great victory over the giant temporarily led to the subjugation of the Philistines by Israel. (The name Mebunnai in 2 Sam. 23:27 may well be a corruption of the Heb. name Sibeccai and may therefore refer to the same Hushathite.)          P.D.G.

**SIHON,** king of the Amorites, first appears in the Bible in Num. 21. The people of Israel were travelling from Egypt northwards to Canaan following a traditional route known as the King's Highway to the east of the river Jordan and along the Dead Sea. They requested permission of Sihon to travel through his territory, promising they would not turn aside into his fields or even stop for water. Sihon refused the request and brought out his entire army to attack the Israelites (vv. 21–23). Israel won the battle and captured all the cities of the Amorites, including Sihon's home city of Heshbon (v. 26; see also Deut. 2:24–36; 3).

This first victory on their way to the Promised Land that God had given the Israelites became very important to them in their history and a point by which events could be dated (e.g. *Deut. 1:4; 4:46*). Immediately after facing Sihon the Israelites were faced with a battle against Og of Bashan. The LORD's words to Moses and the people encouraged them with a reminder of the victory over Sihon and they went on to another great victory (*Num. 21:33–35; Deut. 3:2, 6*). News of the victory quickly spread and drove fear into the hearts of those in Canaan. Rahab, the prostitute of Jericho, was convinced the LORD had power even over that heavily fortified city because she and others had heard of the victory over Sihon and Og (*Josh. 2:10*; also see *9:9–10*). In the period of the Judges, Jephthah recalled the victory in a letter to the Ammonite king who had claimed the territory won from Sihon. The Ammonite king ignored this appeal to the LORD's great power and was himself defeated (*Judg. 11:20–33*). The demonstration of God's faithfulness to his people in defeating Sihon was recounted in the people's praises to the LORD down through the generations (e.g. *Neh. 9:22; Ps. 135:11; 136:19*).

The territory of Sihon and the Amorites was eventually distributed among the tribes of Reuben, Gad and Manasseh (*Num. 32:33; Josh. 13:9–10*)    P.D.G.

**SILAS (SILVANUS)** Like Paul, this leading member of the Jerusalem church was one of the few Jewish Christians in the East known by name who possessed the much-prized Roman citizenship (*Acts 16:38*). He is referred to either by his Semitic name, 'Silas' (by Luke in Acts) or by his Latin *cognomen*, Silvanus (by Paul and Peter). Because he was the 'secretary' who actually copied down *1 Peter*, it is clear from the word order and style of the letter that he was a man who had received a good Greek education. Silvanus would

therefore have been a person who came from a high social register (*cf.* also Apollos).

Silvanus was held in high standing in Jerusalem. The apostles, elders and the whole church chose him, one of the 'leaders among the brethren', to accompany Paul and Barnabas with the letter from the Jerusalem church on that most important matter of the Council's ruling on Gentile Christians. His choice may, in part, have been dictated by his Roman citizenship as well as his position as a Jewish church leader.

In Antioch he was as one of the prophets whose gifts greatly encouraged and strengthened the church (*cf. 1 Cor. 14:1ff.*). The welcome given to the Jerusalem Council's letter and his ministry among them resulted in the soothing of the feelings of Gentile Christians. They had originally been told that unless they were circumcised (equated by the Romans with castration) according to the Mosiac Law they could not be saved (*Acts 15:1*). The success of the mission resulted in them giving the blessing of peace at the end of this ministry.

Silvanus accompanied Paul on his second missionary journey. It was a choice dictated by his gifts (in contrast to Paul's disappointment with Mark's ministry at that stage), his leadership role in the Jerusalem church and also, providentially, his status in an area where his citizenship could well have played an important role in the Roman province of Galatia.

Together in the Roman colony of Philippi they engaged in a ministry to Jewish adherents including Lydia, a high-class business lady in the purple trade. The arrest of these two missionaries as Jewish 'revolutionaries' engaged in teaching anti-Roman practices in a Roman colony excited the attention of the local authorities. The illegality rested with the magistrates who ordered their flogging which was proscribed punishment for

Roman citizens (*Acts 16:22, 37*). Normally three local guarantors were required of those who claimed citizenship who could swear that such claims were true. In this situation no such persons would have been able to bear witness to this fact. Problems involved in securing documentary verification and the delay in prison until the provincial governor heard these serious charges when he came next on his annual assize, may well have persuaded these two missionaries that not only had it been granted to them to believe on his name, but also to suffer for his sake (*Phil. 1:29*). The demand that the magistrates themselves release Paul and Silvanus would have given protection from mob violence both for them and the newly formed church.

The Christian fortitude shown by Paul and Silvanus singing in the inner prison having been beaten and with their feet in stocks, together with the miraculous escape from death (but not custody), of all the prisoners in the earthquake – a pagan author records seismic disturbances that year – had such an effect on the jailer, that he sought, not the destruction of his own life, but the everlasting salvation through belief in Jesus, both for himself and his household (*Acts 16:25–34*).

They left for Thessalonica, where on three successive Sabbath meetings they successfully reasoned from the OT that the Messiah had to suffer and rise from the dead. The converts, including Jews, God-fearers and some women from the social élite formed the new church (*Acts 17:1–3*).

Silvanus remained in Berea, where there was a receptive group of both Jews and prominent Greeks (*Acts 17:10–12*), and subsequently joined Paul in Corinth, from where Paul together with Silvanus and Timothy 'co-authored' *1* and *2 Thessalonians*. Note the way in which Paul included his fellow workers as equals in his ministry and apostolic letters.

The last word about Silvanus is to be found at the conclusion of *1 Peter* where he himself testifies of this letter 'that this is the true grace of God' and commands the recipients 'to stand fast in it'. Silvanus' ministry was unique in that he was not only a leader of the Jerusalem church but also a cross-cultural missionary engaged with Paul in mission to Jews and Gentiles alike. It might well be that his many contacts with the churches enabled *1 Peter* to be directed to such diverse locations (*1 Pet. 1:1*).      B.W.

**SIMEON** (Heb., 'hearing').

**1.** Simeon was the second son born to Leah and Jacob (*Gen. 35:23; 1 Chron. 2:1*). One of the tribes of Israel was therefore named after him. *Gen. 29:33* reveals that Leah called him Simeon 'because the LORD heard that I am not loved' (*Gen. 29:33*). In *1 Chron. 4:24* his sons are listed as leaders of clans in their own right. They included Nemuel, Jamin, Jarib, Zerah and Shaul (variations on these names are given in *Gen. 46:10; Exod., 6:15; Num. 26:12–14*).

Simeon first enters the narrative of Genesis when he and his brother, Levi, decided to avenge themselves for the rape of their sister Dinah by Shechem, son of Hamor (for more detail see *Dinah* and *Shechem*). When Hamor appealed to Jacob and his sons for reconciliation and forgiveness between the two peoples, and asked whether his son could make amends and marry Dinah, the two brothers decided to retaliate through deception. They insisted on the circumcision of all Hamor's people. While Hamor, Shechem, and his people were still sore from the circumcision, Simeon and Levi attacked them and killed all the males of the city (*Gen. 34:25*). The revenge was disproportionate to the crime, and this was noted in Jacob's comments and his blessing on Simeon towards the end of his life (*Gen. 34:40; 49:5*).

When Jacob's sons travelled to Egypt

for food during the famine in Canaan, without knowing who he was, they encountered their brother Joseph who was the prime-minister. Joseph held Simeon prisoner until they brought Benjamin back to see him (Gen. 42:24, 36). When Benjamin did eventually come Simeon was released and Joseph revealed himself to the brothers (Gen. 43:23). Later Simeon travelled with his father to Egypt when they moved there to settle (Exod. 1:2).

Little is known of what happened to the tribe of Simeon in later years. The tribe is mentioned on a number of occasions in Numbers and at one stage had 59,300 men of army age (Num. 1:22–23). The leader of the tribe in Moses' day was called Shelumiel (Num. 2:12; 7:36; 10:19) and the tribe camped beside the tribe of Reuben on the south side of the Tent of Meeting.

This tribe seems not to have inherited any land other than particular cities within the tribal lands of Judah. Scriptures do not make it clear why this should be, although some have speculated that the tribe was so decimated during the wilderness wanderings that there were not enough of them to be given a large area (cf. Num. 1:23 with 26:14; see Josh. 19:1). Perhaps the tribe's demise was linked to the fact that it was Zimri, a Simeonite leader, who introduced a Midianite woman to the Israelite camp against the explicit instructions of the LORD. It was Zimri who was then killed by Phinehas (Num. 25:14–15; see Zimri and Cozbi).

In King David's day the Simeonites still seemed to live in the south. They gathered in Hebron in some numbers from their cities in Judah to fight for David (1 Chron. 12:25).

In spite of the lack of information on the tribe, its name recurs in Rev. 7:7 where people of Simeon will be among those from all the tribes who will be protected and 'sealed' by the Lord for all eternity. The Lord's faithfulness to Abraham, Isaac and Jacob, will thus be seen to be brought to completion despite the unfaithfulness of some Simeonites down through the centuries.          P.D.G.

**2.** One of the devout witnesses to Jesus in the Lucan infancy account is named Simeon (Luke 2:25–35). As an old man, he exemplified one who served the Lord and was content to be used by him until the Lord took him home. Told that he would not see death until he beheld the Lord's Christ, Simeon offered praise to the child and predicted what the newborn's career would be like. The prophet then was ready for the Lord to bring him to heaven, his watch completed with him having served God faithfully. He is the first person in Luke's Gospel to predict that Jesus would be a blessing to Gentiles, as well as Jews, even though he himself was awaiting the deliverance of Israel. He also was the first to predict Jesus' suffering, as he warned Mary of her pain at what Jesus would experience. Simeon was a faithful servant of God who told what God was doing, but did so with compassion and openness to God's working broadly among all types of people.

**3.** Another Simeon is mentioned in Acts 13:1–2. He possessed prophetic and teaching gifts. He helped ordain Saul and Barnabas for their missionary endeavour. His surname was Niger. He may well have been African, although we do not know much about him. He is one of several figures in the NT whose faithfulness is briefly noted. Like so many other servants in the Bible as well as today, their service is seen by God, even though its mention is brief.          D.B.

**SIMON** The name Simon is used as the Gk. form of the Heb. Simeon which means 'hearing'. In the NT there are nine characters with this name.

**1.** Simon Peter, the brother of Andrew. He was one of Jesus' twelve disciples and an apostle. See Peter.

**2.** Simon, a brother of Jesus, is mentioned by name only in *Mark 6:3* and its parallel passage in *Matt. 13:55*. In that narrative, Jesus had arrived in his home town of Nazareth and began to teach in the synagogue. Both Gospels record the astonishment of the crowds at the wisdom displayed by Jesus. People were particularly astonished because they all knew his family who were present with them at the time. In a rhetorical question they asked, ' "Isn't this the carpenter's son? Isn't his mother's name Mary, and aren't his brothers James, Joseph, Simon and Judas? Aren't all his sisters with us? Where then did this man get all these things?" And they took offence at him.' (*Matt. 13:55–57*). Sadly, because of their lack of faith, Jesus did not do many miracles in the area and stated that a prophet was only without honour in his home town.

Elsewhere the brothers of the Lord are seen wanting Jesus to be much more public with his working of miracles and yet still not actually believing in him (*John 7:3–5*). However, they clearly came to faith in Jesus later and were among those 'constantly in prayer' before the Day of Pentecost in *Acts 1:14*. At least some became missionaries in the early church and are referred to in *1 Cor. 9:5*.

Throughout the history of the church the word 'brother' with reference to Jesus' brothers has been interpreted in various ways. Some have argued that these must have been Joseph's sons by a previous marriage, thus helping to maintain what later became known as the doctrine of the perpetual virginity of Mary. Augustine and some notable Roman Catholic writers have argued that the word simply meant 'relatives' or even 'cousins'. However, the texts where the phrase appears read most naturally as referring to the literal brothers of Jesus, born to Mary after she had her 'firstborn' (*Luke 2:7*) son, Jesus (*cf.* also *Matt. 1:25*).

**3.** Simon, a Pharisee, is mentioned only in *Luke 7*. Jesus accepted an invitation to dinner at his home. A woman from the same town 'who had led a sinful life' entered the house and stood 'behind him at his feet weeping, she began to wet his feet with her tears. Then she wiped them with her hair, kissed them and poured perfume on them' (*v. 38*). Clearly this was admitting her sin to Jesus and seeking his blessing and forgiveness. As a Pharisee, Simon was immediately concerned that a 'sinner' was touching Jesus and that he would thus be ceremonially contaminated. Given that Jesus seemed unconcerned, Simon concluded that Jesus could not be a real prophet otherwise he would have understood what was happening. Jesus responded to Simon's unspoken thoughts with a parable. In the parable Jesus contrasted two people who owed money to a money-lender. One owed much and the other little, but both debts were cancelled. He asked Simon which of the two men would love the money-lender more. Simon was thus drawn into the parable and forced to apply it to his own thinking. He replied that the one who had been forgiven the largest debt would love more. Jesus then applied this parable to Simon and the woman. Simon had fulfilled his legal obligations of hospitality to Jesus, but his woman had continued to show her love for him ever since she had entered the house. 'She loved much' and her 'many sins' were forgiven. On the other hand, by implication, Simon loved little for he had been 'forgiven little' (*v. 47*).

Luke draws out two important points from this incident in *vv. 49–50*. First, he continues a theme of his Gospel by showing how the other guests were forced to ask 'Who is this who even forgives sins?' He wanted his readers also to ask this question so they would come to know Jesus for themselves (see also *Luke 4:22, 41; 5:21; 7:16, 19; 8:26; 9:18–20* etc.). Secondly, he concludes the section by showing that it was the woman's response to Jesus that was critical in her receiving forgiveness: 'Your faith has saved you; go in peace.' Therefore, by implication, it will be the readers' response to Jesus that will lead to their forgiveness and salvation.

P. D. G.

**4.** Simon the Zealot is one of the lesser-known apostles of Jesus Christ. His name is recorded in Scripture only in the lists of the apostles in the first three Gospels and in the Upper Room in *Acts 1.*

There are most likely two reasons why this Simon's name is always qualified by 'the Zealot', or like wording. The first of these reasons is so that there would be no confusion with Simon Peter. Both men had the given name of Simon, and there was thus the need to distinguish between them. Jesus gave the more prominent Simon the nickname Peter (*Matt. 10:2; 16:18*). It is not known who first called the other Simon 'the Zealot'.

The second reason for the designation is undoubtedly that it was descriptive of his past or present character or allegiance. Besides family relationships, such additional names were common among the apostles. James and John, the sons of Zebedee, were known as 'Sons of Thunder' (*Mark 3:17*), clearly a commentary on their fiery personalities. Matthew is called 'the tax collector' (*Matt. 10:3*), recalling his background before becoming a disciple of Christ.

The explanation concerning Simon the Zealot could be either personality – character or background. Describing him as 'the Zealot' in a post-resurrection passage (*Acts 1:13*) implies that whatever prompted the designation has continued to that point. If that is correct, it should be understood as 'the zealous one', whether generally, or specifically zeal on behalf of Jesus Christ.

On the other hand, the passages in the Synoptic Gospels (*Matt. 10:4; Mark 3:18; Luke 6:15*) occur at a much earlier point in the earthly ministry of Jesus. At such a juncture, it is slightly more likely that 'Zealot' refers to the nationalistic political party in Judaism in that period. That view is also supported by the Greek word translated as 'Zealot' in *Matt. 10:4* and *Mark 3:18*. It is Cananaios, another term for the Zealot Jewish sect. It is, of course, quite possible that Simon's former nationalistic zeal was translated into intense allegiance to Jesus Christ, in which case both names would be present. In either case, the role of Simon the Zealot as an apostle of the Lord Jesus is a magnificent example of the transforming grace of God as well as how he uses drastically different people to accomplish his purposes.

A.B.L.

**5.** Simon the leper is mentioned only in *Matt. 26:6* and *Mark 14:3*. He is the only leper mentioned by name in the NT. See *Leper.* He provides us with an interesting example of how Jesus was quite able to accept those who were socially outcast in society. In *Mark 14* Jesus had gone to Simon's house in Bethany to a meal. While there a woman entered and poured expensive perfume on Jesus' head. Some in the room thought this a great waste of money and 'rebuked her harshly' (*Mark 14:5*). Jesus reminded those present that the poor were always with them but he would not always be among them. He took the perfume as a prophetic pointer to his death when his body would be prepared with perfumes for burial (*v. 8*). In *John 12:1–8* what is apparently the same incident, also in Bethany, is recounted. The woman is identified as Mary, but no mention is made of Simon the leper.

**6.** Simon Iscariot is only mentioned in the Gospel of John. He was the father of Judas Iscariot, the disciple who betrayed Jesus (*John 6:71; 13:2, 26*). See *Judas Iscariot.*

**7.** Simon of Cyrene was a man who was compelled by the Roman guard to carry Jesus' cross for him to Golgotha where Jesus was to be crucified (*Matt. 27:32; Luke 23:26*). *Mark 15:21* adds that this

Simon was 'the father of Alexander and Rufus' and 'was passing by on his way in from the country'. This may imply that Alexander and Rufus were known to the early church and had later come to faith in Christ.

Cyrene was in north Africa (modern Libya) and seems to have had a large Jewish community (Acts 6:9). It is possible Simon was in Jerusalem for the Passover. Later, on the day of Pentecost, visitors from Cyrene heard the gospel in their own language and were converted (Acts 2:10). People from Cyrene are also mentioned in connection with preaching the gospel to the Gentiles (Acts 11:20) and a certain Lucius of Cyrene was a teacher in the church at Antioch (Acts 13:1).

**8.** Simon the sorcerer lived in Samaria and his sorcery was well known in the community (Acts 8:9). He enjoyed the acclaim of the local people who believed he had a divine power (vv. 10–11). Philip the evangelist preached the gospel in the town and many believed and were baptized. He performed miracles in the name of Christ and cast out demons and the whole city was affected (vv. 4–8). Even Simon was astonished at what was happening through Philip and he himself 'believed and was baptized' (v. 13). Peter and John arrived to see for themselves how many in Samaria had believed in Christ, and they laid hands on the new converts so they would receive the Holy Spirit (vv. 14–17). 'When Simon saw that the Spirit was given at the laying on of the apostles' hands, he offered them money and said, "Give me also this ability so that everyone on whom I lay my hands may receive the Holy Spirit"' (vv. 18–19).

Having been used to being paid for his services of sorcery, he probably saw nothing wrong in this offer of money so he too could have some of the power the apostles had. But the request revealed his sin and lack of understanding. Peter saw through him straightaway and told him that his heart was 'not right before God'

and urged him to repent, seek forgiveness and a change of heart, saying, 'For I see that you are full of bitterness and captive to sin.' Simon asked Peter to pray for him so that he would not be judged (vv. 23–24).

Whether Simon's conversion was ever genuine is not clear from the text. Certainly he was attracted by his experience of signs and wonders as so many have been through the ages. It needed Peter's spiritual maturity to see that an attraction to and belief in the signs was not a true conversion. The implication at the end of the passage is that while his faith may not have been genuine to begin with, in the end, he did seek forgiveness of the Lord.

**9.** Simon the tanner lived by the sea in Joppa (Acts 9:43; 10:6, 17, 32). The house may have been by the sea in order that a trade dealing with dead animals should not ceremonially contaminate the Jewish community. The apostle Peter stayed there 'for some time'. Peter had come to Joppa from Lydda at the request of some disciples because Tabitha, a disciple and woman renowned for her good deeds, had died. Peter prayed and she was raised from the dead (Acts 9:40). It was while on the roof of Simon's house that Peter had his vision in which he was encouraged to eat so-called 'unclean' animals. In this vision the Lord was preparing Peter for his work among the Gentiles and specifically with Cornelius, the centurion, whose men were at that very time on their way to Simon's house to ask Peter to come back with them to Caesarea.          P.D.G.

**SIPPAI** Mentioned only in 1 Chron. 20:4, Sippai, a descendant of Rapha, was killed by Sibbecai in an Israelite battle against the Philistines at Gezer. The incident was of special importance for the Israelites because the victory over the giant temporarily led to the subjugation of the Philistines by Israel. Also see Saph.

**SISERA** was the commander of Jabin's

army and lived in Harosheth Haggoyim. Jabin was a king in Canaan and ruled in Hazor (*Judg. 4:2*). During the period of the Judges there was a considerable period of anarchy in Israel. From time to time godly men were raised up by God to be deliverers of his people from the hands of various groups of Canaanites. The influence of the Canaanites on the Israelites was considerable, causing them to turn away from the LORD and worship idols. After the leaders Ehud and Shamgar had died, the Israelites again did evil and 'the LORD sold them into the hands of Jabin' (*v. 2*). Sisera, his commander, had 900 iron chariots and oppressed Israel for 20 years until at last they cried once again for help to the LORD.

This was the period when Deborah was leading Israel. She was a prophetess. She summonsed Barak and told him that God was commanding him to lead 10,000 men of Naphtali and Zebulun to Mount Tabor. Once there they would lure Sisera into a trap in the valley by the Kishon river (*v. 7*). Barak obeyed, subject to Deborah agreeing to go with him. She agreed to go but prophesied that if she went Barak would not get the glory but 'the LORD will hand Sisera over to a woman' (*v. 9*). The trap worked. Sisera went after Barak (*vv. 12–13*) and 'The LORD routed Sisera and all his chariots and army . . . and Sisera fled on foot', all his men being killed along the way (*vv. 15–16*).

Sisera then sought refuge in the tent of Jael, the wife of Heber the Kenite, with whom Jabin had friendly relations (*v. 17*). She invited him in (*v. 18*) and, while he slept, she hammered a tent-peg through his skull. When Barak arrived he found that indeed the LORD had delivered his enemy into the hands of a woman (*v. 22*). Eventually, under the leadership of Deborah, the prophetess who feared the LORD, the Israelites grew stronger and finally destroyed Jabin. The exploits of Deborah in leading the people are recorded in a song of praise to God which recalls the slaying of Sisera (*Judg. 5:20–30*).

The incident with Sisera is one of many in the book of Judges in which we find the LORD coming to the aid of his people whenever they turned to him and asked him for help. Their sin was that whenever they settled back they forgot the LORD and began to mix in with Canaanites and were drawn into the Canaanite religions. In *1 Sam. 12:9* the problems encountered when the Israelites 'forgot the LORD' are remembered as a warning for future generations. Their subjugation to Jabin and Sisera was to serve as a reminder to remain faithful to the LORD. That faithfulness of God over Sisera when his people repented is remembered with rejoicing in *Ps. 83:9* where David prays that God will once again show his mighty power over his enemies.

**2.** A leader of one of the families of Temple servants whose descendants returned from the Babylonian Exile in the days of Ezra and worked on the Temple (*Ezra 2:53; Neh. 7:55*). P.D.G.

**SISMAI** The son of Eleasah and a leader from the tribe of Judah, he was a descendant of Jerahmeel and the father of Shallum (*1 Chron. 2:40*).

**SITHRI** (Heb., 'protection'). A son of Aaron's uncle, Uzziel. He was a descendant of Levi and a leader among the Kohathites (*Exod. 6:22*).

**SO** Hoshea, the last king of the Northern Kingdom of Israel, had tried to escape from the clutches of the Assyrians by refusing to pay the heavy tribute levied upon the nation and by sending envoys to seek the help of So, king of Egypt (*2 Kings 17:4*). This led to Shalmaneser taking Hoshea prisoner and to an Assyrian invasion. With whom this King So is to be identified is not at all clear. Some scholars have suggested he was Shabaka, who was king in Egypt from about 716 BC, but this would seem to place him too late for the events described, since Hoshea was king between about 732–722 BC. He has also been identified by some scholars with Osorkon IV of Tanis (the biblical Zoan). This view is supported by Isaiah's prophecy against Egypt in which he pointed out that Egypt would be of no help and specifically mentioned the 'officials of Zoan' (*Is. 19:11–15*). Other suggestions have also been made.

P.D.G.

**SODI** was the father of Gaddiel and was from the tribe of Zebulun. Gaddiel was one of the twelve spies sent out by Moses from the Desert of Paran to spy out the land of Canaan (*Num. 13:10*).

## SOLOMON

The name Solomon is associated with the word for 'peace', with which it shares the same consonants. It is also associated with the name of the city of David, Jerusalem with which it also shares three consonants. These two identifications call to mind those aspects of this king of Israel and Judah which are best known: a peaceful reign presided over by a monarch with worldwide fame for his wisdom to maintain that peace; and a prosperous city which attracted the wealth and power of all the surrounding nations and which was epitomized in the constructions of the house of God and the magnificent Temple. These same elements are remembered in the NT, where Jesus referred to the wisdom of Solomon which attracted the Queen of Sheba (*Matt. 12:42; Luke 11:31*) and where the Temple of Solomon was preserved in names given to some parts of Herod's Temple (*John 10:23; Acts 3:11; 5:12*). However, the NT also hints at the disastrous consequences of these glorious aspects of Solomon's life. For all his wealth, Jesus told his listeners, Solomon could not compare with the lily of the valley (*Matt. 6:29; Luke 12:27*). The lily displays a beauty given by its caring and loving heavenly Father. In contrast, Solomon's splendour betrayed a brutal seizure of the throne, apostate support and worship of other national deities, and an oppressive regime which squandered the good will of the northern tribes of Israel and abused the subject peoples of the empire which David had created. The same can be said for the Temple of Solomon. Most significant here, as Stephen observed (*Acts 7:47*), was the dangerous attempt to 'tame' the God of Israel by placing him in a 'box' where the king would have control and could choose to worship and obey him or to worship and obey other deities, as he pleased.

The story of Solomon's life is told in 1 *Kings* 1–11 and in 1 *Chron.* 28 to 2 *Chron.* 9. Both record the glorious aspects of Solomon's reign. However, the account of Kings also demonstrates the gradual slide of the king into apostasy. This is accomplished by punctuating the reign with three pronouncements by God. Each of these introduces a new era in Solomon's life and passes judgment upon what has happened. In order to understand the life and work of this great biblical figure, we will examine the four parts of Solomon's life into which the three divine appearances divide it: the securing of Solomon's throne (1 *Kings* 1–2); Solomon's wisdom and accomplishments (1 *Kings* 3–8); Solomon's international fame and the consequent apostasy (1 *Kings* 9–11:8); and Solomon's opponents (1 *Kings* 11:9–43).

## Securing the throne

Solomon was the tenth son of David, according to the biblical records. He was the son of Bathsheba, whose first son by David died as a judgment for David's sins of adultery and murder of Bathsheba's husband, Uriah (2 Sam. 11). The story of how the older sons of David died before ascending to the throne occupies much of the account of David's later life and death (2 Sam. 10 – 1 Kings 2). In a sense, this material justifies the legitimacy of Solomon as David's successor, even though he was not the eldest son.

The accounts of Solomon's actual choice and coronation in Chronicles and Kings emphasize two different perspectives. In 1 Chron. 28–29 Solomon is anointed king at a public gathering. There he is declared to be the divinely chosen successor to David. However, this is not the view of 1 Kings 1 which describes a very different ceremony, one done quickly and without advance warning. Chronicles shows us what went on in the outward display where Solomon was made king 'a second time'. 1 Kings 1 gives us some idea of what really went on behind the scenes.

With Adonijah taking matters into his own hands to declare himself king, it was necessary to act quickly if Solomon was to become the successor. Bathsheba acted under Nathan's guidance though with her own interests. Her message to David was to show how Adonijah's acts were contrary to David's stated intentions (1 Kings 1:17–21). Nathan's own statement to David argued that Adonijah was challenging David's kingship: 'Long live King Adonijah' (vv. 22–27). However, there are two problems here. First, there is the fact that nowhere before has the story informed us of this promise to Bathsheba. Even in Chronicles, where David refered to Solomon as a divinely revealed choice (1 Chron. 22:9), there was no earlier hint of this. One is left wondering to what extent this was divinely revealed and to what extent it was a suggestion of Nathan. Second, Nathan's claim that people were shouting 'Long live King Adonijah' is not supported by the report in vv. 5–9. This is not quibbling with details, since the other details reported by Bathsheba and by Nathan are confirmed in the description of Adonijah's actions. Although he wanted to be king, we are nowhere told that Adonijah had been proclaimed as king, only that he was making preparations.

Nevertheless, David assented to the requests of Bathsheba and Nathan. Solomon was confirmed as king in a hasty ceremony with David's blessing. This was sufficient to dissolve all opposition. Nathan retained his position and his sons served in key posts in Solomon's kingdom. Adonijah was rebuked. He became one of those who were hunted down and killed by Benaiah at Solomon's instructions (1 Kings 2:13–25). These instructions introduce Solomon's dutiful fulfilment of the last will of his father (1 Kings 2:1–9, 26–46). Even so, 1 Kings 2 is a terrible tale of revenge and butchery. One wonders what kind of king Solomon would become when his reign began with so many murders. That God would appear to Solomon and bless him was not due to any merit on the king's part. It was a manifestation of divine mercy and faithfulness to the covenant given to David and to his descendants with its promise of a dynasty in Jerusalem (2 Sam. 7:4–17). Solomon was heir to this promise.

## His wisdom and accomplishments

Solomon's reign begins with powerful alliances and great building activities in his capital (1 Kings 3:1). Solomon dedicated himself to the service of God (v. 3). He travelled north of Jerusalem. At Gibeon he was met by God in a dream, and offered his choice of gifts. Solomon requested a 'listening heart' (v. 9). The heart was the centre of the will. To have a listening heart was to have one which would hear and respond in obedience to God's Word. It would also hear and respond to the needs of Solomon's subjects. Solomon qualified the request with a reference to the ability to discern 'between good and evil'. More is meant here than knowledge of right and wrong. That is available to everyone. It involved the ability to grasp the essence of a problem and to understand exactly what was going on in the minds of those around him. It involved the ability to respond in all difficult situations, to govern wisely. This seems to contrast with the last days of David and the events of the preceding two chapters. David did not know of Adonijah's rebellion. He did not remember his choice of Solomon. Solomon, thrust into the midst of the brutal politics of the palace, had already begun to play the same game. But here, before God, he sought the ability to change course, to alter the world of politics so that the values of God and of the divine covenant emerge as dominant, rather than values where the strongest win.

God's response was one of approval (vv. 10–14). This was the correct thing to ask for. Instead of selfish requests for length of life or wealth or security, Solomon had asked for that which was appropriate to his calling as a ruler of God's people. For this reason God was pleased to grant discernment and to add the additional blessings for which Solomon did not ask. One proviso was added to the blessings, however, 'if you walk in my ways and obey my statutes and commands as David your father did' (v. 14). This only Solomon was expected to do.

The blessing of a listening heart had already begun to take effect. After all, Solomon's ability to listen to God was demonstrated by his presence at Gibeon and the divine appearance to him. His ability to listen to his people would be demonstrated by the story of the infant son claimed by two women (vv. 16–26). Solomon's famous decision, threatening to divide the child in two and thereby identifying the true mother, demonstrated to all the people that 'he had wisdom from God to administer justice' (v. 28). Additional examples are provided in the following chapters. Solomon organized his prospering kingdom (1 Kings 4:1–21) and his court (1 Kings 4:22–28), and prepared proverbs and other wisdom literature (1 Kings 4:29–34; cf. Prov. 1:1; 10:1; 25:1; S. of S. 1:1; and the title of Pss. 72 and 127).

However, Solomon's greatest demonstration of his wisdom was the building of the Temple to the LORD God of Israel. 1 Kings 5–7 contains elaborate details of the negotiations and preparations for the construction, as well as the building itself. The completion of the work is celebrated with the entrance of the ark of the covenant into the holiest part of the structure (1 Kings 8:1–11). This is followed by Solomon's blessing upon the people and his great dedicatory prayer, wherein he called to mind the promises which God made to David his father and interceded for the welfare of the people and their land (1 Kings 8:12–66).

## International fame and consequent apostasy

God's second appearance follows the Temple dedication and the note that Solomon 'had achieved all he had desired to do' (1 Kings 9:1). This time God's message is laden with warnings of judgment on the people and on the Temple if Solomon and his sons do not follow God wholeheartedly (vv. 6–9). Yet God's blessing remains and is promised for Solomon's faithful obedience and worship (vv. 3–5). Again this is exemplified in Kings by two cycles of narratives which describe Solomon's international, imperial and religious achievements. However, unlike the earlier accounts of Solomon's unqualified success, these now introduce an element of tension. Problems begin to appear, though it is not until the end of the second cycle that the root cause is made explicit.

In the first cycle, Solomon's payment to Hiram, king of Tyre is described as an example of Solomon's international involvements (vv. 10–14). However, Hiram was not pleased with the payment. Imperially, Solomon enlisted the Canaanites left in the land to complete his building projects (vv. 15–24). Here, too, one wonders how this use of slave labour could maintain the peace in the country. Even more worrying is the hint that Canaanites remain in the land long after the command to eradicate them. God had allowed them to remain in order to test the Israelites, whether or not they would remain faithful to him or would worship other deities (Judg. 3:1–4). Would Solomon pass the test? Solomon's religious achievement is summarized in a brief note about how he offered sacrifices at the Temple three times a year (1 Kings 0:25). This is praiseworthy insofar as it fulfilled the command to appear before the LORD three times a year (Exod. 23:14). However, for a ruler to offer burnt offerings in place of God's appointed priest was a sin. Saul had been removed from his kingship for this practice (1 Sam. 13:8–14).

In the second cycle of achievements, Solomon's international relations focus on the visit of the Queen of Sheba (1 Kings 9:26–10:13). While this is a happy scene with the Queen marvelling at the grandeur of Solomon and praising the God he worshipped, it is also a picture of close ties with two rulers of pagan countries, Hiram of Tyre and the queen of Sheba. Such close ties would be condemned by later prophets as leading the kings of Jerusalem into sin (Is. 7). Imperially, Solomon's weath and grandeur are again emphasized with special note of his throne and of the tribute and defences which he possessed (1 Kings 10:14–29). Yet these events, like the earlier discussion of slave labour, foreshadow the requests of the northern tribes for Solomon's son to reduce their load of servitude (1 Kings 12:4). Ultimately, that reason would form the basis for the seccession of the north. Religiously, Solomon's foreign wives turned him away from following after the true God of Israel (1 Kings 11:1–10). The 'listening heart' of Solomon became a 'divided heart' in the end (1 Kings 11:4, 9).

## Solomon's opponents

God's third word to Solomon came as a judgment for his sins (1 Kings 11:11–13). The kingdom was to be divided and removed from the control of David's dynasty. Yet, even in judgment for Solomon's explicit disobedience to God's covenant, God remained merciful. The threat was qualified by promises that it would not happen in Solomon's lifetime and that it would not be the whole kingdom which would be lost. Unlike the other two visits of God, this one is not followed by examples of Solomon's wisdom and glory. The remainder of Solomon's story becomes one of division and loss (1 Kings 11:14–42). The empire began to disappear. To the south, Hadad, an Edomite, was supported by Pharaoh. He fomented rebellion against Solomon. To the north, Rezon, an Aramean, created a rebel army which operated out of Damascus. Within Israel itself, Jeroboam was met by a prophet. Solomon had appointed Jeroboam to oversee the slave labour which came from the northern part of the kingdom. The prophet foretold Jeroboam's future kingship over the north. Solomon tried to kill him, but Jeroboam fled to Egypt and remained there until the king died. Although some of these rebellions may have already begun before the third word from God to Solomon, the books of Kings organize them so as to show their true origin in the rebellion of Solomon's heart against the exclusive loyalty to the God of Israel.

## Summary

Solomon succeeded with the one aspect of a listening heart, that of listening to others to make the wisest of judgments and to render other insights. Solomon did not succeed in the other aspect of a listening heart, that of listening to the voice and will of God. In the end this distorted his life and work. No amount of wisdom or insight or sensitivity to others replaces the heart directed toward God. Solomon was the world's greatest success but his life could not be counted as successful in terms of eternal truths. He is a model, tragically followed again and again, of the failure to remain faithful to God until the end.                                    R.H.

## SONSHIP

Sonship is a multi-faceted idea in the Bible. It includes children in families and metaphorical uses such as referring to the inhabitants of Jerusalem as her 'children'. Most important are the many references in which God is regarded as Father or an individual or a group is regarded as God's child. (Variations between 'sons of God' and 'children of God' seem to be based most often on stylistic, not theological, concerns.)

In a fashion typical of ancient Mediterranean peoples, the Bible occasionally refers to angelic beings as 'sons of God' (Job. 1:6; 2:1; 38:7; Ps. 89:6; but not Gen. 6:4). Because God is their creator and they are under his authority they are called 'sons of God'. Similarly human beings are called the 'offspring of God' (Acts 17:28–29) because God is their creator. This usage, however, is very rare.

### Redemptive sonship

The dominant theme which is at the heart of the biblical presentation is that God is Father by virtue of redemption. Even texts which use the language of creation or begetting (such as Deut. 32:6 and Mal. 2:10) do so metaphorically referring neither to a biological generation of humanity by God (as in pagan religions) nor to creation, but rather to the formation of Israel as God's son, chosen and delivered out of Egypt in the Exodus (*Hos. 11:1*).

In *Is. 63:16* the prophet cries out, 'You, O LORD, are our Father, "Our Redeemer" from of old is your name.' The Father's name is 'Redeemer'. God redeemed Israel and so he is the Father of the nation of Israel. Because the king of Israel was the representative of the nation he also could be regarded as God's son (*2 Sam. 7:14; 1 Chron. 17:13*). The king was God's servant and son (*Ps. 89:20, 26*), the adopted son of God (*Ps. 2:7*). In the intertestamental period this led to the use of the phrase 'son of God' as a Messianic title (*4 Q Florilegium 1:11–13; 4 Q ps Dan A 1:7–2:1*).

### Eschatological sonship

This eschatological use of 'Son of God' as a Messianic title is not surprising but it is not the only eschatological use of sonship motifs. Israel's trust that God would come and meet their needs was expressed by the prophets in the language of the family (*Is. 63:16; 64:8; Jer. 3:19; Hos. 1:10*). In the midst of oppression God's people looked forward to the day of blessing when they would be called 'children of God'.

### Sonship is in Christ

Jesus the Messiah is frequently called the Son of God in the NT. Sometimes the phrase is used simply as a messianic title (*Luke 4:41; John 1:49*). On the other occasions it identifies him as the pre-existent, unique Son of God (*Gal. 4:4; Matt. 22:41–46*). (See *Jesus*.) Others become children of God as they believe in Jesus, the son of God (*John 1:12*). Their adoption into God's family is 'through Jesus Christ' (*Eph. 3:5*; see also *Heb. 2:5–13; Rom. 8:14–19; Matt. 11:27*). More specifically, it is through his sufferings that the Son of God brings others into God's family. *Heb. 1–2* develop Jesus' supremacy as Son. *Heb. 2:10–18* addresses the issue of how the Son of God brings 'many sons to glory' (*2:10*). Clearly (*2:11, 14, 17–18*) it is his suffering and death which is the means by which the Son frees those 'held in slavery' (*2:15*) and brings God's sons, Jesus' brothers, to glory (*2:10–11*). The coming of Jesus the messianic Son of God is the central feature of God's provision of eschatological familial blessings of his people. That is, the familial blessing of God's people is in union with Jesus specifically because he is the messianic Son of God. As the Messiah he brings to realization the hopes of the prophets. This realization includes not only God's sons but God's daughters as well (*Is. 43:6; 2 Cor. 6:18*). The well-known disclaimer 'there is neither male nor female' is the Pauline explanation of the affirmation 'You are all sons of God' (*Gal. 3:26–28*). That is, in biblical language 'sons of God' is not gender specific but is generic.

### The loving call of the Father

Not everyone is a child of God. In *John 8:44* Jesus told his Jewish kinsmen, 'You belong to your Father, the devil.' Similarly the beautiful picture of God's fatherly care in *Ps. 68:5–6* is followed by the clear warning in *v.* 6 that not all are God's children. 'A father to the fatherless, a defender of widows, is God in his holy dwelling. God sets the lonely in families, he leads forth the prisoners with singing; but the rebellious live in a sun-scorched land.' Because everyone is not God's child, Jesus said that in order for someone to see the Kingdom of God, he 'must be born again' (*John 3:3, 7*).

The solution to the plight of the person who is not a child of God begins with the gracious Father. No one comes to recognize Jesus' Sonship unless the Father reveals it (*Matt.* 16:16–17) and the good news of the gospel is that the Father has taken the initiative (*John 6:37, 44–45, 65*). How can one draw near to God? Only if 'your Father is merciful' (*Luke 6:36*), only if 'your heavenly Father will also forgive you' (*Matt. 6:14*). The Father is a gracious, forgiving Father. His loving mercy is the root of his people's sonship (*Jer. 31:9, 20; 1 Pet. 1:3*).

The apostle Paul's distinctive stress on this theme is found in *Eph. 1:3–14*. Two of the major themes of this doxology are the adoption of God's children and God's will or purpose. The latter is expressed with a variety of words: 'will' (*Eph.* 1:5, 9, 11), 'purpose' (*v.* 11), 'plan' (*v.* 11), 'good pleasure' (*vv.* 5, 9), 'predestine' (*vv.* 5, 11), and 'chose' (*v.* 4). The cumulative effect is to stress that adoption into God's family is built on no less a foundation than the heavenly Father himself. (The basic meaning of the word 'adoption' stresses the choice of the adopting Father.)

### Adoption and regeneration

Two metaphors are used in the biblical texts to describe how the Father's loving choice comes to realization and the person who is not a child of God is united with Christ and made a member of God's family: adoption and regeneration. The word 'adoption' which never occurs in the OT and only five times in the NT (always in *Paul, Rom.* 8:15, 23; 9:4; *Gal.* 4:5; *Eph.*1:5), is taken from the socio-legal sphere of the Greco-Roman world. 'Regeneration', which appears primarily in the Johannine corpus, is a biological metaphor.

In spite of distinctive nuances, they both make the basic point that the change involved is a radical change in the entire orientation of life. The old life is gone and a new life begun. Likewise, both metaphors stress that the change is not only radical; it is also sudden. Neither rebirth nor adoption into the family of God is a process. A third shared characteristic of adoption and regeneration is that the change envisioned is a divine change. People become children of God, 'through God' (*Gal.* 4:7). They are 'born of God' (*1 John 3:9; 4:7; 5:1, 4, 18*). Specifically adoption and regeneration are both linked to the work of the Holy Spirit (*John 3:5; Gal. 4:6*).

### The results of sonship

One of the striking features of the biblical use of sonship is the broad range of results with which it is associated. This is predictable because sonship touches the centre of the human existence and extends to every area of life.

**1.** Trust in Father's care. The child of God rests in the Father's omniscience (*Matt. 10:29–30*), omnipotence (*Mark 14:36*), and compassion (*John 16:26–28*). All three are essential to the security of the child. *Matt. 6:19–34* deals from several perspectives with the relation of God's people to the 'stuff' of this world: money, food, and clothing. *Vv. 25–34* focus on the problem of worry about the basic needs of (1) life supporting nourishment, and (2) protection. In both instances the climax is 'your heavenly Father' (*Matt. 6:26, 32*). The child of God rests in the promise of the knowing, powerful, caring Father. (See also *Jer. 31:8–9; Ps. 68:5.*)

The fact that the sonship of God's child is an 'in-Christ' sonship has the result that the present life of the child involves suffering on the path to glory, just as Jesus' Sonship involved suffering on the path of glory. 'We are fellow heirs (by virtue of sonship) with Christ, provided we suffer with him in order that we may also be glorified with him' (*Rom. 8:17*). There is present suffering under the loving control of the Father. It is a suffering which leads to glory with the children of God in conformity to the image of Christ the first-born Son (*Rom. 8:18–30*).

In fact, so far are the trials of life from being signs of abandonment by God; often they are discipling, nurturing gifts of the Father who is shaping and moulding the children he loves. This is the point of *Prov. 3:11–12; Deut. 8:1–5* and especially *Heb. 12:3–11*. One of the results of sonship is the discipline of the Father, 'for our good' (*Heb. 12:10*), for the 'good' (*Rom. 8:28*) of being 'conformed to the likeness of his Son' (*Rom. 8:29–30*).

The child's trust in the Father for provision, protection, and discipline means that she does not worry but commits herself to God. This kind of trust, however, is not to be mistaken for self-confidence. The children of God learn the lesson of *Ps. 103:13–14*. The heavenly Father has compassion on his children and re-members that they 'are dust'. God's child remembers the same thing, recognizes her weakness and trusts in God.

A corollary to trust is patient endurance. God's child is called to labour and not to give up (*Heb. 12:5–13; Rom. 8:24–25*). Trust in God results in selfless, enduring, joyful service of the Father in heaven (*2 Cor. 1:2–5; Deut. 1:29–31; Matt. 5:9*).

**2.** Intimacy. The child of God is a personal creature who has been called into a personal and intimate relationship of openness, concern, and tenderness with the loving heavenly Father. This intimacy is seen in many ways in the Bible, but one of the most significant is in its connection with prayer.

(a) Prayer to Father. Jesus' own intimate relationship with God came to expression in his characteristic address of God as 'Father' in prayer (*Luke 10:21; 22:42; 23:34, 46*). (Note: 'characteristic' not 'unique'. Recent scholarship has put to rest the older claims that Jesus' address of God as 'Father' was lexically or syntactically unique.) In the 'Lord's Prayer' he teaches God's other children to pray, 'Our Father' (*Matt. 6:9*). Because they have been adopted into God's family (*Gal. 4:5*), because God has sent the Spirit of his Son into their hearts (*Gal. 4:6*), they also through the Spirit can pray to God, 'Father' (*Gal. 4:6; Rom. 8:15*).

This kind of intimate prayer relationship with the heavenly Father is (for Jesus) the antithesis of the impersonal, ritual formulas of pagan magic (*Matt. 6:7*). Prayer is not a tool for coercing the powers of the universe. Prayer is coming into the personal presence of God. The prayer of the child of God is also the antithesis of the hypocritical prayer of self-seeking religionists (*Matt. 6:1–6*). Jesus affirms the omniscience of Father and says that the child of God who is secure in God does not seek praise and security from others. The cure for hypocritical prayer (and hypocrisy in general) is the nurture of intimate security with the heavenly Father.

(b) *Family holiness*. Biblical intimacy with the heavenly Father is a comforting, secure relationship. It is not, however, a simple or unchallenging relationship. Biblical sonship brings not only blessings but also demands. In *Deut. 14:1* we read 'You are the children of the LORD your God. Do not cut yourselves or shave the front of your heads for the dead.' Because the Israelites are God's children they must not adopt the religious customs of their pagan neighbours. There is a distinctive lifestyle of the family of God (*Deut. 32:5–6; Mal. 1:6; Is. 63:16; 64:8–9*).

Similarly, the NT develops the ethical responsibilities of Christians in a family-of-God context. The Father is the holy judge who in the future will decide the eternal destiny of humanity (*Matt. 18:35; Mark 8:38; Luke 9:26*). The call for present holiness is also framed in family of God language. 'Do everything without complaining or arguing, so that you may be blameless and pure, children of God' (*Phil. 2:14–15*). In *Heb. 2:11–17* union with Christ and sonship are developed in connection with sanctification, and in *1 John 2:29–3:2* the child of God is called on to purify himself. In this way the biblical model of sonship is radically different from the surrounding Hellenistic religions in which sonship was commonplace but was never tied to personal moral ethics in the way it was in Scripture. In the Bible, it is repeatedly stressed that family membership brings family responsibilities. 'Be imitators of God, as dearly loved children' (*Eph. 5:1*). 'Be perfect as your heavenly Father is perfect' (*Matt. 5:48*). Intimacy with the God of the Bible provides security and demands holiness.

**3.** *The freedom of sons*. Sonship is contrasted with slavery to stress the freedom of God's children. 'You are no longer a slave but a son' (*Gal. 4:7*; also *Rom. 8:21*). The old life was bondage; the new is liberation. As Israel was freed from Egyptian bondage to national sonship so also the Christian is liberated to sonship. Particularly this freedom is described as a freedom from fear. 'For you did not receive a spirit that makes you a slave again to fear, but you received a Spirit of sonship. And by him we cry, "Abba! Father!"' (*Rom. 8:15*). Adoption produces confidence not fear. The child of God is freed from the fear of death (*Rom. 8:12–15; Heb. 2:11–17*). In *Heb. 9:15* it is spelled out clearly that the reason the child of God is certain of her eternal inheritance as God's child is that she has been set free from her sin. The fear of guilt is gone. The child of God is also freed from a directionless life. The work of Jesus (and of the Father) which liberates the children from slavery and makes them sons (*John 8:31–37*) is also the word which marks out the contours of their lives (*vv. 37, 47, 55*). The freedom of sonship is freedom from sin and death and freedom to the life of the family of God.

**4.** *The family of God*. To become a child of God is to become a member of the household of God (*1 Tim. 3:15*). For the biblical writers the liberty of sonship is not a modern, Westernized autonomy. It is a liberty that is found only in relationship with others in the family of God. The family of God is a united household which has no room for pride, bigotry, and self-centredness. Racial, cultural, and societal barriers must give way to humility, love, and concern for others (*Eph. 2:18–19*). The 'Sons of God through faith' are those who have been 'baptized into Christ' (*Gal. 3:26–27*), who have been incorporated into the church of God.

Every NT writer except Jude refers to Christians as 'brothers'. Paul does so 133 times. 'Brother' is a word of deep personal affection denoting friendship, love, and fellowhip in the work of Christ (*1 Cor. 8:11; 1 Pet. 5:9;* 19 times in *1 Thessalonians*). In the midst of a pagan culture, the alien people of God were called on to 'love the brotherhood' (*1 Pet. 2:17*) and were offered in that brotherhood a foretaste of the eternal family banquet (*Jer. 3:19; Luke 20:34, 36; Rom. 8:23; Rev. 19:9*). A.M.

**SOPATER** The son of Pyrrhus, Sopater was from Berea, a town in Macedonia. He joined the apostle Paul on his travels from Greece through Macedonia and on to Jerusalem (*Acts 20:4*). His name is an abbreviation of Sosipater and he may be the 'relative' of Paul referred to in *Rom. 16:21*.

**SOPHERETH** (Heb., 'scribe') was one of Solomon's servants whose descendants returned from the Exile in Babylon in company with Zerubbabel (*Neh. 7:57*). In *Ezra 2:55* he appears as Hassophereth.

**SOSIPATER** (Heb., 'the saving father'). Either a fellow Jew or a blood relative of Paul and one of those who was with him when he wrote his letter to the Roman church (*Rom. 16:21*). He joined Paul, Timothy, Lucius and others in sending the church his greetings. It is likely that he had visited the Christians in Rome either when on business or as an itinerant Christian teacher. He may well have been the man called Sopater in *Acts 20:4* who came from Berea, a town in Macedonia. He joined the apostle Paul on his travels from Greece through Macedonia and on to Jerusalem.

**SOSTHENES 1.** Sosthenes was the ruler or leader in the synagogue in Corinth when Paul was preaching the gospel of Christ in the town (*Acts 18:17*). In accordance with his usual custom, Paul had first gone to the synagogue 'every sabbath' to try to persuade and reason with them about the truth of the gospel. Eventually the Jews became very abusive (*Acts 18:6*) and so Paul left to concentrate on preaching to the Gentiles. He moved in next door to the synagogue in the house of Titius Justus, 'a worshipper of God'. Through Paul's preaching the synagogue ruler, Crispus, was converted and 'believed the Lord' (*v. 8*).

Paul stayed in the town about 18 months and eventually the Jews made a united attack on him and brought him to court before Gallio the proconsul of Achaia. He refused to judge the case because he considered the charges to be about minor internal matters of the Jewish faith and of no real concern to the Roman authorities. The Jews were ejected from the court and 'they all' rounded on Sosthenes and beat him outside the court. Probably this means that the Jews beat him because he had failed to obtain a conviction, but the text might imply that Greeks outside the court beat him because he was a Jew (*vv. 14–17*). Paul stayed on for a while in Corinth, having seen a number of Jews and Greeks turn to Christ.

**2.** A 'brother' called Sosthenes is mentioned in *1 Cor. 1:1* as one who was writing to the Corinthians along with Paul. There is little doubt that in referring to him by name, Paul was using Sosthenes as his scribe or amanuensis. The fact that he is mentioned and called 'brother' suggests he was known to the Corinthians and therefore may well have been the Sosthenes of 1. above, now converted and working at Paul's side, perhaps even given the task of carrying the letter back to the Corinthians. P. D. G.

**SOTAI** was one of Solomon's servants whose descendants returned from the Exile in Babylon in company with Zerubbabel (Ezra 2:55; Neh. 7:57).

**SPIRIT** See Holy Spirit.

**STACHYS** (Gk., 'car of grain'). A man who was a 'dear friend' of the apostle Paul. He lived in Rome and was greeted by Paul in Rom. 16:9. Paul's personal recognition and care for many individuals in different congregations is to be noted in most of his letters.

**STEPHANAS** means 'crown'. A well-known Christian in the church at Corinth, Stephanas and his household were the first to be converted in the province of Achaia (1 Cor. 16:15) and were known for their devotion to the service of the other Christians in the church. Paul urged other Christians in the church to submit to the likes of Stephanas who worked so hard at the Christian service.

We know that Stephanas was baptized by Paul. At Corinth it appears that some people were dividing into groups around certain figureheads. Perhaps some of these divisions went back to people being proud about the leader who had baptized them. Paul claimed he had baptized only about three, among whom were Stephanas and his household. Paul argued that the unity of Christians must be centred on the gospel of Christ crucified, not on who had baptized whom (1 Cor. 1:16–17, 23).

In 1 Cor. 16:17–18 Stephanas is mentioned along with Achaicus and Fortunatus. These men were 'worthy of recognition' for their faithful service to the Lord, specially in bringing news to Paul in Ephesus about the Corinthian church. Perhaps these three had carried a letter from the Corinthians to Paul and they may have carried back the letter we now know as 1 Corinthians. Their faithful service was 'refreshing' to Paul's Spirit. It is a regular feature in Paul's letters that those with a Christian ministry of encouragement are commended. P.D.G.

## STEPHEN

Stephen (Heb., 'wealth' or 'crown') is one of the most attractive characters in the NT, and his speech is the longest in the books of Acts (7:2–53). His life and work are highlighted in Acts 6–7, though his martyrdom and the persecution which followed are noted later in Acts (22:20; 11:19).

Stephen came to prominence in the early days of the Christian church, when the community was developing and experiencing growing pains. One of the tensions that surfaced was the charge that the Hellenistic (Grecian) widows were being neglected in the daily distribution of food (Acts 6:1). In response to this criticism, the twelve apostles called the community together, faced the issue squarely, and proposed a reasonable solution: 'Brothers, choose seven men from among you who are known to be full of the Spirit and wisdom. We will turn this responsibility over to them and will give our attention to prayer and the ministry of the word' (6:3–4). This proposal met with general acceptance in the whole community, and they chose seven men of unblemished reputation to handle the situation. Two of the leading members of this group were Stephen and Philip.

When the remedial action was carried out, the Jerusalem church experienced further growth: 'So the word of God spread. The number of disciples in Jerusalem increased rapidly, and a large number of priests became obedient to the faith' (6:7).

As Luke makes clear, Stephen was deeply involved in this whole church growth movement, particularly in the expansion of the church from Jerusalem to Antioch (Acts 6:1–12:25). Luke devotes considerable attention to the witness of Stephen (6:8–7:60), which he describes in terms of his arrest (6:8–15), his brilliant 'defence' (7:1–53), and his martyrdom (7:54–60).

Stephen was not only a practical man who could deal with the administration of church relief to the needy, but was also interested in the direct communication of the gospel to others. His message was accompanied by forceful demonstrations of the power of God which enabled him to perform 'great wonders and miraculous signs among the people' (Acts 6:8). This gave his preaching a remarkable credibility, but it also aroused opposition from conservative Jewish sources who were suspicious of the new Christian movement and jealous of Stephen's evident popularity and charismatic appeal. Despite their opposition, his enemies were not able to withstand 'the wisdom of the Spirit' which characterized his public witness (6:10). Since they were determined to attack and undermine his work, they instigated a surreptitious campaign to convict Stephen on serious charges of blasphemy 'against Moses and against God' (6:11). Mobilizing the crowd against him and utilizing the evidence of false witnesses, they secured his arrest by twisting his glowing testimony for Christ into something sinister and hostile to Mosaic authority (6:14). The undeniable fact, however, is that Stephen maintained his composure before the Jewish council, and his enemies recognized his transparent saintliness; his face was 'like the face of an angel' (6:15).

Stephen's speech to the council is a remarkable review of Jewish history and a bold defence of the Christian faith before his accusers. He was asked by the high priest if the charges made by the witnesses were true or false. They had blatantly asserted: 'This fellow never stops speaking against this holy place and against the law. For we have heard him say that this Jesus of Nazareth will destroy this place [the temple] and will change the customs that Moses handed down to us' (Acts 6:13–14). Stephen's answer was not an attempt to escape suffering or persecution, but rather a magnificent confession of his faith in Christ against the backdrop of God's dealings with his covenant people throughout their history. The sermon really offers us a 'biblical theology' – an examination of the OT in the light of Christ's coming. It paints a gloomy picture of constant backsliding on the part of God's people, and really points to their rejection of the promised Messiah as the tragic climax of a long history of apostasy and disobedience (7:2–53).

The speech has three main parts, the first being devoted to the patriarchs (Acts 7:2–16), the second to Moses (7:17–43), and the third to the Tabernacle and the Temple (7:44–50). This historical review is followed by his rebuke of their prevailing attitude toward the coming of Christ (7:51–53), their angry response in martyring him (7:54–8:1a), and the dispersal of the Jerusalem church in consequence of the ensuing persecution (8:1b–4).

After asking for their careful attention to what he had to say (*Acts 7:1; cf. 22:1*), Stephen began his account of holy history by going back to God's dealings with the great forefather of the covenant people, Abraham (*7:2–8*). God had spoken to the patriarch and directed him into the land of promise (*Acts 7:3; cf. Gen. 12:1–3*). Abraham had obeyed, leaving the country of the Chaldeans and settling in Haran, where he remained until the death of his father (*Acts 7:4; cf. Gen. 11:31–21:1, 5; 15:7*). God had made wonderful promises to Abraham, even though at that time he was childless (*Acts 7:5; cf. Gen. 12:7; 13:15; 15:2, 18; 16:1; 17:8; etc.*). God told Abraham: 'Your descendants will be strangers in a country not their own, and they will be enslaved and mistreated four hundred years' (*Acts 7:6*). Nevertheless, God would eventually judge their oppressors and lead them safely into the Promised Land where they would worship him (*Acts 7:7; cf. Gen. 15:13–14; Exod. 3:12*). It was in this covenantal context that the rite of circumcision was to be understood (*Acts 7:8; cf. Gen. 17:10–14*), and so in due course 'Abraham became the father of Isaac and circumcised him eight days after his birth. Later Isaac became the father of Jacob, and Jacob became the father of the twelve patriarchs' (*Acts 7:8; cf. Gen. 21:4*).

Similarly the story of Joseph was recounted to remind the people of God's providence and to set the stage for the mighty deliverance of the Exodus under Moses. Both Joseph and Moses experienced jealousy and rejection at the hands of their people (*Acts 7:9, 27, 35; cf. Gen. 37:11; Exod. 2:14; 3:13–14*). Despite this rejection, God used Moses to be the 'ruler and deliverer' of his people (*Acts 7:35*); indeed the divine guidance was seen in the birth of Moses (*7:17–22*), his time in the wilderness (*7:23–29*), his direct commission (*7:30–34*) and the deliverance from Egypt (*7:35–38*), despite Israel's idolatry since Egypt (*7:39–43*).

The final part of the historical overview deals with the contrast between the Tabernacle and the Temple (*Acts 7:44–50*). Stephen clearly opposed a static view of Israel's life in favour of a dynamic view of God's people following him in pilgrimage. The closing rebuke was an attempt to make the Jewish people face up to their hard-heartedness and rebellion against the Holy Spirit (*7:51–53*). It was really a call to repentance and faith which unfortunately fell on deaf ears. He accused his audience of being 'betrayers and murderers' of 'the Righteous One' (Christ), and in a fit of rage they attacked him, dragged him outside the city and put him to death by stoning (*7:54, 58*). He died in the presence of Saul of Tarsus, who was 'giving approval to his death' (*7:60–8:1*). Later Saul became a believer (*9:1–19; 22:1–21; 26:2–23*). Stephen's death was probably one of the 'goads' that turned Paul to Christ (*26:14*).

Several features need to be noted here. First, Stephen, the protomartyr, acted like his Lord. He told the truth in his trial (*Acts 7:51–53; cf. John 18:37*), forgave his enemies (*Acts 7:60; cf. Luke 23:34*), cried with a loud voice (*Luke 23:46*) and committed his spirit (*Acts 7:59; cf. Luke 23:46; Ps. 31:5*). The commitment of his spirit was given a Christ-centred emphasis in Acts which is particularly striking: 'Lord Jesus, receive my spirit' (*Acts 7:59*). Stephen had lived, suffered and died for Christ; now he looked to his Lord for final vindication.

Two other elements may be noted. One is the striking use of the witness theme. In his first volume Luke had recorded the words of Jesus: 'I tell you, whoever acknowledges me before men, the Son of Man will also acknowledge before the angels of God' (*Luke 12:8f.; cf. Matt. 10:32f.*). Stephen at his martyrdom boldly claimed that promise and asked that Jesus, the Son of Man, acknowledge him in heaven as a true disciple in the divine presence. He was granted his request and cried: 'Look, I see heaven open and the Son of Man standing at the right hand of God!' (*Acts 7:56*). The other feature is the fact that Stephen's life is clearly under the full control of the Holy Spirit. This role of the Spirit is evident in Stephen's appointment (*6:3, 5*), his powerful witness to Christ (*6:9–10*), his mighty works and miraculous signs (*6:8*), and his fearless speech before the Sanhedrin (*7:2–53*).

Stephen's heroic stand for his Lord, his courage in facing opponents, and his loving attitude towards his enemies, all mark him out as a worthy model of a faithful disciple, an effective worker, and a noble martyr. His story has relevance today, since the 20th century has seen more martyrdoms than any other century of the Christian era.                                                      A.A.T.

**STOICS** This was one of several Greek philosophical schools in the time of Paul. The apostle encountered this tradition in *Acts 17:18*. The movement was founded by Zeno (340–265 BC) in about 300 BC. Its proponents were pantheists, who argued for the unity of humanity and kinship with the divine. They were dominated by a concern for reason and issues related to the world-state. They divided their philosophy into three parts: the consideration of physical objects, ethics, and logic. Their consideration of ethics also had much to say about human passion and impulses. The goal of life was to live in a way that was harmonious with nature and to perform befitting action, that is, that which reason prevails on us to do. Happiness consists in virtue and a harmonious disposition. So one should seek to be prudent, just, courageous, and temperate. The soul had eight elements: five senses, speech, intellect, and that which the soul generates. Emotion is a reflection of prior judgments, but the wise man is emotionless, not subject to judgments based on the swing of circumstances. Neither is the wise man vain. Stoics did seek to honour the gods, offer prayers, and ask for good things from the gods. Stoics also sought to pursue excellence. Love is expressed in friendliness. Life has three dimensions: the contemplative life, the practical and the rational, of which the last is the most important. God is the reason inherent in matter. So the world is ordered by reason and providence. The philosophy is detailed in Diogenes Laertius' *Life of the Eminent Philosophers*, book 7.                                    D.B.

**SUAH** Mentioned in *1 Chron. 7:36* as a son of Zophah, a chief in the tribe of Asher. He was among the 'brave warriors and outstanding leaders' of the tribe (*v. 40*).

**SUSANNA** is mentioned only in *Luke 8:3*. She was one of the women who supported Christ during his earthly ministry out of her own means.

**SUSI** was the father of Gaddi and was from the tribe of Manasseh. Gaddi was one of the twelve spies sent out by Moses from the Desert of Paran to spy out the land of Canaan (*Num. 13:11*).

**SYNTYCHE** A Christian woman at Philippi who was one of Paul's 'fellow workers' (*Phil. 4:2–3*). In spite of theories to the contrary, the feminine pronouns show that she was a woman. Paul exhorted Syntyche and her co-worker Euodia to be reconciled for the sake of the unity of the church.

# T

**TABALIAH** A Merarite Levite who was the third son of Hosah. He is listed among the gatekeepers chosen by King David, and he also had duties ministering in the Tabernacle worship (1 *Chron. 26:11*).

**TABBAOTH** His descendants were among those who returned from the Babylonian Exile with Nehemiah and Zerubbabel (*Ezra 2:43; Neh. 7:46*).

**TABEEL** (Heb., 'God is good').
**1.** Together with Bishlam and Mithredath, he wrote a letter to King Artaxerxes lodging an accusation against the people of Judah (*Ezra 4:7*). For more detail see *Mithredath*.
**2.** This Tabeel is known only as the father of the man whom Pekah, king of Israel, and Rezin, king of Aram, wanted to set up as king in Judah once they had conquered the territory (*Is. 7:6*). The name occurs in a message from the LORD through the prophet Isaiah to encourage Ahaz king of Judah that this plan would fail. The LORD would not let Judah fall into their hands, even though the invasion did conquer much of the kingdom. For more detail see *Pekah* and *Rezin*.

P.D.G.

**TABITHA** In *Acts 9:36–43* we meet Tabitha, a disciple from Joppa who was always doing good and helping the poor. Tabitha became ill and died, and her friends summoned Peter, believing that he had power to restore Tabitha to life once more. Peter arrived on the scene to find the grieving friends, and he watched as they openly cried and showed him fine clothing their friend had made while still alive. Peter sent everyone from the room, got down on his knees and began to pray. When the time was right, Peter spoke the words, 'Tabitha, get up,' and she did. Tabitha was restored to her friends that day, and many people believed in the Lord because of God's work through Peter. (She was also called Dorcas.) S.C.

**TABRIMMON** (Aram., 'Rimmon [a god] is good'). The son of Hezion and the father of Ben-Hadad. Ben Hadad I was the king of Aram who made an alliance with King Asa of Judah against King Baasha of Israel (1 *Kings 15:18*). See *Ben-Hadad*.

**TAHAN 1.** A son of Ephraim and a leader of the Tahanite clan (*Num. 26:35*).
**2.** This Tahan was a member of an Ephraimite family. He was the son of Telah and the father of Ladan. They are mentioned in 1 *Chron. 7:25* as ancestors of Joshua son of Num (*v. 27*).

**TAHASH** was a son of Abraham's brother Nahor by his concubine Reumah (*Gen. 22:24*).

**TAHATH** (Heb., 'compensation').
**1.** 1 *Chron. 6:24* mentions a Tahath who was a Levite and a descendant of Kohath. He was a son of Assir and the father of Uriel. Given that some names are omitted in these genealogies, it is likely that the Tahath mentioned in *v. 37* (who was also the son of Assir and a Kohathite Levite) was the same person. If this is so, then he was also the father of Zephaniah. He was an ancestor of Samuel (*v. 33*).
**2.** A descendant of Ephraim named

Tahath is mentioned in 1 Chron. 7:20. He was a son of Bered, the father of Eleadah and the grandfather of 3. below.

**3.** Another descendant of Ephraim, son of Eleadah and father of Zabad (1 Chron. 7:20).

**TAHPENES** was an Egyptian queen whose sister was given in marriage by Pharaoh to Hadad (1 Kings 11:19). Hadad had been a member of royalty in Edom but had fled to Egypt when Joab, David's commander, had attacked the Edomites. Pharaoh was pleased with Hadad and so bestowed this great honour on him of marrying into the Egyptian royal family. Tahpenes' sister later bore Hadad a son called Genubath. He was brought up in the royal family by Tahpenes herself (v. 20).

**TAHREA** One of King Saul's descendants and from the tribe of Benjamin, Tahrea was the third son of Micah and grandson of Merib-Baal (1 Chron. 9:41).

**TALMAI 1.** One of three notorious descendants of Anak who lived in Hebron at the time of the conquest of Canaan by Joshua. Caleb led the attack against Hebron, defeating these three giants in battle. As a result he and his family inherited this part of the land of Canaan (Num. 13:22; Josh. 15:14; Judg. 1:10). It is particularly interesting to note how the LORD blessed Caleb in this conquest. It had been he and Joshua alone who had originally returned to Moses after spying out the land of Canaan and who had trusted the LORD sufficiently to believe that such giants could in fact be defeated. His faith was seen to be well-placed and his rewards for that faith were considerable (Num. 13:30; 14:24).

**2.** This Talmai was king of Geshur, a small area to the north-east of the Sea of Galilee (2 Sam. 3:3; 1 Chron. 3:2). He was the father of Maacah, one of King David's wives, who became the mother of Absalom. It was to this area that Absalom later fled after the revenge killing of his brother Amnon (2 Sam. 13:37). P.D.G.

**TALMON** The head of a family of Levitical gatekeepers of the Temple who lived in Jerusalem following the return from the Babylonian Exile (1 Chron. 9:17; Neh. 11:19; 12:25). His descendants continued in the work (Ezra 2:42; Neh. 7:45) which also involved guarding the Temple storerooms at the gates.

**TAMAR** (Heb., 'date tree').

**1.** Tamar was daughter-in-law to Judah and wife to his sons, Er and Onan. When Judah lost both sons during their marriage to Tamar, he became afraid to offer his third son to the young widow. Judah sent Tamar back to her father with the false promise that she would be betrothed to his youngest when the time was right. Tamar learned of Judah's deceit and resolved in her heart to bear his child. Disguising herself as a prostitute, Tamar caught Judah's attention and he slept with her without realizing her identity. Tamar requested a young goat as payment for her services, so Judah left his seal, cord and staff as a symbol of good faith. When Judah's servant could not locate the woman, the matter was suppressed for three months until Judah was told that his daughter-in-law was a prostitute and pregnant. Judah ordered that Tamar be burned to death. However, when she produced the seal, the cord and the staff Judah spared her, confessing his own deceit and proclaiming her more righteous than himself. Tamar gave birth to twin boys, Perez and Zerah (Gen. 38:6, 11, 13, 24; Ruth 4:12; Matt. 1:3).

**2.** This Tamar was David's daughter, the sister of Absalom and the half-sister of Amnon (see 2 Sam. 13:1–22; 1 Chron. 3:9). As a young woman, Tamar was summoned to help care for her sick half-brother. In fact, Amnon was not sick at all, but in love with his half-sister, a beautiful young virgin. Amnon took advantage of Tamar's kindness and vulnerability, and he raped her. He then added insult to his sin by refusing to take her as his wife. We are told that, after raping his sister, Amnon 'hated Tamar more than he had loved her'. Tamar was devastated by the whole situation and lived in desolation in the house of her brother, Absalom. Absalom later took revenge and killed Amnon. David's lack of authority or action in this family tragedy undoubtedly contributed to the contempt that Absalom later showed for his father.

**3.** Another Tamar was the daughter born to Absalom. We are told that she became a beautiful woman (2 *Sam.* 14:27). S.C.

**TAMMUZ** In a prophetic vision, Ezekiel saw many 'detestable' pagan happenings in Jerusalem and the Temple which would bring down the judgment of God on the people. One of the dreadful events he saw was women sitting by one of the gates of the Temple mourning for the Babylonian god of fertility, Tammuz (*Ezek.* 8:14). A month of mourning was part of the cult associated with this god.

**TANHUMETH** (Heb., 'consolation'). The father of Seraiah (2 *Kings* 25:23; *Jer.* 40:8) who lived at the time of Jeremiah and the fall of Jerusalem (see *Seraiah* and *Gedaliah*). He was a Netophathite who remained in Judah after the Exile to Babylon.

**TAPHATH** A daughter of King Solomon who was married to Ben-Abinadab, one of Solomon's twelve district governors (1 *Kings* 4:11).

**TAPPUAH** (Heb., 'apple') was a leader in the tribe of Judah and was a son of Hebron (1 *Chron.* 2:43).

**TAREA** One of King Saul's descendants and from the tribe of Benjamin, Tarea was the third son of Micah and grandson of Merib-Baal (1 *Chron.* 8:35; called Tahrea in 9:41).

**TARSHISH 1.** A great-grandson of Benjamin and a son of Bilhan (1 *Chron.* 7:10).

**2.** A son of Javan, a descendant of Japheth and Noah. He headed a line that gave rise to a 'maritime people' (*Gen.* 10:4–5). The word is later linked with Mediterranean trading and with ships and possibly an area of coast by the same name (e.g. *Ps.* 48:7; *Ezek.* 38:13 etc.).

**3.** A wise man and legal expert consulted by King Xerxes (*Est.* 1:14). For detail see *Memucan*.

**TARTAK** After the Assyrian invasion of the Northern Kingdom of Israel, the Israelites were dispersed to other parts of the empire. Meanwhile foreign groups were settled in Israel and Samaria, bringing with them their own gods. 2 *Kings* 17:24–41 recounts this movement of peoples and the introduction of other gods to Israel. The Avvites were said to have introduced Nibhaz and Tartak. These two names would appear to represent their gods. The passage describes how those people and their descendants continued to try to worship both their own gods and the one they saw as the god of their newly adopted country, 'Yahweh' or 'the LORD' (v. 32). Such worship of course denied the Law of the LORD, the covenant, and the truth of monotheism, so fundamental to the faith of Israel (vv. 34–41). P.D.G.

**TATTENAI** was the governor of Transeuphrates at the time of King Darius of Persia. The return of the Jews to Jerusalem from their captivity in Babylon came under this Persian official's oversight (*Ezra* 5:3). He is mentioned in connection with Shethar-Bozenai and various 'associates'. When he and his associates saw what was happening in Jerusalem, they questioned the returnees, whose response is recorded in *Ezra* 5:11–17.

Together with Shethar-Bozenai, he wrote to King Darius asking whether Zerubbabel and his people genuinely had permission to rebuild the Temple (v. 6). Darius found the original decree signed by Cyrus and ordered that the officials not to interfere with 'the work on this temple of God' (Ezra 6:6–7). Indeed he did much more than this, for Darius ordered Tattenai and Shethar-Bozenai to pay for the work out of the royal treasury. They were even to pay for animals for the sacrifices (vv. 8–12). The two officials and their associates then set about helping the Jews with the building work and carried out Darius' orders 'with diligence' (v. 13).

As the work continued, the book of Ezra notes how the LORD helped at each stage of the work and how thanks continued to be given by the people for the way his providence was seen even in events that were under the authority of the rulers back in Persia.　　　　　P.D.G.

**TEBAH** was a son of Abraham's brother Nahor by his concubine Reumah (Gen. 22:24).

**TEHINNAH** (Heb., 'supplication'). One of the leaders of the tribe of Judah. His father was Eshton and he and his family lived in Recah (1 Chron. 4:12). He was the father of Ir Nahash.

**TELAH** was a member of an Ephraimite family and a son of Resheph. He and his son Tahan are mentioned in 1 Chron. 7:25 as ancestors of Joshua son of Nun (v. 27).

**TELEM** Following the Exile in Babylon, many people from Judah had married foreign women. Once in Jerusalem and under the leadership of Ezra they repented and made a covenant to serve the LORD (Ezra 10:2). Telem was a Levite and Temple gatekeeper who had a foreign wife (v. 24).

**TEMA** A son of Ishmael and grandson of Abraham and Hagar, he was a leader of his clan (Gen. 25:15; 1 Chron. 1:30).

**TEMAH** A leader of one of the families of Temple servants whose descendants returned from the Babylonian Exile in the days of Ezra and worked on the Temple (Ezra 2:53; Neh. 7:55).

**TEMAN** An Edomite leader who was the grandson of Esau and Adah (a Canaanite woman) and a son of Eliphaz (Gen. 36:11, 15, 42; 1 Chron. 1:36, 53).

**TEMENI** Mentioned in 1 Chron. 4:6, he was one of the sons of Ashhur and Naarah of the tribe of Judah.

**TERAH** lived in Ur of the Chaldeans and was a descendant of Shem (Gen. 11:10–26; 1 Chron. 1:26). He was the father of Abra(ha)m and son of Nahor. His other sons included Haran and Nahor (Gen. 11:26–27). Haran, who died quite early on in Ur, had a son called Lot, Abram's nephew who later went to Canaan with him. Terah took his whole family from Ur and set out for Canaan round the fertile crescent, heading north west along the Euphrates (v. 28). However, when they arrived at a place called Haran they settled there. Terah later died there at the age of 205 (vv. 31–32). Later God spoke to Abram and called him to travel to Canaan, a land which would be given to him by God for his own possession.

While Abram's move to Canaan was clearly part of his faith commitment to God and God's call, there is no indication that Terah had heard such a call. Indeed much later Joshua reminded the people of Israel that Terah had lived the other side of the Euphrates and had worshipped 'other gods'. Abram's move to Canaan was certainly regarded as a deliberate move to leave behind the idolatrous past (Josh. 24:2, 15). Terah is later mentioned in the genealogy of Jesus in Luke's Gospel (Luke 3:34)

P.D.G.

**TERESH** One of two gate-keepers who guarded the palace doorway for King Xerxes. Along with his colleague, Bigthana, he 'became angry and conspired to assassinate King Xerxes' (Est. 2:21). The reason for their inclusion in the book of Esther is that it was the Jew Mordecai who exposed them. Haman had arranged to have Mordecai hanged for not bowing down to him. That night the King read in the annals of the kingdom about Mordecai's exposure of the two conspirators and, in the morning, ordered Haman to honour Mordecai.

This recognition of Mordecai by the king eventually led to the salvation of the Jews from the evil designs of Haman. See *Mordecai* and *Esther* for more detail.

P.D.G.

**TERTIUS** (Lat., 'third'). Tertius wrote the letter to the Romans at the dictate of the apostle Paul. He added his own greetings to the church at the end of the letter (Rom. 16:22). However, the final continued greetings may indicate that Paul himself then took up the pen and, as was his custom on other occasions, finished the letter in his own hand (vv. 23–27; see 1 Cor. 16:21–24; 2 Thess. 3:17). We do not know where Tertius originally came from, but his greetings indicate that he was a Christian and may suggest that he came from Rome.

**TERTULLUS** The high priest Ananias and the elders of the Jewish people in Jerusalem employed the lawyer, Tertullus, to help them bring charges against the apostle Paul who was being held captive in Caesarea by Felix (Acts 24:1–2). He may have been a Roman citizen. At least a part of his speech before Felix is recorded in vv. 2–8. It begins with statements of respect and flattery concerning the governor, but continues to argue that Paul was a troublemaker stirring up riots among the Jews. This argument was designed to force the Romans into action against Paul in order to keep the peace in the empire. He suggested Paul was a leader of a sect and had tried to desecrate the Temple. Paul carefully rebutted the complaints (vv. 10–21). For more detail see *Felix* and *Lysias*.

P.D.G.

**THADDAEUS** One of the twelve disciples of Jesus, Thaddaeus is mentioned by this name only in Matt. 10:3 and Mark 3:18. In Luke 6:16 and Acts 1:13 Luke used the name 'Judas the son of James' in his list of disciples. It is probable that Judas was his usual name but, following the disgrace attached to the name of Judas, he became known by an affectionate nick-name; Thaddaeus meaning 'breast' or 'heart'. He therefore may be the person referred to as 'Judas (not Judas Iscariot)' in John 14:22.

## THEOPHANY

The word 'theophany' does not actually occur in the Bible. It comes from two roots which combine to give the literal meaning, 'appearance of God'. In Scripture a theophany is a localized, formal and personal manifestation of God.

Two primary principles provide the context for theophanies: (1) Being omnipresent, God cannot be and is not limited to a particular place and time (1 Kings 8:27; Ps. 139:7–10; Is. 55:8–9). Therefore, theophanies do not abrogate his omnipresence.

(2) The Bible teaches that all of creation reveals God (e.g. Ps. 19:1–6; Rom. 1:20). God has designed and formed the creation in such a way that it mirrors his

attributes, character and person. However, the fallenness of human beings prevents them from interpreting this general revelation properly (*Rom. 1:21ff.*). Therefore God has provided special revelation (Scripture) for the particular purpose of redeeming humanity. Theophanies are phenomena within special revelation.

So seeing God's power in the forces of nature or seeing his beauty in the beauty of creation is not a theophany as such. Theophanies are always accompanied by verbal revelation which clearly identifies God. In theophanies God reveals himself *to be known*, i.e. he is *personal*.

That theophanies are redemptive in character can be seen from the first instance, where God appeared to Adam and Eve in the garden after the Fall (*Gen. 3:8*), and through the final form of Christ, God incarnate (*Rev. 1:13ff.*). Whenever God revealed himself in this manner it indicated some significant event in the advancement of his programme of redemption, such as a renewed pledge of faithfulness (*Gen. 15*), the imminent judgment of his enemies (*Exod. 14*) or the commissioning of his prophet with a message for his people (*Is. 6*).

## The forms of theophanies

Theophanies occur in a variety of forms, including storms, fire and clouds and are usually accompanied by auditory phenomena such as a voice or thunder. There are often tactile accompaniments such as heat, coolness and earth tremors. There are instances in which the form is not described, and all we are told is that God appeared (e.g. *Gen. 12:1; 17:1; 35:9; 1 Sam. 3:21; 1 Kings 9:2; 2 Chron. 7:12*). In these cases, the content of the encounters is the guide to their significance. It is the words of God which, for the reader of Scripture, constitute the importance of the meeting, since the form is not reported to us. However, where the form is indicated, it is an additional pointer to the significance of the encounter (see 'The Angel of the LORD' and 'The glory cloud' below).

Dreams and visions may be considered as both distinct from yet similar to theophanies. Dreams involve an imprint upon the subject which is psychical rather than sensory (e.g. *Gen. 28:10ff.*). Nevertheless, the same principles apply. The form is adapted to the particular purpose of the encounter. Visions, it may be argued, are sensory, but they are in fact distinct from material theophanies. Both dreams and visions are more 'flexible' than theophanies because they are not bound to the space and time limits of material.

## The glory cloud

The two dominant forms of theophanies in Scripture are the glory cloud and the Angel of the LORD. The most vivid appearance of the glory cloud was that which began at Mt Sinai (*Exod. 19:16*), where Moses received the Law of God, and continued through the wilderness period. It must have been massive both in size and effect, for the Israelites 'trembled and stood at a distance' (*Exod. 20:18*). This response was consistent with God's demands in the situation, for the mountain was off-limits to the people (*19:12, 21, 24*). Only Moses and the leaders of Israel could ascend the mountain (24:9ff.). The significance of this can be found in the association which this thunderous, fiery presence would have evoked.

One association would have pertained to common perceptions of deity in Israel's cultural context. The Canaanite deities Baal and El were associated with the thunderstorm and the mountains. As the chief deities in the Canaanite pantheon, they were thought to dwell in the mountains. Critics argue that this association with the God of Israel was an incorporation of pantheistic notions into Israelite religion, but in fact quite the opposite is the case. God, in effect, was co-opting this association to declare himself the God above all gods. It was he, and not Baal, who was the true and living God. Rather than Baal, it was Yahweh (the LORD) who 'makes the clouds his chariot' and 'walks upon the wings of the wind' (Ps. 104:3). It was Yahweh to whom was due exclusive and complete devotion (Exod. 20:3).

A second association with the storm theophany, which constitutes a pervasive OT theme, is between the heavenly courts and the glory cloud. God's throne was regarded as beyond the skies, concealed by the clouds and filled with light. Whenever Scripture provides a glimpse of God's heavenly throne, this conception is affirmed (e.g. Is. 6). The significance is that God had established his throne presence in Israel's midst. The connection was clear when the glory cloud took up abode in the Tabernacle and, subsequently, in the Temple. This presence brought the blessings of divine protection and justice and made ethical demands. Israel's special responsibility to be a kingdom of priests and a holy nation (Exod. 19:6) was directly related to the immediate divine presence in their midst, beginning at Sinai and continuing in their life in the land of Canaan.

This understanding of the glory cloud would have been extended by the Israelites to prior theophanies. In particular we may think of the smoking oven and flaming torch (Gen. 15:17) which passed between the animal pieces as a sign of divine commitment to Abraham. Early Israel, as the original audience of Genesis, would have understood that the God who made the covenant with Abraham was the same God who manifested himself on the mountain and who would accompany them through the wilderness. The pledge, 'To your descendants I have given this land' (Gen. 15:18) would have been theirs too as they moved towards Canaan. The glory cloud theophany is identified functionally with the Holy Spirit (e.g. Neh. 9:19–20; Is. 63:11–14; Hag. 2:5). This identification is confirmed in the consummate descent of God's glory/Spirit upon believers, the new abode of God (1 Pet. 2:5), at Pentecost, constituting the true Israel (Acts 2:1–4).

## The Angel of the LORD

The other dominant form of theophany in Scripture is the Angel of the LORD, the appearance of a human form which is frequently identified as God. Not all appearances of this special angel are so identified (e.g. 2 Sam. 24:16). But in the vast majority of cases the identification is clear, variously made by explicit claims (e.g. Exod. 3:15), possession of divine attributes (Gen. 16:10), receiving worship (Josh. 5:14), accepting sacrifices (Judg. 13:19–23), being called God (Judg. 13:22) and forgiving/remembering sins (Exod. 23:21). Instances of the Angel of the

LORD include Abraham's encounter with the three angels near Sodom and Gomorrah (Gen. 18), Lot's visit in Sodom (Gen. 19), Hagar in the wilderness (Gen. 21:9–21), Abraham at Mt Moriah (Gen. 22:1–19), Jacob at Peniel (Gen. 32:24–32), Moses at the burning bush (Exod. 3:1–6, 13–16), Israel in the wilderness (Exod. 23:20), Balaam on the road (Num. 22), Israel at Bochim (Judg. 2), Gideon at Ophrah (Judg. 6:11–24), Samson's parents (Judg. 13), Elijah in the wilderness (1 Kings 19:1–8), Elijah after Ahab's death (2 Kings 1:3, 15), the Assyrians near Jerusalem (2 Kings 19:35), Zechariah in his night visions and Daniel in the fiery furnace (Dan. 3:25).

The fundamental significance of this figure is in the posture of a warrior, manifested for the protection of God's people and for leading God's army in battle. In the patriarchal period he was a defender on the clan level (Gen. 15:1), but from the period of the Exodus onwards he was the leader of an army (Josh. 5:14). (See Angel of the LORD).

God's condescension to a temporary human form communicated to Israel that he was their defender and protector. They were to see their need to trust in him rather than in the strength of their own numbers. They also were to anticipate the theophany par excellence which was to come in Jesus Christ. The Angel of the LORD as God taking human form quite naturally anticipated the permanent abode in flesh that God would assume at the incarnation. Both Jesus and the Angel are called 'Lord' (Gen. 16:7; John 20:28) and 'God' (Gen. 48:15–16; Heb. 1:8); they both claimed to be 'I AM' (Exod. 3:2–14; John 8:58), lead and guide God's people (Exod. 14:19; Matt. 28:20) and are commanders of the Lord's army (Josh. 5:13–15; Rev. 19:11–14). The parallels are substantial enough that the Angel of the LORD is frequently termed a 'Christophany' – a pre-incarnate, temporary manifestation of the second Person of the Trinity.

### Jesus Christ

Beyond his identification with the Angel of the LORD, Jesus Christ is the consummate theophany in that he is the permanent and complete joining of the divine and human natures in one Person. 'The Word became flesh and lived for a while among us. We have seen his glory, the glory of the one and only Son, who came from the Father, full of grace and truth' (John 1:14). Surpassing all the theophanies of the OT, Christ came as the throne room of God (being the final Temple, John 2:19–21), a full manifestation of God (Col. 2:9) bringing God's consummate Word to humanity (Heb. 1:1–3). As such he saves undeserving sinners, not through their own efforts but through his inestimable grace (Titus 3:4); he makes ethical demands of us to live in accordance with his character (Titus 2:11) and he leads the armies of heaven in the defence of his people and in the defeat of their enemies (Rev. 2:16).

M.J.G.

**THEOPHILUS** Luke dedicated his two volumes to Theophilus (Luke 1:3; Acts 1:1). We know little about him. It is possible, given the respect with which Luke addressed him that he came from a high social class and that, perhaps, he was a financial supporter of Luke's work. It is also debated whether he was a

Gentile, a God-fearer, or a Jew, as well as whether he was a believer or was being evangelized. The types of issues addressed in the book suggest either a God-fearer or a Gentile, and most probably a believer. The fact that he was addressed in the book as needing reassurance (*Luke 1:4*) shows Luke's commitment to him as a person and suggests that Theophilus was under pressure to renounce what he had believed.                                D.B.

**THEUDAS** Peter and the apostles had been preaching in the city and the Temple precincts in Jerusalem, much to the consternation of the religious authorities. Following an arrest from which they had been freed in the middle of the night by an angel of the Lord, they were once more arrested in the Temple courts and made to appear before the Sanhedrin. Here again they refused to stop their preaching, arguing with the Jewish leaders that God had commanded them to preach (*Acts 5:17–32*). Several leaders wanted to put Peter and the others to death, but Gamaliel stood up and argued that they should be let alone to see what happened in due course. Perhaps eventually they and their message would simply disappear from the scene, and in the meantime it was not worth risking going against God if these people were truly from him. Gamaliel appealed to recent history in which one known as Theudas had claimed to be 'somebody' (perhaps claiming to be the expected Messiah). Some 400 men had rallied to him, but it all came to nothing when he was killed and his followers dispersed (*Acts 5:36*). Obviously Gamaliel was convinced this would happen again. He is not to be identified with a Theudas mentioned by Josephus who led a revolt in AD 44.
                                P.D.G.

**THOMAS** The name comes from the Aramaic for 'twin' (Gk. 'Didymus', as in *John 11:16; 20:4; 21:2*). In the NT,

Thomas is one of Jesus' twelve apostles. In Matthew, Mark and Luke, the only times he appears by name are in the list of the Twelve (*Matt. 10:3; Mark 3:18; Luke 6:15*). In each case he is paired with Matthew, perhaps reflecting Jesus' practice of sending out his disciples two-by-two (*Mark 6:7*). In his sole appearance in Acts, Thomas is paired with Philip (*Acts 1:13*).

In John's Gospel, Thomas appears a little more frequently. In *John 11:16*, Thomas impulsively urged his fellow disciples to go to Jerusalem to die with Jesus. In *14:5* he displayed his confusion by asking Jesus the way to the Father. In *21:2* he was simply one of the company of fishermen. The only passage of theological importance, which has given 'doubting' Thomas that famous label, is *20:24–28*. Having not been present for Jesus' previous resurrection appearances, Thomas refused to believe until he had seen and touched Christ. When he did so, he acknowledged Jesus' deity with the striking words (particularly for a monotheistic Jew), 'My Lord and my God' (*v. 28*). Thomas' testimony is one of the strongest evidences of the truth of the resurrection, but John is probably at least as concerned to stress Jesus' response: 'Because you have seen me, you have believed; blessed are those who have not seen and yet have believed' (*v. 29*).

Certain early Christian legends make claims of varying historical probability about Thomas' subsequent ministry; one which might be true is that he founded churches in India. At least three apocryphal writings are falsely attributed to him. Nothing else is known about him.
                                C.B.

**TIBERIUS** is mentioned in *Luke 3:1* as the Caesar who was reigning and in his 15th year when John the Baptist began to preach. See *Caesar*. He ruled from AD 14–37 and was the second emperor of Rome.

**TIBNI** Following the death of King Zimri of Israel, Omri, the commander of the army, was proclaimed king. However, it seems that not all the Israelites immediately rallied behind Omri, and about half of them supported Tibni, son of Ginath, for king (1 *Kings* 16:21–22). However, Omri's troops were the stronger, Tibni was killed, and Omri ruled the whole of the Northern Kingdom, restoring some measure of law and order and calm to the nation. See *Omri*.

**TIDAL** was the king of Goiim and one of four Mesopotamian kings who invaded Palestine at the time of Abraham (see also *Arioch*, *Amraphel* and *Kedorlaomer*; *Gen.* 14:1, 9). The account given in *Gen.* 14 is of particular interest as it highlights both the desirability of the Jordan valley that could attract an alliance of kings from so far afield, and the rapidly advancing influence of Abra(ha)m.

It is clear that the invading alliance was headed by Kedorlaomer (*vv.* 4–5). The invaders had conquered several of the city states of the Jordan valley and areas around the Dead Sea and had ruled the land for 12 years. In the 13th year the local kings of these cities rebelled and fought the invaders (see *Bera*, *Birsha*, *Shinab*, *Shemeber*). Once again, however, they were defeated and fled. The four kings seized a huge area of land including the cities of Sodom and Gomorrah from which they took all the spoil. In this conquest they carried off Abram's nephew, Lot, who was living in Sodom.

This brought Abram into the arena. When he heard what had happened, he went in pursuit of Kedorlaomer, chasing him far to the north. Finally in a clever attack he defeated the alliance and returned with Lot and his family (*Gen.* 14:14–17).

The alliance had come from the same area that had been Abram's home. It is of great significance that Abram's defeat of these kings is seen in *Gen.* 14 as God's victory, and indicates God's establishment of Abram in Canaan and his final and complete separation from his former life. From this point onwards, under God's sovereign plan Abram's influence in the 'promised land' continued to increase.                                  P.D.G.

**TIGLATH-PILESER** (Assyr., 'my trust is in the son of Esharra'). Tiglath-Pileser III was king of Assyria from 745–727 BC, and comes to our attention in Scripture as the monarch responsible for the invasion of the kingdom of Israel and the deportation of many of its citizens. He was also known as Pul (2 *Kings* 15:19; 1 *Chron.* 5:26). He was one of the greatest of Assyrian kings and reigned at a time when the Assyrian empire's boundaries extended far beyond Mesopotamia. He moved west to the Mediterranean, forcing Syria, Philistia and the Northern Kingdom of Israel to pay him tribute.

It was when Menahem was king of Israel (c. 743–738 BC) that Tiglath-Pileser first invaded Israel, according to the biblical data. Menahem quickly exacted huge payments from his people and paid this to the Assyrians thus averting a full-blown war. The Assyrians then withdrew temporarily. The payment of this tribute is also recorded in Assyrian records. But such payment only bought a little time for Israel which was under the judgment of God for its idolatry and sin. Soon the Assyrian campaigns against this western area of their empire began again, and this time it was Pekah who was king of Israel.

'In the time of Pekah king of Israel, Tiglath-Pileser king of Assyria came and took Ijon, Abel Beth Maacah, Janoah, Kedesh and Hazor. He took Gilead and Galilee, including all the land of Naphtali, and deported the people to Assyria' (2 *Kings* 15:29; 1 *Chron.* 5:6, 26). The long prophesied conquest of Israel had begun in earnest. (See *Pekah* for more detail on the difficulties of absolute dating.)

Pekah's response to this invasion was to ally himself with Rezin of Syria and to build a power-base in Palestine. The two kings attacked King Ahaz of Judah because he failed to join them in their plans (2 Chron. 28:5–21). Ahaz appealed to Assyria for help (2 Kings 16:7; 2 Chron. 28:16). When Tiglath-Pileser did come he simply caused Ahaz still more trouble (2 Chron. 28:20), but he did capture Damascus and thus relieve the siege on Jerusalem (Is. 7; 9:8–21). Eventually, probably with the connivance of Tiglath-Pileser, Pekah was assassinated by the pro-Assyrian Hoshea (2 Kings 16:30).

However, what Tiglath-Pileser had started was not to be stopped by Hoshea. He too did evil in the eyes of the LORD (2 Kings 17:1–2) and so Shalmaneser, the next king of Assyria, finished the job, capturing Hoshea and invading the whole land.

In biblical terms Tiglath-Pileser can be seen as the instrument used by God to bring judgment on his people for their sin, specially for their worship of other gods. Having turned to other nations and followed their gods, the true God let those nations invade. Their gods could not save for that was the perogative of the LORD God alone.          P.D.G.

**TIKVAH** (Heb., 'hope').

**1.** The son of Harhas and the father of Shallum. Harhas was the keeper of the king's wardrobe in the days of King Josiah. Shallum was the husband of the prohetess Huldah (2 Kings 22:14).

**2.** This Tikvah was the father of Jahzeiah who lived in Jerusalem at the time of Ezra. Jahzeiah was one of the few to disagree with the plan for those who had married foreign wives to divorce them (Ezra 10:15).

**TILON** Mentioned in 1 Chron. 4:20 as a son of Shimon of the clan of Judah.

**TIMAEUS** was the father of a blind man known as Bartimaeus. The latter's name actually means 'son of Timaeus' (Mark 10:46). See Bartimaeus.

**TIMNA 1.** The first Timna mentioned (Gen. 36:12) was the concubine of Eliphaz, the grandson of Esau. She bore a son to Eliphaz called Amalek. She was the sister of Lotan, a Horite leader (1 Chron. 1:36, 39).

**2.** This Timna was a chief of Edom and was descended from Esau (Gen. 36:40; 1 Chron. 1:51).

**TIMON** was one of seven men appointed to help the apostles who were finding the work of administration in the early Jerusalem church to be too burdensome (Acts 6:5). Many new people were becoming Christians. The new Christians of Greek-Jewish background were falling out with those of Hebrew-Jewish background over the distribution of food to widows. The disciples found that they were spending so much time sorting out these things (v. 2) that they were neglecting the ministry of the Word of God. Seven men were therefore to be appointed and to be chosen as those known to be 'full of the Spirit and wisdom'. The apostles prayed and laid their hands on these men and appointed them to the job of looking after the day-to-day affairs of the church.

This incident is an interesting indication of how early in the church's life there was a recognition of the fact that God gives different people different 'ministries' or gifts. But it also reflects the early recognition by the church that those called to 'the ministry of the Word of God' (v. 2) should not have other preoccupations. V. 7 indicates the success of this division of labour: 'the word of God spread. The number of disciples in Jerusalem increased rapidly.'          P.D.G.

## TIMOTHY

Timothy, a fascinating NT figure, was converted during the apostle Paul's first missionary journey, and became a fellow worker on the second missionary journey which took the gospel across the Aegean Sea into Europe (*Acts 16:1, 3*).

### The man and his family

Timothy came from a mixed family – his mother was a 'Jewish woman who was a believer, but his father was a Greek' (*Acts 16:1*). He learned faith at the knee of his grandmother Lois and his mother Eunice (*2 Tim. 1:5; 3:15*). For Timothy to be useful in Jewish evangelism and accepted as a Jew, it was expedient for Paul to circumcise him, for all the Jews 'knew that his father was a Greek' (*Acts 16:3*). This concession to Jewish sensitivities is to be contrasted with Paul's absolute refusal to circumcise the Gentile Christian worker Titus, for that would have involved a repudiation of the gospel of grace as Paul understood it (*Gal. 2:3, 16*). Some modern commentators have suggested Paul was inconsistent in his policy or that Luke, in writing, simply got it wrong. However, Paul's behaviour is understandable given the different contexts in which he worked. Paul was not prepared to compromise the basic truth that salvation was by grace alone, through faith alone. Thus he refused those who tried to insist that Christians should be circumcised. On the other hand, when no compulsion or violation of Christian principle was at stake, he was prepared to go to great lengths to share the gospel with others: 'To the Jews I became like a Jew, to win the Jews' (*1 Cor. 9:20*). This flexibility is illustrated in the circumcising of Timothy.

### A gospel worker

Timothy worked with Paul and Silas (also called Silvanus) to bring the good news of Christ to Europe. The missionary team preached Jesus as 'the Son of God' (*2 Cor. 1:19*) in such Macedonian cities as Philippi, Thessalonica, and Berea. When Jews from Thessalonica followed Paul and his party to Berea and stirred up the crowds against them, the believers sent Paul off to the coast and brought him to Athens, while Timothy and Silas stayed behind to do further work in Berea (*Acts 17:13–15*). Later Paul went down to Corinth, and Timothy and Silas left Macedonia and joined him there (*18:5*). Paul seems to have been the chief leader and spokesman for the faith, but Silas and Timothy were certainly partners in mission and happy to work with him and under his leadership and direction. In *Acts 19:22* Timothy is described with Erastus as one of Paul's 'helpers' who was sent off to Macedonia while Paul continued to work in the Roman province of Asia.

Similarly, in the Pauline epistles there is a strong recognition of Timothy and others like Silvanus as Paul's fellow workers. Thus when Paul wrote to the churches he naturally included Timothy as one of his colleagues in the opening salutations or greetings (*1 Thess. 1:1; 2 Thess. 1:1; 2 Cor. 1:1; Phil. 1:1; Col. 1:1*). In the case of the Thessalonians, Paul was so concerned about their spiritual welfare that he sent Timothy from Athens 'to strengthen and encourage' the believers there. The veteran missionary spoke affectionately of Timothy as 'our brother and God's fellow worker in spreading the gospel of Christ' (1 Thess. 3:2). The purpose of the visit was to foster Christian faithfulness in the face of persecution and attacks from 'the tempter' (1 Thess. 3:3–5). Fortunately, Timothy's visit brought back encouraging news of their faith, love and kindly regard for the apostle (1 Thess. 3:7). In Paul's view, Timothy could be entrusted with responsible tasks and carry them out satisfactorily.

### A young leader

Evidently Paul believed that Timothy was one of the promising younger leaders in the emerging church who could be called upon to give significant leadership when it was needed. It is striking that Paul in writing to the Romans could say, 'Timothy, my fellow worker, sends his greetings to you' (Rom. 16:21). Similarly, Paul associated Timothy with himself in the opening words of greeting in Philippians by describing them both as 'servants of Christ'. Later in the same letter he paid tribute to Timothy, acknowledging his genuine concern for the Philippians in contrast to the self-centred attitudes of others (Phil. 2:20–21). Paul had the highest confidence in Timothy's fine track record as a Christian worker: 'Timothy has proved himself, because as a son with his father he has served with me in the work of the gospel' (Phil. 2:22).

Paul valued such partnership in the gospel. For example, in 1 Cor. 4:17 Paul stated that he had sent 'Timothy, my son whom I love, who is faithful in the Lord. He will remind you of my way of life in Christ Jesus.' Paul instructed the Corinthians that Timothy was not to be treated with contempt, but was to be warmly welcomed as a genuine Christian worker who was doing the work of the Lord just as Paul was (1 Cor. 16:10–11). Paul clearly expected Christian people to respect young leaders like Timothy: 'Send him on his way in peace, so that he may return to me. I am expecting him with the brothers' (1 Cor. 16:11b).

### 1 and 2 Timothy

It is in this connection that the Pastoral Epistles are so important, for they spell out the instructions that Paul had to give to Timothy and Titus. These writings must be taken seriously as a source of information about Timothy, despite the widespread tendency of modern scholars to disparage their importance or to question the traditional view of Pauline authorship. While the Pastorals (1 and 2 Timothy and Titus) contain guidelines on the expected characteristics of overseers and deacons, they also have personal things to say to these leaders (e.g. 1 Tim. 6:20–21; 2 Tim. 3:10–17; 4:9–22; Tit. 3:12–15). Paul addressed Timothy in endearing tones as 'my true son in the faith' (1 Tim. 1:2). He reminded his young understudy of the things that had been said of him in earlier days: 'Timothy, my son, I give you this instruction in keeping with the prophecies once made about you, so that by following them you may fight the good fight, holding on to faith and a good conscience' (1 Tim. 1:18).

Timothy needed to fulfil the potential which others had seen in him and avoid the disastrous mistakes that Hymenaeus and Alexander, among others, had made (1 Tim. 1:19–20).

In a formal way Timothy was solemnly charged to guard what has been entrusted to him (1 Tim. 4:11–16; 6:20; 2 Tim. 3:10–17; 4:1–5). These personal instructions were to be taken with the utmost seriousness: 'But you, man of God, flee from all this [i.e. false teaching and pursuit of personal riches]; and pursue righteousness, godliness, faith, love, endurance and gentleness. Fight the good fight of the faith. Take hold of the eternal life to which you were called when you made your good confession in the presence of many witnesses' (1 Tim. 6:11–12). In the past Timothy had taken his stand for Christ and confessed his faith in public, probably at his baptism or ordination. He was challenged to remain Christ's loyal soldier to the end. The standards were high, and the call to Christian leadership made exacting demands which could not be avoided.

### Timothy's spirituality

Timothy was plainly told, 'Watch your life and doctrine closely. Persevere in them; because if you do, you will save both yourself and your hearers' (1 Tim. 4:16). Paul insisted that Timothy's personal relationship with God was a matter of the greatest importance both to his own life and to the effectiveness of his ministry. Therefore he explicitly instructed his young colleague to 'train' himself 'in godliness' (1 Tim. 4:7), a virtue which is frequently mentioned in the Pastoral Epistles (eusebeia, 'godliness', is used some ten times in the Pastorals: e.g. 1 Tim. 2:2; 3:16; 4:7–8; 2 Tim. 3:5; note also the use of theosebeia, 'reverence for God', in 1 Tim. 2:10).

Living in close fellowship with God was to provide the foundation for his work among people. Timothy was not to allow people to disparage his ministry because of his youthfulness, but rather to live such a well-rounded, wholesome Christian life that no fault could be found in him (1 Tim. 4:12). His exemplary conduct would give credibility to his witness. As he awaited the eventual arrival and public affirmation of Paul, he was to give attention 'to the public reading of Scripture, to preaching and to teaching' (1 Tim. 4:13). His gifts had been recognized at his ordination when the council of elders had laid hands on him. Now he was urged to cultivate and use these gifts 'so that everyone may see your progress' (1 Tim. 4:14–15). His trustworthiness as a Christian leader must be established beyond reasonable doubt.

As Paul's personal representative, Timothy was asked to remain in Ephesus 'so that you may command certain men not to teach false doctrines any longer, nor to devote themselves to myths and endless genealogies. These promote controversies' (1 Tim. 1:1, 3–4). Obviously, false teachers were active, spreading their dangerous view, and Timothy was called to oppose them (1 Tim. 1:3–11; 6:3–10; 2 Tim. 3:1–9). In place of this type of incipient gnostic teaching which had a Jewish, speculative element, Timothy was to present 'sound teaching' (1 Tim. 1:10; 2 Tim. 4:3; cf. Tit. 1:9; 2:1) using 'sound words' (1 Tim 6:3; 2 Tim. 1:13; cf. Tit. 2:8) which would build up his hearers in the Christian faith and challenge the erroneous views of the false teachers.

Timothy did not enjoy the best of health, for he suffered from stomach trouble and frequent bouts of illness (1 Tim. 5:23). Paul advised him to exercise, and to take normal precautions to protect his health (1 Tim. 4:8; 5:23; cf. 3:8).

In summary, Timothy is an interesting case study in discipleship and Christian leadership. He was converted and carefully discipled by Paul himself. Then he was put to work for Christ and given opportunities to develop his gifts, which included the preaching of the gospel and the strengthening of young converts and new churches. He was somewhat diffident and lacking in self-confidence, so he needed reassurance and support from mature Christian people. He was counselled about the need of experiencing afresh the grace of Christ: 'So you, my son, must keep renewing your strength in the spiritual blessing that comes through union with Christ Jesus' (2 Tim. 2:1, Williams). He was reminded of his Christian heritage, a 'faith which first lived in your grandmother Lois and your mother Eunice and, I am persuaded, now lives in you' (2 Tim. 1:6). This personal encouragement was necessary to bolster a rather insecure person, who was reminded that 'God did not give us a spirit of timidity, but a spirit of power, of love and of self-discipline' (2 Tim. 1:7).

To give strong Christian leadership, Timothy always needed to be in touch with God in a fresh and living way. Accordingly, Paul said, 'fan into flame the gift of God, which is within you' (2 Tim. 1:6). This called for renewed commitment, determination and willingness to suffer and sacrifice. In all this he would have to join Paul in relying on 'the power of God' (2 Tim. 1:8).

Christian service for Timothy was challenging and demanding. There were false teachers presenting subtle and superficially attractive alternatives to the Christian faith. There were also the perennial temptations of materialism and secularism (1 Tim. 6:9–10; 2 Tim. 3:1–5). As a Christian leader Timothy was called to wage a spiritual war against the powers of evil (1 Tim. 1:18; 2 Tim. 2:4; 4:7). The 'snare of the devil' was to be avoided (2 Tim. 2:26).

Timothy had made promises to the Lord, and was called upon to keep them as a loyal soldier of Christ (2 Tim. 2:3–7). Paul himself had provided an excellent model worthy of imitation (2 Tim. 3:10–12). Timothy was expected to maintain his fidelity to the Christian tradition, remembering the noble people who had passed it on to him (2 Tim. 1:5; 3:14–15). The sacred heritage of the Scriptures was to be used 'for teaching, rebuking, correcting and training in righteousness' so that the servant of God might be 'thoroughly equipped for every good work' (2 Tim. 3:16–17). A.A.T.

**TIRAS** The seventh son of Japheth and a grandson of Noah (Gen. 10:2; 1 Chron. 1:5). It is not clear which group of people were descended from him, although some have suggested the people of Tarshish and others the Etruscans.

**TIRHAKAH** is called the 'Cushite king [of Egypt]' (2 Kings 19:9; Is. 37:9). He was a Pharaoh of the 25th dynasty and comes to our attention in the Bible in the accounts dealing with King Hezekiah of Judah. Sennacherib, the king of Assyria, had attacked many of the fortified cities of Judah (2 Kings 18:13). He had laid siege to Lachish (v. 14) and seemed such a threat that Hezekiah sent him money to try and deal with the obvious threat to Jerusalem. Hezekiah had hoped for help from Egypt, but it had not come, and so Sennacherib mocked him (vv. 21–22). Hezekiah realized that it was actually the LORD who was being ridiculed, as his people had refused to trust in the LORD for the help they needed (2 Kings 19:3–4).

Eventually Tirhakah did march out against Sennacherib (2 Kings 19:9), but again Hezekiah was threatened by Assyria. Hezekiah turned to the LORD for help and Isaiah gave the LORD's response. Assyria would be defeated. The LORD inflicted a great death among the Assyrian troops, and so Sennacherib withdrew to Nineveh, where he was killed. What happened to Tirhakah at this point is not recorded in Scripture. Egypt had not been able to save Judah, but when Hezekiah turned to the LORD he, in his great power over the kings of the world, was able to save immediately.

P.D.G.

**TIRHANAH** A son of Caleb the brother of Jerahmeel and his concubine Maacah. He was from the tribe of Judah (1 Chron. 2:48).

**TIRIA** One of the sons of Jehallelel from the tribe of Judah, and a descendant of Caleb son of Jephunneh (1 Chron. 4:16).

**TIRZAH** One of five daughters born to Zelophehad. Zelophehad had no sons. These daughters married cousins on their father's side and were members of the tribe of Manasseh (Num. 26:33; 27:1; 36:1–12; Josh. 17:3). They faced a predicament over their inheritance, for normally inherited land would have been passed on through a son.

They approached Moses at the entrance to the Tabernacle about the problem, asking him to rule that they should be allowed to inherit their father's property, for it would not be right that his name should die out. Moses consulted the LORD about the situation, as a result of which a new law was promulgated allowing daughters to inherit land from their father. Later some of the leaders from the tribe of Manasseh appealed to Moses about the case, pointing out that if these women were now to marry outside the tribe the land would be lost forever to the tribe. The ruling which followed further defined the law of inheritance, insisting that the women should marry into their father's tribe or else lose the inheritance (Num. 36). Hence the daughters married cousins 'on their father's side', thus fulfilling the requirement of the LORD.

When finally the Israelites entered the land of Canaan and the land was divided up among the tribes, the daughters of Zelophehad were duly given their inheritance (Josh. 17:3–4).

**TITIUS** Justus, a resident of Corinth, is mentioned in Acts 18:7 as a 'worshipper of God' into whose house Paul moved when he was expelled from preaching in the synagogue. See Justus.

**TITUS** was one of the major ministry companions of Paul. He was so trusted an aide that Paul left him in Crete and wrote a letter of instruction to him about how to structure the church with meaningful leadership so that it could get back up on its feet. Thus some of the most detailed instruction we possess about elders (Titus 1:5–9), the role of older men (2:2), older women (2:3), young women (2:4–5), young men (2:6–8), and slaves (2:9–10) comes to us through this letter. He also was an able instructor, since Paul urged him to teach sound doctrine (2:1, 15). He must have been a model of character, since those qualities are what Paul desired be taught to this Cretan community.

It is clear that Paul thought much of Titus, since Titus' arrival in aiding Paul brought the apostle so much joy and comfort (2 Cor. 2:13; 7:6). Titus was also helpful to Paul in Corinth, since he left this assistant behind to help the Corinthians in a variety of matters including the raising of funds for other churches in need (2 Cor. 7:13–14; 8:6, 16, 23). In fact, he regarded Titus as a partner and fellow messenger of the church. The term for messenger is 'apostle', not in the technical sense of the Twelve, but in the looser form of missionary, a commissioned servant whose call is to build up the church.

Titus is also well known because he accompanied Paul and Barnabas to a meeting in Jerusalem about the role of Gentiles in the church. Titus was Greek in descent and was not forced to be circumcised by those who held this conference. (Some equate this meeting with *Acts 15*, while others tie it to *Acts 11:29–30*. It is not clear which it is.) Thus Titus became a major illustration of the equal access Gentiles had to the promise of the gospel. They did not have to become Jews to become Christians.

Titus had many qualities of an exemplary servant. He had a long track record of service. He was faithful. He was trustworthy. He could be given assignments and follow through on them. He was organized enough to lead others and set up fresh leadership teams. He was a major asset to the early church.          D.B.

**TOAH** An ancestor of Samuel (*1 Chron.* 6:34). In *1 Sam. 1:1* it would seem the same person is called Tohu, and in *1 Chron. 6:26* his name is given as Nahath. He was a Kohathite Levite and one of the musicians who served at the Tabernacle.

**TOB-ADONIJAH** (Heb., 'the LORD Yahweh is good') lived in the days of King Jehoshaphat of Judah. During the early years of his reign Jehoshaphat served the LORD and sent out various teachers and Levites to teach the people of Judah the Book of the Law. Tob-Adonijah was one of those Levitical teachers (*2 Chron.* 17:8).

**TOBIAH** (Heb., 'the LORD is good').

**1.** The descendants of this Tobiah are listed in *Ezra 2:60* and *Neh. 7:62* as among those who returned to Jerusalem with Nehemiah and Zerubbabel, follow-

ing the Exile in Babylon, but who could not demonstrate that their families were of Israelite origin.

**2.** 'Tobiah the Ammonite official' was probably a representative in Judah of the Persian overlords. Together with Sanballat the Horonite and others, right from the start, he was steadfastly opposed to Nehemiah's work of rebuilding Jerusalem (*Neh. 2:10*). This was probably generated by the fact that Tobiah and his associates had real power in Jerusalem and saw Nehemiah as a direct threat. Although Tobiah had married an Israelite woman (*Neh. 6:18*), he was not of Israelite origin and he could see that only those with a true tribal pedigree would be allowed leadership roles in the rebuilt Jerusalem and Judah. Nehemiah knew his work was God's work and made it clear that Tobiah had 'no share in Jerusalem or any claim or historic right to it' (*Neh. 2:20*).

Tobiah tried to suggest that Nehemiah's work should be regarded as a rebellion against the King of Persia (*v. 19*), and this generally was his chosen method by which he attempted to undermine the rebuilding of the city walls. He also tried to discourage the workers, pouring scorn on their efforts saying: 'What they are building – if even a fox climbed up on it, he would break down their wall of stones!' (*Neh. 4:3*). But the work continued and Tobiah and his associates became very angry (*v. 7*). They intended to attack the walls and the workers and so Nehemiah had to post guards while the work continued (*vv. 10–15*).

Once the walls were almost complete, Tobiah, Sanballat and Geshem accused Nehemiah of setting up a king in Jerusalem, once again trying to persuade Persia to stop the work and suggesting there was about to be a revolt headed by Jerusalem. Nehemiah's response was to turn to prayer and seek the help of God whose desire it was that his people should return to Jerusalem (*Neh. 6:1–14*). Tobiah had many nobles in Judah who gave their allegiance to him and this meant disruption and undermining of Nehemiah's work from within, but God saw to it that the work was eventually completed (*Neh. 6:15–7:1*).

As the work came to an end, the Book of Moses was read publicly. In the Law it was found that Ammonites and Moabites were not to be admitted to 'the assembly of God'. The Israelites thus excluded people of this descent from Israel (*Neh. 13:1–3*). What Nehemiah discovered, however, was the Eliashib, the priest in charge of the Temple storerooms, had secretly given Tobiah a room in the Temple precincts. Nehemiah had him ejected, but the incident reveals just how much power Tobiah wielded among the higher echelons of society in Jerusalem.

Nehemiah's complete dependence upon the LORD God for help against almost impossible odds from within and from outside shines through in his dealings with Tobiah. Nehemiah trusted God's call and his promises and was determined that the rebuilt Jerusalem would worship God with renewed purity, the lack of which had been one of the original causes of God's judgment on Judah and its Exile to Babylon.      P.D.G.

**TOBIJAH** (Heb., 'the LORD is good').

**1.** A Jewish returnee from the Babylonian Exile who gave silver and gold with which to make crowns for the priest Joshua (*Zech. 6:10, 14*).

**2.** A teacher whom King Jehoshaphat of Judah sent to teach the Law throughout Judah (*2 Chron. 17:8–9*).

**TOGARMAH** was the grandson of Japheth and son of Gomer and therefore a direct descendant of Noah. He had two brothers (*Gen. 10:3; 1 Chron. 1:6*).

**TOHU** An ancestor of Samuel mentioned in *1 Sam. 1:1*. In *1 Chron. 6:34* it would seem the same person is called Toah and in *1 Chron. 6:26* his name is given as

Nahath. He was a Kohathite Levite, father of Elihu, and son of Zuph an Ephraimite. For a possible explanation of the link between this Levitical family and the mention of Ephraim see *Jeroham 1*.

**TOKHATH** Mentioned in *2 Chron. 34:22*, he was the father of Shallum the husband of the prophetess Huldah. See *Tikvah*.

**TOLA** (Heb., 'worm' or 'scarlet stuff'; *cf. Ps. 104:18*).

**1.** One of Issachar's four sons (*Gen. 46:13; 1 Chron. 7:1*) who were mentioned as going to Egypt with Jacob (*Gen. 46:13*). Later on they were apparently a leading family in Issachar (*Num. 26:23; 1 Chron. 7:1–2*).

**2.** Tola ben Puah was a judge from the tribe of Issachar who judged Israel for 23 years (*Judg. 10:1–2*). He lived in Shamir, a village of uncertain location in the hill country of Ephraim where he was later buried.

**TOU** was the king of Hamath at the time when David was king of Israel. When David defeated Hadadezer king of Zobah, Tou sent one of his sons to take tribute of silver and gold to David and congratulate him. Tou had also been at war with Hadadezer (*2 Sam. 8:9–10; 1 Chron. 18:9–10*). The mention of Tou in this context adds weight to the reader's understanding of how David's victories were being recognized far and wide. David saw all his victories as the LORD's work and dedicated all the goods and silver and gold he was given to the LORD (*2 Sam. 8:11–13*). Tou's son is called Joram in *2 Sam. 8:10* and Hadoram in *1 Chron. 18:10*.      P.D.G.

**TROPHIMUS** came from Ephesus and was one of the Christian leaders who accompanied the apostle Paul on some of his travels. He is mentioned in *Acts 20:4* as one of a group who went ahead of Paul from Greece to Troas where Paul joined them a few days later. After seven days in Troas the group travelled south by ship stopping at a number of ports where Paul visited Christians and encouraged them. Clearly Trophimus remained with Paul on this quite lengthy trip that eventually took them back to Jerusalem. Once back in Jerusalem Trophimus is again mentioned (Acts 21:29).

Paul was arrested as 'Jews from the province of Asia' tried to stir up the people of Jerusalem against the teaching of the gospel of Jesus Christ (Acts 21:27). They recognized Trophimus as a Gentile (Greek) among Paul's supporters and assumed that Paul had taken him, illegally, into the Temple precincts. This, of course, was a trumped-up charge, but Paul had to be rescued from the crowds by Roman troops (vv. 30–32).

The only other occasion we hear of Trophimus is much later on. Paul was writing his second epistle to Timothy and refers to Trophimus whom he had left 'sick in Miletus'. It is clear that this faithful converted Gentile had remained at Paul's side for several years and had become a faithful and dear friend to Paul in his work. Perhaps his Greek origin had enabled Paul, a Jew, to enter places and speak to people he might otherwise have found hard to reach.                    P.D.G.

**TRYPHENA** (Gk., 'dainty'). One of two women who were greeted by the apostle Paul at the end of his letter to the Romans (16:12). They 'worked hard in the Lord'. Tryphosa's name meant 'delicate'. Their names probably indicate a wealthy background of leisure, but it is clear they had sacrificed this for the sake of the gospel work in Rome.

**TRYPHOSA** See Tryphena (Rom. 16:12).

**TUBAL** The fifth son of Japheth and grandson of Noah (Gen. 10:2; 1 Chron. 1:5). Tubal was probably the founder of a people who settled near the Taurus mountains in modern Turkey. In Ezek. 27:13 the people of Tubal traded in slaves and in bronze artefacts (see Is. 66:19). In Ezekiel's prophecy the people of Tubal were the subject of condemnation for their idolatry and evil ways (Ezek. 32:26; 38:2; 39:1). See also Gog.

**TUBAL-CAIN** This man was the son of Lamech and his wife Zillah (Gen. 4:22). He 'forged all kinds of tools out of bronze and iron' and had a sister called Naamah. It is possible that the suffix (Cain) to the name Tubal meant 'metal-worker'.

**TYCHICUS** (Gk., 'fortuitous'), like Trophimus, was a Gentile convert from Ephesus. He is mentioned in Acts 20:4 as one of a group who went ahead of Paul from Greece to Troas where Paul joined them a few days later. After seven days in Troas the group travelled south by ship, stopping at a number of ports where Paul visited Christians and encouraged them. They eventually went to Jerusalem where Paul was arrested.

He became a close personal friend of the apostle and was with Paul during his first imprisonment in Rome and used in delivering Paul's letters to the Ephesians (Eph. 6:21) and to the Colossians (Col. 4:7–9). As well as delivering the letters, Paul laid on him the duty of 'encouraging' both churches in their faith and commitment to Christ. This work of encouragement, which involved turning people back to Christ and building them up in their knowledge and love of the Lord (Col. 2:2–4; Phil. 2:1:3) was a characteristic of many of those who travelled with the apostle Paul. Clearly Tychicus was highly regarded in this work for Christ, being called 'the dear brother and faithful servant in the Lord' in Eph. 6:21 and 'a dear brother, a faithful minister and fellow servant in the Lord' in Col. 4:7.

Even much later, and perhaps towards the end of Paul's ministry, Paul was still using Tychicus, sending him to help

Titus in his work on Crete (*Titus 3:12*) and later sending him to work back at home in Ephesus thus allowing Timothy to continue his work elsewhere (*2 Tim. 4:12*).

We do not know what became of Tychicus, but he had learned how to encourage Christians with his teaching, how to evangelize and how to serve to the death, at the side of the apostle Paul. It was people like him who took the Asian churches into the next generation, kept them obedient to the apostolic teaching, and led them through the great persecutions. He was indeed a 'faithful servant in the Lord'.                                    P.D.G.

**TYRANNUS** The 'lecture hall of Tyrannus' is mentioned in *Acts 19:9*. When Paul arrived to preach the gospel in Ephesus he went first to the synagogue, but as so often happened in his ministry, he was soon the object of derision and persecution. In Ephesus he moved to this hall for daily discussions which went on for two years (*v. 10*). Nothing further is known about this Tyrannus. His name suggests he may have been a Greek man who had a room used for debate and discussion, but this can only be conjecture.

The move from synagogue to a venue that was more accessible to Gentiles happened in a number of places that Paul visited and reflected Paul's living out in his life the pattern of the gospel message being first for the Jews and then for the Gentiles. The rejection of the gospel by the majority of Jews meant that it was offered to the Gentiles and this pattern was obviously repeated in many towns (see *Acts 13:46–48; 14:1; 17:2; 18:6–7; Rom. 1:16; 2:10*).                     P.D.G.

# U

**UCAL** Various proverbs were addressed to Ucal and Ithiel by Agur son of Jakeh (*Prov. 30:1*). However, scholars are not sure that the Heb. text here has been correctly interpreted. It is possible that the Heb. letters have been mistakenly assumed to be referring to proper names when in fact the text should be read (with the same letters) to mean 'I am weary O God, I am weary O God, and I am consumed'. However, Agur's concern was that his listeners heed the 'word of God [which] is flawless' (*Prov. 30:1, 5*).

**UEL** (Heb., 'the will of God'). A descendant of Bani at the time of Nehemiah (*Ezra 10:34*). After Shecaniah confessed to Ezra that many men of Judah had married wives from other tribes and nations, Ezra and the people repented and made a covenant to serve the LORD (*Ezra 10:2*). Uel was one of those listed as having married a foreign wife.

**ULAM** (Heb., 'the first').
**1.** Rakem was the son of Sheresh, a descendant of Manasseh and a leader in that tribe. He was a grandson of Makir and his wife Maacah (*1 Chron. 7:16–17*).
**2.** The first son of Eshek and listed among the descendants of Benjamin and King Saul. His sons were 'brave warriors' and accomplished archers (*1 Chron. 8:39–40*).

**ULLA** The head of a clan in the tribe of Asher. He had four sons and was a 'brave warrior' and 'outstanding leader' (*1 Chron. 7:39–40*).

**UNNI 1.** After the ark of the covenant had been brought to Jerusalem, the worship of God was properly organized by King David. Unni was one of the family of Merarite Levites who were gatekeepers. The particular job he and his brothers were given was to be musicians and to play the harps and lyres before the ark of the covenant as it was moved to Jerusalem (*1 Chron. 15:18, 20*).
**2.** Mentioned in *Neh. 12:9*, this Unni was a Levite who returned from the Exile in Babylon with Zerubbabel. He seems to have had a senior responsibility for the music of worship. P.D.G.

**UR** (Heb., 'flame') was the father of Eliphal who was one of David's 'mighty men' (*1 Chron. 11:35*).

**URBANUS** (Lat., 'urbane'). A man whom Paul called a 'fellow worker in Christ'. He lived in Rome and was greeted by Paul in *Rom. 16:9*. Paul's personal recognition and care for many individuals in different congregations is to be noted in most of his letters.

**URI** (Heb., 'my light').
**1.** This Uri was the father of Bezalel, and son of Hur from the tribe of Judah (*Exod. 31:2; 35:30; 38:22; 1 Chron. 2:20; 2 Chron. 1:5*). Bezalel was appointed by the LORD to work in the building of the Tabernacle.
**2.** This Uri was the father of Geber who was one of Solomon's twelve district governors (see *Ben-Hur*) in charge of the area of Gilead. This was 'the country of Sihon king of the Amorites and the country of Og king of Bashan' (*1 Kings 4:19*).
**3.** Following the Exile in Babylon,

657

many people from Judah had married foreign women. Once in Jerusalem and under the leadership of Ezra they repented and made a covenant to serve the LORD (*Ezra 10:2*). This Uri was a Levite and Temple gatekeeper who had a foreign wife (*v. 24*). P.D.G.

**URIAH** (Heb., 'the Lord is my flame').

**1.** Uriah the Hittite lived in Jerusalem with his wife during the reign of King David. He was one of David's famous 'Thirty' mighty men (*2 Sam. 23:39; 1 Chron. 11:41*). His house was built somewhere below and not far from the palace. He was a warrior fighting for David under the command of Joab. On one occasion when Uriah was at war, David walked on the roof of his palace and, looking down, he saw Uriah's wife, Bathsheba, bathing. Falling in love with her, David summoned her to the palace where she became pregnant (*2 Sam. 11:1–5*. David recalled Uriah from war in the hope that he would have sex with his wife and the king would avoid a tricky situation (*vv. 6–9*). However, Uriah proved faithful to both God and his king. He refused to take privileges his fellow soldiers did not have and did not return to his house after talking to David, even when David got him drunk. His concern for 'the ark and Israel and Judah' were commendable and showed his commitment to his adopted country and God (*vv. 10–13*).

In exasperation David sent him back to Joab with a message that Uriah be given a front-line position in the siege of Rabbah. In the course of the battle Uriah was killed and David was later able to marry Bathsheba (*vv. 16–27*). Effectively David had murdered Uriah with his order to Joab and 'the thing David had done displeased the LORD' (*v. 27*). Later the prophet Nathan was sent by the LORD to rebuke David. The child of that pregnancy died as a judgment and the sin had lasting consequences for King David (*2 Sam. 12; 1 Kings 15:5*; also see *Nathan, Bath-*

*sheba*). However, in spite of the devastating and lasting consequences of such dreadful sin, the account reveals that God does forgive all who are truly repentant, no matter how serious the sin (*2 Sam. 12:13–14*).

**2.** Another Uriah was a priest at the time of King Ahaz of Judah. Ahaz was being attacked in Judah and Jerusalem by Rezin king of Aram and Pekah king of Israel because he would not join them in an alliance against Assyria. Ahaz appealed to Tiglath-Pileser, the king of Assyria, for help and sent him gifts from the Temple and palace treasuries. Tiglath-Pileser then attacked and conquered Damascus (*2 Kings 16*). King Ahaz visited him there and saw an altar, the plans of which he drew and sent back to Uriah so that a similar one could be built in Jerusalem (*vv. 10–11*). When Ahaz returned he offered sacrifices on the new altar. Uriah moved the position of one of the altars of the Temple to make room for the new one and offered sacrifices according to Ahaz's instructions rather than according to the rules of the Law of Moses (*vv. 12–18*).

Such worship of other gods right at the heart of the Temple that should have been kept holy for the worship of the LORD (Yahweh) clearly indicated how far Ahaz and the priesthood had moved from the true God and his worship. No doubt they thought that perhaps worship of both the LORD and of the gods of Damascus would help them hedge their bets against invasion and destruction (*2 Chron. 28:22–23*). In fact the opposite was true. Had they relied entirely upon the LORD they would have been saved but, in turning to other gods, they were simply storing up for themselves the LORD's judgment (*2 Chron. 28:25; Is. 8:1–2*).

**3.** A man from Kiriath Jearim, this Uriah was son of Shemaiah (*Jer. 26:20*). He was a faithful prophet of the LORD at the same time as Jeremiah. He prophesied at the time of King Jehoiakim and warned of the impending full judgment of God and destruction of Jerusalem by the Babylonians. The king and his officers were furious, believing that such prophecies would undermine the confidence of the people in their leadership. They tried to kill Uriah who fled to Egypt. But Jehoiakim sent Elnathan to Egypt to bring the prophet back. On their return Uriah was put to death (*vv. 21–23*).

**4.** Another priest, son of Hakkoz and father of Meremoth (*Ezra 8:33; Neh. 3:4, 21*). Meremoth was one of those responsible for accounting for the silver and gold brought back from Babylon by those returning from the Exile to Jerusalem.

**5.** This Uriah was among those who stood on Ezra's right-hand side on a high wooden platform as he read the Book of the Law to the people of Israel. As the Law was read the people worshipped and praised God, confessed their sin, and recommitted themselves to the LORD's service (*Neh. 8:4*). P.D.G.

**URIEL** (Heb., 'God is my flame').

**1.** *1 Chron. 6:24* mentions Uriel, a Levite, and a descendant of Kohath. He was son of Tahath and father of Uzziah.

**2.** The Levite leader of the Kohathite clan at the time of King David. He and 120 family relatives were chosen with those from other Levitical families for the task of consecrating themselves and bringing the ark up to Jerusalem (*1 Chron. 15:5, 11*). The ark had been left at Obed-Edom's home for three months after the LORD's judgment had fallen on Uzzah (*1 Sam. 6*). – See *Uzzah*.

**3.** Uriel of Gibeah was the father of Maacah. Maacah was the mother of Abijah king of Judah (*2 Chron. 13:2*).

**UTHAI** **1.** Mentioned in *1 Chron. 9:4* as the son of Ammihud. After the captivity in Babylon, Uthai was among the first returnees to Jerusalem from the tribe of Judah.

**2.** Another Uthai returned from the captivity in Babylon with Ezra (*Ezra 8:14*). He was a descendant of Bigvai.

**UZ** **1.** The first of the four sons of Aram and a grandson of Shem listed in *Gen. 10:23* and *1 Chron. 1:17*.

**2.** The second Uz was a son of Milcah and Nahor (and therefore Abraham's nephew). One of his brothers was called Buz. The names 'Huz and Buz' have become famous over the years, 'Huz' being the AV version of the name Uz (*Gen. 22:21*). Also see *Bethuel*.

**3.** Another Uz was the son of Dishan and brother to Aran. Dishan was leader of the Horite clan and they lived in Edom (*Gen. 36:28; 1 Chron. 1:42*). References to a land called 'Uz' presumably refer to a territory settled by the descendants of one of the above. Many scholars seem to assume that 2. above is the most likely, but there can be no certainty. The land also cannot be definitely identified. However, it may have been in the northwestern part of Arabia (*Job. 1:1; Jer. 25:20; Lam. 4:21*). P.D.G.

**UZAI** The father of Palal who worked under Nehemiah in the rebuilding of the walls of Jerusalem following the return from the Babylonian captivity (*Neh. 3:25*).

**UZAL** A descendant of Shem and son of Joktan, he became a tribal leader (*Gen. 10:27; 1 Chron. 1:21*). Probably his descendants settled in the area that became known as Uzal. However, it is not possible to identify the location of that land (*Ezek. 27:19*).

**UZZA** **1.** A descendant of Benjamin. He was head of a clan and son of Gera. He was an ancestor of Saul and appears in that king's genealogy (*1 Chron. 8:7*).

**2.** The 'palace garden', used as a royal burial ground for Manasseh and Amon kings of Judah, was called the 'garden of Uzza' (*2 Kings 21:18, 26*). He may have been the owner of the garden or the gardener, but nothing more is known of him.

**3.** A leader of one of the families of Temple servants whose descendants returned from the Babylonian Exile in the days of Ezra and worked on the Temple (*Ezra 2:49; Neh. 7:51*).

**UZZAH** **1.** Uzzah was one of the two sons of Abinadab who guided the cart on which the ark (the covenant box) was being carried when King David brought it from Baalah of Judah to Jerusalem (*2 Sam 6:3*). The oxen pulling the cart stumbled. Uzzah put out his hand to steady the cart and touched the ark, something which probably everyone had been strictly forbidden to do (*v. 6; Num. 4:15*). As a result God 'struck him down and he died' (*v. 7*).

David was angry because God had judged in this way and for three months no-one moved the ark any further as all were frightened what might happen to them. David called the place Perez Uzzah (*v. 8*) meaning 'outbreak against Uzzah'. See also *1 Chron. 13:7–11* and *Obed-Edom*.

**2.** A descendant of Merari and a Levite, this Uzzah was the son of Shimei (*1 Chron. 6:29*). P.D.G.

**UZZI** **1.** The son of Bukki and father of Zerahiah, Uzzi is mentioned in the lists of the descendants of Levi in *1 Chron. 6:5–6, 51*. He was an ancestor of Ezra (*Ezra 7:4*).

**2.** A grandson of Issachar and first son of Tola, Uzzi was a family leader and a valiant soldier. He had a son named Izrahiah (*1 Chron. 7:2–3*).

**3.** A grandson of Benjamin and son of Bela, this Uzzi was head of a large family (*1 Chron. 7:7*).

**4.** Mentioned in *1 Chron. 9:8* as the son of Micri and father of Elah. After the captivity, this Uzzi was among the first returnees to Jerusalem from the tribe of Benjamin.

**5.** The son of Bani, this Uzzi was 'the chief officer of the Levites in Jerusalem' following the return of the exiles from Babylon to Judah. He was a descendant of Asaph and served with Nehemiah (*Neh. 11:22*).

**6.** Possibly the same as 7. below. He was the head of Jedaiah's family, and helped in the service of the Temple during Nehemiah's time (*Neh. 12:19*).

**7.** A Levite who was part of the choir that sang at the dedication of the wall. The walls and city had been destroyed by the Babylonians when they took the Israelites into captivity. Under the direction of Nehemiah they were eventually rebuilt amidst great praises to God (*Neh. 12:42*). P.D.G.

**UZZIA** (Heb., 'my strength is the Lord'), 'the Ashterathite' belonged to David's 'Thirty' mighty men who went to battle for him and led the people of Israel to war (*1 Chron. 11:44*).

**UZZIAH** (Heb., 'the Lord is my strength').

**1.** Uzziah king of Judah reigned from around 791–740/39 BC. The longest account of Uzziah is found in *2 Chron. 26* which says he reigned for 52 years. He ruled as co-regent with his father Amaziah whom he later succeeded. For part of Uzziah's early reign it is likely Amaziah was a captive in the Northern Kingdom of Israel. His mother who came from Jerusalem was called Jecoliah. He led Judah through a time of great prosperity into a period of rapid decline. (The passage in *2 Kings 15:1–7* calls him Azariah.)

The Chronicler wants the reader to understand that, as with his father Amaziah, Uzziah had great success 'as long as he sought the LORD' (*v. 5*). Certainly for the first part of his reign he 'did what was right in the eyes of the LORD' (*v. 4*) and this led to blessings from the LORD in battle against the Philistines,

Arabs and Ammonites. During this time he was taught his faith by a prophet called Zechariah who is mentioned only here in the Bible (v. 5). His fame spread even as far as the borders with Egypt (vv. 6–8). He fortified Jerusalem and built outposts in the desert. He drew together an enormous army and equipped it well, even developing new weapons for use on the city walls (vv. 9–15).

However, as with so many who become powerful and famous, he became proud and disobeyed the LORD. He entered the Temple to offer a sacrifice that only the priests were allowed to perform according to God's Law. Brave priests, led by Azariah, stood up to Uzziah and pointed out the evil of what he was doing. While Uzziah's anger burned against the priests he became a leper for 'the LORD had afflicted him' (vv. 16–20). Leprosy meant that a person could not enter the Temple and so was an appropriate penalty for the crime.

2 Kings 15:1–7 recounts little of Uzziah's reign. But, following his affliction with leprosy, it seems he reigned with his son Jotham as co-regent (v. 5). His son later succeeded him to the throne (vv. 13, 30, 32, 34; see also Matt. 1:8–9).

During Uzziah's reign the prophets Isaiah, Amos and Hosea all prophesied (Is. 1:1; 6:1; 7:1; Hos. 1:1; Amos 1:1). Their concern with wealth and pride is evident throughout their prophecy of that period. Judah's rather rapid decline in the last few years of Uzziah was all part of God's judgment that comes upon such pride that ignores God. God also sent an earthquake by way of judgment on the nation. Such was the earthquake that the prophecy of Amos used it to indicate a particular date and the prophet Zechariah later looked back to it as a picture of what God would eventually do in judging the earth (Amos 1:1; Zech. 14:5).

**2.** The son of Uriel and father of Shaul, this Uzziah was a Levite from the Kohathite clan (1 Chron. 6:24).

**3.** The father of a certain Jonathan who was 'in charge of the storehouses' as one of King David's personal overseers (1 Chron. 27:25).

**4.** This Uzziah was a descendant of Harim and one of those in the time of Ezra who had married a foreign wife rather than one from Judah (Ezra 10:21).

**5.** The father of Athaiah and a descendant of Perez from the tribe of Judah. Athaiah settled in Jerusalem on the return from the Exile in Babylon (Neh. 11:4).                    P.D.G.

**UZZIEL** (Heb., 'my strength is God').

**1.** A grandson of Benjamin and son of Bela, this Uzziel was head of a large family and a great warrior (1 Chron. 7:7).

**2.** This Uzziel was one of four sons of Kohath and a grandson of Levi (Exod. 6:18; 1 Chron. 6:2, 18, 38; 23:12). He was an uncle of Moses and Aaron and father of a clan leader among the Kohathites (Lev. 10:4; Numb. 3:19; 1 Chron. 15:10). He led the Uzzielites and his family had care of the ark and other articles used in the sanctuary (Num. 3:27–31). His own sons were Mishael, Elzaphan (called Elizaphan in Num. 3:30) and Sithri (Exod. 6:22). In 1 Chron. 23:20; 24:24, Mishael is called Micah and another son, Isshiah is mentioned.

**3.** A Simeonite who was the son of Ishi and lived in the time of King Hezekiah of Judah. He helped lead an invasion of the hill country of Seir (to the east of the Dead Sea), killing the remaining Amalekites. His people then settled the area (1 Chron. 4:42–43).

**4.** One of the sons of Heman listed among those set apart for the ministry of prophesying and music during the reign of King David. Heman was the king's seer (1 Chron. 25:4).

**5.** A Levite mentioned in 2 Chron. 29:14, he was a descendant of the musician Jeduthun and worked in the

Temple during the revival under King Hezekiah. See *Heman* for more detail.

**6.** The son of Harhaiah, this Uzziel was a goldsmith and helped repair a section of the walls of Jerusalem under the direction of Nehemiah following the return from the Babylonian Exile (*Neh. 3:8*).

P.D.G.

# V

**VAIZATHA** One of ten sons of Haman killed in Susa by the Jews (*Est. 9:9*).

**VANIAH** In *Ezra 10:36* Vaniah is listed among the descendants of Bani. Shecaniah confessed to Ezra that many men and even descendants of the priests of Judah had married wives from other tribes and nations. Ezra and the people repented and made a covenant to serve the LORD (*Ezra 10:2*). Vaniah was one of those who had a foreign wife.

**VASHTI** was queen to Xerxes, the Persian King (*Est. 1*). On the final day of the King's banquet, Queen Vashti was summoned for the purpose of displaying her beauty. Vashti refused the invitation, and this sparked controversy among the King's advisers. Fearing Vashti's disobedience would discredit men throughout the kingdom, the queen was deposed and a new queen was sought to take her place. This opened the way for Esther who was chosen as her successor. The LORD overruled so that Esther was then in position to help save her people, the Jews, from destruction. See *Esther* and *Haman*.                    S.C.

**VOPHSI** The father of Nahbi. Nahbi was one of the twelve spies sent out by Moses from the Desert of Paran to spy out the land of Canaan (*Num. 13:14*). A representative of each tribe was chosen. Vophsi and his son were from the tribe of Naphtali. For further detail on their mission see *Shammua*.

# W

## THE WOMAN AT THE WELL

The account of the Samaritan 'woman at the well' is found only in the Gospel of John. Christ's encounter with this female foreigner is an integral part of the apostle John's overall purpose for writing: to prove that Jesus is indeed the Son of God and that believing in him brings eternal life. Who she was and the conversation they had reveals Christ's supernatural ability to search hearts. Their meeting also confirms his mission to receive and save all who believe in him (*John 1:12*).

It is no accident that John places this encounter with the Samaritan woman directly after Christ's nocturnal conversation with the well-respected Pharisee, Nicodemus. For Jesus told this distinguished religious leader that God so loved the world that he gave his only Begotten Son (*John 3:16*). Thus, the apostle John shows his Gentile readers that this 'world' included the Samaritans, a people who were hated by the Jews. As much as possible, they avoided them at every turn. See *Samaritans* for detail.

Therefore, it is significant enough that Jesus chose to journey through Samaria instead of taking the 'accepted' alternative route along the Jordan river. But to speak to a Samaritan, and a woman at that (for no Jewish rabbi openly had conversation with a woman), was breaking all boundaries! His eccentric behaviour undoubtedly left his disciples shocked and bewildered (*John 4:27*).

However, that woman needed to hear the Saviour's life-changing message. When she heard the good news she believed and immediately reaped the heavenly benefits. For little did she realize that the path which led her to Jacob's well would one day be the doorway to the Kingdom of God. The mundane daily routine of fetching water turned out to be the catalyst that changed her life.

The woman was from Sychar, a small village near Shechem. Jacob's well was about a half a mile walk from her home. It was customary for the women of the village to gather together at a certain time and go to the well to draw water each day. But this woman journeyed to the well alone and at an unusual time ('the sixth hour' was about noon).

When she arrived at the well, she found Jesus sitting there. She was undoubtedly surprised to find a Jew in Samaritan territory. Jesus had sent his disciples to buy some food which left the two of them alone. Ironically, it was physical need (thirst and weariness, *John 4:4–8*) which brought the Son of God and the woman to the same place. This meeting serves as a beautiful picture of the incarnation. Divinity and humanity drawn together to meet human need.

Jesus asked the woman for a drink. Her flippant response clearly reveals the tension that existed between the Jew and the Samaritan (*v. 9*). Jesus, in turn, offered her a drink of 'living water' (v. 10). This offer amazed her because he had no means to draw water from the well.

His empty hands and his generous offer caused her to question his identity. She wondered if he was greater than the patriarch, Jacob (who she referred to as 'our father'; perhaps in order to acknowledge their common ancestry), who founded the well and drank from it himself (vv. 11–12).

Christ's reply was even more puzzling. The living water he offered her would quench her thirst forever. In fact, his water, which is spiritual in nature, would well up in her to eternal life. She would not have to work for this water because it would bubble up from within her (vv. 13–14).

Naturally, she did not understand that his gift of living water was not material, but spiritual. She was thinking only in terms of her physical thirst. This is evident from her response. She wanted his water so that she would no longer thirst or have to come to the well (v. 15).

Then Jesus made a seemingly peculiar request of her. He asked her to return to town and call her husband (v. 16). He probably did this for two reasons. First, it was proper for a man to talk to a woman with her husband present. Secondly, this simple request would expose her spiritual condition and her deep need. It would also give him an opportunity to reveal his true identity as Messiah, the Saviour of the world.

The woman promptly informed Jesus that she had no husband. Christ acknowledged that her statement was true and then supernaturally unveiled her sordid personal history. He spoke of her previous failed relationships and her current adulterous one (vv. 17–18). This parading of her shameful background by the Saviour undoubtedly made her blush.

Christ was not purposely being disdainful. He was exposing her need for the true living water. For she had a thirst that was much deeper than a physical one and only he could provide the means to quench it. She was obviously thirsty for love, but found her desires dashed upon the rocks of broken relationships. Christ was offering her a new beginning through the living waters of eternal life.

In support of the overall argument of his book (John 20:31), the apostle John shows that the Messiah has the supernatural ability to search a person's heart, exposing both its sin and need. Also, John demonstrates that the Christ has the means and authority to grant eternal life.

The Samaritan woman was so astonished by this revealing of her previous life that she changed the subject! Apparently, she sought to divert his attention away from her personal life and towards the subject of religion. So she questioned him about the proper place for worship.

The Jews insisted that worship was to take place at Solomon's Temple in Jerusalem. The Samaritans, on the other hand, claimed that the true worship centre was Mt Gerizim (Jacob's Well was located at the foot of Mt Gerizim). The Samaritans based this assumption on a command Moses gave Israel before they entered the Promised Land.

After crossing the Jordan River, six tribes were to stand at the foot of Mt Gerizim to bless the people. The other six tribes were to stand on Mt Ebal to pronounce curses (Deut. 27:12–13). The Samaritans concluded that this event established Mt Gerizim as the place of worship. The Jews and Samaritans were in bitter controversy over this subject.

However, Jesus would not be drawn into such a debate. Instead, he revealed to her a profound truth about the nature of God. God, who is Spirit and unconfined, is not to be worshipped in any one place. Rather, he desires his true worshippers to have a certain attitude. They are to worship him in spirit and in truth (*John 4:21–24*). True worshippers, whether they are Jews or Samaritans, are to be open and honest with God.

According to Jesus, true worship is from the heart. It requires honesty and transparency from the worshipper. Thus far, the Samaritan woman had been concealing her heart from God. Hence, she responded to these profound truths with yet another theological statement. She informed Jesus that the 'Christ' is coming, the One who will explain everything (*v. 25*).

With a simple statement in return, Jesus revealed to her that he is the Christ, the One she has been waiting for (*v. 26*). Her immediate response to this truth is not recorded, but her actions show that she was finally deeply affected. Leaving her water jar, she returned to her home and told of her experience (*v. 28*).

It is interesting to note what she said to the people upon her return. She was given much spiritual truth in her encounter with Jesus: the true nature of God, the true nature of worship, and Jesus' true identity as the Messiah. But it was the truth about herself that she went back to her village to proclaim.

She implored them to come and see the Man who told her everything she ever did. Then she spoke of his identity as the Christ (*v. 29*). It seems that Christ's ability to search her heart left the lasting impression. She realized her need through her encounter with him. This was her testimony and this is what compelled the Samaritans to come out to him (*v. 30*).

The Samaritans urged him to stay, and he stayed with them two days. They initially believed in him because of the woman's testimony. But when they heard his words themselves, many came to believe that he was the Saviour of the world (*vv. 39–42*).

The apostle John's main point in this account of the Samaritan woman is twofold. The Messiah, who is the Saviour of the world, has the divine ability to search the human heart and reveal God's truth. Those who worship God, regardless of their ethnic background, must do so in spirit and in truth. These two truths support his overall purpose to prove that Jesus is the Son of God and that believing in him brings eternal life.                    K.MC.R

# X

**XERXES 1.** Xerxes I. This king of Persia (called Ahasuerus in many English translations) is mentioned in the book of *Esther* and in *Ezra 4:6*. He was one of the great kings of the Persian empire, ruling from 486–465 BC. He was the son of Darius (I) the Great. An inscription found at Persepolis indicates the extent of his rule. He put down rebellions in his empire most brutally and even attacked Greece, burning the city of Athens in the process. However, the Greeks fought back and around 466 BC managed to push the Persians back into Asia Minor. He was assassinated in 465 BC, having lost much of his empire.

In the book of Esther, Xerxes is portrayed as a king of great power and huge empire with 'provinces stretching from India to Cush' (*Est. 1:1*). This is clearly an accurate description at least of the first quarter of his reign. He reigned from Susa and his queen was called Vashti (*v. 2*). Vashti refused to appear at the king's command and so was stripped of her role (*1:16–19*). Esther was appointed in her place as Queen. The description of the king's anger (*2:1*), attempts to overthrow him (*2:21–23*), his weakness at the hands of his advisers (*1:16; 3:10–11*) etc. all point to a king who gradually lost his way and saw his power diminish. In the midst of his increasing political impotence, God placed Esther and Mordecai in positions around King Xerxes and moved to protect his people, the Jews. Once again the sovereignty of the LORD God over the nations of the world was witnessed as he saved his people from extermination.

**2.** This Xerxes is described as the father of Darius, who was the ruler of Babylon during the time when Daniel and the people of Judah were in captivity there (*Dan. 9:1*).                                        P.D.G.

# Z

**ZAAVAN** was the second son of Ezer, one of the tribal leaders in Seir where Esau settled (*Gen. 36:27; 1 Chron. 1:42*).

**ZABAD** (Heb., 'gift').

**1.** Mentioned in *1 Chron. 2:36–37*, he was the father of Ephlal and son of Nathan. He was a descendant of Judah.

**2.** A descendant of Ephraim, son of Tahath and father of Shuthelah (*1 Chron. 7:21*).

**3.** Zabad, son of Ahlai, was one of David's 'Thirty' warriors (*1 Chron. 11:41*).

**4.** Zabad was son of Shimeath, an Ammonite (*2 Chron. 24:26*). In *2 Kings 12:21* he is called Jozabad. Zabad was one of those who murdered King Joash of Judah. The murder was regarded as judgment from God on Joash who had ordered the righteous priest, Zechariah, killed and who had led the nation away from the LORD and into idolatry (*2 Chron. 24:18–24*). The fact that Zabad's mother was identified as an Ammonite, and the second conspirator was identified as having a Moabite mother, reminds the reader of Chronicles how far the nation had moved from obedience to the Law of God, where such intermarriage was forbidden.

**5.** This Zabad was among the descendants of Zattu. At the time of return from the Exile in Babylon, Shecaniah confessed to Ezra that many men and even descendants of the priests of Judah had married wives from other tribes and nations. Ezra and the people repented and made a covenant to serve the LORD (*Ezra 10:2*). Zabad is listed in *Ezra 10:27* as one who had married a foreign wife.

**6.** Another Zabad living in the time of Ezra, from the descendants of Hashum, who had married a foreign wife (*Ezra 10:33*).

**7.** Another Zabad living in the time of Ezra, from the descendants of Nebo, who had married a foreign wife (*Ezra 10:43*).

P.D.G.

**ZABBAI** **1.** This Zabbai was among the descendants of Bebai. At the time of return from the Exile in Babylon, Shecaniah confessed to Ezra that many men and even descendants of the priests of Judah had married wives from other tribes and nations. Ezra and the people repented and made a covenant to serve the LORD (*Ezra 10:2*). Zabbi is listed in *Ezra 10:28* as one who had married a foreign wife.

**2.** Mentioned in *Neh. 3:20* as the father of Baruch. Baruch helped repair the wall of Jerusalem in the days of Nehemiah. P.D.G.

**ZABDI** (Heb., 'my gift').

**1.** Mentioned in *1 Chron. 8:19* in the genealogy leading from Benjamin to Saul. A son of Shimei.

**2.** A Shiphmite who was an overseer during the reign of King David. He was in charge of the produce of the vineyards from the wine vats (*1 Chron. 27:27*).

**3.** The grandfather of Mattaniah, a Levite. Mattaniah 'led the people in thanksgiving and prayer' as the Temple was being restored in the days of Nehemiah (Neh. 11:17).

**ZABDIEL** (Heb., 'gift of God').

**1.** The father of Jashobeam and a descendant of Perez (1 Chron. 27:2). Jashobeam was a commander in David's army and on duty with his men in the first month of each year.

**2.** This Zabdiel is listed among the priests who returned from the Babylonian Exile and set up house in Jerusalem. His father was Haggedolim. His clan contained 128 'able men' (Neh. 11:14).

**ZABUD,** a priest, was one of King Solomon's personal advisers and officials. He was the son of Nathan, who was perhaps the prophet known in King David's time (1 Kings 4:5).

**ZACCAI** The ancestor of 760 people who returned from the Exile in Babylon with Nehemiah and Zerubbabel (Ezra 2:9; Neh. 7:14).

**ZACCHAEUS** (Heb., 'righteous') was a wealthy chief tax collector who lived in the area of Jericho. His story is recounted in Luke 19:1–10. He was a short man who, when he heard Jesus was passing through the city, climbed a sycamore-fig tree to see over the heads of the crowd. Jesus saw him, addressed him by name, and said 'I must stay at your house today' (v. 5). Such a move angered the crowd who regarded this tax collector as 'a sinner', because of his work for the Romans and the way he took money from his own people. Many tax collectors would have earned their own wealth from their fraudulent requests for more taxes than were due.

For Zacchaeus, however, this visit marked the turning point in his life as he recognized Jesus as his Lord. In demonstration of his repentance he said, 'Here and now I give half of my possessions to the poor, and if I have cheated anybody out of anything, I will pay back four times the amount' (v. 8; see Lev. 6:1–5).

The reaction of Zacchaeus contrasts dramatically with what had happened, perhaps only days earlier, when Jesus had encountered the 'rich young ruler' (Luke 18:18–25). There wealth had been a stumbling block and had stood between the ruler and his commitment to Jesus as Lord. Jesus had commented, 'How hard it is for the rich to enter the kingdom of God!' (v. 24).

For Zacchaeus this encounter with Jesus brought salvation and revealed that true commitment to the lordship of Christ is immediately evidenced in a changed life. Jesus called this change in his life and his entrance into the kingdom, 'salvation'. But this salvation did not begin in Zacchaeus but rather came to him in the person of Jesus. 'Today salvation has come to this house . . . The Son of Man came to seek and to save what was lost' (Luke 19:10). Such is the gracious work of Christ in bringing God's grace, forgiveness and salvation even to those whom society deems to be the worst 'sinners'.

P.D.G.

**ZACCUR 1.** The father of Shammua one of the twelve spies sent out by Moses from the Desert of Paran to spy out the land of Canaan (Num. 13:4). For further detail on their mission see Shammua.

**2.** A descendant of Mishma and son of Hammuel from the tribe of Simeon (1 Chron. 4:26).

**3.** Found in the lists of 1 Chron. 24:27, Zaccur was the son of Jaaziah, the son of Merari, a Levite. These descendants of Merari are listed as serving in the Tabernacle in the time of King David.

**4.** Mentioned in 1 Chron. 25:2, this Zaccur was one of the sons of Asaph. Immediately under Asaph's direction, and on the direct orders of King David (v. 1), he and others were among those who prophesied and led in the ministry of music for worship. He was leader of the third group of Levitical musicians and choirs who ministered in the Temple (v.

10). He is mentioned again in a genealogy in *Neh. 12:35*.

**5.** Another Zaccur returned from the captivity in Babylon with Ezra (*Ezra 8:14*). He was a descendant of Bigvai.

**6.** The son of Imri, this Zaccur was involved in helping to rebuild the walls of Jerusalem following the return from the Exile in Babylon. Under Nehemiah's direction he built the wall in a section next to the place where the men of Jericho were working (*Neh. 3:2*).

**7.** This Zaccur was one of the Levites who joined Nehemiah, following the Babylonian Exile, in witnessing the solemn covenant promising to worship and obey the LORD (*Neh. 10:12*).

**8.** The father of Hanan. Hanan was one of those to whom Nehemiah gave great responsibility, as he was considered 'trustworthy' (*Neh. 13:13*).          P.D.G.

**ZADOK** (Heb., 'righteous').

**1.** The most important figure by this name in the Bible is Zadok son of Ahitub. A Levite and leader among the Aaronites (*1 Chron. 6:50–52; 27:17*), he was a priest during the reign of King David and is often mentioned in connection with another priest, Abiathar. The early chapters of *2 Samuel* describe an Israel under David where most of the Philistines had been subdued and Israel was enjoying considerable prosperity. *2 Sam. 8:14* sums it up: 'The LORD gave David victory wherever he went'. In this context we first hear of Zadok and Ahimelech (Abiathar's father) being priests among a list of David's top army and social leaders (*8:17*).

Later when Zadok and Abiathar were well established as priests, David had to flee Jerusalem with them because of Absalom's conspiracy against him. They took with them the ark of the covenant. David sent them back to Jerusalem with the ark and asked them to work for him in Jerusalem right under the nose of Absalom (*2 Sam. 15:24–29*). With help from Hushai, an adviser to Absalom but in the pay of David, Zadok and Abiathar's sons were able to relay Absalom's plans directly to David (*17:15; 18:19*). Following the fall of Absalom, David asked the two of them to bring him back to Jerusalem to rule (*19:11–14*). Zadok seems to have been totally loyal to David even from the time when he was listed as a Levite who was 'a brave young warrior' and joined David at Hebron when he was fighting Saul (*1 Chron. 12:26–28*).

Zadok was given responsibility by David to bring the ark to Jerusalem and to organize the service of the Tabernacle at Gibeon (*1 Chron. 15:11; 16:39*). He also helped David allocate tasks of service for the Tabernacle and Temple to the Levites (*1 Chron. 24:3, 31*).

On the death of David, Zadok sided with David's desire that Solomon should inherit the throne and was involved in the overthrow of the rebellious Adonijah and the crowning of the new king (*1 Kings 1:8, 26, 32–53; 1 Chron. 29:2*). He remained a chief priest with Abiathar during the early part of Solomon's reign (*1 Kings 4:4; 1 Chron. 29:22*). Zadok's sons and descendants continued to have influential positions in the land probably until the time of the Exile (*1 Kings 4:2; 1 Chron. 6:8, 12; 9:11; 2 Chron. 31:10; Ezra 7:2; etc.*).

The faithfulness of this man of God, who saw that David was God's anointed and followed him, even when it meant persecution, and was faithful throughout to the service of the LORD, meant that he and his descendants were rewarded by God and allowed to keep the priesthood under their control. The prophet Ezekiel regarded the descendants of Zadok as the only God-appointed legitimate heirs to the priesthood (*Ezek. 40:46; 43:19; 44:15*).

**2.** A descendant of 1. above and the father of Shallum (*1 Chron. 6:12*).

**3.** A Levite whose descendants were listed as being among the first to return to live in Jerusalem following the return from the Babylonian Exile (1 Chron. 9:11). He was the father of Meshullam and the son of Meraioth (Neh. 11:11).

**4.** The father of Jerusha who became King Jotham's wife (2 Kings 15:33; 2 Chron. 27:1).

**5.** Zadok son of Baana helped in rebuilding the walls of Jerusalem following the return from the Babylonian captivity (Neh. 3:4).

**6.** Zadok son of Immer also helped in rebuilding the walls under Nehemiah's direction (Neh. 3:29).

**7.** One of the leaders of the people who had returned from Babylon, this Zadok (who may have been the same as either 5. or 6. above) signed Nehemiah's covenant of allegiance to the Lord and his Law (Neh. 10:21).

**8.** A scribe appointed by Nehemiah to have responsibility for the storerooms in which were placed the people's tithes and offerings (Neh. 13:13).

**9.** Another Zadok appears in the genealogy of Christ in Matt. 1:14. He was the father of Akim and the son of Azor.

P.D.G.

**ZAHAM** (Heb., 'loathsome'). One of three sons born to Rehoboam and Mahalath (2 Chron. 11:19).

**ZALAPH** (Heb., 'caper plant'). The father of Hanun. Hanun, Zalaph's sixth son, was involved in helping to rebuild the walls of Jerusalem following the return from the Exile in Babylon. Under Nehemiah's direction he rebuilt a section of the wall near the East Gate (Neh. 3:30).

**ZALMON** the Ahohite was one of David's 'Thirty' mighty warriors who fought at his side (2 Sam. 23:28). It would appear that this is the same person as Ilai in 1 Chron. 11:29.

**ZALMUNNA** One of two Midianite kings who were eventually put to death by

Gideon. See Judge. 8 and Ps. 83:11. For detail see Zebah.

**ZANOAH** A descendant of Ezrah, he was the son of Jekuthiel. He is listed in the genealogy of Judah (1 Chron. 4:18). Zanoah may have been the name of a city which Jekuthiel founded rather than his son (see the inheritance of the tribe of Judah, Josh. 15:20–63, esp. v. 56).

**ZAPHENATH-PANEAH** This was the special name given to Joseph by Pharaoh when he was promoted to be prime-minister 'in charge of the whole land of Egypt' (Gen. 41:44–45). The meaning of the name is not known, but no doubt indicated his rank and status in some way. At the same time as being given the name, Joseph was given Asenath to be his wife. See Joseph and Asenath.

**ZATTU 1.** A family leader whose descendants were counted among those who, in the time of Ezra, returned with Zerubbabel and Nehemiah from the Babylonian Exile. Their number was 945 (Ezra 2:8; 8:5; Neh. 7:13). Some of these descendants were mentioned in Ezra 10:27 as being among those who had intermarried with foreign women.

**2.** Probably a descendant of 1. above or possibly the same person, this Zattu was among the leaders of the people who signed the covenant under Nehemiah in which they promised to worship and obey only the Lord (Neh. 10:14).

**ZAZA** A son of Jonathan and brother to Peleth, Zaza was from the tribe of Judah and a Jerahmeelite (1 Chron. 2:33).

**ZEBADIAH** (Heb., 'the Lord has given').

**1.** One of the sons of Beriah and a leader from the tribe of Benjamin, this Zebadiah lived in Jerusalem (1 Chron. 8:15).

**2.** One of the sons of Elpaal and a leader from the tribe of Benjamin, this Zebadiah lived in Jerusalem (1 Chron. 8:17).

**3.** One of the warriors who deserted Saul to join David at Ziklag. They were ambidextrous in archery and with slings and came from the tribe of Benjamin. This Zebadiah was a 'mighty man' among David's famous and valiant 'Thirty' warriors. He was a son of Jeroham from Gedor (1 Chron. 12:7).

**4.** A Levite from the Korahite clan who is listed as one of the 'gatekeepers' of the sanctuary. He was appointed during the latter part of King David's reign and was the third son of Meshelemiah (1 Chron. 26:2).

**5.** This Zebadiah was one of David's army commanders. As a leader in David's army he was on duty with his men in the fourth month of each year and had 24,000 men in his division (1 Chron. 27:7). He succeeded his father, Asahel the brother of Joab, into the job.

**6.** A Levite, this Zebadiah lived in the days of King Jehoshaphat of Judah. During the early years of his reign Jehoshaphat served the LORD and sent out various teachers and Levites to teach the people of Judah the Book of the Law. Zebadiah was one of those teachers (2 Chron. 17:8).

**7.** Another Zebediah living in the days of King Jehoshaphat was the leader of the tribe of Judah. In his desire to see a restoration of worship of the true God, Yahweh (the LORD), in the nation, Jehoshaphat appointed Amariah to be the chief priest dealing with matters 'concerning the LORD' and Zebadiah to deal with 'any matters concerning the king'. In his commission to these important leaders who would steer the people and the nation back to the LORD, Jehoshaphat encouraged them that the LORD would be with them and that they should 'act with courage' (2 Chron. 19:11).

**8.** One of the heads of family who returned to Jerusalem from Babylon with Ezra. He was a descendant of Shephatiah and son of Michael. He returned with 80 men (Ezra 8:8).

**9.** This Zebadiah was a descendant of Immer and one of the priests in the time of Ezra who had married a foreign wife rather than one from Judah (Ezra 10:20).

P.D.G.

**ZEBAH** (Heb., 'sacrifice') and Zalmunna were two Midianite kings who were defeated by Gideon and the Israelites. In an amazing display of reliance upon and obedience to God, Gideon had attacked the Midianite camp with a mere 300 men (Judg. 7; see Gideon). The Midianites had fled in the dark and Gideon called up Israelites from several different tribes to come and chase them down. People from the tribe of Ephraim captured and killed the leaders Oreb and Zeeb (Judg. 7:25). But Gideon and his men chased after Zebah and Zalmunna. Tired and in need of food, Gideon asked the people of Succoth (8:5–7) and then the people of Peniel for help with their material needs. Unconvinced that Gideon would actually win this battle with the Midianite kings and their huge army (v. 10), they refused to help him. Eventually with his small army, Gideon made a surprise attack on the Midianites and routed them, capturing the two kings (v. 12). Gideon then took the two kings back through Succoth and Peniel, punishing the leaders in both towns for their refusal to help. Gideon himself then killed the two kings in revenge for the way they had killed members of his family at Tabor (vv. 12–21).

Gideon was only too well aware that a victory of this magnitude was God's work (Judge 8:3). As a result of this victory the Israelites wished to make Gideon king but he insisted, in keeping with his faith, 'The LORD will rule over you' (v. 23). Future generations looked back to the victory as an indication of what God could do on their behalf and therefore what they could ask him to do again for them (e.g. Ps. 83:11; Is. 10:26).

P.D.G.

**ZEBEDEE** (Heb., 'gift of the Lord'). The father of two of Jesus' disciples, James and John. He was a fisherman from the Sea of Galilee and was present when Jesus called his sons to be disciples. The sons immediately left their father and followed Jesus. Zebedee owned his own boat and had other hired hands apart from his sons working for him (*Matt.* 4:21–22; *Mark* 1:19–20; *Luke* 5:10). From time to time it would seem that the two sons returned to their fishing and it is quite likely that this reasonably well-established family supported Jesus financially during his ministry. The family appears to have been in partnership with Simon Peter and his family (*Luke* 5:8–10).

By comparing *Matt.* 27:56 and *Mark* 15:40 it is deduced that Zebedee's wife was Salome. Salome's concern for Jesus indicates that it was not just the sons who heard the call of Jesus and wished to follow and serve him. See also *Matt.* 10:2; 26:37; *Mark* 3:17; 10:35; 16:1; *John* 21:2. See *James* and *John*.     P.D.G.

**ZEBIDAH** The daughter of Pedaiah and mother of King Jehoiakim, Zebidah came from Rumah (*2 Kings* 23:36). Jehoiakim became king of Judah at the age of 25.

**ZEBINA** (Heb., 'bought') was among the descendants of Nebo. At the time of return from the Exile in Babylon, Shecaniah confessed to Ezra that many men and even descendants of the priests of Judah had married wives from other tribes and nations. Ezra and the people repented and made a covenant to serve the LORD (*Ezra* 10:2). Zebina is listed in *Ezra* 10:43 as one who had married a foreign wife.

**ZEBUL** (Heb., 'exalted'). The name originally belonged to one of the gods of Canaan but in the Bible belongs to an official in charge of the city of Shechem in the days of the Judges. This Zebul worked under the leadership of Gideon's son,

Abimelech. The people of Shechem did not like this arrangement and, led by Gaal, they rebelled. Zebul informed Abimelech and the two of them organized an ambush of Gaal's forces. Gaal was routed. The following day Abimelech attacked the people of Shechem again but no further information is given about what happened to Zebul (*Judg.* 9:26–41). See also *Abimelech*.     P.D.G.

**ZEBULUN** was Jacob's tenth son and his mother was Leah. Leah was pleased at his birth, largely because of the rivalry between her and Rachel, and so she called him Zebulun in a play on two words one of which meant 'dowry' and the other 'honour'. Thus in *Gen.* 30:19–20: "God has presented me with a precious gift [dowry]. This time my husband will treat me with honour, because I have borne him six sons." So she named him Zebulun.'

Zebulun's own sons were born before he travelled with his father to Egypt (*Gen.* 35:23; 46:14). In Jacob's blessing on him and his descendants he was promised land by the seashore and a border extending towards Sidon (*Gen.* 49:13). The eventual distribution of lands to the tribes gives only an indication of where the tribal boundaries lay. However, the northern and western area of the Valley of Esdraelon was part of the territory and in the east the borders extended towards, but did not reach, the southern part of Lake Galilee. Southwards the land reached Mt Tabor, and in the west it bordered the tribal lands of Asher (*Josh.* 19:10–16). Interestingly, records available do not indicate that access to the sea was available to the tribe. However, people have speculated that Jacob's blessing may have been fulfilled in other ways, perhaps with an unrecorded extension to Carmel, implied by Josephus.

During the wilderness wanderings Zebulun was led by Eliab son of Helon (*Num.* 2:7) and their camp was to be with Judah to the east of the Tabernacle. The judge Elon also came from this tribe (*Judg. 12:11–12*), and Zebulun provided 50,000 men with many weapons to help David when he rallied them at Hebron (*1 Chron. 12:33*). The tribe largely had turned from the LORD in the days of Hezekiah, although some still came to worship in the great revival (*2 Chron. 30:10–11, 18*). The tribe disappeared under the Assyrian invasions of the Northern Kingdom. However, in spite of his awesome judgment, in a lovely testimony to the faithfulness of God to his people, Isaiah prophesied that the 'humbled' lands of Zebulun and Naphtali would again be honoured by God (*Is. 9:1*; see also *Ezek. 48:26–33*). Isaiah's prophecy found its fulfilment, as Matthew demonstrated when, in the midst of their darkness, Christ himself brought them God's light by living in Capernaum (*Matt. 4:13–16*). *Rev. 7:8–9* reminds us that eventually the faithful of Zebulun will join the faithful of the world worshipping at the feet of Christ, the Lamb on the throne.                    P.D.G.

**ZECHARIAH** (Heb., 'the Lord remembers').

**1.** Zechariah the OT prophet. This post-exilic prophet is identified as a son of Berekiah and grandson of Iddo (*Zech. 1:1*). Chronological and genealogical clues suggest that this Iddo is the priest who returned from Babylonian Exile under the leadership of Zerubbabel and Jeshua (*Neh. 12:4, 16*). This would imply that Zechariah was also a priest, specifically one 'of Iddo' (*v. 16*), that is, of the same family. His dual role of priest and prophet is not unique in the OT (see also Samuel, Jeremiah, and Ezekiel) and it explains Zechariah's unusual interest in priestly matters (see *Zech. 3:1–5; 4:1–6, 11–14; 6:9–15; 8:18–19; 14:16–21*).

The prophet carefully dates his oracles, a practice in line with prevailing compositional custom of the time and one that asserts that his ministry was not in the abstract but was related to the times and circumstances of which he was a part. His first public proclamation was in the eighth month of the second year of Darius Hystaspes, King of Persia from 522–486 BC. In terms of the modern calendar the word of Yahweh came to him in October/November, 520. Subsequent chronological notations appear in *Zech. 1:7* (January/February, 520) and *7:1* (December 7, 518). Zechariah's entire documented ministry thus embraces a period of only two years, though many scholars suggest that *Zech. 9–14* may be later.

By 520 BC the return from Babylonian Exile was 18 years underway (see *Ezra 1:1*). By the second month of the second year (April/May, 536) Zerubbabel and Jeshua had led the returnees in laying the foundations of the Temple (*Ezra 3:8–10*), a work that barely began before it was interrupted by the enemies of the Jews who convinced Artaxerxes, predecessor of Darius, to forbid its continuation (*Ezra 4:23–24*). The accession of Darius brought about a reversal of the royal edict and once more the work could be undertaken (*Ezra 6:12–13*).

Not to be overlooked is the role that the prophets Haggai and Zechariah played in the resumption and completion of the work of Temple-building (*Ezra 5:1; 6:14–15*). As suggested already, Zechariah's priestly lineage must have provided extra impetus to his interest in the Temple and the re-establishment of its worship services.

Virtually nothing is known of the personal life of Zechariah. His own prophetic contemporary Haggai fails to mention him and, apart from brief references to him in *Ezra* and *Nehemiah* cited above, the Scriptures are silent as to his life and vocation. This includes the oft-quoted statement of Jesus to the lawyers and Pharisees that they (i.e. their ancestors) had slain the prophets from Abel to Zechariah, 'Whom you murdered between the temple and the altar' (*Matt. 23:35*). Despite the fact that Zechariah is identified by Jesus as the son of Berekiah, he has another Zechariah in view than the canonical prophet. This is evident from the reference to the martyrdom of Zechariah, a fact unattested for the canonical prophet but well-known elsewhere with respect to another Zechariah, namely, the 'son' of Jehoiada who died at the command of King Joash (*2 Chron. 24:20–22*). Thus, prophets from Genesis (Abel) to the end of the Bible (Chronicles in the Hebrew canon) suffered persecution. As for the apparent conflict between Zechariah as 'son of Jehoiada' (*2 Chron. 24*) and 'son of Berekiah' (*Matt. 23*), many scholars suggest that Jehoiada was, in fact, the grandfather of the prophet, his father Berekiah being omitted in the chronicler's record.

Of particular interest in the writings of the prophet is his recording of eight visions filled with dramatic imagery (*Zech. 1:7–21; 2:1–13; 3:1–10; 4:1–14; 5:1–11; 6:1–15*). This imagery and other features of the prophet's work in both the visions and the oracles that follow (*Zech. 9:1–11:17; 12:1–14:21*) are elements of a special kind of prophecy described technically as 'apocalyptic'. These include prevalent use of animal symbolism, dramatic and earth-shaking interventions of Yahweh into human history, bizarre scenes of flying vessels and scrolls, and the like. Apocalyptic had already been employed by Ezekiel and even Isaiah, but no prophet exceeded Zechariah in the use of this vehicle of revelation. The reason, no doubt, was that the horizons of Judah's history had been broadened to the very ends of human civilization under Persian rule. No longer was Yahweh to be understood as the god of only a small Jewish community. Rather, he had already demonstrated his sovereignty over mighty Assyria, Babylonia, and now Persia and so had to be seen in universal, cosmic terms. The contribution of Zec-

hariah to this enlarged understanding of Yahweh's judging and saving work can hardly be overstated.

In proportion to its length Zechariah is the OT book most frequently and fully quoted in the NT. It is especially rich in messianic allusions (*Zech. 9:9* [see *Matt. 21:5; John 12:15*]; *9:11* [see *Matt. 26:28; Mark 14:24; Luke 22:20; 1 Cor. 11:25; Heb. 13:20*]; *11:12* [see *Matt. 26:15; 27:9*]; *12:10* [see *John 19:37*]; *13:7* [see *Matt: 26:31; Mark 14:27*]), suggesting its importance to the early Christian community. Its place near the end of the canon of the prophets and of the OT era gives the book a forward look, one that already anticipates God's saving work in Christ.

**2.** Zechariah, the King of Israel. The last ruler of the wicked dynasty of Jehu (*2 Kings 15:12*), he succeeded his father Jeroboam II (*2 Kings 14:29*) and reigned only six months (753 BC). He was assassinated by Shallum, the next king (*2 Kings 15:8, 10*).

**3.** Zechariah, father of Abi, King Hezekiah's mother, (*2 Kings 18:2*). She is otherwise named Abijah (*2 Chron. 29:1*).

**4.** Zechariah, a descendant of Reuben and the leader of a Reubenite clan (*1 Chron. 5:7*).

**5.** Zechariah, a Levite. A son of Meshelemiah and a Temple gatekeeper at the time of the return from the Babylonian Exile (*1 Chron. 9:21*).

**6.** Zechariah of Gibeon. A descendant of Jeiel of Gibeon and a kinsman of Ner, the grandfather of King Saul (*1 Chron. 9:37*). See Zeker.

**7.** Zechariah, a Temple musician. A Levite appointed by the Levite leadership to a position in the second rank of musicians in David's time (*1 Chron. 15:18*), specifically to play the lyre (*v. 20*; see *16:5*).

**8.** Zechariah, a priest. A musician appointed under David to play the trumpet before the ark of God (*1 Chron. 15:24*).

**9.** Zechariah, a Levite. A descendant of Uzziel through Isshiah who was selected by lot to serve at the Temple in David's time (1 Chron. 24:25).

**10.** Zechariah, a Levite. A son of Meshelemiah and a doorkeeper in the Temple of David's time (1 Chron. 26:2; cf. v. 14); not to be confused with 5. above, who was a returnee from the Babylonian Exile and whose father's name was also Meshelemiah.

**11.** Zechariah, a Levite. A son of Hosah of the clan of Merari who was among the Temple gatekeepers of David's time (1 Chron. 26:11).

**12.** Zechariah, a Manassehite. The father of Iddo, leader of the half tribe of Manasseh in Gilead in David's reign (1 Chron. 27:21).

**13.** Zechariah, an official. A leader whom King Jehoshaphat sent throughout the land to teach the Law to the people (2 Chron. 17:7).

**14.** Zechariah, the father of Jahaziel. A Levite whose son Jahaziel prophesied the deliverance of King Jehoshaphat and Judah from the Ammonites and Moabites (2 Chron. 20:14).

**15.** Zechariah, a son of Jehoshaphat. One of the brothers of King Jehoram, successor to his father Jehoshaphat (2 Chron. 21:2).

**16.** Zechariah, a prophet. A son of the high priest Jehoiada who prophesied against King Joash of Judah and suffered martyrdom for it (2 Chron. 24:20; cf. 26:5); probably the prophet mentioned by Jesus as a victim of Jewish persecution (Matt. 23:34–55). Not the same as 1. above.

**17.** Zechariah, an Asaphite. A Levite who assisted King Hezekiah in the cleansing of the Temple and the ensuing reformation (2 Chron. 29:13).

**18.** Zechariah, a Kohathite. A Levite who helped oversee the restoration of the Temple and the initiation of reformation under King Josiah (2 Chron. 34:12; see 35:8).

**19.** Zechariah, a descendant of Parosh. A Jewish leader who led 150 male descendants of Parosh back from Babylonian Exile (Ezra 8:3; cf. 10:26?).

**20.** Zechariah, a descendant of Bebai. A Jewish leader who, with 28 men, returned with Ezra from Babylonian Exile (Ezra 8:11; cf. v. 16?).

**21.** Zechariah, a Jewish leader. A leader of the post-exilic community who stood on Ezra's left side as he expounded the Law to the people (Neh. 8:4); perhaps the same as 19. or 20. above.

**22.** Zechariah, a Judahite. A grandfather of Athaiah, one of the leaders of Judah who lived in Jerusalem in Nehemiah's time (Neh. 11:4); a descendant of Perez.

**23.** Zechariah, a Judahite. An ancestor of Maaseiah, a leader of Judah who lived in Jerusalem in Nehemiah's time (Neh. 11:5); a descendant of Shelah.

**24.** Zechariah, a son of Pashhur. A Levite(?) who was a leader among the citizens of Jerusalem in Nehemiah's time (Neh. 11:12).

**25.** Zechariah, a priest. The head of the priestly family of Iddo at the time of the return from Babylonian Exile under Zerubbabel and Jeshua (Neh. 12:16).

**26.** Zechariah, an Asaphite. A Levite whom Nehemiah placed on the wall of the newly rebuilt Jerusalem as part of the dedication ceremony (Neh. 12:35, 41).

**27.** Zechariah, a son of Jeberekiah. A witness before whom Isaiah the prophet attested to the naming of his son Maher-Shalal-Hash-Baz (Is. 8:2). E.M.

**28.** A Jewish priest who was the father of John the Baptist. He is found in the Bible only in Luke 1. Zechariah was married to Elizabeth (v. 5), a relative of Mary, who would become the mother of Jesus (v. 36). They were a godly couple, but were beyond the normal child-bearing age and had no children (vv. 6–7) when the events of Luke 1 happened. Zechariah was attending his priestly duties (vv. 9–10) in the Temple in

Jerusalem when an angel of the Lord appeared, terrifying him (*vv.* 10–11). The angel foretold that Elizabeth would have a son, to be named John, who would be 'great in the sight of the Lord' (*vv.* 13, 15) as the forerunner of Jesus Christ. This prophecy was very difficult for Zechariah to believe at his age. Because of his doubt, the angel Gabriel rendered him unable to speak until the baby's birth (*vv.* 18–21).

Soon after Elizabeth became pregnant, taking away her 'disgrace among the people' (*v.* 25) as a barren woman. Zechariah remained mute throughout Elizabeth's term of pregnancy until the baby was born and circumcised (*vv.* 57–64). Even as he wrote out his insistence to the neighbours that the baby be named John (*v.* 63), he regained his speech (*v.* 64) and prophesied (*vv.* 67–79). Much interest was raised throughout Judea in these events and the child, John, who would play a unique role in preparing the way for Jesus Christ (*vv.* 65–66). See *John the Baptist.*                          A.B.L.

**ZEDEKIAH** (Heb., 'the Lord is my righteousness').

**1.** Zedekiah son of Kenaanah was a false prophet who worked in the kingdom of Israel during the reigns of King Jehoshaphat of Judah and King Ahab of Israel. Jehoshaphat and Ahab wanted to regain the city of Ramoth-Gilead from the king of Aram but Jehoshaphat suggested they first consult the LORD to see if he would bless their enterprise (1 *Kings* 22:1–5). Ahab summonsed all the prophets and they advised that the kings should go to war to regain the town. Jehoshaphat, however, asked whether a prophet of the LORD could be found, indicating that the other prophets probably worshipped pagan gods. Reluctantly, because he always seemed to prophesy evil, they sent for Micaiah son of Imlah.

As they waited for Micaiah, Zedekiah prophesied using two iron horns he had made as an illustration: 'With these you will gore the Arameans until they are destroyed' (*v.* 11; 2 *Chron.* 18:10). When Micaiah came he prophesied the defeat of Israel. He also informed the kings that a 'lying spirit' had been put into the mouths of the other prophets in order to lead Ahab and Israel astray. Zedekiah then slapped Micaiah in the face (1 *Kings* 22:24). They went to battle and Ahab was killed and Israel defeated (*vv.* 35–38; also see 2 *Chron.* 18).

The dire consequences for a false prophet were often proclaimed by the true prophets (e.g. *Ezek.* 13:9; *Jer.* 50:36 etc.) and in this case Micaiah prophesied Zedekiah's downfall (2 *Chron.* 18:24). But the consequences for the people of Israel in listening only to the prophets whose message appealed to them, and who they knew did not speak for the LORD, were equally fearful (see 1 *Kings* 22:7).

Throughout the Scriptures those who bring God's truth are often persecuted. Micaiah was put in prison for his words (1 *Kings* 22:27). Centuries later the apostle Paul reminded Timothy (2 *Tim.* 4:3–4) of similar dangers as people would 'gather around them a great number of teachers to say what their itching ears want to hear'.

**2.** Another Zedekiah, about whom we know little, was the son of Jehoiakim and appears in the royal genealogy of Judah (1 *Chron.* 3:16).

**3.** King Zedekiah, the third son of King Josiah (1 *Chron.* 3:15), became the last king of Judah. He came to the throne when 21 years old and reigned in Jerusalem for eleven years. His mother was Hamutal, the daughter of Jeremiah. Right from the start he followed in the evil ways of the previous kings, Jehoiakim and Jehoiachin. He came to the throne as a vassal king under Nebuchadnezzar of Babylon, having been placed on the throne of his nephew who had been deported to Babylon. As a sign of his subservience to the empire his name was changed from Mattaniah to Zedekiah (2 Kings 24:17–18).

In spite of Jeremiah's warning to Zedekiah and the surrounding nations of Edom, Moab and Ammon (Jer. 27:1–11), Zedekiah soon rebelled against Babylon. He probably did this, believing that a coalition of those nations would be successful and urged on in that view by false prophets (e.g. Jer. 28:1–4; 37–38; see also 4. below). This led to the king of Babylon marching on Jerusalem and laying siege to the city (2 Kings 24:20; 2 Chron. 36:13; Ezek. 17:13–18). Vivid descriptions of the terror of the days under siege and the eventual fall of Jerusalem are given in 2 Kings 25, 2 Chron. 36 and Lamentations. However, it is in the writings of the prophets Jeremiah and Ezekiel that more information is gained of these awful days of God's judgment on his rebellious people which was brought to them at the hands of the Babylonian Empire.

Although the king of Babylon briefly withdrew to fight the Egyptians, he soon returned and eventually broke down the walls of Jerusalem, entered the town, killing many and taking others prisoner. Zedekiah and others fled but were soon overtaken. His family was put to death in front of his eyes and then his eyes were gouged out and he was taken away to Babylon. He later died there (Jer. 39; 52:1–10; Ezek. 33; 2 Kings 25 etc. ).

In the prophets the character of Zedekiah is questioned. In the face of such a formidable enemy he proved indecisive and unable to accept the word of the LORD even when he knew that is what he was hearing. On the one hand we read that he did not pay any attention to the words of the LORD through Jeremiah (Jer. 37:3), and yet, on the other, we read that he sent a message to Jeremiah saying: 'Please pray to the LORD our God for us' (v. 3). For a while the people seemed to repent and promised to obey the LORD in freeing their slaves, but very soon they reinstituted slavery and went back on

their desire to serve the Lord (Jer. 34:8–22).

The message from the LORD to Jeremiah and hence to the king and his people was indeed a difficult one for them to bear. Jeremiah had to tell the king that he should accept the fact that the Babylonians would conquer and the people would be exiled (vv. 7–10). Understandably, the king and his advisers believed that Jeremiah was in the pay of the Babylonians and would desert to them and so he was put in prison by Zedekiah (vv. 11–21). King Zedekiah clearly knew Jeremiah's word was the LORD's word, but the truth is often unpalatable and unacceptable, and so it was between Jeremiah and Zedekiah (e.g. Jer. 38:14–18).

In many ways Zedekiah reflected Judah's past, for which she was being judged. It was a history of some acknowledgement of the LORD, at times more and at times less, but always there was a reluctance to rely completely upon God for help. The fall of Jerusalem came as God's judgment on his people and their leaders. The Chronicler sums it up in 2 Chron. 36:14: the Temple had been defiled, the idolatrous practices of the surrounding nations had been followed to the neglect of true worship and all had become unfaithful to the LORD (see also 2 Chron. 24:20).

**4.** This Zedekiah, the son of Maaseiah, lived in Judah and prophesied lies during the time of the Exile. He was roundly condemned by the LORD through the true prophet Jeremiah (Jer. 29:21–22). He was accused along with Ahab son of Kolaiah, of prophesying a quick return of the captives from Babylon and of gross immorality and adultery.

**5.** This Zedekiah joined in witnessing the solemn covenant of obedience to the Law of God in Nehemiah's time in Jerusalem (Neh. 10:1).

**6.** One of the leaders of Judah to whom Jeremiah's scroll was read by Baruch. The scroll warned of God's impending judgment on Judah and Jerusalem (*Jer. 36:12*).                                    P.D.G.

**ZEEB** One of two Midianite leaders who were defeated by Gideon and the Israelites. In an amazing display of reliance upon and obedience to God, Gideon had attacked the Midianite camp with a mere 300 men (*Judg. 7*). The Midianites had fled in the dark and Gideon called up Israelites from several different tribes to come and chase them down. Zeeb was captured and killed at the winepress of Zeeb, probably called that to commemorate the victory (*v. 25*). Gideon was only too well aware that a victory of this magnitude was God's work (*Judg. 8:3*). Future generations looked back to the victory as an indication of what God could do on their behalf and therefore what they could ask him to do again for them (e.g. *Ps. 83:11*).                  P.D.G.

**ZEKER** Mentioned in *1 Chron. 8:31*, this was one of the sons of Jeiel, a Benjamite, and his wife Macah. He is listed in the genealogy leading from Benjamin to Saul and was Saul's great-uncle. In *1 Chron. 9:37* he is called Zechariah.

**ZELEK** Mentioned in *2 Sam. 23:37* and *1 Chron. 11:39*, Zelek the Ammonite was one of David's 'Thirty' mighty men who were warriors fighting at his side.

**ZELOPHEHAD** The son of Hepher, Zelophehad did not have any sons. He belonged to the tribe of Manasseh and had five daughters who were called Mahlah, Noah, Hoglah, Milcah and Tirzah (*Num. 26:33; 27:1*). Their father had died during the wilderness wanderings and yet he had been a faithful Israelite and had not joined Korah's rebellion, so they wanted to get Moses to rule about his inheritance, which would normally have passed to a son (*Num. 27:1–11*). In a significant legal

judgment received from the LORD himself, Moses agreed that they should be allowed to inherit their father's land. The ruling was later slightly modified so that the land could not leave the tribe of Manasseh should one of the women marry into another tribe (*Num. 36:2–12; Josh. 17:3; 1 Chron. 7:15*). This was a landmark law in the defence of women's rights in Israel. The daughters did later fulfil its requirements and obtain their inheritance, and the land stayed within the tribe. See *Mahlah* for detail.     P.D.G.

**ZEMIRAH** A grandson of Benjamin and a son of Beker (*1 Chron. 7:7*).

**ZENAS** was a Christian lawyer who is mentioned by the apostle Paul only at the end of his epistle to Titus (*Titus 3:13*). It is not clear from the letter whether Paul wanted Titus to send Zenas, accompanied by Apollos, to join him at Nicopolis, or whether he was asking Titus to send Zenas and Apollos off on a further mission to teach the gospel, perhaps in Crete or elsewhere. Titus was to see that they were well supplied. It is also far from clear whether Zenas was a Jewish lawyer or a Roman lawyer.

Even though little is known of this man, the passage does provide yet another insight of how different people from many different professions had been converted and were becoming missionaries of the gospel. The movement of Christians around the empire was clearly considerable, even from earliest times, as people committed themselves to Christ and wanted to preach and teach and help others in need (*v. 14*).         P.D.G.

**ZEPHANIAH** (Heb., 'the Lord hides [me?]').
**1.** Zephaniah the prophet. The verb on which this name is based occurs frequently with the idea of being hidden by Yahweh from evil (*Ps. 27:5; 31:20*) or of his saints being his treasured ones (*Pss.*

83:3). Both would be appropriate ways to describe this prophet's relationship to the LORD.

No other prophet is introduced with such a lengthy genealogy (*Zeph. 1:1*). Zephaniah, according to this list of names, is the fourth generation after a certain Hezekiah. Most scholars identify Hezekiah as the king of Judah with that name, an identification that certainly is compatible with chronological requirements. Hezekiah reigned from 729–686 BC and Zephaniah's ministry took place in the period of Josiah's reign, from 640–609. Allowing 25 years for each generation, Zephaniah could have been born as early as 640 and still claim Hezekiah as his great-great-grandfather, even though the prophet's ministry appears to have been focused on the earlier part of King Josiah's tenure. Nineveh had not yet fallen (*Zeph. 2:13*), though the Cushites (or Ethiopians) were already advancing (*2:12*), a movement led by Psammeticus II (664–610 BC). There is no record of Josiah's reformation having yet occurred, an event dated 622 BC. Omission of such information suggests a pre-622 setting, as does reference to the idolatrous practices that the reformation eventually eradicated (*Zeph. 1:2–6; 3:1–7*).

Some object that the Hezekiah mentioned was not the king because he was not known to have a son Amariah. Hezekiah's only named son was Manasseh (696–642) who was succeeded by Amon (642–640) and then Josiah (640–609). It is well known, however, that kings of Israel and Judah often had many children, most of whose names never appear in the record. Clearly Zephaniah could have descended from Hezekiah through one line of sons and Josiah through another. This would, interestingly enough, make Josiah and Zephaniah cousins and would contribute to the view that Zephaniah's preaching had much to do with Josiah's reformation. The very fact that Zephaniah links the

names Hezekiah and Josiah (*Zeph. 1:1*) implies perhaps a family linkage with himself and certainly draws together the two great royal reformers of Judah's history.

Like Joel, Zephaniah is preoccupied with the theme of 'the day of the LORD' (*Zeph. 1:7, 14; 3:11, 16, 20*), that is, the day of wrath and judgment. Most immediately he has in view the coming of the Babylonians against Judah, a conquest culminating in the destruction of Jerusalem and the Temple and the deportation of the population (*Zeph. 1:8–18*). But that day is also at the end of time and brings the promise of salvation as well as retribution (*Zeph. 3:8–20*). Zephaniah's royal lineage gives special poignancy to his message that in that day 'The LORD, the King of Israel, [will be] with you; never again will you fear any harm' (*Zeph. 3:15*). This great biblical theme becomes the basis for the Christian expectation of Christ's return.

**2.** Zephaniah, the father of *Josiah* and *Hen* (see both), described as a Jewish returnee from the Babylonian Exile (*Zech. 6:10, 14*). Not to be confused with the prophet Zephaniah.

**3.** Zephaniah, a priest. The priest second in rank to Seraiah in the time of the Babylonian siege and destruction of Jerusalem; he, with others, was executed in Nebuchadnezzar's presence at Riblah (*2 Kings 25:18–21*; see *Jer. 52:24*).

**4.** Zephaniah, a son of Tahath. A descendant of Levi through Kohath and an ancestor of Heman, he was a leading musician in the Temple worship of David's time (*1 Chron. 6:36*).

**5.** Zephaniah, a son of Maaseiah. A priest in the days of Jeremiah and King Zedekiah (*Jer. 21:1*) who sympathized and shared information with Jeremiah (*29:25–29*) and who solicited Jeremiah's prayer (*37:3*). He may be the same as 2. above.                    E.M.

**ZEPHO** An Edomite leader who was the

grandson of Esau and Adah (a Canaanite woman) and the third son of Eliphaz (Gen. 36:11, 15; 1 Chron. 1:36).

**ZEPHON** The first of seven sons of Gad listed in Gen. 46:16 among those who went with Jacob into Egypt. In Num. 26:15 he is mentioned as the founder of the Zephonite clan.

**ZERAH** (Heb., 'bright, scarlet').

**1.** A grandson of Esau and Basemath, Zerah was a son of Reuel and an Edomite clan chief (Gen. 36:13, 17; 1 Chron. 1:37). Possibly the same as 2. below.

**2.** This Zerah came from Bozrah and was the father of Jobab. He is mentioned in a list of the kings of Edom. Jobab followed King Bela (Gen. 36:33; 1 Chron. 1:44). The writer makes the point that this was before 'any Israelite king reigned' thus implicitly comparing the Edomites unfavourably with the Israelites and Esau unfavourably with Jacob. Gradually the assumption that God alone was the rightful king became part of Israel's understanding of their nationhood and no doubt this is reflected in the writer's comment (see Num. 23:21 and, later, Samuel's concern at the appointment of a king in Israel, 1 Sam. 8:6–7).

**3.** Another Zerah was a twin brother to Perez and son of Judah. He was the founder of the Zerahite clan (Gen. 38:30; 46:12; Num. 26:20; 1 Chron. 2:4; Neh. 11:24). His five sons all became clan leaders in their own right (1 Chron. 2:6). Perez and Zerah were born as a result of an incestuous relationship between their father Judah and his daughter-in-law Tamar. His unusual name was given because of the nature of his birth. When he was about to be born one of the sons' hands appeared and so a scarlet thread was put round the wrist to identify the 'first born'. Zerah can mean 'scarlet'. However, the hand was withdrawn and Perez 'burst forth' ahead of his brother. Perez therefore became the first-born son

whose name was then linked with all the genealogies of Judah, although Zerah is mentioned along with Perez in the genealogy of Christ in *Matt. 1:3*.

This Zerah was also an ancestor of Achan, being the father of Zimri and grandfather of Achan (Josh. 7:1, 18). In Josh. 7:24 and 22:20 Zimri has been omitted from the list of Achan's ancestors. See *Achan*.

**4.** A descendant of Simeon and a leader of the Zerahite clan within the tribe of Simeon (Num. 26:13; 1 Chron. 4:24).

**5.** A descendant of Gershon son of Levi, head of one of the Levitical clans. His father was Iddo (1 Chron. 6:21).

**6.** The son of Adaiah and father of Ethni, he was a Levite who served in the ministry of the Tabernacle in the days of King David (1 Chron. 6:41).

**7.** Zera the Cushite led the Cushites to battle against Asa king of Judah (2 Chron. 14:9). This Zerah probably came from Africa (perhaps Ethiopia). The army he led against Judah was vast. Asa called upon the LORD. His complete trust in the LORD was reflected in his prayer: 'LORD, there is no one like you to help the powerless against the mighty. Help us, O LORD our God, for we rely on you, and in your name we have come against this vast army. O LORD, you are our God; do not let man prevail against you.' In the battle that ensued 'the LORD struck down the Cushites' and the Israelites pursued them as far as Gerar (vv. 10–15). His trust was vindicated in God's victory over their enemies.                P.D.G.

**ZERAHIAH** (Heb., 'the Lord has shone').

**1.** The son of Uzzi and father of Meraioth, Zerahiah is mentioned in the lists of the descendants of Levi in 1 Chron. 6:6, 51. He was an ancestor of Ezra (Ezra 7:4).

**2.** A descendant of Pahath-Moab and father of Eliehohenai who returned to

Jerusalem with Ezra after the Babylonian Exile (*Ezra 8:4*).

**ZERESH** was the wife of Haman, a senior minister in the Persian government of King Xerxes. She had very considerable influence over her husband and did not like to see him embarrassed. When Mordecai, the Jew, refused to kneel down before Haman or pay him honour (*Est. 3:2; 5:9–14*), it was she who advised Haman to ask the king's permission to have Mordecai hanged on a gallows. Later, when Haman's wishes were outflanked by Queen Esther, it was Zeresh who appears to have realized that Haman could not win against the Jews. Perhaps she had come to realize the sovereignty of the Jewish LORD God even over the affairs of their kingdom and family (*Est. 6:13*).                              P.D.G.

**ZERETH** Mentioned in *1 Chron. 4:7*, Zereth was a son of Ashhur and his wife Helah and was of the tribe of Judah.

**ZERI** One of the sons of Jeduthun listed among those set apart for the ministry of prophesying and music during the reign of King David. Jeduthun, with Asaph and Hamen, was directly under the supervision of the king (*1 Chron. 25:3, 6*). Zeri is probably the same person as Izri (*1 Chron. 25:11*) who was the leader of the fourth group of Levitical musicians and choirs who ministered in the Tabernacle.

**ZEROR,** son of Becorath, was the grandfather of Kish who was the father of Saul. Saul became first king of Israel and was from the tribe of Benjamin (*1 Sam. 9:1*).

**ZERUAH** This woman was a widow and the mother of King Jeroboam I. Her husband, from the tribe of Ephraim, was called Nebat (*1 Kings 11:26*). Jeroboam rebelled against Solomon and then against his son Rehoboam. Eventually Jeroboam became the first king of the northern part of the divided kingdom of Israel.

**ZERUBBABEL** (Heb., 'seed of Babylon'). The name suggests his birthplace as a son of either Shealtiel (*Ezra 3:2, 8; Hag. 1:1; Matt. 1:12*) or Pedaiah (*1 Chron. 3:19*), the brother of Shealtiel. Perhaps he was adopted by Shealtiel following Pedaiah's death. He was the first governor of post-exilic Judah, having been appointed as such by either Cambyses or Darius I of Persia. He, with the priest Joshua, led in the reconstruction of the Jerusalem Temple. This was a work under the LORD's direction, designed to give tangible evidence of his continuing covenant faithfulness and to point forward to a still more wonderful reality, namely, Yahweh's personal residence among his people (*Hag. 2:1–9*). Reference to Zerubbabel in the lineage of Jesus in both *Matt. 1:12–13* and *Luke 3:27* is significant in fulfilling the typology of *Hag. 2:23* in which Zerubbabel serves as prototype of Jesus, the 'chosen signet' of the LORD.                              E.M.

**ZERUIAH** was the mother of Joab, Abishai and Asahel who were all commanders in King David's army. She is mentioned many times in *2 Samuel, 1 Kings* and *2 Chronicles*, but always in connection with her sons, and her husband is never mentioned. It is likely that she was a specially prominent and well-known woman. The most we know about her husband was that he had a tomb in Bethlehem where eventually Asahel was buried (*1 Sam. 26:6; 2 Sam. 2:13, 18, 32; 3:39; 8:16; 14:1; 16:9 etc.; 1 Chron. 11:6, 39; 18:12, 15; 26:28 etc.*).

She was either a sister or half sister to King David, since she was Abigail's sister and in *1 Chron. 2:16–17* the two women are identified as sisters of David. For discussion of this see *Nahash* (*2 Sam. 17:25*).                              P.D.G.

**ZETHAM** (Heb., 'olive tree'). One of the Gershonite Levites, a son of Ladan, whose duties were assigned by David towards the end of his reign in anticipation of their work in the Temple. He was given charge of the treasuries of the Temple where all the gifts of the people were kept (*1 Chron. 23:8; 26:22*).

**ZETHAN** (Heb., 'olive tree'). A great-grandson of Benjamin and a son of Bilhan (*1 Chron. 7:10*). He was a leader and warrior among his people.

**ZETHAR** One of seven eunuchs who served King Xerxes (*Est. 1:10*). See *Vashti*.

**ZEUS** was the chief god of the Greek pantheon and was believed to live on Olympus. He was the god of the skies and hence the god of thunder and weather. In Latin he was known as Jupiter. His messenger was known in Greek as Hermes (Latin, Mercury). The name is only mentioned in Scripture in the description of the visit of Paul and Barnabas to Lystra. Paul preached and then healed a man who had been lame from birth. The people immediately assumed that Paul and Barnabas were gods. They called Barnabas Zeus and Paul, because he did most of the speaking and was therefore supposedly the messenger, they called Hermes (*Acts 14:12–13*). The priest of Zeus brought the two missionaries gifts which were immediately refused. (For more detail of Paul's response and teaching on this occasion, see *Hermes*). P.D.G.

**ZIA** A clan leader who was head of one of the seven Gadite clans settled in the area of Gilead and Bashan (*1 Chron. 5:13*).

**ZIBA** was a servant of King Saul who came to prominence after Saul's death. King David summonsed him to give account of what had happened to Saul's family (*2 Sam. 9*). Ziba reminded David of one of Jonathan's sons, Mephibosheth, who was crippled in both feet (*v. 3*). King David wanted to be kind to Mephibosheth for the sake of his earlier friendship with Jonathan, and so Ziba brought him to the royal palace. From that day on, Mephibosheth was allowed to eat the royal food and was waited upon by Ziba and his family. Ziba's family was also required by David to farm Mephibosheth's land for him and bring him the produce (*vv. 9–10*).

During the period of Absalom's rebellion, when David had to flee Jerusalem, Ziba helped provide David with supplies. When David asked after Mephibosheth, Ziba replied that he was still in Jerusalem waiting to be restored to his family's throne (*2 Sam. 16:1–4*). It turned out later that this was a lie and that Mephibosheth had remained loyal to David throughout. However, David, not knowing this, gave Mephibosheth's inheritance to Ziba. It was only later when David was back in control that Mephibosheth was able to put the record straight and David suggested that Ziba and Mephibosheth split the property in two (*2 Sam. 19:17, 26–30*).

Ziba was undoubtedly loyal to King David in spite of his eye for gaining favour, but ultimately he owed his prominence to David's great kindness to the remnants of Saul's household.     P.D.G.

**ZIBEON** (Heb., 'hyena') was a 'Hivite' (*Gen. 36:2*) or Horite and a chief among his people living in Edom. He was the third son of Seir (*Gen. 36:14, 20, 29; 1 Chron. 1:38*). His granddaughter was Oholibamah who was one of Esau's Canaanite wives (*Gen. 36:2*). Zibeon's sons were called Aiah and Anah (*Gen. 36:24; 1 Chron. 1:40*).

**ZIBIA** (Heb., 'gazelle') was the head of a family and a son of Shaharaim and his wife Hodesh. Listed in the genealogy of Benjamin leading to King Saul, he was born in Moab (*1 Chron. 8:9*).

**ZIBIAH** (Heb., 'gazelle') was the mother of King Joash of Judah. She came from Beersheba (*2 Kings 12:1; 2 Chron. 24:1*).

**ZICRI** (Heb., 'remembrance').

**1.** The first Zicri mentioned in the Bible was one of the three sons of Izhar (*Exod. 6:21*). He was a Kohathite Levite.

**2.** The name also seems to have been a regular family name within the tribe of Benjamin. Listed in the genealogy of King Saul, this Zicri was one of the sons of Shimei (*1 Chron. 8:19*).

**3.** Listed in the genealogy of King Saul, this Zicri, another Benjamite, was one of the sons of Shashak (*1 Chron. 8:23*).

**4.** Listed in the genealogy of King Saul, this Zicri, another Benjamite, was one of the sons of Jeroham (*1 Chron. 8:27*).

**5.** The son of Asaph, this Levite was an ancestor of Shemaiah, one of the first Levites to return to Jerusalem following the Babylonian Exile (*1 Chron. 9:15*).

**6.** This Zicri was a descendant of the Levite, Eliezer, and part of a family that had charge of the Temple treasuries (*1 Chron. 26:25*). He was the father of Shelomith.

**7.** The father of Eliezer. Eliezer was an officer over the tribe of Reuben in the days of King David (*1 Chron. 27:16*).

**8.** The father of Amasiah from the tribe of Judah. Amasiah was an army commander in Jerusalem who volunteered with 200,000 men to fight for King Jehoshaphat at a time when Jehoshaphat was obeying the LORD and greatly prospering (*2 Chron. 17:16*).

**9.** This Zicri was the father of Elishaphat. Elishaphat was a commander of 100 men who joined with others of similar standing in a covenant with the priest Jehoiada against Queen Athaliah. Together they killed Athaliah and put the young King Joash on the throne (*2 Chron. 23:1*). For more detail see *Jehoiada* and *Athaliah*.

**10.** Zicri, an Ephraimite warrior, killed Maaseiah who was King Ahaz's son and various of Ahaz's officials. Zicri worked for Pekah (*2 Chron. 28:7*). See *Pekah* and *Ahaz* for more detail.

**11.** The father of a certain Joel who was the chief officer of the Benjamites in Jerusalem following the return from Exile in Babylon (*Neh. 11:9*).

**12.** This Zicri was a leader of the priestly family of Abijah and among those who returned with Zerubbabel from the captivity in Babylon (*Neh. 12:17*). P.D.G.

**ZIHA 1.** Ziha had been a leader among the Temple servants, presumably prior to the Babylonian Exile. Some of his descendants were among those who returned from the Exile with Nehemiah and Zerubbabel (*Ezra 2:43; Neh. 7:46*).

**2.** Another Ziha, probably a descendant of 1., was among those in charge of the Temple servants in the days of Nehemiah (*Neh. 11:21*).

**ZILLAH** (Heb., 'shadow') was one of two wives of Lamech. She was the mother of Tubal-Cain 'who forged all kinds of tools out of bronze and iron' (*Gen. 4:19–22*). Her daughter was called Naamah. Zillah had to listen to Lamech's vengeful boast of murdering those who had wronged him (vv. 23–24) – a reminder of the sin that already so thoroughly permeated the world.

**ZILLETHAI** (Heb., 'the Lord protects').

**1.** Mentioned in *1 Chron. 8:20* in the genealogy leading from Benjamin to Saul. A son of Shimei.

**2.** This Zillethai was one of those great fighting men who deserted Saul and came from the tribe of Manasseh to join David at Ziklag. He led a unit of 1,000 men (*1 Chron. 12:20*). The passage in *1 Chron. 12* makes it clear that the gradual desertion from Saul of such warriors from various tribes was led by the Spirit of God. The last verse of the section (v. 22) says: 'Day after day men came to help David, until he had a great army, like the army of God.'

**ZILPAH** was a servant girl given by Laban to his daughter Leah on her marriage to Jacob (Gen. 29:24). Leah bore children to Jacob but later, when she ceased having children (Gen. 30:9), she gave Zilpah to Jacob so he could have children by her. Legally these would have been considered Leah's children. Leah's desire to have more children to her name than she had actually borne came from the jealousy between Leah and Rachel, Jacob's other wife. Zilpah bore Jacob two sons, Gad and Asher (Gen. 30:10–12; 35:26; 37:2; 46:18).

**ZIMMAH** **1.** A descendant of Gershon son of Levi and head of one of the Levitical clans. His father was Jehath (1 Chron. 6:20). While it is just possible that the 2. and 3. below are the same person, this is most unlikely. The names seem to relate to quite different periods in Israel's history, especially 3. below. However, this name is likely to be another example, of which there are several, where a Levitical family name reappears down through the years. It is probably an indication of how some of the Levitical families did remain faithful to the LORD through the generations.

**2.** The son of Shimei and father of Ethan, this Zimmah was also a Gershonite Levite whose descendants served in the ministry of the Tabernacle and included Asaph (1 Chron. 6:42).

**3.** The next Zimmah was also a descendant of Gershon, son of Levi. His son, Joah, was head of one of the Levitical clans and helped in cleaning and purifying the Temple in the days of King Hezekiah (1 Chron. 6:21; 2 Chron. 29:12).

P.D.G.

**ZIMRAN** The first of Abraham's sons by his wife Keturah (Gen. 25:2). He appears in a list of Abraham's descendants bridging the narratives of the death of Sarah and the death of Abraham (also 1 Chron. 1:32).

**ZIMRI** **1.** While Israel was staying near Shittim during their wanderings in the wilderness, the Israelite men made contact with Moabite women and became involved in sexual immorality with them (Num. 25). Probably they indulged in fertility rites with these women since v. 2 tells us that they were invited to make sacrifices to their gods, the 'Baal of Peor'. The LORD was angry and promised judgment unless Moses put to death all who had participated in this activity.

However, Zimri, son of Salu, the leader of a Simeonite family, compounded the evil by bringing Cozbi, a Moabite woman, back into the Israelite camp with him just as Israel 'was weeping' over the judgment God was inflicting. Phinehas, a grandson of Aaron, determined to vindicate the LORD and to stem any further judgment, immediately took his spear and followed Zimri and Cozbi into their tent and killed them both (Num. 25:14).

The defence of the holiness of the Israelites and their separation from the other peoples for the service of the LORD alone was of the very essence of their calling as a nation. The preservation of such holiness was therefore vital if they were to remain faithful to their covenantal relationship with the LORD.

**2.** The next Zimri mentioned was from the tribe of Judah and was grandson of Judah and Tamar and one of five sons of Zerah (1 Chron. 2:6). When the Israelites eventually entered Canaan under the leadership of Joshua they captured and destroyed the city of Jericho (see Rahab). Some Israelites, contrary to God's commands, took some of the Canaanite spoil and their objects of worship. Zimri's grandson, Achan was one of these and was judged by God for his actions (Josh. 7:1, 17–18). Violation of 'the covenant of the LORD' even at this early stage of

Israel's occupation of Israel was serious indeed. In spite of this clear evidence from the LORD of the seriousness of such sin (covenant violation), time and again the Israelites sinned in just this way and were severely judged by the LORD.

**3.** Another Zimri was an army officer in the Northern Kingdom of Israel in the days of King Baasha and King Elah. He rebelled against Elah who was clearly a drunkard and did not have the support or respect of his people. Zimri killed Elah while he was drunk and became king himself (probably around 855 BC). He immediately began to kill off all of Baasha's family (1 Kings 16:8–11). Another general, Omri, had been leading the Israelites against the Philistines while this was going on. As soon as he heard what Zimri had done he attacked Zimri, who was at Tirzah. Zimri retreated into the citadel of the royal palace where he killed himself, having reigned for only seven days (1 Kings 16:15–18).

Later, Jezebel referred back to Zimri's rebellion by greeting Jehu with some sarcasm, knowing he had come to kill her: 'Have you come in peace, Zimri, you murderer of your master?' (2 Kings 9:31).

The writer of 1 Kings wanted his readers to understand that in all these events God's hand was at work. Elah had followed Baasha in his evil ways. Both had encouraged idolatry. The prophet, Jehu son of Hanani, had prophesied the demise of Baasha and his whole family because of his very great sin and rebellion against the LORD. Thus Zimri's annihilation of Baasha's family was to be seen as God's retribution (1 Kings 16:12–13). However, the fact that God in his sovereignty was able to use Zimri in this way did not mean that Zimri was righteous. Far from it. Zimri too had encouraged Israel to sin and had, presumably, followed the route of idolatry (v. 19) and thus his death too was God's judgment.

**4.** This Zimri, from the tribe of Benjamin, was the son of Jehoaddah and a descendant of King Saul. He is mentioned in Saul's genealogy and was the father of Moza (1 Chron. 8:36; 9:42).

P.D.G.

**ZIPH 1.** The grandson of Caleb and son of Mesha from the tribe of Judah (1 Chron. 2:42).

**2.** One of the sons of Jehallelel and a leader in the tribe of Judah (1 Chron. 4:16).

**ZIPHAH** One of the sons of Jehallelel and a leader in the tribe of Judah (1 Chron. 4:16).

**ZIPPOR** (Heb., 'bird') was the father of King Balak of Moab. Balak lived at the time when Moses and the Israelites were leaving the wilderness and about to enter Canaan. After seeing what had just happened to the Amorite kings, Sihon and Og, Balak 'was terrified' and sought the help of the seer Balaam. But God again intervened to protect his people from the Moabites (Num. 22:2, 4, 10, 16, 18; Josh. 24:9; Judg. 11:25). See Balak, Balaam and Sihon.

**ZIPPORAH** (Heb., 'sparrow' or 'bird') was the daughter of Jethro, a Midianite priest. Moses had to flee from Egypt after killing an Egyptian and settled with Jethro. Jethro gave his daughter Zipporah to Moses for his wife. Their first child was called Gershom and another, Eliezer (Exod. 2:21–22; 18:2–4). See Jethro and Gershom.

When Moses eventually decided he should return to Egypt to see how the Israelites were doing, he set off with Zipporah and their child. When they stopped at a lodging place, Exod. 4:24–26 says that 'the LORD met [Moses] and was about to kill him. But Zipporah took a flint knife, cut off her son's foreskin and touched [Moses'] feet with it. "Surely you are a bridegroom of blood to me," she said. So the LORD let him alone. (At that time she said "bridegroom of blood," referring to circumcision.)' Many have speculated as to exactly what was going on in this incident. It would seem that Moses had not fulfilled the covenant demand for circumcision of his son and, in order to avoid the judgment of God, Zipporah quickly stepped in to perform the circumcision and save her husband. Perhaps Moses' failure to have the child circumcised resulted from his lengthy absence from his own people. The incident must have reminded Moses of the importance of keeping the Abrahamic covenant.                    P.D.G.

**ZIZA**  **1.** A clan leader of the tribe of Simeon, mentioned in 1 Chron. 4:37. He was the son of Shiphi and lived on the outskirts of Gedor.
**2.** This Ziza is mentioned in 1 Chron. 23:10–11 as the second son of Shimei and a Levite. He belonged to the clan of the Gershonites and was appointed by King David to lead his family in their duties at the Tabernacle.
**3.** Mentioned in 2 Chron. 11:20, this Ziza was a son of King Rehoboam and his wife Maacah, who was Absalom's daughter (2 Chron. 11:20).

**ZOHAR** (Heb., 'yellow').
**1.** Zohar the Hittite was the father of Ephron, who sold Abraham a field in which there was a cave suitable for family burials (Gen. 23:8; 25:9). See Ephron.
**2.** The fifth son of Simeon, a clan leader, and listed among those who went to Egypt with Jacob his grandfather (Gen. 46:10; Exod. 6:15).
**3.** A descendant of Judah, Zohar is listed as one of the sons of Helah (1 Chron. 4:7).

**ZOHETH** Mentioned in 1 Chron. 4:20 as a descendant of Ishi of the tribe of Judah.

**ZOPHAH** A tribal leader and a descendant of Asher, he was the son of Helem (1 Chron. 7:35–36).

**ZOPHAI** A descendant of Kohath and a Levite. His father was Elkanah and his son was Nahath. Zophai was an ancestor of Samuel (1 Chron. 6:26). He was also called Zuph. See Zuph.

**ZOPHAR** was one of Job's 'three friends' and is called 'the Naamathite' (Job 2:11). Initially the three friends went to Job to 'sympathize with him and comfort him'. When they saw the appalling troubles Job was facing under God's testing, they were unable to speak at all for a long time. Eventually they began to offer various forms of 'advice'. Only two of Zophar's speeches are recorded, the first in Job 11 and the second in Job 20. He argued strongly with Job that his claim to innocence could not possibly be correct. If Job would only recognize this and repent, God would restore him to a good life (Job 11:13–19). He clearly did not believe Job's claim to righteousness and tried to persuade Job his self-assessment was wrong. There was little compassion in what he had to say.
A similar analysis is repeated in his second speech in Job 20. Increasingly Job had become convinced that God was the source of these troubles and so he had appealed to God to fulfil his responsibilities to his people (Job 19). In a great statement of faith he had looked for his Redeemer to vindicate him (Job 19:25). This was all too much for Zophar who, simplistically, saw trouble as evidence of sin and a good life as evidence of righteousness.
In the end God did vindicate Job and ordered the friends to go to Job and have him offer sacrifices for their forgiveness: 'My servant Job will pray for you, and I will accept his prayer and not deal with you according to your folly. You have not spoken of me what is right, as my servant

Job has' (*Job 42:7–9*).                    P.D.G.

**ZUAR** (Heb., 'little one'). The father of Nethanel, who was the leader of the people of Issachar in the days of Moses (*Num. 1:8; 2:5; 7:18, 23; 10:15*). See *Nethanel*.

**ZUPH** (Heb., 'honeycomb'). Mentioned as an Ephraimite in *1 Sam. 1:1* and listed among the Kohathite Levites in *1 Chron. 6:35*, Zuph was an ancestor of Elkanah and Samuel. Various explanations have been given for his association with two tribes. Perhaps it is possible that he lived in Ephraim as a Levite and was therefore called an 'Ephraimite', but it is not possible to be sure.                    P.D.G.

**ZUR** (Heb., 'rock').
**1.** The Midianite father of Cozbi and a leader in his tribe (*Num. 25:15*). He died in a battle between the Israelites, led by Moses, and the Midianites. The battle was ordered by God (*Num. 31:7–8*) as part of his judgment on the Midianites for their sin in seducing the Israelites into disobeying God (*Josh. 13:21*). While Israel was staying near Shittim the Israelite men had made contact with Moabite women and became involved in sexual immorality with them. Zimri, son of Salu, brought Zur's daughter back into the Israelite camp just as Israel 'was weeping' over the judgment God was already inflicting on them. The immediate death of Cozbi and Zimri at the hands of Phinehas, and the later death in battle of Zur, formed part of God's defence of the holiness of the Israelites. Separation from the other peoples for the service of the LORD alone was of the very essence of their calling as a nation. See *Cozbi* for more detail.

**2.** One of the sons of Jeiel and his wife Maacah. This Zur was a Benjamite who came from Gibeon. He was one of the forefathers of Kish, the father of Saul (*1 Chron. 8:30; 9:36*).                    P.D.G.

**ZURIEL** (Heb., 'my God is a rock'). One of the leaders among the Levites during the wilderness period. This man was head of the Merarite clan which itself included a number of large family clans (*Num. 3:35*). He was the son of Abihail. *Num. 3:33–37* reveals that this clan was responsible for much work outside the Tabernacle, notably caring for 'the frames of the tabernacle, its crossbars, posts, bases, and all its equipment'.

**ZURISHADDAI** (Heb., 'my rock is the Almighty'). The father of Shelumiel, who was the leader of the people of Simeon in the days of Moses (*Num. 7:36*). See *Shelumiel*.

W9-AAE-023

THE FAR EAST

Political Boundaries June 1997

# PACIFIC NIGHTMARE

SIMON WINCHESTER

# PACIFIC
# NIGHTMARE

*How Japan Starts World War III*
*A Future History*

Maps and Charts by Cézanne Wong

A Birch Lane Press Book
Published by Carol Publishing Group

THIS BOOK IS FOR
MISS HELEN RODGERS STEVENSON
OF BROOKLYN AND GENEVA

Copyright © 1992 by Simon Winchester
Maps and charts copyright © 1992 by Cézanne Wong

A Birch Lane Press Book
Published by Carol Publishing Group
Birch Lane Press is a registered trademark of Carol Communications, Inc.

Editorial offices: 600 Madison Avenue, New York, N.Y. 10022
Sales & Distribution Offices: 120 Enterprise Avenue, Secaucus, N.J. 07094

In Canada: Canadian Manda Group
P.O. Box 920, Station U
Toronto, Ontario M8Z 5P9

Queries regarding rights and permissions
should be addressed to Carol Publishing Group
600 Madison Avenue, New York, N.Y. 10022

First published in Great Britain in 1992 by
Sidgwick & Jackson Limited, London

Manufactured in the United States of America
10 9 8 7 6 5 4 3 2 1

Carol Publishing Group books are available at special discounts
for bulk purchases, for sales promotions, fund raising, or
educational purposes. Special editions can be created to
specifications. For details contact: Special Sales Department,
Carol Publishing Group, 120 Enterprise Avenue, Secaucus, N.J. 07094

Library of Congress Cataloging-in-Publication Data

Winchester, Simon.
    Pacific nightmare : how Japan starts World War III, a future
history / by Simon Winchester.
        p.   cm.
    Includes index.
    "A Birch Lane Press book."
    ISBN 1-55972-136-7
    1. World War III—Fiction. 2. Imaginary wars and battles—
Fiction. I. Title.
PR6073.I479P3    1992
823'.914—dc20                                    92-16509
                                                    CIP

# CONTENTS

# THE MAJOR CHARACTERS

## THE AMERICANS

President Benson *The successor to George Bush: elected on a strongly anti-Japanese platform.*

Hugh Rackham Charlesworth III *Assistant Secretary of State for East Asian and Pacific Affairs. Founder of the highly influential HK7 committee.*

## THE BRITISH

Richard Adaire *Private Secretary to Sir John Courtenay.*

George Clovis *Hong Kong Island Regional Commander of police and supplementary forces.*

Sir John Courtenay *Last Governor of Hong Kong.*

James Gahan *Consul for South China at the time of the rebellion.*

Dr John Gurdon *Psychological warfare specialist. Responsible for establishing covert links with the Triad groups.*

General Sir William Harbinson *Commander, British Forces, Hong Kong.*

James Hogge *Secretary of State for Foreign and Commonwealth Affairs.*

Lord Inverdonald *Minister of State for Foreign and Commonwealth Affairs.*

Richard James *Reuters correspondent in Peking.*

Sir Jeremy Longford *Ambassador to Washington.*

Sir Peter MacDuff *Ambassador to Peking.*

Captain Richard Margerison *Intelligence agent. Encouraged and supplied the southern dissident movement before the rebellion.*

Captain James Wilkinson *Intelligence officer with the Gurkha Rifles.*

Peter Williamson *Consul-General, Xianggang.*

# THE CHINESE

## CIVILIAN

Chen Shuqing *Fujian Military District Commissar.*

Duan Keda *Father of Duan Kun and a founding member of the Republican Party.*

Duan Kun *Student leader shot by police in Xiamen.*

Peter Heung Way Yeung *Solicitor's clerk. 'Super 489', overall leader of the Hong Kong Triads and pro-Republican terrorist.*

Li Peng *Premier, head of the State Council (the Chinese Cabinet).*

Mao Ren-chin *Chief Executive of Xianggang SAR after 1997.*

Yang Shankun *President of the PRC.*

Yi Juan Ling *Ex-governor of Guangdong Province. Leader and co-founder of the Republican Party.*

Madame Zhang Xiaodi *Senior spokesman for Sino-European Bilateral Matters at the Foreign Ministry. Later executed for her part in leaking information about Mao Ren-chin's appointment and the possibility of PLA revolt to the press.*

Zhu Senlin *Governor of Guangdong Province.*

## MILITARY

Major-General Chen Cong Da *C-in-C 63rd Group Army. Republican.*

Major-General Hu Dai-fang *CO 111th Infantry Division. Captured Xinggiang. Republican.*

Major-General Lan *CO 123rd Infantry Division. Republican.*

Brigadier Li Guang *Commander of a tank brigade in the 14th Tank Division. Leader of the disastrous attack on Quemoy. Communist.*

Lieutenant-Colonel Li Guo-hong *CO 46th Battalion, 123rd Infantry Division. The first PLA officer to declare for the people. Republican.*

Major-General Lu Chuanzhi *CO 37th Infantry Division. Defender of Xinggiang. Surrendered to General Hu. Communist.*

Lieutenant-General Tang Zhou Hou *GOC-in-C Guangzhou MR. Republican.*

Lieutenant-General Wu *GOC Guangdong MD. Republican.*

Lieutenant-General Yang *CO 15th Group Army. Communist.*

Major-General Yang Xuchu *CO 73rd Infantry Division. Republican.*

# LIST OF MAPS

# FOREWORD

From the endless steppes of Kazakhstan to the fogbound cliffs of the Kamchatka peninsula, the entire immensity that the rest of the world once called the Far East, and which it now prefers to call the West Pacific, is today in turmoil and in flames. Those who take the long view will say it has always been so, and that what is happening today is no more than the latest in an endless procession of irruptions of violence that tell us much about the nature of the Oriental mind.

From the feudal battles of China's warring states of the fourth century BC to the spread of the Mongol empire under Genghis Khan, from the Boxer Rebellion to the Korean War, from the Taiping Rebellions to the bizarreries of the Cultural Revolution, there seems invariably to have been some all-consuming fight going on somewhere in and around China and her satellites, spreading itself with a perverse magnificence over the politicians' and the geographers' maps and thereby changing what is written on them, often for ever.

This latest outbreak of war and insurrection, with the Greek chorus of torture and banditry and execution and rapine sounding all the while, started with the event that some modern historians like to refer to as the East's Sarajevo – the long-awaited, carefully planned and yet ultimately shocking handover of the British Crown Colony of Hong Kong to its rightful owners, the People's Republic of China.

The Chinese behaved, as no British official had ever publicly supposed they might, with a wanton disregard for the agreement that the two parties had earlier signed over the colony's future – and the news of their behaviour became known some few days before the handover itself. The revelation triggered a wave of violence in Hong Kong – which led in turn to violence within China herself, and then, as the whole world is now only too well aware, to the outbreak of full-scale civil war.

That war has raged mercilessly for the past three years, and its pace and ferocity show no signs of easing. In fact, a pattern appears to have been set: border conflict and rebellions are eating away at China's peripheries, full-scale war is gnawing at her vitals, and the leadership in Peking is too frightened and too numbed by the events, and too shaken by its own internal schisms, to know just what to do. In the wake of the mercifully brief outbreak of war in Korea, China is now wholly surrounded by non-Communist countries; and indeed, she remains the only unelected Communist regime anywhere on the face of the globe. The dual imperatives of logic and force of history suggest that the Chinese Communist hierarchy, the Chinese Communist system, cannot be much longer for this world.

But the debilitated state of the Chinese body politic attracted, as was inevitable, the scavengers. In particular the Japanese – the most dangerous of all potential protagonists – became involved. Japan's decision to send troops into China brought, at length, a ferocious response from the United States, and reminded the world how easy it is for great powers to become embroiled in regional matters, for provincial affairs suddenly to become transformed into a global crisis.

This brief outline account of the events that we now know to have followed on from the handover of Hong Kong is, I believe, the first such account to appear. Professional historians may well say that this book – and any book produced at such proximity to the fighting – cannot benefit from the luxury offered by a longer perspective. This is a criticism I anticipate, and am bound to accept. But that is not the point of this book.

I am hoping instead to throw some light, for the benefit principally of readers in the West who are not so closely engaged with the complexities of the East as once they were, on a difficult topic that television viewers and newspaper readers may prefer to ignore. This war, they will say, is far away, it involves people of whom we know little and about whom we care less.

This is an understandable view, but one which I, as one who has chosen to live in lengthy and voluntary exile from my home country, think is profoundly regrettable. That we

have at our disposal the means to examine in detail the lives
of creatures on distant planets, and yet care to know so little
about men and women who live – and now who die – upon
our own, is, to me, a sad consequence of our present-day
materialism, comfort and *richesse*. We read less and less about
the people of the far-away; and I hope I will not sound
hectoring if I say once more that I find this a great pity. We
inhabit a most extraordinary world: the vast war that is
raging on its far side – its dark side, if you like – is the most
extraordinary of events. We should know it better – we
should know its causes, its principals, its participants and
now, as it threatens to spill out to infect us more directly, its
prognosis, too.

There are few disinterested documents on so fresh a conflict, other than the files of newspapers and texts of Short
Wave Broadcasts, still faithfully monitored by the BBC. China
News Analysis, a Jesuit research group new based in Kyoto,
publishes regular lengthy analyses of the twists and turns in
the battling; and I have been lucky enough to have been given
access to a number of confidential British Foreign Office files
relating to the last days of Hong Kong and the first of the new
Special Administrative Region. I have cited the *Report of the
All-Party Parliamentary Inquiry into the Circumstances Surrounding the Final Handover of Hong Kong and Related Developments in
South China* (Cmnd 5611, October 1997, HMSO, London) as a
document that offered a valuable insight into British handling
of the situation. Similar reports have been produced by the
United States and Japanese governments.

Much of the help for this account came from diplomats
who prefer not to be named. The former – and indeed the
last – Governor of Hong Kong, Sir John Courtenay, was
unfailingly helpful, and gave me access to his private diaries;
as did the Commander, British Forces, General Sir William
Harbinson. I have been fortunate enough to have had
several interviews with Mr James Hogge, the former Secretary of State for Foreign Affairs, and his Minister of State at
the time, Lord Inverdonald. Sir Peter MacDuff, still at the
time of writing Ambassador in Peking, was also interesting
on many aspects of British policy and the official Chinese
response to it.

Within China itself I am happy to be able to acknowledge

the help of Miss Zhou Kwan and Mr Cui Ping-dan, who assisted me on my single visit to see General Tang's headquarters in Canton City. Since the Battle of Wuhan was in full flood at the time, the General was away from his base; but I was able to speak with a number of assistants to Governor Yi, and to the father of the slain Xiamen University student, Mr Duan. All spent much time with me, and gave me many insights into the events of mid-July in Canton and Xiamen.

I am grateful to Mr Xing of the Ürümqi Railway Workers' Recreation Club; to former PLA Lieutenant Ma of Heihe, in Heilongjiang Province, who drove me to meet a group of Oroqen rebels near Mohe; and to Miss Lee Hyong-ju of Seoul, who acted as guide and helpmeet on my visits to Panmunjom and, later, to Pyongyang. That she was permitted to visit the former North Korean capital at the same time was, for her, a reward of unbelievable worth. I am grateful on her behalf to those who made it possible. Ambassador Bengt Jacobsen will recognise the assistance he gave to me: not least, the ample supplies of Glenmorangie over which he spent many an evening watching the fires of Pyongyang burn themselves out.

My assistance in Japan comes principally from the writer Nagai Hiromi, whose recent book *Japanese Bully-Boys* investigated the connections between the *yakuza* – the so-called 'Japanese Mafia' – and the right wing of the ruling LDP, and remains a classic analysis of the new reactionary mood that appears to be sweeping through Japan's young people. Others within the *yakuza* organisations prefer not to be named.

I was able to write most of this book in the relative peace and quiet of Kyoto, staying in a small farm north of the city which was loaned to me by my good friend Sakai Yoko during her absence in Europe: my thanks to her for providing the creature comforts that proved so necessary as an antidote to the wretched narrative I had to tell. I then took the manuscript to my temporary home here in Bali, well away from the conflict, and I did the final editing here. Any errors that remain are not, of course, the responsibility of any of those above, named or anonymous, who gave me their time, their help, their coffee or their affection: any such errors must be laid, of course, at my door.

My wife Catherine, who has been as dismayed as I have by all the traumas of the last two years, remains optimistic that, before long, we will be able to return to Hong Kong, where we first met ten years ago and where I first hoped to be able to write this book. Although the new Republican Hong Kong government appears stable enough, the military situation in the city – with Communist Chinese air raids still an occasional occurrence – has dictated otherwise. But my wife's incurable optimism has been justified on so many occasions before that I am tempted to believe her even now.

SBAW – Sanur, Bali
March, 2000.

# AUTHOR'S NOTE

The Chinese language being what it is – and allowing for the innumerable possible transliterations into English script – there may be some confusion in the perception of some of the proper names, particularly Chinese family names, that I have used in this account. This arises from the reality that a man who is named Mr Ng in Canton is named Mr Wu in Peking: the Chinese character that represents his name is pronounced in two totally different ways depending on whether it is read by someone from Canton or Peking, a speaker of Cantonese or of the mainland mandarin, *putong-hua*. Similarly, a speaker of Fukkienese would call the man something else again, as would a speaker of Shanghainese, or Hakka, or Hainanese, or . . .

To minimise this problem for the reader I have given each person in this account the name by which he knows himself or herself – so if Mr Wong is from Canton, then he is called in the book what he calls himself in Cantonese; and if Madame Zhang is from Peking, then she is named in the book by the name she calls herself in the Chinese capital. The given names make for a further complication; but in that most Western readers will pay little heed to them, I have simply presented them in the book as they were presented to me.

I have retained – principally because of their more pleasing sound – the Wade–Giles transliteration of the names Peking and Canton, and I have changed Hong Kong to the *pinyin*\* version, Xianggang, on those few occasions where it seemed appropriate. But all other Chinese place names are as approved by the Government of the People's Republic of China.

---

\**Pinyin* is the phonetic transliteration of Chinese, now widely adopted in mainland China, which uses Roman letters rather than phonetic symbols.

A substantial amount of directly quoted dialogue appears in the narrative. Readers will understand that in most cases it is a reconstruction from third party and other sources. Naturally I am aware of the dangers of using such materials, but stress that I have generally used such dialogue where it seems to add materially to an evocation of a particular event. Similarly, translations from the various Chinese languages and dialects have been the work of specialists in those particular tongues, and there may occasionally be some variance between the English written word and the original Chinese intention. But on the whole both the dialogue and the translations present, I am persuaded to believe, a wholly fair account of the events I have described.

Readers are additionally cautioned that the names used in this narrative are, with certain rather obvious exceptions – Kim Il Sung, Mao Tse-tung among them – wholly fictitious, and bear no resemblance to any individual, living or dead. He is not him, nor is she her, nor they them. The events described are also entirely hypothetical; these things are not necessarily those things. But none the less it is my earnest hope that readers will discern a fair degree of verisimilitude between all of this and all of whatever that may come to be.

## CHAPTER ONE

# TYPHOON WARNING

## WHITEMAN AFB, MISSOURI

### *Wednesday, 24 November 1999*

It was the eve of the last Thanksgiving of the century, and a bitterly cold northerly wind was sweeping down through the Midwest from central Canada, bringing with it the first bad storm of the winter. The forecasts were universally grim, and traffic advisories and snow and freeze warnings had been posted from the international frontier as far south as Little Rock, Arkansas, and the Red River, on the border between Oklahoma and Texas.

Snow started to fall a little before 8 p.m. in western Missouri. At first it was just a thin snow that looked like a yellow mist as it swirled and eddied in the light of the sodium vapour arclamps on the triple perimeter fence that circled Whiteman Air Base. Before long it had turned into a full blizzard. Air Force sentries, their faces hidden by fur collars pulled right up to the dulled steel of their helmets, stamped up and down, snorting steam into the night. Their rifles glinted in the gleam of the lights. On a normal night there would be no more than two of them, with another couple on the gate, and a patrolling team in a Cherokee truck. But tonight there were dozens of rifles, dozens of sentries. If anyone cared to look, Whiteman Air Base – once home to the 351st Strategic Missile Wing, and now America's most secret strategic bomber base – would, on this particular night, look uncannily and ominously different.

But probably no one would care to look over at the three strange aircraft and their sinister huddles of attendants. In

1

this bleak and featureless corner of western Missouri there were few enough passers-by at this time of night anyway. And in this weather, and on the eve of the holiday, hardly a soul was stirring. This lack of interest was a matter of some comfort to every one of the small, tightly secured group of people – from President Benson downwards – who had reason to be acutely concerned about the maintenance of secrecy on this critical night.

The airport over at Kansas City, sixty miles to the west, was still busy, with dozens of late-night jets bringing last-minute holidaymakers in from New York and Chicago and the coastal cities. A few trucks hummed by on Route Fifty, and a freight train clanked and grumbled its way along the old Missouri Pacific tracks from Sedalia and Jefferson City. But otherwise, in just about all of the rest of Johnson County, from Hughesville in the north to Quick City in the south, people were tucked up in their farms and their trailers, staying warm, watching the TV or the flickering of the fire, listening to the howl of the gathering storm and giving thanks – half in preparation for the next day's feast – that they didn't have to be out in it.

Behind the triple cyclone fences, however, the men of the 414th Bombardment Wing, United States Air Force, were busier than they had ever been in their unit's history. Three of the low, sleek Northrop B-2 Stealth bombers assigned, uniquely, to the Whiteman wing had been loaded with fuel. Normally they were filled with enough for a training mission, somewhere over the Mojave desert. But tonight each of them was filled to the brim with eighty tons of aviation spirit, enough to power the four General Electric F-118 turbofans for nearly nine hours of cruising, allowing the three planes to fly to their full range of more than 5,000 miles from base.

More extraordinary still, shortly after nightfall a nuclear weapons technical crew had arrived at the B-2 hangar from the underground ordnance bunker sited behind the earth mounds at the eastern corner of the base. The crew had arrived in a convoy of three heavily armoured vehicles, each of which was driven directly beneath the fuselage (if a B-2 can be said to have a fuselage: its tiny radar cross-section made it look like a flying wing, no more) of each of the

2

planes. They worked silently, behind hessian screens, for more than two hours, departing once they had completed the intricacies of their work. They left the bombers loaded – as the crews assigned to fly them quickly discovered – as no US Air Force plane had been loaded for the previous eight years.

Shortly after 10 p.m., Central Standard Time – 0400 Zulu, Universal Coordinated Time, or GMT – each B-2 bomber was taxiing down the runway between the frozen stubble of Whiteman Air Base, carrying eighty tons of fuel, and two live and primed atomic bombs. More specifically, each plane carried two mark B-61 nuclear fission weapons – each one eight feet long, shaped like a torpedo, with a rounded nose and small guide fins on the tail. Each atom bomb was packed with high explosive and enough precision-machined uranium 235 to create a nuclear explosion that would be equivalent to the detonation of nearly 50,000 tons of TNT.

The three bombers left Whiteman AFB at one-minute intervals, with the lead plane clocked out at 0405 Zulu, 25 November 1999. They swept almost silently up through the Missouri blizzard and climbed steadily to their cruising altitude, nine miles above the eastern edge of the Great Plains. At this moment the six Air Force commissioned officers to whose lot this mission fell, two assigned to pilot each aircraft, had no information about their ultimate destination, nor about the nature of their task. They knew only a very few details.

They knew they were headed on the first leg of their mission – a 4,000-mile, seven-hour flight to Hickam Air Base, Hawaii, where they would land and refuel. They knew they would remain at Hickam for no more than three hours, after which they would take off with another set of new, sealed orders. Depending on a possible third set of fresh orders that would be transmitted through a highly secure airborne satellite data link from the National Command Authorities (President Benson in the White House and the Secretary of Defense at the Pentagon, via the Joint Chiefs and the SAC commander at Offutt Air Force Base in Nebraska) they knew that a single one of the three aircraft would then proceed to execute the mission. All three aircraft would then rendezvous after the attack and would be refuelled by

aerial tankers before returning to Hickam Field, after which the crews would rest and then bring the aircraft back to the headquarters of the 414th BW at Whiteman.

And they knew that the new top-secret attack orders would be transmitted once only at precisely 2200 Zulu on 25 November. If no orders had arrived on the data link by 2201 Zulu, the attack mission would be considered aborted, and all three planes would return immediately to the designated refuelling rendezvous point 'R-3' before returning to Hickam and then to Whiteman. Total radio silence had to be maintained at all times, aside from the five minutes immediately prior to the first landing at Hawaii.

The westbound flight was uneventful. The planes flew high, a mile or so apart, their black and unreflective shapes rendering them nearly invisible to each other, as well as to all the radar devices below and which they were designed to evade. The ice and snow storms eased above the southern Rockies, and by the time the planes had reached Lake Mead the sky was bright and clear, the immense body of water below turned into molten silver by the light of a low full moon. They passed above the Los Angeles basin at around 1.30 a.m., Pacific time: the lights of Hollywood and Pasadena and Burbank were like a clutch of brilliant jewels, the curling freeways like loops of gold chain.

Three and a half further hours spent hurtling southwest over the Pacific and the lead plane spotted Mauna Kea on the Big Island of Hawaii; Major Bill Pringle, the lead pilot, radioed a single message down to Hawaii Oceanic and then to Hickam Control before coming in low around South Cape to Diamond Head, overshooting Hickam and making a smooth and silent approach from the west. He touched down at 1.16 a.m. Hawaii Standard Time, 1116 Zulu, the others a minute or two behind. It was pitch dark, and comfortably warm. Soft trade winds wafted across the runway, with the plangent sounds of late night guitar music, and cicadas carried on the breeze. 'H' hour was now ten hours and forty-four minutes away.

The planes were refuelled at a remote western corner of the field, well away from the freeway bridges. There was no one in sight, and the only signs of life came from one of the warships riding at anchor in the roads, where a party seemed

to be in full swing. Sentries had taken up positions around the three aircraft. An unmarked USAF truck brought in a second technical team to check the bombs, and one of their officers entered a series of numerical codes into the firing devices. Finally, moments before the scheduled take-off time a second truck appeared, with two officers and more sentries. They were from the office of CINCPAC, the Commander in Chief, Pacific, whose headquarters were in Camp H. M. Smith on a hill overlooking Pearl Harbor. They demanded positive identification from all six of the B-52 crew members, and then handed over sealed envelopes of orders which were to be read, they said, once the aircraft were airborne. They saluted and left. The three aircraft taxied back on to the main runway and soared up into the black Pacific sky on schedule, at 4 a.m. local time, 1400 Zulu. 'H' hour was now eight hours away.

Thirty minutes later, once the three machines had reached their cruise altitude, Major Pringle and his two other colleagues alongside opened the stiff manila order envelopes. Inside each was a single sheet of flimsy paper, with a number of lines of machine-readable type which read, in full:

ZCZC CINCSAC OABNE/OPCDRS 33 SQN 414 SBW HABHI 251330Z NOV 99 MSGRDS+++USING GPS PROCEED AT MACH 0.80 AT FL450 TO POSITION GAMMA COORDINATES 30.00.00N 150.00.00E AFTER WHICH DESCEND TO FL 350 AND PROCEED AT FULL SPEED AND IN SECURE STATE THREE TO POSITION DELTA COORDINATES 34.00.00N 140.00.00E EXPECT FURTHER ORDERS 2200 ZULU EX NCA VIA DATALINK CODENAME OPERATION TYPHOON WARNING STOP REFUEL POSITION 'R' PRIOR DESIGNATIONS STOP ENDS+++

The commanders calculated swiftly. It was now 3,100 miles to Position Gamma. At the designated speed, and given the high-altitude weather, it would take the small squadron six hours and eighteen minutes to arrive. Since it was now 1440 Zulu the planes should all reach this first position at 2058 hours. The second position, Position Delta, was a further 620 miles on – one hour and two minutes at full

speed, and in Secure State Three, with all RAM baffles, ECM screens and signal monitoring arrays switched on, and with jamming devices readied. It should thus be possible to be at Position Delta, and probably undetected, at precisely 2200 Zulu – the time at which the final set of orders from the President should come in over the datalink.

It would be idle to think that these orders – if they came – would demand any other course of action than that which was blindingly and horrifyingly obvious. Operation Typhoon Warning, the name by which these orders would now be identified, would almost certainly require one of the three strategic bombers to drop and detonate at least one of its nuclear weapons. It would be the first time that an atomic device had been used in anger since August 1945. Each of the fission weapons in the bomb bays of the B-2s was four times as powerful as the bombs that devastated Hiroshima and Nagasaki. Many scores of thousands of people could be less than seven and a half hours away from a horrible death.

But where were they likely to be? It was the question uppermost in the minds of the six men as they punched their course orders into the INS, and as their planes began to hurtle northwestwards, away from the glow of the American dawn, and towards the deep Pacific night. Just where, each man wondered as he unscrolled his computerised global positioning system map, where exactly on the face of the earth were these two positions?

Position Gamma, it turned out, was in the middle of the ocean, 400 miles northwest of the tiny atoll of Marcus Island, which for the last thirty years – since the Americans handed it back – had supported a small Japanese weather station and a squid-harvesting plant.

Position Delta, 34° 00 N' 140° 00' E, however, was by no means in mid-ocean. It was on the very verge of the Japanese mainland. Ten miles to the west was the island of Miyake-jima. Fifty miles north were the beaches and the pearl divers of the Boso-hanto peninsula. And eighty miles away from Position Delta – ten minutes' flying time – was Tokyo itself.

The realisation dawned suddenly on all six men. Though they would have no way of knowing for certain for another seven hours and an odd few minutes, it seemed well within the bounds of probability that the target for nuclear attack

6

under Operation Typhoon Warning was near, or even directly over, the city of Tokyo.

The scores of thousands who would die would be residents of the capital of the most powerful economic state on the planet – the leaders of whom were currently locked in a seemingly intractable dispute, an irresolvable crisis with the United States.

The dispute, which now seemed about to spin out of control and to culminate in the most terrifying of tragedies, had its origins just two and a half years before in a place that was far from, and formally unrelated to, both of the nations that were now locked so ruinously together. Its origins can be traced, in fact, to the summer of 1997, and to what was then the last British Imperial possession in the Far East – the Crown Colony of Hong Kong. It was then about to be handed back, after 150 years of foreign rule, to its rightful owners, the Chinese.

But the ponderous mechanics by which this transfer was undertaken, and the unanticipated realities of the takeover, were to produce an escalating crisis that has kept the Far East in turmoil almost ever since, and which seemed to these young American pilots, so far from home on this still dark Thanksgiving morning, to be readying itself for the most appalling and unspeakable climax.

# CHAPTER TWO

# DISTANT THUNDER

## THE BRITISH EMBASSY, WASHINGTON, DC

### *Tuesday, 11 June 1996*

The first expression of Washington's serious interest in the coming crisis in Asia – though at this early stage perhaps serious curiosity would be the more accurate phrase – came as the result of a very brief chance encounter between two guests at the most celebrated diplomatic event of 1996, the annual Official Birthday Party in honour of Queen Elizabeth II. The meeting, so short as to be almost perfunctory, involved on the one side an Assistant Secretary of State and, on the other, a middle-ranking British soldier with a noticeably new sun-tan. On the June day that they met it is fair to say there was not even the faintest apprehension of trouble from this quarter of the world. The only apprehension that anyone recalls from the day of this meeting was that of the coming summertime heat.

This hint that yet another of the Potomac Valley's notoriously debilitating summers had settled itself on the American capital caused the half-dozen British Foreign Office functionaries charged with organising the 1996 'QBP' to curse as profusely as they perspired. For it was an unusually large and splendid party they had planned this year, and they were in no mood to see it spoiled, by storm, or humidity, or the insufferable swampy heat.

Two thousand, two hundred and twenty-eight gilt-edged, heavily illuminated and embossed invitation cards had gone out, three weeks before, to the great and the good of Bethesda, Chevy Chase, Cabin John and Alexandria, and to

8

the better addresses in the District of Columbia, most of them found to the west of Rock Creek Park. A variety of factors suggested that perhaps most of those who had been invited would turn up. After all, it was the seventieth anniversary of the building of the embassy itself, *and* the seventieth birthday of Her Majesty: the party would provide a moment for everyone to toast the further survival both of the monarchy and the present monarch, and to recall the astuteness of the Treasury negotiators who in 1926 persuaded the Government of the District of Columbia to hand over this most commodious piece of land on Massachusetts Avenue for the sum of ten dollars (which, subsequent Ambassadors were wont to remark, was admittedly worth a *great deal more* in those days).

There were other reasons. The friendship between the White House and Downing Street had never been stronger, it seemed, and George Bush, in these closing months of his eight-year Presidency, had come to seem a near-avuncular figure to the succession of Prime Ministers who had been thrown up by the minority governments of the post-Thatcher years. (This feature of modern political life was now making Britain almost as curious and fascinating a phenomenon as Italy had been in the Eighties. Not a few of the American journalists who had been invited would come, the Embassy assumed, because of the extraordinary turmoil which Whitehall had suffered during the last two years – turmoil which had been warmly welcomed by all of those who found the peaceful world dreadfully dull.)

Then again, it had also been hinted that there was a very slight possibility of a visit to Washington – and thus the Embassy – from the Princess (who had been sailing with friends off Bequia, in the Grenadines, and was expected to fly home after a brief stop in some American city). The merest suggestion that she might appear had been enough to give half of Georgetown the most acute attack of nerves, and to treble the business of the local couturiers, dressmakers and seamstresses. In addition, the extraordinary good looks of the young – and still single – new British Ambassador counted for a lot. Sir Jeremy Longford had, it was generally agreed, quite a bit of pulling power.

Yes, concluded the perspiring Second Secretaries and

advisers on Protocol and *placement*, all told it was highly likely that most of those who had been asked to come would do so. The Treasury would no doubt grumble again about the ensuing bill: but then the accountants' miserable idea of twenty years before, of staging a mere *vin d'honneur* for only 200 guests, had long gone the way of so many other examples of Cold War-inspired parsimony. One of the more comforting consequences of the so-called Peace Dividend was that British diplomatic parties, all around the world, were now back to being recognised as the best on the circuit. And this one in Washington, to celebrate the dual seventieth birthdays, was due to be one of the grandest of all.

In the event, the Royal Marine security officers later reported a heroic turnout. One thousand, eight hundred and ninety invitations had been presented at the Embassy's Observatory Gate, and a further ninety guests had been welcomed at the door of the Lutyens-designed Residency itself, a mark of special favour for their age, importance, and often both. The substantial acreage of rose-rimmed lawns was thus awash with an immense and multicoloured scrum of people and hats – some of the most remarkable of hats this particular year – tucking merrily into hundreds of pounds of the sweetest of small Norfolk strawberries piled with billows of whipped Devon cream, sipping icy flutes of Krug (though some misguided patriots opted for a rather chalky-tasting Sussex Chardonnay), and chattering over the selections from *The King and I*, *Cats* and the latest London musical, *The Speckled Band*, that were played for them by a visiting Police Band from the Colony of Hong Kong.

The Secretary of State was there, if briefly. So were some fourteen senior figures from Foggy Bottom who were either Assistant Secretaries, Heads of Departments or else enjoyed some especially intimate relationship with Her Majesty's Government. Hugh Rackham Charlesworth III was one such. He was officially listed as Assistant Secretary of State for East Asian and Pacific Affairs (Japan to New Zealand, Singapore to Tonga). But he was rather more than that: he had been at Keble (as a Rhodes Scholar, and an oarsman) along with Jeremy Longford; and it was thought there was a fighting chance that Charlesworth's sister Anne-Marie might one day become Lady Longford (despite the complications

of nomenclature that would then arise for the Countess of the same title).

It was not, however, his perfunctory exchange with Jeremy – *Sir* Jeremy, he said correctly, and with a courtly bow and an amused grin, as he reached the head of the receiving line – that made that June encounter so historically memorable. It was instead a conversation that occurred towards the end of the party that came to assume seminal importance. It was fairly brief, and it took place when Hugh Charlesworth was strolling back towards the Residency steps, and was gazing towards the stolid bronze back of the Churchill statue beyond, wondering if he could now leave without causing offence.

His eye lighted on a fellow of his age, a man whom he had noticed earlier, largely because of his fiercely dark sun tan and the startling cut of his pale linen suit. When Charlesworth saw him for this second time he was being given a light by the conductor of the police band. He drew deeply on a small cigar – probably a Burmese cheroot, Charlesworth thought. The policeman then waved at him cheerily, and got back on with the business of conducting a rather thin version of *I'm Just a Gal Who Can't Say No*.

Charlesworth introduced himself. The stranger, it turned out, was a British soldier, a captain in the Gurkha Rifles, currently on leave and attached to St Antony's College, Oxford. His name was Wilkinson. He spoke Cantonese, he explained – and Police Senior Inspector Tsui, the band conductor, was an old friend. Indeed he had called on Tsui's son in Hong Kong only one week before, when he returned to the colony after a long journey in the Kumon Hills of Northern Burma, and near by. He had flown to the States for his sister's wedding – she was a Secretary in the Embassy's Private Office. Jeremy Longford had invited him to the party. He knew very few people in Washington: his speciality was China – he had read Chinese at Cambridge, and had been on a short posting in Hong Kong three years before to work with the Gurkhas as an intelligence officer, with a particular interest in the handover of the colony to Chinese rule.

'Little more than a year away, isn't it?' remarked Charlesworth.

'A year and' – Wilkinson looked down at his watch, and counted with his fingers – 'and twenty days. And everyone rather nervous, as I expect you know.'

Charlesworth had taken a keen interest in the last year's reporting by the American Consulate at Hong Kong. Things were going none too well, he admitted. There had been demonstrations and some spectacular rioting the previous summer. The gyrations of the local stock and property market had caused more than usual alarm. The flow of emigrants had become remarkable – and indeed there was a memorandum sitting on his desk at that very moment from the Immigration and Naturalisation Service, requesting some advice and forecasts on the likely volume of applicants for immigration to the United States. 'An atmosphere approaching panic' was a phrase he had noted.

The American Chamber of Commerce in the colony had reported its own concern over the continuing drain of competent people, a tapering-off of foreign investment (except from Japan, which was still increasing its investment, though more slowly and prudently than a decade before), and a 2 or 3 per cent decline in the number of American corporate offices in the territory. Most of the latter had moved down to Singapore, though the temptations of Kuala Lumpur and Djakarta had increased since the signing of the Middle East Treaty, and the consequent lessening of tension between America and the more conservative half of the Islamic world.

Relations between the major industrial powers and China, which – with the exception of the eternally prosperous provinces in the south, near Hong Kong – was currently enduring yet another phase of inexplicable barbarism, were very poor: a further reason for everyone to be concerned and dejected about the outlook for Hong Kong, caught in the middle. 'Troubling' was the word most commonly used to describe the colony's prospects. 'But not terminal,' added many of the analysts who were familiar with the resilience and energy of the place. 'Down, but not out.'

The two men strolled towards the Residency steps, the music fading as they moved away from the little band. The late afternoon air was thick and hot, and Charlesworth suddenly wished he was in creased white linen, and not his regulation Brooks Brothers grey. He had long regretted that

he had had little truly foreign experience – not the kind that Wilkinson appeared to have, anyway. His career was based mostly on meetings in embassy offices and on reading mimeographed reports and studying matters of protocol. The man who was strolling beside him seemed by contrast to be making his life a progress through jungles and villages, and into parts of foreign cities that it would be imprudent for a foreign diplomat to visit. He might well hear more – much more – than his colleagues on the conventional circuit. He decided to ask.

'Any ideas about what the Chinese'll do to the place?' It was a casual question, the kind of thing he asked every businessman and foreign envoy and journalist who passed through his office. Most of them replied gloomily. There were guarantees – cast-iron guarantees, the British insisted to everyone else's sceptical amusement – that the system that had made Hong Kong so successful would be permitted to continue for at least half a century more. 'Come on!' they all scoffed. 'The Chinese won't be able to keep their hands off the place.'

'Odd that you should ask,' Wilkinson replied. 'Well – not odd that you should ask – but odd that I'd meet someone here who was interested.

'Yes, I do have an idea or two. It's all very dismal, as you'd probably expect me to say. But I've kept my ears open during the past couple of months. This trip – I wasn't only in the Kumon Hills, actually. I have some friends from Peking who I meet from time to time over in Yunnan Province. They're people I go climbing with. They've got quite interesting jobs. We talk about things. And one of them did say something on this journey that I have to confess I found rather strange.'

Charlesworth paused, fascinated. The buzz of conversation around him seemed to quieten, and the faces that he recognised from time to time blurred into the crowd. They were under a mulberry tree, and there was no one around to overhear.

'You probably know all about the agreement,' Wilkinson continued, 'concerning who exactly is actually going to run Hong Kong, once the British Governor steps down. It'll be a Chinese, of course. But I'm sure you are aware that the

powers that be in Peking were always terribly careful to say that this person, whoever it was, would be from Hong Kong – perhaps even someone who was chosen by the local people. Certainly it would be someone the locals would approve of.

'But from what I hear, that's not going to happen at all. The people in – well, to be frank I'm not sure what ministry they're in, let's just say *some people in Peking* – are getting really rather steamed up about what's happening in South China. They think the place is getting away with itself, becoming too prosperous and falling under all this foreign influence. I'm sure you've read all about it. There are endless pieces in the *Review* and so forth.

'They've put some pretty hard-line people in at the top in the provinces, as you'll have noticed. But they think – rightly, I suppose – that the real trouble comes from Hong Kong. They see it as a sort of illness, if you like. And they want the illness to end – they want to cut it off at source so that the infection, if that is what it is, stops spreading. The best way of doing that is to make absolutely sure that Hong Kong, once it is under their control, is totally ideologically reliable. So what my friends tell me is that they're planning to put one of their real Stalinists in as the new boss. They're going to tear up that part of the agreement – not, I suppose, that anyone thought they'd abide by it in the first place. Remember all that nonsense about "whatever else the Chinese do, at least they stick to their agreements"? How could anyone believe that?

'Anyway, for what it's worth, that's what I'm told. I mentioned it to one or two people in London before I came here. But I don't think they thought much of it. They're not terribly open to that kind of thing back in the Foreign Office. One chap called Cooper took an interest – you might have a chat with him, if you're interested. But the others – they seem to assume I go climbing with the wrong sort of people.'

Charlesworth grinned, and thanked Wilkinson for the tip, and promised to keep in touch; and then the pair made their separate ways towards the exit. Longford was waiting, looking with some exasperation over the shoulder of Diane Forgiss, the somewhat overdressed social editor of the *Standard*. He spotted Charlesworth and with relief cried:

'Hugh – how good to see you! Come over here. There's something I want to say to you,' and edged him over to the marquee.

'Christ that woman's a bore. Got to pay my dues, they say. Full page in the Style section, or whatever it is. My press chap seems to think it's a good idea, give us more visibility, after all the damage my predecessor is supposed to have done on the social scene. Thank God you rescued me.'

'But was there something?' asked Charlesworth, who had a six o'clock with the Indonesian Ambassador, and ought not to be late. 'I'm sorry to be so abrupt.'

'Not at all, Hugh. Yes, there was one thing. Did you meet a fellow called Wilkinson? I had a mind that I saw the two of you talking. Well, I gather from a person in Policy Planning in London that he's really rather good. He's attached to St Antony's, as you may know. So his credentials – and his connections – are obviously pretty impressive. And I gather that he may have some interesting views on what the Chinese are up to. Not that I'd know. I can't stand them. No interest at all. But I rather liked Hong Kong, at least for a day or two. Quite a nice bunch of people there, people who work in Swires,* all very civilised.

'Jimmy Wilkinson seems to think it is all going to go wrong, and that are people aren't taking it seriously enough. He talked to me about it the other day, and I thought he should pop along here and see if he could interest anyone. His view is that the appointment of the chief executive has all sorts of implications, that will go a lot further than Hong Kong itself. He thinks it'll set off – or that it could set off – all manner of problems.

'Something about his manner I rather like. I'd heard a bit about him from one of our Defence Liaison people. He's quite a character: hard but wise if you know what I mean.

'Anyway – you've got to go. I'm seeing your sister tomorrow night. We'll catch up after that. But my advice to you for now is – even if we are pooh-poohing Wilkinson's ideas, you might think about it a bit more carefully. You don't have the blinkers, or the baggage. Think about what he said. Keep it at the back of your mind.'

---

*John Swire & Co. Ltd, one of the biggest trading firms in Hong Kong, owned by a British family of the same name.

At this time of the evening the traffic on Rock Creek Parkway was northbound only, taking the commuters back to the Maryland suburbs. Charlesworth thus had to drive down 22nd Street, and got stuck in a jam near M Street. He was frustrated, and he was fuming by the time he arrived and discovered that Mr Thayeb was already in the Ambassadors' Waiting Room, and had been there for ten minutes.

But the delay had convinced him of the need to take Longford's advice seriously – and to make a note to thank him for passing Wilkinson on to him. He, too, had liked the young soldier. He had no way of deciding whether what he had said was true or not; but he was certain that if it was true, then it had profound implications not just for Hong Kong, but for China, and even for China's neighbours. Precisely what these implications were needed to be established. A group ought to be established to monitor the situation, and to report up, perhaps regularly, for the Department.

The EAPAC Hong Kong Transition Working Group – or the Charlesworth 'HK 7' Committee as it soon became known – was formally convened two weeks later, meeting for its first session in the Assistant Secretary's private office. There were seven members: two from the People's Republic of China Bureau, one from the Taiwan Coordination Staff, one from the Office of Japanese Affairs, one from the Office of Korean Affairs, a representative from the Central Intelligence Agency and another specialist on Hong Kong and colonial affairs attached to the Bureau of European Affairs. It had a part-time secretarial staff of one, and a telephone number. It was to meet monthly, and to prepare regular study papers on 'the likely impact on the East Asian region of the retrocession of the British Crown Colony of Hong Kong on 30 June 1997, with particular reference to matters of United States political, commercial and national security interests.' It would report to the Assistant Secretary, who would in turn file the reports with the Office of the Secretary of State.

The Committee's monthly meetings, viewed with the benefit of hindsight, provided a thread of continuity to American policy towards the Far East in the late Nineties that would prove invaluable both to the outgoing Bush administration and to that of President Benson, who won his sur-

16

prise electoral victory that November largely on the basis of a wave of Far Eastern – or, more specifically, anti-Japanese – interest.

When the regional troubles that Charlesworth's group accurately predicted in the summer of 1996 came to a head, and then in turn precipitated the global crisis of the autumn of 1999, the HK7 meetings became ever more important to the inner circle of Presidential advisers. Hugh Charlesworth is regarded by contemporary historians as the principal architect of US policy towards China, Japan and Korea – perhaps not wholly surprisingly, given his official Assistant Secretaryship. But it is an impressive aspect of the affair, none the less, that senior White House officials, NSC chairmen and the chairmen of the Joint Chiefs of Staff have deferred so often and so uncomplainingly in this matter to the authority and knowledge of a single individual.

The Assistant Secretary himself has simply replied to the publicity he has received as a consequence by saying that 'good committee work' seems to have underlain the decision-making process – a reply that appears to have guaranteed him a secure position in the US bureaucracy for some time to come.

## CHAPTER THREE

# RECESSIONAL

## GOVERNMENT HOUSE, HONG KONG

*Saturday, 28 June 1997*
EARLY MORNING

The Foreign Office telegram number 97/54658/GHK, sent over the name of James Hogge, Secretary of State for Foreign and Commonwealth Affairs, was timed at 1845 Zulu, and was dated 27 June 1997. It was heavily coded, was classified Top Secret and marked Flash. It was addressed for 'The Personal Attention of His Excellency the Governor of Hong Kong', and was copied to Her Britannic Majesty's Ambassadors in Peking, Washington and to the United Nations, and also, with a number of addenda, to the Commander, British Forces, Hong Kong.

The classification of a British diplomatic telegram as Flash carries the implicit instruction that all intended recipients are to be alerted immediately to its arrival, whatever the time of day or night; and so in Government House Hong Kong, where the time of its initial receipt was logged as 0300 local – when it was pitch dark, on the hot and soundlessly stormy Saturday morning of 28 June – the duty cipher clerk at the Communications Centre telephoned up to Richard Adaire, Private Secretary to the Governor.

Adaire, whose post in the Hong Kong government allowed him handsome official quarters in a block of flats on Mount Nicholson Gap Road, had for the past six weeks of the Diplomatic Emergency been living in Government House itself, in a poky *pied-à-terre* beneath the eaves of what had long been called the Japanese Tower. He was lying half awake, listening to the subsiding rumble of the night-time riots, when the clerk's call came through. 'I'll be down in a second. Tony,' he said quietly; and by two minutes past three

18

he was indeed down in the basement Centre, watching as the clerk worked at his IBM terminal to strain some sense from the cryptographic soup that had poured down the line from London.

He was good at his job, and it took him just three minutes to produce a copy of the message that was clean enough to read and to present to His Excellency. Leaving aside all the salutational flummery and the distribution lists, the text, Adaire noted, was very brief. But however spare the prose, the implications were profound. The message, the first formally recorded apprehension of a tide of events that would soon wash across world history with as much power as either of the century's two earlier conflicts, was marked by a lack of both elegance and persiflage:

HMG CONFIRMS STATE COUNCILLOR MAO REN CHIN APPOINTED CEXG STOP PRC AUTHORITIES AGREEING TO WITHHOLD STATEMENT UNTIL 1559 ZULU MONDAY 30 JUNE STOP CIVIL ORDER IMPLI-CATIONS INDICATE CLEAR NEED FOR CONTINUING DISCRETION STOP CONTINGENT PRECAUTIONS NECESSARY STOP TWO BATTALIONS CURRENTLY BSB THOUGH FCO REGARDS UTILISATION DECIDEDLY IMPRUDENT FURTHER DETAILS IN ANNEXES FOR CBF STOP +++ HOGGE

Adaire read the message, shook his head and whistled in disbelief. 'Make sure you copy it and all the annexes to Tamar,' was all he said at first. He picked up the telephone and punched 211. It was answered immediately. Sir John Courtenay, who was in any case a light sleeper, was half expecting a message from London, and had probably lain awake as well.

'Flash telegram, sir – I'll bring it up right away,' said Adaire, fighting to keep his voice calm. He paused. The Governor asked him for a *précis*. 'Basically it says that Mao's been appointed, just as they thought. I'm having the text copied to the General. I've got the summary with me now, and Tony says he'll have the lot by half-past three. I'll come right up.'

Sir John was in the dressing-room when Adaire arrived,

perspiring slightly. He took the flimsy paper from the scarlet folder marked Top Secret and read through it, frowning occasionally. He walked down the stairs to his study and sat at his desk, rubbing his eyes. He picked up the right hand of the three telephones on his desk, which gave him a direct connection to General Sir William Harbinson, the Commander, British Forces.

'Morning, Willy,' he said. 'You won't have seen the cable yet, but Adaire here says you'll get it in a minute or two. Once you've read it all, come right up here, will you? I'm afraid it looks like trouble. *Big* trouble. You'd better bring Tomsett, too. Let's say an informal meeting at zero four hundred hours. My study.'

He hung up, took off his spectacles and rubbed his eyes once again. Adaire thought that for a moment the Governor looked particularly old – though it was probably no more than weariness, and the wretched hour of night.

The caught each other's gaze. Then Sir John shook his head, slowly. 'What bloody, bloody fools these Chinks can be. You'd never imagine they'd make such madness. A rod for their own backs – that's what this is. Why? Can anybody tell me why?'


# 12TH FLOOR, HMS *TAMAR*, HONG KONG

### EARLY MORNING

The three Operations Requirements Departments at the Ministry of Defence had clearly had a hand in the preparation of the annexes to FCO Flash Telegram 97/54658/GHK which Squadron Leader Bates, the Military Assistant, handed to General Harbinson at 0332 on the Saturday morning. They were voluminous, and detailed, and they talked extensively about the diversion and possible deployment of men, ships, jets, transport planes and helicopters. The General, who like the Governor was half awake when Bates telephoned for permission to bring him the telegram, put them to one side to read in the car on the way up to Government House; his attention was held by his skimming

of the single sheet of flimsy that held the main message.

If the news that Mao Ren-chin was to be installed as China's first Chief Executive of the Special Administrative Region of Xianggang did not exactly surprise Harbinson – who was a wily ex-Gurkha who had served some tours in the colony and thus had some foreknowledge of Peking's ways – it most certainly did appal him. Like Sir John he whistled softly with incredulity.

'Betrayal' was the word that came to mind. There had, after all, been an explicit assurance given by the Chinese nearly fourteen years before, that the first Chief Executive of what in *putonghua* was called Xianggang would be drawn from within the Hong Kong community. Whoever it was would be – or would probably be, for this, it had to be admitted, was never stated specifically – a person of Cantonese stock. But this Mr Mao of the telegram, far from being Cantonese, far from having any links at all with the Hong Kong community, far from being in any sense the choice of the five million who still lived in the territory, was a total outsider.

Mao Ren-chin came from Dalian, in Liaoning province, south Manchuria. He spoke not a word of the Cantonese dialect. He was seventy-four years old, a former soldier, reputed to be a hard-line member of the Party. He had done much, it was reliably reported, to help organise the suppression of the Chinese student movements in 1976, 1989, 1993 and 1996. He was, in short, the very antithesis of the kind of person that Hong Kong, even in its politically emasculated state at the time of the handover, wanted to have preside over its first months and years of post-colonial life. It was an appointment, Harbinson felt sure, that would lead to disaster.

He instructed Bates to awaken his deputy, Brigadier Rex Tomsett, and the young Major, Julian Berry, who had been sent from London six months before to help organise the handover ceremonial this coming Monday night. The General was in no mood for small talk. 'Meet me at my car at zero three fifty,' he told each man as he came to the phone. 'We have a problem. There is a meeting at Government House at four. Top Secret Rules apply. That is all.'

The three men met downstairs, outside the steel grilles of

21

the gates to the Prince of Wales Building. The two junior officers saluted the General, who climbed into the back seat of the armoured Jaguar. Tomsett, who carried a sheaf of briefing papers, sat beside him. The driver, a corporal from the 6th Gurkha Rifles, the General's former regiment, shut the car's door, and waited while Berry got himself and his briefcase into the front seat. Then, checking to see that all the bullet-proof windows were properly closed, he drove off through the triple chicanes, past the sentries and the sand-bags that marked the perimeter of Tamar, and out into the confusion – ebbing somewhat, given the hour – of the Hong Kong night.

The city did look in a hellish state. There was little enough traffic about, except for army and police vehicles. But small groups of agitated people were still milling around the Star Ferry concourse, spilling out of the MTR* exits – not that the trains themselves were running – and were joining groups already in Statue Square and the streets around the old Legislative Council building. A few held up banners, and chanted. From one group came an eerie, ugly growl of anger. Suddenly this group charged as one towards a police car which, with the sound of screaming tyres, promptly sped away. A water-cannon lay in wait up an alley by the Bank, with helmeted troops beside it. Some were smoking. A few looked half asleep.

Even with the windows closed, the onion-smell of tear gas filtered in through the car's air conditioning system, and the eyes of the four occupants began to smart. And there was another more acrid smell of burning tyres. A number of fires had been set. Half-way up Garden Lu a police LandCruiser was on its side in flames, and from the flyover the group could see the orange glow of fire from shops and offices at the base of Furama House and on top of the car park at Murray Road. There had once been secret police offices there – 'J' branch had worked from above the park in its early years – and there were said to be files and computer tapes stored in what had become a big police godown. Prob-ably that was why it had been set alight. In fact, as the officers all knew, most of the files were on computer disc, stored in

*Mass Transit Railway, the Hong Kong version of the Underground.

the vaults out at Chung Hom Kok, where the old GCHQ monitoring station had been; in the coming days they were supposedly to be loaded on to a destroyer that would be waiting behind Po Toi – doubtless the Annexes to the night's message had some further details from London about that. Exactly what would be done with the files was anyone's guess. Someone had estimated that 3 million personal records had been accumulated by 'J' branch in the past two years: doubtless there would be some great material for an entire battalion of historians and blackmailers.

The Jaguar, its two-star general's badge gleaming in the light of the fires, turned into Upper Albert Road and pushed its way through the crowds that, for the previous week, had assembled nightly beyond the barricades in front of the Government House walls. There was a series of checks and searches here, even for so well-known a group of visitors as these. The sergeant who performed the final inspection was, his cap badge declared, a member of the 2nd Battalion, The Queen's Regiment – the final British unit that London had seen fit to have garrisoned down at Stanley Fort.

It was a decision that had prompted some wry comment in a number of Messes and in a letter to *The Times* about the irony – a deliberately contrived coincidence, it was thought sure. For the Second Battalion, a complicated amalgam of other units that was first formed as a consequence of the end of Empire, and then made even more necessary by the steady reductions in the number of soldiery after the end of the Cold War, had subsumed into its immensity a relic of what was once called the Royal East Kent Regiment – a unit that was once rather better known simply as the Buffs. And this regiment had listed among its battle honours (though not in bold type, for in truth it was no great victory) '*Pekin, 1860*'. The Buffs and their sepoys had, under the command of Lord Elgin, taken part in the sacking of the Chinese emperor's Summer Palace – an adventure in which *The Times* correspondent, Bowlby, had been captured, and died (a point which, the letter writer felt certain, would see his miss-ive into print). To send as its final military gesture to Hong Kong a unit that had been intimately involved in the destruc-tion of old Peking was, if nothing else, cheeky. If, that is, it had been deliberate.

Furthermore, Brigadier Tomsett was a Royal Scot – and back in the days when the Scots were dignified by the title of First of Foot, the Scotsmen too had been making war on Peking. A Brigadier and a battalion – it was too much of a coincidence, *The Times* letter writer had suggested.

This was no time to ponder on such an amusing twist. Once the sergeant had, unsmiling, scrutinised all the passes and saluted those whom he now was certain were his superiors, there was a short wait while unseen hydraulic jacks pushed down the anti-terrorist blocks, after which the car drove through the great white gates and around the lawn. Richard Adaire was waiting, grim-faced. The general nodded for him to lead the way, and the three soldiers went in to the study.

Gentlemen,' began Sir John, once everyone was seated. 'I am afraid what we have here' – and he tapped the paper on his desk – 'looks very much like the beginning of the end. I don't mean to sound dramatic, but I'm angry. And frankly, I'm afraid of the implications of this. Not just for Hong Kong but for China herself. And not even just for China. I fear, quite candidly, for the whole region. The implications of a decision like this are very grave indeed. As I assume you all agree?'

The soldiers nodded. The men were briefly silent. Outside the sound of shouts and cries and breaking glass had died – dawn, after all, was less than an hour away. But the weather radar at Tamar had shown thick clouds boiling up from the east, and this night would be peculiarly long, and dark. A sudden crump of thunder sounded in the distance: the beginnings of the storm that threatened to spoil the ceremonial which would mark the beginning of true Chinese rule over this tiny territory. The Governor looked up at the sound, as did the General. They grinned at one another, but sardonically.

# QUEEN'S ROAD EAST, HAPPY VALLEY, HONG KONG

### BEFORE DAWN

During the night some thirty-six men were assigned to be visibly guarding the red marble entrance to the New China News Agency on Queen's Road East. This had been the People's Republic's centre of operations in Hong Kong – its embassy, if you will – since the early Eighties, and it was to be guarded rigorously from any threat to which the Hong Kong government might unwittingly play host. Its head was an Ambassador, in both rank and regard: if the offices had ever housed a true News Agency, then it and its editors and writers had long gone to more down-at-heel quarters far away.

On this particular night the guards were especially vigilant. A small detachment of British infantrymen formed the outer ring – there had been bamboo knife-rest barricades set up on Queen's Road itself, and others with razor-wire trimmings established on the approaches from Wanchai and the Aberdeen Tunnel. Large blue signs propped up by sandbags ordered night-time motorists to extinguish their headlights and submit to searches and ID checks. A short line of cars waited: drivers were warned that they could spend some minutes waiting too, while a young infantryman from the London suburbs tried to work his way around the linguistic complexities involved in persuading a Cantonese driver to offer some proof of who he was and why he was abroad at this hour.

Beyond the lines of soldiers, and assigned specifically to the task of checking on any pedestrians who might be making for the eleven-storey building, was a detachment of ten men from the Hong Kong Supplementary Force. There were 3,000 such individuals now assigned to duties around the territory. They had been recruited in Britain in 1995 after the manning levels in the Royal Hong Kong Police had fallen to what was considered a dangerous low. According to the Kirby Inquiry's Report on the 1995 riots, those recruited for the HKSF 'are not men who had derived over-much benefit from their training, if indeed they undertook it at all',

and, moreover, 'were drawn generally from that seemingly bottomless pool of security employees who had, for one reason or another, failed to qualify for entry into any United Kingdom police force.' One newspaper, seeing them in action at a political rally a year before had called them 'louts', and compared them unfavourably to the 'B' Specials, Protestant bully-boys who had once been attached to the Royal Ulster Constabulary, called out to whack Catholic heads in times of trouble in and around Belfast.

The men of the HKSF, known generally as 'Suppers' and kitted out in dark blue serge tunics and battledress trousers, lounged against the Agency's walls. Each held a long truncheon and carried a gas-gun in a holster; from each belt dangled a tear-gas mask and every man wore a dark blue helmet, the visor down. On this occasion they were not carrying side-arms: these would only be drawn from the armouries at moments of extreme emergency. But both individually and collectively the men of the HKSF looked tough, and full of menace.

Behind them, standing actually at the Agency's iron-bound gate, were four regular police officers – their jungle-green uniforms crisp, their silver badges of rank glittering in the street lamps, their radios chattering and squawking with the noise of distant messaging. All were Chinese: the last Britons to take junior operational posts within the RHKP had been eased out the year before. Pressure from Peking, it was said. Senior officers were permitted to remain until retirement, though the Commissioner had by agreement been a post reserved for a Chinese since 1988. The only remaining Britons in senior posts were the Regional Commanders in Hong Kong Island and the New Territories, five of the District Commanders and eleven Divisional Commanders. There were no junior British officers other than in administration and training.

The men's uniforms had been changed at China's request too. The dark blue winter wear and the pale desert khaki of the summer strip had given way to a uniform that was chromatically consonant with that worn by the men of the People's Armed Police across the border, though the men of Hong Kong were distinguished by the immeasurably better cut of their tunics, by their possession of radios and badges

of rank, and by their caps, on which the old dragon-and-pearl icon of Hong Kong had been allowed to remain. The prefix 'Royal' had been officially dropped six months before: it would cease to be used in all official communications from midnight on the final day of June. The fact that the word was still in common unofficial usage stemmed partly from custom, partly from defiance.

At this time of night – it was shortly before five, and a faint stain of morning could be seen on the clouds looming over Mount Collinson – neither the police, nor the Suppers, nor the infantry had a great deal of work to do. Earlier, things had been quite active. The remains of a stolen sixteen-seat minibus still smouldered on its side in the roadway, the rubber of its tyres reduced to smoking white powder. Shards of glass and broken masonry littering the road were being kicked aimlessly into the gutters by soldiers. There were also dozens of empty gas cartridges, lying as testimony to the volleys that were fired some six hours before, when a mob had roared up from Wanchai, well on in drink, its members – all Cantonese, and probably part of the local Triad gangs – eager to get their hands on any of the Chinese mainland officials who had long since retreated behind the marble bastions of Agency protection.

At five-thirty, a careful observer would have noticed, there came a sudden increase in the volume and frequency of radio transmissions to and from the four police officers. Almost simultaneously the lieutenant in charge of the army platoon ordered the opening of one of the barricades; and within moments of that having been accomplished the iron blast doors at the front of the Agency were unhasped and opened wide. Then, over the brow of the low hill by the Ruttonjee Sanatorium, came a stream of police motorcycles and Land-Rovers, their blue lights flashing, their sirens uncannily silent. Four motorcycles, headlights blazing; then three, four, five white police cars – and then a lone black Mercedes, with darkened windows, flying two flags of the People's Republic from its front bumpers. Further police cars brought up the rear.

The convoy sped down the hill, through the chicanes. The army lieutenant turned towards the cars, and saluted. Beside the Agency the police vehicles braked to a sudden stop,

fanning out to afford still further protection while the Mercedes itself eased to a stop beside the gates. For a few seconds there was total silence, and nothing moved – not a man, not a car, not a light, not a door.

But then, like a snake flicking its tongue from above its fangs, a small Chinese man darted suddenly from inside the Agency and opened the rear door of the car. The Hong Kong Police moved forwards, perhaps to protect the recording of this scene from any inquisitive telephoto lens. All that could be glimpsed was the momentary passing from car to building of the type of blue cloth cap commonly worn by Chinese senior cadres and, for an instant, the grey-haired head of an elderly man. And then the car's door was slammed, and the car and escort vehicles started for base. the twin iron gates of the Agency were clanged shut, and one could hear bolts being rammed home, and keys twisted in the locks. The policemen stepped away, the Suppers commenced their lounging once again, and the men of the 2nd Battalion, The Queen's Regiment, shifted the barricades back into position.

A number of lights were snapped on in adjoining rooms on the building's eighth floor – a floor invariably reserved, according to Security Branch Intelligence, for the truly senior of their visitors. The events in Queen's Road East on that hot Saturday morning had seen the arrival, unnoticed by almost all, of the man who had just become known to the Foreign Office as the next Chief Executive of Hong Kong. Mr Mao had come down from Peking to take up his post a few days early. Now he was installed, and not a soul knew of it.

# THE MINISTRY OF FOREIGN AFFAIRS, PEKING

## MID-MORNING

Madame Zhang was a little late, her assistant said, and would Mr James like to wait in her office? The Reuters man, who had long since had his breakfast, agreed to tea, and watched

idly as the assistant unplugged the soft old cork from the vacuum flask and sloshed near-boiling water on to a layer of black leaves in a cracked mug. The leaves rose, forming an island of vegetation, through which the tea now had to be drunk. Strange, he mused, that the inventors of the drink can never make it properly. He waved away a cigarette from the cylindrical tin of fifty.

He was not entirely sure why he had been summoned. Zhang Xiaodi was the senior spokesman for Sino-European Bilateral Matters at the Foreign Ministry, had held her post for the past three years, and was popular with the five other Europeans – excluding the Tass, *Pravda* and *Izvestia* correspondents, who had their own briefing officer – who remained to work as journalists in Peking. (The clamp-down on the foreign press in 1993 had drastically reduced the number of Western news representatives resident in Peking, from more than ninety to less than twenty. The number of academics and students at Chinese universities and institutes had been similarly slashed, all in the name of limiting foreign influences on Chinese attitudes.)

Since Madame Zhang's given name *Xiao* meant 'little' and *Di* 'flower', they called her Daisy, and the man from Agence France Presse was reputed to have briefly enjoyed a near-liaison with her. Shortly after this it was made known that she had been divorced from a chemical engineer who, those who had met him at Great Hall cocktail parties reported, smelled strongly of green onions, and rarely shaved. She was still, however, known as Madame, and was generally thought of as untouchable.

But as to why her office had called to summon him, and him alone, Richard James did not know. He had to assume it had something to do with Hong Kong which, after all, was only three days away from repossession. The BBC had reported a fairly rough night, and the Reuters wire spoke of three deaths in a shooting incident at Tuen Mun. But there had been no suggestion of behaviour by the British, at least, that warranted criticism. So why this meeting? An appointment to be made? Not that of the Chief Executive, though: there had been a well-reported leak just the week before that it was likely to be David Lam, the Chairman of the Bank of North Asia, and matters had briefly stabilised once the

reports had gained wide enough currency. Lam, a rather colourless man who sat on the boards of a dozen of the colony's *hongs*,* and who belonged to all the right clubs and had all the proper connections, was the ideal choice. There could be no question of the Chinese attempting to veto that.

While Richard James, two years as the Reuters news agency man in China, and with just another one in Peking to go, pondered on all these matters, staring out on to the shadowless greys of the street beyond, the door opened quietly and Madame Zhang and one other man, in uniform, filtered in. He heard her, fortunately, and stood: he was startled to see that she was dressed in deep grey, and that she looked almost frumpish, and was not smiling. He decided not to refer to her as Daisy. She bade him sit down and followed suit. The uniformed man, who looked like a People's Liberation Army officer, did not.

'I hope they have given you tea. We are sorry to ask you to come here so early this morning. I shall now explain. This is an official meeting, but one the occurrence of which you will not report, Mr James.' She paused, and looked at him. He nodded.

'I have a brief statement to make to you, and I will then offer you some background guidance. You will not take notes. I will have no further explanation. There will be no questions. It is to be firmly understood that you will not report the sources of the following remarks, and that you will make no report of the contents of the remarks until thirteen hours, local time, today. I have to ask you if you understand these rules?' She looked up again.

'I accept them, Madame Zhang,' Richard James replied, embarrassed and puzzled by the formality.

'Are you using a tape recorder?' she asked, suddenly.

'No,' he said. But he took a small Sony from his pocket – it was switched off – and laid it on the table. The uniformed figure stepped out from the shadows and picked it up. 'It will be returned later,' the man said, stepping back into a dark corner of the room.

*The big trading companies such as Swires, Jardines, Hutchison, Inchcape, etc. Not to be confused with the 'Hong' of Hong Kong which means fragrant (Kong means harbour).

Madame Zhang cleared her throat, spitting into a brass pot beside the sofa. She put on a pair of dark-rimmed spectacles.

'This, then, is the text of the Statement. "The Hong Kong and Macau Affairs Office of the State Council of the People's Republic of China is pleased to announce the appointment of State Councillor Mao Ren-chin to the post of Chief Executive of the Special Administrative Region of Xianggang – Hong Kong – with effect from 1 July 1997. Mr Mao, who is seventy-four, presently advises the Council on legal and constitutional matters. He is a Hero of the Revolution, and has a distinguished career spanning many decades. The Foreign Ministry joins with the Hong Kong and Macau Affairs Office in offering Mr Mao its salutations for this most auspicious post, in which he will be aided nobly by all compatriots in the new S.A.R.' That is the end of the Statement.

'I now have a few words of guidance to add.' Madame Zhang spoke shakily. Richard thought she sounded nervous, almost frightened.

'It may come as a surprise for you to learn of Mr Mao's appointment.' Richard James nodded his assent, vigorously. 'I believe our Hong Kong compatriots had been expecting that Lin Zhou-ming* would be appointed. But after considerable thought it has been decided that it would be more appropriate to appoint a man who is distinguished throughout China, rather than a man who, however notable his achievements, is known principally for his work in and around your colony – or rather your former colony, as it will soon be. There are other considerations too. But it was felt that in the interests of a fuller dialogue between Beijing and the newly re-acquired Region, the appointee should have a direct line, if you will, to the State Council in the capital, as well as a presence in the Region itself. The custom for the last two decades has been to appoint a representative with strong Beijing connections to the Xinhua – the News Agency – office. It has also been the custom to select senior representatives holding similar qualifications to act as provincial governors. The Government of the People's Republic is thus

*The Chinese character which in the Cantonese dialect is pronounced *Lam* sounds like *Lin* when spoken in Madame Zhang's tongue, *putonghua*. Lin Zhou-ming is the same person as David Lam.

maintaining a tradition of governance of many years, and is extending it to cover the special situation in our newly regained region of Xianggang.'

Madame Zhang took off her spectacles and looked across at the correspondent. 'That is by way of background. I will have nothing further to say on this matter.' She rose.

Richard said: 'There are a number of questions,' but Madame Zhang waved him down.

'That is all I can say – really,' she replied, looking across at the soldier, who was readying himself to escort her from the room. 'You must understand. These are sensitive times.'

The soldier handed Richard his tape recorder, then stood at Madame Zhang's side and led her quickly out into the corridor. By the time Richard reached the door the passage was dark and empty, except for a cleaner who was aimlessly buffing the floor with a five-foot mop. Mustering his primitive Chinese he asked the woman if she had seen a soldier and a female cadre pass by a few seconds before, but the woman grunted and kept her face to the ground, pushing the dirt back and forth, grinding it still further into the cement.


# JIANGUOMENWAI, PEKING

## BEFORE NOON

Ten minutes later the correspondent was in the Embassy. He had asked the Press Secretary for an urgent and immediate meeting with Sir Peter MacDuff, the ambassador, and was not surprised to be shown upstairs and into the private office without delay. He related to the two men, and the Military Attaché, whom Sir Peter had invited, the gist of what he knew. He asked for some further information, some guidance.

There was a long and pregnant silence. The ambassador looked at his watch. It was fifteen minutes before noon, China summer time. He looked at the carpet, then at his Press Secretary, then at Richard. He cleared his throat.

'I cannot, of course, expect you to tell me how you heard this information?' he asked. Richard shook his head.

'Of course. I will draw my own conclusions. I will assume for the purpose of what I now have to say that it came as a secret briefing from an official of the Foreign Ministry. I don't expect you to confirm or deny this. But we are all well aware that some departments in the Ministry take a view somewhat at variance with the official one. I will expand on this in a moment or two.

'What I have to say first – indeed, everything I will say to you now – is completely and utterly off the record. Is that understood? I mean, seriously understood?'

Richard nodded, adding, for posterity and formality, 'Yes, of course, Sir Peter.'

'Right. I'm going to have to speak to London about this – though it looks as if I'll not get any sort of sensible answer before you file your piece. And on this point I've got to be candid with you – I'd be very much obliged if you'd delay filing this for another couple of hours. Perhaps you'd tell me whether you're able to at the end of what I have to say. I know I'm in no position to ask. But there are considerations – lives at stake, basically. A delay would be helpful.

'But whatever. This appointment is something we've known of for about three days. That an appointment might be made along these general lines is something we have known for almost a year, and which we have lobbied hard to reverse. In vain, seemingly. I am not permitted to tell you exactly how we heard first. If I say that we are well connected in Washington, and that the new President, Mr Benson, has trenchant views on the situation in this corner of the world, you might understand. If in addition I say Cheltenham, and if I remind you that we have a station in Hong Kong at Chung Hom Kok, then perhaps you can draw your own conclusions. But anyway – we heard, and we confronted the Chinese Ambassador in London with what we knew.

'You can imagine what we said. Direct contravention of the letter and the spirit of the 1984 Declaration, the 1991 Agreement, and the 1993 Letter. A move likely to cause serious social disorder. A move which, if known about before the handover, when getting out might be possible, would cause panic. And all kinds of other implications. We told Ambassador Li how we felt about it, in no uncertain terms.

33

'We were given a formal reply about ten hours ago. This confirmed what GCHQ and the Americans had said. It also went on to say that in view of the probability of social disorder in the territory if the announcement was made before the moment of handover, no announcement would be made until the moment of the change of sovereignty itself, on Monday night.

'Her Majesty's Government then took certain prudent and precautionary measures, including one that I will only tell you as background and which you must absolutely not report.' He looked pointedly at Richard.

The Reuters man winced. 'I think you know the rules, sir. If you tell me, I must report it. All I can do is accept what you say as unattributable. That's how it is, I'm afraid.'

'Well, in that case I can't tell you what the precaution might be; you will have to speculate. I suppose it is more a matter for the history books, anyway.

'I was formally informed of these decisions about seven hours ago. So was Sir John Courtenay. So was General Harbinson. So were our embassies in Washington and at the UN.

'Frankly, I had expected the Chinese side to stick by their agreement not to make any announcement. But now they appear, by their briefing of you, to have broken that agreement. They have, of course, sought to distance themselves from the briefing by winning your assurance of confidentiality and have informed you as a representative of Reuters. I will have to inform the government, and steps will have to be taken. If you report this now, it will have the most severe consequences for the people of Hong Kong. That is all I can say on that matter.'

Richard looked pained. 'Once again, sir, I know you know the rules. Of course I will have to report what I've been told, and on time. That's my job. Of course I know it is yours to try to persuade me otherwise. But we have different tasks here. You have to deal with trouble. I just have to report it. And anyway – you get a knighthood and a fancy house for that sort of thing.' He got on well enough with Sir Peter to be able to say so, though on this occasion, with the ambassador in what seemed the grimmest of tempers, he thought he might be sailing close to the winds. The Press Secretary, a rather weak-chinned man named Treadwell, stepped forward in protest. Sir Peter waved him back.

'You're right, to an extent. But I want you to consider one other matter – something the Sinologists will make much of in the next few days. And that is what I was talking about at the start of this lecture – *just why did they choose to announce it?*

'It is difficult for me to guess, since you won't tell me who told you. But let me suppose, as I did at the start, that it came from a branch of the Foreign Ministry. Let me suppose that this particular branch is in some way closely connected with the army. There might have been some army involvement in your briefing – yes?'

Richard said nothing, and tried to look as impassive as a poker player with a single pair and a great deal in the pot.

'Be that as it may. One has to begin with the single presumption that there is going to be one hell of a lot of trouble in Hong Kong as a result of this move. The Cantonese will be furious, blindly furious, at being let down this way. By tonight there'll be riots the like of which you've never seen before. I expect that within half an hour of your bulletin going out on the radio, there'll be a dozen people dead.

'Now who will those people be? If the announcement was kept until next Tuesday, then the whole thing is a matter for the Chinese alone. *They'll* have to clean up. If anyone tries to play the heavy-handed law enforcement card, it's the Chinese.

'But now, with the statement coming out on Saturday, who'll be there to take the brunt of it all? Right – *we will be.* Who have we got down there – a battalion of infantry, some Gurkhas, some reservists, the Suppers, the police? They'll be in the middle. They'll be firing the gas grenades. They'll be smashing in a few heads. And if the mob gets angry at anyone – who'll they be getting angry at? Why – *us*, of course. And that'll give the Chinese a bit of breathing space. Not much, mind you. But for a moment or two, a day or so, the British colonialists will be the villains, and the Chinese won't be. Even though they really are the villains – appointing a northern Chinese to run Hong Kong! They're just asking for trouble.

'And when I say trouble, I mean real trouble. I mean civil war type trouble. This is really big stuff. You know how angry the Cantonese are, how vicious they can get. Well, this

kind of a decision is going to whip them up – and not just in Canton. They'll be angry in Canton and Xiamen and Guilin and Macau and Kunming. Everywhere in the south, they'll be angry and anti-north. It really has the makings of major trouble.

'So someone, some branch within the Foreign Ministry is wanting to head it off. Someone – I'm still assuming you were told about this by the Ministry, and probably by that little girl, Daisy Zhang or whatever you call her – someone wants the British to be blamed, not the Chinese. Someone, in other words, realises what's going to happen. Someone, in other words, is a pragmatist.

'And if there's war, it is going to be pragmatists against the dogmatists. So you can see the splits developing. Right under their very noses. Right here in a senior ministry. And you can bet they leaked it to you to show you that there was a split. After all they could have simply put out a statement over Xinhua. No need for anyone to be personally involved doing it that way. So ask yourself for a moment why they didn't.

'I only wish you'd tell me if there was a soldier present. I wish you'd give me some idea of which one, so I can get some idea of where the army stands on this? Not that it would tell me much. It'd just be a hint.'

But Richard remained mute. He looked at his watch. It was just after noon. He had to leave, and he had to file.

And so Sir Peter showed him out, promising him there'd be no hard feelings about the meeting. 'Only just think how well you'd have been treated if I were Chinese. But here I am showing you out – nearly even offered you a glass of sherry. If I were a Chinese official asking one of your Xinhua colleagues for information, and he refused, it'd be round the back with a bullet in the neck, don't you think?'

Back in the empty office Richard James wrote his story. He switched on his computer terminal, punched in his access code, and typed a crisp and effortless 300 words, as he had done countless times before in a career that had already covered eight countries. He slugged it for the urgent attention of the Foreign Duty Editor in London:

PROMELUNSKY FOREIGN

EXJAMESPEKING 280350z note embargo 280400z strict

FLASH FIRST PARA

In a surprise move the Chinese government today appointed the Long March veteran Mao Ren-chin to be the first Chief Executive of Hong Kong, which passes into mainland control on Monday night.

ENDFLASH PARA RESUME

Mr Mao's appointment, made known through highly placed sources in the Chinese capital, is expected to provoke a serious adverse reaction in Hong Kong. The British government, which has known about the appointment for the past three days, is said to be taking 'prudent and precautionary steps' to limit any consequential disturbances in the colony. There have been serious anti-British and anti-Communist demonstrations and riots in the past week.

Mr Mao, who is seventy-four, comes from Dalian city, in southern Manchuria. A State Councillor and adviser to the Chinese leadership on legal and constitutional affairs, he is reputed to have assumed a strong stance against students involved in the various anti-corruption and pro-liberty movements in China in the last ten years. He is known to have been personally behind the public execution of the so-called 'Shanghai Six' after the Shanghai University disturbances of 1995. (++NB TO PIX EDITOR: MAO SEEN IN FRONT ROW OF EXECUTION AUDIENCE ON 13 AUGUST 95 REUTERS STAFF PICTURES AVAILABLE++)

Hong Kong had expected the popular 53-year-old North Asia Bank chief David Lam to be appointed as first Chief Executive. Mr Lam is not only well liked and respected in Hong Kong, but has the ear of the Chinese ruling élite. He is Cantonese – which Mr Mao is not. The 1984 Joint Declaration signed by the British and Chinese leaders spoke of the need to appoint the territory's Chief Executive 'from within the local community', and, until today, it had been assumed that the Peking government would stick to this undertaking. The British government is expected to make its feeling known to the Chinese ambassador in London later today.+++

SVCMELUNSKY +++Analysis piece follows in fifteen minutes. Above should do for the flash+++

RGDS JAMES PEKING

Richard looked over the piece, tinkered with it briefly, then set his machine into XMIT mode. He looked at the clock. It was ten minutes to one. Outside the sky was leaden. The streets were empty, except for a few cyclists and the occasional passing bus. Four members of the People's Armed Police, assigned to guard the entrance to the compound, stood at attention by the gate. The clock's second hand swept up to mark nine minutes before one, China summer time – nine minutes before four in the morning, Greenwich Mean Time, nine minutes before noon, Hong Kong. Richard pressed the green transmit message key.

A box flashed onto the screen, with a dial indicating how long it took the story to be sent, and to arrive, checked for transmission errors, on Jacob Melunsky's desk. Four seconds, the dial said.

And nine minutes after that the message was dispatched around the world. Down in the Hong Kong Reuters office, over in the London offices of a dozen newspapers, across in New York, and down in Sydney, the same clangour of ten bells would announce the arrival of a major story. It arrived back in Peking, too, with barely a word changed:

FLASH FLASH FLASH+++0400gmt 28 June
Mao Named First Chinese Hong Kong Governor
By Richard James, Peking, Saturday 28 June
In a surprise move the Chinese government today . . .

Richard James sat back in his chair and lit a cigarette. He inhaled one long, deep breath. And now, he said to himself, all hell breaks out.

## QUEEN'S ROAD, HONG KONG
### MID-AFTERNOON

Twenty of the protected two-ton Bedford trucks, dark blue, with their steel grilles clicked down over all the windows, had been deployed in the rain down every side-street by two o'clock, after urgent orders had been transmitted from

Police Headquarters in North Wanchai. Four hundred constables from the regular police and 200 additional Suppers, issued with side arms and, in a few cases, with automatic rifles, were at the ready. Two police helicopters, flying high, were overhead. The windows of the New China News Agency were shuttered, and the doors were firmly closed.

The Reuters dispatch had been broadcast first by the Chinese-language pirate commercial station, the Catholic-Church-backed Radio Freedom, *Chi Yao Ding Toi*, at three minutes past twelve. By half past the hour – by which time even the government-controlled radio and TV stations were (somewhat reluctantly, it was later said) issuing statements about Mao's appointment – small crowds were out on the streets. The Xinhua office in Sha Tin, which was not well guarded, had been briefly attacked by a pair of young men wielding crowbars and choppers. The doors of the offices of the Ever Light Company in Yuen Long, a trading concern with long-established connections across the frontier, were spattered with black paint. The police and army were fully expecting trouble directed at any mainland Chinese institution – the New China News Agency being a natural prime target – and they believed themselves to be well prepared.

The speed and efficiency of the organisation of the subsequent vocal and violent opposition to Mao's appointment led to the assumption by police intelligence – a correct assumption, as it later turned out – that it was principally the work of Hong Kong's major Triad gangs, acting in concert.

Before relating the particular effects of the Triad-led disturbances in the territory during the closing days of British rule, it is perhaps appropriate to offer some brief background information.

For the previous two years, ever since the signing of the so-called Warwick Accord in April 1995 between the Sun Yee On and the 14K gangs after their meeting at the Warwick Hotel on Cheung Chau Island, the Triads had emerged as a powerful political force – the only powerful political force, in fact – in the territory. The various democratic organisations that had been founded with such optimism in the early part of the decade had all foundered,

their early antipathy to China becoming ever more muted, their popular support in consequence becoming ever more limited. The only groups who were consistently regarded by the ordinary working-class Hong Kong Chinese as having both the muscle and the willpower to stand up for the entre-preneurial 'rights' of the Hong Kong public, and to be stand-ing firmly against the sombre tenets of Marx and Mao were, as it happened, utterly illegal: this network of rigidly organ-ised and historically romanticised gangs of criminals, loan sharks, drug-peddlers and racketeers, who had been a run-ning sore on the face of most Chinese communities around the world for many decades, but who had only achieved a degree of cohesion, and the consequent political muscle, here in Hong Kong.

Although for the previous half century all of the Triad societies in Hong Kong had directed their individual ener-gies towards crime (while at the same time enjoying the same kind of cosy, seemingly respectable relationship with slum society as was projected by the Sicilian Mafia) their leader-ship had reason to remember that their roots had little to do with thievery and pimping. The very name, Triad, is a sem-antic contraction of the organisation's original title, *The Heaven and Earth League* – in Chinese an ideographic trinity forged of the characters for words pronounced in Cantonese as *San, Ho* and *Hui* and standing for heaven, earth and man. And the original purpose of the group thus gilded was – two centuries ago – the extirpation of the hated Manchus, the barbarous foreigners who had ruled China since 1644.

Such a grouping had, of necessity, to be utterly secret; the numerous clones met in covens: their members were the subject of witchhunts and victims of terrible revenge. The political ambitions of the League within China were not to be realised until the revolution of 1912; and those of its brother organisations continued long after. The 14K, which was to flourish quite openly (though illegally) in Hong Kong until the end of British rule, had been established in Canton City as a nakedly political operation, aimed at consolidating popular support behind the Kuomintang of Chiang Kai-shek, and against the growing power of Mao Tse-tung. It was only when the members of 14K realised they had failed in this particular aim (Chiang having being forced by the over-

whelming military superiority of Mao to run to Taiwan and establish his nationalist government there) that the gang moved down from Canton to Hong Kong and, preserving their secrecy, their rituals and their symbols, started on the more infamously predatory side of their career.

A survey early in 1996 showed there were some forty-three Triad societies at work in Hong Kong. This was well down from the fifty-four whose existence was acknowledged by a police study in 1991 – an indication, the police then concluded erroneously, that they were 'winning the war' against what they considered to be the most nefarious of organisations. But rather than 'winning' any war, the police – who years before had managed not only to infiltrate the Triads, but who had then actually been a singularly corrupt extension of them – were becoming progressively less and less competent to understand them, or even to find them. Police informers within the gangs were brutally dealt with: one such young man who was found dead in an alley in Sham Shui Po in the late summer of 1995, after the signing of the Accord, had been skinned and scalped. A deafening silence thereafter protected the organisations from the police. The Accord, which involved the signing of blood oaths by some thirty-eight of the major groups, similarly protected most of the gangs (for they had been, of course, arch-rivals) from each other.

The hierarchy within any of the major Triads – the Sun Yee On, the Wo Sing Wo, the Won On Lok, the Big Circle Boys, the 14K, the Four Seas, the Bamboo Union – is invariably the same. The leading members are given titles that are both evocative and, hinting to many foreigners at the strangeness of Chinese society, numerical. The clan chief is known as the Dragon Head or, in this more familiar terminology of the streets, the 489. Beneath him is the Second Marshal, the 438. Below him in status, the Red Pole, Number 426 – the man to whom is allotted the disagreeable tasks of skinning and scalping and meting out other punishments for members' acts of malfeasance, treachery, or worse. And then the White Paper Fan, 419, and the Straw Sandal, 432 (who is a less than amiable individual usually involved in protection rackets). Finally come the legions of junior members known as the 49 Boys who are recruited direct from school, and who

are on probation awaiting their ritual tattooing, their granting of passwords and all the rest of the paraphernalia that goes with the *lam dang long*, the so-called *hanging of the blue lantern*, the youngsters' formal initiation into the tribe.

The numbers of Triad members grew almost exponentially following the signing of the Warwick Accord. Under this agreement all of the individual 'regiments' in the Triad pantheon would remain, recruiting where they were best known, carrying out their own internal disciplinary functions, indulging in the relatively small-scale activities that kept their income streams flowing healthily. The individual regiments would, however, cease all competition between one another, and borders for the individual gangs' territories were rigidly set by the rulings of an official Boundary Commission. (The head of this Commission, a 426 in the Sun Yee On named Mr Law, had previously worked as an Assistant Registration Officer in the Constitutional and Electoral Affairs Division of the Government Secretariat, and thus had some experience in these matters. Police intelligence concluded that he did not give any obvious favours to his own gang, which in any case had innumerable territorial claims in most of the major urban areas and housing estates.)

In addition to these arrangements for internal regimental management, the Accord resulted in the promotion of a senior hierarchy of members who would coordinate the political activities of all of the membership. This new leadership, well aware of the fate that would befall identified members once the mainland Chinese had established their rule, remained shadowy indeed. Few names have ever been credibly reported. British intelligence was in this respect somewhat more accurate and reliable than that provided by the Hong Kong Police Special Branch, who were caught wrong-footed on many of the Triad developments after the signing of the Accord. The one name that emerged was that of one Peter Heung Way Yeung, who had as his cover job that of solicitor's clerk in a firm of Kowloon tax lawyers. Mr Heung is thought to have been appointed the 'Super 489', with overall political authority over the Hong Kong Triad membership, with some limited authority to define policy and, in an emergency, to order the deployment of regiment members.

By the beginning of 1997 it was thought that 245,000 men and boys aged sixteen and over had been recruited into the forty-three known Triad gangs. The 14K was still the most prominent, with an estimated membership of 47,000, and an annual income in excess of $1.8 billion. The total amount of money taken in by the various illegal organisations in 1996, the last year for which reliable figures are known, was $4.7 billion.

One further factor needs to be explained. In the immediate aftermath of the signing of the Warwick Accord Mr Heung and a number of his most politically adroit lieutenants sought a meeting in Shenzhen City, immediately across the border fence, with senior officials in the Guangdong Provincial Administration. In particular they had asked for an interview with W. Y. Yip, the Administration's political officer, to see if some measure of cooperation might be achieved once the British authorities had vacated the territory of Hong Kong. It was assumed that the enthusiasm for corruption found among middle levels of the Chinese bureaucracy would enable such an alliance – informal or otherwise – to be founded. But in the event Mr Heung's group was rebuffed. No meeting ever took place, and radio intercepts and wiretaps on both sides of the border suggest that any desire for union or association remained moribund. Observers in Hong Kong and London have long regarded this as puzzling; although one possibility, that the Cantonese-speaking officials who were approached by the Heung team were fearful of having their complicity discovered by those Peking-based cadres who were assigned to the Guangdong Administrative Service, was thought to provide a reasonable explanation.

It is against this complicated background that the involvement of the Triads in the final days of Hong Kong's British administration needs to be regarded.

News of the appointment of Mao was first given to Peter Heung at 1215, at his headquarters on the penthouse floor of a new commercial building at 230 Shanghai Street, Kowloon. A number of his 49 Boys had heard the broadcast on

the Catholic station, and had relayed it back through their various Straw Sandals. Heung, knowing the extent of the wiretaps on his phones and radio intercepts on his mobile phones, sent alarm messages, in a specially developed code, to his deputies by fax. The first messages were sent at 1255, and were dispatched to gang deputies in Aberdeen, Shek O, Wanchai, Kennedy Town, Western, Causeway Bay and to that very small group in Repulse Bay on the South Side of Hong Kong Island.

This signal, which was duly intercepted by Special Branch engineers working at the facsimile switching centre in Causeway Bay, said simply, and in Chinese characters, DRAGON MOUTH EIGHT. There was no great difficulty to the decoding: the phrase DRAGON MOUTH clearly signified the headquarters of the New China News Agency; and EIGHT was, in line with the Thai linguistic conceit of adding six to everything, an indication that something would happen there either at two, or in two hours.

The Branch Senior Duty Analyst concluded that, given the logistical difficulty that various Second Marshals might have of rounding up significant numbers of members in just sixty-five minutes, the number related to two hours. A signal marked Most Immediate was thus sent to the Police Operations Room, the HQ Police Tactical Unit (Fan Ling), the HQ Supplementary Force (Hong Kong Island) and to the Royal Hong Kong Regiment's barracks at Happy Valley, where a number of regular soldiers from 3 Queen's were billeted, advising them of the probability of a confrontation near the New China News Agency on Queen's Road East at 3 p.m. Commanders were then advised by secure telephone that there could well be serious violence, and that all available defensive means should be taken to minimise it.

A subsequent directive to the Commander British Forces and the Police Commissioner, marked 'For Your Eyes Only' and sent from the Political Adviser's Office at Government House, timed at 1330 local, underlined the need for the police, the supplementary force members and all army units, both local Volunteers and the British garrison, to maintain discipline and to exercise restraint.

'There is the possibility,' the directive concluded, 'that this news has been deliberately leaked in Peking by factions,

presently unknown to us, who would not react unfavourably to the British and colonial disciplined services becoming intimately involved in last-minute disturbances. It is our desire to keep our involvement in any civil disorder problems to a minimum.

'However, in view of the potential new dangers to life and property, and in view of the possible instability and questionable loyalty of the RHKP in dealing with this particular problem, and in view of possible discipline problems within the HKSF, two army battalions equipped for civil order work, 1KOSB and 2 Para, which are presently standing by at the airfield at Bandar Seri Begawan, Brunei, can be made available to you at short notice. It is our hope that deployment of additional forces will not prove necessary. It cannot, however, be impressed upon unit commanders too firmly that the necessity to protect key personnel and buildings in these final few hours of British Administration remains paramount.'

Helicopters, flying low because of heavy clouds and mist, reported the first significant gatherings of crowds near the Aberdeen Tunnel and in Central District, and then of a very large crowd – of as many as 3,000 people – massing on Hennessey Road, Wanchai, and still growing. Police spotters on the roofs of nearby buildings said most were young men, often with red bands tied around their foreheads. Many pushed or pulled small handcarts on which were piled bottles – probably Molotov cocktails – and fragments of paving stone. The carts, of a type well known for their use in making local deliveries, appeared to have been stored, awaiting such a moment. A few banners were in evidence, all of them outspokenly condemning the mainland Chinese. These, too, appeared to have been prepared beforehand: none specified the appointment of Mao as central to the popular disquiet. The organisation of the coming riot – for there could be no doubt that the confrontation would result in rioting – was clearly most sophisticated.

The police and Supplementary Force units took up their positions around the NCNA building. Three companies of soldiers were held in reserve, waiting for the Governor's

permission before they could be called in formally to assist the civil power in the suppression of a riot. On many occasions in the past two years such sanction had been given: there seemed little likelihood it would be withheld today, and so the company commanders had already broken out the tear gas and the live ammunition, and the soldiers were waiting fully equipped to do battle.

Advance picquets of police across the approach roads confronted the crowds of demonstrators as they came within a quarter of a mile of their target. Officers with megaphones formally warned them, in English and Cantonese, that they were breaking the law, specifically the Public Order Act, and that they should cease their illegal assembly and disperse quietly. The warnings had little effect. By 3 p.m. a crowd of men estimated to number 6,000 had converged on the scene: 4,000 had come up Morrison Hill Road from Wanchai, 800 had spilled out from the tunnel entrance and were descending the flyover exit ramps, and a further 1,000 were streaming down Stubbs Road and along Queen's Road.

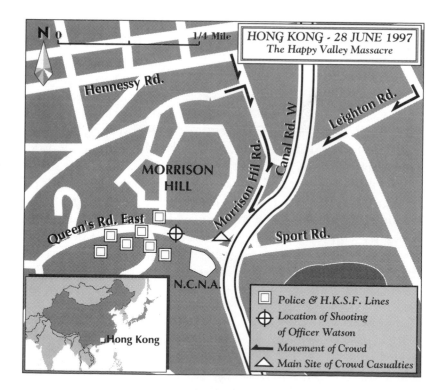

The police and Supplementary Force units, numbering no more than 600 armed men, had to face in three directions an angry crowd that outnumbered them by ten to one. The Hong Kong Island Regional Commander, George Clovis, a man widely known for his trenchant views and his bushy moustaches, was to say later that it would be difficult to heed the Political Adviser's warning about the need to keep use of force to a minimum.

'This was a huge Triad-organised mob that was bent, quite simply, on sacking the news agency and on tracking down Mr Mao, whom they had good reason to believe was inside the building. Our use of minimum force, in compliance with the advice of a Foreign Office official who had little experience in operational matters, would only have served to frustrate and delay the efforts of the mob.

'I believed at the time and still believe today* that to delay and frustrate a mob organised by Mr Heung's group would have enraged them to such an extent that there would have been many casualties among the disciplined forces guarding the building.

'Accordingly, I instructed the individual force commanders to make use of such means as they deemed necessary to protect the building and its occupants, and to protect the force members themselves; and I further requested that the regular army would be deployed only in the event that the building was itself under direct threat. I felt, in short, that we would handle matters satisfactorily providing we were permitted to employ proper firepower.

'I regarded any political consequences of our success in handling this temporary emergency as being of secondary importance, compared with my immediate need to protect life and limb. Besides, it was clear that any political considerations for the British side would inevitably be limited by time: at the moment of the outbreak of violence outside the NCNA on the

*Commander Clovis's remarks were part of a deposition made before the All-Party Parliamentary Committee Inquiry into the circumstances surrounding the final handover of Hong Kong and related developments in south China, and were published in the Committee's final report (Cmnd 5611, October 1997, HMSO).

Saturday Britain had just fifty-seven hours' of tenure remaining. So my decision to use deadly force was, in my view, correct.'

Strong popular support for Mr Clovis was expressed in Britain at the time of the Parliamentary Inquiry, and no vote of censure for his conduct was thought necessary. John Wildways, a Conservative Member of Parliament who had not sat on the Committee, remarked that 'We made a mistake with General Dyer. We weren't going to make the same mistake again.'

By the time the three mobs had assembled, the rain that had started the day had eased and the weather was warm and misty. 'Good tear-gas weather,' as police were wont to say. Accordingly, tear-gas launchers mounted on Land-Rovers, and Supplementary Force officers armed with gas guns, were pushed to the front of the defensive lines. Loud-hailer announcements exhorted the crowds to disperse, but were shouted down.

A number of speakers – young, vocal, well-educated – then began to harangue the 'colonial forces' for conspiring, as they put it, to prevent the crowds of Hong Kong people 'making clear their feelings about having a Communist from Peking' as their new governor. With each of a series of emotive phrases, the speakers began to whip the mood of the mob into one of extraordinary anger, and experienced police officers were later to say they had rarely witnessed such passion among any group of the Hong Kong citizenry. The mood during the pro-communist riots of 1967 seemed muted, compared with the fury that was building on this Saturday afternoon.

'There was a feeling of bitter desperation,' one of Clovis's junior officers told the inquiry. 'I had seen anger before – anger at the British, at the local government, over building projects, over a variety of decisions announced since the Joint Declaration. But the mobs' attitudes and actions had always had a sort of Confucian respectability to them – rather as if this was the crowd's duty to show the govern-

ment the error of its ways. This was something very, very different. It was naked fury.'

The first missiles began to rain down on police lines at 3.50 p.m. – bricks, paving stones, pieces of iron, marbles, ball-bearings fired from catapults. All lines held until 4 p.m., when the first of a wave of petrol bombs was launched – huge numbers of bombs, coming from all three crowds, exploding with near simultaneity, and causing severe disruptions. Clovis ordered a massive cannonade of tear gas, and during the first half hour of the confrontation more than 400 canisters of gas were fired into the crowd or lobbed behind it with grenade launchers to cause maximum confusion.

But the gas essentially failed to move the mob – particularly the Wanchai crowd which, according to helicopter estimates, had grown to some 5,000 by 4 p.m. And the missile batteries increased furiously, with wave after wave of axe-heads, iron bars, chunks of concrete and glass spikes rained down on the men. By 4.10 p.m. some thirty-one police and Supplementary Force members had been injured; and it was at 4.12 p.m., according to later reports, that the first indication came of the employment of firearms by the rioters – with the corollary that some firmer action was going to have to be taken.

In this incident a Special Supplementary Officer, Patrick Watson, attached to 'B' platoon, 3rd HKSF, was hit in the chest by a 9 mm bullet and died almost immediately. The reaction from within the Force was immediate. Their commander, John Oakes, demanded through the police senior officer on site, who was the District Officer (Eastern District), that his men be permitted to use live ammunition to repulse further attacks. This police officer, who was later to report noticing some reluctance on the part of the younger Chinese recruits to be involved in a serious confrontation with the rioters, supposed that a wholly British-manned unit would have, as he stated later, 'more fire in its belly', and would probably deal positively with the disturbance. He then gave immediate assent to the request, as he had the notional authority to do, and as a matter of record and courtesy passed his decision up the line to Commander Clovis.

The shootings that occurred as a direct consequence of this District Officer's explicit instruction can be regarded,

with the benefit of today's hindsight, as the true beginning of the wave of violence that was to engulf China for the following years. If not exactly the first shot of China's still continuing civil war, it was certainly the first exchange of fire of any consequence, and one that precipitated a series of actions, political, diplomatic and military, that have brought China and its neighbours to their present parlous state.

Because of the enormity of the consequences of his action, the District Officer himself, who is married to a Hong Kong Chinese woman, has never been officially named. But records published at the time identify the DO (Eastern) as a Mr Christopher Green; and a Mr Green of the same age and background is now known to be working as a police adviser to a former British colonial possession in West Africa.

Immediately upon receipt of the order – some accounts suggest some minutes before its receipt – men of 'B' platoon opened fire on the mob in Morrison Hill Road with their automatic rifles. Ten men of this platoon fired continuously, reloading several times; and they were joined by men of 'C' and 'D' platoons shortly thereafter.

In all, over a period of the eight minutes between 4.15 p.m. and 4.23 p.m., some 431 rounds of high-velocity ammunition were fired directly into the crowd. Although the firearms training of the Supplementary force was limited, at best, the concentration of fire and the enormous size of the crowd which retreated in panic down a narrow road dictated the very considerable scale of casualties. A total of 102 males, many of them little more than schoolchildren, were shot dead; a further 240 were injured – some badly burned after a trolley-load of petrol bombs was hit and caught fire. Almost all the casualties, save for those hit in the very opening moments of the firing, were shot in the back.

By 4.25 p.m., when all shooting had stopped, the streets in the immediate vicinity of the NCNA building were cleared, though Morrison Hill Road itself was the scene of terrible carnage. Scores of bodies lay where they had fallen, and the pitiful cries of the wounded, dragging themselves to shelter, were especially affecting.

The Supplementary Force members were ordered not to take part in clearing-up operations, but were to remain guarding the NCNA from a now much-diminished threat of

attack. Heavily armed police, who summoned dozens of first-aid units to the scene, moved cautiously down into Wanchai, sealing off roads as they did so, and taking care of survivors as best they could. The British Army remained scrupulously in the background, the battalion commander reasoning that members of the Chinese population 'would not welcome the sight of any more white faces,' as he put it, 'because of what we are now going to be accused of having done.'

## WEST KOWLOON

### EVENING

The Colonel's decision was founded on a shrewd judgement but one that was to prove, mercifully for the British, somewhat shortsighted. Later that night, as renewed rain lashed down on the territory, the leaders of the united Triad organisations met in the Shanghai Road offices of Mr Heung, to review the situation. They all, with a solemnity and concern that others might find uncharacteristic of loan sharks and drug dealers, professed themselves stunned by the enormity of the tragedy. They seemed particularly puzzled that the British, who now had little more than two days of administrative tenure left to run, would commit so grave a tactical error. 'They seem to be siding with Beijing,' was a remark heard and echoed many times. 'They feel obliged to protect this Mao, and are willing to kill large numbers of us to do so. What a terrible end to their rule here. What strange ways they have of saying farewell.'

But Peter Heung, their supreme leader, took a different view, one which coincided, not entirely unexpectedly, with the view being taken during similar analysis sessions held late that evening at Government House, at Police Headquarters and, over pre-lunch sherries, across in Downing Street in London. It was a degree of insight and foresight that showed just why the Warwick Accord signatories had named him as their principal spokesman and policymaker.

'The events of this afternoon,' he told his brother office-holders in carefully measured tones, 'were indeed tragic.

51

The scale of the killing appears to have been extraordinary. At the time the figures were not fully known; it was thought that more than 80 bodies had been recovered, and the local hospitals had accounted for 156 living casualties. The total may have exceeded the casualty figures from the Tienanmen Square incident of 1989, and of the Wuhan People's Park incident of 1993. There will no doubt, be hostile commentaries from Beijing, and I have to assume there may even be an offer from the Chinese to bring troops or People's Armed Police into the territory before the handover, to protect the citizens from the British.

'But my belief is that all this has been contrived by the mainland government – or at least by sections of the Chinese government – with two principal aims. First, they want to blacken the names of the British just as they are leaving, to ensure that international opinion reacts positively to the Chinese takeover. They want to have the British leave with the reputation of imperialists, with all that that implies. And second, they want to divert public hostility away from themselves. For just remember why we organised the marches this morning. Who were we opposing? Was it the British? No, it was not. Was it the Hong Kong Government? No, it was not. It was China – the mainland Chinese. They had broken the agreement. They had decided to appoint this old communist to rule over us. So we decided to get our people out on the streets to show them how we felt.

'Now if we had only learned of Mao's appointment on Tuesday, when we were probably expected to, we would have done the same thing – made a protest – but we would be up against the Chinese authorities. *They* would have been guarding the NCNA or Government House, or wherever Mao chose as his headquarters. But in fact, as we all now know, we learned of his appointment three days early. And that being the case, we had to deal with the *local* authorities, the colonial authorities, who were bound by duty to guard the premises of the Chinese.

'Now, under ordinary circumstances, if only the police and the British were on the streets, matters might have ended peacefully. There would have been a riot. They would have operated with a lot of gas, a lot of arrests, and everything would be over. We would have made our point. The tele-

vision would have covered it. The Chinese would be condemned for that they had done, for how they had broken their word, and that would be that.

'But instead we had these part-time soldiers – a lot of scum, recruited from the worst parts of Britain, men who wouldn't care how many of us they shot. And they reacted badly, and fired at us. So we had a massacre – done by the British. So now we all hate the British again, and we've forgotten that it's the Chinese who caused it all!

'So whoever leaked that story to the press this morning in Beijing was acting very shrewdly. It was a clever move. It was one that worked exactly as they had wanted. We've now got to think more cautiously about our next response. We've played into their hands once. We mustn't be caught like this again. We made a mistake, Brothers – next time, we'll be more clever.'

## GOVERNMENT HOUSE

### EVENING

The Emergency Committee convened at 7 p.m., in the main conference room on the ground floor. As throughout most of the mansion, evidence of impending departure was all around: paintings had been taken down from walls, tea-chests filled with books lay everywhere, much of the non-essential furniture was covered with dustcloths. But Government House continued to function with decorous efficiency. Richard Adaire was on hand beneath the *porte-cochère* to meet the individual participants: General Harbinson; Brigadier Tomsett; the Police Commissioner Sir K. H. Poon; the Director of Special Branch Leung Ping-lok; the Information Services Director Mary Chung; the Political Adviser Robin Moore; and a representative from Composite Signals Organisation, who was, as usual, unnamed. The seven arranged themselves around the conference table; they stood when Sir John arrived shortly after 7.15 p.m.

The meeting was brief. It opened with a discussion of the casualties that had been tallied on both sides: the civilian

death toll was now known to have been finalised at 102; there was one known death among the KHSF, Patrick Watson from Toxteth, Liverpool; and a further twelve casualties caused by fire bombs and a single pipe bomb which exploded near the picquet outside the Sikh gurdwara on Queen's Road.

Commissioner Poon, who had overall responsibility for civil order in the territory, expressed his formal regret for what he called the 'mishandling' of the situation. He did not name the District Officer (Eastern) for giving permission for the Supplementary Force platoons to open fire; but in his defence he noted that the officer was unaware that one of the platoons had taken a casualty, and that the mood of the men could be fairly described as 'vengeful'. He accepted that Commander Clovis, a man of much experience in colonial police conduct, was only told of the permission after the fact; and that the Commander had informed him that, had he been asked for permission, rather than presented with a *fait accompli*, he might have been reluctant to give it.

'Rather shutting the door after the horse has bolted, don't you think, Commissioner?' said Sir John. 'There's not a great deal of point in justifying what has happened, or analysing the events on the ground. What's happened has happened. We've got to work out what to do next.'

The discussion that followed considered various possibilities. Central to the options was the fact that two fully equipped army battalions were presently waiting for orders at the Brunei international airport. They could be brought in at night, landed at Sek Kong in the centre of the New Territories, and deployed at various key posts before dawn. The Police Commissioner was eager for this to be done, and argued that it would take some of the pressure off his men, who were suffering from severe morale problems, and amongst whom there were already mumblings of grave discontent.

'I have to report,' he said, 'that there has been actual mutinous talk. The Messes at Yau Ma Tei, Ho Man Tin and Kwun Tong Districts are filled with disgruntled men who are muttering about their unwillingness to fight Chinese in the streets. And the commanders both in Frontier District and the Border Division are reporting actual attempted defection

– men going north across the fence and into Shen Zhen, to get away from what is happening. I regret I cannot offer you the comfort of a police force which is necessarily going to be able to hold the line. It depends on the task we are set. If we have to guard key posts, if we remain a final line of defence, then I think maybe we can do it. If we are to be used offensively against our own people, against people as well organised as Mr Heung's, then I am afraid we will break. It is as well you know this.'

Sir John gave, very briefly, what those who knew him well recognised as a slightly contemptuous smirk. He neither liked nor admired Commissioner Poon, and he had opposed his being given a knighthood. But Downing Street had countermanded; honouring the Commissioner would be a device for displaying British faith in the police force at a time of crisis, a private memorandum had said.

But the sardonic expression faded rapidly from the Governor's face. He waved down any further comment from Poon. He looked instead to the end of the table. 'Let's hear of the situation to the north of the border. The gentleman from CSO: perhaps you would give us the benefit of your knowledge to date.'

The Composite Signals Organisation maintained a number of foreign signals intelligence-gathering stations around Britain and around the world, all reporting to GCHQ, Cheltenham, and with selected reports passed on to the National Security Agency in Fort Meade, Maryland. Since the late 1970s the principal Far Eastern collection station had been sited on the headland of Chung Hom Kok in southern Hong Kong island. Arrangements had been made in 1996 for the dismantling of the major receiving antennae and radios and associated computers, and their shipment to Darwin, in Northern Australia.

However, it had been decided by the Joint Services Intelligence Evaluation Committee (JSIEC) in London that a small but selected array of equipment would remain in place, for the monitoring of events in China and North Korea, until the end of British administration. According to this arrangement a number of Royal Navy helicopters would remove the final equipment and files to a waiting destroyer, which had been on station in southern Hong Kong waters for the previous week.

London had insisted that it wished to enjoy maximum intelligence-gathering abilities for as long as was practically possible: a number of cryptographers and Chinese-language specialists were already on the ship, HMS *Dorsetshire*, and were decoding signals passed between all the major Chinese organisations. GCHQ's pride in being able to monitor telephone conversations held by members of the Chinese leadership in their command headquarters at Zhongnanhai, beside the Forbidden City in Peking, was undiminished by the lowering of activity at Chung Hom Kok.

The CSO officer was able to report what both Sir John and General Harbinson wished to hear: there was absolutely no indication of any new military activity in the Guangdong Military District, nor of any particular heightened activity throughout the whole of the Guangzhou Military Region. Indeed, the only significant developments in the region had come in April, when the Political Commissars at Regional Headquarters in Canton City, and at Divisional Headquarters there and in Guangxi, Hunan and Hainan Island, had been changed, all at the same time. This had been a puzzling development, and the CSO representative was not able to offer any explanation – certainly none that would have any likely bearing on the incidents that had just taken place in Hong Kong.

'Our only suggestion of a development that may be of real interest is that from Zhanjiang. Some of you may remember this place – it is a port on the gooseneck of southern Guangdong Province, down near Hainan Island. You may remember when it was a French treaty port named Fort-Bayard. Anyway, we hear this afternoon that Vice-Admiral Gao, the Commander of the South Sea Fleet, has ordered a number of his transports and a number of commandeered passenger vessels – we think eight, but we are waiting for the pictures – to be moved closer to Hong Kong waters.

'Our suspicion is that these vessels are loaded with troops and vehicles, and members of the Armed Police and the Auxiliary Police. We also feel that they are bound for Hong Kong, although they are keeping radio silence. We have a

P. & O. container ship, the *Cape Carmarthen*, near by and on a parallel track, and she has been asked to listen out with particular care. She is also looking for light-signalling between the flagship and the convoy.

'We had always suspected that this would happen. The emotive impact of Chinese troops and vehicles coming across the frontier itself would have been too great. We have anticipated that they would establish themselves by sea: they could make landings in small boats at the outer islands – on Lantau, Lamma, Peng Chau, Cheung Chau – and secure those places; and they could land at the airport, in Aberdeen, at Kwun Tong, at Castle Peak, at Tai Po, and secure much of the island, Kowloon and the New Territories. No one would be much the wiser. Only when they wanted to stage something public would they need to moor one of their vessels at Stonecutters Island, or by the Star Ferry landing, or at Ocean Terminal, or down the road at HMS *Tamar*; they would have a great deal more control of the impact of the changeover, and they would be able to gain real control that much more quickly.

'So we don't see anything particularly sinister. Not even the timing. The departure from Zhanjiang began at 1600 local time – that was 3 p.m., Hong Kong time – and they are about a day's sailing away. Our information is that they will stand off Fan Lau lighthouse, in the Pearly River estuary, until about 9 p.m. on Monday night. Then they'll move.

'I would like to stress one thing – to the extent that SIGINT officers like myself can stress anything without committing *lèse majesté*.' The Governor motioned to him to continue.

'We do not think the dispatch of this force – if we can call it such a thing – is in any way connected with the events this afternoon. We do not think it is linked in any way with the Foreign Ministry's decision to brief the Reuters man in Peking. We think this move has been long planned, and has been fully approved by the Central Military Commission. Unlike the briefing, which we do not think had the approval of the CMC. We don't know about that. We're still checking.

'So in our opinion – and I suspect you will find that this is the opinion of the JCIEC – the reaction of the civil order institutions in Hong Kong should not take these developments into account. We should not react, lady and gentlemen. This is irrelevant to our immediate problems.

'And my second suggestion is simply that we do not allow this news to be publicised. If we add the news to that of Mr Mao's appointment, local feelings are sure to be inflamed still further. Nothing, I think, need be said, or even alluded to, suggesting Chinese naval manoeuvres.' Here the CSO man, and indeed all the conferees, looked across at Miss Chung, the tough and respected former head of Radio Television Hong Kong, who now headed the entire information department of the colonial government. (She would be leaving on Monday night, for retirement in Vancouver.)

'I will of course do my best,' Miss Chung replied, acidly. 'But if Peking decides to leak this one too, there's not a great deal that I can do.'

The CSO officer took off his glasses, and rubbed his eyes. 'Which brings me to one final point. And before I go on, may I express the wish that everyone here will forgive me for what I accept is a particularly gross example of a signals officer exceeding his remit. It is simply that I am currently in possession of particular and particularly sensitive information, of which I need to inform you. I believe I am right to doubt whether, under these most exacting of circumstances, matters of departmental protocol will prevent my forwarding this information to the committee and commenting on what my training suggests is its significance. May I, despite the lapse, go on?' He glanced around the room. The Governor signalled at him to continue.

'Very well then. We in the community do not believe that this news will be announced, publicly or privately, until after the handover is complete. We believe the Chinese will wish to keep it a total secret, to avoid any complications. We base our assumption on a small piece of information we received less than thirty minutes ago, from an operative in Peking.

'We understand that the official in the Chinese Foreign Ministry who summoned the Reuters reporter was a Madame Zhang Xiaodi, the Western European Senior Desk Officer. Madame Zhang was well known to our Embassy in Peking, had travelled to London on a number of occasions and had, moreover, developed a reasonably intimate personal relationship with our present Minister of State, Lord Inverdonald – and Lady Inverdonald, I might add. We have considered her to be a friend of the British, though no more than that.

'At first we found her decision to leak the information on the Mao appointment somewhat perplexing. It would deflect criticism of the move from China, and towards ourselves – which is just what has happened. Why she – a friend of ours, as I mentioned – should do such a thing, was, as I say, perplexing.

'But we considered the longer-term implications, as she and on whoever's behalf she was acting must have considered too. And we concluded, as they probably did, that the reaction in Hong Kong to what has happened today would in fact calm, very quickly. Our suspicion is that Mr Heung's groups will not cause trouble tomorrow, but will wait until we leave. They will reserve their fire, if they have any, for those who are coming, not those who are leaving. Madame Zhang's group, if I may call them that, and whoever they are, seem to have counted on that too.

'They assumed it would alert the Hong Kong population to the duplicity of the mainland Chinese, and it would give them fair warning; and that the price in lives that they – and us, the British – would have to pay would be worthwhile, hey thought, so long as the ultimate goal, that of enabling the groups to coalesce and to marshal their anger while they could still do so, was achieved. So long as Heung's officers are thinking along the same lines as we are, then a formidable anti-Mainland resistance group has been born today, and will provide the nucleus for further activity in Hong Kong and south China in the months to come.

'That, I believe, is why the news was leaked. The army officer who was in the room with her – we have seen all the Reuters service messages to London, of course – was probably part of the group that, we guess, wants there to be an anti-Mainland organisation set up and working inside Hong Kong. In other words, Madame Zhang's act was, in the eyes of any shrewd and dogmatically loyalist cadre in Peking, one of profound disloyalty.

'It seems, lady and gentlemen, that there are indeed shrewd and dogmatically loyalist men in Peking. We heard half an hour ago that Madame Zhang had been removed from her office, summarily tried, and that she has now been shot. We have no information on the army officer who was with her. But she, poor woman, is definitely dead.'

## CHAPTER FOUR

# ENTR'ACTE

### THE GOLDEN DEER RESTAURANT
### SHAM SHUI PO, HONG KONG

*Sunday, 29 June 1997*

DIM SUM

Peter Heung, who had remained in the Shanghai Road offices all night (a bunk had been set up for him in an inner office after the long nights of the previous year's rioting) had received a telephone call shortly after dawn. It came from a man he knew quite well, a British Army captain named Richard Margerison.

The two had first met socially two years before, at a cocktail party given by a local insurance agent named Derek Thomas, who had connections deep within the territory's government. (His father had been a senior Appeals Court justice; his stepmother was a member of the Legislative Council, and sat on many company boards.) Thomas and Margerison were old friends; and Thomas knew Heung (and Margerison was aware of this) because of the latter's job as a solicitors' clerk with Appleby, Rowling and Munke, the tax lawyers.

Margerison knew, in addition, about Heung's other connections. Richard Margerison was a very considerable enigma in the British Army. He held an American green card (but, not being a citizen, was permitted to serve in an army loyal to his late father's nationality). He had as one of his principal homes a large dairy farm south of Watertown in upstate New York, and he had a socially celebrated sister who worked as a fashion model with the Click! agency, and lived in Greenwich Village. He was said to be comfortably well-off, was handsome, a bachelor of remarkable eligibility,

60

and he spoke several languages including Korean, which had helped when he asked to be posted as temporary head of the United Nations Honour Guard that accompanies the Commander-in-Chief of UN and US Forces in South Korea.

There had never been any certainty about his precise duties either in Korea or in Hong Kong. In the colony he occupied offices on the twelfth floor of HMS *Tamar*, conveniently close to those of the Commander, British Forces, to whom he was said to be an adviser. He did not answer to the Foreign Office men who worked three floors above, and who were the colony's more visible spies. He travelled frequently, and those with whom he socialised said he was often away for inexplicably long periods, in countries and places of which he spoke little.

And he knew a great deal, as it happened, about Peter Heung and the Warwick Accord. The party at which he expected that Heung would be present took place just three weeks after the signing: Margerison thought, very much on his own initiative as subsequent papers have indicated, that he might strike up a relationship with Heung to find out something, however little, about the agreement between the 14K and the Sun Yee On – to see whether it encompassed other Triad groups, and whether it presaged the birth of a real political entity. It was Margerison's report, dated 14 July 1995, that gave Her Majesty's Government its first insight – an insight that the Hong Kong government was never able to duplicate, nor was ever told – into the rapidly growing new power structure in the territory, and beyond into south China. It was this report that laid the basis for the development of a whole new sense of *realpolitik* among the British: the development of an unspoken assumption, and one that was never to be translated formally into a policy, that these gangsters were, in fact, to be regarded both as spokesmen for the working people of Hong Kong and as a group with whom Britain, however distasteful it might seem, could do some kind of business.

This change of heart, this development, this recognition of a certain political congruency came about largely because Richard Margerison did indeed strike up a friendship with Peter Heung. It would be idle to say they two were intimate:

61

there was too little trust between the two sides in those years for close friendship to develop. But it was evident that there could be, in time, a communion of interests, if not of spirit, and the two men were content to deal on that basis. Both sides had a common foe in the mainland Chinese; both sides had indifferent relations with the Hong Kong government, which they regarded as contemptibly inept; both sides claimed they favoured the retention of the capitalist system in the territory, and its extension well beyond, into all of the China that wished to enjoy its benefits.

But it was here, in matters of interpretation, that they differed. Margerison wished for the full flowering of the free-market system to be nurtured within the framework of law (though he was willing to debate the philosophical implications of that wish); Heung had bolder, more ambitious, less scrupulous means of making money – means that not unnaturally included the comfortable feathering of his own nest.

The two men saw each other every two or three months, usually alone, usually in restaurants. Those who saw them and did not recognise them took them for homosexuals, for there was a certain furtiveness in their manner. But Heung invariably saw to it that lieutentants were near by, and on call, so within the Chinese community it was probably fair to say that the relationship was one that was known about, and probably approved. One must assume that the mainland Chinese, whose agents were well positioned throughout the territory (though probably not deep within Heung's organisations: the scalpings and skinnings appeared to have taken care of that), knew of the relationship as well.

Very early on Sunday morning, 29 June 1997, Margerison was briefed by the General. The details of this briefing have never been fully discussed: one can only speculate on the basis of what happened subsequently. The first direct consequence of the briefing came at 8.15 a.m. when Margerison telephoned Heung and arranged to meet in the Golden Deer Restaurant, over early dim sum. Heung, heavily guarded, was the first to arrive. He left four of his men outside the restaurant, and scattered another three at other tables. He was reading the *Ta Kung Pao* when the officer walked in – a small joke between the two of them, since *Ta Kung Pao* was a

rabidly left-wing paper, espousing views with which neither man was in accord.

On this occasion neither man was disposed to be amused. Heung, after all, had lost a great number of his young recruits during the shootings of the previous afternoon, and he was under considerable street pressure to have his forces retaliate against those Britons who had perpetrated the killings. That he should instead be sitting down and dining with one of these very people would, in ordinary circumstances, seem heretical, wholly incredible. But Peter Heung was a man of considerable authority over his troops. Those lieutenants who knew of the meeting with Margerison were the same men who had attended the previous evening's strategy session, and who thus knew – and approved – of the more cautious and restrained approach that they were planning to take in the final remaining hours of British administration. They acknowledged that the mainland government – or some unidentified group within the mainland government, acting for reasons they could not entirely fathom – had tricked them into the fight with the British. And they knew they would not be so tricked again.

So although these lieutenants did not know the full extent of Heung's relationship with Margerison, they were content with what they knew. They supposed that such discussions as had taken place before, as well as these brief discussions scheduled at the Golden Deer today, would prove to be of ultimate benefit to the organisation, and through the organisation, to the people of Hong Kong. Such synergies may have seemed improbable had they been revealed at the time: from today's perspective – when there is universal recognition of the commonality of enemies – they seem rather more credible.

The meeting was brief, and simple. Since both men had anticipated, in a very non-specific sense, the possibility of some serious breakdown in civil order on the eve of the handover, and since Margerison had the sympathetic ear of thinking British diplomats when he insisted on the importance of the Warwick Accord, some 'arrangements', as the Foreign Office had instructed, had been made. Margerison was here to tell Heung of the nature of those arrangements.

They were far from generous. A few dozen Chinese-made

automatic rifles. A hundred or so side-arms, all, via round-about sources, from North Korea. A quantity of a reliable Pakistani-made plastic explosive, and a quantity of detonators. Sufficient ammunition from a supplier in Israel to keep a few small cells going for a month, at most. No radios. No codes. No names of any contacts.

Margerison gave Heung a list of six-figure numbers, the grid references of the points where the twelve packages had been cached, some days before. Most were concealed in the network of old British trenches that had been dug into hillsides all around the territory during the Forties, just before the Japanese invasion. Although some thought had been given to transferring the arms directly, and so ensuring that they got into the right hands, this method ensured secrecy – that no connection between donor and recipient could be discovered. The only link was this Golden Deer meeting, and the slip of paper with the grid references, which would become an irrelevance once the caches had been found and removed. And this, Margerison suggested, should happen quickly – within hours. The trench hiding-places would be easy for Heung's men to find; the weapons dumps were individually of sufficiently small quantities to ensure that they could be moved with ease and without suspicion.

'But is that really all?' Heung asked, once Margerison had told him the news. 'We have a massive task. You know how massive. We are dealing with a hugely powerful force, one with excellent intelligence, with vast networks of spies and informers. To have any hope of dealing effectively, we need many weapons. What you have arranged is simply not enough.'

Margerison had anticipated the man's plaint. There was no possibility of obtaining more, he explained. Downing Street knew of the arrangement, and had given its assent on the firm assurance that all involved would be at pains to see that no possible connection to the British authorities could ever be either suspected or established – this instruction being surely understandable, he said to Heung, who nodded. To meet this requirement, the weapons had all to have originated in places that would arouse no suspicions if the mainland Chinese did ever discover them, before or after

they had been collected from the caches. And collecting weapons and explosives from North Korea and Pakistan was not a matter wholly lacking in complication, Margerison went on. Only limited numbers could be found and brought into Hong Kong without either the Hong Kong government or the mainland intelligence operators coming to know.

'All told, you'll have to accept that we've done the best we can. You know how to turn these into many more. You don't have to be a genius. You just have to be tactically shrewd. But I can't say any more. I won't say any more. You have the references. I leave it up to you.'

Margerison got up to leave, and extended his hand to the Dragon Head. 'A great deal depends on what you do now. I wish some of us were staying behind to give you a hand. But we can't. So I'll just wish you all the best. I dare say I'll read about you. Stay out of trouble. They'll be looking for a reason to pull you in – ten minutes after they've taken over, I expect. I'd keep low. Very low.'

Margerison left, walked to the MTR stop, and merging into the crowds took a train back to Tamar. Heung pretended to study the *Ta Kung Pao* for a few moments more, and then left for Shanghai Road. He was on the telephone for the next ten minutes, and then disappeared.

## CHAPTER FIVE

# RECESSIONAL

## (CONCLUSION)

### CENTRAL HONG KONG

*Monday, 30 June 1997*
LATE EVENING

The green Bedford trucks grumbled slowly through the city, halting at their prearranged points to collect the men and their belongings for shipment home. The task of clearing the barracks, formally set in motion some weeks before, had been completed a few hours earlier. Four transport ships on three-month charter to the Royal Navy and one ammunition supply ship were assembled in the harbour to take on the last remaining stocks and men. The thirty trucks that would take the final sentries and their equipment to the docks would be handed over to the Hong Kong government.

The Chinese authorities had been firm in demanding that the British military make what they termed a 'proper' exit from Hong Kong. By this, they had told the Joint Liaison Group, they meant that no weapons or ammunition or 'militarily significant equipment' of any kind could be left in the territory by the departing British forces. Furthermore, the 1,000 men of the Royal Hong Kong Regiment, known in the territory as the Volunteers and regarded in British operational terms as part of 38th Gurkha Rifles, would have to be disarmed. This was a suggestion that was greeted with dismay in the territory (dismay that was reinforced by the seeming alacrity with which the British agreed to the demand), and there were angry demonstrations outside Government House when the rules were promulgated in the summer of 1996.

Most of the protesters were elderly expatriates – even

though the Volunteers were overwhelmingly Chinese – who saw in the Hong Kong Regiment a relic of Empire that, they felt, should not be permitted to wither and die. An army unit without weapons was valueless, they said; and a wreath of white roses was suspended outside the main gate to the Happy Valley barracks, the headquarters of the Volunteers for the previous forty years. The commanding officer did not order it to be removed; but pressure from Government House, to whom complaints had been made by the New China News Agency, saw that it was taken down after a day.

The result of these agreements with the Chinese was the arrival in early June of the ammunition ship HMS *Andromeda*, which remained in the Dangerous Goods Anchorage taking on cargo and mysterious crates day and night for the duration of her stay. The British authorities never allowed the mainland Chinese to know precisely what equipment was maintained at the various British barracks, nor at the two small Ordnance Stores at Stonecutters Island and at Sek Kong. Nor did the Chinese balk at the refusal of their request, since they had consistently agreed to the sovereign status of British military bases on Hong Kong soil.

But the Chinese did post observation craft alongside *Andromeda*, ostentatiously taking photographs and filmed records as the boxes and crates were loaded aboard. The nature of some of the cargo surprised even such members of the Hong Kong public who came to know of the loadings: a number of heavy artillery pieces, three self-propelled howitzers, ten armoured personnel carriers and six small tanks were taken aboard the ship on the first day – equipment that was testimony to a rather more considerable amount of firepower than had ever been suspected. Hong Kong, after all, was officially described as only 'a small garrison, akin to those in Cyprus, the Falklands and Belize'.

The ammunition boxes were counted out daily by the unsmiling and assiduous Chinese observers, as were the jeeps and lorries and engine parts and helicopters and bowsers and small cranes, rubber boats and radio transmitters and receivers and uniform stores and NAAFI equipment and all the other accoutrements of empire and far-flung military power. By the morning of 30 June, all was safely squirreled away in holds and under canvas awnings on deck.

The quartermasters reported to the Commander, British Forces, on 'the satisfactory clearance of the Hong Kong garrison', and 4,200 of the remaining forces had, on that final Monday morning, been put aboard ten Royal Air Force flights for Brize Norton, and redeployment. The Supplementary Forces had also embarked on fleets of chartered British Airways jets; by 9 p.m. all were said to be outside colonial jurisdiction, having been paid off, and given a letter formally thanking them for their duties.

Those wounded on Saturday afternoon were taken aboard one of the transport ships, which had excellent medical facilities. The coffin holding the body of Warrant Officer Patrick Watson, late of 3HKSF, was in the hold of one of the aircraft. He was to be the only British fatality of the handover, and though his widow and two children naturally regarded his death as the most dreadful of tragedies, it was to be the considered judgement of British military historians that, all things considered, the British side 'got off pretty lightly'.

By 10 p.m., little remained of a British presence in Hong Kong. The offices and barrack-blocks were empty, guarded by groups of police and awaiting the anticipated inspection of the mainland Chinese. And all the while, during this eerie period, the old British Bedford lorries ground slowly from depot point to depot point, collecting the last groups of men and their kitbags, dismantling the barricades, or handing over the sentry duties to the men of the Hong Kong Police who were, it is worth noting, permitted to continue to wear their side-arms.

Occasionally small groups of Chinese civilians would gather beside the sandbag emplacements in the streets to bid farewell to the British soldiers – farewells that were more notable for the nervousness with which they were expressed than for their particular warmth. The small public gatherings were illustrative, however, of the profound change of mood that had seized the territory over the previous twenty-four hours: a Chinese population that could have been expected to rise up and attack and destroy all that was British, as revenge for the mayhem of Saturday, was now reported to be docile, almost submissive, almost friendly.

The explanation, it is now known, was quite simple: the Heung officers had put out the word to their men and boys

that there should be no further reaction to the killings and the violence of Saturday afternoon, and that word was being almost universally obeyed (a degree of compliance that was helped to no small degree by the activities of large numbers of Straw Sandals directed to police the order). Moreover, there was no evidence of any 'freelance' reaction from Chinese unconnected with the Saturday disturbances. Once again, members of the Triad group worked to ensure calm throughout the territory's population, those associated with their political aims and those who were not. There had been a brief upsurge of activity in Kowloon late on Saturday night, when a police barracks was burned to the ground and two Hong Kong policemen were killed. But a force of Suppers firing tear gas had put paid to that by 3 a.m. on Sunday, since when there had been no reports of significant violence directed against either the British or the mainland Chinese. In a report to the Governor made at mid-morning on Monday – his last officially scheduled commentary since the General Declaration of Emergency three months before – Commissioner Poon noted with surprise the passing of 'one of the most serene nights Hong Kong has known in the past thirty years', and went on to mention with wistful irony how pleasing it would have been if the colony had always been so tranquil.

As had been decided on Saturday, Government House had made no announcement about the Chinese naval convoy that had left Zhanjiang that afternoon. However, in view of the contact made between Captain Margerison and Mr Heung, and in view of the likelihood that large numbers of mainland Chinese would soon be deployed throughout the territory, a further and final discreet connection was made in which the British side made it clear that no time should be lost by Heung's organisers in the collection of the various packages located at the grid reference points. The British side was relieved to be assured that all the collections had indeed been made, that the packages were in safe custody and that the paper with the grid references had been destroyed. Mr Heung's associates wondered aloud why the urgency, and one was reported to have asked a British representative direct if the hurry related to the likelihood that the Chinese would arrive *en masse*, perhaps by helicopter or by sea. The British representative replied that he assumed that

under the terms of a gentlemen's agreement reached at the Joint Liaison Group meeting in March, the very small number – 'a token force' – of Chinese PLA (People's Liberation Army) and PAP (People's Armed Police) members who would be stationed in Hong Kong would arrive by land over the Lo Wu, Lok Ma Choi and Sha Tau Kok border crossing points. The reply was disingenuous; but was apparently believed.

Meanwhile the Marine Department, with the assistance of coded radio signals from the *Carmarthen Bay*, had been tracking the Chinese fleet continuously since Saturday. It had not, as expected, waited off Fan Lau light on Lantau Island, just beyond the limit of Hong Kong waters that was closest to its point of departure. (Passengers on commercial boats passing between Hong Kong and Macau knew Fan Lau well: they knew that once the light was square on their starboard beam, they could commence gambling since they were no longer under colonial jurisdiction; similarly, on the return journey, the appearance of Fan Lau on the port beam meant that the chips had to be cashed in, the roulette wheel silenced and the playing cards shelved for another day.)

Instead of parking there the convoy of four naval transports and eight former passenger ships, including an old Danish-built cruise ship that had for many years been used as a floating hotel off the city of Xiamen, had divided into three, and had manoeuvred into position at noon on Monday. One transport and four liners – designated Group Alpha – had turned north up the Pearl River, and then had wheeled about and had held position off the Castle Peak power station. Group Beta, consisting of two transports and two liners, had heaved to and was lying uncomfortably in very choppy waters behind the Waglan Island lighthouse at the eastern approach to the territory. The remainder of the force, Group Gamma, was off Lamma Island, to the south.

At 10.30 p.m. the Marine Department telephoned to inform Government House – which was now preparing for the flag-lowering ceremony – that the three groups of vessels had simultaneously passed into territorial waters and were steaming rapidly towards their supposed landing-points. Group Alpha had passed down the Urmston Roads and was lying off the main container base at Tsing Yi; Beta was

about to pass through the Lei Yue Mun gap and could be expected to be off Kai Tak airport runway by 11 p.m.; and Gamma had moved in close to the Aberdeen typhoon shelter. Observers in accompanying small vessels had reported that a number of Chinese Army and Navy Mi6 Mikhail heavy transport helicopters were visible on the converted afterdecks of the liners, and that their rotors were turning in evident preparation for take-off.

Protocol officers from the British and Chinese sides had met three weeks before to decide on the detailed provisions for the final ceremonial. Perhaps the most important practical result of the talks was that the British had been given six extra hours after the official handover deadline – which was midnight local time; 1 a.m. Chinese Daylight Saving Time; 5 p.m. British Daylight Saving Time in London; and 4 p.m. GMT – to clear up and leave. This meant that the final collection of sentries, the destruction of papers, the establishment of radio links and so forth could continue past the actual deadline. The legality of doing so and the necessary indemnifications had been covered both by a Note from the Chinese Embassy in London and the passage of a brief Enabling Act at Westminster: the British expressed their gratitude to the Chinese for their forbearance.

The ceremony surrounding the lowering of the Union flag and the raising of its Chinese counterpart was said to have been adapted from that used at the end of British rule of their last Chinese colony, that at Port Edward in Shandong Province in 1930. At that time the British flag was left flying at sunset on the evening of the retrocession; at midnight the Chinese flag was raised alongside it; and by dawn the British flag had been taken down and all British diplomatic and military personnel had been embarked on a battleship, which then bade its farewell with sirens at sunrise, and set sail for the Royal Navy base at Esquimault in Canada.

Much the same was supposedly due to happen in Hong Kong. The British and Hong Kong flags flew together in the garden at Government House, without having been struck at dusk as was customary. The Chinese flag was due to be raised at midnight, in the presence of a group of dignitaries who would arrive from the New China News Agency a few moments beforehand. Sir John and Lady Courtenay would

then fly to the cruiser HMS *Manchester*, and the support staff would fly on a later Navy helicopter to the destroyers HMS *Calliope* and HMS *Hermione*, which were waiting in Junk Bay, ready for a speedy departure. It had been arranged that all remaining military personnel would be embarked at the same time, and that all British military men and materials – and vessels – would have cleared what would then be Xianggang Chinese territorial waters by 6 a.m. on Tuesday, 1 July.

In the event the ceremonial was even less ornate an affair than the stripped-down version approved by the protocol officers; and the departure by the British was hurried and – according to participants – undignified. The following reconstruction comes largely from the diaries of the author, who was permitted access to much of the closing formalities. A British newspaper journalist, a Mr Ralph Upton, supplied additional details.

The Governor and Lady Courtenay walked out of the Government House kitchen and through the empty dining-room. A couple of naval ratings were collecting the last boxes and bundling them up to go off on the tender to the *Manchester*, the cruiser which would speed the senior colonial officers out to sea. The pair emerged into the brightly lit foyer, looked around for the last time at the paintings that had been left behind – nothing of note, someone had assured them – and went out into the heat of the night.

The three klieg lamps which local television had set up to provide coverage for the BBC immediately flared into life, dazzling the group. Six Royal Marines – a lieutenant and five of his men – came to attention. The officer saluted as the group emerged: Lord Inverdonald (the Foreign Office Minister of State with Special Responsibilities for Hong Kong), then Sir John and Lady Courtenay, General Harbinson, Brigadier Tomsett and Richard Adaire.

Inverdonald stepped up to the podium. The rest of the party stood grouped around him. The Marine lieutenant barked a command, and from beneath the monkey-puzzle tree stepped a soldier in full Highland dress with bagpipes. Pipe-Major Duncan Kennedy, from the band of the 2nd

Battalion, Royal Scots, had been flown from Edinburgh only days before, to perform the simple act of playing the lament *St Kilda*. It must have been evident to those who were watching the broadcast that Lady Courtenay, who was of Scots origin, found this lament – a soliloquy on the abandonment of another small and distant island – intensely painful. She and her husband looked straight ahead, almost at attention, willing the piper to stop. Which he did, at three minutes before the hour, with a trailing note left in the air, swept away by the wind, and the sound of Inverdonald clearing his throat. He looked in the direction of the main gate. He had but two simple sentences to utter.

'In the name of Her Majesty, and of the people of Hong Kong, I invite our honoured guests to join us in the celebration of arrival. Please enter these precincts, as welcome friends.'

And with that, and with a strangely menacing silence that was punctuated only by the sound of twenty-four motor tyres crunching on to gravel and the occasional grating of branches against one another in the wind, six long black Mercedes limousines moved slowly in through the gates. They had been parked on Upper Albert Road for the past few minutes, protected by a detachment of British troops. Each of the cars had darkened windows, and each flew two red flags of the People's Republic of China. The convoy moved around clockwise, behind the television camera, heading towards the podium, the lead car coming to rest beside the main doorway of the house.

The Royal Marine lieutenant opened the passenger door of this car, and his men, each of whom had been assigned to stand at a point where each following car would halt, opened the doors of the others. From the lead car stepped two men: Zhang Nan, the rather disagreeable negotiator who had been head of the News Agency for the past seven years, and a small, plump, busy-looking man with bushy eyebrows and bad teeth which were displayed in a fixed grin. He was unknown by sight to many of the party. But the BBC commentator knew, and the commentary could be heard coming from a television set somewhere near by.

'... and now, confirming all the rumours of the last few hours, we see stepping from the first car, the man all Hong

Kong has feared to see appointed as its new Chief Executive – 74-year-old Mao Ren-chin. The agreement of thirteen years ago had spoken specifically of the people here having some influence over the choice of their immediate ruler. But this man, who comes from Dalian in northeastern China, who speaks English but no Cantonese and who is known as a diehard party member with enormous influence in the ruling hierarchy, would never have been selected by the people of Hong Kong. If, as we suspect, Zhang Nan is going to introduce him as Chief Executive – in effect, the replacement for Sir John Courtenay – we can expect the new territory to become, rapidly, a very different place . . .'

From the other cars stepped two dozen or more Chinese men, some familiar, some not, some in Western suits, some in baggy outfits of dark blue serge or grey duck. Two soldiers and a sailor from the People's Liberation Army were among the throng too – unarmed, as the orders had specified. They moved towards the podium.

Lord Inverdonald grasped Zhang Nan's hand and shook it warmly, then took, with considerably less warmth, the hand proffered by Mr Mao. He made to introduce the others, but Mao waved him down. 'No time,' he said. 'Raise the flag.'

Sir John looked down at his watch. A minute to go. The Royal Marine lieutenant – history records his name as Roger Moorcock, a 24-year-old bachelor from Kendal, in Westmorland – then stepped forward and took from a leather box beside the front steps, and with due reverence, a single and apparently very large Chinese flag. Aided by Sergeant Michael Firth, Corporal Peter Ransome and by the unidentified Chinese sailor, he then clipped the flag to its halyard, secured all, and waited.

From a radio set inside the doors the chimes of Big Ben, 6,000 miles away in London, sounded the preamble to sixteen hours, Greenwich Mean Time, seventeen hours, British Summer Time, and midnight, Hong Kong time. The sixteen notes tumbled out of the ether, pleasing in their primitive melody, raising the tension to an unbearable quivering, as though every soul and every mind and every heartbeat was touched by a tuning fork, humming with expectation.

The first peal of the great thirteen-ton bell finally crashed out of the silence. A shouted command, one in Cantonese,

one in English, and the huge Chinese flag was rushed effortlessly up to the top of the pole, and the halyards lashed and knotted below to assure its security. Everyone looked upwards as the hot winds swiftly unfurled it and sent it waving lazily, even in the gale, with a vast imposing dignity, beside the jauntily tattered Union Jack a few feet beyond. Inverdonald, the Courtenays, the General, his ADC and Rex Tomsett stood with respectful rigidity, while the remaining peals of the bell thundered through the night.

And then they stopped, and from down below in the streets came a sudden huzzah of activity: a surge like the roar of an immense wave, sucking back the beach before it came crashing down again. It seemed to be a mixture of cheering and wailing, of distant firecrackers and explosions, of gunfire and sirens and the sound of tyres turning at high speed. It was not, in short, a pleasant sound, nor one that augured well for a night of peace.

Then another sound started from beside the tennis courts. The sudden low whine of the starter motor, and the slow thwack of a Sea King's rotor blades, as the Governor's helicopter fired up, ready to take Sir John and his party off to the waiting *Manchester*.

The party, including Ambassador Zhang and Mr Mao, walked around to the perimeter of the helicopter pad. As they waited, Sir John tried small talk. 'We've prepared a small gift for you, Mr Zhang,' he said, and turned to let Richard Adaire hand him a flat red morocco case, about the size of a large magazine, with a royal crest engraved in gold. 'It's an original Chinnery, a watercolour, a picture of Hong Kong in 1841, the year we – well, the year that this ceremony seeks to have forgotten.' He handed it to Zhang. 'I hope you like it, sir. And may I congratulate you both – congratulate you all.'

Zhang waved his gesture away, and grunted at an aide to take the box. Mao then said, in surprisingly good English: 'You won't want to miss your machine, I think,' and with a gesture more usually reserved for bouncers in Kowloon nightclubs, made as though to usher the Governor across the tennis court to where the helicopter crew was waiting to board them.

And so, with a few kisses and handshakes of farewell, but

with less real ceremonial than has probably ever attended the concluding moments of any part of the British Empire save perhaps that of the island of Southern Thule, in Antarctica, His Excellency the Governor, Lady Courtenay, the Minister of State at the Foreign and Commonwealth Office and the Commander and Deputy Commander, British Forces, clambered into the helicopter with as much dignity as the wind and height of the Sea King's steps permitted them, and, at precisely 300 seconds into Chinese rule, left the soil that they so recently had governed.

At first the dark blue machine clattered upwards just a few feet, then it moved forward, then back, put its nose down and began to move ahead and upwards out over the tennis courts, before turning left over Upper Albert Road. At a height of no more than fifty feet it hovered above the flag-poles, setting the two banners streaming wildly. The machine then rose again, with a deafening roar, until it was level with the top of the Japanese turret above the Governor's study, climbed high above the azalea bushes of the great gardens, and finally, its red lights winking on and off, looped up and away over the huge skyscrapers of Central to where HMS *Manchester* was even now steaming at ten knots, down the western roads. Soon the sky was silent, with just the lights twinkling on and off; and then these, too, had vanished into the darkness. The Colonial Presence, in the persons of this small group of men and a woman, had left for ever.

The agreement with Peking had the British governor and his party beyond the limits of territorial waters within ninety minutes of the raising of the Chinese flag. London had insisted that all would be done strictly by the book, and that matters of pride were no longer of any consequence. 'Leave in a timely fashion with dignity,' was the order of the day.

Meanwhile some thirty men had poured from the other cars and had swarmed inside Government House within moments. Sentries – by now well armed, with machine-guns – took up positions by the doorway. Two trucks drew up outside, and two dozen more men in fatigues, carrying rifles with fixed bayonets, took up positions along the driveway. There was the crackle of instructions shouted over the radio – in *putonghua*, not Cantonese. Five more soldiers were posted at the outer gate, and in the sentry-boxes from which

they were already hustling the British soldiers into their own Bedford trucks. 'All right, you bastard,' Upton heard one voice say, in broad Lancashire. 'I'm getting out as fast as I can. Don't bloody push me or I'll clout you.'

Two soldiers came quickly across to the flagpoles, looked upwards to see from which the Chinese flag was flying, and undid the halyards of the other. One of the remaining Britons tried to protest, but a third soldier blocked his way. 'You stay – no interfere,' said the man, an officer. The Union Jack came down, and a soldier took it away, presumably as a souvenir. Another soldier was seen with the royal crest, torn from the lectern.

There came the clattering of rotor blades again, sounding directly above the remaining party. It was only twenty past – and the first of the helicopters due to take the ancillary parties to sea were not due until twenty *to*. What on earth was happening?

The leading soldier caught up to *The Times'* correspondent. 'Mister Upton,' he said roughly. 'Mister Adaire? This helicopter for you. You must go now. No time for more. You must leave. This official residence.'

Those final five minutes remain confused in the minds of all who took part. The helicopter settled down, the door was thrown open. Chinese sentries were pushing people roughly towards the Lynx, pulling them down under the rotor blades. Hands reached out of the helicopter doors and hauled the last pair on board. Even as they did so the machine was lifting up and turning around, blowing some of the Chinese soldiers to the ground. There was shouting, anger, confusion.

They flew high above Central, the Fleet Air Arm pilot cool and composed. 'Six-oh-one turning for *Hermione* now with six souls aboard, ETA one six three five Zulu.'

'Roger six-oh-one, *Hermione*. New orders received, so we are presently under way some two nautical miles east of Junk Bay. Come direct to our beacon and prepare for under-way landing.'

'Roger and Wilco, *Hermione*, see you soon.'

From the air the city was as staggeringly beautiful as ever, with the orange fires and the blue flashing lights of emergency vehicles adding immeasurably to the scene. But the machine was speeding out over water, and before long the lights of

Central and Kowloon were well behind them, and the airport approach light gantries slipped below, and then the islets to the east, and finally, picked out in the blackness of the open sea, they saw the running lights of the little frigate, heading as rapidly as possible away from Hong Kong. The pilot was well trained, and put them down on the after-deck with little fuss. By twenty minutes to one they were in the wardroom, being handed large glasses of gin by the captain.

'My apologies,' he said. 'Bit of a fright all round. They changed the rules the moment they took charge, it seems. They weren't going to have an ambiguous night where no one knew where they stood – not with all the bother in the city. So we got orders, exactly one minute after midnight, telling us to be out of their waters no later than *Manchester* – and she's got until one-thirty, I believe.' He looked across at a lieutenant, who nodded his assent.

'They warned us they might shoot at us if we didn't so we had to scrap all the best plans and get out. All sorts of things have happened. Radio's off the air. They shut down the BBC feed. We don't have a working consulate for another week. And I was just told they've cut the phones, so we can't patch in to any of our friends who're still there. We just won't know what's going on until they've secured things.'

Everyone then gathered under the soft red nightlights of the bridge, and gazed out into the blackness. Waglan Island Lighthouse – the Light at the End of the Empire, it had once been called – slipped by to starboard. The captain ordered a turn, to a southeasterly course, and rang down for full speed ahead both.

Richard Adaire stepped out on to the starboard bridge wing. Hong Kong was but a reddish glow on the horizon now, aside from a few islets that loomed up blackly against the beam of the lights. They passed a shoal of fishing junks, and a small cargo ship, inbound. But otherwise, as the colony slipped ever further astern, the sea darkened and became more deserted still. And a swell, struck up by the passing storm, began to lift the little ship up, and dump her down heavily. It was going to be an uncomfortable night.

Then there was a cry from the bridge. 'Vessel dead ahead one mile, stopped in the water.' The captain ordered a cut in speed to half ahead, and a turn of ten degrees to starboard.

He came on to the wing. 'The sentry boat. Just making sure we're out the door on time. And we will be!'

The captain looked at his watch, the luminous figures pulsing in the dark. It was twenty-five minutes past. He peered ahead, holding on to a stanchion to keep his balance as the vessel turned into the swells. There was a black shape ahead, probably the guardship. He could just make out the faint riding lights, before suddenly an Aldis lantern came on, and he could hear the shutters rise and snap shut, as they tapped out their morse signal.

The lookout read off the letters. 'They're saying farewell, sir,' he said, and read out: 'Have safe voyage. Don't come back. This belongs to China now. Goodbye.'


At the same time, and with the same apparent speed, the soldiers and police of the People's Republic came ashore to retake their longest-sought possession. The huge Mikhail troop-carrying helicopters and landing craft brought men to all the piers and docks in and around Hong Kong and Kowloon, in Aberdeen and Silvermine Bay and Tai Po and Tuen Mun and Yuen Long and at every village on Lamma and Lantau and Cheung Chau and Ma Wan and every other centre of population reckoned to be of potential challenge. By three in the morning there were sentries posted at all the major junctions in Central, Tsim Sha Tsui, Mong Kok, Sham Shui Po and Sha Tin; all the British Army barracks were secure; the airport was closed; the Navy was in full control of the waters and there were political officers manning the radar rooms at the Marine Department. Government House, from which flew the red banner with its golden stars, was protected by scores of soldiers; and on Queen's Road East the lights blazed fiercely from the red marble building that now sported a brass plaque reading 'Central Organising Offices – Xianggang Special Administrative Region'.

A guard had also been placed outside the offices at 230 Shanghai Street, Kowloon, and a search made of the premises. But, as might be expected of a small China trading company at three in the morning during this most turbulent time in the Region's history, there was nobody to be found in the office; nor were there any documents to be found that

79

were of any interest to the detectives from the People's Armed Police who conducted a thorough search.

# ROOM 4231, DEPARTMENT OF STATE WASHINGTON, DC

*Thursday, 3 July 1997*

It was the eve of the long Fourth of July weekend, and everyone in every quarter of the United States government – like everyone else in the country – was wanting to get away early. Mercifully for most of the people at State, the world was in a generally placid mood – except, that is, for the troubles in Hong Kong, which had kept everyone in the East Asia Department awake for the past week or so. These people were not, by the looks of things, going to be able to get away early.

The events in South China had been the principal story on CNN every day since the Happy Valley riots. Some of the racier aspects of the story had even made it onto the network shows. Moreover the BBC coverage of the handover ceremony had been watched live by many millions of enthralled people – even though noon, Eastern Time, on a summer Monday was not the best time to catch the American public in front of its televisions.

But then China – and the plight of Hong Kong – had captured the American imagination once again. It was a peculiar phenomenon: the apparently imperturbable villainy of the Chinese Communist leadership was political anathema to all Americans, of course. But China, as in Cathay, Old China, the Middle Kingdom, the land of Imperial Yellow, of concubinage, of bound feet, of silk, of Squeeze and Face – that was something different, and America was currently infatuated with it. All over the country there were now China Tea Clubs, decorated in the style of Thirties Shanghai. Cantonese dining was back in fashion, and people were rediscovering the small triumph of eating with chopsticks. The *cheongsam* had come back into some sort of vogue. Mature women in suburban Dallas and Grosse Pointe and Westchester Country were spending afternoons playing mah-jong, and there were said

to be fan-tan tables in Atlantic City and down on Paradise Island. The novels of Amy Tan were all the rage, and late night television was managing to offend everyone by showing Charlie Chan and Fu Manchu mysteries, and being accused of presenting a stereotypical China, which the viewing public naturally loved. The May 1997 issue of *Vanity Fair* had written a cover story on the television star Pu Ching, who lived in Los Angeles and who laid claim (accurately, genealogists concluded) to being the Empress of China-in-waiting. Barber shops in Los Angeles reported that the queue had taken over from the ponytail, for men.

Many analysts said the phenomen had much to do with – and was indeed a reaction to – the wave of anti-Japanese sentiment that had begun to sweep the country in the early and middle Nineties, and which had led to the abrogation of the US–Japan Mutual Security Treaty in June 1994. (That American troops, airmen and warships had been withdrawn from their bases in Japan during 1995 was inconvenient – and would prove decidedly so during the mounting of Operation Eastern Union, the defence of South Korea, in February 1998. The leadership on both sides of the Pacific agreed, however, that in the face of ugly domestic realities in their respective countries, annulling the Treaty had become an absolute political necessity.)

Contacts between an increasingly aggressive Japan and an economically battered United States remained correct and formal during the latter half of the decade, despite the abrogation of the Treaty. But the old intimacy had evaporated. And with this intimacy went part of a grand and historic American connection with the Orient – a connection that had been a part of American life ever since the establishment of the first Chinatowns in San Francisco, ever since Lieutenant Pinkerton met Cho-cho-san in Nagasaki City.

Hence, it is thought, the deliberate rediscovery of an idealised China. It was of no consequence that today's China was still ruled by the Communist gerontocracy. What the American of the late Nineties needed was to assuage the thirst that had been caused by the departure of Japan. An obsession with China, in some shape or form, and with things Chinese, did just that.

But obsession or not, it was irritating in the extreme to the

members of the HK7 Committee when, as they had each feared, the call came at noon on Thursday from the Assistant Secretary of State's office, scheduling an extraordinary meeting of the Committee in the fourth-floor conference room at five that evening. Most were planning to leave town: one – the man from the European Affairs Bureau – had been scheduled to leave on the 7 p.m. Air Russia flight to Moscow, for a long weekend with his fiancée.

It was an ill-tempered group that assembled under the portraits of President Benson and Secretary Crowther that evening. Hugh Charlesworth recognised the mutinous mood, and apologised.

'I really would not have scheduled this meeting, ladies and gentlemen, had I not felt it to be most urgent. But I had a telephone call today from Miss Waters at the Agency. She is to blame, if anyone is. She feels she has something to report.'

Jillian Waters, who had been the CIA representative on the HK7 Committee for nine of the last twelve regular meetings, was both well-liked and well-respected by the group. She was young, with an impressive clutch of degrees from Yale and Stanford and one of the first doctorates to be granted at the new Shaw Institute of Chinese Studies at Oxford. Her special subject at Langley was the tracking of political personalities in China, and her analyses were said by all who received them to be invariably factually spot-on and analytically shrewd. The looks of ill-temper thus slowly faded from the faces of her six colleagues, to be replaced by expressions of keen interest.

'I have rather little to say in terms of facts. But the little I have gleaned sounds kind of interesting.' Miss Walters glanced up, and looked around the room over the top of her spectacles. 'This meeting is, by the way, classified Top Secret. We all know that. But it is perhaps worth repeating on this occasion.

'I have firm information that suggests three things. First: within the next few days we are going to see the outbreak of a full-scale campaign of social disruption waged in Southern China. There will be strikes, riots, assassinations – and the forces that are organising the campaign are well equipped, and will soon be better equipped. Second: at least three well-known political personalities in southern China now

82

believe they have enough latent popular support to encourage an attempt to break away from the main Chinese union.

'And last – and this will cause problems for the sceptics among you – is that I have what I believe to be good and reliable information that elements of the People's Liberation Army based in the region are becoming unstable. They could prove unreliable in the event of a major outbreak of disorder. Their loyalty to central authority, in short, is in question.'

Peter Chin, Deputy Director of the People's Republic of China Bureau, laughed incredulously. The other five looked stunned, well aware of the implications of Miss Watson's news. There was a sudden barrage of questions. Hugh Charlesworth raised his hand for silence.

'Peter is right to doubt this information,' he said. 'I found it difficult to believe. But I think it is fair to say that your reporting from Canton City has been rather poor of late' – Peter Chin nodded in response, and remarked that he had had nothing to do with the appointments to the Consulate-General there – 'and these reports all come from Canton, or thereabouts, and from impeccable sources.

'They need to be checked, but using all the normal procedures that will not alert anyone to the suggestion that we have any information whatsoever. This – if it is true – is for the development of policy. Not for the development of reaction. So no word to our missions in China, or elsewhere. This is one for Washington – and it would be as well if Canton and all the Chinese missions are allowed to be surprised by whatever happens. Maybe nothing will. But if it does, and if their normal diplomatic channels have told them nothing, then I want them caught off-guard. We don't want anyone in Peking having any idea of the level of our information.

'So, everyone – go back and double-check with your own sources. I'll expect a report in forty-eight hours. And after that, if it's good, it's for the National Security Council. This deserves an airing in the White House. Things could get out of hand in China pretty quickly. And the implications of that – the implications for Japan, for instance – well, I'm sure I don't have to spell it out.'

Thus was the Fourth of July weekend spoiled for seven American bureaucrats and their families, and for a young

woman, a Russian translator living in Moscow. By the Monday, however, a report was on Charlesworth's desk; it was on Secretary of State Crowther's desk by mid-afternoon; and by evening had been circulated to the core personnel on the National Security Council's East Asia Coordinating Committee. A copy was also sent to the NSC's Interdepartmental Groups for Defense Policy, Foreign Policy and Emergency Planning.

The United States government was, in other words, fast becoming aware – and at the very highest level of policy making – of the gathering storms in China. A complex series of policy options for dealing with a number of long-term eventualities was constructed. Very few of these options have ever been made public.

It is significant to note, however, that at a meeting held in late August 1997, members of the Joint Chiefs of Staff were briefed secretly on matters relating to southern China and its neighbours, and that as a result they ordered the formal commencement of Phase I of the Joint Chiefs of Staff Crisis Action System. Under the Crisis Action System Phase I order, a military plan would now be developed for the management of one or two of the most likely outcomes of the China situation – a plan that would involve the possible deployment of American forces into the region.

It is of further significance to note that, according to available records (and there are very few, since all these operations were conducted under a need-to-know Top Secret basis) the staff who were assigned to the Crisis Action System planning effort included, as well as the expected specialists on China and Taiwan, a number of intelligence and military analysts who were familiar with three other nations not presently involved – South Korea, North Korea and, somewhat surprisingly, Japan.

The inference is clear: that even as early as the late summer of 1997, the United States was beginning to express concern at the possibility, however slight, that Japan might in the longer term become a party to the gathering crisis; and, further, that the United States of America might have to exercise some kind of military option to prevent such a situation from developing uncontrollably.

# CHAPTER SIX

# INTIMATIONS OF ANGER

## CANTON CITY
### *Thursday, 10 July 1997*

China is a country where superstition still plays a vital role in the lives of its 1.5 billion inhabitants, and in the summer of 1997, to judge by contemporary accounts in the *People's Daily*, there was much to be superstitious about.

The astrologers, whose utterances are still given considerable weight, especially in rural China, had all long before predicted adverse combinations of astral conjunctions, planetary alignments and elemental combinations. A cow with two heads had been born on a farm outside Zhuhai. There was a mysterious wave of sickness, which involved the eruption of unsightly boils, among the ferrymen who worked on the lower reaches of the Pearl River. On 9 March there was, for the first time in scores of years, a total solar eclipse, which could be seen from Mongolia to Manchuria. And, in early July, a typhoon which had threatened to dampen Hong Kong's midnight handover celebrations recurved, as the Western Pacific's summer storms are apt to do, and struck the southern Guangdong coast with immense ferocity, drowning an estimated fifty-two people, bringing down several hundred houses and matsheds, and spoiling the stores of rice in a score of riverside godowns.

The first sign of real trouble came in Canton City, on the morning of 10 July. A young and recently arrived member of the People's Armed Police named Wan Zhu'er was bicycling to his point duties when he was shot through the head in the main city market, as he passed the edible birds section. It

was said that the owls, which were on hand to be trussed for the pot, since a particular variant of the brown fish owl is regarded as a great delicacy in southern China, boiled in soup, gazed down with interest at the body. The constable died quickly, and though his bicycle was left untouched his gun, a small automatic pistol, a Type 54 copy of the Russian Tokarev made in Shanghai, was taken from its holster. A clip of 7.62 mm ammunition was taken as well.

Constable Wan had been assigned to surveillance and guard duties close to an unmarked Party building beside the Shamian north bridge. But it was not his specific duties that lay behind his violent death. That, as subsequent developments confirmed, came about partly because of who he was, but principally because of where he came from.

His colleagues said he was from a village up in Shandong province, near the town of Weifang in northeastern China. He spoke heavily accented Mandarin, and some Cantonese. He had been assigned six weeks before to guard duties in Canton City because, firstly, he was tall and looked daunting, and secondly because there was an official campaign – fruitless, as it later turned out – to persuade northern PAP officers to take assignments in the south to learn the dialects of southern China.

The truck drivers who passed Comrade Wan at his post seemingly knew, or had a fair suspicion, that he was a northener. The people of Canton City had long been accustomed to seeing northerners in their midst, and were well able to recognise them. As a provincial capital city, Canton sported scores of official institutions that were laden with *bak fong yan*, as those bureaucrats from 'the north direction' were known. All the locally-posted officials of the central government were from *bak fong*, as were most of those who worked administering the railways, many of the officers in the army and the police, the senior men in the telegraph offices, banks and customs houses. And all these hundreds had, until quite recently, been tolerated by the Cantonese of Canton – not exactly liked, but accepted as part of the enormous patchwork quilt that was China, and which had been stitched into some semblance of a harmonious whole by the efforts of the Party.

In recent years, however, that tolerance had started to

wear a little thin. More and more often the classic veiled insult – 'you steamed bread eaters' – was heard snarled at northerners.* It was a development that was both slow and subtle, and which requires some background explanation.

For a long while there had been some suspicion and distaste – others might claim it could be more properly described as a downright loathing – expressed for the northerners by the Cantonese *of Hong Kong*. These, it should be remembered, are not the same as the Cantonese people generally. They are a people who, thanks in part to the astonishing economic prosperity of their colonial home, steadily developed marked differences in attitude and outlook from their ethnically and linguistically similar colleagues who lived to the north of what in colonial times was the border fence. (This fence, built by the British to keep would-be immigrants out of the colony, still existed for a long time after the handing-back of the territory, though the subsequent events that are retold in these pages rendered it a wholly irrelevant structure; a second, electrified, chain-link fence some miles further into China had also been built by the Chinese as further insurance against the contagions of Hong Kong ever entering the ideologically uncorrupted bloodstream of China proper: it, too, was to prove quite useless.)

As long ago as the Seventies the residents of Hong Kong began to be referred to by their Chinese compatriots, by politicians, even by anthropologists, as *Hong Kong-ese* people, a group who were now so different from the Cantonese that they had become almost a distinct and separate race. They were taller, heavier, healthier, they lived longer lives, and immense new lexicons had intruded into their (already very colourful, slang-filled) mother-tongue. They were, indeed, a race apart – and it was this race who, in the Seventies and

---

*The reference is to the climatically induced diet of northern Chinese, which tends to be based on dry-farmed wheat – hence buns, bread and noodles. Southern China, on the contrary, is wet and hot – hence rice. Since southerners tend also to be darker and shorter than northerners, the reverse epithet is 'southern monkeys'.

Eighties, began to run out of trust and patience for their fellow Chinese from the north.

For the rest of the world and China, a great many things may well have been true. In the years following the Great Proletarian Cultural Revolution, after the death of Mao Tse-tung, the arrest of the Gang of Four and the ascension of the seeming pragmatism and openness of Deng Xiaoping, it may have been true that the whole world trusted the northern Chinese. It may have been true that the Americans, the French, the Germans, the Italians – everyone of consequence, in fact – accepted without question that some great sea-change had come over China, and that she had, after all, returned herself to the community of nations for ever. It may have been true that the British, who were after all renowned for their diplomatic wisdom and caution, had decided that they could place their trust in the essential goodness of the Peking Chinese. And it may have been true that in this spirit they dealt away the future of their tiny colony of Hong Kong, and gave it into the hands of the Pekingese with little more than a fond hope that all would be well.

It may have been that all these things were true for the rest of the world. But for the Hong Kong people they were never true. The Hong Kong people never gave the Chinese their trust. Communist China was, after all, the country and the system from which they had fled. Communist China was the country which they remembered only too well, which they knew only too well, and which seemed to them to behave still with pitiless inconsistency. Torture, assassination, massacre, official corruption – a whole catalogue of sins of which Hong Kong had been mercifully purged still flourished in China. And Hong Kong wanted none of it.

So while the rest of the world took comfort in the appearance, as they saw it, of the 'new' China, and of an entity with whom they could do business and treat as an equal, so the Hong Kong people became steadily more and more cynical. They tried to fall in with the rest of world opinion. They tried optimism, and buoyancy, and – being from Hong Kong, where the dollar was an all-powerful ju-ju – they tried to make as much money in business as they could before the deadline as they saw it, of 1997. But underlying all of their attempts was a profound sense of unease, mistrust, and distaste, all of which

they expressed by the simple expedient of leaving the colony, in huge numbers. 'Voting with our feet,' they called it.

This exodus began as a trickle in the Eighties, soon after the publication of the Joint Declaration. Perhaps 100 people were leaving every week. It was a relatively insignificant figure regarded by the government as statistically insignificant, and was little noticed. But a decade later the stream had widened to a flood. In 1992 people were fleeing Hong Kong at the rate of 1,000 a week, for Canada, Australia, the United States. By 1995 some 300 of them were leaving every day – most of them skilled professionals, the qualified, the intelligent. By now they were going anywhere that would take them – to Tonga, Belize, Singapore, Uruguay. The people who had hoped, who had done their best to try to trust those who would soon take them over, now just wanted to get out, to somewhere that offered them and their children some suggestion of stability. The unskilled and the ill-educated who were left behind soon became easy prey, as we have already seen, for the blandishments of the territory's well-organised and politically adroit criminal gangs.

But also during the Eighties there came, unrecognised at first, a further stealthy development, and one of profound importance to the way in which China was later to disintegrate to its present anarchic state.

The suspicion, the distaste, the distrust, the loathing – whatever it was; a precise characterisation of the antipathy expressed towards the northern Chinese comes very much from the reading of individual sets of runes – was up until that point peculiar to, wholly restricted to the Hong Kong people. It was almost wholly non-existent in China itself. To the north of the border fence the Chinese, whether they were Cantonese or Pekingese, Manchu or Szechuan, were of essentially similar outlook, one conditioned by decades of propaganda. It was an outlook which had little in common with that of the people of Hong Kong.

The Hong Kongers may have been ethnically Cantonese, but they were spiritually capitalists. The phrase 'running dogs' was often used by ordinary Chinese to describe them, those greedy semi-barbarians south of the fence. And up until this point during the Eighties there was no apparent mistrust – at least, no mistrust that was ever publicly

expressed, though Sinologists have claimed to have detected it many years before – ever expressed by the Cantonese of China for their northern compatriots. There was, in fact, much more mistrust for those to the south, in Hong Kong.

The date of a shift in attitude can hardly be fixed, but it probably started to occur between the time of the Joint Declaration in September 1984, which dealt with Hong Kong's future, and the Tienanmen Square incident of five years later. At any rate, some time during the mid-point of the decade the mood started to change and the suspicion that was being expressed by the Hong Kong people started to infect the minds and attitudes and expressions of their colleagues over the border, the 80 million inhabitants of Guangdong Province.

Slowly a new kind of cross-border sympathy began to be forged, one that conjoined these people into a broad ethnic and ideological communion. At first it was the Hong Kongers with just their Cantonese-speaking confrères, and then with those who lived in the provinces near by, in Fujian, Guangxi and Hunan. There were many reasons for the development. There was prosperity, for a start: ever since the formation of the Shenzhen Special Economic Zone in 1980, and of its three neighbour zones along the coast at Zhuhai, Xiamen and Shantou, there had been a tremendous influx of foreign money and foreign ideas. Skyscrapers had been built, with revolving restaurants on top, in which *cheongsam*-clad waitresses would bring bottles of Burgundy to the table. A huge four-lane expressway had been built to link Canton City to Hong Kong. Most southern Chinese watched Hong Kong television, and those who could not at least listened to Hong Kong radio.

It was still true that the peasantry of Qinghai Province, the farmers of Heilongjiang Province, and the desert-nomads of Xinjiang had no knowledge of such developments, and were thus insulated against the influences of capital and greed. But in general the provinces of southern China were fast gaining a solid apprehension of the world outside, and of the possibilities that could be open to their own people. South of the Yangtze River there was indeed a 'new' China developing – but one that was evolving not, as Party cadres once had hoped, into an immense ideological communion, but into an

ethnic whole that was united by a common hope for modernism and prosperity and individual freedom. South of the Yangtze River, in short, the Chinese people wanted what they saw their colleagues in Hong Kong already had.

The Cantonese were, of course, at the forefront of these developments. By the early Nineties, under the relentlessly seductive influences of Hong Kong, the Province of Guangdong had become, in the view of Party ideologues in Peking, 'tainted'. The word first appeared in a commentary in the *People's Daily* of 26 December 1993 – the centenary of Mao Tse-tung's birth. The paper's editors wrote at length about the legacy of the esteemed founder of the People's Republic, and concluded that there was much of which all China could be proud. But the condition of the nation was judged by the editor still to be, in some quarters, imperfect:

There is concern, however, at recent anti-progressive trends that have been detected among certain uninformed quarters of Guangdong and Fujian Provinces, where the triple contagions of avarice, corruption and landlordism are once more rearing their heads. These pathetic human traits have long been known to exist – and indeed to have been fostered by the colonial elements – among our compatriots in Hong Kong. Now, in part because of the huge infrastructural developments that physically link Hong Kong to our mainland provinces, we have seen some of these evil tendencies start to taint the less personally courageous of our people in Guangdong. It will take bold action on the part of our glorious Party to root out this evil. But the Party has never flinched from its duty, and there is great confidence among the guiding influences of our nation that these cancers can be purged from our midst. It is important that, in the coming months of this struggle, we all be on our guard and see that, while work is being undertaken to rid these influences from our midst, they not be permitted to infect other nearby quarters of our glorious nation. The imperialist capitalist-roaders who will soon, and mercifully, be absolutely gone from our shores must not be allowed to leave influences behind that may pose a danger to our nation and its people, and lead them to practise the decadent ways that will yet prove and accelerate the downfall of these aged imperial states.

This warning, blunt and uncompromising though it seemed, was taken less seriously than it perhaps should have been. The Hong Kong newspapers wrote about it at length; the local stockmarkets (including the market established in Shenzhen in 1991 – another indication of 'taint') fell heavily.

But a day or two later Mr Gilbert Hu, a Hong Kong based businessman with immense interests in building new roads and rail links in southern China (he had built the four-lane Canton–Hong Kong Highway, for example, and was involved in a consortium to build the Canton City Beltway) made a series of reassuring statements on local television (which he knew would be heard throughout Guangdong Province) to the effect that the success of southern China in no way threatened the primacy of the nation's political system, and that the economic benefits that proximity to Hong Kong brought to southern China would inevitably trickle through to the entire country, helping to make the nation as a whole richer and more up to date. Mr Hu's remarks, which were reaffirmed by the Provincial Governor, Zhu Senlin, helped to stabilise the situation; and for more than two years following there was no further public statement from Peking, and no signs in southern China that anyone had taken notice of the remarks.

In the summer of 1995, however, there were further signs that all was not well in relations between the ruling north and the ideologically wayward south. Governor Zhu, an amiable but compliant figure who had been appointed to his post four years before, came into a heated and public confrontation with his immediate predecessor, Mr Yi Juan Ling.

Mr Yi was, crucially, a native of Guangdong province. (Technically he was a Hakka, but he was on record as saying that his heart was in Guangdong.) He was the son of Yi Jianying, a venerated Marshal in the Chinese Army and a Long March hero. He had been appointed by Peking in 1993 to run Guangdong Province: by all statistical reckonings he had succeeded fabulously. He was much liked, too – and not least because of his local roots.

Too often a Chinese provincial governor was, like the commanding general of a military region or his political commissar, a figure deliberately selected to be from ethnic and linguistic stock far removed from the province he was

governing or the army he was commanding. While this rarely produced any actual resentment among the population, who were either persuaded by propaganda or too cowed by other means to think of protest, they were never exactly exultant about it. But in 1993 the people of Guangdong had reason to celebrate: Yi Juan Ling was one of their own, rewarded for meritorious service in the trenches by being given command over people he knew, and who drew pride from his appointment.

But after only a few months Peking started to worry: the very success that Yi was overseeing was producing, they thought, a cuckoo in the nest. Internal memorandums – many of them intercepted by the SIGINT interceptors at Chung Hom Kok – showed that conservative elements in Peking were becoming increasingly concerned at the way Governor Yi seemed to be building a 'mountain stronghold' in south China. There were privately expressed fears that he might be creating a power base for himself, that he was becoming, in short, the economic version of a warlord.

So after only a year Governor Yi was retired, and his post was taken by a man from a more traditional, conservative and non-Cantonese (actually Shanghainese) background: Mr Zhu Senlin. Mr Yi, however, refused to move out of his mansion near Canton City, arguing that, as an old man of great distinction, it was both improper and inconvenient for him to leave.

The situation was at first of little consequence. Governor Zhu was found a palace of equivalent splendour, and Mr Yi was generally ignored. Or would have been ignored had he not embarked on a strenuous programme of self-promotion by giving, over the following three years, a series of lengthy interviews to the Hong Kong press, in each of which he drew attention to the scale of his success, based, as he put it, on the 'keen friendship' which he was able to enjoy with 'my local people'. He expressed his concern that the same intimacy might not develop with the 'less well-connected' Zhu regime. He pointed out that all the reforms he had instituted in Guangdong were carried out with the full support of the Peking government – he was thus at pains to demonstrate that there never had been any intention on his part to create a 'mountain stronghold' – but went on to issue what others

interpreted as veiled protests at what seemed to be a gradual easing of the pace of reform in the south.

'I am naturally fully supportive of the great leaders of our nation,' he told *Asia Week*. 'Those who think otherwise have been indulging in incorrect speculation based on certain superficial phenomena. The tide of events in our nation has changed, that is true. It is naturally unwise to check the flow of that tide. I have no doubt this view is shared by the great majority of those who are placed in positions of great trust by the people, and whose wisdom is central to the successful management of our ancient and complicated nation.'

Few would take issue with such remarks. But in the summer of 1995 Governor Zhu did, and challenged his predecessor in a signed article in the Canton City *Workers' Daily*.

There are those no longer in public office who shared the responsibility for taking our region of China along perilous pathways. Now that the folly of their ways has been demonstrated, now that the tainting of our way of life has been treated and the restlessness which briefly characterised our country has been stilled, it would be as well if such former office-holders were to keep their own counsel. It would be most unfortunate if the passions which once gripped our people are permitted to visit us again: should they do so, those former office holders who speculate on such matters and who wish for the old days and the old ways would have to be held responsible.

Mr Yi left public view three days after the publication of this editorial, and was not seen again for some months. Signals Intelligence reports indicated that he had been briefly placed under house arrest. By September he was released from whatever privations he suffered, and though he gave no further interviews with any member of the press, and became somewhat difficult to see (diplomats from Hong Kong had long been in the habit of taking tea with him as part of their scouting ventures into the south Chinese hinterland) he was said to be alive and well, still in his old house, and a figure of some note on what passed for the Canton social scene. The fact of his silence was taken as a victory for Peking, but a sign as well that the anxiety over the 'tainting'

of the region had not eased. Peking was indeed still very much on its guard.

This was the situation that prevailed when Constable Wan Zhu'er was shot dead on 10 July 1997.

It has to be remembered that the shooting of a policeman in China is an event of extraordinary rarity. The premeditated defiance, in any form, of the state, of authority, is extremely infrequent. Chinese people do not, generally speaking, go on strike. They do not carry banners of protest. They do not walk out of public meetings. Heckling is a virtually unknown phenomenon. Graffiti is rare. Vandalism never takes place. Instructions are followed. Orders are obeyed. The individual never acts alone. Only the mob turns mean.

Many times in recent years the mob has tried to defy authority. In Peking in 1976, Shanghai in 1987, in Peking again in 1989, in Wuhan four years later, crowds of students, joined later by workers, did battle with the police and, in the two last incidents, with the soldiers of the PLA as well. The demonstrators always came off much the worse, and retreated to lick their wounds and think again about mounting other protests at a later date. Scores of them died or were injured in the confrontations; and while it was true that in several of the incidents police and soldiers and other authority figures died and were injured as well, it can fairly be said that they died or they suffered at the hands of the mob, in the heat of battle, and that their fate was decided in an impromptu fashion and never once premeditated. Although Chinese records on the committing of individual acts of criminal violence are difficult to discover, it seems likely that Constable Wan was the first policeman to die by an assassin's hand in a decade, at least. His murder caused, without a doubt, a major sensation – one that echoed all the way to Peking.

Within minutes of the shooting, which was logged as having taken place at 7.17 a.m., police from the depot on Shamian Island sealed off the road where Constable Wan lay. In addition other police and security men closed all the entrances and exits to the Qingping Market. Crowds of housewives and workers who were making early morning visits on their way to their factories and offices, or who were

buying the ingredients for their lunch, began to build up in front of the police barricades. Long lines of cars and buses accumulated on Liuersan Lu, the road running along the waterfront between the market and Shamian.*

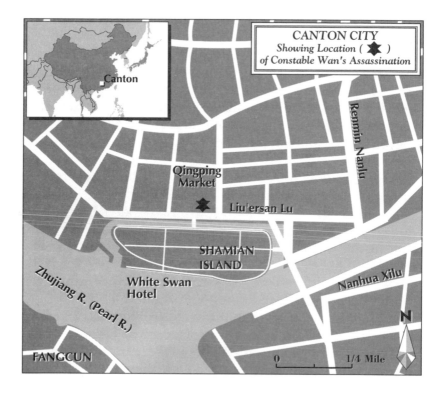

The noise of car horns, the shouts of angry drivers, the querulous protests of the gathering crowds, the insufferable heat of a damp July Thursday – all of this led to a growing fractiousness, and a potential for trouble that was quickly spotted by Police Commissioner Zhou. But instead of attempting to placate the crowd by reopening the market,

*The name Liuersan Lu, '6-23 Road', commemorates the shooting of striking Chinese workers by British and French soldiers on 23 June 1925, an incident that did much to strengthen the hand of the anti-Imperialist movement and the so-called United Front coalition of Communists and Kuomintang. There is no evidence that those stranded in the traffic jam more than seven decades later were aware of how history was repeating itself.

say (for the scene of the crime occupied only a very small section of its outer rim, just off Qingping Lu) or devising a detour for the stranded motorists, the Commissioner ordered a large detachment of armed police into the area to impress the crowd into silence and forbearance. By mid-morning there was an uneasy standoff: some 20,000 people in the side streets around the market, some 600 vehicles caught between the barricades and, surrounding them all, two battalions of the PAP, armed with rifles and side-arms and in no mood to let the situation get further out of hand.

The investigation into the shooting, meanwhile, had produced some interesting facts. Constable Wan took the single bullet in the right side of his face: it had entered below his cheekbone and spun upwards through his brain, emerging through the scalp and blowing almost all of the top left side of his head away. He would have died instantly. The single bullet used in the attack was a 9mm Parabellum, and from comparisons with photographs of other bullets it was speedily agreed among the police that it was a bullet that had been manufactured in Israel. The weapon that fired it was probably, the detectives then concluded with surprising rapidity, an Uzi sub-machine-gun, set to fire single shots.

Given the trajectory of the bullet and the characteristics of the weapon – which was somewhat difficult to aim, and best fired at close range – it was likely that the assassin was hiding in a car or a lorry parked on Qingping Lu. The bullet's upward path suggested that the assassin was lower than the target, probably in a car, rather than a lorry. Investigators thus began questioning all those who were in the market at the time. Had they heard the shot? Had they seen a vehicle – probably a car – leave the area in a hurry, after the shooting? In fact, had they seen anything at all unusual that morning?

Qingping Market is a place where a Western visitor would regard almost everything as unusual. That the constable was shot while cycling just beside the parade of owls – eagle owls and brown fish owls being the most favoured for the pot – hints at the menagerie beyond. On a normal day one can find, in the slimy alleyways of Quingping, such delights as leopard, golden monkey, the seven-banded civet cat, pangolins rolled tight into defensive balls, the slow loris, the giant salamander, a bagful of banded kraits, a cage of Peking

robins, and legions of unremarkable cats and dogs, all waiting to be butchered, skewered and served up roasted for dinner.

Against such a background – of strange animal cries, the pandemonium of the crowds of shoppers, the traffic noise and the thunderclaps (for the day had begun with a vicious summer storm) – could anyone be expected to remember hearing a gunshot, or seeing a car lurch off in an unexpected hurry or the constable fall to the ground? At least, such were the excuses that those questioned all offered. After four hours, during which the crowds grew larger and more restless and more angry, it turned out that no one had seen or heard anything. No one in the market that morning was able to help the police carry the investigation any further than their own forensic examinations had taken them. There was, it seemed to the frustrated and irritated officers, almost a conspiracy of silence abroad. One detective even claimed to his superiors later that he had heard two men in the market laugh and say they were glad that the policeman had died. 'Wretched scum from Peking,' was the phrase that was used – a remark that may have been geographically inaccurate (since the constable had come from Shandong Province, 300 miles south of Peking), but which probably summed up the sentiment of the crowd.

By lunchtime the mood on both sides was dangerously hostile. The detectives had achieved nothing, and under pressure from their officers to find some clues to the killing their questioning was growing ever harsher. The shoppers and passers-by, who were by now clearly unwilling to be of any help to the police, had been detained for much longer than any one of them was willing to tolerate. The crowds outside the police barricades began to jeer at the police, and to shout sympathetically to those detained inside.

Then suddenly half a dozen of those who were being held for questioning decided that they had had enough, and broke away from their questioners. They ran at full speed through the slippery halls of the market and straight into the backs of the policemen who were keeping the curious crowds out. Their speed and determination allowed them to break the police line and, in the momentary confusion, they succeeded in getting through to their colleagues outside. A huge

cheer went up, and the crowd began to pelt the police with vegetables and chunks of sugar cane and the contents of dozens of large straw baskets of refuse that were waiting for collection in a gutter.

Two companies of armed police were ordered to hurry around to the northern side of the market, where this irruption of violence had broken out, and to take up defensive positions. They were ordered, as a precautionary measure, to fix bayonets; the sight of this formidable array of men marching towards the alleys where the mob had accumulated caused immediate panic and dismay. 'Another Wuhan!' a woman screamed, and there was a chorus of anger from the mob. 'You cowards!' 'Why turn your guns on us?' 'Have you no shame?'

However, the boiling black clouds which had been circling the city all morning chose this particular moment to explode in thunder and lightning, and great drops of rain began to pelt down. A brief but violent tropical storm lashed down on the city once again, as it had earlier that morning. Within five minutes the streets were awash with torrents of dirty water coursing its way down to the canal and the Pearl River. The crowds melted away home and the tension was instantly relieved.

The Police Commissioner, after consulting his officers on the spot, decided there would be little value in pursuing further interviews, and allowed all those remaining in the market to go home as well, once they had given their identity card numbers and their addresses to the officers.

But Peking was not satisfied. Later that evening Commissioner Zhou – who had made a full report on the incident to his superiors, and to the office of Governor Zhu Senlin – was telephoned personally by an (as yet unidentified) official at the headquarters of the Public Security Bureau. The precise contents of the message have never been revealed, but it is believed that it was made brutally clear to the Commissioner and his senior colleagues that such signs of potential disorder as had manifested themselves in Canton City that morning and afternoon should be dealt with immediately, the results promulgated with equal speed, and the population left in no doubt that neither the central, provincial nor city governments would tolerate such aberrant behaviour.

The Commissioner did indeed act swiftly. Late that evening he ordered two dozen men from the PSB to enter, by force if necessary, a number of rooming houses in a slum area close to the market at Zhoutouzui Wharf, from where the Pearl River boat services to and from Hong Kong are operated. The houses, gloomy and foetid places notorious for harbouring smugglers and drug users and the cheaper kinds of prostitutes, were often raided when politicians demanded a quick arrest or a scapegoat for an unsolved crime, and the police were confident, on this occasion as in the past, of netting someone on whom they could pin this killing.

By midnight three men were in custody. Two – Leung Ka Tan and Leung Wan – were from Hong Kong; the third, Lam Wang Fook, was from the city of Foshan, about twenty miles west of Canton. None of the three had satisfactory identification papers, the police said later, and one of the Leungs was in possession of a rusty automatic pistol which might have been fired recently. It was of 7.62 mm calibre, and so could not be directly linked to the murder of Constable Wan.

None the less the men were taken early next morning to a public hearing of the Canton City People's Court. Each of the men was held tightly by the arms – which were handcuffed behind the back – by two members of the PAP. They looked dazed, and several observers in court said later they appeared to have been drugged.

A tribunal of judges sitting for twenty minutes heard the evidence against them. Eyewitness accounts were read out, indicating that all three men had been seen in a red Toyota, evidently a former Hong Kong taxicab, parked in Qingping Lu at 6.45 the previous morning. Forensic tests were read out, showing that wax impression samples taken from the hands of suspect Lam showed evidence of cordite burns that matched the known chemical characteristics of the type of cordite used in Israeli-manufactured ammunition. A scrawled note was produced with the characters for 'police' and 'Qingping Market' and a time '7 a.m.' clearly legible. All this evidence, a prosecuting lawyer said, proved beyond a shadow of doubt that these three men had conspired to murder Constable Wan. It was regrettable, the lawyer told

the court, that the eyewitnesses were unable to be present that morning, and that the forensic scientist who had conducted the tests on Lam's hands had been ordered to another case in southern Guangdong; the calligraphy expert who had compared the characters on the handwritten note with samples of Leung Ka Tan's writing, pronouncing them 'of identical origin', could be called back from holiday if necessary. The tribunal replied that it did not feel such drastic measures were called for. The three men were clearly, on the basis of the evidence so painstakingly assembled, guilty as charged, and would be sentenced to death by shooting.

Accordingly later that morning, a hot and sunny Friday, the three men were placed, standing, in the back of three open police trucks, to be driven to their place of execution. The chosen spot was a small park named Dongshanhu to the east of the city. During the five-mile journey from the courts on Jeifang Beilu, in the north of the city, loudspeaker announcements informed pedestrians and motorists and the crowds of cyclists that the men responsible for the appalling crime of the morning before had been successfully apprehended, and were being dealt with according to law. Large posters hung around each man's neck also stated, in large red characters, the nature of the crime and his guilt. Since the journey was a slow one it is estimated that in the order of 1 million people came to know of the impending act of retribution.

The act itself came at five minutes after noon – nearly twenty-nine hours after the murder. The lorries bumped across the waste ground into the park. The backs of the lorries were opened, the men were pulled down and marched to a spot on a small hillock near the riverside. They were forced to kneel beside each other.

The policemen guarding them moved back, and one senior officer stepped forward with a pistol. He went up to Mr Lam, placed the snout of the pistol beneath his right ear, angled upwards, and fired. Lam fell forward, dead. The officer then moved to the two Leungs, and did the same. Another officer with a stethoscope examined the three for any sign of life and, finding none, ordered the bodies placed in the back of one of the open trucks. The policemen then left the scene. A park attendant with a brush of bamboo strips tidied up the area and brushed earth over the pools of blood.

Later that day large posters went up outside the city police stations with the names of the three men, an account of their crimes, the court's verdict, and the nature of the sentence. Across each of the names was drawn a distinctive red tick mark, indicating that the sentence had, in all cases, been carried out. Justice had both been done and, as was most important in what the Police Commissioner was later to say were 'these volatile times', had been seen to be done. The people of south China had been warned.

## CHAPTER SEVEN

# ONSET
# OF RAGE

## THE SOUTH COAST OF CHINA
### *July 1997*

The southern Chinese summer grew steadily hotter and more sultry, and an unusual number of powerful storms battered the coastal towns and villages. The rains spread into central China too, the Yangtze and the Yellow Rivers flooded catastrophically, and hundreds of people were reportedly drowned in Sichuan and Hubei Provinces, which suffered this year even more miserably than was customary.

Hundreds of thousands of refugees (perhaps scores of millions, the number could never be reasonably estimated) joined the annual trek south – workless and hungry peasants leaving their hardscrabble farms and their mud-ruined fields in search of work, or even for the opportunity to beg, in the industrial cities of Guangdong. Such unfortunate people could be seen everywhere in the city: they were smaller and darker skinned than their Cantonese comrades. They were invariably dressed in rags, showed no shame in their appearance, and had an almost feral energy for hard and dirty manual work, for panhandling, or for villainy.

Outside the main railway station, which was in any case perpetually thronged with masses of filthy, sweaty and unkempt men and women, hundreds of such refugees would lie in wait for arriving or departing passengers. One young woman, who serves as an example of the mood of economic desperation of the times, would sit outside the Main Line exit from dawn until late at night, an undersized and almost lifeless baby clutched firmly to her naked and shrivelled

breast. Any passenger who evidenced even the slightest hint of prosperity – by carrying a suitcase instead of a sack, or if one article of his clothing that he wore looked clean, or even moderately new, or if he carried a newspaper or a magazine or some other sign of having recently parted with small change – any such hapless individual was her invariable and immediate target.

She would launch herself at him with the speed and venom of a snake. She would fasten herself to him with a single bony claw, and she would screech at him in some barely comprehensible rural tongue, demanding that he part with a few *renminbi* for the child she held clamped tight under her other arm. He invariably would look bewildered, disgusted and embarrassed by turn. He would try to beat her away, as would a man enveloped in a swarm of bees. But it was of no avail. She would shout even more loudly, and she would berate him for his lack of decency, his lack of charity, and for his assault on her and her defenceless child. And eventually, under so withering a barrage, he would give in, and dig deep into his pockets for one or two from a small bundle of creased and dirty notes that he was in no position to afford to waste, and he would hand them to the woman who, without even a word or a gesture of gratitude, would sidle back into the crowds, and wait for her next victim, the next unsuspecting arrival in the city of Canton.

By 1995, according to a study made available from the American Embassy in Peking, there were no fewer than 340 million peasants – more people, in other words, than lived in all of the United States – who could officially be classified as so deeply underemployed that by Western standards they would be regarded as literally unemployed. And in 1997, driven by poverty, hunger, frustration, desperation, anger – and then the floods – they were on the move. It mattered little to such people that China had strict rules to limit labour mobility – rules that prohibited anyone moving to another town without a Residency Permit, a document rarely granted, and then only to those with a guaranteed job (which, as might be expected of so controlled a state, could not be acquired without the production of a Residency Permit). These people moved in an unstoppable flood, and when they arrived in the chosen city – Chongqing, or Changsha, or Canton – they knew they had

already flouted the rules, and were thus outlaws, and could suffer no worse than imprisonment, which would at least ensure them a small amount of daily food, work, and shelter.

The social order of Canton, rarely stable in the best of times, and maintained in less good times by strict policing and force of arms, was to deteriorate sharply in the summers of the Nineties. As the numbers of workless peasants increased, as their summer migrations accelerated in scale and boldness, as climatic conditions forced more and more of a deeply dissatisfied rural population to infiltrate the city populations, so the distemper of the city became ever more pronounced. An Oriental version of Boyle's law seemed to operate: the temperature went up, the numbers of people climbed, the volume available for their accommodation remained unchanged, and so the pressure increased steadily, inexorably, fatally. Sooner or later something was bound to burst.

Hindsight shows us now that the events of 10 and 11 July 1997 – the assassination, and the hurried retribution – provided the needle that was to release this pressure. But other contributory factors were to come into play in the following days, ensuring that the explosion, when it finally came at the end of the month (to coincide, not unexpectedly, with the celebrations called to mark the 76th anniversary of the First Congress of the Chinese Communist Party) was all the more extreme.

The principal factor was the knowledge both in Peking and Canton that the three men hauled from their shacks near the Zhoutouzui wharf had nothing at all to do with the shooting of Constable Wan. The public security apparatus felt that the execution of the three men might still any latent local volatility, and remind any dissident forces of who exactly was in control. But the act was only an expedient. The reality remained that some vestigial anti-social organisation now existed in Canton, and that it was an organisation equipped with, at the very least, an Uzi sub-machine-gun from Israel and sufficient ammunition from the same source, and was possessed of a car, a willing driver and a good marksman, together with the constable's own side-arm and a clip of 7.62 mm bullets. This unit alone, if it remained

undetected, could be dangerous: the likelihood was that many more members, and many more weapons, were secreted around the city. The police had to find them, and find the source of both the men and *matériel*, and put a swift and decisive halt to whatever anti-social agency had started to operate.

Emergency conferences held by senior PSB officers during mid-July drew on their very limited resources of street intelligence (which had gone unaccountably silent in recent weeks) and concluded that the most probable source of the trouble was Hong Kong. However, a Policy Directive from Peking dated 4 July ordered that the 'serious social unrest' that had followed the departure of the British (and which had resulted in fires, destruction of many buildings and the deaths of some 300 people evenly divided between the civilian and armed populations) 'should now be allowed to dissipate'. Thus any 'interference in Hong Kong's internal government', which invariably led to 'grave expressions of anger among the local population', should be 'kept at a minimum for the time being, to permit Chief Executive Mao to enjoy a period of stability'.

The corollary to this instruction was that officials from the PSB should not undertake major criminal investigations inside the territory, other than with the permission of Mao's office. A formal approach seeking such permission was turned down flat. A senior PSB officer from Canton accordingly flew to Peking to win the sanction of higher authority. He returned on 17 July with permission to send his officers, in plain clothes, into the Special Administrative Region and to make 'such discreet investigations as are deemed vitally necessary'. Before his men left he added a warning to the effect that 'the normal procedures used by the Bureau to conduct investigations may not be wholly suited to the sensitivities of the people of Hong Kong'.

The next day twelve Bureau officers travelled by train to Kowloon and, to use the slang of the time (and completely ignoring the warning from Peking) 'slapped some beancurd' in the slums of Mong Kok. The arrest and subsequent torture – for this is what the 'slapping' implied – of three men whose names were in the Mong Kok police files of known arms smugglers produced little that was of use or interest,

other than to confirm that Uzi sub-machine-guns had been freely available 'shortly before the end of July', and that a number were known to be circulating now.

The dealers themselves had not seen any of these weapons, though they admitted under severe 'slapping' that they could provide suitable 9 mm American-made Parabellum ammunition from stock. But none had been ordered in the previous week, the dealers said: everyone 'in the business' was clearly intimidated by the Chinese Communist presence, which was much larger and more overwhelming than had ever been expected.

The leader of the PSB group, fearing that their continued stay in the Region would leak out and further excite local passions and embarrass the local leadership, then ordered a retreat. To limit any likelihood of the news of their questioning becoming public, the three arms dealers were promptly strangled to death in circumstances that made the killings appear to be the result of criminal rivalry.

On their return to Guangdong Province the police ordered strict new controls to be placed on all movements through the two barriers. At the southern frontier – the old Hong Kong border – there would henceforth be a thorough inspection of all northbound vehicles and their occupants, all of whom would now have to disembark and be subjected to a body inspection; the northern frontier, which had recently been equipped with electric fencing on which two young men (trying to get into the Zone from the north) had already died, was thought to be adequately secure, though new mirror-sticks were to be provided to vehicle inspectors to ensure that no goods were smuggled into China underneath any northbound cars or trucks.

Peter Heung had by this time vanished underground. To maintain his invisibility he had a simple set of rules. He would not spend successive nights at the same address. He never used the telephone. He communicated with his lieutenants in code, on scraps of paper. Such meetings as he attended were called at short notice, with those attending ignorant of which of their colleagues was likely to be present.

But in spite of these inconveniences he was still surprisingly able to organise his White Fans and his 49 Boys to perform the bidding of the gang hierarchy. The three nights of heavy rioting that greeted the arrival of the Chinese and the departure of the British colonial administrators was testimony to his tactical genius. Furthermore, there was no indication that Chinese intelligence knew either his name or his whereabouts: as part of the agreement with Margerison struck some weeks before, all Special Branch files relating to the Warwick Accord had been either destroyed or removed to vaults in London.

It did not take Heung very long to find out about the visit of the PSB officers from Canton City, nor to ascertain the 'release' (to use bandit slang once again) of the three men they had interrogated. He and his colleagues had expected the visit, and had expected they would lose men as a consequence of it. That only three had suffered was not, in the group's view, particularly distressing since these particular three had no knowledge of the Margerison arrangements, and no knowledge (aside from the inevitable rumours) of the fate of the new weapons.

As it happened, more than 80 per cent of the weapons had already been sent into Chinese territory. They had gone, by train, by car, in individual pockets and in plastic luggage bags, during the chaos of those first few days of July. Border security for southbound travellers was exacting; but for northbound visitors there was very little. (It only became strict in the immediate aftermath of Constable Wan's death on 10 July, and then again following the visit of the PSB officers on 18 July. For the first week of July the searching of passengers and vehicles passing up to Shenzhen and beyond was perfunctory at best.)

Heung's view of the need for such movement of arms stemmed from two thoughts: first, his uncertainty that he could maintain the total operational security of his Hong Kong forces, and second, and most important of all, his and his colleagues' firm belief that, in the long term, *it was more valuable for his organisation to try to help foment discord and trouble in Canton in southern China than it was for him to reinforce the resentment and dissent that already existed in Hong Kong.*

The task of turning the population against the northern

Chinese was, as has been explained above, already complete in the former British territory. But the growing dissatisfaction in the main cities of Guangdong and Fujian Provinces – Canton in particular, but in Zhuhai, Foshan, Huiyang, Shantou, Zhanzhou, Xiamen and Quanzhou as well, as outlined in the previous chapter – suggested to Heung's group that there was sufficient potential to produce, one day, and with their help, a pan-Cantonese, pan-Fukkienese political communion, a southern resistance axis, or whatever else one might term it: in short, a coalition of men and forces south of the Yangtze who perhaps might, one day, be able to help direct all of southern China along the same path that had, until very recently, been followed by the people of Hong Kong.

Captain Margerison had mentioned the point to him idly some months before. Now, with the acquisition of a limited amount of weapons, there was the opportunity. He could perhaps help nudge his colleagues across the frontier in the proper direction. So he directed both the bulk of the weapons, the explosives and the ammunition and more than a hundred of his best men, all of them former natives of Canton City or of Xiamen, and frequent visitors to their relatives there, with orders to blend into the population and await detailed instructions.

Their general occupation in the meantime was to arrange and complete a small number of assassinations, as a way of testing the authorities' mettle and competence (an order which they started to carry out – with the shooting of Constable Wan – with dispatch); and to assist in finding and organising groups who might, at appropriate moments, stage acts of disobedience and defiance to excite and irritate the authorities. Only after these probing devices had been completed and their effects noted would more serious and concerted activities begin.

The second and third of such 'probing' incidents took place simultaneously early on the evening of Tuesday, 22 July. Both took place in Fujian Province, a coastal region to the east of Guangdong which enjoyed a prosperity similar to that of the Pearl River delta area. According to Heung's

operations officers in China there was an important tactical purpose in staging the events in these two separate areas: firstly, it would enable the rebels to gauge the level of popular sympathy in two ethnically dissimilar but equivalently prosperous and 'tainted' parts of south China; and secondly, it would enable a comparison of the government's response to incidents staged in two adjoining military regions, for although Guangdong and Fujian Provinces are linked by a common border, and are, like all provinces, separate military districts, they happen also to belong to different Military Regions. Guangdong Province is a part of Guanzhou Military Region, which – commanded by a full general based on the outskirts of Canton City – includes six Military Districts, each commanded by a lieutenant-general. These six are Guangdong, Guangxi, Hainan Island, Hubei, Hunan and, since 1 July, Yianggang. Fujian, on the other hand, is part of the Nanjing Military Region, which has its headquarters in the city of Nanjing. The Region administers five districts, which include Fujian, Anhui, Zhejiang, Jiangxi and Jiangsu and is associated with the Shanghai Military Garrison Command, which (like Peking and Tianjin Garrisons) has a high degree of military autonomy.

It is important to note also that Fujian Military District has notional responsibility for 'protecting' the mainland from Taiwan. The forces there had, ever since the Fifties, been on the alert for any hostile acts that might be mounted by the forces of the Republic of China, which lies directly east of Fujian – and indeed of Xiamen City – across the 100-mile-wide Taiwan Strait. So Heung's group supposed that the response, if any, of the Fujian military commander to what he might see as an incipient rebellion, would be likely to be very much more robust – because of the perceived 'foreign threat' from Taipei – than would be the response to similar problems arising elsewhere in any other districts. (Although it was perhaps true that the action of commanders in Tibet and the extreme north of Manchuria, who would have reason to suspect foreign threats of a different kind from the Tibetans, the Nepalese, India, forces loyal to the Dalai Lama, or the Russians, respectively, might be equally swift and strong.)

Which makes the boldness of the Xiamen incident of 22

July, and the tenor of the reaction, all the more interesting.

It will be recalled that in late July the country was scheduled to celebrate the seventy-sixth anniversary of the staging of the First Congress of the Chinese Communist Party. The anniversaries were generally lavish affairs, with each provincial capital vying with its rivals in the scale and grandeur of its parades, with special editions of the newspapers, adulatory documentary films on television and in cinemas, and self-congratulatory banquets where the local party grandees would toast the achievements of the past year and look forward with professed enthusiasm to the triumphs awaiting.

This year the celebrations were due to be even more heart-felt, since the Party could now give thanks for the welcoming into its fold of one further piece of real estate – Hong Kong – and a further 6 million new comrades, to take the total population of China over the almost unimaginably massive figure of 1500 million. It remained only for the Portuguese-held enclave of Macau to join the family – an event which was formally due to happen in two years' time – and then for Taiwan, which it surely would, but at some date as yet unstated – before the entire realm of the Middle Kingdom could all be safely joined into an ideological one. This anniversary, therefore, would be particularly joyful, marking the first of the final steps that the nation was taking towards becoming the state for which all the Chinese yearned.

There were two dozen elderly Party cadres in Xiamen and the neighbouring counties who were due to be singled out for honours at the 1997 celebrations. The formal banquet at which citations were to be read and plaques presented was due to take place on Friday, 25 July in the famous Bagua Lou, 'The Building of the Eight Diagrams' on the island of Gulangyu. The building, with its distinctive dome, had been a merchant's mansion; during the cultural revolution it had been an electrical factory; and then in the Seventies it had been restored, and opened as a museum of Xiamen history in 1993. It was the finest building in the city, the natural setting for a ceremony of this splendour.

A final planning meeting was organised for the evening of the Tuesday before. It would be attended by the Assistant Party Secretary, Mr Wei Chunwa, four of his secretariat, and

a group of ten officials from the Xiamen Municipality and from Hui'an County, who were planning to stage a tableau. This meeting, which had been little publicised, was also to take place in a grand building – in this case the former trader's mansion complex that had been taken over by the Municipality in 1978 and was now known as the Gulangyu Guesthouse. This assembly of three large houses lay in a park, once the old Foreign Concession Parade Ground, near the northern end of the little island, and suitably close to the much-visited museum to Koxinga*, the region's favourite son.

The guesthouse, once owned by a businessman named Mr Huang, had managed to keep all its old furniture – old clocks (one made by Hamilton in New York in 1911), a fine billiard table (made by a company in London's Soho Square in 1925), leather Chesterfields and grimy oil paintings. The place had the look and feel of a rather down-at-heel gentlemen's club – and with the fine old banyan trees and the scrubby lawns, a colonial watering-hole in some distant corner of the tropics.

The men arranged themselves around the main dining table at 6 p.m. Mr Wei, who was the guest of honour, was seated at the head of the table; two of his four assistants were beside him, the other two at the far end of the table. The men from Hui'an and Xiamen were in between. At 6.07 p.m. – the hands of the Hamilton clock stopped at this point – there came a huge explosion. A bomb, estimated to contain at least four pounds of a plastic explosive, exploded beneath the table no more than two feet from where Mr Wei was sitting. He was almost decapitated, and died instantly, as did his two closest assistants, three of the men from Xiamen

---

*Koxinga was the nickname for the famous and revered General Zhen Chenggong, who used Xiamen as his base for his numerous fruitless attacks on the Manchus after the fall of the Ming Dynasty in 1644. But his defeat at the hands of the northerners is less well remembered by modern Chinese than is his single triumph – his attack on the Dutch in Taiwan, and his success in driving them unceremoniously off to Japan. Koxinga's little army – strong men, selected, it was said, only if each could lift a 600 lb stone lion on to his back – is an army of heroes, even today. And among the gifts that each of the cadres was due to be given at the Friday celebration dinner was a small stone lion, an exact hand-carved replica of that still kept in an honoured place in the Gulangyu shrine.

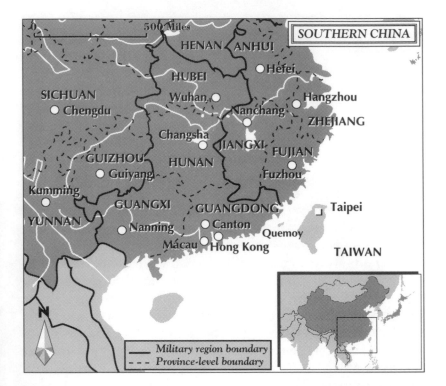

Municipality, a waiter who had been pouring Mr Wei's tea, and another unidentified man. The remaining members of the group were all savagely injured, with two of them requiring the amputation of both legs, and all suffering severe abdominal injuries.

Devastation in the room was extraordinary, and the fact that two large crossbeams were blown out and crashed down on the injured delayed the removal of the men to a hospital. In addition, none of the clinics on the island was capable of handling such an emergency, and the injured had to be taken by boat across to the city's piano-shaped tourist pier, and sped to Xiamen Number Four Hospital. It was not until midnight that the injured had all been removed from the ruined building, and forensic examination did not start until dawn.

There had been an initial suspicion that a liquefied gas bottle from the kitchen, inadvertently left beneath the table, had somehow caught fire and exploded. But the discovery, shortly after first light, of the remains of a timing device,

with a Seiko digital watch seemingly used as part of the triggering mechanism, indicated beyond doubt that the incident was an act of sabotage. One, moreover, of which its organisers could be justly proud: seven men, five of them leading local members of the Chinese Communist Party, had died. It was probable that the Friday celebrations would have to be cancelled.

This probability increased further when local police were told of another unprecedented outrage that had occurred in the nearby town of Shitsze, also known by its nickname of Xiao Xianggang, or 'Little Hong Kong'.

The town, which ten years before had been no more than a gaggle of crude shacks, had blossomed into one of the country's most astonishing success stories. It had neither a railway nor a port, and until 1995 had been connected to the rest of Fujian Province by a single-lane track. And yet – for reasons which were never explained, but were thought to have been due to a large measure of official corruption, and the fact that a very large number of the local residents had wealthy relations living abroad in the Philippines and the United States – it boomed, like nowhere else in South China, with more than 10,000 privately owned businesses.

It was possible to obtain anything in Shitsze City. There were BMW cars for sale, and Honda motorcycles, CDs of the latest Japanese pop singers, CDI players, cases of Australian Chardonnay, pornographic holograms, See's chocolates, Love Flower Brand silk underwear (which was made in a privately owned factory), Jade Horse Brand Cigars (owned by the Tabaqueria Filipiniana of Manila, and exported around the world) and Xiao Xianggang Brandy, rebottled as 'Tall Man' French VSO, and marketed very successfully in Macau.

Occasionally the local authorities were ordered, by Public Security Ministry fiat from Peking, to try to clamp down on the plethora of illegality in the town. Such clampdowns usually manifested themselves as executions, which followed widely publicised show trials. Such a trial had taken place on 20 July, when two men, a Mr Hua and a Mr Dong, were put on show in Shitsze's half-completed basketball stadium, accused of smuggling Hitachi television sets from a Manila-registered freighter which was, at the time of its supposed sighting, hove to ten miles east of Quemoy Island.

114

The men were duly sentenced to death and were marched off to a patch of waste ground a mile outside town. However, as they were being helped down from their transport there was a brief and efficient ambush: five armed men stepped from an unmarked van and, according to eyewitness reports, spoke to the police escorts. One of the policemen clearly objected, there was a struggle, and a single shot was fired. The policeman fell to the ground, injured. The remaining officers dropped their weapons and fled, whereupon Mr Hua and Dr Dong, collecting up the half-dozen rifles and pistols left behind, were bundled into the van and driven away. The policeman who had been injured had not been badly hurt, and survived: he said later he believed the assailants had Hong Kong accents. The other policemen, at the time news of this incident was telegraphed to Xiamen, had not been found.

The authorities were, in essence, panic-stricken. The police and Public Security Bureau had long been under standing orders to notify the army if anything untoward and 'of possibly Taiwan-inspired origin' occurred in the area. Acting under these instructions the Xiamen authorities informed the Fujian Military District Commissar, Chen Shuqing, at his headquarters camp near Drum Mountain, east of the provincial capital city of Fuzhou. Chen conferred both with his military commander, General Shen, and by telephone with Region HQ in Nanjing City. They concluded that enemy interference was probably behind the two incidents, and suitable precautions had therefore to be taken.

The Drum Mountain Early Warning Station was thus put on full alert. Two squadrons of Shenjang J8 fighter aircraft based at Xiamen and Fuzhou were told to be ready for immediate action. Armed patrol vessels of the East Sea Fleet were ordered to set out from Dinghai Island near Shanghai, and from Xiamen naval dockyard, and to stand to in the Taiwan Straits. Two Anshan-class destroyers were ordered to proceed north from Hong Kong, to join the patrol vessels.

In addition, two entire infantry divisions from the 63rd Integrated Group Army based near Quanzhou were ordered into full battle gear, and six coastal artillery batteries were

issued with quantities of 155 mm ammunition and instructed to be on close watch for any potential invaders from across the Straits. The two islands of Quemoy and Matsu, the former so near that observers on Gulangyu could see the Taiwanese flag with only moderately powered glasses, were kept under particular surveillance.

It was against this background of the most extraordinary military readiness that the Fujian Provincial PSB began the investigation into the most serious acts of criminal violence and defiance to have occurred in China for twenty years.

For the Gulangyu inquiry the island was completely sealed off: the ferry-boat that normally shuttled to and from the mainland was halted, and only official police boats were permitted to land. The fishing harbour was shut. Policemen fanned out over the island, telling all residents to remain indoors.

A number of clues were found in the debris. Fragments of the Seiko digital watch timer were dug from the mess of plaster and brick soon after dawn. Then a number of charred fragments of paper were found which were cylindrically curved, probably wrappers from sticks of explosive. The detectives were able to recognise two types of writing on the paper, one English, the other probably Urdu. More careful examination that followed the piecing-together of a number of these paper fragments indicated that the explosives had come from a well-known but illicit munitions factory in a town called Darra, in Pakistan's North-West Frontier Province. To import from such a source would not be difficult: ever since the opening, ten years before, of the Karakoram Highway between Gilgit and Kashgar there had been justifiable anxiety about the possibility of what were called 'tribal guns' being brought into China. One of the consequences of the Gulangyu investigation was an immediate tightening of the frontier inspection, much as had been ordered on the Hong Kong–Shenzhen border: the dangers of allowing weapons into the country were self-evident.

Other clues emerged later in the day. A worker in the grounds of the old Catholic church – not a Catholic himself, but a gardener who had long been in the pay of the PSB and had been assigned to keep an eye on the activities of the elderly priest – reported that a week before he had seen

three men, who at the time he assumed were tourists, talking in hushed tones to a man known to be a cleaner from the guesthouse. He assumed the men were tourists because they were speaking in Cantonese, a language which he did not understand.

Enquiries showed that the cleaner, whose name was Li, had left the island by boat on the afternoon of the explosion. The guesthouse manager said he had been working in the main dining-room that afternoon. He also reported that Li was from Canton City, and that while he spoke *putonghua* and some Fukkienese, his mother tongue was Cantonese.

All of this information had been gleaned before noon on 23 July, the Wednesday. It seemed clear to the investigators that the conspiracy involved at least four men of whom at least three came from either Canton or Hong Kong. The word 'tourist', when used by a Chinese, usually refers to someone from an evidently very different community – someone whose appearance and dress and manner look most unfamiliar. The fact that the three men who spoke to the cleaner were evidently very different in appearance from the cleaner – who did come from Canton – suggested to the investigators that they were looking for a group from Hong Kong.

Messages were sent to all hotels and guesthouses to check their records. Surveillance at airports and liner ports was stepped up. Xiamen University, which was still open for summer classes, was ordered closed, and the students told to remain on campus. The single bridge linking Xiamen to the mainland at Jimei was cordoned off by troops. Later that afternoon house-to-house searches were ordered in two districts of the city known to be favoured by overseas Chinese – particularly the Taiwanese who trickled up from Hong Kong, and those who lived in Manila, and returned to see relations in the region.

The only effect of this hurriedly and clumsily organised cordon and search operation was to alienate at least two sectors of the local population – the students and the fishermen. Neither of these groups of people, amounting to nearly 4,000 each, was permitted to leave. By early evening the students had become dangerously restless and the leader of the student body, a third-year anthropologist named Duan

Kun, organised a protest march out of the university grounds. The march got under way at 7 p.m. and had reached Daxue Lu, the main coast road that leads to the city, when it was confronted by a double line of men from the People's Armed Police.

At about the same time, and one has to assume by pure coincidence, a crowd of several hundred squid-fishermen whom police had forbidden to take their craft out for the night also gathered on Daxue Lu about a third of a mile west from where the students were facing their lines of policemen. Here a similar double line of PAP, all armed with rifles, halted the fishermen. There was then a great deal of shouted protest from both groups – protest which might have ebbed away during the evening had not one of the more observant students, alerted by the noise of distant shouting, noticed, some few hundred yards down the hill, the lines of police and the distant crowd of brother protestors.

The students then took up the cry of the fishermen, and within minutes hundreds of them had broken through the police lines and had run down the incline to confront the other police line from the rear. The fishermen began to push against the policemen from the front; students were jeering and catcalling from the back; and the PAP officer in charge, finding that his radio did not work and that he had little chance of calling in reinforcements, panicked. He screamed to the front line of his men, who had fixed bayonets, to stand firm; and to the rear line to reverse and, if necessary, to ward off the students with force.

For a few moments this tactic worked, and the students retreated. But Duan Kun, aware of the power of his rhetoric, climbed up on a boulder and started to scream an attack on the authorities. He had just shouted the current student rallying-cry of 'Remember Wuhan!' when one of the soldiers, probably acting without orders and fearing for his life, fired a single shot at him, hitting him square in the chest. Mr Duan spun backwards from the rock and landed on his head in a jumble of sharp granite riprap that made up the footwall at the rear of the bathing beach.

The fishermen, seeing the shooting, roared into action as one, and began to fight the policemen with their bare hands, tearing the rifles from their grip, punching, pulling hair,

kicking, biting. The rear line of police turned to help their colleagues, whereupon the students rushed at them, laying about them and disarming all of the police in a matter of minutes. Before night had fallen the thirty policemen had been stripped of weapons, ammunition, uniforms and the broken radio, and were standing forlornly by the roadside in their underwear. Two of them, however, marched off with the victorious students, three others with the exultant fishermen.

These five men will come to be remembered in history books throughout the world as the first of the turncoats, in what was to become – from the point of view of the Chinese authorities – a summer of traitorous and disastrous behaviour. And one that essentially began with a night of ugliness and mayhem in a city that was shortly to become wayward and virtually ungovernable.

Crowds of students and factory workers roamed through the city streets all that night. There was one major organised protest, when the body of Duan Kun – for the young man

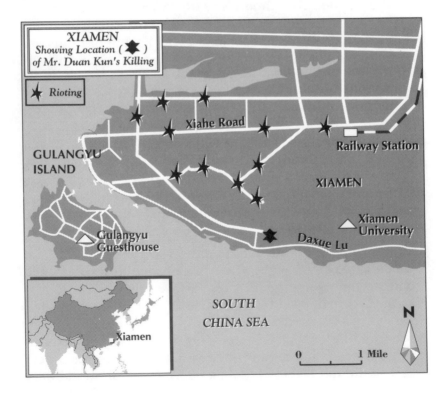

119

never responded to treatment, and died at 8.30 p.m. in the University medical department – was carried in procession along Xiamen Road, towards the railway station. The students took the longer route in an attempt to generate as much local sympathy and publicity as they could. Hundreds of other workers, alerted by swiftly spreading rumours, joined the cortège and followed it to the Municipal Court, and there set up a huge, impromptu protest rally.

Large four-character posters denounced the authorities' actions in shooting at the student, and other observers recorded seeing banners attacking in turn the corruption and anti-Chinese attitudes of the local Party leaders, the insulting behaviour of the police, the selfish outlook of the Municipal officials, the lack of press freedom and freedom to stage public meetings, and – perhaps most interesting of all – the swingeing measures that had been taken against 'our fraternal partners in the newly liberated territory of Hong Kong'.

Police patrols were spat at and insulted, and one police car near the Xiamen Guesthouse was overturned and set on fire, its occupants forced to flee and to leave their weapons behind. Indeed, it has to be said with the benefit of hindsight that an unusually large proportion of the police and public security officials who were caught up in most of these early incidents seemed to flee, almost without hesitation.

The conclusion that has to be drawn from the alacrity with which they fled, especially in the light of subsequent events, is that many in the rank and file of the police both recognised the feelings of the mob and, moreover, were in many cases not wholly out of sympathy with them. China's police forces and their less well-organised bands of auxiliary colleagues were by custom nearly all recruited locally (the appointment of the late Constable Wan Zhu'er in Canton being part of a nationwide programme to attempt to reverse this policy). In Xiamen City on the night of 23 July and, to judge from the mood at the Qingping Market days earlier, these locally recruited guardians of authority harboured feelings that were in broad accord with those of the people they policed. By the middle of that July week no single unit had broken. But it was becoming perilously clear to the local commanders that it would not be long before a police battalion would defy

its officer cadres, and defect to the students and workers against whom they now stood guard.

The temper of that Wednesday evening grew ever more ferocious. By midnight some sixteen shops and offices had been set alight by the mob, and trucks had been used to barricade entrances to the grounds of the ten-year-old ultra-luxurious Xiamen Guesthouse, which the students decided to sack and occupy as their temporary headquarters.

A small group of leaders, all anthropology students and friends of their slain colleague, decided to use the long-distance telephones in the hotel's management office to help rally support. Calls were made to studer: colleagues in Canton (Duan Kun's home town: the students were asked to convey the news of his death to his parents, who lived in a suburb to the west of the city), in Shanghai and Peking. In addition the Xiamen students telephoned the office of the Reuters correspondent, Richard James, who was known locally since he visited the university campus during the last period of unrest two years before. James, who was unable to obtain any confirmation of the events from the university authorities, was none the less able to file a short story based on what the students had said, on his telephone calls to a Swedish factory official staying at the Xiamen Mandarin Hotel, and on his own sources in the diplomatic community. After detailing the night's events his piece continued:

A spokesman for the Xiamen Municipality was not available for comment last night. In Peking a spokesman for the Ministry of Public Security said there had been reports of a minor outbreak of 'hooliganism' which had been dealt with appropriately.

Meanwhile there were persistent reports from within the diplomatic community in the Chinese capital that units of the country's armed forces had been put on heightened alert following an unexplained 'event' that also happened in Xiamen yesterday. The Defence Ministry denied that any forces were at an unusually high state of readiness, and accused foreign embassies who were repeating such reports of 'mischief-making'. The ambassadors of Pakistan and the United Kingdom were both summoned to the Ministry during the day, but both described their visits as 'routine'.

There were firm denials also that there had been any 'incident' in Xiamen on Tuesday; nor that another reported 'breakdown in discipline' – notified by students in Peking – had taken place at the small town of Shitsze, also called 'Little Hong Kong', some eighty miles east of Xiamen. 'Such reports are quite without foundation,' the Public Security Ministry spokesman said. 'The only report I have that might be of interest is that an execution of three convicted smugglers in the town of Shitsze, due to have taken place on Tuesday, has been postponed. New evidence in the case has been put forward to the Examining Magistrate, and a decision on the men's future will be made in a day or two. With that single exception there is nothing taking place in Fujian Province that would be of any interest to the outside world.

The Reuters desk in London, interested in the disruption of public order on the streets of Xiamen, was however insistent on having further news of troop alerts. These, after all, had potential international consequences. Within minutes of his sending his first story Richard James received an urgent service request:

PROJAMES PEKING EXFOREIGN DNE 231730ZULU MOST URGENT: FCO HERE CONFIRMING STATE OF READINESS ALERT BY SELECTED TROOPS AIR AND NAVAL UNITS IN NANJING MILITARY REGION STOP THIS SUGGESTS IMMINENT ATTACK BY TAIWAN STOP ADVISE US LEAD SOONEST STOP ENDS MELUNSKY+++

By 3 a.m., when the rioting in Xiamen had started to subside, Peking – which had become aware of the Reuters request – decided to make a statement in order to clarify a matter that now seemed to be of such urgent interest to foreign embassies. Since it seemed evident to Peking itself that there was no actual threat from the Kuomintang on Taiwan, and thus there was nothing occurring in southeastern China that had any international consequences, it was thought important to say so. Accordingly – and with an eye on the timing of the London and New York newspaper first editions – Pang Weiqang, a spokesman for the Foreign

Ministry, summoned reporters to a 4 a.m. briefing, at which he read out, without elaboration or taking questions, the following hastily written single paragraph:

> The Government of the People's Republic of China, wishing to allay any unjustified concern, is pleased to confirm that, for a period of eighteen hours yesterday, a limited number of troops, patrol vessels and fighter aircraft attached to the Nanjing Military region and the East Sea Fleet took part in a routine training exercise in and off the coasts of Fujian and Zhejiang Provinces. These exercises have now been successfully completed, and the results are being evaluated. The troops and associated forces will remain at training readiness during the evaluation period. There is no reason for alarm at any of these moves, which are purely intended to test and examine the strength and capabilities of the forces of the People's Republic of China.

The only puzzling matter, Richard James was later to write, was that Madame Zhang had not given the briefing. This was normally her task, even at this unseemly hour of the morning. Mr Pang, of whom he knew little, declined to answer any questions, either about the status of troops or, during those normally friendly, off-camera moments that follow a briefing, about Madame Zhang. 'I know nothing of her,' was all he said and left the room.

Later that same morning the body of Duan Kun was driven to his parents' house in Canton City.

There was no mention of the 'routine training exercise' in Thursday morning's vernacular papers. There was, however, one significant paragraph tucked away at the bottom of the main news page in the Canton City *Workers' Daily*. It referred to the actions of certain *liu mang* – the word means hoodlums – in Xiamen city, who had been on a 'drinking spree' after the success of a local football team. A small crowd

of these 'drunken and carousing young men' carried out 'a limited number of wanton acts of vandalism' before being 'apprehended by socially responsible members of society and handed over to the authorities'. It was likely, the newspaper concluded, that the courts would deal strictly with this outbreak of 'youthful boisterousness'.

The customary code words and phrases – 'hoodlums', 'vandalism', 'socially responsible members of society' – were all there, readily apparent to those few foreign readers who had developed the cryptological skills necessary for the full appreciation of the Chinese press. But it has to be assumed, too, that the paragraph was principally designed to be read by any potential *liu mang* in Canton. The local police, the item was clearly warning them, would crack down harshly on any further disturbances. Canton City was where the authorities anticipated the next rebellious blow would fall.

They were entirely accurate. The rebel leadership met late on Wednesday night in a safe house in Shenzhen – conveniently close to the Hong Kong frontier, but with excellent road communications both north and east, to both Canton and Xiamen. They decided that the arrival of Duan's body and the rites associated with his funeral could provide the necessary excuse for a massing of crowds. Some incident, it was felt, would almost certainly occur between the crowd and the authorities who were sent to police them; if not, the leaders decided, then there should be agents present who could easily ensure an outbreak of trouble.

The Duan family, who were Christian and by Chinese standards quite comfortably off, lived in the *xiguan*, the western quarter of the city. Mr Duan senior was by all accounts a most remarkable man, seen in retrospect as one of the quiet heroes of modern China.

Like so many notables, from the famous Admiral Cheng Ho onwards, he was not a Han Chinese. (Admiral Cheng, whose fourteenth-century sailing fleet reached as far as Mogadishu in East Africa, was a Muslim, and moreover a eunuch.) Mr Duan came from Kunming, in western China, and he belonged to a Tibeto-Burman minority group, the *yi*. He looked different from the majority of those around him. He was not a strong believer in such Confucian concepts as 'face'. And he was extremely clever mathematically, having

won a doctoral degree from the Shanghai Mathematical Institute. At the time of these events he held a post as the local under-manager of a Hong Kong-based bank.

It would have been incorrect to describe Mr Duan as politically active. It would have been folly for a man in his position, and one who had that cherished privilege of a passport, to have voiced his opinions or to have become involved in any group that was under the watchful eye of the PSB. But he was evidently a man who harboured strongly held views about what he saw as the injustices of contemporary Chinese rule. He had long been a strong private supporter of what were regarded as the 'young' reformers in Peking – men like Hu Yaobang and Zhao Zhiyang – and he had been bitterly angered by the crushing of the Tienanmen and Wuhan protests. He maintained a good personal friendship with his former patron, the elderly former Guangdong governor, Yi Juan Ling. But other than this vaguely 'dangerous' association – for Yi, as has been mentioned, was something of a maverick figure in Canton City society – Mr Duan said and did nothing, except to counsel his children on his long term hopes for an improved China.

His frequent visits to Hong Kong before the British hand-over had convinced him of the merits of the free-market economy – though it was remarked unkindly in the Hong Kong Special Branch files that he was thought to have developed a particular friendship with a junior bank official in the territory, a relationship which may have accounted in a large part for his fondness for the place. He told his children that he had been disillusioned by the way that China had dealt with both Hong Kong and Britain over the future of the territory, and he had rightly regarded both the Joint Declaration of 1984 and the Memorandum of Understanding of 1991 as allowing China almost unfettered rule there.

He was accordingly not in the least bit surprised when Peking announced that Mao Ren-chin had been appointed to the post of Chief Executive; but he was sufficiently diplomatic to hold his tongue, and he said nothing untoward during his only post-handover visit to Hong Kong in early July.

Both he and his wife had encouraged their son's student enthusiasms, and while they were devastated by his death,

they saw him as very much of a martyr for a cause which they and their late son had so vigorously espoused.

The couple were, in short, and fortuitously, everything that Peter Heung's group could possibly hope for. It was no surprise to learn that the Duan family were thus visited by two members of the group early on that Thursday morning. And although details of the conversation have never been made available, subsequent events suggest that it took little persuading for them to agree that Duan should address the protest rally planned for later that afternoon and evening.

The bank reacted sympathetically when he telephoned to say he would not be coming to work that day. The rebel leaders, together with Mr Duan and, through the good offices of a child messenger, old Mr Yi himself, were thus locked in meetings all day. They were planning the direction of protests later that evening – protests that were to assume a profound importance in the development of modern China.

It is useful at this point to summarise the positions of the various sides as they were known to stand at noon on Thursday, 24 July 1997.

Thus far three cities in two provinces of China were affected by the disturbances – Canton, the capital of Guangdong Province, and Xiamen and Shitsze, both situated in Fujian Province. (Disturbances were also continuing sporadically in Hong Kong; but the focus of the rebels' activities, as had been made clear by Peter Heung's meeting in early July, was to be south China itself. Events in Hong Kong, though historically seminal in their early stages, were now of less immediate relevance.)

In all three cities there had been as massive call-out both of police and People's Armed Police. In Fujian Province – which came under the authority of the Nanjing Military Region – there had also been what can be reasonably described as a fairly comprehensive alert of troops and naval units, to meet what was suspected of being a Taiwanese threat.

There were three Integrated Group Armies assigned to Nanjing, the 1st, 12th and 63rd, under the leadership of the elderly General Nie Kuiji, a man brought in to command in

1994 and reputed to be of strict conservative bent. The political commissars in headquarters – certainly the chief commissar and his two senior deputies – were also men of considerable age and seniority who had no known sympathy with any reform group. The same was also thought to be true of the military command in Fujian Military District, although there had been some suspicion voiced in Western embassies that one of the deputy commanders, the 56-year-old Major-General Chen Shengkun, held political views that were not wholly in tune with those of his senior colleagues in Nanjing and Peking.

The military situation in Guangdong was, from the point of view of the Peking political authorities, considerably less certain. The reorganisation of the PLA that followed the 1993 Wuhan Incident, and various border problems with India (1992), Turkestan (1994), Mongolia (1994) and Laos (1995), the ever-present potential for problems with Taiwan and the continuing internal security disruptions in Xizang (Tibet) had prompted the dispatch of the most experienced and hard-line commanding generals to the western and southern border areas and the southeastern coast, as well as to Hubei, where the Wuhan students were still in an occasionally rebellious mood.

Hubei, it should be recalled, is in the Guangzhou Military Region, and outsiders might therefore have thought it logical that those men selected as commanders of the region should have been particularly resolute individuals who would deal firmly with any disturbances or threats of disturbance in this northern outpost. But due to some oversight – or perhaps to a deliberate act of policy in Peking – it was thought that while the commanding general in Hubei Military District itself should be such a strong and uncompromising figure, the rest of Guangzhou – and indeed, the overall Guangzhou leadership – need not be so restrictive. After all, recruiting was performed locally: to maintain a high level of morale among Cantonese soldiers, and to keep them in good fighting trim, it was thought more suitable to appoint a Cantonese commanding general, even if he occasionally erred on the side of ideological flexibility. Should he ever be found to be doctrinally wanting, his ideological needs would be supplied by a team of firm Peking-approved political commissars.

This, as it turned out, was to prove a fatal error of judgement. General Tang Zhu Hou, a Cantonese who had been transferred down from the cold plains of northern Manchuria six months before, was a man whose divided loyalties became swiftly apparent. His chief commissar, a Shanghainese named Gu Zhi, had once been chief of the political department of the Peking Garrison, and was known to be excessively hard-line. But Mr Gu aside, all the ranking officers down the chain of command were southerners. This included most of the influential figures at Guangzhou regional headquarters, the generals and the brigadiers and staff colonels in the Canton City district headquarters, and the great majority of the field officers out at regimental and battalion level. This particular set of forces – and in particular the 40th Integrated Group Army based outside Canton itself – was almost entirely led by men from South China, men who were theoretically liable to be 'tainted'.

It has never been wholly clear just why Peking permitted this situation to develop – for it evolved over a number of years, rather than resulted from a sudden change in policy. It can only be surmised that the posts which these southerners filled were not thought by the Peking authorities to be vital to the defence or the internal security of the realm. The politically hard-line officers, those who could be sure of keeping the revolutionary flame alive, were needed in Tibet and Turkestan. The men who were, or were suspected of being, of marginally more flexible stance could be kept in 'soft' posts like those in the relatively risk-free south. The error – the fatal flaw in this thinking – was the supposition that Guangzhou and its neighbouring southern provinces were in any way 'soft'.

In Canton, on the hot and sunny afternoon of Thursday, 24 July, approximately 2,500 police and PAP auxiliaries were on street duty. The Police Commissioner had warned General Tang of the possibility of civil disorder in the city, and that his men should be prepared for a call-out request. Accordingly, three battalions of the 123rd Infantry Division and most of the 44th Light Armoured Regiment were put on standby in the barracks.

Across in Fujian the military alert of the previous day was still in force. But the situation on the streets was quiet, and the general assumption among the field officers was that they would soon be stood down. Peking, indeed, was about to order such a relaxation of duty, to allay the international anxiety which was still simmering. The General Political Department of the Ministry of National Defence cautioned, however, that it might be more prudent to wait to see how matters developed in Canton, in case any military assistance was to be needed there. Hindsight shows that was about the only prudent move that the Ministry was to make during the next twenty-four hours.

Crowds began to gather in mid-afternoon at the Memorial Garden to the Martyrs of the Canton Uprising, on Zhong-shan Lu. The Duan family, and the Heung rebel organisers, thought this an ideologically suitable venue. The gardens commemorate those Cantonese activists who, led by Sun Yat-sen, organised the first proper uprising against the ruling Manchu dynasty in April 1911. It was an insurrectionary act that failed (seventy-two young rebels died) but for the Qing forces who routed the small force it was very much a Pyrrhic victory. They themselves were swept from power just six months later. The seventy-two Cantonese fighters of 1911 are regarded as heroes still: it was Peter Heung's view that the Cantonese fighters of 1997 would earn a reputation that would be just as glorious, and might enjoy an even longer life.

Chinese Communist authorities – like communists in most countries – have rarely been fully competent to deal with public demonstrations other than by the sudden deployment of disproportionately massive amounts of force. Dealing with the curious routines and feints and diversionary tactics of sophisticated street opposition, such as that being planned by the Heung rebels, presented an acute problem for the police, for they lacked the relevant skills and in consequence made many blunders. The first blunder of this particular incident came early in the afternoon when Police Commissioner Zhou decided to send the bulk of his forces to entirely the wrong location.

129

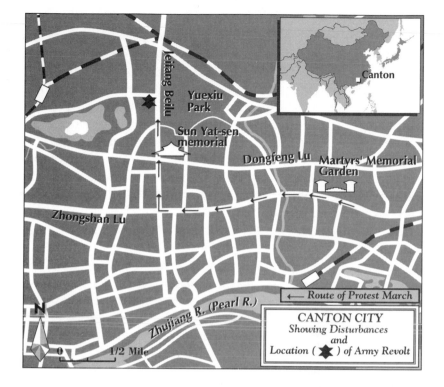

He supposed, for no obvious reason, that the demonstrations – which were ostensibly planned to offer public sympathy for the Duan family, and to condemn the killing of their
young son by the Xiamen police force – would be staged in
Yuexiu Park. This large expanse of grassland to the north of
the city was the site of the much-visited Sun Yat-sen Memorial,
and traditionally attracted the few government-approved rallies that took place in the city.

Zhou had accordingly placed the bulk of his men there, and
it was nearly 5 p.m. before radio messages from Zhongshan Lu
alerted him to the need for a change of plan. By the time the
bulk of his forces arrived and were properly deployed on
Zhongshan and Lingyuan Roads, and by the time barricades
had been erected at the front and east gates of the park so that
police could check that no weapons were being brought inside,
at least 25,000 people had assembled. It was thought, on the
basis of information from the plain-clothes surveillance
officers who had issued the alert, that some of those already in
the park carried weapons and stocks of Molotov cocktails.

The mood of the crowd, once the police vehicles were heard and then seen approaching, became increasingly militant. Marshals inside the park had to urge restraint on a number of young tearaways, who wanted immediately to launch an attack on the police before they were sufficiently well organised to repulse it. By 5.30 p.m., however, calm of a sort prevailed, and organisers were able to bring Mr and Mrs Duan in through the front gate – though not until the police had searched and (Mrs Duan complained later) insulted the couple for 'mingling with agitators and troublemakers'.

When it became known that the Duans were in the garden there was a giant roar of approval. There was an even greater roar of appreciation when a young man climbed to the podium that had been erected in front of the Martyrs' Memorial and announced that he had been asked to broadcast a message of sympathy for the bereaved family from no less a luminary than the former Guangdong Provincial Governor, Yi Juan Ling.

There were several minutes of almost uncontrollable cheering, and shouts of 'Marshal Yi's son can see the good sense of our ways!', 'The old governor is a fine champion of our rights!' and 'The people respect your attention to their problems!', before the crowd organisers, urging the mob to be respectful to the memory of the fallen student, caused a hush to fall on the huge assembly. Hundreds more protestors were still filtering in through the police lines: by 5.45 p.m. probably 40,000 demonstrators were jammed in front of the memorial.

Two Gazelle helicopters stuttered overhead, presumably with Army observers aboard. Outside the railings hundreds of city police looked on, unsmiling; behind them were scores of helmeted Armed Police in close order formations, each man with his rifle, bayonet unfolded, clasped tight before his chest.

The young man placed a small tape recorder in front of the microphone, and the unmistakable voice of Governor Yi, speaking in Cantonese, thundered out over the stifling evening air. It was a brief address. But it had a heretical, accusing tone that few who heard it would ever forget. The crucial final passage, which triggered burst after burst of loud and wild cheering, has been translated as follows:

131

The events of these past few weeks have saddened all the people of southern China. Our compatriots in Hong Kong have been betrayed. Citizens of our own city have been snatched from their beds and punished savagely for crimes they have not committed. Our friends in Xiamen have suffered much, and there are parents here with us tonight who have lost a young son, a man whose brilliant future was snuffed out by the arrogant action of unprincipled men of power.

There comes a time in a people's history when they must begin to realise that they, the people, have the power, and that the state, those who claim to have the power, do not deserve to have it and to wield it with such cruelty and barbarism. It has become clear to me and to many of you in recent months and years that the hopes and aspirations of those of us who have the good fortune to live in the warmth and rains of southern China have the potential to enjoy a good and happy life, with prosperity brought about as the direct result of our own labours.

Sadly there are those in authority in China today – those who have been in such authority for many, many years – who will not believe that a people have a right to enjoy a good and happy life based on the fruits of their own labours and the expenditure of their own energies. But I believe, and I hope that many of you believe, that this right does exist. I believe that this is a right worth struggling for. I believe that we should light a beacon here, a beacon that will be seen by all our friends along the whole of the southern coast of this wonderful land, so that they will rise up and turn back the repressive forces that seek to deny us what is no more and no less than a God-given right.

And I use the phrase 'God-given' advisedly. Many of us here in this city are not, or have not been permitted to be, followers of a God. But the young man in whose memory we meet, Duan Kun, was a follower of the Christian God. His father and mother, who are here in this time of sorrow, find strength in that same Christian God as well. They believe that their God instils certain rights in the human spirit – rights to be free, to be happy, to live without fear. I believe in those rights too, and I hope you will also. And I believe and hope that you young people of Canton, and of all the neighbouring

cities that will sight the beacon we light today, will strive for this belief and for all these beliefs in the right of the individual – and will fight for these beliefs and for these rights. If this fight is undertaken by you, and if you prevail as prevail you must, then young Duan Kun will not have given his life for nothing. Rise up! Overturn the tyranny! Rise up!

The student switched off the machine and stepped down from the podium, and the park erupted in an ocean of sound. Cheers, cries of 'Rise Up!, Rise Up!' and 'You are with us!', and jeers at the watching policemen rang out for more than ten uninterrupted minutes. Outside the park the streets were now thronged with the curious, people drawn as if by magnetism to the vast and endless roaring sound. They were the ordinary Canton citizenry, passers-by and shoppers, and workers on their way home from the factories in east Canton.

The police tried to move them on, the officers becoming ever more desperate to avoid having their men trapped, caught between two mobs. Just outside the East gate a burly middle-aged policeman was very nearly run down by a cyclist who – like so many Chinese cyclists – was looking at the view and not the road. The officer lashed out with his rifle butt, knocking the cyclist to the ground. Six or more others – including two middle-aged women workers – crashed into the first. Within seconds an angry knot of people had crowded around the policeman cursing him for his clumsiness, his lack of concern for the people. Other police rushed to help him, and soon a boiling mob of police and cyclists and housewives and shoppers and schoolchildren and ever more curious bystanders had accumulated in the centre of Zhongshan Lu. People were shouting and waving their fists, and at the outside of the mob young men could be seen pushing and shoving.

Across in the park Mr Duan had begun to speak, and after the exuberance that was stimulated by Governor Yi's address, a respectful silence had fallen on the crowd. But Duan, despite his soft voice and the curiously pleasing *yi*-accented Cantonese, turned out to be something of an orator as well. The deeply felt nature of his grief, his passionate denunciation of the 'cruel and wanton actions' of the Xiamen

police, his simple, intelligently stated sincerity all roused the crowd once again. And when Duan, too, began to take up the cry 'Rise up! Rise Up!', the mobs, both the vast one inside the iron fence and now the fast-gathering crowd outside, started to howl their protest, and catcall and jeer at the police.

The first of the inevitable hail of missiles were thrown not from the rebel crowds in the park, but by the workers out in the street. The knot of men and women who had gathered in front of the park entrance withdrew – shouts urging them to do so were heard coming from an alleyway that ran south-wards down to Donghua main road. Parked in the alley, it turned out, was a construction lorry, and beside it a pile of cobblestones that had been ripped from the street earlier in the month. The men in the crowd seized hungrily at the larger stones and began to pelt the policemen, aiming par-ticularly at the burly officer who had first knocked the man from his bicycle.

The police tried to run, but were hemmed in by stone-throwing crowds. They looked terrified, huddling together against the park's iron bars, cowering as fusillade after fusil-lade of jagged chunks of granite and concrete rained down on them. One had a radio and could be seen shouting into it before he was knocked to the ground by a stone. But he had evidently managed to get his message across, for no more than a minute had passed when, jogging silently from another side street, came at least a hundred Armed Police, helmeted, wearing white gloves. They streamed out, running in a perfect loping lockstep until, with a cry that sounded like a war-whoop, they suddenly began to sprint forward, directly towards the main stone-throwing group.

The mob broke and scattered back into the alley. The police stopped their running and, turning briefly back to their previously surrounded colleagues, ordered them to run back to the protection of the main police group, 200 yards to the west. This they did, carrying their injured away with them.

At the same time, however, crowds of excited youngsters who had been at the park meeting began to stream out of the exits and on to Zhongshan Lu. Here they joined up with the workers who, as they became bolder, poured out of the alleyways and doors in which they had been sheltering. The

police reserve surprise squad who had just been brought in to break them up now melted back westward, having completed their assigned task of rescuing their trapped colleagues. The pattern of confrontation was thus now quite simple: a mass of police and Armed Police were at the southwest corner of the Memorial Gardens, near the junction with Lingyuan West Road; and the rebels and their worker colleagues occupied all of Zhongshan Lu. And it was from here that the rebels decided to advance. With ten young men in the lead, all wearing red headbands bearing the characters 'Rise Up!', and with Mr and Mrs Duan behind them, the first of what must now have been 80,000 people, angry, excitable and unpredictable, began to march westwards, towards the building they had now declared as their goal – the headquarters of Canton Public Security at Number 863, Jeifang Beilu.

'We must destroy in order to rebuild!' one of the hastily scrawled banners proclaimed. The police who made the initial attempt to stop the mob reported back to their commanders that the final line of defence would probably have to be the PSB office. 'It is not possible to hold back so many angry people with the forces we have available,' a police commander was recorded as having shouted into his radio. 'You will have to hold the PSB office as a last resort, and with much force of arms.'

At the park's corner the police did their best to halt the progress of the mob. Two Russian-made water cannon that had been brought up from the police barracks in the north of the city, and which had not been used for more than a decade, fired into the centre of the slowly moving tide of people. But this was a hot, unbearably sticky evening: the cool clouds of water – even the jets that, at close range, knocked down a few of the young men – seemed refreshing, and only spurred the crowd to greater enthusiasm. And when the police fired tear-gas, the youngsters were ready for it.

Within the mob was an extraordinarily sophisticated degree of good tactical organisation. At every tenth row of marchers there was one strong young man designated to carry a large red nylon bag filled with strips of vinegar-soaked cloth. At the moment that the first platoons of PAP gas-gunners

appeared at a street corner near Yuexiu Park, the marchers stopped briefly. Each of the red bags was opened, the cloth strips were handed out, and by the time that the first volleys of gas canisters and grenades thundered down on the mob the rebels were prepared. Only a few young men and women broke rank and ran away from the billowing white clouds: the police, falling back into the park reported with astonishment that as the smoke cleared away the march continued steadily, menacingly. Four drummers had by this time joined the head of the procession, and they beat out a steady and sinister rhythm. It was, one Western observer later remarked, 'like hearing the procession of the tumbrils. It was terrifying. The atmosphere was electric. You knew this could never end peacefully.'

Shortly before 9 p.m. the head of the march turned north into Jeifang Beilu, and approached the PSB headquarters. The marchers had moved slowly and deliberately through the city, their leaders occasionally stopping to exhort them to 'defy and destroy the vicious apparatus of the state machine , urging them to meet the enemy – the police, the Armed Police, the Army – with 'a firm eye and a straight back'. They made their steady progress westward despite frequent police attacks with gas-guns and water cannon, and despite the speedy erection of more than a dozen barbed-wire barricades that were swept away by the crowds as though they were made of balsa wood.

It was 9.15 p.m., and by now dark and still very hot, when the leading demonstrators finally ordered the procession to halt. Before them, looming up like a vast impregnable medieval border fort, with turrets and razor wire and spiked railing, was the PSB headquarters. Scores of powerful searchlights illuminated its tall, faceless walls, and cast an eerie white light back down on to the tens of thousands of faces in the crowd.

The light also caught in sharp silhouette the figures of what seemed hundreds upon hundreds of helmeted figures, each showing his bayonet up above his left shoulder. The men stood with imperturbable immobility. These, as antici-

pated, were the men of the Chinese Army – men whom regimental history now records as belonging to the 46th Battalion of the 123rd Infantry Division, based at Xicun Barracks in the northwest of the city.

They had been brought into the city by truck three hours before after Commissioner Zhou had formally requested General Tang Zhou Hou to provide support for the civil power because of 'an urgent and imminent threat to the city's security'. The soldiers, mostly young men from the rural rice-growing areas of the province, had been instantly deployed to protect the PSB headquarters. They were under command of a Lieutenant Colonel Li Guo-hong, a man whose role in his country's history will not easily be forgotten.

Two entire companies of troops had been deployed to guard the PSB offices, and a third was held in reserve. A line of open Army trucks could be seen in the background, near the China Hotel and across from the Statue of Five Rams. Beside them, in the centre of Jeifang Beilu, was a group of six armoured personnel carriers, the Type YW 309 ICVs that had been in use for the past decade, and could carry eight men at speeds of 30 m.p.h. for more than 300 miles. Each armoured car had a small machine-gun and a much larger 73 mm cannon, and three of them had multiple tear-gas grenade-launchers. They looked menacing under the bright street lamps, with their diesel engines revving up and blowing clouds of blue smoke into the street. Helmeted soldiers stood in each turret, seemingly waiting for the order to move.

The immediate attention of the demonstrators was focused, however, on the solid phalanx of soldiers who blocked their way. There were three lines of them, all carrying automatic rifles. Most had the new light Norinco CQ guns, which fired 5.56 mm bullets at a rate of three a second, in ten bursts. Others carried the more traditional Type 68 assault rifles, while up on the roof of the PSB were marksmen with Dragunov sniping rifles and light-machine-guns. It was certainly a formidable demonstration of firepower, and there was no question that it checked the advance of the marchers. They gathered silently under the lights, the massed marchers behind them coming to a halt so that,

within a few minutes, the street was filled with a vast mass of silent humanity. Perhaps 100,000 were now involved. To the helicopters still stuttering overhead the confrontation must have appeared especially dramatic: a throng of humanity kept at bay by three thin lines of green, and six small toy-like armoured cars.

The rebel leaders decided that, for the moment at least, further northward progress would be imprudent. Their goal, the hated PSB office, was within shouting range and probably Commissioner Zhou was inside. So they would give voice to their dispute, and shout their protests over the heads of the soldiers, hoping that Zhou and his fellow intelligence officers would hear, and, as a student was later to say, 'Be properly ashamed of what they have done.' The leaders set up a chorus of shouts – 'Rise Up!', 'Shame on the forces of repression!', 'Down with the old men!' – until the voices of the mob swelled into an immense cathedral roar, peppered only with the bass thrumming of the helicopters 200 feet overhead.

The soldiers stood stony-faced, their rifles tightly clutched before them. Their officers, who were identified by their shoulder flashes and by the fact that they held 9 mm machine-pistols (snub-nosed black guns with folding stocks that were now snapped into the ready position) stood beside their men, looking over to the command post, where Colonel Li stood waiting for his orders. The noise of the crowd grew thunderous, intolerable. A few stones soon began to rain down – all of them thrown into high arcs so that they went above the heads of the soldiers and crashed into the PSB compound.

The helicopters swooped lower. The radios crackled ever more urgently. Sounding over the roar of the mob there came a sudden electric hum, then a buzz, and the roar of stentorian voices from several loudspeakers began to echo down and along the street.

'Comrades, be attentive. This is an urgent message to you all!' A chorus of hisses and catcalls greeted the introduction. 'We are not your comrades!' one voice returned. 'Crawl back into your holes, you cowards!' screamed another. And '*diu lei lo mou*' – you motherfucker! The Cantonese have access to the coarsest of all Chinese vocabularies, and the crowd made ample use of this talent that night.

But the loudspeakers boomed still louder, until the voice

seemed less than human, more some terrible feral howl. 'Go back to your homes, dear comrades. Go back now!

'This demonstration of yours is absolutely forbidden. Some of you have behaved most irresponsibly. A small number of you have committed wanton acts of destruction. By doing this you have insulted the dignity of the Party. The Party is the people. You are insulting the people of China. You must stop these insults.

'You must now go peacefully to your homes, or else a terrible tragedy will befall you all. This is your last warning.

'The People's Army is here to protect our dear city from any further acts of vandalism, and it will use its might to protect the city as instructed.

'The People's Army is your friend, and the people love their Army. Only deranged people do not love the People's Army. This is China. This is not some foreign nation, where the people behave with stupidity. This is our dear country, and it must be orderly.

'So take urgent notice of this announcement, dear comrades. There will not be another. You must go to your homes, or else dreadful and unforgettable things will happen here tonight!'

The loudspeakers then buzzed for a few moments more, and there was a sudden loud burst of martial music, crackling with interference and the burning of overloaded cables. A rattle of sharp detonations set off a wild frenzy near one edge of the crowd: someone had thrown a string of firecrackers, and they popped and fizzed and banged their way across the roadway. Some of the soldiers instantly levelled their rifles towards the disturbance, and glanced with fright towards their commanders, waiting for the order to go.

Then, without warning, all the lights in the street went out. The music from the speakers faded and died. A strange and eerie calm descended, as if the entire crowd and the forces opposing them were collectively holding their breath. From the rear of the mob came the sound of flagstones being broken, the better to make ammunition. And from the very front on the left there was a sudden flash of flame as the rags of four petrol bombs were lit from a match. The four bombs soared up into space and crashed, spreading huge gobbets and pools of fire at the base of the walls of the PSB compound.

But then the scene fell silent, and dark once again; the street breathed in, and echoed with the vague thump of a huge communal heartbeat.

Suddenly there was more radio noise – quick, urgent commands being given, their staccato echoing between the buildings. The sounds became more and more confused, there was the amplified noise of argument, then a strange screeching, followed by the thump of scores of steel-shod boots, but not in unison.

The rebel leaders were accustomed now to the blackness that had fallen since the failure of the power. They supposed the police had cut it deliberately, as had been the case in Tienanmen Square in Peking, and on the Wuchang Bridge in Wuhan, a precursor to the rampage and the killings. So the young men were prepared to have to run, to dodge and weave through a hail of bullets and the roaring chase of armoured cars. They expected it to begin at any moment; but instead there was some apparent discord in the lines in front of them, and whatever the movement of soldiery presaged was not an attack on the students. They could see vaguely now: the soldiers had moved back 100 feet, and some were facing – it scarcely seemed possible – were facing backwards, *towards* the PSB.

In a fraction of a second they realised what seemed the unimaginable enormity of what had happened. *The soldiers had changed sides.* This single unit of the People's Liberation Army, perhaps amounting to the three companies of the 46th Battalion, 123rd Infantry, had rebelled. For some then quite inexplicable reason they had turned against the men of the Public Security Bureau and the People's Armed Police, they had turned against Commissioner Zhou and his men. *They had taken the side of the students and the workers: they were in open rebellion against the government of China.*

For a few moments, while the rumour went racing wildly through the body of protestors, there was confusion, suspicion, doubt and fear. The crucial question was the extent and solidity of the rebellion: was it just the men who had mutinied? Did the officers acquiesce? Did they, perhaps, foment the rebellion? The answer came dramatically, moments later.

The buzz of the loudspeakers was heard. The lights

snapped on up and down the street. The PSB office, now surrounded by scores of soldiers, all pointing their rifles towards its walls and up at its sentry-posts, was illuminated by searchlights once again. The speakers crackled into life.

'People of Canton,' said an unfamiliar voice, quavering with nervousness at first, but rapidly gaining strength and authority, 'do not be afraid. This is a night of victory!

My name is Li Guo-hong. The post I have the honour to hold is commanding colonel of the 46th Battalion of the 123rd Infantry Division of the People's Liberation Army. We have been sent in to Canton City to give support to the civilian forces of law and order. As you see, we have been assigned to give protection to the senior officers' headquarters of the Public Security Bureau.

Fifteen minutes ago we were given very solemn news. We were issued with orders to attack you people and drive you back towards the river. We were told to use any methods of force to make you return to the river and go to your homes. We were ordered to fire our guns at you to make you move your position.

But I have now to tell you that, in my position as commanding colonel of this battalion, and being a son of Guangdong, and commanding men who come from this province of ours, I could not order the firing of guns at my Guangdong compatriots and comrades. I conferred briefly with my company and platoon commanders, and they graciously informed me that this decision would be well received by the men in my battalion. I therefore ordered them not to fire at you. I am ashamed to report that I disobeyed my commanders. This is a Cantonese unit. It will not fire on Cantonese people.

The crowd, stunned by what they were hearing, cheered wildly, but were cut off immediately as Colonel Li continued to speak.

I therefore informed the Police Commissioner, Comrade Zhou, that I would not carry out the order he had transmitted to me. I also sent a radio message to the Commanding Generals of the Guangzhou Military Region and the

141

Guangdong Military District, informing them of my decision.
I have had no reply from them. But I have just been informed
by radio that at least three of the Municipal Police groups who
have been monitoring the progress of this protest demonstration of yours have agreed to join with me!

I cannot speak for long. The situation is very dangerous.
But I have to tell you that the only way for us to succeed is to
rally behind an organised army. This situation will never
improve if the rule is placed in the hands of the masses. There
must be leadership. There must be direction. There must be
discipline. All I say to you now – in words which the heroic
Mao Tse-tung declared in other, very different circumstances
– is this: To rebel is justified! Bombard the Headquarters! Let
us now go forward and do these things!

The crowd surged forward, hugely excited, the popular
mood suddenly stoked with adrenalin. But sentries with
loudhailers urged them back. 'This is a task for the soldiers.
This is too dangerous for the people. Let them fight. Let
them succeed.'

The two helicopters that had been circling above all the
while suddenly gunned their motors and raced northwards,
presumably to the Army air base out near Baiyun airport.
The six armoured cars raced their engines, too, and a thick
cloud of blue smoke suddenly obscured them. Between them
and the crowd, the soldiers were busily taking up positions
on the east side of the road, taking cover behind the trees
that grew thickly in this part of Yuexiu Park. Only when all
the soldiers had vanished, and the PSB office, brightly lit,
was quite isolated, did the megaphone start broadcasting.
This time it was a different voice, and it was speaking in
*putonghua*, not Cantonese. Those with authority inside the
building were men from Peking: these were the architects of
the policy that had brought Constable Wan Zhu'er and his
like to Canton, a policy which provided the first excuse, if
excuse were needed, for the terrible instability of this seemingly endless hot July.

'The People's Liberation Army wishes you to know that
your barrack block is quite surrounded,' the voice
announced, slowly and calmly. 'It would be wise for you to
come to our side, to put down your weapons and to permit

our forces to take you into custody. You will come to no harm. You will be sent back to your homes in Peking. If you do not do as we wish and as is undoubtedly wise, you will be fired upon. The forces on our side have an overwhelming superiority. Come out now, and surrender. In the name of China, come!'

The answer was a single burst of rocket fire. With a tremendous whoosh! an anti-tank grenade shot out from a lower-floor window. It smashed into the front of the leading armoured car, there was a huge explosion, the car was thrown violently up into the air and landed, a flaming ball, a dozen feet back. Soldiers rushed forwards out of the trees and tried to beat back the flames; but there then came volley after volley of rifle fire from windows at the same level. Two of the soldiers fell, their steel helmets clattering on to the road, while the rest withdrew.

Colonel Li's forces soon struck back. Two machine-guns mounted in the woods started to fire, the bullets raking the front of the PSB, smashing glass, tearing chunks of masonry from the walls, shattering wood. At the same time the five remaining armoured cars moved in and began firing their 73 mm cannon, their commanders aiming them at the upper windows and the roof. There was a small forest of radio antennas on the flat roof of the building, probably being used at this very moment, relaying sounds and news of the disaster back to Regional Command and then on to Peking itself.

The radio aerials fell within seconds, their support structures smashed apart by the fusillade of cannon-fire. At the same time, a shell from another APC smashed through an upper-floor window, and flames began to lick hungrily from within. There were angry shouts and cries from the men who had been in the room, and figures could be seen at the windows, frantically trying to get out. But heavy steel bars, tangled from the gunfire, prevented their escape, and the crowds could only watch as the men clawed frantically, flames spouting around them, until they slumped back, out of sight.

Machine-guns inside the PSB started to chatter in reply, and from a courtyard at the rear, mortar shells began to rain down on the roadway, exploding in bursts of orange and

143

green. But the barrage was not intense, and not strong enough to halt the steady onrush of the remaining armoured cars, which chugged their purposeful way across the wide expanse of road and up to the heavy steel gates of the compound. The small convoy halted momentarily. There was a sustained burst of firing from the two lead cars, and a huge hole was blown in the roadway and, behind it, the gates. The cars headed into the crater, tipped down, then up, and pushed through the broken entrance. Within seconds they were all safely inside the compound, within the wall, and hundreds of Colonel Li's men were running fast behind them.

The remaining action lasted less than two minutes. There was another burst of cannon-fire from the APC, and a few replying rifle shots. But only a very few. The crowd, who had by now pressed right up to the limit set by the sentries, and were watching the drama with rapt but disciplined fascination, could hear the battle tailing away. When silence fell the crowd pushed forward, straining to hear anything – cries, running footfalls, radio messages, licking flames, the crunch of heavy tyres on broken glass. And then a sudden cheer went up. A single phrase in Cantonese was being repeatedly shouted from an upstairs window. '*Ngau dei tau hong – ngau dei tau hong!* (They've surrendered – they've surrendered!). The PSB men have given themselves up. The first battle is over. The first battle is won.'

His cry came shortly before midnight on Thursday, 24 July. In a few moments more it would be Friday, and the nation would be marking with joy and tears, with fireworks and parades (or so the China News Agency had forecast) the anniversary of that first Communist Party Congress, more than three quarters of a century before.

In Peking and Shanghai, Lanzhou, Shenyang and Kunming – in every Chinese city, from Mohe in the icy north of Manchuria to Yulin in the tropic south of Hainan, from Kashgar among the deserts and peaks of the west to Tongjiang, thousands of miles away in the birch forests of the east – everywhere across this immense nation of 1,500 million people, the Party would be celebrating. Everywhere across the

vast expanse of China – except, now, for this one southern city.

For the Party would not be celebrating in Canton. The city where the Chinese revolution had first really begun, nearly ninety years before, and where the first blows were struck against the despots and the tyrants of the Qing regime – this city was now about to see the birth of a new Chinese revolution. On the eve of the anniversary of Communism's Chinese birth this city and thousands, perhaps even millions, of her people were busily and eagerly putting Chinese Communism to its death. What started with the death of a single Christian student – who did not even come from Canton – turned into a massed protest of an angry people. The protestation of this anger turned, in a matter of a few short hours, into the rebellion of a single Army regiment. The conversion of just this one of the People's Army units – however small and insignificant it was in terms of numbers, however fated its action was to be the later cause of destruction and tragedy – in its turn released a flood of pent-up disaffection among the other forces of discipline and the State.

Within hours, quite literally hours, the Canton Municipal Police force had fallen in with the wishes of the crowd, had turned away from its leadership. The People's Militia, and most of the rank and file of the People's Armed Police had, with a speed and scale not witnessed since the Eastern European revolutions of ten years before, reversed their loyalties and become a mirror image of themselves. And overnight, this city of 4 million people became a tiny island of freedom, a pinpoint of light in the grey miasma of Maoism that had spread over China for the previous forty-eight years. Its immediate fate was certain: the fate of the nation and the system that surrounded it has not been settled yet. The only certainty of that heady Thursday night lay behind the cry of the victorious infantryman, hauling down the red flag from in front of the police headquarters.

'The first battle is over,' he had cried. The battle for Canton may indeed have been won on that steamy night, but it was certainly only the first of very many battles yet to come, not all of which would be won by these same victors.

## CHAPTER EIGHT

# DESCENT INTO CHAOS

## CANTON

### *July – August 1997*

The rebels in Canton consolidated their hold on the city with a remarkable swiftness matched by the tardiness with which Peking reacted to the crisis. The State Council did not meet to discuss the situation until Saturday, and a series of bitter and complex internal wranglings, which will be discussed in more detail later, delayed a decision for almost a full week. During these final days of July the revolution, once secured in Canton, was able to spread to nearby towns and cities, so that by the beginning of August almost all of Guangdong Province and parts of neighbouring Hunan and – crucially – Fujian Provinces were affected as well.

The speed with which the Republicans – for this was the name the rebels gave to themselves – took hold of the administration of their southern bastion was so great, and there was such widespread confusion, that an accurate reconstruction of the events has proved difficult. The account that follows, though falling victim on occasion to these limitations, is probably a reasonably reliable, if brief, narration of the historic days that followed the attack on the PSB on Jeifang North Road.

The heroes of 24th July were Colonel Li Guo-hong, the eloquent father of the slain student, Mr Duan Keda, and, from his sickbed, the former Provincial Governor Yi Juan Ling. Shortly after midnight, while patrols of soldiers from the 46th were securing the PSB, and while the crowds of demonstrators were still roaming the streets in search of any

counter-revolutionary activity, these three men, accompanied by three young student leaders, a Mr Gu, a Mr Ng and a Miss Wong, organised a brief meeting to discuss what to do next.

The meeting was held at Governor Yi's home, the former gubernatorial mansion from which he had declined to move following his dismissal three years before. A maid served scalding cups of chiu-chow tea in an effort to keep everyone awake. The old man, who was described later as 'excited but calm', sat up in his bed, and acted as chairman. The four other men sat at the foot of the bed with Miss Wong taking the role of secretary.

Her notes serve as the basis for this short account: she remarks at the opening of her record that the meeting, convened at Colonel Li's request, took place on the morning of a day that was reckoned by the Communist Party to be most auspicious. She had crossed out the character for auspicious, and replaced it with the word 'unlucky'.

There was little time for formality. Colonel Li, grim-faced and grimy from the brief fight, outlined the military situation as best he knew it. He first explained that in and around Canton City itself – he nodded across to Governor Yi, who would already know these details from his terms in office – there were now approximately three infantry divisions. Four more divisions made up the total strength of the Military Region. The total number of men under arms in the Region (which stretched 1,000 miles from the sea to the mountains of northern Hubei) thus amounted to some 100,000. Colonel Li's battalion, from which the headquarters company had been detached to remain in the Xicun barracks that night, had a strength of no more than 600 men.

The arithmetic, Li went on, was sobering. Just one half of 1 per cent of the Army in just one of the seven regions of China were with them. As a fraction of the total Chinese Army the numbers would have seemed still more depressing; just two hundredths of 1 per cent had turned. Miss Wong noted: 'Members assumed expression of great misery.'

But the young colonel brightened. Before he left the barracks that afternoon, he explained, he had been summoned to a private interview with his divisional commander, a Major-General Lan. Like the colonel and most of the other

147

senior line officers in the District, Lan was a southerner, born in Zhuhai. He had distinguished himself fifteen years before in the border war with the Vietnamese, and bore a vivid scar across his right cheek as testimony to the ferocity of the battles.

Lan, who conducted the brief meeting in his private quarters, spoke somewhat elliptically – nervous, as Li soon realised, that the political commissars who were attached to the division might have some means of listening in to the conversation. The message, however, was abundantly clear to Li, who had worked under Lan for some years, and knew of his private disaffection from the Peking leadership.

'Should you decide,' Lan said, 'to permit your battalion to side with those whom you have been ordered to subdue, then you may count on full practical support from me, from my division, and in all probability from the divisions commanded by Generals Hu Dai-fang and Yang Xuchu as well. Whether you decide to use this occasion to stage a rebellion is wholly up to your political and tactical judgement. We have discussed this subject on many occasions during the last year: you may decide, such is the ferment of the city at present, that this is the moment to strike.'

It was left simply to work out a simple and unambiguous set of signals that would need to be sent to Xicun Barracks and then on to the Baiyun Divisional Headquarters if indeed the rebellion had taken place. General Lan decided that three messages should be prepared, each one of them plausible in its own right and unlikely to draw the attention of the commissars monitoring the signals traffic. 'Returning to barracks immediately' would denote an attempt that had failed or was clearly about to fail. 'Delayed by unexpected opposition' would indicate that help was needed, but that with such help there was little doubt that the revolt would succeed. 'Operation concluded' would tell Lan and his brother generals that the battalion had managed both to revolt and to defeat those limited number of forces arrayed against it in the police and public security barracks.

'I naturally sent the message "Operation concluded" at 2344 hours,' Li said. 'It was acknowledged with congratulations and a foreign phrase, "three cheers". While I have had no time for confirmation I have taken this message to mean

that all three divisions are now ours. I believe that the security of Canton City is thus internally absolute. Our principal threat is now from outside. Our purpose at this meeting will be to decide on our short-term strategy. Long-term is not my business. We have concluded a small victory. We have effective support. We need to know we can survive, before we establish how we can fight.'

Governor Yi smiled. 'This is the beginning of a very interesting period in our country's history,' he said. 'I am only sorry that this opening meeting is taking place in such insalubrious quarters. The Communists, I think, did rather better in that regard when they first met in Shanghai.' Everyone laughed, their mood lighter now that they realised there would be relatively few problems within the city itself. The testing time would come in a day or so – though at this meeting no one was aware of exactly how much time would elapse before the first response from Peking. No one knew there was likely to be any breathing space.

'We need to secure the city,' the Governor said, warming to the theme, suddenly assuming his old mantle of authority. 'First, all the obvious. The radio station. Television station. All transmitters. The power stations. The Party headquarters. Railways. Civil airport. Military air bases. That means a large number of soldiers and police. The deployment should begin immediately. We need a spokesman – either me or Duan here. We need to tell the people what has happened, and ask for their support. I suggest we secure all points now, then make a radio broadcast at 5 a.m. and repeat it every fifteen minutes thereafter. We need to have a curfew, a state of emergency, and the closing of all roads in and out of the city. If we have your colleagues, Colonel Li, this will be quite easy to organise. We can manage without but their help will be of inestimable value. And of course, not having them fighting us is of inestimable value too.' There was a gale of good-humoured laughter once again. The mood was optimistic; there was a scent of triumph in the air.

Duan Keda volunteered to be the spokesman. It was arranged that he would travel, under police escort, to the broadcasting station, and prepare an address for the early morning. He would stress in his speech that he was simply a conduit for information, and that the leaders of the rebellion

149

would appear later, once the situation had become more stable. According to Miss Wong's notes, Duan then asked what the movement should be called? 'We must have a name. We must be able to say in whose name, under what ideological flag we fight. What do I say this morning?'

Governor Yi smiled. 'I hope we can all agree that we shall call ourselves – the Republicans. Our name must be simple. It must mean, as our friend Mr Duan remarks, exactly what we stand for. And it must be recognisable as an idea around the world. For one thing must be understood here: our movement, which has its beginnings in this small room, will be known throughout the world. We will be spoken of in America and England and in faraway places. We must be known by something that they know too. And I have one further thing to say on this subject too – but may we first agree? We are the Republican Party of China? Yes?'

One of the student representatives, Mr Gu, rose, his face flushed with tension. 'But we should be the Kuomintang, surely? We follow the path of Sun Yat-sen. We have our origins in the south. We started our demonstrations at the Martyrs' Memorial Garden. Are we not fighting in the traditions of the Nationalist Party? Should we not call ourselves this?'

His was a lone protest, and the force and eloquence with which it was rebutted suggests, from scrutiny of the historical documents, that he may well have been required to ask the question so as to provide an opportunity for a policy statement to be placed firmly on the record. The argument that both Governor Yi and Mr Duan put to the young man was simple: the very concept of nationalism was, to this new entity, intellectually repugnant. Mr Yi then went on to explain, in a speech which Miss Wong was to capture in full, and which remains the most eloquent testimony to the early ideas of the Republican Party – almost, one might say, the Party Manifesto:

> I have thought about all these questions at length in the years that I have been away from centre stage. I and a few of my colleagues who you will come to know in the months ahead have considered this before. We have known this day would come. We suspected it would come, just as it has done,

in the aftermath of the return to us of our beloved Hong Kong. We have had contacts with men and organisations there who share our ideas, even if they organised themselves along lines that seemed to some of us to be ethically unacceptable. But that is no matter now. They have helped put us where we are now. You will meet them soon.

My argument is basically this: if we accept nationalism as our by-word, as the guiding light of the movement we have started here today, then our policies would be directed by the idea of nationalism, and this idea is one that would lead us and our nation into further chaos.

I say further chaos, because we must all understand that what has happened today is certain to lead to chaos within China, a total breakdown of all our established ways, for what could be many months and years. There are old hatreds in this land of ours. There are old hatreds in the lands that surround ours. People exploit hatred. They exploit weakness. Nations that are in chaos are weak. There may be attempts at exploitation from both within and without. All of the old wounds will be bound to flare up. Old scores will have to be settled. That is all inevitable, and it is important that we recognise what is going to happen.

I am an old man. I may not live to see this through. But you are younger. You have the power. You must also have the vision and the wisdom to know just what it is that you have started, and to have the courage to fight on, no matter how great the damage to you and all you have known and loved. For you must recognise what I believe Sun Yat-sen realised, but which few have been able to realise since – and that is that you, us, this idea *has right on its side*. Has, if you like [and here he looked over at Mr Duan, whom he knew to be a Christian] *God on its side*.

So there will be a terrible chaos. But we can try to alleviate it, even though it is us, and our ideas, that have begun it. We can try, I believe, by at least assuming a mantle of moderation. And that is why I believe that the concept of republicanism is right for us – simply because it is and always has been a neutral, moderate concept. What does it mean? It simply means that the people are sovereign, and that the nation is theirs, and that there is no figurehead promoted to leadership by divine right, or by tradition, or by reasons of class or

cleverness or wealth. The people say who is their leader, and they are thus the masters of their nation.

Nationalism, on the other hand, would place us instantly in conflict – with the outside world, with all the new nations that have been born on our frontier. Or else there would be attempts at union, at the forging of links between people beyond and inside our frontiers to form yet new nations, still unknown. So our border would be in turmoil for many years to come.

Within our nation, especially such a richly complex nation as ours, the idea of nationalism would be sure to lead to racism. See what has happened in India, a neighbour with whom we have better relations than once before. All their religious and racial groups have sought national status. They are at each others' throats. They fight in the name of nationalism, and have become Balkanised, weakened, impoverished. Look at the Balkans today, the terrible break-up of Yugoslavia, the difficulties in Italy, in Ireland, even in America again. No, my friends, nationalism promotes sectarianism, and we need the wisdom to be able to see that now, and not fall into a trap of naming ourselves after the idea.

The world has changed greatly since the collapse of Communism in Eastern Europe in the late 1980s, and we have seen with horror and dismay how the spectre of nationalism has risen to replace it – particularly in Yeltsin's short-lived Commonwealth. We have seen so many new nations that have risen, and in some cases fallen, with frightening speed, as people after people, freed from the crushing yoke of Communism, have declared their nationalistic ideals, their desire to be 'free', to be 'themselves'. In China, the danger is the same. There could be a Manchu nation. A *yi* nation, Mr Duan. A Tibetan nation. A Cantonese nation. This, surely, is what we all want to avoid. But it will be difficult to do so.

I see the nightmare of banditry rising again – and I, you must know, remember what the time of the bandits was like. I see warlordism. I see a civil war of terrifying proportions and length. But I see us, those of us in this little group, as being in possession of another force, and that is the force of moral leadership. Because although it will be said that we are just southerners fighting against northerners, you know, I know, that we are much, much more than that.

The south is rising not because it is southern, but because it, more than any other region of China, has some knowledge of the power and possibilities of freedom. There are people in this area of our nation who have seen and tasted its goodness. There are people who have seen it in Hong Kong. You have seen it, Mr Duan. You have been there, and you have seen how much finer life is down there, how backward our people, our attitudes, our lives are here. It may be changing. It probably is. We must start our movement here to help to rescue it, before it is too late.

I have seen the workings of freedom. I have been overseas, and I have seen Paris and London, and I have seen Hong Kong. So I know what is possible. I know what happens in a system where any man is allowed to try to reach his own potential, to strive for any heights his abilities and his energies permit. And it is for these ideas, rather than the fact of our being southern Chinese people, that we fight.

To call ourselves nationalists, to align ourselves from the beginning of our movement with our compatriots in Taiwan, is to make, in my view, a fatal mistake in what the outside world knows as public relations. What we stand for is freedom and the people – all the people of China. The people must be sovereign. The people must be free. The party must be the Republican Party of China. Republicanism must be our guiding principal. And this the name we must adopt.

Of course, there will be much more substantive meetings than this. We have only been in a state of rebellion for a matter of hours – though some of us have been considering such a move for many months and years. It is impossible to chart a path for an organisation that is but a few hours old. All I have just said is to give some direction and impetus – some sense of organisation, if you will – to our young movement. For unless we know where we are going, even those few of us who are here, then this movement, like any directionless movement, will filter away into the sand. So nothing I have said is carved in stone. Proper meetings, with debate and discussion, and elections and votes, will decide our ultimate direction. This is just to get matters under way. I hope you respect and understand that approach.'

Mr Yi then fell back on his pillow, exhausted. He took a sip of tea. Mr Gu, who had stood throughout this oration, his

153

expression changing from dejection to elation as he listened to the old man speak, clapped his hands in a sign of appreciation, and sat down. He had been defeated, or converted – the notes do not reveal, though as we have seen, Miss Wong noted his appearance, which is suggestive.

Colonel Li spoke next: 'If that matter is settled – and I take it we all agree – then we have some things to attend to urgently. I shall make contact with my senior officers and return with some of my men to Baiyun headquarters, to ascertain the situation. No doubt we shall be ordering the police under our control to take the various actions you recommend, Governor. Mr Duan, as spokesman I wish you formally to notify the foreign consulates in this city of the situation. We will draft a brief statement here, and we shall make sure the foreign powers are aware of the development. We may need assistance. I also recommend that we make contact now with our compatriots in Hong Kong, to inform them of the situation and to open a channel of communication with them. We are unaware so far of the loyalty of the border security forces at Shenzhen. It is my expectation that they will not be on our side of the argument, and there may have to be some fighting. We shall also make contact with our colleagues across in Fujian Province.

'From now on, gentlemen and Miss Wong, I shall fade into the background. I am, after all, only a colonel, in charge of one very small percentage of the Army – although a percentage that has been at a pivotal point in our nation's history. From now on the decisions in this conflict will be made by the general officers and their staffs, and by the political leadership. I believe you will regard it as appropriate, Governor Yi, if there is no resurgence of the cult of personality that has so often sullied our nation's record. My name will be remembered, perhaps. But from now I will return to my regiment and, until some future appropriate moment, to my rank.

'Our tasks are clear, then? Mr Duan – to write the statement, to deliver it, and to broadcast it. You will have an escort of soldiers to guarantee your security. Mr Gu and Mr Ng will go to the telephone exchange and attempt to make contact with Hong Kong, telling them of the situation. Miss Wong will remain here and write a record of these events, and provide a central telephone number which any of us may call to relay

messages to one another. And Governor Yi, dear Governor Yi, you may now try to go to sleep. It will have been a very testing day for you. You have done much to bring this movement to life. You will be able to watch it grow. But I hope you will be able to do so in some comfort and peace.'

The colonel rose, clicked his heels in what Miss Wong took to be a most un-Chinese fashion, and left the room. His escort was waiting, and those remaining in the Governor's bedroom listened to the APCs' engines roar into life, remaining silent as the soldiers took off into the city.

The brief statement – which was written in English as well as in Chinese – took them only a few moments to prepare. When Miss Wong had completed writing it, on a single sheet of white vellum, it was datelined 'Canton – 25 July 1997', and read as follows:

The Republican Party of China has today been established, and has taken control of the city of Canton as a first step to gaining control of all of China. The aim of the Party is to restore to the people of our great and beloved nation the freedoms and happiness and prosperity that are common to most other nations in the world, and which have been taken away by the evil machinations of the Chinese Communist Party. The Republican Party recognises the sovereignty of all the people of China, and is against only those who are the enemies of the freedom of those sovereign peoples. The Party has already been given the unqualified support of the People's Liberation Army and the People's Armed Police, the People's Militia and the Municipal Police of the city of Canton. The Party will seek to make contact, probably through third parties, with the Communist authorities in Peking, to ascertain the position of the leadership in our nation's capital. The Republican Party of China calls on the nation to support its aims in the coming struggle, and asks respectfully for the sympathy and understanding and succour of like-minded nations around the world who, it is hoped, will support our goals in our nation's coming time of need. All honour and blessings to the people of China!'

The statement was signed and dated, with a red ink chop-mark, simply 'Yi Juan Ling, for the Republican Party of China.'

James Gahan, Her Majesty's Consul for South China, had not slept at all that night. The disturbances in town during the previous afternoon and evening had, he later confessed, caught him somewhat by surprise. He had, of course, been aware of the Reuters report of an outbreak of violence the day before in Xiamen, and he knew that the body of the dead student would be brought back to Canton for the funeral. He had also heard rumours that the violence in Xiamen had been the consequence of a ham-fisted police investigation into an apparent explosion on the island of Gulangyu – an explosion in which, he had heard, a number of Communist Party officials had been injured, or had died. But he had not reckoned on any kind of popular demonstration in Canton City – and certainly not a popular uprising on the scale that he was shortly to learn had taken place.

He was later to say (and the Foreign Office was sympathetic to his explanation) that he had only just taken up his post, sixteen days before. There had never been a Canton Consulate: this office had been established as a direct result of the retrocession of Hong Kong, and was a subsidiary of the Consulate-General that had been set up in Hong Kong itself, to monitor the passport situation of those British subjects and protected persons who remained in the Special Administrative Region. The Chinese had gained two new consular offices in the United Kingdom as a result: where now the British had offices in Peking, Shanghai, Hong Kong and Canton, so the Chinese had consular offices in London, Cardiff, Glasgow and Belfast – the first being the Embassy, the last being a Consulate, and the two others being formal Consulates-General.

Mr Gahan, a 50-year-old trade specialist who had not had a China post before, but had been, successively, a Middle East Floater, Third Secretary Djakarta, Third, later Second, Secretary Madrid, Second Secretary (Commercial) Caracas and had then been seconded to the Department of Trade and Industry in London immediately before his Canton posting, had been given a Chinese interpreter-cum-secretary. But because of the perceived relative unimportance of the post, he had been given few other tools with which to carry out an effective intelligence-gathering mission in this part of China.

The *Parliamentary Inquiry into Circumstances Surrounding the Final Handover of Hong Kong and Related Developments in South China* (op. cit. – HMSO Report Cmnd 5611, October 1997) was later to be severely critical of what members regarded as 'this severe lack of foresight in British planning policy for UK-China relations'.

Mr Gahan, despite his lack of information that night, was awake when the Consulate's doorbell rang. He assumed there was no security problem: the police guard outside the Consulate was impressive, and had been doubled the previous night. Whoever had managed to penetrate it at this time of night – his bedside clock said 3 a.m. which he automatically calculated was 6 p.m. in London, on Thursday – would be bound to be on business. So without hesitation he went downstairs, and opened the door to find Mr Duan Keda, a man he had not previously encountered but whose name he knew as that of the father of the dead Xiamen University student. Mr Duan was holding a message clipped to a board.

He was to say later that he found Mr Duan a most impressive individual – stoic, dignified, sincere and, crucially, very credible. The visitor handed him the single sheet of paper, and asked the Consul if he could possibly either photocopy it – since Miss Wong had only typed the one sheet – or transcribe it in longhand. He said he understood that at this hour it would be unlikely that a secretary would be on duty. Gahan accordingly sat down at his study desk and painstakingly copied out the statement. He handed it back to Mr Duan, who checked it for accuracy. Mr Duan then thanked him, said he would have to make a similar visitation to the United States Consulate, and left.

Once he had gone, Gahan tried to telephone Peking, but found that the lines were inexplicably down. It was the same with Hong Kong, and with London and, most irritating of all, he found he could not get through to the American Consulate. The telephones were still working, but there seemed to be some fault on all the lines he tried. He telephoned the White Swan Hotel, to check: the operator there said that a city-wide emergency had been declared, but did not know why. He then decided to walk to the American Consulate but when he turned into Zhongshan Lu – the Consulate was on the outskirts of Liwan Park, in the west of

the city, close (as it happened) to the pleasant suburban area where the Duan family lived – he found to his astonishment a constant stream of armoured cars grinding into the city from across the Pearl River Bridge. Heavily armed soldiers were taking up positions at street corners. Large guns – they looked to him rather like anti-aircraft weapons – were being set up in the park, with soldiers piling sandbags around their supports.

Before he had made 100 yards an infantryman pointed a sub-machine-gun at him and shouted angrily. The soldier was joined by two others, all wearing helmets, and the three gestured at him. He fancied he heard the words: 'Go your home!'; but even if he had not, Her Majesty's Consul had to assume that some kind of curfew had been put into effect and it would probably be imprudent for him to go further. He turned tail and scuttled back into the Consulate, heading for the radio room.

Here, thanks to the rapidly reducing costs of modern technology, was his single – though unsecured – link to London: a Casio hand-held satellite link radio-phone, with a long-life battery and a small dish aerial. He took the device on to the lawn, examined the built-in compass to find north, and then pointed the tiny dish aerial east forty-one degrees and south thirteen degrees, and switched on the power. Tiny motors then aligned the dish ever more finely, until it was locked on to the Marisat III Pacific satellite, hovering in geostationary orbit 22,000 miles above Hawaii and, on securing an answering signal from the Marisat's Foreign Office transponder, demanded 'Dial Number'.

It was 3.25 a.m. in Canton – 6.25 p.m. at the Foreign Office. Given the likelihood that the Far East Department had left for the evening, and adding to that the uncertainty over the radio-phone's batteries and the possibility, however remote, that the consulate's garden might at any moment be overrun with Chinese soldiers (a terrifying prospect for most people, let alone a man recently on secondment to the DTI) Gahan decided to speak directly to the Resident Clerk. The Clerk – one of six First Secretaries who took turns to work a week of night shifts in a flat at the top of the Foreign Office, in case of a faraway crisis just like this – began his duties at 6 p.m., and remained beside his bank of phones and faxes and

telex machines until 10 a.m. the next day. He effectively directed the running of British Foreign Policy from the apartment overlooking the Horse Guards: he could telephone almost anyone at the core of the British establishment; he had the illusion of near-total power.

He picked up the telephone instantly. 'Resident Clerk here,' he said.

'This is Gahan, Consulate-General Canton,' said the diplomat, unsteadily, and then added the word 'China', for good measure. 'I am speaking on a non-secure line. We have a situation here that I believe is very grave. So I am going to give you a brief report. We may be cut off.'

'Wait a moment, Mr Gahan,' replied the Clerk. He tried to assume a reassuring tone. Here, he realised swiftly, was a low-flying diplomat who was probably out of his depth, alone, and frightened. But at the same time, in a tradition that went back to the days of Richard Burton and beyond, he was being resourceful, and probably trying to do his very best. Goodness knows how he was managing to send this report. (The Clerk was a suave man named Woodhead who was said to be in line for the post of Head of Chancery in Paris. He was not to find out for many more months that a colleague he would never come to know intimately was at the time kneeling by a radio transmitter on a muddy lawn, with the screech of armoured-car tyres, the grinding of tank-tracks and the occasional rattle of sub-machine-gun fire coming from all around. But he said that his measured response that night stemmed from his belief that 'Gahan was probably in a rather tight situation', and it would be 'sensible to listen carefully to everything he said, and then to thank him most sincerely for his efforts and let him know that we cared'.) 'I'm just going to switch on the recorder, so I don't miss a word. Right – go ahead.'

Gahan, sounding more reassured by the pleasant voice at the other end of the (remarkably clear) line, then reported what he knew. He spoke of the telegrams he had sent the day before, and of the growing tension that he had felt in the city ever since the shooting of Constable Wan Zhu'er two weeks before. (That incident – with its probable Hong Kong connections – had happened just two days after he had taken up his post. A China specialist at the US mission and an old

friend at the Hong Kong Consulate-General had told him of the immense significance of the shooting and the authorities' violent reaction to it: he had written a telegram two days later that forecast severe trouble that summer in the city – a telegram that would stand him in good stead during the Parliamentary Inquiry later that year, and which would do his career prospects no harm either.)

He went on to outline with speed the events in Xiamen and such additional rumoured details of the explosion in the Galangyu Guesthouse as he had omitted from his telegram. (He had not originally said that any Party officials had died, but the rumours had been ever stronger during the Thursday, and so he repeated them now: the line was good enough for him to be able to hear Woodhead's rapid intake of breath.) He spoke of Wednesday's riot at Xiamen University, the confusing events of Thursday, the visit of Mr Duan and the apparent founding of a new political entity named 'The Republican Party of China'.

'In summary, though I say this with the benefit of a little more than a fortnight in this country, it seems to me as though Canton is in the grip of a serious insurrection involving instruments of armed authority at the very highest levels. It would perhaps be accurate to say that there has been, in this part of southern China, if I may mix my languages rather inelegantly, a *de facto coup d'état*. I can only imagine now that Peking will seek to reverse this situation with speed and resolution. Depending on the ability of these Republicans to muster the support of the people and of other forces in adjoining regions, we may have the makings of a major disruptive situation in this country. I hesitate to use the words civil war. But you should be aware of the potential for some grave events here.'

Gahan then went on briefly to mention the communications difficulties, and that he was unable to copy this message to Peking or Hong Kong, nor to raise his colleagues in other missions. He knew that Duan, who was escorted by a number of police, would be making a similar visit to the US Consulate-General, and assuming that he made it safely through the streets he would imagine that a report similar to his own would at that moment be arriving in Washington. He told Woodhead that he was physically all right, that the

Consulate had stocks of food and water and its own generator (although he doubted that any staff would make it to work next day), that the Republicans were unlikely to be hostile to the presence of foreigners in their territory, and that he felt certain he could manage to man the office without problems for some while. He knew of 128 British citizens who had registered as living in the consular region and he would attempt to get in touch with them as the situation allowed. His own advice was that they remain at home and keep out of sight, and he wondered if such a message could be broadcast by the World Service.

Finally he asked that the Clerk telephone Mrs Gahan in Gillingham in Dorset to inform her of the situation and to suggest that she postpone her planned arrival in China until the situation clarified itself. At this state the Battery Low light on the transmitter began to blink, and the transmission of the first report made to the outside world of these remarkable events in Chinese history – and, it was to turn out, in world history – came to an end.

Although it would be unsurprising to learn, in view of Mr Gahan's very recent posting, that the British were the last to learn of the uprising they were, in fact, the first. This had much to do with Mr Duan's choice of the British as the first to receive a copy of the Republican Party Statement, which in turn had to do with the closeness of the Consulate to Governor Yi's house and to the fact that, as a worker in a Hong Kong bank Mr Duan had had cause to visit the new Consulate only three days before. He had gone not to see Mr Gahan, as it happened, but to ask advice from a clerk about a quantity of funds that had been frozen in Hong Kong by the new Chinese Banking Commissioner there, under the complicated new Exchange Control rules. The clerk had not been able to help, but had been sympathetic.

The relative speed with which London knew of the uprising also had much to do with circumstances at the US Consulate, which had recently moved to a large compound near its old offices in the Dong Feng Hotel and very close to the PSB. Its staff, unlike Mr Gahan, had a fair appreciation

of the situation – or at least, of the call-out of the Army to deal with the protest march. They had not however, heard the statement from Colonel Li (despite his announcement being made no more than 200 yards from the Consulate wall: the State Department was later to blame 'unfavourable wind conditions' for the statement's lack of audibility) and were unaware of the storming of the PSB headquarters by Colonel Li's battalion. Telephone and telex communications were then cut, and all Canton was able to report to Washington over its own portable cellular network was that there had been 'serious disturbances' in the city, with a considerable amount of gunfire from a 'bewildering variety' of weapons.

By the time Mr Duan arrived at the Consulate gates – even though he arrived with a police escort and other trappings of formality – the Marine guards refused to let him in. From behind their bulletproof windows the pair on duty (normally only one was stationed at the entrance, but the guard had been doubled in the wake of the disturbances, with the rest of the eight-man squad armed and in a ready-room inside the building) ordered Mr Duan and his party to be escorted away from the Consulate's walls, and they refused to accept the proffered piece of paper. It was not until one of the marines called a duty political officer to inform him that 'a suspicious individual escorted by a number of uniformed and armed men' was waiting on Liuhua Road and refusing to leave that some attention was paid to him. The letter was eventually accepted and, as Mr Duan insisted, photocopied and returned to him.

The Consul-General, a long-serving career officer named Meisel, was on the radio-telephone to Washington for more than an hour during this period and it was only when he finally broke the connection, after being assured of further security assistance from Peking, that he was asked to assess Duan's photocopied statement. Not having seen Duan himself, and relying only on reports from his Marines, he did not at first pay much attention; it was only after the Department had radioed back to alert him to reports from both the US Embassy in London and from the NSA's own intercepts from Fort Meade, Maryland, that he reread the statement, considered anew its signature, and reacted with the energy that such a development warranted. He was later to be reprimanded, and was not to serve in an overseas post again.

In London, the Foreign Secretary James Hogge was holding a reception for a visiting Iraqi trade delegation at his official London residence in Carlton Gardens. Peter Woodhead had, as protocol demanded, tracked down the relevant Minister of State for the region, Lord Inverdonald – he was at a reception as well, for the departing South Korean ambassador – and told him of the news from Canton.

Inverdonald, who had presided over the flag-lowering ceremony in Hong Kong just four weeks before and whose experience allowed him readily to appreciate the likelihood of a major breakdown in civil order in both Hong Kong and South China, immediately called Hogg, and suggested a meeting. Together with such other assistants as were found – including the Head of the Far Eastern Department Robert ffolkes, the Head of News Department Peter Mayhew and the Head of Defence Department Roger Whittham – an emergency meeting was held in the Foreign Secretary's office just two hours later at 9 p.m., when presumably dawn was breaking in southern China.

Details of the meeting have remained highly classified. Certain relatively trivial facts have emerged, some from a special meeting of diplomatic correspondents that was called just before midnight. These include the fact that after a series of unexplained disturbances involving the People's Liberation Army, communications appeared to have broken down inside China, and that the British missions in Peking and Shanghai had been told of a particularly critical situation that had developed overnight in Canton by means of radio messages direct from London; that the British subjects resident throughout China – including the newly constituted Xianggang SAR ('which Correspondents will recall', said the Head of News, with a sardonic grin, 'was until lately the Crown Colony of Hong Kong') – were being asked to keep off the streets, and to listen to the World Service for instructions since messages to this effect had been passed for broadcast to Bush House; that two of the British warships that had taken part in the evacuation of Hong Kong and which had then proceeded to Australian waters, HMS *Manchester* and HMS *Hermione*, were being called back north to await orders while on what the diplomat quaintly referred to as 'the China station'; that other Allies, who were unaware of the China

development, had been informed; and that from the evidence of the last two weeks in Canton and from around the rest of China, with additional recent information about possible 'serious and possibly profound disagreements' breaking out inside a number of key ministries in Peking, including Defence, Foreign Affairs and Internal Security, China appeared to be headed for a period of 'serious instability'. It was, therefore, probable that a meeting of the major Western powers and the Russian Federation would be called within the coming days to assess the situation: the American Secretary of State Mr Richard Crowther and his Moscow counterpart, Mr Akhrimov, had both been informed that night.

What was never made clear in the briefing with the correspondents was exactly what Britain's policy might now be. Neither was it made clear whether there was any probability of a common allied policy – and if there was, what that was likely to be.

But some hints of a possible British attitude – which heavily influences today's general Western thought on the calamitous situation in the region – could be discerned some months before. Close reading, for instance, of the proceedings of a confidential Chatham House Conference entitled *The Political Structure of North-East Asia in the Twenty-First Century*, held the previous January, and attended by Lord McLean, a former Permanent Under-Secretary at the Foreign Office, and now Professor Emeritus of Asian Studies at the University of Leeds, would have enabled a reasonably astute analyst to have drawn a fair outline of at least the potential for new ideas; and the *New York Times* was actually bold enough to recognise and to write, albeit briefly, about a new 'tilt' in Western attitudes suggested by the similarly close scrutiny of a series of lectures given at Harvard in the spring of 1997 by Professor the Lord Wilson, the Director of the Shaw Institute of Chinese Studies at Oxford, a former British diplomat and acknowledged specialist on modern Chinese political history.

Both McLean and Wilson, who, as advisers to the British government were the principal navigators of this new direction, appeared to hold, basically, that in the event of any conflict within China's borders, the Western powers should display a discreet tendency *to favour the hopes and aspirations of*

*the southern Chinese* over those of the Communist old guard in the north.

There was no doubt, the pair reiterated in separate interviews early in the year (stressing at the same time that both were retired, and were now officially 'out of the loop') that the failure of Communism in Europe and the former Soviet Union, and the resulting fragmentation of both blocs into quarrelsome micro-states, would eventually happen in China. The fact that Communism had survived for so long in both China and North Korea was a puzzle, and had many probable reasons. It was, for instance, a measure of the relative lack of public discontent in both countries – of the existence of a bovine acceptance of the *status quo* that arose from the enduring sub-Confucian trait of respect for authority and the popular acceptance of the wisdom of elders, as well as from the very poor communications, the absolute control of the press, radio and television and of popular movement within the two countries, and from the extremely harsh and imaginatively cruel public penalties that were imposed on any would-be rebels within the system.

Banishment, exile, bamboo slivers under the finger-nails – the spectrum of punishment was vast, and appalling. 'While both the Chinese and the North Koreans can be the most gentle and kindly people in the world,' one of those attending the Chatham House conference wrote, 'there is a capacity for cruelty and repression within both societies that is quite chilling. It is nothing like the animal savagery of Amin's Uganda, nor is it akin to the crazed butchery of some of the Middle Eastern despots we have seen in recent years. In China and in North Korea those in power appear to sit down and think: how exactly do we inflict the most awful pain on a man? How many volts do we give him, where, and for how long? How finely should the wire be sharpened before we insert it? To how many degrees do we heat the iron bar? For how long can we strangle someone before we release the noose, and then start it up again? The cruelty here is precise, it is measured to a fine art, it is carried out coldly and with clinical ritual. It is therefore infinitely more terrifying than any cruelty based on anger. People know what is coming to them if they stray – and they know that they never know how dreadful it is going to be. So they almost never stray. Just to

be afraid to imagine what will happen is enough to keep a society straight.'

But having said that, the academics concluded, there was a weak spot in the Chinese armour – the influence, steadily growing in the south of the country since the late 1970s, of the entrepreneurial ways of life that had proved so successful for the southern Chinese in Hong Kong. The potential for the 'tainting' of sub-Yangtze China by the 'triple contagions of avarice, corruption and landlordism' and other capitalist excesses had been condemned by the Peking authorities as far back as 1993, in the famous *People's Daily* editorial written on the centenary of Mao Tse-tung's birth. (Further details of the extent of this influence, and of the dismay of the Communist authorities, were outlined in Chapter 4.)

In the eyes of the West – particularly in the eyes of Western commercial interests – it was these same capitalist influences that offered the chance for the making of some massive fortunes. Businesses in the West had, of course, looked hungrily at the possibilities offered by a China that, since the opening up of the country to foreigners in the early 1970s, had nearly doubled its population of potential customers. It was a delightful coincidence that personal liberties and democracy tended to go hand in hand with market-led economies. From the simple view of the unreconstructed business leaders in the West, for China to be turned capitalist – to be tainted by the southern influences, in other words – would be little short of ideal.

The British academics naturally enough shared this view, and took it further by hoping for the encouragement of personal freedoms in China. And, finding little resistance to this view within the infamous 'China Mafia' of the Foreign Office, it became an essential plank – though a very secret one – of British and then American foreign policy. The 'infection' of southern China was thus, during the remaining years of British rule in Hong Kong, to be systematically encouraged; limited but significant assistance was to be given, *sub rosa*, to a would-be dissident movement that seemed likely to have the ability both to grow in Hong Kong and to become, eventually, rooted in Guangdong and Fujian Provinces (hence the meetings between Captain Margerison and Peter Heung, outlined above); and, if such a

movement produced a serious rebellion, it should be supported.

The procedures are very delicate whereby a foreign power is able to support a rebel movement, without seeming to violate that cardinal rule of international diplomacy which forbids meddling in a nation's internal affairs. Under conditions of the greatest secrecy, weapons and ammunition can be supplied. Men can be trained. Your own soldiers, specially schooled, can be inserted. Where diplomatic breakdown can be risked, rebel governments-in-exile can be harboured. Regional regimes newly established in captured enclaves can be recognised. Leaders can be welcomed. Conferences can be organised. Mediation can be offered. Peace can be brokered. Support can be given to the stripling regime.

Britain – and, it was to be assumed, the United States – almost certainly favoured a comprehensive approach to the Canton rebellion, following this basic outline of what has become known as the McLean Formula. Since the situation in China has not yet been wholly clarified it is not possible to be certain. But the covert foreign military support given to the Republicans has been considerable. Republican leaders have been ostentatiously welcomed in London and Washington and there is a distinct iciness in relations between London and Peking.

But to enlarge on these matters is to skip ahead too far in the narrative: suffice to say that at the first meeting of what was soon to become known as the China Crisis Committee, the CCC, the decision to tilt in favour of the Republican Party of China was probably made. (Similar recommendations had already been made by Mr Charlesworth's HK7 Committee in Washington.) The success which the Party and its military allies has subsequently enjoyed is owed in large measure to the decisions that were initiated, on the one hand by Hogge, Inverdonald and ffolkes – the so-called 'Holy Trinity' – after taking advice from the 'Heavenly Twins' of Wilson and McLean, and on the other by Hugh Charlesworth, and his ebullient new Secretary of State.

However, other grave events in the Western Pacific have

recently taken place, all undoubtedly consequent upon the situation in China. Whether responsibility for those events, can be laid at the door of any Western government's China policy, is a matter that will have to debated for many years to come.

By dawn on Friday Canton was almost totally secure. The Guangdong Communist Party headquarters had proved troublesome, and it took several hours of negotiation – though no gunfire – to persuade a group of diehards to give themselves up and to hand over their weaponry and, more crucially, their files, to the rebel leaders. But, as Colonel Li suspected from his 'three cheers' message, the three divisional commanders, Lan, Hu and Yang, had all pledged allegiance to Governor Yi and, moreover – and in the most significant shift of the latter part of that crucial night – so had General Tang Zhu Hou, the General Officer Commanding Guangzhou Military Region.

Discussion on the matter had been mercifully brief. General Lan, who it will be remembered had spoken to Colonel Li in his quarters immediately before the skirmish outside the PSB barracks, had – without the company of his political commissar – visited his brother generals shortly afterwards, to tell them of the situation. He was careful to see that their ever-vigilant commissars were not present at the meeting either. He took care to say, truthfully, and in case there was any surreptitious monitoring of the conversation, that he had not specifically conspired with Colonel Li to persuade him to 'turn' his battalion.

His view was that the other major-generals, although broadly sympathetic to the aspirations of the Cantonese non-Communists, would not be so disloyal to the tenets of a proud and disciplined army as to incite junior officers to treasonable behaviour. Such a move should come from below – from the colonel level, invariably the locus of discontent in any army. The colonels were close enough to the rank and file to detect the popular mood, and they were on terms of sufficient intimacy with the staff to be able to transmit that mood upwards.

All that General Lan had done, he told Hu and Yang with great care, was to indicate to the colonel that if in his duties

that night he detected a mood among his men that might persuade him to disobey an order or orders that were genuinely repugnant to him as a patriotic Chinese, then any act of defiance that he committed would in all probability not encounter disfavour at staff level and above.

General Hu and General Yang agreed, instantly. It remained now to neutralise the commissars – by cutting off their communications links rather than by the drastic but possibly necessary means of killing them, it was thought – and to alert the two most senior officers in the chain, Lieutenant-General Wu, GOC Guangdong Military District (who was in any case on leave) and, most important of all, General Tang, the GOC-in-C of Guangzhou Military Region. These two latter officers were based at the Army headquarters near Baiyun airport: to get Tang's *imprimatur* was vital to the military success of the coming operation.

The two black Red Flag limousines that left Xicun barracks for Baiyun at 1.30 a.m. that Friday morning took only fifteen minutes to complete the vitally important journey. General Tang was in any case expecting them: his commissar Gu Zhi, had received a coded message from a subordinate at Xicun, warning him of the possibility of trouble within the senior ranks of the local detachments. As the three divisional commanders were announced, Gu was in the process of angrily lecturing his general – in *putonghua*, which was both Gu's and Tang's second language, Gu being from Shanghai, Tang from Zhuhai – on the lunacy, as he put it, of the move.

'Of course, like you, I am aware of the discontent that has been spreading. I am not blind, nor am I unfeeling. But to take a step like that which has been reported to me is madness. It is also, if I may say so, quite extraordinarily insulting timing. Today, as you know, is the anniversary of the Party's first congress. Next week is the seventieth birthday of our glorious People's Liberation Army. Yet now I hear that you are seriously thinking of acquiescing to the demands of a small clique of back-sliders, of corrupt and greedy criminals, influenced by gangsters in Hong Kong ...'

General Tang motioned him to be quiet, and welcomed his three junior officers into his study. 'I have heard what is going on. I have been monitoring the radio traffic. I believe Colonel Li is about to send you a message from Jeifang Beilu.

The signaller will bring it to us presently. Meanwhile my friend Mr Gu here is raising objections. He accuses me of being a traitor, of not having enough patience. That last is indeed true. But we need not talk of this now.'

The Army signaller entered, with a handwritten note. Tang glanced at the name of the addressees, and handed the paper to General Lan. The General read it, then instructed the soldier to make a reply to Colonel Li immediately. It was to read 'Your message acknowledged. Felicitations on your achievement.' It was to be signed simply 'Lan, Commander 123rd Infantry'. Then, just as the signaller was leaving, Lan called him back, and instructed him to add the phrase 'three cheers' to the message. 'He will appreciate the significance,' he said, and looked pointedly at his two colleagues and at their senior commander.

Commissar Gu then tried to leave the room, but was stopped by a sentry. 'You will be placed under arrest, I regret to say, along with all your fellows,' said Tang. 'You must not be permitted to make any attempts to communicate with other units of the Liberation Army or with other cadres. Should you succeed in doing so by any means, you will be shot. There is to be no question about this. This movement will succeed. We have right on our side, whatever you may say.' More sentries were called, and Gu, screeching abuse in Shangainese, was led away to the cells. Others later joined him; telephone messages to the Xicun barracks and the remaining camps in and around Canton City instructed line officers there to locate all the political commissars and place them under close arrest.

In the meantime the two remaining infantry battalions and the single armoured unit that had already been placed on alert, the 37th and 38th Infantry Battalions and the 44th Light Armoured Regiment, all of which were attached to the 123rd Division, were ordered to deploy with immediate effect to the Baiyun civil and military airports, to the main railway station and the port and to the Communist Party headquarters and, in liaison with Colonel Li of the 46th Infantry, to carry out the procedures which they knew all too well, having studied in great detail the document *Standing Instructions for the Comprehensive Security of the City*. (The circumstances in which they were now putting the *Instructions*

into effect were, however, somewhat different from those which had been assumed by the document's authors.)

Hundreds of soldiers and light armoured cars then started to pour into the city and its outskirts. By dawn the operation was essentially complete. Canton City was, except for a few small pockets of resistance, in the hands of the Republican Party, and was now waiting for the rest of China to flex its mighty muscles and strike back.

## PEKING

### *Friday, 25 July 1997*

No comprehensive account of what took place inside the Chinese leaders' apartments in Zhongnanhai during this critical period is ever expected to be published. The old men gathered around the equally elderly and enfeebled President Yang Shankun are unlikely to write their memoirs; nor are there allies – like the Bulgarians, in the old days – who were privy to the internal machinations of the Chinese power élite, and who would, at some later date, recount what they knew. Peking and P'yongyang were almost wholly isolated in the world – a handful of minor African states and a cluster of unvisited island nations were their only friends; and though both France and Germany supplied weapons and defence technology to China, its diplomats were never among the intimates who enjoyed real access to those at the centres of power.

The events in Peking that followed the rebellion in Canton can only be sketchily reconstructed from the reports of some Western diplomats, the few journalists operating in the city, and from that most useful of information sources, the electronic intelligence intercepts captured from the three satellite monitoring stations at Darwin in Australia's Northern Territories, at Wakkanai in northern Hokkaido, Japan, and the recently completed monitoring base operating under the cover of the new BBC short-wave transmitter near Chiang Mai, in Thailand.

The British Ambassador at Peking, Sir Peter MacDuff,

had been told of the apparent rebellion in a Flash telegram which arrived shortly before dawn. He tried to call Gahan in Canton, but was told by the Embassy operator the lines were said to be 'temporarily down'. He then convened an immediate meeting in his study with the Military Attaché, Colonel Robert Strange, and with his Political Counsellor, Simon Hughes-Lockhart. He told them of Gahan's extraordinary report to London – which, he now gathered, had been confirmed by a much later but apparently substantially similar report passed to the State Department by their Canton consular office. The entire military organisation based in Canton City had seemingly rebelled, and had pledged its loyalty to an organisation about which nothing was known save its name, the Republican Party of China, and its titular leader, the former provincial governor Yi Juan Ling. He declined to say what British policy was likely to be in the event of a full-scale Chinese civil war. This was clearly a major crisis, one which threatened the stability of the region and perhaps the world. He asked if either of his colleagues had any further news or thoughts.

Hughes-Lockhart was able to report on what he thought was the development of schisms in a number of Peking Ministries. He had, in fact, been writing a minute on the subject in the office the day before, and was due to present it to the Ambassador that very morning.

He had discovered that there were in particular, in his phrase, 'ominous cracks' developing within the Ministry of Foreign Affairs. That something exceedingly peculiar was happening had become clear in the wake of the summary execution by shooting of Madame Zhang three weeks before. Exhaustive interviews with the Reuters correspondent, Richard James, and attempts to have him recognise from Colonel Strange's massive library of mug-shots the Army officer who had accompanied Madame Zhang to that fateful last interview, had eventually produced a name: the soldier was in all probability a Captain Wong Hao-tian, an English-language specialist who was working as a documents translator at the Chinese Military Academy at Shijiazhuang, south of Peking. Captain Wong had been seconded from a post in an infantry regiment attached to the 123rd Division, based in Canton.

Colonel Strange nodded, adding that the Chinese captain had not been seen since, and it was assumed that he had returned to his original post in Canton. (He certainly did not return to Shijiazhuang Academy that Saturday afternoon, and an informer working for a British government agency at Peking airport hinted that he may have been spotted boarding a jet of China South Air Lines later that afternoon.) The Military Academy had been closed to all foreign visitors, diplomats included, for the previous month.

It was not known exactly why the officer had accompanied Madame Zhang to the meeting with James, though the natural assumption within the Embassy was that the directive for leaking the news of Mr Mao's appointment as Chief Executive of Xianggang SAR (Hong Kong) came not from within the Ministry of Foreign Affairs itself but from a rebel group within the Army, and, moreover, one that had powerful connections inside the Ministry.

The Political Counsellor had been able to find out who had authorised the execution of Madame Zhang. The Head of the General Political Department of the PLA, Mr Yang Baibang, who was the younger step-brother of the Chinese President, Yang Shankun, conducted a swift investigation once he heard of the release of the news. He summoned the Foreign Affairs Minister, who angrily denied all knowledge of the maverick news leak: the scapegoat was Madame Zhang, and she was picked up by PAP officers at 5 p.m., taken to the Political Department fifteen minutes later, then taken to a remote spot behind the Daiyuotai Guest House and shot in the back of the neck.

Hughes-Lockhart said he had learned that a small group of middle-ranking Western specialists – all of them former colleagues of Madame Zhang – had been removed from their posts and sent to a language training school in Shenyang, in Manchuria. Day-to-day contacts between the Ministry and a number of European countries had been badly affected as a result. Three ambassadors – those to Iceland, Tadzhikistan and Sri Lanka – had been recalled in the past week; and there was a rumour circulating among the diplomatic compounds of Sanlitun and Jianguomenwai that the Deputy Foreign Minister, Li Jiwei, had been removed from office.

'My conclusion,' Hughes-Lockhart went on, 'is that a group of Ministry officials knew of this coming Army rebellion, and supported its aims. Some of these people have been slowly and quite carefully removed from positions of influence. At least one – Madame Zhang – has been executed, as an example to others. But I expect that this dissident movement within the Ministry is in fact quite large, and I very much doubt that the powers that be have the ability to contain it. Not now, at least.'

Colonel Strange, who had only been on-post for three months, admitted that he was not well enough grounded to have heard much about dissidence within the PLA. He had followed up the disappearance of Captain Wong, as Simon Hughes-Lockhart had just noted; and he had been aware of 'mutterings' among reformist officers, most of them assigned to forces based in southern China, that were suggestive of serious unease within the PLA command structure. He had anticipated trouble – indeed, a minute from his predecessor, Colonel Peterman, had indicated the 'mutterings' among a reform group of younger officers had begun in the aftermath of the violence of the Wuhan Incident. But neither Peterman nor he, Strange, had the slightest idea that matters were to move with such speed. All he could do now was to sketch, very broadly, the known military dispositions, and, from the point of view of a disinterested foreign military officer, advise the Ambassador on how matters could possibly develop. He looked at the Ambassador for agreement, and Sir Peter nodded.

'The Chinese have, ever since the breakdown of Communism in Russia and her satellites, been most fearful for the security of their national borders. As everyone now knows, the country is surrounded on all sides but one by non-socialist countries – some of them old, some others of them very new and the consequence of the explosion of nationalism that followed the collapse of the Marxist experiment. With the single exception of the Yalu River boundary, where China abuts on to her lone ideological friend and ally North Korea, the entire length of her land border is inhabited by non-Communists who, in most cases, have ethnic connections with the people living as neighbours across inside China.

'Consider. Vietnam has not been Communist since 1994, and Laos held popular elections last year. Myanmar, Burma, is in the hands of a military clique, but one that is now aggressively right wing, and which no longer subscribes to the beliefs of Ne Win, who is generally thought of as a madman. India, of course, is perpetually troublesome, but is no longer specifically non-aligned and nowadays generally sides with the United States. Bhutan and Nepal are manifestly non-socialist, and have been since their two monarchs offered democratic reforms to their people – there was some flirtation with Marxism in 1991, it is true, but it was pretty short-lived.

'Pakistan and Afghanistan are of course rabidly anti-socialist in their outlook. The Kazakh Federation is brutally militaristic, and the neighbouring state of Tadzhkistan is unstable and illiberal. Kirgizia is free and independent again. Even old Tannu Tuva is back on her feet again. The Mongol Republic is heartily anti-Marxist, though barely stable. The Russian republic, with the exceptions I have noted, is stable, though there have lately been stirrings, as you know, among several of the ethnic groups in Eastern Siberia – most notably the Buryat groups east of Irkutsk, who have been forging links with the Oroqen minorities of northern Manchuria.

'The Chinese have good reason to be worried about their frontiers. There are Vietnamese and Lao and Burmese minority groups living in Yunnan and Guangxi Provinces. There is quite a strong Yao opposition group in Yunnan, particularly. Then again, Xizang – Tibet – is terribly unstable, and there is much cross-border assistance from the Nepalese and the Indians. There are various Turkic groups in Xinjiang who have much to do with their brothers and sisters across in the Federation. The people of Inner Mongolia are being stirred up by those in Outer Mongolia. The Manchus are reviving their strength in Dongbei – the three North East provinces – and are being egged on by the Siberians and the Buryats and the other minority groups.

'So the Peking authorities have seen fit to handle this by placing their best Armies and their best men out in the frontier regions. The élite corps are there – the 2nd and the 67th Armies in Chengdu, dealing with the Vietnamese and the Burmese; the 21st and the 65th in Lanzhou, dealing with

### The Chinese People's Liberation Army

### Basic Organization

The Chinese Army, the Chinese Navy, the Second Artillery (the strategic nuclear forces) and the Chinese Air Force are known generically as the forces of the People's Liberation Army. While they are technically subordinate to the Ministry of National Defence they come under the overall supervision of the two Central Military Commissions, that of of the Communist Party and (since 1982) of the National People's Congress. The Army is thus regarded as a force that 'belongs', as it were, both to the Party and to the People.

The Army itself, which had a strength (in 1997) of 2,450,000 (of which 1,400,000 were conscripts) is organized into some 24 Integrated Group Armies and, geographically, into seven Military Regions (MRs), 29 Military Districts (MDs) and three Garrison Commands.

The Military Regions (indicated on the map below) are each headed by a full General, with a Political Commissar of equivalent rank serving alongside. The Military Districts and Garrison Commands are headed by Lieutenant-Generals. Each of the Integrated Group Armies, commanded by a Lieutenant-General, is approximately equivalent in size to a US Army Corps, with a strength of about 44,000 troops. A Group Army usually has three infantry divisions, as well as associated tank, artillery and air defence units. Armies are assigned to the various Military Regions as required. Defence ministry recruitment policy attempts to discourage 'regionalization' of fighting units, though this has not always been successful, especially (and crucially) in South China.

The upper chart on the next page shows the regional and district organization of the PLA in July 1997, with a further indication of the identity - where known - of the Group Armies (GAs) and some Divisions assigned to various geographical units.

The lower chart shows in rather more detail the situation that obtained in two of the more acutely affected PLA units by mid-1999, with the units and the unit leaders who were known to have gone across to the Republican government, or played some otherwise interesting part in the story, indicated.

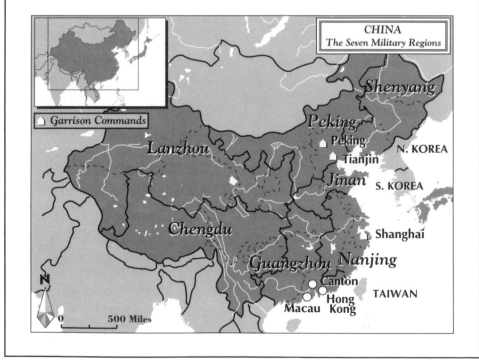

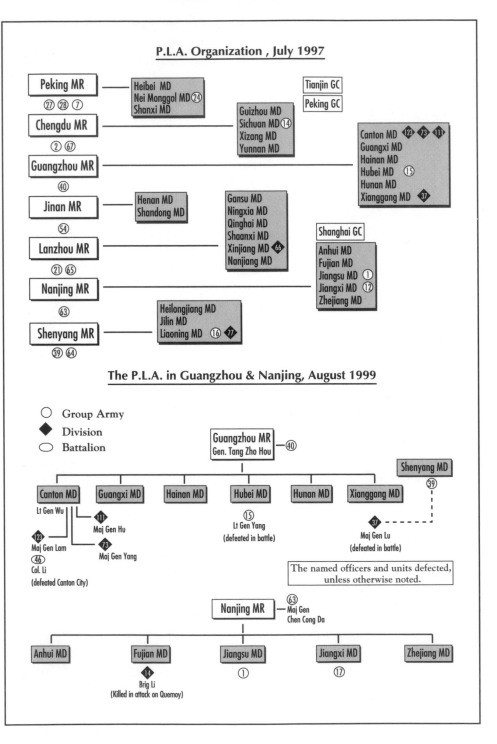

## P.L.A. Organization , July 1997

## The P.L.A. in Guangzhou & Nanjing, August 1999

177

the Tibetans and the Tadjiks; the 24th in Inner Mongolia; the 16th, 39th and 64th in Manchuria; and four whole Armies in and around Peking, just in case there's any assault on the capital.

'But the Armies that are not so hot, and particularly the commanders that are not so totally reliable, have been assigned to the centre and the south – where the trouble has broken out. The 15th and the 40th in Guangzhou Region – commanded by General Tang? It's difficult to know why he got the job. There have always been mutterings about him, ever since Tienanmen Square, when he was an armoured brigade commander. He did as he was told. But it was always rumoured that he did it with bad grace, and he was out of the picture for four or five years.

'Then again, the 1st Army in Nanjing – buttressed admittedly by the 12th and the 63rd – seems to have its fair share of troubles. General Nie, who runs the show, is a tough old man, a real died-in-the-wool conservative. But he's old, that has to be remembered. Not entirely with it. And one of his deputies who was operational commander of the three divisions of the 63rd Army based at Quanzhou has long been suspect. He was involved in the call-out the other day, when Peking thought the Taiwanese were stirring up trouble in Xiamen. He was at Sandhurst for a while, if that means anything.

'Speaking off the top of my head, then, we have a situation where the upper echelons of two of the lesser southern Armies have rebelled. I don't know for sure that all of the troops under General Tang's command are with him. I have strong reservations, for instance, about the airborne divisions based at Wuhan, part of the 15th Army in Hubei. I know the general in Wuhan, a wild man named Yang, and I think there's a fair chance he'll side with Peking, no matter what his Regional command orders him to do.

'But I would imagine that some of the Nanjing Military Region officers will come over to the side of the rebels. By the end of the next few days we will probably see four and maybe five armies, more or less totally on the side of the Republicans. Who will attack whom, I can't rightly say.

'Then I would expect some of the new independent states on the Russian side of the frontier to stir up trouble, and the

Indians to do the same on theirs, so that the border armies will be too occupied to be able to deal with this insurrection. Peking will thus have to use its capital forces to attack. That probably means the 27th Army, which is the most loyal of all, and has a great deal of internal air support and a great deal of mobility. But to move forces out of the capital – well, for the old leaders here it is a risk, a very grave risk.

'From the rebels' point of view there is one thing that must be done, and I imagine they can do it, and will want to do it quickly. And that is secure Hong Kong and bring it into the fold.

'If they have Hong Kong on their side, then they'll have the port, the airfields, the railways links – the perfect logistical tail for whatever they do. They'll probably get their hands on the Shenzhen airport, which will be useful for them. It would be nice for them to have the ports and airfields in Shantou and Xiamen as well, but Hong Kong is the crucial one. I can't pretend to know what British policy is. I think I know what I'd like it to be. But if there was any possibility of us siding with the rebels, then the fact of Hong Kong being in rebel hands would clearly make it a great deal easier for us to help, with covert resupply and that sort of thing.

'We know two things about the military situation in Hong Kong. The first, obviously, is that the population is going to be very much on the side of the rebels. And the second is that the troops which have been sent down to occupy the place are detached from the 39th Army, from Manchuria. They're really tough – real so-and-sos. They've seen a lot of fighting. Their commanders are true died-in-the-wool conservatives. Their troops are peasant boys from the remotest and roughest of regions, and they have been taught to loathe the Cantonese. I suspect they'll put up quite a fight.

'But the Republicans have got to engage them, and quickly, and gain those airfields and ports. It is absolutely vital. So I'd imagine that the fighting will begin in earnest inside Hong Kong within the next few hours. I could be wrong – but if I were a betting man . . .'

Later in the day there were reports of 'unusual activity' within Zhongnanhai compound, with many vehicles entering and leaving through the gate beside the Forbidden City. However, the complicated network of tunnels beneath Peking – many of the tunnels restricted to the use of senior members of the Chinese government – would have enabled officials to ply between the various ministries and commissions without ever being seen by the public; it has to be assumed, given the magnitude of the crisis, that the 'unusual activity' seen at the surface was but a fraction of that actually experienced.

Among those few who were both seen entering the compound and were recognised was General Li Huan, the Commander of the Second Artillery Corps. Since the Corps is the division in charge of all China's atomic weapons delivery systems it is assumed that the leadership was trying to make certain that, no matter what happened between the land forces in southern China, no rebel group managed to lay its hands on atomic weapons. The Political Commissar attached to the Second Artillery, a Mr Yin, was also called in to the meeting. What was said can only be surmised.

The Commander of the Chinese Air Force was believed to be in Hong Kong at the time of the rebellion. His deputy, a General Ri, is thought to have attended the Zhongnanhai meeting.

A brief statement was then issued through the China News Agency that Friday evening, over the dual signatures of – somewhat unexpectedly – the Ministry of Railways and the Director of the Civil Aviation Administration. Referring to 'unauthorised disruptive acts' by 'a limited number of hooligans and mobsters' in 'a small segment of Guangdong Province', it had been decided with immediate effect to halt all rail and air traffic links between Canton City on the one hand and the cities of Peking, Shanghai, Nanjing, Wuhan, Kunming and Xian on the other; and, in a second case, between the city of Xiamen on the one hand and Shanghai, Peking and Nanjing on the other. Moreover, frontier security police at the road crossings between the Provinces of Hunan and Hubei, Anhui, Zhejiang and Jiangxi, and Guangxi and Guizhou were being instructed to make strict checks on all vehicles and people passing between provinces;

and it was suggested that, to minimise personal inconvenience, citizens in the affected regions stay at home 'until a
normal situation has been restored'.

Two things that might have been expected to happen on
that Friday did not, however. First, there was no formal
convening of either the thirteen-man State Council, nor of
the Central Military Commission, the rather smaller and
more exclusive body that acts, during events of the utmost
gravity, as the supreme authority in matters relating to the
nation's civil discipline.

The only explanation to be put forward by those Peking-
based diplomats who make a study of the minutiae of
Chinese politics was a rather colourful one: that the problems clearly affecting the middle-level bureaucrats within the
Ministry of Foreign Affairs were now leaching into the
upper echelons of the highest policy-making bodies of the
nation. Dissent within either the CMC or the State Council
was unheard of since the days before the Cultural Revolution; but at the same time, there was an apparent lack of firm
and decisive action that day, and although later events suggest that the two bodies have since pulled themselves
together (and that there have been several rumoured
changes in the membership of the CMC), only dissent could
have accounted for the dithering.

The second event that did not take place that Friday was
the staging of any attempt to reverse the deteriorating military situation. The cancellation of domestic air travel, the
closure of selected airports and the shutdown of most of the
southern railway system admittedly did clear the way for the
rapid movement of soldiers if and when that was reckoned to
be necessary. But none was actually moved. None of the
main northern Group Army commands, so far as could be
ascertained, was even put on special alert. Moreover – and in
view of the developments of the next few hours, crucially –
no signal was sent (or at least, none was ever intercepted: and
all intercept stations had been ordered to listen intently for
code traffic out of Peking)] to the Commander, PLA Sub-
Regional Headquarters, Xianggang.

Major-General Lu Chuanzhi, who had his temporary
headquarters at the former Royal Naval base on what used to
be Hong Kong's Stonecutters Island, was wholly ignorant of

the developments in Canton. He was thus caught quite unprepared by the events of the few hours between breakfast and dinnertime on the following, highly eventful, Saturday.

## XIANGGANG SAR

### FRIDAY MORNING TO SATURDAY NIGHT

The rebel generals had acted precisely as Colonel Strange had anticipated. At their barracks meeting early on the Friday morning they had mapped out their immediate stratagems. They had two principal concerns. The first was based on the lack of response to radio messages from General Yang up in Wuhan. All of the other military district commanders and the scores of various outpost commands within the massive Guangzhou Region had been told during the night of the developments; and all had reacted enthusiastically to the situation, giving their unqualified backing to Governor Yi and the Republican cause. All, that is, except General Yang, Commander of the 15th Group Army. Not a word had come from him, and further attempts to make contact even with his signals units had been in vain.

General Yang, who was reportedly the son-in-law of the President of the Supreme People's Court, and was from Shaanxi Province, had a particularly mobile force at his disposal. He had paratroopers and transport aircraft, and – coming under his tactical command in time of crisis – he had two squadrons of modern, Russian-built MiG 29 jet fighters, which were given by Moscow in 1992 after the Chinese pledged several hundred million dollars' worth of construction loans to the then crippled Commonwealth of Independent States. The fighters were normally assigned to the Chengdu Military Region, to assist troops in the event of cross-border skirmishes in the southwest; but they had been seconded to General Yang's territory three months before to enable him to stage a series of exercises.

If Yang decided to stay loyal to Peking, his forces would surely be the first to be utilised to weaken Tang's hold on the

far south – and in Tang's view, they would present a formidable problem. Orders thus went out to ensure that the rebel units and key locations were given full anti-aircraft protection, including the deployment of all of the region's available batteries of surface-to-air missiles.

The second concern expressed that morning at Baiyun was the need to acquire, and quickly, the shortest of supply lines, and to accomplish this by seizing a port.

The obvious choice was Hong Kong. The other possible candidates, Shantou and Xiamen, both fell under the operational control of the Nanjing Military region which, in the aftermath of the mysterious events on Gulangyu, had been ordered to effect a wide-ranging programme of alerts against possible actions by – fanciful though it now sounds – the forces in Taiwan. One effect of this order was to ensure that the coastal and anti-aircraft defences of both cities would be much more active than usual; and in addition warships from the East Sea Fleet would be on patrol in the Straits.

Of course, it was always possible that the Nanjing command would pass to the rebels – Tang had good enough contacts to suppose that this would, in time, happen. But he could not be sure, and so reasoned that to attack Shantou or Xiamen now would be imprudent and premature and, though the prize was very great, would present a very considerable risk.

By contrast, Hong Kong was exceptionally lightly guarded against outside attack. That, the authorities had mistakenly believed, was a near-total improbability. The troops who had been selected for posting to the SAR were there principally to maintain civil order. They were men from the far north of China; they had been told that the Cantonese who they were there to guard were troublesome, awkward, anti-Chinese. Their foremost task was to subdue the local population, to bully them if necessary, to keep them cowed, and thus to ensure by force of arms and numbers their continued loyalty to the regime of their new Chief Executive, Mr Mao.

It will be recalled that troops had been dispatched to the former colony by ship. They had been taken by rail to Zhanjiang in southwestern China, and then embarked on a fleet of vessels – both warships and commandeered passenger craft.

The actual landings on Hong Kong territory, made either by small craft or from helicopters, were comprehensive, sophisticated and well-organised. Nearly one complete division was involved in the operation – and all from the lightly armed 37th Infantry, a unit originally assigned to the 39th Army in Harbin, in north Manchuria. They, in particular, had been selected because of their unfamiliar ethnic origin, and because of their near-total ignorance of the ways and the language of the people they had to police. But the price that the designers of this cunningly unpleasant form of suppression had to pay was that they were very lightly armed. They were not equipped to deal with what was least expected – an attack by heavily armed and airmobile divisions of rebel soldiers, coming from a few miles to the north.

A plan for the attack on Hong Kong had to be devised quickly, before any messages of warning or, more dangerously, any suitable reinforcements, were sent from Peking. Accordingly General Tang directed that the attack be made by Major-General Hu Dai-fang's 111th Division; that a formal plan be devised and agreed by that evening; and that the operation be commenced on Saturday morning and completed by Saturday evening.

Hu and his staff officers spent the rest of the day in secret conclave, emerging at about 4 p.m. to brief General Tang. Approval was formalised at 5.30 p.m., whereupon the first detachments of infantrymen – all wearing bright Imperial-yellow arm-bands – were sent south, by truck, and told to await orders on the Shenzhen airfield. Operations would commence at first light. Tang's principal concern was now whether the 15th Army would mount an aerial attack on him in Canton while he was one division short, and before he had the supply-lines he needed. He doubled and trebled the radio and radar watch, searching for any signs of activity from the barracks in Hubei Province; he slept little on Friday night, though all was quiet.

Sunrise officially came to Shenzhen airport at 6.36 a.m., China summer time. General Hu's men had been moving fast for more than an hour before first light, and most of

their trucks and their eighty medium tanks had been massed among the skyscrapers of Shenzhen City by the time startled workers started to trickle in to the factories and offices.

The plan was simple enough, and depended on speed and surprise and sudden annihilation. Given the need to keep the local population on the Republicans' side, orders had been issued to all platoon and section leaders to use their weapons selectively and to cause only the very minimum of collateral damage and casualties. If it were possible to confuse the opposition and to force a surrender without a shot being fired, so much the better.

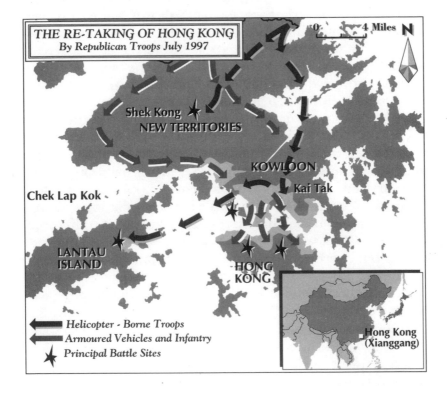

THE RE-TAKING OF HONG KONG
By Republican Troops July 1997

Helicopter - Borne Troops
Armoured Vehicles and Infantry
Principal Battle Sites

During the night the very small number of Type 77 amphibious vehicles that were available to General Hu had been used to ferry all 135 members of the 111th Division's Reconnaissance Company across to the Mai Po marshes. From here they had fanned out across the territory, using stolen and commandeered vehicles and a variety of other

special forces' tactics, and by 6 a.m. were already comfortably close to various key points, from where they were due to mount a series of sudden ambuscades. At 5.55 a.m. specialists from the signals battalion had cut all communications lines with Hong Kong, and had set up portable electronic jamming equipment to frustrate the internal communications of the Manchurian infantrymen – the frequencies having already been determined during the night by the Recon force.

The attack proper began at 6.15 a.m., with the launch of three separate operations. First, a force of twenty-two Mi6 Mikhail troop-carrying helicopters – each capable of carrying thirty men and their equipment – flew low over the New Territories with the three goals of securing the Kai Tak airfield, surrounding the main northern regimental headquarters in the countryside at Sek Kong, and, most symbolically important of all, reinforcing the special forces troops who were scheduled to commence their attack on Government House at 6.40 a.m.

The first wave of machines crossed the eastern edge of the border near the village of Sha Tau Kok, and apparently escaped detection. The first ten helicopters then swung right and landed in the grounds of the Sek Kong barracks, where they arrived at 6.35 a.m. The men – approximately two companies' strength – then deployed tactically towards the HQ building, but meeting no resistance approached in force, behind a Chinese flag. The four gate sentries challenged them, but were summarily disarmed, and thirty of the invading soldiers fanned out inside the building, capturing the radio room and the armoury, and locating the detachment commander, a Colonel Chin. The headquarters was thus totally secure by 7 a.m., and the men of the 111th spent the following hour collecting prisoners and detaining them in the barracks stockade.

Capturing the Kai Tak airfield proved to be an equally easy task. The helicopters flew below the radar shield and landed on the apron – five beside the cargo building, five near the control tower. Sentries guarding the tower were disarmed with astonishing speed, and by 7.15 a.m. Kai Tak was safely in rebel hands. (The much larger Chek Lap Kok airport, which had been the source of so much delay and argument in the 1990s, was still not complete at the time of

the invasion. The island itself, well secured by razor-topped airport fencing, was to be used later that day for detaining the prisoners from the 37th Infantry Division).

These two victories were secured without the need for the firing of a single shot. The same was not true, however, of the raid on Government House. As had been planned, some fifty men from the Recon battalion made their first contact with the enormous number of guards close to the front gate at 6.15 a.m. Resistance here was far stronger than had been imagined. An élite unit, later determined to be men of the 37th's fabled 104th Mechanised Light Infantry, had been assigned to guard the territory's Chief Executive, and they fought hard, using a large number of very sophisticated weapons.

The Republican soldiers, a section of whom were also spotted by sentries (or by electronic warning devices; it was not made clear in the Report) as they approached Government House from the northeast corner, took a huge amount of automatic weapons fire. During the first two minutes of the fight they were hit by no fewer than eight fragmentation grenades. Six men were killed outright and four others were gravely wounded: the remainder withdrew.

A few minutes later the two remaining helicopters from the twenty-two that had set off from Shenzhen settled on the rear lawn – under heavy automatic gunfire that the Recon battalion had not been able to prevent – and disgorged some sixty well-armed troops. One of the helicopters was hit by a lucky bullet and caught alight – creating a massive pall of smoke from behind which, fortunately, the invading troops were able to mount a swift operation to get inside the mansion itself.

Once there they fought, hand to hand, with the Manchurian defenders. There was much use of the bayonet and, in one case, of a portable phosgene gas generator, which sent some 100 defending troops retching and screaming out into the fresh air. The remaining men from the Recon unit had by this time also regrouped, and mounted an attack on the sentries by the Government House front gate.

By 7.30 a.m. rebel soldiers had fought their way up to the third-floor bedroom of Chief Executive Mao Ren-chin, had broken down the door with their rifle butts and placed Mao –

so terrified he was about to be shot that he was reportedly found cowering beneath his bed – under arrest. Mao Ren-chin, the man from Manchuria whose appointment had caused such turmoil and, already, so much suffering, had ruled over the Special Administrative Region of Xianggang for just 25 days. The best that could be said about his tenure was that it had stimulated this particular revolution: in the eyes of those who care for the future of China, however, whether that Revolution was to be a good or an evil thing depended essentially upon its outcome. If it ever succeeded, then Mao Ren-chin would probably become at least a foot-note, though probably nothing more in the long history of the nation.

At the same time as the helicopter and Recon battalion attacks, three very large convoys, each comprised of approximately sixty lightly armoured cars and trucks, sped down the three main highway links from China into Hong Kong. The regiments involved secured in turn the Lo Wu to Tai Po Highway, the Castle Peak Elevated Road and the Canton Expressway Feeder Road, and then poured southwards in strength. Some, about 4,000 men, would peel off to secure areas of Kowloon; helicopters would ferry smaller detach-ments – perhaps a total of 1,000 – to clean up the pockets of loyalist resistance in the outer islands, particularly on Lan-tau; the remainder, 2,000 soldiers, would continue south until they reached the mouths of all three of the Cross Harbour Tunnels. Tanks would follow, and some 3,000 infantrymen behind them, marching in double-quick time.

With both the Sek Kong regional headquarters seized, and the territory's Chief Executive under arrest, there seemed little point in resistance. But the Manchu-based soldiers are tough men, and they fought hard to retain some redoubts – especially, and at first somewhat mysteriously, an area of central Hong Kong Island between two mountains, which in colonial times were called Jardine's Lookout and Mount Butler.

The Republican troops were first aware of this resistance when, shortly before noon, one of their convoys was moving

slowly up Wong Nai Chung Gap Road. The battalions were under orders both to secure the communities of Aberdeen and Repulse Bay, to take control of the satellite earth stations at Stanley and Chung Hom Kok, and to install (two engineer companies were accompanying the infantry) a set of coastal defence and air defence batteries to secure the colony from any surprise attack from the South China Sea. But as the vehicles ground their way up the steep hill, they suddenly and catastrophically came under heavy artillery fire from the east.

At least five trucks were hit by what was almost certainly 152 mm shellfire, probably from the most modern Type 66 towed artillery; as many as eighty soldiers were killed. It was a brutally disruptive attack – the more so because the regiment's officers could not exactly understand what the Manchu artillery was attempting to defend at the top of this ridge. Close scrutiny of the maps showed an essentially barren hillside, with one area of granite quarries, now disused.

General Hu's men promptly regrouped, and summoned up elements of the artillery regiment, which were equipped with fast-moving howitzers. Spotters in a number of Gazelle helicopters – which had been taken on the ground at Kai Tak airport – located the enemy as being well dug in just to the north of the ridge at Jardine's Lookout, where there were a maze of trenches and tunnels dug by British defenders in 1941. It could take a considerable time to prise the men from their grasp of the hillside – for whatever reason, they were clinging on to it.

Heavy bombardment of the enemy positions began at 1 p.m., with the eight howitzers lobbing shells into the hillside at the rate of one every five seconds. The enemy replied fitfully – clearly they had little ammunition, and were probably out of contact with their battalion headquarters, which had almost certainly been seized. But they did not give up easily: by 3 p.m. machine-gun and sniper fire was still raking the hillside, and the howitzers were unable to make their way across the ravines and dense undergrowth that covers so much of the Hong Kong countryside. Shortly before 4 p.m. the regimental commander ordered in the infantry for mopping-up, together with a chemical company equipped with flamethrowers: an hour later the hillside was quiet.

Inspection of the area quickly showed what the artillery had been trying to protect. Immediately below the quarry was the entrance, closed by heavy concrete gates, to a series of large chambers that had been tunnelled into the base of Mount Butler. Originally the chambers had been constructed by the Royal Hong Kong Police Force, and were used to store emergency vehicles, ammunition, tear-gas, communications equipment and other vital spares for use in times of emergency. But since the arrival of the mainland troops – by which time all these items had been removed, and had been loaded on to HMS *Dorsetshire* together with the secret decryption equipment from the CSO station at Chung Hom Kok – all manner of other paraphernalia were stored there.

The engineers placed demolition charges on the gates. Troops entering the caverns found vast quantities of costly goods, apparently looted from museums and private houses all around the territory. Some were in the midst of being crated before, presumably, being sent up into mainland China itself. Twenty civilian workers were discovered, and were arrested. There were large quantities of jade, porcelain, paintings and calligraphy scrolls, as well as high quality antique furniture, jewellery and precious stones. Papers indicated other collections that were due for confiscation: several names of prominent Hong Kong businessmen and elderly aristocrats who had decided to remain in the territory and welcome the 'return' of the mainland Chinese, were indicated – marks against some identified the type of collection in which each was known to have specialised.

There were other small pockets of resistance, though the fighting was not so savage as at Jardine's Lookout, given the relatively low value of the positions the soldiers had been instructed to protect. On Lantau Island there was a spirited firefight at the old Shek Pik prison on the southern coast; on taking it the Republican soldiers discovered that some forty Chinese men and women had been detained there under the terms of what they said were hastily imposed security regulations. All the prisoners were Taiwanese. Then again, in a former Vietnamese refugee detention camp near the High Island reservoir, Republican troops came across a bedraggled and demoralised group of more than 300 Indian nationals.

190

They were apparently all Sindhis, and were among the small number of Indian passport holders who, for one administrative reason or another, had not managed to obtain alternate passports or residency permits before the Chinese took over. They had thus been officially classed as stateless persons and, the Manchurian troops not taking too kindly to them, they were placed in detention camps while the new administration decided their fate.

They expected to be eventually deported to Pakistan, where they or their parents had originally come from (though when they first journeyed to Hong Kong, or when their parents had taken jobs in Shanghai, there was no such entity as Pakistan). Nearly all of them were Hindus: it would be 'socially impossible', as they had kept insisting to their Chinese captors, for them to return to a nation that had been established on the basis of being almost wholly Islamic.

Their experiences in the previous month had been horrendous. Almost all of them spoke Cantonese, and a few had some Mandarin or *putonghua*. But the new soldiers, who were different in appearance and in manners, spoke none of these languages – or else their *putonghua* was heavily accented, and almost unrecognisable. They were most unfriendly, and seemed to regard the Indians as beneath contempt until many of them had begun to fear for their lives.

Now, while they were in the depths of depression, they were to be still more confused by the sudden appearance at the camp gates – and after a brief exchange of gunfire with their sentries – of a new detachment of Cantonese-speaking troops, all of whom were wearing yellow flashes on their uniform sleeves. General Hu's orders to keep good relations with the civilian population were also being rigorously observed so the Indians were given rations, and told that they would be free to return home after a few days of administrative checks. The relief on their faces was evident – all the more so when one of the Republican soldiers told them of the rebellion in Canton, and that in his view 'we will now see the end of Communism in China'.

As the mopping-up operations continued, so contact was initiated between Peter Heung and his organised triad groups. One might wonder why contact was not made at an earlier stage – perhaps even during the planning of the

operation to take the territory. The group would have proven most useful in providing local knowledge to the invaders, and in taking part in psychological operations and sabotage, to help the arriving troops. But it was not until late on Saturday that contact was made, and it appears from the records that the contact came from Heung's group to the men of the 111th Division, and not vice versa. The explanation offered by General Hu is certainly plausible.

His incoming army certainly knew some details of the existence of the Triad group. The Guangdong provincial government, through its agents working in colonial Hong Kong, had had access for the better part of a year to intelligence reports relating to the Warwick Accord. But these reports were confusing and inconclusive, and in retrospect they seem to have been deliberately contaminated with locally generated black propaganda.

It is now known that a top-secret unit buried deep within Headquarters British Forces, identified only by the number of the room from which it operated, G-13, did disseminate confusing information in selected quarters of the territory, in the hope that it would be picked up, and then confuse, the mainland Chinese. A Ministry of Defence 'D' notice was issued in June 1997 asking editors of British newspapers to refrain from discussing even the existence of this unit. No such obligation rests with the present author, however; and it is now possible to reveal that the unit had six members, all fluent Chinese speakers, and headed by a psychological warfare specialist from the Ministry, Dr John Gurdon. Dr Gurdon had been placed in the colony some five years before, under the cover of 'Attached Commander British Forces Hong Kong' and with the public position of adviser on cross-border developments to the various brigadiers who headed the colony's small garrison. He made particular efforts to cultivate excellent relations with local left-wing groups, leaders and newspapers in the territory; he was on notably good terms with one of the writers on one such opinion-forming paper, the *Ta Kung Pao*. He is believed to have given misleading information on the identities of the signatories of

the Warwick Accord, as well as on the group's aims and abilities; he is known to have fomented rivalries between two groups of left-wing publishers; and he is said to have given to a Taiwanese journalist, whom he suspected of being a double agent, a series of bogus tape-recordings that he said resulted from telephone taps between the New China News Agency and a Western reporter. His record for spreading confusion and dissent among the large army of Chinese secret service personnel working under a variety of covers in Hong Kong in the closing months of British administration was, London colleagues later admitted, most impressive.

It was a testimony, therefore, either to the excellent security of Heung's group – who were well practised in the local version of *omerta* – or to a signal degree of G-13-assisted incompetence on the part of the Chinese agents, that little specific was known about the Heung group. General Hu had no knowledge, for instance, of the meetings between Heung and Margerison, nor of the small arms dumps left behind by the British forces. There is no indication that the Chinese forensic scientists working either on the cases of the murder of Constable Wan, the explosion at the Gulangyu Guest-house, or the escape of the men due to be executed in the town of Shitsze, had any proof of links with any gangs operating in Hong Kong, or with any arms or explosives left behind by the departing British. The extent to which this lack of progress by the Guangdong and Fujian authorities was due to their local incompetence, or whether they were in any way further frustrated by G-13 or similar groups, is still unknown. It remains singularly fortunate, from the point of view of the Republican rebels, that no such discoveries were made during the days before the events outside the Canton City PSB headquarters.

The contact made between the 111th Division officers and Heung's men was cordial, and produced an informal agreement that men of the latter group would be able to play a part in assisting with the policing of the territory, with identifying and locating locals who had collaborated with the Manchu forces, and with agents of the Peking government who had been operating before the British departure. The agreement seemed a convenient one at the time; but local Hong Kong residents have since complained that the unto-

ward degree of graft and corruption that has plagued the territory since the date of the Republican takeover indicates that it was an imprudent move, and may limit the possibilities of a swift return to real democracy in the territory.

The final fight – which was mercifully brief – was at the Stonecutters Island Garrison headquarters. General Hu wished to lead this assault himself. The Xianggang Commander, Lu Chuanzhi of the 37th Division, was known to him as a classmate, though not as a particular friend. They had served in adjoining regiments twenty years before during the Vietnam border wars, and General Lu had taken part in many of the suppression operations in Tibet.

He had also played a prominent role in the 1989 Tienanmen Incident – it was indeed believed, though it was never confirmed, that he was the officer who, from a helicopter hovering above Fuxingmenwai and West Changan Avenues, gave orders for those soldiers then advancing to clear the Square of protesters to fire at will. PLA files on the incident had apparently been destroyed less than a year after the event, and other senior Army officers had conspired to protect the identity of those who were directly responsible for the killings. Persistent rumours had long connected General Lu to those orders: since Hu Dai-fang had lost a niece – a student of Peking Normal University – in the massacre, he had long felt a sense of acute bitterness about the affair. It could fairly be said that it was Tienanmen, and the later Wuhan Incident, that first triggered the sentiments that led him to take part in the Canton Rebellion: taking General Lu's surrender here would, therefore, have a particular sweetness to it.

In the event the confrontation was neither prolonged nor spectacular. The 37th Infantry Division's headquarters held about 1,200 troops, with a 120-strong guard company, a small number of armoured cars and machine-guns. There had never been any expectation of an attack from the north: such defences as there were assumed either insurrectionary activity from the local population, or an attack from the air or water by enemy forces assembled in the South China Sea.

194

Two companies from an anti-aircraft battalion and a number of fast patrol boats moored beside the base offered protection from such eventualities.

Opposing them on this Saturday afternoon was a highly organised force, in high good spirits. One half of the force had moved southwards, down the main highway from the Kwai Chung container base – once the world's busiest – and the other had come from the east via the main Boundary Street Expressway. The force was comprised of some 60 tanks, 40 armoured cars, two dozen self-propelled howitzers, dozens of pieces of towed artillery and any number of mortars, and some 5,000 heavily armed infantrymen. To have resisted would have been pointless, as General Hu pointed out in a megaphone address to the loyalist troops. He had sufficient foresight to have a graduate of Shenyang Foreign Languages Institute, a former resident of Heilongjiang Province, address the headquarters troops in their own dialect. The young man, standing atop a personnel carrier, spoke as follows:

'As you may know from foreign broadcast sources, forces loyal to the former governor of Guangdong Province, Mr Yi Jaun Ling, have lately taken control of the city of Canton and of the surrounding region. These troops, our brothers in arms, are committed to assisting Governor Yi and other democratically minded people to restore liberty and the rights to personal happiness to the people of all of our dear country.

'The entire civilian population of Canton is with us. And we have received messages from all over southern China, from Yunnan in the west to Jiangxi in the east, indicating that we now have the masses on our side. I am now pleased to be able to inform you that the armies based in all of the Guangzhou and Nanjing Military Regions have come over to Governor Yi's view. Our position is therefore impregnable.

'Our military leaders recently arrived at the wise and understandable decision that, to enable our troops to have at their disposal the very best possible logistical advantage, it was necessary for us to take control of a major port and aviation centre. We were aware that the indigenous population of the Special Administrative Region of Xianggang –

which is to be formally known again now by the name by which its inhabitants have long called it, Hong Kong – was likely to concur with Governor Yi's view of the developments in southern China. We felt it prudent, therefore, to make as one of our movement's priorities the securing of Hong Kong to our cause.

'A strong force of men led by the heroic General Hu Dai-fang thus crossed into Hong Kong this morning. In the past ten hours we have succeeded in securing the city and its key positions and in detaining the entire 37th Infantry Division, all of whom are now on their way to a detention centre off Lantau Island.

'In the name of Governor Yi Juan Ling, and in the fervent hope of a peaceful and dignified end to this conflict, I thus call upon you men, on your officers and on your general officer commanding, to come forward without delay and indicate by customary means your total surrender to our forces. I can offer the assurances that all will be well-treated, and that you will be permitted to return without delay to your homes, providing the situation permits it. I look to the immediate display of a white flag of truce, and to receiving emissaries from your leadership. That is all.'

There was an uneasy pause. Then an upstairs window was opened in the main headquarters building, and two soldiers could be dimly seen draping a white sheet from the sill. There was a ripple of pleasure from the waiting troops, and one or two of the tank commanders turned off their diesel engines, thickening the silence of the evening.

A door opened, and three Army officers, each carrying a white banner, marched out across the parade ground and up to the triple wire fence. 'We have come to offer the surrender of the entire remaining force of the 37th Infantry Division,' their senior officer, a major, announced stiffly. 'Emissaries from your group will be welcome. Our men prefer not to engage in battle with other compatriots, no matter from which part of China they come. Our desire is for a peaceful end to this struggle.'

By dusk the entire headquarters battalion had formally surrendered and laid down their arms, and General Hu's soldiers were consolidating their position. Yellow quarantine signal flags – for now the only flags available to the Repub-

licans, and to be their symbol for the coming several weeks of
the campaign – were hoisted above the barrack blocks;
another had been raised over Government House, from
where temporary administrators were already working,
principally to see if there were records of any further
detainees who had been picked up by the soldiers of the
37th.

Radio Television Hong Kong had been secured early in
the afternoon, and its transmitters had been putting out a
steady diet of Cantonese popular music. But at 8 p.m.
General Hu appeared in a simultaneous radio and television
broadcast. Speaking in Cantonese he announced the establishment of the Republican Party of China, the need for the
speedy capture of the territory and the success of his mission.
Everyone who co-operated would be safe, he said. Furthermore, the establishment of 'a civilian Administration that
finds favour with the local people' would be carried out
promptly. He would be holding urgent talks later that night
with the British Consul-General, Peter Williamson, and with
officials from the US Consulate, to ask for advice on the
running of the territory. And he went on to make a further
series of reassuring remarks, to the effect that the new
administration would abide by the letter and the spirit of the
major promises that had been made thirteen years before in
the Joint Declaration on the Future of Hong Kong. But then
he added some further words, which must have sent a chill
down the necks of many of his listeners.

As all of you who have lived here in the last thirteen years
must be aware, the British colonial government placed many
restrictions on the citizens of Hong Kong in the closing period
of their rule to ensure that the people did or said nothing that
was likely to insult or to anger the Communist government of
the People's Republic of China. Many times British officials
made statements declaring that Hong Kong 'will not be used
as a base for subversion' against the People's Republic. It was
regarded by the British as crucially important that relations
between China and Hong Kong were, on the surface at least,
amicable.

From today, all of that is to change. The illusion of ami-
cability ends here. The Republican Party of China has been

established specifically to rid China of the scourge of Communism. The movement has as its emotional base the City of Canton – a city that has played so vitally important a role in revolution and rebellion in the past.

Now, however, we need a practical base – a site with peerless communications, with access to high technology and transport, with expertise and knowledge. Hong Kong is the natural centre of such excellence. From today onwards, therefore, all talk of Hong Kong's unwillingness to assist in the overthrow of the Communist régime ceases. This is the paramount headquarters. From this single bastion of capitalism and freedom will grow a revolution that will inevitably spread across the face of the entire nation. For the first time we can say with pride that the Cantonese people, and especially the Cantonese people who live along the banks of the Pearl River between the two mighty cities of Canton and Hong Kong, will take up the torch and the sword, and fight for a new China. We have the energy, the pride and the will. We will not stop, until China is free!

The broadcast was monitored in Peking that night. The State Council was called into emergency session in the Zhongnanhai Compound just before midnight. The telephone call summoning the thirteen members warned that decisions of the utmost gravity, relating to matters of national and international importance, had to be taken without delay.

In the West, too, a sudden air of emergency gripped the leadership. In London a Cabinet meeting was called for Sunday morning, local time. In Washington there was an emergency secret meeting of the Charlesworth Committee and, at the urging of Secretary of State Crowther, a meeting of the National Security Council's Deputies Committee late in the evening. Both meetings were scheduled to hear disturbing evidence of strange and inexplicable warnings about other, seemingly unrelated military activities that were now affecting two of China's eastern neighbours.

## CHAPTER NINE

# DOMINIONS
# OF FURY

## PEKING

### *Sunday, 27 July 1997*

News of the loss of Hong Kong, and the stated intention of its interim rulers to permit a speedy return to democracy and freedom, triggered a sudden and terrified panic among the elders in Peking. The State Councillors – the nation's cabinet, headed by the premier, Li Peng – converged on the Zhongnanhai Compound in the small hours of the morning. One member who has since crossed to the Republican side, the 61-year-old Shanghainese hero of the Vietnam War, Li Lizhi, later described the scene.

The meeting took place underground, in a room harshly illuminated by neon tubes and guarded by helmeted sentries from the élite Peking Garrison Command. The men who assembled from their homes to the north and west of the city came through a steel door that led into the network of tunnels running below the city. None came in from the lift that led from the upstairs world. The attendees were all ashen-faced, angry and puzzled.

The premier and the Ministers for Defence, State Security and Civil Affairs led the brief discussion. The situation was offered in outline: the Army in Canton had rebelled, and had gained control of Hong Kong; there was a growing likelihood that Army units in Fujian Province, and perhaps throughout Nanjing Region, would join the rebellion. The People's Republic of China was facing the greatest threat ever known to its internal stability. Harsh measures needed to be taken quickly to stamp out the

rebellion, before it was allowed to infect the rest of the nation.

A little-known councillor, Qian Hanxiong, who had been gazetted head of the equally unfamiliar Bureau for the Establishment of Correct Socialist Attitudes, an offshoot of the State Security Ministry, was first asked to make remarks about the identities of those who were known to have seized power. He said that in his view the ringleaders of the operation were Governor Yi, General Tang and three or four of his subordinate generals, together with a number of figures in Hong Kong including 'figures well-known in organised anti-socialist criminal movement', including the colony's best-known barrister and former political activist, Martin Lee Chu-ming. Subsequent information has shown that particular surmise to be incorrect: it is probable, once again, that the propaganda put out by the British G-13 unit had had some influence on Peking's muddled thinking.

Qian announced that he had already instructed Radio Peking and its foreign language satellites to commence broadcasts denouncing these men individually and by name, and for all national radio and television stations to commence immediately a programme of massive discreditation of 'these guilty individuals and bandits'. He was confident, he said, that 'among the peasants and workers at least, any temptation to believe the lies of these southern monkeys will vanish quickly', such was the persuasive nature of the broadcasts his Bureau had formulated.

The Minister of Defence angrily waved him down. 'Propaganda is not what is needed right now,' he said, thumping his fist on the table. 'We have a crisis that could spread to critical units of our beloved Army in a matter of days. It must be halted by military means immediately. The peasants are for the moment irrelevant in all of this. The key is the loyalty of the Army.

'We have atomic missile units that are close to the rebels, and it is vital to our nation that they be secured and protected. There are many institutions holding weapons of unparalleled ferocity – and if they fall into the hands of these vandals and outlaws, the country will be in even greater peril.

'I have information, gentlemen, that this rebellion has been fomented by Kuomintang forces in Taiwan.' There was a chorus of shouts of disbelief and anger from many of the

assembled councillors. Some of the older men present, survivors of the Long March and of the brutal civil war against
Chiang Kai-shek's armies, bayed from their wheelchairs,
hammering their sticks against the floor. It was some minutes
before the Premier was able to restore order, and the
Defence minister could continue.

'I urge our Council to give me the necessary permission to
go after the source of this insurrectionary madness, by
striking at the heart of the Kuomintang military machine
itself.' There was a further eruption of shouting, with cries of
'Yes, let him do it! Kill the traitors of the Kuomintang! End
the division of our country! Kill all those who are loyal to the
bandit Chiang!'

'Our brave forces in Fujian,' he went on, rising to the
mood of the occasion, 'who at this moment are being subjected to the most brutal propaganda attacks by the rebel
forces, should be allowed the honour of making the strike
against the capitalist warmongers in Taipei. But if those
forces are of uncertain loyalty – and this may happen, councillors should be fully prepared – then we must make use of
the Shanghai Garrison Command and the destroyers of the
East Sea Fleet to make the attack.

'This is for you to decide, as it is a matter of foreign policy,
and may have repercussions that go far beyond these concrete walls. But whatever you do instruct, I must first have
your immediate unanimous agreement and authorisation to
move regiments by air to protect the nuclear forces of our
Second Artillery, and to take similar steps to protect the
chemical and biological warfare bases and nuclear research
institutes that have been set up in a number of distant provinces known to you all.

'Secondly I request permission for an immediate air and
paratroop assault on the rebel headquarters at Baiyun and
Hong Kong. I am pleased to be able to tell you that the
airborne elements of the 15th Army in Wuhan have
remained loyal, and the officers and men, to whom I spoke
only a few minutes before coming down to this meeting, are
now eagerly awaiting permission to strike at the cowards and
desperadoes who are in control of the southern part of the
nation. That operation must begin now, this very night.

'And thirdly, I request permission to begin planning for

this recommended assault on the Kuomintang force. Such an assault will have, in my view, a dual effect – both of neutralising the source of this rebellion and of providing a stimulus for our patriotic people, a symbol of our resolve around which they can rally in this time of uncertainty.'

Several councillors rose. The premier waved them down, and stood himself. 'There must be no argument. I authorise immediate moves to secure the atomic and chemical weapons bases. I authorise an immediate airborne attack on Baiyun and Hong Kong. I also instruct you to make contact with our forces in Fujian to see if there are officers sufficiently reliable and loyal to add to this attack, so that the Canton forces find themselves under fire from two separate army groups.

'But I cannot give sanction yet to a move against our compatriots in Taiwan. Only after the most exhaustive proof of their complicity in this rebellion, and which I would wish to have demonstrated before the United Nations Security Council, can I engage in warfare with the Kuomintang. You know full well of my hatred for these villainous people. My own father was murdered by them when I was a small child. But the consequences of our attacking them now without the proof that I demand would be too horrendous to contemplate. So for that, I cannot give permission.'

A storm of shouting and bellowing broke out, and so many members who were able to stand, did so, and started waving fists at one another in argument that sentries entered the room to ensure that the rebellion itself had not penetrated this supposed fastness of loyalty. The premier struggled to calm his deputies and, gesturing to the soldiers to leave the room, eventually succeeded in doing so.

'Gentlemen,' he said finally, 'we have work to do. Let us meet again in forty-eight hours' time. By then, I feel sure, I and our colleague Ministers will have encouraging news for you all. But for now, we have work to do. The nation must be composed. The Army must be stabilised. The crisis must not be permitted to spread. To achieve all of these goals we need to act, not to argue. So let us go from here in agreement, and meet in two days' time, and see where the actions we have taken this day have themselves taken us.' He looked directly at each of the councillors – the more particularly at those, mostly seated, who represented the troublesome old guard

of the Party, those who feared most that their grip on power might be faltering. 'Have no fears,' he said to one, whose face was suffused with anxiety. 'We will prevail. We shall see each other again in two days' time.'

It was in fact nearly two weeks before the State Council was to meet again, so dire and fast-moving were the developments of the following days. It would be misleading to assign a particular priority to the occurrences, since all of them contributed in one way or another to the beginning of the awful ebb and flow of a classically complicated civil war. The order in which the events are recounted here is not necessarily chronological: all had their beginnings in the August of the war's first year, but each incident overlapped in time and had eventual effects on the outcome of each of the other incidents – as, once again, the occurrences of war are likely to do. The picture that emerges from this *tour d'horizon* does present the quiddity of the situation that summer – of a nation decaying rapidly into uncontrollability, fast presenting that phenomenon that has terrified world-watchers' nightmares for centuries past: China – on the loose.

# FUJIAN PROVINCE –
# THE COAST OF THE TAIWAN STRAIT

On the beach road not far from the city of Xiamen, where so many of the events that triggered the first battles of the civil war took place, is a small bluff, topped by a structure known as the Huli Mountain Fortress. This is a venerable and not unlovely complex of brick barrack and granite battlement, a sort of Chinese Martello Tower. It was built in 1823, at a time when the Ching emperors were starting to become restive at the way that foreigners – particularly the British – were landing huge quantities of Indian opium at their seaports. The drug was seriously debilitating to the Chinese peasantry, and the Forbidden City was grumbling, quite properly, that so vile a trade should be halted.

The construction of Huli Mountain Fort, from which cannon could be trained across the mouth of Amoy Bay and

so restrict ships' access to the port that was then known as Amoy (but which is now Xiamen) just predated the appearance on the political scene of Canton's infamous Commissioner Lin, the bureaucrat whose formal campaign against the British export of the drug to the Pearl River ports started the Opium Wars – which had such disastrous and humiliating repercussions for all of China.

So it is yet another pleasing historical irony – like the commencement of Canton's July riots at the Martyrs' Memorial – to find that this very same fort, which was built to help in a war that then itself decimated China and the dynasty that ran it, and helped in no small way to found and aid the early prosperity of the Colony of Hong Kong, should play a part, nearly two centuries later, in events that were so savagely to injure the nation on which it stood. China, though, is so rich in historical association, and has so long a lineage, that barely an event can take place, nor a site be chosen for one, that has not played a part in the story before. And Huli Mountain Fortress played a part of no small significance in the summer of 1997.

Since the mid 1980s the fortress had been abandoned. The barracks were empty, their windows broken, their doors broken from their hinges. But at the cliff's edge, protected by embrasured buttresses of yard-thick cement, was a huge old gun. It had been made by Krupp in 1895, and could hurl half-ton shells for twenty miles. But in the early summer of 1997 it stood as it had for nearly fifteen years, silent and rusting, locked on a trajectory of fifty-two degrees, and a bearing of 92 degrees, a fraction south of east.

It had been one of a number of guns that, just twenty years earlier, had been active almost beyond an artilleryman's imagination. A glance through the rusting gunsights would explain why. Not five miles away from the Huli Mountain Fortress, and on a bearing of 092° magnetic from its gun, is a rocky island, perhaps eight miles long and, so the maps indicate, seven miles wide. There is a small port at the southern end called Shuitou, and near by a town of 40,000 people – the town of Quemoy. And though the dialect names of the island are various – Chinmen Tao, or Kinmen Tao are those most commonly heard in Xiamen City – the world knows the island by the name of its tiny capital, Quemoy.

For although Peking will not tolerate the remark, the island is legally not a part of the People's Republic of China. It may be only five miles away from the coast; it may be possible, on a calm day, to hear conversations from fishermen on the coast, or hear music wafting from radios in the island villages; but this island of Quemoy basks under the invigilation of a red flag quartered with blue, with a twelve-pointed white star. The flag, in other words, of the Republic of China, of Taiwan. The flag of the Kuomintang, fluttering within easy sight of a child's spyglass, just a short swim across the Bay of Amoy.

Back in the 1950s, the sight and sound of the hated Kuomintang – for more powerful glasses would reveal Taiwanese soldiers patrolling the Quemoy beaches – so very close to the Chinese mainland was utter anathema to the loyalists of the Communist government. No matter that Taiwan and the few offshore islands held by Chiang Kai-shek were visible signs of his defeat – a reminder to all Chinese people that a man who had once wanted his flag to fly from Manchuria to the Annamese border, could fly it only on a few chunks of rock off the nation's eastern coast. To the diehards, the very sight of the flag was too insulting; and so a violent campaign to purge the vision was initiated.

Every day during the mid and early 1950s heavy guns – of which the Krupp monster at Huli Shan was one – pounded and pounded away at Quemoy (and at Matsu, a similar though smaller island off the town of Fuzhou, to the north). The Taiwanese responded both with anger, and *sang-froid*: they protested in 1954 that they would demand implementation of the terms of the newly ratified defence treaty with the United States (and indeed the 7th Fleet was deployed, and the world was briefly plunged into a diplomatic crisis); and at the same time they ordered their soldiers on the outpost to plaster immense banners along the most visible beaches, bearing the ideographs, in red on white, of one of Sun Yat-sen's best-known aphorisms: 'people's democracy, people's rights, people's livelihood.'

The crisis eventually stilled. The mainland Chinese, under discreet pressure from the Great Powers, lost interest in the islands; most of the guns were hauled away for other tasks, or for scrap; and the Krupp cannon at Huli Shan Fortress

which had been manned by full-time soldiers of the PLA, was then handed over to ratings from the Navy's East Sea Fleet. In 1984 it was abandoned, and left to the wind and the damp oxidising agents it carried to reduce it – like the idea of the forcible conquest of Taiwan – to history.

All of which would have probably continued, had not a Brigade Commander named Li Guang, based with his troops in the barracks just a few hundred yards from Huli Shan, decided to attempt to revivify a patriotic fascination with the fate of the island of Quemoy. He was in command of a tank brigade, part of the battle-hardened 14th Tank Division. He planned to use his not inconsiderable military assets for what he thought would be one grand and splendid patriotic act – a move that would unite all China behind him and enable it to purge, at a stroke, those elements of cowards and madmen who, he understood, were now trying to destroy the fabric of the nation.

Brigadier Li was manifestly part of no gerontocracy, being just forty-seven years old. He had, none the less, something very much in common with the old men of the Central Committee and of the Central Military Commission: a per-fervid enthusiasm for the Communist system, one that had brought him many times to the notice of the authorities and of his senior officers. Long before he had won the First Grade of the Wartime Hero and Model Soldier Medal, for what the citation proclaimed were 'patriotic actions beyond the call of duty during the Counter-Attack for Self-Defence against Vietnamese Aggression along the China-Vietnam Border'. Precisely what those actions were has never been revealed.

But it is known that Brigadier Li, when still a young captain, was head of the 'Lei Feng Squad' that had been formed within his tank battalion. He was its natural leader: he had long been well-known for trying to follow Mao's instructional slogan 'Learn from Lei Feng', and his barracks room was awash with well-thumbed copies of biographies and magazine articles about the famously courageous little soldier Lei, whose exploits – although quite probably fictitious – did so much to stimulate patriotism and zeal within the ranks of the Chinese Army. And Brigadier Li is said by his men to have followed the example of Lei Feng in

at least one particular respect – by offering to wash out the socks of soldiers who had become fatigued by the jungle fighting. But it was always hinted that some particular act of military heroism, and not his enthusiasm for laundry-work, had won him the Wartime Hero and Model Soldier Medal. It remains something of a mystery that the Chinese authorities chose never to publicise it.

One explanation perhaps lies in the acute embarrassment – not to say the heavy military loss – that was suffered by the Chinese authorities as a direct consequence of Brigadier Li's extraordinary and unilateral actions of August 1997. For, taking a far more extreme and improbable step than even Lei Feng's biographer might imagine, Li Guang decided to take it upon himself to do what no Chinese had tried to do seriously since 1958 – to liberate Quemoy from Taiwanese hands.

He had planned his move to come shortly after the celebrations – which were naturally cancelled this year because of the crisis – that were scheduled to mark the seventieth anniversary of the Founding of the PLA. He had planned with some care: and he began with placing sixteen men from his signals battalion – fourteen soldiers and two officers – inside the offices of the local branch of Xiamen Central Radio. They informed the quite credulous station director that they had been dispatched there to act as additional sentries, bolstering the existing Militia force to help guard the station and its transmitter against possible seizure by Cantonese rebels.

Leaving a statement behind with his signallers, and a series of precise instructions for its broadcast on receipt of a pre-arranged signal, Brigadier Li then ordered the placement, under cover of a moonless night, of more than a dozen of his heavy artillery pieces and 140mm rocket launchers, into positions along the coast between Xiamen City and Huli Shan, and for a mile beyond. He also, for what is assumed to have been emotional reasons, arranged for ammunition to be brought from the reserve armoury for the old Krupp cannon, enabling that ancient weapon to be added to his notional list of assets for the planned bombardment.

It needs to be said that he took all of these remarkable steps entirely on his own initiative, without reference either

to his divisional commander (who in any case had been summoned up to Nanjing for 'urgent consultations' about the fast-developing situation), nor to his political commissar, who accepted the unusual number of movements of men and *matériel* from the barracks as part of an 'emergency exercise' that had been ordered in response to the heightened tension in the Taiwan Strait.

The guns and rockets were all zeroed in on the well-identified targets – gun emplacements, barracks, a small communications centre and (for its symbolic value) the huge Taiwanese flag that could be seen along Quemoy's western coast. They could not be seen at night, of course; but the aiming coordinates had already been constructed in Li's planning department some days before, and the gun crews had simply to ratchet their weapons to predesignated compass bearings and trajectories, to be certain their ammunition would do the necessary damage.

At the same time he ordered some 2,000 of his most skilled and courageous infantrymen to embark on a flotilla of landing craft and zodiac boats that had been driven down to the shore just after dusk. By midnight he was ready for his daredevil operation; and shortly thereafter, following the firing of a series of green flares, he ordered his artillerymen to commence a withering cannonade, all directed at enemy positions in Quemoy. A coast that had been quiet for the previous forty years erupted in a sea of flame and fury as the shells and rockets arced out over the water with furious frequency. The roar and shudder of the guns was like the beginnings of an earthquake. In Xiamen near by, and in towns as far away as Jimei and Shitsze – which had itself played a small part in the events leading to this catastrophe – residents were rudely shaken awake, many reportedly thinking that this was the end of the world.

The barrage went on for more than an hour. All the while, under cover of the streaking gold parabolas of shellfire, the boats and landing craft sped forward at full tilt. By the time they were within hailing distance of the coast the gunfire slackened, then stopped. It remained only for them to gain the shore and, so Li's brother officers had planned, the island of Quemoy would be theirs. Resistance had surely been crushed like eggshells: no force could withstand so

fierce a bombardment, especially without a breath of warning.

And so, as the scores of ships manoeuvred into position to wait for the flares ordering the landing of their soldiers, the signal – somewhat unimaginatively, a telephone call and the uttering of the name 'Lei Feng' – went out to the radio station. The 'sentries' then took control of the station and its transmitters; and one of the officers, speaking in perfect *putonghua*, made the following announcement:

> People of Fujian. People of China. This special announce-ment, a matter of pride and joy for you all, is made with the authority of the People's Liberation Army stationed in Xiamen City.
>
> For the last forty-eight years, as you all will know, the treacherous bandits of the Kuomintang have grasped with cowardly hands our beloved island of Chinmen Tao, and have waved in our faces the wretched flag of their bastard-like nationhood. For forty-eight years our People's Republic has borne with valour and stoicism this gross insult, and we have watched with pain and torment the flying of the symbol of their treachery across so short a stretch of sea.
>
> But today, after an heroic struggle that was mercifully brief and cost our glorious fighters little by way of sacrifice, I am honoured to announce to you that moves are even now under way to recover the island of Chinmen Tao, and return it to its natural place alongside all the other lands and dominions that are so dear to all our hearts.
>
> By the time the golden sun rises over our nation tomorrow, this dear island and our compatriot brothers and sisters will have been freed from the corrupt tyranny of their evil gaolers, and will be welcomed back into the arms of the motherland. All praise and honour to our glorious fighting men, and to the bold and imaginative plan that has enabled them to right this most despicable wrong of recent history.

The Brigadier had given orders that this message was to be broadcast every fifteen minutes, throughout the night, and that it was to be replaced at dawn by an even more stirring announcement of triumph. But in the event it was only to be heard three more times during that night; and no other message of similar bent ever replaced it. For within one

further hour, and with tragic results, the Taiwanese military struck back.

Within moments of the halting of the artillery barrage, dozens of F-5E fighters came roaring south of the Quemoy headland and fired salvoes of Sidewinder missiles directly into the mass of boats beneath them. The pilots were clearly using laser aiming devices and other smart electronic homing aids, for within no more than ten minutes the attacking force was in total disarray, with over twenty boats sunk or sinking, and the waters thick with struggling and screaming men. Machine-guns on the shore opened up, firing into the blackness at near point-blank range, adding to the carnage in the water. Sheets of flame occasionally illuminated the scene; but otherwise there was total darkness, with the terrifying sound of the waves of jets screeching down for their attack runs, the explosion of anti-personnel bombs and ship-destroying shells, and the fearful yelling of the injured and frightened men in the sea.

At the same time scores of newly developed Green Bee coastal defence missiles were fired from batteries on Quemoy's west coast, all designed to home in on the now quiet emplacements of Brigadier Li's artillery force. The Green Bee had been perfected only two years before at Taiwan's Chungshan Institute of Science and Technology, and had been designed specifically to neutralise night-time artillery barrages.

That it took more than an hour to order the Green Bee platoons to retaliate was quite deliberate, a Taiwanese Defence Department spokesman was quoted as saying the next day. Their emplacements on Quemoy had been so wholly encased in concrete as to render them almost perfectly secure from the effects of mainland gunfire; and so long as they could survive the barrage it was regarded as 'likely to be of much greater military effect' if the Communists could be lulled into sending their boat-borne infantrymen into deep and unfamiliar waters, before attacking them so brutally from the air.

It was a tactic that worked brilliantly. The shore batteries were knocked out in their entirety (though not the Krupp: a technical problem meant that it was never fired, and so did not offer an infra-red signature to the Green Bee spotters on

Quemoy), and of the 2,000 men sent to invade the island, only sixty-three made it back.

For good measure the Taiwanese Air Force made a number of sorties over Xiamen itself, and one jet placed a smart bomb through an air vent in the radio transmitter main hall, and brought to an end an attempted fourth transmission of the so-called Victory Broadcast – which was probably as well, since the supposed victory had turned into a sudden, decisive and humiliating defeat.

Brigadier Li himself was killed in the onslaught, as were most of his planning officers. The political commissars attached to both the Brigadier's unit and to the 14th Tank Division both committed suicide the next day. Morale within the units remaining fell to a devastating low. There were mutinous mutterings over the coming weeks about the apparent inferiority of the mainland Chinese weapons, the lack of discipline and training, the fact, as many junior officers were wont to say, that 'we don't know exactly what we are fighting for'.

By the end of the autumn the situation within the entire 63rd Army based at Quanzhou had become untenable. An entire tank brigade had been lost. Morale in its most important tank division, the 14th, had fallen to the point where there was open talk of mutiny. The political commissars – replacements had been sent from Lanzhou and Peking – were men of intolerably harsh political views, unwilling to yield even fractionally in their devotion to the 'Lei Feng Way', despite the humiliating backwash from the most recent occasion when it had been put into practice. And so it was not a matter of total surprise when General Tang, while fighting hard on many fronts in Canton, heard through intermediaries that the operational commander of the 63rd Army Group, Major-General Chen Cong Da, had agreed to put all of his men and his equipment in with the Republican camp.

Not a shot was ever fired between the two armies. There was a last-minute attempt by General Nie in Nanjing to have Major-General Chen either arrested or shot before he sent the fatal message and announced the decision to his men – who came out in the barrack blocks by the thousands, cheering the

decision and wishing 'Long Life to Governor Yi Juan Ling and his Republican Party'. But the attempt backfired badly: the assassination squad drawn from the 1st Army itself rebelled, and killed two of General Nie's staff officers, thereby indicating that the Republican infection had begun to spread even within the utterly loyal 1st Group Army.

By mid-autumn, therefore – and due in so no small part to the fervent lunacy of the Lei Feng Movement – the Republican rebellion had grown to sizeable proportions. China was beginning to spin rapidly, and horribly, out of control.

# THE DZUNGARIAN GATE, NORTHERN XINJIANG

*December*

The winter cold of China's western Dzungarian Basin is almost unimaginable. The great Altai Mountain chain rises to the north, the jagged peaks of the Tien Shan to the south, and in between is a flat and featureless plain, dry as a bone, with howling winds in winter and weather that is equally inhospitable in the summer – the Dzungarian Basin.

There are a few lakes, and some marshy lowlands. There is scrubland and steppe. And there are patchy outcrops of sand that hint at the proximity of the great Taklamakan Desert lying over the Tien Shan to the south. Dzungaria is not a desert in the strict sense. There is some rainfall – 1 foot a year. There are some rivers – the Bortala, the Ulungur, the Ili and the Ertix, which flows west into what once was Russia (but which by 1997 was independent Turkestan) and thence on up into the Arctic Ocean – thus becoming China's only riverine connection with the icefields of the North Pole. That it rises in Dzungaria seems only appropriate for so harsh and cheerless a place.

The main towns are as bleak and ugly as their setting. Ürümqi, all factories and pollution and blocks of workers' flats. Turfan, an oasis by the great depression of the same name, is far from being as splendid as its name suggests. And the other towns – Karamay, Kuytun, Shihezi – are as undis-

tinguished and unattractive as only modern Chinese towns can be. Only the people – a vast mixture of Central Asian ethnic types, some blue-eyed, looking almost Nordic, others nomadic Kazakhs or Uighurs of Turkic stock with a smattering of Han Chinese – and the history, give the place its due fascination.

Today the province of which Dzungaria is the northwestern part is that known as Xinjiang, or Sinkiang – the so-called Chinese New Territories, sharing the name with the northern portion of British Hong Kong. But here is no back garden of low hills and rice paddies, hastily annexed to protect a naval base. This is instead a massive and barely settled tract of country, three times the size of France, and yet with a total population not much larger than that of greater New York, and all wrested from the hands of the Russian and Ottoman Empires and made part of China instead of what it would otherwise have been, a country or a province named East Turkestan.

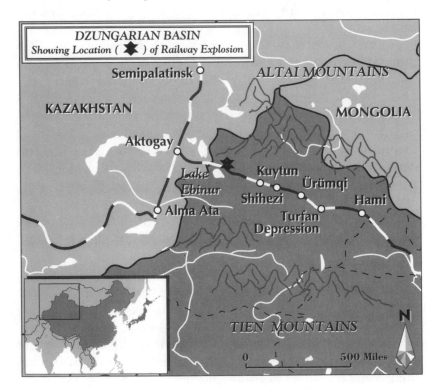

And Dzungaria has played its part in the world's politics before, just as it has begun to do once again. In particular there was the occasion when, for almost all of the 1870s, Russia took control of a part of western Dzungaria, along the valley of the Ili River, and refused to hand it back until the Ching emperor paid a handsome bounty. That the Czar managed to do such a thing was indicative of the weakness of China in the wake of the Opium Wars and the Taiping Rebellion: another echo of the past in the events of today. For what happened by the Dzungarian Gate in the winter of 1997 and 1998 amply illustrates the weakened state of China in the wake of the 1997 Canton Rebellion. The tendency that China's neighbours have to gnaw away at her sickened carcass has been evident yet again.

There were specific triggers for both sets of troubles, too; and it is probably worth diverting briefly from the modern narrative to offer an outline of the Victorian problems, to indicate how similar they are to the events of more recent times.

In the last century, the beginnings of the particular afflictions of Xinjiang came about as a result of rebellions among the Muslims. Small outbreaks of trouble between Han Chinese self-defence groups and those Muslims who followed a peculiarly virulent form of imported Sufism known as the 'New Faith' led, by the 1860s, to concerted mayhem throughout the province. The breakdown of order was exploited by a number of adventurers – and in particular by a memorable figure from Tashkent called Yakoob Beg. From his 'capital' of Kashgar on the western edge of the Taklamakan Desert, Yakoob ruled a kingdom he came to call Kashgaria; and indeed the Ottoman Sultan declared Yakoob the Emir – the King of Kashgaria.

The Russians promptly took advantage of the disorder and seized parts of the Ili River valley, just to the south of the Dzungarian Gate and immediately (and to the outrage of the Manchu Emperor in far-away Peking) entered into a commercial treaty with Yakoob. The British, eager to see the emergence of a buffer state between the Russian Empire and their own territories in India, did the same, giving Kashgaria legitimate international recognition, and thus existence.

Kashgaria did not last long. The Chinese Emperor dis-

patched to the region his most seasoned military scholar-hero, Tso Tsung-tang. General Tso was a brilliant strategist. Within a year the rebels were either captured (and sentenced to death by the charmless Imperial means of slicing) or run to earth and (as in Yakoob's case) persuaded to commit suicide. By 1877 Xinjiang was clear of rebellion; it remained only for the Russians to be forced to leave Ili and sneak back through the Dzungarian Gate.

This they eventually did, but only after a briefly farcical interlude, a further humiliation for the Chinese Court. In 1879 an Imperial Chinese delegation, headed by one Chung-hou, was sent to St Petersburg to ask the Russians to vacate the Ili valley. The Russian court was on holiday in the seaside town of Livadia, and demanded the Chinese see them there. A treaty was eventually signed, whereby the Russians agreed to move out – but since Chung-hou had no idea of the geography of the disputed area, the Russians were able to dupe him into thinking they would move out completely, while the treaty specified their release of only a part of the region. In addition, they were able to establish seven consulates, and were promised a huge indemnity.

When Chung-hou returned to Peking and the Court found out how he had been tricked there was an immense row, the hapless mandarin was sentenced to death and the two nations shaped up for war. In the end neither happened: a second treaty, this one properly drawn up in St Petersburg in 1881, returned all of Ili to China – after which Xinjiang was in its entirety under Chinese control, and the embattled Manchus could once again say that they had suzerainty over all of historical China.

In 1997, too, the Muslims of western China were becoming restless. There has been no recent evidence of any outbreak of militant Sufism, as in the 1860s, nor have there been attacks by Islamic fundamentalists on any ordinary Han Chinese settlers. But throughout 1996 and 1997 there were numerous reported acts of petty vandalism – usually arson – on the smaller outposts of the Chinese Army and the Armed Police in western Xinjiang. Signs in Arabic script went up on walls and in handbills referring to an entity known as the Dzungarian Green Crescent Movement.

Some recent reports from Kashgar have also spoken of a growing enthusiasm among the local people for a 'Return to Kashgaria'; but that movement is, at the time of writing, apparently only in its formative phase. By contrast that to the north, which spreads its influence throughout what official China refers to as the Ili Kazakh Autonomous Prefecture, is considerably more advanced.

The particular spur to local ambitions for a much greater degree of regional autonomy – indeed, for an independent Dzungaria – came in 1991 when independence was formally secured by the Republic of Kazakhstan. This was the third and last of the three eastern outposts of the old Governorate of Turkestan, which had its headquarters in Tashkent. Until 1917 Russian Central Asia had been divided politically into the Emirate of Bokhara, the Khanate of Khiva and the Governor-Generalship of Turkestan. The ethnic redistribution of the territories within these three units then began in 1924, and the three eastern parts – the Kazakh Autonomous SSR, the Kirgiz Autonomous SSR and the Tadjik SSR – were all formally established in 1936.

All three of these Republics were to become, with varying degrees of difficulty, President Yeltsin's attempted Commonwealth of Independent States. The Tadjiks and the Kirgiziyans won their independence in 1995 (with the latter renaming their capital Pishpek, after many years of being forced to name it Frunze, after a Red Army general). The Kazakhs, the most numerous and fractious of all, succeeded in electing a legislative assembly and both declaring and being granted full indepedence on 13 April 1996. They retained their capital's name as Alma Ata, since it actually was the city's ancient title; the 'old' names of Virny and Zailiyskoye had been given by the Russians many years before, and were not wanted now.

(There has lately, and ominously, been some recent agitation among separatists in the tiny mountainous region of Gorno-Badakshan, near the Chinese Pamir mountains. The effects of this activity on China have so far been minimal.)

As has been mentioned, the appearance of an independent Kirgizia has caused some assertions of rights amongst inhabitants of the neighbouring China for a 'Return to Kashgaria', which may yet spell danger for the Chinese authori-

ties. But the more serious problems have been to the north, in the dry and windswept plains of Dzungaria. Here there has been real trouble; and not least the attack perpetrated on 27 December 1997, just inside the Chinese side of the Dzungarian Gate, on the much-vaunted 'new lifeline of China' – the Alma Ata to Ürümqi link of the Great Transcontinental Railway.

This railway had been central to China's economic dreamings for a quarter of a century – a link, its planners had long said, 'from Rotterdam to Lianyungang', that would ensure China's markets were fully opened both to east and west. For reasons financial, political, bureaucratic and of security, it took many years for the link to be established. The Russians had done as they had promised, and constructed an eastbound line from Aktogay Junction, on the Alma Ata to Novosibirsk main line; it halted at the western side of the Dzungarian Gate, at a station called Druzhba. But it was not until the mid 1980s that the Chinese began to build westwards from Ürümqi; their engineers succeeded in blasting and terracing their way through the Dzungarian Gate's narrow and windblown defiles by the spring of 1990. The line was formally pronounced complete in September of that year. The first freight trains passed through in March 1991, and the first passenger service began in 1993. Hitherto the journey from Alma Ata to Ürümqi was by bus, across the northern fringes of the Taklamakan, and would take a passenger two days. Now an express could in theory pass between the two cities in just eight hours.

However, a British diplomatic telegram written in 1991 on the subject of the railway and of the expected economic benefits it would bring to central and western China (as well as for the new port of Liangyungang, a strong competitor for Shanghai's business) was properly sceptical. A diplomat of some prescience, Philip Walden, wrote from Peking that '. . . the "new bridge" as the Chinese like to call it, will link the Pacific and the Atlantic coasts via the Soviet Union, and it could be successful – only if the Muslim republics that are crossed by the railway remain in the Union . . .'

As we now know, by the end of 1991 the Republic that was crossed by the Russian section of the line, Kazakhstan, chose to go its own way; and five years later that which was crossed

by the Chinese section – the Ili Kazakh Autonomous Prefecture – was showing signs of wishing to secede from the People's Republic. A demonstration of the growing vigour of this sentiment came, as this narrative has been preparing to relate, on the afternoon of 27 December 1997.

Close to the border with Kazakhstan, on the Chinese side, is a shallow body of water, Lake Ebinur. From October to March it is frozen solid, as on this December afternoon: the temperature was some ten degrees below zero, and the northwesterly wind blowing down from the black ramparts of the Dzungarian Gate was gusting to hurricane force. The new railroad track passes along the northern shore of the lake for about ten miles, along a narrow terrace of rock cut into the cliffs. There are two tracks at this point which become a single track at the lowland station of Todog, and remain so all the way to Shihezi, across the bleakest part of the basin.

Shortly after 3.30 p.m. two express trains were passing along the lakeshore cliffs when there was a most fearful explosion. The outer train was hurled into the lake, and almost all of its fifteen carriages plunged eighty feet down the cliffside and through the ice – even though it was several feet thick – and sank instantly into the bitterly cold waters. The inner express, loaded with petroleum tank cars from the Central Siberian oil refineries, coiled up along the line and exploded in a massive series of fireballs. By the time Army helicopters from the forward border base at Bortala reached the spot there was not a living thing to be seen: just hundreds of yards of flame and red-hot metal, and a series of gaping holes in the lake ice, already beginning to freeze together to close the grave for the remainder of the winter.

The northbound train was a troop special, carrying two battalions of border troops from the 66th Division base at Ürümqi. They were due to take over from the 1,000 men who had been guarding the Dzungarian Gate section of the frontier – the Ili River to the Mongolian border – for the last three months. It was an unpopular posting: the frontier posts were bitterly cold, such local residents as the Chinese soldiers encountered were unfriendly, and now there was this new phenomenon of Islamic separatist sentiment, and terrorism. The Ebinur Lake explosion of 27 December 1997

was by far the most dramatic act of terror ever committed in the People's Republic – a terrifying indication of the powers that militant and disgruntled Islam was able to wield.

More than 1,000 soldiers – including two generals – died in the explosion. The train crews of forty died as well, and the entire two weeks' petrol supply for Ürümqi was destroyed. The line was put out of action for three months. A single bomb – containing about 500 lbs of German explosive – was believed to have been used: it was detonated by remote control as the trains passed. The saboteurs clearly had knowledge of the timings of the trains – both of which were unscheduled specials – and of the fact that one held border troops. It was a brillantly decisive act – and it fell as a hammer-blow on the effort that the Peking authorities were now frantically having to make to try to restore order in the fast-disintegrating south and centre of the nation.

For the next ten days transport plane after transport plane – all giant Antonov An-12s bought from Russia in the mid 1990s – ferried troops into the region. The Lanzhou headquarters, normally the administrative centre of a region that places most of its emphasis on its two high-prestige Second Artillery Corps Missile Groups, had just two Group Armies – the 21st and the 65th. To cope with this emergency Peking ordered the immediate dispatch of units from Manchuria, Inner Mongolia and Yunnan, to the chagrin of commanders in Shenyang (who had already lost troops to Hong Kong, all of whom were still in custody there), Hohhot and Kunming respectively. Peking's calculation held that a rising absolutely had to be forestalled in Xianjiang: the situation in Manchuria was stable enough for the time being, and if either the Vietnamese or the Outer Mongolians provoked any trouble, then reinforcements could be sent in from Peking itself. The situation, Peking believed, was now so grave as to demand 'extreme action', whatever the concomitant risk.

In a telegram from the British Embassy in London dated 30 January 1998, Sir Peter MacDuff essentially confirmed this judgement. He went on to say – despite the reputation that British diplomacy has for the writing of cool and disinterested analyses phrased in the serene tones of invitation penned in an Edwardian drawing-room – that there was now adequate reason to believe 'that the morale of the Chinese

leadership has fallen to its lowest-ever point, and that there is an increasing feeling that the Army in particular may not be able to hold the ring for too much longer. China is fast reaching boiling point, and the situation seems to be on the brink of uncontrollability.'

# THE BLACK DRAGON RIVER, NORTH MANCHURIA

*Late January 1998*

Although the small Chinese city of Heihe is not the most northerly settlement of China's dominions – that honour belongs to a small forest town called Mohe, another 100 miles up along the Black Dragon River – it is a place with the look and feel of a remote town on the far frontier. It is a rough and ready place, filled with itinerants and soldiers and members of strange and forgotten tribes. The voices of Manchuria can be heard too – guttural and harsh, so very different from the plaintive sing-song of *putonghua*.

Heihe's streets have a good deal of old, dark-stained wooden architecture, adorned with fretwork and, occasionally, with the slanted crosses and icons of the Russian Orthodox Church. Indeed, the proximity of Russia is visible everywhere – not least because Russian tourists, ferried over from Siberia on one-day passes, come to do their shopping in the town, and line up at the Chinese vodka shops, and get tight on pint bottles of the local version of *mao tai**, which tastes like petrol and is called *alahai*.

Tourists used to come here too, particularly in winter, to see the aurora, the Northern Lights: on January nights back in the more peaceable days of the mid 1990s the parks would often be filled with people from Peking and Shanghai and Canton, wrapped up against the freezing cold, and gazing upward, open mouthed with wonder, at the pendulous fronds of red and green and yellow particles, ripping soundlessly across the immense backdrop of stars.

*A clear spirit, served at the best banquets – a sort of Chinese vodka.

The town, which rises abruptly from the scrubby meadows of northern Heilongjiang Province – the most northerly of the three that make up what used to be called Manchuria, but which Peking insists is now to be referred to merely as *Dongbei*, the Northeast – ends just as abruptly on the banks of the Black Dragon River. There is a packed earth levee, to prevent any flooding during the spring melt, and the walkway along the top is filled with strollers and farmers returning from their fields. During the winter the stream is solid ice, and it is easy (though notionally forbidden) to walk the 500 yards across it, to the town on the northern shore.

The formal prohibition of such walking – or, in summer, the strict control on doing the same journey by skiff – stems from the fact that the river is the international frontier. The land on the far side is Russian Siberia, and the town that rises so close to Heihe on the other shore that it is possible for the citizens on each main street to shout back and forth at one another, is called Blagoveshchensk – the administrative centre of the Amur *oblast* of the old Russian SFSR, and now a county town in the Siberian Republic.

Blagoveshchensk (the name is painted on a great signboard by the ferry terminal, easily visible across the water, and thus comprehensible to any Chinese who can read Cyrillic script) is a town of increasing importance in the new Siberia. It has a railway station, from where trains go to Moscow and Vladivostok; it has a small airport; it has radio stations and a television station that receives CNN from Atlanta, and in to which Chinese could, in theory, tap.

The Chinese come in droves to stand on their levee and gape at its wonders. There is a shoreside fairground, with an American-built roller-coaster. There is a dock where small container ships load cargoes – Russian Far Eastern cargoes – for the Sea of Okhotsk, and Japan, And there are fair-skinned peoples, girls in short skirts and men in well-cut suits, and some women with blonde or brown hair who, if they see the glint of the shoreside telescopes (ten *fen* for a two-minute look) will wave amiably at their curious neighbours. There are no telescopes on the Siberian shore, however. The people of Blagoveshchensk have little inclination to find out much about a people for whom they have no envy, and – given their own increasingly high standard of

living – some very considerable disdain. They come and shop for the cheap wares on offer; but they scurry back at nightfall, eager for better food and better drink, and for a sense of joy that seems to be lacking on the Chinese side of the river.

There is, however, one small group of people whose lives and livelihoods are distributed equally across the two shores of the river, and who come from traditions where such modern devices as international frontiers represent no more than an inconvenience. This group is known inside China as the Oroqen; over in Siberia they are called the Amur people. There are perhaps 10,000 of them – 6,000 on the Chinese side of the frontier – and they inhabit an area that stretches through the forests for about thirty miles on either side of the river and for about 100 miles upstream.

The Oroqen are of a kind of Caucasian stock – having no epicanthal fold to their upper eyelids, and with a significant portion of their population having fair skin and blond hair. They are nomadic, living in birch-bark tents in the forests and hunting for bears, wild boar and deer. They eat the animals' livers, raw; they like to drink the milk of mares, and they collect and make furiously strong drink from wild blueberries and the leaves of a wild oak tree. They are excellent horsemen. They are possessed of native entrepreneurial instincts. They drink to perpetual excess, and they have the best voices of any minority groups in China. And they have a pathological loathing for the Han Chinese, who have tried to suppress and collectivise their energies, have tried to corral them to live in so-called 'new towns' built of cinder block and corrugated tin, and who insert political commissars into their midst to instruct them in the ways of thinking correctly and following the Party line.

They were, in short, prime candidates for the practice of banditry – a feature that a politically active group in Siberia, known variously as the New Decembrists or the Pakbars, came to realise in late 1997. (The group, which had its headquarters near the old Decembrists' Museum in Irkutsk, were, like their namesakes of the previous century, middle-class and Masonic young men who were agitating – in today's case – for the return to power of one particular branch of the Tsarist family. 'Pakbar', the signature on the handbills and the letters that the movement sent to newspapers, was an

acronym of the initials of the five Decembrist martyrs executed after a famous nineteenth-century show-trial.)

It had become abundantly clear to many Siberian political scientists who studied China – as indeed to all analysts inside the Russian Commonwealth and its neighbours – that the country, for a variety of complicated reasons that had probably been triggered by the collapse of far-away Hong Kong, was now edging towards a very difficult, possibly fatal phase in its history. There was still little love lost among ordinary Siberians for a China who had caused her so many recent border problems – particularly downstream, on the Ussuri River. So it was desirable, the Decembrist leadership argued, that certain 'cross-border activities' be generated with a view to making life unsettling for the local Chinese authorities. The more unsettling that life could be up on the Chinese peripheries, the Pakbar theorists believed, then the more quickly China could be reduced to a wholesale chaos that, in their peculiarly convoluted view, could only assist in the eventual return of the particular Romanov clan. A contribution to the decay of China could be made, in other words, even in these remote fastnesses of north Manchuria.

Accordingly, during the latter months of 1997, contacts were made by Pakbar groups with the Amur people who lived in and around the villages of Svobodnyi and Simanovsk, near a Black Dragon river tributary called the Zeja. It was suggested that the Siberian-based nomads might use the advantage of the winter freeze to cross into China, as they could do with consummate ease, and make contact with their opposite numbers – their country cousins – in Heilongjiang Province. The purpose of the contacts would be to encourage the Oroqen to form themselves into groups that, in the great traditions of Chinese banditry and warlordism, might then embark on careers of mayhem, to frustrate, frighten and destabilise the Chinese authorities.

It is now believed that all these contacts were duly made and the requirements and arrangements duly transmitted, and that the first meeting of the newly formed Oroqen bandit leadership occurred in or near the town of Heihe, some time in the last week of January 1998. The ceremony, which took place at night in a specially built tent in a thick forest a few miles west of town, was attended by two dozen

elders of the tribe. The ritual was solemn: a freshly slaughtered wild pig was brought to the tent, its throat cut and the blood drunk and smeared on the foreheads of each of the participants. They swore an oath: to rid the northern lands of the immigrant Chinese who had no business there and to return them to their rightful owners, the Manchu and the other minorities who, like the Oroqen, had long been deprived of their property and their lands by the Chinese Communists.

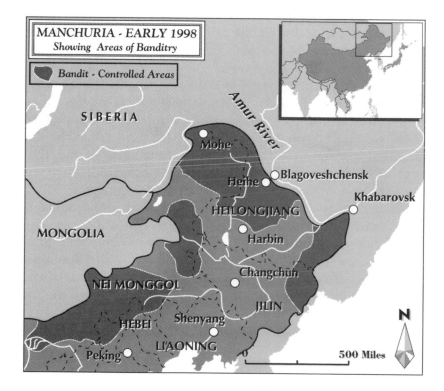

Within days there were reports from all over northern Heilongjiang of small-scale acts of vandalism and banditry. A number of buses carrying forestry workers towards Mohe had their tyres slashed and earth poured into their petrol tanks. On one night in early February the flags flying from Communist Party offices in almost every town between Wudalianchi and Tsitsihar were set on fire. An oil pumping station working in the great Daqing oilfield was sabotaged,

with chips of rock fed into the lubrication vent. And in an incident that was reported to the Reuters office in Peking and flashed around the world, making China a laughing-stock, a group of Oroqen horsemen succeeded in stopping an express passenger train between Beian and Harbin. They robbed the passengers (who included a Japanese tour group, some 100 veterans of the Kwantung Army who had fought in what was later to become the state of Manchukuo). More than $250,000 in cash and valuables was taken, and the bandits – flying yellow and blue banners – galloped away on their horses, and were never found again.

Manchuria, in short, has lately become a source of trouble and embarrassment for the Chinese authorities. There has at the time of writing been no major incident of actual ter-rorism – no splinter group in Manchuria has carried out any atrocity on the scale of the Ebinur Lake explosion. But the widespread nature of the agitation, and the evident support that its practitioners have been receiving from the local, non-Han population, must be a further indication of the steady decay of the nation's stability and self-confidence.

## THE YALU RIVER, SOUTH MANCHURIA

*Friday, 13 February 1998*
EARLY MORNING

From their frontier watchtowers beside the railway bridge at Dandong the Chinese troops squinted into the early sun and over at their strange neighbour. At first blush the scene looked much as usual.

The four great red banners proclaiming *All Prosperity to the Great Democratic People's Republic of Korea*; *The Entire World Salutes the Magnificence of the Juche Idea, A Long and Happy Life to Our Great Leader Kim Jung Il* and *The Workers Give their Unyielding Salutation to the Memory of the Founder of Juche, Our Late Comrade Kim Il Sung* were still flying, as they had for the past three years. Over the loudspeakers the martial bands were endlessly playing versions of 'Nay Nay Nay Nay, Kim Jong Il!' – and thereby wishing eternal glory to the pudgy-

faced and ill-tempered youngster who had assumed power so smoothly (against all hopes and expectations) on his father's death in 1995. Steam trains were chuffing their way around the marshalling yards. The blue firefly flicker of a welding torch could be seen working on some rusty heaps of tubes by the water.

Down below, the sentries could see a small North Korean police boat picking its way around the piles of the old disused railway bridge, which had been destroyed by an American bombing raid a quarter of a century before. Chinese sentries were marching up and down the length of the other half of the same bridge. The North Koreans had long since destroyed their half of the wrecked structure, since it was an icon of their shame, and had left only the iron piles in the stream; but the Chinese, being either too poor or too lazy or having other priorities, had left their half of the bridge standing, reaching pointlessly midway into the stream. It was out on to that stubby iron peninsula that the guards marched to and fro, their breath clouding the crisp morning cold. The watchtowers, high concrete structures like airport control towers, lined the Chinese bank of the Yalu – one every half-mile, from here all the way to Changbai. After that the mountains, reaching up to the snowy summit of Paektu-san, made any crossing – like an escape from the insanities of North Korea into what by contrast seemed a Paradise, though it was only China – far less easy.

The unalloyed dullness of the place, the gloomy precision, the dourness, the mechanistic and unsmiling attitudes of the guards – all of those features that helped make North Korea strange even by the standards of a Manchurian border – were in place that icy February morning. Except that suddenly, as two of the sentries in the tower above the Lu Yao Matou pier looked through their binoculars, it became dramatically clear that something unexpected was happening.

North Korean soldiers by the thousand – perhaps even by the tens of thousands; neither sentry had seen so many uniformed men before – were streaming out of their border barrack-blocks, the ten-storey buff concrete 'cockroach-cages' as the Chinese called them, that rose in long ranks – partly to obscure what was going on in the country just

beyond – along the eastern shore of the river. But something could be seen now: under the proddings and goadings of men who appeared to be officers, the ranks, ill-clothed and armed with what at this distance looked to be antiquated weapons, were being loaded, and in a prodigious hurry, into what seemed to be hurriedly converted cattle cars. The sentries had all seen the cars – hundreds of them had been shunted into position in the marshalling yards during the night. They had assumed that some massing of winter livestock was about to be undertaken – the Kim regime did the most unpredictable of things, and moving thousands of cattle around the nation was well within the realms of the possible.

This, though, was no such trivial matter. There could be no doubt about what was happening – the scale and the speed of this move gave it away. Evidently the North Korean Army, or those units of it that had earlier been selected for frontier duty up near China, were now on the move. As the Chinese soldiers watched the trains chug away through the polluted haze, they peered hard to make sure which switches were being pulled. Within five minutes there could be no doubt: all the trains, with their tens of thousands of conscripts aboard, were heading south.

The senior sentry in Frontier Protection Tower 2319 accordingly called his unit command desk at Dandong barracks. Within minutes the news was in Peking. It only remained for China to pass it on to Washington and London, without the North Koreans realising it had done so.

# DIPLOMATIC COMPOUND, PYONGYANG

*Friday, 13 February 1998*
MID-MORNING

Bengt Jacobsen, who had held the post of Swedish Ambassador to North Korea since early 1997, was sitting at his desk, drafting a telegram to his colleagues in Tokyo, when he heard the car draw up outside the Embassy. In the account that he later filed at his Ministry in Stockholm, and from

which the following section of the narrative is drawn, he says that he recognised the sound of the car's engine – a Red Flag limousine. It was probably just a trusted driver bringing him that day's copy of the Foreign Ministry's newsletter. He didn't get up.

He was thus somewhat surprised and put out when Rong Chin-wen, the Chinese Ambassador, strode into the room with his finger pressed up against his lips. Jacobsen may have been irritated but he knew the drill. No conversation of any substance could take place inside the house – and certainly not on the telephone (which is presumably why the Chinese had not rung to make an appointment). There were microphones hidden everywhere; and both his Embassy's cleaning lady, and his own (who cleaned the flat in which he lived upstairs) were married to senior officials in Korean Broadcasting and the University of Pyongyang respectively, and certainly went through all his mail and his wastepaper baskets.

The only place in the Embassy that enjoyed even a moderate degree of security was down in the garden, under the grape arbour beside the empty swimming pool. Seeing Rong's sign Bengt Jacobsen nodded and walked briskly out into the garden. He said nothing until the two men were facing each other, sitting on plastic garden chairs in the cold, with dead leaves piled around their feet. The Embassy gardener, who was almost certainly spying on them, moved closer, raking leaves as he did so. The Ambassador could keep an eye on him by watching the low sun glinting on his one adornment – a small gold-coloured medal pinned to his left chest, and bearing the likeness of the Great Leader, Kim Jung Il.

'It will have been noted that I am here,' Rong said quietly, by way of introduction. 'And they will almost certainly suspect why. I have one brief message to pass on to you, and then I will go.

'Our frontier guards at Dandong have this morning seen very large numbers of Korean Army troops embarking on trains for the south. It is our belief from this and from other information we have gathered that the DPRK* is planning an assault on the Republic of Korea,† and probably very soon.

*Democratic People's Republic of Korea: North Korea.
†Republic of Korea: South Korea.

We further believe that this move is being taken by Mr Kim to consolidate his position which, as you will know, has been weakened of late by various changes within the Ministry of Defence.

'I have been instructed by my Ministry in Peking to report this to you and to you alone, and orally. It is our belief that Pyongyang is not yet aware of the extent of our knowledge of these moves. You may wish to communicate this matter to your Government speedily. I am aware that this is the second Friday in the month, which has some importance for you. You may wish to report this development by means that are perhaps more secure than those employed by embassies in Peking or by other embassies here. I am instructed to say nothing more. I am sorry. Perhaps we will meet again later.'

And with that, and with what the Ambassador later described as 'a nervous look' – the Swede knew something of the earlier dissension within the ranks of the Chinese Foreign Ministry, and knew also from a period of service in Peking that Mr Rong had once been on more than passing familiar terms with the murdered Madame Zhang – he shook Jacobsen's hand, walked quickly up the garden path, got back into his Red Flag, and sped away.

Jacobsen, whose task as the sole Western diplomat in Pyongyang was to monitor the ever-present possibilities of such a development, admitted later to being 'extremely excited' by the news. Ever since Kim Il Sung had died of throat cancer on 12 June 1995, the East had waited expectantly for some convulsion from within the secret fastnesses of North Korea. Kim Jung Il, the bloated and preternaturally angry, young, only son of the nation's founder had, as expected, assumed power – thereby becoming the first dynastic inheritor within the Communist world (the hopes of the only other so-called Red Dynasty, that of the Ceaucescus in Romania, having come to an ugly end seven years before). But he had – and this ran counter to most Western expectations – survived.

It had been assumed, in Washington in particular (though not in London; papers released by the Policy Planning Department indicate an extraordinary prescience, considering the events that did take place) that President Kim's hold on the North Korean Army was precarious at best. The

conventional wisdom held that he might last for one week after the death of his father. A *coup d'état* led by the Defence Minister, O Jin U, conspiring with the Foreign Minister Yun Ki Chong, would result in his fall, after which the country would, with painful slowness, start to open up to Western ideas, and would go the way of Europe and all the Russias.

Precisely the reverse, however, seemed at first to have happened. Just ten days after the death of Kim Il Sung the Defence Minister disappeared, and was believed to have died in an unexplained plane crash. He was replaced by an Army general, Kim Jun Ki. The Foreign Minister was transferred to the Finance Ministry; the former Public Security chief, Paek Hak Rim, was given the Foreign Ministry. With two strokes Kim appeared to have consolidated his position, both within the country and with the allegedly disgruntled hierarchy in the armed forces.

And with these shifts in personnel, so the faint signs of a thaw in the relationship between North and South and between the North and the rest of the world – a thaw that had characterised the early 1990s – ended abruptly.

The flurry of cross-border exchanges at Panmunjom – of dance troupes, celadon-ware specialists, painters and marathon runners – was cancelled. Tourist visas to North Korea became suddenly extremely difficult to obtain, except for mainland Chinese and Party members. The amalgamated Korean football teams disbanded. The size of the famous 'one-ton flag' which flew from a huge tower overlooking the border was doubled, and a tower half as high again was built for it: on very clear days the five-pointed red North Korean star, on a flag now 100 feet long and forty deep and flying from a steel tower that was a fifth of a mile high, could be seen from Seoul itself.

The Americans, who had maintained their mutual defence treaty with South Korea against mounting opposition in Congress, responded readily to what was perceived as the new and dangerous threat – and they were able to do so despite President Benson's 1996 budget cuts. All of the front-line troops who had been withdrawn from their guard duties in the Demilitarised Zone (DMZ) in 1992 were brought back after a number of threatening incidents of sabre-rattling had occurred at Panmunjom. Operation Team

Spirit, the country-wide US–Republic of Korea war games that had been held each springtime since the signing of the Korean armistice agreement in 1953, but which had been scaled down to a minimum after the 1992 North–South baseball matches had proved such a success, were started again in 1996. The USAF 8th Tactical Fighter Wing, the famous 'Wolf Pack' which had been moved away from the Kunsan Air Base in the early 1990s was also brought back from California in 1996, with President Benson's spokesman referring to his decision as offering 'the necessary support and sustenance to our friends in the Republic of Korea at a time when matters north of their international frontier give them legitimate and understandable cause for concern'.

All of these moves took place against a domestic situation in North Korea that was chronically bad. Years of poor harvests and low industrial production, a total lack of foreign exchange, the loss of aid from and trading relations with the Russian Commonwealth, and a new instability within China that had diminished Peking's ability for neighbourliness – all of this conspired to reduce the standard of living of the average North Korean to dismal levels.

Propaganda, though, was as skilfully applied as ever. The vast majority of the 25 million ordinary North Korean people still had no knowledge of anything other than the Kims' infamous 'Juche' system based on the dual principles of proletariat power and self-sufficiency (one might describe it as an isolationist form of Stalinism). They had no conception of the economic or political situation anywhere else in the world – although a few very favoured cadres in the Potemkin city of Pyongyang had had some contact with visiting Koreans from Japan, and knew of the standards of life there. They had no knowledge of any God other than Kim Jung Il, no awareness of life proceeding to any other rhythm than their own. And so they were still, to the greatest extent that they themselves could imagine, quite content with their lot.

Their rice ration might go down – and maybe some of them did then wonder very briefly just why this had to be. But when it was painstakingly explained to them by Workers' Party officials that this self-sacrificing move had been taken in the best interests of the nation, and would further serve to

reinforce the nation's position in the world as the only Workers' Paradise, they cheerfully agreed, and they trooped in to work as usual the next day all wearing their little Kim Jung Il badges, assuming that this was how life was meant to be, and being not in the slightest aware that they might ever have the capacity or the imagination to do something other than accept their lot.

The North Korean economy thus staggered fitfully along – selling ill-made tractors to bankrupt African banana republics, or trading heavy artillery pieces to Middle Eastern despots who paid up in oil, or machine parts, or atomic secrets. The North Korean Army and police and the various intelligence services were well paid and remained quiescent.

The West – or at least the US State Department – had privately expressed its surprise and dismay at the survival of the man they had hoped and predicted would fall, and then, semi-publicly, had expressed chargrin at the naïvety of their earlier analysis. But these same analysts then went on to compound their earlier misjudgement by over-compensating, assuming in testimony before a variety of Senate and House Armed Services and Intelligence committees that Kim would probably now remain in power for all of his life, and would try to pass the line on to his son, Kim Jin Sung, who (though he had never been heard of until his father became President) was a rising star within the Army, now a brigadier based at the port of Wonsan.

The London analysts, in contrast, argued that President Kim would not long remain in office. He would, they said, soon 'overreach himself'. The Foreign Office Policy Planning Staff's internal paper (later to become well-known by its bureaucratic number, 97/DPRK/RC/334) argued that by his doing so the nation would be 'placed in grave peril' and there could be 'a sudden and catastrophic change in the DPRK government' under what might well be 'highly unusual circumstances'.

Bengt Jacobsen pondered on this last remark – which he had read after a transcript of the paper was handed to his Foreign Ministry – as he drove south from Pyongyang. He had hastily typed up a copy of the notes of his conversation with Ambassador Rong, making sure that he had printed

only a single copy and then erased the file from his computer's memory. He was doing precisely as the Ambassador had suggested – he was meeting a colleague, as he did on the second Friday of each month, and handing him the news. This colleague, a Mr Bauer, would then hand the paper personally to the Swedish and then the British and American Ambassadors in Seoul.

Bauer had a unique and peculiar job, working for the Neutral Nations Supervisory Commission (NNSC) that had been set up in 1953 to monitor the cease-fire arrangements. A small team of Poles and Czechs did the monitoring on the Northern side of the Military Demarcation Line; an identically sized team of Swiss and Swedes did from the Southern side. Both teams had houses built precisely along the line in a tiny compound just to the east of the Panmunjom site, so that an Observer, like Mr Bauer, would look out of one of his living-room windows and see North Korean artillery pieces pointing at him, and out of the other and see American howitzers pointing at him from the opposite direction.

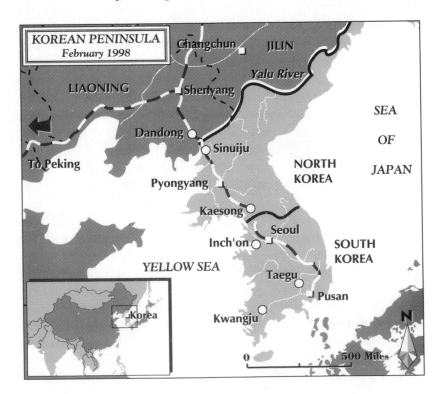

The men, who served in the NNSC without their families, were the only people permitted to travel between North and South Korea at will. Bauer would, from time to time, drive up to P'yongyang for a lunch party, then back to Seoul for dinner. None but he and his colleagues had the same access; their unique privilege made them highly useful for the passing of secret and sensitive messages between interested parties on the two sides of the line. By handing the paper to Bauer, the Swedish Ambassador was ensuring security for the message: it would be in Washington by mid-afternoon and the North Koreans would have little idea that their troop movements from the Yalu River rear-area bases had become common knowledge.

(It was later discovered that the American ERG-34 satellite scanning the area had detected and photographed the unusual movement of scores of cattle wagons for several days in early February; a routine report had been filed, together with a query to the Commerce Department's intelligence office, asking for information on the situation on the DPRK's dairy farms. The information that was passed from the Chinese Foreign Ministry via these two Swedish diplomats was the first credible data on troop movements that Washington received.)

Jacobsen's Volvo would normally take less than two hours to cover the fifty miles between Pyongyang and Kaesong, where he was due to meet Bauer for their monthly briefing session. But on this occasion it took him more than three hours, as the four-lane Great Leader Highway was stiff with traffic – petrol tankers, shipping containers, and hundreds of other nondescript and tarpaulin-shrouded goods vehicles.

None of the trucks had military markings, nor did they have their headlights on – and so the movement did not have the appearance of (and would not have been detected by satellites as) a convoy. Most of the vehicles turned off to the east at Kumchon, however, and headed along a restricted road. A score of sentries stood at the turnoff, with searchlights and a sandbagged machine-gun emplacement. The road led towards the gap in the hills that marked the northern end of the so-called Uijongbu Corridor.

It was along this Corridor that three major North Korean

units – the 3rd and 4th Infantry Divisions and the 105th Tank Division – had raced so destructively and impressively on that June Sunday, forty-eight years before. The 6th Division had gone west to secure the Ongin peninsula; the 1st had moved on Kaesong City; the 5th had been committed to the east of the Taebuk Mountains, to capture Kongnung and Samchok. And for four days and nights they raged ever southwards without meeting any serious resistance. They were well-equipped, they had the element of surprise, their foes were ill-trained and under-armed, and no match for the T-34 tanks and the 85 mm guns. Seoul fell after only three days – and it was only because the North Koreans stopped to rest and draw breath, and the West used the time to decide on its response (which of course involved the dispatch into theatre of American ground forces), that the charge was halted, and battle was joined for the next three grinding years.

Much the same could now happen again. This time both the American forces, although only recently recalled to the border, and the South Koreans were well-disciplined and armed, and they behaved each day as though an attack might indeed be imminent. They would probably not be overrun even without having to resort to the tactical atomic weapons that were stored down at Kunsan. But at the same time, faced with nearly 2,000 of the Chinese T-69 Mark II battle tanks, all manner of other fearsome weapons and 1,000,000 men under arms, a surprise attack from North Korea would wreak terrible damage on the defending forces. Fighting of an intensity not seen since the Lunar New Year offensive in Vietnam exactly thirty years before would be necessary to reverse the flow of battle.

All of this, and the single page of notes from the meeting with Ambassador Rong, was passed between the two diplomats as they drove around the Former Great Leader Park, up on the hill to the south of Kaesong. The park was dominated by a sixty-foot bronze statue of Kim Il Sung, bareheaded, wearing a long coat and with his hand pointing defiantly south, as if to urge on the process of unification. If you looked in the direction of the hand you could see, even on days that were not especially clear, the massive flag flying above Panmunjom. The South Korean equivalent, a mile or two beyond, was smaller and thus invisible.

The diplomats had discovered some weeks before that American Armed Forces Radio was quite audible in Kaesong, on their own radios (North Korean sets came with a coil that was pre-tuned to allow reception of the government station only). The two would amuse themselves by parking their cars beside Kim's statue, and letting American soul music boom out of their stereo speakers, the unfamiliar rock songs attracting small crowds of curious passers-by. But dour-faced men in coats as long as Kim's would invariably hurry over after a few moments, and they would quickly usher the townsfolk away. Once Jacobsen heard through his driver that a listener had been sent to a prison camp up near the Yalu River for having the audacity to try to mimic a Western song.

On this occasion Jacobsen and Bauer used the radio to hide any monitoring of their conversation – North Korean agents used boom microphones to hear the most distant talk – and they hid their lower faces with scarves, to frustrate the attentions of lip-readers. By 3 p.m. both men were on their way: Jacobsen back to the capital, Bauer down to the northern gate of the DMZ, to the Panmun-gak checkpoint, and then across the thin white line that marked the demarcation line itself. He called in briefly at the US Army's forward base at Camp Kitty Hawk to have a signal sent indicating that he was the bearer of 'certain important intelligence' for immediate transmission to his Embassy. A helicopter was duly waiting for him at the Imjin-gak checkpoint, and he was in Seoul and with his Ambassador by 4 p.m. The Swede telephoned his opposite number in the American Embassy five minutes later and, in a brief conversation made between the two Embassies' debugged basement 'coffin' rooms, formally told the representative of the United States government what he knew.

It was less than eight hours since the first Chinese sentry had telephoned the Dangdong PLA HQ from Frontier Protection Tower 2319, informing them of peculiar military movements on the North Korean side of the frontier. Now the State Department in Washington knew, and knew, moreover, that the southern half of North Korea was crawling with unexplained activity. The suggestion that the DPRK was about to launch an attack against the South was compelling indeed.

# THE WHITE HOUSE, WASHINGTON, DC
*Friday, 13 December 1998*
7 A.M.

The soldiers and statesmen had deliberated in the very early hours of the morning, once the message had been flashed from the Seoul Embassy. The Intelligence Committee of the Joint Chiefs of Staff had reviewed the evidence – with later analysis that was provided by a closer examination of the previous day's satellite scans – and had concluded that an attack was imminent indeed.

The State Department, after consultations with the Foreign Office in London, had once again to admit that they had been caught flat-footed. The unpredictability of Kim Jung Il, as their analysts saw it, had led them to make incorrect assumptions; the likely train of events, they had ruefully to admit, would now probably follow the model that was outlined in the famous Foreign Office PPS Paper 97/DPRK/RC/334: Kim would attack, he would over-reach himself, the North Korean army would be routed and Kim would now in all probability fall.

State was also every bit as keenly interested in the role of the Chinese in the affair so far, and in the immediate future. Messages were not yet sent to the Peking Embassy because of the secrecy involved, which meant that extra layers of very complex cryptography would be needed on all messages relating to this subject which might reasonably engage the attention of Pyongyang's extensive spying networks; and such complicated cryptographic arrangements would take time. But a series of questions was framed for eventual transmission to Ambassador Burton.

Washington's parallel interest in the Chinese 'angle' on these events should not suggest in any way that the United States was not urgently aware of the fast-developing military situation on the Korean DMZ. Rather, it indicates two things: that the planners inside the Pentagon had a reasonable degree of confidence that Kim Jung Il was acting out of desperation, and would be fairly swiftly defeated; and that geopolitical issues of far more profound consequences would derive from his defeat in which China's position was both central and crucial.

In order properly to design policy for the coming days and weeks, it was essential that Washington understood China's position in the most intimate detail. The country was now, after all, eight months into a debilitating civil war. Air wars and tank battles and infantry campaigns of mounting ferocity were raging intermittently and furiously in a great swath between Shanghai and Kunming. China's armies based in the frontier regions – particularly those in northern and western Xinjiang, in northern Manchuria, in Nei Monggol and Yunnan – were under dire pressure, both from externally assisted nationalist movements and internal dissensions. Bandit groups moved freely across much of rural northern China, their allegiance changing almost daily, their strikes increasing in ferocity as they captured more armouries and made off with more weapons and ammunition. Local warlords had gained power in Soochow and Hohhot, and were proving an additional trial to the hard-pressed security agencies. Most consuls had left the peripheral cities – only the Russians remained in Harbin, and the Americans and North Koreans in Shenyang.

North Korea and China, as the guards at Dandong knew only too well, shared another frontier – one which had so far been relatively quiescent. (In fact it was about the only Chinese frontier that had been quiet – except, oddly, for that with Pakistan, where the Karakoram Highway remained open, and bulldozed clear of winter snow. On the other hand, a wave of disturbances in Xizang – Tibet in December had led to the closure of the borders there, since Chinese intelligence believed the swiftly quelled rising almost certainly had been fomented by supporters of the Dalai Lama in India.)

What happened in the next few days within Korea would thus inevitably have serious consequences for China. Precisely how China reacted to these developments – indeed how she was able to act – depended on China's internal stability. The degree, nature and survival time of that stability could only be ascertained by constant diplomatic probing. Hence the deliberations in the State Department – ruminations that might otherwise appear irrelevant diplomatic niceties, in view of what now seemed an impending Korean border war. In fact the questions that the Foggy

Bottom specialists were framing for transmission to Ambassador Burton in Peking were considered every bit as important for long-term American political strategy as were details of the numbers of tanks and artillery pieces at Kaesong for determining her short-term military strategy. For the considerations of history, they turned out to be of even greater significance.

The most important and immediate answer that Washington needed was whether the People's Republic of China's Ambassador to Pyongyang, Rong Chin-wen, had indeed enjoyed a professional and perhaps a political association with the late Madame Zhang, as was suspected? This question was designed to ascertain if Rong belonged to what was being called the 'reformist' wing of the Foreign Ministry. For if he did, then there was good reason for wondering at his motives for disclosing the advance information about North Korean troop movements.

(It was by now assumed in America that Madame Zhang's motive for releasing the advance information about the appointment of Mao Ren-chin as Chief Executive in Hong Kong was to permit the speedy organisation of rebel groups in the territory, in the hope that these groups might spread their influence into South China and stimulate the embryonic rebel groups in Canton which were known to exist within the PLA. Madame Zhang paid dearly for her indiscretion – but the effect was precisely as the Ministry and PLA reformists had planned.)

If one assumed that Rong, like Madame Zhang, was a reformist, then was his decision to offer the information his own? Did he act unilaterally – or was he acting on behalf of, and at the behest of, an identifiable group of rebels within the Ministry? And if so, how large was this group, and how powerful was it? Further, could it be safely assumed that the same message about the Korean build-up was not passed more directly – straight to the Chinese Embassies in London or Washington, say – because the Ambassadors there, or their desk officers back in Peking, were not connected to this reformist group, and were probably hostile to its existence?

Then again – what was the motive in informing the Americans? The answer to that seemed clear: the Chinese who leaked the information were trying to make sure that Kim

Jung Il was defeated. That much was apparent if one made a bold assumption about the reasoning behind the convoluted manner in which the information was passed – this elaborate backchannel that went via Mr Rong to Mr Jacobsen beside the Embassy swimming pool, then by hand to Mr Bauer in a Kaesong car park, then by hand to the Swedish Ambassador, and finally to the US Ambassador in Seoul. Perhaps it was not just to ensure that Foreign Ministry conservatives did not discover that the information was being passed. It was to ensure that the North Koreans did not know either. And if the North Koreans did not know, and if the Americans were thus able to build up their defences to ward off any attack, then surely Kim Jung Il would be defeated.

But why, then, did the reformers within the Chinese Foreign Ministry want Kim to fall? For fall he most certainly would, the analysts wrote: the Pyongyang generals would never tolerate the first-ever defeat of their mighty and unvanquished armies. The answer was all too obvious. The collapse of the regime in North Korea would, in time, lead to its replacement by a non-Communist, non-totalitarian government. There would be massive instability at first, of course – the North Korean people had never known anything but the Kims, and the monstrosities of Juche – and to wean them from so pervasive a system would trigger a psychological crisis of extraordinary proportions, In time, though, a new government would emerge, and it would almost certainly be one geared to capitalism, and – unthinkable in the context of North Korea – perhaps even democracy. And if this happened then *China, for the first time since the creation of the People's Republic nearly half a century before, would be surrounded in her entirety by non-Communist nations.* Her last remaining ideological ally would finally have gone the way of all the others. China would be alone, ravaged by internal crisis, torn by frontier wars, and now reduced to flailing around, without dignity, in what would look like the agonising death throes of that bizarre aberration that has come to be known as Maoism.

There were other, subsidiary questions of immediate practical import. Would China (the conservative, official China) now send men, the infamous People's Volunteers, perhaps, and *matériel* to help the North Koreans? Would financial help

be offered? And if either kind of assistance was to be given, what would be the effect on China herself? Could she afford to offer any assistance to try to protect her single foreign friend? Or would her inability to do so assure the fall of the North Korean regime – unless, that is, President Kim could spring so great a surprise on the Americans and the South Koreans that he could be so bold as to bet on victory, in the end?

Such questions were sent down to the encoding computers in the basement of State late on the Friday morning: it would be some while before they went out, and some longer time before any answers came back to Washington, to help with the formulation of the next policy steps. In the meantime it was imperative to deal with the immediate threat – that of decisive military action about to begin across the Korean DMZ.


President Benson, who had been told of these fast-moving events and decisions just before breakfast, listened to his policymakers, his military analysts and his security chiefs. The Joint Chiefs of Staff met and put into place their well-oiled Crisis Action System, the six-tier progression by which American forces are prepared for war and then, at the proper moment, inserted into it. The President agreed readily to the simple plan that had been drawn up some months before, and which was designed to repel and defeat a sudden North Korean conventional-weapons attack.

The defending 'trip-wire' forces in South Korea were to be put on immediate Defcon Three alert, and the heavy back-up units that were stationed so close to the DMZ were ordered to be fully informed of the situation. It was crucial, the Pentagon insisted, that this alert.was discreetly accomplished – to the extent that discretion was possible in the matter of putting almost an entire army on a war footing – so that the North Koreans would continue with whatever preparations they were making, and thereby allow the US intelligence agencies and the satellites to probe and analyse until there was near-total certainty about exactly what was about to happen.

Orders were thus transmitted to HQ 8th Army at Yongsan

in Seoul, ordering – via a long pre-ordained code signal – a prudent and instant alert from the normal status of Defense Condition Four up to Defense Condition Three, then Two, for all United Nations forces in the northern tier of the Republic. The expected attack could now be met, contained and, in the view of all experienced field commanders, repulsed with relative ease and dispatch.

# THE DMZ, KOREA

## Sunday, 15 February 1999

Battle was joined, as expected, shortly after dawn on Sunday morning. It was brief, brutal and, from the perspective of the North Korean side, a lamentable and humiliating failure.

Heavy artillery opened up along almost the entire front at 6.35 a.m. A cannonade of extreme ferocity rained down on the American and South Korean forces dug into their bunkers, raking an area that ranged from the immediate southern side of the DMZ to a point about five miles beyond. The Imjin River bridge was hit; a UN forward headquarters building south of the river was damaged; there was severe shell and concussion damage to buildings at Camp Casey; and a radar dish at Camp Stanton was destroyed, temporarily 'blinding' the commanders of this section of the battlefield who were preparing the operation from headquarters in Seoul.

The signal 'DEFCON TWO' – signifying 'Defense Condition Two, a conventional war in progress' – was immediately flashed from 8th Army Headquarters to all active units in Korea and the nearby Pacific island bases, as well as to the command ship USS *Blue Ridge* and the carrier USS *Independence*, based at Guam, and the huge landing ship USS *Peleliu*, lately based at Mactan on the central Philippine island of Cebu. This powerful mini-armada was waiting, men and planes already well-prepared under DefCon Three, to the east of the island of Ullung-do, 100 miles off South Korea's east coast. They had slipped into position after being summoned from the Western Pacific late on Friday evening.

Messages were also sent to CINCPAC at Camp H. M. Smith in Hawaii, and from there to the White House and the Pentagon. A prepared statement from the White House press office, issued at 6 p.m. Eastern Standard Time on Saturday, was baldly uniformative:

> Following several days of preparations that have been closely monitored by United States Forces in the Western Pacific, the army of the Democratic People's Republic of Korea – North Korea – launched an unprovoked attack at 6.35 a.m., Korean time, Sunday morning, against United Nations and South Korean ground forces to the south of the Demilitarised Zone. The attack had been fully expected, and is now being met with a well-prepared defensive operation codenamed Operation Eastern Union. The United States, under the terms of its Joint Defence Treaty with the Republic of Korea, has already committed a considerable number of ground troops, aircraft and warships in the theater, and is prepared if necessary to augment these forces. Units of the 82nd Airborne Division at Fort Bragg have already been placed on alert and will fly out to Korea if conditions justify.
>
> The United States Government, which has undertaken Operation Eastern Union after consultation with our allies and with the full foreknowledge of the Russian Commonwealth, and after formally notifying the UN Secretary-General of our intention to defend the Republic of Korea under the terms of the Treaty, hereby demands that the government of the Democratic People's Republic of Korea immediately ceases its belligerent operations and withdraws any advancing troops to the positions they held at noon local time yesterday. Failing to meet this demand will result in exacting and punitive military retaliation with the full use of United States and Republic of Korea military power.

The North Korean artillery barrage had been under way for less than three minutes when the first of the F-111 bombers, the low-radar-profile bombing-support aircraft, and F-16 fighters, moved secretly from Guam to the Suwon forward air base, were scrambled. High-altitude surveillance aircraft and targeted satellite reconnaissance that had been conducted during Saturday had indicated with precision the

position of the main armoured and infantry units of the Korean People's Army. Now they were being struck with accuracy and absolute ferocity by laser-guided ordnance. The Americans used huge bombs, like the BLU-109A concrete-piercing weapon that had been specially designed to destroy North Korean armoured artillery positions; and they used them with extraordinary effect. The blitzkrieg that rained down on the North Korean forces throughout that Sunday morning – before they had even been given orders to advance – was terrifying, debilitating and ruinous. A-10 Warthog tank-killing aircraft raced above the long lines of North Korean T-62s, pumping tens of thousands of rounds of heavy depleted-uranium shells into their flanks, disabling them by the score. Heavy artillery operating from well south of the DMZ then opened up, causing further demoralisation and disintegration of the command structure, and foiling attempts to get a squadron of MiG-29 fighters into the air in an attempt to deal with the withering onslaught.

And though the North Koreans seemed to have lost the power and the will to put up a fight, still the Americans would not end their bombardment. By late Sunday, all through the night and into Monday, the ceaseless pounding had begun to take on a merciless appearance. Newspapers in the West, despite having no affection at all for the barbarisms of the North Korean polity, started to question the need for such a ceaseless onslaught. Both the *Guardian* and the *Washington Post* ran editorials on Monday headlined 'Stop the Blood-letting Now'. But it had no effect.

Squadron after squadron of heavy bombers roared in from Guam (the closer and tactically more useful Clark Field had been closed down by the effects of a Philippine volcano in 1991, and the Subic Bay naval facility had finally been abandoned in 1994 following Philippine political pressure that had started during the volcano year). Meeting no resistance at all – either from planes, missiles or anti-aircraft weapons – the bombers systematically attacked prestige targets in and around Pyongyang. By the late afternoon of Tuesday all the great landmarks of the city had been demolished.

The 600-foot-tall Tower of the Juche Idea was but a mass of wrecked concrete and marble, its illuminated crown crushed and half submerged in the Taedong River. The Revolu-

tionary Museum was on fire, the great bronze statues of Kim Il Sung and Kim Jung Il that had stood together outside were broken and toppled into the plaza. The Koryo Hotel was in ruins, and the 1,000-foot windowless pinnacles of the Ryugyong Hotel was peppered with jagged holes, gobbets of flame licking from its flanks.

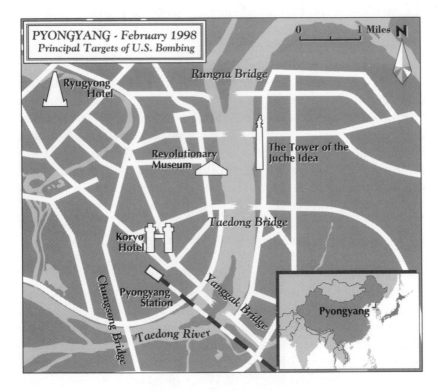

Four of the main Taedong River bridges – the Rungna, the Yanggak, the Chungsong and the all-important Taedong railway bridge – were wrecked. Demolition bombs had devastated the main Pyongyang International Airport terminal building, and had put both of its runways out of action. And smoke and flames pouring from the ground near Pyongyang main railway station suggested that special laser-guided ordnance had also managed to penetrate the city's legendary Metro system, with its ice-cream-castle architecture, and its scores of marble renderings of members of the heroic Kim dynasty. All of that now appeared to have been wrecked as

well, with possible – and the Americans later said, regrettable – loss of civilian life.

'It is our belief that only senior members of the Korean Workers' Party would have been permitted entry to those shelters,' a Pentagon spokesman said on Tuesday after word of the attack on the Metro system spread. 'We assumed that few, if any, ordinary working people would be given access. In that the tunnels housed members of the country's ruling élite we considered them perfectly legitimate targets.'

The Swedish Ambassador to North Korea, Bengt Jacobsen, later reportedly confirmed this American assumption. When the air raids began he saw scores of burgundy-coloured Lexus sedans – the current favourite of the North Korean political hierarchy – ferrying families from the senior cadres' apartment blocks on Changgwang Street and Haebangsan Street, across to the main Metro entrances. At the same time helmeted policemen were preventing passers-by entering these same stations, Jacobsen said. Instead they were forced to run and take cover in parking garages and basements of nearby office buildings. In the event they were the lucky ones: the privileges of senior membership of the Korean Workers' Party proved in the end to be of dubious benefit.

At the same time heat-seeking surface-to-surface missiles directed from mobile rocket launchers hit a variety of military targets around Pyongyang: a storage depot for strategic weapons parts close to the atomic power plant at Yongbyon, sixty miles north of the capital; a terrorism school and explosives store near Wonsan; the Wonsan naval base itself; and the early stages of the construction of a large 'offensive dam' on the Upper Han River that Kim had started building for the sole purpose of creating a Damoclean lake that would threaten the very existence of Seoul, which lay further down the river. All the launch sites for the so-called 'Super-Scud' that North Korea was said to have been developing were located and destroyed, a Pentagon spokesman said.

All of these targets, and more, were hit and damaged or destroyed within seventy-two hours of the first North Korean artillery salvoes. Not a single North Korean soldier had penetrated the northern wire of the DMZ. There were just three casualties on the Allied side – an American obser-

ver in a forward radar base was killed by shrapnel on Sunday morning, and two Koreans assigned to an American obstacle-clearing unit were killed when their M728 Combat Engineering Vehicle overturned into a shell crater, crushing them.

There was, at first, total silence on the diplomatic front. The Chinese apparently made an abortive attempt to move elements of the 39th Group Army towards the border, and their defensive radar sites in Central Manchuria were turned around to detect any possible overflying of their territory by enemy warplanes scouting the Yalu Valley (although American pilots were under strict orders to keep at least ten miles south of the Chinese border at all times). The local commanders appeared, however, to have problems of their own: satellite photographs of the Shenyang region showed a series of apparent explosions in a barracks that were believed to house the 77th Mechanised Infantry Division, and an anti-aircraft missile site south of Tonghua was reportedly sabotaged. The US Consulate in Shenyang spoke later of unconfirmed rumours of intense bandit activity in the border area in the immediate aftermath of the first skirmishes.

The Chinese media made no reference to the fighting in its domestic broadcasts. The Voice of America and Radio Japan transmitters both, as was the usual case, increased their regional broadcasting hours to provide coverage of the conflict; the BBC, which had abandoned its Korean language service in the 1980s, found itself unable to compete for listeners among Korean speakers, though it commanded its traditionally faithful audiences within China itself. (The BBC had in any case a considerably enlarged following among educated Chinese, since it had reported the shifting events in the Chinese civil disturbances very comprehensively. Its listenership had benefited considerably from the rebel-inspired destruction of a Chinese Broadcasting Ministry jamming transmitter in southern Fujian that had been interrupting BBC broadcasting throughout southern China. The Chinese had shut down the Hong Kong transmitter as soon as they took over the territory in July 1997; but once the rebel forces had taken control they were able to restart broadcasts, with the full co-operation of Bush House in

London. The Communists responded by trying to jam the signal, but with only limited effect.)

Listeners to the international coverage of the Korean conflict noted with keen intrest the tone of reporting from NHK, the Japanese government radio system. Although the English-speaking reporting was eminently even-handed, in line with traditional NHK policies, the Japanese and Korean language versions presented a rather different picture.

References were made to the unstable situation that now obtained both in the Korean peninsula and, more ominously, in China; comparisons were offered between the situation of today, and the 'very much more agreeable and assured situation that obtained in the 1930s', in the words of the announcer. Foreign diplomats and analysts at the Caversham Listening Service in England wrote later that the tone of these broadcasts from Tokyo was the first of a series of indications – usually subtle – that Japan was beginning to take an alarmed interest in developments among the countries on her western flank.

An internal PPU document circulated six months later within the Foreign Office in London concluded, with an uncharacteristic literary flourish, that 'there will be those who wonder whether, in some extremist and perhaps even not-so-extremist circles within Japan, there are men who even now are looking back fondly to the times when their own Empire was able to embrace and envelop those nearby countries that seemed to be suffering in such a dire manner. Echoes of the Japanese *Manchukuo**, and of the Japanese *Chosun*†, are being heard and felt ever more strongly in certain circles in Tokyo today. That the noble and august NHK, so closely and intimately linked to the Japanese establishment, has chosen also to broadcast a political tune that will find so many distant harmonies from within these groups, is both understandable and, to those who have had to deal with Nipponese expansion and tyranny before, both

*The name given by Japan to Manchuria after 1931 once she had conquered it and was running it as her own, with the last Emperor of China, Henry Pu Yi, as its puppet ruler. Only two countries ever recognised Manchukuo: El Salvador and the Vatican.
†The old name for Korea and, in this context, the name given to Korea by Japan when she ran it as a colony from 1910–45.

regrettable and alarming. Japan should perhaps be prevailed upon by the international community to insist that she harbours no designs on her much weakened and long-suffering neighbours.'

But neither the Japanese nor the Chinese governments said anything, publicly, about the conflict. There was a long and worrying silence, but one that was interrupted finally when the Pentagon announced a two-hour bombing pause at 5 p.m., local time, on Tuesday 17 February. They had been told, via another complicated backchannel once again involving the Swedish government, that the Democratic People's Republic of Korea was about to make a brief but important statement to the nation and, through the International Service of Radio Korea, to the world.

The statement was exceptionally difficult to hear. The radio transmitters had clearly taken a pounding, and the electricity supplies, even to central government offices in Pyongyang, were fitful. The National Security Agency, using enhancement techniques, managed to have the text translated and broadcast on US and British radio networks by 6.15 p.m. (9.15 a.m. GMT). The statement was read by a hitherto unknown Mr Kim Hyun Hwee, who described himself as 'an official with the Information Department of the Provisional North Korean Government, speaking on behalf of the North Korean Armed Forces' and Citizens' Committees' – significance already being attached by Western analysts to the phrase 'North Korean', which had never been in use in the country before. The brief text was as follows:

Fellow Koreans! You will all be aware that many tragic events have befallen our beloved country in the last three days. Foreign soldiers and airmen, mainly from the United States of America, but with the assistance of our brothers from the Republic of South Korea, have mounted a series of cruel attacks on our people and our cities. Much of our nation has been destroyed and devastated, and many of our people have died. This is indeed a sad, sad day for all Koreans, everywhere.

But there are those among us who feel that our leadership

has not been wholly without blame in these matters. The brutal attacks made against us have come about in response to a wholly unauthorised series of attacks which our armed forces were ordered to make on our brother Koreans living south of the 38th parallel on Sunday morning last. There was no need whatsoever for this military action; and whilst the ferocity of the response is, in our view, quite unjustified, the former leadership of this nation has to bear much responsibility for the events of the past days.

Accordingly, some ten hours ago, senior members of the Korean Armed Forces, on whose behalf and with whose authority I have the honour and privilege to address you this evening, took control of this nation's government. The fate of former members of the leadership will be made known in due course, after a fair and public examination of their conduct while in office.

The first decision that has been taken by the North Korean Armed Forces' and Citizens' Committee is that the fighting must come to an immediate stop. I therefore announce that our Armed Forces will agree without reservation to meet all conditions announced by the Government of the United States and the United Nations Command on Sunday, 15 February 1998. A cease-fire has been ordered among all members of the North Korean Armed Forces. Senior members of our armed forces are prepared to meet members of the United Nations Command in the Joint Security Area at Panmunjom, under the auspices of the Neutral Nations Supervisory Committee, at any time after 1000 GMT today. Following the signing of certain documents, members of the United Nations Command are at liberty to make inspection tours within our nation, and to station personnel to ensure compliance with the demands of these agreements.

Dear Korean people. You have suffered much in recent days – and in recent years. Your suffering is now at an end. Much will be happening in the days and months to come. There will be trials ahead. But the interests of our beloved country will come first once again, after many years when that has not, regrettably, been true.

I leave you now with the music that unites all of our country, in the hope that the events of these last days may

hasten the time when the Korean peninsula is, at long last, a whole nation once again.

The strains of the love-song 'Arirang' could then be heard, faintly, before the broadcast ended. Solemn Western classical music followed. There was no further mention made of any member of the Kim family.

All American hostile operations were halted forthwith. The Panmunjom meeting took place at 1030 GMT, with the Eighth Army Commander, General Hotchkiss, signing a brief document headed 'Cessation of Hostilities', on behalf of the United Nations. General O Sik Yong, Commander-in-Chief, North Korean Land Forces, signed on behalf of the Forces' and Citizens' Committee of North Korea. After which the two generals got into an American Humvee and sped off, with escorts, to dinner at a hastily reopened restaurant in Kaesong. Both men returned to their barracks in high good humour: it was evident that the situation on the Korean peninsula was changed for ever.

It was later reported by the North Korean News Agency that Kim Jung Il had been sentenced to death by a 'People's Court' on Thursday, 19 February, and that the sentence had been carried out immediately. Other members of his family were said to have died in an unexplained traffic accident on the outskirts of Pyongyang a day later. All statues of Kim Jung Il were removed from public view within a week after his death. The massive statue of Kim Il Sung that stood on he hill at Kaesong was left standing, however, 'as a memorial'; the huge flag on its 1,000-foot tower just to the north of the DMZ was taken down within a further week; and work started on clearing the minefields of the DMZ, and cutting down the wire fences, in April.

This latter task – which was being undertaken by the Samsung Construction Company – was not expected to be completed until the end of the year, at least. There was a lone protest entered by the World Wildlife Fund, which argued that the half-century of total inactivity within the DMZ had allowed thousands of specimens of the previously

rare Manchurian Crane to breed between the two wire barricades. A professor from Wisconsin was brought over to
supervise the demolition in those parts of the DMZ where
the cranes lived, All were said to have been saved.

## CHAPTER TEN

# DAYDREAMS OF SAMURAI

## TOKYO AND WASHINGTON, DC

*Early 1999*

The situation within China, watched intently by diplomats and military planners across the world, became ever more confused and desperate during the ensuing weeks and months.

The traumatic, mercifully brief, events on the Korean peninsula in the early part of the year took some time to wreak their inevitable direct effect on the Manchurian border regions. A significant proportion of the hundreds of thousands of ethnic Koreans living in Jilin and Liaoning Provinces, close to the Korean frontier, took part in anti-Chinese demonstrations. There was a steady increase, probably linked to this phenomenon, in the audacity and the scale of banditry in the region

The detonation of a large bomb outside a PLA munitions dump south of Harbin in June, and the derailing of no fewer than nineteen goods and passenger trains travelling on Manchurian routes between Dalian, Shenyang, Harbin and at the Shanhaiguan Gap – where the Great Wall nears the sea – continued to cause major headaches for the administration of north-east China. It was some small comfort to the central government, however, that the region's three Group Armies – which were all headed by politically conservative generals – remained loyal to Peking during the year. But then again, there had been losses, and there were still acute military problems.

The total strength of loyal forces in the Chinese north-east

253

had been attenuated since June 1997 by the dispatch of the soldiers of the 37th Division to Hong Kong, and by their subsequent rout and imprisonment following the recapture of the territory by Republican forces. (Most of these former Shenyang-based soldiers were reportedly still penned by Republican troops – though now under Red Cross supervision – on the island that had been reclaimed as a site for the former colony's proposed new airport). In addition, the military commanders were plagued by trouble in a variety of guises that was initiated by Oroqen and other Manchu bandit groups along the length of the Amur River valley. There were almost daily reports of assassinations, kidnappings, bank robberies and arson (huge forest fires were being regularly set, many of them as large and destructive and as difficult to handle as the immense accidental blazes of the mid-Eighties). The remaining Armies might be loyal, but it was a loyalty that was now, the commanders agreed, somewhat less of an asset, and more of an absolute necessity. If it faltered, then the control of the entire north-east of China would be put in jeopardy.

If the practical effects of the Korean situation on China were inconvenient, the symbolic consequence of the fall of the Kim dynasty was devastating. There could be no doubt, all Western embassies reported throughout the year, that the loss to China of her sole remaining political ally in Asia – even so perverse and erratic an ally as Kim Jung Il and his father had been – was distressing in the extreme. Those few Peking-based diplomats still in contact with the Chinese leadership – and it has to be recalled that the political divisions within the Foreign Ministry made it exceptionally difficult for these envoys to know who was speaking for whom – reported that the defeat of the North Korean regime had a grave psychological impact on the battered and demoralised leadership in Peking.

The debilitating effect it had on morale further exacerbated the apparently pathological inability of the Chinese leaders to deal decisively with the deteriorating situation in the nation. Rebel leaders in the south, bandit groups on the peripheries, and a variety of foes both actual and potential seemed at this stage to take an almost perverse delight in exploiting the tragic situation of this wounded giant. An

analyst for a leading American brokerage house, writing an almost sympathetic-sounding internal end-of-year memorandum in December 1998, compared (if in somewhat purple phrases) China's appalling present situation with that of a victim of that most awful of Imperial punishments – slicing.

> First the executioners start with the hands and the feet. Their tiny razors are wielded with menacing precision, taking away millimetre-thin layers of flesh each time. They make almost imperceptible lesions, but wounds that suddenly, when an artery is nicked or a nerve is cut, gush blood or trigger some massive muscular crisis. Before the victim knows, an entire arm is unusable, or a leg is utterly gone – and the brain suddenly and chillingly comes to the realisation that before long the heart is just not going to be able to cope. The brain, itself quite undamaged, begins to suffer from the perception that it, too, is ultimately doomed – that it will receive the final cuts, and that having lost control of those areas of the body that might have been able to put up some resistance, it can do little to halt the terrible progress of the little flashing knives. And so it is at this moment that the organs of the head, which has been deliberately left untouched so that it can observe the whole slow process of dying, begin to howl with dismay and pain. China is just now beginning to howl – because she knows that nothing can be done any longer to save her from extinction. She can only hope that in the way of the Oriental soul, the rebirth of this wretched ancient will bring forth a stronger and more determined China, a nation and a people who will never let such punishment befall her again.

The razors were at their devilish work throughout the year. Huge tank and infantry battles raged at places whose names will soon pass into the convoluted history of the region, once again sounding echoes from earlier fights at the very same places. The Battle of Wuhan was fought out as expected in March: the long-awaited showdown between the two bitterly opposed armies, between the Republican General Tang and the loyalist General Yang, resulted in the eventual defeat of the 15th Army. Wuhan was secured for the Republicans, and sufficient of the hinterland was captured and a sufficient protective barrier of anti-aircraft positions was established for

the city to house the administrative and military headquarters for the entire rebel-held region.

Central to the undoing of General Yang's battle plan for
Wuhan was in any case the wholesale defection of the
leadership of the Air Force's crack MiG-29 squadron, which
had been expected to protect the loyalist tank formations
from Republican bombers. In the event the bombers managed time and again to penetrate all air defences and pummel
Yang's forces, leaving the way open for heavy artillery to slug
it out across the Yangtze and then, after the northern banks
had been stormed, for the Republican infantry to take and
secure Wuhan City. The battle took three weeks from start to
finish: it is estimated that 56,000 men died in the fighting.

The Wuhan victory was hard won, with the loyalist forces
putting up a remarkable fight. In psychological terms the
result was crushing for the morale of the northern leaders –
who then had to look on in dismay and horror as a formally
constituted Provisional Mainland Chinese Republican
government was established in the city on 10 October, 1998.
Taiwan immediately recognised this new government –
though it has been, at the time of writing, still the only major
country to do so. It set up a small Embassy in Wuhan, and
the PMCR Government set up an office in Taipei.

The British and Americans, who had briefly closed their
Consulates in Canton and Hong Kong in the spring,
reopened them in mid-summer, once the threat of air raids
had diminished in both cities, and once the remaining Communist cells had been rooted out and eliminated.

The reestablishment of these missions necessitated some
complicated diplomatic manoeuvres, since neither government wanted a total breach in relations with the People's
Republic, however serious her situation might be. Thus both
governments stated publicly in late October that they would
not, for the time being, establish diplomatic relations with
the PMCRG – it was, they explained, only 'provisional' – and
that they would not, for the time being, open missions in
Wuhan City. Their diplomats in Hong Kong and Canton
were, Washington and London insisted, still officially accre-
dited to the People's Republic government in Peking.

But since there was now no physical contact or communication between Canton and Hong Kong on the one side, and

Peking and other 'loyal' cities on the other, and since it was known that the Consuls saw and privately entertained members of the Republican government, it was generally agreed that the accreditation was a diplomatic fiction, and one that cannot be sustained indefinitely.

Peking did not, however, object publicly to the slight. A Western spokesman commented in November that the Chinese side, in preferring not to create a diplomatic incident over the matter of the southern Consulates, was reacting with 'considerable grace' under the pressure of the times.

But if China restrained itself in its dealings with the West, it took a wholly different approach in dealing with its most important and most deeply feared neighbour, Japan.

For although only Taiwan actually recognised the PMCRG, a small number of other nations, including the Japanese, did invite the rebel leaders to secret talks; and a number of medium-level Japanese and Korean diplomats flew to Hong Kong in mid-November to discuss 'matters of mutual interest'. These matters were believed to include the present and future status and protection of the Nissan and Hyundai car-assembly factories that had been built in the mid 1990s in Changsha and Fuzhou – cities that were now both firmly in Republican hands – as well as those of the Mitsubishi Heavy Industries plants in Baoshan, north of Shanghai – a city that was still, for the most part, held by forces loyal to the Peking government.

In the aftermath of these Hong Kong talks it was reported, though it has still not been confirmed, that during the meeting the Japanese government had requested permission of the Republican leadership to be allowed to send a small detachment of its lightly armed Self-Defence Force troops to protect their plant and personnel in Changsha 'during this period of difficulty'.

This was a request that was, of course, heavy with symbolism. The Chinese, of whatever temporary stripe, would never allow themselves to forget the enmity that had dogged relations between the two countries for centuries past, and which flared at regular intervals into real and terrible conflict. This past century alone has seen the two ancient empires clash repeatedly, and with a violence and a vehemence unknown

between other neighbours anywhere on the planet (though the venom displayed within the Indian subcontinent since Partition may develop in a similar way – a depressing thought indeed). The Sino–Japanese war at the turn of the century, the Japanese occupation of Manchuria in the 1930s, and the full-scale war between the two countries that raged after the Marco Polo Bridge incident of 1937 until the defeat of Japan in 1945 – all of these were vicious conflicts, peppered with unforgettably horrific episodes.

The eight years of the last Sino-Japanese war took an estimated 40 million dead – 3 million in the actual fighting, and more than twelve times that number who perished from starvation and in flooding that might have been avoided in conditions of peace. Lin Yutang, a novelist of the period, said the war was 'the most terrible, the most unhuman, the most brutal, the most devastating' in all of Asia's history.

The powers that were pitted against one another – those led by Peking (its characters representing Northern Capital) and Tokyo (or Dongjing, its characters meaning Eastern Capital) – represented in that war, and in the conflicts before, the colliding ambitions of tradition and development, the confrontation between popular power and technological power, a contest that was rooted in national pride, the pride of being Asian and the pride that would be gained by the inheritance of Asian leadership.

Which Empire, which people were truly emblematic of the region that the Assyrians had long since named Asia, *the place in the world that sees the rising of the sun*? Was it China: the country that first gave the region its linguistic and cultural underpinnings, the nation that was immeasurably more vast and populous than any other on the face of the earth and had enjoyed or suffered or patiently endured 5,000 years of what was once the most advanced of civilisations?

Or was it Japan, the small and fog-bound group of islands to the east of the Chinese landmass that could trace two millennia of unbroken imperial lineage from the Sun Goddess? The islands whose people are, unlike their neighbours on all sides, ethnically and linguistically and culturally fused into one seamless whole? A people whose economic and mercantile success has been unparalleled in world history, whose triumphs have always been accom-

plished with unprecedented speed and in a manner that the rest of civilisation has long envied, and attempted to emulate? A nation that has never caved in to white imperialism, and which, according to its own reckoning, had fought a world war with America in an effort to bring pride back to an Asia ruined by the despoliation and humiliation of centuries of Western colonial dominion?

The impertinence of the Japanese request to station soldiers inside Republican China, seen in such a context, is all the more grotesque. The earlier conflicts between the two countries had been accompanied by the most frightful atrocities, committed largely by the Japanese side. While the Japanese have managed, conveniently, almost to erase them from popular memory, they have never been forgotten by the Chinese, where they remain peculiarly and intensely painful. It was thus not surprising that the Republican Chinese refused the request – or this 'offer for limited military assistance' as it was reported by two Western correspondents based in the Japanese capital – point blank.

But though there was a predictably cool response from the Republican camp, a far more hostile reaction was to come from the Communists, leading to regional and global consequences that have become all too familiar.

The first suggestion of Japanese proposals for sending troops into China had appeared simultaneously in the Friday 13 November editions of the Baltimore *Sun* and the London *Daily Telegraph*, both of which papers had experienced and well-connected correspondents in Tokyo. The Japanese Prime Minister, Mr Tanaka, under extreme pressure from the vocal right wing of the ruling Liberal Democratic Party, reportedly sent an envoy to Hong Kong to consult Governor Yi about stationing troops at the threatened factories. The Governor, using the excuse that the factories and such Japanese supervisors as had remained were well-protected by Republican troops, declined the offer politely. It was reportedly his courtesy, as much as anything, that made the North blow its top.

Radio Peking, which immediately seized on the story of the Changsha troops demand, was almost hysterical in its hostility. The language of its commentary, which was repeated several times on all the domestic and foreign

services, was filled with the rhetoric of the Cultural Revolution, and was highly inflammatory, to say the very least:

It is beyond belief that these running-dogs and scabs who have temporarily seized a small number of our southern cities would even contemplate talking to the swinish Japanese. It was only sixty years ago that those wretched dregs of humanity, the Japanese invading army, behaved with fearful, unforgivable and unforgettable depravity in our country, committing barbarisms which, though possibly allowable under the bankrupt moral codes of Nippon, are unacceptable in all civilised nations throughout the rest of the world.

Have the foul traitors in Wuhan forgotten what terror the Japanese wrought in Nanjing? Have they conveniently overlooked how the vile incursionists stole vast tracts of our country, how they bombed our cities, raped our women, machine-gunned our peasants, and committed the most terrible of barbaric acts against millions of our people?

Even to think of inviting more soldiers, the heirs of such inhuman behaviour, back on to China's hallowed ground – just who are the filth who imagine doing such a thing? What rights have they to even dream of issuing such invitations, or to bow before such typically revolting Japanese demands? Does this not show, to all the rest of the people of China and to the world, that these traitorous swine are mere animals, greedy for their own benefit, while at the same time peddling the birthright of our nation to the beasts who tried so viciously to ruin and ravage it only so very short a time ago?

This broadcast, read in a number of languages (including Japanese), will probably be remembered as one of the more incautious and unwise examples of megaphone diplomacy ever to have been conducted. And once Japanese analysts had concluded that the text was indeed genuine, and that it did in fact represent the official thinking of at least the loyalist wing of the Chinese Foreign Ministry, it triggered a result that could well have been predicted.

Within hours, the Chinese Ambassador to Tokyo was summoned by the Ministry of Foreign Affairs and was told in no uncertain terms that Japan was 'insulted' and 'absolutely outraged' by the Chinese government's sentiments and by

the choice of words it had chosen to authorise for use on its radio stations. The Japanese Foreign Minister, Mr Abe, was angry and upset, and upbraided the Ambassador for more than thirty minutes – an unprecedented length of time. But the Chinese Ambassador had evidently been told to stand his ground. Indeed, he repeated his government's assertion that it would be 'criminal' (as the Tokyo press statement said the next day) to permit the stationing of Japanese soldiers on Chinese soil again – 'now, tomorrow, or ever again'. And according to the same press briefing, having delivered that terse message, he then stormed angrily out of the meeting.

The Japanese Ambassador to Peking was promptly summoned back to Tokyo for 'discussions', and at the time of writing he has not returned. His functions were from that moment on performed by a First Secretary.

Meanwhile, within Japan itself there was a nationwide outpouring of anger expressed at the Radio Peking broad-cast – anger which, significantly, was not on this occasion confined to the right-wing extremist groups who had first urged the Prime Minister to send troops to the PMCRG-controlled region. These groups had, until now, been in the vanguard, fomenting anti-Chinese sentiment inside Japan. In the wake of the Radio Peking broadcast, the reaction of the mainstream Japanese was precisely as they had hoped. Indeed, the scale of the reaction provided persuasive evidence that their campaign to achieve such a result had been planned with thought, foresight and much sophisti-cation.

The first indications of the campaign's success had come some nine months before when, it will be recalled, eye-brows had been raised around the world at the tone of the Japanese radio and television coverage of the brief Korean conflict.

The NHK commentators had on several occasions (and with the presumed sanction of the Japanese government), remarked on the uneasy state of the Korean peninsula and on the similarly unstable and unpredictable nature of contemporary China. Remarks about the relative tranquillity of this part of the world in the 1930s were made in several broadcasts. Remarks that were widely regarded as suggesting ominously that the world situation had somehow been rather

better sixty years before, when both Korea and Manchuria were controlled by Japan – and when Japan also had obvious and increasing designs on China as a whole.

Perhaps, foreign relations specialists around the world wondered out loud, Japan did once again have designs on China – now that the latter was so weakened and exhausted, and overrun with refractory and disloyal soldiers, administrators and warlords. In Washington the HK7 Committee, which was still meeting regularly under the chairmanship of Assistant Secretary of State Hugh Charlesworth, made a particular point of voicing its concerns during the months following the Korean liberation, and of ensuring that these concerns were heard in the most senior levels of the Administration.

The White House later acknowledged that four times, in March and October 1998, in the immediate aftermath of the Baltimore *Sun* story in November, and once again in March 1999, the potential for some degree of active Japanese involvement in the situation was discussed by the full National Security Committee. Meetings during the spring, summer and autumn of 1999 were then held regularly as the momentum of the crisis gathered. In June 1999 the Joint Chiefs, working under the terms of their Joint Operations Planning System, drew up a series of options for President Benson to consider – options which were designed to prevent any Japanese involvement in the deteriorating situation.

The crisis should be seen in the context of severe strains in US–Japanese relations which had begun in the mid-1990s. President Benson had little doubt for example that his stunning election victory in November 1996 over his Democratic Party challenger, Tom Harkin, was due in no small measure to his ceaseless rhetorical attacks on Japan and all things Japanese. President Bush had bowed to the necessity of abrogating the Mutual Security Treaty two years before; and the early stages of the 1996 Presidential campaign coincided with the final withdrawal of American forces from their bases in Japan, with the emotional impact of the ending of an occupation that had been in place for more than half a century.

On Okinawa, in particular, the impact of the US Forces' departure was enormous, for both sides. Kadena Air Base was vacated, to be reoccupied by Japanese Air Self-Defence Force. Camps Courtney, Hansen and Schwab were closed. The Marine Artillery Regiment was withdrawn from Zukeran, the airborne special forces group left Torii for Korea. The island of Okinawa had been all but an American protectorate – traffic drove on the right until the mid-Seventies, to satisfy American, not Japanese, motoring habits. Every other restaurant in Naha seemed to be a Burger King or a Pizza Hut. The Stars and Stripes flew from almost every building in town. There was a formidable number of mixed marriages, and in the wake of the treaty abrogation a similarly formidable number of divorces and broken homes. And now, at a stroke, it was all ended, with the marines and the soldiers and airmen pulling out amidst a torrent of anti-American rhetoric and ill-feeling.

The situation was far worse on the mainland, with noisy demonstrations and angry protests at the alleged tardiness of the US withdrawal. The US Army headquarters at Zama was firebombed, and demonstrators fouled the screws of the carrier USS *Independence* in mid-summer, preventing her from leaving her home port of Yokosuka bound for her new base near Guam. An American child was kidnapped on his way to school north of Yokohama, with a right-wing group demanding a ransom payment which the Tokyo Metroplitan Government agreed to pay – to the official fury of Washington.

By the time the last detachment of Army clerks and senior officers left the country in early October 1996 after a hastily organised flag-lowering ceremony at Yokota Air Base, relations between the two countries were at a post-war low point – making it all the easier for Mr Benson to trounce his opponent a month later for being, allegedly, 'soft on Japan'.

Benson took forty-nine of the states, and the government of the United States which assembled in mid-January 1997 had a complexion that commentators described as more obviously right-wing in its views – particularly in its international views – than any since President Nixon's second administration of the early Seventies. And the new Secretary of State, Richard Crowther, made an early point of letting the *Washington Post* know that his grandfather had died at the hands of the Japanese, at Guadalcanal.

It therefore came as no surprise to learn that the official policy line devised by the Benson administration was wholly opposed to any interference by Japan in the China crisis. Diplomatic niceties were observed, however: in the immediate wake of the Baltimore *Sun* story the on-the-record State Department briefings were restrained, and simply offered the view that any such interference would be manifestly 'unhealthy' and inimical to regional stability. But the background briefings went rather further. The growing apprehension in Washington and in Europe was that the competition between American and Japanese economic and political interests in the Pacific was now coming to a head, and Washington would regard with 'great disfavour' any attempt on the part of Tokyo to adopt a hegemonic approach to the current regional disorder.

'The Japanese should be persuaded to remember,' said a Department of State memorandum that was considered by the NSC, and a précis of which was leaked to the *New York Times*, 'that their exploitation of the weakened state of China in the 1930s led them on to pursue an escalating series of ambitions that resulted, eventually, in the attack on Pearl Harbor. To permit such ambitions to be pursued again would have serious implications, and the United States should look to its responsibilities to see that such a massively destabilising situation *is not permitted* to come to pass [author's italics].

The Joint Chiefs also considered one further aspect of this possible development: whether, if the Japanese did decide to send troops into China, they would meet any significant resistance from the Chinese. The conclusion was exceptionally alarming. It was estimated that the weakened state of the Chinese military machine was such that the Japanese could, in fact, and without meeting resistance, land soldiers in certain areas – Manchuria, in particular – in which they had commercial and industrial installations that they needed 'to protect'. But the Chinese would eventually retaliate: and when they did so, all intelligence reports indicated, they would do so *with atomic weapons*.

'It has been noted with some admiration,' a study carried out for the Joint Chiefs remarked, 'that the Chinese Communists have so far restrained any temptation to make use of

their Second Artillery strategic assets or of any of their tactical atomic weapons to deal with the various troubling military situations that beset them. Precisely why they have been so restrained remains unclear – and the threat that some elements within the People's Liberation Army may in desperation resort to the use of these weapons in a domestic scenario is ongoing. However, diplomatic contacts in Peking suggest that it is most unlikely that nuclear weapons will be used in the conflict.

'The same cannot be said, however, in the event of any kind of unwarranted interference by an outside Power. In particular, the tone and tenor of Chinese antipathy to the possibility of Japanese involvement in their internal crisis suggests that theatre atomic weapons might well be deployed against Japanese forces.

'The United States, which has privately stated its opposition to any Japanese interference in China's internal troubles, thus has an additional reason to be concerned with Japan's current alleged intentions.'

But these 'alleged intentions' were in fact quite firmly rooted, and not simply 'current'. During the months that followed the Korean conflict, during which, as has been noted, the situation inside China progressively deteriorated, there had been a disturbing number of rallies, marches and protests inside Japan, all suggesting precisely what had been feared. The old, moribund and until lately little-regarded right-wing groups – the Cherry Blossom Society, the Black Dragon Society and the ludicrous *Ketsumeidan*, the Blood Brotherhood, prominent among them – were in the forefront, lobbying politicians, staging demonstrations, placing advertisements in the popular press.

All chanted the same essential message: the collapse of Communism in Europe and Russia, and its now inevitable collapse in China, was about to bring a period of utter chaos to the Far East – chaos that would be similar in scale and extent to, but far greater in perilous consequence than, the instability of seventy years ago. The only nation that was capable of restoring order to the region, of acting as regional policeman and disciplinarian, was the nation that had acted in this role once before, albeit in an effort that was misguidedly thwarted and attenuated by the white colonial powers: Japan.

265

Japan, these groups all chorused, should therefore intervene at once in China, both to protect her own considerable investments in the country, and also to prevent further bloodshed and to assist in stabilising the neighbour-nation. 'It is our duty as patriots,' a spokesman for the Cherry Blossom Society said in an interview on NHK. 'We are deeply disappointed at China's weakness, his seeming inability to deal with his internal problems. China is our own nation's dearest brother, and we have an obligation to go to his assistance in this, his hour of need. We go to his side not out of anger at his actions, but with sorrow at his lack of fortitude and decisiveness, and with deep fraternal sadness for his prodigal ways.'

China protested angrily at the increasing frequency of such remarks and demonstrations, and few were the weeks during the spring and summer of 1998 when the Chinese Ambassador to Tokyo did not have cause and occasion to interview Japanese ministers to complain.

He was especially furious at his own treatment. Beginning in March, convoys of huge sound-trucks had been constantly circling his residence, blasting humiliating insults at him in *putonghua*, reminding him of the Sino-Japanese War, the Twenty-One Demands, the Mukden Incident, the Marco Polo Bridge Incident, the bombing of Shanghai and the Rape of Nanjing and a hundred and one other waystations in Japan's half-century of infamous behaviour within the bounds of the Middle Kingdom.

The laws relating to free speech in Japan generally permitted such noisy demonstrations, although the city police had in the past usually prevented any disturbance to foreign ambassadors, citing some special but unspecified provisions of Japanese Diplomatic Regulations. In the particular case of the PRC Embassy in the summer of 1998, however, the city police took no action, and the Ambassador spent several sleepless nights before being forced to move to a hotel.

Even so it was not long before he was run to ground – first at his penthouse suite at the Imperial, then at the Okura, then the Shinjuku Hilton, from each of which he was obliged to leave in turn when the management complained that other 'innocent' guests were being deprived of their rest by the blasting and screeching from the sound-trucks. In the

end the hapless diplomat had no course other than to return to his Embassy, and, while continuing his daily and duly ignored protests at the Ministry, to take liberal quantities each evening of a well-known Chinese herbal sleeping-draught.

The tone of the broadcast on Radio Peking in November provided a heaven-sent opportunity for those right-wingers to intensify their demands for some form of Japanese intervention in China. But on this occasion it was not simply the old reactionaries of tradition who led the assault, but the underworld gangs – the infamous *yakuza* and their violent motorcycling cousins, the *bosozuka*. The leaders of these tightly disciplined groups of hoodlums and swindlers announced they had formed themselves into the vanguard of a wholly new organisation, to be called the Young Officers' Association. The name itself was significant – a throwback to the more 'romantic' age of the Japanese right wing, when patriotic swells in the Imperial army tried to instigate a coup to overthrow what they contemptuously regarded as the weak-willed and complaisant government of the day.

The involvement of the *yakuza*, whose network of influence reached right into the heart of the nation – or at least, if not into the Imperial Palace, then with certainty directly into the National Police and, most importantly, into the Army – suddenly triggered a large-scale outpouring of national frustration. Young people in particular were known to have expressed themselves as feeling exceptionally jaded and disillusioned by the affluence and flabbiness, as their leaders put it, of the Japanese middle class. 'The nation must return to its traditional posture of disciplined asceticism,' said one poster that became popular on Japanese university bulletin-boards. 'Only by this means can we achieve the respect that is necessary for resuming the leadership of Asia, of the Pacific and, as is our due, of the entire world.'

In contrast to the situation in President Benson's United States, where everything Japanese was reviled, Japan's virulent anti-American rhetoric which had been such a hallmark of the mid-1990s, and which had become the rallying-cry of most Japanese right-wing groups, had cooled. Once it had achieved its results – the abrogation of the Mutual Security Treaty and the withdrawal of all of the remaining

US military personnel – that particular aspect of the movement had essentially quietened. A year later and there was
actually some nostalgic yearning – and not only, as cynics
suggested, in the brothels of Yokohama – for the Americans
to return. Such antipathy as had precipitated the crisis was
confined now to the American side.

But if anti-American sentiment no longer drove the
Japanese right, other forces did. Their other dominant
anxiety in the late Nineties seemed to centre on what they
saw as the laxity and informality of the present Imperial
Court. The Emperor Showa (or Hirohito as he had been
known in life) was their chosen hero, and there was much
private disquiet expressed at the attempts of his son and
successor Akihito to demystify the whole Imperial system,
and make it accessible to the Japanese public. The moves,
these strident students declared, were just further indications that Japan, under foreign influence, had abandoned
her sacred responsibility to exert her cultural and moral
influence on her people and her region. The much-vaunted
'demystification' of the sacred and unbroken chain of two
millennia of Japanese emperors was an 'unnecessary and
insulting intrusion, forced on Japan by her foreign con-
querors of half a century before'. It should have been resisted then; it should and it could be resisted now.

Talk like that went down well among the young members
of the Japanese élite of the late 1990s. Once the *yakuza*, who
were given discreet support by such right-wing politicians as
realised the jingoistic possibilities that could be stimulated by
the Radio Peking broadcast, had taken up the call, so the
message began to penetrate the ranks of the ordinary Japanese with extraordinary and alarming rapidity. By the end of
1998 the nation was in ferment: the leadership of the Liberal
Democratic Party, still in power in Tokyo as it had been since
the end of the Second World War, was now forced to accept
that in order to continue to remain in office, it had to move
swiftly to accommodate the fast-developing national mood.
In a sense, developments forced on the nation by events
helped to foster such changes.

The most profound change was perhaps related to Japan's
attitude to her own post-war constitution. The Japanese
Navy's peripheral involvement in the Gulf War of 1991 was

the harbinger of this change. There was initial resistance to the sending of ships, but it was a resistance that was soon and quite painlessly overcome. And once it was overcome so it was felt, both inside and beyond Japan, that the most critical element of Japan's modern psyche – the principle enshrined in Article Nine of the Constitution, which essentially held that war was outlawed as an instrument of Japanese policy, and that Japanese forces should never be used for any purpose than the defence of the realm, strictly construed – had been fatally damaged.

It was not too much longer before the Article's effectiveness as a self-disciplinary check on the hallowed spirit of *bushido** vanished completely in 1993, when Japanese ground forces were sent to Cambodia to try to restore peace there, and were drawn into a shooting war with the Khmer Rouge – in which, as it happens, they performed with tremendous efficiency and courage.

The principle is still written into the Constitution – Article Nine still exists – but it is generally agreed that it is no longer regarded as binding upon the activities of the military. The regional situation has long since changed, Japan argues. In any case, as an editorial in January 1999 in the influential conservative American journal the *National Review* was to point out, Japan 'has a lengthy history of disregarding what were once seen as the most hallowed of international treaties and conventions and protocols. Tokyo's current expressed disdain for even so sacred a document as an article of their nation's very own constitution should hardly cause a ripple of moral concern, nor even a momentary stab of conscience . . .'

It was in this context that, during the first three months of 1999, there were significant changes in the siting of the Japanese armed forces throughout the islands of the nation. The troop movements caused immediate concern in Washington, and resulted in Secretary of State Crowther summoning the Japanese Ambassador for an explanation –

*Bushido is the Japanese code of chivalry, practised by the *samurai*.

269

which essentially went as follows. The Director-General of the Japanese Defence Agency had explained, the Ambassador told Crowther, that: 'the changing conditions that have followed the Russian Republic's decision to hand over the Southern Kurile Islands in 1995 have altered the priorities for the siting of our self-defence forces. There is no more sinister interpretation that needs to be placed upon what is, in any case, the internal affair of a sovereign nation. That an explanation is being demanded at all appears to the Japanese people to be a serious discourtesy on the part of the United States. That the Director-General has deigned to offer this explanation indicates the sincerity of the Japanese nation, which is at variance with the current posture of the United States Government – a posture which we trust will soon be reversed.'

Russia's decision to give back the four groups of contested islands in 1995 ended more than half a century of argument between Tokyo and Moscow. It also meant that, for the first time since the end of the Second World War, Japan could afford to lower its guard on the northern island of Hokkaido, off the coast of which the Russian-held islands lay. Until then the Army – which had been at least 15 per cent under-strength, but which by 1997 was, given the prevailing mood, winning recruits at a record rate – had concentrated its strength in the north, as well as in the far south (the latter to cope with any threat from North Korea).

From March 1999, the Japanese indicated, matters would be reversed. The build-up on Hokkaido would be ended, and the forces on Kyushu would be augmented further, and quickly. It was this latter aspect, the speed of the redeployment of so much of the Northern Army, and of its precipitate relocation in Kyushu – which has two naval ports, Kagoshima and Sasebo, that were *less than a full day's steaming from Shanghai* – that led promptly to Washington's questions about the real intent behind the move.

The shifts that were announced in January 1999 placed a formidable amount of Japanese manpower and firepower conveniently close to the coast of China, leading to a series of interpretations that Tokyo was not, despite its initial 'explanation', over-eager to deny. Under the new arrangements the existing 4th and 8th Infantry Divisions, the 1st

270

Combined Brigade and the 3rd Artillery Group, all on the island of Kyushu, were joined by the 2nd, 5th and 7th Infantry Divisions and the 1st Artillery Brigade – meaning that within a matter of months the numerical strength in the Japanese Army bases closest to China had risen from 16,000 to 45,000, and included 600 of the new high-performance T-90 tanks.

Two entire Fleet Escort Flotillas, including three of the four 7,200-ton brand-new AEGIS super-fast destroyers – ships that since the early Nineties had been regarded as having far greater power than was necessary for the simple 'self-defence' of the country – were at the same time moved to Kyushu, to be home-based at Sasebo near Nagasaki, and at Kagoshima. The 4th and 5th Fleet Air Wings were also moved to a new base outside Sasebo.

The 83rd Air Wing and 5th Air Defence Missile Groups at Naha in Okinawa were to be strengthened, and an additional Wing – the 2nd, previously based at Chitose, near Sapporo – was be moved south to augment the 5th and 8th, near the city of Fukuoka.

All told, by the early spring of 1999, more than a quarter of Japan's land forces, nearly half of her navy and a third of her air force were stationed on or near Kyushu – in easy striking distance of China. The specific purpose was not to be stated for several more months, but by late August the Washington planners had little doubt. Contingency orders were thus set in place to implement one of the three principal plans that had been drawn up: in particular, an operation, all details of which were Top Secret and which were passed to no other foreign government, that was to be named Operation Typhoon Warning.


As part of the plan, a series of urgent but discreet messages were passed by friendly third-country diplomats, as well as by the usual more direct diplomatic channels, warning Tokyo against precipitate and unilateral action. The United States, together with the overwhelming majority of its allies, was implacably opposed to any Japanese intervention in the China crisis. Suggestions that had been voiced in some sections of the Tokyo press in recent months, to the effect

that Japanese troops should be airlifted into those parts of China in which vital Japanese-owned industrial plants were situated, were now being taken seriously in Washington. Such moves would not, the messages all said in unison, be tolerated.

The United States would not permit the landing of troops or of men or *matériel* by Japan on any part of China for any pretext; any attempt by the government of Japan to follow such a course of action would be met with resistance of the greatest magnitude.

There was no indication that Japan paid any heed to these warnings. In early November a flotilla of troop ships was reported to have left Kagoshima port for Naha, Okinawa, with elements of two infantry divisions embarked. The men would reportedly spend the next two weeks on Okinawa 'in training'. At the same time the 1st and 3rd Tactical Airlift Divisions of the Air Self-Defence Force's Support Command were dispatched to Kadena from their existing bases at Komaki and Miho respectively.

The United States took a steadily more aggressive tone as November wore on, demanding that the Japanese premier make a statement 'clarifying' the reasons for the unusual troop movements. But there was no statement from Tokyo, and the White House recalled its Ambassador to Tokyo for consultations, and to offer a further sign of its displeasure.

In China, meanwhile, the fighting continued without respite, although without major advances or retreats on either side. There was a lengthy battle for control of a bridge across the Huang He – the Yellow River – at Jinan, which was eventually repulsed by well-reinforced Communist troops; and Wuhan was again seriously bombed and shelled by loyalist forces, suggesting to Governor Yi that it might be prudent to move the seat of his provisional government back to the relative safety of Canton. But otherwise, central and southern China was simply beset by the ebb and flow of inconclusive fighting, with a mounting toll of casualties and refugees and ruined cities providing graphic testimony to the utter futility and tragedy of yet another Chinese civil war.

And then, late on the night of Sunday, 21 November, there was an incident in Harbin, a northern Manchurian industrial city that had so far been little scarred by the fight-

ing. It was an incident that suddenly and decisively changed the course of history.

A mysterious – and still unexplained – dynamite explosion severely damaged the administrative office building of the Sumitomo Metals Company's chromium smelter. An entire corner of the building was destroyed, collapsing all of the seven floors of the structure. Normally the building would, at that time on a Sunday, have been deserted; but on this occasion there was one employee on duty. He was Mr Shimizu Tokuya, a Sumitomo accountant who had been asked to work late on a special and urgent financial project. His office was sited directly above the bomb's blast core, and he was killed instantly. His wife and three small children were on home leave at the time in the northern Japanese city of Niigata: they were informed of his death by an emissary from the Foreign Ministry in Tokyo, after news of the incident had been passed from the Chinese.

Angry crowds – whose anger Western diplomats later agreed appeared to have been somewhat orchestrated – promptly gathered both outside Mrs Shimizu's house in Niigata, and next morning outside the Japanese Diet and other public buildings in Tokyo. They protested loudly at the continuing 'instability' of China, they pointed to the evident danger of leaving unprotected the many Japanese industrial installations that were still functioning there, and they condemned the prudence of permitting Japanese workers to continue to do business in China without 'proper security measures'.

The Tokyo demonstrations continued throughout Monday well into the evening. Hundreds of National Riot Police were brought in to try to calm the crowds, but in fact only succeeded in exacerbating the situation, which then erupted into a number of running battles fought along Showa-dori and in the back streets of Ginza, with some casualties sustained by both sides, and a great deal of fires and property damage.

The Japanese Prime Minister went on national television the next day in an additional effort to calm the people. Towards the end of his short speech he made his long-awaited, long-feared announcement.

In accordance with the urgent need for security, Tanaka

said, that was now being felt by the owners and operators of some 26 major and 145 standard-sized Japanese industrial installations inside China, and in order to protect the lives and livelihoods of some tens of thousands of Japanese workers inside the country, he had authorised the immediate dispatch to China of some 6,000 lightly armed Japanese troops.

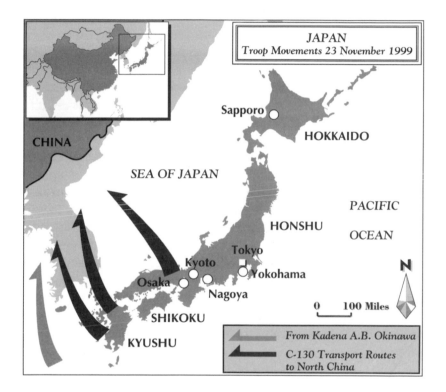

These troops would, the premier insisted, 'and as a reassurance to our foreign friends', operate only as defensive forces, and would uphold to the letter the principles enshrined in Article Nine of the 1947 Constitution. The relevant passage continues:

Our men are travelling today in the name of the Emperor to be deployed to a number of places within China in an effort to guard and to protect our nation's property. That is the sole reason they are going to China. There is no state of war.

There will not be a state of war. We have no argument with any nation and any people – and least of all with our ancient friends, the people of China. We only wish for the stability of our assets, and for the protection of our people.

We are, in short, simply trying to do today what we attempted but failed nearly seven decades ago – and that is to bring calm and stability to a region that is still beset by historical feuds and ancient enmities. We all have to realise that the troubles that afflict the region today came as a direct consequence of foreign imperialism and adventurism in south China. Our role in this limited action, and in possible future actions, is to return Asia to the influence of the Asian peoples, and not to the colonial influences of the whites. Our cause is therefore just, and noble, and we ask the entire world to support us in our endeavour.

A seemingly endless procession of fully laden Japanese Lockheed C-130H troop transport planes, with fighter escorts, took off during the early morning of Tuesday, 23 November from the former US Air Force Base at Kadena and from other tactical bases in western Kyushu and northern Honshu. Most of the planes were making for airfields in Manchuria – to Harbin, where the explosion had taken place, to Changchun and Shenyang; but other aircraft were later discovered to have landed at Jinan, Xian, Shanghai and Chengdu, where there were Japanese-owned car factories, computer-chip assembly plants, steel mills and coal processing plants.

By late afternoon, China time – early Tuesday morning in Washington – all of Japan's troops were in place. There had been no resistance from the Chinese: no anti-aircraft fire, no interference on the ground. The aircraft had landed at the destination airfields, the troops had deployed to their target installations and set themselves up inside the buildings or in tented encampments, and had begun immediate high-visibility patrolling to ensure, as a press statement had it, 'that there are no further incidents that might affect the smooth running of our commercial operations in China'.

A grim-faced President Benson addressed the American nation later that afternoon.

What he said was short, and to the point. He said that for the past nine months there had been growing indications that Japan wished to become involved in the steadily deteriorating situation in China, so as to be able to 'exploit' the country's disarray 'for Japan's own territorial ambitions'. The rest of the world, which had once before this century experienced the effects of such action on the part of Japan, could not and would not tolerate such a step. Diplomatic pressure was applied to dissuade Japan from doing so, but to no avail. All approaches had been ignored or rebuffed.

'Last Sunday night,' the President continued, 'there was an incident in Harbin, a remote town in the cold wastes of northern Manchuria, in which a Japanese factory was damaged, and an employee of the plant, a Japanese national, was killed. It is not known whose hand was behind this fatal explosion. But one should learn from history. One should remember the infamous incident in 1931 that prompted Japan to send troops to Manchuria in almost precisely similar circumstances to these: it has always been assumed that agents working for Japan staged that earlier incident to provide Japan with an excuse to deploy her army. It is not too far-fetched to suppose that this incident too may have been staged, so as to offer Tokyo an excuse to send in her soldiers.

'Whatever the precise origins of this deployment, only history will be able to judge. But as the United States and its allies have made repeatedly clear, this deployment, this interference in the affairs of the world's most populous nation, will not be permitted. The United States is resolved to use all and any means at its disposal to ensure that Japan's troops are removed from the People's Republic of China.

'Accordingly I hereby announce that the United States has set a deadline of 5 p.m. Eastern Standard Time on Thursday – just over two days from now – by which we must have firm evidence that the troops are withdrawing to their home bases. Failing satisfactory and unambiguous evidence that such return movement is taking place, the United States will take extreme measures to ensure compliance. There will be no further warning, no further announcement.

'It is as simple as I have stated. All of Japan's troops must be on their way out of China by 5 p.m. on Thursday, 25 November – Thanksgiving Day. The time is equivalent to 6 a.m. on Friday in China, and 7 a.m. on Friday in Tokyo. If the troops are not out, or on their way out, then I have to say, as calmly and as firmly as I am able, that there will be no holds barred in the actions of this nation to enforce the wishes of the rational world.

'At this exceptionally difficult time I ask for your prayers, that all may be accomplished in peace and with wisdom and good will. God bless the United States of America.'

## CHAPTER ELEVEN

# NIGHTMARE

## POSITION DELTA, FLIGHT LEVEL 350
### *Wednesday, 24 November 1999*

### 2159 ZULU

The three aircraft reached the assembly point precisely on schedule, at one minute before seven in the morning, local time. The flight commanders verified their status with the Global Positioning System computers, and immediately slowed, as ordered, to cruising speed. There was, to the relief of all six crewmen, no indication that their arrival had been noticed. Despite the excellence of Japan's air defences – all on full alert since President Benson's television address – the B-2s were all but invisible to any of the detection technology that was available to the Japanese pilots and ground radar sites.

The skies were to all intents and purposes empty. Radio traffic indicated just a couple of early-morning freighters inbound from Europe, and a single passenger plane taking off from Haneda, heading for Osaka. Otherwise, nothing.

To the west – to the left of the aircraft – it was still quite dark. Ahead and to the right, barely visible on the horizon in the early dawn glimmer, was Cape Nojima, the southern tip of the Boso-hanto peninsula. Directly ahead, and only visible on the radar, was the small island of Miyake, with its 2,400-foot volcano, Mt. Oyama. Beyond that were the cliffs of Cape Iro, and the Izu Peninsula.

In daylight it would have been a breathtaking sight. Iro-zaki and Nojima-zaki were the twin gateways to Tokyo Bay, and between their gaunt cliffs, each day and night, scores of mighty ships would be sailing, bringing in the raw materials, taking out cars and televisions and lawnmowers and steel bars. Even now Bill Pringle could look down six miles from

278

his lead aircraft and see the tiny firefly sparkles of a couple of ships heading southwards, out into the Pacific Ocean. Another tiny streak of light near Nojima-zaki indicated early morning traffic on the coast freeway, Route 16: the cars and trucks were heading north towards the junction with the new Kanto Skybridge – the world's longest, it was said – where they would cross the entire sweep of Tokyo Bay to the factories at Kawasaki and Yokohama.

But the pilots had little time to consider the view, nor the implications of what might lie ahead. The only question was whether the orders – any orders – would be transmitted. Operation Typhoon Warning indicated with absolute precision that an Execute Order would be transmitted at 2200 Zulu. If it was not transmitted within sixty seconds of that time, the planes would all return to Refuelling Position 'R', and then return to Hawaii and home.

The clocks snapped up to 2200 and instantly the screen of the satellite data link terminal lit up. A message was indeed being transmitted. The President in Washington had decided to give the Execute Order. The planes were now going to attack. The pilots felt the sudden rush of adrenalin, and then, equally suddenly, the awful calm that years of relentless training can bring – a calm that has the effect of turning each man into an emotionless, dedicated, intelligent machine for the critical moments of the bombing mission.

The message was brief. It ordered a single aircraft, designated Chase Bravo, to descend immediately to 5,000 feet and to fly directly at full speed towards the target position at 35° 23'N, 139° 47'E and to release on target a single B-61 nuclear weapon.

Technicians in Hawaii had already preset the bomb to burst at sea level – in part to reduce very slightly the effects on surrounding population centres, and structures, but principally to maximise the demonstratory nature of a medium-range atomic blast. The Operation was not called Typhoon Warning for nothing: the purpose of this most dreadful of detonations was to warn, not to destroy – although a weapon of this size and type would bring an immense amount of destruction in its wake, no matter what cosmetic precautions might be taken.

Major Pringle wiggled his plane's massive single wing as a

279

message to his colleagues – who turned away into a holding position – and then began his dive towards Sagami Bay, to the west of the main Tokyo Bay. As the altimeter started to spiral downwards he punched the target coordinates into the weapons delivery computer, and added figures relating to the windspeed, atmospheric pressure and other crucial data about the target.

He reached his designated flight level at six minutes after seven, local time, and swept northwards towards his target. The computer beeped softly. To ensure that he was nowhere near the blast effect when the weapon exploded he would execute a 'toss-and-loft' manoeuvre some five miles short of the target: he would begin a steep climb, release a single bomb as he was doing so and then, as soon as it was indicated to him that he was clear of the weapon, he would extend his turn into a backward loop and clear the area as rapidly as possible.

At eleven minutes after seven, having levelled out and completed his targeting procedures, he had a few seconds to notice where he was, and where his bomb would land. The Global Positioning System computer was now linked into his automatic pilot, and it was steering him relentlessly towards his goal. He glanced at his map: the target was at the mouth of Tokyo Bay itself, at about its widest point, midway between Yokohama on the west and the reclaimed land by Kisarazu airfield in Chiba prefecture on the east.

He began to climb rapidly as he passed beside Yokosuka, the former headquarters of the US Naval Forces, Japan. A few seconds later, having checked the datalink for any indication of a countermand order, Major Pringle assumed his place in history by lifting the plexiglass flap and punching the bright red Execute button.

The weapons-delivery computer then took control of the system, and at precisely 7.15 a.m. the Major heard the distinct clicks of the bomb-bay latches snap open, and a few seconds later felt the small but perceptible relief from the plane's four engines as a third of a ton of steel and high explosive and uranium and electronic weaponry tumbled from the belly of his aircraft, first up, then along and then finally free-falling down towards the designated Ground Zero in the centre of the Bay.

The confirmation that the weapon had been released came within a further second. Major Pringle immediately gunned his engines, climbed vertically for two miles – little caring if at this point the Japanese fighters spotted his heat trails and found reflections from his turbine blades, though the infrared suppressors and RAM baffles fitted to the engines should confuse them for several more minutes, at least.

Once at 20,000 feet he set in motion a long, fast overhead loop and roll, and then climbed steadily back up to the rendezvous point. He was just in sight of his two colleagues when he felt the distant detonation of the bomb.

All three planes had switched on their light-sensitive cockpit shield protectors, which had the effect of enclosing the aircraft in enormous non-reflective polarising sunglasses. Even so, the flash of pure white light was impressive – a searing, scorching dazzle that was followed seconds later by an upward-roaring fireball and a cigar-shaped plume of water and steam and – if the dark adornments to its sides could be said to have solidity – the vaporised carcasses of half a dozen cargo ships that had been caught in the blast.

The electromagnetic pulse, the high energy radio waves that can wreak such havoc on electronics, hit briefly. It caused, as planned, just a momentary flicker in the instruments – a flicker that was easily compensated for by the lightweight surge suppressors and the Faraday-caged backup computer. And then, as expected, came the blast – manifesting itself as a huge and sudden shove in the back, a lurch that hurled the planes forward briefly, and set them rocking in the sky – alarmingly, but not dangerously.

The training had covered all of this, and none of the pilots expressed any concern. The small squadron flew on, resuming its flight level of 45,000 feet, until the giant tankers from Hickam came into view. They broke radio silence at this point, connected their drogues, refilled their tanks with aviation spirit and continued down normally towards Hawaii.


In Tokyo, however, nothing continued, and nothing was normal any more. The relatively small bomb which Major Pringle had dropped had been specifically designed to inflict

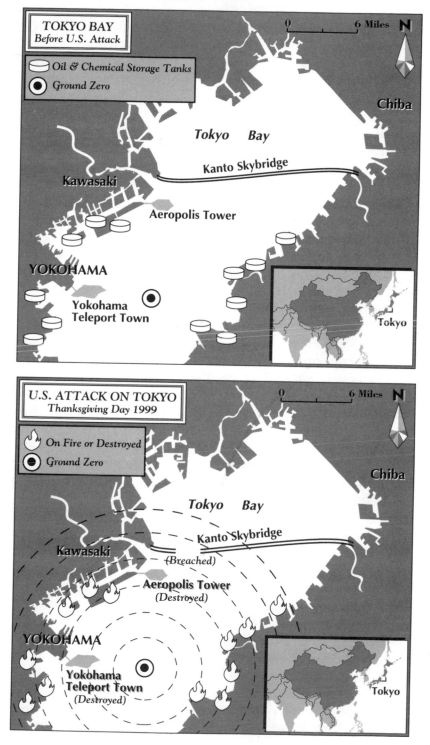

some damage to the industrial structures that lined Tokyo Bay, and to knock out some of the high-prestige constructions that had been built in the Bay during the construction frenzy of the early Nineties. But the people of Tokyo itself, which was some 18 miles from Ground Zero, were, as had also been planned, essentially safe from a 50-kiloton explosion – and though the shock wave blew out some few thousand windows and blinded a few score of people unlucky enough to have been looking out of their windows towards the Bay entrance, there were few enough casualties, and no disruption of the government and rescue services.

The real damage was done to ships in the Bay, to the Chiba-Kawasaki Sky Bridge (one third of a mile of which vanished into the sea), and to the two ultra-high-prestige constructions that had been started in early 1998 – Yokohama Teleport Town, a 50,000-unit apartment complex that was being built on an artificial island near Sarushima, and the 500-storey Aeropolis Tower, a mile and a quarter high, which had been started on a tiny island seven miles from Ground Zero.

The tower, which had been designed by the Ohbayashi Corporation and was expected to be the most spectacular and 'intelligent' building on the planet – the Emperor had laid the foundation stone in 1997 – had already reached 180 storeys when Major Pringle dropped the bomb. When the fire and smoke had cleared the stunned residents of Yokohama could see that Aeropolis, which had become a familiar landmark, had been almost completely demolished.

Much damage was done to a number of vital electronic components factories in Kawasaki. In addition there was severe destruction around the so-called 'poison necklace' of inflammable and noxious chemical storage depots near the various city docks, and which, when on fire and mixed into one another, form a cocktail of the most lethal pollution. The fires that raged in plants belonging to Sumitomo Chemicals, Nippon Oil, Tokyo Gas, Mitsui Petrochemicals and Mobil Oil raged for days. A southerly winter wind brought the clouds over the city, and blanketed Tokyo with a fine rain of filthy black chemicals that lingered for weeks. Radiation from the bomb was, however, light: the Department of Defense had called for a 'clean' weapon, and it was not their concern that

the subsequent fires caused the air over Tokyo to be chokingly filthy for weeks to come.

The final casualty figures were relatively light: 810 dead, 12,604 suffering from a variety of injuries – though very few of the injuries were flash burns, as had been experienced in Hiroshima and Nagasaki fifty years before. The city hospitals found themselves generally well able to cope with the emergency. Aside from the Sky Bridge, all of the city's major infrastructural links had remained intact; and although the population was stunned and demoralised by what had happened, all of the affected areas – even Yokohama and Kawasaki, which were the closest to the explosion – were functioning more or less normally within two weeks.

The psychological effect was incalculable, however, and profound. The Civil Defence authorities quickly established that the destruction caused by the bomb was manageable, but warned that the Americans could well send in their planes once again and engage in far more devastating attacks. The politicians and senior members of the military assimilated this message with equal rapidity, and by mid-morning a message of conciliation was ordered sent by diplomatic cable to the American government. President Benson made mention of the receipt of such a message when he broadcast to the American people at 9 p.m. Washington time, informing them of Operation Typhoon Warning, and of the fact that an atomic weapon had been dropped, once again, on Japan.

Emperor Akihito then broadcast to his nation on radio and television an hour later, at 11 a.m., Tokyo Time. Wearing a dark suit and a black tie, and with his Empress sitting by his side, he spoke firmly and softly for ten minutes about the tragedy that now afflicted both Japan and China, and which, he admitted 'might to some degree have been of our own making'.

He continued: 'It may be that the decision to send members of our Land Self-Defence Forces into Chinese territory has not worked wholly to our nation's advantage. Accordingly I am announcing the agreement of my government to comply with the request made three days ago by President Benson. I have instructed force commanders in this matter,

moves are already under way, and I am assured that the request will have been fully complied with by midnight tonight, Japan Standard Time . . .'

News of the beginning of the Japanese withdrawal from China was broadcast to the American people shortly before midnight on Thursday. President Benson made the formal announcement, and was not slow to point out that he was able to do so, just, on what on the East coast was at the very close of Thanksgiving Day. It was not the end of the day in the rest of America, he went on: perhaps some appropriate gratitude might be expressed.

Reports from police traffic departments across the United States soon confirmed that many in the nation took their President's advice. Soon after the broadcast scores of roads were clogged with a rush of late-night churchgoers, all of them apparently wishing to offer their thanks in person for the satisfactory ending of this chapter in the crisis – and, the pastors later said, to pray for all of the victims, so far away, whose leaders had so very nearly brought their conflict to engulf the entire world.

The commonly held view all across the United States that night was that since the spectre of so terrible a war had, at the very last moment, been averted, so it seemed right and proper to consider the implications in the quiet and private world of Church, at the close of the very last Thanksgiving of the American century.

# EPILOGUE

The world was stunned by the enormity of events, horrified at the seemingly uncontrollable speed of developments in the Far East and, almost universally, appalled by what President Benson had ordered done. That the United States had decided, in secrecy and without any apparent prior consultation, to unleash an atomic bomb against a country with whom it was not itself at war and which had made no threatening gesture towards the United States or any of its possessions or interests, was condemned on all sides. The UN Security Council was called into emergency session, and a resolution of the General Assembly excoriating the United States for its unilateral use of nuclear weaponry was passed by an overwhelming vote.

Four days later, with what seemed a somewhat weary and condescending calm, the United States commenced a campaign to explain the rationale behind its action. Robert Upshaw, the Under-Secretary for the US Air Force, held a news conference at the Pentagon on the Monday afternoon, an event timed to coincide with the main BBC World Service television news for Europe, the Americas and West Asia. He announced, to widespread astonishment, that he was staging the conference in his capacity as Director of the National Reconnaissance Office, and that he would produce evidence to indicate just how close the world had come to total catastrophe.

The National Reconnaissance Office was an organisation whose very existence had only rarely been confirmed. The first indication that there was such an intelligence-gathering bureau buried deep inside the Pentagon came, mistakenly, in a 1973 Congressional budget report. For years following that error – and even during the early post Cold War period, when the need for obsessive secrecy seemed to have declined in proportion to the strength of the perceived threat from

287

Moscow – the NRO remained a 'black' programme, rarely discussed, never publicly acknowledged, its funding and staff kept wholly classified.

Its basic function, however, was known to be the management of satellite reconnaissance and intelligence-gathering programmes. Mr Upshaw's news conference was called to give details of what were code-named 'Ruff' images – ultra high definition three-dimensional photographs – that had been transmitted during the previous week from the NRO's new synthetic aperture radar-imaging satellite, a four-ton high-performance monster that had been launched from the Cape York Satellite Centre the previous July under the number Keyhole-16, and to which the Pentagon had given the Byeman designation Lacrosse V. The Lacrosse satellites were in low Earth orbits – about 300 miles up – and took photographs of any one portion of the planet at 90-minute intervals. Lacrosse V had been specifically tasked to cover northern China.

The Lacrosse Ruff images, which Upshaw showed on a series of wall-to-ceiling screens, were in full colour and were of incredible clarity – far more impressive than even the best of the high-definition televisions that had been in use in the US for the past two years. They depicted an area of northern China to the northeast of the Manchurian city of Harbin and were shown in rapid sequence, the series beginning on Monday morning, 22 November. The pictures, despite being taken in five-minute bursts by a variety of cameras and lenses trained down during each of the passes at 90-minute intervals, were shown in such a way as to take on the appearance of a moving film. They were also accompanied by a commentary – a translation of the so-called 'Zarf' signals intelligence intercepts from a geostationary satellite code-named Magnum 9, which had been ordered to listen to (and if possible to decode) all signals emanating from the Chinese military forces in the areas under surveillance.

The satellite operators working on Lacrosse V could use wide-angle shots, or close-ups. In the latter the imaging systems could show parked vehicles and their number plates, Chinese Army personnel and their shoulder-badges, the rescuers working in the damaged Sumitomo Metals building in Harbin City, the expressions on the faces of the bystanders –

whether Harbin was in darkness, or bathed in the light of the late autumn sun. The technological triumph of the system was evident (something of which the Hughes Aircraft Company, the Lacrosse V's manufacturers, were later to make much). But it was the wide-angle pictures that were much more dramatic, in terms of illustrating just how close the world had come to the brink: it was on those – some fifty separate images – that Secretary Upshaw spent most of the news conference.

Twelve Japanese transport aircraft were shown landing on the Tuesday morning at an airfield five miles north of Harbin. Men and vehicles – mostly Japanese, though with some commandeered PLA troop-carriers in the convoys – were then to be seen securing the Sumitomo plant, established in a tented encampment beside the frozen Sungari River, constructing defences. Orders from the operational headquarters in Hakata were decoded and translated: the Japanese, it seemed, were bent on remaining in Harbin for an indefinite period, and reinforcements were due within the week.

The Lacrosse cameras were then switched to a Chinese air base at Suihua, fifty miles further north. It was here, Secretary Upshaw insisted, that direct and critical evidence first emerged of what would have happened next.

The pictures showed bleak hillsides, their northern flanks covered with snow. At the centre of the screen was the Suihua base, close to a small town of the same name. There was evidently extreme security around the base: a sanitised area two miles wide completely surrounded the airfield and the pod-shaped structures that were ranged beside the runway. Triple fences ringed both the cordon and the base itself; there were watchtowers and, visible even from 300 miles, scores of guard dogs.

The Suihua base was home to the 453rd Strategic Rocket Unit of China's Second Artillery, Upshaw explained. The twelve pods beside the main runway each housed a single CSS-7 medium-range ballistic missile, each with a cone-shaped warhead, a copy of a Russian design of the late 1980s, that held ten individual targeted nuclear-fission bombs. Each one of these weapons had a yield of 500 kilotons-equivalent: they were in short powerful, dirty and extremely dangerous nuclear missiles.

When the Suihua base was first opened in the mid-1970s

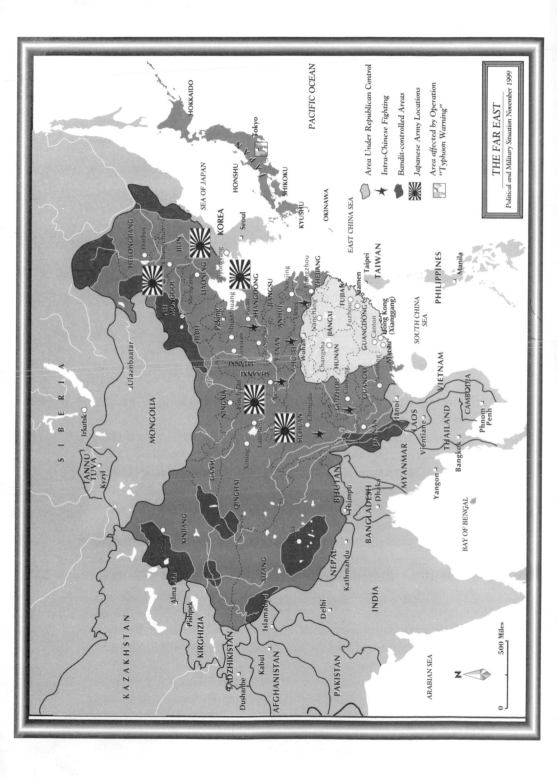

THE FAR EAST
Political and Military Situation November 1999

Area Under Republican Control
Intra-Chinese Fighting
Bandit-controlled Areas
Japanese Army Locations
Area affected by Operation "Typhoon Warning"

PACIFIC OCEAN

HOKKAIDO

Tokyo
JAPAN
HONSHU
SHIKOKU
KYUSHU
SEA OF JAPAN
OKINAWA
EAST CHINA SEA

KOREA
Seoul
Pyongyang

SIBERIA
Irkutsk
Ulaanbaatar
MONGOLIA

HEILONGJIANG
Harbin
Changchun
JILIN
LIAONING
Shenyang
NEI MONGGOL
HEBEI
Peking
Shijiazhuang
Taiyuan
SHANXI
SHAANXI
Xi'an
Luoyang
NINGXIA
Yinchuan
GANSU
Lanzhou
QINGHAI
Xining
SICHUAN
Chengdu

SHANDONG
Ji'nan
JIANGSU
ANHUI
Hefei
Nanjing
Nanchang
JIANGXI
HUBEI
Wuhan
Changsha
HUNAN
GUIZHOU
Guiyang
GUANGXI
Nanning
ZHEJIANG
Hangzhou
FUJIAN
Fuzhou
Xiamen
GUANGDONG
Canton
Hong Kong (Xianggang)
Macau

TAIWAN
Taipei

SOUTH CHINA SEA

PHILIPPINES
Manila

VIETNAM
Hanoi
LAOS
Vientiane
MYANMAR
THAILAND
Bangkok
CAMBODIA
Phnom Penh
Yangon

XINJIANG
Ürümqi
XIZANG
Lhasa
YUNNAN

NEPAL
Kathmandu
BHUTAN
Thimpu
BANGLADESH
Dhaka
INDIA
Delhi

TANNU TUVA
Kyzyl

KAZAKHSTAN
Alma-Ata
KIRGHIZIA
Pishpek
TADZHIKISTAN
Dushanbe
AFGHANISTAN
Kabul
PAKISTAN
Islamabad

ARABIAN SEA
BAY OF BENGAL

500 Miles
0
N

the weapons were kept in first-rate condition and the teams who were trained to fire them were kept under constant training. The weapons themselves were programmed to be fired either at targets in Alaska or Siberia, since both the United States and the then USSR were regarded in Peking as presenting apparent dangers to China. But with the lessening of global tension two decades later the base – like most of the Second Artillery's bases and weapons – had become of rather less potential use. There had been reported talk in Peking of standing the missile crews down and of removing the active warheads. But the turmoil within China halted that debate, and at the time when the NRO's Lacrosse V satellite was ordered to take an active interest in the Suihua base, all the missiles' firing stations were secured and manned ready for immediate action.

While the camera steadied on a series of pictures of the base, journalists in the Pentagon briefing room – and, via the BBC and CNN cameras, scores of hundreds of millions of viewers around the world – listened to the decoded transcripts of the signals proceeding to and from, and conversations proceeding within the headquarters buildings at the centre of the screen.

This signal traffic began with routine reports of the arrival of the Japanese troops in Harbin, and of their deployment. (Alert messages concerning the Japanese intrusion on Chinese airspace had already come in from the Chinese Air Force's defensive tracking station of Taiyuan in Shanxi Province; the more useful station, considering the direction of the planes' approach, would have been that at Changle in Fujian Province but this had fallen into Republican hands some months before, and its reports were presumably being given only to the Republican force commanders down in Wuhan, Canton and Hong Kong. This, the Pentagon said, was the essential reason for the lack of Communist Chinese air defence activity during the Japanese incursion.)

Later in the morning and in the early afternoon signals were sent from the base to the Commander, Heilongjiang Military District, in Harbin, to the Commander, Shenyang Military Region, and to the Commander, Second Artillery, asking – with some asperity – what response, if any, should

come from the missiles of the 453rd. But there was no reply for the following seven hours.

Just before midnight another flurry of messages was intercepted, going up the line from the Suihua commander. One reply came on this occasion, from the Shenyang commander, who insisted on his belief that the Japanese would probably leave Harbin within a matter of days, and that there was probably no need for 'any kind' of military response from China. However, at about this time it became evident that Suihua was also given the stark news that the Japanese had not just landed their troops near by, in Harbin, but that their men were also now present in strength at Jinan, Xian, Chengdu and, most ominously of all, outside Shanghai itself. All China, it seemed, was under threat.

It was at this point – identified both on the Lacrosse images and through the transcripts collected by the Magnum 9 – that the Suihua base commander (who was since identified as a Brigadier Deng, a veteran of the Vietnam border war) decided he had had enough of the battle-weary indecision which, he must have judged, was now infecting his senior colleagues in Peking and Shenyang. The Magnum intercepts report the Brigadier taking over the camp's public address system and announcing to all his personnel on the base that, in view of what he called the 'brutal invasion of our nation by the vile armies of Japan', the 453rd Strategic Rocket Unit would now take 'an appropriate and unilateral response'.

All twelve of the missiles under his command would now be targeted on military, industrial and communications centres in Japan, he said. The re-assigning of targets would take the base technicians three days to complete. 'If there is no clear undertaking from Japan that they will remove their troops and aircraft from our soil. by midday, Friday,' Brigadier Deng continued, 'then the Suihua base will launch a full nuclear strike against Japan, one that will have the most dreadful consequences.'

The next sequence of satellite pictures, all taken during the night, showed dozens of special vehicles moving out to the various pods, the lids of these pods being opened, the orange warheads of the weapons poking up through the snow, scores of men swarming over the weapons, or begin-

ning complex fuel-replacement and countdown operations in the bunkers dotted along the northern edge of the airstrip.

One of the Lacrosse pictures that Upshaw displayed was taken with a zoom lens: it showed one of the open nose-cones and, poking through, ten bulbous objects arrayed in splayed cluster, as though in some monstrous piece of botany. Each of the bulbs, four feet long and two wide, contained enough nuclear material to destroy the centre of Tokyo, or turn every wooden temple within a ten-mile radius of Kyoto into a pile of ashes.

Secretary Upshaw turned off the screens, and ordered the transcript tape halted. The lights came up in the briefing room. The audience was quite silent.

'The last series of intercepts came in to the NRO action room at 3 p.m. last Tuesday afternoon, our time. There was no doubt in our minds that Base Commander Deng had both the intention and the ability to release his weapons at targets in Japan, and that he would do so without compunction or concern for the consequences. The implications for the Japanese people would have been incalculable, of course. The implications to the world economy of the destruction or decimation of Japan's manufacturing ability would have been equally profound. It was thus imperative that we acted to halt the Japanese before a freelance Chinese commander such as Brigadier Deng or other like-minded commanders with whom we know he was planning to make contact acted unilaterally to do the same thing – but with much more frightening consequences.

'The United States naturally regrets having to take the action it did, in dropping a single nuclear gravity weapon over Tokyo Bay. It naturally regrets the loss of life and the destruction of property. But I trust, however, that you will find credible the evidence that we have presented here today – evidence that indicates beyond any reasonable doubt that, had we not taken the action that we did, Japan would be in far worse shape than she is today, and the entire world economy would have been put at risk. It is true that our relations with Japan are currently very poor, and our strike this week will inevitably have made them much poorer. It is not for a military man to become engaged in diplomatic

matters. It is my hope, however, that the government of Japan, too, will one day come to realise that the attack by the United States, while achieving its short-term objective, succeeded also in averting a situation that was immeasurably more terrible than that which befell the people of Tokyo and Yokohama.'

Diplomatic relations between the United States and Japan were restored early in 2000 – an indication that the Ministry of Foreign Affairs in Tokyo, probably under pressure from the Imperial Palace, was persuaded to see the sense in the argument that was initially advanced so bluntly by Air Force Secretary Upshaw. There was, in addition, a good deal of American domestic sympathy for the Japanese victims of the Yokohama bomb – sympathy which went some long way to reverse the tide of anti-Americanism that had marked President Benson's first term. At the time of writing the US President was expected to visit Tokyo, to inspect repairs and to see if the United States could offer any assistance.

There was talk also of a joint US-Japanese-Russian mission to calm the civil war that was continuing to disrupt life inside China herself. But virtually all the countries on China's immense periphery had taken the attack on Tokyo as a warning that they, too, should keep aloof from their neighbour's internal problems. The cross-border skirmishing and terrorism in the far north and west was thus soon largely stilled, and the incidence of banditry grew steadily less disruptive.

Elsewhere in the region a sense of cautious optimism began to return. In Korea – the newly united Korea – democratic elections were held in February 2000. The residents of what had been North Korea took to the idea of voting with alacrity – voter turnout in Pyongyang was far greater than in Seoul, for example – with the result that a left-leaning slate of candidates, the Social Democratic Union, was elected into office. The new Korean premier, Lee Chun-ok – in a remark that underscored the notion that the newly united nation would rapidly become a formidable economic and political power – immediately offered his good offices as well, to help

bring about an end to the Chinese conflict. There was no immediate reply, however, from either Canton or Peking.

The Hong Kong provisional government, which had occupied itself repairing the city in the wake of the fighting, also announced elections – the first in which all citizens on the rolls would have the opportunity to vote for their local leadership. Foreign investment, which had drained away to nothing in the months leading up to June 1997, began to seep back into the city: the first notable infusion of foreign money was a two-billion-dollar reclamation scheme in western Lantau that was financed entirely by Korean banks and which was due to be constructed by a subsidiary of Daewoo corporation, based in the former North Korean port city of Nampo. Hong Kong, in summary, appeared to be recovering with characteristic swiftness from its two years of travails.

In November 1999 the world's great powers clashed suddenly, briefly, violently, horribly. It could all, however, have been so very much worse. Millions could have died, where only thousands fell. The dull background roar to which China's internal battling has now faded could have continued at full pace for decades yet to come, with still many more dead, and the attendant possibility of the rest of the world – neighbours, allies, friends, foes, or those with ill-defined 'interests' – becoming embroiled again and again and again.

But a single bombing mission, performed in secret by three mysterious aircraft based in the icy hills of western Missouri, appears to have changed all that. Instant history, like that contained in this account, can only offer an instant judgement, with all the attendant imperfections. More sober and serious documents will soon be written, no doubt, and the benefit of perspective will permit others to analyse and debate and draw more considered conclusions on the tide of events. And there will be no shortage of material: for there can be little doubt that the implications of Operation Typhoon Warning, like the sound of the explosion itself, will reverberate for decades around the nations of the world, and will echo down the years for as long as history continues to be written.

# INDEX

Page numbers in *italics* refer to maps. n = footnote. Chinese
and Korean names are indexed by first element of name

S I B E

Irkutsk O

TANNU
TUVA
Kyzyl

KAZAKHSTAN

MONGOL

Ürümqi O

Alma Ata

XINJIANG

Pishpek

GANSU

KIRGHIZIA

NIN

TADZHIKISTAN

QINGHAI

Dushanbe

Xining O

Lanzhou

Kabul

Islamabad

XIZANG

SICHUAN

AFGHANISTAN

Lhasa

Cher

Delhi

NEPAL

BHUTAN

C

PAKISTAN

Kathmandu

Thimpu

Kunming

YUNNAN

INDIA

BANGLADESH

Dhaka

Han

MYANMAR

LAOS

ARABIAN SEA

Vientiane

Yangon

THAILAND

N

Bangkok

CA

BAY OF BENGAL

Phnom
Penh

0          500 Miles